Decision Support Systems and Intelligent Systems

DECISION SUPPORT SYSTEMS AND INTELLIGENT SYSTEMS

SIXTH EDITION

EFRAIM TURBAN

CITY UNIVERSITY OF HONG KONG

JAY E. ARONSON

THE UNIVERSITY OF GEORGIA

with contributions by

NARASIMHA BOLLOJU

CITY UNIVERSITY OF HONG KONG

Prentice
Hall

Upper Saddle River, New Jersey

Turban, Efraim.
    Decision support systems and intelligent systems / Efraim Turban, Jay E. Aronson.—
6th ed.
        p.   cm.
    Includes bibliographical references and index.
    ISBN 0-13-089465-6
    1. Management—Data processing. 2. Decision support systems. 3. Expert systems
(Computer science) I. Aronson, Jay E. II. Title.
HD30.2.T87 2000
658.4′03′0285633—dc21   00-037324

Editor-in-Chief: Mickey Cox
Senior Editors: David Alexander and Robert Horan
Editorial Assistant: Erika Rusnak
Associate Editor: Kyle Hannon
Senior Marketing Manager: Sharon Turkovich
Permissions Coordinator: Suzanne Grappi
Media Project Manager: Nancy Welcher
Director of Production: Michael Weinstein
Manager, Production: Gail Steier de Acevedo
Production Coordinator: Kelly Warsak
Manufacturing Buyer: Natacha St. Hill Moore
Associate Director, Manufacturing: Vincent Scelta
Cover Design: Blair Brown
Full Service Composition: Carlisle Communications
Printing and Binding: Hamilton Printing

10 9 8 7 6 5 4 3 2
ISBN 0-13-089465-6

Dedicated to
my wife Lina,
and my daughters Daphne and Sharon
with love

and to
my wife Sharon,
and my children Marla, Michael, and Stephanie
with love

Efraim Turban (M.B.A., Ph.D., University of California Berkeley) is a visiting professor at City University of Hong Kong. Prior to this he was on the staff of several universities including Lehigh University, Florida International University, and the University of Southern California. Dr. Turban is the author of about 100 refereed papers published in leading journals such as *Management Science, MIS Quarterly,* and *Decision Support Systems.* He is also the author of 20 books including *Electronic Commerce: A Managerial Perspective* and *Information Technology for Management.* He is also a consultant to major corporations worldwide. Dr. Turban's current areas of interest are Web-based decision support systems, using intelligent agents in electronic commerce systems, and collaboration issues in global electronic commerce.

Jay E. Aronson (M.S.E.E., M.S.O.R., Ph.D., Carnegie Mellon University) is a professor of Management Information Systems in the Terry College of Business at The University of Georgia. Prior to this he was on the faculty at Southern Methodist University. Dr. Aronson is the author of about 50 refereed papers that have appeared in leading journals including *Management Science, Information Systems Research,* and *MIS Quarterly.* He is the author of two books and contributes to several professional encyclopedias. He is also a consultant to major international corporations and organizations. Dr. Aronson's current areas of research include knowledge management, collaborative computing, and parallel computing.

BRIEF CONTENTS

CONTENTS

OVERVIEW

As we begin the 21st century, we observe major changes in how managers use computerized support in making decisions. From primarily a personal support tool, as more and more computers become networked, DSS is quickly becoming a *shared commodity* across the organization. Organizations now can easily use intranets and the Internet to deliver high value performance analysis applications to decision makers around the world. Corporations are developing distributed systems, *intranets* and *extranets,* that enable easy access to data stored in multiple locations, and collaboration and communication worldwide. Various information systems are being integrated with each other and/or with other automated systems. Some integration even transcends organizational boundaries. Managers can make better decisions because they have more accurate information at their fingertips.

Today's DSS tools can also create a key interactive user interface that allows users to view and process data and models with standard Web browsers with great flexibility, efficiency, and ease. The easy to use and readily available capabilities of executive information, knowledge, and other advanced systems have migrated to the PC and personal digital assistants (PDAs). Managers can communicate with computers and the Web with a variety of handheld wireless devices, including the cell telephone. Through these devices, managers access important information and useful tools, and collaborate. *Data warehouses* and their analytical tools, such as *online analytical processing* (OLAP), dramatically enhance information access across organizational boundaries. Decision support for groups continues to improve with major new developments in *group support systems* for enhancing collaborative work, anytime and anywhere. *Artificial intelligence* methods are improving the quality of decision support and are becoming embedded in many applications ranging from toasters to intelligent Web search engines. *Intelligent agents* perform routine tasks, freeing up decision makers' time to devote to important work. Developments in *organizational learning* and *knowledge management* deliver the entire organization's expertise to bear on problems anytime and anywhere. The Internet and intranet information delivery systems are enhancing all of these decision support systems.

The purpose of this book is to introduce the reader to these technologies, which we call collectively, *management support systems* (MSS). This book presents the fundamentals of the techniques and the manner in which they are developed and used.

The theme of this totally revised edition is "enterprise decision support, the Web and the role of knowledge management." In addition to the traditional DSS applications, this edition introduces the reader to the world of the Web by providing examples, products, services, and exercises, and by discussing Web-related issues throughout the text. The book is supported by a Web site (www.prenhall.com/turban) that contains additional readings, relevant links, and other supplements. In the specific changes of this sixth edition, most of the improvements concentrate in three areas: knowledge management, supply chain decision support, and Web DSS. Despite the many changes, we preserved the text's comprehensiveness and user friendliness that made it a market leader. We also reduced the book's size by eliminating generic IT material and by moving material to the book's Web site. Finally, we present accurate and updated material not available in any other text.

DSS and ES courses and portions of courses are recommended jointly by the Association for Computing Machinery (ACM), Association for Information Systems (AIS), and Association of Information Technology Professionals (AITP, formerly DPMA) (see *Data Base,* Vol. 28, No. 1, Winter 1997). This course is designed to cover the decision support and artificial intelligence components of the IS'97 Model Curriculum for information systems. It actually covers more than what is recommended. This text also covers the decision support and artificial intelligence components of the Information Systems 2000 Model Curriculum draft (www.is2000.org). Another objective is to provide the practicing manager with the foundations and applications of DSS, GSS, knowledge management, ES, neural computing, intelligent agents, and other intelligent systems.

THE SIXTH EDITION

The sixth edition of this book presents a major departure from the previous editions conducted for the purpose of improving the text. The major improvements include the following:

- A new chapter on knowledge management (Chapter 9) describing this exciting new decision support methodology.
- Replacing the chapter on executive information systems (EIS) with a new chapter on enterprise decision support systems (Chapter 8) that centers on supply chain management.
- Combining the chapters on artificial intelligence and expert systems into a single chapter.
- Creating a single chapter from those on networked decision support and group support systems (Chapter 7).
- Eliminating the chapter on user interface and moving some of its content to the book's Web site and to other chapters.
- Creating a new section on the use of intelligent agents in electronic commerce.
- Updating a chapter on data warehousing and its role in decision support (Chapter 4).
- Expanding the theoretical material on decision making in Chapter 2. This includes material on alternative decision-making models and personality temperament types.
- Including new, real-world case applications in many of the chapters. These include the IMERYS case applications of Chapters 2, 5, and 6.
- Expanded coverage of the LP packages, Lingo, Lindo, and Solver in Chapter 5.
- Major updating and streamlining of the DSS development process in Chapter 6.
- A new section on distance learning in Chapter 7.
- Moving the updated creativity and idea generation material into Chapter 7.

- Major updating and streamlining of the intelligent systems development process in Chapter 14.
- Including examples of neural network computer runs in BrainCel and BrainMaker in Chapter 15.
- Improving the material on genetic algorithms and fuzzy logic in Chapter 16. This includes an example of an Evolver (genetic algorithm) run.
- Moving the material on qualitative reasoning from knowledge representations to the one containing advanced artificial intelligent systems and applications (Chapter 16).
- Reducing the number of chapters from 21 to 19.

Other improvements and refinements are as follows:

- Moving the book to the Web age. Throughout the book you will find many discussions and references to the Internet, intranets, Web, and other network computing.
- A Web site supports this book: www.prenhall.com/turban. The Web site includes cases, software information, appendices, additional exercises, and more.
- Internet exercises for each chapter. A diversity of exercises provides the students with extensive, up-to-date information and a better sense of reality.
- Hands-on exercises provide opportunities to build decision support applications.
- Expanded group exercises and term projects. These enhance the learning experience by providing activities for small groups and longer term activities. Some term projects involve building systems for real organizations (we have used this approach very successfully for over 15 years in our teaching).
- Updated research findings and references.
- More real-world examples.

THE INSTRUCTIONAL MATERIALS

The instructional package consists of several components (check the Web site for updates).

- **Instructor's Manual and Test Item File (0-13-040633-3).** The *Instructor's Manual* includes learning objectives for the entire course and for each chapter, answers to the questions and exercises at the end of the chapters, teaching suggestions (including instructions for projects), and a software guide. The test item file includes multiple-choice questions for each chapter with answers and many test exercises for both DSS and intelligent systems with solutions.
- **Prentice Hall Test Manager for Windows (0-13-040634-1).** The *Prentice Hall Test Manager* is a computerized test generator with an optional grade book and available online testing.
- **Web site: www.prenhall.com/turban.** The Web site includes additional materials such as pointers to available software and documentation, data files, appendices, cases, additional exercises, and more.

ACKNOWLEDGMENTS

Many individuals provided suggestions and criticisms since the initiation of the first edition. Dozens of students participated in class testing of various chapters and problems and assisted in collecting material. It is not possible to name all of the many who participated in this project; thanks go to all of them. However, certain individuals made significant contributions, and they deserve special recognition.

First, those individuals who provided formal reviews of the first through sixth editions are Robert Blanning, Vanderbilt University; Warren Briggs, Suffolk University; Charles Butler, Colorado State University; Sohail S. Chaudry, University of Wisconsin, LaCrosse; Woo Young Chung, University of Memphis; Pi'Sheng Deng, California State University-Stanislaus; Joyce Elam, Florida International University; George Federman, Santa Clara City College; Joey George, Florida State University; Paul Gray, Claremont Graduate School; Orv Greynholds, Capital College (Laurel, MD); Ray Jacobs, Ashland University; Leonard Jessup, Indiana University; Jeffrey Johnson, Utah State University; Saul Kassicieh, University of New Mexico; Anand S. Kunnathur, University of Toledo; Shao-ju Lee, California State University at Northridge; Hank Lucas, NYU; Jane Mackay, Texas Christian University; George M. Marakas, University of Maryland; Dick Mason, SMU; Ido Millet, Pennsylvania State University–Erie; Benjamin Mittman, Northwestern University; Larry Moore, Virginia Polytechnic Institute and State University; Marianne Murphy, Northeastern University; Roger Alan Pick, University of Missouri–St. Louis; W. "RP" Raghupaphi, California State University–Chico; Loren Rees, Virginia Polytechnic Institute and State University; David Russell, Western New England College; Steve Ruth, George Mason University; Vartan Safarian, Winona State University; Jung P. Shim, Mississippi State University; Randy Smith, University of Virginia; James T. C. Teng, University of South Carolina; John VanGigch, California State University at Sacramento; David Van Over, University of Idaho; Paul J. A. van Vliet, University of Nebraska at Omaha; B. S. Vijayaraman, University of Akron; Diane B. Walz, University of Texas at San Antonio; Paul R. Watkins, University of Southern California; Randy S. Weinberg, Saint Cloud State University; Jennifer Williams, University of Southern Indiana; and Steve Zanakis, Florida International University.

Second, several individuals contributed material to the text or the supporting material. Major contributors include the following: independent consultant Lou Frenzel, whose books *Crash Course in Artificial Intelligence* and *Expert Systems and Understanding of Expert Systems* (both published by Howard W. Sams & Company of New York, 1987) provide considerable material; Larry Medsker (The American University), who contributed substantial material on neural networks; Dave King and Mark Wood (Comshare, Inc.), who contributed to the EIS material; Narasimha Bolloju (City University of Hong Kong), who updated Chapters 13 and 18; and Stephen Ives (Hong Kong University of Science and Technology), who assisted in updating Chapters 11 and 12.

Third, the book benefited greatly from the efforts of many individuals who contributed advice and interesting material (such as problems), gave feedback on material, or helped in class testing. These individuals are Warren Briggs (Suffolk University), Frank DeBalough (University of Southern California), Alan Dennis (Indiana University), George Easton (San Diego State University), Janet Fisher (California State University, Los Angeles), David Friend (Pilot Software, Inc.), Paul Gray (Claremont Graduate School), Dustin Huntington (Multilogic Inc.), Dave King

(Comshare, Inc.), Ben Mortagy (Claremont Graduate School of Management), Jim Ragusa (University of Central Florida), Elizabeth Rivers (Nova Southeastern University), Alan Rowe (University of Southern California), Steve Ruth (George Mason University), Linus Schrage (University of Chicago), Antonie Stam (University of Missouri), Ron Swift (NCR Corp.), Dan Walsh (Bellcore), Merril Warkentin (Northeastern University), Paul Watkins (University of Southern California), Richard Watson (The University of Georgia), and the many instructors and students who have provided feedback.

Fourth, several vendors cooperated by providing development and/or demonstration software. They are CACI Products Company (LaJolla, CA), California Scientific Software (Nevada City, CA), Cognos, Inc. (Ottowa, Canada), Comshare, Inc. (Ann Arbor, MI), DS Group, Inc. (Greenwich, CT), Expert Choice, Inc. (Pittsburgh, PA), Idea Fisher Systems, Inc. (Irving, CA), Lindo Systems Inc. (Chicago, IL) Multilogic, Inc. (Albuquerque, NM), Palisade Software (Newfield, NY), Pilot Software, Inc. (Cambridge, MA), Promised Land Technologies (New Haven, CT), Ward Systems Group, Inc. (Frederick, MD), and Wordtech Systems (Orinda, CA). Also, the Defense Systems Management College (Fort Belvoir, VA) provided its PMSS.

Fifth, many individuals helped us in administrative matters and in editing, proofreading, and preparation. The project began with Jack Repcheck (a former Macmillan editor), who initiated this project with the support of Hank Lucas (New York University). Initial editing was done by Efraim Turban's daughter, Sharon. A major "thank you" goes to Eleanor Loiacono (Worchester Polytechnic Institute) and Anthony Napolito, Franck Schmiedt and Henry Webb (The University of Georgia) for their countless hours in tracking down library material, Web sites and other information. Thanks, also, to Yasmeen Fadel, Tom Hoover, Sebrena Mason, Tony McDonald, Nada Morris, Connie McEver, Karen Turner, and Amy Walker for their help and expertise. And finally, Judy Lang, who played a major role in many tasks including the preparation of the book, the *Test Bank,* and the *Instructor's Manual.*

Finally, the Prentice Hall team is to be commended: David Alexander and Erika Rusnak, who orchestrated this project; Carol Dean, who copyedited the manuscript; the production team including Kelly Warsak, Suzanne Grappi, and the staff at Carlisle Communications, including Larry Goldberg, who transformed the manuscript into a book; our associate editor, Kyle Hannon; and our media project manager, Nancy Welcher.

We would like to thank all these individuals and corporations. Without their help the creation of this book would not have been possible.

E.T.
J.E.A.

DECISION MAKING AND COMPUTERIZED SUPPORT

Management support systems (MSS) are collections of computerized technologies used to support managerial work and decision making. In Part I, we present two topics. An overview of the book, including the rationale for the technologies and a brief description of each, is given in Chapter 1. In Chapter 2, we present the fundamentals of decision making, including terminology and an overview of the decision-making process.

MANAGEMENT SUPPORT SYSTEMS: AN OVERVIEW

This book is about emerging and advanced computer technologies for supporting the solution of managerial problems. We are already seeing evidence that these technologies are changing the manner in which organizations are structured, reengineered, and managed. This introductory chapter provides an overview of the book and covers the following topics:

1.1 OPENING VIGNETTE: DECISION SUPPORT AT ROADWAY PACKAGE SYSTEM[1]

The market of business-to-business small package delivery is extremely competitive. Large corporations such as United Parcel Service (UPS) are competing with dozens of medium and small companies. Therefore, the first decision a new company must make is *where* to open its first hubs and terminals. There are many alternatives. Placing hubs and terminals costs money. Using the wrong sites can result in large losses and even endanger the life of a newcomer like Roadway Package System (RPS), which started operations in March 1985.

There were many uncertainties. How do you attract customers? Will competitors reduce their fees? What new services will competitors offer, and what should you do in response? It was obvious that the company would have to make many decisions, quickly and continuously. Also, the importance of both updated external and internal data has been recognized.

To solve its initial location problem, RSP developed a quantitative locational model using software (from SAS Institute, Inc.). The parent company of RPS had used the SAS software package before, mainly for report generation. Now RPS uses it for decision support.

With the help of computerized **decision support systems (DSS[2]),** RPS has grown from 3 hubs and 36 terminals to 21 hubs and over 300 terminals in 10 years. About 50 decision support applications are provided in three critical areas: market and research planning, operations planning, and sales support. Some examples of DSS applications are

- *Market planning and research.* DSS applications include pricing decisions for each customer. These are based on shipping patterns recognized by statistical tools used to analyze data collected daily. This provides a competitive advantage because discounts can be offered to valuable customers, yet large profits can be realized. Another DSS application is forecasting. Here, each product's growth pattern is analyzed using forecasting models. The appropriate decisions about termination or expansion of each product and service can be made. Customer satisfaction levels are also analyzed using DSS models.
- *Operation and strategic planning.* DSS is used to support both short-term and strategic planning for monitoring, analyzing, and reporting on the subtle market trends that determine where the computer hub satellite network needs to expand to take advantage of growing markets (e.g., by identifying the fastest-growing markets).
- *Sales support.* An **executive information system (EIS)** provides support for top management by generating daily sales summaries and details by region, division, salesperson, and product. The reports identify lost business, rescued business, and new business, and they can be generated on demand in addition to periodic reports. The special reports are customized, and comparisons and trend analysis can be provided to managers. The reports are useful in identifying problems and opportunities.

All data needed for the DSS/EIS are extracted from the regular **transaction processing system (TPS).** With the use of bar codes, data are scanned several times between the

---

[1]Compiled from "Keeping an Eye on the Road Ahead," *SAS Communication,* SAS Institute, Inc., Second Quarter, 1994, and from www.shiprps.com, Jan. 2000.
[2]The acronym *DSS* is used as both singular and plural throughout this book. Similarly, other acronyms such as *MIS* and *EIS* designate both plural and singular forms.

initial pickup and the final delivery. The company collects the data rapidly and monitors the whereabouts of every package, almost in real time.

The information generated by the DSS is useful not only to corporate managers but also to customers. Customers have direct online access to some corporate information which they can download on demand. Self-tutoring and help functions are also available online to all users.

In the shipping industry, information processing is vital to survival. Marketing, for example, is considered to be the management of customer information and extraction of value. DSS and EIS applications help management make timely and effective decisions by providing reliable and relevant information in the correct format and at the right time. Furthermore, DSS and EIS applications help end users conduct any necessary *analysis* easily and quickly by themselves. Now, nontechnical people have easy access to a special decision support database called a *data warehouse* (Chapter 4). This gives people considerably more power at their fingertips. It is not necessary to be an information system (IS) wizard to run DSS applications. All in all, a DSS helps a company to extract the data required to understand the market better and compete successfully on price, quality, timeliness, and customer service.

Now a subsidiary of Federal Express, RPS (www.shiprps.com) has become the second-largest U.S. business-to-business small package carrier. Using the Internet, RPS offers complete customized solutions to its customers. The company even provides free DSS software to customers for report generation and work monitoring.

❖ QUESTIONS FOR THE OPENING VIGNETTE

1. Identify the specific decisions cited. Why do such decisions need computerized support? (Be specific and provide an answer for each decision.)
2. It is said that the DSS/EIS helped the company to compete on prices, quality, timeliness, and service. Visit a competing company such as UPS (check the company's Web site) and explain the importance of this type of competition.
3. Find information about RPS (use the Internet). Find the volume of their business in terms of packages delivered and their financial statements (you can check this information at the Federal Express Web site). How successful is this company? Why?
4. It is said that decision support tools empower employees and customers. Can you identify such empowerment?
5. It is said that the TPS is separate from the DSS/EIS. What kind of TPS can you envision in this type of shipping company? Why is it different from the decision support systems?

1.2 MANAGERS AND DECISION MAKING

The Opening Vignette illustrates how decision support is provided to RPS, a relatively young company that operates successfully in an extremely competitive market. Some of the points demonstrated by this vignette are as follows:

- The nature of the competition in the shipping industry makes it necessary to use computerized decision support tools to succeed and to survive.
- End users and even customers can work with the system by themselves.
- The system is based on data organized in a special data warehouse. This allows easy processing and manipulation by end users.

- Two major technologies provide support: DSS, which supports managers and marketing analysts in making decisions such as pricing, and EIS, which helps top managers monitor sales and identify problems and opportunities.
- The DSS is used in making a variety of decisions, ranging from a strategic decision about where to open the initial terminals and hubs to day-by-day pricing decisions for individual customers.
- Decision support is based on a vast amount of internal and external data.
- DSS applications are separate from the TPS, yet they use much of the TPS data.
- Statistical and other quantitative models are used in DSS applications.
- The managers ultimately are responsible for all decisions.
- The company now uses the World Wide Web extensively, including DSS Web applications.

The vignette demonstrates that to run an effective business today, in a competitive environment, computerized decision support is essential. How this is done is demonstrated throughout this text.

THE NATURE OF MANAGERS' WORK

To better understand the support information systems can give managers, it is useful to look at the nature of managers' work. Mintzberg's (1980) study of top managers and several later replicated studies suggest that managers perform 10 major roles, which can be classified into three major categories: interpersonal, information, and decisional (Table 1.1).

TABLE 1.1 Mintzberg's 10 Management Roles

Role	*Description*
Interpersonal	
Figurehead	Symbolic head; obliged to perform a number of routine duties of a legal or social nature
Leader	Responsible for the motivation and activation of subordinates; responsible for staffing, training, and associated duties
Liaison	Maintains self-developed network of outside contacts and informers who provide favors and information
Informational	
Monitor	Seeks and receives a wide variety of special information (much of it current) to develop a thorough understanding of the organization and environment; emerges as the nerve center of the organization's internal and external information
Disseminator	Transmits information received from outsiders or from subordinates to members of the organization; some information factual, some involving interpretation and integration
Spokesperson	Transmits information to outsiders on the organization's plans, policies, actions, results, and so forth; serves as an expert on the organization's industry
Decisional	
Entrepreneur	Searches the organization and its environment for opportunities and initiates improvement projects to bring about change; supervises design of certain projects
Disturbance handler	Responsible for corrective action when the organization faces important, unexpected disturbances
Resource allocator	Responsible for the allocation of organizational resources of all kinds—in effect the making or approving of all significant organizational decisions
Negotiator	Responsible for representing the organization at major negotiations

Source: Adapted from Mintzberg (1980) and Mintzberg (1993).

To execute these roles, managers need information that is delivered efficiently and in a timely manner by computers. In addition to obtaining information necessary to better perform their roles, managers can use computers to directly support and improve decision making, a task that is involved in most of these roles.

1.3 MANAGERIAL DECISION MAKING AND INFORMATION SYSTEMS

We begin by examining two important topics: managerial decision making and information systems.

Management is a process by which organizational goals are achieved through the use of resources. These resources are considered to be inputs, and attainment of goals is viewed as the output of the process. The degree of success of the organization and the manager's job is often measured by the ratio of outputs to inputs. This ratio is an indication of the organization's **productivity.**

Productivity is a major concern for any organization because it determines the well-being of the organization and its members. Productivity is also one of the most important issues at the national level. National productivity is the aggregate of the productivity of all organizations and individuals, and it determines the standard of living, the employment level, and the economic well-being of a country.

The level of productivity, or the success of management, depends on the performance of managerial functions such as planning, organizing, directing, and controlling. To carry out these functions, managers are engaged in a continuous process of making decisions.

All managerial activities revolve around decision making. The manager is first and foremost a decision maker (see DSS in Focus 1.1). Organizations are filled with decision makers at various levels.

For years, managers have considered decision making a pure art—a talent acquired over a long period of time through experience (learning by trial and error). Management was considered an art because a variety of individual styles could be used in approaching and successfully solving the same types of managerial problems. These styles are often based on creativity, judgment, intuition, and experience rather than on systematic quantitative methods grounded in a scientific approach.

However, the environment in which management operates today is changing very rapidly. Business and its environment are more complex today than ever before, and the trend is toward increasing complexity. Figure 1.1 shows the changes in major factors that have had an impact on managerial decision making. As a result, decision making today is more complicated than it was in the past. It is more difficult to make decisions for several reasons. First, the number of available alternatives is much larger today than ever before because of improved technology and communication systems, especially the availability of the Internet and its search engines. Second, the cost of making errors can be very large because of the complexity and magnitude of operations, automation, and the chain reaction that an error can cause in many parts of the organization. Third, there are continuous changes in the fluctuating environment and more uncertainty in several impacting elements. Finally, decisions must be made quickly.

DSS IN FOCUS 1.1

ABILITY TO MAKE DECISIONS RATED FIRST IN SURVEY

In almost any survey of what constitutes good management, you are likely to find the ability to make clear-cut decisions when needed prominently mentioned.

It is not surprising, therefore, to hear that the ability to make crisp decisions was rated first in importance in a study of 6,500 managers in more than 100 companies, many of them large blue-chip corporations.

As managers entered a training course at Harbridge House, a Boston-based firm, they were asked how important it was that managers follow certain management practices. They also were asked how well, in their estimation, managers performed these practices.

From a statistical distillation of these answers, Harbridge ranked making clear-cut decisions when

needed as the most important of 10 management practices.

From these evaluations they concluded that only 20 percent of the managers performed very well on any given practice.

Ranked second in managerial importance was getting to the heart of problems rather than dealing with less important issues, a finding that shows up in similar studies. Most of the remaining eight management practices were related directly or indirectly to decision making.

Although this large-scale survey was done more than a decade ago, the situation has not changed much as shown in recent surveys published in *CIO, Datamation,* and *Information Week.*

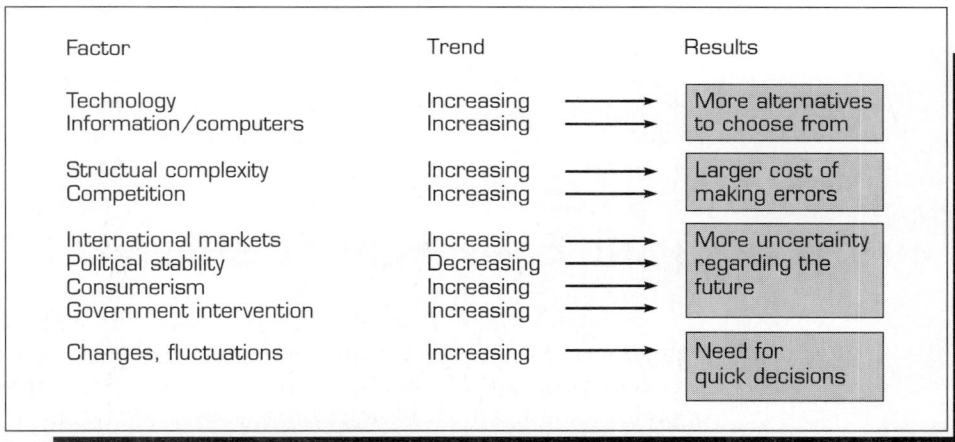

FIGURE 1.1 FACTORS AFFECTING DECISION MAKING

As a result of these trends and changes, it is very difficult to rely on a trial-and-error approach to management, especially for decisions involving the factors shown in Figure 1.1. Managers must become more sophisticated: They must learn how to use new tools and techniques that are being developed in their fields. Some of these tools and techniques are the subject of this book. Using them to support decision making can be extremely rewarding in making effective decisions. For an example of technology assisting in effective decision making, see DSS in Action 1.2.

DSS IN ACTION 1.2

TRW LAUNCHED ITS INTRANET FOR INFORMATION PUBLISHING BUT NOW RECOGNIZES IT AS A CRITICAL APPLICATION ARCHITECTURE

A manager at a TRW automotive manufacturing plant has just received an unexpected order from a major supplier of car engines. The customer needs valves, and fast. But he is also exerting considerable pressure for low prices. The manager runs a check on companies providing goods to other portions of TRW's massive automotive business with a Web browser and accesses the Supplier Data Warehouse, a repository of vendor and product information available on TRW's intranet. He chooses one of the top 10 suppliers. Because of the other business that TRW does with one of the suppliers, the manager can leverage and negotiate a great deal, despite the fact that he personally has had no prior relationship with the supplier. He passes the good price on to the customer, who is pleased with the quality and price of the valves.

TRW's intranet team considers the Supplier Data Warehouse one of the more mission-critical applications on the corporate Web. It helps TRW reduce costs by helping managers select suppliers having long-term relationships with other parts of the organization. The TRW intranet carries not only Web information (such as information about personnel and projects, and up-to-date technical documentation) but also mission-critical data such as production information for all TRW manufacturing units.

Source: Modified from B. Schultz, "Shooting for the Stars," *Intranet—A Network World Supplement,* Dec. 1996, pp. 28–34.

1.4 MANAGERS AND COMPUTERIZED SUPPORT

The impact of computer technology on organizations and society is increasing as new technologies evolve and existing technologies expand. Interaction and cooperation between people and machines are rapidly growing to cover more and more aspects of organizational activities. From traditional uses in payroll and bookkeeping functions, computerized systems are now penetrating complex managerial areas ranging from the design and management of automated factories to the evaluation of proposed mergers and acquisitions. According to Caldwell (1995), nearly all business executives say that information technology is vital to their business and that they use technologies extensively.

Computer applications are moving from transaction (or backroom) processing and monitoring activities to problem analysis and solution applications. Topics such as data access, online analytical processing, and use of the Internet and intranets for decision support are becoming the cornerstones of modern management as we enter the twenty-first century. There is a trend toward providing managers with information systems that can assist them directly in their most important task: making decisions (see DSS in Focus 1.3).

DSS IN FOCUS 1.3

THE WIDE USE OF COMPUTERS IN BUSINESS

Nine of 10 senior executives say U.S. companies have successfully made computers a vital part of their business.

Interviews with 320 chief executives, chief operating officers, and strategic planners, conducted in 1991 under the sponsorship of Digital Equipment Corporation, indicate that computers are now an integral factor in major U.S. corporations.

The results of the survey show that top executives believe that computers play significant roles throughout their enterprise. Moreover, executives believe that they personally have a role in the management of their company's computers as a strategic resource. Among highlights of the poll:

- Nine of 10 respondents said U.S. companies have been somewhat or very successful in integrating computer technology into all areas of their business.

- An overwhelming majority—98 percent—said senior executives *must* understand computers and their business impact.

- Eighty-one percent said computer networks are critical to doing business abroad.

- Eighty-eight percent said they are using computers to increase communications, and 87 percent said computers have already cut the time needed to develop products.

Source: Based on information provided by Digital Equipment Corporation.

1.5 THE NEED FOR COMPUTERIZED DECISION SUPPORT AND THE SUPPORTING TECHNOLOGIES

A computerized decision support system may be needed for various reasons. Here are some common ones:

- *Speedy computations.* A computer allows the decision maker to perform large numbers of computations very quickly and at a low cost. Timely decisions are critical for many situations, ranging from a physician's decision in an emergency room to that of a stock trader.
- *Increased productivity.* Assembling a group of decision makers, especially experts, may be costly. Computerized support can reduce the size of the group and enable the group members to be at different locations (saving travel costs). Also, the productivity of staff support (such as financial and legal analysts) may be increased.
- *Technical support.* Many decisions involve complex computations. Data can be stored in different databases and at Web sites possibly outside the organization. The data may include sound and graphics, and there may be a need to transmit them quickly from distant locations. Computers can search, store, and transmit needed data quickly and economically.
- *Quality support.* Computers can improve the quality of the decisions made. For example, more alternatives can be evaluated, risk analysis can be performed quickly, and views of experts (some of whom are in remote locations) can be collected quickly and at a lower cost. Such expertise can even

be derived directly with the use of a computer system. Using computers, decision makers can perform complex simulations, check many possible scenarios, and assess diverse impacts quickly and economically. All these capabilities lead to better decisions.

- *Competitive edge: business process reengineering and empowerment.* Competitive pressures make the job of decision making difficult. Competition is not just on price but also on quality, timeliness, customization of products, and customer support. Organizations must be able to frequently and rapidly change their mode of operation, reengineer processes and structures, empower employees, and innovate. Decision support technologies such as expert systems can create meaningful empowerment by allowing people to make good decisions quickly, even if they lack some knowledge. Decision support systems are used in business process reengineering: Research into competitors' activities, customization of products, and customer services can be facilitated by computerized voice systems (Turban et al., 1999).

- *Overcoming cognitive limits in processing and storage.* According to Simon (1977), the human mind is limited in its ability to process and store information. Also, people may have difficulty in recalling information in an error-free fashion when it is needed.

COGNITIVE LIMITS

An individual's problem-solving capability is limited when diverse information and knowledge are required. Pooling several individuals may help, but problems of coordination and communication may arise in workgroups. Computerized systems enable people to quickly access and process vast amounts of stored information. Computers can also improve coordination and communication for group work, as demonstrated in Chapters 7–9.

DECISION SUPPORT TECHNOLOGIES

Decision support can be provided by one or more decision support technologies (tools). The major decision support technologies are listed in DSS in Focus 1.4 together with the relevant chapter in this book. They are described briefly in this chapter. Which of these technologies should be used depends on the nature of the problem and the specific decision support configuration (Chapter 3).

In this text, the term **management support system (MSS)** refers to the application of any technology, either as an independent tool or in combination with other information technologies, to support management tasks in general and decision making in particular.

DSS IN FOCUS 1.4

MANAGEMENT SUPPORT SYSTEM TECHNOLOGIES (TOOLS)

- Decision support systems (DSS) (Chapter 3)
- Group support systems (GSS) (Chapter 7)
- Enterprise (executive) information systems (EIS) (Chapter 8)
- Supply chain management (SCM) (Chapter 8)
- Knowledge management (KM) (Chapter 9)

- Expert systems (ES) (Chapter 10)
- Artificial neural networks (ANN) (Chapters 15 and 16)
- Hybrid intelligent support systems (Chapter 16)
- Intelligent decision support systems (IDSS) and agents (Chapters 6 and 18)

1.6 A FRAMEWORK FOR DECISION SUPPORT

Before describing specific management support technologies, we present a classic framework for decision support. This framework provides us with several major concepts used in forthcoming definitions. It also helps us cover several additional issues, such as the relationship among the technologies and the evolution of computerized systems. This framework, shown as Figure 1.2, was proposed by Gorry and Scott Morton (1971), who combined the work of Simon (1977) and Anthony (1965). The details of this framework follow.

The left side of Figure 1.2 is based on Simon's idea that decision-making processes fall along a continuum that ranges from highly structured (sometimes called *programmed*) to highly unstructured (*nonprogrammed*) decisions. **Structured** processes are routine, and typically repetitive problems for which standard solution methods exist. **Unstructured** processes are fuzzy, complex problems for which there are no cut-and-dried solution methods. Simon also describes the decision-making process with a three-phase process of intelligence, design, and choice (for details see Chapter 2).

Intelligence: searching for conditions that call for decisions
Design: inventing, developing, and analyzing possible courses of action
Choice: selecting a course of action from those available

An *unstructured problem* is one in which none of these three phases is structured. Decisions in which some but not all of the phases are structured are called **semistructured** by Gorry and Scott Morton.

In a *structured problem,* the procedures for obtaining the best (or at least a good enough) solution are known. Whether the problem involves finding an appropriate inventory level or choosing an optimal investment strategy, the objectives are clearly defined. Common objectives are cost minimization and profit maximization. The manager can use the support of clerical, data processing, or management science models. Management support systems such as DSS and ES can be useful at times. In an *unstructured problem,* human intuition is often the basis for decision making. Typical unstructured problems include planning new services, hiring an executive, or choosing a set of research and development (R & D) projects for the next year, only part of the unstructured problem can by supported by advanced decision support tools such as intelligent decision support systems (IDSS), expert systems (ES), and knowledge management systems (KMS). *Semistructured problems* fall between structured and unstructured problems, having some structured elements and some unstructured elements. Solving them involves a combination of both standard solution procedures and human judgment. Keen and Scott Morton (1978) give the following examples of semistructured problems: trading bonds, setting marketing budgets for consumer products, and performing capital acquisition analysis. Here, a DSS can improve the quality of the information on which the decision is based by providing not only a single solution but a range of alternative solutions. These capabilities, described later, allow managers to understand the nature of problems better so that they can make better decisions.

The second half of this framework (Figure 1.2, top) is based on Anthony's (1965) taxonomy, which defines three broad categories that encompass all managerial activities: *strategic planning,* defining long-range goals and policies for resource allocation; *management control,* the acquisition and efficient use of resources in the accomplishment of

Type of Decision	Type of Control			Technology Support Needed
	Operational Control	Managerial Control	Strategic Planning	
Structured	Accounts receivable, order entry **1**	Budget analysis, short-term forecasting, personnel reports, make-or-buy **2**	Financial management (investment), warehouse location, distribution systems **3**	Management information system, operations research models, transaction processing
Semistructured	Production scheduling, inventory control **4**	Credit evaluation, budget preparation, plant layout, project scheduling, reward system design **5**	Building new plant, mergers and acquisitions, new product planning, compensation planning, quality assurance planning **6**	DSS, KMS
Unstructured	Selecting a cover for a magazine, buying software, approving loans **7**	Negotiating, recruiting an executive, buying hardware, lobbying **8**	R & D planning, new technology development, social responsibility planning **9**	IDSS, ES, neural networks
Technology Support Needed	Management information system, managment science	Management science, DSS, ES, EIS, SCM	EIS, ES, neural networks, KMS	

FIGURE 1.2 DECISION SUPPORT FRAMEWORKS

organizational goals; and *operational control*, the efficient and effective execution of specific tasks.

Anthony's and Simon's taxonomies are combined in a nine-cell decision support framework. In Figure 1.2 the right-hand column and the bottom row indicate the technologies needed to support the various decisions. Gorry and Scott Morton suggested, for example, that for semistructured and unstructured decisions, conventional **management information systems (MIS)** and management science approaches are insufficient. They proposed the use of a supportive information system, which they called a decision support system (DSS).

The more structured and operational control-oriented tasks (cells 1, 2, and 4) are performed by low-level managers, whereas the tasks in cells 6, 8, and 9 are the responsibility of top executives and/or highly trained specialists. This means that IDSS, KM, neural computing, and ES are more often applicable for people tackling specialized, complex problems.

The Gorry and Scott Morton framework is used for classifying problems and selecting appropriate tools. However, modifications may be needed because of special characteristics. For example, Murphy (1993) amended the framework by adding *novelty* and *specificity* as dimensions. Also, a combination of tools may be used.

CHAPTER 1 MANAGEMENT SUPPORT SYSTEMS: AN OVERVIEW **13**

COMPUTER SUPPORT FOR STRUCTURED DECISIONS

Structured and some semistructured decisions, especially of the operational and managerial control type, have been supported by computers since the 1960s. Decisions of this type are made in *all functional areas,* especially in finance and production (operations management).

Such problems, which are encountered fairly often, have a high level of structure. It is therefore possible to abstract and analyze them and classify them into prototypes. For example, a make-or-buy decision belongs in this category. Other examples are capital budgeting, allocation of resources, distribution problems, procurement, planning, and inventory control. For each type of problem, a prescribed solution was developed through the use of quantitative formulas or models. This approach is called **management science (MS)** or **operations research (OR).**

MANAGEMENT SCIENCE

The management science approach adopts the view that managers follow a fairly systematic process in solving problems. Therefore, it is possible to use a scientific approach to automate portions of managerial decision making. The systematic process involves the following steps:

1. Defining the problem (a decision situation that may deal with some trouble or with an opportunity).
2. Classifying the problem into a standard category.
3. Constructing a mathematical model that describes the real-world problem.
4. Finding potential solutions to the modeled problem and evaluating them.
5. Choosing and recommending a solution to the problem.

The above process is centered around modeling. Modeling involves transformation of the real-world problem into an appropriate prototype structure (model). There are computerized methodologies that help find solutions to this model quickly and efficiently. Less structured problems can be handled only by a DSS that includes customized modeling capabilities. For example, Parker et al. (1994) provide an example of why materials requirements planning (MRP) is not sufficient for labor scheduling and DSS is needed.

1.7 THE CONCEPT OF DECISION SUPPORT SYSTEMS

In the early 1970s, Scott Morton first articulated the major DSS concepts. He defined DSS as "interactive computer-based systems, which help decision makers utilize *data and models* to solve unstructured problems" (Gorry and Scott Morton, 1971). Another classic definition of DSS, provided by Keen and Scott Morton (1978), is as follows:

Decision support systems couple the intellectual resources of individuals with the capabilities of the computer to improve the quality of decisions. It is a computer-based support system for management decision makers who deal with semistructured problems.

Note that DSS, like MIS and other MSS technologies, is a content-free expression; that is, it means different things to different people. Therefore, *there is no universally accepted definition of DSS.* The major definitions of DSS will be presented in Chapter 3.

DSS AS AN UMBRELLA TERM

DSS is used by some as a specific tool. The term DSS is also sometimes used as an umbrella term to describe any and every computerized system used to support decision making in an organization. An organization might have an executive information system for its top executives, separate DSS for marketing, finance, accounting, a supply chain management (SCM) system for production, and several expert systems for product repair diagnostics and help desks. DSS encompasses them all. In contrast, a narrow definition refers to a specific technology whose definition is covered in Chapter 3.

DSS in Action 1.5 demonstrates some of the major characteristics of a DSS. The initial risk analysis was based on the decision maker's definition of the situation using a management science approach. Then, the executive vice president, using his experience, judgment, and intuition, felt that the model should be scrutinized. The initial model, although mathematically correct, was incomplete. With a regular simulation system, a modification would have taken a long time, but the DSS provided a very quick analysis. Furthermore, the DSS was flexible and responsive enough to allow managerial intuition and judgment to be incorporated into the analysis (see Chapters 4–6 for details).

How can a thorough risk analysis, such as that found in DSS in Action 1.5, be performed so quickly? How can the judgment factors be elicited, quantified, and worked into a model? How can the results be presented meaningfully and convincingly to the executive? What are "what-if" questions? The answers to these questions are provided in Chapters 3–9.

WHY USE A DSS?

The expected benefits of DSS and their determinants were studied by Udo and Guimaraes (1994) in 201 U.S. corporations. The perceived benefits discovered are higher decision quality, improved communication, cost reduction, increased productivity, time savings, and improved customer and employee satisfaction. Factors such as degree of competition, type of industry, size of the company, and user-friendliness of the DSS were found to be highly correlated with the perceived benefits of DSS.

DSS IN ACTION 1.5

THE HOUSTON MINERALS CASE

Houston Minerals Corporation was interested in a proposed joint venture with a petrochemical company to develop a chemical plant. Houston's executive vice president responsible for the decision wanted analysis of the risks involved in the areas of supplies, demands, and prices. Bob Sampson, manager of planning and administration, and his staff built a DSS in a few days by means of a specialized planning language. The results strongly suggested that the project should be accepted.

Then came the real test. Although the executive vice president accepted the validity and value of the results, he was worried about the potential downside risk of the project: the chance of a catastrophic outcome. As Sampson tells it, his words were something like this: "I realize the amount of work you have already done, and

I am 99 percent confident with it. However, I would like to see this in a different light. I know we are short of time and we have to get back to our partners with our yes or no decision."

Sampson replied that the executive could have the risk analysis he needed in less than an hour. Sampson concluded. "Within 20 minutes, there in the executive boardroom, we were reviewing the results of his 'what-if?' questions. Those results led to the eventual dismissal of the project, which we otherwise would probably have accepted."

Source: Based on unpublished information provided by Execucom Corporation, now Comshare, Inc.

Surveys conducted in the 1980s and 1990s identified the following reasons why major corporations started to develop large-scale DSS:

Companies work in an unstable economy.
There are difficulties in tracking the numerous business operations.
Competition has increased.
Electronic commerce has emerged.
Existing systems do not support decision making.
The IS department is too busy and cannot address all management inquiries.
Special analysis of profitability and efficiency is needed.
Accurate information is needed.
DSS is viewed as an organizational winner.
New information is needed.
Management mandates a DSS.
Timely information is provided.
Cost reduction is achieved.

Another reason for the development of DSS is the end-user computing movement. End users are not programmers, and so they require easy-to-use construction tools and procedures. These are provided by DSS.

The overall results of using a DSS can be very impressive, as indicated by the Atlantic Electric Company case (see DSS in Action 1.6).

1.8 GROUP SUPPORT SYSTEMS

Many major decisions in organizations are made by groups. Getting a group together in one place and at one time can be difficult and expensive. Furthermore, traditional group meetings can take a long time, and the resulting decisions may be mediocre.

DSS IN ACTION 1.6

HELPING ATLANTIC ELECTRIC COMPANY SURVIVE

Atlantic Electric Company of New Jersey was losing the monopoly it once held. Some of its old clients were already buying electricity from a new, unregulated brand of competitor: an independent cogenerator that generates its own electricity and sells its additional capacity to other companies at low prices. The competitor finds easy-to-serve commercial accounts. Atlantic Electric Company was even in danger of losing its residential customer base because the local regulatory commission was about to rule that these customers would be better served by another utility.

To *survive,* the company had to be the least expensive provider in its territory. One way to do this was to provide employees with the information they need to make more up-to-date and accurate business decisions. The old information technology included a mainframe and a corporate network for mainframe access. However, this system was unable to meet the new challenge. It was necessary to develop user applications, in a familiar format, and to do it rapidly with minimum cost. This required a PC-based DSS that currently runs on the corporate intranet.

Some of the applications are

- A decision support system for fuel-purchasing decisions
- A DSS for customized rates, based on a database for customers and their electricity usage pattern
- A DSS for substation design and transmission
- A cash management DSS for the finance department.

The implementation of these and other DSS applications helped the company to survive and by 1997 to successfully compete in its field. By 2000 the company had deployed the DSS applications on its intranet (see www.atlanticelectric.com).

Attempts to improve the work of groups with the aid of information technology have been described as groupware, electronic meeting systems, collaborative systems, and group decision support systems. Of special interest in this book are **group support systems (GSS)** (see Chapter 7 and DSS in Action 1.7).

1.9 EXECUTIVE INFORMATION (SUPPORT) SYSTEMS

Executive information systems (EIS) are developed primarily for the following objectives:

- Provide an organizational view of operations
- Serve the information needs of executives and other managers
- Provide an extremely user-friendly interface compatible with individual decision styles
- Provide timely and effective corporate level tracking and control
- Provide quick access to detailed information behind text, numbers, or graphics
- Filter, compress, and track critical data and information
- Identify problems (opportunities).

Executive information systems, which started in the mid-1980s in large corporations, have spread around the globe, have become affordable to smaller companies, and are serving many managers as enterprise-wide systems (Watson et al., 1997; Gray and Watson, 1998). In the late 1990s the focus of stand-alone EIS moved from "executives" to "enterprise" usually in which a Web-based support system serves *everyone* in the organization. (See Chapter 10.)

DSS IN ACTION 1.7

GROUPSYSTEMS ENHANCE POLICE TRAINING OF THE HONG KONG POLICE FORCE (HKPF)

THE PROBLEM

The HKPF runs management skills training courses for its officers. These involve deliberation of topics central to police work, with officers expected to reach a decision and develop an action plan. The police have traditionally used face-to-face discussion and "butcher paper" for these sessions but found that discussions lacked depth and that a minority of "loud" officers dominated many sessions.

THE SOLUTION

The course director, turned to GroupSystems software (Chapter 7) to enhance the quality of the training provided. Officers, in groups of five to eight, brainstormed issues online before voting on key solution components and developing action plans. Topics include the repatriation of Vietnamese migrants and combating CD-ROM piracy. The course director (a senior officer) used GroupSystems to inject his own contributions into the discussions as they were in progress, modifying the problem context and increasing the realism of the ma-

terial, officers being expected to incorporate these new challenges on the fly.

THE RESULTS

The officers, despite their lack of familiarity with GroupSystems, expressed general approval of the software, believing that their learning experience had been significantly enhanced and that their skills in eliciting and discussing critical issues had been developed remarkably. The course director was similarly satisfied, acknowledging that more had been accomplished than would normally be possible given session constraints. No officer rated the sessions negatively, even though some admitted their computer phobia and inability to type effectively. All used the system to contribute valuable ideas, and the dominance of individual officers was much reduced.

Source: Contributed by Robert Davison, City University of Hong Kong (Jan. 2000). Used with permission.

1.10 EXPERT SYSTEMS AND INTELLIGENT AGENTS

When an organization has a complex decision to make or a problem to solve, it often turns to experts for advice. These experts have specific knowledge about and experience in the problem area. They are aware of the alternatives, the chances of success, and the benefits and costs the business may incur. Companies engage experts for advice on such matters as what equipment to buy, mergers and acquisitions, and advertising strategy. The more unstructured the situation, the more specialized (and expensive) the advice. Expert systems attempt to mimic human experts.

Typically, an **expert system (ES)** is a decision-making or problem-solving software package that can reach a level of performance comparable to—or even exceeding—that of a human expert in some specialized and usually narrow problem area.

The basic idea behind an ES, which is an applied artificial intelligence technology, is simple. **Expertise** is transferred from the expert to a computer. This knowledge is then stored in the computer, and users call on the computer for specific advice as needed. The ES can make inferences and arrive at a specific conclusion. Then, like a human consultant, it advises nonexperts and explains, if necessary, the logic behind the advice (Jackson, 1998). Expert systems are used today in thousands of organizations, and they support many tasks [see Chapter 10 and AIS (Artificial Intelligence Systems) in Action 1.8]. Expert systems are often integrated with or even embedded in other information technologies.

AIS IN ACTION 1.8

HOW EXPERT SYSTEMS CAN PERFORM USEFUL TASKS

Suppose you manage an engineering firm that bids on many projects. Each project is, in a sense, unique. You can calculate your expected cost, but that is not sufficient to determine your bid. You have background information on your likely competitors and their bidding strategies. Something is known about the risks: possible technical problems, political delays, material shortages, or other sources of trouble. An experienced proposal manager can put all this together and, generally, arrive at a sound judgment concerning terms and bidding price. However, you do not have that many experienced proposal managers. This is where expert systems become useful. An expert system can capture the lines of thinking the experienced proposal managers can follow. It can also catalog information gained on competitors, local risks, and so on, and can incorporate your policies and strategies concerning risk, pricing, and terms. It can help your inexperienced proposal managers develop an informed bid consistent with your policy.

Suppose you are a life insurance agent and you are a very good one; however, your market has changed. You are no longer competing only with other insurance agents. You are also competing with banks, brokers, money market fund managers, and the like. Your com-

pany now carries a whole array of products, from universal life insurance to venture capital funds. Your clients have the same problems as ever, but they are more inquisitive, more sophisticated, and more conscious of tax avoidance and similar considerations. How can you give them advice and put together a sensible package for them when you are more confused than they are? Why not try an expert system for support?

Financial planning systems and estate planning guides have been part of the insurance industry's marketing kit for a long time. However, sensible financial planning takes more skill than the average insurance agent has or can afford to acquire. This is one reason why the fees of professional planners are as high as they are. A number of insurance companies have been investing heavily in artificial intelligence techniques in the hope that these techniques can be used to build sophisticated, competitive, knowledge-based financial planning support systems to assist their agents in helping their clients.

Source: Condensed from a publicly disclosed project description of Arthur D. Little, Inc.

SUMITOMO CREDIT SERVICE—AN EXPANDING WORLD MARKET

With close to 18 million cardholders and 1,800,000 merchants nationwide, the Sumitomo Credit Service Co., Ltd., is the leading credit card issuer in Japan in 2000. Sumitomo Credit Service is recognized as an innovator in the Japanese consumer credit industry, both for its international business strategy and its early adoption of technical advances in card processing.

When credit card fraud became a critical issue in the Japanese market in 1996, Sumitomo Credit Service decided to implement Falcon, a neural network-based system from HNC Corporation. The system excelled in identifying a fraud pattern that had gone undetected before. HNC had never before implemented a Japanese version of Falcon, complete with features specific to the Japanese market such as the double byte architecture necessary for Japanese characters.

Sumitomo Credit Service was the first issuer in Japan to implement predictive software solutions, and the enhanced power to predict fraud has become Sumitomo Credit Service's competitive advantage in the security and risk management area. A neural network, as we will see in Chapters 15 and 16, uses historical data to predict the future behavior of systems, people, and markets to meet the growing demand for predictive analysis to provide effective consumer business strategies.

_____

Source: Compiled from www.hnc.com, 2000.

INTELLIGENT AGENTS

Intelligent (or software) agents are used to help in automating various tasks, increasing productivity and quality manyfold. Most intelligent systems include expert systems or another intelligent component. Intelligent agents play an increasingly important role in electronic commerce (EC) (Murch and Johnson, 1999).

1.11 ARTIFICIAL NEURAL NETWORKS

Application of the previously mentioned technologies was based on the use of explicit data, information, or knowledge, which was stored in a computer and manipulated as needed. However, in the complex real world we may not have explicit data, information, or knowledge. Thus, people must make decisions based on partial, incomplete, or inexact information. Such conditions are created, for example, in rapidly changing environments. Decision makers use their experiences to handle these situations; that is, they recall similar experiences and *learn* from these experiences what to do with new similar situations for which *exact* replicas are unavailable. This approach is known as **machine learning,** and its primary tools are case-based reasoning and artificial neural computing.

Neural computing or **artificial neural networks (ANN)** use a pattern recognition approach to problem solving and have been employed successfully in many business applications (Haykin, 1999; Trippi and Turban, 1996a; Ainscough et al., 1997) (see AIS in Action 1.9).

1.12 KNOWLEDGE MANAGEMENT SYSTEMS

It is often possible to use past knowledge and expertise to expedite decision making. It does not make sense to reinvent the wheel each time a decision is made. The knowledge accumulated in organizations over time can be used to solve identical or similar problems. Several issues are involved in such a strategy: where to find knowledge, how to

DSS IN ACTION 1.10

XEROX CORPORATION'S KNOWLEDGE BASE HELPS THE COMPANY SURVIVE

With decreasing demand for copying, Xerox Corporation has been struggling to survive the digital revolution. Championed by Cindy Casslman, the company pioneered an intranet-based knowledge base in 1996, with the objective of delivering information and knowledge to the company's employees. A second objective was to create a sharing virtual community. Known as the first knowledge base (FKB), the system was designed initially to support salespeople so that they could quickly answer customers' queries. Before FKB it frequently took hours of investigation to collect information to answer one query. Since each salesperson had to deal with several queries simultaneously, clients sometimes had to wait days for a reply. Now, a salesperson can log onto the intranet and in a few minutes provide answers to the client. Customers have similar questions, and when a solution to an inquiry is found, it is indexed so it can be quickly found when needed by another salesperson. An average saving of 2 days per inquiry was realized. In addition to improved customer service, the accumulated knowledge is analyzed to learn about products' strengths and weaknesses, customer demand trends, and so on. Employees now share their knowledge and help each other. The major problem that Xerox had to solve in introducing the FKB was to persuade people to share and contribute knowledge as well as to go on the intranet and use the knowledge base. This required a cultural change that took several years to implement. The knowledge base is still evolving, solidifying and expanding rapidly. People in almost any area in the company, worldwide, are now making much faster and frequently better decisions.

classify it, how to ensure its quality, how to store it, how to maintain it, and how to use it. Furthermore, it is important to know how to motivate people to contribute their knowledge, since much knowledge is usually not documented. The technology that deals with these issues is called **knowledge management (KM)** (Liebowitz, 1999). The knowledge is organized and stored in an **organizational knowledge base.** Then, when a problem is to be solved, or an opportunity to be assessed, the relevant knowledge is extracted from the knowledge base using technologies such as intelligent agents.

Knowledge management systems appear in a variety of formats, and they can be used to support decision making in several ways, as will be illustrated in Chapter 9. One such application is demonstrated in DSS in Action 1.10.

1.13 SUPPORTING ENTERPRISE RESOURCES PLANNING AND SUPPLY CHAIN MANAGEMENT

Strong global competition is driving companies to find ways to reduce costs, improve customer service, and increase productivity. One area where substantial savings are realized is the steamlining of the various activities conducted along the supply chain, both inside a company and throughout the extended supply chain which includes suppliers, business partners, and customers (Handfield and Nichols, 1999). Using various information technologies and decision support methodologies, companies attempt to *integrate* as many information support systems as possible. Two major concepts are involved. First, **enterprise resources planning (ERP)** tries to integrate, within one organization, repetitive transaction processing systems such as ordering, producing, packaging, costing, delivery, and billing. Such integration involves many decisions that can be facilitated by DSS or provide a fertile ground for DSS applications. Second, **supply chain management (SCM)** attempts to improve tasks within the various segments of the supply chain, such as manufacturing and human resource management, as well as along the entire extended chain. SCM can be enhanced by the previously described decision support tools. SCM involves many nonroutine decisions. These topics are related to enterprise systems such as organizational decision support systems, EIS, and intranet applications. They are also related to interorganizational systems and concepts such as **customer relationship management (CRM),** extranets, and virtual organizations.

Interrelated with the above is the emerging field of **electronic commerce (EC),** (Turban et al., 2000), which includes not only electronic markets but also interorganizational electronic systems, Web-based customer services, intraorganizational applications, and business processes reengineering. Web-based EC is described in Chapter 8.

1.14 HYBRID SUPPORT SYSTEMS

The objective of a **computer-based information system (CBIS),** regardless of its name or nature, is to assist management in solving managerial or organizational problems faster and better than is possible without the use of computers. To attain this objective, the system may use one or more information technologies. The benefits of integrating technologies were investigated by Forgionne and Kohli (1995), who found significant improvements when integrated systems were used.

A useful analogy is the repair of a machine. The repairperson diagnoses the problem and looks for the best tools to use to make the repair. While one tool may be sufficient, it is often necessary to use several tools to get better results. Sometimes there are no standard tools. Then, special tools must be developed.

The managerial decision-making process described in DSS in Action 1.11 illustrates the possible need for several MSS technologies in the solution of a single problem.

DSS IN ACTION 1.11

SUPPORTING PLANNING IN CHINA'S PUBLIC SECTOR

The World Bank and the Chinese State Planning Commission developed an MSS for coal production, transportation, and consumption (in producing electricity). Coal is an important resource in China. However, insufficient production, transportation bottlenecks, and worsening air pollution are major problems.

The MSS consists of a management science optimization model, a geographical information system, and custom-made decision support models, resulting in a large-scale *hybrid support system.*

The core model included 26,100 variables and 6,400 constraints. It is designed to find the optimal type, location, scale, and timing of investment projects; the optimal coal and electricity distribution and flows; the optimal use of existing mines; the predicted locations of bottlenecks and shortages; system-wide cost; and amounts of ash and sulfur in the delivered coal.

The support system could help China solve one of its most critical problems, which is threatening to curtail China's growth, by increasing coal production from 1.1 billion tons in 1991 to 6.4 billion tons in 2005. The complexity of the problem requires a hybrid support system where several tools are incorporated in a large-scale model. Preliminary results reported in *China Daily,* Jan. 21, 1996, indicated the success of the plan in significantly increasing coal production.

Source: Condensed from M. Kub et al., "Planning China's Coal and Electricity Delivery Systems," *Interfaces,* Jan./Feb. 1995.

Indeed, many complex problems require several MSS technologies, as illustrated in the Opening Vignette and throughout this book. When a problem solver uses several tools, he or she can employ them in different ways. The following are some possible approaches:

- Use each tool in an independent way to solve a different aspect of the problem.
- Use several tools that are loosely integrated. Such an approach mainly involves transferring data from one tool to another (e.g., from an ES to a DSS) for further processing.
- Use several tools in a tightly integrated manner. That is, the tool appears as one hybrid system to the user.

Note that the key is the *successful solution* of managerial problems, not the use of a specific tool or technique.

In addition to performing different tasks in the problem-solving process, tools can support each other. For example, an expert system can enhance the modeling and data management of a DSS. A neural computing system or a GSS can support the knowledge acquisition process required for building an expert system. Expert systems and artificial neural networks are playing an increasingly important role in supporting other MSS technologies (making them "smarter"). It is becoming increasingly feasible economically to build all kinds of hybrid MSS. The components of such systems include not only MSS but also management science, statistics, and a variety of computer-based tools. These tools can be provided by different vendors. Improved capabilities of networks and of the major operating systems facilitate the process of quickly and accurately building MSS.

1.15 THE EVOLUTION AND ATTRIBUTES OF COMPUTERIZED DECISION AIDS

Computers have been used as tools to support managerial decision making for over four decades. Table 1.2 presents a summary of the development of computerized procedures used as aids in decision making. The support to specific questions provided by DSS is illustrated in Table 1.3.

There are several opinions about the evolution of management support tools and their relationship to the other systems. A common view is that the recommendations and advice provided by MSS to the manager can be considered information needed for final decisions made by humans. If we accept this approach, we can consider MSS sophisticated, high-level types of information systems that can be used in addition to traditional transaction processing systems, office automation, and MIS.

The evolutionary view of computer-based information systems (CBIS) has a strong logical basis. First, there is a clear-cut sequence through time: Transaction processing systems appeared in the mid-1950s, MIS followed in the 1960s, office automation systems were developed mainly in the 1970s, and DSS was a product of the 1970s that was expanded in the 1980s. Commercial applications of expert systems and executive information systems emerged in the 1980s. In the 1990s, we saw group support systems and neural computing emerging, as well as many **hybrid (integrated) computer systems.** Entering the twenty-first century, we see a trend toward Web-based applications, use of a knowledge management approach, and incorporation of

TABLE 1.2   Aids in Decision Making

Phase	Description	Examples of Tools
Early	Compute "crunch numbers," summarize, and organize.	Calculators, early computer programs, statistical models, simple management science models.
Intermediate	Find, organize, and display decision-relevant information.	Database management systems, MIS, filing systems, management science models.
Current	Perform decision-relevant computations on decision-relevant information; organize and display the results; query-based and user-friendly approach; what-if analysis; interact with decision makers to facilitate formulation and execution of the intellectual steps in the process of decision making.	Financial models, spreadsheets, trend exploration, operations research models, computer-assisted design (CAD) systems, decision support systems. Expert systems, executive information systems.
Just beginning	Complex and fuzzy decision situations, expanding to collaborative decision making and machine learning. Using ERP software, the Web, and electronic commerce.	Second-generation expert systems, group support systems, neural computing, knowledge management, Fuzzy logic, intelligent agents, SAP.

TABLE 1.3   The Support Provided by DSS*

DSS Provides	Answers to Questions
Raw data and status access	What is . . . ?
↓	
General analysis capabilities	What is/why . . . ?
↓ ↑	
Representation models (financial statements), causal models (forecasting, diagnosis)	What will be . . . ?
↓	Why . . . ?
Solution suggestions, evaluation	What if . . . ?
↓	Why . . . ?
Solution selection	What is best/what is good enough . . . ?

*DSS may provide several types of support. The structure above is based on Alter (1980). Each level of support contains and adds to the previous level (but may also contribute to the previous level).

decision support capability in supply chain management and ERP. Second, there is a common technology linking the various types of CBIS: the computer, which itself has evolved considerably over time. And third, there are systemic linkages in the manner in which each system processes data into information. Additional support for the evolutionary view is presented in Figure 1.3. This figure lists the attributes

Dimension	Transactions Processing Systems (TPS)	Management Information Systems (MIS)	Decision Support Systems (DSS)	Expert Systems (ES)	Executive Information Systems (EIS)	Neural Computing	(KMS)
Applications	Payroll, inventory, recordkeeping, production and sales information	Production control, sales forecasting, monitoring	Long-range strategic planning, complex integrated problem areas	Diagnosis, strategic planning, internal control planning, strategies	Support to top management decisions, environmental scanning	Complex, repetitive decisions; diagnosis, control investment	Complex decisions in a changing environment
Focus	Data transactions	Information	Decisions, flexibility, user-friendliness	Inferencing, transfer of expertise	Tracking, control, drill-down	Pattern recognition	Reusability of best practices
Database	Unique to each application, batch update	Interactive access by programmers	Database management systems, interactive access, factual knowledge	Procedural and factual knowledge; knowledge base (facts, rules)	External (online) and corporate, enterprise-wide access (to all databases)	Historical cases, provide learning	Organizational knowledge repository
Decision Capabilities	No decisions	Structured routine problems using conventional management science tools	Semistructured problems, integrated management science models, blend of judgment and modeling	System makes complex decisions, unstructured; use of rules (heuristics)	Only when combined with a DSS	Mainly predictions, based on historical cases	Complex, including enterprise level
Manipulation	Numerical	Numerical	Numerical	Symbolic	Numeric (mainly), some symbolic	Numeric needs preprocessing	Numeric, qualitative, symbolic
Type of Information Generated	Summary reports, operational	Scheduled and demand reports, structured flow, exception reporting	Information to support specific decisions	Advice and explanations	Status access, exception reporting, key indicators	Forecasts, classification to patterns	Advice, knowledge, know-how
Highest Organizational Level Served	Submanagerial, low-level management	Middle management	Analysts and managers	Managers and specialists	Senior executives (only)	Specialists, managers	Managers, specialists
Impetus	Expediency	Efficiency	Effectiveness	Effectiveness and expediency	Timeliness	Expediency	Effectiveness, expediency

FIGURE 1.3 ATTRIBUTES OF THE MAJOR COMPUTERIZED SUPPORT SYSTEMS

of the major CBIS classified into several dimensions. Only the most sophisticated attributes of each level are listed. Most CBIS have several lesser attributes which are not listed.

The relationships among these and other technologies (not shown in Figure 1.3) can be summarized as follows:

- Each technology can be viewed as a unique class of information technology (IT).
- The technologies are interrelated, and each supports some aspects of managerial decision making.
- The evolution and creation of newer tools help expand the role of information technology for the betterment of management in organizations.
- The interrelationship and coordination among these tools is still evolving.

1.16 PLAN OF THIS BOOK

The 19 chapters of this book are organized in six parts (Figure 1.4).

Part I: Decision Making and Computerized Support
This part includes two chapters. In Chapter 1, an introduction, definitions, and an overview are provided. In Chapter 2, the process of managerial decision making and modeling is described.

Part II: Decision Support Systems
This part includes four chapters. Chapter 3 provides an overview of DSS and its major components. Chapter 4 presents the topics of databases, data warehouses, data analysis, and visualization. Chapter 5 deals with modeling and analysis. Here, a discussion is presented about structured models as well as about modeling tools and languages for creating nonstructured models. Chapter 6 describes the process of developing DSS both by IS professionals and by end users.

Part III: Collaboration, Communication, and Enterprise Support Systems
This part contains four chapters. Chapter 7 deals with the support provided to groups working in the same room or at different locations, and the role of the Web is highlighted. Chapter 8 covers the topic of enterprise-wide systems, including the topics of integration, SCM, ERP, and decisions along the supply chain. The last chapter in this part provides a discussion of knowledge management at the enterprise level.

Part IV: Fundamentals of Expert Systems and Intelligent Systems
The fundamentals of artificial intelligence and expert systems are the subject of Chapter 10. Methods of knowledge acquisition are considered in Chapter 11, and representation and inference techniques are the subjects of Chapters 12 and 13. The process of developing intelligent systems is described in Chapter 14.

Part V: Advanced Intelligent Systems
This part is divided into three chapters. Chapters 15 and 16 cover artificial neural computing and its applications, respectively. In addition, Chapter 16 covers genetic algorithms, fuzzy logic, qualitative reasoning, and hybrid intelligent systems. The role of intelligent agents in decision support in general and in decisions related to electronic commerce in particular, is the subject of Chapter 17.

Part VI: Implementation, Integration, and Impacts
This concluding part contains two chapters. The integration and implementation of MSS are described in Chapter 18. Finally, MSS organizational and societal impacts are considered in Chapter 19.

WEB SITE
This book's Web site, www.prenhall.com/turban, contains a wealth of supplemental material organized by chapters. These include: PowerPoint presentations, teaching notes, appendices, cases, links to cases, software links, demo links, data files, uniform resource locators (URLs) for many resources, additional problems, and late-breaking developments in MSS.

❖ CHAPTER HIGHLIGHTS

- The rate of computerization is increasing rapidly, and so is its use for managerial decision support.

FIGURE 1.4 PLAN OF THIS BOOK

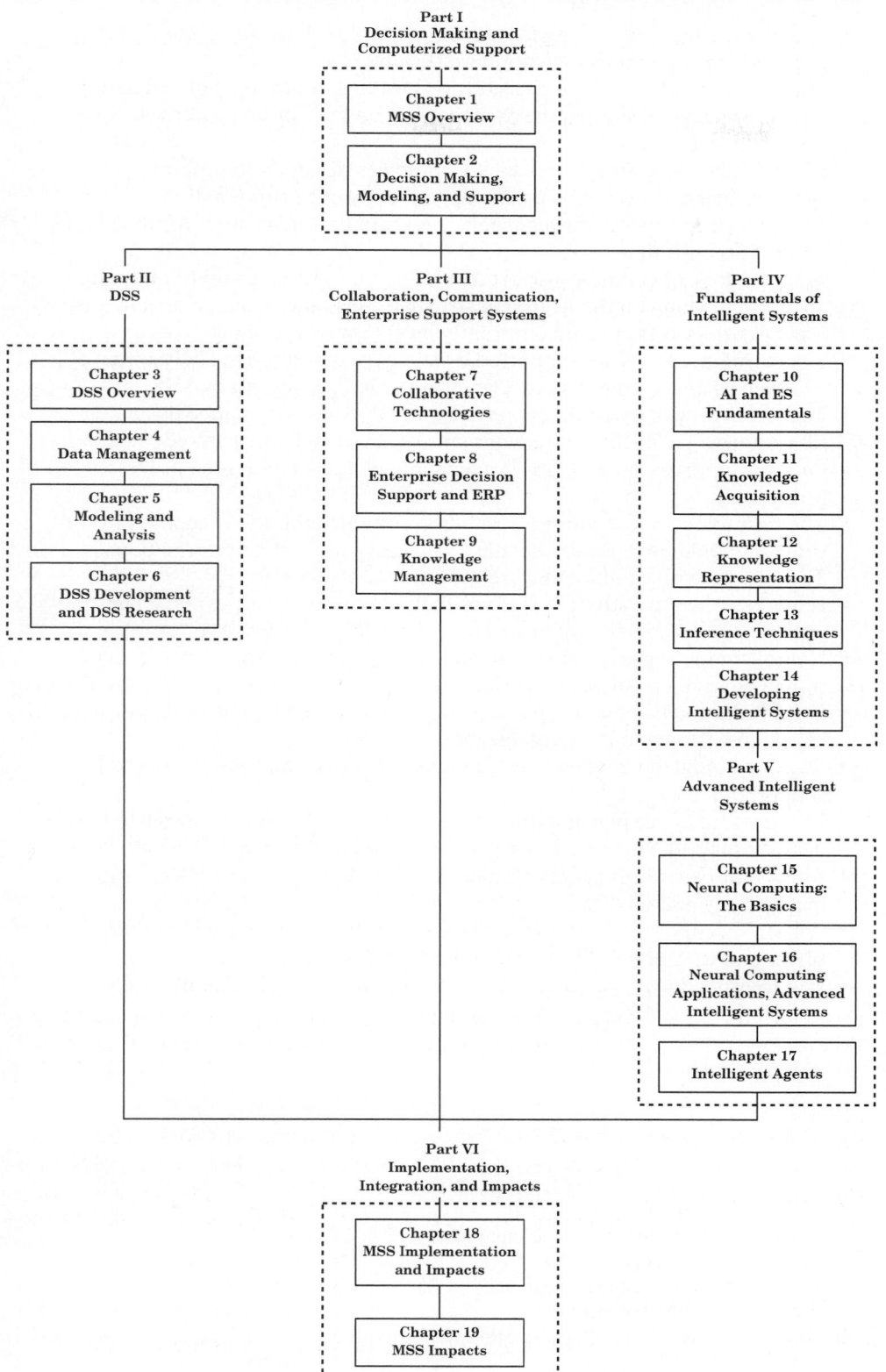

- Managerial decision making is becoming complex. Therefore, intuition and trial-and-error methods may not be sufficient.
- The time frame for making decisions is shrinking, whereas its global nature is expanding, necessitating the development and use of computerized decision support systems.
- Management support systems are technologies designed to support management work. They can be used independently or in combination.
- Computerized support for managers is essential, in many cases for the survival of organizations.
- A framework of decision support divides decision situations into nine categories, depending on the degree of structuredness and managerial activities. Each category is supported differently by computers.
- Structured decisions are supported by standard quantitative analysis methods such as management science and capital budgeting and by MIS.
- The technology of decision support systems (DSS) uses data, models, and possibly knowledge for the solution of semistructured and unstructured problems.
- Group support systems (GSS) is a technology that supports the processes of group work.
- The technology of executive information systems supports executives by providing them with timely, detailed, and easy-to-visualize information. These have evolved into enterprise information systems.
- Expert systems are advisory systems that attempt to mimic experts. The main feature of expert systems is the application of knowledge.
- Neural computing is a technology that attempts to exhibit pattern recognition by learning from past experiences.
- Knowledge management systems capture, store and disseminate important know-how throughout an organization.
- Organizational knowledge bases contain knowledge that can be reused to support complex decisions.
- Enterprise resource planning and supply chain management are correlated with decision support, electronic commerce, and customer relationship management.
- Intelligent (software) agents automate mundane tasks, thereby increasing productivity and quality.
- All MSS technologies are interactive and can be integrated among themselves and with other CBIS, resulting in hybrid systems.
- The Internet, intranets, and extranets facilitate the development, dissemination, and use of MSS.

❖ KEY WORDS

- Artificial neural networks (ANN)
- Cognitive limits
- Computer-based information system (CBIS)
- Customer relationship management (CRM)
- Decision support systems (DSS)
- Electronic commerce (EC)
- Enterprise resource planning (ERP)
- Executive information system (EIS)
- Expert system (ES)
- Expertise
- Group support systems (GSS)
- Intelligent agent (IA)
- Hybrid (integrated) computer systems
- Knowledge management (KM)
- Machine learning
- Management information system (MIS)
- Management science (MS)
- Management support system (MSS)
- Operations research (OR)
- Organizational knowledge base
- Productivity
- Semistructured decisions
- Structured decisions
- Supply chain management (SCM)
- Transaction processing system (TPS)
- Unstructured decisions

❖ QUESTIONS FOR REVIEW

1. What caused the latest revolution in management use of computers? List at least two causes.
2. What is a computer-based information system (CBIS)?
3. List and define the three phases of the decision-making process (according to Simon).
4. Define DSS.
5. Discuss the major characteristics of DSS.
6. List five major benefits of DSS.
7. Management is often equated with decision making. Why?
8. Discuss the major trends that affect managerial decision making.
9. Define management science.
10. Define structured, semistructured, and unstructured decisions.
11. Categorize managerial activities (according to Anthony).
12. Define expert system.
13. Define knowledge management.
14. List the major benefits of ES.
15. Trace the evolution of CBIS.
16. Define intelligent agents.
17. Define group support systems.
18. Relate DSS to SCM, ERP, and the Web.
19. Define neural computing.
20. What is a hybrid support system?

❖ QUESTIONS FOR DISCUSSION

1. Give additional examples for the content of each cell in Figure 1.2.
2. Design a computerized system for a brokerage house that trades in securities, conducts research on companies, and provides information and advice to customers (such as "buy," "sell," and "hold"). In your design, clearly distinguish seven parts: TPS, MIS, DSS, EIS, ANN, ES, and KMS. Be sure to deal with input and output information. Assume that the brokerage company is a small one with only 20 branches in four different cities.
3. Survey the literature of the last 6 months to find one application of each MSS technologies. Summarize the applications on one page and submit it with a copy of the articles.
4. Observe an organization with which you are familiar. List three decisions it makes in each of the following categories: strategic planning, management control (tactical planning), and operational planning and control.
5. What capabilities are provided by ANN and not by another MSS?
6. Describe how hybrid systems might help a manager in decision making.
7. Indicate which MSS can be used to assist a manager in fulfilling Mintzberg's 10 management roles. How and why can they help?
8. Why is the role of KM so important for decision support? Discuss an example of how the two can be integrated.
9. Why is electronic commerce related to ERP and decision support?

❖ Exercise

1. Write a report describing how your company, or a company you are familiar with, currently uses computers and information systems in any decision making. Then, considering the material in this chapter, describe how you could use such support systems if they were readily available (which ones are available to you and which ones are not?).

❖ Group Exercises

1. Find information on the proactive use of computers to support ad hoc decisions versus TPS. Each member of the group chooses an application in a different industry (such as banking, insurance, or food). The group summarizes the findings and points out the similarities and differences of the applications.

2. Use as sources companies where students are employed, trade magazines, Internet newsgroups, and vendor Web sites. Finally, prepare a class presentation on the findings.

❖ Internet Exercises

1. Search the Internet for material regarding the work of managers, the need for computerized support, and the role decision support systems play in providing such support (use elibrary.com, infoseek.com, and cio.com). What kind of references to consulting firms, academic departments, and programs do you find? What major areas are represented? Pick five references in one area and report your findings.

2. Enter dssresources.com. Explore the site and prepare a list of the major available resources. You will need to use this site frequently.

3. Enter this book's Web site: www.prenhall.com/turban; go to the DSS book and familiarize yourself with the site. Prepare a list of major resources available.

4. Enter www.sap.com and www.peoplesoft.com and find information on how ERP software helps decision makers. Also, examine the relationship with the Web.

5. Enter www.intelligententerprise.com. For each topic cited in this chapter find some interesting development reported on the site and prepare a report.

MANUFACTURING AND MARKETING OF MACHINE DEVICES

PART A: THE 1998 CRISIS

Durapart is a medium-sized manufacturer of specialized mattel (metallic) devices in southern California. The company has had a reputation for excellent quality and customer service. The company formerly made about 30 different products and sold them to several hundred clients, mainly in the food processing industry. The company was successful in competing against several Japanese competitors.

However, the situation changed drastically in the mid-1990s. While demand weakened because of the slow economy, customers' requirements for low prices and customized products increased. Durapart found itself changing products constantly. In 1997 the number of products grew to 58, and in 1998 to 119. In both years, the company reported losses. Furthermore, competing Japanese companies decreased their prices and Durapart lost market share.

The company's problems were created because of two major factors: First, it was difficult to forecast demand because of the frequent introduction of new and modified products. Second, it was difficult to schedule production and change it quickly enough to meet changing market requirements. Attempts to increase productivity and reduce costs failed.

In an emergency meeting conducted on July 1, 1999, the company decided, as a last resort, to try applying some Web-based MSS. As Jim West, the CEO, put it, "After all, these neural machines and gigabytes should certainly help us to survive, especially when implemented on the Web."

Nancy Chen, the IS director, was less optimistic. She explained that there are different MSS from many vendors and that the technologies are fairly new. She said that it would take several months before a plan could be completed and that it would take an additional year to implement it.

CASE QUESTIONS

1. Which MSS technique is most likely to be selected by Ms. Chen, and why? (If several techniques can be used, rank them by a descending order of likelihood of success and explain your ranking.)
2. Should MSS tools be used in this situation at all?

PART B: THE YEAR 2000 SITUATION

John Morgan was known as a top production manager in the industry. Mr. Morgan, age 65, retired at the end of 1998 and moved to Long Beach, CA, to enjoy sailing and golf. He had over 40 years of experience working for three companies, including Durapart. He played golf with Jim West on a regular basis. When Jim told him about the company's problem, he came up with the following suggestion: "Listen, Jim, between you and me, you are heading for bankruptcy. What if you hire me on a part-time basis to help you solve the problem?"

Mr. Morgan started his mission in early 2000. In a few months, he had changed the situation drastically. Not only was he able to predict market demand better than anyone else, but he also was able to flexibly schedule production.

At that time he requested an advance of several hundred thousand dollars against his salary for the next 5 years.

An emergency management meeting was called again.

MR. WEST: I think that we should give John the money and stop messing around with the idea of computers. John promised me that, within several years, he can train two or three of our employees so they can take over his job when he is ready for full retirement.

MS. CHEN: What if he drops dead?

MR. WEST: We will insure him so that we will get back the money advanced.

MS. CHEN: I am not worried about the advance, but I am worried about the fate of the company in the event that Mr. Morgan dies before his replacements are trained. I feel that we must evaluate the feasibility of MSS technologies. We will be too dependent on one person who may not be around for a long time. Also, today's Web technologies makes it cheaper and easier to acquire and disseminate knowledge electronically.

CASE QUESTIONS

1. Evaluate the following three alternatives:
   a. Hire Mr. Morgan; forget MSS.
   b. Accelerate the evaluation of MSS technologies; forget Mr. Morgan.
   c. Combine alternatives (a) and (b).
2. Discuss the pluses and minuses of each alternative. Which one would you select and why?
3. Which of the MSS techniques is (are) most likely to be selected by Ms. Chen, and why?
4. How can the Web be utilized?

DECISION MAKING, SYSTEMS, MODELING, AND SUPPORT

The major focus of this book is the computerized support of decision making. The purpose of this chapter is to describe the conceptual foundations of decision making and the systems approach, and how support is provided. This chapter covers

2.1 OPENING VIGNETTE: HOW TO INVEST $10 MILLION

When Grandpa Sam passed away at the age of 91, he left a pleasant surprise for his seven grandchildren. Unknown to the family, Grandpa Sam was a skillful investor in the stock market and kept this hobby to himself. The family knew that he was investing in stocks, however, no one suspected that he had accumulated substantial equity.

According to his will, after taxes were paid, his grandchildren would receive more than $10 million. The will contained one stipulation: The money could not be divided for 20 years. It was the responsibility of the grandchildren (whose ages ranged from 18 to 43) to manage the investment collectively. Grandpa Sam wanted the family "to preserve its unity and work together for everyone's well-being."

When the surprised grandchildren met to discuss how to manage the money, it became apparent that Sam's hoped-for unity preservation would not be easy. Here is the discussion that occurred at the first family investment meeting:

BRIAN: I really don't know much about investing. Could we put the money in a mutual fund? It should do pretty well.

BOB: That's silly. First off, there are thousands of different funds, and second, most of them perform badly.

BRIAN: But I just heard on the news that several high-tech Internet-based mutual funds outperformed the market because they aggressively sought out IPOs, whatever those are.

DAVE: I disagree. I think we should buy only real estate. Why risk the money in the stock market? Remember, Uncle Harold had that big farm and made his fortune by selling it to those condo developers!

JUDY: I disagree. He bought that farm when land was only pennies per acre. Why don't we just buy CDs? They're really safe investments.

SHARON: But, in the long run, stocks always do much better than CDs.

JUDY: Can you *guarantee* that this situation will occur once we enter the market? What if the historical trend reverses?

SHARON: The President mentioned in yesterday's news that the economy will be stronger than ever.

DAVE: Get real! You can't trust a politician! *Ever!*

CARL: Why don't we invest in old paintings and antiques. My wealthy brother-in-law buys and sells them and told me that this is the best investment right now. He'd be willing to help us out.

JUDY: Sure! And he'd collect a commission on each item. You all want to be speculators! I want a really safe investment. My kids will be going to college soon, and I'll need to use the income for tuition. And by the way, how are we going to predict the success of any of these speculative investments? Markets always fluctuate.

BOB: I don't want to sacrifice potential profit for safety. I think we should assume *some* risk to get better returns than from CDs. This isn't speculation, is it? Let's buy some stocks and see what happens.

JUDY: But which stocks? I think you're crazy! We shouldn't do this. We could lose lots of money just waiting to see what happens. This happened to my college fund 20 years ago when the market kept dropping and our broker said, "Keep buying, it'll go up soon!"

BRIAN: Hey guys, I'm the youngest, and I'm really confused. Do any of you know how serious investors make this decision? I'm pretty sure they don't do what we're doing. I wonder how Grandpa did it?

KAREN: Hmmm. I agree with Brian. Let's find out how serious investment decisions are made by expert investors. I suggest we first get the money into a bank account to start accruing interest. Then we should contact Grandpa's financial advisor! I'll call Grandma!

All the grandchildren agreed, and they lived happily, and wealthily, ever after.

❖ QUESTIONS FOR THE OPENING VIGNETTE

1. Identify the conflicting objectives.
2. Identify the uncertainties.

3. Identify the alternative courses of action (can they be combined?) and the criteria that should be considered in making a decision.

4. What are the possible results of the decision? Why might the results be difficult to predict?

5. What kind of risk is associated with the decision? What were the decision makers' different attitudes toward risk? How could they influence the decision?

6. Can the decision be changed if the economic environment changes? How hard or easy would it be to change the decision once it is made? What could it cost?

7. What kinds of problems in the decision-making process is the family encountering because they currently lack good information and expertise?

8. What kinds of problems in the decision-making process is the family encountering because a group is involved in the decision? How could you eliminate or at least minimize these problems?

9. What decision would you make and why?

2.2 DECISION MAKING: INTRODUCTION AND DEFINITIONS

The Opening Vignette demonstrated some aspects of a typical business decision:

- The decision may be made by a group.
- Group members may have biases.
- Groupthink (buy-in by group members without any thinking) can lead to bad decisions.
- There are several possibly conflicting objectives.
- There may be many (hundreds or even thousands) of alternatives to consider.
- The results of making a business decision usually materialize in the future. No one is a perfect predictor of the future, especially in the long run.
- Many decisions involve risk. Different people have different attitudes toward risk.
- There may not be sufficient information to make an intelligent decision.
- Gathering information and analyzing the problem takes time and is expensive. It is difficult to determine when to stop this and make a decision.
- There may be too much information available (information overload).
- Decision makers are interested in evaluating what-if scenarios.
- Experimentation with the real system (i.e., investing and seeing what will happen—trial and error) may result in a loss.
- Experimentation with the real system is possible only for one set of conditions at a time and can be disastrous.
- Changes in the decision-making environment may occur continuously, leading to invalidating assumptions about the situation.
- Changes in the decision-making environment may impact on decision quality by imposing time pressure on the decision maker.

To determine how real decision makers make decisions, we must first understand the process and the important issues of decision making. Then we can understand appropriate methodologies for assisting decision makers and the roles that information systems can play. And only then can we develop decision support systems to help decision makers. We address these topics next.

This chapter is organized along the three key words that form the term *DSS: decision, support,* and *systems.* Support is provided through a rational modeling approach that simplifies reality and provides a relatively quick and inexpensive means of experimenting with various alternative courses of action.

DECISION MAKING

Decision making is a process of choosing among alternative courses of action for the purpose of attaining a goal or goals. According to Simon (1977), *managerial decision making is synonymous with the whole process of management.* Consider the important managerial function of planning. Planning involves a series of decisions: What should be done? When? How? Where? By whom? Hence, planning implies decision making. Other functions in the management process, such as organizing and controlling, also involve making decisions.

DECISION MAKING AND PROBLEM SOLVING

A problem occurs when a system does not meet its established goals, does not yield the predicted results, or does not work as planned. Problem solving may also deal with identifying new *opportunities.* Differentiating between the terms **decision making** and **problem solving** can be confusing. One way to distinguish between the two is to examine the phases of the decision process. These phases are (1) intelligence, (2) design, (3) choice, and (4) implementation (Section 2.5). Some consider the entire process (phases 1–4) as problem solving, with the choice phase as the real decision making. Others view phases 1–3 as formal decision making ending with a recommendation, whereas problem solving additionally includes the actual implementation of the recommendation (phase 4). We use the terms *decision making* and *problem solving* interchangeably.

DECISION-MAKING DISCIPLINES

Decision making is directly influenced by several major disciplines, some behavioral and some scientific in nature. We must be aware of how their philosophies can impact our ability to make decisions and provide support. Behavioral disciplines include

- Philosophy
- Psychology
- Sociology
- Social psychology
- Law
- Anthropology
- Political science.

Scientific disciplines include

- Economics
- Statistics
- Decision Analysis
- Mathematics
- Management science/operations research
- Computer science.

Each discipline has its own set of assumptions about reality and methods. Each also contributes a unique, valid view of how people make decisions. See Harrison (1999) for

DSS IN ACTION 2.1

THE 75 GREATEST MANAGEMENT DECISIONS EVER MADE

Management Review asked experts for their nominations of the 75 greatest management decisions ever made. The resulting list is both eclectic and eccentric. All the decisions were *successful* and had *major impact.* Here is a sample:

- Walt Disney listened to his wife, Lillian, and named his cartoon mouse Mickey instead of Mortimer. Entertainment was never the same after Mickey and Minnie debuted in *Steamboat Willie* in 1928.

- As ambassador to France in the 1780s, Benjamin Franklin spent his time encouraging the emigration of skilled workers to the United States—an early instance of poaching staff.

- Around 59 B.C., Julius Caesar kept people up to date with handwritten sheets that were distributed in Rome and, it is suspected, with posters that were placed around the city. The greatness of leaders has been partly measured ever since by their ability to communicate.

- Ignoring market research, Ted Turner launched the Cable News Network in 1980. No one thought a 24-hour news network would work. It did.

- During World War II, Robert Woodruff, president of Coca-Cola, committed to selling bottles of Coke to members of the Armed Services for a nickel a bottle. Customer loyalty never came cheaper.

- In 1924 Thomas Watson, Sr., changed the name of the Computing-Tabulating-Recording Company to International Business Machines. The company had no international operations, but it was a bold statement of ambitions.

- In 1981 Bill Gates decided to license MS/DOS to IBM, while IBM ceded control of the license for all non-IBM PCs. This laid the foundation for Microsoft's huge success and IBM's fall from grace.

- The Chinese Qin Dynasty (221–206 B.C.) produced the Great Wall—a fantastic feat of both management and engineering. They also developed what is reputed to be the first reliable system of weights and measures, thereby aiding commercial development.

- In the nineteenth century, Andrew Carnegie decided to import British steel and steelmaking processes to America to build railway bridges made of steel instead of wood. The imported skills ignited the U.S. steel industry, and Carnegie became a steel baron.

- Queen Isabella of Spain decided to sponsor Columbus' voyage to the New World in 1492— the ultimate in R&D.

Source: Adapted from Anonymous, "Top 75: The Greatest Management Decisions Ever Made," *Management Review,* Vol. 87, No. 10, Nov., 1998, pp. 20–23; and S. Crainer, "The 75 Greatest Management Decisions Ever Made" *Management Review,* Vol. 87, No. 10, Nov. 1998, pp. 16–19.

more details. Finally, there is much variation in what constitutes a successful decision in practice. To examine this variation, we provide a sample of the "75 greatest management decisions ever made" in DSS in Action 2.1.

2.3 SYSTEMS

The acronyms *DSS, GSS, EIS,* and *ES* include the term *systems.* A **system** is a collection of objects such as people, resources, concepts, and procedures intended to perform an identifiable function or to serve a goal. For example, a university is a system of students, faculty, staff, administrators, buildings, equipment, ideas, and rules with the goal of educating students, producing research, and providing service to the community (another system). A clear definition of the goal is a critical consideration in MSS design. For example, the purpose of an air defense system is to protect ground targets, not just to destroy attacking aircraft or missiles.

The notion of levels (a hierarchy) of systems reflects that all systems are actually subsystems because all are contained within some larger system. For example, a bank includes subsystems such as a commercial loan department, a consumer loan department, a savings department, and an operations department. The bank itself may also be a branch that is part of a collection of other banks, and these banks may collectively be a subsidiary of a holding corporation, such as the Bank of America, which is a subsystem of the California banking system, which is part of the national banking system, which is part of the national economy, and so on. The interconnections and interactions among the subsystems are called **interfaces.**

THE STRUCTURE OF A SYSTEM

Systems (Figure 2.1) are divided into three distinct parts: inputs, processes, and outputs. They are surrounded by an environment and often include a feedback mechanism. In addition, a human decision maker is considered part of the system.

INPUTS
Inputs are elements that enter the system. Examples of inputs are raw materials entering a chemical plant, students admitted to a university, or data input into a computer.

PROCESSES
Processes are all the elements necessary to convert or transform inputs into outputs. For example, a process in a chemical plant may include heating the materials, using operating procedures, using a material-handling subsystem, and using employees and machines. In a university, a process may include holding classes and performing library work. In a computer, a process may include activating commands, executing computations, and storing information.

FIGURE 2.1 THE SYSTEM AND ITS ENVIRONMENT

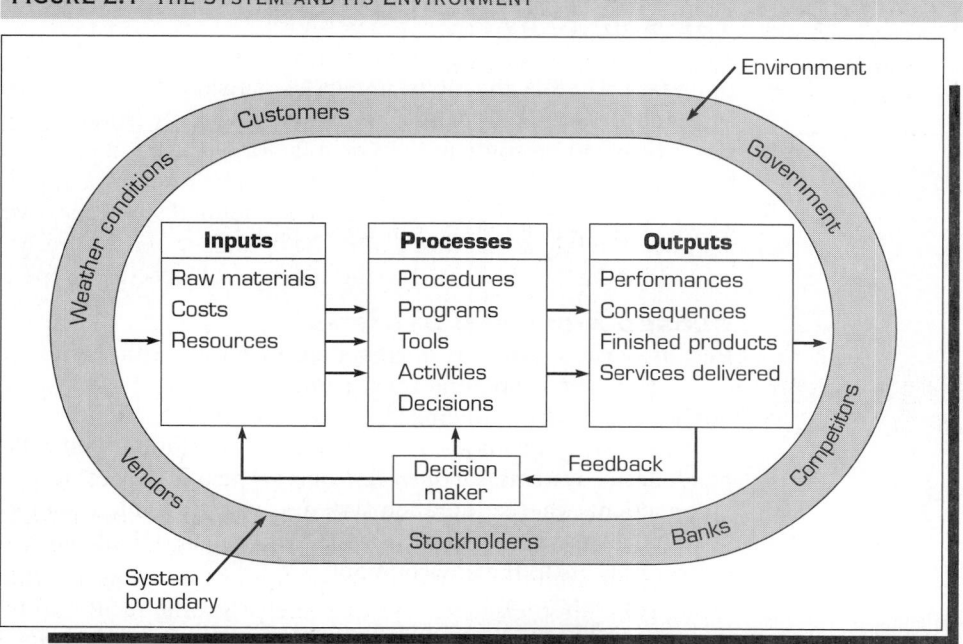

Outputs

Outputs are the finished products or the consequences of being in the system. For example, fertilizers are one output of a chemical plant, educated people are one output of a university, and reports may be the outputs of a computer system.

Feedback

There is a flow of information from the output component to the decision maker concerning the system's output or performance. Based on the outputs, the decision maker, who acts as a control, may decide to modify the inputs, the processes, or both. This information flow, appearing as a closed loop (Figure 2.1), is called feedback. This is how real systems monitoring occurs. The decision maker compares the outputs to the expected outputs and adjusts the inputs and possibly the processes to move closer to the output targets.

The Environment

The environment of the system is composed of several elements that lie outside it in the sense that they are not inputs, outputs, or processes. However, they affect the system's performance and consequently the attainment of its goals. One way to identify the elements of the environment is by posing two questions (Churchman, 1975):

- Does the element matter relative to the system's goals?
- Is it possible for the decision maker to significantly manipulate this element?

If and only if the answer to the first question is yes, and the answer to the second is no, is the element in the environment. Environmental elements can be social, political, legal, physical, and economical. Often they consist of other systems. For a chemical plant, the suppliers, competitors, and customers are elements of the environment. A state university may be affected by rules and laws passed by the state legislature, but for the most part the legislature is part of the environment since the university system has no impact on it. (In some cases, they may interact, though, and the environment is redefined.) A DSS designed to set tuition rates would not then normally interact with the state government.

The Boundary

A system is separated from its environment by a *boundary*. The system is inside the boundary, whereas the environment lies outside. A boundary can be physical (e.g., the system is a department with a boundary defined by Building C or the boundary is your skin), or it can be some nonphysical factor. For example, a system can be bounded by time. In such a case, we can analyze an organization for a period of only 1 year.

The boundary of a system is usually defined when narrowing a system's scope to simplify its analysis. In other words, the boundary of a system, especially a DSS, is by design. Boundaries are related to the concepts of closed and open systems.

Closed and Open Systems

Because every system is a subsystem of another, the system analysis process might never end. Therefore, one must confine the system analysis to defined, manageable boundaries. Such confinement is called *closing* the system.

A *closed system* is at one extreme of a continuum that reflects the degree of independence of systems (an *open system* is at the other extreme). A closed system is totally independent, whereas an open system is very dependent on its environment. An open system accepts inputs (information, energy, materials) from the environment and may deliver outputs to the environment.

When determining the impact of decisions on an open system, we must determine its relationship with the environment and with other systems. In a closed system, we need not do this because the system is considered to be isolated. Many computer systems, such as transaction processing systems (TPS), are considered closed systems. Generally, closed systems are fairly simple in nature.

A special type of closed system called a *black box* is one in which inputs and outputs are well defined, but the process itself is not specified. Many managers are not concerned with how a computer works. Essentially, they prefer to treat them as black boxes, like a telephone or an elevator. Managers simply use these devices independent of the operational details because they understand how the devices function and their tasks do not require them to understand the way they really work (this concept lead to the development of commercially successful expert systems).

Decision support systems attempt to deal with systems that are fairly open. Such systems are complex, and during their analysis one must determine the impacts on and from the environment. Consider the two inventory systems outlined in Table 2.1. We compare a well-known inventory model, the economic order quantity (EOQ) model for a fairly closed system, with a hypothetical DSS for an inventory system for an open system. The closed system is very restrictive in terms of its assumptions and thus its applicability.

SYSTEM EFFECTIVENESS AND EFFICIENCY

Systems are evaluated and analyzed with two major performance measures: effectiveness and efficiency.

> **Effectiveness** is the degree to which goals are achieved. It is therefore concerned with the outputs of a system (such as total sales or earnings per share).
> **Efficiency** is a measure of the use of inputs (or resources) to achieve outputs (e.g., how much money is used to generate a certain level of sales).

Peter Drucker proposed an interesting way to distinguish between the two terms. He makes the following distinction:

> Effectiveness is doing the right thing.
> Efficiency is doing the thing right.

An important characteristic of MSS is their emphasis on the effectiveness, or "goodness," of the decision produced, rather than on the computational efficiency of obtaining it—usually a major concern of a transaction processing system.

Measuring many managerial systems' effectiveness and efficiency is a major problem. This is especially true for systems that deliver human services (education, health, recreation), which often have several qualitative and conflicting goals and are subject to much external influence because of funding and political considerations.

TABLE 2.1   A Closed Versus an Open Inventory System

Factor	*Management Science: EOQ (Closed System)*	*Inventory DSS (Open System)*
Demand	Constant	Variable—influenced by many factors
Unit cost	Constant	May change daily
Lead time	Constant	Variable, difficult to predict
Vendors and users	Excluded from analysis	May be included in analysis
Weather and other environmental factors	Ignored	May influence demand and lead time

INFORMATION SYSTEMS

An information system collects, processes, stores, analyzes, and disseminates information for a specific purpose. Information systems are often at the heart of most organizations. For example, banks and airlines cannot function without their information systems. With the advent of electronic businesses (e-businesses), if there is no information system, then there is no business. Information systems accept inputs and process data to provide information to decision makers and help them communicate their results. Now, a World Wide Web presence and activities are expected by consumers and decision makers. So, information systems have become critical for many organizations that in the past did not rely on them.

2.4 MODELS

A major characteristic of a decision support system is the inclusion of at least one model. The basic idea is to perform the DSS analysis on a model of reality rather than on the real system itself.

A *model* is a simplified representation or abstraction of reality. It is usually simplified because reality is too complex to describe exactly and because much of the complexity is actually irrelevant in solving the specific problem.

The representation of systems or problems by models can be done with various degrees of abstraction; therefore, models are classified into three groups according to their degree of abstraction: *iconic, analog,* and *mathematical.*

ICONIC (SCALE) MODELS

An **iconic model**—the least abstract model—is a physical replica of a system, usually on a different scale from the original. An iconic model may appear in three dimensions, such as that of an airplane, car, bridge, or production line. Photographs are two-dimensional iconic scale models.

ANALOG MODELS

An **analog model** behaves like the real system but does not look like it. It is more abstract than an iconic model and is a symbolic representation of reality. These models are usually two-dimensional charts or diagrams. They can be physical models, but the shape of the model differs from that of the actual system. Some examples include

- Organization charts that depict structure, authority, and responsibility relationships
- Maps on which different colors represent objects such as bodies of water or mountains
- Stock market charts that represent the price movements of stocks
- Blueprints of a machine or a house.

MATHEMATICAL (QUANTITATIVE) MODELS

The complexity of relationships in many organizational systems cannot be represented by icons or analogically because the representation quickly becomes cumbersome and its use becomes time-consuming. Therefore, more abstract models are described mathematically. Most DSS analyses are performed numerically with **mathematical** or other **quantitative** models.

THE BENEFITS OF MODELS

An MSS uses models for the following reasons:

- Models enable the compression of time. Years of operations can be simulated in minutes or seconds of computer time.
- Model manipulation (changing decision variables or the environment) is much easier than manipulating the real system. Experimentation is easier to conduct and does not interfere with the daily operation of the organization.
- The cost of modeling analysis is much less than the cost of a similar experiment conducted on a real system.
- The cost of making mistakes during a trial-and-error experiment is much less when models are used rather than real systems.
- The business environment involves considerable uncertainty. With modeling, a manager can estimate the risks resulting from specific actions.
- Mathematical models enable the analysis of a very large, sometimes infinite, number of possible solutions. Even in simple problems, managers often have a large number of alternatives from which to choose.
- Models enhance and reinforce learning and training.

Recent advances in computer graphics have led to an increased tendency to use iconic and analog models to complement MSS mathematical modeling. For example, visual simulation (Chapter 5) combines all three types of models.

2.5 A PREVIEW OF THE MODELING PROCESS

EXAMPLE: HOW MUCH TO ORDER?

The Ma-Pa Grocery is a small neighborhood grocery store south of Pittsburgh. Bob and Jan, the owners, are very sensitive to their customers' needs. They are also concerned with the financial viability of the store. These two objectives have to be "balanced." Bread is one of their major products; and it gives them headaches. Some days, they don't have enough; other days, they have so much extra that they have to sell it at a loss the next day. Their problem is to determine how much bread to stock each day. They have already identified the problem (so have their customers) and taken charge of it (ownership). They have some notions of how to solve the problem. They decide to explore a few possible approaches since their friends' daughter, Marla, is taking a DSS course at the Graduate School of Industrial Administration (GSIA) at nearby Carnegie Mellon University and they can get free advice.

Bob and Jan can apply several approaches to solving the problem. Four potentially viable approaches are trial and error, simulation, optimization, and heuristics.

TRIAL AND ERROR WITH THE REAL SYSTEM

In this approach, the owners try to learn from experimentation on the real system. Namely, they change the quantities of bread stocked and observe what happens. If they find they are short on bread too often, they increase the quantities ordered. If they find that too much bread is left over, they decrease the quantities ordered. Sooner or later they will home in on how much bread to order (if they don't go out of business first).

Although this approach may be very successful for Bob and Jan, it may fail in other cases. Trial and error may *not* work if one or more of the following is true:

- There are too many alternatives (trials) to explore.
- The cost of making errors (part of the trial-and-error approach) is very high.
- The business environment keeps changing (e.g., demand could change over time—and probably does). Therefore, learning from experience may be difficult or even impossible. By the time they have experimented with all the alternatives, the environmental conditions could change and the results become invalid.

Fortunately, Jan and Bob can try modeling approaches. Instead of manipulating the real system, they can develop a reasonable model to represent it. Three common types of modeling approaches that they can develop are simulation, optimization, and heuristics.

SIMULATION

In this case, Jan and Bob play a make-believe game. The results depend on the demand, which may be constant or vary (be stochastic). **Simulation** based on historical and projected data applies to both situations. Jan and Bob first examine their bread sales for a year (fortunately they built a small data warehouse and have these data readily available). The data includes estimates of the unsatisfied demand. They develop a probability distribution for their daily demand. Then, they then ask themselves, "If we order 300 loaves of bread, what will happen?" They randomly generate demands and calculate results. They replicate the experiment several (hundred) times, and look at the statistical results for bread: the total profit (or loss), the unmet demand, and the number of leftover loaves. Next, Jan and Bob change the order quantity to 350, 400, 200, and 250 and attempt to home in on the best decision alternative. They "run the store" on a computer several times with each daily order quantity over several months and calculate the results. Finally, they compare the results of each order quantity and decide how much to order. Thus, rather than using trial and error on the real system, they capture the salient features of the real system in the simulation model and use a trial-and-error approach on the model.

A major advantage of simulation modeling is that years of operations can be simulated in seconds on a computer (which is very important when modeling a production system or transportation system) (see the online visual simulation demo of the Orca Visual Simulation Environment at the Orca Computer, Inc., Web site, www.orcacomputer.com). Another advantage is that there are special languages (e.g., Simula II) and spreadsheet add-ins (e.g., @Risk) that assist in the model development and execution process.

A major problem with the simulation approach is that once the experiment is completed there is no guarantee that the selected daily order quantity is the best (optimal) one. It is probably the best of all those tested, but it is possible that the true best level (the optimal one) is 675, a level not tried. Another problem with the simulation is that Jan and Bob may need professional help to design the simulation study, program it on a computer, and interpret the statistical results (or perhaps Marla could make it a DSS class project). The cost of creating and testing the model may not be worth the benefits obtained. Actually, the more details incorporated in a model, the more expensive it is to construct and test. The marginal value of capturing and representing the finer details of the system in the model may not be worth the marginal cost.

OPTIMIZATION

A more sophisticated approach to solving the problem is to develop an **optimization** model. Ideally such a model generates an optimal (best) order level in seconds.

Fortunately, inexpensive, user-friendly optimization software packages for conducting such an analysis for many structured situations are readily available. The limitation of optimization is that it works only if the problem is structured and, for the most part, deterministic (nonrandom). An optimization model defines the required input data, the desired output, and the mathematical relationships in a precise manner. Obviously, if reality differs significantly from the assumptions used in developing the model, optimization cannot be used.

Recall that a DSS deals with unstructured problems. This does not preclude using optimization because many times a problem can be decomposed into subproblems, some of which are structured enough for applying optimization. Also, optimization can be combined with simulation for the solution of complex problems. Two advantages of optimization are that the expressions that represent the problem are based on algebraic notation and that there is readily available, robust optimization software (e.g., Lindo, Lingo) some including spreadsheet add-ins (e.g., Solver). A disadvantage is that a particular problem may not fit the framework of optimization or that it is too complex to be solved to optimality. In these cases, we can sometimes use heuristics.

HEURISTICS

Jan and Bob could develop and use some rules on which to base the order quantity. For example, they could stock today the average daily quantity demanded over the last 7 days. Another rule that they could use is to stock each day the quantity demanded on the same day 1 week earlier. The rules may be provided by experts or even derived by trial and error. Heuristics can be effective, but there is no guarantee of obtaining an optimal solution.

PHASES OF THE DECISION-MAKING PROCESS

To better understand modeling, it is advisable to follow a systematic decision-making process, which, according to Simon (1977), involves three major phases: *intelligence, design,* and *choice.* A fourth phase, implementation, was added later. Monitoring can be considered a fifth phase, however, we view monitoring as the intelligence phase applied to the implementation phase. *Simon's model is the most concise, and yet complete characterization of rational decision making.* A conceptual picture of the decision-making process is shown in Figure 2.2.

There is a continuous flow of activity from intelligence to design to choice (bold lines), but at any phase there may be a return to a previous phase (feedback). Modeling is an essential part of this process. The seemingly chaotic nature of following a haphazard path from problem discovery to solution by decision making can be explained by these feedback loops.

The decision-making process starts with the **intelligence phase,** where reality is examined and the problem is identified and defined. Problem ownership is established as well. In the **design phase,** a model that represents the system is constructed. This is done by making assumptions that simplify reality and by writing down the relationships among all variables. The model is then validated, and criteria are set for evaluation of the alternative courses of action that are identified. Often the process of model construction identifies potential alternative solutions, and vice versa. The **choice phase** includes selection of a proposed solution to the model (not to the problem it represents). This solution is tested to determine its viability. Once the proposed solution seems to be reasonable, we are ready for the last phase: **implementation.** Successful implementation results in solving the *real* problem. Failure leads to a return to an earlier phase of the process. In fact, we can return to an earlier phase during the execution of any of the latter three phases. We next discuss the process in detail.

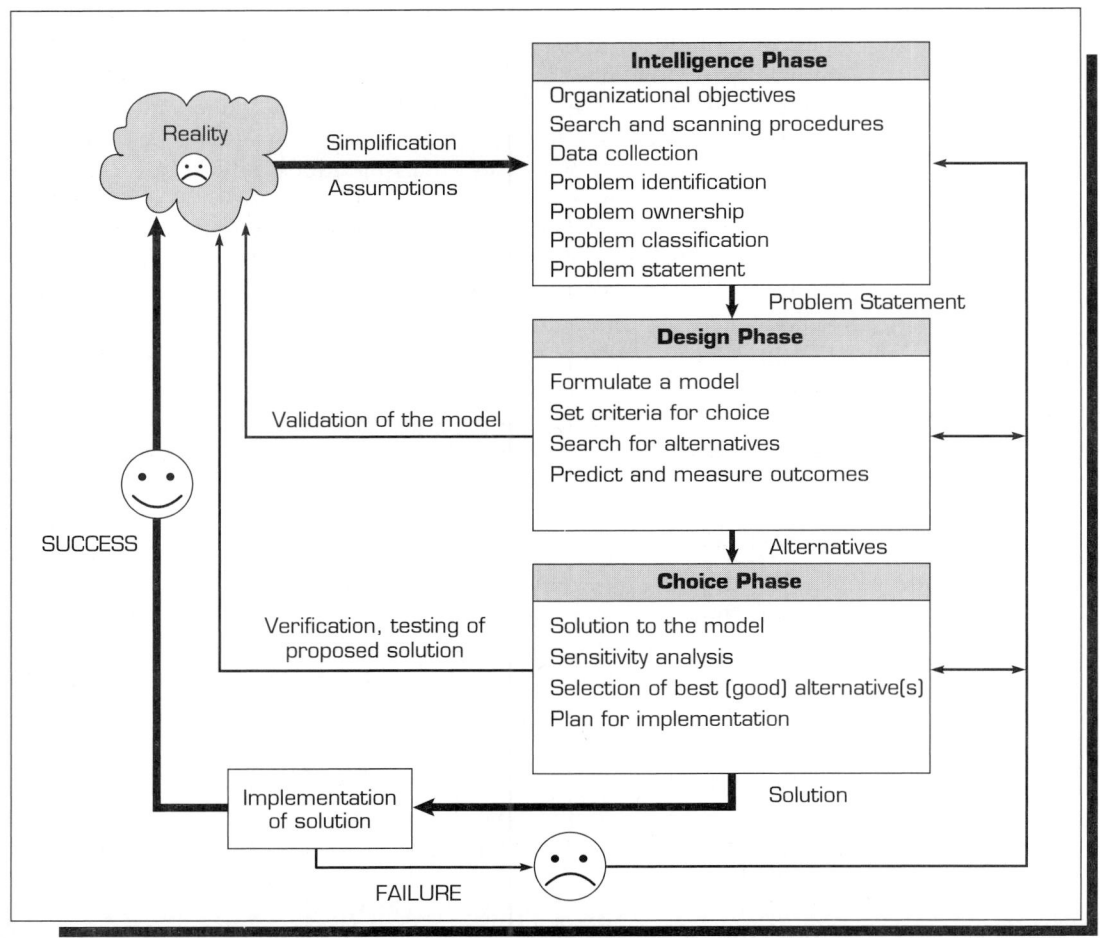

FIGURE 2.2 THE DECISION-MAKING/MODELING PROCESS

2.6 DECISION MAKING: THE INTELLIGENCE PHASE

Intelligence in decision making involves scanning the environment, either intermittently or continuously. It includes several activities aimed at identifying problem situations or opportunities. (It may also include monitoring the results of the implementation phase of a decision-making process.)

PROBLEM (OR OPPORTUNITY) IDENTIFICATION

The intelligence phase begins with the identification of organizational goals and objectives related to an issue of concern (e.g., inventory management, job selection) and determination of whether they are being met. Problems occur because of dissatisfaction with the status quo. Dissatisfaction is the result of a difference between what we desire (or expect) and what is occurring. In this first phase, one attempts to determine whether a problem exists, identify its symptoms, determine its magnitude, and explicitly define it. Often, what is described as a problem (such as excessive costs) may be only a symptom (measure) of a problem (such as improper inventory levels). Because real-world problems are usually complicated by many interrelated factors, it is sometimes difficult to distinguish between the symptoms and the real problem.

The existence of a problem can be determined by monitoring and analyzing the organization's productivity level. The measurement of productivity and the construction of a model are based on real data. The collection of data and the estimation of future data are among the most difficult steps in the analysis. Some issues that may arise during data collection and estimation, and thus plague decision makers, are

- Data are not available. Potentially inaccurate estimates must be made and relied on in the model.
- Obtaining data may be expensive.
- Data estimation is often subjective.
- Important data that influence the results may be qualitative.
- There may be too many data (information overload).
- Outcomes (or results) may occur over an extended period of time. As a result, revenues, expenses, and profits will be recorded at different points in time. To overcome this difficulty, a present-value approach should be used if the results are quantifiable.
- It is assumed that future data will be similar to historical data. If not, it will be necessary to predict the nature of the change and include it in the analysis.

Once the preliminary investigation is completed, it is possible to determine whether a problem really exists, where it is located, and how significant it is.

PROBLEM CLASSIFICATION

Problem classification is the conceptualization of a problem in an attempt to place it in a definable category, possibly leading to a standard solution approach. An important classification is according to the degree of structuredness evident in the problem.

PROGRAMMED VERSUS NONPROGRAMMED PROBLEMS

Simon (1977) has distinguished two extremes regarding the structuredness of decision problems. At one end of the spectrum are well-structured problems that are repetitive and routine and for which standard models have been developed. Simon calls these **programmed problems.** Examples of such problems are weekly scheduling of employees, monthly determination of cash flow, and selection of an inventory level for a specific item under constant demand. At the other end of the spectrum are unstructured problems, also called **nonprogrammed problems,** which are novel and nonrecurrent. For example, unstructured problems may include merger and acquisition decisions, undertaking a complex research and development project, evaluating an electronic commerce initiative, and selecting a job. Semistructured problems fall between the two extremes.

PROBLEM DECOMPOSITION

Many complex problems can be divided into subproblems. Solving the simpler subproblems may help in solving the complex problem. Also, some seemingly poorly structured problems may have some highly structured subproblems. Decomposition

DSS IN FOCUS 2.2

KNOWLEDGE CAN STRUCTURE
AN UNSTRUCTURED PROBLEM

A decision maker must recognize that problems can be unstructured when the level of knowledge and information about them are minimal or nonexistent. Developing knowledge about a problem can add structure to unstructured or semistructured problems. This is partly why the prototyping development process for DSS has proven successful in practice (Chapter 6). This also explains the difference between being an expert and being a novice in a particular field. For example, if you know little about the restaurant business, except that you want to open a new restaurant, determining an appropriate location for your first restaurant is unstructured. If you seek out expert knowledge and demographic information, you will add structure to the problem through learning. Alternatively, if you are responsible for choosing locations for a large chain of restaurants, determining where to put the 2,000th restaurant is a very structured problem to which known data and models from your organization are applied.

DSS IN ACTION 2.3

EXPERT CHOICE SUPPORTS ERP SOFTWARE SELECTION

The Norfolk Navy Shipyard used TeamEC (the collaborative version of Expert Choice) to help determine source selection evaluation criteria for a major enterprise resource planning software purchase. Lieutenant Commander Mark Bracco said

the process allowed us to reach consensus among group members who represent widely varying viewpoints. The resulting model was one that all could support. Without it, I don't think we would have ever reached any agreement

and our resulting product (by other methods) would have been inferior. The TeamEC output should strengthen our source selection process from internal criticism and external protest. I think I made believers out of many who thought the process wouldn't work.

———————

Source: Condensed from "Success Stories: TeamEC Supports ERP Software Selection," Expert Choice, Inc., www.expertchoice.com, 2000.

also facilitates communication among decision makers. Decomposition is one of the most important aspects of the Analytical Hierarchy Process (AHP), (Saaty, 1999) which helps decision makers incorporate both qualitative and quantitative factors into their decision-making models. See DSS in Action 2.3.

PROBLEM OWNERSHIP

In the intelligence phase, it is important to establish **problem ownership.** A problem exists in an organization only if someone or some group takes on the responsibility of attacking it and if the organization has the ability to solve it. For example, a manager may feel that he or she has a problem because interest rates are too high. Because interest rate levels are determined at the national and international levels and most managers can do nothing about them, high interest rates are the problem of the government, not a problem for a specific company to solve. The problem companies face is how to operate in a high interest rate environment. For an individual company, the interest rate level should be handled as an uncontrollable (environmental) factor.

When problem ownership is not established, either someone is not doing his or her job or the problem at hand has yet to be identified as belonging to anyone. It is then important for someone to either volunteer to "own" it or assign it to someone.

The intelligence phase ends with a formal problem statement.

2.7 DECISION MAKING: THE DESIGN PHASE

The design phase involves finding or developing and analyzing possible courses of action. These include understanding the problem and testing solutions for feasibility. Also, a model of the decision-making problem is constructed, tested, and validated.

Modeling involves conceptualization of the problem and its abstraction to quantitative and/or qualitative forms. For a mathematical model, the variables are identified and the relationships among them are established. Simplifications are made, whenever necessary, through *assumptions*. For example, a relationship between two variables may be assumed to be linear even though in reality there may be some nonlinear effects. A proper balance between the level of model simplification and the representation of reality must be obtained because of the benefit/cost trade-off. A simpler model leads to a lower development cost, easier manipulation, and a faster solution but is less representative of the real problem and can lead to inaccurate results.

The process of modeling is a combination of art and science. As a science, there are many standard model classes available, and with practice an analyst can determine which one is applicable to a given situation. As an art, a level of creativity and finesse is required when determining what simplifying assumptions can work, how to combine appropriate features of the model classes, and how to integrate models to obtain valid solutions. We present the following topics of modeling as they relate to quantitative models (mathematical, financial, and so on):

- The components of the model
- The structure of the model
- Selection of a principle of choice (criteria for evaluation)
- Developing (generating) alternatives
- Predicting outcomes
- Measuring outcomes
- Scenarios.

Decision makers sometimes develop mental models, especially in time pressure situations. These mental models help frame the decision-making situation. (See cognition theory in Section 2.13.)

THE COMPONENTS OF QUANTITATIVE MODELS

All models are made up of three basic components (Figure 2.3): **decision variables, uncontrollable variables** (and/or **parameters**), and **result (outcome) variables.** Mathematical relationships link these components together. In a nonquantitative model, the relationships are symbolic or qualitative. The results of decisions are determined by the decision made (value of the decision variables), the factors that cannot be controlled by the decision maker (in the environment), and the relationships among the variables.

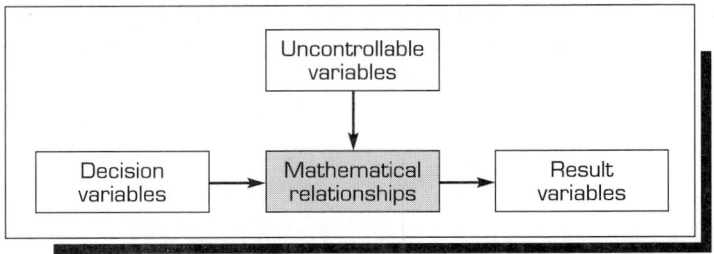

FIGURE 2.3 THE GENERAL STRUCTURE OF A QUANTITATIVE MODEL

TABLE 2.2   Examples of the Components of Models

Area	Decision Variables	Result Variables	Uncontrollable Variables and Parameters
Financial investment	Investment alternatives and amounts How long to invest When to invest	Total profit, risk Rate of return (ROI) Earnings per share Liquidity level	Inflation rate Prime rate Competition
Marketing	Advertising budget Where to advertise	Market share Customer satisfaction	Customers' income Competitors' actions
Manufacturing	What and how much to produce Inventory levels Compensation programs	Total cost Quality level Employee satisfaction	Machine capacity Technology Materials prices
Accounting	Use of computers Audit schedule	Data processing cost Error rate	Computer technology Tax rates Legal requirements
Transportation	Shipments schedule Use of *smart cards*	Total transport cost Payment float time	Delivery distance Regulations
Services	Staffing levels	Customer satisfaction	Demand for services

RESULT VARIABLES

Result variables reflect the level of effectiveness of the system; that is, they indicate how well the system performs or attains its goals. These variables are outputs. Examples of result variables are shown in Table 2.2. Result variables are considered *dependent variables.*

   Note: A dependent variable implies that for the event described by such a variable to occur, another event must occur first. Result variables depend on the occurrence of the decision and the uncontrollable **independent variables.**

DECISION VARIABLES

Decision variables describe alternative courses of action. The levels of these variables are determined by the decision maker. For example, for an investment problem, the amount to invest in bonds is a decision variable. In a scheduling problem, the decision variables are people, times, and schedules. Other examples are listed in Table 2.2.

UNCONTROLLABLE VARIABLES OR PARAMETERS

In any decision-making situation, there are factors that affect the result variables but *are not under the control* of the decision maker. Either these factors can be fixed, in which case they are called parameters, or they can vary (variables). Examples are the prime interest rate, a city's building code, tax regulations, and utilities prices (others are shown in Table 2.2). Most of these factors are uncontrollable because they are in and determined by elements of the system environment in which the decision maker works. Some of these variables limit the decision maker and therefore form what are called the *constraints* of the problem.

INTERMEDIATE RESULT VARIABLES

Intermediate result variables reflect intermediate outcomes. For example, in determining machine scheduling, spoilage is an intermediate result variable, and total profit is the result variable (spoilage is one determinant of total profit). Another example is employee salaries, which is a decision variable for management. It determines employees' satisfaction (intermediate outcome), which determines the productivity level (final result).

THE STRUCTURE OF QUANTITATIVE MODELS

The components of a quantitative model are linked together by mathematical (algebraic) expressions—equations or inequalities.

One very simple financial model is $P = R - C$, where P = profit, R = revenue, and C = cost. The equation describes the relationship among these variables.

Another well-known financial model is the simple present-value cash flow model:

$$P = \frac{F}{(1 + i)^n}$$

where P = present value, F = a future single payment in dollars, i = interest rate (percentage), and n = number of years. With this model, one can readily determine the present value of a payment of $100,000 to be made 5 years from today, at a 10 percent (0.1) interest rate, to be

$$P = \frac{100,000}{(1 + 0.1)^5} = \$62,092$$

We present a more interesting, complex mathematical model next.

EXAMPLE: THE PRODUCT-MIX MODEL

MBI Corporation makes special-purpose computers. A decision must be made: How many computers should be produced next month at the Boston plant? Two types of computers are considered: the CC-7, which requires 300 days of labor and $10,000 in materials, and the CC-8, which requires 500 days of labor and $15,000 in materials. The profit contribution of each CC-7 is $8,000, whereas that of each CC-8 is $12,000. The plant has a capacity of 200,000 working days per month, and the material budget is $8 million per month. Marketing requires that at least 100 units of the CC-7 and at least 200 units of the CC-8 be produced each month. The problem is to maximize the company's profits by determining how many units of the CC-7 and how many units of the CC-8 should be produced each month. Note that the data in the problem statement could possibly take months to determine in a real-world environment, and that while gathering the data, the decision maker would no doubt uncover facts about how he or she would structure the model to be solved. This was true for the situation described in IMERYS Case Applications 2.1 and 2.2.

MODELING

A standard mathematical modeling technique called **linear programming (LP)** is applicable (see DSS in Focus 2.4). It has three components:

Decision variables:
X_1 = units of CC-7 to be produced;
X_2 = units of CC-8 to be produced

Result variable:
Total profit = Z. The objective is to maximize total profit: $Z = 8,000X_1 + 12,000X_2$

Uncontrollable variables (constraints):
Labor constraint: $300X_1 + 500X_2 \leq 200,000$ (in days)
Budget constraint: $10,000X_1 + 15,000X_2 \leq 8,000,000$ (in dollars)
Marketing requirement for CC-7: $X_1 \geq 100$ (in units)
Marketing requirement for CC-8: $X_2 \geq 200$ (in units)

This information is summarized in Figure 2.4.

The model also has a fourth, hidden component. Every linear programming model has some internal intermediate variables that are not explicitly stated. The labor and budget constraints may each have some "slack" in them when the left-hand side is strictly less than the right-hand side. These slacks are represented internally by slack variables that indicate excess resources available. The marketing requirement constraints may each have some "surplus" in them when the left-hand side is strictly greater than the right-hand side. These surpluses are represented internally by surplus variables indicating that there is some room to adjust the right-hand sides of these constraints.

DSS IN FOCUS 2.4

LINEAR PROGRAMMING

Linear programming is perhaps the best known optimization model. It deals with the optimal allocation of resources among competing activities. The allocation problem is represented by the model described as follows:

The problem is to find the values of the decision variables X_1, X_2, and so on, such that the value of the result variable Z is maximized, subject to a set of linear constraints that express the technology, market conditions, and other uncontrollable variables. The mathematical relationships are all linear equations and inequalities. Theoretically, there are an infinite number of possible solutions to any allocation problem of this type. Using special mathematical procedures, the linear programming approach applies a unique computerized search procedure that finds the best solution(s) in a matter of seconds. Furthermore, the solution approach provides automatic sensitivity analysis (Section 2.9).

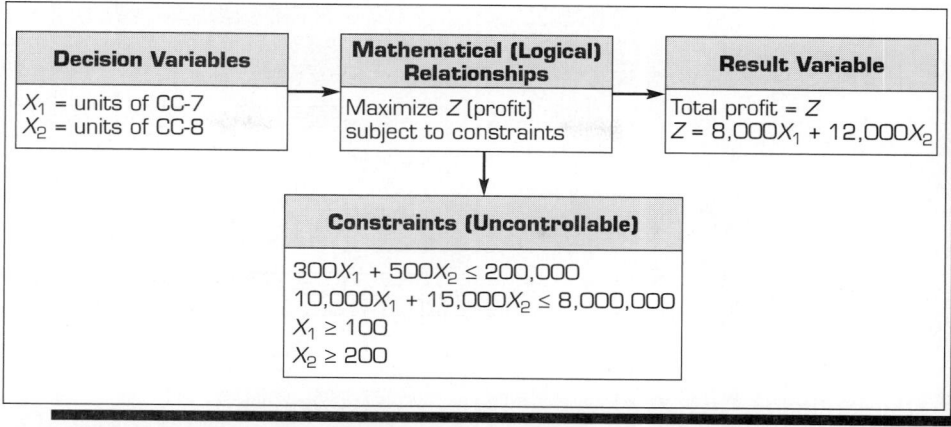

FIGURE 2.4 MATHEMATICAL MODEL OF A PRODUCT MIX EXAMPLE

These slack and surplus variables are intermediate. They can be of great value to the decision maker because linear programming solution methods use them in establishing sensitivity parameters for economic what-if analyses.

The product-mix model has an infinite number of possible solutions. Assuming that a production plan is not restricted to whole numbers—a reasonable assumption in a monthly production plan—we want a solution that maximizes total profit—an optimal solution.

Fortunately, Excel comes with the add-in Solver that can readily obtain an optimal (best) solution to this problem. We enter these data directly into an Excel spreadsheet, activate Solver, and identify the goal (set Target Cell equal to Max), decision variables (By Changing Cells), and constraints (Total Consumed elements must be less than or equal to Limit for the first two rows and must be greater than or equal to Limit for the third and fourth rows). Also, in Options, activate the boxes Assume Linear Model and Assume Non-negative and then *solve* the problem. Solve, then select all three reports—Answer, Sensitivity, and Limits—to obtain an optimal solution of $X_1 = 333.33$, $X_2 = 200$, Profit = \$5,066,667 as shown in Figure 2.5. Solver produces three useful reports about the solution. Try it.

The most common optimization models are

- Assignment (best matching of objects)
- Dynamic programming
- Goal programming
- Investment (maximizing rate of return)
- Linear and integer programming
- Network models for planning and scheduling
- Nonlinear programming
- Replacement (capital budgeting)
- Simple inventory models (e.g., economic order quantity)
- Transportation (minimize cost of shipments).

The evaluation of alternatives and the final choice depend on the type of criteria we want. Are we trying to find the best solution? Or will a "good enough" result be sufficient? This issue is discussed next.

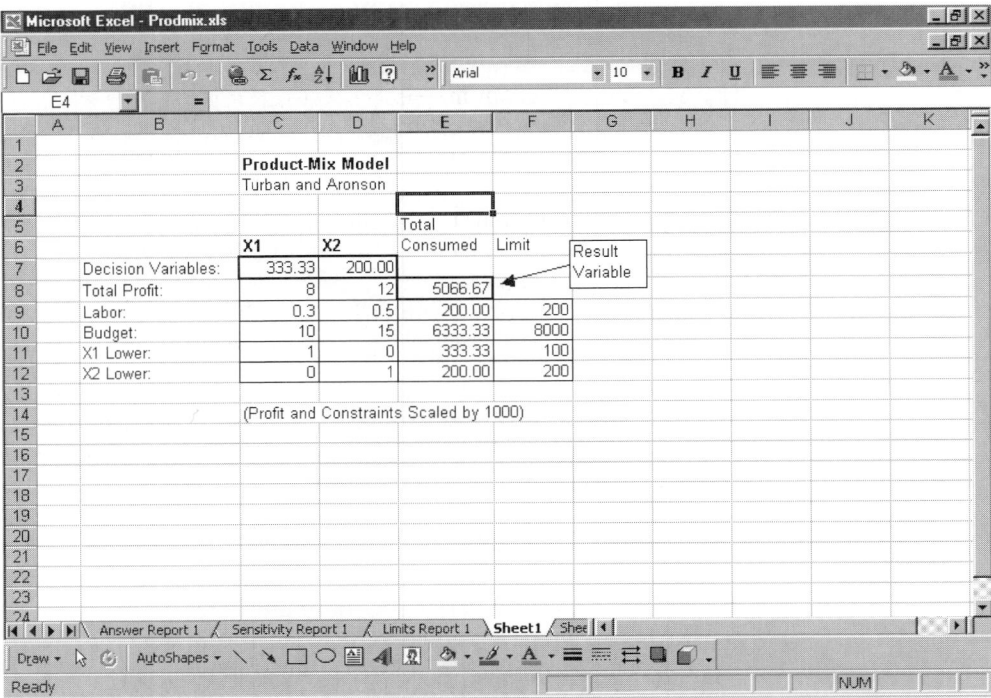

FIGURE 2.5 EXCEL SOLVER SOLUTION TO THE PRODUCT-MIX EXAMPLE

SELECTION OF A PRINCIPLE OF CHOICE

A **principle of choice** is a criterion that describes the acceptability of a solution approach. [It is important to remember that selecting a principle of choice is not part of the choice phase but rather involves how we establish our decision-making objective(s) and how it is (they are) incorporated into the model(s).] Are we willing to assume high risk or do we prefer a low-risk approach? Are we attempting to optimize or satisfice? Of the various principles of choice, two are of prime importance: *normative* and *descriptive*.

NORMATIVE MODELS

Normative implies that the chosen alternative is demonstrably the best of all possible alternatives. To find it, one should examine all alternatives and prove that the one selected is indeed the best, which is what one would *norm*ally want. This process is basically *optimization*. In operational terms, optimization can be achieved in one of three ways:

- Get the highest level of goal attainment from a given set of resources. For example, which alternative will yield the maximum profit from an investment of $10 million?
- Find the alternative with the highest ratio of goal attainment to cost (e.g., profit per dollar invested) or maximize productivity.
- Find the alternative with the lowest cost (or other resources) that will meet an acceptable level of goals. For example, if your task is to build a product to certain specifications, which method will accomplish this goal with the least cost?

Normative decision theory is based on the following assumptions of rational decision makers:

- Humans are economic beings whose objective is to maximize the attainment of goals; that is, the decision maker is rational. [More of a good thing (revenue, fun) is better than less; less of a bad thing (cost, pain) is better than more.]
- For a decision-making situation, all viable alternative courses of action and their consequences, or at least the probability and the values of the consequences, are known.
- Decision makers have an order or preference that enables them to rank the desirability of all consequences of the analysis (best to worst).

Are decision makers really rational? See DSS in Focus 2.5, Schwartz (1998), and Halpern and Stern (1998) for anomalies in rational decision making. Though there may be major anomalies in the presumed rationality of financial and economic behavior, we take the view that they could be caused by incompetence, lack of knowledge, multiple goals that are framed inadequately, misunderstanding of a decision maker's true expected utility, and time pressure impacts.

SUBOPTIMIZATION

By definition, optimization requires a decision maker to consider the impact of each alternative course of action on the entire organization because a decision made in one area may have significant effects (positive or negative) in other areas. Consider a production department that plans its own schedule. Ideally and independently, the department should produce only a few products in extremely large quantities to minimize manufacturing costs. However, such a plan may result in large, costly inventories and marketing difficulties caused by the lack of a variety of products.

Using a systems point of view assesses the impact of all decisions on the entire system. Thus, the production department should make its plans in conjunction with other departments. However, such an approach may require a complicated, expensive, time-consuming analysis. In practice, the MSS builder may close the system within narrow boundaries, considering only part of the organization under study (the production department in this case), and incorporate relationships into the model that assume away certain complicated relationships describing interactions with and among the other departments. The other departments can be aggregated into simple model components. Such an approach is called **suboptimization.**

DSS IN FOCUS 2.5

ARE DECISION MAKERS REALLY RATIONAL?

Some researchers question the rationality concept. There are countless cases of individuals and groups behaving irrationally in real-world and experimental decision-making situations. For example, suppose you need to take a bus to work every morning and the bus leaves at 7:00 A.M. Therefore, if it takes you 1 hour to wake up, prepare for work, and get to the bus stop, you should always awaken at or before 6:00 A.M. However, sometimes (perhaps many times) you may sleep until 6:30, knowing that you will miss breakfast and not perform well at work. Or you may be late and arrive at the bus stop at 7:05, hoping that the bus will be late. So, why are you late? Multiple objectives and hoped-for goal levels may lead to this situation. Or your true *expected utility* for being on time might simply indicate that you should go back to bed most mornings!

If a suboptimal decision is made in one part of the organization without considering the details of the rest of the organization, then an optimal solution from the point of view of that part may be inferior for the whole.

However, suboptimization may still be a very practical method, and many problems are first approached from this perspective. It is possible to reach some tentative conclusions (and generally usable results) by analyzing only a portion of a system without getting bogged down in too many details. Once a solution is proposed, its potential effects on the remaining departments of the organization can be tested. If no significant negative effects are found, the solution can then be implemented.

Suboptimization may also apply when simplifying assumptions are used in modeling a specific problem. There may be too many details or too many data to incorporate into a specific decision-making situation, and so not all of them are used in the model. If the solution to the model seems reasonable, it may still be valid for the problem and thus be adopted. For example, in a production department, parts are often partitioned into A/B/C inventory categories. Generally, A items (large gears, whole assemblies) are expensive (say, $2,000 or more apiece), built to order in small batches, and inventoried in low quantities; C items (nuts, bolts, screws) are very inexpensive (say, less than $1) and ordered and used in very large quantities; and B items fall in between. All A items can be handled by a detailed scheduling model and physically monitored closely by management; B items are generally somewhat aggregated, their groupings are scheduled and management reviews these parts less frequently; and C items are not scheduled but are simply acquired or built based on a policy defined by management with a simple EOQ ordering system that assumes constant annual demand. The policy might be reviewed once a year.

Suboptimization may also involve simply bounding the search for an optimum (e.g., by a heuristic) by considering fewer criteria or alternatives or by eliminating large portions of the problem from evaluation.

The suboptimization approach fits well with the iterative (step-by-step) development approach to DSS.

DESCRIPTIVE MODELS

Descriptive models describe things as they are, or as they are believed to be. These models are also mathematically based. Descriptive models are extremely useful in DSS for investigating the consequences of various alternative courses of action under different configurations of inputs and processes. However, because a descriptive analysis checks the performance of the system for a given set of alternatives (rather than for *all* alternatives), there is no guarantee that an alternative selected with the aid of a descriptive analysis is optimal. In many cases, it is only satisfactory. Simulation is probably the most common descriptive modeling method. Simulation has been applied to many areas of decision making. Computer and video games are one form of simulation. An artificial reality is created, and the game player lives within it. Virtual reality is a form of simulation as well. The environment is simulated, not real. A common use of simulation is in manufacturing. Again, consider the production department of a firm. The characteristics of each machine in a job shop can be described mathematically. Relationships can be established via how each machine physically runs and relates to others. Given a trial schedule of batches of parts, they flow through the system, and the utilization statistics of each machine are measured. Alternative schedules may then be tried, and the statistics recorded, until a reasonable schedule is found. This is a primarily experimental modeling method.

Other descriptive models include

- Information flow
- Scenario analysis
- Financial planning
- Complex inventory decisions
- Markov analysis (predictions)
- Environmental impact analysis
- Simulation (alternative types)
- Technological forecasting
- Waiting line (queuing) management.

There are a number of nonmathematical descriptive models for decision making. One is a cognitive map (Ackermann et al., 1996; Eden and Ackermann, 1998). A cognitive map can help a decision maker sketch out the important, qualitative factors and their causal relationships in a messy decision making situation. It helps the decision maker (or decision-making group) focus on what is relevant and what is not, and the map evolves as more is learned about the problem. The map can help the decision maker understand issues better, focus better, and reach closure. One interesting software tool for cognitive mapping is Decision Explorer (Banxia Software Limited, Glasgow, Scotland, UK, www.banxia.com; a downloadable demo is available).

Another descriptive decision-making model is the use of narratives to describe a decision-making situation. A narrative is a story that, when told, helps a decision maker uncover the important aspects of the situation and leads to better understanding and framing. It is extremely effective when a group is making a decision and can lead to a more common frame. Courtroom trials by jury typically use narrative-based approaches in reaching verdicts (Beach, 1997).

GOOD ENOUGH OR SATISFICING

According to Simon (1977), most human decision making, whether organizational or individual, involves a willingness to settle for a satisfactory solution, "something less than the best." In a **satisficing** mode, the decision maker sets up an aspiration, goal, or desired level of performance and then searches the alternatives until one is found that achieves this level. The usual reasons for satisficing are time pressure (decisions may lose value over time), the ability to achieve optimization (solving some models could take longer than until when the sun is supposed to become a supernova), as well as recognition that the marginal benefit of a better solution is not worth the marginal cost to obtain it. (This is like searching the Web. You can look at only so many Web sites until you run out of time and energy.) In this regard, the decision maker is behaving rationally, though in reality he or she is satisficing. This is directly related to the concept of suboptimization, where an optimum is known to exist but is difficult, if not impossible, to attain.

Related to satisficing is Simon's idea of *bounded rationality*. Humans have a limited capacity for rational thinking; they generally construct and analyze a simplified model of a real situation. Their behavior with respect to the simplified model may be rational. However, the rational solution for the simplified model may not be rational for the real-world problem. Rationality is bounded not only by limitations on human processing capacities but also by individual differences such as age, education, knowledge, and attitudes. Bounded rationality is also why many models are descriptive rather than normative.

DEVELOPING (GENERATING) ALTERNATIVES

A significant part of the process of model building is generating alternatives. In optimization models (such as linear programming), the alternatives may be generated automatically by the model. In most MSS situations, however, it is necessary to generate alternatives manually. This can be a lengthy process that involves *searching* and *creativity.* It takes time and costs money. Issues such as when to stop generating alternatives can be very important. Generating alternatives is heavily dependent on the availability and cost of information and requires expertise in the problem area. This is the least formal aspect of problem solving. Alternatives can be generated with heuristics. The generation of alternatives from either individuals or groups can be supported by electronic brainstorming software.

Note that the search for alternatives usually comes after the criteria for evaluating the alternatives are determined. This sequence can reduce the search for alternatives and the efforts involved in evaluation of the alternatives, though identifying potential alternatives can sometimes aid in identifying criteria.

PREDICTING THE OUTCOME OF EACH ALTERNATIVE

To evaluate and compare alternatives, it is necessary to predict the future outcome of each proposed alternative. Decision situations are often classified on the basis of what the decision maker knows (or believes) about the forecasted results. Customary, we classify this knowledge into three categories (Figure 2.6), ranging from complete knowledge to total ignorance. These categories are

- Certainty
- Risk
- Uncertainty.

DECISION MAKING UNDER CERTAINTY

In decision making under *certainty,* it is *assumed* that complete knowledge is available so that the decision maker knows exactly what the outcome of each course of action will be (as in a deterministic environment). It may not be true that the outcomes are 100 percent known, but often this assumption simplifies the model and makes it tractable. The decision maker is viewed as a perfect predictor of the future because it is assumed that there is only one outcome for each alternative. For example, the alternative of investing in U.S. Treasury bills is one for which there is complete availability of information about the future return on the investment. Such a situation occurs most often with structured prob-

FIGURE 2.6 THE ZONES OF DECISION MAKING

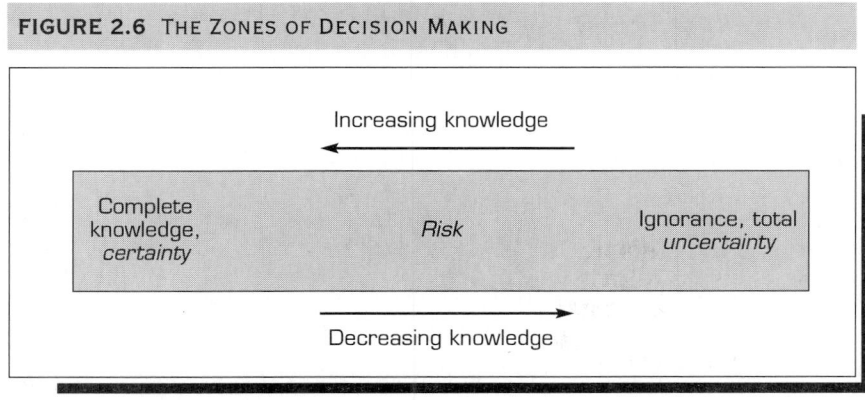

lems with short time horizons (up to 1 year). Another example is that every time you park downtown, you get a parking ticket because you exceed the time limit on the parking meter—although once it did not happen. This situation can still be treated as one of decision making under certainty. Some problems under certainty are not structured enough to be approached by analytical methods and models; they require a DSS approach.

DECISION MAKING UNDER RISK (RISK ANALYSIS)

A decision made under risk[1] (also known as a probabilistic or stochastic decision making situation) is one in which the decision maker must consider several possible outcomes for each alternative, each with a given probability of occurrence. Also, the long-run probabilities of the occurrences of the given outcomes are assumed known or can be estimated. Under these assumptions, the decision maker can assess the degree of risk associated with each alternative (called *calculated* risk). **Risk analysis** can be performed by calculating the expected value of each alternative and selecting the alternative with the *best* expected value.

DECISION MAKING UNDER UNCERTAINTY

In decision making under **uncertainty,** the decision maker considers situations in which several outcomes are possible for each course of action. In contrast to the risk situation, in this case the decision maker does not know, or cannot estimate, the probability of occurrence of the possible outcomes.

Decision making under uncertainty is more difficult because of insufficient information. Modeling of such situations involves assessment of the decision maker's (or the organization's) attitude toward risk.

MEASURING OUTCOMES

The value of an alternative is evaluated in terms of goal attainment. Sometimes an outcome is expressed directly in terms of a goal. For example, profit is an outcome, profit maximization is a goal, and both are expressed in dollar terms. An outcome such as customer satisfaction may be measured by the number of complaints, by the level of loyalty to a product, or by ratings found by surveys.

SCENARIOS

A **scenario** is a statement of assumptions about the operating environment of a particular system at a given time, that is, a narrative description of the decision situation setting. A scenario describes the decision and uncontrollable variables and parameters for a specific modeling situation. It also may provide the procedures and constraints for the modeling itself.

Scenarios originated in the theater. The term was then borrowed for war gaming and large-scale simulations. Scenario planning and analysis is a DSS tool that can capture a whole range of possibilities. A manager can construct a series of scenarios (what-if cases), perform computerized analyses, and learn more about the system and decision-making problem as he or she analyzes it.

A scenario is especially helpful in simulation and in what-if analysis. In both cases, we change scenarios and examine the results. For example, one can change the anticipated demand for hospitalization (an input variable for planning), thus creating a new scenario. Then, one can measure the anticipated cash flow of the hospital for each scenario.

---

[1]Our definitions of the terms *risk* and *uncertainty* were suggested by F. H. Knight of the University of Chicago in 1933. There are other, comparable definitions in use.

Scenarios play an important role in MSS because they

- Help identify potential opportunities and problem areas
- Provide flexibility in planning
- Identify the leading edges of changes that management should monitor
- Help validate major modeling assumptions
- Allow the decision maker to explore the behavior of a system through a model
- Help to check the sensitivity of the proposed solutions to changes in the environment as described by the scenarios.

POSSIBLE SCENARIOS

There may be thousands of possible scenarios for every decision situation. However, the following are especially useful:

- The worst possible scenario
- The best possible scenario
- The most likely scenario
- The average scenario.

The scenario determines the context of the analysis to be performed.

ERRORS IN DECISION MAKING

Since the model is the critical component in the decision-making process, it is possible to make a number of errors in its construction and use. It is critical to validate the model before it is used. Gathering the correct amount of information, with the right level of precision and accuracy, to incorporate into the decision-making process is also critical. Sawyer (1999) describes the "seven deadly sins of decision making," most of which are behavior- or information-related. We summarize these "sins" in DSS in Focus 2.6.

DSS IN FOCUS 2.6

THE SEVEN DEADLY SINS OF DECISION MAKING

Sawyer (1999) describes what she calls "the seven deadly sins of decision making." These are all common pitfalls of decision making that decision makers often unwittingly encounter. They are all interrelated. The seven deadly sins are

1. Believing that you already have all the answers (no attempt is made to seek outside information or expertise)

2. Asking the wrong questions (you need the right information to make an informed decision)

3. The old demon ego (a decision maker feels he or she is right and refuses to back down from a bad policy or decision)

4. Flying-by-the-seat-of-your-pants saves money— doesn't it? (by not seeking out information, an organization saves money—and makes bad decisions)

5. All aboard the bandwagon: if it works for them, it'll work for us (copying someone else's ideas really involves understanding why and how they work)

6. Hear no evil (discourage and ignore negative advice—kill the messenger with the bad news)

7. Hurry up and wait: making no decision can be the same as making a bad decision (procrastination is not necessarily a good management technique).

Of course, all these lead to faulty decisions that lead to unnecessary and high costs for firms and individuals (including getting fired). Many of these "sins" clearly involve behavioral issues and lack of information and expertise that leads to less objectivity in the decision-making process.

Source: Based on D. C. Sawyer, *Getting It Right: Avoiding the High Cost of Wrong Decisions,* Boca Raton, FL: St. Lucie Press, 1999.

2.8 DECISION MAKING: THE CHOICE PHASE

Choice is the *critical act* of decision making. The choice phase is the one in which the actual decision is made and where the commitment to follow a certain course of action is made. The boundary between the design and choice phases is often unclear because certain activities can be performed during both the design and choice phases and because one can return frequently from choice activities to design activities. For example, one can generate new alternatives while performing an evaluation of existing ones. The choice phase includes search, evaluation, and recommendation of an appropriate solution to the model. A solution to a model is a specific set of values for the decision variables in a selected alternative.

Note: Solving the model is not the same as solving the problem the model represents. The solution to the model yields a recommended solution to the problem. The problem is considered solved only if this recommended solution is *successfully implemented.*

SEARCH APPROACHES

The choice phase involves a search for an appropriate course of action (among those identified during the design phase) that can solve the problem. There are several major search approaches, depending on the criteria (or criterion) of choice. These search approaches are shown in Figure 2.7. For normative models, either an analytical approach is used or a complete, exhaustive enumeration (comparing outcomes of *all* alternatives to each other) is applied. For descriptive models, a comparison of a limited number of alternatives is used, either blindly or by employing heuristics. Usually the results guide the decision maker in his or her search.

ANALYTICAL TECHNIQUES

Analytical techniques use mathematical formulas to derive an optimal solution directly or to predict a certain result. Analytical techniques are used mainly for solving structured problems, usually of a tactical or operational nature, in areas such as resource allocation or inventory management. Blind or heuristic search approaches are generally employed for solving more complex problems.

ALGORITHMS

Analytical techniques may use algorithms to increase the efficiency of the search. An **algorithm** is a step-by-step search process (Figure 2.8) for arriving at an *optimal* solution. Solutions are generated and tested for possible improvements. An improvement is made whenever possible, and the new solution is subjected to an improvement test based on the principle of choice (objective value found). The process continues until no further improvement is possible.

BLIND AND HEURISTIC SEARCH APPROACHES

In conducting a search, a description of a desired solution may be given. This is called a *goal.* A set of possible steps leading from initial conditions to the goal is called the *search steps. Problem solving* is done by searching through the space of possible solutions. Two search methods are considered: blind search and heuristic search.

FIGURE 2.7 FORMAL SEARCH APPROACHES

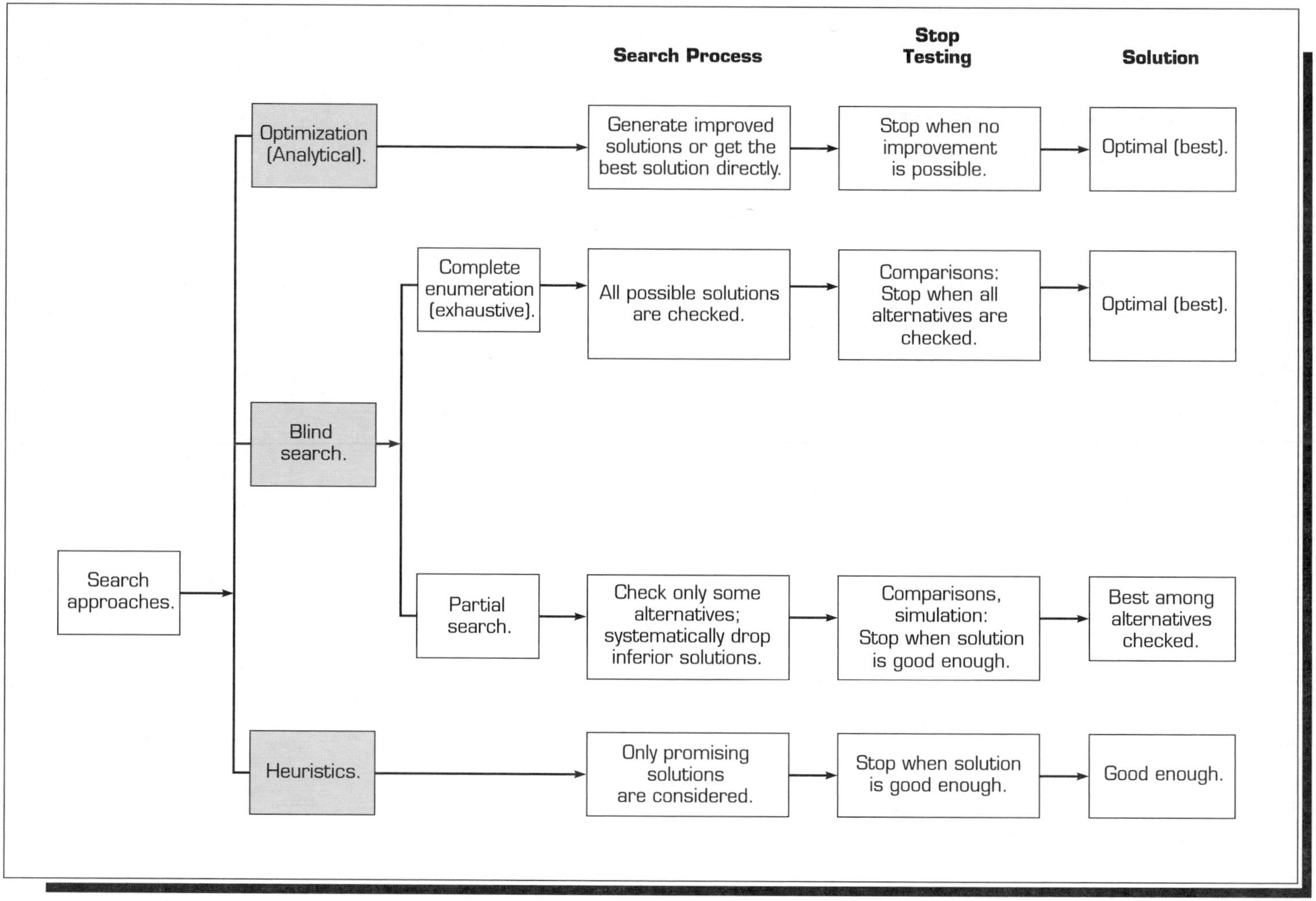

Search Process	Stop Testing	Solution

Search approaches. → Optimization (Analytical). → Generate improved solutions or get the best solution directly. → Stop when no improvement is possible. → Optimal (best).

Blind search. → Complete enumeration (exhaustive). → All possible solutions are checked. → Comparisons: Stop when all alternatives are checked. → Optimal (best).

Blind search. → Partial search. → Check only some alternatives; systematically drop inferior solutions. → Comparisons, simulation: Stop when solution is good enough. → Best among alternatives checked.

Heuristics. → Only promising solutions are considered. → Stop when solution is good enough. → Good enough.

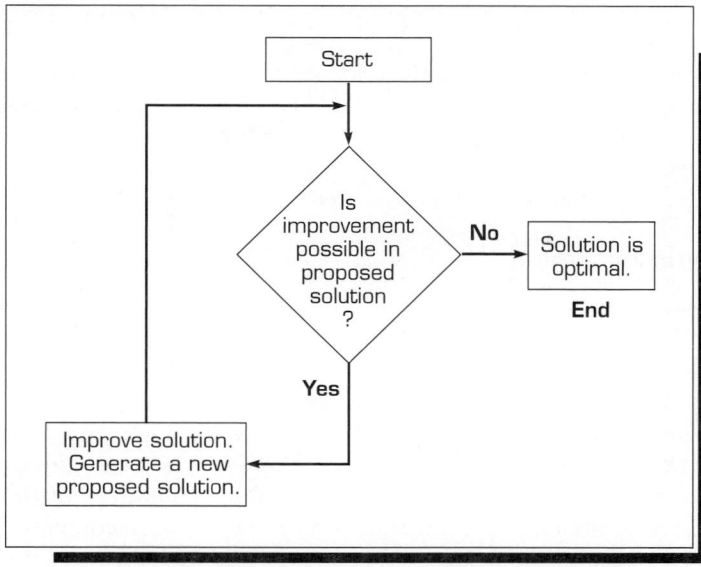

FIGURE 2.8 THE PROCESS OF USING AN ALGORITHM

BLIND SEARCH

Blind search techniques are arbitrary search approaches that are not guided. There are two types of blind searches: a *complete enumeration,* for which all the alternatives are considered and therefore an optimal solution is discovered; and an *incomplete,* partial search which continues until a good enough solution is found. The latter is a form of sub-optimization.

There are practical limits on the amount of time and computer storage available for blind searches. In principle, blind search methods can eventually find an optional solution in most search situations, and in some situations the scope of the search can be limited; however, the method is not practical for solving very large problems because too many solutions must be examined before an optimal solution is found.

HEURISTIC SEARCH

For many applications, it is possible to find rules to guide the search process and reduce the amount of necessary computations. This is done by heuristic search methods.

Heuristics (from the Greek word for *discovery*) are decision rules governing how a problem should be solved. Usually, heuristics are developed on the basis of a solid, rigorous analysis of the problem, sometimes involving designed experimentation. In contrast, guidelines are usually developed as a result of a trial-and-error experience. Some heuristics are derived from guidelines. *Heuristic searches* (or *programming*) are step-by-step procedures (like algorithms) which are repeated until a satisfactory solution is found (unlike algorithms). In practice, such a search is much faster and cheaper than a blind search, and the solutions can be very close to the best ones. In fact, problems that theoretically can be solved to optimality (but with a very long solution time) are in practice sometimes solved by heuristics that can guarantee a solution within a few percent of the optimal objective value. For details, see Camm and Evans (1996) and Schwartz (1998). Examples of heuristics are given in Table 2.3. For the role of heuristics in MSS, see Chapters 5 and 10.

TABLE 2.3   Examples of Heuristics

Sequence jobs through a machine	Do the jobs that require the least time first.
Purchase stocks	If a price-to-earnings ratio exceeds 10, do not buy the stock.
Travel	Do not use the freeway between 8 and 9 A.M.
Capital investment in high-tech projects	Consider only projects with estimated payback periods of less than 2 years.
Purchase of a house	Buy only in a good neighborhood, but buy only in the lower price range.

Decision makers use heuristics or rules of thumb for many reasons, some more reasonable than others. A decision maker may use a heuristic if he or she does not know the best ways to solve a problem or if optimization techniques have not yet been developed. A decision maker might not be able to obtain all the information necessary, or the cost of obtaining the information or developing a complex model may be too high.

It is critical to realize that heuristics provide time-pressured managers and other professionals with a simple way of dealing with a complex world, producing correct or partially correct judgments more often than not. In addition, it may be inevitable that humans will adopt some way of simplifying decisions. The only drawback is that individuals frequently adopt. . . heuristics without being aware of them. (Bazerman, 1998)

2.9 EVALUATION: MULTIPLE GOALS, SENSITIVITY ANALYSIS, WHAT-IF, AND GOAL SEEKING

The search process described earlier is coupled with evaluation. Evaluation is the final step that leads to a recommended solution.

MULTIPLE GOALS

The analysis of management decisions aims at evaluating, to the greatest possible extent, how far each alternative advances management toward its goals. Unfortunately, managerial problems are seldom evaluated with a single, simple goal like profit maximization. Today's management systems are much more complex, and one with a single goal is rare. Instead, managers want to attain *simultaneous goals,* where some of them conflict. Therefore, it is often necessary to analyze each alternative in light of its determination of each of several goals.

For example, consider a profit-making firm. In addition to earning money, the company wants to grow, develop its products and employees, provide job security to its workers, and serve the community. Managers want to satisfy the shareholders and at the same time enjoy high salaries and expense accounts, and employees want to increase their take-home pay and benefits. When a decision is to be made, say, about an investment project, some of these goals complement each other while others conflict.

Many quantitative models of decision theory are based on comparing a single measure of effectiveness, generally some form of "utility" to the decision maker. Therefore, it is usually necessary to transform a multiple-goal problem into a single-measure-of-effectiveness problem before comparing the effects of the solutions. This is a common method for handling multiple goals in a linear programming model. For example, see DSS in Action 2.7, in which we have modified the MBI model into a *goal programming* model.

DSS IN FOCUS 2.7

THE GOAL PROGRAMMING MBI MODEL

In a goal programming model, all goals are represented as constraints that have target values for the left-hand side. For example, the labor constraint has a target value of 200,000 days. If the target is met, there is no penalty. If we use more than 200,000 days of labor, we are over our goal, and there is a penalty for the deviation. If we are under our goal (we use less labor than the target amount), there may also be a penalty, perhaps wages must be paid for no production. The same is true of the budget constraint. In this model, we convert the objective of maximizing profit to a goal of profit meeting or exceeding a target level of $5 million. If we are under our goal, there is a penalty; but if we are over our goal, there is no penalty. Penalties are imposed by weights indicating the importance of each of the multiple objectives and the importance of each being over or under our goal. The marketing constraints here are not goals, but required limits.

Profit goal: $8000X_1 + 12{,}000X_2 - OVER_1 + UNDER_1 = 5{,}000{,}000$

Labor goal: $300X_1 + 500X_2 - OVER_2 + UNDER_2 = 200{,}000$

Budget goal: $10{,}000X_1 + 15{,}000X_2 - OVER_3 + UNDER_3 = 8{,}000{,}000$

Marketing requirement for CC-7: $X_1 \geq 100$

Marketing requirement for CC-8: $X_2 \geq 200$

The objective is to minimize a weighted sum of the *OVER* and *UNDER* variables. For a particular solution, the UNDER and OVER variables indicate the amount the left-hand side of the goal constraint value varies from the target. Below is a Lingo model and solution. The budget is right on target (it had the highest weights in the objective). The profit is outstanding. We produce 500 units of CC-7 ($=X_1$), and 200 units of CC-8 ($=X_2$). We exceeded the $5 million by $1.4 million ($= OVER_1$), which leads to a total profit of $6.4 million, which is $1.3 million greater than before. But because $OVER_2$ is 50,000, we are using an additional 50,000 hours of labor. Since the weight in the objective for $OVER_2$ reflects the marginal cost of obtaining additional labor, this solution is an improvement over the standard linear programming one.

```
! Lingo Goalprodmixsimple Model ;
MIN   =   0 * OVER1 + 1000 * UNDER1 +
         50 * OVER2 +   10 * UNDER2 +
        100 * OVER3 +   20 * UNDER3 ;
[PROFIT] 8000 * X1 + 12000 * X2 - OVER1 + UNDER1 = 5000000 ;
[LABOR]   300 * X1 + 500 * X2 - OVER2 + UNDER2 = 200000 ;
[BUDGET]  10000 * X1 + 15000 * x2 - OVER3 + UNDER3 = 8000000 ;
[MARKET1]   X1 >= 100 ;
[MARKET2]   X2 >= 200 ;
<<< Lingo Goalprodmixout Solution (Variables only) >>>
     Variable         Value        Reduced Cost
       OVER1        1400000.         0.0000000
      UNDER1       0.0000000         1000.000
       OVER2        50000.00         0.0000000
      UNDER2       0.0000000         60.00000
       OVER3       0.0000000         101.5000
      UNDER3       0.0000000         18.50000
          X1        500.0000         0.0000000
          X2        200.0000         0.0000000
```

Here is a list of some of the difficulties that occur when analyzing multiple goals:

- An explicit statement of the organization's goals is usually difficult to obtain.
- The decision maker may change the importance assigned to specific goals over time or for different decision scenarios.
- Goals and subgoals are viewed differently at various levels of the organization and within different departments.
- Goals themselves change in response to changes in the organization and its environment.
- The relationship between alternatives and their determination of goals may be difficult to quantify.
- Complex problems are solved by groups of decision makers, each with his or her own agenda.
- Various participants assess the importance (priorities) of the various goals differently.

Several methods of handling multiple goals can be used when working with MSS. The most common ones are

- Utility theory
- Goal programming
- Expression of goals as constraints using linear programming
- A point system.

Some methods even work interactively with the decision maker in searching the solution space for an alternative that provides for required attainment of all goals while searching for an "efficient" solution. DSS in Action 2.8 contains an example. For more on multiple-goal decision making, see Chapter 5 and Tamiz et al. (1998).

SENSITIVITY ANALYSIS

A model builder makes predictions and assumptions regarding the input data, many of which deal with the assessment of uncertain futures. When the model is solved, the results depend on these data. **Sensitivity analysis** attempts to assess the impact of a change in the input data or parameters on the proposed solution (the result variable).

Sensitivity analysis is extremely important in MSS because it allows flexibility and adaptation to changing conditions and to the requirements of different decision-making situations; it provides a better understanding of the model and the decision-making situation it attempts to describe; and it permits the manager to input his or her data so that confidence in the model increases. Sensitivity analysis tests relationships such as

- The impact of changes in external (uncontrollable) variables and parameters on outcome variable(s)
- The impact of changes in decision variables on outcome variable(s)
- The effect of uncertainty in estimating external variables
- The effects of different, dependent interactions among variables
- The robustness of decisions under changing conditions.

Sensitivity analyses are used for

- Revising models to eliminate too large sensitivities
- Adding details about sensitive variables or scenarios
- Obtaining better estimates of sensitive external variables

SELECT A COLLEGE WITH AN INTERACTIVE MULTIPLE-GOAL DSS

One way to decompose and solve a multiple-goal problem with qualitative and quantitative criteria is to use the Analytical Hierarchy Process (AHP), especially as implemented in Expert Choice software. In January 2000 we consulted with a senior-level DSS class at The University of Georgia to build a DSS to help a decision maker, typically a high school senior, select a college. We planned to capture the decision-making problem in a model. All the class members were familiar with the problem (and perhaps just a little biased).

The goal was to select a college. Clearly, selecting a college involves many criteria (possibly hundreds) and many decision alternatives (thousands). Our first task was to examine potential criteria. After much discussion, we came up with the four most important (we eliminated four others): (1) distance (from home); (2) cost (including cost of living and the impact of state scholarships); (3) reputation (of the university), and (4) size (total number of students). Again, after a discussion, to limit the work we came up with five viable decision alternatives (choices) (students considered from 1 to 12 choices in practice): (1) The University of Georgia (UGA); (2) Georgia Tech (GATECH);

(3) Georgia State University (GSU); (4) the University of Tennessee (TENN); and (5) the University of Virginia (UVA). The model is an inverted tree, starting with the goal, underneath which are the criteria, and underneath these are all five choices. The Expert Choice model appears below.

As a group, the class made pairwise comparisons of all criteria, and then for each, the choices. Both verbal and graphic comparison modes were used. The criteria weights that resulted were distance at 0.094, cost at 0.545, reputation at 0.321, and size at 0.041. We estimated these weights beforehand as 0.2, 0.36, 0.35, and 0.09 respectively. Clearly, cost was the major consideration followed by reputation. Size and distance accounted for less than 15 percent of the decision weight. Satisfied that we had captured the correct criteria and weights, we moved to pairwise comparison of the choices relative to each criterion. At this point, a number of interesting issues arose. Some students prefer large-sized universities (Tennessee), while others prefer small ones (Georgia Tech). The model is robust enough so that each decision maker's preference can be captured and used individually or in a group setting with

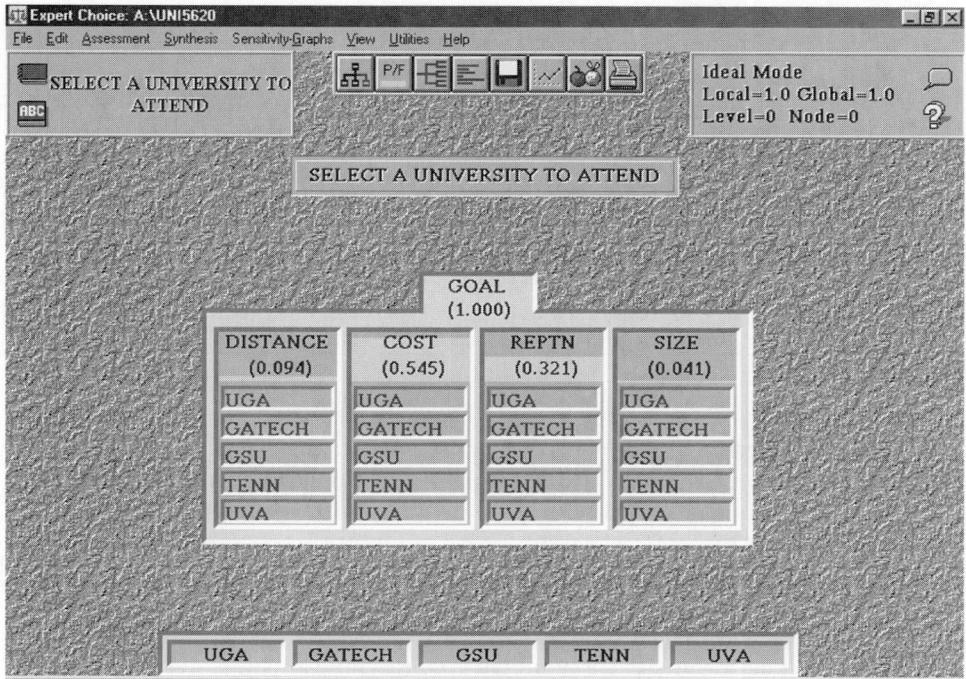

By permission of Expert Choice Inc.

TeamEC. Another interesting issue involved distance. Most students were from the Atlanta area. Being close to home was least preferred, but being far from home was not preferred very much either. Being relatively close was preferred. This gave the University of Georgia an edge in that it is about 70 miles (about 100 kilometers) from Atlanta, while Georgia Tech and Georgia State University are in Atlanta and Tennessee and Virginia are relatively far away. The cost criterion was influenced by the Georgia HOPE Scholarship Program, which grants every Georgia high school student *free* tuition and fees for 4 years to any state college if he or she graduates from high school with and maintains a B average in college. When synthesized, the weighted results, divided up the total weight of 1.000 as follows: the University of Georgia, 0.292—a clear winner; Georgia State University, 0.209; Georgia Tech, 0.197; the University of Virginia, 0.170; and the University of Tennessee, 0.132 (as shown below). The overall inconsistency index was 0.09, indicating that the class was quite rational in establishing their preference structure. For more details on the AHP and Expert Choice, see Saaty (1999), www.expertchoice.com of Expert Choice, Inc., and Case Application 2.3.

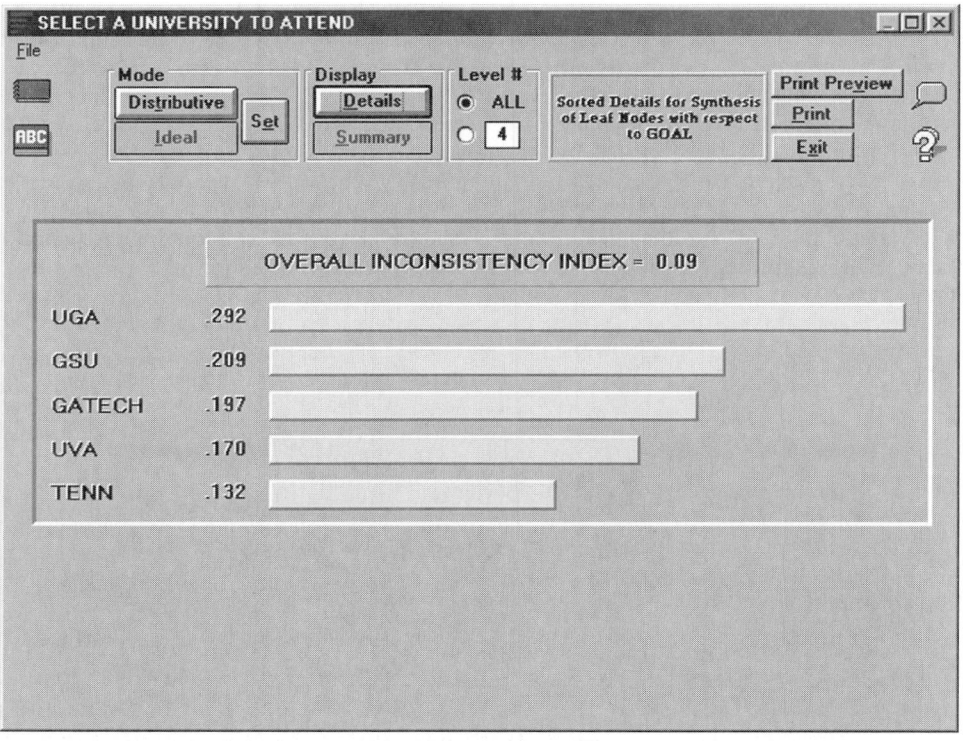

- Altering the real-world system to reduce actual sensitivities
- Accepting and using the sensitive (and hence vulnerable) real world, leading to the monitoring of actual results continuously and closely.

The two types of sensitivity analyses are automatic and trial and error.

AUTOMATIC SENSITIVITY ANALYSIS

Automatic sensitivity analysis is performed in some standard quantitative model implementations such as linear programming. For example, it reports the range within which a certain input variable or parameter value (such as unit cost) can vary without making any significant impact on the proposed solution. Automatic sensitivity analysis is usually limited to one change at a time, and only for certain variables. However, it is very powerful because of its ability to establish ranges and limits very fast (and with little or no additional computational effort). For example, as part of the linear programming (LP) solution report (see this book's Web site at www.prenhall.com/turban) for the solution files for the MBI Corporation product-mix problem described earlier. If the right-hand side of the marketing constraint on CC-8 could be decreased by one unit, then the net profit would increase by $1,333.33. This is valid for the right-hand side decreasing to zero. For details see Wagner (1995).

TRIAL AND ERROR

The impact of changes in any variable, or in several variables, can be determined through a simple trial-and-error approach. One changes some input data and re-solves the problem. When the changes are repeated several times, better and better solutions may be discovered. Such experimentation, which is easy to conduct when using appropriate modeling software like Excel, has two approaches: what-if analysis and goal seeking.

WHAT-IF ANALYSIS

What-if analysis is structured as What will happen to the solution if an input variable, an assumption, or a parameter value is changed?
Examples include the following:

- What will happen to the total inventory cost if the cost of carrying inventories increases by 10 percent?
- What will be the market share if the advertising budget increases by 5 percent?

Assuming the appropriate user interface, managers can ask the computer model these types of questions easily and get immediate answers. Furthermore, they can perform multiple cases and thereby change the percentage, or any other data in the question, as desired. All this is done directly, without a computer programmer.

Figure 2.9 shows a spreadsheet example of a what-if query for a cash flow problem. The user changes the cells containing the initial sales (from 100 to 120) and the sales growth rate (from 3 percent to 4 percent per quarter). The computer immediately recomputes the value of the annual net profit cell (from $127 to $182). What-if analysis is common in expert systems. Users are given the opportunity to change their answers to some of the system's questions, and a revised recommendation is found.

GOAL SEEKING

Goal-seeking analysis calculates the values of inputs necessary to achieve a desired level of an output (goal). It represents a backward solution approach. Some examples of goal seeking are

- What annual R&D budget is needed for an annual growth rate of 15 percent by 2000?
- How many nurses are needed to reduce the average waiting time of a patient in the emergency room to less than 10 minutes?

An example of goal seeking is shown in Figure 2.10.

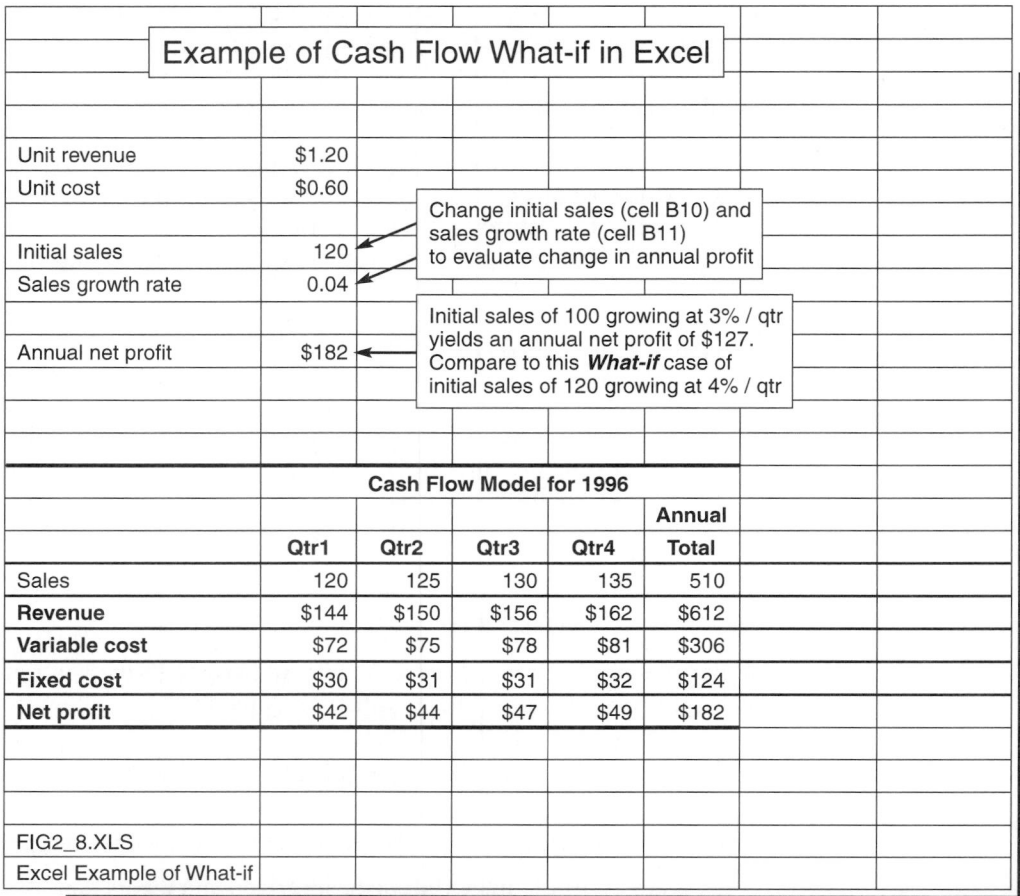

Example of Cash Flow What-if in Excel					
Unit revenue	$1.20				
Unit cost	$0.60				
Initial sales	120	Change initial sales (cell B10) and sales growth rate (cell B11) to evaluate change in annual profit			
Sales growth rate	0.04				
		Initial sales of 100 growing at 3% / qtr yields an annual net profit of $127. Compare to this *What-if* case of initial sales of 120 growing at 4% / qtr			
Annual net profit	$182				

Cash Flow Model for 1996

	Qtr1	Qtr2	Qtr3	Qtr4	Annual Total
Sales	120	125	130	135	510
Revenue	$144	$150	$156	$162	$612
Variable cost	$72	$75	$78	$81	$306
Fixed cost	$30	$31	$31	$32	$124
Net profit	$42	$44	$47	$49	$182

FIG2_8.XLS
Excel Example of What-if

FIGURE 2.9 EXAMPLE OF "WHAT-IF" ANALYSIS DONE IN EXCEL WORKSHEET

Initially, initial sales were 100 growing at 3 percent per quarter yielding an annual net profit of $127. By changing the initial sales cell to 120 and the sales growth rate to 4 percent, the annual net profit rose to $182.

COMPUTING A BREAK-EVEN POINT USING GOAL SEEKING

Some modeling software packages can directly compute break-even points, an important application of goal seeking. This involves determining the value of the decision variables (e.g., quantity to produce) that generate zero profit. For example, in a financial planning model in Excel, the internal rate of return is the interest rate that produces a net present value of zero.

In many decision support systems, it can be difficult to conduct sensitivity analysis because the prewritten routines usually present only a limited opportunity for asking what-if questions. In a DSS, the what-if and the goal-seeking options must be easy to perform.

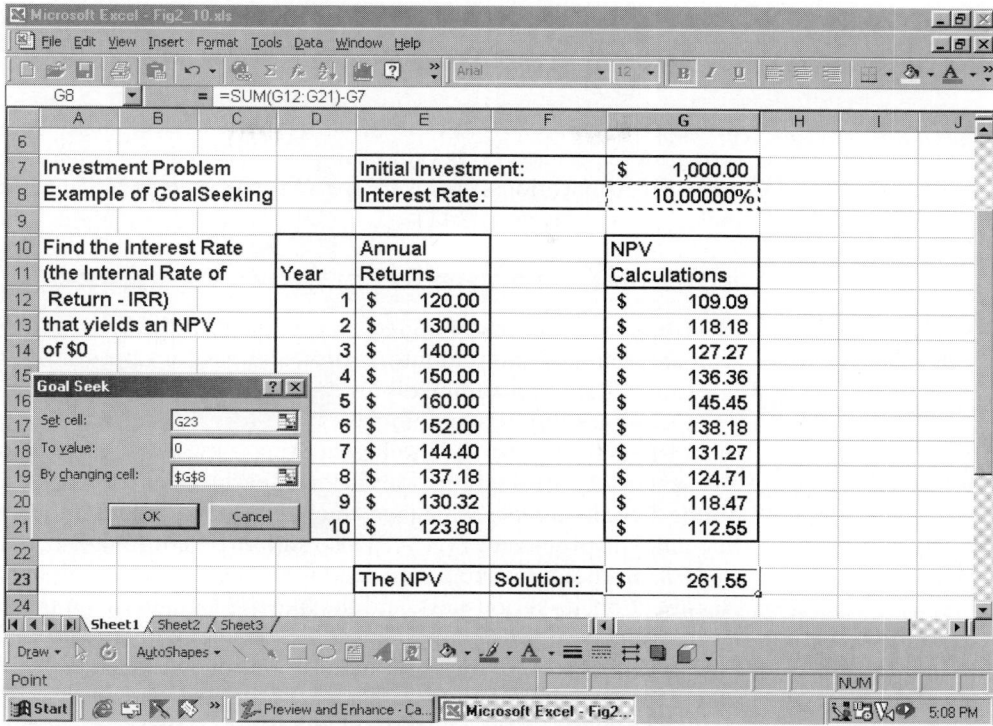

FIGURE 2.10 GOAL-SEEKING ANALYSIS

The goal to be achieved is NPV equal to zero, which determines the internal rate of return (IRR) of this cash flow including the investment. We set the NPV cell to value 0 by changing the interest rate cell. The answer is 38.77059 percent.

2.10 DECISION MAKING: THE IMPLEMENTATION PHASE

In *The Prince,* Machiavelli astutely noted more than 400 years ago that there was "nothing more difficult to carry out, nor more doubtful of success, nor more dangerous to handle, than to initiate a new order of things." The *implementation* of a proposed solution to a problem is, in effect, the initiation of a new order of things or the introduction of *change.* And, change must be managed. User expectations must be managed as part of change management.

The definition of implementation is somewhat complicated because implementation is a long, involved process with vague boundaries. Simplistically, *implementation* means putting a recommended solution to work. Many of the generic issues of implementation, such as resistance to change, degree of support of top management, and user training, are important in dealing with MSS. Implementation of MSS is discussed in detail in Chapter 18. The decision-making process described in Sections 2.6–2.10, though conducted by people, can be improved with computer support, the subject of the next section.

2.11 HOW DECISIONS ARE SUPPORTED

In Chapter 1 we discussed the need for computerized decision support and briefly described some decision aids. (For examples of MSS decision making, see DSS in Action 2.9 and Case Applications 2.1–2.3.) Here we relate specific MSS technologies to the decision-making process (Figure 2.11).

SUPPORT FOR THE INTELLIGENCE PHASE

The primary requirement of decision support for the intelligence phase is the ability to scan external and internal information sources for opportunities and problems and to interpret what the scanning discovers.

Decision support technologies can be very helpful. For example, the major purpose of an EIS is to support the intelligence phase by continuously monitoring both internal and external information, looking for early signs of problems and opportunities. Similarly, data mining (which may include expert systems and neural networks) and on-line analytic processing (OLAP) also support the intelligence phase.

ES, on the other hand, can render advice regarding the nature of the problem, its classification, its seriousness, and the like. ES can advise on the suitability of a solution approach and on the likelihood of successfully solving the problem. One of the primary areas of ES success is interpreting information and diagnosing problems. This capability can be exploited in the intelligence phase.

Another area of support is reporting. Both routine and ad hoc reports can aid in the intelligence phase. For example, regular reports can be designed to assist in the problem-finding activity by comparing expectations with current and projected performance.

The intelligence phase is a primary target for DSS and for other computer-based information systems that deal with nonstructured problems (Lucas, 1995).

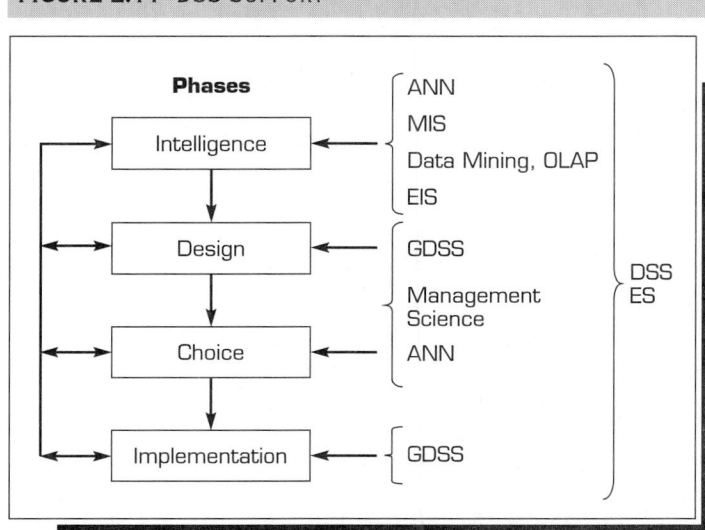

FIGURE 2.11 DSS SUPPORT

Source: Based on Sprague, R. H., Jr., "A Framework for the Development of DSS." *MIS Quarterly,* Dec. 1980, Fig. 5, p. 13.

DSS IN ACTION 2.9

TRACKING SALES AT CONAGRA

ConAgra Frozen Foods in Omaha, NE, uses MyEureka! software from Information Advantage to provide data on demand to their marketing staff. MyEureka! allows companies to access, organize, and analyze large data sets. It is quick and flexible so that users can get the information they need in the form that they want. For example, the ConAgra database tracks information so that a marketing analyst can determine the relationship between trade promotions and sales to gauge their effectiveness immediately.

This online analytical processing (OLAP) system allows a marketing analyst to determine the effectiveness of promotions fast and make quick decisions on what works in what market and why. Also, users can generate reports to obtain needed information, bypassing involvement with the MIS staff, saving time, and getting exactly what they need.

Source: Based on A. Horowitz, "Smart Decision Making," *Intelligent Enterprise,* June 1, 1999, p. 59.

SUPPORT FOR THE DESIGN PHASE

The design phase involves generating alternative courses of action, discussing the criteria for choice and their relative importance, and forecasting the future consequences of using various alternatives. Several of these activities can use standard models provided by a DSS (such as financial and forecasting models). The generation of alternatives for structured problems can be provided through the use of either standard or special models. However, the generation of alternatives for complex problems requires expertise that can be provided by a human, brainstorming software, or an expert system. Most DSS have quantitative analysis capabilities, and an internal ES can assist with qualitative methods as well as with the expertise required in selecting quantitative analysis and forecasting models. If the problem requires brainstorming to help identify important issues and options, a GSS may prove helpful. Also, tools that provide cognitive mapping can help.

SUPPORT FOR THE CHOICE PHASE

In addition to providing models that rapidly identify a best or good enough alternative, a DSS can support the choice phase through the what-if and goal-seeking analyses. Different scenarios can be tested for the selected option to reinforce the final decision. An ES can be used to assess the desirability of certain solutions as well as to recommend an appropriate solution. If a group makes the decision, a GSS can provide support.

SUPPORT FOR THE DECISION IMPLEMENTATION

Interviews conducted by Mittman and Moore (1984) suggest that the DSS benefits provided during implementation are often as important as or even more important than those in the earlier phases. Respondents reported many uses of DSS in implementation activities such as decision communication, explanation, and justification.

Implementation phase DSS benefits are partly due to the vividness and detail of the analysis and displayed output. For example, one chief executive officer (CEO) gives employees and external parties not only the aggregate financial goals and cash needs for the near term but also the calculations, intermediate results, and statistics used in determining the aggregate figures. In addition to communicating the financial goals unambiguously, the CEO signals other messages. Employees know that the CEO has thought through the assumptions behind the financial goals and is serious about their importance and attainability. Bankers and directors are shown that the CEO was personally involved in analyzing cash needs and is aware of and responsible for the implications of the financing requests prepared by the finance department. Each of these messages improves decision implementation in some way.

All phases of the decision-making process can be supported by improved communication in group decision making. Computerized systems can facilitate communication by helping people explain and justify their suggestions and opinions. Quantitative support can also be quickly provided for various possible scenarios while a meeting is in session.

Decision implementation can also be supported by ES. An ES can be used as an advisory system regarding implementation problems (such as handling resistance to change). Finally, an ES can provide training that may smooth the course of implementation.

2.12 ALTERNATIVE DECISION-MAKING MODELS

Many decision-making processes are described in the MIS, behavioral, and scientific literature along with many real-world applications to which they have been applied. Some are more theoretical in nature and have been empirically tested, while others are more applied and involve the use of very practical tools to guide the decision-making process. There are more similarities than differences among these processes, and it is instructive to examine and compare the steps in each, as well as their theoretical underpinnings and how they work. Here we review a sample of these methods and provide a brief description.

The Paterson decision-making process [adapted, see Van den Hoven (1996)] consists of the following five steps:

1. Problem identification
2. Generation of alternatives
3. Choice
4. Authorization
5. Implementation.

Note the similarity to the Simon four-phase model.
Kotter's process model (Dearden, 1983) consists of two fairly complicated steps:

1. Agenda setting (stating loosely connected goals and plans addressing a wide range of financial, product/market, and organizational issues)
2. Network building (developing cooperative relationships with all the people who may play a role in providing information for developing and implementing the agenda).

Pounds' (1969) flowchart of managerial behavior has eight steps. The first four involve *problem finding,* while the last four involve *problem solving.* The steps are

1. Choose a model
2. Compare to reality
3. Identify differences
4. Select a difference
5. Choose a model
6. Compare to reality

7. Identify differences
8. Select a difference.

Step 8 returns to step 1. The often chaotic nature of decision making is not captured by this model because the steps do not allow the decision maker to return to earlier steps until the last one is taken.

The Kepner–Tregoe (1965) method is a more widely used rational decision-making approach. It involves three main steps (which are subdivided into many smaller ones). They are

1. Problem analysis, which includes preparing a deviation statement and a hypothesis of possible causes, testing the hypothesis for logical consistency with the specifications, selecting the most probable cause, and verifying for true cause
2. Decision analysis
3. Potential problem analysis, which includes developing an action plan statement (implementation plan) and anticipating specific potential problems.

Because the tools and methods are readily available from Kepner–Tregoe, Inc., many decision makers have adopted this approach.

Hammond et al. (1998) provide a set of core ideas for making better decisions. There are eight key elements for making smart choices. Sometimes a single one can resolve an issue, but all eight should be considered. They are as follows:

1. *Problem.* Define your decision problem to solve the right problem.
2. *Objectives.* Clarify what you're really trying to achieve with your decision.
3. *Alternatives.* Create better alternatives from which to choose.
4. *Consequences.* Describe how well each alternative meets your objectives.
5. *Trade-offs.* Make tough compromises when you can't achieve all your objectives at once.
6. *Uncertainty.* Think about and act on uncertainties affecting your decision.
7. *Risk tolerance.* Account for your appetite for risk.
8. *Linked decisions.* Plan ahead by effectively coordinating current and future decisions.

These key elements provide a solid foundation for decision making. Each can be explored in depth, depending on the decision-making situation.

Cougar (1995, 1996) describes a creative problem-solving (CPS) concept and model based partly on the Simon four-phase model and on other CPS. His variant of the CPS model includes, starting with a stimulus:

1. Opportunity delineation, problem definition
2. Compiling relevant information
3. Generating ideas
4. Evaluating, prioritizing ideas
5. Developing implementation plan

leading to an action. Cougar also describes a variant of this CPS model that allows the stages to be performed out of sequence.

There are many tools and methods that can assist decision makers in problem solving. These include brainstorming methods, interviews, creative visualization, idea evaluation methods, priority setting, change management methods, and so on. See Cougar (1995), Altier (1999), and Pokras (1989) for details.

Pokras (1989) describes a very direct, simple methodology for problem solving, along with tools and worksheets to assist the decision maker. His steps and their results include the following:

1. *Recognition:* agreement that an issue needs resolution
2. *Label:* an agreed-on statement of the problem
3. *Analysis:* unanimous identification of the root cause that needs correcting
4. *Options:* a complete list of possible solutions
5. *Evaluation:* a firm joint decision on the chosen solution
6. *Action plan:* a complete step-by-step roadmap for translating the decision into reality.

The first three steps are considered the *problem definition process,* while the last three steps are considered the solution *decision-making process.*

Bazerman (1998) describes the "anatomy of a decision." There are six steps that must be taken when performing rational decision making:

1. Define the problem
2. Identify the criteria
3. Weigh the criteria
4. Generate alternatives
5. Rate each alternative on each criterion
6. Compute the optimal decision.

These steps are based on the Simon model and fit well into the structure of the Analytical Hierarchy Process (Saaty, 1999). This process fits Case Application 2.3 in which a key grip must decide on which movie projects to work.

In a more theoretical framework, Harrison (1999) describes four different interdisciplinary approaches to decision making. These models are not mutually exclusive and are simplified. They are the rational, organizational, political, and process models. The rational (classical) model is concerned with a maximized outcome. It is highly structured in nature and considered a judgmental decision-making strategy. The organizational (neoclassical) model involves satisficing outcomes. It is a judgmental decision-making strategy. The political (adaptive) model searches for acceptable outcomes. It clearly includes multiple objectives of multiple stakeholders. There are often many qualitative aspects of this type of decision-making approach, and compromise or bargaining is used in the process. Finally, the process (managerial) model has an objectives-oriented outcome. It is a judgmental decision-making strategy with selective use of computation and compromise. Also see Shapira (1997).

From a psychological and economic point of view, Beach (1997) describes several *naturalistic decision theories.* Naturalistic decision theory has an almost exclusive focus on how decisions are actually made instead of on how they *should* be made, which is the focus of prescriptive decision theories (the methods are supposed to be used, and so they are prescribed). Some people see naturalistic decision theory as a development of behavioral decision theory. However, it goes beyond it both in how decisions are described and in explaining decision implementation. *Recognition models* include the following:

1. *Policy.* Includes standard operating procedures; though very efficient and easy to follow, these are very inflexible.
2. *Recognition-primed decision model.* With new situations, a decision maker develops a mental simulation (directed visualization) for imagining the results of selecting certain choices. If problems occur, the actions are modified and another simulation is run.

Narrative-based models are very descriptive. They include

1. *Scenario model.* Creates a reasonable narrative to generate forecasts of what might happen.
2. *Story model.* Juries usually make decisions based on this model. The decision maker creates a story from the decision-making situation. This is an ancient method for organizing knowledge (like a parable).

Argument-driven models consist of walking through a logical argument to reach an appropriate solution. They include the argument-driven action (ADA) model.

Incremental models involve observing public policy decisions and evaluating how options are evaluated before making a decision.

Image theory involves using a set of stored knowledge (images) to set standards that guide decisions about what to do (goals) and how to do it (plans). Goals and plans that are incompatible with existing standards are dropped, and the best of the survivors is chosen. There is a separate version for individuals and organizations. See Weatherly and Beach (1996) for details.

2.13 PERSONALITY TYPES, GENDER, HUMAN COGNITION, AND DECISION STYLES

PERSONALITY (TEMPERAMENT) TYPES

Many studies indicate that there is a strong relationship between personality and decision making. Personality type influences general orientation toward goal attainment, selection of alternatives, treatment of risk, and reactions under stress. It also affects a decision maker's ability to process large quantities of information, time pressure, and reframing. It also influences the rules and communication patterns of an individual decision maker. For example, see Harrison (1999).

People are not alike. In the 1920s, Carl Jung (1923) described how people are fundamentally different, though they all have the same set of instincts that drive them internally. Actually, **personality (temperament) types** were described in ancient Greece by Hippocrates (Keirsey and Bates, 1984). In the 1950s, Myers and Briggs revived Jung's research and developed the well-known Myers–Briggs Type Indicator (Quenk, 1999), along with an interpretation of each type (Berens and Nardi, 1999; Myers and Myers, 1999). The specific Myers–Briggs temperament types are described briefly in DSS in Focus 2.10.

There is a long, detailed Myers–Briggs test that can be administered only by a professional counselor; however, Keirsey and Bates (1984) have published a shorter, readily available questionnaire to determine one's type, along with a detailed description of the types and how they are motivated, act, and interact.

Birkman (1995) developed a personality typing called a "True Colors" (be aware that there are several different "colors" types in books and on the Web). His personality typing follows the basic Jungian structure, however, the establishment of one's personality type requires answering 16 simple, true/false questions. One author has used this personality typing in his classes since 1998, and of the more than 500 students who have been typed, less than 10 have claimed that the types did not match their own sense of their personalities. These color types can be quickly established, discussed, and used to build teams in classes and, more importantly, in decision-making environments. Birkman's True Colors typing is briefly described in DSS in Focus 2.11.

DSS IN FOCUS 2.10

MYERS–BRIGGS TEMPERAMENT TYPES

Myers–Briggs temperament types are characterized along four dimensions, four pairs of so-called preferences. They are

- Extraversion (E) to Intraversion (I)
- Sensation (S) to Intuition (N)
- Thinking (T) to Feeling (F)
- Perceiving (P) to Judging (J).

There are 16 main types (combinations) and an additional 32 mixed types. Types do change over time and depend a bit on mood and situation. Some simple words that describe people of each type are

- Extraversion: sociable
- Introversion: territorial
- Sensation: practical
- Intuition: innovative
- Thinking: impersonal

- Feeling: personal
- Perceiving: open
- Judging: closure.

And, if one examines the entire population, the types are distributed approximately as

- Extraversion (75 percent) to Intraversion (25 percent)
- Sensation (75 percent) to Intuition (25 percent)
- Thinking (50 percent) to Feeling (50 percent)
- Perceiving (50 percent) to Judging (50 percent).

According to Jung, one need not be one or the other of each pair but can exhibit traits of both. Also, through learning, it is possible for an introvert to behave as an extrovert (as do many college faculty), and for an extrovert to behave as an introvert (as do many college students).

Source: Based partly on Keirsey and Bates (1984).

DSS IN FOCUS 2.11

TRUE COLORS TEMPERAMENT TYPES

True Colors temperament types are Red, Green, Yellow, and Blue. The colors have no formal meaning but are simply used to differentiate among the types. These colors appear on the following grid:

Red	Green
Yellow	Blue

Some traits are shared up and down the columns (Red and Yellow, Green and Blue), while others are shared across the rows (Red and Green, Yellow and Blue). Diagonal colors have little in common in their makeup. Green types like to communicate directly and work with people. They like to work in groups and to get people excited about what they are doing. Marketing specialists have a tendency to be Green. Red types also like to communicate directly but stay focused on the task at hand, as do Yellow types. Red types tend to volunteer to be group leaders and stay excited about and focused on getting a job done. Yellow types are most comfortable with indirect communication and like to deal with details (they make great accountants and programmers), while Blue types also prefer indirect communication and are innovative, introspective, and creative but are easily distracted and may need people nearby to provide their creative spark. Blue types make great researchers but often have to be reminded about the projects they are working on. When a team is formed with members of all different color types, the team tends to be very creative and productive.

Source: Based partly on Birkman (1995).

Temperament types help describe how one can best attack decision-making problems because certain activities are better handled by each type. They also indicate how each type relates to each of the other types, describing positive communication patterns, work patterns, and so on. This information can be helpful in determining the best way to interact with your significant other. The most important issue to understand in identifying and using temperament types is that there is no right or wrong, or good or bad, type. People simply have different personality types. People of different types act and react differently in different situations (e.g., under stress, under normal conditions), have different motivational needs and values, conceptualize differently, and readily adopt certain roles in the decision-making process. Each type has preferred ways of learning and explaining (important for college careers and training). Each type is communicated with in different "best" ways, and hence there are differences in the way they work in teams, in the way they lead teams, in how they frame problems, and also in their cognitive and decision styles. Since each type can be best reached differently, it is important in developing shared frames to use an appropriate approach for each type. Finally, it is important to have a balanced team made up of various types to best get the work done. Some types are better "thinkers," while others are better "doers," and so on. Each type can contribute actively to teamwork. Personality type clearly influences one's cognitive style and decision style. See DSS in Action 2.12.

For more information on the Myers–Briggs Type Indicator, see Keirsey and Bates (1984); for more information on True Colors typing, see Birkman (1995).

GENDER

Psychological empirical testing sometimes indicates that there are gender differences and gender similarities in decision making, including factors such as boldness, quality, ability, risk-taking attitudes, communication patterns, and so on.

> Powell and Johnson (1995) observe that decision-support systems are designed assuming no gender differences, but that they may take decisions in different ways and have different information style preferences. Their extensive review of the recent literature suggests that gender differences are associated with abilities and motivation, risk attitude and confidence, as well as decision style. Men are more inclined to take risks than women, in a variety of situations, a difference which does not stem from differences in the perceived probability of success. (Smith, 1999.)

Where gender differences do exist (i.e., have statistical significance) they are very small (Smith, 1999). The results are essentially inconclusive, and so it is unwise to attempt to characterize either males or females as better or worse in decision making.

DSS IN ACTION 2.12

TEMPERAMENT DOES INFLUENCE DECISION STYLE

The influence of a manager's decision style in strategic decision making was examined in an experimental setting. Simulated decisions were used for 79 executive-level hospital managers and 89 hospital middle managers. They first took a Myers–Briggs (1963) type indicator test to determine their decision style. Then the managers received a set of projects keyed to their individual styles to evaluate. Decision style influenced their views of adoption and risk. The decisions of top executives were more style-dependent than those of middle managers. The judicial top executive was found to be action-oriented, and the systematic top executive was found to be action-averse. The speculative and heuristic top executives took nearly identical, neutral positions. Top executives with a sensate style were similar to top executives with a pure systematic style, and top executives with a feeling style were similar to top executives with a pure judicial style.

Source: Modified from P. C. Nutt, "Strategic Decisions Made by Top Executives and Middle Managers with Data and Process Dominant Styles," *Journal of Management Studies,* Vol. 27, No. 2, Mar. 1990, pp. 173–194.

COGNITION THEORY

Cognition is the set of activities by which a person resolves differences between an internalized view of the environment and what actually exists in that environment. In other words, it is the ability to perceive and understand information. Cognitive models are attempts to explain or understand various human cognitive processes. For instance, they explain how people revise previous opinions to conform with a particular choice after they have made that choice.

COGNITIVE STYLE

Cognitive style is the subjective process through which people perceive, organize, and change information during the decision-making process. Cognitive style may be important because in many cases it determines a person's preference for the human–machine interface. For example, should data be raw or aggregate, or should they be tabulated or presented as graphs? Furthermore, cognitive styles affect preferences for qualitative versus quantitative analysis as well as preferences for decision-making aids. In this way, cognitive style affects the way an individual "frames" a decision-making situation to help him or her understand it better. Simply put, a frame "provides the context within which information is used, and different frames put the focus on different kinds of information" (Beach, 1997). In other words, a frame is the decision maker's interpretation of the situation. A frame provides a mental model for the decision maker. As a problem is analyzed, it can be reframed in light of new information. When a group is involved in decision making, it is desirable to have shared frames, which involves some level of common organizational culture. If frames are not shared sufficiently, the group will have trouble developing a consensus.

Research on cognitive styles is directly relevant to the design of management information systems. MIS and transaction processing systems tend to be designed by people who perceive the decision-making process to be systematic. Systematic managers are generally willing to use such systems; they are typically looking for a standard technique and view the system designer as an expert with a catalog of methods. However, such systems do not conform to the natural style of a heuristic decision maker. For such an individual, a system should allow for exploration of a wide range of alternatives, permit changes in priorities or in processing, allow the user to shift easily between levels of detail, and permit some user control over the output form (visual, verbal, graphic, and so on). This is precisely what a DSS attempts to do (Table 2.4).

Although cognitive style is a useful concept, it may be overemphasized in the MIS literature. It can be difficult to take cognitive style into consideration for information systems and decision making. For one thing, cognitive style is a continuous variable. Many people are not completely heuristic or analytic but are somewhere in between. Related to cognitive style are the concepts of personality (temperament) type and decision style.

DECISION STYLE

Decision style is the manner in which decision makers think and react to problems. This includes the way they perceive, their cognitive response, and how values and beliefs vary from individual to individual and from situation to situation. As a result, people make decisions differently. Although there is a general process of decision making, it is far from linear. People do not follow the same steps of the process in the same sequence, nor do they use all the steps. Furthermore, the emphasis, time allotment, and priorities given to each step vary significantly, not only from one person to another but also from one situation to the next. The manner in which managers make decisions (and the way

TABLE 2.4 Cognitive-style Decision Approaches

Problem-solving Dimension	Heuristic	Analytic
Approach to learning	Learns more by acting than by analyzing the situation and places more emphasis on feedback	Employs a planned sequential approach to problem solving; learns more by analyzing the situation than by acting and places less emphasis on feedback
Search	Uses trial and error and spontaneous action	Uses formal rational analysis
Approach to analysis	Uses common sense, intuition, and feelings	Develops explicit, often quantitative, models of the situation
Scope of analysis	Views the totality of the situation as an organic whole rather than as a structure constructed from specific parts	Reduces the problem situation to a set of underlying causal functions
Basis for inferences	Looks for highly visible situational differences that vary with time	Locates similarities or commonalities by comparing objects

Source: G. B. Davis. *Management Information Systems: Conceptual Foundations, Structure, and Development.* New York: McGraw-Hill, 1974, p. 150. Reproduced with permission of McGraw-Hill, Inc.

they interact with other people) describes their decision style. Because decision styles depend on the factors described earlier, there are many decision styles.

In addition to the heuristic and analytic styles mentioned earlier, one can distinguish autocratic versus democratic styles; another style is consultative (with individuals or groups). Of course, there are many combinations and variations of styles. For example, one can be analytic and autocratic, or consultative (with individuals) and heuristic.

For a computerized system to successfully support a manager, it should fit the decision situation as well as the decision style. Therefore, the system should be flexible and adaptable to different users. The ability to ask what-if and goal-seeking questions provides flexibility in this direction. Graphics are also a desirable feature in supporting certain decision styles. If an MSS is to support varying styles, skills, and knowledge, it should not attempt to enforce a specific process. Rather, it should help decision makers use and develop their own styles, skills, and knowledge.

Different decision styles require different types of support. A major factor that determines the type of required support is whether the decision maker is an individual or a group.

2.14 THE DECISION MAKERS

Decisions are often made by individuals, especially at lower managerial levels and in small organizations. There may be conflicting objectives even for a sole decision maker. For example, in an investment decision, an individual investor may consider the rate of return on the investment, liquidity, and safety as objectives. Finally, decisions may be fully automated (only after the decision is made by a human decision maker to do so!).

DSS IN ACTION 2.13

GROUP CONSENSUS: THE 23-MILES-PER-HOUR SPEED LIMIT

Consensus by a group can lead to the implementation of unusual and potentially unrealistic solutions. For example, there is a condominium complex in Lake Worth, FL, where the residents could not agree on a "reasonable" speed limit. They finally came to a consensus that was a compromise value close to the average of the group members' individual suggestions. The speed limit was set to 23 mph (13.8 kph), whereas 20 mph (12 kph) or 25 mph (15 kph) would have been generally considered an acceptable and especially anticipated solution by most drivers.

The discussion of decision making in this chapter essentially focused on an individual decision maker. However, the Opening Vignette described a group making a decision. Most major decisions in medium and large organizations are made by groups. Obviously, in a group decision-making setting, there can often be conflicting objectives. Groups can be of variable size and may include people from different departments or from different organizations. Also, collaborating individuals may have different cognitive styles, personality types, and decision styles. Some clash, whereas others enhance each other. Consensus can be a difficult, political problem (see DSS in Action 2.13). Therefore, the *process* of decision making by a group can be very complicated. Computerized support (Chapter 7) can greatly enhance group decision making. Computer support can be provided at even a broader level, enabling members of whole departments, divisions, or even entire organizations to collaborate online. Such support has evolved over the last few years into enterprise information systems and include forms of GSS, enterprise resource management (ERM), and enterprise resource planning (ERP) systems. For details, see Chapter 8.

❖ CHAPTER HIGHLIGHTS

- Managerial decision making is synonymous with the whole process of management.
- Problem solving is also opportunity evaluation.
- A system is a collection of objects such as people, resources, concepts, and procedures intended to perform an identifiable function or to serve a goal.
- Systems are composed of inputs, outputs, processes, and decision makers.
- All systems are separated from their environment by a boundary which is often imposed by the system designer.
- Systems can be open, interacting with their environment, or closed.
- DSS deals primarily with open systems.
- A model is a simplified representation or abstraction of reality.
- Models are used extensively in MSS; they can be iconic, analog, or mathematical.
- Models enable fast and inexpensive experimentation with systems.
- Modeling can use optimization, heuristic, or simulation techniques.
- Decision making involves four major phases: intelligence, design, choice, and implementation.
- In the intelligence phase, the problem (opportunity) is identified, classified, and decomposed (if needed), and problem ownership is established.

- In the design phase, a model of the system is built, criteria for selection are agreed on, alternatives are generated, results are predicted, and a decision methodology is created.
- There is a trade-off between model accuracy and cost.
- In the choice phase, alternatives are compared and a search for the best (or a good enough) solution is launched. Many search techniques are available.
- In implementing alternatives, one should consider multiple goals and sensitivity analysis issues.
- What-if and goal-seeking approaches are the two most common methods of sensitivity analysis.
- Computer systems can support all phases of decision making by automating many of the required tasks.
- Human cognitive styles may influence human–machine interaction.
- Personality types may influence decision-making capabilities and style.
- Human decision styles need to be recognized in designing MSS.
- There are inconclusive results on how gender differences influence decision making and computer use in decision making.
- Decisions made by individuals or by groups can be supported by MSS.

❖ KEY WORDS

- algorithm
- analog model
- analytical techniques
- choice phase
- cognitive style (cognition)
- decision making
- decision style
- decision variables
- descriptive models
- design phase
- effectiveness
- efficiency
- goal-seeking analysis
- heuristics
- iconic model
- implementation phase
- independent variables
- inputs
- intelligence phase
- interfaces
- linear programming (LP)
- mathematical (quantitative) model
- nonprogrammed problem
- normative models
- optimization
- parameters
- personality (temperament) type
- principle of choice
- problem ownership
- problem solving
- programmed problem
- result (outcome) variable
- risk analysis
- satisficing
- scenario
- sensitivity analysis
- simulation
- suboptimization
- system
- uncertainty
- uncontrollable variables
- what-if analysis

❖ QUESTIONS FOR REVIEW

1. Review what is meant by decision making versus problem solving. Compare the two and determine whether or not it makes sense to distinguish between the two.
2. Define a system.
3. List the major components of a system.
4. Explain the role of feedback in a system.
5. Define the environment of a system.
6. Define open and closed systems. Give an example of each.
7. What is a black box?
8. Define efficiency, define effectiveness, and compare and contrast the two.
9. Define the phases of intelligence, design, choice, and implementation.
10. Distinguish a problem from its symptoms.

11. Define programmed (structured) versus nonprogrammed (unstructured) problems. Give one example in each of the following areas: accounting, marketing, and human resources.
12. List the major components of a mathematical model.
13. Define optimization and contrast it with suboptimization.
14. Compare the normative and descriptive approaches to decision making.
15. Define rational decision making. What does it really mean to be a rational decision maker?
16. Why do people exhibit bounded rationality when problem solving?
17. Distinguish between decision making under certainty, under risk, and under uncertainty.
18. What is the major advantage of optimization?
19. What is the major disadvantage of complete enumeration?
20. Define heuristics.
21. Why do decision makers use heuristics?
22. Compare simulation and optimization.
23. Define sensitivity analysis.
24. Why is a heuristic search superior to a blind search?
25. How can a DSS support the implementation of a decision?
26. Discuss the various types of computerized support.
27. Define what-if analysis and provide an example.
28. Define goal-seeking analysis and provide an example.
29. Define implementation.
30. Define a scenario. How is it used in decision making?
31. What is a personality type? Why is it an important factor to consider in decision making.
32. Define cognition and cognitive style.
33. Define decision style.
34. Describe some potential gender differences in decision making.
35. Compare and contrast decision making by an individual with decision making by a group.

❖ QUESTIONS FOR DISCUSSION

1. Specify in a table the inputs, processes, and outputs of the following systems. Also determine what is required for each system to be efficient and to be effective.
   a. Post office
   b. Elementary school
   c. Grocery store
   d. Farm
2. List possible kinds of feedback for the systems in the previous question.
3. A hospital includes dietary, radiology, housekeeping, and nursing (patient care) departments, and an emergency room. List and describe four system interfaces between pairs of these departments.
4. How would you measure the productivity of
   a. A letter carrier
   b. A salesperson
   c. A professor
   d. A social worker

   e. A student
   f. A farmer

5. Give an example of five elements in the environment of a university.

6. Analyze a managerial system of your choice and identify the following:
   a. The components, inputs, and outputs
   b. The boundary
   c. The environment
   d. The processes
   e. The system's goals
   f. The feedback

7. What are some of the measures of effectiveness in a toy manufacturing plant, a restaurant, an educational institution, and the U.S. Congress?

8. What are some of the controllable and uncontrollable variables in the following systems: automotive manufacturing, hospital, courthouse, airline, restaurant, hotel, bank, oil refinery, nuclear power plant, and farm? Specify a typical decision in each one.

9. Assume that a marketing department is an open system. How would you *close* this system?

10. What could be the major advantages of a mathematical model used to support a major investment decision?

11. Your company is considering opening a branch in China. List typical activities in each phase of the decision to open or not to open (intelligence, design, choice, implementation).

12. Many farm equipment manufacturers have had major losses in recent years because farmers have had no money to purchase new farm equipment. What problems are the manufacturing companies faced with?

13. You are about to sell your car. What principles of choice are you most likely to use in deciding about accepting or rejecting offers? Why?

14. You are about to decide whether to drive to work via the freeway or via the parallel road. There is no immediate traffic information. Is your decision under certainty? Under risk? Under uncertainty? Why?

15. There are $n!$ (n factorial) ways to schedule jobs through one machine. You have 50 jobs to schedule. You must decide which job to run first, second, and so on. There is no analytical solution to the problem. How many feasible solutions exist? What type of search would you use in your analysis and why?

16. You are about to buy a car. Follow Simon's four-phase model and describe your activities at each step.

17. How is the term *model* used in this text? What are the strengths and weaknesses of modeling?

18. List five heuristics in use in your company, your university, a bank, or a fast-food restaurant.

19. Compare the basic ideas that underlie simulation to video games. Identify similarities and differences.

20. A hospital administrator wants to know what level of demand for services will guarantee an 85 percent bed occupancy. What type of sensitivity analysis should the administrator use and why?

21. The use of scenarios is popular in computerized decision making. Why? For what types of decisions is this technique most appropriate?

22. What is the major advantage of a goal-seeking over a what-if analysis?

23. Explain, through an example, the support given to decision makers by computers in each phase of the decision process.

24. Some experts believe that the major contribution of DSS is to the implementation of the decision. Why is this so?

25. Explain how personality type, gender, cognitive style, and decision style are related. How might these concepts affect the development of decision support systems?

26. Table 2.4 shows the major differences between heuristic and analytic cognitive styles.
    a. Do you consider yourself heuristic or analytic? Why?
    b. Assume you are making a presentation to two managers—one heuristic, the other analytic—regarding a decision about adding a service by the bank you work for. How would you appeal to their cognitive styles? (Be specific.)

27. Decision-making styles vary from analytic to heuristic-intuitive. Does a decision maker consistently use the same style? Give examples from your own experience.

28. Most managers are capable of using the telephone without understanding or even considering the electrical and magnetic theories involved. Why is it necessary for managers to understand MSS tools to use them wisely?

❖ EXERCISES

1. Consider the "75 greatest management decisions ever made" described in DSS in Action 2.1. From the articles, examine a subset of 5 decisions. Compare and contrast them: Identify the similarities and differences. How do you think the intelligence phase was handled for each?

2. Consider a situation in which you have a preference for where you go to college; you want to be not too far away from home and not too close. Why might this situation arise? Explain how this situation fits in with rational decision making behavior.

3. Some decision support models may be simple and others may be complex, but they all may describe the same decision-making problem. Models can be implemented on different computing platforms (PC, mainframe, workstation, and so on) and even with different software. These factors often dictate the structure and type of model developed and used and also dictate applicable solution procedures. Some solution procedures involve more human intervention and activity than others and thus may be error-prone to different degrees. Furthermore, there may be a trade-off in the effort required to develop a model and solve it. Some models may even provide additional information about the problem that the decision maker may want but not know how to request. Consider the simple present-value model described earlier: $P = F/(1 + i)^n$. If $F = \$1000$, $i = 12$ percent, and $n = 6$ years, determine the present value P in the following ways. Compare the results found, as well as the difficulty in developing and solving the model, using the platform and using the software.
    a. Make a guess (i.e., use a mental model and apply a heuristic—often used under time pressure). How close were you to the correct answer found below?
    b. Use a simple four-function calculator to determine P directly.
    c. Use the built-in financial functions (or subroutines) in a financial calculator.
    d. Write, debug, and run a computer program in a third-generation programming language (such as BASIC, C, COBOL, or FORTRAN).
    e. Use a spreadsheet (such as Excel) to solve the problem directly, without using its built-in financial functions.
    f. Use a spreadsheet (such as Excel), but this time use its built-in financial functions.

4. Consider a more advanced financial model to determine the net present value P of an initial investment I that has end-of-year cash returns F_k at the end of each of m years:

$$P = \sum_{k=1}^{m} F_k/(1 + i)^k - I$$

Suppose the initial investment is $I = \$1,000$, the interest rate is $I = 12$ percent, the project lasts $m = 10$ years, and the annual cash return over the 10 years is $F_k = \{\$200, \$300, \$300, \$200, \$250, \$300, \$400, \$400, \text{ and } \$400\}$.

a. Model and solve this problem using the methods and models outlined in Exercise 3.

b. Determine the payback period (the year in which the project breaks even, $P = 0$) and internal rate of return (the interest rate for which $P = 0$) for this project. Which models helped you determine the payback period and internal rate of return the easiest? Why? (*Hint:* In the Excel spreadsheet, try trial and error (what-if) first, then use goal-seeking, and then compare the two.)

5. Suppose that in Exercise 4 the end-of-year cash returns are initially $200 and increase by 10 percent per year. Which of the models you created in Exercise 3 is easiest to modify to solve this problem? Choose one of the methods and solve this problem. What if the increase in end-of-year cash flows changes from 10 percent per year to 8 percent per year? Which implementation is easiest to modify and why? Do so and solve the problem.

6. Given the situation described in Exercise 5, suppose we are seeking a net present value of $800. What initial end-of-year cash return is required to reach this goal? (The end-of-year cash returns increase by 10 percent per year.) Compare the methods of trial and error and goal-seeking in the spreadsheet model.

7. Solve the MBI product-mix problem described in the chapter (use either Excel's Solver or a student version of a linear programming solver such as Lindo or QSB. Lindo is available from Lindo Systems, Inc., at www.lindo.com; others are also available—search the Web. Examine the solution (output) reports for the answers and sensitivity report. Did you get the same results as those reported in this chapter? Try the sensitivity analysis outlined in the chapter; that is, lower the right-hand side of the CC-8 marketing constraint by one unit from 200 to 199. What happens to the solution when you solve this modified problem? Eliminate the CC-8 lower bound constraint entirely (this can be done easily by either deleting it in Solver or setting the lower limit to zero) and re-solve the problem. What happens? Using the original formulation, try modifying the objective function coefficients and see what happens.

8. You are about to buy a car. What criteria are important? What specific choices do you have and how will you limit your choices? Read Case Application 2.3 and structure your problem within the AHP framework. Does this make intuitive sense? Explain why it does or does not.

9. Comment on Simon's (1977) philosophy that managerial decision making is synonymous with the whole process of management. Does this make sense or not? Explain. Use a real-world example in your explanation.

10. Consider the A/B/C parts inventory management and scheduling situation described in the Section 2.7 (under Suboptimization). Discuss how management of the A items might be viewed as a nonprogrammed (unstructured or least-structured) problem, management of the B parts might be viewed as a semistructured problem, and management of the C parts as a programmed (structured) problem.

11. Stories about suboptimization issues abound in some formerly centrally planned national economies in which the output of factories was measured by seemingly useful measures with unexpected and disastrous results. Specifically, a ball bearing factory's output was measured by the total weight of the ball bearings produced, and so the plant manager decided to produce one very large ball bearing each month. There was also a shoe factory where output was measured by the number of left shoes, and so (you guessed it) the plant manager decided to make only left shoes to double the factory's official output. Explain in detail how the measure of the result variable (output) of a subsystem can lead to bad decisions that lead to suboptimized results for the entire system, and what the consequences might be. This is not unique to centrally planned economies but can happen in any organization. Give an example from your personal or professional life in which this happened.

12. Read the paper by S. K. M. Ho, entitled "Problem Solving in Manufacturing" in *Management Decision,* Vol. 3, No. 7, 31–37, 1993 (available on ABI Inform) to see how the Kepner–Tregoe decision-making method was applied to a pager manufacturer case. In the context of this case, compare the Kepner–Tregoe method to the Simon four-phase method. Which do you think is better and why?

13. Compare the results for gender differences and similarities described by Smith (1999) and Leonard et al. (1999) with the case of gender differences described by R. L. Fox, and R. A. Schuhmann in "Gender and Local Government: A Comparison of Women and Men City Managers" in (*Public Administration Review,* Vol. 59, No. 3, May/June, 231–242, 1999). Do the results for city managers match those found in the other literature? In what ways?

❖ GROUP EXERCISES

1. Interview a person who was recently involved in making a business decision. Try to identify
   a. The scope of the problem being solved
   b. The people involved in the decision (explicitly identify the problem owners)
   c. Simon's phases (you may have to ask the person specific questions such as how he or she identified the problem)
   d. The alternatives (choices) and the decision chosen
   e. How the decision was implemented
   f. How computers were used to support the decision making or why they were not used.
   Produce a detailed report describing an analysis of the above and clearly state how closely the real-world decision-making process compares to Simon's suggested process. Also, clearly identify how computers were used or why they were not used.

2. Have everyone in your group perform a personality type test—either the Myers–Briggs (Keirsey and Bates, 1984) or the True Colors (Birkman, 1995) type. Compare the results and see if they match up well with each member's general *modus operandus.* For each member, how does their type describe the way they make decisions? Is the group made up of different or similar types? How will this help or hinder the group's ability to function? Based on the types, what will each member be able to bring to the table for better functioning? What special things will the group need to consider to enhance communication in the group so it will function effectively?

3. Develop a cognitive map of the decision-making problem of selecting a job, or a university program using Decision Explorer (Banxia Software Ltd., www.banxia.com). Describe your thought processes and what you did to develop the map.

❖ INTERNET EXERCISES

1. Search the Internet (World Wide Web) for material on managerial decision making. Take a sample of 10 sites. What general classes of materials can you identify?

2. Many colleges and universities post their course catalogs, course descriptions, and syllabi on the Web. Identify a sample of 10 decision-making courses that are posted and compare their topical material. What is the major focus of these courses? What percentage of them cover computerized support? In which departments or colleges are they typically found?

3. Search the Web for companies and organizations that provide computerized support for managerial decision making. Take a sample of 5 software vendors and characterize their products based on specific functional market area (marketing, manufacturing, insurance, transportation, and so on), on managerial level of support (strategic, tactical, operational, transactional), and on type of computerized tool (such as DSS, EIS, ES, or ANN). Take a sample of 10 nonvendors. What kinds of support do they provide?

4. Some companies and organizations have downloadable demo or trial versions of their software products on the Web so that you can copy and try them out on your own computer. Others have online demos. Find one that provides decision support (Chapter 5), try it out, and write a short report about it. You should include details about the intended purpose of the software, how it works, and how it supports decision making.

5. Perform a Web search for business shareware (software that can either be freely copied and used or freely copied and used for a short period of time after which a licensing fee must be paid). Categorize the software in terms of the type of support it provides. Download and try the DSS-oriented ones and report your findings.

CASE APPLICATION 2.1

CLAY PROCESS PLANNING AT IMERYS: A CLASSICAL CASE OF DECISION MAKING

PART 1: THE GO/NO GO DECISION FOR THE PROCESS OPTIMIZATION (POP) DSS

INTRODUCTION

IMERYS [formerly English China Clay International (ECCI)] in Sandersville, GA, mines crude kaolin (China) clay and processes it into a wide variety of products (dry powders, slurries, and so on) that add gloss to paper, cardboard, paint, wallpaper, and so on. Kaolin clay is also used to make ceramics, tableware, sculptures, and so on. It can also be used for processing aluminum, for making toothpaste, and as a medication for soothing stomach upset (yes, the crude clay is edible right from the ground). Between 50 and 100 million years ago, during the Cretaceous and Tertiary geological periods, kaolin deposits formed on the Atlantic seacoast along the Fall Line that crosses central Georgia. In 1880 the first clays were mined and processed, and since then the industry has expanded dramatically. The total annual economic impact in Georgia was $824 million in 1996. The total Georgia kaolin production capacity was 8.6 million tons in 1998, which represented the bulk of kaolin processing in the United States. Major deposits are also mined in Brazil, China (Peoples Republic of China), the Czech Republic, France, Germany, and the United Kingdom, totaling an estimated capacity of about 4.3 million tons in 1998. The middle-Georgia kaolin deposits are the largest in the world. Hence, Sandersville is known as the "kaolin capital of the world." See the China Clay Producers Association (www.kaolin.com), ECCI (www.ecc.com and www.ecci.co.uk), IMERYS (www. imerys.com), and Dry Branch Kaolin Company (www. dbkminerals.com) Web sites for more information on the geology, history, mining, products, and economic impacts of kaolin clay.

THE SITUATION

In late 1998, as part of a continuous improvement initiative, ECCI managers, engineers, and IS analysts met to determine the feasibility of applying mathematical programming (optimization) to clay mining and production. The need to process lower-quality crude clays, the depletion of higher-quality crude clays, and some new processing methods prompted a fresh look at the various aspects of clay processing and scheduling.

Several members of the continuous improvement initiative team had previously been involved in the development of complex and large linear and mixed-integer programming models for kaolin clay production planning at other organizations (the models were used mostly for capacity planning and had several thousand relationships and variables). None of these models had taken the clay all the way from the mines to the customer in the detail that would ideally be required now. Also, the problems involved in determining blends of clays had never been modeled before.

DECISION MAKING: DECISION NUMBER 1: GO/NO GO

The initial decision-making process began with the continuous improvement team recognizing that there was an opportunity, exploring potential impacts, and taking ownership of the problem (intelligence). The ECCI team was charged with exploring any potential improvement methodology. Such improvements could include making better decisions, making faster decisions, and so on. Initially, there was no way to know that such an approach would really work, however, some team members were familiar with mathematical programming and knew that it was certainly worth exploring because it had produced favorable results for other problems in other organizations with which they had been associated. The next step was to seek out additional knowledge, information, and expertise and establish the likelihood of success. This included meeting with managers and other potential users who need accurate production plans in order to determine what new sales can be accepted and how they can be made. The decision to pursue the development of a system was based on mental models and past experience (design). Influencing the decision was the fact that the IS department was implementing a forecasting model that was part of a staged development enterprise resource planning (ERP) system. Given a set of forecasts, this new mathematical programming model, as part of a decision support system, could potentially drive the ERP in overall organizational planning. This was decision making under uncertainty, where the risk of failure (or success) had to be as-

sessed. Analysts find these problems most challenging because they eventually may have to build a system that has never been developed before. Following a workshop, the team decided that the initiative had merit, and recognizing that the project would be a major initiative requiring substantial resources in personnel and money, they reached a consensus and decided to proceed with development of the system (choice). The implementation phase involved assembling a formal team to move forward with development of the decision support system. The consequences of the decision follow in the narrative.

And so ECCI committed resources to developing a decision support system to assist members of the organization in decision making. This began a new initiative for the decision-making model. The development team now had to understand how clay is processed and develop a methodology to assist the decision makers in their work. The scope of the project evolved as new information was learned.

CASE QUESTIONS

1. Why did the continuous improvement team start exploring the use of mathematical programming for clay process planning?
2. Why do you think that earlier models and systems developed to solve similar types of problems were not directly applicable in this case?
3. For this first go/no go problem, describe how the decision was made. Do you think that this was a crucial decision in light of this project?

CASE APPLICATION 2.2

CLAY PROCESS PLANNING AT IMERYS: A CLASSICAL CASE OF DECISION MAKING

PART 2: THE DECISIONS OF THE PROCESS OPTIMIZATION (POP) DSS

KAOLIN PROCESSING

Kaolin production involves mining followed by a number of purification, grinding, separation, heating, blending, and other steps. Different crude clay recipes can be used to produce similar and different final products; and, at a number of points in production, alternate blends can be used in creating final products with identical properties (brightness, gloss, and so on). Some processes can be performed on alternate pieces of equipment, and sometimes there are several units of similar equipment that can be aggregated into a single one (for modeling purposes).

Further complicating the decision-making situation, different initial crude blends may require different rates for several pieces of equipment used for different processes. For example, a lower percentage of a "fines" (smaller-particle-size) crude clay blended with "coarse" clays generally requires additional time (a slower rate) to crush the coarser clay sufficiently for further processing. Costs per hour, costs per ton, recovery factors (which may vary by clay), and rates (in tons per hour) are specified for each process for each clay for each recipe (blend). These data are estimates because the times vary with subtle changes in the clay, depending on the mine, and the particular pit in the mine from which the clay is extracted.

ALTERNATE RECIPES AND NEW PROBLEMS

One of the problems facing ECCI in late 1999 was that some of the mines with high-quality crude clays were almost depleted. Alternative crude recipes, process adjustments, and new processes had to be instituted to produce final clays identical in quality to existing products. New final clay products (pure and blends) are continually being developed as well. The clays also follow different step orderings through the production process, depending on their major "class" of products. One class of clays is wet; the other is dry. Within each major class are several pure finished products and hundreds of blends of these are needed to obtain the desired properties required by customers in the global marketplace. Kaolin (dry) clays have three major products with about 20 final blends, while hydrous (wet) clays have six major products with several hundred final blends. Clays may also be processed at alternative plants. There are transfers of clays from other plants, some of which were initially modeled in this phase of the project, while others are on hold. Some crude clays and finished clays can be purchased in the open market, while others cannot be (these are uniquely produced by ECCI in Sandersville). Chemicals are added at a number of different steps in the process. There is a direct relationship between chemical use and the processing rates of several pieces of equipment. The use of more chemicals may typically require less processing time.

ECCI ships finished products to customers on every inhabited continent of the world. They also maintain warehouses on several continents.

Clearly, there are many decisions to be made, hence many decision variables. There are many constraints due to time and tonnage capacity limits, and these vary depending on the rates. There are many constraints that simply relate the flows from each piece of equipment to the others. There are many intermediate variables representing the amount of clay that flows from the output of one process to the input of another. There are many combinations of clays, dramatically increasing the number of decision variables. The result variable is *profit*, which is to be maximized. Also, certain assumptions that bound rationality must be made to be able to develop a reasonable-sized model that can be solved in a finite amount of time. For example, the model can be assumed to be linear, within the normal operating parameters of the plants, however, the engineers and scientists who design and run the processes have indicated that there are some subtle nonlinearities.

DECISION MAKING: DECISION NUMBER 2: OPTIMAL CLAY PROCESSING

The primary goal is to determine the optimal way (i.e., maximizing net profit) to process clays all the way from the mines to the customers. This model can determine how the clays should be optimally blended, and at which stages, and which equipment should run at capacity. Later, capacity expansion can be added to the model to determine which equipment should have additional production capacity, again to maximize profit. The model can also determine which demand from the open market has to be met if existing capacity proves insufficient.

The overall decision-making problem is: Given a set of demands for final clay products (possibly obtained from a forecasting system), determine how to process the clay optimally (at maximum profit). This involves determining

- A time horizon (1 year or less)
- Which mines to use, which clays from these mines to extract, and how much to extract
- Which crude blends to use
- Which processes to run the clays through and at which rates
- Chemicals to be used and where they should be used
- Which intermediate blends to use
- How best to blend the finished products.

These decisions involved establishing standard rates and costs for equipment for the various clays, as well as determining which specific pieces of equipment could be utilized for specific clays. Because a new process was coming online in late 1999, it was modeled as well, along with discontinuing use of the old crude clays as they would soon be depleted, and activating a new one.

Given a set of demands for finished clay products, specific decisions included

1. How much of each kind of crude clay to mine (before and after the depletion of high-quality grades)
2. What crude blends (recipes) to use (which impacts certain equipment process rates)
3. Which production processes to use for crude clay blends
4. How to further blend processed crude clay blends into intermediate clays (which impacts certain equipment process rates)
5. Which specific processes to use on intermediate clays
6. How to recycle coproducts back into the production stream

7. How to blend intermediate clays into final clays
8. What demands to really meet
9. How much clay should be purchased from external sources to blend into intermediate and final products
10. How much of each chemical should be used (more processing often means less use of chemicals, and vice versa)
11. Which final processes to use on final clay blends
12. Which final demands should be met by external market purchases or should be met by production at other plants in the organization.

A linear programming model can support this kind of decision making within a DSS. Data gathering for the model could prove difficult and time-consuming. Development of the Process OPtimization (POP) linear programming model and the DSS are described as case applications in Chapters 5 and 6.

THE PROTOTYPING APPROACH

Early in the project it was decided that a DSS prototyping approach would be used. One small calcine (dry) plant would be modeled first to develop the necessary features, familiarize the team members with the tools and methodologies, and establish the database structures that would guide the rest of the system development.

NEW COMPLICATIONS

Impacting directly on the POP project, in early 1999 IMATEL, a French mining consortium purchased ECCI and merged it into their holdings under the name IMERYS in late 1999. These holdings included the Dry Branch Kaolin Company located in Dry Branch, GA. The European Community (EC) approval agency quickly approved the purchase, but the U.S. Justice Department added some restrictions: some of the ECCI plant processing operations had to be quickly sold to obtain approval.

CASE QUESTIONS

1. Why was it important for the model to be able to handle blends and recipes?
2. *To think about:* The linear programming model to be developed will describe several plants and be rather large. The version of the model that represented two plants had on the order of 10,000 constraints and 40,000 variables. How does one go about verifying that the model is correct, that is, getting the right answer? How can one "manage" the data? Who should be allowed to update the model structure? Update the demands? Update other aspects? Why?
3. Pick three decisions listed and explain their importance to the company.
4. What approach was used to develop the model and why?
5. How could the "external event" of the merger (purchase) of ECCI by IMATEL into IMERYS affect the model and the system development? Why is this an important event with regard to the DSS and the model?
6. Why was a prototyping (evolutionary design) approach adopted by the team? Did this make sense? Why or why not?
7. The mining and materials processing industries, in general, lag other industries in the development and use of DSS and modeling. Why do you think this is so, and what can be done to advance these industries so that they can and will use advanced tools?

KEY GRIP USES THE ANALYTICAL HIERARCHY PROCESS APPROACH TO SELECT FILM PROJECTS[2]

INTRODUCTION

In the motion picture industry, a grip is "intelligent muscle on set," since grips are responsible for setting up lights, cameras, and other materials on the set. Not just muscle is required, however. Grips must be able to make decisions as to how best to do setups, which can be quite complex. In fact, many grips have a B.A. or M.A. degree in theater. The *key grip* is responsible for all the grips on the set and is essentially their manager, as well as a liaison between the other grips and the production company. The primary concern of the key grip is safety on the set.

Charles N. Seabrook, of Charleston, SC, is a key grip, an important role in the filmmaking industry. Charles has been in the business for nearly 20 years and has an excellent reputation. He is one of the best. Consequently, he often has problems deciding which job offers (movies) to accept. Even when there are no competing offers, he sometimes has to decide whether or not he wants to work a particular job.

The Analytical Hierarchy Process (AHP) (Saaty, 1999) is an appropriate method for selecting competing activities using distinct criteria. The criteria can be quantitative or qualitative in nature, and even quantitative criteria are handled by a decision maker's preference structure rather than by the actual numbers. To develop a DSS to solve Mr. Seabrook's recurrent (institutional) problem, we developed an AHP model in Expert Choice (Expert Choice, Inc., www.expertchoice.com; downloadable demo versions are available at the Web site). Our decision-making approach fits the Simon four-phase model. Additionally, the method and the structure of the model lend themselves well to the Bazerman (1998) "anatomy of a decision," description. We decided to use the Ratings Module of Expert Choice to formulate a model to aid Mr. Seabrook in the decision-making process.

CRITERIA

Our first step was to interview Mr. Seabrook regarding the general aspects of his professional life and how he goes about making decisions. Then, we interviewed him to establish the important criteria for job selection. Initially, he stated the following eight potential criteria:

- Location of filming — The distance from Mr. Seabrook's home in Charleston, SC.
- Time away from family — Mr. Seabrook is dedicated to his family and prefers not to spend long periods of time away from home.
- Reputation of the production company — The company producing the film plays an important part in how well people get along on the set and how well the filming is organized.
- Film budget — Often, if a film has a low budget, there are problems in obtaining equipment and general dissatisfaction among the crew.
- Pay — Obviously, the hourly rate paid to Mr. Seabrook is a high priority.
- Union involvement — If the union is involved in the film, working conditions are usually better and, more importantly, employee benefits are paid.
- Quality of best boy available — The best boy is the key grip's assistant and is heavily involved in the large amount of paperwork required on the set. Having a reliable best boy is crucial to the film. However, this does not apply because Mr. Seabrook does not accept a film if his regular best boy, Jack Gilchrist, is not available.
- Quality of grips available for hire — A film often functions as a virtual company with technically qualified individuals hired to do a particular job. If there a lack of competent grips available, the key grip's tasks become much more difficult.

After further discussion, the criteria were reduced to a more manageable set of five, for which further expansions of their definitions were developed. The final five were

- Location of filming — This implies that there will be time away from family, as the distance from home determines the amount of time he is away.
- Pay.
- Working conditions — This factor includes how lenient the budget is, as well as how many days per week and hours per day are required. Because this also determines how much overtime is available, it is closely tied to pay as well.
- Union involvement.
- Reputation of production company.

Note: In developing the criteria, we did not discuss specific alternative choices.

[2]Contributed by the MAccAttack student team: M. Adams, P. Lambeth, C. Maxwell, and M. Whitmire, The University of Georgia, Athens, GA, December 1999.

AHP: EXPERT CHOICE MODELS AND DEVELOPMENT

The structure of an AHP model as implemented in Expert Choice is that of an inverted tree. There is a single *goal* node at the top that represents the goal of the decision-making problem. One hundred percent of the weight of the decision is in this node. Directly under the goal are leaf nodes representing all the *criteria,* both qualitative and quantitative. The weight of the goal must next be partitioned among the criteria nodes. There are several methods built into Expert Choice to do this. All are based on comparing all pairs of criteria to establish how the weight of the goal is to be distributed. The software also provides a measure of the inconsistency of the comparisons. So, if the decision maker prefers criterion 1 to criterion 2 at a certain preference level (say, moderate) and compares criterion 1 to criterion 3 identically, then for consistency in decision making, he or she should compare criteria 2 and 3 as equally preferred. After the decision maker completes the comparisons, the weight of the decision-making problem is distributed among the criteria in accordance with the preference structure derived from the pairwise comparisons. Expert Choice provides an inconsistency ratio indicating how *consistent* the decision maker is in his or her judgments.

Next, there are two ways to build the model. If the problem is ad hoc (occurs one time) and there are few alternatives (say, seven plus or minus two), then the decision maker enters his or her *choice nodes* (alternatives) beneath the first criterion and replicates them to all its peers (the other criteria). Then the decision maker pairwise compares the choices under the first criterion, under the sec-

ond one, and so on, until all are compared. From each set of comparisons, Expert Choice divides the problem's weight in the specific criterion among the choices and calculates an inconsistency ratio. Once all the choices have been compared, the results are synthesized, the choice with the most weight becomes the "expert choice," and the inconsistency ratio indicates how trustable the decision is.

If the problem is recurring or there are many alternatives to select among, the ratings model can be used. The leaf nodes below each criterion describe the *scale* for each criterion. For example, working conditions might be characterized as excellent, good, fair, or poor. The decision maker pairwise compares these scale characterizations just like choices. Excellent is clearly preferred to good, good to fair, and fair to poor. The weights of these characterizations establish a scale for a specific movie project.

Once all the criteria have their scales and have been pairwise compared, we switch to the ratings model where each choice is represented by the rows of a spreadsheet-like framework and each criteria is represented by a column. The decision maker then clicks on the appropriate rating for each criterion for each movie. The decision maker may decide to accept movies only if they meet a certain minimum level or may sort the choices and select the most highly rated one.

MODEL BUILDING

The goal and five criteria were entered into our Expert Choice model, and a rating scale was determined for each of the criteria by Mr. Seabrook. The screen shot in Figure 2.12 shows the goal (Which movie to choose?), the five criteria, and the scale for each.

FIGURE 2.12 EXPERT CHOICE MODEL SHOWING THE CRITERIA AND THEIR RATING SCALES

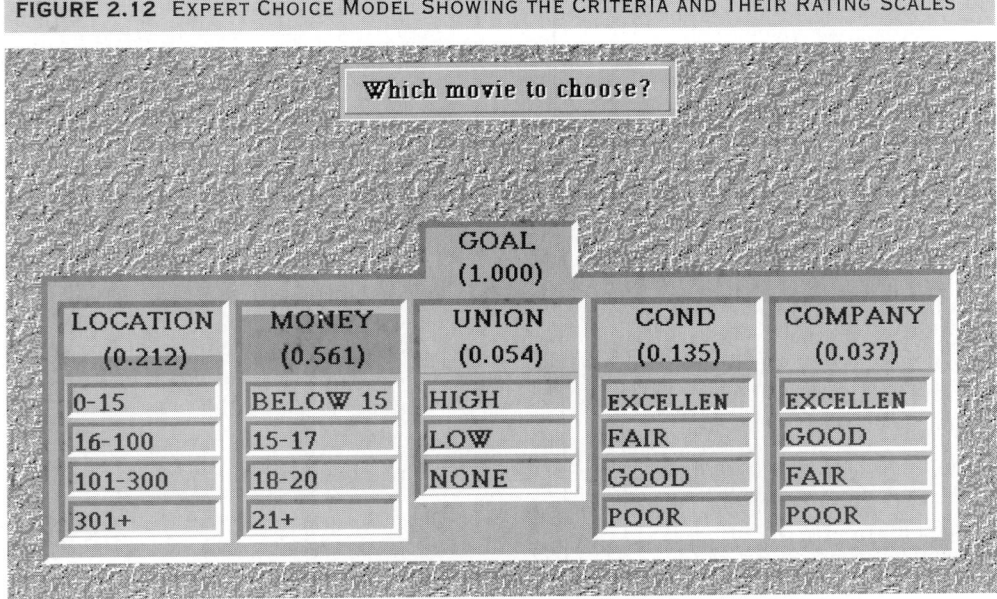

By permission of Expert Choice Inc.

A pairwise comparison analysis was then performed, and the priorities were determined. At this point, another conference with Mr. Seabrook allowed us to fine-tune the priorities, and the results are shown in the screenshot in Figure 2.13 and also in the weights in the criteria nodes in Figure 2.12. Note the overall inconsistency ratio of 0.07. Attempts to reduce this number led to priorities that Mr. Seabrook felt did not match his preferences, and so we returned to the presented results. Generally, if the ratio is less than 0.1, the comparisons can be considered consistent.

Next, we pairwise compared the ratings scales beneath each criterion. Finally, we moved the model into the Ratings Module of Expert Choice and contacted Mr. Seabrook again to obtain a set of usable real-world data on movies he had considered in the past to validate the model. We prepared a survey form for him to rate the last four jobs he had been offered. It was a simple, circle-the-correct-response survey, and once we received the results, the data were entered into the model with the ratings results shown in Figure 2.14.

FIGURE 2.13 EXPERT CHOICE RESULTS OF PAIRWISE COMPARISONS FOR THE CRITERIA

Note that money has about 56 percent of the weight.

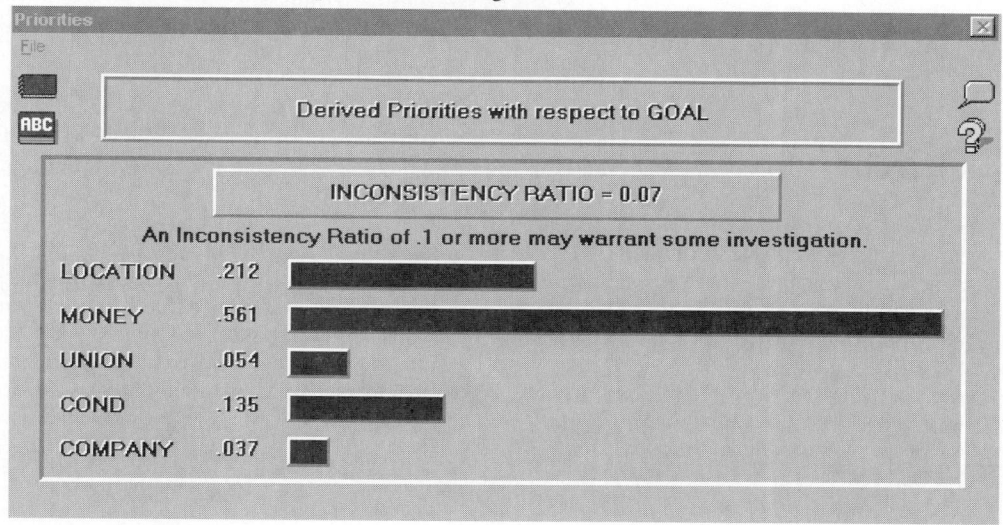

By permission of Expert Choice Inc.

FIGURE 2.14 EXPERT CHOICE RATINGS MODEL WITH SAMPLE, REAL-WORLD DECISION MAKING RESULTS

LOCATION

0-15	16-100	101-300	301+
1 (1.000)	2 (.637)	3 (.212)	4 (.066)

	Alternatives	TOTAL	LOCATION .2123	MONEY .5610	UNION .0537	COND .1355	COMPANY .0374
1	Movie 1	0.279	16-100	15-17	NONE	GOOD	GOOD
2	Movie 2	1.000	0-15	21+	HIGH	EXCELLEN	EXCELLEN
3	Movie 3	0.399	16-100	18-20	HIGH	GOOD	GOOD
4	Movie 4	0.409	0-15	BELOW 15	NONE	EXCELLEN	EXCELLEN
5							
6							
7							
8							
9							
10							

By permission of Expert Choice Inc.

RESULTS

The names of the movies were omitted for confidentiality, but the results matched Mr. Seabrook's decisions. Movie 1, with a rating of only 0.279, was rejected by both the model and by Mr. Seabrook. Mr. Seabrook accepted all of the other three movies and, as a result, felt that the ideal cut-off rating should be set to 0.4 since the lowest rated accepted movie was only 0.001 points less than that. This level may change once Mr. Seabrook adopts the model and begins to use it for future decisions, as he will be able to adapt the model as his priorities change. One month following the initial model and system development, Expert Choice was installed on Mr. Seabrook's computer and training sessions were provided to ensure that he could use the model to its fullest potential. He is very pleased with the system and has incorporated it into his decision-making process for use when his next job offer arrives.

CONCLUSION

Through this project, Mr. Seabrook can now use a DSS tool that provides assistance in the rational decision-making process to determine which job offers he should accept or reject. In the past, he used the same criteria as described earlier, but with a mental model in which it can be difficult, if not impossible, to consider all criteria while simultaneously weighing the importance of each. Using the AHP through Expert Choice to transfer his knowledge and preferences into a formal decision-making model leads to more consistent and higher-quality decision making. In the past,

Mr. Seabrook generally made decisions based on one factor that was overwhelmingly good or bad. Now, he is able to weigh the importance of *all* the factors in a rational way.

CASE QUESTIONS

1. Do you think that Mr. Seabrook really used *all* eight criteria in his decision making before this DSS was developed? Why or why not? How much information would be needed if he were selecting from among 12 movies and used all eight criteria? Is this a feasible way to go about working with information? Why or why not?
2. Describe how the process and model fit into the Simon four-phase decision-making model.
3. Describe how the decision-making process and model fit into the Bazerman "anatomy of a decision" structure.
4. Explain the differences between the "standard" AHP model with goal/criteria/choices and the ratings AHP model with goal/criteria/ratings scales/choices.
5. Why was it more appropriate to use the ratings model approach than to use the standard one?
6. How did the AHP Expert Choice model assist Mr. Seabrook in providing a more rational framework in his decision making?
7. Do you think that this project would have been as successful if the development team had not worked closely with the decision maker? Why or why not?

DECISION SUPPORT SYSTEMS

In Part II, we concentrate on decision support methodology, technology components, and construction. Chapter 3 provides an overview of DSS: the characteristics, structure, use, and types of DSS. The major components of DSS are presented in Chapter 4 (Data Management) and Chapter 5 (Modeling and Model Management). Chapter 6 deals with the development process of DSS.

CHAPTER 3

DECISION SUPPORT SYSTEMS: AN OVERVIEW

In Chapter 1 we introduced DSS and stressed its support in the solution of complex managerial problems. The methodology of decision making was presented in Chapter 2. In this chapter we show how DSS superiority is achieved by examining its capabilities, structure, and classifications. The following sections are presented:

3.1 OPENING VIGNETTE: EVALUATING THE QUALITY OF JOURNALS IN HONG KONG

BACKGROUND

Universities, government agencies, and research institutions all over the world frequently need to assess the quality of academic and professional journals such as *Harvard Business Review* and *Decision Support Systems*. Such an assessment is needed for several purposes. First, personnel decisions, such as promotions and salary increases, for authors of papers published in such journals are frequently made by reviewing where the authors publish. Second, requests for funding research projects are evaluated by observing in what journals the investigators have published in the past

94

and where the results of their current projects are most likely to be published. Finally, material published in quality journals can be used to develop guidelines and plans of organization.

The government of Hong Kong is conducting a formal evaluation of all major scientific journals in dozens of disciplines. This evaluation is done by teams of experts. The major purpose of the evaluation is to determine how many quality researchers, called active researchers (ARs), are at each of the universities and research institutions in the country. Then, budgets are allocated in accordance with the number of ARs at each institution.

THE PROBLEM

It is very difficult for a team to assess the quality of a journal. It is very likely that different team members have different opinions regarding a journal's quality. Also, individual evaluators are not always sure which grade they should assign to the journal. In Hong Kong, the possible grades are A, B, C, or ungraded. Frequently, a member feels that the journal is in between two grades (e.g., less than A, yet more than B). Currently, a team is established for each academic discipline, and the team evaluates several dozen related journals. The teams have complete freedom regarding the procedures they use. However, they must submit one and only one grade for each journal.

The teams who conduct face-to-face meetings usually use one of two well-established approaches. Either they employ an objective measure, such as looking at the number of times a journal is cited during a certain time period, or they use mostly subjective perception. There are frequent disagreements within the teams and complaints from outsiders about poor grading.

THE SOLUTION

The decisions of the teams can be facilitated by a Web-based computerized system. The basic idea is to integrate the objective and the subjective methods, deriving the best aspects of the two approaches.

The system allows each team member to make a qualitative and/or quantitative evaluation in front of a PC, rather than at a face-to-face meeting. Using Web links, the members can access any needed information. A formal decision is made regarding how much weight to assign to objective information (e.g., how many times a journal has been cited in other academic journals during the past 2 years), as well as how to value subjective information. Members' opinions are consolidated using a mathematical model. The system is flexible and user-friendly. A consensus is attempted online, and only if no consensus is reached is a face-to-face meeting called. How this is done and why it is necessary to use the Web and computers will be described later in this chapter.

THE RESULTS

Preliminary studies indicate that the system support resulted in a less biased final consensus. The team members save 20–70 percent of their time, as well as travel expenses to the meeting place. Full implementation is expected by 2002.

❖ QUESTIONS FOR THE OPENING VIGNETTE

1. What are the major difficulties in evaluating quality of journals?
2. How did the DSS solve the difficulties listed in your answers to question #1?
3. Discuss the role of the Web in this system.

3.2 DSS CONFIGURATIONS

The Opening Vignette illustrates the versatility of a DSS. Specifically, it shows a support system with the following characteristics:

- It supports individual members and an entire team.
- It is used repeatedly and constantly.
- It has two major components: data and models.
- It is Web-based.
- It uses subjective, personal, and objective data.
- It is used in the public sector.

This vignette demonstrates some of the potential diversification of DSS. Decision support can be provided in many different configurations. These configurations depend on the nature of the management decision situation and the specific technologies used for support. These technologies are assembled from four basic components (each with several variations): *data, models, knowledge,* and *user interface.* Each of these components is managed by software that either is commercially available or must be programmed for the specific task. The manner in which these components are assembled defines their major capabilities and the nature of the support provided. For example, models are emphasized in a model-oriented DSS. Such models can be customized with a spreadsheet or a programming language or can be provided by standard algorithm-based tools such as linear programming. Similarly, in a data-oriented DSS, a database and its management play the major roles. In the situation in the Opening Vignette, as will be shown later, both approaches were used.

In this chapter we will explore all these and related topics, but first we revisit the definitions of a DSS.

3.3 WHAT IS A DSS?

The early definitions of a DSS identified it as a system intended to support managerial decision makers in semistructured decision situations. DSS were meant to be an adjunct to decision makers to extend their capabilities but not to replace their judgment. They were aimed at decisions where judgment was required or at decisions that could not be completely supported by algorithms. Not specifically stated, but implied in the early definitions, was the notion that the system would be computer-based, would operate interactively online, and preferably would have graphical output capabilities.

The early definitions were open to several interpretations. Soon several other definitions appeared that caused considerable disagreement as to what a DSS really is. We discuss these definitions next.

DSS DEFINITIONS

Little (1970) defines DSS as a "model-based set of procedures for processing data and judgments to assist a manager in his decision making." He argues that to be successful, such a system must be simple, robust, easy to control, adaptive, complete on important issues, and easy to communicate with. Alter (1980) defines DSS by contrasting them with traditional electronic data processing (EDP) systems on five dimensions, as shown in Table 3.1.

TABLE 3.1   DSS Versus EDP

Dimension	DSS	EDP
Use	Active	Passive
User	Line and staff management	Clerical
Goal	Effectiveness	Mechanical efficiency
Time horizon	Present and future	Past
Objective	Flexibility	Consistency

Source: Based on Alter (1980).

TABLE 3.2   Concepts Underlying DSS Definitions

Source	DSS Defined in Terms of
Gorry and Scott-Morton (1971)	Problem type, system function (support)
Little (1970)	System function, interface characteristics
Alter (1980)	Usage pattern, system objectives
Moore and Chang (1980)	Usage pattern, system capabilities
Bonczek et al. (1989)	System components
Keen (1980)	Development process

Moore and Chang (1980) argue that the structuredness concept, so much a part of early DSS definitions (i.e., that DSS can handle semistructured and unstructured situations), is not meaningful in general; a problem can be described as structured or unstructured only with respect to a particular decision maker or a specific situation (i.e., structured decisions are structured because we choose to treat them that way). Thus, they define DSS as extendible systems capable of supporting ad hoc data analysis and decision modeling, oriented toward future planning, and used at irregular, unplanned intervals.

Bonczek et al. (1980) define a DSS as a computer-based system consisting of three interacting components: a language system (a mechanism to provide communication between the user and other components of the DSS), a knowledge system (a repository of problem domain knowledge embodied in DSS as either data or procedures), and a problem-processing system (a link between the other two components, containing one or more of the general problem manipulation capabilities required for decision making). The concepts provided by this definition are important for understanding the relationship between DSS and knowledge.

Finally, Keen (1980) applies the term *DSS* "to situations where a 'final' system can be developed only through an adaptive process of learning and evolution." Thus, he defines a DSS as the product of a developmental process in which the DSS user, the DSS builder, and the DSS itself are all capable of influencing one another, resulting in system evolution and patterns of use.

These definitions are compared and contrasted by examining the various concepts used to define DSS (Table 3.2). It seems that the basis for defining DSS has been developed from the perceptions of what a DSS does (such as support decision making in unstructured problems) and from ideas about how the DSS's objective can be accomplished (such as components required, appropriate usage pattern, and necessary development processes).

Unfortunately, the formal definitions of DSS do not provide a consistent focus because each tries to narrow the population differently. Furthermore, they collectively ignore the central purpose of DSS, that is, *to support and improve decision making.* In later DSS definitions, the focus seems to be on inputs rather than outputs. A very likely

reason for this change in emphasis is the difficulty of measuring the outputs of a DSS (such as decision quality or more confidence in the decision made).

A DSS APPLICATION

A DSS is usually built to support the solution of a certain problem or for evaluation of an opportunity. As such it is called a **DSS application.** In DSS in Focus 3.1 we provide a working definition that includes a range from a basic to an ideal DSS application. Later in this chapter the various configurations of DSS are explored. However, it is beneficial first to deal with the characteristics and capabilities of DSS, which we present next.

3.4 CHARACTERISTICS AND CAPABILITIES OF DSS

Because there is no consensus on exactly what a DSS is, there is obviously no agreement on standard characteristics and capabilities of DSS. The list in Figure 3.1 is an ideal set, some members of which were described in the definitions as well as in the Opening Vignette.

The major DSS capabilities, per Figure 3.1, are the following:

1. DSS provide support for decision makers mainly in semistructured and unstructured situations by bringing together human judgment and computerized information. Such problems cannot be solved (or cannot be solved conveniently) by other computerized systems or by standard quantitative methods or tools.
2. Support is provided for various managerial levels, ranging from top executives to line managers.
3. Support is provided to individuals as well as to groups. Less structured problems often require the involvement of several individuals from different departments and organizational levels or even from different organizations.
4. DSS provide support to several interdependent and/or sequential decisions. The decisions may be made once, several times, or repeatedly.
5. DSS support all phases of the decision-making process: intelligence, design, choice, and implementation.
6. DSS support a variety of decision-making processes and styles.
7. DSS are adaptive over time. The decision maker should be reactive, able to confront changing conditions quickly, and able to adapt the DSS to meet

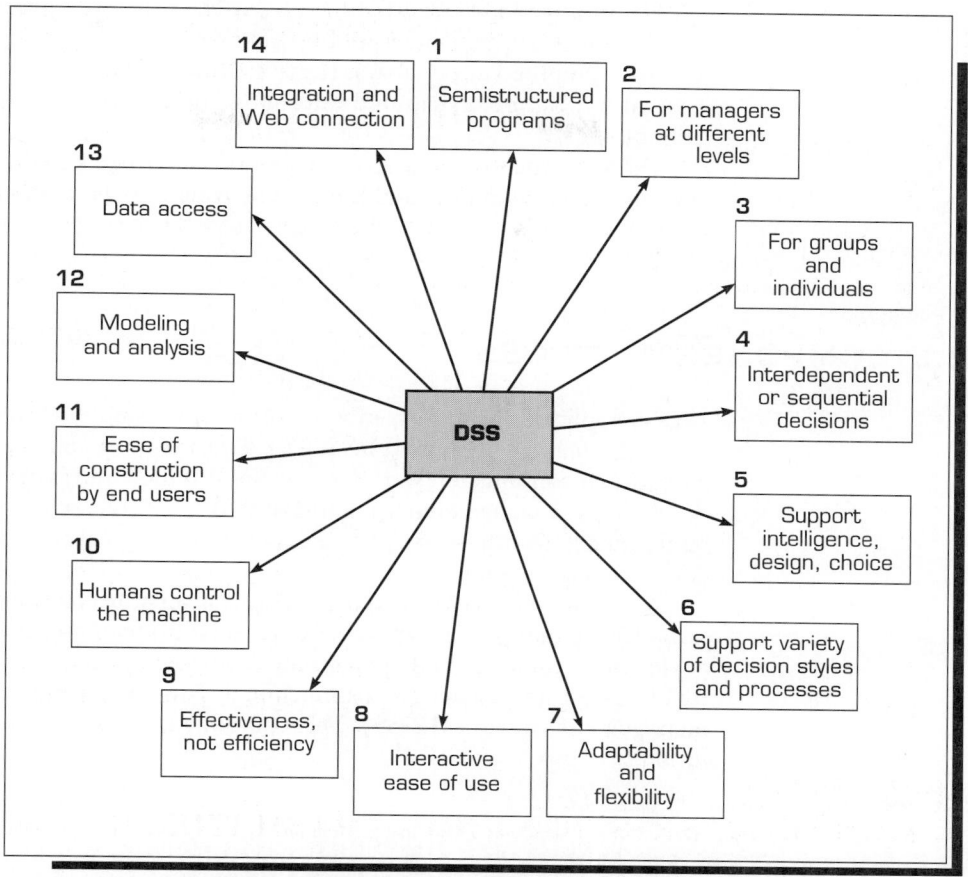

FIGURE 3.1 THE IDEAL CHARACTERISTICS AND CAPABILITIES OF DSS

these changes. DSS are flexible, and so users can add, delete, combine, change, or rearrange basic elements.

8. Users must feel at home with DSS. User-friendliness, strong graphical capabilities, and an English-like interactive human–machine interface can greatly increase the effectiveness of DSS.

9. DSS attempt to improve the effectiveness of decision making (accuracy, timeliness, quality) rather than its efficiency (the cost of making decisions).

10. The decision maker has complete control over all steps of the decision-making process in solving a problem. A DSS specifically aims to support and not to replace the decision maker.

11. End users should be able to construct and modify simple systems by themselves. Larger systems can be built with assistance from information system (IS) specialists.

12. A DSS usually utilizes models for analyzing decision-making situations. The modeling capability enables experimenting with different strategies under different configurations.

The DSS should provide access to a variety of data sources, formats, and types, ranging from geographic information systems (GIS) to object-oriented ones. A DSS can be employed as a stand-alone tool used by an individual decision maker in one location, or it can be distributed throughout an organization and in several organizations along the supply chain. It can be integrated with other DSS and/or applications, and it can be distributed internally and externally, using networking and Web technologies.

These characteristics allow decision makers to make better, more consistent decisions in a timely manner, and they are provided by the DSS major components, which we describe next.

3.5 COMPONENTS OF DSS

A DSS application can be composed of the subsystems shown in Figure 3.2.

Data management subsystem. The data management subsystem includes a database, which contains relevant data for the situation and is managed by software called the **database management system (DBMS).**[1] The data management subsystem can be interconnected with the corporate **data warehouse,** a repository for corporate relevant decision-making data.

Model management subsystem. This is a software package that includes financial, statistical, management science, or other quantitative models that provide the system's analytical capabilities and appropriate software management. Modeling languages for building custom models are also included. This software is often called a **model base management system (MBMS).** This component can be connected to corporate or external storage of models.

---

[1]DBMS in both singular and plural (system and systems), as are many similar acronyms in this text.

FIGURE 3.2 A SCHEMATIC VIEW OF DSS

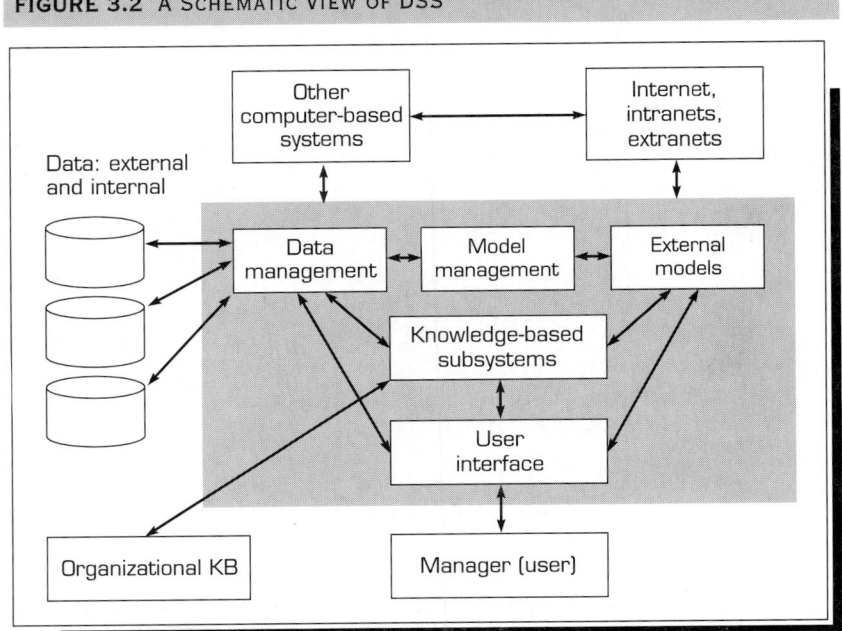

Knowledge-based management subsystem. This subsystem can support any of the other subsystems or act as an independent component. It provides intelligence to augment the decision maker's own. In can be interconnected with the organization's knowledge depository, which is called the **organizational knowledge base.**

User interface subsystem. The user communicates with and commands the DSS through this subsystem. The user is considered part of the system. Researchers assert that some of the unique contributions of DSS are derived from the intensive interaction between the computer and the decision maker.

These components form the DSS application system, which can be connected to the corporate intranet, to an extranet, or to the Internet. The schematic view of a DSS and the above components shown in Figure 3.2 provides a basic understanding of the general structure of a DSS. Next, we present a more detailed look at each component; later we provide details in Chapters 4–7.

3.6 THE DATA MANAGEMENT SUBSYSTEM

The data management subsystem is composed of the following elements:

- DSS database
- Database management system
- Data directory
- Query facility.

These elements are shown schematically in Figure 3.3 (in the shaded area). The figure also shows the interaction of the data management subsystem with the other parts of the DSS, as well as its interaction with several data sources. A brief discussion of these elements and their function follows; further discussion is provided in Chapter 4.

THE DATABASE

A **database** is a collection of interrelated data organized to meet the needs and structure of an organization and can be used by more than one person for more than one application. There are several possible configurations for a database. For some DSS, data are ported from the data warehouse. For other DSS applications, a special database is constructed as needed. Several databases can be used in one DSS application, depending on the data sources.

The data in the DSS database, as shown in Figure 3.3, are extracted from internal and external data sources, as well as from personal data belonging to one or more users. The extraction results go to the specific application's database or to the corporate data warehouse (Chapter 4), if it exists. In the latter case, it can be used for other applications.

Internal data come mainly from the organization's transaction processing system. A typical example of such data is the monthly payroll. Depending on the needs of the DSS, operational data from functional areas, such as marketing, might be included. Examples of other internal data are machine maintenance scheduling or budget allocations, forecasts of future sales, costs of out-of-stock items, and future hiring plans. Sometimes internal data are made available through Web browsers over an **intranet,** an internal Web-based system (see Bayles 1996 and Stone-Gonzalez 1998).

External data can include industry data, marketing research data, census data, regional employment data, government regulations, tax rate schedules, or national economic data. These data can come from the U.S. government, trade associations, marketing research

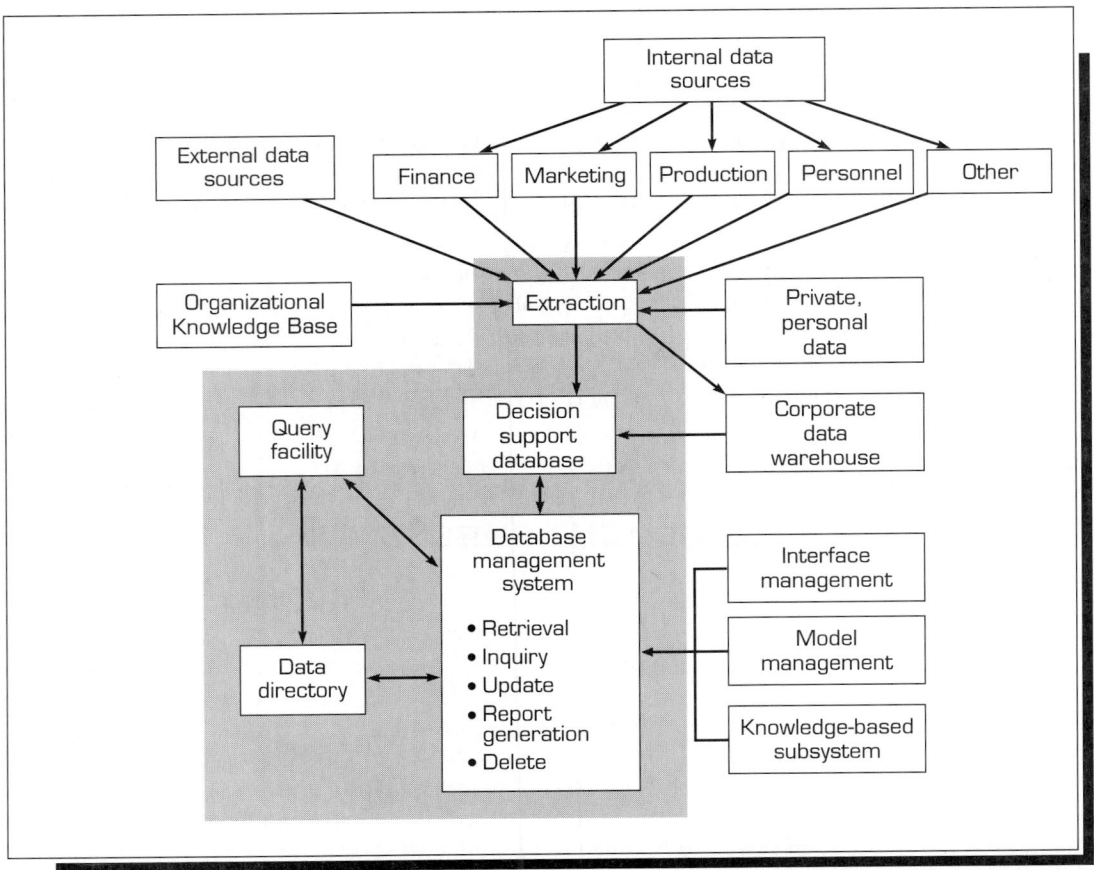

FIGURE 3.3 THE STRUCTURE OF THE DATA MANAGEMENT SUBSYSTEM

firms, econometric forecasting firms, and the organization's own efforts at collecting external data. Like internal data, external data can be maintained in the DSS database or accessed directly when the DSS is used. External data are provided, in many cases, over the **Internet** (e.g., from computerized online services or as picked up by search engines).

Private data can include guidelines used by specific decision makers and assessments of specific data and/or situations.

DATA ORGANIZATION

Should a DSS have a stand alone database? It depends. In small ad hoc DSS, data can be entered directly into models sometimes extracted directly from larger databases. In large organizations that use extensive data, such as Wal-Mart, AT&T, and United Air Lines, data are organized in a data warehouse and used when needed (Gray and Watson, 1998; Inmon, 1996; Poe, 1996). Some large DSS have their own fully integrated, multiple-source DSS databases. A separate DSS database need not be physically separate from the corporate database. They can be stored together physically for economic reasons.

A DSS database can also share a DBMS with other systems. A DSS database can include multimedia objects (such as pictures, maps, or sounds) (Burger, 1995; Ghafoor, 1995; Larson, 1995). An object-oriented database is found in some recent DSS (Chen, 1996; Wolf, 1994).

EXTRACTION

To create a DSS database or a data warehouse it is often necessary to capture data from several sources. This operation is called **extraction.** It basically consists of importing of files, summarization, standardization filtration, and condensation of data. Extraction also occurs when the user produces reports from data in the DSS database. As will be shown in Chapter 4, the data for the warehouse are extracted from internal and extranal sources. The extraction process is frequently managed by a DBMS.

DATABASE MANAGEMENT SYSTEM

A database is created, accessed, and updated by a DBMS. Most DSS are built with a standard commercial relational DBMS that provides capabilities such as those shown in DSS in Focus 3.2.

An effective database and its management can support many managerial activities; general navigation among records, support for creating and maintaining a diverse set of data relationships, and report generation are typical examples. However, the real power of a DSS occurs when data are integrated with its models.

THE QUERY FACILITY

In building and using DSS, it is often necessary to access, manipulate, and query data. The **query facility** performs these tasks. It accepts requests for data from other DSS components (Figure 3.3), determines how these requests can be filled (consulting the data directory if necessary), formulates the detailed requests, and returns the results to the issuer of the request. The query facility includes a special query language. Important functions of a DSS query system are selection and manipulation operations (e.g., the ability to follow a computer instruction such as "Search for all sales in zone B during June 2000 and summarize sales by salesperson").

THE DIRECTORY

The data **directory** is a catalog of all the data in the database. It contains data definitions, and its main function is to answer questions about the availability of data items, their source, and their exact meaning. The directory is especially appropriate for supporting the intelligence phase of the decision-making process by helping to scan data and identify

---

DSS IN FOCUS 3.2

THE CAPABILITIES OF A RELATIONAL DBMS IN A DSS

- Captures or extracts data for inclusion in a DSS database
- Updates (adds, deletes, edits, changes) data records and files
- Interrelates data from different sources
- Retrieves data from the database for queries and reports (e.g., using SQL)
- Provides comprehensive data security (such as protection from unauthorized access and recovery capabilities)

- Handles personal and unofficial data so that users can experiment with alternative solutions based on their own judgment
- Performs complex data manipulation tasks based on queries
- Tracks data use within the DSS
- Manages data through a data dictionary

problem areas or opportunities. The directory, like any other catalog, supports the addition of new entries, deletion of entries, and retrieval of information on specific objects.

3.7 THE MODEL MANAGEMENT SUBSYSTEM

The model management subsystem of the DSS is composed of the following elements:

- Model base
- Model base management system
- Modeling language
- Model directory
- Model execution, integration, and command processor.

These elements and their interface with other DSS components are shown in Figure 3.4. The definition and function of each of these elements are described next.

MODEL BASE

A **model base** contains routine and special statistical, financial, forecasting, management science, and other quantitative models that provide the analysis capabilities in a DSS. The ability to invoke, run, change, combine, and inspect models is a key DSS ca-

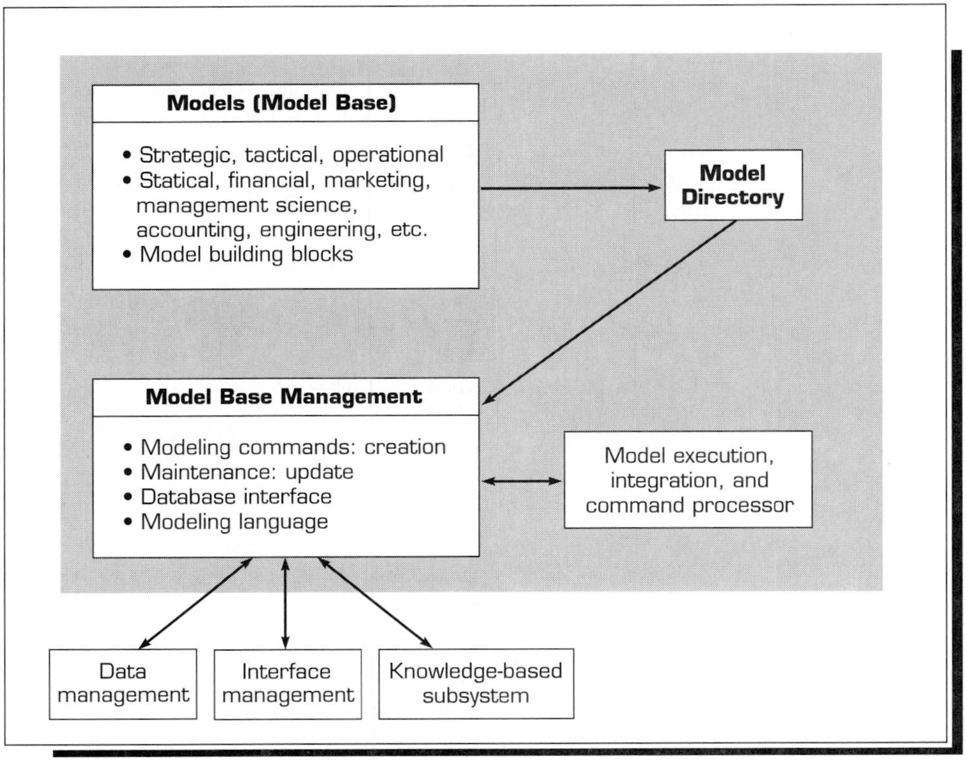

FIGURE 3.4 THE STRUCTURE OF THE MODEL MANAGEMENT SUBSYSTEM

pability that differentiates it from other CBIS. The models in the model base can be divided into four major categories: strategic, tactical, operational, and analytical. In addition, there are model building blocks and routines.

Strategic models are used to support top management's strategic planning responsibilities. Potential applications include developing corporate objectives, planning for mergers and acquisitions, plant location selection, environmental impact analysis, and nonroutine capital budgeting. An example of a DSS strategic model can be found in the GLSC Corporation case which is posted on the book's Web site (www.prenhall.com/turban) Chapter 3.

Tactical models are used mainly by middle management to assist in allocating and controlling the organization's resources. Examples of tactical models include labor requirement planning, sales promotion planning, plant layout determination, and routine capital budgeting. Tactical models are usually applicable only to an organizational subsystem such as the accounting department. Their time horizon varies from 1 month to less than 2 years. Some external data are needed, but the greatest requirements are for internal data. The Hong Kong Opening Vignette includes some tactical models for its budget allocation.

Operational models are used to support the day-to-day working activities of the organization. Typical decisions involve approval of personal loans by a bank, production scheduling, inventory control, maintenance planning and scheduling, and quality control. Operational models support mainly first-line managers' decision making with a daily to monthly time horizon. These models normally use only internal data.

Analytical models are used to perform some analysis on the data. They include statistical models, management science models, data mining algorithms (see Chapter 4), financial models and more. Sometimes they are integrated with other models, such as strategic planning models.

The models in the model base can also be classified by functional areas (such as financial models or production control models) or by discipline (such as statistical models or management science allocation models). The number of models in a DSS can vary from a few to several hundred. Models in DSS are basically mathematical; that is, they are expressed by formulas. These formulas can be preprogrammed in DSS development tools such as Excel. They can be written in a spreadsheet and stored for future use, or they can be programmed for only one use.

MODEL BUILDING BLOCKS AND ROUTINES

In addition to strategic, tactical, and operational models, the model base can contain **model building blocks** and routines. Examples include a random number generator routine, a curve- or line-fitting routine, a present-value computational routine, and regression analysis. Such building blocks can be used in several ways. They can be employed on their own for applications such as data analysis. They can also be used as components of larger models. For example, a present-value component can be part of a make-or-buy model. Some of these building blocks are used to determine the values of variables and parameters in a model, as in the use of regression analysis to create trend lines in a forecasting model. Such building blocks are available in DSS commercial development software, such as functions in Excel.

MODELING TOOLS

Because DSS deal with semistructured or unstructured problems, it is often necessary to customize models using programming tools and languages. Some examples of these are C+ and Java. For small and medium-size DSS or for less complex ones, a spreadsheet is usually used. We will use Excel throughout this book.

THE MODEL BASE MANAGEMENT SYSTEM

The functions of model base management system (MBMS) software are *model creation* using programming languages, DSS tools and/or subroutines, and other building blocks; *generation of new routines* and reports; *model updating* and *changing;* and *model data manipulation.* The MBMS is capable of interrelating models with the appropriate linkages through a database (see DSS in Focus 3.3.)

THE MODEL DIRECTORY

The role of the model directory is similar to that of a database directory. It is a catalog of all the models and other software in the model base. It contains model definitions, and its main function is to answer questions about the availability and capability of the models.

MODEL EXECUTION, INTEGRATION, AND COMMAND

The following activities are usually controlled by model management. *Model execution* is the process of controlling the actual running of the model. *Model integration* involves combining the operations of several models when needed (such as directing the output of one model to be processed by another one) or integrating the DSS with other applications.

A *model command processor* is used to accept and interpret modeling instructions from the user interface component and route them to MBMS, model execution, or integration functions.

An interesting question for a DSS might be which models should be used for what situation? Such model selection cannot be done by the MBMS because it requires expertise and therefore is done manually. This is a potential automation area for a *knowledge component* to assist the MBMS.

DSS IN FOCUS 3.3

MAJOR FUNCTIONS OF THE MBMS

- Creates models easily and quickly, either from scratch or from existing models or from the building blocks
- Allows users to manipulate models so that they can conduct experiments and sensitivity analyses ranging from what-if to goal seeking
- Stores, retrieves, and manages a wide variety of different types of models in a logical and integrated manner
- Accesses and integrates the model building blocks

- Catalogs and displays the directory of models for use by several individuals in the organization
- Tracks model data and application use
- Interrelates models with appropriate linkages with the database and integrates them within the DSS
- Manages and maintains the model base with management functions analogous to database management: store, access, run, update, link, catalog, and query
- Uses multiple models to support problem solving

DSS IN ACTION 3.4

INTELLIGENT DSS AT ECKERD DRUG

Prescription drugs can be subject to significant amounts of theft by the employees who work around them (about 8 percent of sales). Eckerd Drug, one of the largest chains of drugstores, is fighting the problem with intelligent decision support software. Using the Data Interpretation package from IBM, the system downloads all drug-related sales and shipment data from mainframe store and warehouse systems. Loss prevention analysts use automated intelligent procedures to detect both shipping discrepancies and store theft. The system tracks each item sold by store and by National Drug Code number. Furthermore, it can distinguish between generic and branded medication, allowing Eckerd to more narrowly categorize its losses. In its first year of operation, the system discovered 147 cases of suspected theft.

Source: Condensed from R. Pastore, "To Catch a Thief," *CIO*, July 1994; and Anonymous, "Shrinking Shrink at Eckerd," *Chain Store Age Executive,* Apr. 1994.

3.8 THE KNOWLEDGE-BASED MANAGEMENT SUBSYSTEM

Many unstructured and even semistructured problems are so complex that they require expertise for their solution. Such expertise can be provided by an expert system or other intelligent system. Therefore, more advanced DSS are equipped with a component called a *knowledge-based management subsystem.* This component can supply the required expertise for solving some aspects of the problem and providing knowledge that can enhance the operation of other DSS components.

An example of the role of the knowledge subsystem is provided by Silverman (1995), who suggests three ways to integrate knowledge-based expert systems (ES) with mathematical modeling: knowledge-based decision aids that support the steps of the decision process not addressed by mathematics; intelligent decision modeling systems that help users build, apply, and manage libraries of models; and decision analytic expert systems that integrate theoretically rigorous methods of uncertainty into expert system knowledge bases.

The knowledge component consists of one or more intelligent systems. Like data and model management software, knowledge management software provides the necessary execution and integration of the intelligent system.

A decision support system that includes such a component is called an intelligent DSS, a DSS/ES, an expert support system, active DSS, or knowledge-based DSS (see DSS in Action 3.4). For example, the current generation of data mining applications (systems that identify potentially profitable patterns in data) include intelligent systems (Bort, 1996; Newquist, 1996).

3.9 THE USER INTERFACE (DIALOG) SUBSYSTEM

The term **user interface** covers all aspects of communication between a user and the DSS or any MSS. It includes not only the hardware and software but also factors that deal with ease of use, accessibility, and human–machine interactions. Some MSS experts feel that the user interface is the most important component because much of the power, flexibility, and ease-of-use characteristics of MSS are derived from this component (Sprague and Watson, 1996a). Others state that because the user sees only this part of the MSS, to him or her the user interface *is* the system (Whitten and Bentley, 1997). An inconvenient user interface is one of the major reasons why managers have not used computers and quantitative analyses to the extent that these technologies have been available. Lately, the Web browser has been recognized as an effective tool for a DSS interface.

MANAGEMENT OF THE USER INTERFACE SUBSYSTEM

The user interface subsystem is managed by software called the **user interface management system (UIMS).** The UIMS is composed of several programs that provide the capabilities listed in DSS in Focus 3.5. The UIMS is also known as the dialog generation and management system.

THE USER INTERFACE PROCESS

The user interface process for an MSS is shown schematically in Figure 3.5. The user interacts with the computer via an action language processed by the UIMS. In advanced

FIGURE 3.5 SCHEMATIC VIEW OF THE USER INTERFACE SYSTEM

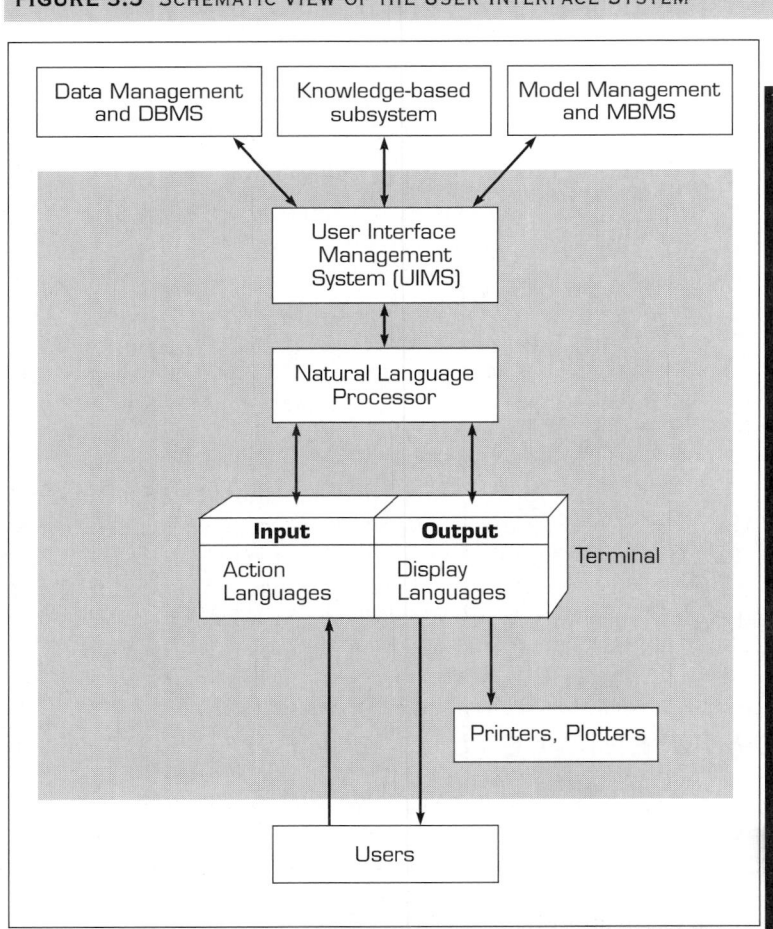

MAJOR CAPABILITIES OF THE UIMS

- Provides a graphical user interface, frequently using a Web browser
- Accommodates the user with a variety of input devices
- Presents data with a variety of formats and output devices
- Gives users help capabilities, prompting, diagnostic and suggestion routines, or any other flexible support
- Provides interactions with the database and the model base
- Stores input and output data
- Provides color graphics, three-dimensional graphics, and data plotting

- Has windows to allow multiple functions to be displayed concurrently
- Can support communication among and between users and builders of MSS
- Provides training by example (guiding users through the input and modeling process)
- Provides flexibility and adaptiveness so the MSS can accommodate different problems and technologies
- Interacts in multiple, different dialog styles
- Captures, stores, and analyzes dialog usage (tracking) to improve the dialog system; tracking by user is also available

systems, the user interface component includes a natural language processor or can use standard **objects** (such as pull-down menus, buttons, and Internet browser) through a **graphical user interface (GUI).** The UIMS provides the capabilities listed in DSS in Focus 3.5 and enables the user to interact with the model management and data management subsystems. A DSS user interface can be accessed from a cell telephone via either voice or the display panel.

3.10 THE USER

The person faced with the decision that the MSS is designed to support is called the *user,* the *manager,* or the *decision maker.* However, these terms fail to reflect the heterogeneity that exists among users and the usage patterns (Alter, 1980) of MSS. There are differences in the positions that users hold, users' cognitive preferences and abilities, and ways of arriving at a decision (decision styles). As discussed in Chapter 2, the user can be an individual or a group.

An MSS has two broad classes of users: managers and staff specialists. Staff specialists, such as financial analysts, production planners, and marketing researchers, outnumber managers by about 3 to 2 and use computers by a much larger ratio. When designing an MSS, it is important to know who will actually have hands-on use of it. In general, managers expect systems to be more user-friendly than do staff specialists. Staff specialists tend to be more detail-oriented, are more willing to use complex systems in their day-to-day work, and are interested in the computational capabilities of the MSS. Often, staff analysts are the intermediaries between management and the MSS.

An **intermediary** allows the manager to benefit from the decision support system without actually having to use the keyboard. Several types of intermediaries reflect different support for the manager:

1. **Staff assistant.** This person has specialized knowledge about management problems and some experience with decision support technology.
2. **Expert tool user.** This person is skilled in the application of one or more types of specialized problem-solving tools. An expert tool user performs tasks that the problem solver does not have the skill or training to perform.
3. **Business (system) analyst.** This person has a general knowledge of the application area, a formal business administration education (not in computer science), and considerable skill in using DSS construction tools.
4. **Facilitator in group support system.** This intermediary controls and coordinates the use of software to support the work of people working in groups. The facilitator also is responsible for the conduct of work group sessions.

Even within the categories of managers and staff specialists, there are important subcategories that influence MSS design. For example, managers differ by organizational level, functional area, educational background, and need for analytic support. Staff specialists differ in areas such as education, functional area, and relationship to management.

3.11 DSS HARDWARE

Decision support systems have evolved simultaneously with advances in computer hardware and software technologies. Hardware affects the functionality and usability of the MSS. Although the choice of hardware can be made before, during, or after the design of the MSS software, the hardware choice is often determined by what is already available within the organization. Typically, MSS run on standard hardware. The major hardware options are the organization's mainframe computer, a workstation, a personal computer, or a client/server system. Distributed DSS runs on various types of networks including the Internet, intranets, and extranets.

3.12 DISTINGUISHING DSS FROM MANAGEMENT SCIENCE AND MIS

The characteristics and the components of DSS distinguish it from other computer-based information systems. In Chapter 1, a brief distinction was made between DSS and management science. Keen and Scott-Morton (1978) attempted to compare DSS with management science and with management information systems. The modified comparison is shown in Table 3.3 and is still valid.

MIS can be viewed as an IS application that can generate standard and exception reports and summaries, provide answers to queries, and help in monitoring and tracking. It is usually organized along functional areas. Thus, there are marketing MIS, accounting MIS, and so on. A DSS, on the other hand, is basically a problem-solving tool

TABLE 3.3	The Major Characteristics of MIS, MS/OR, and DSS

Management Information Systems (MIS)
- The main impact has been on structured tasks, where standard operating procedures, decision rules, and information flows can be reliably predefined.
- The main payoff has been in improving efficiency by reducing costs, turnaround time, and so on, and by replacing clerical personnel or increasing their productivity.
- The relevance for managers' decision making has mainly been indirect (e.g., by providing reports and access to data).
- MIS application is routine and done periodically.

Management Science/Operations Research
- The impact has mostly been on structured problems (rather than tasks), in which the objective, data, and constraints can be prespecified.
- The payoff has been in generating better solutions for general categories of problems (e.g., inventory).
- The relevance for managers has been in the provision of detailed recommendations and new methods handling complex problems.
- Application are nonroutine, as needed.

Decision Support Systems
- The impact is on decisions in which there is sufficient structure for computer and analytic aids to be of value but where the manager's judgment is essential.
- The payoff is in extending the range and capability of managers' decision processes to help them improve their effectiveness.
- The relevance for managers is in the creation of a supportive tool, under their own control, that does not attempt to automate the decision process, predefine objectives, or impose solutions.
- DSS applications are nonroutine, as needed.

Source: Keen and Scott Morton (1978), pp. 1–2.

and is often used to address ad hoc and unexpected problems. An MIS is usually developed by the IS department because of its permanent infrastructure nature. A DSS is frequently an end-user tool; it can provide decision support within a short time. An MIS can provide quick decision support only in situations for which the models and software have been prewritten.

Because of its unstructured nature, a DSS is usually developed by a "prototyping" approach (Chapter 6). An MIS, on the other hand, is often developed by a structured methodology such as the system development life cycle (SDLC).

EXAMPLE: MARKETING DSS

An example of a marketing DSS framework is shown in Figure 3.6. On the left side of the figure are the data and the knowledge. In the center are the standard and the customized marketing models. Electronic commerce tools such as Web site evaluators and intelligent search and computational agents are shown on the right. The DSS generates different evaluations and recommendations, such as the level of advertisement budget by media (television, Internet newspaper, and so on). An MIS can use some standard models and periodically produce marketing reports, but it cannot provide ad hoc evaluations and recommendations. A specific application of a marketing DSS is presented in DSS in Action 3.6.

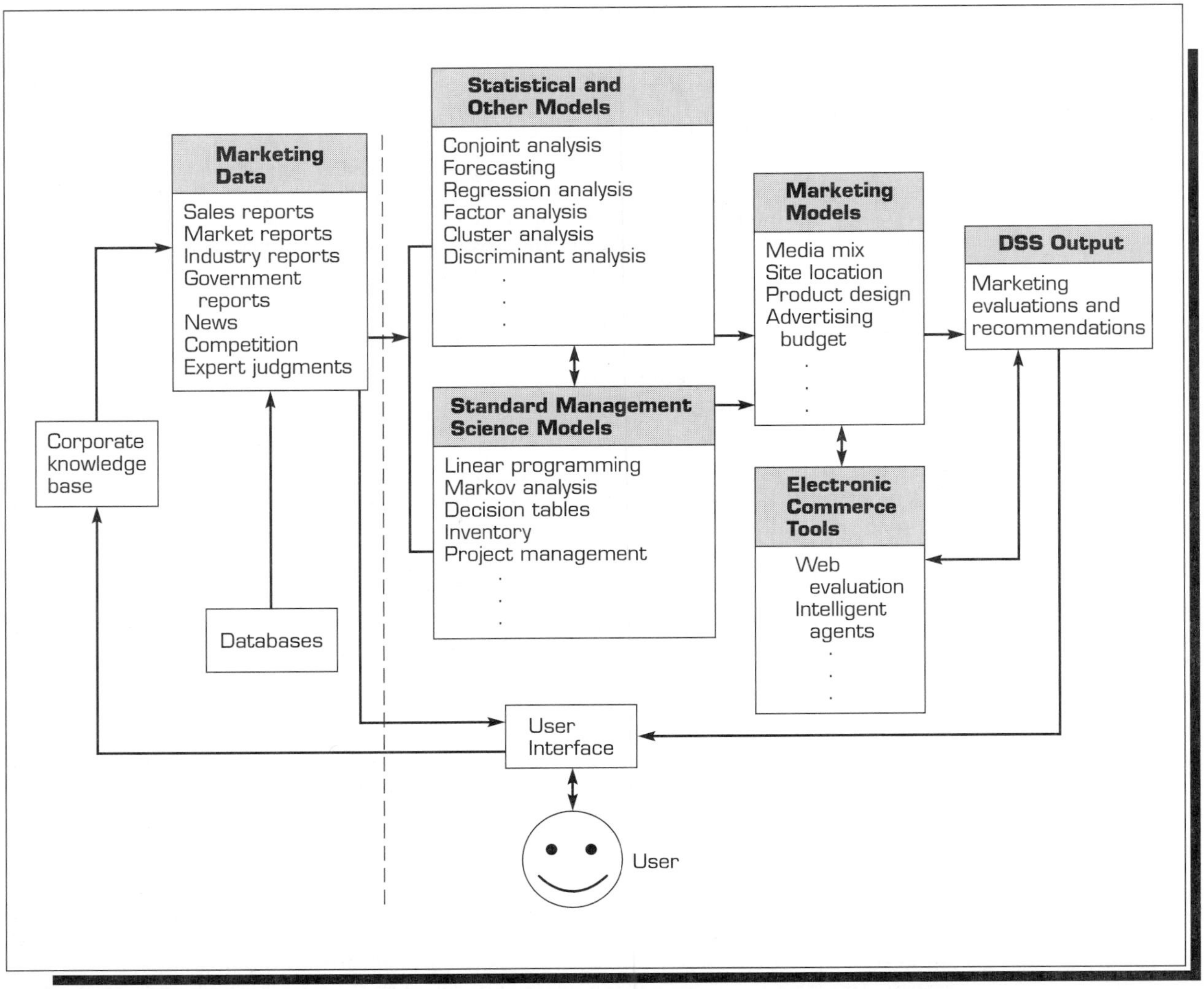

Statistical and Other Models

Conjoint analysis
Forecasting
Regression analysis
Factor analysis
Cluster analysis
Discriminant analysis
.
.
.

Marketing Data

Sales reports
Market reports
Industry reports
Government reports
News
Competition
Expert judgments

Marketing Models

Media mix
Site location
Product design
Advertising budget
.
.

DSS Output

Marketing evaluations and recommendations

Corporate knowledge base

Standard Management Science Models

Linear programming
Markov analysis
Decision tables
Inventory
Project management
.
.

Electronic Commerce Tools

Web evaluation
Intelligent agents
.
.

Databases

User Interface

User

FIGURE 3.6 A MARKETING DSS FRAMEWORK

Source: Based on P. Kotler, *Marketing Management,* 8th ed. Englewood Cliffs, NJ: Prentice Hall, 1994.

DSS IN ACTION 3.6

MARKETING DSS

Retail IS professionals are keeping busy during the holiday season, using target-marketing techniques and decision support systems to bolster sluggish yuletide sales. Many retailers are tapping their information system departments to provide key information on their most frequent customers and biggest spenders during the busy holiday sales push. Barneys New York, an upscale fashion apparel chain with 20 shops throughout the United States, captures customer information on Fujitsu-ICL Systems Inc., Atrium 9000 point-of-sale terminals every time a customer makes a purchase during Barneys' annual winter sale. Other retail outfits have looked to outsourcing to help them segment their customer information. Retailers such as Land's End Inc. and Caswell-Massey Company Ltd. are developing innovative marketing DSS (Bustamente and Sorenson, 1994).

Source: Condensed from T. Hoffman and M. Wagner, "Visions of Holiday Sugarplums," *ComputerWorld,* Dec. 4, 1995, pp. 3, 147.

3.13 DSS CLASSIFICATIONS

There are several ways to classify DSS applications. The design process, as well as the operation and implementation of DSS, depends in many cases on the type of DSS involved. However, remember that not every DSS fits neatly into one category. We present representative classification schemes next.

ALTER'S OUTPUT CLASSIFICATION

Alter's (1980) classification is based on the "degree of action implication of system outputs" or the extent to which system outputs can directly support (or determine) the decision. According to this classification, there are seven categories of DSS (Table 3.4). The first two types are *data-oriented,* performing data retrieval or analysis; the third deals both with data and models. The remaining four are *model-oriented,* providing simulation capabilities, optimization, or computations that suggest an answer.

HOLSAPPLE AND WHINSTON'S CLASSIFICATION

Holsapple and Whinston (1996) classify DSS into the following six frameworks: text-oriented DSS, database-oriented DSS, spreadsheet-oriented DSS, solver-oriented DSS, rule-oriented DSS, and compound DSS.

TEXT-ORIENTED DSS

Information (including data and knowledge) is often stored in a textual format and must be accessed by decision makers. Therefore, it is necessary to represent and process text documents and fragments effectively and efficiently. A text-oriented DSS supports a decision maker by electronically keeping track of textually represented information that could have a bearing on decisions. It allows documents to be electronically created, revised, and viewed as needed. Information technologies such as Web-based document imaging, hypertext, and intelligent agents can be incorporated into text-oriented DSS applications. DSS in Action 3.7 describes a typical Web-accessible document-based DSS for customers to access shipping data in the transportation sector. For further discussion, see Chapter 9 in Holsapple and Whinston (1996) and Bieber (1992, 1995).

DATABASE-ORIENTED DSS

In this type of DSS the database organization plays a major role in the DSS structure. Early generations of database-oriented DSS mainly used the *relational* database configuration. The information handled by relational databases tends to be voluminous, descriptive, and rigidly structured. A database-oriented DSS features strong report generation and query capabilities. For an example, see DSS in Action 3.8. For details, see Stamen (1993).

SPREADSHEET-ORIENTED DSS

A spreadsheet is a modeling language that allows the user to write models to execute DSS analysis. These models not only create, view, and modify procedural knowledge[2] but also instruct the system to execute their self-contained instructions. Spreadsheets are widely used in end user–developed DSS. The most popular end user tool for developing DSS is Microsoft Excel. Excel includes dozens of statistical packages, a linear programming package (solver), and many financial and management science models.

---

[2]Procedural knowledge is generic knowledge regarding problem-solving procedures. In contrast, descriptive or declarative knowledge relates to the specific knowledge domain of the problem to be solved.

TABLE 3.4   Characteristics of Different Classes of Decision Support Systems

Orientation	Category	Type of Operation	Type of Task	User	Usage Pattern	Time
Data	File drawer systems	Access data items	Operational	Nonmanagerial line personnel	Simple inquiries	Irregular
	Data analysis systems	Ad hoc analysis of data files	Operational analysis	Staff analyst or managerial line personnel	Manipulation and display of data	Irregular or periodic
Data or Models	Analysis information systems	Ad hoc analysis involving multiple databases and small models	Analysis, planning	Staff analyst	Programming special reports, developing small models	Irregular, on request
Models	Accounting models	Standard calculations that estimate future results on the basis of accounting definitions	Planning, budgeting	Staff analyst or manager	Input estimates of activity; receive estimated monetary results as output	Periodic (e.g., weekly, monthly, yearly)
	Representational models	Estimating consequences of particular actions	Planning, budgeting	Staff analyst	Input possible decision; receive estimated results as output	Periodic or irregular (ad hoc analysis)
	Optimization models	Calculating an optimal solution to a combinatorial problem	Planning, resource allocation	Staff analyst	Input constraints and objectives; receive answer	Periodic or irregular (ad hoc) analysis
	Suggestion models	Performing calculations that generate a suggested decision	Operational	Nonmanagerial line personnel	Input a structured description of the decision situation; receive a suggested decision as output	Daily or periodic

Source: Condensed from Alter (1980), pp. 90–91.

Because packages such as Excel can include a rudimentary DBMS or can readily interface with one, they can handle some properties of a database-oriented DSS, especially the manipulation of descriptive knowledge. Some spreadsheet development tools include what-if analysis and goal-seeking capabilities, and they are revisited in Chapter 5. A spreadsheet-oriented DSS is a special case of a solver-oriented DSS.

SOLVER-ORIENTED DSS
A solver is an algorithm or procedure written as a computer program for performing certain computations for solving a particular problem type. Examples of a solver can be

TEXT-ORIENTED DSS: APL DEPLOYS A KEY ENTERPRISE-WIDE DOCUMENT MANAGEMENT APPLICATION

To communicate better with its customers, APL developed a key enterprise-wide application for reaching customers in the transportation sector. Information access is very document-intensive and paper-intensive. With a fleet of 22 container cargo ships and a worldwide trucking and rail network, the company may have 150,000 containers shipping goods at any one time. To move that massive paperwork load onto the intranet, APL uses Web-integrated versions of WorkFlo Business System and its Windows client, WorkForce Desktop from FileNet Corporation.

APL went live with about 500 customers in October 1996. In addition to providing Web access to active documents, the software also lets customers view archived data on past shipments. This application is accessible through an icon on APL's public Web site.

Source: Adapted from C. Wilder, "Reaching for the Web," *InformationWeek,* Aug. 26, 1996, p. 48.

DATABASE-ORIENTED DSS: GLAXO WELLCOME ACCESSES LIFE-SAVING DATA

When Glaxo Wellcome revealed that a combination of two of its drugs, Epivir and Retrovir, was effective in treating AIDS, doctors began writing prescriptions en masse almost overnight. Such a tidal wave of demand could have resulted in lower inventories to pharmaceutical wholesalers and shortages.

But thanks to a data warehouse application, market analysts at Glaxo Wellcome were able to track the size and sources of demand and generate reports within hours, even minutes. The result: Wholesalers around the world never ran out of Epivir and Retrovir.

Called GWIS (Glaxo Wellcome Information System), the data warehouse application was built with MicroStrategy Inc.'s DSS relational online analytical processing (ROLAP) technology. GWIS works directly with data stored in a relational database management system, integrating internal data with data from external sources.

The application was rolled out in June 1996 to 150 employees in Glaxo Wellcome's marketing analysis department. Now, users can analyze sales, inventory, and prescription data for drugs on the fly, helping Glaxo Wellcome streamline its distribution process and cut operational costs. An additional IS benefit is that users can access information from various databases and computers. They no longer create local databases on their PCs which ultimately interfere with data integrity or require IT support. GWIS helps the IT organization design and manage the disparate data sources.

Source: Condensed from B. Fryer, "Fast Data Relief," *InformationWeek,* Dec. 2, 1996, pp. 133–136; and www. microstrategy.com/customersuccesses, Jan. 2000.

an economic order quantity procedure for calculating an optimal ordering quantity or a linear regression routine for calculating a trend. A solver can be commercially programmed in development software. For example, Excel, includes several solvers, which are called *functions*. The DSS builder can incorporate the solvers in creating the DSS application. Solvers can be written in a programming language such as C++; they can be written directly in or can be an add-in tool in a spreadsheet, or they can be embedded in a specialized modeling language such as Lingo. More complicated solvers such as linear programming, used for optimization, are commercially available and can be incorporated in a DSS.

RULE-ORIENTED DSS

The knowledge component of DSS described earlier includes both procedural and inferential (reasoning) rules, often in an expert system format. These rules can be qualitative or quantitative, and such a component can replace quantitive models or can be integrated with them. For example, Bishopp (1991) describes the integration of an assignment algorithm implementation (a form of linear programming) (Chapter 5) with that of an expert system for redirecting in-flight airplanes, flight crews, and passengers in the event that a major hub airport is knocked out of commission.

COMPOUND DSS

A compound DSS is a hybrid system that includes two or more of the five basic structures described earlier. See DSS in Action 3.9 for an example of a compound DSS.

INTELLIGENT DSS

The so-called intelligent or knowledge-based DSS has attracted a lot of attention. The rule-oriented DSS which we described above can be divided into six types: descriptive, procedural, reasoning, linguistic, presentation, and assimilative. The first three are termed "primary" types, and the remainder are derived from them. Mirchandani

---

DSS IN ACTION 3.9

COMPOUND DSS: FINANCIAL REPORTING, DECISION SUPPORT, AND EIS HELP T&N PREDICT THE FUTURE

T&N is a leading world supplier of high-quality automotive components, as well as engineering and industrial materials. The company has an annual turnover of more than $4.1 billion and employs 43,000 people throughout the world. The company formed an independent finance advisory division to improve company performance.

Operating units wanted detailed information at product level; product groups wanted broader detail; management wanted strategic, high-level summary and exception information (requiring three systems: financial reporting, decision support, and executive information), but all data had to be consistent.

A comprehensive MSS was initiated in the mid-1990s. Data are transmitted by e-mail to the Manchester (England) headquarters for the production of group accounts. This includes all accounting data, profit and loss, analysis of expenditure, cash flow, and balance sheets.

T&N also stores explanation text within the database. The DSS is installed at all main consolidation points in the group, allowing rapid collection and aggregation of the data. The data are not seen simply as historical information, however. They are increasingly being used to help predict the future. T&N uses financial models and such techniques as simulation, stochastic forecasting, and statistical analysis of variance based on accurate information. This enables the firm to track resources more directly.

The success of the DSS led to the completed implementation of an EIS.

Source: Based on material extracted from www.comshare.com.

and Pakath (1999) divided and identified four intelligent DSS models: sybiotic, expert-systems-based (learn through indiction), adaptive, and holistic. Details on this topic can be found in Chapters 6 and 18.

OTHER CLASSIFICATIONS OF DSS

There are several other classifications of DSS, such as the following.

INSTITUTIONAL AND AD HOC

Institutional DSS Donovan and Madnick (1977) deal with decisions of a recurring nature. A typical example is a portfolio management system (PMS), which has been used by several large banks for supporting investment decisions. An institutionalized DSS can be developed and refined as it evolves over a number of years because the DSS is used repeatedly to solve identical or similar problems. See DSS in Action 3.10 for a description of an institutional DSS.

DSS IN ACTION 3.10

INSTITUTIONAL DSS: THE UNIVERSITY OF GEORGIA USES A WEB-BASED DSS FOR THE COURSE APPROVAL PROCESS

When The University of Georgia moved from the quarter to the semester system in 1998, there was a need to revamp the entire curriculum. Every course had go through the entire course approval process involving a lengthy paper trail with approve/modify/reject decisions made at every step. This workflow clearly needed to be automated, and decision making embedded in the process. The Course Approval Process Automatic (CAPA) system was developed to support semester conversion issues with a work coordination and automation solution that used specific technology. Its objectives were to coordinate a process that involves multiple committees, dean's offices, departmental offices, the graduate school, and the vice president of academic affairs.

CAPA is a Web-based (intranet) system. It uses a two-tiered architecture. The Web server provides information to the users, and the SQL database runs on another system in the background. Comments, approval, denial, or more work decisions are made every step of the way, and the results are recorded in the database.

The reason for using a Web server was so that the university could freely provide Web browsers for clients (access software for PCs on the various local area networks on campus). No additional hardware or software costs would be incurred by individual colleges and departments.

The principal benefits of CAPA are as follows:

- CAPA saves time and is cost-effective, especially for users.
- CAPA is flexible enough to support various related applications and is extensible, to support additional requirements.
- CAPA requires little or no user training and no new hardware or software.
- CAPA addresses long-term maintenance, management, and upgrade issues.

Appropriate information on courses can be accessed from the database to assist decision makers at the departmental, college, and university levels. Information is current, and decisions on the courses are based on current information. The CAPA system is the only course approval process at the university; no paper course applications are used. A variation of the system is now in permanent use in course management.

DSS IN ACTION 3.11

AD HOC DSS: VISUAL BASIC HELPS CLOSE THE DEAL

No one needs to convince real estate agent Jim Rauschkolb about the value of information technology. A bad math error in 1980 turned him into a computer programmer and forever changed the way he sells property. In 1980 he sold a family's home and calculated, with a pencil and paper at their dining room table, what they were going to net. At the closing, he discovered that his calculations were off by $1,800, which came out of his pocket. When this happened, Rauschkolb set out to develop a computer system that would remember every line item that needed to be calculated, do the math, and manage the increasingly complex interdependencies between details such as the net gain from the sale of a home and the down payment on a new property. He learned how to program and built an ad hoc DSS. By using the software, he found that it was much easier to get people to sign a contract. He could show customers all the financial details up front in an easy-to-understand fashion, including whether they qualified for a mortgage. Furthermore, the calculations were done quickly and accurately. Rauschkolb,

now a vice president in the Century 21 office in Orinda, CA, continued to use DSS and computers. In the late 1990s he needed to integrate applications and port them to a client/server development environment. Rauschkolb has ported three of his applications to Visual Basic (VB), with more on the way. One application, which is copyrighted, calculates the accurate cost of buying a house by analyzing sale price, equity, down payments, monthly mortgage, interest, income, and other factors. This process takes some agents hours to complete; Rauschkolb's program delivers accurate results in minutes. Having ported his applications to VB, Rauschkolb is now making the next logical move: distributing his programs to other agents for their PCs. He packaged several of his applications with Web capabilities. What started as revenge against a math error ended as an outstanding Web DSS application.

Source: Condensed from R. Levin, "Visual Basic Helps Close the Deal," *InformationWeek,* Nov. 4, 1996, pp. 16A–17A.

Ad hoc DSS deal with specific problems that are usually neither anticipated nor recurring. Ad hoc decisions often involve strategic planning issues and sometimes management control problems. Justifying a DSS that will be used only once or twice is a major issue in DSS development. See DSS in Action 3.11 for a description of an ad hoc DSS.

PERSONAL, GROUP, AND ORGANIZATIONAL SUPPORT
The support given by DSS can be separated into three distinct but interrelated categories (Hackathorn and Keen, 1981):

Personal Support   Here the focus is on an individual user performing an activity in a discrete task or decision. The task is fairly independent of other tasks. See DSS in Action 3.11.

Group Support   The focus here is on a group of people, all of whom are engaged in separate but highly interrelated tasks. An example is a typical finance department in which one DSS can serve several employees all working on the preparation of a budget.

Organizational Support   Here the focus is on organizational tasks or activities involving a sequence of operations, different functional areas, possibly different locations, and massive resources.

INDIVIDUAL DSS VERSUS A GROUP SUPPORT SYSTEM (GSS)
Several DSS researchers and practitioners (such as Keen, 1980) point out that the fundamental model of a DSS—the lonely decision maker striding down the hall at high

noon to make a decision—is true only for minor decisions. In most organizations, be they public, private, Japanese, European, or American, most major decisions are made collectively. Working in a group may be a complicated process, and it can be supported by computers in what is called a **group support system (GSS)** (see the Opening Vignette).

Note: The term *group support* introduced earlier should not be confused with the concept of GSS. In group support, the decisions are made by individuals whose tasks are interrelated. Therefore, they check the impact of their decision on others but do not necessarily make decisions as a group. In GSS, each decision (sometimes only one decision) is made by a group.

CUSTOM-MADE SYSTEMS VERSUS READY-MADE SYSTEMS

Many DSS are custom-made for individual users and organizations (e.g., the real estate DSS application in DSS in Action 3.11). However, a comparable problem may exist in similar organizations. For example, hospitals, banks, and universities share many similar problems. Similarly, certain nonroutine problems in a functional area (such as finance or accounting) can repeat themselves in the same functional area of different organizations. Therefore, it makes sense to build generic DSS that can be used (sometimes with modifications) in several organizations. Such DSS are called *ready-made* and are sold by various vendors. For example, the Visual Basic (VB) applications described in DSS in Action 3.11 can be viewed as a ready-made DSS. Recently, we have seen an increased number of ready-made DSS because of their flexibility and low cost. An example of such a system is given on this book's Web site at www.prenhall.com/turban.

In 1999 several ERP and SCM companies started to offer DSS applications online. For a description see Chapter 10.

DSS AND THE WEB CONNECTION

Two recent developments in computer technology provide a fertile ground for new or enhanced DSS application. The first one is Web technologies (Internet, intranet, and extranets), and the second one is enterprise software such as ERP and SCM (Chapter 10).

The Web–DSS connection is divided into two categories: DSS development (Chapter 7) and DSS use.

DSS DEVELOPMENT

The Web can be used for collecting both external and internal (intranet) data for the DSS database. The Web can be used for communication and collaboration among DSS builders, users and management. In addition, the Web can be used to download DSS software, or to use DSS applications provided by the company, or to buy online from application service providers (ASPs).

DSS USE

The DSS is used on the Web in several ways. First, users can go on the intranet and activate ready-made DSS applications. Namely, all they have to do is to enter some data, or specify dates and other information. The DSS is then run and they can see the results. Second, they can get online advice and help on how to use the DSS applications. Third, they communicate with others regarding the interpretation of the DSS results. Finally, they can collaborate in implementing solutions generated by the DSS model.

3.15 THE BIG PICTURE

So far we have introduced the fundamentals of DSS. We started the chapter with a discussion of the Hong Kong journal evaluation vignette. Now that you have learned about the components of a DSS, we can superimpose the details of the vignette on the general structure of a DSS (Figure 3.2). The result is shown in Figure 3.7. A similar situation is provided on this book's Web site in the GLSC case. Also, we have summarized the major capabilities of DSS components (excluding the knowledge component) in Figure 3.8. For further details, see Daniel Power's DSS Web tour at dss.cba.uni.edu/tour/dsstour.html.

FIGURE 3.7 THE STRUCTURE OF THE JOURNAL-EVALUATION DSS IN HONG KONG

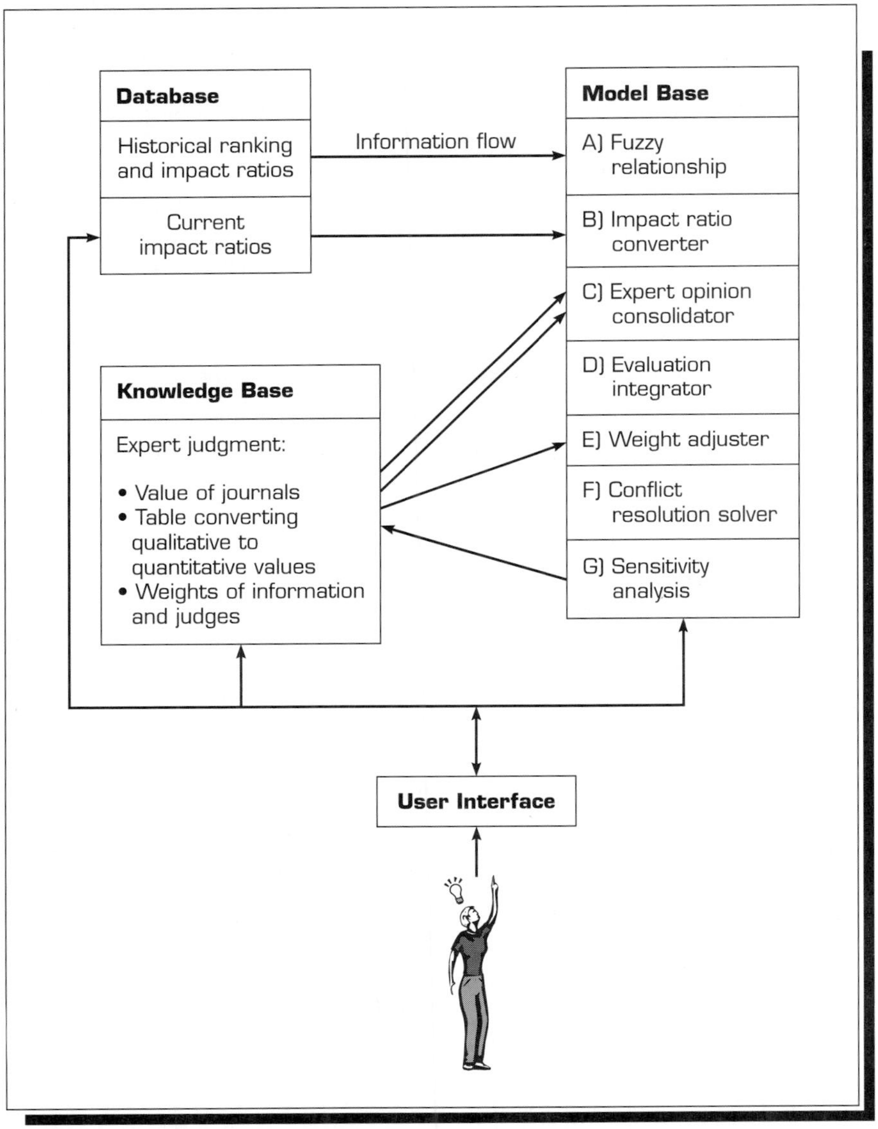

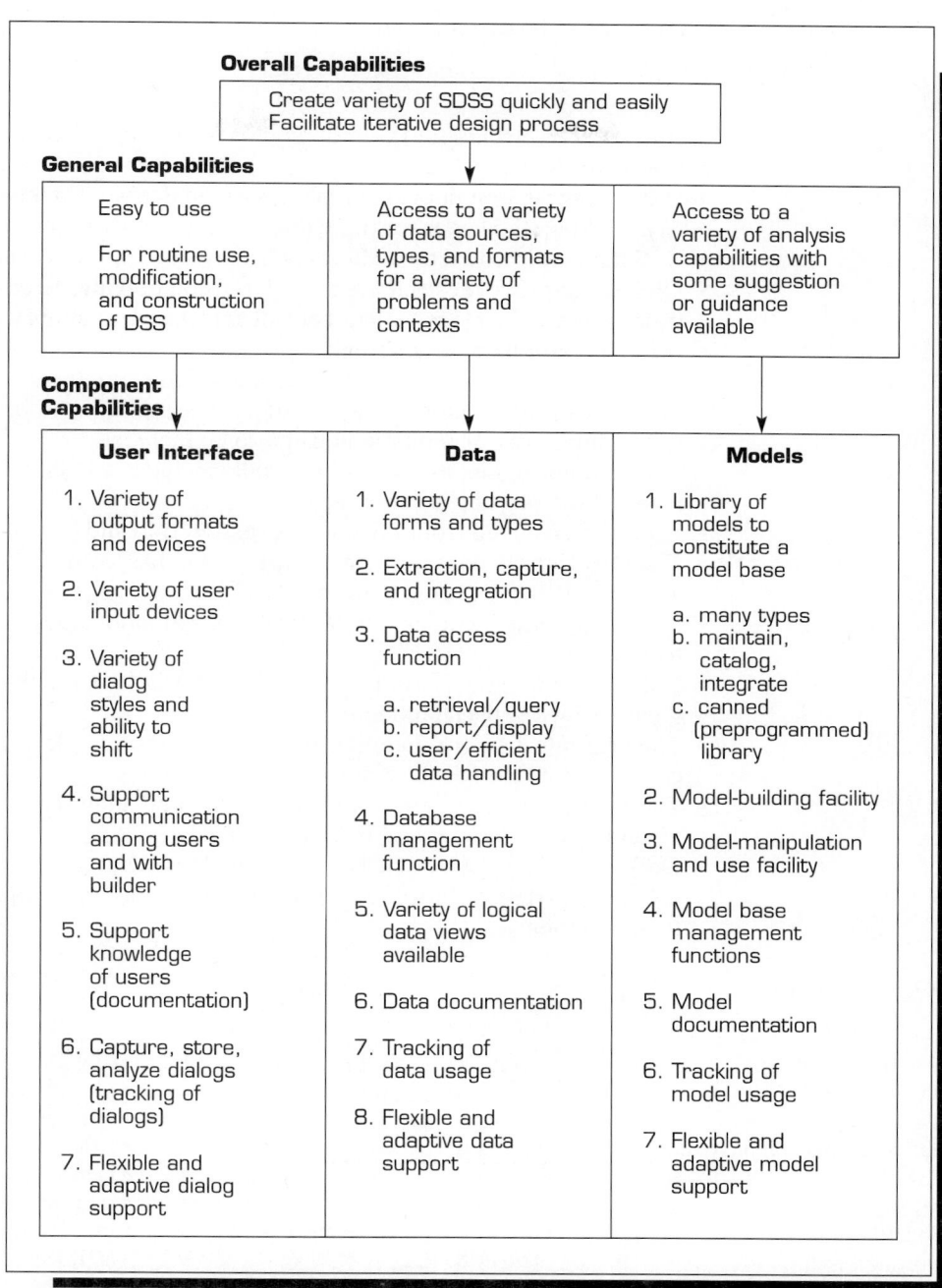

Overall Capabilities

> Create variety of SDSS quickly and easily
> Facilitate iterative design process

General Capabilities

Easy to use	Access to a variety	Access to a
For routine use, modification, and construction of DSS	of data sources, types, and formats for a variety of problems and contexts	variety of analysis capabilities with some suggestion or guidance available

Component Capabilities

User Interface	Data	Models
1. Variety of output formats and devices	1. Variety of data forms and types	1. Library of models to constitute a model base
2. Variety of user input devices	2. Extraction, capture, and integration	a. many types b. maintain, catalog, integrate
3. Variety of dialog styles and ability to shift	3. Data access function a. retrieval/query b. report/display c. user/efficient data handling	c. canned (preprogrammed) library
4. Support communication among users and with builder	4. Database management function	2. Model-building facility 3. Model-manipulation and use facility
5. Support knowledge of users (documentation)	5. Variety of logical data views available	4. Model base management functions
	6. Data documentation	5. Model documentation
6. Capture, store, analyze dialogs (tracking of dialogs)	7. Tracking of data usage	6. Tracking of model usage
7. Flexible and adaptive dialog support	8. Flexible and adaptive data support	7. Flexible and adaptive model support

FIGURE 3.8 SUMMARY OF DSS CAPABILITIES

Source: Ralph Sprague and Eric Carlson, *Building Effective Decision Support Systems,* 1982, p. 313. Reprinted by permission of Prentice-Hall, Inc.

❖ CHAPTER HIGHLIGHTS

- There are several definitions of DSS.
- A DSS is designed to support complex managerial problems that other computerized techniques cannot. DSS is user-oriented, uses data, and often uses models.
- DSS can provide support in all phases of the decision-making process and to all managerial levels for individuals, groups, and organizations.
- DSS is a user-oriented tool. Many applications can be constructed by end users.
- DSS can improve the effectiveness of decision making, decrease the need for training, improve management control, facilitate communication, save effort by the user, reduce costs, and allow for more objective decision making.
- The major components of a DSS are a database and its management, a model base and its management, and a user-friendly interface. An intelligent (knowledge-based) component can also be included.
- The data management subsystem usually includes a DSS database, a DBMS, a data directory, and a query facility.
- Data are extracted from several sources, internal and external.
- The DBMS provides many capabilities to the DSS, ranging from storage and retrieval to report generation.
- The model base includes standard models and models specifically written for the DSS.
- Custom-made models can be written with third- and fourth-generation languages or with special modeling languages.
- The user interface (or dialog) is of utmost importance. It is managed by special software that provides the needed capabilities.
- The DSS can be used directly by managers (and analysts), or it can be used via intermediaries.
- DSS applications can be delivered on the Web. Thus, it is possible to distribute them to remote locations. Also, it is possible to lease applications rather than buy them.

❖ KEY WORDS

- ad hoc DSS
- business (system) analyst
- data warehouse
- database
- database management system (DBMS)
- directory
- DSS application
- expert tool user
- extraction
- facilitator (in GSS)
- graphical user interface (GUI)
- group support system (GSS)
- institutionalized DSS
- intermediary
- Internet
- intranet
- model base
- model base management system (MBMS)
- model building blocks
- object
- operational models
- organizational knowledge base
- query facility
- staff assistant
- strategic models
- tactical models
- user interface
- user interface management system (UIMS)

❖ QUESTIONS FOR REVIEW

1. Provide two definitions of DSS. What do they have in common? What features differentiate them?
2. Why do people attempt to narrow the definition of DSS?
3. Give your own definition of DSS. Compare it to the definitions in Question 1.
4. List the major components of DSS and briefly define each of them.

5. What are the major functions (capabilities) of DBMS?
6. What is extraction?
7. What is the function of a query facility?
8. What is the function of a directory?
9. Models are classified as strategic, tactical, or operational. What is the purpose of such a classification? Give an example of each.
10. List some of the major functions of the MBMS.
11. Compare the features and structure of the MBMS to those of the DBMS.
12. Why is model selection for DSS difficult?
13. What is the major purpose of the user interface system?
14. Define the term *ready-made DSS*.
15. Define a text-oriented DSS.
16. What are the major functions of a dialog (interface) management system?
17. List and describe the major classes of DSS users.
18. What types of support are provided by DSS?
19. Define a procedural computer language and contrast it with a nonprocedural one.
20. Compare a custom-made DSS with a ready-made DSS. List the advantages and disadvantages of each.
21. Search for a ready-made DSS. What type of industry is its market? Why is it a ready-made DSS?

❖ QUESTIONS FOR DISCUSSION

1. Review the major characteristics and capabilities of DSS. Relate each of them to the major components of DSS.
2. List some internal data and external data that could be found in a DSS for selecting a portfolio of stocks for an investor.
3. List some internal and external data in a DSS that would be constructed for a decision regarding a hospital expansion.
4. Provide a list of possible strategic, tactical, and operational models for a university, a restaurant, and a chemical plant.
5. Show the similarities between DBMS and MBMS. What is common to both and why? What are the differences and why?
6. Compare an individual DSS to a group DSS.
7. What are the benefits and the limitations of Holsapple and Whinston's classification approach?
8. Why do managers use intermediaries? Will they continue to use them in the future? Why or why not?
9. Explain why the user is considered a component of the DSS.
10. Examine the Excel spreadsheet in Microsoft Office (or any other Windows-based software package). Identify and describe the different user interface features there.
11. Discuss the potential benefits that a DSS application can derive from the Web.

❖ EXERCISES

1. Susan Lopez has been made director of the transportation department at a medium-size university. She controls the following vehicles: 17 sedans, 15 vans, and 3 trucks. The previous director was fired because there were too many complaints

concerning the nonavailability of vehicles when they were needed. Susan was told not to expect any increase in the budget for the next 2 years (meaning no replacement or additional vehicles). Susan's major job is to schedule vehicles for employees and to schedule the maintenance and repair of these vehicles. All this was accomplished manually by her predecessor. Your job is to consult with Susan regarding the possibility of using a DSS to improve this situation. Susan has a top-end PC and the newest version of Microsoft Office, but she uses the computer only as a word processor. She has access to the university's intranet and to the Internet. Answer the following questions:

   a. Can the development and use of a DSS be justified? (That is, what can the DSS do to support Susan's job?)
   b. What will be included in the data management, model management, and interface?
   c. What type of support do you expect this DSS to render?
   d. How would you classify this DSS?
   e. Does it make sense to have a knowledge component?
   f. Should the DSS be built or should one be rented online? Why?
   g. Should she disseminate the DSS to others on the intranet? Why or why not?

2. Consider the following two banking situations.

   A bank's marketing staff realizes that check-processing data—which banks too often purge after a short period (60–90 days)—could yield valuable information about customers' loan payment patterns and preferences. The bank starts to retain these data using information discovery tools running on an advanced parallel-processing system to sort through checking account activity data to identify home-owner customers who pay mortgages by check on the fifth, sixth, or seventh day of the month. The bank targets these customers with a special home equity loan to consolidate debts, with automatic payment for the loan and the mortgage on the first of the month.

   The bank uses data mining tools to study levels of activity by affluent users over time in multiple channels: branches, automated teller machines (ATMs), telephone centers, and point-of-sale systems throughout all the regions the bank serves. It then takes the analysis to a second level: determining the profitability per transaction in each channel.

   Based on this initiative, the bank undertakes a comprehensive reengineering effort. Discovering that ATM and telephone banking are increasingly active and profitable, the management decides to focus resources and marketing efforts in expanding these channels. It decides to close full-service branches with low activity but replaces some with stand-alone ATM machines to continue providing customer service. Because some branches are still highly profitable and heavily used, management decides to expand the services offered at these locations.

   In both situations, identify the DSS applications that are used and classify them according to the Alter scheme and according to the Holsapple and Whinston scheme.

3. Find literature about an actual DSS application, (professional journals, ABI Inform, customer success stories in DSS vendors' sites, or the Internet for your search). In this application, identify the reasons for the DSS, the major components, the classification (type) of the DSS, the content of the model, and the development process and cost. *Note:* try www.microstrategy.com for good applications.

❖ GROUP PROJECT

Design and implement a DSS for either the problem described in Exercise 1 or a similar real-world problem. Clearly identify data sources and model types and document the problems your group encountered while developing the DSS.

❖ INTERNET EXERCISES

1. Search the Internet for literature about DSS (use google.com, e-library, or Yahoo).

2. Identify an electronic group (newsgroup or interactive Web page) about DSS. Post a message, conduct communication, and prepare a brief report.

3. Identify a DSS software vendor. Communicate electronically with the vendor to obtain further information. Write up your findings about their products in a report.

4. On the World Wide Web, find a DSS software vendor with downloadable demo software. Download the software, install it, and test it. Report your findings to the class and demonstrate the software's capabilities.

5. Find a student, at another college or university who takes a DSS course and exchange ideas about his or her course and yours. Communicate by e-mail and report your results by including both your messages and those of the other student.

6. On the World Wide Web, identify a course syllabus and materials for a DSS course at another college or university. Compare the course description to that of your own. Repeat this assignment using a DSS course syllabus from a university outside your native country. Use www.isworld.org.

7. Access Prentice Hall's Web site (www.prenhall.com) and explore material related to DSS books.

CASE APPLICATION 3.1

DECISION SUPPORT FOR MILITARY HOUSING MANAGERS[5]

THE PROBLEM

The U.S. Department of the Army often enters into agreements for long-term leasing or even for building appropriate housing facilities close to or on military bases. The decision about where, what, when, and how to build or lease is a complex one, and it requires a formal segmented housing market analysis (SHMA) that costs about $50,000 to prepare and whose purpose is to justify the decisions. The SHMA must meet not only the available budget but also the requirements of several auditing agencies. Furthermore, the analysis takes into account the economy around each base and the existing housing market (e.g., availability of rental units that the military can use). The problem is even more complex because there are 20 military ranks (the higher your rank, the nicer accommodations you can get, of course). Housing is available in six sizes, ranging from a studio to a five-bedroom unit. A family's size is also a determining factor. The SHMA uses several quantitative models, including econometric models. The execution of such computations for each of the 200 military installations is lengthy and is subject to errors, especially when done manually.

THE SOLUTION

The DSS was developed in the interactive financial planning system (IFPS) modeling language. It runs on a PC and can support the SHMA. A simplified diagram of the DSS is shown in Figure 3.9.

THE COMPONENTS OF THE DSS

On the left side of the figure, two basic components are listed: a database and a model base. The database consists of

Off-post data: economic characteristics of the area around the military installation

On-post data: profiles of the military personnel seeking housing. Sources for the internal data are internal databases and reports. Sources for the external data are Rand McNally's *Places Rated Almanac,* statistical abstracts of the United States, chambers of commerce, banks, real estate boards, and online databases.

The model base consists of two parts:

- *Regional econometric model (RECOM) for the area.* This model uses many variables and

---

[5] Condensed from G. A. Forgionne, "HANS: A Decision Support System for Housing Managers," *Interfaces,* Nov./Dec. 1991.

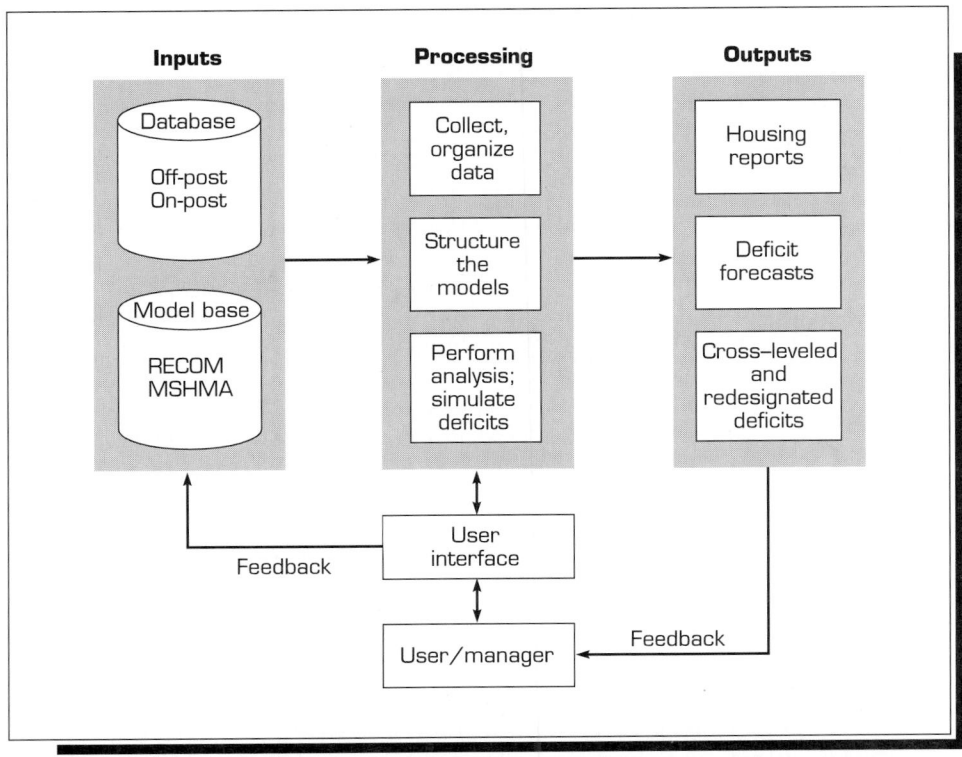

FIGURE 3.9 THE HOUSING MANAGEMENT DSS

constraints (such as value of housing, consumer price index, median rent, median per capita income, annual utility bill, and military allowances).

- *Modified segmented housing market analysis (MSHMA).* This model has many variables, and it also uses on-post and off-post data. The on-post data include the military share of the housing market, housing available at the base (post), housing occupancy levels, demographics of military people, and housing needs. The off-post data are derived from RECOM sources, consisting of median selling price, taxes paid, household income, and total population.

OPERATION

The user receives the DSS on a disk (including all the documentation). The processing starts with data entry. The data are recorded on forms supplied in manuals. The DSS organizes the database, structures the model, and performs analysis (using simulation). All this is done interactively in a user-friendly environment.

The DSS performs all the calculations requested by the housing manager (several options are available). The user can review and modify values as needed.

OUTPUTS

Three major outputs are produced: housing reports as desired by army managers (e.g., reports that identify market conditions), housing deficit (demand over supply) forecasts, and cross-leveled and redesignated deficit forecasts. These outputs are synthesized into two major reports. The output of tested cases was found to be accurate 95 percent of the time.

FEEDBACK

Decision making is a continuous process. Managers learn from reality. Thus, corrective actions can take place. As shown in Figure 3.9, there is feedback from the manager's actions (processing) to the database and the models (adjustment, changes). The second feedback goes from the outputs to the decision maker so that processing can be improved. This feedback can include sensitivity analysis. The

DSS can also be used to determine how much SHMA is required (from "needed" to "strongly needed").

SENSITIVITY ANALYSIS

The IFPS model provides what-if analysis and goal-seeking capabilities. When there is a change in the situation being examined, what-if questions are posed to the model. If targeted goals are required, they are performed with goal seeking.

BENEFITS

The system provides both monetary and managerial benefits.

- *Monetary benefits.* Savings are estimated at about $16,500 per housing project that runs SHMA (or about $2 million per year for the U.S. Army). In addition, there may be savings of about $1 million per year as a result of reduced training requirements.
- *Managerial benefits.* The tedious manual procedures that often resulted in inaccurate, incomplete, and redundant data have been eliminated.

The decision-making process has been considerably improved by quicker analysis of the housing market, impact analysis, error-free computation, and rapid sensitivity analyses. In addition, the auditing process has been standardized, and it is done faster, resulting in an earlier release of funds and the alleviation of housing shortages in many locations.

ENHANCEMENTS

The DSS has been enhanced with an intelligent component, a market-share model, and an improved DBMS.

CASE QUESTIONS

1. Why was this DSS needed?
2. What factors, in your opinion, contributed to the success of the DSS?
3. Discuss the role of forecasting in this DSS.
4. Discuss the role sensitivity analysis may play in this DSS.
5. Discuss how the system might evolve to handle additional related decision-making situations.

DATA WAREHOUSING, ACCESS, ANALYSIS, MINING, AND VISUALIZATION

Data are the foundation on which MSS applications are constructed. Where data come from, how they are organized for decision support, and how they are used are the subjects of this chapter. Data for MSS are treated differently from data for transactions processing. Such treatment is known as business intelligence, and it involves topics such as data warehousing, online analytical processing, data mining, and multidimensionality.

The outline of this chapter is as follows:

4.1 OPENING VIGNETTE: OBI MAKES THE BEST OUT OF THE DATA WAREHOUSE[1]

OBI Inc. (Germany) is the largest home improvement multinational retailer in Europe, with about 500 stores in most European countries and several in China. The number of items in stock is about 300,000, about 70,000 of which are physically available on aver-

---

[1]Based on information published in *DM Review Magazine,* July 1998, by OBI's CEO, and publically available corporate information (in Germany, 2000).

age in each store. The company sells both material and services (installation); you can even buy a complete home (with financing!).

OBI's most important business strategy is to develop one-to-one relationships with each of their customers, learning as much as possible about their needs and purchasing patterns in order to serve them better. This has been a pressing requirement because the customer base is changing dramatically. A significant increase in the number of single-adult households and dual-income families, combined with changing family dynamics, is bringing more women into OBI's stores. As a result, OBI has to incorporate women's styles and preferences into store displays and product assortments—without turning away loyal male customers.

In the mid-1990s, OBI recognized that managing the franchise expansion, the growth in SKUs, and the wider assortment of products demanded the help of a data warehouse. But as the company began collecting data, it quickly pushed the existing system's limits of manageability. Tandem, a Compaq company, proved to OBI management that it could build a data warehouse with the scalability, price performance, and manageability needed to handle the massive amounts of data required for inventory and vendor management. OBI realized that the same data warehouse could also help meet the goals of one-to-one marketing by helping OBI better understand its new customer base.

OBI has begun implementation of an enterprise-wide information system that links transaction detail (where, when, and which items) with customer information (demographics, history, and purchasing patterns). This wealth of information opens the door to product, service and customer profitability analysis, assortment planning, one-to-one marketing programs, replenishment management, and other day-to-day management and service improvements.

OBI launched its data warehouse with approximately 60 gigabytes of raw data which quickly grew to 250 gigabytes. While OBI previously had been able to store only aggregated sales data for an item, the new data warehouse stores every point-of-sale (POS) transaction. Data are extracted from the operational systems and refreshed nightly.

By 2000 more than 25,000 employees were using the data warehouse regularly with the help of access, analysis, and visualization decision support software from Microstrategy (DSS Agent, DSS Web).

The results were gratifying:

- The company improved its competitiveness and profitability.
- The one-to-one marketing program was launched (customers have "virtual loyalty" cards).
- Marketing strategies were refined, and in-store product assortments were optimized for specific stores' demographics.
- Store turnover has increased 10–15 percent.
- Inventory costs were cut by 10–30 percent for many items.
- Vendors were linked to the system and assigned a responsibility for just-in-time deliveries.
- Customer service has improved drastically, with the retail staff responding quickly to customer queries. For example, using a Web browser interface, staff can tell a customer immediately whether an item is available, is on order, or is available at a nearby store.

❖ QUESTIONS FOR THE OPENING VIGNETTE

1. Explain how the data warehouse supports inventory control, vendor management, and CRM.
2. Identify the driving forces that led to creation of the data warehouse.

3. Comment on the benefits derived.
4. Identify decisions supported by the data warehouse.
5. How is customer information used to improve vendor management?

4.2 DATA WAREHOUSING, ACCESS, ANALYSIS, AND VISUALIZATION

The opening vignette demonstrates a scenario in which a multinational company uses a centralized database called a *data warehouse* to support decision making, customer service, and supply chain management. The necessary data for many decisions were located in several countries, and so it was difficult to access the data when they were needed. This situation resulted in higher costs and reduced effectiveness. Now the centralized database contains data from different sources organized so that they are easily accessible from user desktops with Web browsers. Dramatic improvements in customer service and profitability have been realized.

Organizations, private and public, are continuously collecting data, information, and knowledge at an accelerated rate and storing them in computerized systems. Updating, retrieving, using, and removing this information becomes more complicated as the amount increases. At the same time, the number of users interacting with the information increases because of the Internet and other networks, end-user computing, and reduced costs of information processing. Working with multiple databases is becoming a difficult task that requires considerable expertise.

Information overload is threatening to drown organizations. The problem is especially acute in the **client/server architecture,** where connectivity and incompatibility factors may further aggravate the situation.

One solution to the problem is found in the concept of *business intelligence* and the related topics of *data warehousing, data access and mining, online analytical processing,* and *data visualization.* These topics have been considered top issues in IT management since the mid-1990s, and the relationships among them are demonstrated in Figure 4.1.

The data needed for MSS applications are extracted from several sources and organized in a data warehouse (using summarization and relational data organization). End users access the warehouse using different tools that depend on the reason for the

FIGURE 4.1 THE ACTIVITIES OF BUSINESS INTELLIGENCE

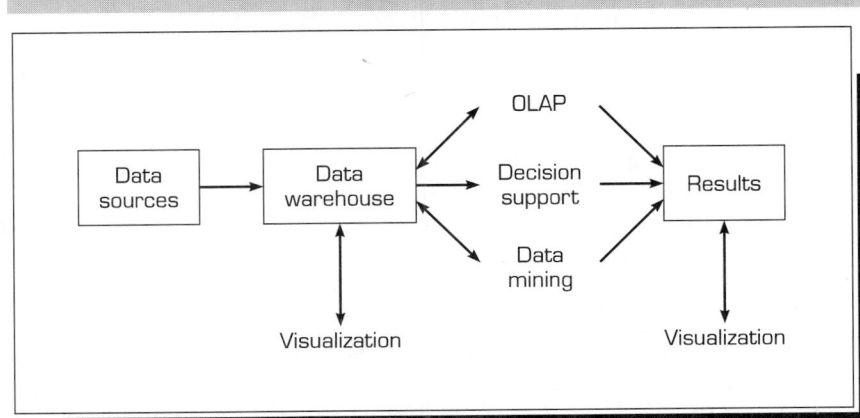

access. For example, in a DSS, one can use query tools or optimization; in EIS one can use data monitoring and data mining tools. The accessed data must be analyzed and presented to the users. Tools for data analysis, visualization, and presentation are available at various steps of the process sometimes referred to as **business intelligence.** Business intelligence results in improved decisions and the creation of knowledge. It is executed with several tools which are presented in Sections 4.8–4.12. But before describing basic data warehousing, its use, and related concepts, we will discuss some fundamental issues related to data acquisition.

4.3 THE NATURE AND SOURCES OF DATA

All decision support systems use data, information, and/or knowledge. These three terms are sometimes used interchangeably and may have several definitions. A common manner of looking at them is as follows:

- *Data.* Data items about things, events, activities, and transactions are recorded, classified, and stored but are not organized to convey any specific meaning. Data items can be numeric, alphanumeric, figures, sounds, or images.
- *Information.* Information is data that have been organized so that they have meaning for the recipient. They confirm something the recipient knows, or may have "surprise" value by revealing something not known. An MSS *application* processes data items so that the results are meaningful for an intended action or decision.
- *Knowledge.* Knowledge consists of data items and/or information organized and processed to convey *understanding, experience, accumulated learning,* and *expertise* as they apply to a current problem or activity. Knowledge can be the application of data and information in making a decision.

MSS data can include documents, pictures, maps, sound, and animation. These data can be stored and organized in different ways before and after their use. They also include concepts, thoughts, and opinions. Data can be raw or summarized. Many MSS applications use summary or extracted data that come from three primary sources: internal, external, and personal.

INTERNAL DATA

Internal data are stored in one or more places. These data are about people, products, services, and processes. For example, data about employees and their pay are usually stored in the corporate database. Data about equipment and machinery can be stored in the maintenance department database. Sales data can be stored in several places: aggregate sales data in the corporate database, and details at each region's database.

An MSS can use raw data as well as processed data (such as reports and summaries). Internal data are available via an organization's intranet or other internal network.

EXTERNAL DATA

There are many sources of external data. They range from commercial databases to data collected by sensors and satellites. Data are available on CD-ROMs, on the Internet, as films, and as music or voices. Government reports are a major source of external data, most of which are available on the Web today. Chambers of commerce, local banks, research institutions, and the like, flood the environment with data and information, resulting in information overload for the MSS user. Data can come from around the globe. Most external data are irrelevant to a specific MSS. Yet much external data must be monitored and captured to ensure that important items are not overlooked. As we will see later, using intelligent scanning and interpretation agents may alleviate this problem.

PERSONAL DATA AND KNOWLEDGE

MSS users and other corporate employees have expertise and knowledge that can be stored for future use. These include subjective estimates of sales, opinions about what competitors are likely to do, and interpretations of news articles.

4.4 DATA COLLECTION, PROBLEMS, AND QUALITY

The need to extract data from many internal and external sources complicates the task of MSS building. Sometimes it is necessary to collect raw data in the field. In other cases, it is necessary to elicit data from people or to find it on the Internet. Regardless of how they are collected, data must be validated and filtered. A classic expression that sums up the situation is "Garbage in, garbage out" (GIGO). Therefore, *data quality (DQ)* is an extremely important issue which will be discussed later.

METHODS FOR COLLECTING RAW DATA

Raw data can be collected manually or by instruments and sensors. Representative data collection methods are time studies, surveys (using questionnaires), observations (e.g., using video cameras), and soliciting information from experts (e.g., using interviews; see Chapter 11). In addition, sensors and scanners are increasingly being used in data acquisition.

The need for reliable, accurate data for any MSS is universally accepted. However, in real life, developers and users face ill-structured problems in "noisy" and difficult environments. There is a wide variety of hardware and software for data storage, communication, and presentation, but much less effort has gone into developing methods for MSS data capture in less tractable decision environments. Insufficient methods for dealing with these problems may limit the effectiveness of even sophisticated technologies in MSS development and use. Arinze and Banerjee (1992) proposed a framework for detecting, preventing, and correcting errors in data specifically collected for DSS use.

DATA PROBLEMS

All computer-based systems depend on data. The quality and integrity of these data are critical for the MSS to avoid the GIGO syndrome. MSS depend on data because compiled data that make up information and knowledge are at the heart of any decision-making system.

The major DSS data problems are summarized in Table 4.1 along with some possible solutions. Data must be available to the system or the system must include a data acquisition subsystem. Data issues should be considered in the planning stage of system development. If too many problems are anticipated, the MSS project should not be undertaken. For suggestions on how to use DSS data properly, see Rubenfeld et al. (1994).

TABLE 4.1   Data Problems

Problem	Typical Cause	Possible Solutions
Data are not correct.	Data were generated carelessly. Raw data were entered inaccurately. Data were tampered with.	Develop a systematic way to enter data. Automate data entry. Introduce quality controls on data generation. Establish appropriate security programs.
Data are not timely.	The method for generating data is not rapid enough to meet the need for data.	Modify the system for generating data. Use the Web to get fresh data.
Data are not measured or indexed properly.	Raw data are gathered inconsistently with the purposes of the analysis. Use of complex models.	Develop a system for rescaling or recombining improperly indexed data. Use a data warehouse. Use appropriate search engines. Develop simpler or more highly aggregated models.
Needed data simply do not exist.	No one ever stored data needed now. Required data never existed.	Predict what data may be needed in the future. Use a data warehouse. Generate new data or estimate them.

Source: Based on Alter (1980), p. 130. Alter, S. L. (1980). *Decision Support Systems: Current Practices and Continuing Challenges.* Reading, MA: Addison-Wesley.

DATA QUALITY

Data quality (DQ) is an extremely important issue because quality determines the usefulness of data as well as the quality of the decisions based on them. Data in organizational databases are frequently found to be inaccurate, incomplete, or ambiguous. The economic and social damage from poor-quality data costs billions of dollars (Redman, 1998).

Strong et al. (1997) conducted extensive research on DQ problems and divided these problems into the following four categories and dimensions:

- *Contextual DQ:* Relevancy, value added, timeliness, completeness, and amount of data
- *Intrinsic DQ:* accuracy, objectivity, believability, and reputation
- *Accessibility DQ:* accessibility and access security
- *Representation DQ:* interpretability, ease of understanding, concise representation, consistent representation.

Strong et al. (1997) developed a framework that presents the major issues and barriers in each of the categories and have suggested that once the major variables and relationships in each category are identified, an attempt can be made to find out how to better manage the data. Some of the problems are technical ones, such as capacity, while others relate to potential computer crimes. For a comprehensive discussion, see Wang (1998).

One of the major issues of DQ is **data integrity.** Older filing systems may lack integrity. That is, a change made in the file in one place may not have been made in the file in another place or department. This results in conflicting data. Data quality specific issues and measures depend on the application of the data. In the area of the data warehouse, for example, Gray and Watson (1998) distinguish the following five issues:

- *Uniformity.* During data capture, uniformity checks ensure that the data are within specified limits.
- *Version.* Version checks are performed when the data are transformed through the use of metadata to ensure that the format of the original data has not been changed.
- *Completeness check.* A completeness check ensures that the summaries are correct and that all values needed to create the summary are included.
- *Conformity check.* A conformity check makes sure that the summarized data are "in the ballpark." That is, during data analysis and reporting, correlations are run between the value reported and previous values for the same number. Sudden changes can indicate a basic change in the business, analysis errors, or bad data.
- *Genealogy check or drill down.* A genealogy check or drill down is a trace back to the data source through its various transformations.

4.5 THE INTERNET AND COMMERCIAL DATABASE SERVICES

External data are pouring into organizations from many sources. Some of the data come on a regular basis from business partners. A major source of data is the Internet.

- *The Internet.* Many thousands of databases all over the world are accessible through the **Internet.** A decision maker can access the home pages of vendors, clients, and competitors; view and download information; or conduct research. The Internet is the major supplier of external data for many decision situations.
- *Commercial data banks.* An **online (commercial) database** service sells access to specialized databases. Such a service can add external data to the MSS in a timely manner and at a reasonable cost. Several thousand services are currently available, many of which are accessible via the Internet. Table 4.2 lists several representative services.

The collection of data from multiple external sources may be complicated. Products from leading companies, such as Oracle, can transfer information from external sources and put it where it is needed, when it is needed, in a usable form.

Since most external data sources are now usually on the Web, it makes sense to use intelligent agents for collecting and possibly interpreting external data. For an example of how this is accomplished, see Liu et al. (2000).

THE WEB AND CORPORATE DATABASES AND SYSTEMS

Developments in **document management systems (DMS)** include use of Web browsers by employees and customers to access vital information. Other Web developments include Pilot Software's Decision Support Suite (www.pilotsw.com) combined with BlueIsle Software's InTouch (www.blueisle.com) and group support systems deployed via Web browsers (Lotus Notes-Domino and TCBWorks), and database management

---

TABLE 4.2   Representative Commercial Database (Data Bank) Services

CompuServe (compuserve.com) and The Source. Personal computer networks providing statistical data banks (business and financial market statistics) as well as bibliographic data banks (news, reference, library, and electronic encyclopedias). CompuServe is the largest supplier of such services to personal computer users.

Compustat (compustat.com). Provides financial statistics about tens of thousands of corporations. Data Resources Inc. offers statistical data banks for agriculture, banking, commodities, demographics, economics, energy, finance, insurance, international business, and the steel and transportation industries. DRI economists maintain a number of these data banks. Standard & Poor's is also a source. It offers services under the U.S. Central Data Bank.

Dow Jones Information Service. Provides statistical data banks on stock market and other financial markets and activities, and in-depth financial statistics on all corporations listed on the New York and American stock exchanges, plus thousands of other selected companies. Its Dow Jones News/Retrieval System provides bibliographic data banks on business, financial, and general news from the *Wall Street Journal, Barron's,* and the Dow Jones News Service.

Lockheed Information Systems. The largest bibliographic distributor. Its DIALOG system offers extracts and summaries of hundreds of different data banks in agriculture, business, economics, education, energy, engineering, environment, foundations, general news publications, government, international business, patents, pharmaceuticals, science, and social sciences. It relies on many economic research firms, trade associations, and government agencies for data.

Mead Data Central (www.mead.com). This data bank service offers two major bibliographic data banks. Lexis provides legal research information and legal articles. Nexis provides a full-text (not abstract) bibliographic database of hundreds of newspapers, magazines, and newsletters, news services, government documents, and so on. It includes full text and abstracts from the *New York Times* and the complete 29-volume *Encyclopedia Britannica.* Also provided are the Advertising & Marketing Intelligence (AMI) data bank and the National Automated Accounting Research System.

---

systems that provide data directly in a format that a Web browser can display with delivery over the Internet or an intranet. Pilot's Internet Publisher is a stand-alone Web product, as is DecisionWeb for Comshare (www.comshare.com).

The "big three" relational database management system vendors—Informix, Oracle, and Sybase—have reworked their core database products to accommodate a world of client/server and Internet/intranet applications that incorporate nontraditional, or rich, multimedia data types. Oracle's Developer/2000 is able to generate graphical client/server applications in PL/SQL code, Oracle's implementation of structured query language (SQL), as well as in COBOL, C, and HTML. For details see the July/Aug. 1999 issue of *Oracle Magazine.* Other tools provide Web browser capabilities, multimedia authoring and content scripting, object class libraries, and OLAP routines (Gill, 1996a). Also, Microsoft has many products related to business intelligence.

Sybase is also readying software—the Internet Development Toolkit for PowerBuilder, an add-on to the PowerBuilder Windows application tool—for deploying Web-enabled client/server applications.

Web site and database integration suppliers include Spider Technologies (spidertech.com), Hart Software (hart.com), Next Software Inc. (next.com), NetObjects Inc. (netobjects.com), Oracle Corporation (oracle.com), and OneWave Inc. (onewave.com).

The use of the Web has a far-reaching impact on collaborative computing in the form of groupware (Chapter 7), executive information systems (Chapter 8), document management systems (Section 4.11), and the whole area of interface design development.

4.6 DATABASE MANAGEMENT SYSTEMS IN DSS

The complexity of most corporate databases and large-scale independent MSS databases sometimes makes standard computer operating systems inadequate for an effective and efficient interface between the user and the database. A **database management system (DBMS)** is designed to supplement standard operating systems by allowing for greater integration of data, complex file structure, quick retrieval and changes, and better data security, to mention a few advantages. Specifically, a DBMS is a software program for adding information to a database and updating, deleting, manipulating, storing, and retrieving information. A DBMS combined with a modeling language is a typical system development pair used in constructing DSS or other MSS. DBMS are designed to handle large amounts of information. Often, data from the database are extracted and put in a statistical, mathematical, or financial model for further manipulation or analysis. Large DSS often do this.

The major role of DBMS is to manage data. By *manage,* we mean to create, delete, change, and display the data. DBMS enable users to query data as well as to generate reports. For details, see Ramakrishnan and Gehrke (1999).

Unfortunately, there is confusion regarding the appropriate role of DBMS and spreadsheet programs. This is because many DBMS offer capabilities similar to those available in an integrated spreadsheet such as Excel, enabling the DBMS user to perform DSS spreadsheet work with a DBMS. Similarly, many spreadsheet programs offer a rudimentary set of DBMS capabilities. Although such a combination can be valuable in some cases, it may result in lengthy processing of information and often inferior results. The add-in facilities are not robust enough, and they are often very cumbersome. Finally, the computer's available RAM may limit the size of the user's spreadsheet. For some applications, DBMS work with several databases and deal with much more data than a spreadsheet can.

For DSS application, it is often necessary to work with both data and models. Therefore, it is tempting to use only one integrated tool such as Excel. However, interfaces between DBMS and spreadsheets are fairly simple, facilitating the exchange of data between independent more powerful programs.

Small to medium DSS can be built either by enhanced DBMS or by integrated spreadsheets. Alternatively, they can be built with a DBMS program and a spreadsheet program. A third approach to the construction of DSS is to use a fully integrated DSS generator (Chapter 6).

4.7 DATABASE ORGANIZATION AND STRUCTURES

The relationships between the many individual records stored in a database can be expressed by several logical structures (McFadden et al., 1999). DBMS are designed to use these structures to perform their functions. The three conventional structures are relational, hierarchical, and network and are shown in Figure 4.2.

RELATIONAL DATABASE

The relational form of DSS database organization—described as tabular or flat—allows the user to think in terms of two-dimensional tables, which is the way many people see data reports. Relational DBMS allow multiple access queries. Thus, a data file consists

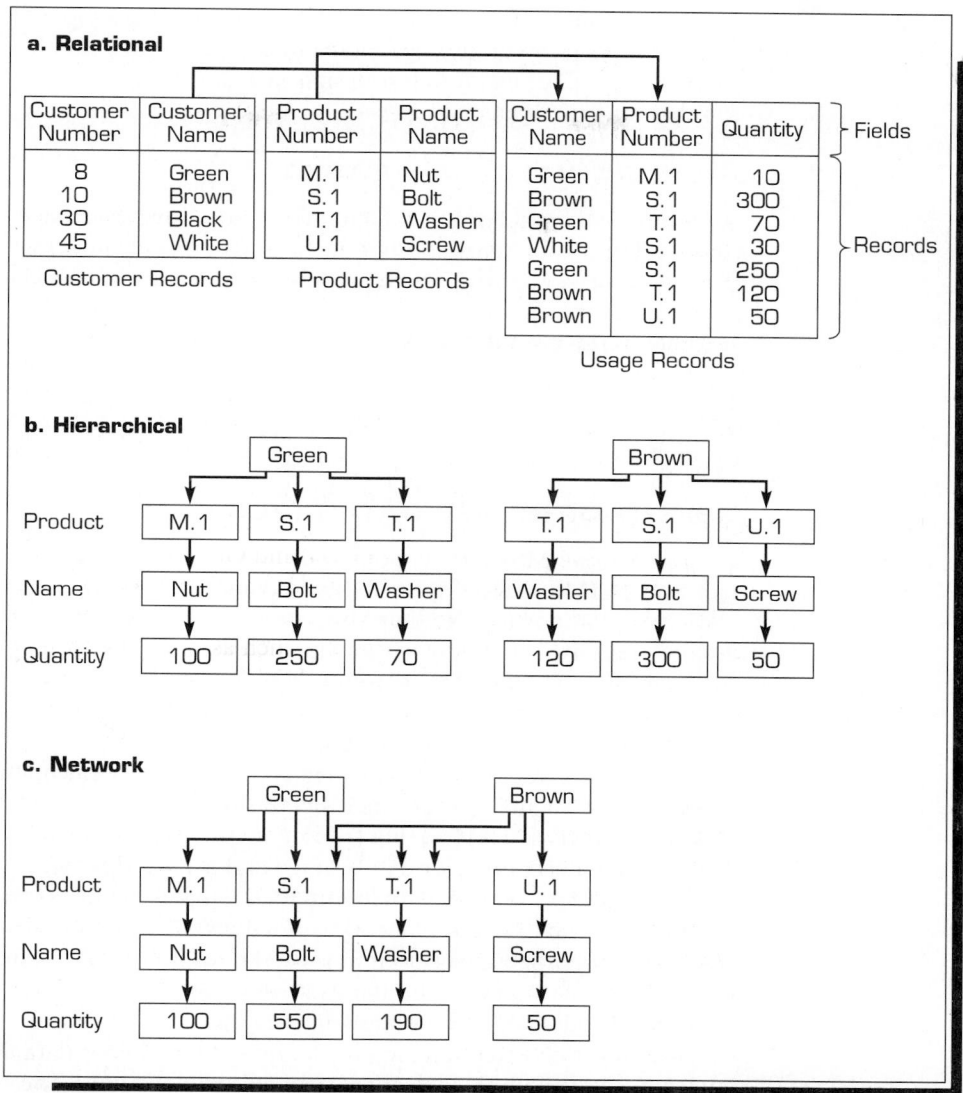

FIGURE 4.2 DATABASE STRUCTURES

of a number of columns proceeding down a page. These columns are considered individual fields. The rows on a page represent individual records made up of several fields. This is the same design used by spreadsheets. Several such data files can be related by means of a common data field found in the two (or more) data files. These common fields must be spelled exactly alike and must be the same size (the same number of bytes) and type (e.g., alphanumeric or dollar). For example, in Figure 4.2 the data field Customer Name is found in both the customer and the usage files, and they are thus related. The data field Product Number is found in the product file and the usage file. It is through these common linkages that all three files are related and in combination form a **relational database.**

The advantage of this type of database is that it is simple for the user to learn, can be easily expanded or altered, and can be accessed in a number of formats not anticipated at the time of the initial design and development of the database. Many data warehouses are organized this way.

HIERARCHICAL DATABASES

A hierarchical model orders data items in a top-down fashion, creating logical links between related data items. It looks like a tree or an organization chart. It is used mainly in transaction processing where processing efficiency is a critical element.

NETWORK DATABASES

This structure permits more complex links, including lateral connections between related items. This structure is also called the CODASYL model. It can save storage space through the sharing of some items (e.g., in Figure 4.2 Green and Brown share S.1 and T.1).

OBJECT-ORIENTED DATABASES

Comprehensive MSS applications, such as those involving computer-integrated manufacturing (CIM), require accessibility to complex data, which may include pictures and elaborate relationships. Neither hierarchical, nor network, nor even relational database architectures, which mainly use an alphanumeric approach, can efficiently handle such situations. Even when SQL is used to create and access relational databases, the solution may not be effective. For such applications a graphical representation, such as the one used in objected-oriented systems, may be useful.

Object-oriented data management is based on the principle of object-oriented programming (see details on this book's Web site). Object-oriented database systems combine the characteristics of an object-oriented programming language such as Smalltalk or C++ with a mechanism for data storage and access. The object-oriented tools focus directly on the databases. An **object-oriented database management system (OODBMS)** allows one to analyze data at a conceptual level that emphasizes the natural relationships between objects. Abstraction is used to establish inheritance hierarchies, and object encapsulation allows the database designer to store both conventional data and procedural code within the same objects.

An object-oriented data management system defines data as objects and encapsulates data along with their relevant structure and behavior. The system uses a hierarchy of classes and subclasses of objects. Structure, in terms of relationships, and behavior, in terms of methods and procedures, are contained within an object. Object-oriented database managers are especially useful in distributed DSS for very complex applications. Object-oriented database systems have the power to handle the complex data used in MSS applications (see DSS in Action 4.2 and Chaudhri and Loomis, 1998).

MULTIMEDIA-BASED DATABASES

Multimedia database management systems (MMDBMS) manage data in a variety of formats, in addition to the standard text or numeric fields. These formats include images such as digitized photographs or forms of bit-mapped graphics such as maps or .PIC files, hypertext images, video clips, sound, and virtual reality (multidimensional images).

The majority of all corporate information resides outside the computer in documents, maps, photos, images, and videotapes. For companies to build applications that take advantage of such rich data types, a special database management system with the ability to manage and manipulate multiple data types must be used. They store rich mul-

DSS IN ACTION 4.1

OBJECT-ORIENTED DATABASE AT ALCOA
(WWW.ALCOA.COM)

Modern aluminum rolling mills are highly automated. Therefore, a key factor for smooth operation is taking appropriate action to ensure high quality and low downtime of equipment. Alcoa's Tennessee rolling mill (in Alcoa, TN) has 1,500 sensors and 2,000 alarms. The relationship between alarms and sensors is often highly abstract. Troubleshooting requires fast access to an integrated body of data, information, and knowledge. Conventional DBMS and artificial intelligence were too slow. The solution: G-Base (from Graphael, Waltham, MA), an object-oriented data-base combined with a relational DBMS, which is used for information retrieval. The system includes 4,000 objects. G-Base stores information as objects and manipulates them independently of the data structure, allowing the structure to be modified at any time. The operator can locate information in seconds instead of hours. The system is also equipped with hypertext access to 30,000 pages of documentation. Last, but not least, using the system is very simple, requiring only minimal training.

DSS IN FOCUS 4.2

MULTIMEDIA DATABASE MANAGEMENT
SYSTEMS: A SAMPLER

IBM developed its DB2 Digital Library multimedia server architecture for storing, managing, and retrieving text, video, and digitized images over networks. Digital Library consists of several existing IBM software and hardware products combined with consulting and custom development (see www.ibm.com). Digital Library will compete head to head with multimedia storage and retrieval packages from other leading vendors.

MediaWay Inc. (mediaway.com) claims that its multimedia database management system can store, index, and retrieve multimedia data (sound, video, graphics) as easily as relational databases handle tabular data. The DBMS is aimed at companies that want to build what MediaWay calls "multimedia cataloging applications" that manage images, sound, and video across multiple back-end platforms. An advertising agency, for example, might want to use the product to build an application that accesses images of last year's ads stored on several servers. It is a client/server implementation. MediaWay is not the only vendor to target this niche, however. Relational database vendors, such as Oracle Corporation and Sybase Inc., are incorporating multimedia data features in their database servers. In addition, several desktop software companies are promoting client databases for storing scanned images. Among the industries that use this technology are health care, real estate, retailing, and insurance.

Source: Condensed from various vendors' Web sites and publically advertised information.

timedia data types as binary large objects (BLOBS). Database management systems are being modified to provide this capability (McFadden et al., 1999) (see DSS in Focus 4.2). For Web-related applications of multimedia databases, see DSS in Action 4.3 and Maybury (1997), and multimedia demonstrations on the Web: the macromedia's products, and a Visual Intelligence Corporation (affinity.com).

Some computer hardware (including the communication system with the database) may not be capable of playback in real time. A delay with some buffering might be necessary (e.g., try RealAudio at www.realaudio.com). Intel Corporation's Pentium chip released in early 1997, and later versions, incorporate multimedia extension (MMX) technology for processing multimedia data for real-time display (see DSS in Focus 4.4). This technology is embedded in many current chips.

DSS IN ACTION 4.3

VIRTUAL NEWSSTAND DEBUTS ONLINE

Southam New Media (www.southam.com), one of the largest newspaper chains in Canada (part of Hollinger Inc.), has created and instituted a multimedia database called a virtual newsstand. The Southam interactive database (SID) allows the entry, filing, and retrieval of data in all formats used by Southam: wire service text, newspaper and magazine text, classified ads, photographs, graphics, television, video and sound, software programs, and Web content. Any unit of data can be bound and has identifying attributes that can be stored and retrieved through a single access point. Southam's initial investment was only $500,000—much, much less than if their newspapers were paginated on different systems. According to Peter Irwin, president of Southam New Media, there is a single access window for retrieval and input, with one export button where content can be exported onto the Web or, for example, a commercial service provider such as America Online

or the Microsoft Network. Basically, what the development team did was to write software that enables extraction of content from all Southam's newspapers online and tries to make sense of what is in a story. The information was then put into an Oracle database, which allows flexibility, and the whole system was set up on Southam's intranet. Currently, Southam is merging its system with the Web. Southam owns *Business World,* a Canadian television show. The company plans to put video from the program into the database using standard video capturing technology. The video can then be bound to any story.

Future applications for SID include full electronic distribution of Southam's content.

Source: Condensed from J. B. Cohen, " 'Virtual Newsstand' Debuts Online," *Editor & Publisher,* Vol. 129, No. 24, June 15, 1996, pp. 86–87.

DOCUMENT-BASED DATABASES

To alleviate paper storage and shuffling, document-based databases were developed. These are also known as electronic document management (EDM) systems (Haskin, 1998). They are used for information dissemination, form storage and management, shipment tracking, expert license processing, and workflow automation. EDM uses both object-oriented and multimedia databases, and so document-based databases are included in the previous two sections. What is unique to EDM are the implementation and the applications. McDonnell Douglas Corporation distributes aircraft service bulletins to their customers around the world using the Internet. The company used to distribute a staggering volume of bulletins to over 200 airlines, using over 4 million pages of documentation every year. Now it is all on the Web, saving money and time both for the company and for its customers.

Motorola uses DMS not only for document storage and retrieval but also for small group collaboration and company-wide knowledge sharing. They have developed virtual communities where people can discuss and publish information, all with the Web-enabled DMS.

INTELLIGENT DATABASES

Artificial intelligence (AI) technologies, especially expert systems (ES) and artificial neural networks (ANN), can make the access and manipulation of complex databases simpler. One way to do this is to enhance the database management system by providing it with an *inference capability,* resulting in a so-called **intelligent database.** Al-Zobaidie and Grimson (1987) provide three possible architectures for such a coupling. They also explain how the efficiency and function of the DBMS can be enhanced. The contribution of an ES to a database can be further increased if it is coupled with a nat-

CPU SPEEDS UP MULTIMEDIA PROCESSING

Because some computer hardware (including the system that communicates with the database) may not be capable of playback in real time, delays with some buffering might be necessary. Intel Corporation's (Santa Clara, CA, www.intel.com) Pentium chip, released in early 1997, incorporates multimedia extension (MMX) technology for processing multimedia data for real-time display. This PC processor chip has a single-instruction multiple-data (SIMD) parallel processing design. It is designed to take advantage of the most common characteristics of multimedia applications. These include small-integer data types, frequent multiply-and-accumulate operations, small repetitive loops, and highly parallel operations. In tests, Intel says it has seen performance improvements of 50–400 percent, depending on the application. This enhanced graphics performance eliminates the need for three-dimensional graphics accelerator cards. (*Authors' note:* Most of the chips released by Intel since 1997 incorporate the MMX circuitry.)

Source: Condensed from J. Piven, "Multimedia Enhanced Pentium Boosts Power, Cuts Costs," *Computer Technology Review,* Vol. 16, No. 10, Oct. 1996, pp. 1, 12, 16.

ural language processor. For a description of the integration of a database, DBMS, ES, and natural language processors, see Chapter 18.

Difficulties in connecting ES to large databases have been a major problem even for large corporations. Several vendors have recognized the importance of such integration and have developed software products to support it. An example of such a product is the Oracle relational DBMS, which incorporates some ES functionality in the form of a *query optimizer* that selects the most efficient path for database queries to travel. In a distributed database, for example, a query optimizer recognizes that it is more efficient to transfer two records to a machine that holds 10,000 records than vice versa. (The optimization is important to users because with such a capability they need to know only a few rules and commands to use the database.) Another product is the INGRES II Intelligent Database.

One of IBM's main initiatives in commercial AI is providing a knowledge processing subsystem to work with a database and enable users to extract information from the database and pass it to an expert system's knowledge base in several different knowledge representation structures.

Databases now store pictures, sophisticated graphics, and other media. Therefore, access to and management of databases are becoming more difficult and so are the accessibility and retrieval of information. For a discussion of intelligent object-oriented databases, see Parsaye and Chignell (1993) and Maybury (1997).

The use of intelligent systems in database access is also reflected in the use of natural language interfaces which can be used to help nonprogrammers retrieve and analyze data.

4.8 DATA WAREHOUSING

Two contradictory forces are evidenced in modern business. First, there is a need for specialized, localized hardware and software solutions. Second, there is a need for a cost-effective means of *uniting* these information resources into a manageable business asset.

As managers respond to this challenge, they must cope with the explosive growth in the number and diversity of devices and systems. Enterprise systems are becoming profoundly more complex. Organizations today have a mixture of older, centralized systems and newer, distributed systems; a wide variety of technologies is provided by an even larger number of vendors. Facing this environment, managers must use new concepts in managing information technologies. One such concept is *data warehousing* (Singh and Singh, 1998; Gray and Watson, 1998).

THE DATA WAREHOUSE CONCEPT

The definition of a data warehouse begins with the physical separation of a company's operational and decision support environments. At the heart of many companies lies a store of *operational data,* usually derived from critical mainframe-based online transaction processing (OLTP) systems such as order entry applications. OLTP systems are built with COBOL, and they operate in a customer information control system (CICS) environment. OLTP systems for financial and inventory management and control, for example, also produce operational data. In the operational environment, data access, application logic tasks, and data presentation logic are tightly coupled together, usually in nonrelational databases. These nonrelational data stores are not very conducive to data retrieval for decision support applications. However, decision support information must be made accessible to management.

The goal of a **data (or information) warehouse** is to establish a *data repository* that makes operational data accessible in a form that is readily acceptable for decision support and other user applications. As part of this new accessibility, a process must transform detail-level operational data to summaries in a relational form, which makes them more amenable to decision support processing. Oracle Corporation defines a data warehouse as a collection of corporate information derived directly from operational systems and some external data sources. Its specific purpose is to support business decisions, not business operations.

Only the data needed for decision support processing in a variety of MSS applications are carried over from the operational environment to the data warehouse, where they are transformed or integrated into a consistent structure. The data are then placed directly in a data repository at the current level of detail, where they are eventually summarized, archived into the older detail data level, or purged. Data warehouses also allow for the storage of **metadata,** which are data about data. Metadata provide information about the content of the warehouse (like a directory); they include a guide to moving data to the warehouse, rules for summarization, business terms used to describe data, technical terminology, and rules for data extraction.

Moving MSS information off the mainframe presents a company with an opportunity to restructure its MSS strategy. Companies can reinvent the way in which they shape and form their MSS data. They have an opportunity to make it very amenable to widespread use for decision support. For example, any kind of EIS requires having good summarized data in different forms. Old-fashioned EIS and DSS applications often failed because the underlying data were difficult or impossible to access. A data warehouse overcomes this problem.

IMPLEMENTING DATA WAREHOUSING

A data warehouse combines various data sources into a single resource for *end-user* access. End users can perform ad hoc querying, reporting, analysis, data mining, and visualization of warehouse information. Data warehousing typically involves combining a variety of vendors' products into an integrated solution. This process is known as the "best of the breed" approach. There can be several data warehouses and variants such as data marts in one company.

USERS, CAPABILITIES, AND BENEFITS

The major end users are analysts, managers, executives, administrative assistants, and professionals. A data warehousing solution should provide ready access to critical data, insulate operation databases from ad hoc processing that can slow TPS systems, and provide high-level summary information as well as data drill-down capabilities. These properties can improve business knowledge, provide competitive advantage, enhance customer service and satisfaction, facilitate decision making, improve worker productivity, and help in streamlining business processes (see DSS in Action 4.5).

ARCHITECTURE AND PROCESS

There are several basic architectures for data warehousing. Two common ones are two-tier and three-tier architectures, but sometimes there is only one tier. Gray and Watson (1998) distinguished among these by dividing the data warehouse into three parts:

1. The data warehouse itself, which contains the data and associated software
2. Data acquisition (back-end) software which extracts data from legacy systems and external sources, consolidates and summarizes the data, and loads it into the data warehouse
3. Client (front-end) software, which allows users to access and analyze data in the warehouse (e.g., a DSS engine).

In three-tier architecture operational systems contain the data and the software for data acquisition in one tier (server), the data warehouse is another tier, and the third tier includes the decision support engine (i.e., the application server) and the client. The advantage of this architecture is separation of the functions of the data warehouse, which eliminates resource constraints and make it possible to easily create data marts.

DSS IN ACTION 4.5

GTE EMPOWERS DECISION MAKERS

To determine the viability of a new service or product, a product manager must get an answer to requests such as this: List all Hispanic households with a median income of less than $40,000 per year that generated more than $50 per month in telephone toll revenue during the third quarter of 1999. To get an answer, the product manager used to wait days or even weeks. The data were in different sources and had to be accessed and compiled. Today, such information is provided in minutes or even seconds at GTE, a large telephone company in California (www.gte.com), by using a data warehouse. The company feels that the data warehouse is essential because of the intense competition in telecommunication services.

The warehouse was created because the company felt that their then existing system, sufficient for day-to-day transaction processing (TPS), was not sufficient for strategic decision making. Decision making usually requires integration of data across multiple subject areas, such as customers and network usage. Also, GTE needed to tap external sources of information. Online

query and analysis tend to be unpredictable with respect to computer resource use, placing high demands on the system and disturbing efficient operation of the TPS. It was decided to provide infrastructure, one for the TPS and the other for decision support, including a data warehouse.

Additional reasons for creating a data warehouse were that it could supplement some of the routine operational (transaction processing) applications. Furthermore, the efficiency of both the IT and the business units has increased. Today, GTE uses fewer subcontractors to handle peak computer resource demands. The cost reduction enables GTE to reduce its fees and to be more competitive.

Finally, the time spent on querying has been reduced substantially. Now, decision makers can ask what-if questions and get immediate replies. GTE also can respond quickly to the need for accurate, comprehensive data.

Source: Condensed from "Data Warehousing," *ComputerWorld,* Sept. 4, 1995, and www.gte.com (2000).

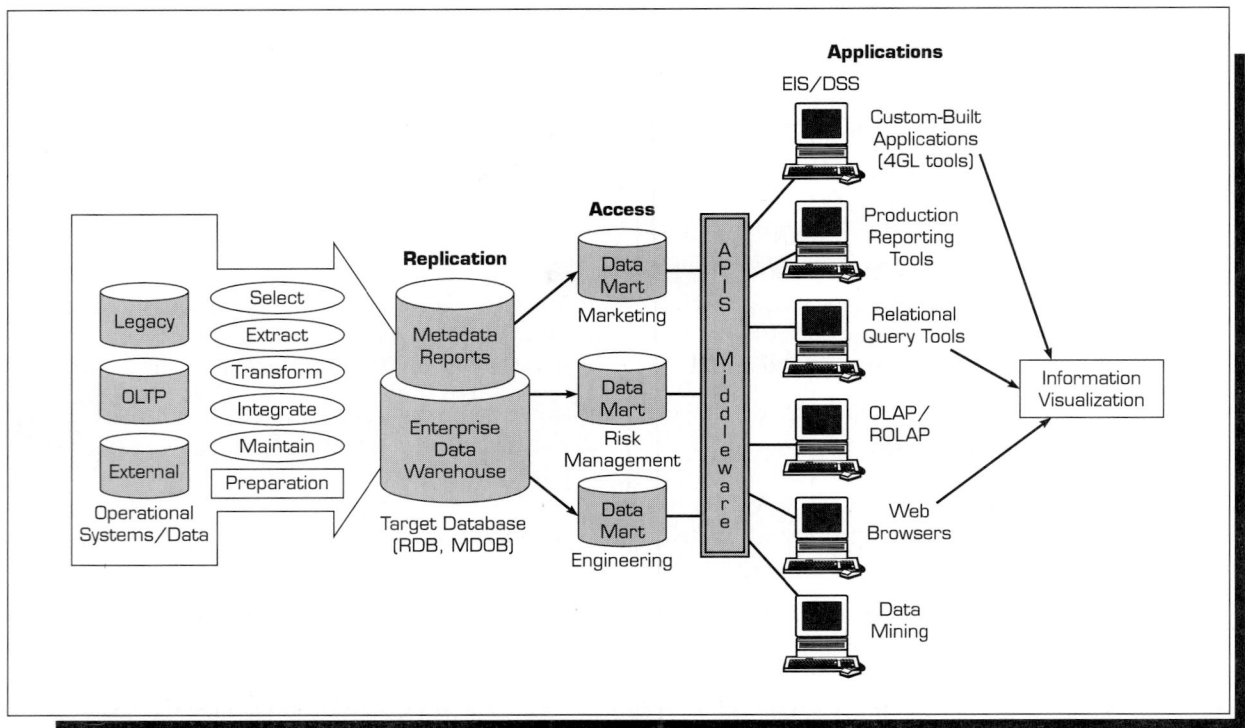

FIGURE 4.3 DATA WAREHOUSE FRAMEWORK AND VIEWS

In a two-tier architecture, it is possible to have the DSS engine on the same platform as the warehouse. Therefore, it is more economical than the three-tier structure. For further details, see Gray and Watson (1998).

The basic data warehouse architecture is shown in Figure 4.3. The possible data sources are on the left. The data warehouse software is used to process the data to the enterprise warehouse. Several data marts (which will be described soon) are shown in the middle, and the applications appear on the right.

COMPONENTS

The major components of the data warehouse are

- *A large physical database.* The data warehouse is basically a large database. Data for the data warehouse are gathered, along with metadata and the processing logic used to scrub, into a physical database where they are organized, packaged, and preprocessed for end-user access.
- *A logical data warehouse.* This component contains all the metadata, business rules, and processing logic required to scrub, organize, package, and preprocess the data. In addition, it contains the information required to find and access the actual data wherever they reside.

Data Marts   The high cost of data warehouses limits their use to large companies. An alternative used by many firms is creation of a lower cost, scaled-down version of a data warehouse called a **data mart.** A data mart is a small warehouse designed for a strategic business unit (SBU) or a department. The advantages of data marts are the following:

- The cost is low (prices under $100,000 versus $1 million or more).
- The lead time for implementation is significantly shorter, often less than 90 days.
- They are controlled locally rather than centrally, conferring power on the using group.
- They contain less information than the data warehouse and hence have more rapid response and are more easily understood and navigated than an enterprise-wide data warehouse.
- They allow a business unit to build its own decision support systems without relying on a centralized IS department.

There are several types of data marts:

1. *Replicated (dependent) data marts.* Sometimes it is easier to work with smaller parts of the warehouse. In such cases one can replicate functional subsets of the data warehouse in smaller databases, each of which is dedicated to certain areas as shown in Figure 4.3. In this case the data mart is an addition to the data warehouse.
2. *Stand-alone data marts.* A company can have one or more independent data marts without having a data warehouse. In such cases there is a need to integrate the data marts. This can be done only if each data mart is assigned a specific set of information for which it is responsible. The IS department specifies the rules to the metadata so that the information kept by each mart is compatible with that provided by all the other marts. When this is not done, the data marts are difficult to integrate, creating potentially serious fragmentation problems for the organization.

Operational data stores An operational data store is a database for transaction processing systems that use data warehouse concepts to provide clean data. That is, it brings the concepts and benefits of the data warehouse to the operational portions of the business. It is used for short-term decisions involving mission-critical applications rather than for the medium- and long-term decisions associated with the data warehouse. These decisions depend on much more current information. For example, a bank needs to know about all the accounts for a given customer who is calling on the phone. The operational data store can be viewed as situated between the operational data (legacy system) and the data warehouse. A comparison between the two is provided in Table 4.3.

Multidimensional databases In some cases an additional database is built containing data from the data warehouse which are organized to support multidimensional analysis, as discussed in Section 4.11.

TABLE 4.3 Comparing an Operational Data Store and a Data Warehouse

Operational Data Store	*Data Warehouse*
Subject-oriented data	Subject-oriented data
Integrated data	Integrated data
Volatile data	Nonvolatile data
Data updated as they change	Data remain fixed
Only current data	Current and historical data
Short time between data refreshing	Longer time between data refreshing
Detailed data only	Detailed and summary data
Used for short-term decisions	Used for planning purposes

Source: Gray and Watson (1998), p. 109. Gray, P., and H. Watson (1998), *Decision Support and the Data Warehouse.* Upper Saddle River, NJ: Prentice-Hall.

SUITABILITY

Data warehousing is most appropriate for organizations where

- The data are stored in different systems.
- An information-based approach to management is in use.
- There is a large, diverse customer base.
- The same data are represented differently in different systems.
- Data are stored in highly technical, difficult-to-decipher formats.

Often the development of a data warehouse is driven by a specific organizational need, such as expanding sales by discovering relationships in customer data.

CHARACTERISTICS OF DATA WAREHOUSING

The major characteristics of data warehousing are as follows:

- *Subject oriented.* Data are organized by detailed subject (e.g., by customer, policy type, and claim in an insurance company), containing only information relevant for decision support.
- *Integrated.* Data at different source locations may be encoded differently. For example, gender data may be encoded 0 and 1 in one place and "m" and "f" in another. In the warehouse they are changed to one format so that they are standardized and consistent.
- *Time-variant (time series).* The data do not provide the current status. They are kept for 5–10 years and are used for trends, forecasting, and comparisons.
- *Nonvolatile.* Once entered into the warehouse, data are read-only, they *cannot* be changed or updated. Obsolete data are discarded, and changes are recorded as new data.
- *Summarized.* Operational data are aggregated, when needed, into summaries.
- *Not normalized.* Data can be redundant.
- *Metadata.* Metadata are included.
- *Sources.* Both operational and external data are present.

PARALLEL PROCESSING

Because of the large size of the data warehouse, some firms use a parallel computing architecture, in hardware and software, to speed data retrieval and processing.

The problem with parallel processing is its cost. Also, there is a shortage of skilled programmers. Nevertheless, parallel computing is now standard for many data warehouses. For details on implementation, see Gray and Watson (1998).

4.9 OLAP: DATA ACCESS, QUERYING, AND ANALYSIS

For many years IT concentrated on building mission-critical systems that mainly supported corporate transaction processing. Such systems must be virtually fault-tolerant and provide rapid response. An effective solution was provided by online transaction processing (OLTP), which centers on a distributed relational database environment. The latest developments in this area are the utilization of ERP and SCM software for transaction processing tasks, and the integration with Web-based technologies and intranets. Many tools were created for developing OLTP applications; the INFORMIX OnLine Dynamic Server (www.informix.com) is an example of an effective tool.

Access to data is often needed by both OLTP and MSS applications. Unfortunately, trying to serve both types of requests may be problematic (Gray and Watson, 1998).

Therefore, some companies elect to segregate databases into OLTP types and OLAP types. The OLAP type is based on the data warehouse.

The term **online analytical processing (OLAP)** refers to a variety of activities usually performed by end users in online systems (see DSS in Action 4.6). There is no agreement on what activities are considered OLAP. Usually one includes activities such as generating queries (see DSS in Focus 4.8), requesting ad hoc reports, conducting statistical analyses, and building DSS and multimedia applications. Some include executive information systems and data mining. To facilitate OLAP it is useful to work with the data warehouse (or with the data mart or a multidimensional warehouse) and with a *set of OLAP tools.* These tools can be **query tools,** spreadsheets, data mining tools, data visualization tools, and the like. (For a list of OLAP tools, see Dresner (1993), Tyo (1996), and periodic reviews in the software sections of *Datamation, PCWeek, DM Review,* and *Software Review.*) The major vendors of such tools are Oracle, Microstrategy Corporation, Computer Associates, Cognos, Hyperion Software Corporation, Information Builders, Comshare, SAS Institute Inc., Software A&G, Business Objects Inc., Intersolve, and Platinum Technology. The major data warehouse vendors are Carleton, IBM, Informix, NCR, Oracle, Red Brick, and Sybase.

USING SQL FOR QUERYING

Structured query language (SQL) is a standard data language for data access and manipulation in relational database management systems. It is an English-like language consisting of several layers of increasing complexity and capability. SQL is used for online access to databases, DBMS operations from programs, and database administration functions. It is also used for data access and manipulation functions of some leading DBMS software products (such as ORACLE, IBM's DB2, and INGRES II).

SQL is nonprocedural and fairly user-friendly, and so many end users can use it for their own queries and database operations. SQL can be employed for programs written in all standard programming languages; thus, it facilitates software integration. Support of DSS and EIS is accomplished in the warehouse with products from vendors such as Brio, Business Objectives, Cognos, Pilot Software, Platinum Technology, and SAS.

SS IN ACTION 4.6

SIMON & SCHUSTER IMPLEMENTS OLAP

Simon & Schuster, a major publisher, developed a data warehouse and implemented OLAP in its elementary education division. The $2 billion division produces thousands of books every year, including software products. More than 600 employees work with computers and need to interact with databases constantly. It was necessary to teach SQL to all employees, many of whom were not computer-literate. The solution was to build a data warehouse and use OLAP. Using a system from Business Objectives Corporation, Simon & Schuster developed a user-friendly OLAP. Now employees can access information directly without dedicated support from the IS group. With a client/server architecture, the system increased productivity at a lower cost than could be done on the old mainframe system. Now even the most difficult queries can be answered quickly. In addition, the system provides an effective and efficient inventory control mechanism. The mainframe is now completely occupied with the transaction processing system. Overall, the new system is viewed as a great success.

Source: Condensed from *InfoWorld,* June 10, 1996.

OLAP TOOLS AND DATA MINING

Using SQL and other conventional data access and analysis tools is helpful, but not sufficient, for OLAP. In OLAP a special class of tools is used, known as decision support front ends, data access front ends, database front ends, and visual information access systems. These tools are intended to empower users, as will be described next. For details of these tools, see Gray and Watson (1998) and Berson and Smith (1997). Of these tools we will discuss here only data mining.

4.10 DATA MINING

Traditional data analysis is done by inserting data into standards or customized models. In either case, it is assumed that the relationships among various system variables are well known and can be expressed mathematically. However, in many cases, relationships may not be known. In such situations, modeling is not possible and a data mining approach may be attempted.

Data mining is a term used to describe knowledge discovery in databases. It includes tasks known as knowledge extraction, data archaeology, data exploration, data pattern processing, data dredging, and information harvesting. All these activities are conducted automatically and allow quick discovery even by nonprogrammers (see DSS in Action 4.7). The following are the major characteristics and objectives of data mining:

- Data are often buried deep within very large databases, which sometimes contain data from several years. In some cases, the data are consolidated in a data warehouse.
- The data mining environment is usually that of a client/server architecture.
- Sophisticated new tools—including advanced visualization tools—help to remove the information "ore" buried in corporate files or archival public records. Finding it involves massaging and synchronizing these data to get the right results. Cutting-edge data miners are also exploring the usefulness of "soft" data (unstructured text stored in places such as Lotus Notes databases or text files on the Internet or a corporate-wide intranet).
- The miner is often an end user, empowered by data drills and other power query tools to ask ad hoc questions and obtain answers quickly with little or no programming skill.
- "Striking it rich" often involves finding an unexpected result and requires end users to think creatively.
- Data mining tools are easily combined with spreadsheets and other software development tools. Thus, the mined data can be analyzed and processed quickly and easily.
- Because of the large amounts of data, it is sometimes necessary to use parallel processing for data mining.

HOW DOES DATA MINING WORK?

Intelligent data mining, according to Edelstein (1996), discovers information within data warehouses that queries and reports cannot effectively reveal. Data mining tools find patterns in data and may even infer rules from them. These patterns and rules can be used to guide decision making and forecast the effect of these decisions. Data mining can speed analysis by focusing attention on the most important variables. The dra-

---

DSS IN ACTION 4.7

EMPOWERING WORKERS WITH DATA MINING AT ROCKWELL INTERNATIONAL

Rockwell International's air transport division (Cedar Rapids, IA) needed to access the corporate database frequently. For many years, only a few MIS personnel had the technical know-how to dig corporate data out of the mainframe. However, executives and managers increasingly demanded access to information stored in the mainframe. Frustration and delays in providing information were common. The MIS department operated under a heavy workload. Furthermore, because of the priority given to top management, other employees had to wait days or even months to get the information

they needed. Today, managers can get most of the data they need by themselves easily and quickly.

The solution was provided by creating a special database on a server in a client/server environment. Managers can develop their own applications with LightShip (from Pilot Software, www.pilotsw.com). Managers can go right after the information they need without being programmers, resulting in less frustration and backlog and in happy employees at Rockwell.

Source: Condensed from public information provided by Pilot Software Inc., www.pilotsw.com.

---

matic drop in the cost/performance ratio of computer systems has enabled many organizations to start applying the complex algorithms used in data mining techniques. Five common types of information can be obtained by data mining:

- *Classification:* infers the defining characteristics of a certain group (e.g., customers who have been lost to competitors)
- *Clustering:* identifies groups of items that share a particular characteristic (clustering differs from classification in that no predefining characteristic is given)
- *Association:* identifies relationships between events that occur at one time (e.g., the contents of a shopping basket)
- *Sequencing:* similar to association, except that the relationship exists over a period of time (e.g., repeat visits to a supermarket or use of a financial planning product)
- *Forecasting:* estimates future values based on patterns within large sets of data (e.g., demand forecasting).

For further details see Berry and Linoff (1997) and Weswphal and Blaxton (1998).

DATA MINING TOOLS

The main types of tools used in intelligent data mining are the following:

- *Case-based reasoning.* Using historical cases, the case-based reasoning approach can be used to recognize patterns. For example, customers of Cognitive Systems Inc. use such an approach for help desk applications. One customer has a 50,000-query case library. New cases can be matched quickly against the 50,000 samples in the library, providing more than 90 percent accurate, automatic answers to queries. For more on case-based reasoning, see Chapter 13.
- *Neural computing.* Neural computing is an approach by which historical data are examined for pattern recognition. Thus, one can go through large databases and, for example, identify potential customers for a new product (see DSS in Action 4.8) or companies whose profiles suggest that they are heading for bankruptcy. Many applications are in financial services (Trippi and Turban, 1996b) and in manufacturing. For further discussion see Chapters 15 and 16.

DSS IN ACTION 4.8

DATA MINING AT MARRIOTT

Marriott Club International (www.marriot.com), the nation's largest seller of vacation time-share condos, had a problem. The company has a database with millions of names. They used to send advertisements to all of them at great expense, but the response was minimal. The company decided to identify the customers on their list who were more likely to respond. Marriott uses neural computing technology in their data mining, whose objective is to detect patterns by combing through the digitized customer lists.

Marriott started with names, mostly of hotel guests. Digging into a trove of motor vehicle records, property records, warranty cards, and lists of people who have bought by mail or on the Web, a computer program enriches the prospect list. It adds such facts as the customers' ages, their children's ages, their estimated income, what cars they drive, and whether they play golf. The Marriott system then identifies who is most likely to respond to a mailed flier.

Using these clues, Marriott is able to cast its net a little more narrowly and catch more fish. Data mining has increased the response rate to Marriott's direct mail time-share pitches by 33 percent. In addition, they have reported significant savings on their mail costs. The same approach is being considered for Internet advertisement.

Source: Condensed from J. Novack, "The Data Miners," *Forbes*, Feb. 12, 1996, and www.marriotclub.com.

- *Intelligent agents.* One of the most promising approaches to retrieving information from databases, especially external ones, is the use of intelligent agents. As vast amounts of information are becoming available through the Internet, finding the right information is becoming more difficult. This topic is discussed in Chapter 17.
- *Other tools.* Several other tools can be used. These include decision trees, rule induction, and data visualization.

TEXT MINING

Text mining is the application of data mining to nonstructured or less structured text files. Data mining takes advantage of the infrastructure of stored data to extract additional useful information. For example, by data mining a customer database, an analyst might discover that everyone who buys product A also buys products B and C, but 6 months later.

Text mining, however, operates with less structured information. Documents rarely have a strong internal infrastructure, and when they do, it is frequently focused on document format rather than document content. Text mining helps organizations to

- Find the "hidden" content of documents, including additional useful relationships
- Relate documents across previous unnoticed divisions, for example, discover that customers in two different product divisions have the same characteristics
- Group documents by common themes, for example, all the customers of an insurance firm who have similar complaints and cancel their policies.

EXAMPLE

Pfizer, a large pharmaceutical company uses text mining to look for parallels in pharmaceutical testing in the extremely large database that the National Institutes of Health uses to catalog medical research. The text mining project targets biomedical documents extracted from various external sources such as

MedLine, a medical research literature service provided by the National Institutes of Health.

The Pfizer system searches the database of documents and extracts a set of documents characterized by simple search criteria based on a combination of keywords. Next, the set of documents is further segmented into topics. Topics are characterized by lists of keywords extracted from the free-format text contained in the documents. The scientists choose topics of interest by examining keyword lists. Pfizer has realized several benefits. First, the company has discovered that text mining is not only a technology for the categorization of information. The results of text mining also permit the building of new applications for further navigation of data and decision support.

SAMPLER OF DATA MINING APPLICATIONS

Data mining can be very helpful, as shown by the following representative examples. Note that the intent of most of these examples is to identify a business opportunity to create a sustainable competitive advantage.

- *Marketing:* predicting which customers will respond to Internet banners or buy a particular product; segmenting customer demographics
- *Banking:* forecasting levels of bad loans and fraudulent credit card usage, credit card spending by new customers, and which kinds of customers will best respond to new loan offers
- *Retailing and sales:* predicting sales and determining correct inventory levels and distribution schedules among outlets
- *Manufacturing and production:* predicting when to expect machinery failures, finding key factors that control the optimization of manufacturing capacity
- *Brokerage and securities trading:* predicting when bond prices will change, forecasting the range of stock fluctuation for particular issues and the overall market; determining when to trade stocks
- *Insurance:* forecasting claim amounts and medical coverage costs, classifying the most important elements that affect medical coverage, predicting which customers will buy new policies
- *Computer hardware and software:* predicting disk drive failure, forecasting how long it will take to create new chips, predicting potential security violations
- *Government and defense:* forecasting the cost of moving military equipment, testing strategies for potential military engagements, predicting resource consumption
- *Airlines:* capturing data not only on where customers are flying but also the ultimate destination of passengers who change carriers in midflight. Then, airlines can identify popular locations that they do not serve to add routes and capture lost business
- *Health care:* correlating demographics of patients with critical illnesses; using data mining, doctors can develop better insights on symptoms and how to provide proper treatments.
- *Broadcasting:* predicting what programs are best shown during prime time and how to maximize returns by inserting advertisements
- *Police:* tracking crime patterns, locations, criminal behavior, and attributes to help crack criminal cases.

For the capabilities of data mining and a comparison of data mining tools, see Berson and Smith (1997), Wesphal and Blaxton (1998), and Cabena (1997).

4.11 DATA VISUALIZATION AND MULTIDIMENSIONALITY

Online analytical processing includes not only obtaining and analyzing data and information but also presenting it to the user and interpreting it. We discuss this topic next.

DATA VISUALIZATION

Visual technologies make pictures worth a thousand numbers, and decision support applications more attractive and understandable to users. **Data visualization** refers to technologies that support visualization and sometimes interpretation of data and information at several points along the data processing chain (Figure 4.1). It includes digital images, geographic information systems, graphical user interfaces, multidimensions, tables and graphs, virtual reality, three-dimensional presentations, and animation. Visualization software packages offer users capabilities for self-guided exploration and visual analysis of large amounts of data. People have reported that by using visual analysis technologies, they have spotted problems that have gone undetected by standard analysis methods for years. See DSS in Action 4.9. These technologies can be integrated to create different information presentations. In Chapter 5, we discuss visual spreadsheets and visual interactive simulation.

Data visualization is easier to implement when the necessary data are in a data warehouse, or better yet in a multidimensional server. Our discussion here is focused mainly on the concept of multidimensionality. In the next section we present a brief description of geographic information systems and virtual reality.

NEW DIRECTIONS IN DATA VISUALIZATION

Since the late 1990s data visualization has been moving both into mainstream computing, being integrated with decision support tools and applications, and into intelligent visualization which includes data (information) interpretation.

The following are some interesting areas:

- Interactive graphs and models that let users drill down into the underlying data to reorganize and compare data so that its meaning is clearer. Visualization tools can be useful in three areas: (1) statistical analysis, (2) graphical presentation tools, and (3) analytic applications.
- WatchMark Corporation, a subsidiary of Lucent Technologies uses a sophisticated data visualization tool for wireless network operators. WatchMark Pilot Release 1.3 incorporates an innovative video replay engine with VCR-like controls, which enables network operators to quickly review the events that preceded a network problem, much like viewing an instant replay of a televised sporting event.
- Comshare Inc. provides OpenViz so that users can interact with images and data in meaningful ways. This reaffirms the notion that sophisticated visualization solutions now belong on the desktops of business professionals. OpenViz is a suite of components—supporting both Microsoft Common Object Model (COM) and JavaBean models—that enable IT developers to extend commercial and custom-developed business intelligence solutions to encompass business-class data visualization.
- Identitech Inc. has developed Graphical Interface for Information Cognition, a data visualization tool designed to support business decision making. This

| DSS IN ACTION 4.9 |

DATA VISUALIZATION FOR FINANCIAL DATA

To prevent systems from automatically identifying meaningless patterns in data, chief financial officers (CFOs) want to make sure that the processing power of a computer is always tempered with the insight of a human being. One way to do this is through data visualization, which uses color, form, motion, and depth to present masses of data in a comprehensible way. Andrew W. Lo, director of the Laboratory for Financial Engineering at Massachusetts Institute of Technology's Sloan School of Management, developed a program in which a CFO can use a mouse to "fly" over a three-dimensional landscape representing the risk, return, and liquidity of a company's assets. With practice, the CFO can begin to zero in on the choicest spot on the three-dimensional landscape: the one where the trade-off among risk, return, and liquidity is most beneficial. Lo says, "The video-game generation just loves these 3-D tools."

So far, very few CFOs have cruised in three-dimensional cyberspace. Most still spend the bulk of their time on routine matters such as generating reports for the Securities and Exchange Commission. But that's bound to change. Glassco Park president Robert J. Park says, "What we have in financial risk management today is like what we had in computer typesetting in 1981, before desktop publishing."

Source: Condensed from P. Coy, "Higher Math and Savvy Software are Crucial," *Business Week,* Oct. 28, 1996.

---

software can be programmed to map data to sets of rectangles whose colors symbolize different levels of conditions, such as normal, high, and low.

- Analogous to a "visual spreadsheet" (Chapter 5) Visual Insights ADVIZOR allows users to find and understand patterns and trends hidden in complex data. It combines ease of use, industry-standard data access, and the power of interactive data visualization to create the next-generation user interface for business decision making.

- There is a new, emerging category of enterprise data visualization applications, termed *on-line visualization for an enterprise (OLIVE)*. OLIVE systems are chart-centric applications that deliver visual business intelligence to the enterprise. There are 12 attributes that an enterprise charting application tool should have to qualify as an OLIVE tool, including (1) chart definition language and (2) a lifecycle process [see Craig (1998) for details].

Most major OLAP vendors offer three-dimensional visualization tools with their decision support tool. For example, Forest Tree 6.0 is a Web-enabled development tool with a three-dimensional visualization version that enables users to visualize and easily manage multiple dimensions of data in a single view.

MULTIDIMENSIONALITY

Spreadsheet tables have two dimensions. If one needs to present information with three or more dimensions, he or she can use a set of two-dimensional tables or a fairly complex table. In decision support, an attempt is made to make information presentation simple and to allow the user to easily and quickly change the structure of tables so that they will be more meaningful (e.g., by flipping columns and rows or by combining several rows and columns).

MULTIDIMENSIONAL PRESENTATION

Summary data can be organized in different ways for analysis and presentation. An efficient way to do this is called **multidimensionality.** The major advantage of multidimensionality is that data can be organized the way managers like to see them rather than the way that system analysts do. Further, different presentations of the same data can be arranged easily and quickly. Three factors are considered in multidimensionality: *dimensions, measures,* and *time.*

- *Examples of dimensions:* products, salespeople, market segments, business units, geographic locations, distribution channels, countries, industries
- *Examples of measures:* money, sales volume, head count, inventory profit, actual versus forecasted
- *Examples of time:* daily, weekly, monthly, quarterly, yearly.

A manager may want to know the sales of a product in a certain geographic area, by a specific salesperson, during a specified month, or in terms of units. The answer to such a question can be provided regardless of the database structure, but it can be provided much faster, and by the user, if the data are organized in multidimensional databases or if the query or related software products are designed for multidimensionality. In either case users can navigate through the many dimensions and levels of data via tables or graphs and are able to make quick interpretations such as uncovering significant deviations or important trends.

Multidimensionality has some limitations, according to the Gartner Group research report (Dresner, 1993; Gray and Watson, 1998):

- The multidimensional database can take up significantly more computer storage room than a summarized relational database.
- Multidimensional products cost significantly more percent wise than standard relational products.
- Database loading consumes system resources and time, depending on data volume and number of dimensions.
- Interfaces and maintenance are more complex than in relational databases.

Multidimensionality is available in different degrees of sophistication. Therefore, there are several types of software from which multidimensional systems can be constructed at different price levels. Multidimensionality is especially popular in DSS and EIS *executive information and support systems* (such as Decision Web from Comshare Inc., www.comshare.com, and Pilot Analysis Server from Pilot Software Inc., www.pilotsw. com). Tools with multidimensional capabilities often work in conjunction with database query systems and other OLAP tools. These include Brio Enterprise (www.brio.com), PowerPlay (www.cognos. com), and Business Objects (www.businessobjects.com) (see these companies' Web sites) (Tyo, 1996; Gray and Waston, 1998).

4.12 GEOGRAPHIC INFORMATION SYSTEMS AND VIRTUAL REALITY

GEOGRAPHIC INFORMATION SYSTEMS

A **geographic information system (GIS)** is a computer-based system for capturing, storing, checking, integrating, manipulating, and displaying data using digitized maps. Its most distinguishing characteristic is that every record or digital object has an identified geographic location. By integrating maps with spatially oriented (geographic location) databases (called *geocoding*) and other databases, users can generate information for planning, problem solving, and decision making, and increasing their productivity and the quality of their decisions [e.g., see Dennis and Carte (1998)], as many banks have done.

Banks use GIS for displays that support

- Determining branch and ATM locations
- Analyzing customer demographics (e.g., residence, age, income level) for each product of the bank
- Analyzing volume and traffic patterns of business activities
- Analyzing the geographic area served by each branch
- Finding the market potential for banking activities
- Evaluating strengths and weaknesses against those of the competition
- Evaluating branch performance.

A GIS is used as a geographic spreadsheet that allows managers to model business activities and perform what-if analyses (what if we close a branch or merge branches? What if a competitor opens a branch?). Each map consolidates pages of analysis. Representative pioneering banks are First Florida Banks (Tampa, FL) and NJB Financial (Princeton, NJ).

For many companies, the intelligent organization of data within a GIS can provide a framework to support the process of decision making and of designing alternative strategies [e.g., see Swink and Speier (1999) and Grimshaw (1999)]. Some examples of successful GIS applications are provided by Bidgoli (1995), Hamilton (1996b). Other examples of successful GIS applications are summarized in Table 4.4.

TABLE 4.4 GIS Applications

Company	*Application of GIS*
Pepsi Cola Inc., Super Value, Acordia Inc.	Used in site selection for new Taco Bell and Pizza Hut restaurants; combining demographic data and traffic patterns
CIGNA (health insurance)	Uses GIS to answer such questions as How many CIGNA-affiliated physicians are available within an 8-mile radius of a business?
Western Auto (a subsidiary of Sears)	Integrates data with GIS to create a detailed demographic profile of store's neighborhood to determine the best product mix to offer at the store
Sears, Roebuck & Co.	Uses GIS to support planning of truck routes
Health maintenance organizations	Tracks cancer rate and that of other diseases to determine expansion strategy and allocation of expensive equipment in their facilities
Wood Personnel Services (employment agencies)	Maps neighborhoods where temporary workers live to locate marketing and recruiting cities
Wilkening & Co. (consulting services)	Designs optimal sales territories and routes for their clients, reducing travel costs by 15 percent
CellularOne Corporation	Maps its entire cellular network to identify clusters of call disconnects and to dispatch technician accordingly
Sun Microsystems	Manages leased property in dozens of places worldwide
Consolidated Rail Corporation	Monitors the condition of 20,000 miles of railroad track and thousands of parcels of adjoining land
Federal Emergency Management Agency	Assesses the damage of hurricanes, floods, and other natural disasters by relating videotapes of the damage to digitized maps of properties
	Combines GIS and GPS as a navigation tool
Toyota (and other car manufacturers)	Directs drivers to destinations via the best route

GIS AND THE INTERNET/INTRANET

Most major GIS software vendors provide Web access, such as embedded browsers, or a Web/Internet/intranet server that hooks directly into their software. Thus, users can access dynamic maps and data via the Internet or a corporate intranet (Jacobs, 1996). Big Horn Computer Services (Buffalo, NY) uses a Web-adapted GIS to develop a custom application for a national television network that wants its affiliate stations to be able to access an intranet containing demographic information about their viewers. Using a Web browser, employees at each station can view thematically shaded maps analyzing their market (Swenson, 1996).

A number of firms are deploying GIS on the Internet for internal use or for use by their customers. For example, Visa Plus, which operates a network of automated teller machines, has developed a GIS application that lets Internet users call up a map to locate any of the company's 257,000 ATM machines worldwide. As GIS Web server software is deployed by vendors, more applications will be developed. Maps, GIS data, and information about GIS are available over the Web through a number of vendors and public agencies. Note that related to this is the inclusion of spatial data in data warehouses [see Theodore (1998)], for later use with Web technology.

VIRTUAL REALITY

There is no standard definition of **virtual reality (VR).** The most common definitions usually imply that virtual reality is interactive, computer-generated, three-dimensional graphics delivered to the user through a head-mounted display. Defined technically, virtual reality is an "environment and/or technology that provides artificially generated sensory cues sufficient to engender in the user some willing suspension of disbelief." So in virtual reality, a person "believes" that what he or she is doing is real even though it is artificially created.

More than one person and even a large group can share and interact in the same environment. VR thus can be a powerful medium for communication, entertainment, and learning. Instead of looking at a flat computer screen, the virtual reality user interacts with a three-dimensional computer-generated environment. To see and hear the environment, the user wears stereo goggles and a three-dimensional headset. To interact with the environment, control objects in it, or move around within it, the user wears a computerized behavior-transducing head-coupled display and hand position sensors (gloves). Virtual reality displays achieve the illusion of a surrounding medium by updating the display in real time. The user can grasp and move virtual objects.

HOW DOES VIRTUAL REALITY WORK?

In a typical virtual reality system, the user views the virtual world either with a head-mounted display or on a screen (with or without three-dimensional shutter glasses). Delivered over headphones or speakers, three-dimensional sound provides realistic audio. A tracking system receiver and one or more transmitters tell the computer where the user is looking and where the three-dimensional controller is in space. These connect to the computer through either a serial port or a special interface card. The computer contains a graphics subsystem, a spatialized audio subsystem, databases of the geometry of the objects in the virtual world, a world database (which defines the environment and how objects in it relate to each other), and a sound database.

Sophisticated virtual reality systems are interactive and usually simulate real-world phenomena. They often simulate sight, sound, and touch and combine these senses with computer-generated input to users' eyes, ears, and skin. By using a head-mounted display, gloves, and a bodysuit, or large projected images in simulator cabs, users can "enter" and interact with virtual or artificially generated environments.

VIRTUAL REALITY AND THE INTERNET/INTRANET

A platform-independent standard for VR called **virtual reality markup language (VRML)** (Goralski et al., 1997) makes navigation through online supermarkets, museums, and stores as easy as interacting with textual information. VRML allows objects to be rendered as an Internet user "walks" through a virtual room. At the moment, users can utilize regular browsers, but VRML browsers will soon be in wide circulation.

Extensive use is expected in marketing (Burke, 1996). For example, Tower Records offers a virtual music store on the Internet where customers can "meet" each other in front of the store, go inside, and preview CDs and videos. They select and purchase their choices electronically and interactively from a sales associate. Applications in other areas are shown in Table 4.5.

Virtual supermarkets could spark greater interest in home grocery shopping. In the future, shoppers will enter a virtual supermarket, walk through the virtual aisles, select virtual products, and put them in their virtual cart. This could help remove some of the resistance to virtual shopping. Virtual malls are designed to give the user a feeling of walking into a shopping mall.

Virtual reality is just beginning to move into many business applications. A three-dimensional world on the Internet should prove popular because it is a metaphor to which everyone can relate.

TABLE 4.5   Examples of Virtual Reality Applications

Industry	Application
Manufacturing	Training
	Design testing and interpretation of results
	Safety analysis
	Virtual prototyping
	Engineering analysis
	Ergonomic analysis
	Virtual simulation of assembly, production, and maintenance
Architecture	Design of building and other structures
Business	Real estate presentation and evaluation
	Advertisement
	Presentation in electronic commerce
	Presentation of financial data
Medicine	Training surgeons (with simulators)
	Interpretation of medical data
	Planning surgeries
	Physical therapy
Research and education	Virtual physics lab
	Galaxy configurations
	Representation of complex mathematics
Amusement	Virtual museums
	Three-dimensional race car games (on PCs)
	Air combat simulation (on PCs)
	Virtual reality arcades
	Virtual reality parks
	Ski simulator

VIRTUAL REALITY AND DECISION MAKING

Most VR applications to date have been used to support decision making indirectly. For example, Boeing has developed a virtual aircraft mock-up to test designs. Several other VR applications for assisting in manufacturing and for converting military technology to civilian technology are being utilized at Boeing. At Volvo, VR is used to test virtual cars in virtual accidents; Volvo also uses VR in its new model design process. British Airways offers the pleasure of experiencing first-class flying to its Web site visitors.

Another VR application area is data visualization. VR helps financial decision makers make better sense of data by using visual, spatial, and aural immersion virtual systems. For example, some stock brokerages have a VR application in which users surf over a landscape of stock futures, with color, hue, and intensity indicating deviation from current share prices. Sound is used to convey other information, such as current trends or the debt/equity ratio. VR allows side-by-side comparisons with a large assortment of financial data. It is easier to make intuitive connections with three-dimensional support. Morgan Stanley & Co. uses VR to display the results of risk analyses (see *Computerworld,* Feb. 1996, p. 65).

4.13 BUSINESS INTELLIGENCE AND THE WEB

Business intelligence activities—from data acquisition, through warehousing, to mining—can be performed with Web tools or are interrelated with Web technologies and electronic commerce. Users with browsers can log onto a system, make inquiries, get reports, and so on, in a real-time setting. This is done through intranets, and for outsiders via extranets (see www.informationadvantage.com; also, for a comprehensive discussion of business intelligence on the Web, see the white paper at www.businessobjects.com).

Electronic commerce software vendors are providing Web tools that connect the data warehouse with the EC ordering and cataloging systems. One such example is Tradelink, a product of Hitachi (www.hitachi.com). Hitachi's EC tool suite combines EC activities such as catalog management, payment applications, mass customization, and order management with data warehouses (marts) and ERP systems.

Data warehousing and decision support vendors are connecting their products, or creating new ones to connect, with Web technologies and EC. Examples are Comshare's DecisionWeb, Brio's eWarehouse (www.brio.com), Web Intelligence from Business Objects, Cognos's DataMerchant, and Hyperion's Appsource "Wired for OLAP" product that connects OLAP with Web tools. Pilot's Internet Publisher incorporates Internet capabilities within the Pilot Decision Support Suite. IBM's Decision Edge and MicroStrategy's DSS Web are other tools that offer OLAP capabilities on the Intranet from anywhere in the corporation using browsers, search engines, and other Web technologies. MicroStrategy offers DSS Agent and DSS Web for help in drilling down for detailed information, providing graphical views, pushing information to users' desktops, and more.

Bringing interactive querying, reporting, and other OLAP tasks to many users (company employees and business partners) via the Web can also be facilitated by using Oracle's Financial Analyzer and Sales Analyzer, Hummingbird Bi/Web and Bi/Broker, and several of the products cited above.

Data marts are becoming much more popular in the Web environment. For example, Bell Canada uses its intranet extensively for fast data access to its multiple data marts (over 300 analysts; see *PCWeek,* July 28, 1997), and at Nabisco, the large food company, financial analysts track the profits and losses of 8,000 products using Web browsers, saving millions of dollars (*InfoWorld,* Sept. 28, 1998).

4.14 THE BIG PICTURE

Data for decision making come from a variety of sources, both internal and external. Because the data management system is one of the major components of most management support systems, it is important to be familiar with the latest developments in the field. Organizations are recognizing that their data contain a gold mine of information if they can dig it out. Consequently, they are warehousing and mining data for users to obtain information on their own (through a variety of analysis tools and new enterprise-wide system architectures) and to establish relationships that were previously unknown (through data mining). OLAP tools provide on-the-fly data analysis for identifying problems and opportunities.

The object-oriented approach to systems analysis, design, and implementation may create an incredible opportunity for simplified representations of systems along with more code reuse. A wide variety of data formats are becoming available as multimedia database management systems are developed and deployed. Internets and intranets are providing universal interfaces, including query capabilities, with database systems. Finally, built-in artificial intelligence methods can be used to enhance data search and analysis.

❖ CHAPTER HIGHLIGHTS

- Data exist in internal, external, and personal sources.
- External data are available on thousands of online Web sites, commercial databases, directories, reports, and so on.
- Data for MSS must be collected frequently in the field using one or several methods.
- MSS may have data problems such as incorrect data, nontimely data, poorly measured and indexed data, too many data, or no data.
- Commercial online databases such as CompuServe and Dow Jones Information Service can be major sources of MSS data.
- The Internet is becoming a major external data source for MSS.
- Intranets are providing internal data for MSS.
- Most major databases have Web links to enable direct query via Web browsers on client workstations.
- Data are usually organized in relational, hierarchical, or network architectures. For many MSS, the relational type is preferable.
- Structured query language (SQL) is a standard means of access for querying relational databases.
- Multimedia databases are becoming increasingly more important for decision-making applications.
- Object-oriented databases are easy to use and can be accessed very quickly. They are especially useful in distributed MSS and complex DSS.
- One of the most critical objectives is to make databases intelligent so that users can find information quickly by themselves.
- A data warehouse is a specially constructed data repository where data are organized so that they can be easily accessed by end users for several applications.

- Data marts contain data on one topic (e.g., marketing). They can be a replication of a subset of data in the data warehouse. It is a less expensive solution that can be replaced or supplement the data warehouse.
- Online analytical processing (OLAP) is a set of tools for timely data analysis. It is becoming increasingly important in MSS applications.
- Data mining is the discovery of knowledge in databases. It is often done on data in data warehouses.
- Data multidimensionality enables people to view data quickly in different dimensions, even if the data are in different files and databases.
- Geographic information systems (GIS) capture, store, check, manipulate, and display data using digitized maps. GIS is used for decision support because it simplifies the presentation of complex data.
- Virtual reality can be used not only for presentation but also to facilitate decision making.

❖ KEY WORDS

- business intelligence
- client/server architecture
- data
- data mart
- data integrity
- data mining
- data quality (DQ)
- data visualization
- data (or information) warehouse
- database management systems (DBMS)

- document management systems (DMS)
- geographic information systems (GIS)
- information
- intelligent database
- Internet
- knowledge
- metadata
- multidimensionality

- object-oriented database management system (OODBMS)
- online analytical processing (OLAP)
- online (commercial) databases
- query tools
- relational database
- structured query language (SQL)
- virtual reality
- virtual reality markup language (VRML)

❖ QUESTIONS FOR REVIEW

1. Define data, information, and knowledge. Identify two examples of each.
2. Describe the role of the Internet in MSS data management.
3. Define a data warehouse and list some of its characteristics.
4. What is SQL?
5. List the major categories of data sources for an MSS.
6. Describe the benefits of commercial databases.
7. Describe OLAP.
8. Define object-oriented database management.
9. Define data multidimensionality and a multidimensional database.
10. Define data mining and list its major technologies.
11. What are intelligent databases and why are they so popular?
12. Why is ES needed as an interface to commercial databases?
13. Define a data mart.
14. Describe the role that a data warehouse can play in MSS. List its benefits.
15. Describe a GIS and its major capabilities.
16. Define document management.
17. Define virtual reality.

❖ QUESTIONS FOR DISCUSSION

1. Relate data warehousing to OLAP and data visualization.
2. Discuss the relationship between multiple sources of data, including external data, and the data warehouse.
3. Explain the relationship between SQL and a DBMS.
4. Compare OLTP to OLAP.
5. Define and describe a commercial database (online) service. Name one or two with which you are familiar.
6. Explain the relationship between OLAP and data mining.
7. Describe multidimensionality and explain its potential benefits for MSS.
8. Identify a commercial DBMS provider. Prepare a short report that describes the services offered, the fees, and the process for obtaining the service.
9. It is said that a relational database is the best for DSS (as compared to hierarchical and network structures). Explain why.
10. Explain the issue of data quality and some of the measures one can take to improve it.
11. It is said that object-oriented DBMS are the best solutions to a complex (especially distributed) DSS. Explain.
12. What is a data warehouse and what are its benefits? Why is Web accessibility important?
13. Why is the combination of GIS and GPS becoming so popular? Examine some applications.
14. Describe the major dimensions of data quality.
15. Discuss the benefits of DMS.
16. Explain what GIS is used for and how it supports decision making.
17. Distinguish data mining from other analytic tools.
18. Discuss the major features of virtual reality and explain how they can be used to facilitate decision making.

❖ EXERCISES

1. A university is installing a DSS for budget preparation, expense monitoring, and financial planning. There are four schools at the university and 18 departments. In addition, there are two research institutions and many administrative services. Prepare a diagram that shows how the DSS will be distributed to all users. Comment on data and its sources for such a DSS. Suggest what decisions could be supported at each managerial level.
2. Typically, data on a university campus are stored in different physical locations for different purposes. For example, the registrar's office, the housing office, the individual departmental offices, the personnel office, the staff benefits office, and the fund-raising and development office may maintain separate unintegrated databases with student (and faculty) records.
   a. Explain what problems can occur in obtaining data to support complex decisions.
   b. Explain how a data warehouse might help solve these problems.
   c. Discuss some of the behavioral (political) and technical problems that can occur in developing and implementing a data warehouse in such an environment.

   d. Visit or call several offices and departments at your university (or at your place of business) and determine how basic data on students and faculty (or customers and employees) are stored, maintained, and manipulated. Find out whether they have multiple databases and what chronic problems they encounter.

3. Review the list of data problems in Table 4.1. Provide additional suggestions for each category.

4. The U.S. government spends millions of dollars gathering data on its population every 10 years (plus some mid-decade adjustments). Census data are critical in determining the representation of each state in the House of Representatives and the number of Electoral College votes to which each state is entitled in presidential elections. More importantly, census data provide information about U.S. markets. The demographics indicate family and gender makeup, income, education level, and other information for states, metropolitan statistical areas (MSAs), and counties. Such data are available from various sources including books, disks, CD-ROMs, and the World Wide Web (see Internet Exercise 6). In this exercise, we take a real-world view of external but readily available data.

   a. Find an electronic source of standard census data files for states and MSAs (check this book's Web site).

   b. Access the data and examine the file structures. Do the contents and organization of each make sense? Why or why not? If not, suggest improvements.

   c. Load the state P1 data population table into a spreadsheet file (Excel if possible) and into a database file (Access if possible). How difficult was this? How could this have been made easier? Don't forget to delete the comments and U.S. totals (if present) at the top, for later use. Note that Washington, DC, is listed as well. Print the table.

   d. Using the state P1 population data, sort the data based on population size. What are the five most populated states and the five least populated states? Which five states have the largest and smallest population densities? Which state has the most males and which state has the most females? Which three states have the most people living on farms, and which state has the fewest lonely people? Which file type (spreadsheet or database) did you use and why? What features made it easy to do these analyses?

   e. Load the state basic Table P6 (household income) into a spreadsheet or database file. Which five states have the most people earning $100,000 or more per year? Which five states have the highest percentages of people earning $100,000 or more per year? Combine these data with data from Table P1 to determine which five states have the most people per square mile earning $100,000 or more per year? Which file type (spreadsheet or database) did you use and why? What features made it easy to do these analyses?

   f. Data warehousing and data mining are used to combine data and identify patterns. Use data (load and save them in spreadsheet or database files) from the following files: P1: Population; P3: Persons by Age; P4: Households by Size; P6: Household Income; P8: Other Income Measures; and P9: Level of Education. Synthesize these tables into a usable set and determine whether there are any relationships at the state level between

     i. Population per square mile and education
     ii. Income and age
     iii. Household size and education.

   Can you think of any other relationships to explore? If you can, do so. What made this task difficult or easy? Explain.

   g. Examine the MSA data tables and see whether any of the relationships found for the state data above hold.

   h. How does the profile of your MSA (or the one closest to where you live) compare with your state's census profile and with that of the entire United States? How did you determine this?

5. Given the following list of employees in a manufacturing company, use DBMS software or a spreadsheet to
   a. Sort the employees by department
   b. Sort the employees by salary in an ascending order
   c. Sort the employees by department and sort the employees of each department by age in an ascending order
   d. Calculate the average salary
   e. Calculate the average salary of female employees
   f. Calculate the average age in Department A
   g. List the names of females who were hired after December 31, 1995
   h. Show the age distribution graphically (use a 5-year grouping) as a pie chart
   i. Compute the linear regression relationship of salary versus age for all employees
   j. Compute the relationship for females and males independently. Is there a significant difference?

Name	Gender	Age	Date Hired	Dept.	Salary
Martin Dean	M	28	06 Jan. 88	A	$22,000
Jane Hanson	F	35	15 Mar. 96	D	$33,200
Daniel Smith	M	19	06 Dec. 90	C	$18,500
Emily Brosmer	F	26	10 Jan. 88	B	$27,000
Jessica Stone	F	45	26 May 83	A	$38,900
Tom Obudzinski	M	38	01 Dec. 98	B	$29,800
Kathleen Braun	F	32	18 Apr. 92	B	$35,600
Lisa Gregory	F	48	03 Sept. 91	C	$32,400
Timothy Parker	M	29	03 Aug. 93	A	$21,200
Jessica Hibscher	F	53	30 July 94	D	$38,900
Adam Handel	M	62	29 Nov. 97	A	$40,250
Melissa Black	F	42	01 Dec. 89	B	$26,400
Ray Ernster	M	29	02 July 87	C	$23,200
Daniel Baim	M	38	26 Feb. 88	C	$31,000
Amy Melnikov	F	45	30 Apr. 86	A	$36,400
Adrienne Cammizzo	F	30	15 June 86	A	$25,400
Steven Knowless	M	48	22 Oct. 85	D	$33,200
Patricia Salisbury	F	56	26 Feb. 84	B	$42,600
Matthew Broekhuizen	M	44	01 Jan. 88	C	$45,400
Sarah Parent	F	64	01 Jan 99	A	$38,200

6. Investigate the integration of data warehouse and GIS. Start with Theodore (1998), www.mapinfo.com, and Coddington et al. (1999).

7. Take a test drive of demos of DecisionWeb (Comshare) and of business intelligence from sterling.com, Brio, and Cognos. Do not miss Sybase's free interactive CD on business intelligence (hosted by soccer star Alexi Lalas). Prepare a report.

❖ **INTERNET EXERCISES**

1. Surf the Internet to find information about data warehousing. Identify some newsgroups that have an interest in this concept. Explore ABI/Inform in your library, e-library, and Yahoo for recent articles on the topic, including the areas of data mining, multidimensionality, and OLAP. Begin with www.dw-institute.org and the major vendors: www.sas.com, www.oracle.com, and www.ncr.com. Also check www.cio.com, www.dmreview.com, www.dssresources.com, and pwp. starnetic.com.

2. Survey some data mining tools and vendors. Start with www.nestor.com, www.hnc.com, and www.inference.com. Also consult dmreview.com.

3. Contact some of the DBMS vendors listed on this book's Web site and obtain information about their products. Special attention should be given to vendors that

provide tools for multiple purposes, such as Cognos, Software A&G, SAS Institute, and Oracle. Free demos are available from some of these vendors over the Web (e.g., www.brio.com). Download a demo or two and try them. Write a report describing your experience.

4. America Online, stock brokerages, and portals provide a free service that shows the status of investors' stock market portfolios, including profits (losses) and prices (with a 15-minute delay or even in real time). How is such individualized information retrieved so quickly?

5. What economic data are available from government agencies? Who provides what types of data? How easy are these data to access, download, and use? (Provide 10 examples.)

6. Search the Internet to identify sources of U.S. government census data files. Download and examine some of the files. Are they flat ASCII text data files, spreadsheet files, or database files (and what are their formats)? Were they compressed or archived? If so, how easy was it to extract the data? Which tables (files) would be useful and what kinds of analyses could be performed with such data (e.g., for a consumer product marketing firm, a financial services firm, an insurance company, and a real estate developer)?

7. Survey GIS resources such as www.mapinfo.com, www.geo.ed.ac.uk, and www.geoplace.com and use search engines. Identify recent applications.

8. Identify successful applications of virtual reality in electronic commerce (marketing) in real estate and in quality control.

9. Find recent cases of successful business intelligence applications. Try www.briefingbook.co.za/cases/cases. Also find customers' success stories on the Web sites of various vendors.

❖ GROUP EXERCISES

1. One of the most difficult tasks in any large city is traffic law enforcement. According to *PCWeek,* Nov. 13, 1993, p. 63, a solution to the problem can be found in a client/server-based data warehousing system. In addition, GIS and GPS can be helpful. Read the article and then visit your local traffic enforcement agency.
   a. Review the current information system.
   b. Identify problems in the existing system.
   c. Explain how a system like the one described in the *PCWeek* article can help your local agency.

2. Each group member will check a major DBMS vendor (Oracle, Sybase, Informix, and so on). Examine their major Web-related products. Explain the connection of the databases to data mining and to electronic commerce.

3. Data visualization is offered by all major data warehouse vendors, as well as by other companies such as www.ilog.com. Students are assigned one to each vendor to find the products and their capabilities [For a list of vendors, see Gray & Watson (1998) and www.dw-institute.org.] Each group summarizes the products and their capabilities.

MODELING AND ANALYSIS

In Chapter 4 we introduced the first major component of DSS: the database and its management. In this chapter, we describe the second major component: the model base and its management. We present this material with a note of *caution:* Modeling can be a very difficult topic and is as much an art as a science. The purpose of this chapter is not necessarily for the reader *to master the topics* of modeling and analysis. Rather, the material is geared toward *gaining familiarity* with the important concepts. We walk through some basic concepts and definitions of modeling before introducing the influence diagram, which can aid a decision maker in sketching a model of a situation and even solving it. We next introduce the idea of modeling directly in spreadsheets. Only then do we describe the structure of some successful time-proven models and methodologies: decision analysis, decision trees, optimization, heuristic programming, and simulation. We next touch on some new developments in modeling tools and techniques and conclude with some important issues in model base management. Since modeling and model management software evolve rather rapidly, we have placed most of the information on modeling and model management software on this book's Web site. The outline of this chapter is as follows:

5.1 OPENING VIGNETTE: DUPONT SIMULATES RAIL TRANSPORTATION SYSTEM AND AVOIDS COSTLY CAPITAL EXPENSE[1]

DuPont used simulation to avoid costly capital expenditures for rail car fleets as customer demands changed. Demand changes could involve rail car purchases, better management of the existing fleet, or possibly fleet size reduction. The old method of analysis, past experience, and conventional wisdom led managers to feel that the fleet size should be increased. The real problem was that DuPont was not using its specialized rail cars efficiently and effectively, not that there were not enough. There was immense variability in production output and transit cycle time, maintenance scheduling, order sequencing, and so on. This made it difficult, if not impossible to handle all the factors in a cohesive and useful manner leading to a good decision.

The fleets of specialized rail cars are used to transport bulk chemicals from DuPont to manufacturers. The cost of a rail car can vary from $80,000 for a standard tank car to more than $250,000 for a specialized tanker. Because of the high capital expense, effective and efficient use of the existing fleet is a must.

Instead of simply purchasing more rail cars, DuPont developed a ProModel (ProModel Corporation, Orem, UT, www.promodel.com) simulation model that represented their entire transportation system. A simulation model can provide a virtual environment in which experimentation with various policies that impact on the physical transportation system can be performed before real changes are made. Changes can be made quickly and inexpensively in a simulated world because relationships among the components of the system are represented mathematically. So, purchases of expensive rail cars need not be made to determine the effect.

ProModel allowed the company to construct simulation models easily and quickly (the first one took just 2 weeks to develop) and to conduct **what-if analyses.** It also included extensive graphics and animation capabilities. The simulation involved the entire rail transportation system. Many scenarios were developed, and experiments were run. DuPont experimented with a number of conditions and scheduling policies. Development of the simulation model helped the decision-making team understand the entire problem (also see Eldabi et al., 1999; Agatstein and Rieley, 1998). The ProModel simulation accurately represented the variability associated with production, availability of tank cars, transportation times, and unloading at the customer site.

With the model, the entire national distribution system can be displayed graphically (visual simulation) under a variety of conditions—especially the current ones and forecasted customer demand. The simulation model helped decision makers identify bottlenecks and other problems in the real system. By experimenting with the simulation model, the real issues were easily identified. The results convinced decision makers that a capital expense was unjustified. In fact, the needed customer deliveries could still be made after downsizing the fleet. Simulation drove this point home hard. As a consequence, DuPont saved $480,000 in capital investment that year.

Following the proven success of this simulation model, DuPont has started performing logistics modeling on a variety of product lines, crossing division boundaries and political domains. Simulation in ProModel improved DuPont's logistics dramati-

---

[1] Adapted from "ProModel Saves DuPont $480,000," ProModel Corporation, Orem, UT, www.promodel.com, 1999.

cally. Future work will focus on international logistics or logistics support for new market development. Savings in these areas could be substantially higher.

❖ QUESTIONS FOR THE OPENING VIGNETTE

1. Why did the decision makers initially feel that fleet expansion was the right decision?
2. How do you think the decision makers learned about the real system through model development? As a consequence were they able to focus better on the structure of the real system? Do you think their involvement in model building helped them in accepting the results? Why or why not?
3. Explain how simulation was used to evaluate the operation of the rail system before the changes were actually made.
4. How could the time compression capability of simulation help in this situation?
5. Simulation does not necessarily guarantee that an analyst will find the best solution. Comment on what this might mean to DuPont.
6. Once the system indicated that downsizing was a viable alternative, why do you think that the managers bought into the system? Do you think that this is why the development team continues to work on further logistics problems?

5.2 MODELING FOR MSS

The Opening Vignette illustrates a complex decision-making problem for which conventional wisdom dictated an inferior decision alternative. By modeling the rail transportation system, decision makers were able to experiment with different policies and alternatives quickly and inexpensively. *Simulation* was the modeling approach used. The DuPont simulation model was implemented with commercial software, which is typical.

The simulation model was used to learn about the problem at hand, not necessarily to derive new alternative solutions. [Also see Eldabi et al. (1999), who describes how simulation can be similarly used in health care decision making.] Simulation models can enhance an organization's decision-making process and enable it to see the impact of its future choices (Agatstein and Rieley, 1998).

The simulation approach saved the company a substantial amount of money. Instead of investing in expensive rail cars and then experimenting with how best to use them (also quite expensive), all the work was performed on a computer. Before the first flight to the moon, the National Aeronautics and Space Administration (NASA) performed countless simulations. It is extremely easy to change a model of the operation of a physical system with computer modeling.

Modeling is a key element in most DSS and a *necessity* in a model-based DSS. There are many classes of models, and there are often many specialized techniques for solving each one. Simulation is a common modeling approach, but there are several others. For example, look at the Procter and Gamble (P&G) Case Application 5.1. P&G's DSS for its North America supply chain redesign includes several models:

- A generating model (based on an algorithm) to make transportation cost estimates. This model is programmed directly in the DSS.
- A demand forecasting model (statistically based).
- A distribution center location model. This model uses aggregated data (a special modeling technique) and is solved with a standard linear/integer optimization package.

- A transportation model (specialization of a linear programming model) to determine the *best* shipping from product sources to distribution centers (fed to it from the previous model) and hence customers. It is solved using commercially available software and is loosely integrated with the distribution location model. These two problems are solved sequentially. The DSS must interface with commercial software and integrate the models.
- A financial and risk simulation model that takes into consideration some qualitative factors that require important human judgment.
- A geographic information system (effectively a graphical model of the data) for a user interface.

The P&G case demonstrates that a DSS can be composed of several models, some standard and some custom built, used collectively to support strategic decisions in the company. It further demonstrates that some models are built directly in the DSS software development package, some need to be constructed externally to the DSS software, and others can be accessed by the DSS when needed. Sometimes a massive effort is necessary to gather or estimate reasonable model data (about 500 P&G employees were involved over the course of about a year), that the models must be integrated, that models may be decomposed and simplified, that sometimes a suboptimization approach is appropriate, and finally, that human judgment is an important aspect of using models in decision making.

As is evident from the P&G case, modeling is not a simple task. The model builder must balance the model's simplification and representation requirements so that it will capture enough of reality to make it useful for the decision maker.

Some of the major modeling issues are problem identification and environmental analysis, variable identification, forecasting, the use of multiple models, model categories (or appropriate selection), model management, and knowledge-based modeling.

IDENTIFICATION OF THE PROBLEM AND ENVIRONMENTAL ANALYSIS

This issue was discussed in Chapter 2. One important aspect that bears discussion is **environmental scanning and analysis,** which is the monitoring, scanning, and interpretation of collected information. No decision is made in a vacuum. It is important to analyze the scope of the domain and the forces and dynamics of the *environment.* One should identify the organizational culture and the corporate decision-making processes (who makes decisions, degree of centralization, and so on). It is likely that environmental factors have created the current problem. The problem must be understood, and all those involved should share the same frame of understanding because the problem will ultimately be represented by the model in one form or another (as was done in the Opening Vignette). Otherwise, the model will not help the decision maker.

VARIABLE IDENTIFICATION

Identification of the model's variables (decision, result, uncontrollable, and others) is critical, as are their relationships. Influence diagrams, which are graphical models of mathematical models, can facilitate this process. A more general form of an influence diagram, a cognitive map, can help guide a decision maker toward developing a better understanding of the problem, especially of variables and their interactions.

FORECASTING

Forecasting is essential for construction and manipulation of models because when a decision is implemented, the results usually occur in the future. DSS are typically designed to determine what will be, rather than as traditional MIS, which report what is or what was (Chapter 3). There is no point in running a what-if analysis (sensitivity) on the past because decisions made then have no impact on the future. In Case Application 5.3, the IMERYS clay processing model is "demand-driven." Clay demands are forecasted so that decisions about clay production that affect the future can be made. Further details on forecasting can be found on this book's Web site (www.prenhall.com/turban).

MULTIPLE MODELS

DSS can include several models (sometimes dozens, each of which represents a different part of the decision-making problem). For example, in Case Application 5.1, the P&G supply chain DSS includes a location model to locate distribution centers, a product-strategy model, a demand forecasting model, a cost generation model, a financial and risk simulation model, and even a GIS model. Some of the models are standard and built into DSS development generators and tools. Others are standard but are not available as built-in functions. Instead, they are available as freestanding software that can interface with a DSS. Nonstandard models must be constructed from scratch. The P&G models were integrated by the DSS, and the problem had multiple goals. Even though cost minimization was the stated goal, there were other goals, as was evident in the way the managers examined solutions by taking political and other criteria into consideration when the final decisions were to be made.

MODEL CATEGORIES

Table 5.1 classifies DSS models into seven groups and lists several representative techniques for each category. Each technique can be applied to either a static or a dynamic model (Section 5.3), which can be constructed under assumed environments of certainty,

TABLE 5.1 Categories of Models

Category	Process and Objective	Representative Techniques
Optimization of problems with few alternatives (Section 5.7)	Find the best solution from a small number of alternatives	Decision tables, decision trees
Optimization via algorithm (Section 5.8)	Find the best solution from a large or an infinite number of alternatives using a step-by-step improvement process	Linear and other mathematical programming models, network models
Optimization via an analytic formula (Section 5.8)	Find the best solution in one step using a formula	Some inventory models
Simulation (Sections 5.10 and 5.13)	Finding a good enough solution or the best among the alternatives checked using experimentation	Several types of simulation
Heuristics (Section 5.9)	Find a good enough solution using rules	Heuristic programming, expert systems
Other models	Solve a what-if case using a formula	Financial modeling, waiting lines
Predictive models (Web site)	Predict the future for a given scenario	Forecasting models, Markov analysis

uncertainty, or risk (Section 5.4). To expedite model construction, one can use special decision analysis systems that have modeling languages and capabilities embedded in them. These include fourth-generation languages (formerly financial planning languages) such as Cognos PowerHouse.

MODEL MANAGEMENT

To maintain their integrity and thus their applicability, models, like data, must be managed. Such management is done with the aid of model base management systems (Section 5.14).

KNOWLEDGE-BASED MODELING

DSS uses mostly quantitative models, whereas expert systems use qualitative, knowledge-based models in their applications. Some knowledge is necessary to construct solvable (and thus usable) models. We defer the description of knowledge-based models until later chapters.

CURRENT TRENDS

There is a current trend toward making MSS models completely transparent to the decision maker. In some cases, such as with multidimensional modeling, data are generally shown in a spreadsheet format, with which most decision makers are familiar. Many decision makers used to slicing and dicing data cubes are now using online analytical processing (OLAP) systems that access data warehouses. However, though these methods may make modeling palatable, they also eliminate many important and applicable model classes from consideration, and they eliminate some important and subtle solution interpretation aspects. Modeling involves much more than just data analysis with trend lines and establishing relationships with statistical methods. The subset of methods do not yet capture the richness of modeling, some of which we touch on next and in the three detailed real-world case applications at the end of this chapter.

5.3 STATIC AND DYNAMIC MODELS

DSS models can be classified as static or dynamic.

STATIC ANALYSIS

Static models take a single snapshot of a situation. During this snapshot everything occurs in a single *interval*. For example, a decision on whether to make or buy a product is static in nature (see the Scott Housing decision-making situation in Case Application 5.2). A quarterly or annual income statement is static and so is the investment decision example in Section 5.7. The IMERYS decision-making problem in Case Application 5.3 also is static. Though it represents a year's operations, it occurs in a fixed time frame. This time frame can be "rolled" forward, but it is nonetheless *static*. The same is true for the P&G decision-making problem in Case Application 5.1. However, in the latter case, the impacts of the decisions may last over several decades. Most static decision-making situations are presumed to repeat with identical conditions (see the BMI linear programming model in Chapter 2). For example,

   process simulation begins with *steady-state,* which models a static representation of a plant to find its optimal operating parameters. A static representation assumes that the flow of materials into the plant will be continuous and unvarying. Steady-state simulation is the main tool for process design, when engineers must determine the best trade-off between capital costs, operational costs, process performance, product quality, environmental and safety factors. (Boswell, 1999)

During a static analysis, stability of the relevant data is assumed.

DYNAMIC ANALYSIS

There are stories about model builders who spend months developing a complex, ultra-large-scale, hard-to-solve static model representing a week's worth of a real-world decision-making situation like sausage production. They deliver the system and present the results to the company president who responds, "Great! Well, that handles 1 week. Let's get started on developing the 52-week model."[2]

Dynamic models represent scenarios that change over time. A simple example is a 5-year profit-and-loss projection in which the input data, such as costs, prices, and quantities, change from year to year.

Dynamic models are *time-dependent*. For example, in determining how many checkout points should be open in a supermarket, one must take the time of day into consideration because different numbers of customers arrive during each hour. Demands must be forecasted over time. The IMERYS model can be expanded to include multiple time periods by including inventory at the holding tanks, warehouses and mines. Dynamic simulation, in contrast to steady-state simulation, represents what happens when conditions vary from the steady state over time. There might be variations in the raw materials (such as clay) or an unforeseen (even random) incident in some of the processes. This methodology is used in plant control design (Boswell, 1999).

Dynamic models are important because they use, represent, or generate *trends* and patterns over time. They also show averages per period, moving averages, and comparative analyses (such as profit this quarter against profit in the same quarter of last year). Furthermore, once a static model is constructed to describe a given situation, say, product distribution, it can be expanded to represent the dynamic nature of the problem (e.g., IMERYS). For example, the transportation model (a type of network flow model) describes a static model of product distribution. It can be expanded to a dynamic network flow model to accommodate inventory and back-ordering (Aronson, 1989). Given a static model describing 1 month of a situation, expanding it to 12 months is conceptually easy. However, this expansion typically increases the model's complexity dramatically and makes it harder, if not impossible, to solve.

5.4 TREATING CERTAINTY, UNCERTAINTY, AND RISK[3]

The concepts of **certainty, uncertainty,** and **risk** were introduced in Chapter 2. When we build models, any of these conditions can occur, and different kinds of models are appropriate for each case. We turn to some important modeling issues for each condition.

---

[2]Thanks to Dick Barr of Southern Methodist University, Dallas, TX, for this one.
[3]Parts of Sections 5.4, 5.5, and 5.7–5.10 have been adapted from Turban and Meredith (1994).

CERTAINTY MODELS

Certainty models are relatively easy to develop and solve and can yield optimal solutions. Many financial models are constructed under assumed certainty, even though the market is anything but 100 percent certain. Problems that have an infinite (or a very large) number of feasible solutions are extremely important and are discussed in Sections 5.8 and 5.9.

UNCERTAINTY

Unfortunately, not all decision-making problems fit the assumptions of certainty. Managers do attempt to avoid uncertainty as much as possible, even to the point of assuming it away. Instead of dealing with uncertainty, they attempt to acquire more information so that the problem can be treated under certainty (because it can be "almost" certain) or under calculated (assumed) risk. If more information is not available, the problem must be treated under a condition of uncertainty, which is less definitive than the other categories.

RISK

Most major business decisions are made under assumed risk. Sometimes the actual probabilities of events occurring in the future are known, and we have decision making under risk. Other times, we have decision making under uncertainty, where we make estimates of the risk and presume that the risk situation occurs. Several techniques can be used to deal with risk analysis. They are discussed in Sections 5.7 and 5.10.

5.5 INFLUENCE DIAGRAMS

Once a decision-making problem is understood and defined, it is time to analyze it. This can best be done by constructing a model. Just as a flowchart is a graphical representation of computer program flow, an **influence diagram** is a map of a model (effectively a model of a model). An influence diagram is a graphical representation of a model used to assist in model design, development, and understanding. An influence diagram provides visual communication to the model builder or development team. It also serves as a framework for expressing the exact nature of the relationships of the MSS model, thus assisting a modeler in focusing on the model's major aspects, and can help eliminate the less important from consideration. The term *influence* refers to the dependency of a variable on the level of another variable. Influence diagrams appear in several formats. Bodily (1985) suggested the following convention:

$\square$ Rectangle = decision variable

$\bigcirc$ Circle = uncontrollable or intermediate variable

$\bigcirc$ Oval = result (outcome) variable: intermediate or final

The variables are connected with arrows, which indicate the direction of influence (relationship). The shape of the arrow also indicates the type of relationship. The following are typical relationships:

- Certainty

- Uncertainty

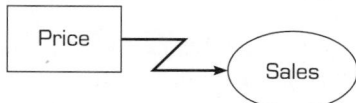

- Random (risk) variable: place a tilde (~) above the variable's name.

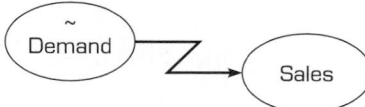

- Preference (usually between outcome variables): a double-line arrow ⇒. Arrows can be one-way or two-way (bidirectional), depending on the direction of influence of a pair of variables.

Influence diagrams can be constructed with any degree of detail and sophistication. This enables the model builder to map all the variables and show *all* the relationships in the model, as well as the direction of the influence.

Example
Consider the following profit model:
Profit = income − expenses
Income = units sold × unit price
Units sold = 0.5 × amount used in advertisement
Expenses = unit cost × units sold + fixed cost

An influence diagram for this simple model is shown in Figure 5.1.

SOFTWARE

There are several software products that create and maintain influence diagrams. The solution process of these products transforms the original problem into graphical form. Representative products are

- *Analytica* (Lumina Decision Systems, Los Altos, CA, www.lumina.com; demo available). Analytica supports hierarchical diagrams, multidimensional arrays, integrated documentation, and parameter analysis.
- *DecisionPro* (Vanguard Software Corporation, Cary, NC, www.vanguardsw.com; demo available). DecisionPro builds near-influence diagrams. The user decomposes a problem into a hierarchical tree structure (thus defining the relationships among variables) where, at the bottom, the variables are assigned values that can be randomly generated.

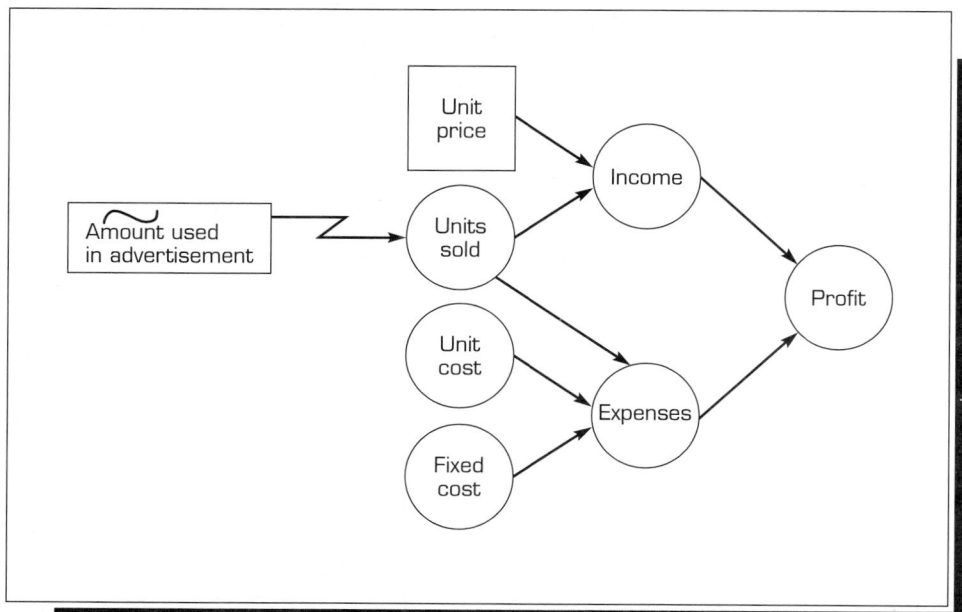

FIGURE 5.1 AN INFLUENCE DIAGRAM FOR THE PROFIT MODEL

- *DATA Decision Analysis Software* (TreeAge Software Inc., Williamstown, MA, www.treeage.com; demo available). DATA includes influence diagrams, decision trees, simulation models, and others.
- *Definitive Scenario* (Definitive Software Inc., Broomfield, CO, www.definitivesoftware.com; demo available). Definitive Scenario creates influence diagram-based decision models with bidirectional integration with Excel spreadsheets. The models can go directly from influence diagrams to Monte Carlo methods.
- *PrecisionTree* (Palisade Corporation., Newfield, NY, www.palisade.com; demo available). PrecisionTree creates influence diagrams and decision trees directly in an Excel spreadsheet.

All these systems create models with a treelike structure in such a way that the model can be easily developed and understood. Influence diagrams help focus on the important variables and their interactions. In addition, these software systems can generate a usable model and solve it. For example, Analytica lets the model builder describe blocks of the model and how they influence the important result variables. These *submodel* blocks are disaggregated by a model builder constructing a more detailed model, and so on. Finally at the lowest level, variables are assigned values (see the Lumina Decision Systems Web site). In Figure 5.2a, we show an example of a marketing model in Analytica. This model includes a price submodel and a sales submodel, which appear in Figures 5.2b and 5.2c, respectively.

DecisionPro incorporates many solution tools such as linear programming, Monte Carlo simulation, decision trees, and so on. (see the Vanguard Software Corporation Web site). Once you develop a model with an influence diagram, you can solve it directly without converting it for solution by a specialized tool. Because of these capabil-

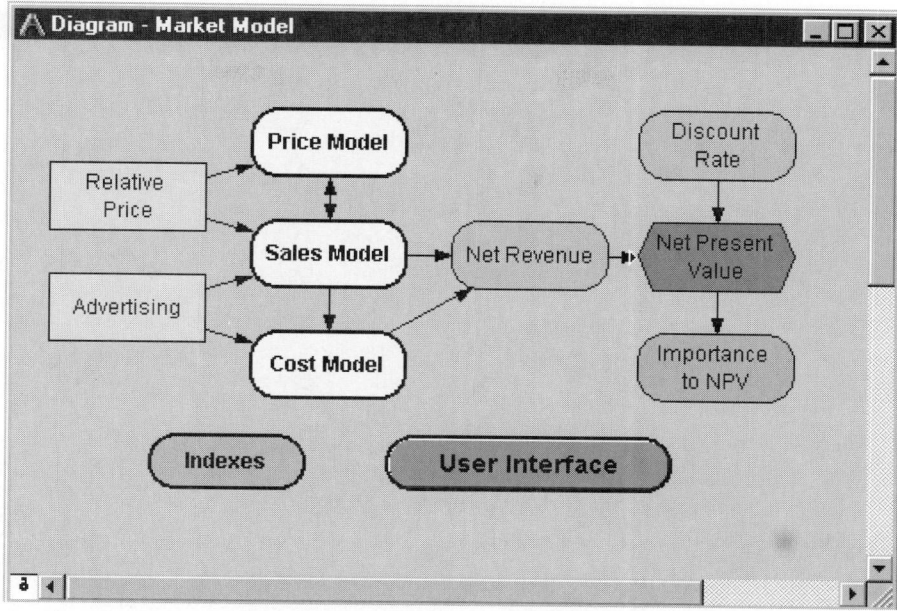

FIGURE 5.2A ANALYTICA INFLUENCE DIAGRAM OF A MARKETING PROBLEM:
THE MARKETING MODEL

Courtesy of Lumina Decision Systems, Los Altos, CA.

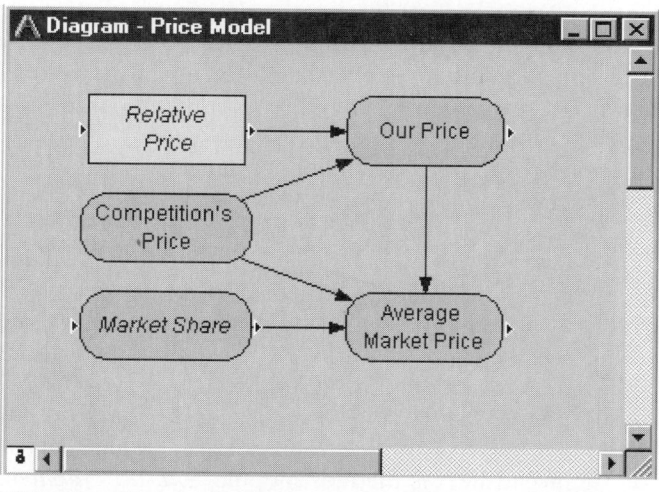

FIGURE 5.2B THE PRICE SUBMODEL

Courtesy of Lumina Decision Systems, Los Altos, CA.

ities and many built-in functions and routines, the use of visual spreadsheets and financial planning models has decreased dramatically.

See Buede (1998) for a survey of decision analysis software that includes influence diagrams. We next turn to an implementation vehicle for models: the spreadsheet.

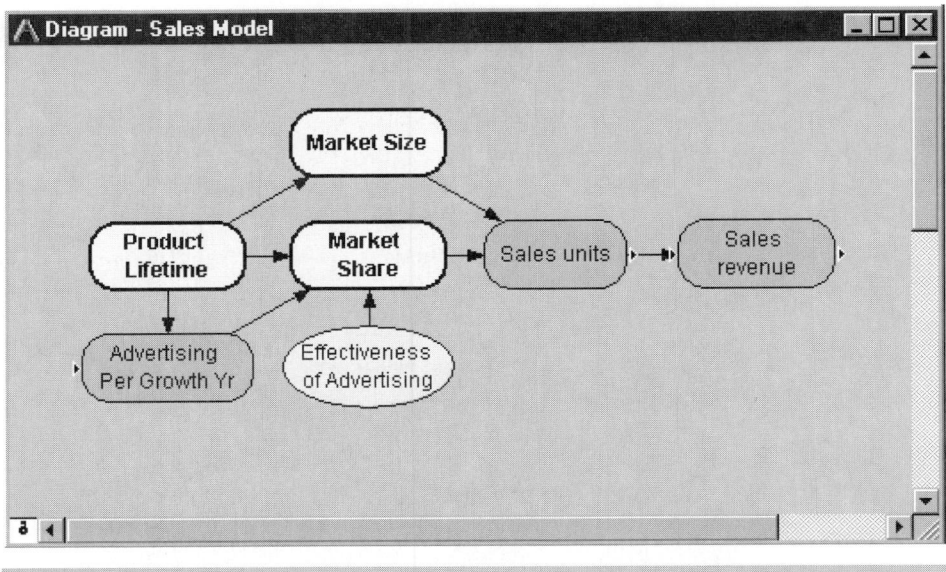

FIGURE 5.2c THE SALES SUBMODEL

Courtesy of Lumina Decision Systems, Los Altos, CA.

5.6 MSS MODELING WITH SPREADSHEETS

Models can be developed and implemented in a variety of programming languages and systems. They range from third-, fourth-, and fifth-generation programming languages to CASE systems and other systems that automatically generate usable software. We focus primarily on *spreadsheets* (with their add-ins), modeling languages, and transparent data analysis tools.

With their strength and flexibility, spreadsheet packages were quickly recognized as easy-to-use implementation software for the development of a wide range of applications in business, engineering, mathematics, and science. As spreadsheet packages evolved, add-ins were developed for structuring and solving specific model classes. These add-ins include Solver (Frontline Systems Inc., Incline Village, NV) and What'sBest! (a version of Lindo, Lindo Systems Inc., Chicago, IL) for performing linear and nonlinear optimization, and @Risk (Palisade Corporation, Newfield, NY) for performing simulation studies. Because of fierce market competition, the better add-ins were incorporated directly into the spreadsheets in later releases (e.g., Solver in Excel is the well-known GRG-2 nonlinear optimization code).

Now, the spreadsheet is the most popular *end-user modeling tool* (Figure 5.3) because it incorporates many powerful financial, statistical, mathematical, and other functions. Spreadsheets can perform model solution tasks like linear programming and regression analysis. The spreadsheet has evolved into an important tool for analysis, planning, and modeling.

Other important spreadsheet features include what-if analysis, goal seeking, data management, and programmability (*macros*). It is easy to change a cell's value and immediately see the result. Goal seeking is performed by indicating a target cell, its desired value, and a changing cell. Rudimentary database management can be performed, or parts of a database can be imported for analysis (which is essentially how OLAP

	A	B	C	D	E	F	G	H
1								
2								
3			**Simple Loan Calculation Model in Excel**					
4								
5								
6		Loan Amount			$150,000			
7		Interest Rate			8.00%			
8		Number of Years			30			
9								
10		Number of Months			360	= E8*12		
11		Interest Rate/Month			0.67%			
12								
13		Monthly Loan Payment			$1,100.65	= E7/12		
14								
15						= PMT (E11,E10,E6,0)		
16								
17								

FIGURE 5.3 EXCEL SPREADSHEET STATIC MODEL EXAMPLE OF A SIMPLE LOAN

works with multidimensional data cubes). The programming productivity of building DSS can be enhanced with the use of templates, macros, and other tools.

Most spreadsheet packages provide fairly seamless integration by reading and writing common file structures allowing easy interfacing with databases and other tools. Microsoft Excel and Lotus 1-2-3 are the two most popular spreadsheet packages.

In Figure 5.3 we show a simple loan calculation model (the boxes on the spreadsheet describe the contents of the cells containing formulas). A change in the interest rate (performed by typing in a new number in cell E7) is immediately reflected in the monthly payment (in cell E13). The results can be observed and analyzed immediately. If we require a specific monthly payment, goal seeking can be used to determine an appropriate interest rate or loan amount.

Static or dynamic models can be built in a spreadsheet. For example, the monthly loan calculation spreadsheet shown in Figure 5.3 is static. Although the problem affects the borrower over time, the model indicates a single month's performance which is replicated. A dynamic model, on the other hand, represents behavior over time. The loan calculations in the spreadsheet shown in Figure 5.4 indicate the effect of prepayment on the principal over time. Risk analysis can be incorporated into spreadsheets by using built-in random number generators to develop simulation models (see Section 5.10 and the examples on this book's Web site, www.prenhall.com/turban, where we describe an economic order quantity simulation model under assumed risk and a spreadsheet simulation model of cash flows).

Spreadsheets were developed for personal computers, but they also run on larger computers. The spreadsheet framework is the basis for multidimensional spreadsheets and OLAP tools, which are described later.

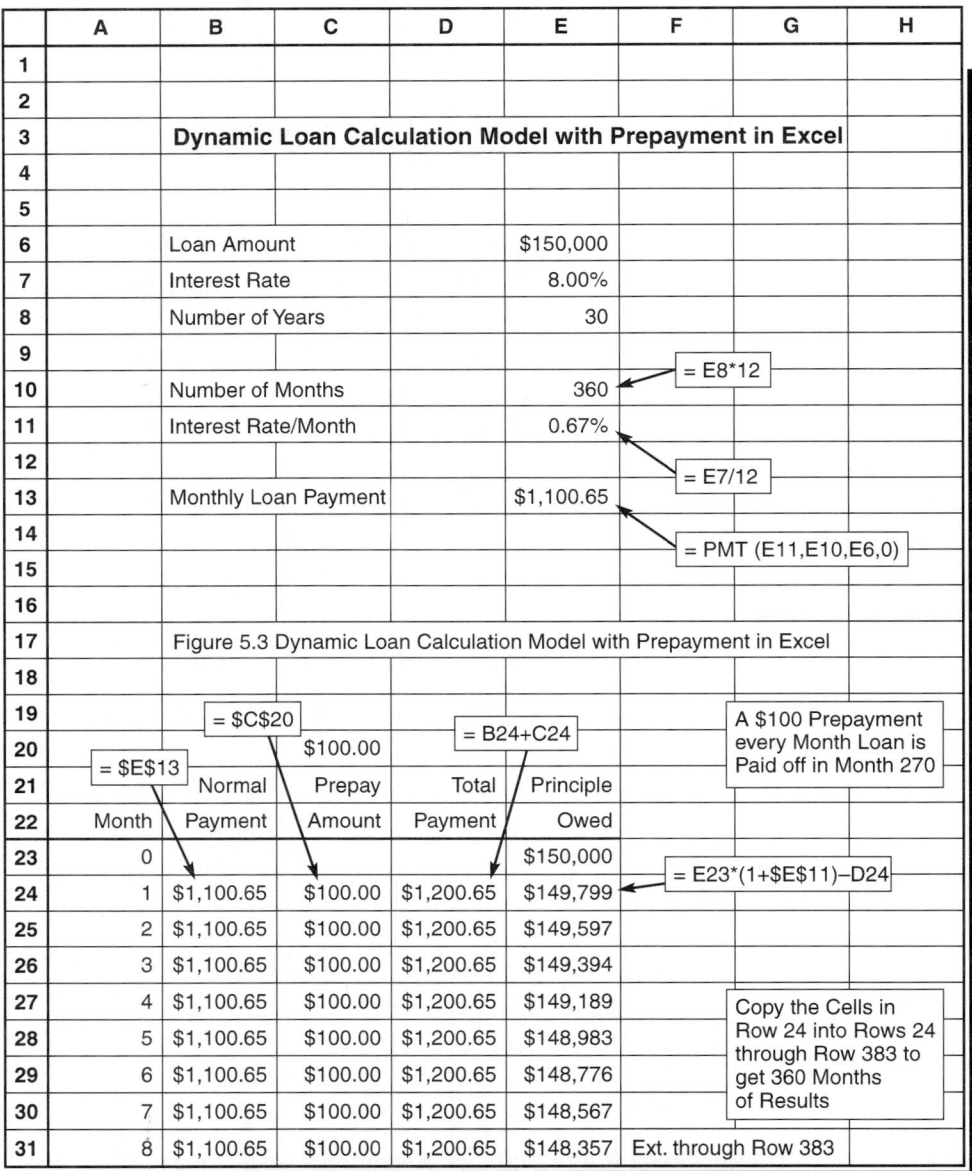

Dynamic Loan Calculation Model with Prepayment in Excel

	A	B	C	D	E	F	G	H
6		Loan Amount			$150,000			
7		Interest Rate			8.00%			
8		Number of Years			30			
10		Number of Months			360	= E8*12		
11		Interest Rate/Month			0.67%			
13		Monthly Loan Payment			$1,100.65	= E7/12		
						= PMT (E11,E10,E6,0)		

Figure 5.3 Dynamic Loan Calculation Model with Prepayment in Excel

= C20 : $100.00 = B24+C24 A $100 Prepayment every Month Loan is Paid off in Month 270

= E13

	Month	Normal Payment	Prepay Amount	Total Payment	Principle Owed			
23	0				$150,000	= E23*(1+E11)−D24		
24	1	$1,100.65	$100.00	$1,200.65	$149,799			
25	2	$1,100.65	$100.00	$1,200.65	$149,597			
26	3	$1,100.65	$100.00	$1,200.65	$149,394			
27	4	$1,100.65	$100.00	$1,200.65	$149,189	Copy the Cells in Row 24 into Rows 24 through Row 383 to get 360 Months of Results		
28	5	$1,100.65	$100.00	$1,200.65	$148,983			
29	6	$1,100.65	$100.00	$1,200.65	$148,776			
30	7	$1,100.65	$100.00	$1,200.65	$148,567			
31	8	$1,100.65	$100.00	$1,200.65	$148,357	Ext. through Row 383		

FIGURE 5.4 EXCEL SPREADSHEET DYNAMIC MODEL EXAMPLE OF A SIMPLE LOAN

5.7 DECISION ANALYSIS OF A FEW ALTERNATIVES (DECISION TABLES AND DECISION TREES)

Decision situations that involve a finite and usually not too large number of alternatives are modeled by an approach called **decision analysis,** in which the alternatives are listed with their forecasted contributions to the goal(s), and the probability of obtaining the contribution, in a table or a graph. They can be evaluated to select the best alternative.

Single-goal situations can be modeled with **decision tables** or **decision trees.** Multiple goals (criteria) can be modeled with several other techniques described later.

DECISION TABLES

Decision tables are a convenient way to organize information in a systematic manner. For example, an investment company is considering investing in one of three alternatives: bonds, stocks, or certificates of deposit (CDs). The company is interested in one goal: maximizing the yield on the investment after 1 year. If it were interested in other goals such as safety or liquidity, the problem would be classified as one of *multicriteria decision analysis.*

The yield depends on the state of the economy some time in the future (often called the *state of nature*), which can be in solid growth, stagnation, or inflation. Experts estimated the following annual yields:

- If there is solid growth in the economy, bonds will yield 12 percent, stocks 15 percent, and time deposits 6.5 percent.
- If stagnation prevails, bonds will yield 6 percent, stocks 3 percent, and time deposits 6.5 percent.
- If inflation prevails, bonds will yield 3 percent, stocks will bring a loss of 2 percent, and time deposits will yield 6.5 percent.

The problem is to select the one best investment alternative. These are assumed to be discrete alternatives. Combinations such as investing 50 percent in bonds and 50 percent in stocks must be treated as new alternatives.

The investment decision-making problem can be viewed as a two-person game. The investor makes a choice (a move) and then a state of nature occurs (makes a move). The payoff is shown in a table representation (Table 5.2) of a mathematical model. According to the definition in Chapter 2, the table includes *decision variables* (the alternatives), *uncontrollable variables* (the states of the economy, e.g., the environment), and *result variables* (the projected yield, e.g., outcomes). All the models in this section are structured in a spreadsheet framework.

If this were a decision-making problem under certainty, we would know what the economy will be and could easily choose the best investment. But this is not the case, and so we must consider the two cases of uncertainty and risk. For uncertainty, we do not know the probabilities of each state of nature. For risk, we assume we know the probabilities with which each state of nature will occur.

TREATING UNCERTAINTY

There are several methods of handling uncertainty. For example, the *optimistic approach* assumes that the best possible outcome of each alternative will occur and then selects the best of the bests (stocks). The *pessimistic approach* assumes that the worst possible outcome for each alternative will occur and selects the best one of those (CDs).

TABLE 5.2 Investment Problem Decision Table Model

Alternative	State of Nature (Uncontrollable Variables)		
	Solid Growth (%)	Stagnation (%)	Inflation (%)
Bonds	12.0	6.0	3.0
Stocks	15.0	3.0	−2.0
CDs	6.5	6.5	6.5

See Clemen (1996) or Golub (1997). There are serious problems with every approach for handling uncertainty. Whenever possible, the analyst should attempt to gather enough information so that the problem can be treated under assumed certainty or risk.

TREATING RISK

The most common method for solving this **risk analysis** problem is to select the alternative with the largest *expected value*. Assume that the chance of solid growth is estimated to be 50 percent, that of stagnation 30 percent, and that of inflation 20 percent (estimated by experts). Then the decision table is rewritten with the known probabilities (Table 5.3). An expected value is computed by multiplying the results (outcomes) by their respective probabilities and adding them. For example, investing in bonds yields an expected return of 12(0.5) + 6(0.3) + 3(0.2) = 8.4 percent.

However, this approach can be a dangerous strategy, because the "utility" of each potential outcome may be different from the "value." Even if there is an infinitesimal chance of a catastrophic loss, the expected value may seem reasonable, but the investor may not be willing to cover the loss. For example, suppose a financial advisor presents you with an "almost sure" investment of $1,000 that can double your money in 1 day. Then he says, "Well, there is a .9999 probability that you will double your money, but unfortunately there is a .0001 probability that you will be liable for a $500,000 out-of-pocket loss." The expected value of this investment is

$$.9999 (\$2,000 - \$1,000) + .0001 (-\$500,000 - \$1,000) = \$999.90 - \$50.10 = \$949.80$$

The potential loss could be catastrophic for the investor unless he or she is a billionaire. Depending on an investor's ability to cover the loss, there are different expected utilities of the investment. Remember that the investor makes the decision only *once*.

DECISION TREES

An alternative representation of the decision table is a decision tree. A decision tree (1) shows the relationships of the problem graphically, and (2) can handle complex situations in a compact form. However, a decision tree can be cumbersome if there are many alternatives or states of nature. DATA (TreeAge Software Inc., Williamstown, MA, www.treeage.com) and PrecisionTree (Palisade Corporation, Newfield, NY, www.palisade.com) are powerful, intuitive, and sophisticated decision tree analysis systems. There are several other methods of treating risk which are discussed later in the book. They include simulation, certainty factors, and fuzzy logic.

MULTIPLE GOALS

A simplified investment case of **multiple goals** is shown in Table 5.4. The three goals (criteria) are yield, safety, and liquidity. This situation is under assumed certainty; that is, only one possible consequence is projected for each alternative (the more complex cases of risk or uncertainty could be considered). Some of the results are qualitative (such as low and high) rather than numeric.

Tavana and Banerjee (1995) discuss a multicriteria DSS for strategic planning. Their method captures the decision maker's beliefs through a series of sequential, ra-

TABLE 5.3   Decision Under Risk and Its Solution

Alternative	Solid Growth, .50(%)	Stagnation, .30(%)	Inflation, .20(%)	Expected Value (%)
Bonds	12.0	6.0	3.0	8.4 (maximum)
Stocks	15.0	3.0	−2.0	8.0
CDs	6.5	6.5	6.5	6.5

TABLE 5.4	Multiple Goals		
Alternative	*Yield (%)*	*Safety*	*Liquidity*
Bonds	8.4	High	High
Stocks	8.0	Low	High
CDs	6.5	Very high	High

tional, and analytic processes. They used the Analytic Hierarchy Process (AHP) (Saaty, 1995, 1996, 1999; Palmer, 1999). Raju and Pillai (1999) apply a multicriteria model to river basin planning. Another example of a DSS designed for handling multiple-goal decision making is described by Murthy et al. (1999). They developed a fairly complex paper manufacturing and scheduling DSS that saved a substantial sum of money annually. There are many decision analysis and multicriteria decision-making software packages, including DecisionPro (Vanguard Software Corporation, www.vanguardsw.com), Expert Choice and TeamEC for groups (Expert Choice Inc., www.expertchoice.com), Hipre and Web-Hipre (Systems Analysis Laboratory, Helsinki University of Technology, www.hipre.hut.fi), and Logical Decisions for Windows and for Groups (Logical Decisions Group, www.logicaldecisions.com; demo available). Demo software versions of all these systems are available on the Web. See DSS in Action 5.1, Case Application 5.2, and this book's Web site (www.prenhall.com/turban).

DSS IN ACTION 5.1

SOLVING MULTICRITERIA PROBLEMS

Multicriteria (goal) decision making was introduced in Chapter 2. One of the most effective approaches is to use weights based on decision-making priorities. However, soliciting weights (or priorities) from managers is a complex task, as is calculation of the weighted averages needed to choose the best alternative. The process is complicated further by the presence of qualitative variables. One method of multicriteria decision making is the Analytical Hierarchy Process developed by Saaty (1996, 1999) (also see www.expertchoice.com, Palmer (1999), and this book's Web site). Here we present two representative examples in which the method proved effective.

The replacement of several milling machines at Deutsche Aerospace Airbus, Germany, required the development of a strategic plan to address both automation of manufacturing systems and machinery replacement. It was necessary to develop and explore different planning alternatives ranging from extending the life of existing machinery to total replacement with a new manufacturing system and to evaluate these alternatives through economical and technological criteria. Quantitative (financial and technological) and qualitative (intangible) benefits of investments in new manufacturing systems were to be considered. The company used commercial packages (AutoMan and Expert Choice) to conduct the planning.[†]

Expert Choice is used by a leading bank to evaluate lending risks and opportunities in foreign countries. This bank had previously used research reports to weigh economic, financial, and political considerations. Although the bank was satisfied with the quality of the reports, both the bank and the consultant preparing the reports felt that the information was not being put to best use. The complex data and decision-making process often resulted in too much or too little weight being placed on various aspects of the decision process. The bank's credit committee also had difficulty integrating the expert information into the deliberation process. Consequently, the bank's consultant prepared an Expert Choice model, enabling the credit committee to use the most recent information in making comparisons among factors. Without any prior exposure to personal computers or Expert Choice, the bankers began to use the software and evaluate the subject country within a matter of minutes.[‡]

[†]*Source:* Based on Oeltjenbruns et al., "Strategic Planning in Manufacturing Systems," *International Journal of Production Economics,* Mar. 1995.

[‡]*Source:* Condensed from material provided by Expert Choice Inc., Pittsburgh, PA.

See Golub (1997) or Clemen (1996) for more on decision analysis. Although quite complex, it is possible to apply mathematical programming (Section 5.8) directly to decision-making situations under risk (Sen and Higle, 1999).

5.8 OPTIMIZATION VIA MATHEMATICAL PROGRAMMING

Optimization was introduced in Chapter 2, where a linear programming example was developed. **Linear programming (LP)** is the best-known technique in a family of optimization tools called **mathematical programming.** It is used extensively in DSS (see DSS in Action 5.2). Linear programming models have many important applications in practice. For example, an assignment problem (a type of linear programming problem) determined the best snow disposal method for the City of Montreal (see DSS in Action 5.3).

MATHEMATICAL PROGRAMMING

Mathematical programming is a family of tools designed to help solve managerial problems in which the decision maker must allocate scarce resources among competing activities to optimize a measurable goal. For example, the distribution of machine time (the resource) among various products (the activities) is a typical allocation problem. LP allocation problems usually display the following characteristics.

LP Characteristics

- A limited quantity of economic resources is available for allocation.
- The resources are used in the production of products or services.
- There are two or more ways in which the resources can be used. Each is called a solution or a program.
- Each activity (product or service) in which the resources are used yields a return in terms of the stated goal.
- The allocation is usually restricted by several limitations and requirements called constraints.

DSS IN ACTION 5.2

EFES' MALT PLANT LOCATION OPTIMIZATION

Efes Beverage Group (Efes), a beer company in Turkey, wanted to determine the best locations for new malt plants. In an earlier project, Efes had used a mathematical programming model to determine where to locate new breweries. As some of these new breweries were being constructed, Efes managers asked the same team to help.

Various sites were evaluated as potential locations for new malt plants. An economic analysis revealed the inferiority of some alternatives that some managers championed. To evaluate the remaining possibilities, a mixed-integer programming model was developed that considered both the location of new malt plants and the distribution of barley and malt. It considered the long-run effects of the decisions and minimized the present value of total costs. The model readily identified locations for the new malt plants. With the user-friendly optimization software, sensitivity analyses were conducted to determine the impact of forcing the selection of certain favored sites. Some were deemed acceptable, while others caused large increases in the optimal overall system cost (about $19 million). Efes used the model for distribution decisions. As a next step, the location and distribution decisions can be linked (as in Case Application 5.1).

Source: Condensed and modified from M. Koksalan and H. Sural, "Efes Beverage Group Makes Location and Distribution Decisions for its Malt Plants," *Interfaces,* Vol. 29, No. 2, Mar./Apr. 1999, pp. 89–103.

MATHEMATICAL PROGRAMMING MODEL HELPS DISPOSE OF MONTREAL'S HEAVY SNOW

Snow removal and disposal are expensive winter activities that affect the quality of life and the environment in cities throughout the world. To facilitate traffic flow in urban regions that receive heavy snowfalls, snow is first plowed from streets and sidewalks and then hauled to disposal sites. A city is typically divided into many sectors that are cleared of snow concurrently. An assignment problem that assigns snow removal sectors to snow disposal sites can be formulated as a multiresource, generalized assignment problem, a kind of mathematical programming problem, or more specifically, a large-scale combinatorial (integer programming) problem.

There are 60 sectors and 20 disposal sites in the City of Montreal, and an average of 300,000 truckloads (7 million cubic meters) of snow are hauled away each year by 660 trucks. Transporting snow is expensive: the average cost is $0.24 (Canadian) per cubic meter of snow. This is an important strategic problem.

By using the straight-line distance from the center of each sector to each disposal site, the goal is to find an assignment that minimizes the sum of the distances from the center of the sectors to the disposal sites, given the hourly capacity of each disposal site and the capacity of the trucks.

Solution of the integer model to optimality took too long. So a fast heuristic method was developed to convert a more easily found linear programming solution into an integer solution. The system quickly found objective values that were within a few percent of the optimum, along with sensitivity results. Satisfied with these results, the decision makers performed many what-if analyses to determine whether a heavy winter would necessitate the opening of new snow disposal sites. The consequences of closing a site were also evaluated; the objective degraded a mere 0.15 percent in cost, with each truck traveling, on average, only an additional 14 meters. The tested scenarios minimized snow removal and disposal costs and improved the quality of life in Montreal.

Source: Condensed from J. F. Campbell and A. Langevin, "The Snow Disposal Assignment Problem," *Journal of the Operational Research Society,* Vol. 46, 1995, pp. 919–929.

The LP allocation model is based on the following rational economic assumptions.

LP Assumptions

- Returns from different allocations can be compared; that is, they can be measured by a common unit (such as dollars or utility).
- The return from any allocation is independent of other allocations.
- The total return is the sum of the returns yielded by the different activities.
- All data are known with certainty.
- The resources are to be used in the most economical manner.

Allocation problems typically have a large number of possible alternative solutions. Depending on the underlying assumptions, the number of solutions can be either infinite or finite. Usually, different solutions yield different rewards. Of the available solutions, at least one is the *best,* in the sense that the degree of goal attainment associated with it is the highest (i.e., the total reward is maximized). This is called an *optimal solution,* and can be found by using a special algorithm.

LINEAR PROGRAMMING

In Chapter 2 we presented a simple product-mix problem and formulated it as an LP problem. Every LP problem is composed of *decision variables* (whose values are unknown and are searched for), an *objective function* (a linear mathematical function that relates the decision variables to the goal and measures goal attainment and is to be optimized), *objective function coefficients* (unit profit or cost coefficients indicating the contribution to the objective of one unit of a decision variable), *constraints* (expressed in the form of linear inequalities or equalities that limit resources and/or requirements; these relate the variables through linear relationships), *capacities* (which describe the upper and sometimes lower limits on the constraints and variables), and *input–output (technology) coefficients* (which indicate resource utilization for a decision variable).

Linear programming models (and their specializations and generalizations) can be specified directly in a number of user-friendly modeling systems. Two of the best known are Lindo and Lingo (Lindo Systems Inc., Chicago, IL, www.lindo.com; demos of both are available directly from the Web) (Schrage, 1997). Lindo is a linear and integer programming system. Models are specified in essentially the same way that they are defined algebraically. Based on the success of Lindo, the company developed Lingo, a modeling language that includes the powerful Lindo optimizer plus extensions for solving nonlinear problems. The IMERYS DSS (Case Application 5.3) was implemented using Lingo as its model generator and solver. Lindo and Lingo models and solutions of the product-mix model of Chapter 2 are shown in DSS in Focus 5.4 and 5.5, respectively.

The uses of mathematical programming, especially of linear programming, are fairly common in practice. There are standard computer programs available. Optimization functions are available in many DSS tools such as Excel. Also, it is easy to interface other optimization software with Excel, database management systems, and similar tools. Optimization models are often included in decision support implementations, as shown in DSS in Action 5.2 and 5.3. More details on linear programming, a description of another classic LP problem called the *blending problem,* and an Excel spreadsheet formulation and solution can be found on this book's Web site.

DSS IN FOCUS 5.4

LINDO EXAMPLE: THE PRODUCT-MIX MODEL

Here is the Lindo version of the product-mix model described in Chapter 2. Note that the model is essentially identical to the algebraic expression of the model.

```
<<The Lindo Model:>>

MAX      8000 X1 + 12000 X2
SUBJECT TO
   LABOR)        300 X1 + 500 X2 <= 200000
   BUDGET)     10000 X1 + 15000 X2 <= 8000000
 MARKET1)     X1 >=    100
 MARKET2)     X2 >=    200
END

<<Generated Solution Report>>

LP OPTIMUM FOUND AT STEP        3

       OBJECTIVE FUNCTION VALUE

     1)      506667.00

  VARIABLE          VALUE          REDUCED COST
        X1       333.333300             .000000
        X2       200.000000             .000000
```

```
          ROW      SLACK OR SURPLUS      DUAL PRICES
       LABOR)             .000000        26.666670
      BUDGET)     1666667.000000          .000000
     MARKET1)         233.333300          .000000
     MARKET2)             .000000     -1333.333000


   NO. ITERATIONS=          3

   RANGES IN WHICH THE BASIS IS UNCHANGED:


                          OBJ COEFFICIENT RANGES
    VARIABLE          CURRENT       ALLOWABLE        ALLOWABLE
                       COEF         INCREASE         DECREASE
        X1        8000.000000        INFINITY      799.999800
        X2       12000.000000     1333.333000        INFINITY


                         RIGHTHAND SIDE RANGES
     ROW              CURRENT       ALLOWABLE        ALLOWABLE
                       RHS          INCREASE         DECREASE
     LABOR      200000.000000    50000.000000     70000.000000
    BUDGET     8000000.000000        INFINITY   1666667.000000
   MARKET1         100.000000      233.333300        INFINITY
   MARKET2         200.000000      140.000000      200.000000
```

LINGO EXAMPLE: THE PRODUCT-MIX MODEL

Here is the Lingo version of the product-mix model described in Chapter 2. Note the specialized modeling language commands, SET definitions, and DATA definitions. Though this model is much more complex than the Lindo version, it is much more powerful in that additional computers or resources can be added by simply augmenting the DATA and SET sections. The model itself is unchanged. In models that interact with databases, the data in the database are simply modified and the entire model file is unchanged. This approach was used in the IMERYS Case Application 5.3.

<<The Model>>>

```
MODEL:
! The Product-Mix Example;
SETS:
COMPUTERS / CC7, CC8 / : PROFIT, QUANTITY, MARKETLIM ;
RESOURCES / LABOR, BUDGET / : AVAILABLE ;
RESBYCOMP (RESOURCES, COMPUTERS) : UNITCONSUMPTION ;
ENDSETS
DATA:
PROFIT MARKETLIM =
  8000, 100,
 12000, 200;
AVAILABLE = 200000, 8000000 ;
```

```
UNITCONSUMPTION =
 300, 500,
 10000, 15000 ;
ENDDATA
MAX = @SUM (COMPUTERS: PROFIT * QUANTITY) ;
@FOR ( RESOURCES ( I):
  @SUM( COMPUTERS( J):
     UNITCONSUMPTION ( I,J) * QUANTITY (J)) <=
AVAILABLE( I)) ;
@FOR( COMPUTERS( J):
     QUANTITY (J) >= MARKETLIM( J)) ;
! Alternative
@FOR( COMPUTERS( J) :
  @BND (MARKETLIM(J), QUANTITY (J) , 1000000)) ;
```

<<(Partial) Solution Report>>

```
 Global optimal solution found at step:          2
 Objective value:                     5066667.
               Variable          Value       Reduced Cost
              PROFIT( CC7)      8000.000        0.0000000
              PROFIT( CC8)      12000.00        0.0000000
            QUANTITY( CC7)      333.3333        0.0000000
            QUANTITY( CC8)      200.0000        0.0000000
           MARKETLIM( CC7)      100.0000        0.0000000
           MARKETLIM( CC8)      200.0000        0.0000000
           AVAILABLE( LABOR)    200000.0        0.0000000
           AVAILABLE( BUDGET)   8000000.        0.0000000
  UNITCONSUMPTION( LABOR, CC7)  300.0000        0.0000000
  UNITCONSUMPTION( LABOR, CC8)  500.0000        0.0000000
  UNITCONSUMPTION( BUDGET, CC7) 10000.00        0.0000000
  UNITCONSUMPTION( BUDGET, CC8) 15000.00        0.0000000

                     Row    Slack or Surplus      Dual Price
                      1        5066667.            1.000000
                      2        0.0000000           26.66667
                      3        1666667.            0.0000000
                      4        233.3333            0.0000000
                      5        0.0000000          -1333.333
```

5.9 HEURISTIC PROGRAMMING

The determination of **optimal solutions** to some complex decision problems could involve a prohibitive amount of time and cost or may even be impossible. Alternatively, the simulation approach (Section 5.10) may be lengthy, complex, inappropriate, and even inaccurate. Sometimes under these conditions it is possible to obtain *satisfactory* solutions more quickly and less expensively by using **heuristics.**

The heuristic process can also be described as developing rules to help solve complex problems (or intermediate subproblems to discover how to set up these subproblems for final solution by finding the most promising paths in the search for solutions), finding ways to retrieve and interpret information on the fly, and then developing methods that lead to a computational algorithm or general solution.

Although heuristics are employed primarily for solving ill-structured problems, they can also be used to provide satisfactory solutions to certain complex, well-structured problems much more quickly and cheaply than optimization algorithms (e.g., large-scale combinatorial problems with many potential solutions to explore) (Sun et al., 1998). The main difficulty in using heuristics is that they are not as general as algorithms. Therefore, they can normally be used only for the specific situation for which they were intended. Another problem with heuristics is that they may produce a poor solution. We do want to point out that heuristics are often stated like algorithms. They can be step-by-step procedures for solving a problem, but there is no guarantee that an optimal solution will be found.

Heuristic programming is the approach of using heuristics to arrive at feasible and "good enough" solutions to some complex problems. Good enough is usually in the range of 90–99.9 percent of the objective value of an optimal solution.

Heuristics can be quantitative, and so they can play a major role in the DSS model base (see DSS in Action 5.3, where heuristics were used to solve a complex integer programming problem). They can also be qualitative, and then they can play a major role in providing knowledge to expert systems.

METHODOLOGY

Heuristic thinking does not necessarily proceed in a direct manner. It involves searching, learning, evaluating, judging, and then re-searching, relearning, and reappraising as exploring and probing take place. The knowledge gained from success or failure at some point is fed back to and modifies the search process. It is usually necessary to redefine either the objectives or the problem or to solve related or simplified problems before the primary one can be solved.

Tabu search heuristics (Glover and Laguna, 1997; Sun et al., 1998) are based on intelligent search strategies to reduce the search for high-quality solutions in computer problem solving. Essentially, the method "remembers" what high-quality and low-quality solutions it has found and tries to move toward other high-quality solutions and away from the low-quality ones. The tabu search methodology has proved successful in efficiently solving many large-scale combinatorial problems (such as the fixed-charge transportation problem (Sun et al., 1998). **Genetic algorithms** start with a set of randomly generated solutions and recombine pairs of them at random to produce offspring (modeled on the evolution process). Only the best offspring and parents are kept to produce the next generation. Random mutations may also be introduced. Genetic algorithms are described in depth later in this book.

WHEN TO USE HEURISTICS

Heuristic application is appropriate in the following situations:

- The input data are inexact or limited.
- Reality is so complex that optimization models cannot be used.
- A reliable, exact algorithm is not available.
- Complex problems are not economical for optimization or simulation or consume excessive computation time.
- It is possible to improve the efficiency of the optimization process (e.g., by producing good starting solutions).
- Symbolic rather than numerical processing is involved (as in expert systems).
- Quick decisions are to be made and computerization is not feasible (some heuristics do not require computers).

ADVANTAGES AND LIMITATIONS OF HEURISTICS

The major advantages of heuristics are the following:

- They are simple to understand and therefore easier to implement and explain.
- They help train people to be creative and develop heuristics for other problems.
- They save formulation time.
- They save computer programming and storage requirements.
- They save computational time and thus real time in decision making. Some problems are so complex that they can be solved only with heuristics.
- They often produce multiple acceptable solutions.
- Usually it is possible to state a theoretical or empirical measure of the solution quality (e.g., how close the solution's objective value is to an optimal one, even though the optimal value is unknown).
- They can incorporate intelligence to guide the search (e.g., tabu search). Such expertise may be problem specific or based on an expert's opinions embedded in an expert system or search mechanism.
- It is possible to apply efficient heuristics to models that could be solved with mathematical programming. Sometimes heuristics are the preferred method, and other times heuristic solutions are used as initial solutions for mathematical programming methods.

The primary limitations of heuristics are the following:

- An optimal solution cannot be guaranteed. Sometimes the bound on the objective value is very bad.
- There may be too many exceptions to the rules.
- Sequential decision choices can fail to anticipate the future consequences of each choice.
- Interdependencies of one part of a system can sometimes have a profound influence on the whole system.

Heuristic algorithms that function like algorithms but without a guarantee of optimality can be classified as follows (Camm and Evans, 1996):

- *Construction heuristics.* These methods build a feasible solution by adding components one at a time until a feasible solution is obtained. For example, in a traveling salesperson problem, always visit the next unvisited city that is closest.
- *Improvement heuristics.* These methods start with a feasible solution and attempt to successively improve on it. For example, in a traveling salesperson solution, attempt to swap two cities.
- *Mathematical programming.* This method is applied to less constrained (relaxed) models in hope of obtaining information about an optimum to the original one. This technique is often used in integer optimization.
- *Decomposition.* This approach involves solving a problem in stages. See the P&G Case Application 5.1, where the distribution problem was solved and then used in solving the product-strategy problem.
- *Partitioning.* This method involves dividing a problem up into smaller, solvable pieces and then reassembling the solutions to the pieces. This technique can be applied to large traveling salesperson problems. The country can be divided into four regions, each problem solved, and then the solutions connected together.

Vehicle routing has benefited from the development and use of efficient heuristics (e.g., Liu and Shen (1999) and Gendreau et al. (1999)). Karaboga and Pham (1999) and Rayward-Smith et al. (1996) discuss modern heuristic methods (tabu search, genetic algorithms, and simulated annealing).

5.10 SIMULATION

To *simulate* means to assume the appearance of the characteristics of reality. In MSS, **simulation** is a *technique for conducting experiments (such as what-if analyses) with a computer on a model of a management system.*

Typically there is some randomness in the real decision-making situation. Because DSS deals with semistructured or unstructured situations, reality is complex, which may not be easily represented by optimization or other models but can often be handled by simulation. Simulation is one of the most commonly used DSS methods.

MAJOR CHARACTERISTICS OF SIMULATION

Simulation is not strictly a type of model; models in general *represent* reality, whereas simulation typically *imitates* it. In a practical sense, there are fewer simplifications of reality in simulation models than in other models. In addition, simulation is a technique for *conducting experiments.* Therefore, it involves testing specific values of the decision or uncontrollable variables in the model and observing the impact on the output variables. In the opening vignette, the DuPont decision makers had initially chosen to purchase more rail cars, whereas an alternative involving better scheduling of the existing cars was developed, tested, found to have excess capacity, and saved money.

Simulation is a *descriptive* rather than a normative method. There is no automatic search for an optimal solution. Instead, a simulation model describes or predicts the characteristics of a given system under different conditions. Once the characteristics' values are computed, the best among several alternatives can be selected. The simulation process usually repeats an experiment many, many times to obtain an estimate (and a variance) of the overall effect of certain actions. For most situations, a computer simulation is appropriate, though there are some well-known manual simulations (e.g., a city police department simulated its patrol car scheduling with a carnival game wheel).

Finally, simulation is usually used only when a problem is too complex to be treated by numerical optimization techniques. **Complexity** here means that the problem either cannot be formulated for optimization (e.g., because the assumptions do not hold), the formulation is too large, there are too many interactions among the variables, or the problem is stochastic in nature (exhibits risk or uncertainty).

ADVANTAGES OF SIMULATION

Simulation is used in MSS for the following reasons:

- The theory is fairly straightforward.
- A great amount of *time compression* can be attained, giving the manager some feel as to the long-term (1- to 10-year) effects of many policies quickly.
- Simulation is descriptive rather than normative. This allows the manager to pose what-if questions. Managers can use a trial-and-error approach to

problem solving and can do so faster, cheaper, more accurately, and with less risk with simulation (see the Opening Vignette).

- The manager can experiment to determine which decision variables and which parts of the environment are really important, and with different alternatives.
- An accurate simulation model requires an intimate knowledge of the problem, thus forcing the MSS builder to constantly interact with the manager—desirable for DSS development. By doing so, both the developer and manager gain a better understanding of the problem and the potential decisions available (Eldabi et al., 1999) (see the Opening Vignette).
- The model is built from the manager's perspective.
- The simulation model is built for one particular problem and typically cannot solve any other problem. Thus, no generalized understanding is required of the manager; every component in the model corresponds to part of the real system.
- Simulation can handle an extremely wide variety of problem types, such as inventory and staffing, as well as higher-level managerial functions such as long-range planning.
- Simulation generally can include the real complexities of problems; simplifications are not necessary. For example, simulation can use real probability distributions rather than approximate theoretical distributions.
- Simulation automatically produces many important performance measures.
- Simulation is often the only DSS modeling method that can readily handle relatively unstructured problems.
- There are some relatively easy-to-use (Monte Carlo) simulation packages. These include add-in spreadsheet packages (@Risk), the influence diagram software mentioned earlier, and the visual interactive simulation systems to be discussed shortly.

DISADVANTAGES OF SIMULATION

The primary disadvantages of simulation are the following:

- An optimal solution cannot be guaranteed, but relatively good ones are generally found.
- Simulation model construction can be a slow and costly process, though the newer modeling systems make it easier than ever.
- Solutions and inferences from a simulation study are usually not transferable to other problems because the model incorporates unique problem factors.
- Simulation is sometimes so easy to explain to managers that analytic methods are often overlooked.
- Simulation software sometimes requires special skills because of the complexity of the formal solution method.

THE METHODOLOGY OF SIMULATION

Simulation involves setting up a model of a real system and conducting repetitive experiments on it. The methodology consists of the steps shown in Figure 5.5.

PROBLEM DEFINITION
The real-world problem is examined and classified. Here we specify why a simulation approach is appropriate. The system's boundaries, environment, and other such aspects of problem clarification are handled here.

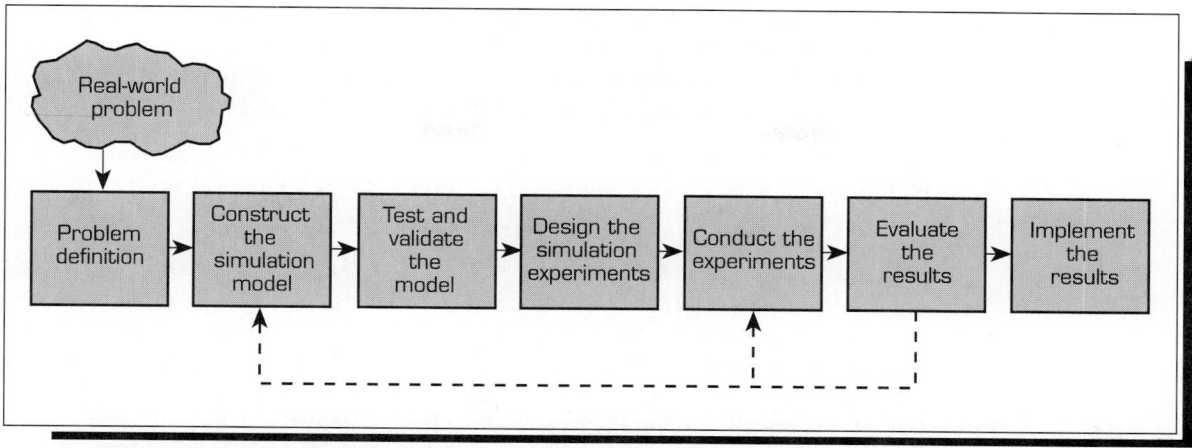

FIGURE 5.5 THE PROCESS OF SIMULATION

CONSTRUCTION OF THE SIMULATION MODEL

This step involves determination of the variables and their relationships, and data gathering. Often the process is described by a flowchart, and then a computer program is written.

TESTING AND VALIDATING THE MODEL

The simulation model must properly represent the system under study. Testing and validation ensure this.

DESIGN OF THE EXPERIMENT

Once the model has been proven valid, an experiment is designed. Determining how long to run the simulation is part of this step. There are two important and conflicting objectives: accuracy and cost. It is also prudent to identify typical (mean and median cases for random variables), best-case (e.g., low-cost, high-revenue), and worst-case (e.g., high-cost, low-revenue) scenarios. These help establish the ranges of the decision variables and environment in which to work and also assist in debugging the simulation model.

CONDUCTING THE EXPERIMENT

Conducting the experiment involves issues ranging from random-number generation to result presentation.

EVALUATING THE RESULTS

The results must be interpreted. In addition to standard statistical tools, sensitivity analyses can also be used.

IMPLEMENTATION

The implementation of simulation results involves the same issues as any other implementation. However, the chances of success are better because the manager is usually more involved in the simulation process than with other models. Higher levels of managerial involvement generally lead to higher levels of implementation success.

TYPES OF SIMULATION

PROBABILISTIC SIMULATION

In probabilistic simulation one or more of the independent variables (such as the demand in an inventory problem) are probabilistic. They follow certain probability distributions, which can be either discrete distributions or continuous distributions.

- *Discrete distributions* involve a situation with a limited number of events (or variables) that can take on only a finite number of values.
- *Continuous distributions* are situations with unlimited numbers of possible events that follow density functions such as the normal distribution.

The two types of distributions are shown in Table 5.5. Probabilistic simulation is conducted with the aid of a technique called *Monte Carlo,* which was used in the Opening Vignette situation.

TIME-DEPENDENT VERSUS TIME-INDEPENDENT SIMULATION

Time-independent refers to a situation in which it is not important to know exactly when the event occurred. For example, we may know that the demand for a certain product is three units per day, but we do not care *when* during the day the item is demanded. Or, in some situations, time may not be a factor in the simulation at all, such as in steady-state plant control design (Boswell, 1999). On the other hand, in waiting line problems, it is important to know the precise time of arrival (to know whether the customer will have to wait). This is a *time-dependent* situation.

SIMULATION SOFTWARE

There are hundreds of simulation packages for a variety of decision-making situations (Section 5.13).

VISUAL SIMULATION

The graphical display of computerized results, which may include animation, is one of the more successful developments in computer–human interaction and problem solving. We describe this in Section 5.12.

OBJECT-ORIENTED SIMULATION

There have been some recent advances in the area of developing simulation models using the object-oriented approach (Briccarello et al., 1995; Ninios et al., 1995; Yun and Choi, 1999). Yun and Choi (1999) describe an object-oriented simulation model for container-terminal operation analysis. Each piece of equipment at the terminal maps into an object representation in the simulation model. SIMPROCESS (CACI Products Company, www.caciasl.com) is an object-oriented process modeling tool that lets the user create a simulation model with screen-based objects. Unified modeling language (UML) is a modeling tool that was designed for object-oriented and object-based systems and applications. Since UML is object-oriented, it could be used in practice for modeling complex, real-time systems. UML is particularly well suited for modeling. A real-time system is a software system that maintains an ongoing, timely interaction with its environment, e.g., many DSS and information and communication systems (Selic, 1999).

TABLE 5.5   Discrete Versus Continuous Probability Distributions

Daily Demand	*Discrete Probability*	*Continuous Probability*
5	.10	Daily demand is
6	.15	normally distrib-
7	.30	uted with a mean
8	.25	of 7 and a stan-
9	.20	dard deviation of
		1.2.

SIMULATION EXAMPLES

We show an example of a spreadsheet-based economic order quantity simulation model and a spreadsheet simulation model for evaluating a simple cash-flow problem on this book's Web site. DSS in Action 5.6 describes a case study of applying simulation to IT network design. CACI Products Company now provides COMNET III, a simulation system specifically for analyzing these types of IT network design problems.

DSS IN ACTION 5.6

PACIFIC BELL USES SIMULATION TO DESIGN AN IT NETWORK

Decision support simulation software for networks and networked applications can be used to experiment with multiple what-if scenarios. Then, IT can determine a best solution before making blind commitments or sinking resources into large projects without a thorough understanding of the expected outcome. Simulations help IT determine how the infrastructure would react to a given scenario such as increased network traffic, new transport technologies, topology changes, and new prioritized applications like ERP and voice-over Internet protocol (IP). The value of a decision support tool is its ability to deliver reliable, timely, and verifiable data about result variables, leading to confident, resource-saving decisions—critical during initial IT system design and implementation, when trade-offs can be weighed and cost considerations examined before committing heavily to a project.

Pacific Bell, a subsidiary of SBC Communications, Inc. (SBC), recently collaborated with a large government agency in southern California to design a network to support more than 80,000 employees at hundreds of sites.

Throughout the southern California project, SBC and the government utilized a modeling and simulation tool from Washington, DC-based MIL 3 Inc. called IT DecisionGuru.

The challenge for the SBC/government team was to design a network backbone to link thousands of nodes at every site into a network capable of supporting data, video, and voice and to support future growth. The design team first built a baseline model of projected "typical" network activity. Then it used its simulation software to explore the relative performance gains offered by various architecture options. This process enabled the design team to *visualize* all relevant network performance indicators.

After running several simulations, it was determined that a network consisting of only ATM OC-3 links would have very low utilization. While perfectly acceptable from a performance perspective, it would be very expensive. But, a network with only T1 links performs poorly at a lower cost. The best solution combined the cost efficiency of T1 lines with the bandwidth of ATM links as the simulation indicated. This middle-of-the-road strategy saved a lot of money and avoided potentially costly impacts from poor performance.

The most critical issue was the sizing of the dedicated wide area network (WAN) links. There was a trade-off between overprovisioned service, for which excess capacity would cost hundreds of thousands of dollars unnecessarily, and underprovisioning, which could cause unacceptably poor network performance. By simulating the key decision elements, the SBC/government team designed an efficient architecture to handle anticipated bandwidth needs at an acceptable cost. Without sacrificing service levels, the government reduced its expected WAN costs by more than 25 percent, translating into millions of dollars saved per year.

SBC also benefited in much the same way that any internal IT organization can benefit from simulation. It built credibility with business decision makers by providing quantifiable data to support its recommendations, making government decision makers much more comfortable that SBC could deliver the service levels it promised.

Source: Based on S. Toborg and M. Cohen, "Benefits and Savings Accrue with Simulation," *Communications News,* Vol. 36, No. 9, Sept. 1999, pp. 34–36.

5.11 MULTIDIMENSIONAL MODELING—OLAP

The concept of multidimensionality was introduced in Chapter 4 from the data point of view. Here we discuss multidimensionality from a spreadsheet and analysis perspective.

The original spreadsheets were two-dimensional. Decision makers sometimes need to work with data with three or more dimensions. For example, sales data may be needed by region, by product, by month, and by salesperson all on the same screen. And such data need to be manipulated (e.g., by what-if analyses) or analyzed directly with standard tools, or automatically by data mining methods that attempt to identify relationships. This can be done with *multidimensional modeling tools*. Many data warehouses permit multidimensional access of data for analysis with multidimensional modeling systems. Most multidimensional analysis systems are embedded in online analytical processing (OLAP) systems.

The goal of OLAP is to capture the structure of real-world data and provide support to the decision maker. There is a natural coupling between data modeling, symbolic modeling, and the what-if analysis aspects of a decision support system (DSS). Koutsoukis et al. (1999) explain how OLAP manipulation and presentation of online data cubes relate to an underlying decision support model. They describe a way to create and use knowledge at the organizational level.

OLAP reports are interactive reports that are highly formatted, easily deployed, and effortless to use. They are especially effective for key performance indicator (KPI) reporting, business performance measurement reporting, and scorecard-style reporting—important metrics for decision makers who want a robust reporting environment in which to work (Cognos, 2000).

To illustrate **multidimensional modeling,** we show the results of a Cognos (www.cognos.com) PowerPlay multidimensional analysis run (interactively on the Web) in Figure 5.6. With PowerPlay, a nonprogrammer moves from one view of the data to another via a mouse click, selecting from a menu of dimensional choices. The user adjusts the cube dimensions by slicing and dicing, drilling down, and changing graphical views. Switching from data to charts and back can be done with the click of a button. A downloadable demo and several Web-running demos of PowerPlay are available on the Cognos Inc. Web site. Also see Cognos (2000).

EXAMPLE

The Multidimensional OLAP Sales Report is shown in Figure 5.6

Clicking on a dimension performs drill down. The display is automatically updated to reflect the action. Slicing is performed by selecting different dimensions to display. All selections are in drop-down boxes.

In Figure 5.6a, the entire data cube resulting from a query is shown. The set of dimensions are Years, Products, Geography, Customer Types, Margin Ranges, Revenue, and more (which are to the right but are not shown). The cross-tabulated display shows Revenue by Value for the two Years (rows) for the Products (columns), with totals for the rows and columns. Any two dimensions can be displayed in the slice by selecting a dimension from the drop down boxes. In Figure 5.6b, we show one available graphical display of the screen in Figure 5.6a. In Figure 5.6c, we show the results for the Environmental Line of Products by drilling down into the data. In Figure 5.6d, we have drilled deep into the data and show the results for Current Month and Water Purifiers only in North America. It is also possible to change the displayed amounts. For example, we can select Quantities Sold as Values rather than Revenue.

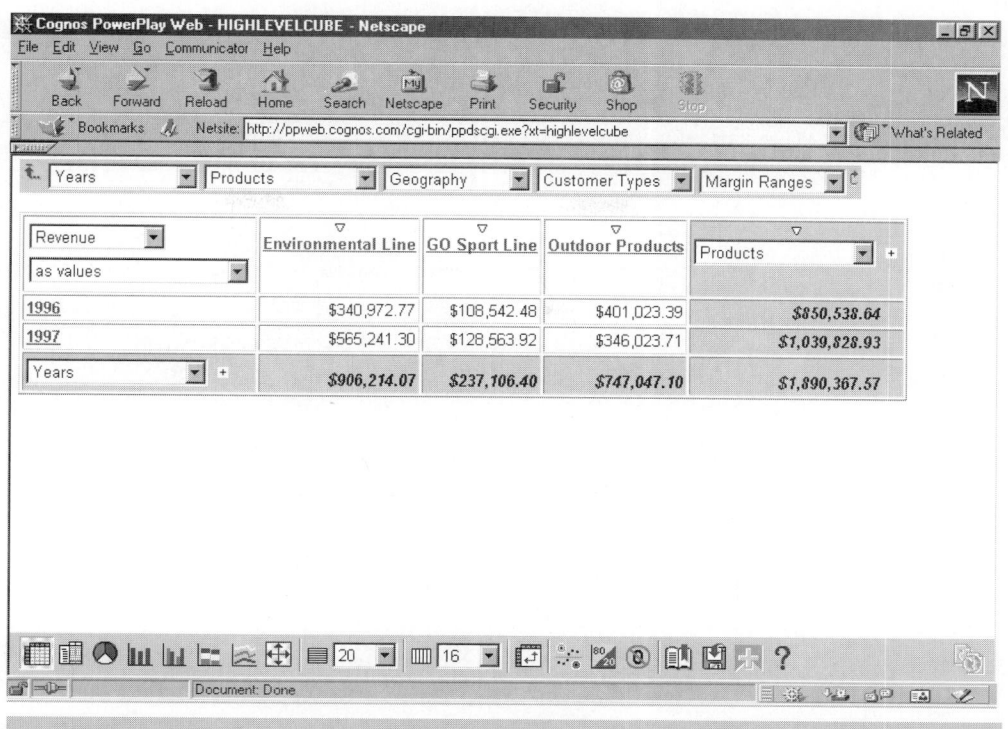

FIGURE 5.6A MULTIDIMENSIONAL OLAP SALES REPORT—ENTIRE DATA CUBE RESULTING FROM QUERY

Courtesy Cognos, Inc.

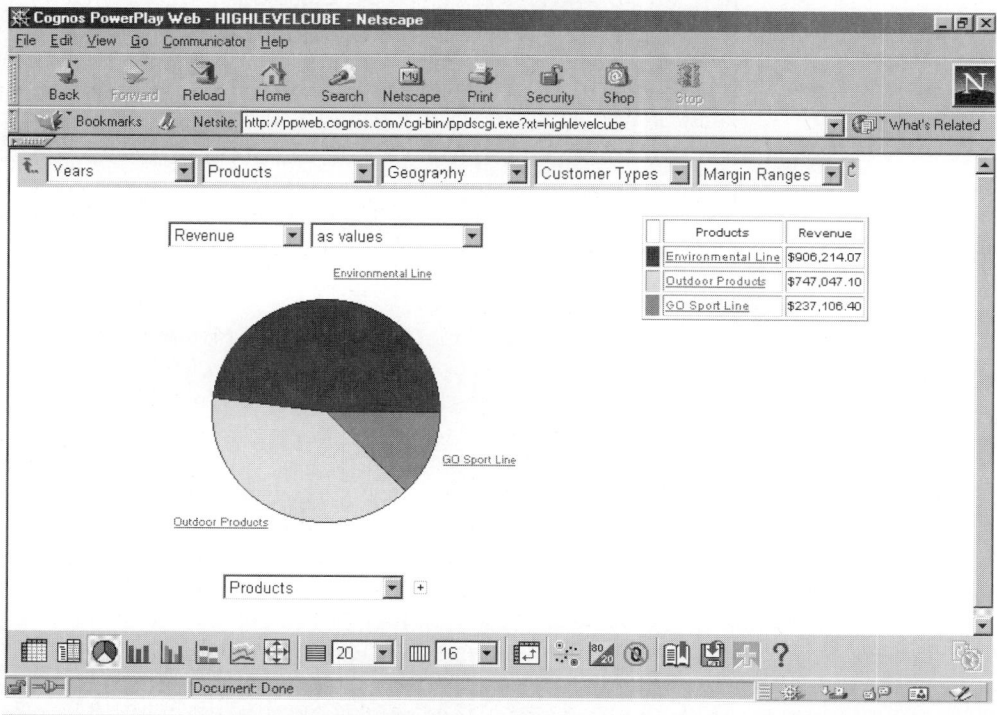

FIGURE 5.6B ONE AVAILABLE GRAPHICAL DISPLAY OF SCREEN IN FIGURE 5.6A

Courtesy Cognos, Inc.

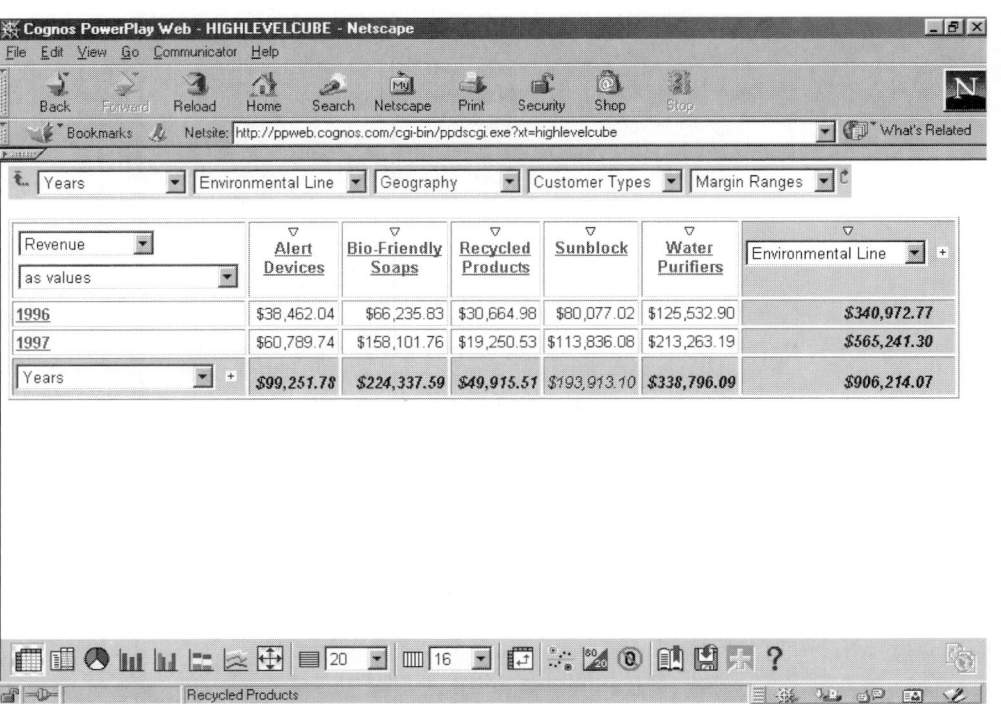

FIGURE 5.6C RESULTS FOR ENVIRONMENTAL LINE OF PRODUCTS

Courtesy Cognos, Inc.

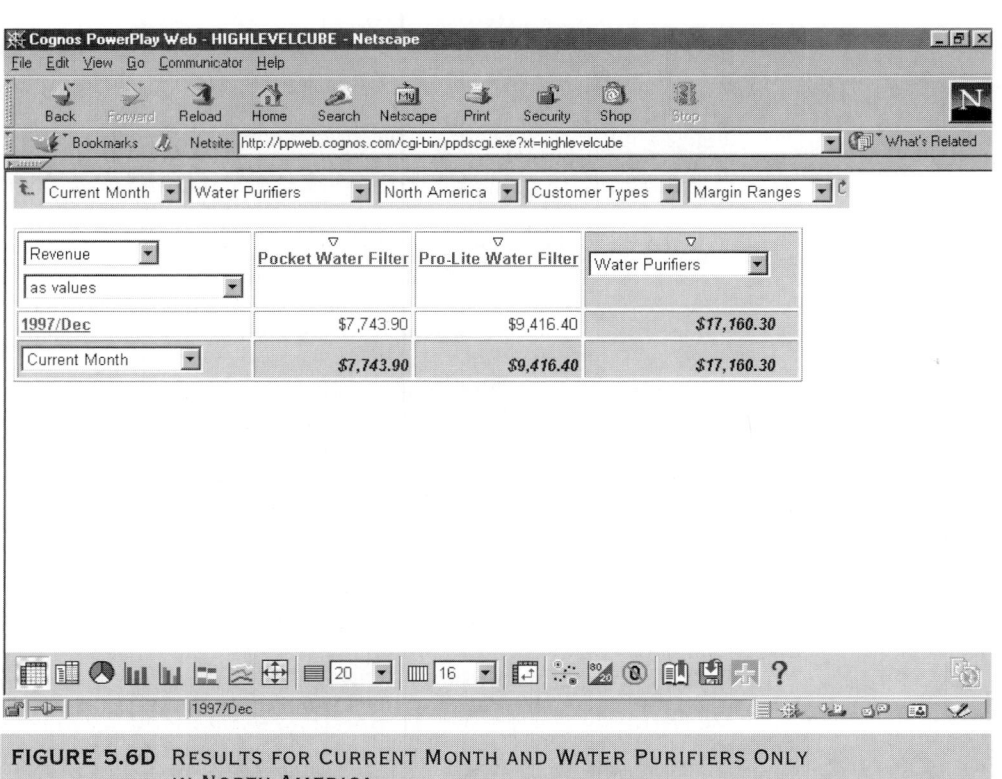

FIGURE 5.6D RESULTS FOR CURRENT MONTH AND WATER PURIFIERS ONLY
IN NORTH AMERICA

Courtesy Cognos, Inc.

OLAP is very effective, as illustrated by Del Taco in DSS in Action 5.7.

Many of the features of executive information systems (customized multiple-data views, drill down, data slice and dice) and other advanced graphically oriented systems have been incorporated into seamless operation in the current generation of OLAP and data mining systems. These tools also have modeling and optimization features, but they are typically transparent to the user, who is often not a trained specialist in applying the tools. In this way, a decision maker without experience with optimization or simulation methods can access powerful analytic methods without the help of a trained analyst. These methods are called **business intelligence tools.** Users simply access a data warehouse and direct the software to show the data in interesting ways and automatically build models to establish sought-after relationships among the data.

Many of these tools are available from database, ERP, data warehouse, and OLAP vendors. These systems include Visionary (Informix Corporation, www.informix.com), Broadbase (Broadbase Information System Inc., www.broadbase.com), BI/Suite (Hummingbird Communications Ltd., www.Humingbird.com), Aclue Decision Supportware (Decisionism, www.decisionism.com), Analytic Application Server (WhiteLight, www.whitelight.com), Decision Support Suite and Balanced Scorecard (Pilot Software Inc., www.pilotsw.com), Business Intelligence Product Suite (MicroStrategy, www.microstrategy.com), PowerPlay and Impromptu (Cognos Inc., www.cognos.com), and Intelligent Miner (IBM, www.ibm.com). Some are designed specifically to analyze and report on ERP data, for example, Baan Decision Support Solution (Baan Company, www.baan.com), Brio ONE including Brio Enterprise (Brio Technology Inc., www.brio.com), and Decision Master and Enterprise Performance Management (EPM)/(PeopleSoft, www.peoplesoft.com). Most of these systems use Web browser-based user interfaces.

DSS IN ACTION 5.7

DEL TACO SATISFIES MANAGERS' HUNGER FOR DATA WITH OLAP AND DSS MODELS

Even before Del Taco's financial turnaround, the firm wanted to analyze field labor, but there were some data integrity issues involving the individual units. Field reports did not always match reality. This problem was corrected with a unified data warehouse.

Working with top-level executives and field-level management, Del Taco's MIS group, headed by Dan Campbell, embarked on a phased approach to deliver a *decision support system* to let end users query a set of multidimensional databases through OLAP. The labor model was developed first. Using a dedicated server to run Hyperion Essbase OLAP tool from Hyperion Solutions Corporation, end users can query the database to compare salaries paid with hours worked and to quantify labor costs on a per-employee basis and segment them by day part. Campbell described the system as a kind of "labor optimization tool" because management can quickly learn when, for example, labor ex-

penses at one unit are trending up or down and when worker hours should be extended or shortened. Next, Campbell plans to expand the OLAP by developing and deploying a product model to let Del Taco analyze promotions and refine combo meal offerings to create "upsell" opportunities.

The product-mix module will help end users identify which menu items are selling best at which stores, during which day parts, and in which geographic areas. "Our marketing folks are very data-hungry," Campbell said. Fortunately, the OLAP system has satiated the area directors' hunger for reliable and more timely store-level data.

Source: Condensed and modified from E. Rubinstein, "Del Taco Taps OLAP System to Optimize Labor, Other Store-level Metrics," *Nation's Restaurant News,* Vol. 33, No. 20, May 17, 1999, p. 84.

As part of the efforts of software vendors to provide better visualization and analysis tools, several have replaced the spreadsheet with a view of the data from a data warehouse in any format that the user desires. With a Web portal interface, these systems can provide data as tables, maps, graphs, video, audio, landscapes, and so on. And the system itself recommends a format. Like other OLAP, analysis tools are transparent and are activated by the decision maker with the touch of a button. The system prepares the data in a format that the analysis tool needs. Visionary (Informix Corporation), along with its multidimensional spreadsheet, has many of these capabilities. Finally, Dimensional Media Associates (DMA) is developing a three-dimensional display that requires no special goggles. Multiplanar Volumetric Display is a room (like *Star Trek*'s holodeck). It could potentially assist financial analysts in visualizing trends based on enormous amounts of data. (*PC Magazine,* 2000). This could have some ramifications for the future of visual interactive modeling and simulation, which we discuss next.

5.12 VISUAL INTERACTIVE MODELING AND VISUAL INTERACTIVE SIMULATION

CONVENTIONAL SIMULATION

Simulation is a well-established, useful method for gaining insight into complex MSS situations. However, simulation does not usually allow decision makers to see how a solution to a complex problem evolves over (compressed) time, nor can they interact with it. Simulation generally reports statistical results at the end of a set of experiments. Decision makers are thus not an integral part of simulation development and experimentation, and their experience and judgment cannot be used directly in the study. If the simulation results do not match the intuition or judgment of the decision maker, a *confidence gap* in the use of the model occurs.

One of the most exciting developments in computer graphics is **visual interactive modeling (VIM)** (see DSS in Action 5.8). The technique has been used for DSS in the area of operations management with great success (Chau and Bell, 1994, 1996). Decision makers who had used VIM in their decision making were surveyed and found to have a high level of support for and interest in these models (Bell et al., 1999).

This technique has several names and variations, including *visual interactive problem solving, visual interactive modeling,* and *visual interactive simulation.*

Visual interactive modeling uses computer graphic displays to present the impact of different management decisions. It differs from regular graphics in that the user can adjust the decision-making process and can see the results of the intervention. A visual model is a graphic used as an integral part of decision making or problem solving, not just as a communication device. The VIM displays the effect of different decisions in graphic form on a computer screen as was done through the GIS in the P&G supply chain redesign through optimization in Case Application 5.1. Some people respond better to graphical displays, and this type of interaction can help a manager learn about his or her decision-making situation.

VIM can represent a static or a dynamic system. Static models display a visual image of the result of one decision alternative at a time. Dynamic models display systems that evolve over time, and the evolution is represented by animation. A snapshot example of a generated animated display of traffic at an intersection from the Orca Visual Simulation Environment (Orca Computer Inc., Blacksburg, VA, www.orcacomputer.com) is shown

---

DSS IN ACTION 5.8

VISUAL INTERACTIVE SIMULATION: U.S. ARMY HOSPITAL USES ANIMATED SIMULATION OF A FAMILY PRACTICE CLINIC

The U.S. Army Hospital in Heidelberg, Germany, used animated simulation to develop viable alternatives for their family practice clinic. The clinic was attempting to examine different staffing alternatives, determine the best patient and staff flow scheme, and increase productivity to provide sufficient capacity. An animated simulation model was developed. The current environment as represented by the status quo model could not provide the needed capacity of outpatient visits. Alternative models were developed, two of which were good possibilities. The two alternative models, an all-physician model (the "physician model") and a combination model with both physicians and nonphysician providers (the "combo model"), were run and compared, and neither could handle the patient load. A process change in parallel patient screening was developed to increase patient throughput and to increase capacity. Then both models could meet clinic capacity requirements, both in the newly planned clinic and in the current one. Based on the simulation, the physician and combo models were selected for the health care operation in a phased-in plan from the former to the latter.

The simulation gave the decision makers insight into provider and support staff use rates, down time,

and small but significant process improvements. The all-physician model was recommended as a short-term arrangement after considering cost, supervisory issues, and provider availability. Changes at the clinic were to take place in the near future, and phasing in the nonphysician providers would take some time.

Although the physician model was selected as a short-term arrangement to meet the needs of the community and health care system, the simulation model showed that much more work and evaluation of patient wait times had to be conducted to decrease the wait for customers. Management had determined the number of physicians and staff members needed to meet patient capacity needs, the necessary size of the waiting area, the necessary provider scheduling changes, and the process changes necessary to meet the capacity requirement, patient expectations, and organizational goals via simulation. The move to the renovated area was successful and had the additional results of empaneling the beneficiaries in the community. A migration plan was adopted based on further simulation runs.

Source: Based on Ledlow et al. (1999).

---

in Figure 5.7. The Orca Web site shows several animations that were generated by its simulation system.

VISUAL INTERACTIVE SIMULATION

Visual simulation is one of the most exciting dynamic VIMs. It is a very important DSS technique because simulation is a major approach in problem solving. **Visual interactive simulation (VIS)** allows the end user to watch the progress of the simulation model in an animated form on graphics displays.

The basic philosophy of VIS is that decision makers can interact with the simulated model and watch the results develop over time (see the online Web demos at Orca Computer Inc., www.orcacomputer.com). The user can try different decision strategies online. Enhanced learning, both about the problem and about the impact of the alternatives tested, can and does occur. Decision makers can also contribute to model validation. They will have more confidence in its use because of their own participation in its development and use. They are also in a position to use their knowledge and experience to interact with the model to explore alternative strategies.

Ledlow et al. (1999) describe how the U.S. Army Hospital in Heidelberg, Germany, used animated simulation to develop viable alternatives for their family practice clinic (see DSS in Action 5.8).

FIGURE 5.7 EXAMPLE OF A GENERATED IMAGE OF TRAFFIC AT AN INTERSECTION FROM THE ORCA VISUAL SIMULATION ENVIRONMENT

Courtesy of Orca Computer, Inc., Blacksburg, VA

Animated VIS software systems are provided by Orca Computer, Inc., GPSS/PC (Minuteman Software), and VisSim (Visual Solutions). See this book's Web site (www.prenhall.com/turban) for a representative list of VIS software with animation. The latest visual simulation technology is coupled with the concept of virtual reality, where an artificial world is created for a number of purposes, from training to entertainment to viewing data in an artificial landscape.

VISUAL INTERACTIVE MODELS AND DSS

VIM in DSS has been used in several operations management decisions (Chau and Bell, 1996) (see this book's Web site). The method consists of priming a visual interactive model of a plant (or company) with its current status. The model then runs rapidly on a computer, allowing management to observe how a plant is likely to operate in the future.

Waiting-line management (queuing) is a good example of VIM. Such a DSS usually computes several measures of performance (such as waiting time in the system) for the various decision alternatives. Complex waiting-line problems require simulation. VIM can display the size of the waiting line as it changes during the simulation runs and can also graphically present the answers to what-if questions regarding changes in input variables.

The VIM approach can also be used in conjunction with artificial intelligence. Integration of the two techniques adds several capabilities that range from the ability to build systems graphically to learning about the dynamics of the system.

High-speed parallel computers such as those made by Silicon Graphics Inc. (CA) make large-scale, complex, animated simulations feasible in real time (the movie *Toy Story* and its sequel were essentially long VIMs).

General-purpose commercial dynamic VIM software is readily available. For a representative list of packages with animation, see this book's Web site. Also see The IMAGE Society Inc. Web site, www.public.asu.edu, and the Society for Computer Simulation International Web site, www.scs.org).

PHYSICAL SIMULATION

Winarchick and Caldwell (1997) describe a physical simulation approach to manufacturing design problems. This particular procedure involves building workstation models and testing them out, rather than constructing the real layout—a potentially expensive proposition. If the layout is deemed inefficient, it can be adjusted quickly and easily with the right building blocks. This approach has been used in a number of other fields. For example, helicopter simulators, spacecraft simulators, and other flight simulators have been constructed as physical representations (from the point of view of the pilot) of the real craft. Also, many materials processing operations have pilot plants to test ideas before they are moved to full production.

5.13 QUANTITATIVE SOFTWARE PACKAGES—OLAP

Some DSS tools offer several built-in subroutines for constructing quantitative models in areas such as statistics, financial analysis, accounting, and management science. These models can be called up by one command, such as

- *MOVAVG.* This function calculates a moving average estimated forecast of a time series of data. It might be embedded in a production planning model to generate demand.
- *NPV.* This function calculates the net present value of a series of future cash flows for a given interest rate. It could be part of a make-versus-buy model.

In addition, many DSS tools can easily interface with powerful standard quantitative stand-alone software packages. A DSS builder can increase his or her productivity by using **quantitative software packages** (preprogrammed models sometimes called "ready-made"), rather than "reinvent the wheel." Some of these models are building blocks of other quantitative models. For example, a regression model can be part of a forecasting model that supports a linear programming planning model (as in the P&G Case Application 5.1 and the IMERYS Case Application 5.3). Thus, a complicated model can easily be integrated with many sets of data. The Lingo modeling language described earlier for optimization problems can be designed with a SET definition section and a DATA section. The sets and data can be fed from a database, while the actual Lingo model lines do not explicitly state any dimension or data aspects. While spreadsheets have the same capability, data must be carefully inserted. For a comprehensive resource directory of these types of systems, see *OR/MS Today* (1999).

STATISTICAL PACKAGES

Several statistical functions are built into various DSS tools; for example, typical functions are mean, median, variance, standard deviation, kurtosis, *t*-test, chi-square, various types of regression (linear, polynomial, and stepwise) correlations, and analysis of variance.

Regression analysis is a powerful statistical curve-fitting technique. An example of an SPSS run that quickly analyzed a set of data can be found on this book's Web site. The run was triggered with a single click of a button, the results were clearly delineated in the report, and the report was automatically formatted. These features can readily enhance a DSS developer's capabilities.

More power can be obtained from stand-alone statistical packages, some of which can be readily interfaced with spreadsheets (Excel). Typical packages include SPSS and Systat (SPSS Inc., Chicago, IL, www.spss.com), Minitab (Minitab Inc., State College, PA, www.minitab.com), SAS (SAS Institute Inc., Cary, NC, www.sas.com), and TSP (TSP International, Palo Alto CA, www.tspintl.com). StatPac Inc. (www.statpac.com Minneapolis, MN) includes survey analysis software in their StatPac package. Most spreadsheets also contain sophisticated statistical functions and routines.

Now statistical software is considered more a decision-making tool than a sophisticated analytical tool in the decision-making process. It is even embedded in data mining and OLAP tools, and so the user is unaware that sophisticated statistical methods are being used. This subtle change in the user's focus has occurred because of the maturity of well-accepted technology and the low cost and high performance of computers. This has lead to a greater acceptance of statistical methodologies (Studt, 1998).

MANAGEMENT SCIENCE (ANALYTICAL MODELING) PACKAGES

There are several hundred management science packages on the market for models ranging from inventory control to project management. Several DSS generators include optimization and simulation capabilities. Lists of representative management science packages can be found in management science publications (such as *OR/MS Today* and INFORMS OnLine, www.informs.org). Lionheart Publishing Inc. (www.lionhrtpub.com) has software surveys on its Web site on statistical analysis, linear programming, simulation, decision analysis, nonlinear programming, forecasting, vehicle routing, and spreadsheet add-ins. QSB+ (Chang, 1997) is an example of a fairly comprehensive, and robust academic management science package. Lindo and Lingo (Lindo Systems Inc.), IBM's Optimization System Library (OSL), and CPLEX (CPLEX Optimization Inc.) are commercial ones. Simulation packages include GPSS (and GPSS/PC), ProModel (ProModel Corporation), SLAM (Pritsker Corporation), and SIMULA and SIMSCRIPT (CACI Products Company). Many academic packages are available directly from their authors and via the Web (see the Society for Computer Simulation International Web site, www.scs.org).

REVENUE MANAGEMENT (YIELD MANAGEMENT)

A new and exciting application area for DSS modeling has developed along with the service industries. Revenue management (yield management) involves models that attempt to stratify an organization's customers, estimate demands, establish prices for each category of customer, and dynamically model all. Until a flight takes off, an airline seat is available, but once the flight leaves, the seat cannot be inventoried. Through revenue management methods, an airline might have as many as 200 different fares for its coach seats on a single flight. Part of revenue management involves knowing when to turn away a customer because a "better" (higher-fare-paying) customer will appear with a significantly high enough probability. See Boyd (1998) and Kelly (1999) for discussions of revenue management in the airline industry. For an example in the hotel industry, see Baker and Collier (1999).

OTHER SPECIFIC DSS APPLICATIONS

The number of DSS application software products is continually increasing. A number of these are spreadsheet add-ins such as What'sBest! (linear programming, Lindo Systems Inc., Chicago, IL, www.lindo.com), Solver (linear programming, Frontline Systems Inc., Incline Village, NV, www.frontsys.com), @Risk (simulation, Palisade Corporation, Newfield, NY, www.palisade.com), BrainCel (neural network, Promised Land Technologies Inc., New Haven, CT, promland.com), and Evolver (genetic algorithm, Palisade Corporation). Sometimes it is necessary to modify the source code of the package to fit the decision maker's needs. Some actually produce source code from the development language. For example, many neural network packages can produce a deployable version of their internal user-developed models in the C programming language. Examples are listed on this book's Web site (www.prenhall.com/turban).

5.14 MODEL BASE MANAGEMENT

In theory, a **model base management system (MBMS)** is a software package with capabilities similar to those of a DBMS. Although there are dozens of commercial DBMS packages, unfortunately there are no comprehensive model base management packages on the market. Limited MBMS capabilities are provided by some spreadsheets and other model-based DSS tools and languages.

There are no standardized MBMS for a number of reasons:

- While there are standard model classes (like standard database structures: relational, hierarchical, network, object-oriented), there are too many of them, and each is structured differently (e.g., linear programming versus regression analysis).
- Each model class may have several approaches for solving problems in the class, depending on problem structure, size, shape, and data. For example, any linear programming problem can be solved by the simplex method, but there is also the interior point method. Method specializations can work better than the standard methods if they match the model.
- Each organization uses models somewhat differently.
- MBMS capabilities (e.g., selecting which model to use, how to solve it, and what parameter values to use) require expertise and reasoning capabilities, which can be made available in expert systems and other artificial intelligence approaches.

An effective model base management system makes the structural and algorithmic aspects of model organization and associated data processing transparent to users of the MBMS (e.g., P&G Case Application 5.1; IMERYS Case Application 5.3) (Orman, 1998). The MBMS should also handle model integration (model to model integration; like a forecasting model feeding a planning model; data to model integration; and vice versa).

Some desirable MBMS capabilities include the following:

- *Control.* The DSS user should be provided with a spectrum of control. The system should support both fully automated and manual model selection, depending on which seems most helpful for an intended application. The user should also be able to use subjective information.

- *Flexibility.* The DSS user should be able to develop part of the solution using one approach and then be able to switch to another modeling approach if desired.
- *Feedback.* The MBMS should provide sufficient feedback to enable the user to know the state of the problem-solving process at any time.
- *Interface.* The DSS user should feel comfortable with the specific model from the MBMS in use. The user should not have to laboriously supply inputs.
- *Redundancy reduction.* Sharing models and eliminating redundant storage as in a data warehouse can accomplish this.
- *Increased consistency.* This can occur when decision makers share the same model and data (designed into the IMERYS DSS).

To provide these capabilities, it appears that an MBMS design must allow the DSS user to

- *Access and retrieve existing models*
- *Exercise and manipulate existing models,* including model instantiation, model selection, model synthesis, and the provision of suitable model outputs
- *Store existing models,* including model representation, model abstraction, and physical and logical model storage
- *Maintain existing models* as appropriate for changing conditions
- *Maintain standard cases* for models as appropriate for changing conditions
- *Construct new models* with reasonable effort when they are needed, usually by building new models using existing models as building blocks.

There are a number of additional requirements for these capabilities. For example, there must be appropriate communication and data changes among models that have been combined. In addition, it must be possible to analyze and interpret the results obtained from using a model in a standard way. This can be accomplished in a number of ways (e.g., by OLAP or by expert systems).

MODELING LANGUAGES

There are a number of specialized modeling languages that act as front ends to software that actually performs optimization or simulation. They essentially front-end the working or algorithmic code and assist the manager in developing and managing models. Some popular mathematical programming modeling languages include Lingo, AMPL, and GAMS.

RELATIONAL MODEL BASE MANAGEMENT SYSTEM

As is the case with a relational view of data, in a **relational model base management system (RMBMS)** a model is viewed as a virtual file or virtual relation. Three operations are needed for relational completeness in model management: execution, optimization, and sensitivity analysis.

OBJECT-ORIENTED MODEL BASE AND ITS MANAGEMENT

Using an object-oriented DBMS construct, it is possible to build an **object-oriented model base management system (OOMBS)** that maintains logical independence between the model base and the other DSS components, facilitating intelligent and stabilized integration of the components. Essentially, all the object-oriented concepts embedded in the GUI can apply to model management. See Briccarello et al. (1995) and Ninios et al. (1995).

MODELS FOR DATABASE AND MIS DESIGN AND THEIR MANAGEMENT

Models describing efficient database and MIS design are useful in that the deployed systems will function optimally. These models include data diagrams and entity-relationship diagrams, which are managed by computer-aided systems engineering (CASE). They graphically portray how data are organized and flow in a database design and work much like the situation described in the Opening Vignette. A model is developed to describe and evaluate an untried alternative. Then, when the decision is implemented, the real system behaves as if the decision makers have had many years of experience in running the new system with the implemented alternative. Thus, the model building and evaluation are training tools for the DSS team members. Models for database and MIS design include those of Cerpa (1995) and Kilov and Cuthbert (1995). Also see Cook (1996).

❖ CHAPTER HIGHLIGHTS

- Models play a major role in DSS. There are several types of models.
- Models can be either static (a single snapshot of a situation) or dynamic (multiperiod).
- Analysis is conducted under assumed certainty (most desirable), risk, or uncertainty (least desirable).
- Influence diagrams graphically show the interrelationships of a model. They can be used to enhance the presentation of spreadsheet technology.
- Influence diagram software can also generate and solve the model.
- Spreadsheets have many capabilities, including what-if analysis, goal seeking, programming, database management, optimization, and simulation.
- Decision tables and decision trees can model and solve simple decision-making problems.
- The Analytic Hierarchy Process (e.g., Expert Choice software) is a leading method for solving multicriteria decision-making problems.
- Mathematical programming is an important optimization method.
- Linear programming is the most common mathematical programming method. It attempts to find an optimal allocation of limited resources under organizational constraints.
- The major parts of a linear programming model are the objective function, the decision variables, and the constraints.
- Heuristic programming involves problem solving using general rules or intelligent search.
- Simulation is a widely used DSS approach involving experimentation with a model that represents the real decision-making situation.
- Simulation can deal with more complex situations than optimization, but it does not guarantee an optimal solution.
- Multidimensional modeling through OLAP allows users to easily create models, display the results in different ways, and conduct sensitivity analysis.
- Many DSS development tools include built-in quantitative models (financial, statistical) or they can easily interface with such models.
- Visual interactive modeling is an implementation of the graphical user interface (GUI). It is usually combined with simulation and animation.
- Visual interactive simulation (VIS) allows a decision maker to interact directly with the model.
- VIS can show simulation results in an easily understood manner.

- Model base management systems perform tasks analogous to those performed by DBMS.
- Unlike DBMS, there are no standard MBMS because of the many classes of models, their use, and the many techniques for solving them.
- Artificial intelligence techniques can be effectively used in MBMS.
- Models are useful for creating information systems.

❖ KEY WORDS

- business intelligence tools
- certainty
- complexity
- decision analysis
- decision table
- decision tree
- dynamic models
- environmental scanning and analysis
- forecasting
- genetic algorithms
- heuristic programming

- heuristics
- influence diagram
- linear programming (LP)
- mathematical programming
- model base management system (MBMS)
- multidimensional modeling
- multiple goals
- object-oriented model base management system (OOMBMS)
- optimal solution
- quantitative software packages

- regression analysis
- relational model base management system (RMBMS)
- risk
- risk analysis
- simulation
- static models
- tabu search
- uncertainty
- visual interactive modeling (VIM)
- visual interactive simulation (VIS)
- what-if analysis

❖ QUESTIONS FOR REVIEW

1. What are the major types of models used in DSS?
2. Distinguish between a static model and a dynamic model. Give an example of each.
3. What is an influence diagram? What is it used for?
4. What is an spreadsheet?
5. What makes a spreadsheet so conducive to the development of DSS?
6. What is an expected value?
7. What is a decision table?
8. What is a decision tree?
9. What is an allocation problem?
10. List and briefly discuss the three major components of linear programming.
11. What is the role of heuristics in modeling?
12. Define visual simulation and compare it to conventional simulation.
13. Define multidimensional modeling.
14. Define visual interactive modeling (VIM).
15. Define multidimensional spreadsheets and explain why OLAP systems have them embedded within.
16. What is a model base management system?
17. Explain why the development of a generic model base management system is so difficult.

❖ QUESTIONS FOR DISCUSSION

1. What is the relationship between environmental analysis and problem identification?

2. Identify in the literature a misapplication of a model, a fallacy in modeling, a disastrous application, or a modeling misconception. Describe what went wrong, as well as what it would take to build a successful decision model in this case.

3. What is the difference between an optimistic approach and a pessimistic approach to decision making under assumed uncertainty?

4. Explain why solving problems under uncertainty sometimes involves assuming that the problem is to be solved under conditions of risk.

5. Explain how a problem under uncertainty can be transformed into one under certainty or risk.

6. Explain the differences between static and dynamic models. How can one evolve into the other?

7. Explain why an influence diagram can be viewed as a model of a model.

8. Excel is probably the most popular spreadsheet software for the PC. Why? What can you do with this package that makes it so attractive?

9. Review the latest capabilities of Excel. Compare them with the capabilities of an ideal DSS generator as discussed in Chapter 3. How wide is the gap? Be specific.

10. What is the difference between decision analysis with a single goal and decision analysis with multiple goals (criteria)?

11. Why are allocation problems so difficult to solve?

12. Explain how linear programming can solve allocation problems.

13. What are the advantages of using a spreadsheet package to create and solve linear programming models? What are the disadvantages?

14. What are the advantages of using a linear programming package to create and solve linear programming models? What are the disadvantages?

15. Give examples of three heuristics with which you are familiar.

16. Describe the general process of simulation.

17. List some of the major advantages of simulation over optimization.

18. What are the advantages of using a spreadsheet package to perform simulation studies? What are the disadvantages?

19. List some advantages of optimization over simulation.

20. Compare the methodology of simulation to Simon's four-phase model of decision making. Does the methodology of simulation map directly into Simon's model? Explain.

21. Compare an OLAP system with multidimensional data and analysis views to a standard spreadsheet. What are the major advantages of the former? Are there any disadvantages?

22. What features make an OLAP system useful for decision makers?

23. Several computer games, such as Flight Simulator, DOOM, and GATO, can be considered visual simulation. Explain why.

24. Explain why VIM is particularly helpful in implementing recommendations derived by computers.

25. Explain why it might be useful to construct a physical interactive simulation of a system.

26. Compare the linear programming features available in spreadsheets (e.g., Excel Solver) to those in quantitative software packages (e.g., Lindo).

27. There are hundreds of DBMS packages on the market. Explain why there are no packages for model base management systems (MBMS).

28. Does Simon's four-phase decision-making model fit into most of the modeling methodologies described? How or how not?

❖ **EXERCISES**

1. Create the spreadsheet models shown in Figures 5.3 and 5.4.
   a. What is the effect of a change in the interest rate from 8 percent to 10 percent in the spreadsheet model shown in Figure 5.3?
   b. For the original model in Figure 5.3, what interest rate is required to decrease the monthly payments by 20 percent? What change in the loan amount would have the same effect?
   c. In the spreadsheet shown in Figure 5.4, what is the effect of a prepayment of $200 per month? What prepayment would be necessary to pay off the loan in 25 years instead of 30 years?

2. *Class exercise.* Build a predictive model. Everyone in the class should write their weight, height, and gender on a piece of paper (no names please!). If the sample is too small (you will need about 20–30 students), add more students from another class.
   a. Create a regression (causal) model for height versus weight for the whole class, and one for each gender. If possible, use a statistical package like SPSS and a spreadsheet (Excel) and compare their ease of use. Also, produce a scatterplot of the three sets of data.
   b. Do the relationships appear linear (based on the plots and the regressions)? How accurate were the models (how close to 1 is the value of R^2)?
   c. Does weight *cause* height, does height *cause* weight, or does neither really *cause* the other? Explain.
   d. How can a regression model like this be used in building or aircraft design? Diet or nutrition selection? A longitudinal study (say, over 50 years) to determine whether students are getting heavier and not taller, or vice versa?

3. It has been argued in a number of different venues that a higher education level indicates a greater average income. The real question for a college student might be, Should I stay in school?
   a. Using U.S. Census data from Census Tables P8 and P9 (USSTXP8.XLS and USSTXP9.XLS) for the 50 states and Washington, DC, develop a linear regression model (causal forecasting) to see whether this relationship is true. (Note that some data massaging might be necessary.) How high was the R^2 value (a measure of quality of fit)? Don't forget to scatterplot the data.
   b. Does the relationship appear to be linear? If not, check a statistics book and try a nonlinear function. How well does the nonlinear function perform?
   c. From this study, do you believe that a higher average education level tends to "cause" a higher average income? Explain. Which five states have the highest incomes, and which five states have the highest average education levels?
   d. If you have studied (or will study) neural networks, using the same data, build a neural network prediction model and compare it to your statistical results.

4. Set up spreadsheet models for the decision table models of Section 5.7 and solve them.

5. *Model building.*
   a. Construct an Excel spreadsheet version of the model represented by the influence diagram in Figure 5.1. Set AMOUNT USED IN ADVERTISING = 10000, UNIT COST = 10, UNIT PRICE = 20, and FIXED COST = 50,000.
   b. Keep everything else constant and set AMOUNT USED IN ADVERTISING to be random: normally distributed with a mean of 10,000 and a standard deviation of 1,000. Do 10 runs and compute the mean and standard deviation of the runs. After each run, copy the value of the result to another location in the spreadsheet.
   c. Implement the random run in the Excel add-in @Risk (you can download a demo from the Palisade Corporation Web site, www.palisade.com). What parameters worked best? Try different values for AMOUNT USED IN ADVERTISING.

    d. Make the random model dynamic. Set up the model over 10 years (1 year is defined previously) and set UNIT COST to increase 5 percent per year, UNIT PRICE to increase 7 percent per year, FIXED COST to increase 5 percent in the first year and 9 percent every year thereafter, AMOUNT USED IN ADVERTISING to increase 10 percent per year, and the discount rate to 8 percent. The decision variable is AMOUNT USED IN ADVERTISING in each year.

    e. Set up the above models and solve them in DecisionPro (if available), starting with developing the influence diagram structure. Compare the DecisionPro approach with those of Excel and @Risk.

6. Your client is considering an investment of $1,000 in a new product venture that will cause an immediate increase of $400 in the client's annual gross sales. It is assumed that the usefulness of this new product will end after 5 years, that its sales will increase by 15 percent per year for years 2 and 4, and that sales in the final or fifth year will be half those of year 4. Although this illustrative exercise involves only a few trivial calculations, use formulas throughout your model that could easily be extended over more time, with more complex relationships, thus showing the power of spreadsheets.

    The incremental variable costs for this new product are estimated at 40 percent of sales. The estimated incremental annual fixed costs begin at $30 for year 1, increase by $5 during each of the remaining 4 years of the new product's useful life, and then end. The initial investment, all during year 1, includes $400 of expenses that are immediately deductible from the firm's taxable profits. The remaining $600 of the investment is capitalized and charged out as depreciation expense over several years, starting during year 1. The income tax rate applicable to the incremental net profit contribution of this new product is 45 percent for all years and all amounts. Because a reported accounting loss on this new product reduces other taxable profits, a cash savings on taxes payable of this same percentage will occur for years that show an accounting loss.

    a. Develop a spreadsheet model for these proposed expenses, taxes, and net profit for each of the 5 years. Assume the $600 capitalized part of the investment is depreciated in equal amounts ($150 per year) over years 1–4.

    b. Now extend the spreadsheet model of part (a) to include the incremental cash flow for each of the 5 years and the cumulative cash flow for each year. Cash flow includes all investments, expenses, and taxes as outflows, and revenues as inflows.

    c. Extend part (b) to show the net present value, at a 20 percent annual discount factor, of the incremental cash flow for this proposed 5-year investment venture. If possible, also show the internal rate of return, or yield, of this investment.

    d. The time period and calculation method for charging the depreciation expense of an investment against incremental taxable income can influence the cash-flow pattern, and hence the attractiveness, of an investment. Extend the spreadsheet of part (c) to examine the impact on periodic net cash flow and on the total net present value and internal rate of return of the following different depreciation options:

        i. Current option of equal allocation of the $600 total over 4 years, that is, a straight-line depreciation schedule over 4 years.

        ii. Then show straight-line depreciation over 5 years.

        iii. And show straight-line depreciation over 3 years.

        iv. Finally, use the sum-of-year's-digits method over 4 years. Notice that the digits 1, 2, 3, and 4 sum to 10; hence first-year depreciation is 4/10 of the total capitalized investment, and the following years are 3/10, 2/10, and 1/10, respectively.

7. Many managers know that a small percentage of customers contribute to most of their sales. Similarly, much of the wealth in the world is concentrated in the hands of a few. This phenomenon is called the 80-20 rule, the A-B-C, and the value volume, and it is attributed to the famous economist Pareto. How can this phenomenon be used in modeling? What kind of approach is this—optimization, simulation, or heuristic?

8. Assume that you know that there is one irregular coin (either lighter or heavier) among 12. Using a two-pan scale, you must find that coin (is it lighter or heavier?) in no more than three tests. Solve this problem and explain the weighing strategy that you use. What approach to problem solving is used in this case?

9. Use a roadmap of the United States (or your own country). Starting from where you are now, identify a location on the other side and plot out a route to go from here to there. What (heuristic) rules did you use in selecting your route? How does your route compare to published distances (if available) between the locations?

10. Use Expert Choice software to select your next car. Evaluate cars on ride (from poor to great), looks (from attractive to ugly), and acceleration (from seconds to 60 mph). Consider three final cars on your list and develop each of the items in parts (a)–(e).
   a. A problem hierarchy
   b. A comparison of the importance of the criteria against the goal
   c. A comparison of the alternative cars for each criterion
   d. An overall ranking (a synthesis of leaf nodes with respect to the goal)
   e. A sensitivity analysis
   f. Maintain the inconsistency index lower than 0.1. If you initially had an inconsistency index greater than 0.1, what caused it to be that high? Would you really buy the car you selected? Why or why not?
   g. Develop a spreadsheet model using estimated preference weights and estimates for the intangible items, each on a scale from 1 to 10 for each car. Compare the conclusions reached with this method to those found using the Expert Choice model. Which one more accurately captures your judgments and why?

11. Build an Expert Choice model to select the next president of the United States (if it is not an election year or you do not live in the United States, use a relevant election). Whom did you choose? Did your solution match your expectations?

12. *Job Selection using Expert Choice.* You are in the job market (use your imagination if necessary). List the names of four or five different companies that have offered you a job (or from which you expect to get an offer). (As an alternative, your instructor may assign graduate or undergraduate program selection.) Write down all the factors that may influence your decision as to which job offer you will accept. Such factors may include geographic location, salary, benefits, taxes, school system (if you have children), and potential for career advancement. Some of these factors (criteria, attributes) may have subcriteria. For instance, location may be subdivided further into climate, urban concentration, cost of living, and so on.
   If you do not yet have a salary figure associated with a job offer, you should guess a reasonable figure. Perhaps your classmates can help you determine realistic figures.
   a. Model this problem in a spreadsheet (Excel) using some kind of weighted average methodology (you set the criteria weights first) (see the current Rand-McNally *Places Rated Almanac* for an example).
   b. Construct an Expert Choice model for your decision problem and use the pairwise comparisons to arrive at the best job opportunity.
   c. Compare the two approaches. Do they yield the same results? Why or why not?
   d. Write a short report (one or two typed pages) explaining the results, including those of the weighted average methodology, and for Expert Choice, explain each criterion, subcriterion (if any), and alternative. Describe briefly which op-

tions and capabilities of Expert Choice you used in your analysis and show the numerical results of your analysis. For this purpose, you may want to include printouts of your AHP tree, but make sure you circle and explain the items of interest on the printouts. Discuss the nature of the trade-offs you encountered during the evaluation process. You may want to include a meaningful sensitivity analysis of the results (optional).

To think about: Was the Expert Choice analysis helpful in structuring your preferences? Do you think it will be a helpful aid in your actual decision-making process? Comment on all these issues in your report.

13. For the last few multicriteria decision making exercises, set each up and solve it using Web-Hipre (www.hipre.hut.fi, Systems Analysis Laboratory, Helsinki University of Technology, Helsinki, Finland), a Web-enabled implementation of the Analytic Hierarchy Process. How does Web-Hipre compare to Expert Choice in functionality and use?

14. Solve the blending problem described on this book's Web site at www.prenhall.com/turban (use either Excel's Solver tool or a student version of a linear programming solver such as Lindo or QSB+. (A useful version of Lindo is available at www.lindo.com). In a spreadsheet model, use trial and error to obtain an answer. Record your best effort. Solve it with the optimizer. Did you get the same results as those reported on the Web site? Examine the solution (output) reports for the answers and sensitivity report. Lower the right-hand side of the first constraint by one unit. What happens to the solution when you solve this modified problem? Using the original formulation, try modifying the objective function coefficients (try lowering the first one by 0.32 and then by 0.34) and examine what happens. What item in the solution reports indicates the change in the solution?

15. *Heuristic study: the traveling salesperson problem.* On a map of the United States mark all the state capitals in the continental United States (exclude Hawaii and Alaska but include Washington, DC). Starting from any state capital, identify the paths you would follow to visit each of the cities exactly once with a return to the starting capital while attempting to minimize the total distance traveled. How can you do this? What would you do differently if you were allowed to visit each city more than once. If you can find the distances in a table (e.g., on a roadmap of the United States), try to do the same using the 49×49 entry table. How hard is it to get the data and organize it? Can you eliminate some data? If so, how or why? If not, why not? Which approach is easier? Do you appreciate the graphic approach more? What does this tell you in terms of developing DSS models for managers?

❖ GROUP PROJECTS

1. *Software demonstration.* Each group is assigned a different state-of-the-art DSS software product to review, examine, and demonstrate in class. The specific packages depend on your instructor and the group interests. You may need to download the demo from a vendor's Web site, depending on your instructor's directions. Be sure to get a running demo version, not a slide show. Do a half-hour in-class presentation, which should include an explanation of *why the software is appropriate* for assisting in decision making, a *hands-on demonstration* of selected important capabilities of the software, and your *critical evaluation* of the software. Try to make your presentation interesting and instructive to the whole class. The main purpose of the class presentation is for class members to see as much state-of-the-art software as possible, both in breadth (through the presentations by other groups) and in depth (through the experience you have in exploring the ins and outs of one particular software product). Also, write a report (5–10 pages) on your findings and comments regarding this software. Include screen shots in your report. Would you recommend this software to anyone? Why or why not?

2. *Expert Choice software familiarity.* Have a group meeting and discuss how you chose a place to live when you relocated to start your college program (or relocated to where you are now). What factors were important for each individual then and how long ago was it? Have these criteria changed? As a group, identify the five to seven most important criteria used in making the decision. Using the current group members' living arrangements as choices, develop an Expert Choice model describing this decision-making problem. Do not put your judgments in yet. You should each solve the EC model independently. How many of the group members selected their current home using the software? If so, was it a close decision or was there a clear winner? If some group members did not choose their current homes, what criteria made the result different (spouses of group members are not part of the home)? Or did the availability of better choices that meet their needs become known? How consistent were your judgments? Do you think that you really prefer to live in the winning location? Why or why not? Finally, average the results for all group members (by adding up the synthesized weights for each choice and dividing by the number of group members). This is one way TeamEC works. Is there a clear winner? Whose home is it and why did it win? Were there any close second choices? Turn in your results in a summary report (up to two typed pages), with copies of the individual Expert Choice runs.

❖ **MAJOR GROUP TERM PROJECT 1**

Identify a decision-making problem in a real organization and apply the Analytic Hierarchy Process Method via Expert Choice software to it. Find a business or organization, preferably one where you (or someone in your group) are working, used to work, or know an employee or owner. Otherwise, you might consider campus organizations or departments with which you are affiliated. Essentially, you need a contact willing to spend a little time with your group. The problem should involve clear choices (you may need to identify these) and some intangible aspects (not all factors should be strictly quantitative). You will have to spend some time learning about the problem at hand. Interview the decision maker, identify important criteria and choices, and build an Expert Choice model. Try your judgments in solving the problem with the prototype (record the results). Then, use the expert's (the decision maker's) judgments and get his or her opinion of how the software helped or hindered the decision-making process. This project has worked very well in practice: students and decision makers have expressed the opinion that they were very satisfied with the activities and results (see Case Application 5.2).

The four deliverables are as follows:

1. *One-page proposal.* Turn in a one-page proposal describing the Expert Choice project you intend to do. Indicate the project title, the client, and the expected results. This proposal should be due no later than 5 weeks before the final due date for the project.

2. *Intermediate progress report (maximum—two pages typed).* In this short report, describe the nature of your application and indicate how far along you are. Experience shows that you may be in trouble if you wait too long to work on this group project, so start working seriously on it as soon as you can. The short report should be due 3 weeks before the final due date for the project. Your instructor may require additional intermediate progress reports.

3. **and 4.** *Final project presentation and report (maximum—10 typed pages excluding appendices with screen shots).* This report must include a letter (on a letterhead) from the client indicating his or her opinion of the project and interaction with your group (two sentences are sufficient). Will they use the method or the software? Does the client believe the choice? Why or why

not? Can they save money by implementing the suggestion? Do they obtain other benefits by doing so? How closely does the suggestion match what the client is doing (or wants to do)? What, if any, were the limitations imposed by the software? How did they affect your ability to do the project? What was the most difficult part of working on the project? The group presentations (20 minutes per group) should be scheduled during the last week of the course, with the report due at the same time.

❖ MAJOR GROUP TERM PROJECT 2

With the outline provided for the first project, use a decision support methodology and a software package that your instructor provides or recommends. This could involve developing an optimization-based DSS, a database-based DSS, a document-based DSS, or a Web-based DSS.

❖ MAJOR GROUP TERM PROJECT 3

Develop a real-world DSS that links a database to a transportation (or other type of linear programming) model through a user interface (Lingo and Microsoft Access are recommended, as are Excel with Solver and Access). The database should contain raw data about the potential transportation routes, along with supply and demand points. The database should also handle the user interface and provide managerially meaningful descriptions of the routes after the optimization system is called.

❖ INTERNET EXERCISES

1. Search the Internet and identify software packages for linear programming, simulation, inventory control, project management, statistics, and financial modeling. What types of organizations provide these packages? Are any free?

2. Investigate ProModel (or a similar simulation package) on the Web. What features do you think DuPont used in their modeling and analysis (as discussed in the Opening Vignette)? Download the demo version and implement the cash flow simulation model on this book's Web site. How does it compare to the Excel version?

3. Repeat Exercise 2 using @Risk.

4. Search the Web for the newest software packages and books on DSS modeling. What appears to be the major focus of each? Prepare a short report.

5. Do a Web search to identify companies and products for decision analysis. Find at least one demo package, download it (or try it online if possible), and write a report on your experience.

6. Use the Internet to obtain demo software from management science or statistics vendors (try the SAS Institute Inc., SPSS Inc., CACI Products Company, and Lindo Systems Inc.). Also, be sure to look for shareware (fully functional packages that can be tried for a limited time for free). Try some of the packages and write a report on your findings.

7. Identify a company involved in animation or visual interactive simulation over the Web. Are any of the products Web-ready? Do any of them provide virtual reality capabilities or real-time online simulations? Try one if you can and write a brief report on your experiences.

8. Run an online demo of Cognos PowerPlay on the Cognos Web site (www.cognnos.com). How does it compare to trying to do the same analysis with Excel?

9. Search the Web for the latest developments of OLAP. Pick three OLAP tools and answer the following: What analytic tools do vendors typically embed in their

OLAP systems? What kinds of data warehouses can they access? What kinds of database features do they have? What kinds of multidimensional or other views do they provide?

❖ DEBATE

Some people believe that managers do not need to know the internal structure of the model and the technical aspects of modeling: "It is like the telephone or the elevator; you just use it." Others claim that this is not the case and that the opposite is true. Debate this issue.

❖ TERM PAPER

Select a current DSS technology or methodology. Get your instructor's approval. Write a report detailing the origins of the technology, what need prompted development of the technology, and what the future holds for it over the next 2, 5, and 10 years (the number of pages is up to your instructor). Use electronic sources, if possible, to identify companies providing the technology. If demo software is available, acquire it and include the results of a sample run in your paper.

CASE APPLICATION 5.1

PROCTER & GAMBLE (P&G) BLENDS MODELS, JUDGMENT, AND GIS TO RESTRUCTURE THE SUPPLY CHAIN[4]

INTRODUCTION

Procter & Gamble (P&G, Cincinnati, OH) produces, markets and distributes more than 300 brands of consumer goods worldwide in more than 140 countries. P&G has operating units (plants, divisions, facilities) in 58 locations around the globe. In 1995 worldwide sales were $33.5 billion with earnings of $2.64 billion.

The company has grown continuously over the past 159 years. To maintain and accelerate the growth experienced continuously since the early 1800s, P&G performed a major restructuring called strengthening global effectiveness (SGE) to streamline work processes, drive out non-value-added costs, eliminate duplication, and rationalize manufacturing and distribution. As a consequence of this program, there were major impacts on P&G, which wrote off more than $1 billion in assets and transition costs. The program affected more than 6,000 people and saved $200 million annually before taxes. It involved hundreds of suppliers, more than 50 product lines, 60 plants, 10 distribution centers, and hundreds of customer zones.

A major component of the initiative was to look carefully at the North American *product supply chain,* specifically to investigate plant consolidation. Before, there had been hundreds of suppliers, more than 50 product categories, more than 60 plants, 15 distribution centers (DCs), and more than 1,000 customers. As P&G became global in terms of brands, common formulas, and packages, there were economies of scale and fewer operations. Thus, plants needed to be closed to cut manufacturing expense and working capital, to improve speed to market, and to help avoid capital investment. P&G also wanted to deliver better consumer value by eliminating non-value-added costs; thus, they wanted to develop more efficient linkages with trade customers, reduce customer inventory, and eliminate the least productive sizes. The decision to restructure the supply chain seemed like the right approach.

P&G wanted to restructure the supply chain because

- Deregulation of the trucking industry had lowered transportation costs.
- A trend toward product compaction allowed more product to be shipped per truckload.

[4]Adapted from J. D. Camm, T. E. Chorman, F. A. Dill, J. R. Evans, D. J. Sweeney, and G. W. Wegryn (1997, Jan./Feb.), "Blending OR/MS, Judgment, and GIS: Restructuring P&G's Supply Chain," *Interfaces,* Vol. 27, No. 1, pp. 128–142.

- Recent focusing on total quality had led to higher levels of reliability and increased throughput at every plant.
- Product life cycles had decreased to about 18–24 months instead of 3–5 years over a few decades.
- Several corporate acquisitions had given P&G excess capacity.

So executives focused on product sourcing: choosing the best site and operation level for manufacturing each product. The production scope at a given site is limited to products relying on similar technologies. Producing too many products at a site can be too complex. But large, single-product plants can be risky (if demands shift). Since plant locations affect raw materials supply costs and the distributing of finished products, the distribution system had to be considered. The scope of the project was defined by these factors.

DSS PROJECT ORGANIZATION

Many teams were formed from multiple business functional areas to handle product sourcing options and the DC location options with customer assignments and transportation decisions (one team). Early in the project, P&G executives recognized that mathematical programming models would be needed to examine the potentially millions of possible alternatives and select a reasonable set of scenarios to investigate. More than 500 P&G employees were involved in this supply chain restructuring.

It took months to collect and analyze data (plant closings had to include the "people factor"). A team from the University of Cincinnati joined the company's operations research/management science (OR/MS) team to provide analytical support and objective input to the decision-making process. The combined OR/MS team was responsible for developing a DSS for the product-strategy and distribution teams to use to obtain the best options for more detailed analysis.

MODELING

The structure of the teams followed the organizational structure of P&G in terms of a brand management philosophy. Each product-strategy team was familiar with its product category, and so all reasonable options for that brand would be investigated. This provided a natural decomposition in the modeling effort. The distribution team could work on DC choices based on its knowledge of the consolidations being considered by each of the product-strategy teams. Given the product-strategy teams' possible consolidation plans, the distribution team could analyze changes for the DC network to support the complete consolidation plans. This could, however, lead to suboptimization because the entire system was not considered at once. However, similar projects at other firms had taken years to

develop comprehensive supply chain and distribution models. This project had a tight time limit (1 year). A prototyping approach was used to develop the DSS. As teams required new features (as team members better understood the problem), they were added incrementally. As data became available, they were encoded and built into the software modules that were added to the system anticipating the data "arrival."

The OR/MS team's objectives were to

1. Provide models and decision support for the product-strategy teams
2. Provide support to a team of experts in transportation and distribution for solving warehousing, distribution, and customer allocation problems
3. Obtain a best, complete supply chain solution across product-strategy and distribution teams.

P&G had been using a successful comprehensive logistics optimization model to support its sourcing decisions for multiple product categories and multiple echelons for a few years. But it ran on a mainframe, took a long time for each run, and required a long cycle time to obtain an answer in a managerially meaningful report. There were a number of other weaknesses related to data display and access. Because of the many what-if cases the product-strategy teams had to run, an interactive tool with a quick turnaround time was critical for project success. Following the decomposition structure of the teams, the supply chain model was also decomposed into (1) a distribution location problem and (2) a set of product-sourcing problems (one for each product category).

DISTRIBUTION CENTER LOCATION MODEL

The team *aggregated* trade customer demand into 150 customer zones to determine the correct location of 5–12 facilities (plants and DCs) in the supply chain. The major considerations influencing the choice of DC locations were customer location, customer service, and sole sourcing. The DCs had to be close enough to customer zones to maintain customer service levels. The model was an ordinary uncapacitated facility location model for finding optimal DC locations and assigning customers to DCs, while minimizing the cost of all DC–customer zone assignments. There were 17 possible locations for DCs, both existing locations and reasonable alternatives based on earlier studies and analyses. Alternatives with 5–13 DCs for the 123 customer zones were considered. The models had about 2,000 variables (only 17 binary, meaning 0 or 1 values) and 2,200 constraints.

Families of optimal and near optimal solutions for each case were found and stored in a database for later access by the product-sourcing model. Near-optimal solutions give the decision makers more options from which to choose. Furthermore, there may be other considerations not built into a model that can lead to the selection of a near-optimal solution. This also helped when working with the product-sourcing options in that the near-optimal solutions expanded the solution space, giving the analysts and decision makers a larger set from which to choose and a sense that the solution would be optimal (or at least closer to the global optimum value).

THE PRODUCT SOURCING MODEL

The product-sourcing model (PSM) was a simple *transportation model* for each product category. The product-strategy teams specified plant location and capacity options to investigate, while each DC was a demand representing the total aggregated demand from its customer zones. Since manufacturing costs were the most important in the product-sourcing decision, good estimates were developed. Real data were used (when available) or a simple model generated the cost for shipping between two points. The generating algorithm was validated using existing costs.

The transportation models were solved with a readily available, fast computer code (an out-of-kilter algorithm). Thus, options could be evaluated in real time.

INTEGRATION WITH A GEOGRAPHIC INFORMATION SYSTEM

The product-strategy teams wanted a powerful, flexible decision support system that could display and manipulate solutions for ease of interpretation. So, the product-sourcing model was integrated with a geographic information system (GIS), Mapinfo. Mapinfo had a readily customizable user interface through its Mapbasic programming language. The GIS provided the capability to make quick changes, run new scenarios, and compare the results. The whole system runs in seconds on a standard laptop PC. File manipulation is used to ship data from Mapinfo to the optimization software and back. The user interface provided by the GIS led to user acceptance of analytic techniques. The product-strategy team members interacted directly with the optimizers but created scenarios directly with the GIS and saw the results there as well. Often, insights given by the spatial visualization led to new and better options. The model acted as a laboratory in which product-strategy teams tested ideas and developed insights.

The spatial visualization also readily identified database errors that could have gone undetected; that is, links between DCs and customers had to look reasonable. If a DC was linked to a customer in the middle of the ocean, the error could be seen.

DSS OPERATION

The solutions to the DC model were inputs to the product-sourcing model. The product-strategy teams chose the con-

sistent potential plant locations, capacities, and manufacturing costs and solved the product-sourcing model. An optimal manufacturing-and-distribution plan was then found. Given the solution, the product-strategy teams created a new case, re-solved the model, and repeated this sequence until they were satisfied. This rapid process lead to the teams working in more than 1,000 sessions to evaluate alternatives. (Often DSS leads to extra analysis because the tools are so good.) It was felt that the objective value of any solution was within 10 percent of the real value because *demands and costs were forecasted* and some estimates were made. The model was validated to be within 2 percent of the optimum using existing data, even though it was designed to represent the state of P&G in the year 2000.

Once the teams had established reasonable alternatives, they focused on collecting data needed to select an optimal long-term solution based on risk-adjusted net present-value analysis. This was a *simulation model* of a net present-value analysis built in a spreadsheet. It was solved with @Risk, a spreadsheet add-in.

While evaluating options, the OR/MS team discovered that the best product-sourcing options were indeed independent of DC locations, thus justifying the decomposition made initially. Manufacturing costs dominated transportation costs in alternatives of product-sourcing options.

INTEGRATION OF HUMAN JUDGMENT

The distribution and product-sourcing models were integrated and solved. Using the models, each category team developed a number of potential sourcing options, varying from 2 to 12, rejecting some. During this process, they included many subjective considerations, including the minimum number of plants, which DCs to consider, and whether to use cross-border sourcing.

They used the product-sourcing model to find the best options for each product category and then subjected these options to a more thorough *financial and risk analysis*. This analysis took into account costs including taxes, interest rates, labor rates, and utilities over a number of years into the future. The risk analysis considered the possibility of earthquakes, hurricanes, and so on. Political considerations were also considered in some of the site selections.

Expert human judgment was considered a critical part of the DSS approach. Difficult problems like this need a hybrid approach which closely links expert human judgment and mathematical optimization. The GIS and consideration of qualitative factors lead to the system's success.

DSS BENEFITS

Two years after completion of the DSS, P&G closed 12 sites and wrote off more than a billion dollars worth of assets and people-transition costs. The new North American manufacturing and distribution system is saving more than $250 million (pretaxes) annually. Most savings have resulted from lower manufacturing costs, because of fewer plants with less staff, and from a more efficient supply chain. Because there are fewer sites, delivery expenses have indeed increased. Regardless of the DSS, P&G would have closed plants and improved its operations. The OR/MS team feels that it was directly responsible for 10 percent of the total savings ($25 million). In addition, the solution implemented affected about 6,000 people because of changes in the product supply system. One-third retired early, another third were relocated, and the last third were retrained and hired by other companies. P&G treated these people fairly, with respect and dignity.

Because of the project's success, P&G now requires that all future sourcing decisions be based on analytic methods. P&G has also used the model to conduct competitive analyses. Tools similar to the model have gained widespread acceptance, with demand for their use in domestic, regional, and global sourcing studies. P&G has es-

tablished a new internal Center for Expertise in Analytics for solving business problems.

CASE QUESTIONS

1. Why is the visual system with a graphical interface provided by a GIS an ideal workbench for analyzing distribution scenarios?
2. Why do you think so many people were involved in the P&G supply-chain restructuring effort?
3. Describe the different models and types that were developed for the DSS. How were they integrated?
4. Why was the decision to decompose the product-sourcing problem from the distribution center locations problem reasonable?
5. Why was it reasonable to aggregate the customers into a single customer zone?
6. Why was it important to take human judgment into consideration?
7. How well do you think P&G would have done without an analysis of this type?
8. Explain why this DSS project was a success.

CASE APPLICATION 5.2

SCOTT HOMES CONSTRUCTS AN EXPERT CHOICE MULTICRITERIA MODEL-BASED DSS FOR SELECTING A MOBILE HOME SUPPLIER[5]

INTRODUCTION

Mr. Jesse Scott is the owner of Scott Housing Inc., a mobile home sales firm in Sylvania, GA. The decision facing Mr. Scott involved selecting potential manufacturers of mobile homes. The nature of the problem was to decide which suppliers could best ensure customer satisfaction and a profitable bottom line for Scott Housing through the quality of their products and other factors. This multiple-criteria (multiple goals, multiple objectives) decision-making problem is an ideal one to solve with the aid of Expert Choice, an implementation of the Analytic Hierarchy Process (AHP).

THE ANALYTIC HIERARCHY PROCESS

The Analytic Hierarchy Process, developed by Thomas Saaty [1995, 1996], is an excellent modeling structure for representing *multicriteria (multiple goals, multiple objec-*

tives) problems—with sets of criteria and alternatives (choices)—commonly found in business environments. The decision maker uses AHP to decompose a decision-making problem into relevant criteria and relevant alternatives. The AHP separates the analysis of the criteria from the alternatives, which helps a decision maker focus on small, manageable portions of the problem. The AHP manipulates quantitative and qualitative decision-making criteria in a fairly structured manner, allowing a decision maker to make trade-offs quickly and "expertly."

Expert Choice (Expert Choice Inc., Pittsburgh, PA, www.expertchoice.com; a functional demo version is available directly from their Web site) is an excellent commercial implementation of the AHP. A problem is represented as an inverted tree with a goal node at the top (Figure 5.8). All the weight of the decision is in the goal (1.000). Directly beneath and attached to the goal node

[5]Contributed by the MASK Innovation DSS Class Team: Avryl Alvarez, Candace Kemp, Wakeelah Moore, and Veneetia Smith, Terry College of Business, The University of Georgia, Athens, GA.

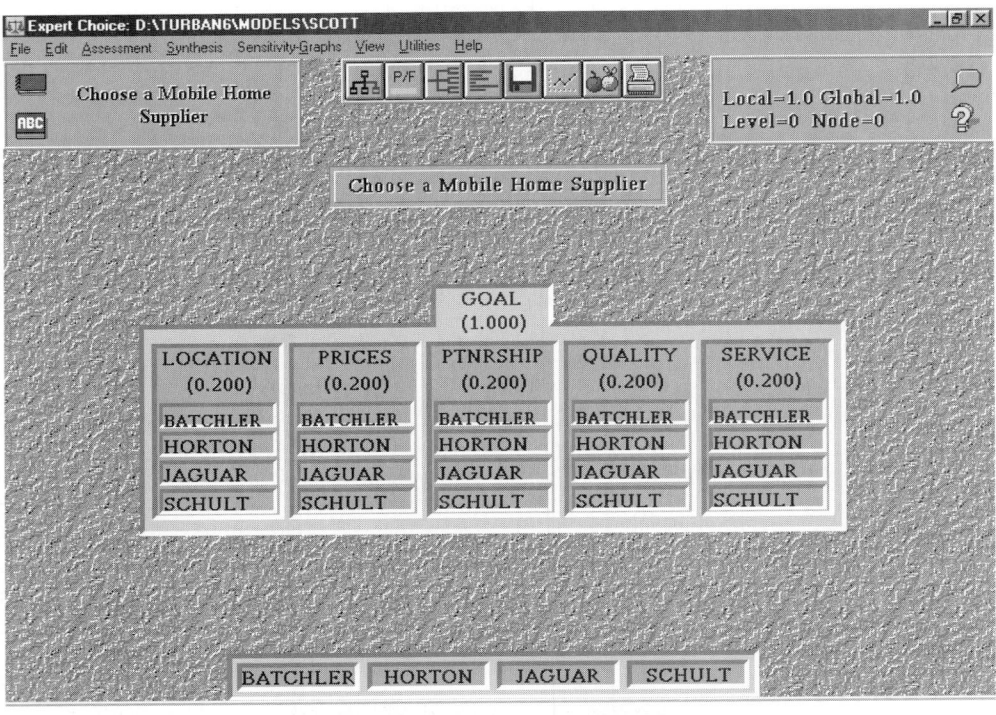

FIGURE 5.8 THE EXPERT CHOICE SCOTT MOBILE HOME MODEL OF THE DECISION PROBLEM BEFORE PAIRWISE COMPARISONS

At the top is the goal, the next layer contains criteria, and the bottom layer contains choices.

By permission of Expert Choice Inc.

are the criteria nodes. These are the factors that are important to the decision maker. The goal is decomposed into criteria, to which 100 percent of the weight of the decision from the goal is distributed. To distribute the weight, the decision maker pairwise compares the criteria: first criterion to second, first to third, . . ., first to last; then, second criterion to third, second to third, . . ., second to last; . . .; then, next to last criterion to the last one. In doing so, he or she establishes the importance of each criterion, that is, how much of the weight of the goal is distributed to each criterion or how *important* each criterion is. This objective method is performed by internally manipulating matrices mathematically. The manipulations are transparent to the user because the operational details of the method are *not* important to the decision maker. Finally, an inconsistency index indicates how consistent the comparisons were, thus identifying inconsistencies, errors in judgment, or simply errors. The AHP method is consistent with decision theory.

The decision maker can make comparisons verbally (e.g., one criterion is moderately more important than another), graphically (with bar and pie charts), or numerically (with a *matrix*—comparisons are scaled from 1 to 9).

Students and business professionals generally prefer to use the graphical and verbal approaches to the matrix one (based on an informal sample).

Beneath each criterion are the same set of choices (alternatives) in the simple case described here. Like the goal, the criteria decompose their weight into the choices, which capture 100 percent of the weight of each criterion. The decision maker pairwise compares the choices in terms of *preference* as they relate to the specific criterion under consideration. Each set of choices must be pairwise compared as they relate to each criterion. Again, all three modes of comparison are available, and an inconsistency index is derived for each set and reported.

Finally, the results are synthesized and displayed on a bar graph. The choice with the most weight is the correct choice. However, the correct decision may not be the correct one under some conditions. For example, if there are two "identical" choices that split the weight (e.g., if you are selecting a car for purchase and you have two identical cars, they may split the weight and neither will have the most weight). Also, if the top few choices are very close, there may be a missing criterion that could be used to differentiate among these choices.

This case is a simple decision-making situation with important ramifications for the decision maker. We did not use some of the more advanced features of Expert Choice, which is very flexible. Subcriteria can be incorporated into a model. There is a Ratings Model (see Case Application 2.3), useful for when there are more than seven choices or for recurring decisions (like hiring employees). Expert Choice has a sensitivity analysis module. And, there is a group version called TeamEC that synthesizes the results of a group of decision makers using the same model.

Overall, the AHP as implemented in Expert Choice attempts to derive a decision maker's preference (utility) structure in terms of the criteria and choices and help him or her make an expert choice. See Case Application 2.3 for additional details about the AHP and Expert Choice.

THE SCOTT HOUSING AHP MODEL

During an interview Mr. Scott and the team determined that the following criteria were the most important in his decision process: price, customer service, quality of materials, supplier location, timing of delivery, special relationship with the supplier, and how long the supplier has been in the market.

Currently Mr. Scott purchases mobile homes from two regular suppliers (Horton Homes and Jaguar) and is considering purchasing from two new suppliers (Schult and Batchlor). He is very much interested in how the model will look and how Schult and Batchlor will stack up against Horton Homes and Jaguar.

THE CRITERIA

Quality decision making requires identification of the proper criteria, and we worked closely with Mr. Scott to determine these. The six important criteria are price, customer service, quality of materials, supplier location, length of time in business, and special relationship with the supplier.

Supplier location is a major concern of our decision maker. A closer supplier means lower freight costs and faster deliveries. This criterion was weighted highest of all at 30.9 percent.

Price is the second criterion. We originally thought that price would be the most important and recognized that location has an indirect relationship to the total cost of a mobile home. The price of the mobile home is of great importance when calculating profits. The price weight was 21.3 percent.

Other criteria. Scott Housing Inc has had a reputation for providing excellent *customer service* and *high-quality materials.* It was reasonable that these criteria be included in the model. Great customer service is defined as being dependable, being accessible, and having a concern for customers. The pairwise comparison step yielded a weight of 15.5 percent. It was also important to Mr. Scott that *length*

of time in business (older is better) and *special relationships with the supplier* be included in the model to impact on the decision.

THE SUPPLIERS (CHOICES)

Horton Homes is located in Eatonton, GA, and has been in business since 1970. Their dramatic growth is directly linked to their commitment to offering the consumer an attractive, affordable home designed and built with modern technological advances. Horton Iron Works uses the latest in welding technology. I-beam frames are manufactured for extra strength and support, adding to the quality of the home. Horton manufactures accent moldings such as baseboards, door casings, and crown and chair rail moldings in various sizes, styles and colors. Horton owns more than 100 trucks to ensure the prompt and courteous delivery of homes to retail sales centers. Adhering to minimum standards higher than those recommended for site-built homes, Horton Homes builds to the federal safety and construction standards set by the Department of Housing and Urban Development (HUD). This guarantees that each home meets or exceeds strict federal regulations for such factors as design, construction, energy efficiency, wind and fire safety, ventilation, durability, and installation procedures. This is their way of ensuring a quality home.

Jaguar Homes specializes in the design and building of luxurious one- and two-story homes. They have been in business for 35 years building single-family homes, apartments, and commercial properties in the Los Angeles, CA, area. Recently they have expanded their business to the east coast, particularly the Virginia area.

Schult Homes was founded in 1934 and has prided itself on giving customers quality, craftsmanship, and service and having a solid relationship with retail dealers. Schult offers a wide variety of models, floor plans and prices to meet the customer's needs. Production efficiency resulting from the Schult manufacturing process can save a homebuyer up to 30 percent per square foot over a site-built home while offering the same amenities and appearance.

Batchlor Supply has been in the business of manufacturing homes for approximately 20 years. They are located in Raleigh, NC, and are a fairly new potential vendor for Scott Housing Inc. Batchlor Supply prides itself on quality customer service and economical pricing.

THE MODEL AND THE RESULTS

We constructed an Expert Choice model with the six criteria and four choices outlined above (Figure 5.8). After completing pairwise comparisons for the six criteria and for the four choices under each criterion (seven comparison sets in all), we synthesized the results (Figure 5.9).

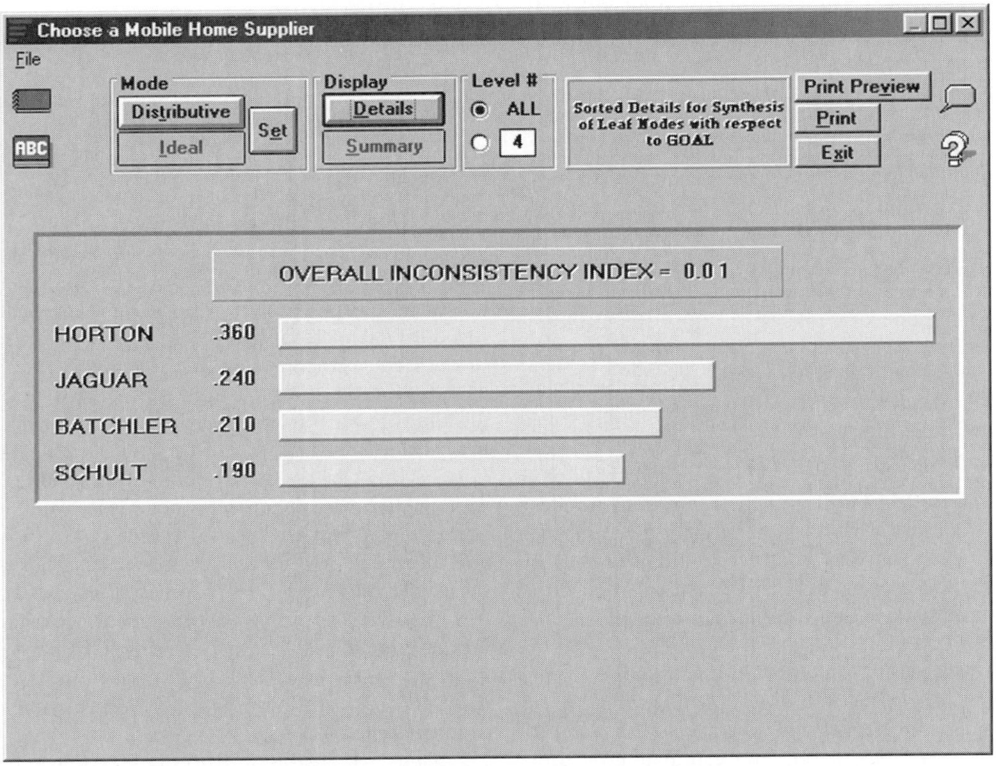

FIGURE 5.9 SYNTHESIS OF THE RESULTS OF THE EXPERT CHOICE SCOTT MOBILE HOME
DECISION MODEL

By permission of Expert Choice Inc.

Horton Homes was a clear winner with a total score of 0.360, Jaguar came in second with a score of 0.240, Batchlor received a score of 0.210, and Schult received a score of 0.190. Location overwhelmingly drove the model to this solution because it is the most important criteria by a wide margin. The inconsistency index was remarkably small—equal to 0.01. Mr. Scott agreed with these results and was impressed with the accuracy of Expert Choice. As he stated in a letter:

It was my pleasure to work with The MASK Innovation on their project for their decision support class. I did not know that decision support software was so easily available (i.e., over the Internet). Amazingly, the group's judgments matched mine and, in the future, I may consider using Expert Choice as a tool in my decision making.

Development of the DSS helped Mr. Scott in making a strategic decision, and the effectiveness of his decision making was increased. Tools like ExpertChoice truly enhance the quality of the decision-making process.

CASE QUESTIONS

1. This is a multicriteria problem. What are the specific goals?
2. What are the criteria? Discuss why they are important.
3. How were the choices "guided" by the criteria?
4. How did Expert Choice enhance Mr. Scott's ability to make a decision?
5. Download the demo version of Expert Choice and build a model similar to Mr. Scott's for practice using the software. Use your own judgments. How close are they, and the solution, to Mr. Scott's? Why are they similar or different?

CLAY PROCESS PLANNING AT IMERYS: A CLASSICAL CASE OF DECISION MAKING

PART 3: THE PROCESS OPTIMIZATION MODEL

INTRODUCTION

This case application continues the effort described in Case Applications 2.1 and 2.2. The Process OPtimization (POP) development team at English China Clay International (ECCI/IMERYS) in Sandersville, GA, developed a large-scale mathematical programming model that describes their clay processing from the mines to the finished product. Here we describe the structure of the POP model: a large-scale, generalized, multicommodity network flow model with side constraints. We further describe how the data and model are managed. Finally, we describe how the model is and will be used. The prototyping development process followed in developing the POP DSS is described in detail in Case Application 6.1.

THE PLANTS

Originally, the scope of the first phase of the project called for developing an integrated model representing four plants—two hydrous plants, a large calcine plant, and a small calcine plant—but did not initially represent the mines (calcine is dry clay and hydrous has more moisture; different products are made from each, and almost any set of clays can be blended to generate a final product with unique properties). While development of the model for the small calcine plant was underway, ECCI was purchased by IMATEL (France), and eventually one hydrous plant, about one-fifth of the large calcine plant, and the small calcine plant were sold per a U.S. Justice Department ruling. As outlined in Case Application 6.1, we had completed development of the model of both calcine plants at that time. For validation purposes, we kept the plants in the model until it became operational. The POP DSS model deployed in late 1999 represented one hydrous plant and both the large calcine and the small calcine plants.

THE MODEL BUILDING BLOCKS

The decision variables include which mines to excavate, how much and what kind of crude clays to extract from each one, how to blend crude clays, which equipment to process the clay on, what speed to process the clay at, what intermediate blends (recipes) to use, which final blends to use, which demands to meet (or not meet if necessary), which final clays to purchase from the open market, and others.

Fortunately, the multicommodity network flow problem represents flow problems of many commodities (e.g., dif-

ferent clays) through common links (arcs) that generally have capacity limits. The model can be represented graphically, making it easy to sketch and understand. Ours is a generalized model; that is, each link that allows flow has a multiplier (a recovery factor for a process) between 0 and 1 indicating how much of the flow actually reaches the node at the end of the link. This is used to model "losses" that result from chemical and physical transformation of the clays. In addition, there are some side constraints that enforce blends and enforce mutual capacities on the links (e.g., the total flow through each arc for all commodities cannot exceed the capacity in terms of flow or time). This is a static model.

Developing a standard set of building blocks made it easier for the team to develop and implement the model. Given a particular clay, there are several model building blocks, but the most important one is the *process*. These are entities that represent a type of equipment processing the clay. For example, transporting the clay from a mine to a particular plant is a process. Another process is grinding. Other building blocks, such as a holding tank, follow naturally from the process definition. Some processes are simply represented as nodes: a source (a supply, e.g., a mine), a sink (the demand for a finished clay), or a link that allows flow between pairs of such building blocks. Every process has a set of clays that can flow through it. For each clay flowing through a process, the following data must be specified: the rate of flow (in tons per hour, which varies by clay), a unit cost per ton for processing, a unit cost per hour utilized, a recovery factor (the multiplier between 0 and 1), a capacity limit on the flow, and a capacity limit on the processing time.

The basic building block of a simple process consists of two nodes and a single arc. The first node is the feed node. Any preceding processes can feed the clay into the process through this node. The second node is the product node. This is where the processed clay arrives and is ready for transport to its next destination. The decision variable is to determine the flow through the process (on the arc). A simple process looks like

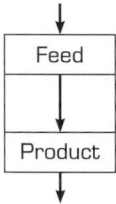

Complex processes have two or more distinct products (e.g., a categorizing process divides clay into small particle and large particle sizes, each of which is processed differently afterward; so each product has a different recovery factor, while the rate and unit costs of processing are unchanged. A complex process has an intermediate node (the process set node), a product node for each one, and arcs to link them. It looks like

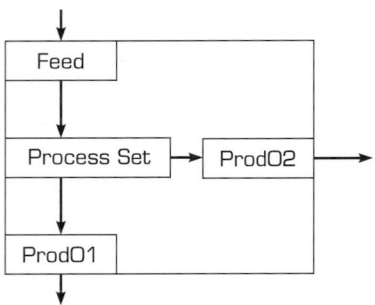

Chemicals that alter the clays' properties are added to the clays in different processes. The amount used is proportional to the flow (in pounds per ton) and, depending on the rate that the process uses, different chemical amounts can be involved. Also, alternate processing for the same clay may lead to the use of different chemicals.

Clays can flow from plant to plant, from the "economy" into the plant, from mine to plant, and so on. The model is then built by connecting these processes with arcs that transport the clays. These arcs represent any transporting of clays. There are five families of hydrous clays and three main calcine products. Though few in number, these clays can be combined with each other and with clays obtained from other plants or on the open market to produce several hundred different final clays. There are hundreds of ways to blend the crudes to form any of the hydrous family clays. Also, the families each go through the production process in several different ways. There are different ways to process each particular clay, and different blends and chemical amounts can be used. The model was to determine the optimal blends to use.

The model, when solved, determines the clay flows (decision variables, in tons) and can then determine the time consumed for each clay in each process. These values are capacitated, and the total flow and total time consumed are also capacitated, both because of physical limitations of the processing equipment and the required characteristics of the finished products. The recipes used, and which processes are running at capacity are of great interest to the company for planning purposes. The mining operations are also a "process," as is meeting the demand for each clay.

The objective is to maximize profit. Each finished product clay has a unit price for every form of it that is sold (slurry, bulk, bag, and so on). More than 2.3 million tons of crude clay processing in a year was modeled.

MODELING DIFFICULTIES

What made this model difficult to construct and interesting was the large size (more than 8,000 constraints and 35,000 variables) and the fact that several different process characteristics were estimated because the processes had not yet been constructed. There were also points in the processing where by-products were fed back into the system to an earlier step (clay recoveries).

Once the small calcine plant and a portion of the large calcine plant were sold, the flows into these portions of the model were turned off by setting the capacity of the calcining process equal to zero. The second hydrous plant was never modeled.

THE LINGO MODELING LANGUAGE AND THE ACCESS DATABASE INTEGRATION

The model was developed in Lingo (a modeling language from Lindo Systems Inc., www.lindo.com), which integrates directly with a Microsoft Access database of more than 10 relational tables through the Microsoft @ODBC interface. The Lingo model lines are specified independently from the data link statements (links). The Process OPtimization Lingo model is populated with data from the database, generates the model, solves it, and loads the solution directly back into the database automatically. Lingo model lines generally look like shorthand for the algebra of mathematical programming, thus providing a familiar vehicle for model building. For example, the Lingo model line for the supply constraints of a transportation problem (from factories to customers) might be

@FOR(FACTORY(I):
    @SUM(CUSTOMER(J): FLOW(I, J)) <=
    CAPACITY(I));

which means: For every FACTORY(I), SUM all the flows from I to J over all CUSTOMER(J) (all customers), (FLOW(I,J)), and set that value to be less than or equal to the available CAPACITY(I) at FACTORY(I). There are special data statements specifying all necessary data to identify the sets FACTORY, CUSTOMER, and CAPACITY. The POP model's mining portion looks very much like a modified transportation problem. Limits on blends can be specified (e.g., between 80 and 95 percent of clay B must be used in the blend).

POP DSS USE

The DSS, written as a menu-oriented Access database table, handled the data in the system. A particular scenario is set

222

222

up in the Access tables through a friendly graphical user interface (GUI) screen. The user sets the demands, makes other adjustments to the processes, and then activates Lingo with the click of a button. Lingo automatically generates the entire model from its compact representation and the data as specified in the database, and solves it. Lingo loads its solution back into the database and returns control to the menu-oriented GUI. Access programs then produce managerially meaningful graphs of utilization and reports on clay extraction and processing. Trouble spots are identified, the case can be saved, and another scenario can be run.

For a fixed time period (1 year, one quarter, 2 weeks, and so on), the solution to the model indicates which mines are active, how much clay is mined from each mine, to which processing unit the clay is shipped from the mines, and the appropriate crude blends (recipes) to be used. It determines all the clay flows throughout the entire system and which clays to purchase from the market. The model quickly identifies which processes are running at capacity and indicates the potential increase in profit that could be obtained if these capacities could be increased (through sensitivity analysis). Sometimes there are underutilized processes that could handle some of the load of the limited processes but are somewhat inefficient at doing so. Plant managers are reluctant to use these processes but now are carefully reexamining them and sometime activate them for these clays.

The model also indicates how to handle the situation now that some of the higher-quality clay mines have become depleted and new processes have been introduced. Finally, underutilization of some processes has indicated that some final products, normally produced at other plants (not yet in the model), could be produced at the plants represented by the model. One such clay has already been successfully added to POP.

The most interesting aspect of the model is that the engineers and managers who structure the plants were doing an excellent job of keeping them fine-tuned without access to these analytical tools. The model did recommend using different mines from time to time, and it has provided guidance in how to manage the mines through the next decade. The total amount of clay being processed is on the same order of what the model solution recommends,

and this certainly helped to validate the model. What the model is best used for is determining how to handle the resources that are 100 percent utilized and how to handle new and unexpected situations such as new clays, new demands, and new processes. It also provides answers quickly and easily, thus guiding managers and engineers in their decision making.

As mentioned in Case Application 2.2, the cost of operating a new process was determined, thus helping with budgeting decisions for the next fiscal year. The model is being used for next year's planning. It is also being used in the short term for scheduling specific large orders in with the forecasted demands.

SUMMARY AND CONCLUSIONS

The POP model as part of the POP DSS at IMERYS is helping to guide planning on an annual, quarterly, and even weekly basis. It helps decision makers determine which options are most viable in terms of meeting clay demand at a maximum profit.

Planning for millions of tons of clay processing is not a trivial task, and the POP DSS handles it readily and quickly. Plans are under way to expand POP to include the other plants in central Georgia. The POP DSS is a success.

CASE QUESTIONS

1. What is the POP DSS used for?
2. What are the benefits of using a network-based model?
3. What are the benefits of the POP DSS?
4. How can what-if cases (scenarios) be used to determine whether to add extra processing equipment instead of adjusting existing processes and chemical use?
5. Could other firms that process materials use a system like this? Why or why not?
6. How could a demand forecasting model be integrated with POP? (A question to think about—not in this case application.)
7. How could the results of the POP DSS guide an enterprise resource planning (ERP) system? (A question to think about—not described in this case application.)

6

DECISION SUPPORT SYSTEM DEVELOPMENT

Up until now, we have presented the basic concepts and components of decision making and decision support. Now we must learn how to construct a DSS. Unfortunately, acquiring a DSS is not as simple as obtaining productivity software like a word processor. DSS are usually designed to handle complex situations, and so few are available right off the shelf. Instead, DSS must usually be custom-designed, developed, and implemented for each specific application. We present the DSS development process through the following sections:

6.1 OPENING VIGNETTE: OSRAM SYLVANIA THINKS SMALL, STRATEGIZES BIG—DEVELOPS THE INFONET HR PORTAL SYSTEM[1]

A *business portal* is a central aggregation point for corporate data, tools, and links accessed through a browser interface. Portals appeal to organizations whose information and business processes are scattered across many different reports, applications, systems, and geography. Thinking small when building a first portal seems to make sense.

---

[1]Adapted from Rudenstein (2000).

Rather than trying to create a megaenterprise portal for everyone and everything, companies are focusing on first building a small, specialized portal that solves a *pressing problem* in a particular department or business function—a prototype. The small, motivated team of IT and business staff at Osram Sylvania approached HR InfoNet, a portal focused on *human resources,* this way. The North American division of Osram GmbH of Germany, has $3.7 billion in sales and 12,500 employees in 30 locations. Osram Sylvania manufactures and markets lighting and precision materials and component products.

HR is strategic to Osram Sylvania. The lighting industry is highly competitive. Finding, recruiting, and hiring specialized scientists, engineers, and hourly staff is a major challenge. Employee benefits administration was accomplished with an expensive outsourcing solution. The recruitment problem needed a faster solution than the existing paper-based system which had a slow, tedious workflow.

An interactive Web portal for employee self-service benefits would improve employee service. With the existing system, employees could not do what-if comparisons or even see the cost of the programs they chose (it was voice-actuated). Another problem was that the system did not perform routine life status changes (e.g., adding a child to a family's benefits). These requests were handled manually. Improvement was clearly necessary.

Bringing job requisitions and benefits enrollment online was the initial goal of HR InfoNet. While the IT requirements were relatively straightforward, there were two internal issues. The first was that only about one-third of the employees had computers. The other issue was that the head of the project, Roger Rudenstein, was hired in 1995 to head up the PeopleSoft system group, a team of three, to maintain and extend the PeopleSoft HR system and the interface with the new payroll system. They were so busy with the payroll conversion that they could not start the HR portal until early 1996. There was a sense from earlier projects that an intranet (an internal internet) was *the* appropriate technology platform for the HR system. This first decision, to build an intranet, was adopted.

Roger championed the project from the IT side, and Geoff Hunt, vice president of human resources, and Nancy Dobrusin and Julie Thibodeau, his counterparts in the HR department, championed it from the business side. They also had ongoing support from Michelle Marshall and the corporate communications department throughout the process.

The team adopted the strategy *think small, strategize big.* Resources were minimal for developing HR InfoNet. There were no dedicated staff, no funds to hire consultants, and *no budget,* despite the fact that this was a crucially strategic project. Roger targeted a solution that they could make workable. *Think small* meant that it was necessary to conserve both money and precious time. *Strategize big* meant that the development platform and solution architecture had to handle current solutions, as well as future applications, as the portal grew in capability. Essentially, it was almost a given that in-house technology was to be used. This cut down on IT staff training and licensing.

After a few suggestions from several coworkers, and some evaluation of potential systems, the team adopted the Lotus Notes/Domino Server. They developed their experience by *just doing it.* Within 3 months, they had successfully deployed a portal application for posting job requisitions in LotusScript and Notes/Domino databases with agents. This validated the technology, and so they continued with the next application, allowing employees to examine and correct their benefits online. For employees without computers, they developed kiosks that used standard browsers with special security features. Hourly employees were given network IDs and training.

The next step of the job requisition application process was to create an intranet-based workflow to allow managers to describe job openings and route them to the correct HR person using online forms. Now, these postings can be submitted directly to the corporate Web site. After successfully creating the initial HR InfoNet portal, they expanded it to include more HR benefits and compensation information.

In early 2000, the portal allowed employees to view their benefits, compare the costs of different programs, access information to help make their benefits decisions, change benefits enrollment, and perform many HR management duties, such as developing plans for salary reviews, management bonus programs, head count reports, and retirement packages. By then, the portal served as the focal point for the firm's job postings, requisitions, and hiring workflow, as well as the interface with HR benefits for all employees.

Employee feedback on the new HR capabilities has been extremely positive. Recruiting cycle time has improved, and HR productivity is higher. HR benefits administration is much more user-friendly, and even kiosk users have embraced the system. By taking benefits administration in-house, the company saves $500,000 annually—an excellent return on the project.

Instead of thinking big and trying to solve every problem at once, which is how traditional systems analysis works, the team used a focused approach, tackling the *key problem* first and then moving on to the next one. This evolutionary development (iterative development) is known formally as prototyping. Thinking big can lead to million-dollar budgets, hiring staff, preparing thousands of pages of specifications, and so on. Instead, they *strategized big* by developing a plan and technology strategy to achieve some quick successes, while offering a solid foundation on which to build the future. The *think small, strategize big* prototyping approach led to a major success for the HR InfoNet portal at Osram Sylvania. We present their practical insights into applying this philosophy in DSS in Focus 6.1.

Success leads to success, and so the team is developing more applications within and like HR InfoNet. HR InfoNet proved the validity of the portal concept. They will continue to develop new applications in succession planning, performance management process (PMP), and time and attendance. Over 3 years, Osram Sylvania estimates a 251 percent return on investment (ROI) and a savings of $1.5 million.

❖ **QUESTIONS FOR THE OPENING VIGNETTE**

1. What was the strategic business need? What were the benefits of the completed HR InfoNet system? Explain.
2. Why was it important to have an IT champion, a functional business (HR) champion, and an executive champion involved in the project?
3. Who were the users? What decisions did the system assist the users in making?
4. How were the users involved in the system development? How was management involved?
5. Do you feel that if the development team had "thought big," that is, tried to design and develop a total solution over a long period of time, they would have succeeded? What could have gone wrong? Do you think they knew this in advance?
6. What technology issues, behavioral issues, and implementation issues had to be worked through in developing the HR InfoNet system?
7. What implementation approach was adopted? Why?
8. Comment on how success breeds success in DSS development.

GUIDELINES FOR A "THINK SMALL, STRATEGIZE BIG" IMPLEMENTATION

Here are some practical insights for applying the *think small, strategize big* philosophy as outlined in the Osram Sylvania HR InfoNet development described in the Opening Vignette.

- *Draw on "hidden" talent.* Osram Sylvania used a small group of staff involved in another project at virtually no cost. Management gave them a challenge and interesting, exciting extra work. They also had the strong support of the IT infrastructure staff, which was critical to their success.

- *Partner with the business staff.* Roger Rudenstein was already working with his functional counterparts in HR business systems, benefits, and compensation. He had an office near them and helped in joint planning and collaboration. He worked hard to determine their needs and make suggestions on how IT could meet these needs. Successful IT projects involve the users throughout the entire development process.

- *Use an iterative process.* Prototyping was critical. The team did not have all the details before starting development but were able to refine on the fly. They used an iterative process, where they sat down with the business staff and worked out an agreement that described what they were trying to do. Then they developed a prototype, and the many ongoing iterations evolved into the application, quickly moving the project along. Employee

feedback via focus groups and other means helped them stay on track and kept the users involved, which helped lead to success.

- *Choose the right technology tools.* Notes/Domino was chosen because the company was already using it, and so it was free. After becoming familiar with it, they realized it would meet their current and future needs. The fact that all its applications are integrated was also a critical factor. Cementing the system together was relatively easy, and there was a common interface—a Web browser.

We add the following:

- *Enlist a champion in higher management.* The full support of an executive sponsor leads to resources for a project.

- *Build a user training program into the system release.* This leads to better adoption and satisfaction. It also leads to fewer problems with noncomputer specialists using the system in the second year.

- *Align the project with business needs.* Without this, it is difficult to get an executive sponsor. The benefits of the project were clear at the outset. New benefits unfolded as the project evolved. There was a critical need for the project.

Source: Partly adapted from Rudenstein (2000).

6.2 INTRODUCTION TO DSS DEVELOPMENT

The HR InfoNet system illustrates a number of important DSS development and implementation issues. It was built with an important DSS development approach called *prototyping* (see DSS in Action 6.2). Prototyping is one adaptation of the traditional **system development life cycle (SDLC).** The development team started small and expanded the system over time. They developed the system sequentially in modules. As each module was completed, it was refined and deployed to users. Then the next module was developed, refined, and added to the system; then the next; and so on. The system evolved as more and more subsystems could be feasibly developed within the

DSS IN ACTION 6.2

USER INTERFACE PROTOTYPING LEADS TO DSS SUCCESS

Several years ago, I worked for an international consulting firm in Pittsburgh, PA. I visited a large midwestern tractor manufacturer to determine their needs for an assembly line balancing method and to propose a decision support system. If they accepted the proposal, I would implement it. Though there are many methods for solving assembly line balancing problems, this situation was different. Even though I was familiar with published work on line balancing, I discovered that their industrial engineers had developed a unique, remarkable, effective approach that utilized information from their manufacturing methods database. I did not push existing methods on them. Instead, I developed specifications for a unique system and included as a major portion of the proposal a *prototype of the user interface*—a set of menus, displays, and reports—so the industrial engineering chief could see how the system would look and work (many users view the user interface as the entire system).

With the interface prototype, the client saw what he was going to get. The prototype enhanced user and managerial involvement. It was a focal point that led users and managers to feel that the proposed system would be exactly what they had needed for several years. The proposal was accepted, and the project was initiated and successfully completed on time and under budget. The user interface prototype also was very useful to me as a system development guide.

Source: Jay E. Aronson.

---

budget and on time. And, as the team and managers learned more about business problems by working with users and managers throughout the development process, they were able to refine the way the older subsystems worked and use their new-found knowledge in developing the new modules [e.g., see Baer (1998)]. The IMERYS Case Application 6.1 was developed in much the same manner. As more was learned about the structure of the real system from DSS users and experts, the new knowledge was incorporated into the newer modules and the older ones were either updated or scheduled to be updated.

The large-scale HR InfoNet system was developed quickly by using a common in-house technology platform. HR InfoNet was created by a team consisting of IS specialists and HR specialists. This was an institutional DSS designed to be used on a recurring basis by many employees, some of whom were not computer-literate. Finally, the system continues to evolve because its success led managers and the team to see new ways to apply the ideas developed to other decision-making situations.

Development of a DSS, especially a large one, is a complicated process. It involves issues ranging from technical (e.g., hardware selection and networking) to behavioral (e.g., user interfaces and the potential impact of DSS on individuals, groups, and the entire organization). This chapter concentrates mainly on DSS software development issues.

Because there are several types and categories of DSS, there is no single best approach to DSS development. There are many variations because of the differences in organizations, decision makers, and the DSS problem area. Some DSS are designed to support a one-time decision like the Scott Housing decision in Case Application 5.2, whereas the IMERYS DSS in Case Application 6.1 was developed for recurrent use. Some systems can be developed in a few days in a spreadsheet or with another tool, while others, like the Osram Sylvania HR InfoNet took several months and will continue to evolve over the next several years. We now explore issues involving DSS development time, managerial aspects, change management, and more.

6.3 THE TRADITIONAL SYSTEM DEVELOPMENT LIFE CYCLE

Development is a very deliberate and orderly approach to making a system a reality. A methodology is needed to provide structure to system development. There are many "traditional" system development life cycles (SDLCs) for information systems, including DSS. Each computer-aided software engineering (CASE) tool has adopted a variation. Further complicating matters, each organization that develops systems can create in-house variations to suit specific needs. Each methodology emphasizes different steps in different ways. But all of the SDLCs that make intuitive and practical sense generally must follow certain guidelines and processes.

Ideally, some kind of need starts the process, and a completed system is its result. A traditional SDLC consists of four fundamental phases—planning, analysis, design, and implementation—which lead to a deployed system (Figure 6.1). It is a cycle because it is possible to return to any phase from any other, though an ideal progression is to follow each phase in order. All projects must go through these phases. Each phase consists of a series of steps, which rely on techniques that produce deliverables. We have adopted the SDLC described by Dennis and Wixom (2000). In Table 6.1, we show the fundamental phases, the steps, and the deliverables for each step. The SDLC presentation appears linear, though at any time the project can be halted or can return to an earlier step in any phase. We now discuss the phases and steps.

FIGURE 6.1 THE TRADITIONAL SYSTEM DEVELOPMENT LIFE CYCLE (SDLC)

Ideally, the project "flows" down and to the right. The upward arrows indicate that changes while developing a system can return the process to an earlier stage. This is also known as *waterfall development*.

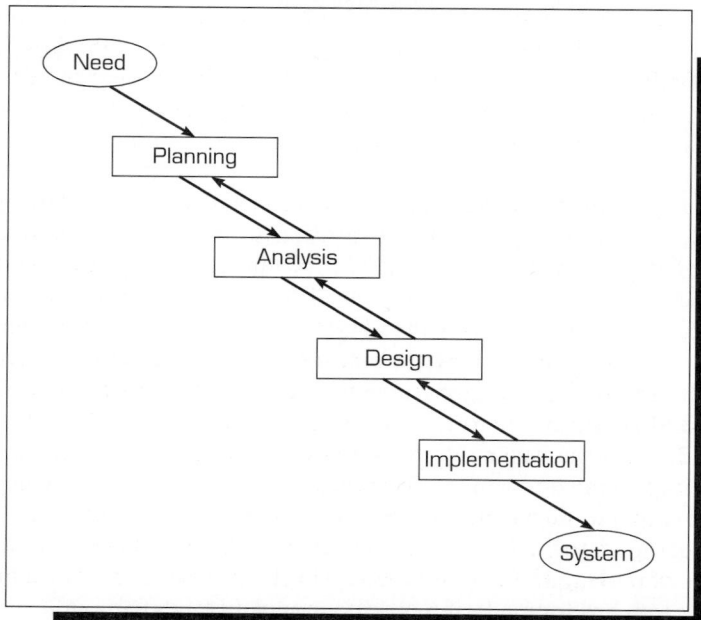

TABLE 6.1   The Traditional System Development Life Cycle

Major Phase	Minor Step	Deliverable
Planning: Why build the system?	1. Identify business value	System request
	2. Analyze feasibility	Feasibility study
	3. Develop work plan	Work plan
	4. Staff project	Staffing plan
		Project charter
	5. Control and direct project	Project management tools
		CASE tool
		Standards list
		Project "binders" or files
		Risk assessment
Analysis: Who, what, when, and where will the system be?	6. Analyze problem	Analysis plan
	7. Gather information	Information
	8. Model process(es)	Process model
	9. Model data	Data model
Design: How will the system work?	10. Design physical system	Design plan
	11. Design architecture	Architecture design
		Infrastructure design
	12. Design interface	Interface design
	13. Design database and files	Data storage design
	14. Design program(s)	Program design
Implementation: System delivery	15. Construction	Test plan
		Programs
		Documentation
	16. Installation	Conversion plan
		Training plan

Source: Based on Dennis and Wixom (2000).

1. *Planning.* The *planning phase* starts with a business need not being met. This includes possible opportunities identified through environmental scanning. Is there a problem that needs to be solved? Project initiation involves a system request that is decided on. If it appears worthwhile, a feasibility analysis is conducted. The feasibility analysis considers whether the idea is viable. Questions concerning technical feasibility, cost feasibility, and organizational feasibility are answered here. If the project is approved, a project manager is assigned, and he or she creates a work plan, staffs the project, and adopts methods for managing it.

2. *Analysis.* The *analysis phase* is like a journalist's interview. It asks and answers the important questions: Who will the users be? What will the system accomplish? Where and when will it run? This phase starts with the development of an analysis strategy or a plan to guide the project. If there is an existing system, it is analyzed, along with ways of moving to the new system. This leads to further information gathering, leading up to the development of a process model and a data model.

3. *Design.* The *design phase* indicates how the system will work, considering all the details of the hardware, software, network infrastructure, user interface, and so on. In this phase, the user interface, forms, displays, reports and programs, databases, and files are specified. In the design strategy, the amount of the system to be purchased or contracted (versus built in-house) is decided on. This leads to the architecture design, which leads to the database and file design, which in turn leads to the program design. Collectively, these are the system specifications.

4. *Implementation.* The *implementation phase* brings it all together. This is where the system is built or purchased. Construction involves not only building the system but also testing it to verify that it works. Better planning can typically lead to systems with fewer bugs. Installation is the last step and involves actually getting the system up and running.

In Figure 6.1, we illustrate the four steps in the structure of an SDLC, which are sometimes referred to as the *waterfall model* (Swanson et al., 1999). Water and everything in it have a tendency to move downward, however, if there is a need to return to an earlier step, it is possible to hop up the waterfall against the effects of gravity.

The process of system analysis, design, and implementation creates *organizational change,* which must be managed. DSS development and implementation involve implementing change—change in an organization or in an individual's work. (See DSS in Focus 6.3.) Throughout the development process, there are a number of factors that must go right or the system will fail (and there may be other, often overlooked factors as well). User expectations must be managed, users and managers must be involved,

---

DSS IN FOCUS 6.3

SUCCESSFUL STRATEGIC SYSTEMS DEVELOPMENT LESSONS AT ARTHUR ANDERSEN

Many lessons were learned in developing and implementing Arthur Andersen's global best practices (GBP) knowledge base. In one year, the GBP grew in size about threefold, the number of personnel involved in the system almost doubled, and the number of users grew dramatically as well. Bob Hiebeler, the managing director of KnowledgeSpace has refined a set of lessons learned about implementing changes that shift a company's culture and the way it does business. We loosely modify these as follows:

1. *Begin before you're ready.* (Just do it!) Don't wait to get started. Get your feet wet and learn while doing.

2. *Commit to a rapid release schedule.* Maintain a sense of urgency and organization but don't overcommit.

3. *Plan to dazzle your customers.* Make the system easy to use and keep the interface simple.

4. *Keep it in prototype longer than you should.* Or better yet, keep it in perpetual prototype. Changes in the environment impose changes in

the system; therefore, there is no such thing as a finished system. You are always improving it.

5. *If you must train, be clever about it.* Align the resources with job tasks so that the system becomes part of the daily life of your employees. Embed the system in their tasks. Get users *excited.*

6. *Force technology to deliver business value.* In other words, keep everyone focused on delivering what the customer wants, not what you think he or she wants.

7. *Rely on fuzzy feedback before hard measures.* This is common in DSS, where effectiveness is the goal. It is hard to estimate the value of a manager feeling better about a decision, but qualitative benefits are very common.

8. *Choose speed and specificity over size and generality.* Use a real example of what the customer wants rather than speaking in general terms. It makes the system real for the customer.

Source: Modified from D. Pearson, "Where Are They Now?" *CIO,* May 15, 1998, pp. 58–64.

executive and IT sponsors must be established, and communication with them all must be open. We list a number of common implementation headaches in DSS in Focus 6.4.

CASE TOOLS

For complex projects, the SDLC should be managed with computer-aided software engineering (CASE) tools. These tools are essentially information systems for systems analysts and can help manage every aspect of developing a system.

CASE tools that assist in the analysis phase in creating system diagrams are called *upper CASE,* CASE tools that manage the diagrams and generate code for the database tables are called *lower CASE,* and *integrated CASE (I-CASE)* tools do both. Some CASE tools are designed to handle strictly object-oriented systems by supporting the constructs of the universal modeling language (UML) (Krutchteen, 1998). For details on how well object-oriented analysis and its performance levels are accepted by systems analysts as compared to traditional methods, see Fedorowicz and Villeneuve (1999) and Morris, et al. (1999).

Though CASE tools may seem to impose many restrictions on the creative aspect of system development, they handle a lot of the system checking as the system is being built. For example, an analyst may try to use a specific data column, but if it is not defined in advance in the CASE tool framework, the tool will not allow its use. These data and others are stored in the CASE *repository,* which helps to ensure *logical consistency*

DSS IN FOCUS 6.4

SYSTEM IMPLEMENTATION HEADACHES

Sources of implementation headaches include management expectations, customization and process issues, resource shortages, and technology integrations. The following is a list of some warning signs of a troubled implementation and what can go right:

1. No project team or management support (or, no players, no game). But a strong project team of empowered managers and technical staff helps ensure realistic objectives, a sound project plan, the right resources, and the necessary buy-in.

2. Hazy purpose, no defined schedule, a ballooning scope. The project needs a clear understanding at the start. A phased development approach (prototyping) on a schedule can keep a project going, provide feedback, and because of the lessons learned while developing the system, keep the scope of the project within reasonable bounds.

3. Unclear aspects of make-versus-buy decisions. The team must determine how much of the project should be developed, how much should be purchased, and how much of the purchased part should be modified. The scope of the project impacts on these factors, as well as the development team's capabilities and available time.

4. Few product integrations are functional right out of the box. Set realistic expectations for standardized software and plan to modify it.

5. Qualitative benefits, some benefits (and costs) are *fuzzy.* Not all benefits can be measured in dollars. Some involve "feeling good" about a decision. Gather data about them and use them to justify your work.

6. No user buy-in. Users must be part of the development process from the start. Include them and get them excited.

7. Poor project management skills. The project manager must have good project management skills to complete the project successfully.

8. No accountability and no responsibility. The development team is held neither accountable nor responsible for what they do or don't do. Use good management skills to enforce accountability and responsibility.

Source: Partly based on A. R. Starck, "How to Implement Like a Pro," *Support Management,* May/June 1998; and D. Slater, "Business Line Backers," *CIO Enterprise,* March 15, 1998.

within the new system and maintain the system's *documentation*. Some versions of CASE tools can even be considered groupware because of the way system developers can collaborate while developing the system.

Some well-known CASE tools are Oracle Enterprise Development Suite, Rational Rose (Rational Software), Paradigm Plus (Platinum Technology), Visible Analyst (Visible System Corporation), Logic Works Suite, AxiomSys, and AxiomDsn (Structured Technology Group Inc.), V32 and X32 (Blue River Software), and Visual Studio (Microsoft). Figure 6.2 is a screen shot of a diagram from Visible Analyst.

PROJECT MANAGEMENT

Many DSS development projects are large-scale systems. Such systems are developed by teams, and the team leader must have good project management skills. Standish Group International Inc. (Johnson, 1999) indicates some surprising facts about IS/IT projects. Though IT project success rates are up and cost and time overruns are down, in 1998 only 26 percent of all projects surveyed (out of 23,000 application projects at large, medium, and small U.S. companies) succeeded outright (28 percent failed outright, while 46 percent were challenged (i.e., did not do well because of major cost or time overruns or major changes in scope). Large companies have lower success rates (24 percent) than medium (28 percent) and small (32 percent) companies. But the success rates in 1994 were much worse (only 9 percent for large, 16 percent for medium, and 28 percent for small). The dollars wasted on IT projects declined from $150 billion in 1994 to a mere $97 billion in 1998. Basically, IT projects are doing better but could improve. Project management is a key area that needs major improvement. Johnson

FIGURE 6.2 SCREENSHOT FROM VISIBLE ANALYST

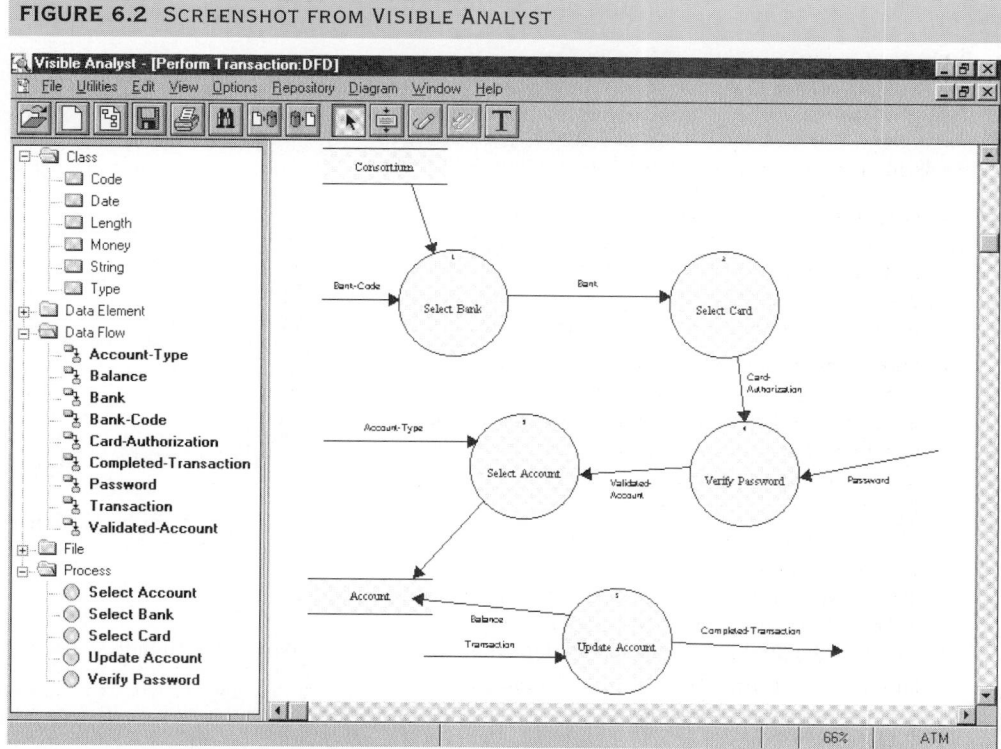

Courtesy Visible System Corporation.

(1999) reports that chief information officers (CIOs) desire the following skills in a project manager: technology and business knowledge, judgment, negotiation, communication, and organization. They emphasize the business side rather than the technical side, and softer skills like diplomacy and time management seem to be valued most. Many firms are making project management skills a core competency. They view them as the future of IT. For example, FMI Corporation was able to reduce its IS staff by 20 percent with a rise in productivity of 30 percent because of a new project management focus (and an SAP implementation) that helped the IT people develop a broader skills set and understood how the software was related to the business (Fryer, 1997).

Along with the managerially oriented skills set, there are software tools to assist project managers in their tasks. They include Microsoft Project, PlanView (PlanView Inc.), and ActiveProject (Framework Technologies Corporation). Many of these tools are Web-enabled to allow collaborative teamwork online over time and distance.

IMPLEMENTATION FAILURE

In closing this section, we want to call attention to a data warehouse implementation failure so that we can learn from someone else's mistakes. The most important factors were no user involvement, no clear objectives stated early, and no real executive sponsorship. These were a few of the key indicators that the project was in trouble from the start. See DSS in Focus 6.5 for more details. The work of Jiang et al. (1998, 1999) may help in identifying some causes of failure at the inception of a project. Their approach is based on the "orientations" of the systems analysts and their perceptions of failure.

DSS IN FOCUS 6.5

ANATOMY OF A DATA WAREHOUSE IMPLEMENTATION FAILURE

Here are several important red flags that popped up early in a real-world data warehouse implementation project. They were leading indicators predicting that the project was headed for failure. To their credit, when the pilot project failed, executives cut their losses and canceled the project.

- No prelaunch objectives or metrics
- Many major systems projects underway simultaneously
- CEO set budgets and deadlines before the project team was on board
- No insider presence on the data warehouse project team
- Overburdened project manager
- Source data availability unconfirmed at the outset
- No user demand for sophisticated data analysis
- No routine meetings of executive sponsors and project manager

- No initial involvement of business managers
- Failure of the pilot project.

Some lessons learned from the failure include the following:

- Executive sponsorship and partnership with IS are the most critical success factors for developing a data warehouse. If possible, establish dual leadership by business and IS executives for the project or pick a project manager from the business side.
- Don't let the project proceed without a clear understanding of the business objectives and how they will be measured.
- Do an incremental pilot project to determine if you can obtain the projected benefit.
- Expect to make a major investment in ongoing management of the data warehouse.
- When all else fails, cut and run.

Source: Adapted from L. G. Paul, "Anatomy of a Failure," *CIO Enterprise,* Nov. 15, 1997, pp. 55–60.

6.4 ALTERNATE DEVELOPMENT METHODOLOGIES

PARALLEL DEVELOPMENT: A TRADITIONAL METHODOLOGY

There are several alternate development methodologies, all of which are based on the traditional SDLC [see McConnell (1996) for a comparison]. The one most closely resembling the SDLC is *parallel development.* In parallel development, following the analysis phase, the design and implementation phases split into multiple copies, each of which involves development of a separate subsystem or subproject. They all come together in a single implementation phase, in which a systems integrator puts the pieces together in a cohesive system. Part of DSS implementation is handled in this manner; the four components, database, model base, user interface, and knowledge, can essentially be developed in parallel.

RAPID APPLICATION DEVELOPMENT METHODOLOGIES

Rapid application development (RAD) methodologies adjust the SDLC so that parts of a system can be developed quickly and users can obtain some functionality as soon as possible. These include methods of *phased development, prototyping,* and *throwaway prototyping.*

The **phased development** methodology involves breaking a system up into a series of versions that are developed sequentially. Each version has more functionality than the previous one, and they evolve into a final system. The advantage is that users gain functionality quickly; the disadvantage is that the systems with which users start to work are incomplete by design.

We now turn to the major methodology under which DSS is developed: prototyping.

Prototyping involves performing the analysis, design, and implementation phases concurrently and repeatedly (Figure 6.3). System prototypes are quickly developed and demonstrated to users, whose input is used to refine them. The main advantage is that systems are quickly provided to users, even though they may not be ready for institutional use. Feedback is obtained, and the system can be modified on moving to the next prototype. Further analysis may need to be performed as well. One disadvantage is that changes are introduced quickly and that there is no attempt to correct design decisions early on. Instead they are repaired as the system evolves. This is like the development of the Chevrolet Monza (an automobile), which initially required that the engine be dropped out to change two of the spark plugs during a tune-up. Customers bought the car and eventually, in later designs, the problem was fixed by inserting panels so the plugs could be reached. On the other hand, if prototyping is done carefully with good design practices, it is very effective (see DSS in Focus 6.6). For example, the IMERYS Case Application 6.1 model was developed by starting with a small plant to gain understanding. More complex plants and more functionality were added to the system over time.

Throwaway prototyping is similar to both prototyping and the traditional SDLC (Figure 6.4). As in the SDLC, the analysis phase is thorough, but design prototypes are developed to assist in understanding more about the system being developed, especially when it is not clearly understood. Often throwaway prototypes are developed as pilot tests on simpler development platforms to learn about user requirements and the final system to be deployed. For example, it is possible to work out calculation methods in Excel to map out the functionality of a program before committing to the formal

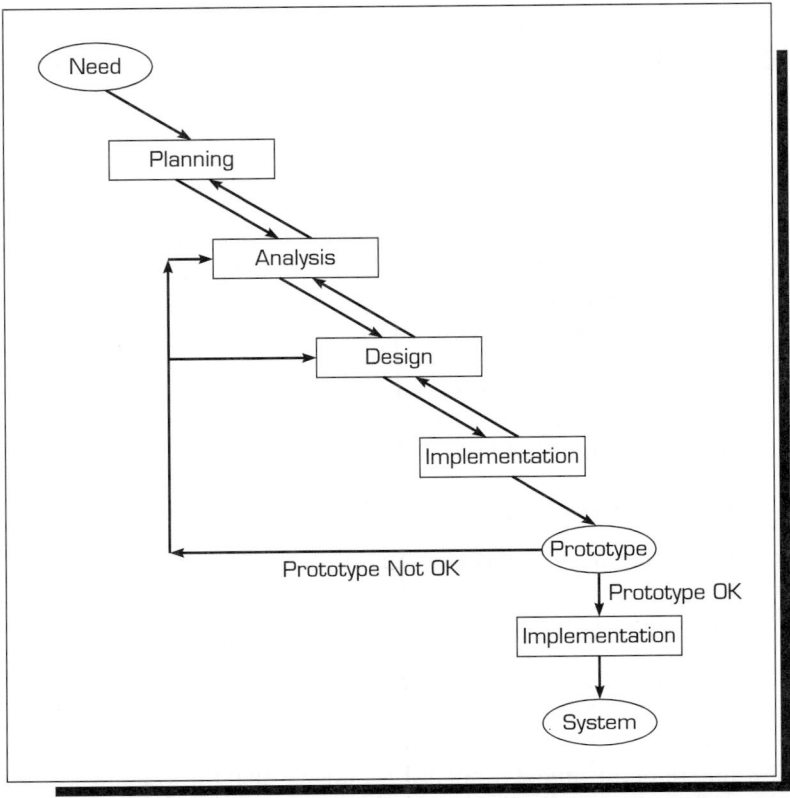

FIGURE 6.3 PROTOTYPING DEVELOPMENT PROCESS: A RAPID
APPLICATION DEVELOPMENT (RAD) METHOD

DSS IN FOCUS 6.6

PROTOTYPING WORKS BECAUSE . . .

Here are some ways to ensure success using a prototyping approach to DSS development.

- Gain the unshakable support of the company's
  top business executive to obtain the proper visibility and resources committed to the project.

- Align new systems across several business
  processes, not just one. This yields a broader level
  of support for the project.

- Slice up a project into pieces. This allows you to
  manage the project better by staying on track.

- Deliver results in phases, not at the end. Early deliverables allow managers and users to see the
  benefits without having to wait for the big bang
  (especially if it doesn't do what is needed; this
  prototyping process encourages user input for
  correction and refinement).

Source: Based on B. Caldwell, "Taming the Beast,"
InformationWeek, March 10, 1997.

---

development in a programming language. (If you do not fully understand what you are
trying to develop, we encourage this approach.) Once the pilot test is successful, the
prototype is discarded and a preliminary design of the real system takes place. After
that, the DSS is completed using the SDLC or prototyping approach.

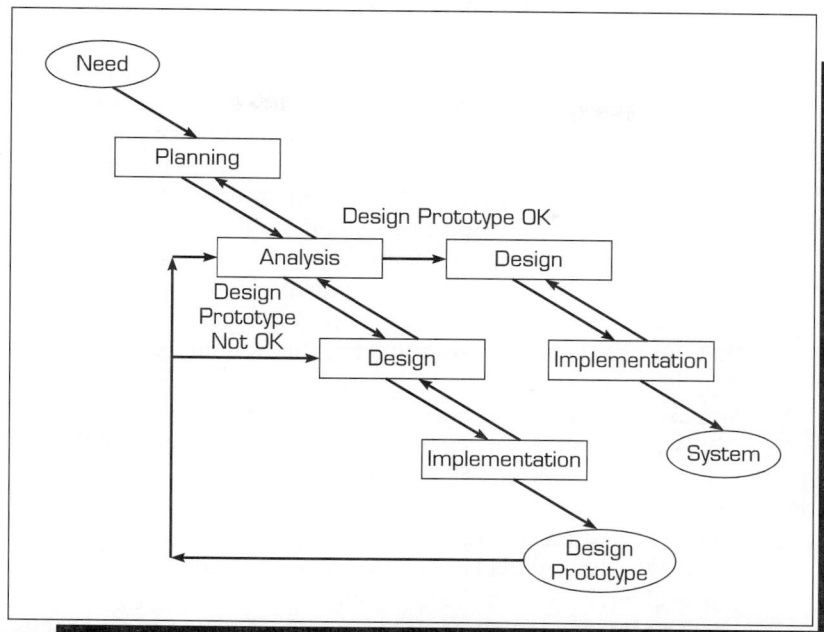

FIGURE 6.4 THROWAWAY PROTOTYPING DEVELOPMENT PROCESS: ANOTHER RAPID APPLICATION DEVELOPMENT METHOD

The design prototype helps the team work out details used in the system that is developed.

6.5 PROTOTYPING: THE DSS DEVELOPMENT METHODOLOGY

Because of the semistructured or unstructured nature of problems addressed by decision support systems, it is quite unlikely that managers and DSS developers have a complete understanding of the decision-making problem. They may not understand the scope of the problem, the types of appropriate models or technologies to apply, and/or the information needs. So most DSS are developed through the prototyping process. Prototyping is also known as **iterative design** or **evolutionary development.** (Other names are *middle-out process, adaptive design,* and *incremental design.*)

The prototyping development methodology aims at building a DSS in a series of short steps with immediate feedback from users to ensure that development is proceeding correctly. Therefore, DSS tools must be flexible to permit changes quickly and easily.

We show the details of the prototyping methodology in Figure 6.3. Prototyping is a process of building a "quick and dirty" version of a system. The *evolutionary* approach starts with overall DSS planning and some analysis. Users and managers, as well as an executive sponsor, must be involved. Other factors, critical for success or leading to failure, are mentioned in the Opening Vignette and several of the DSS in Action and DSS in Focus boxes.

Next, the analysis, design, and prototype implementation phases are iteratively performed until a small prototype is sufficiently developed (decided on jointly by the developer(s), managers, and users). Then the final implementation of this part of the system takes place. Simultaneously, further iterations occur in the loop of analysis-design-implementation-system prototype as other subsystems or capabilities are added to the deployed system until a fairly stable, comprehensive system evolves. This is how the systems both in the Opening Vignette and in Case Application 6.1 were developed.

The first major decision involves which subproblem to build first. The user and the developer jointly identify a subproblem for which the initial DSS prototype is to be implemented. This early joint effort sets up initial working relationships between the participants and opens the lines of communication. The subproblem should be small enough that the nature of the problem, the need for computer-based support, and the nature of this support are clear or quickly established. It should be of high interest value to the decision maker. In the Opening Vignette, it was the employee benefits subsystem that provided intense visibility for the system because *everyone* used it. For Case Application 6.1, it was the small calcine plant. This approach helps to excite managers and users about the potential of the system they want.

A prototype is ideally a small but usable system for the decision maker. No major system analysis or feasibility analysis is involved. In fact, the developer and the user go through all the steps of the system development process quickly, though on a small scale. The system should, out of necessity, be simple.

As the system evolves, it must be evaluated continuously. At the end of each cycle it is evaluated by both the user and the developer.

The interaction among the user, the developer, and the technology is extremely important in this process. There is a balance of effort and cooperation between the user and the developer: The user takes the lead in the use and evaluation activities, and the developer is stronger in the design and implementation phases. The user plays an active role, in contrast to the situation in conventional system development, where the user often operates in a reactive or passive role. Note that the specification of needed data or information evolves as the prototype evolves along with user and developer experience.

Evaluation is an integral part of the development process and is the control mechanism for the entire iterative design process. The evaluation mechanism is what keeps the cost and effort of developing a DSS consistent with its value. At the end of the evolution, a decision is made on whether to further refine the DSS or to stop.

If the prototype is OK, we move to formal implementation of the DSS, which could include all the user training, and so on. Subsequent cycles expand and improve the original version of the DSS. All the analysis, design, construction, implementation, and evaluation steps are repeated in each successive refinement.

Years ago, under the traditional SDLC, the analyst obtained information requirements and other data from the user and went away for a long period of time to develop a system. Over time, the business environment, the organization, the users' needs, and even the users might change. When the system was delivered, it might not meet anyone's needs. In prototyping, looping back to early stages implies that the initial analysis was incomplete, as is expected.

The iterative design approach produces a specific DSS application. The process is fairly straightforward for a DSS designed for personal support. The process becomes more complicated, although not invalid, for a DSS that provides group support or organizational support. Specifically, there is a greater need for mechanisms to support communication among users and developers. There is also a need for mechanisms to accommodate personal variations while maintaining a common core system that is standard for all users.

Most DSS are developed with the prototyping methodology. One reason is that prototyping allows the developers to get a usable (perhaps partial) system up and running relatively fast. And if one views DSS as never being complete, but always in a state of evolution, prototyping is an ideal methodology (see DSS in Focus 6.7). Some prototyping of non-DSS is performed with the same software packages with which the DSS is developed, including DSS generators and DSS tools like report generators, GUI generators, and spreadsheets. An application generator is often nothing more than a collection of prototyping tools that enables a full range of system development activities and is very similar to a DSS generator.

Specifically, DSS development is done through prototyping for the following reasons:

- Users and managers are involved in every phase and iteration. The iterative nature allows users to be involved in system design, which is important for DSS. This approach stems from a need for user expertise in the design and recognizes that successful implementation is more easily achieved with active involvement. Sometimes this involvement is called the *joint application development (JAD) method.*
- Learning is explicitly integrated into the design process. Since the users are involved in system design, both users and system developers learn about the decision making, the ill-structured, complex problem, and the technologies that can potentially be applied to it (Steiger, 1998).
- Prototyping essentially bypasses the formal life-cycle substep 7— information requirement definition (see Table 6.1). Requirements evolve as experience is gained. This strategy assumes that the requirements are only partially known at the beginning of system development, and it attempts to clarify users' needs by actively involving them in a low-cost, fast-feedback development process.
- A key criterion associated with prototyping is the short interval between iterations. The feedback must be fast. This criterion results from the required learning process: Accurate and timely feedback is a prerequisite to effective learning.
- The initial prototype must be low-cost. It must fall below the minimum threshold of capital outlays requiring formal justification. The development of a prototype may be a risky decision, particularly for a DSS. However, because the benefits of a DSS are often intangible, relating to such issues as improved decision making or better understanding, a high initial investment may result in a decision not to proceed (see DSS in Focus 6.5).

DSS IN FOCUS 6.7

HOW COMPANIES SPEED IT DEPLOYMENT

Here are some concepts that can move a project from impulse drive to warp drive. Many of them involve aspects of the prototyping development methodology.

1. Target small, tactical applications
2. Make application deployment iterative and open to customization
3. Use commodity hardware
4. Use object technology

5. Devolve big projects already under way
6. Break major projects into manageable deliverable chunks
7. Use packaged applications
8. Employ IT service providers

Source: J. Hibbard, "Time Crunch," *InformationWeek,* July 13, 1998, pp. 42–52.

ADVANTAGES OF PROTOTYPING

Some of the major advantages of prototyping are

- Short development time
- Short user reaction time (feedback from user)
- Improved user understanding of the system, its information needs, and its capabilities
- Low cost.

DISADVANTAGES AND LIMITATIONS OF PROTOTYPING

When such an approach is used, the gains obtained from cautiously stepping through each of the system's life-cycle stages might be lost. These gains include a thorough understanding of the information system's benefits and costs, a detailed description of the business's information needs, an easy-to-maintain information system design, a well-tested information system, and well-prepared users. However, this could be avoided by using a CASE tool to enforce consistency.

6.6 DSS TECHNOLOGY LEVELS AND TOOLS

The classification of **technology levels** is important not only for understanding the development of DSS (also of ES) but also for developing a framework for their use. Sprague and Carlson (1982) describe a framework that defines the classes of development platforms. There are three **DSS technology levels:** DSS primary tools, DSS integrated tools (generators), and specific DSS.

DSS PRIMARY TOOLS

At the lowest level of DSS technology are the primary tools. These fundamental elements facilitate the development of either a DSS generator or a specific DSS. Examples of **DSS tools** are programming languages, graphics, editors, query systems, and random-number generators.

A **DSS integrated tool (generator or engine)** is an integrated development software package that provides a set of capabilities for building a specific DSS quickly, inexpensively, and easily. A generator has diverse capabilities ranging from modeling, report generation, and graphical display to performing risk analysis. These capabilities are integrated into an easy-to-use package. A popular PC-based generator is Excel. Fourth-generation languages, such as Cognos PowerHouse QUICK, are also integrated tools capable of accessing and manipulating data in a modeling framework. OLAP systems should certainly be viewed as DSS integrated tools. Even a linear programming modeling language like Lingo should be considered an integrated tool. Lingo was used by IMERYS (Case Application 6.1). In a highly data intensive environment, most integrated tools can be accessed via standard Web browser technology.

SPECIFIC DSS (DSS APPLICATIONS)

The final product, or the DSS application that actually accomplishes the work, is called a **specific DSS (SDSS).** Two examples are the HR InfoNet system (Opening Vignette) and the IMERYS POP DSS (Case Application 6.1).

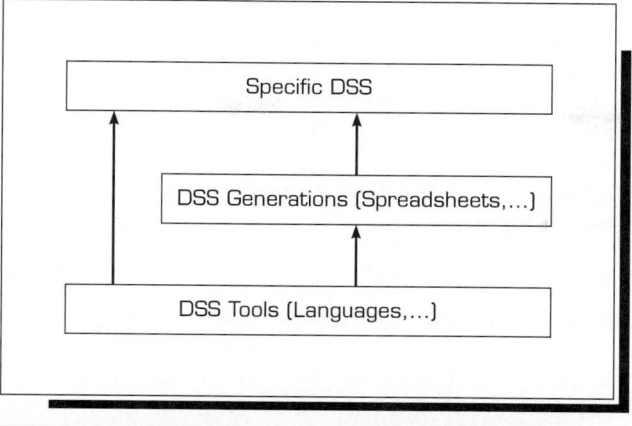

FIGURE 6.5 DSS TECHNOLOGY LEVELS

Each box represents the entire set of the items. Specific DSS may
be developed using either DSS tools, or DSS generators; while
DSS generators may only be developed in DSS tools.

RELATIONSHIPS AMONG THE THREE LEVELS

The relationships among the three levels are illustrated in Figure 6.5. **DSS primary tools**
are used to construct integrated tools, which in turn are used to construct specific DSS.
However, primary tools can also be used to directly construct specific DSS. In addition
(not shown), there may be simpler tools for constructing more complicated tools.

DSS generators or integrated suites are extremely helpful in constructing specific
DSS and in providing flexibility to adapt quickly to changes. Using generators can save
a significant amount of time and money, thus making a DSS financially feasible.
Developing DSS with only primary tools can be very time-consuming and expensive,
especially if the primary tools must be developed. Most early DSS were developed without generators, while new ones are almost exclusively developed with them.

6.7 DSS DEVELOPMENT PLATFORMS

Based on the technology levels described in the previous section, there are several basic DSS development software platforms. The most important ones are the following:

- *Write a customized DSS in a general-purpose programming language such
  as Visual Basic or COBOL.* Although this strategy was viable in the 1980s
  and throughout the 1990s, very few organizations do this. Sometimes,
  though, ultra-large-scale DSS, with many interfaces to other CBIS, are constructed this way.
- *Use a fourth-generation language (4GL).* There are several classes of
  4GL, such as data-oriented languages, spreadsheets, and financial-
  oriented languages. These tools can boost programmers' productivity by a
  magnitude of 10 or even more over general-purpose languages. Even the
  new OLAP systems have embedded 4GLs, for example, Cognos

PowerHouse 4GL QUICK. For the most part, these languages have been replaced by direct OLAP use on multidimensional data cubes and spreadsheets.

- *Use OLAP with a data warehouse or a large database.* Online analytical processing engines not only create multidimensional data cubes but also provide analysis tools that effectively function as "decision support suites." If a manager wants to establish relationships in his or her data but prefers not to know how it is done, data mining methods can hide the methods while producing reasonably effective results.
- *Use a DSS integrated development tool (generator or engine).* An integrated package eliminates the need to use multiple 4GLs. The best known are Excel and Lotus 1-2-3. Generators are more efficient than a collection of individual 4GLs, but they are subject to more limitations.
- *Use a domain-specific DSS generator.* Domain-specific DSS generators are designed to build a highly structured system, usually in a functional area. They include OLAP systems specifically designed for analysis in areas such as retailing, manufacturing, and so on.
- *Develop the DSS using CASE methodology.* As explained in Section 6.3, systems are developed by following a traditional life cycle, and CASE tools can assist in developing large, complex systems. So, CASE tools can be used in developing DSS. CASE tools enforce consistency so that a prototype cannot use nonexistent data, and so on (see DSS in Action 6.8).
- *Develop a complex DSS by integrating several of the above approaches.* This approach is especially suitable for complex DSS. For example, prototypes can be developed with programming languages and generators while managing the project with a CASE tool.

Most of these platforms have integrated links to the Web, and many use Web browser interfaces.

DSS IN ACTION 6.8

SOUTHWESTERN BELL MAKES A CASE

Southwestern Bell provides telephone services to 15.7 million land subscribers and 5.2 million wireless telephone subscribers, each with dozens of options, in Texas, Arkansas, Kansas, Missouri, and Oklahoma. Southwestern Bell needed to construct a large-scale, complex sales negotiation tool to make the process of data organization for customer services more efficient. They needed clear documentation of both the process and the benefits of object-oriented design. They adopted the Rational Rose CASE tool to build this large-scale, complex application framework.

They also needed the ability to convey complex design information to people with little technological experience. Rose was effective because of its graphical depictions of objects, which are easy to manipu-

late. Furthermore, Rose is enhanced through the use of team-enabling features (for collaboration—a GSS). They also used Rose's code generation capabilities so that changes in design would immediately be reflected in the final product. Through the Rose CASE tool, analysis moves directly into design and into implementation via code, while maintaining system documentation.

The features of this CASE tool helped make abstract concepts communicable both to team members and to interested external parties.

Source: Adapted from "Southwestern Bell Makes a Rational Call," Rational Software Corporation, www.rational.com, Feb. 2000.

6.8 DSS DEVELOPMENT TOOL SELECTION

There are many commercially available DSS tools and generators at a wide variety of prices. Some of the software runs only on large mainframes, while other software runs only on PCs. Some software runs on the Web.

Several interdependent questions must be addressed by an organization intending to use DSS tools, including which tools to use, which hardware to run them on, which operating system to use, and which networks to run them on.

HARDWARE SELECTION

DSS run on platforms ranging from an individual PC (a simple Excel application) to the largest multiprocessor computers like the ones that the National Oceanic and Atmospheric Administration (NOAA) uses to run national U.S. weather forecasts. Some run on networks of Unix workstations, while others use PCs as Web clients attached to a Web server. Usually the existing hardware architecture of an organization and its availability to the users (see the Opening Vignette) govern the choice of hardware.

SOFTWARE SELECTION

Selecting the DSS tools or generator is a complex process because

- At the time when selection must be made, DSS information requirements and outputs are not completely known.
- There are hundreds of software packages on the market.
- Software packages are updated very rapidly.
- Price changes are frequent.
- Several people may be involved in the evaluation team.
- One language can be used in the construction of several DSS. Thus, the required capabilities of the tools may change from one application to another.
- Portions of a large DSS may have to be developed with different tools.
- The selection decision involves dozens of criteria against which competing packages are compared. Several criteria are intangible; others are in direct conflict with each other.
- Technical, functional, end-user, and managerial issues are all considered.
- Commercially available evaluations conducted by companies such as Data Decisions, Data Pro, and Software Digest Inc., and the buyer's guides in trade journals such as *eWeek* and *InfoSystems,* are subjective and often superficial, especially for tools that are also used for non-DSS applications.
- The desirability of staying with a few vendors and the nonavailability of client/server open system environments that allow mixing and matching of products from multiple vendors must be considered.

THE SELECTION OF A DSS GENERATOR

When an organization has a DSS generator in-house, it is generally the most likely one to be selected for DSS applications (e.g., Lotus Notes at Osram Sylvania in the Opening Vignette). However, firms do not necessarily use only one generator. Some DSS generators are better for certain types of applications than others. Thus, organizations typically use several generators and may need to purchase a new DSS generator at times. Since there are many criteria, some of which are qualitative, and often

DSS IN ACTION 6.9

HOW I CHOSE HELP DESK SOFTWARE

When Leonard Lopez obtained funding to purchase new software for his help desk, he developed a logical, rational, reasonable approach. He decided that he needed (1) a logical process for help desk software selection that would include gathering requirements, analyzing data, and making a decision; (2) an implementation of this process that would work with a limited budget within a limited time frame; and (3) a good final decision. Along the way, he defused many political and behavioral issues including staff members forming camps in favor of one product over another, aggressive vendor salespersons, and outsourcing part of the process to a knowledgeable consultant.

His aggressive 16-week selection process plan was as follows:

Week(s)	Function(s)
1	Determine and contact key participants
2	Establish a process for requirements-gathering sessions
3 and 4	Conduct requirements-gathering sessions
4 and 5	Compose requirements in RFP format
6 and 7	Distribute RFPs to potential vendors (allow at least 2–3 weeks for a reply)
8 and 9	Gather revisions for requirements; publish and communicate requirements
10 and 11	Collect and summarize RFP data
12	Select RFP short list; advise participants
13	Set short list interviews and demonstrations
14	Accumulate interview findings; make selection of primary and secondary choices
15	Negotiate contract details with primary selection
16	Finalize selection contracts; set implementation plan in place

Mr. Lopez developed a decision-making model as part of this process to develop and weight criteria.

He concluded that some of the important issues that must be dealt with in software selection are the following:

- The software selection affects future use. You are investing in future upgrades not yet created.
- Conduct negotiations with vendors with a *partnership* in mind to get the support or flexibility you'll need further down the road.

- To ensure full participation in your selection efforts, budget for participants from other departments.
- The architecture you purchase *must* be technically compatible with your environment. Make sure you select a compatible product.

Source: Modified from L. Lopez, "How I Chose Help Desk Software," *Support Management,* March 1998, pp. 16–28.

many alternatives, a decision aid such as Expert Choice (Expert Choice Inc.) can greatly improve the selection process (Chapter 5). See DSS in Action 6.9 for an example involving software selection.

6.9 TEAM-DEVELOPED DSS

A **team-developed DSS** requires a substantial effort, though the team may consist of only a few people like the team that developed the HR InfoNet in the Opening Vignette. Team-developed DSS need extensive planning and organization. The planning and organization depend on the specific DSS, the organization in which it will be used, and so on. Certain activities are generic and can be performed by any team.

A complex DSS requires a group of people to build and manage it. The number of people in the group depends on factors such as the size of the effort and the tools used. Some companies have initiated a DSS effort with as few as 2 or 3 people; others have employed as many as 12–15 people.

The organizational placement of the DSS development group varies. Some typical locations are within the IS department, as a highly placed executive staff group, or within a functional group such as finance, accounting, marketing, and so on.

The process that a DSS team follows depends on the specific application. The group may be temporary, created for a specific DSS, or it may be permanent, in which case the group members are assigned to specific DSS projects.

Many of the DSS developed from the 1980s to the mid-1990s were large-scale, complex systems designed primarily to provide organizational support. Such systems are still under development for complex problems and for company-wide applications. These systems are constructed by a team composed of users, intermediaries, DSS developers, technical support experts, and IS personnel. Because there can be several people in each category, these teams can be large and their composition may change over time. Developing a DSS with a team is a complex, lengthy, costly process.

6.10 END USER–DEVELOPED DSS

PCs have diffused throughout organizations, communication with data servers (mainframes and others) has improved, and software tools have improved in capability, quality, price, and user-friendliness. Consequently, users now have the necessary tools to develop their own DSS.

Broadly defined, **end-user computing** (also known as **end-user development**) is the development and use of computer-based information systems by people outside the formal information system area. This includes *all* users in all functional areas at all skill levels at all levels in an organization: managers, executives, staff, secretaries, and others.

User-developed DSS has a more narrow definition. It includes decision makers and professionals (knowledge workers, like financial or tax analysts and engineers) who build or use computers directly to solve problems or enhance their productivity (see DSS in Action 6.10). OLAP tools for multidimensional data cube analysis fall into this category.

We next turn to the advantages and risks of end user–developed DSS.

USER-DEVELOPED DSS: ADVANTAGES AND RISKS

There are several important advantages why users want to develop their own DSS:

- Delivery time is short. There is no wait for an IS development team to schedule and carry out development.
- The prerequisites of extensive and formal user requirements specifications are eliminated. These specifications are often incomplete or incorrect in DSS because of such issues as users' inability to specify the requirements or communication issues between analysts and users. It sometimes takes a long time to develop these specifications.
- Some DSS implementation problems are reduced.
- The cost is usually very low.

DSS IN ACTION 6.10

OLAP GIVES SERVICE MERCHANDISE END-USER DSS

In the late 1980s discount stores forced most catalog showrooms under. Companies like Service Merchandise Company knew nothing about their customers' buying habits or how to target marketing campaigns precisely to help them react quickly enough to reverse the downward slide. Sales and profits declined over 6–7 years.

Because Service Merchandise already had deployed a 500-gigabyte data warehouse, managers decided to use the data to analyze their customers' purchasing habits.

They used DecisionMaster (Intrepid Systems Inc.), a relational OLAP tool, to slice and dice the data and find patterns in sales and inventory by region, store, and individual items. Individual managers can now track marketing campaigns to determine what works and what doesn't. They can then adjust the campaigns for each market. And, if necessary, the OLAP helps target underperforming stores as candidates to be closed.

"When we recognize trends we can act much faster," said Michael Presley, Service Merchandise's di-rector of buying and inventory management. "Before we had this in place, we had to do it all by ad hoc (data-base) requests, which were limited and slow." Presley now transfers chunks of data to his own spreadsheets and manipulates them directly.

Whole new analytic worlds have opened for Presley with the ability to slice and dice and analyze data for individual stores, items, product classes, and supply vendors. "I have more data now than I ever imagined," Presley said.

Postscript. Service Merchandise went into involuntary Chapter 11 bankruptcy in early 1999. Service Merchandise closed 134 underperforming stores in early 1999 as part of its out-of-court restructuring. The retailer had a successful 1999 retail holiday season, in part due to the DSS.

Source: Adapted from Stewart Deck, "Analysis May Help Retailer End Slump," *Computerworld,* Vol. 32, No. 38, Sep 21, 1998, pp. 57–58; with information from "Service Merchandise Announces Intention to Close Up to 134 Stores," *BusinessWire,* Feb. 9, 1999.

Some serious end user–developed DSS risks include the following:

- User-developed DSS can be of poor quality. Lack of formal DSS design experience and the tendency of end users to ignore conventional controls, testing procedures, and documentation standards can lead to low-quality systems (see DSS in Focus 6.11).
- There are three categories of potential quality risks: substandard or inappropriate tools and facilities used in DSS development; risks associated with the development process (e.g., the inability to develop workable systems or the development of systems that generate erroneous results); and data management risks (e.g., loss of data or use of stale, inappropriate, or incorrect data).
- Security risks may increase because of users' unfamiliarity with security measures.
- Lack of documentation and maintenance procedures may cause problems, especially if the developer leaves the organization.

REDUCING THE RISKS OF END-USER COMPUTING

Because most *personal DSS* and many *organizational DSS* are developed by end users, it is important to manage and reduce the risk associated with end user–developed DSS. Experienced development teams use a variety of tools and languages to build DSS. However, end users typically use a **DSS integrated tool** like Excel. They usually follow the "I only own a hammer" approach to problem solving: "When all you own is a hammer, every problem you have looks like a nail."

DSS IN FOCUS 6.11

UH-OH: USER-DEVELOPED DSS RISK

An oil and gas company in Dallas lost millions of dollars in an acquisition deal, and several executives were fired because of an error in a spreadsheet model. The executives had made their decisions based on inaccurate spreadsheet data.

Such errors are common. Few spreadsheet disasters have been published, but consultants and independent audits have found errors in as many as 30 percent of the spreadsheet models created with off-the-shelf spreadsheet systems. A company might have tens of thousands of spreadsheet models in use. What would the impact be if even only 1 percent of them have errors? Decision makers rely on spreadsheet analyses, many of which have never been checked for errors.

Source: Adapted from R. Panko, "Finding Spreadsheet Errors—Most Spreadsheet Models Have Design Flaws That May Lead to Long-term Miscalculations," *CommunicationsWeek,* May 29, 1995, p. 100.

Many spreadsheet applications pose considerable risk to an organization because they support important tasks like financial analysis, budgeting, and forecasting applications. If logical errors or poor documentation create misinformation or make the spreadsheet difficult to interpret, the risk of using incorrect data for financial decisions is great. The cost of an erroneous business decision based on poor data can be enormous (see DSS in Focus 6.11). Quality issues are the most troublesome. How can the work of an end user be validated when the end user develops and uses his or her own system?

There have been several studies that address the issue of risks and controls in end-user development. Some factors contributing to spreadsheet errors include developer inexperience, poor design approaches, application types, problem complexity, time pressure, and the presence or absence of review procedures (Janvrin and Morrison, 2000). Other factors including gender, application expertise, and work group configuration can influence spreadsheet error rates. Janvrin and Morrison (2000) propose applying a structured design approach to developing systems in spreadsheets. This development approach reduced errors significantly in two experiments. Schultheis and Sumner (1994) determined that a number of controls are being applied in practice to spreadsheet applications. Developers use more controls in high-risk spreadsheet applications. Also see Panko (1998; 1999).

Survey data show that spreadsheet errors are common. Freeman (1996) reports in a survey that about 90 percent of spreadsheets with over 150 rows contained at least one significant formula mistake. Overconfidence is perhaps the most serious aspect of spreadsheet errors because it reduces the extent to which end users validate their models before using them to make important decisions. These errors can cost companies millions of dollars in new projects and other business decisions (Berglas and Hoare, 1999).

Whittaker (1999) suggests two simple, obvious, often-skipped approaches to minimizing spreadsheet errors: (1) understand the nature and dynamics of the problem being modeled; and (2) spend time reviewing the spreadsheet model. He also mentions that there are spreadsheet audit tools (Spreadsheet Professional, Operis Analysis Kit, Spreadsheet Detective) available to help identify formula assumptions.

The structure that CASE tools enforce on system analysts, designers, and implementers can indeed force an end user to adhere to methods that create logical consistency in a specific DSS. Also, the issue of level of experience with the development platform and the decision-making problem can influence the quality of a DSS. The upshot is that an organizational unit must take the responsibility to ensure that end user–developed DSS meet rigid quality standards. The data must be accurate, timely, and appropriate, and the system must get the right answers. The system also must be documented and maintained. The unit that ensures these risk factors might be part of an IS center or even a DSS team.

One approach that works well in practice is to *license* end user–developed applications. When a new end-user DSS application is to be created, the user can develop it with an organizationally approved methodology (say, structured design). At the inception, the basic features must be outlined in a one-page report to the DSS licensing group—call it the DLG. A member of the DLG assists the developer by providing appropriate tools and data, as well as methods to access data if they reside on other systems. In this way, security is also preserved. When the DSS is completed, it must be documented, and the DLG must approve its use. The documentation must be good enough so that if the developer leaves the organization, the system can be maintained by the DLG. The DSS is then approved for the individual to use. A copy of all the material is stored with the DLG, and the information about the DSS is cataloged in a knowledge base available to all members of the organization. This practice promotes software reuse. Employees in other departments can search for DSS related to their own work and can ask to use or expand someone else's system on an experimental basis. DSS can be licensed for individual use, several individuals' use, work group use, departmental use, organizational use, or interorganizational use. Each level up requires even tighter restrictions on quality and documentation to ensure that risks in DSS use are minimized.

6.11 DEVELOPING DSS: PUTTING THE SYSTEM TOGETHER

Development tools increase the productivity of developers and help them construct a DSS responsive to users' needs. The philosophy of development tools and generators is based on two simple yet very important concepts: the use of highly automated tools throughout the development process, and the use of prefabricated pieces in the manufacturing of a whole system whenever possible (e.g., component reuse) (Yongbeom and Stohr, 1998). The first concept increases the productivity of the developer in the same way that an electric saw improves the productivity of a carpenter who formerly used a hand saw. The second concept increases productivity analogous to the way a prefabricated wall increases the productivity of a carpenter building a house. Fortunately, when a component is used, it is not "consumed" like the wall is. It can be used again and again.

As the components of a DSS are developed, care must be taken so that they fit together (like the components of a house—the plumbing must fit inside the walls but must link the outside water supply to the sinks and tubs, and so on).

A DSS is more than just the DBMS, MBMS, user interface, and knowledge component. There are interfaces among the components and with outside systems. Typically DSS databases must be refreshed regularly from other, source databases. There may be special tools for a number of necessary functions like report generation. There may be several databases and models, each of which is constructed and used differently; and there may be many people involved in the development in terms of data gathering (refer to the P&G supply chain redesign in Case Application 5.1). Not only do the components have to be constructed, but the specific tools and generators for development also must be selected, installed, and managed.

The system core includes a development language or a DSS generator. Some of the necessary capabilities mentioned above are integrated into DSS generators. Others can be added as needed. These components can be used to build a new DSS or update an existing one. The construction involves the combining of software modules. Fortunately, the newer object-oriented operating systems provide a consistent, user-friendly environment for DSS development. Tools and generators that run in them can easily share results and data. Since a consistent, user-friendly interface can be developed quickly (say, in Microsoft Visual Basic), component interfacing problems are generally minimal. In fact, GUI interfaces are commonly used to front-end legacy DSS and databases instead of rewriting the whole system.

6.12 DSS RESEARCH DIRECTIONS AND THE DSS OF THE FUTURE

We expect to see some of the following major developments in DSS over the next several years:

- Developments in artificial intelligence (expert systems, neural networks, genetic algorithms, fuzzy logic, and other forms of logic) will enhance DSS.
- Specific DSS will include more artificial intelligence. But, the AI will be embedded so that the user will typically be unaware of its presence. Starting from the base of intelligent databases developed in the mid-1990s, AI is now embedded in all the components. Intelligent agents help in searching for needed data and in *sensemaking* of textual and other data. Expert systems help in searching, especially in help desk applications. Neural computing is used in speech recognition and in the handwriting recognition systems employed in small, hand-held PCs like the Palm Pilot. This feature permits different forms of input for the user interface. And of course, model management benefits from expert systems and fuzzy logic in helping to select models and solution methods behind the scenes. Data mining methods that select models based on AI are already in use.
- AI may enhance the development process of DSS. See Bui and Lee (1999), who investigated the possibility of using intelligent agents to support decisions by developing DSS.
- By using AI, future DSS can be more creative. AI can enhance creative work directly (Chapter 7). For example, intelligent software agents can be facilitators in electronic brainstorming sessions of group support systems (GSS).
- Computer technology continues its fast-paced evolution. Capabilities are increasing dramatically, and costs are decreasing. This will lead to more capabilities being embedded in DSS. Faster computers mean that larger, more complex models can be solved to optimality. Exact methods can be employed instead of heuristics. For example, large-scale multidimensional data analysis through OLAP evolved because this was occurring in the 1990s. Larger databases can also be handled relatively easily. This trend will lead to DSS access by more decision makers at lower costs.
- The Web is enhancing collaborative computing. More and better collaboration tools are being developed. The new ones combine collaborative work areas like "whiteboards" with video conferencing. This is one relatively new form of GSS.

- GSS will proliferate through collaborative computing (Chapter 7).
- GSS will see more asynchronous mode use. The different time/different place mode of GSS will be used more frequently, for example, in distance learning environments.
- Enterprise resource management/enterprise resource planning (ERM/ERP) systems, though extremely expensive, are proliferating (Chapter 8). These often provide and incorporate DSS methods for improved decision making. One future development of the IMERYS model (Case Application 6.1) will be to use its results to drive a new ERP.
- An important form of collaboration, knowledge management, is proliferating (Chapter 9).
- Graphical user interfaces are improving in quality. Scanners are cheap and widespread. Digital photography and video are approaching photographic quality at the time this book goes to press. By the end of 2000, digital photography should match or exceed traditional photography quality at comparable prices.
- Better telecommunication is enhancing much of what DSS does.
- Improved DSS should be able to deal with more unstructured problems such as those that affect overall organizational efficiency and effectiveness.
- Theories must continue to be developed in organizational decision making and group decision making.
- Research on developing new concepts of decision making continues. The area of sensemaking is receiving considerable attention.
- Research continues on determining the best approaches to conducting collaborative work online, and on what is gained and lost. New results will impact on how we conduct meetings and how GSS capabilities will evolve.
- Research on what differentiates an expert systems analyst from a novice is important. It helps determine what skills are needed for expert-level performance (Schenk et al., 1998).
- Research on the causes of system development failure is important, especially based on the percentage of projects that fail and the dollar volume of waste in IS projects. Theories such as task–technology fit (Goodhue, 1998) should be explored.
- Organizational learning concepts as they apply to DSS must be explored.
- As new DSS methodologies and approaches are developed, they are studied for their effectiveness (e.g., knowledge management) and how they impact on organizations, and vice versa.
- New methods are being explored for validating DSS results. These include scenarios (Dzida and Freitag, 1998).
- Research on gender issues, cognitive issues (Siau, 1999), and decision style issues as they relate to decision making and DSS continues.
- Research on system success metrics other than pure costs and benefits continues because not all benefits and costs can be quantified.
- Research on change management also continues. The important organizational culture aspects of change and change management have yet to be completely understood.
- DSS applications could be enhanced by the inclusion of values, ethics, and aesthetics. But the problem is how to do this. It will require a broader range of variables that are difficult to measure or even define.

❖ CHAPTER HIGHLIGHTS

- The traditional system development life cycle (SDLC) is a structured approach for managing the development of information systems.
- The four fundamental phases of the traditional SDLC are planning, analysis, design, and implementation.
- The SDLC has many small steps, each with its own techniques and deliverables.
- Computer-aided software engineering (CASE) tools are useful for managing large information system development.
- There is a need for good project management skills in system development team leaders.
- In practice most information systems do not succeed. It is important to understand the factors that lead to failure so that they can be recognized early.
- DSS are usually developed by prototyping (iterative design, evolutionary development) development methodology.
- Prototyping is a rapid application development (RAD) methodology.
- Prototyping consists of rapid cycles through the fundamental phases of the SDLC, with user feedback guiding system modifications. [This is a form of joint application development (JAD)]. Typically DSS developed with prototyping continue to evolve following deployment.
- Iterative prototyping methodology is most common in DSS development because information requirements are not precisely known at the beginning of the process.
- Prototyping helps the user understand the decision-making situation as the system evolves.
- DSS technology levels are DSS primary tools, DSS integrated tools (generators, engines), and specific DSS.
- DSS are typically constructed with a DSS generator consisting of an integrated set of development tools.
- Selecting DSS software and hardware is difficult because it involves both quantitative and qualitative factors.
- There are many DSS tools and generators on the market. The appropriate ones for building a specific DSS must be selected carefully.
- DSS can be built by teams or by individuals.
- A team building a DSS must follow a structured process.
- Most end-user DSS developed with an integrated tool like an Excel spreadsheet are used for personal support.
- The major benefits of end users developing their own DSS are short delivery time, users' familiarity with their needs, low cost, and easier implementation.
- End user–developed DSS can be of poor quality. Appropriate controls based on system development methods can improve quality. The two primary ones are (1) to understand the model of the problem, and (2) to review the model carefully.
- Assembling a DSS can involve many components and their interfaces.
- The future challenges of DSS include actively incorporating artificial intelligence methods, developing better collaboration systems (GSS), and exploiting the Internet.
- DSS research will focus on a number of areas including developing a better understanding of the various aspects of decision making and human behavior, understanding the effectiveness of DSS, and understanding the causes of DSS success and failure.

❖ Key Words

- DSS generator (engine)
- DSS integrated tool
- DSS primary tools
- DSS technology levels
- DSS tools
- end-user computing
- end-user development

- evolutionary development
- feasibility study
- iterative design
- phased development
- prototyping
- rapid application development (RAD)

- specific DSS (application)
- system development life cycle (SDLC)
- team-developed DSS
- technology levels (of DSS)
- throwaway prototyping
- user-developed DSS

❖ Questions for Review

1. List and describe the fundamental phases and minor steps of the traditional system development life cycle (SDLC).
2. Define computer-aided software engineering (CASE). Why is it important?
3. List the reasons why good project management skills are needed by DSS development team leaders.
4. List the reasons why information systems fail in practice.
5. Define prototyping.
6. Describe how the phases of prototyping relate to those of the traditional SDLC.
7. Compare a throwaway (design) prototype to a system prototype.
8. List the reasons why prototyping is the method of choice for developing most DSS.
9. List the three technology levels of DSS.
10. Define DSS integrated tools (generators) and discuss their objectives.
11. List the DSS development platforms.
12. List some of the difficulties in selecting DSS software.
13. List the differences between team-developed DSS and end user–developed DSS.
14. Define *end user* and *end-user computing*.
15. List the major advantages of end user–developed DSS.
16. List the potential quality risk areas in end user–developed DSS.
17. List methods for improving the quality of DSS developed in spreadsheets.
18. List all the different components that a DSS might have. Explain why it is sometimes hard to cement them together.
19. List the major trends in DSS.

❖ Questions for Discussion

1. Describe how the fundamental phases of the SDLC match Simon's four phases of decision making. Compare Simon's definition of implementation to the SDLC definition.
2. Explain how CASE tools can enforce standards in system development.
3. Why is the traditional SDLC an inappropriate methodology for developing most DSS?
4. Explain why prototyping is also known as evolutionary development.
5. Describe the similarities between prototyping and the traditional SDLC. Describe how they are different.

6. Compare prototyping software to prototyping consumer products (say, automobiles). What is similar and what is different?

7. Explain the reasoning behind prototyping a user interface (see DSS in Focus 6.2).

8. How does the iterative process secure more user input than conventional development approaches?

9. How does the user develop a better understanding of the decision-making problem through the iterative process?

10. What are the disadvantages of not having complete specifications for a DSS but instead letting it evolve from a small prototype?

11. How can a CASE tool be used in DSS development through prototyping?

12. Describe how the three DSS technology levels interact.

13. Explain how the classification of technology levels can improve understanding of the DSS development process.

14. Give two examples each of specific DSS, DSS generators, and DSS primary tools not mentioned in this text.

15. Explain how an OLAP package can be a DSS generator.

16. Discuss how to select DSS software. What makes it so difficult?

17. Explain how OLAP running on multidimensional data cubes is an end user–developed DSS.

18. Discuss the reasons why end user–developed DSS can be of poor quality. What can be done to improve the situation?

19. Comment on the statement "When all you own is a hammer, every problem you have looks like a nail" as it relates to end-user developed DSS. Investigate some ways that this issue can be managed properly.

20. How has the World Wide Web changed our views of cementing the components of a DSS together?

❖ EXERCISES

1. Identify the latest developments in CASE tools and methods in the academic and trade literature. Explain how these improvements can impact DSS development.

2. Identify critical issues in the academic and trade literature on information system project management. Describe the five most important issues and what industry is doing to solve them.

3. You have been assigned the task of redesigning the interface for the automatic teller machine at your bank. Describe how you will approach this problem.[2]

4. *Throwaway prototype.* It is possible to use a spreadsheet package like Excel to map out the functionality of a program before committing to a formal development in a programming language. Do this for a problem that your instructor gives you.

5. Identify three OLAP systems specifically designed for analysis in functional business areas such as retailing, manufacturing, and so on. Describe their basic features and recommended use.

6. *Situation evaluation.* Many hours and much expense were involved in developing a DSS to assist a manager in making an important decision. The prototyping approach was used, and so the decision maker and the system developers worked together (and were paid). When it came time for the manager to make the decision, she queried the system, discarded the advice, and made an alternative deci-

---

[2]Adapted from Dennis and Wixom (2000).

sion. How could this happen? Could the system still have been beneficial to the manager? Why or why not? If so, how? Could the system still be beneficial to the organization? Why or why not?

❖ INTERNET EXERCISES

1. Explore CASE tools on vendors' Web sites. Select a single CASE tool, download the demo, and try it. Make a list of the important features of the tool. Is this CASE tool upper CASE, lower CASE, or I-CASE? Why? Report your findings to the class.

2. Explore project management software on vendors' Web sites. Select a single-project management package, download the demo, and try it. Make a list of the important features of the package. Report your findings to the class.

3. Search the Web and recent literature for information on object-oriented database and model base development software. (*Hint:* UML.) For a reasonable sample of 10 sites, answer the following questions: What vendors are there and what products do they offer? How do these products differ from the traditional packages? How can they be used for DSS development?

❖ GROUP EXERCISE

Software selection. Build an Expert Choice (AHP) model to help you evaluate and select a DSS generator package to solve a specific problem (see Chapters 2 and 5 for appropriate software examples). Develop criteria, and so on, in terms of a particular decision-making application. Explain which package you would choose and why.

❖ GROUP PROJECT

Continue developing the DSS Term Project from Chapter 5. Focus on the system development issues. What major problems is your group encountering? How are you resolving them? Finish the project and report your results to the class.

CASE APPLICATION 6.1

CLAY PROCESS PLANNING AT IMERYS: A CLASSICAL CASE OF DECISION MAKING

PART 4: DEVELOPMENT AND IMPLEMENTATION OF THE PROCESS OPTIMIZATION DSS[3]

INTRODUCTION

In Case Applications 2.1, 2.2, and 5.3, we presented some of the decision-making processes, the decisions, the linear programming model, and the database requirements of the Process OPtimization (POP) DSS. In this case application we discuss the process by which the entire system was developed and implemented.

THE POP DSS APPROACH

In November 1998, an analyst/consultant attended a one-day meeting in which the feasibility of the approach was discussed. It was determined that a decision support system could be built and that it would be wise to spend some time canvassing the market for an appropriate mathematical programming language (a DSS generator)

---

[3]Contributed by the initial POP development team: Jay E. Aronson, Chris Hutchings, Teresa A. Rhodes, C. Allen Orr, John Brooker, and Trish Layton.

that could solve problems on the order of magnitude expected (very large because of the complexity of the operations), would be relatively easy to understand (close to English), and could link to standard database systems such as Access (for an easy-to-use interface and data storage). In December the team held a workshop to cover the basic and advanced features of linear programming (the model type) and to discuss how *optimization modeling languages* work, as well as the strengths and weaknesses of the leading systems. Several commercial packages were evaluated at that time, and of them, the team selected Lingo (Lindo Systems Inc., www.lindo.com) because of its fairly natural problem statements, its automatic linking to databases, its ability to solve problems of unlimited size, and some familiarity with Lindo, its predecessor. Embedded in Lingo is a set of robust solvers (Lindo for linear programming problems, Gino for nonlinear programming problems), problem size is limited only by real system memory, the language runs on a variety of platforms from PC to RISC workstation to mainframe, and it links to Access and other database systems directly through the Windows object data base control (@ODBC) method. The PC platform was selected based on its uniform availability throughout the organization, and specific managers (mine managers, plant managers, and the sales forecasting manager) were contacted and informed about the project to gain support and because they would be contacted later for information and their knowledge about the clay processes being modeled.

By the end of December, a small DSS POP team was formed. It consisted of the manager of the project, the manager of the small calcine plant selected for initial modeling, two IS specialists, an accounting specialist, and a mathematical programming analyst/consultant.

At this point, much was unknown about the project, but it was felt to be worth investigating. The idea seemed viable, and the payoff in terms of better planning and scheduling was worth the risk.

SYSTEM DEVELOPMENT— PROTOTYPING: A LEARNING EXPERIENCE

The prototyping approach had proven very successful in the past and was deemed appropriate for this project. Over time, as the team members learned more and more about clay processing, the structure of the model became more complex, the size became quite large, and the model itself became more accurate. Simple models that grew in complexity were in turn examined and discarded until a workable approach evolved. As the model evolved, with the help of users and managers, new potential uses of the system were developed, leading to model refinements and new system queries and reports.

PROJECT INITIATION

In January 1999, the team began to analyze process flowcharts of the small calcine (dry clay processing) plant and developed a very unstructured, direct model that did not utilize database interaction. At that time, IMATEL tendered an offer for ECCI, which led to the team leader temporarily leaving the team and making the manager of the small plant the team leader. This potential buyout led directly to changes in the priorities of the plants to be modeled because different company plants (specific plants were not known but were projected) would not be part of the new, yet to be formed company (per U.S. Justice Department approval), while other plants would be brought in from other companies. Some of these plants were part of the Dry Branch Kaolin Company, which was already owned by IMATEL. As a consequence, work on some processing plants that initially were to be modeled was put on hold, while other models required completion fairly quickly.

There were several factors that complicated the progress of the project. The mathematical programming analyst/consultant was available for only 2–3 days per week. Members of the team had other, full-time responsibilities. For example, the new team manager still ran her plant, one IS analyst was developing the firm's demand-forecasting system, the other was still working on quality-issue projects, and the accounting specialist still continued his other full-time activities. Not knowing how the plants would be divided up and sold off, the team proceeded as planned with the small plant and developed mock-up prototypes of proposed interfaces (screens and reports) with which it felt managers would be the most comfortable. The team also worked closely with several users to get a sense of the kinds of screens and reports that would be useful. An annual time period would be modeled, but the ability to create versions of the model for various time horizons would be designed into the system. The POP DSS was developed and deployed on an IBM PC-compatible notebook computer.

THE FIRST MODEL—THE SMALL CALCINE PLANT

By late March, the team had developed a fairly accurate, but not database-linked, model of the small calcine plant. Its accuracy was demonstrated to the larger, continuous improvement initiative team, and the POP team was directed to continue its efforts because management and users could see large potential benefits in assisting decision making and in profitability. (At each step of the way, the team apprised the managers and potential users of its progress to keep communication lines open and to seek advice.) At this time, one IS analyst determined a way to link the database to the model, and a new, simpler modeling approach was considered and developed. The multi-commodity, near-network model is described in Case Application 5.3.

MODEL AND DATABASE INTERFACING

The new model structure could be readily stored directly in an Access database, and Lingo, through the Windows @ODBC interface mechanism, could link the two together. Lingo models can be defined by sets, both primitive (e.g., clay, plant) and derived (e.g., link, linksum) (Chapter 5). Each set can be represented by a table in a relational database, while each entry in the set maps into a column. These sets include model data to be fed directly from the database into the Lingo model as well as the values of the decision variables found by the Lingo optimizer, which are automatically fed back into the database. The Lingo model itself appears as a series of statements indicating its mathematical definition and the data definitions and their source. Using the set concept, coupled with Lingo's ability to manipulate data, the mathematical programming analyst quickly developed a new structure for the model. The basic design of the database was quickly worked out once the multicommodity, near-network model was developed. The team quickly converted the small model to the new structure and validated it.

SYSTEM DEVELOPMENT BEGINS

From this point onward, it was relatively easy to modify the Lingo model because of the general set structure, and so the team was able to focus on the data, screens, and reports.

Given input parameters and solution entries in the POP database tables, a menu system was created to manage the generation of cases, queries, and solution reports, which could be solved and stored in the tables of the POP database. Early in this part of the process, a *process utilization report* was prepared which included a bar graph showing all clay processes and their utilization. The equipment running at 100 percent capacity could be examined more closely in the model to verify that the plants were running as efficiently as possible. This report was instrumental in the managers being able to *visualize* how the summarized results could be used in practice. This one report was key in obtaining a buy-in by management teams and analysts in the organization.

Over the next several months, the IS specialists worked with users and the mathematical programming analyst to develop a prototype of a complete menu system (along with methods for demand management) and useful queries and reports. The analyst continued to gain an understanding of the clay processing steps so that any structural changes made to the Lingo model (e.g., shared processing equipment and capacities) were immediately communicated to the IS specialists.

START OF THE MINING MODEL

The idea of developing a mining model either independently or as part of the POP model was suggested in May 1999. Much brainstorming took place so that the team could conceptualize how to do this. However, modeling of this portion of the operation was not quite clear this early in the project. Thus, it was put on hold, as was modeling of the more complicated plants that soon might be sold.

THE SECOND PLANT: THE LARGE CALCINE (DRY) PLANT

In June 1999, the team completed the small calcine plant model and started work on the next plant, a calcine (dry) plant. The front-end operation of this plant involved several steps that took clay from crude sheds (where it was piled up after extraction from the mines) and purified it. It then followed a series of initial steps and blends before it went through one of five separate calcine procedures that paralleled the process steps for the small calcine plant. In fact, the small calcine plant was fed from this larger one and functioned as a sixth calcine unit. The complexity of the model increased in that several different clays were fed into the plant to blend into a number of different products, while other clays left to be processed elsewhere. In some cases, clays left to return later in a different form. And some coproducts (by-products) of production were recycled back into the system at various stages). All these aspects were handled over time, as the team examined flow sheets and interviewed the plant manager and assistant manager. As the complexity of the processes grew, the team wanted a graphical representation of the entire clay processing operation, which they viewed as a precursor of the LP model. This was relatively easy to develop because the POP model is essentially a network flow problem. It was easier to focus on this picture of the plants than to look at 15 or more clay flow sheets. Many of the clays in a family usually follow a common set of processing steps, but the variations were hard to follow until the graphical representation was created. In some cases, the flow sheets were out of date, and so as soon as updated information was learned, it was added to the graphical model and the DSS model.

In late June, the team met with the mining manager to learn a bit more about mining operations. The plant's operations were modeled, and the model merged with the model of the small plant's operations in mid-July. Testing indicated interesting features about which sets of equipment the model recommended using. Also, some new final clay products and intermediate processing of clays from other plants were identified, which lead to a data and a model update. The objective at this stage was to incorporate as much as possible about clay production. This portion of the model handled on the order of hundreds of thousands of tons of calcine clay annually.

MODEL DEVELOPMENT CONTINUES—INFEASIBILITY IS NOT AN OPTION

As the model was validated thus far, the modeling team noticed that occasionally it "went infeasible" when demands in excess of production capacity were needed. When a linear programming model becomes infeasible, very few of the solution results are useful to a manager. In fact, normally an analyst must debug the model to determine the cause of the problem. However, the users were managers, not analysts. The model was updated to allow for "feasible infeasibility." For a penalty cost per ton, the demand for almost any clay could be met from an external source that really did not exist. This set of dummy clay sources supplied the unmet demand. This allowed the model to obtain a solution, put a cost on not meeting demand, and let a manager determine what could be done to correct the situation (perhaps defer some demand) by setting up a new scenario (a what-if case) and running it. This form of multicriteria decision making has an objective that imposes a cost for not meeting demand targets and another for maximizing net profit.

MODEL DEVELOPMENT CONTINUES—JUSTICE PREVAILS

Once this portion of the model was running, the U.S. Justice Department ruled that the amount of calcine capacity that had to be sold summed up to that of one of the five calcine units and the small calcine plant. Also, the hydrous (wet clay) portion of this plant (which was to be modeled next) was to be sold. Given this development, the model's demands were adjusted, the capacities of the soon to be sold portions of the plants were zeroed out in the model, and some of the demand was moved to the other plant. Also, the model was restructured to break the demand out of the plant so that any plant could be used to meet the demand if it produced that clay. The ability to restrict demand to a plant remained in the model because some customers prefer this.

THE THIRD PLANT: THE HYDROUS PLANT

Since the hydrous portion of the first major plant that was modeled (the calcine portion) was to be sold, the team skipped creating its model and moved to the complete hydrous plant in the Sandersville area. This plant can produce over 1 million tons of finished clay annually. It is much more complex than the previously modeled calcine plants because six different classes of clay are processed and each follows a different path through the process. Some processes are skipped by some clays. There are several hundred blends that include finished calcine clays (from the second plant) and clays from other plants not yet mod-

eled. Different recipes for crude clays from the mines are used for each clay class, some of the clays have coarse and fine components blended from crude clays, and even different recipes of crude clays and intermediate clays can be used to produce finished products with identical properties. Different chemicals mixed in different blends can also produce clays with identical properties. Each finished clay had a unique flow sheet and a few blends that were recommended. Some had alternate final processing steps.

At the start of the hydrous plant modeling, the team worked out the details for an accurate, integrated mining model. This model portion would prove invaluable by determining which crude clays to mine, and from where, in addition to how to blend and process the clays. The mining model portion required no new modeling structures.

Toward the end of this phase, access to the open market, in terms of purchasing finished clay products, was modeled to give the DSS flexibility in terms of what it recommended—processing or purchasing. This contributed to keeping the solution feasible. Also, transfer operations were modeled as clays are transported from plant to plant in several stages of processing. Transfers can be by truck, rail, or pipeline.

THE POP DSS IS "FINISHED"

The graphical model made it possible to work through the complex details of the hydrous plant and mines. Through the fall of 1999, the team poured over flow sheets and worked with the plant manager, the mining manager, and several very knowledgeable specialists. In October, the manager of the small calcine plant left the team (her plant was no longer part of the company) and the two IS specialists worked part-time to complete the last of phase 1 of the POP development. Another IS specialist was brought on board as the POP administrator. In early November 1999, the POP system was validated and deployed. It was immediately used to determine which clays were to be substituted for the ones that were becoming depleted at this point in time. It also identified the appropriate substitute equipment to be used when a major piece of equipment was to be down for a major overhaul. POP was used to prepare the next year's production plan and budget. All in all, POP was a success.

CONCLUSION—NOT!

Two well-known sayings in DSS development circles are There is no such thing as a finished DSS and Success breeds success. Successful DSS are continually evolving. Another clay family was added to the POP DSS in late November 1999. Plans were underway in the winter of 2000 to expand the POP DSS to include several more plants, the calcine mines and blends, additional crude clay quality factors, more access to the open market, shipping clay products all the way to customers, incorporating additional plants around the globe, and ultimately making the model dynamic by modeling inventory management.

CASE QUESTIONS

1. Compare the steps (fundamental phases and minor steps) of prototyping described in the chapter to the development approach used for POP. How similar are they?
2. Comment on how prototyping helped the team and the users develop a solid understanding of the processes being modeled.
3. Identify the POP DSS components: the model base, the database, and the user interface.
4. What capabilities of Lingo and Access made the POP DSS a success?
5. Comment on the statements "DSS continuously evolve" and "Success breeds success" in terms of the POP DSS.

PART
III

COLLABORATION, COMMUNICATION, ENTERPRISE DECISION SUPPORT SYSTEMS, AND KNOWLEDGE MANAGEMENT

The DSS concepts outlined in Chapters 1–6 are used by millions of people and thousands of organizations worldwide to successfully support their decision making. Individuals do not work in a vacuum. Generally, groups of people work together. Very effective computerized methods have evolved to support the complex situations and settings of work groups. Part III describes collaborative computing in several key frameworks: group support systems (Chapter 7), enterprise-wide DSS (Chapter 8), and knowledge management (Chapter 9). These frameworks are more methodologies than DSS classifications.

The first true form of collaborative computing in practice was group support systems (GSS). GSS enabled the concept of the *electronic meeting (e-meeting)*. Now, GSS are used routinely by many organizations in asynchronous modes (different times and different places) for a variety of purposes, including distance learning. New, expensive, large-scale, enterprise-wide support systems, enterprise resource planning (ERP) also known as enterprise resource management (ERM) systems, are changing the landscape of modern organizations by bringing many complex business functions together under a single umbrella. And knowledge management, a relatively new form of collaborative computing, makes any needed knowledge of an organization available in a meaningful form to anyone, anyplace, and anytime. Knowledge management provides an exciting new paradigm with the potential to revolutionize the way we view and use computing. The Internet (World Wide Web) is impacted by and impacts these collaborative computing methodologies directly. The Internet is the platform that enables collaborative computing: sharing data, information, and knowledge.

COLLABORATIVE COMPUTING TECHNOLOGIES: GROUP SUPPORT SYSTEMS

Groups make most complex decisions in organizations. People work together. The increase in organizational decision-making complexity increases the need for meetings and for groupwork. Supporting groupwork where team members may be in different locations and working at different times emphasizes important aspects of communications, computer technologies, and work methodologies. Group support is a critical aspect of this century's decision support systems. Effective computer-supported cooperative work (CSCW) systems have evolved to provide gains (and losses) in task performance and processes. CSCW includes group support systems (GSS), electronic meeting systems, and electronic conferencing systems. Many readers may currently use distance learning, an important form of collaborative computing. Finally, we discuss creativity and how collaborative computing can enhance it. The sections of this chapter are as follows:

7.1 OPENING VIGNETTE: CHRYSLER SCORES WITH GROUPWARE[1]

THE CHRYSLER SCORE PROGRAM

Chrysler Corporation has met the challenge of reducing supply costs while improving suppliers' profitability through its supplier cost reduction effort (SCORE) initiative. SCORE challenges suppliers in Chrysler's extended enterprise to continuously seek out and identify opportunities to reduce costs. SCORE is Chrysler's way of documenting cost reductions and quality enhancements in a variety of areas including design, manufacturing, logistics, sourcing, and administrative transactions.

The cost-cutting program began in 1989 on paper when Chrysler took the unprecedented step of offering its suppliers a cut of whatever cost savings they could achieve. In 1994 Chrysler moved the program online. Three years after going online, Chrysler went from an overall net loss of $2.6 billion to a net gain of $3.5 billion in 1996. The SCORE program, a precursor of electronic commerce has had a remarkable return on investment.

Chrysler is pursuing efficiency, quality, and affordability while enhancing its suppliers' profit margins. Chrysler works with its suppliers as partners, not adversaries, with a goal of finding ways to improve efficiency and to mutually reduce costs. A supplier's incentive is significant; it can be half of the total savings. In a recent independent report, automotive suppliers ranked Chrysler number one in terms of their business relationships with them. The feeling is mutual. In 1997 Chrysler presented 13 of its suppliers with its highest honor, the Platinum Pentastar Award for outstanding overall performance. Chrysler wants to be its suppliers' best customer because the best customers always get the best service.

THE SCORE SYSTEM

In 1989 paper-based SCORE business processes were developed and deployed. The goal was to identify waste in the value chain and eliminate it. The paper-based system was moderately successful. To enhance communication and collaboration and speed up the process, Chrysler moved from a paper-based system to a groupware environment.

The business process was already in place, and by 1994 appropriate technology had evolved to support it. The first online SCORE was a single, pure Lotus Notes application database with hundreds of Notes clients. Suppliers had access to the Chrysler SCORE system via the Internet or via a modem. They used an online Notes form in which they described the cost savings. With a push of a button, this cost savings/quality improvement proposal was submitted to Chrysler. The information about a proposed savings is collected in one spot, reviewed by a buyer, and if it has merit, is sent to all team members (finance, purchasing, engineering) who then collaborate on it. About 70 percent of all suggestions have been adopted. The second-generation online system, SCORE2, supported automated procurement functions and e-mail. SCORE2 also contained user profiles, system intelligence enablers, database reports, and bilingual support. SCORE2 involved reengineering the successful business process for smoother operation.

---

[1] Adapted from D. Walker, "Supply Chain Collaboration Saves Chrysler $2.5 Billion and Counting," *Automatic I.D. News*, Vol. 14, No. 9, Aug. 1998, p. 60; J. Fontana, "Chrysler's $2B Score," *InternetWeek*, Mar. 9, 1998, pp. 1, 90; J. Fontana, "Chrysler Saves Big Online," *CommunicationsWeek*, Apr. 28, 1997, pp. 1, 84–85; J. T. Landry, "Supply Chain Management: The Case for Alliances," *Harvard Business Review*, Vol. 76, No. 6, Nov./Dec. 1998, pp. 24–25; and K. M. Carrillo, "Tools Address Different Ends of the Supply Chain," *InformationWeek*, No. 699, Sept. 7, 1998, p. 26.

By 1998 SCORE had become a company standard for dealing with suppliers, adding all procurement to the previous focus on goods used only in the production of automobiles. With the latest release, SCORE3, there were 1,000 suppliers online. SCORE3 is fully Web-based. It allows users to access the program through Automotive Network eXchange (AN, AutoChain), an *extranet* that is a collaborative effort among the Big Three automakers and hundreds of their suppliers. AN became operational in 1998, and Chrysler required its top three tiers of suppliers to connect to it by mid-1999.

SCORE BENEFITS

Chrysler's benefits are enhanced relationships with suppliers and better-quality purchasing practices, which yield a better-quality product. SCORE lets Chrysler use its suppliers' expertise to become a better company. The initiative has yielded substantial dollar savings: $2.5 billion through 1998, including more than $1 billion in 1997 and $1.2 billion in 1998. The benefits to suppliers include identifying quality methods and reaping identical cost benefits from shared cost savings. The main benefit to customers is simple and obvious: a higher-quality product at an equal or lower price.

By the year 2000, Chrysler plans to save $2 billion per year and have *all* its suppliers online.

COMMENTS

Paul Lawrence, at the Harvard Business School, and Ranjay Gulati, at Northwestern University, studied the supply relationships at two of the largest U.S. manufacturers, Chrysler and Ford. They interviewed executives and surveyed the purchasing experts for each of the major components of an automobile.

Their work indicates that to build more flexible and efficient supply chains, manufacturers need to forge close, long-term ties with their suppliers. They need to work together to refine products and components, to respond to shifts in demand, and to unclog bottlenecks, while sharing sensitive information. High-trust relationships can be achieved through alliances with outside suppliers—if both sides take certain steps to foster a collaborative environment.

"Manufacturers often get the best of two worlds when they form strong supplier alliances," says Gulati. "They get to work with independent, flexible companies able to specialize in a given component, and they also achieve the close integration thought to be possible only with in-house divisions." Building a high-trust alliance requires a great deal of time and effort. "For managers willing to invest in relationships," comments Lawrence, "the real choice is not the old 'make versus buy' but 'make, buy, or ally.'"

Chrysler's extended enterprise system demonstrates that managing a company's supply chain is just as important as managing its plants or distribution system. If it is done well in collaboration with its suppliers, the company gains a major strategic advantage over its competitors.

For Lotus, Chrysler's SCORE system has become a showcase example of its groupware platform. "It clearly is one of the best quantifications of value the industry has seen this starkly," says Jeff Papows, president and CEO at Lotus.

"Chrysler is giving us a sense of what's to come when you combine groupware, standards and interenterprise communication," comments Gary Rowe, a principal with Rapport Communication. "This is the value of having organizations invest in that type of infrastructure."

According to Tom Stallkamp, executive vice president of procurement and supply, "What we're doing is pursuing efficiency, quality and affordability without eroding our suppliers' profit margin."

"I've never had negative feedback from a supplier about SCORE. They all love it," says Bernie Bedard, manager of the supplier continuous improvement team, "It's basically a win-win, a way to work together in partnership and demonstrate that you're committed to see them grow as well as see Chrysler grow."

❖ QUESTIONS FOR THE OPENING VIGNETTE

1. What prompted Chrysler to investigate development of a collaborative business process with its suppliers?
2. Explain how the supply chain works and how Chrysler uses technology to enhance communication between itself and suppliers within the supply chain construct.
3. Explain why Chrysler migrated from a paper application to a groupware application.
4. Describe the collaboration that SCORE allows between the suppliers and the company, and within the company.
5. Describe the benefits for suppliers and for Chrysler.
6. How would you improve on SCORE?
7. Check the literature and/or the Web to see how SCORE has evolved since this book was written. What additional features does it have? What are the annual savings?

7.2 GROUP DECISION MAKING, COMMUNICATION, AND COLLABORATION

The Opening Vignette illustrates how computerized support can be provided to people who work effectively in groups for the benefit of their organizations. The SCORE system involves collaboration between groups at Chrysler and their vendors and also collaboration of groups within Chrysler. People make decisions, they design and manufacture products, they develop policies and strategies, they design software, and so on. They collaborate and communicate—people perform **groupwork.** Some characteristics of groupwork include the following:

- A group performs a task, sometimes decision making, sometimes not.
- Group members may be located in different places.
- Group members may work at different times.
- Group members may work for the same or for different organizations.
- The group can be permanent or temporary.
- The group can be at any managerial level or span levels.
- There can be synergy (process and task gains) or conflict in groupwork.
- There can be gains and/or losses in productivity from groupwork.
- The task might have to be accomplished very quickly.
- It may be impossible or too expensive for all the team members to meet in one place.
- Some of the needed data, information, or knowledge may be located in many sources, several of which are external to the organization.
- The expertise of nonteam members may be needed.

When people work in teams, especially when the members are in different locations and may be working at different times, they need to communicate, collaborate, and access a diverse set of information sources in multiple formats.

For groups to collaborate effectively, appropriate communication methods and technologies are needed. The Internet and its derivatives, intranets and extranets, are the platform on which most communications for collaboration occur. The **Internet** (**World Wide Web** or **Web**), a network of computer networks, supports interorganizational decision making through collaboration tools and access to data, information, and knowledge from inside and outside the organization. Intraorganizational networked decision support can be effectively supported by an **intranet,** basically an internal Internet. It allows people within an organization to work with Internet tools and procedures. Specific applications can include important internal documents and procedures, corporate address lists, e-mail, tool access, and software distribution. An intranet operates safely behind a company's **firewall,** which isolates it from inappropriate external access. A good example of an intranet application is the Osram Sylvania HR InfoNet described in the Chapter 6 Opening Vignette. An **extranet** links a work group like an intranet for group members from several different organizations. Several automobile manufacturers have involved their suppliers and dealers in extranets to help them deal with customer complaints about their products. Other extranets are used to link teams together to design products, where several different suppliers must collaborate on design and manufacturing techniques. And extranets like the AutoChain are used by entire industries to link companies and suppliers (see the Opening Vignette).

Even in hierarchical organizations, decision making is usually a shared process. A group may be involved in a decision or in a decision-related task, such as creating a short list of acceptable alternatives or choosing criteria for evaluating an alternative. The following activities and processes characterize meetings:

- A meeting is a joint activity engaged in by a group of people typically of equal or near-equal status.
- The outcome of the meeting depends partly on the knowledge, opinions, and judgments of its participants.
- The outcome of the meeting also depends on the composition of the group and on the decision-making process used by the group.
- Differences in opinion are settled either by the ranking person present or, more often, by negotiation or arbitration.

Many computerized tools have been developed to provide group support. These tools are called **groupware** because their primary objective is to support groupwork. The work itself may be known as **computer-supported cooperative work (CSCW).** (The literature uses the word *cooperative,* and we adhere to it, though a more accurate and general term might be *collaborative.* For example, consider two or more groups involved in negotiations.) A list of groupware tools is provided on this book's Web site: www.prenhall.com/turban.

Telecommuting, teleconferencing, supply chain management, and electronic commerce (Turban et al., 2000) are *all* enabled through communication and collaboration technologies. Distance learning is a fast-developing area of **collaborative computing.** And groupware can enhance creativity in the decision-making process.

Groups and groupwork (teams and teamwork) in organizations are proliferating. Consequently, groupware continues to evolve to support effective groupwork.

7.3 COMMUNICATION SUPPORT

Communication is a vital element for decision support. *Without communication, there is no collaboration.* Individual decision makers must communicate with colleagues, experts, government agencies, customers, vendors, business partners, and so on. They also need data and information (and *knowledge*) from many locations around the globe. Groups of decision makers must communicate, collaborate, and negotiate in their work. Most organizations would quickly become nonfunctional without their communication systems. Effective electronic commerce is possible only via modern communication technologies.

Modern information technologies provide *inexpensive, fast, capable, reliable* means of supporting communications. (See DSS in Focus 7.1 for some unsupported aspects of communication.) Networked computer systems, like the Internet, intranets, and extranets, are the enabling platforms that support communication. Historically, these systems began with the telegraph, the telephone, radio, and television. Technologies that followed built upon them. Within about 100 years, we have developed fax machines, electronic mail (e-mail), chat programs, newsgroups, listservs (electronic mailing lists), electronic bulletin boards, and inexpensive, effective desktop videoconferencing systems [see DSS in Action 7.2, Burden (1999), and Davids (1999) for effective uses and the benefits of videoconferencing]. Desktop videoconferencing systems are expected to grow by 60 percent per year through 2003 (Davids, 1999). Most of these technologies operate on the Internet (World Wide Web). Because they have become common in modern enterprises and even at home, we will not discuss the details here. We next turn to collaborative technologies that include the latest communication developments of **electronic meeting systems (EMS)** and electronic conferencing systems and services, generally using the Internet for connecting decision makers.

As Davids (1999) comments in reference to videoconferencing, we note that the following advantages apply to all improved communications methods in organizations: (1) improving employee productivity, (2) involving more people in key decision making, (3) blurring geographic boundaries, (4) creating a consistent corporate culture, and (5) improving employees' quality of life.

DSS IN FOCUS 7.1

COMMUNICATION PROBLEMS

Communication can be problematic in general, but computerized communication methods do not transmit most of our nonverbal cues, which are important in establishing the richer meaning of a message by adding context. A large percentage of our meaning (perhaps exceeding 50 percent) is conveyed via nonverbal cues. Facial expressions, body language, voice tone, expression, inflection, touching, and distance are but a few. (For example, it has been possible to accurately determine who will win a U.S. presidential election by measuring the average rate of the candidates' eye blinking. The one who blinks the least has won the election from the Kennedy–Nixon debate through 1996.) There are cross-cultural aspects and language subtleties that are not easily transmitted through computer-mediated communication channels.

Emoticons were a first attempt to include nonverbal cues in text-based e-mail (e.g., this is a happy face called a smiley:), and, using all capital letters means you are SHOUTING!)

Some aspects of communication such as the frequency of touching and the interpersonal distance between participants are difficult to capture through technology. However, video technology can show facial expressions and some body language. Researchers are attempting to develop collaborative systems that capture more of this imprecise nature of human communication that makes the meaning of the message received more precise.

DSS IN ACTION 7.2

VIDEOCONFERENCING IS READY FOR PRIME TIME

Videoconferencing technology can cut travel expenses and increase a company's productivity. Dan Denardo, manager of global videoconferencing at Dow Chemical Company (an $18 billion per year firm), says that videoconferencing vastly improves customer service and helps Dow deliver products to the market faster. "We know it can decrease cycle time since we can hold more meetings in the same amount of time," Denardo says. Dow has about 160 video cameras at their Midland, MI, headquarters and has an estimated annual travel cost savings of more than $7 million. At Dow, the technology is advancing from in-house conference rooms to customer sites. "It is fairly cheap hardware, the customers really like it and it sets us apart," Denardo comments. By July 1999, Dow had linked six customers.

Quantum Corporation (a $4.9 billion per year storage vendor) saves about $500,000 per month in travel expenses, lost time, and productivity according to Albert Villarde, a network analyst. Quantum has over 20 video-equipped conference rooms around the globe. The primary business advantage is the speed-up in information sharing.

Estimates vary, but Pat Conway, product marketing manager at videoconferencing vendor VTEL Corporation, estimates that videoconferencing should reduce a firm's travel budget by about 15 percent. The most significant savings come from the increased velocity of information delivery because of more frequent, impromptu meetings.

Technology varies from PC desktop video to stand-alone conference rooms. Most companies use ISDN lines because of the higher bandwidth. Three lines are sufficient to provide full-motion video. Videoconferencing is an economical way to cut travel costs and boost productivity.

Source: Adapted from L. Wood, "Videoconferencing Shows It's Ready for Prime Time," *InternetWeek,* July 12, 1999, p. 26.

7.4 COLLABORATION SUPPORT: COMPUTER-SUPPORTED COOPERATIVE WORK

In modern organizations, people collaborate. Groups make most major decisions in organizations. Solving complex problems requires that people work together, necessitating the formation of workgroups.

While communication primarily transmits information from a sender to a receiver, collaboration is much deeper. Collaboration conveys meaning or knowledge among group members. Material is actively worked on during collaboration. Collaboration includes sharing documents, information, and knowledge, as well as such activities as brainstorming and voting. Collaboration implies people actively *working together* and requires collaborative computing support tools that build on communication methods. These computer-supported cooperative work (CSCW) systems are known as group support system (GSS) or groupware. They include electronic meeting systems and electronic conferencing systems.

TIME/PLACE FRAMEWORK

The effectiveness of a collaborative computing technology depends on the location of the group members and on the time that shared information is sent and received. A framework for classifying IT communication support technologies was proposed by DeSanctis and Gallupe (1985, 1987). Communication is divided into four cells, which are shown together with representative computerized support technologies in Figure 7.1. The four cells are organized along the two dimensions of *time* and *place*.

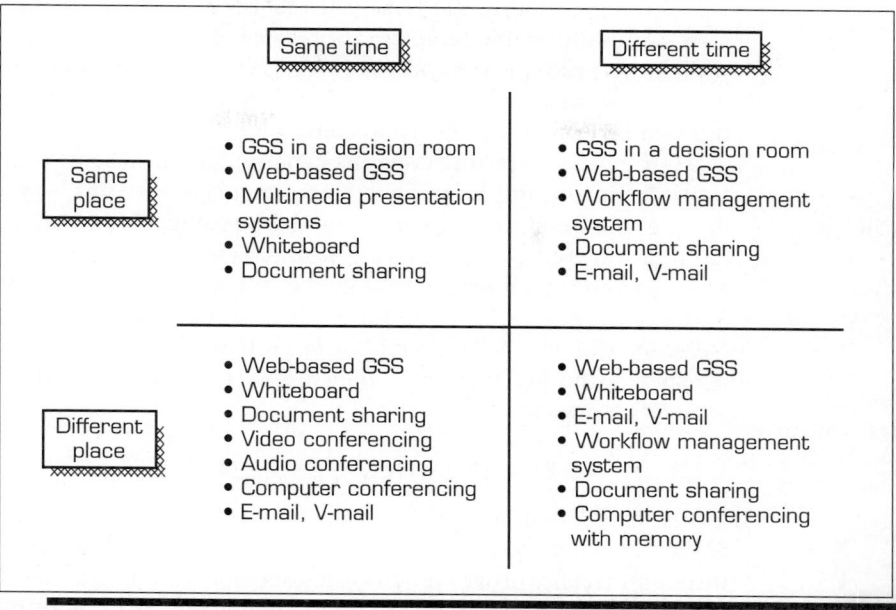

FIGURE 7.1 TIME/PLACE COMMUNICATION FRAMEWORK AND SOME COLLABORATIVE COMPUTING SUPPORT TECHNOLOGIES

- *Time.* When information is sent and received almost simultaneously, the communication is **synchronous.** Telephones, televisions, and face-to-face meetings are examples. **Asynchronous** communication occurs when the receiver receives the information at a different time than it was sent.
- *Place.* The senders and the receivers can be in the same room or not.

The four cells of the framework are as follows:

- *Same time/same place.* Participants meet face-to-face in one place at the same time, as in a traditional meeting or decision room.
- *Same time/different place.* Participants are in different places, but they communicate at the same time, for example, with videoconferencing.
- *Different time/same place.* People work in shifts. One shift leaves information for the next shift.
- *Different time/different place.* Participants are in different places. They send and receive information at different times. This occurs when team members are traveling, have conflicting schedules, or work in different time zones.

GROUPWARE

The term *groupware* refers to software products that provide collaborative support to groups. Groupware provides a mechanism for teams to share opinions, data, information, knowledge, and other resources. Different collaborative computing technologies support groupwork in different ways, depending on the time/place category in which the work occurs, the purpose of the group, and the task. New tools are evolving to support *anytime/anyplace* meetings.

There are thousands of packages that contain some elements of groupware. Some have only rudimentary collaboration capabilities (e.g., voting; see DSS In Action 7.3), while others provide support for every aspect of collaboration (full **electronic meetings** with videoconferencing). Almost all utilize Internet technology for the consistent Web browser-style user interface and communication protocols.

Groupware typically contains capabilities for at least one of the following: **electronic brainstorming,** electronic conferencing or meeting, group scheduling, calendaring, planning, conflict resolution, model building, videoconferencing, electronic document sharing (e.g., screen sharing, whiteboards, or liveboards), voting, and so on. There are electronic meeting services like WebEx, where anyone can start a meeting for a fee. Some groupware such as Lotus Notes/Domino Server, Microsoft NetMeeting, Netscape Collabra Server, and GroupSystems (Groupsystems.com) are fairly comprehensive in the activities that they support. We next briefly describe some popular groupware systems.

LOTUS NOTES/DOMINO SERVER

Lotus Notes/Domino Server was the first widely used groupware. Lotus Notes/Domino Server enables collaboration by letting users access and create shared information through specially programmed Notes documents. For example, Chrysler's SCORE system in the Opening Vignette and the Osram Sylvania HR InfoNet enterprise portal in the Chapter 6 Opening Vignette were programmed in Lotus Notes/Domino Server. Notes provides online collaboration capabilities, workgroup e-mail, distributed databases, bulletin whiteboards, text editing, (electronic) document management, workflow capabilities, consensus building, voting, ranking, and various application development tools, all integrated into one environment with a graphical menu-based user interface. Notes fosters a virtual corporation and creates interorganizational alliances. By the end of 1999, there were more than 50 million Notes users ("Lotus Announces Over 50 Million Users of Lotus Notes," www.lotus.com, Jan. 17, 2000).

Many applications have been programmed (written) in Lotus Notes. This includes Learning Space, a **courseware** package for supporting distance learning.

Lotus Development Corporation also provides TEAMROOM, to which decision makers can subscribe for online conferencing, and both QuickPlace and Sametime Collaboration, which have instant virtual meetings, whiteboarding, live documents, application sharing, and one-to-one instant messaging.

DSS IN ACTION 7.3

INTERNET VOTING

Collaborative technologies that include voting mechanisms operating over the Internet have enhanced groupwork. Voting for public office may be the ultimate form of groupware use. A hot topic in the United States in early 2000 was whether or when states will permit public elections over the Internet. Texas was the first state to permit voting over the Internet, but it was tightly regulated. The resident had to be in orbit in the space shuttle. In 2000 Alaska permitted straw polling via the Internet for residents living in isolated regions. Straw polling is a formal part of the Alaska presidential primary process. The state of Washington allowed any registered voter to use the Internet in the 2000 presidential primary. In 2000 several other states were considering how to establish Internet polling. There are problems with anonymity and with voter validation, but they seem to be no worse than some of the polling practices known to have occurred in Chicago some years ago.

NETSCAPE COLLABRA SERVER

Netscape Collabra Server, a component of SuiteSpot, provides collaboration services through discussion groups, shared multimedia documents, and a Web browser interface. Anytime/anyplace virtual meetings can be structured within Collabra. It includes open e-mail, groupware, editing, calendaring, document access, and Web browsing. Like most groupware, Communicator does not include seamless embedded databases. However, all major database systems provide HTML documents for querying and dynamic Web-based reporting.

MICROSOFT NETMEETING

Microsoft NetMeeting is a real-time collaboration package that includes whiteboarding (relatively free-form graphics to which all participants can contribute simultaneously), application sharing (any Microsoft Windows application document), remote desktop sharing, file transfer, text chat, data conferencing, and desktop audio- and videoconferencing. This application sharing is a vast improvement over what was called simply *whiteboarding* a decade ago. The NetMeeting client is included in Windows 98 and 2000. See DSS in Action 7.4 for an example of the successful use of NetMeeting.

NOVELL GROUPWISE

Novell GroupWise groupware combines document management and sharing, messaging, e-mail, group calendaring and scheduling, task management, imaging, and workflow in a tightly integrated package.

GROUPSYSTEMS

GroupSystems (for Windows and the Web, Groupsystems.com) was one of the first comprehensive same time/same place electronic meeting packages and set the pace for the industry. One version runs on the Web in asynchronous mode (anytime/anyplace).

DSS IN ACTION 7.4

NETMEETING PROVIDES A REAL-TIME ADVANTAGE

Jack O'Donnell is CEO of O'Donnell & Partners, a corporate interior contracting firm in Manhattan with branch offices in Chicago, London, and Milan. Until recently, O'Donnell felt the need to be on-site when any project was in its crucial stages. "Phone calls weren't enough, nor was e-mail—especially when you're dealing with a team of architects, designers and contractors who speak different languages and all have their own professional jargon," he says. "Add to that the need for working on plans, sketches and blueprints together at meetings, and my partners and I found we were spending most of our time at airports."

Microsoft NetMeeting provides collaborative computing support for groupwork, including application sharing through its Remote Desktop Sharing feature. It also provides real-time video. Now O'Donnell and his team members meet online. "Everyone can prepare a presentation that shows and doesn't just tell the progress of their part of the project," says O'Donnell. "We can work on files together, as if we were sitting across from each other at a conference table. And we can see each other's expressions, so it feels more like a real meeting." (See DSS In Focus 7.2.)

O'Donnell estimates that Web conferencing saved his company at least a half-million dollars in travel costs in 1999. And that did not include the benefit of having fewer people out sick with whatever virus they picked up on their last plane trip.

Source: Adapted from M. Delio, "Power Meetings in Cyberspace, *Knowledge Management,* Vol. 2, No. 12, Dec. 1999, pp. 77–78.

GroupSystems online is a subscription service from which an organization can rent electronic meeting "space" and access it via the Web. We describe the capabilities of this and similar types of groupware later in this chapter.

TCBWORKS

TCBWorks (Dennis et al., 1998) is one of the first relatively complete examples of Web-based groupware. It contains agenda setting, idea generation, voting, ranking, and so on. Its access and use are free, and it runs on the Web at tcbworks.terry.uga.edu. Try it! TCBWorks runs under Unix on a Web server and can be accessed through Netscape Communicator (a browser). TCBWorks effectively supports inexpensive anytime/anyplace meetings. A screen shot of a TCBWorks electronic brainstorming session is shown in Figure 7.2.

WEBEX

WebEx (WebEx.com) is a pay-per-use CSCW site. It provides a low-cost, simplified way to share documents and applications over the Web. Meeting time and space are rented and accessed over the Web. WebEx runs a limited subset of ActiveTouch Web Meeting Center for users on a low-fee basis.

FIGURE 7.2 EXAMPLE OF ELECTRONIC BRAINSTORMING WITH WEB-BASED TCBWORKS GROUPWARE

The participant types his/her ideas in the large box in the middle. Then, he/she clicks the send button. The idea is then added to the threaded discussion and appears above the box (e.g., as idea 89).

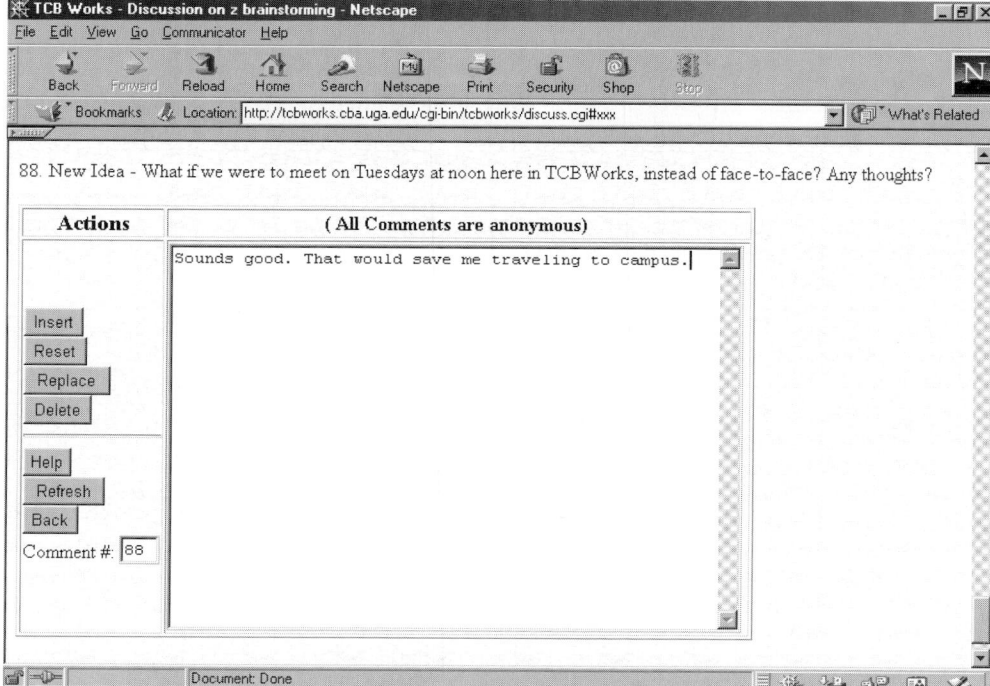

REMARKS

See this book's Web site at www.prenhall.com/turban for a list of current groupware. Successful **enterprise-wide collaboration systems** like Lotus Notes/Domino Server can be expensive to develop and operate. To obtain the full benefits of such groupware, a well-trained, full-time support staff is required to develop applications and operate the system.

7.5 GROUP SUPPORT SYSTEMS

Most groupwork takes place in meetings. Despite the many criticisms of the effectiveness and efficiency of meetings, people still get together in groups to discuss issues and to work. Meetings can be effective despite the fact that up to 80 percent of what is discussed in a meeting is either forgotten or remembered incorrectly.[2] See DSS in Focus 7.5 for a description of what does and does not work in meetings. 3M Corporation's 3M Meeting Network (www.3m.com/meetingnetwork) and the Center for Rural Studies (crs.uvm.edu) have information, surveys, and tips about how to run a more effective meeting.

The goal of groupware, as it was specifically developed as group support systems (GSS), is to support the work of groups throughout every work activity—including meetings.

Despite the inefficiency of meetings, groupwork can and does provide some benefits, and some dysfunctions. In DSS in Focus 7.6, we identify a set of some potential benefits, or **process gains,** of collaborative work. Even so, collaborative work can often be plagued with dysfunctions called **process losses** (see DSS in Focus 7.7).

The goal of GSS is to increase some of the benefits of collaboration and eliminate or reduce some of the losses. Researchers have developed methods for improving the *processes* of groupwork, and some of these methods are group dynamics. Two representative methods are the **nominal group technique (NGT)** and the **Delphi method.** These methods are manual approaches to supporting groupwork. See Lindstone and Turroff (1975) and this book's Web site for details.

The limited success of methods such as the NGT and the Delphi method led to attempts to use information technology to support group meetings. The major technology is called a **group support system (GSS).** At the start of the 1990s, this term was coined to replace *group decision support system (GDSS)* because researchers recognized that collaborative computing technologies were doing more than supporting decision making.

A group support system (GSS) is any combination of hardware and software that enhances groupwork. GSS is a generic term that includes all forms of collaborative computing. GSS evolved after information technology researchers recognized that technology could be developed to support the many activities normally occurring at face-to-face meetings (idea generation, consensus building, anonymous ranking, voting, and so on).

Though a complete GSS is still considered a specially designed information system, since the mid-1990s many of the special capabilities of GSS have been embedded in productivity tools. For example, Microsoft NetMeeting Client is part of Windows. Most GSS are easy to use because they have a Windows GUI or a Web browser interface. Most GSS are fairly general and provide support for activities like idea generation, conflict resolution, voting, and so on.

---

[2]This makes one wonder about the effectiveness of the traditional classroom setting.

THE SEVEN SINS OF DEADLY MEETINGS AND SEVEN STEPS TO SALVATION

Since meetings can be ineffective, unproductive, and unending (to say the least), it helps to understand what can go wrong and what can go right. Bad meetings can be a source of negative messages about an organization and its members. Because more work is becoming groupwork, the number of meetings will likely increase. There are a variety of tools and techniques, that, along with common sense, can make meetings less painful, more productive, and maybe even fun. The following is a summary of the "seven sins" of deadly meetings and seven approaches to making meetings more productive.

Sin 1: People don't take meetings seriously. They arrive late, leave early, and spend most of their time doodling.

Salvation: Adopt a mind-set that meetings are real work. Disciplined meetings are about mind-set—a shared conviction among all the participants that meetings are real work.

Sin 2: Meetings are too long. They should accomplish twice as much in half the time.

Salvation: Time is money. Track the cost of meetings and use computer-enabled simultaneity to make them more productive. Meetings should last no longer than 90 minutes. Often people don't appreciate how expensive meetings really are. Bernard DeKoven (Institute for Better Meetings, Palo Alto, CA) developed the Meeting Meter. It is a taxilike meter that tallies the meeting's total cost (excluding travel time and illness; there is a version running on the Web). One quick look at the numbers, and its back to work, quickly. Groupware can provide parallelism, especially in brainstorming, cutting meeting time down.

Sin 3: People wander off the topic. Participants spend more time digressing than discussing.

Salvation: Get serious about agendas and store distractions in a "parking lot." Make sure you have an agenda. This involves *planning the meeting.*

Sin 4: Nothing happens once the meeting ends. People don't convert decisions to action.

Salvation: Convert from "meeting" to "doing" and focus on common documents. When people leave meetings, they may or may not remember what happened or what is supposed to happen next. The capacity for misunderstanding is unlimited. Group memory is needed. Shared documents must be created. This is the most powerful role for technology: people should leave with real-time minutes.

Sin 5: People don't tell the truth. There's plenty of conversation but not much candor.

Salvation: Embrace anonymity. People may not feel secure enough to say what they really think. GSS that provide anonymity can help.

Sin 6: Meetings are always missing important information, and so they postpone critical decisions.

Salvation: Get data, not just furniture, into meeting rooms. Again, GSS can help in providing a means for capturing and maintaining data.

Sin 7: Meetings never get better. People make the same mistakes over and over again.

Salvation: Practice makes perfect. Monitor what works and what doesn't and hold people accountable. At Charles Schwab & Company, someone serves as an "observer" and creates a Plus/Delta list for virtually every meeting. This list records what went right and what went wrong, and it becomes part of the minutes. Over time, both for specific meeting groups and for the company as a whole, these lists create an agenda for change.

How much can meetings improve? Bernard DeKoven says, "People don't have good meetings because they don't know what good meetings are like. Good meetings aren't just about work. They're about fun—keeping people charged up. It's more than collaboration, it's 'coliberation'—people freeing each other up to think more creatively."

Source: Adapted from E. Matson, "The Seven Sins of Deadly Meetings," *Fast Company,* No. 2, Apr. 1996, p. 122.

An **electronic meeting system (EMS)** is a form of groupware that supports anytime/anyplace meetings. Group tasks include, but are not limited to, communication, planning, idea generation, problem solving, issue discussion, negotiation, conflict resolution, system analysis and design, and collaborative group activities such as document preparation and sharing (Dennis et al., 1988, p. 593). Typically EMS include desktop videoconferencing.

GSS settings range from a group meeting at a single location for solving a specific problem (e.g., building design; see DSS in Action 7.4) to multiple locations held via telecommunication channels for the purpose of considering a variety of problems (e.g.,

---

DSS IN FOCUS 7.6

SOME BENEFITS OF GROUPWORK (PROCESS GAINS)

- It provides *learning*. Groups are better than individuals at understanding problems.
- People are held accountable for decisions in which they participate.
- Groups are better than individuals at catching errors.
- A group has more *information* (knowledge) than any one member. Groups can combine this knowledge to create new knowledge. More and more creative alternatives for problem solving can be generated, and better solutions can be derived (*stimulation*).

- It may produce *synergy* during problem solving.
- Working in a group may stimulate the creativity of the participants and the process.
- A group may have better and more precise communication working together.
- Group members have their egos embedded in the decision, and so they will be committed to the solution.
- Risk propensity is balanced. Groups moderate high-risk takers and encourage conservatives.

DSS IN FOCUS 7.7

POTENTIAL DYSFUNCTIONS OF GROUPWORK (PROCESS LOSSES)

- Social pressures of conformity may result in **groupthink** (people begin to think alike and not tolerate new ideas—yielding to *conformance pressure*).
- It is a time-consuming, slow process (only one member can speak at a time).
- Lack of coordination of the meeting work and poor meeting planning.
- Inappropriate influences (domination of time, topic, opinion by one or few individuals; *fear of contributing* because of the possibility of *flaming*, and so on).
- Tendency of group members to rely on others to do most of the work (free-riding).
- Tendency toward producing compromised solutions of poor quality.
- Nonproductive time (socializing, preparing, waiting for late-comers—*air time fragmentation*).

- Tendency to repeat what was already said (because of failure to remember or process).
- High cost of meeting (travel, participation, and so on).
- Tendency of groups to make riskier decisions than they should.
- Incomplete or inappropriate use of information.
- Too much information (*information overload*).
- Few information cues.
- Incomplete or incorrect task analysis.
- Inappropriate or incomplete representation in the group.
- Attention blocking.
- Attenuation blocking.
- Concentration blocking.
- Slow feedback.

---

a class over distance learning; see Case Application 7.1). GSS can operate in asynchronous mode (different times), but new, effective methods, though good, are still evolving.

GSS can be considered in terms of the common group activities that can benefit from computer-based support: *information retrieval,* which includes access of data values from an existing database and retrieval of information from other group members; *information sharing,* which is the display of data for the whole group on a common screen or at group members' workstations for viewing; and *information use,* which involves the application of software technology (such as modeling packages or specific application programs; see DSS in Focus 7.8), procedures, and group problem-solving techniques for reaching a group decision.

DSS IN FOCUS 7.8

MODELS IN GROUP DECISION MAKING—TEAMEC

Based on the Analytic Hierarchy Process (AHP) decision-making methodology implemented as Expert Choice (Chapter 5), TeamEC helps group members define objectives, goals, criteria, and alternatives and then organize them into a hierarchical structure. Using hand-held radio calculator-style keypads or a PC, participants compare and prioritize the relative importance of the decision variables. TeamEC then synthesizes the group's judgments to arrive at a conclusion and allows individuals to examine how changing the weighting of their criteria affects the outcome.

TeamEC imitates the way people naturally make decisions: gathering information, structuring the decision, weighing the variables and alternatives, and reaching a conclusion (Chapters 2 and 5). The strength of TeamEC is that it supports the decision process. The group structures an AHP decision hierarchy for the problem as members perceive it; members provide the judgments, and members make the decision.

Source: Partly adapted from Expert Choice Inc., Pittsburgh, PA, http://www.expertchoice.com, Mar. 2000. Used by permission.

DSS IN FOCUS 7.9

GSS PROCESS GAINS

- Supports parallel processing of information and idea generation.
- Enables larger groups with more complete information, knowledge, and skills to participate.
- Permits the group to use structured or unstructured techniques and methods.
- Offers rapid and easy access to external information.
- Allows parallel computer discussions.

- Helps participants frame the big picture.
- Provides for multiple ways to participate in instant, anonymous voting.
- Provides structure for the planning process to keep the group on track.
- Enables several users to interact simultaneously (conferencing).
- Records all information presented at the meeting (organizational memory).

The goal of GSS is to provide support to meeting participants to improve the productivity and effectiveness of meetings by speeding up the decision-making process (efficiency) or by improving the quality of the results (effectiveness). GSS attempts to increase process and task gains and decrease process and task losses. Specific GSS process gains are listed in DSS in Focus 7.9. Overall, GSS has been successful in practice; however, some process and task gains may decrease while some process and task losses may increase.

Improvement is achieved by providing support to group members for the exchange of ideas, opinions, and preferences. Specific features such as **parallelism** and **anonymity** produce this improvement. Many experiments, field studies, and surveys have been done to determine the effectiveness of GSS (e.g., Fjermestad and Hiltz, 1998). After a few decades of GSS experience, it is clear that GSS is a winner. Saved travel time (especially when using the Web) and parallelism have led to decreased costs, while anonymity leads to the generation of more ideas and more creative ideas. For examples, see Case Applications 7.1 and 7.2 and DSS in Action 7.10, where collaborative computing led to dramatic speed-ups in process and cost savings.

DSS IN ACTION 7.10

EASTMAN CHEMICAL BOOSTS CREATIVE PROCESSES WITH GROUPWARE

THE PROBLEM

Eastman Chemical wanted to use creative problem-solving sessions to process ideas. Customers would present any number of problems, and they would use flip charts and Post-it notes to come up with better solutions. But organizing and studying the notes took far too long. They needed more ideas and better methods to meet customers' needs. Traditional methods were not effective. The process was extremely unproductive and time-consuming.

THE SOLUTION

Eastman Chemical chose GroupSystems to support their problem solving. First, they defined the problem and framed it. Then they brainstormed ideas to develop potential solutions to the problem, trying for "outside-the-box" thinking using creativity techniques. Recently, it was claimed that 400 ideas were generated by nine people in a 2-hour session (through the parallelism feature). After categorizing similar items, the team established common decision criteria to pick the top three ideas using the Alternative Analysis tool. Results were then copied into an Excel spreadsheet to develop an action plan.

In addition, Eastman ran 100 R&D managers through sessions to determine top strategies. They defined eight opportunities, with an action plan to establish the top three—after generating 2,200 ideas!

THE RESULTS

Henry Gonzales, manager of the polymer technology core competency group at Eastman states, "We found that with GroupSystems, we had more unusual ideas, a richer pool to choose from, and we got to the point a lot faster. I did a study and calculated that the software saved 50% of people's time, and projected a cost savings of over $500,000 for the 12 people during a year's time." Consequently, Eastman Chemical bought a second license and upgraded to another facility so that more people could use the groupware.

Source: Adapted from "GroupSystems Case Studies," GroupSystems.com, www.groupsystems.com, Mar. 2000.

7.6 GROUP SUPPORT SYSTEMS TECHNOLOGIES

There are three options for deploying GSS technology: (1) in a special-purpose **decision room,** (2) at a multiple use facility, and (3) as Web-based groupware with clients running wherever the group members are.

Historically, GSS were installed in customized, expensive, special-purpose decision rooms (electronic meeting rooms) with PCs with sunken displays hidden under desks and a large public screen at the front of the room. The original idea was that only executives and high-level managers would use the facility. The software in this special-purpose electronic meeting room usually runs over a local area network, and these rooms are fairly plush in their furnishings. Electronic meeting rooms can be constructed in different shapes and sizes. A common design includes a room equipped with 12–30 networked personal computers, usually recessed into the desktop (for better participant viewing). A server PC is attached to a large-screen projection system and connected to the network to display the work at individual workstations and aggregated information from the facilitator's workstation. Break-out rooms equipped with PCs connected to the server may be adjacent to the decision room in which small subgroups can consult. The output from these subgroups can also be displayed on the large public screen.

Organizations still use electronic decision rooms, and these rooms very ably support same time/same place meetings (e.g., at The University of Georgia—shown on this book's Web site, at the University of Arizona, and at many other universities, companies, and government agencies). One school district even built a "portable" facility in a bus (the driver's seat turns around to become the facilitator's seat). There is still a need and a desire for groups to meet face to face even when supported by collaborative technology. A facility like this can conveniently double as a videoconferencing room or a distance education facility.

A second option is to construct a multiple-use facility, sometimes a general-purpose computer lab that doubles as a less elegant but equally useful GSS room (Jessup and van Over, 1996). For example, at The University of Georgia, in the Terry College of Business' Sanford Hall, there is a 48-seat lab/computer classroom with GroupSystems for Windows installed. This room also "triples" as a distance learning classroom in that it contains the latest academic videoconferencing software and hardware. Since a decision room might not be used 100 percent of the time for groupwork, this is an effective way to cut or share costs.

For the first and second options, a trained facilitator is necessary to coordinate the meetings. The group leader works with the facilitator to structure the meeting. The success of a GSS session depends largely on the quality, activities, and support of the facilitator (Miranda and Bostrom, 1997). For details on facilitator support, an important but often neglected aspect of GSS, see Ngwenyama et al. (1996).

Since the late 1990s, the most common approach has been the third option: using Web-based or local area network (LAN)-based groupware that allows group members to work from any location at any time (e.g., Lotus Notes). This groupware often includes videoconferencing. The availability of relatively inexpensive groupware (for purchase or for rent) combined with the power and low cost of capable PCs makes this type of system viable. Also, the high cost of constructing a facility and finding an experienced facilitator, and the need to have participants connect from other locations at any time, led to less need for the first two approaches. The Web provides flexibility in running meetings, and it creates interesting issues about how one facilitates such meetings. Generally, for an anytime/anyplace meeting, time deadlines are imposed for each phase of the meeting. These deadlines are set to allow for time zones and travel. Another issue for non-face-to-face meetings is that participants want to see with whom they are working. Some systems have access to still pictures, while videoconferencing enhances some meeting aspects by showing some body language.

GSS EXAMPLES

As mentioned before, two excellent, comprehensive GSS are GroupSystems (GroupSystems.com, Tucson, AZ, www.groupsystems.com) and TCBNET (tcbworks. terry.uga.edu). Since TCBWorks is free, try it. A comprehensive list of relevant GSS can be found on this book's Web site. Next, we describe some of the features and structure of a comprehensive GSS through GroupSystems.

7.7 GROUPSYSTEMS

GroupSystems is comprehensive groupware that supports a wide variety of group processes. (Other versions in use include a Web-based version, GroupSystems Online—a rentable version—and a DOS version.) An overview of the tools and their relationship to the major GSS activities is shown in Figure 7.3. *Agenda* is the control panel for

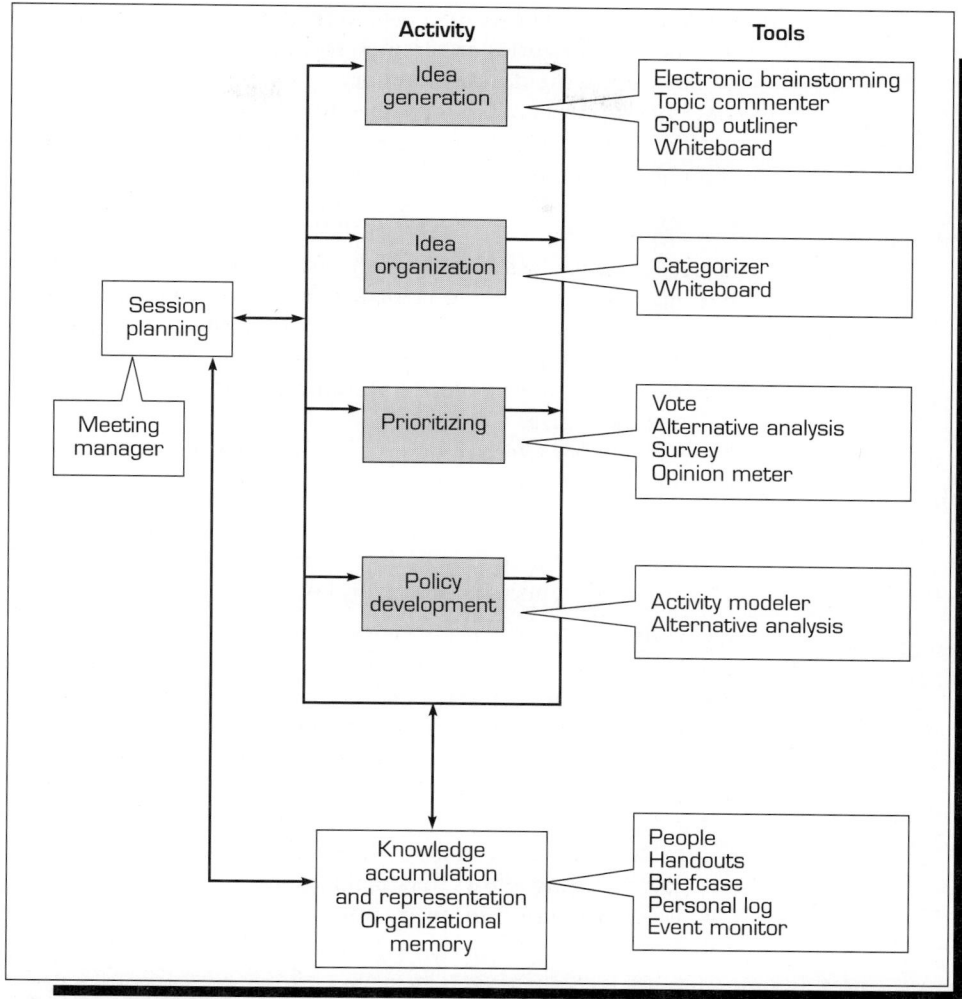

FIGURE 7.3 STRUCTURE OF GROUPSYSTEMS FOR WINDOWS

scheduling and running GroupSystems activities. The tools in GroupSystems are divided into standard tools and advanced tools.

GroupSystems for Windows *standard tools* support group processes including brainstorming, list building, information gathering, voting, organizing, prioritizing, and consensus building:

- *Electronic Brainstorming* gathers ideas and comments in an unstructured manner. Groups work rapidly in generating a free flow of ideas. Participants contribute simultaneously (parallelism) and anonymously.
- *Group Outliner* allows the group to create and comment on a multilevel list of topics in a tree or outline structure. At each level of the outline, participants can attach comments. Comments are integrated and collaborative.
- *Topic Commenter* allows participants to comment on a list of topics. This idea generation is more structured than that of Electronic Brainstorming but less structured than that of Group Outliner.

- *Categorizer* allows the group to generate a list of ideas and supporting comments. Categories are created for the ideas, and participants can drag the ideas into the desired category.
- *Vote* supports consensus development through group evaluation of issues. Several voting methods are provided. Results are tabulated electronically and displayed statistically or graphically.

GroupSystems *advanced tools* include add-ins for analysis, surveys, and modeling:

- *Alternative Analysis* allows the group to weight or rate a list of alternatives against a list of criteria because collaborative decisions require the evaluation of multiple perspectives and ideas. The group can test what-if assumptions by adjusting the weighting of the criteria.
- *Survey* allows the creation, administration, and analysis of an online questionnaire.
- *Activity Modeler* provides user-friendly group support for simultaneous business process reengineering modeling.

Agenda (the control panel) supports the facilitator. Through Agenda, the facilitator plans and runs the meeting and captures and saves session reports and data.
GroupSystems includes several other group resources:

- *People* contains a list of participants with background information.
- *Whiteboard* is a group-enabled drawing and annotation tool.
- *Handouts* are reference materials for group viewing.
- *Opinion Meter* is a fast, simple version of the vote tool for gauging opinions.

The following *individual resources* improve individual productivity:

- *Briefcase* allows access to commonly used applications (word processing, calculators, and e-mail).
- *Personal Log* allows personal note taking.
- *Event Monitor* informs members of new activities and information.

7.8 THE GSS MEETING PROCESS

Face-to-face, same time/same place electronic meetings generally follow a common progression. First, the group leader meets with the facilitator to plan the meeting (this is critically important), select the software tools, and develop an agenda. Second, the participants meet in the decision room, and the leader poses a question or problem to the group. Third, the participants type their ideas or comments (brainstorm), and the results are displayed publicly. Because the participants can see what others are typing on their own monitors, they can provide comments or generate new ideas. Fourth, the facilitator, using idea organization software, searches for common themes, topics, and ideas and organizes them into rough categories (key ideas) with appropriate comments (new research is attempting to automate this part of the electronic meeting). The results are publicly displayed. Fifth, the leader starts a discussion, either verbal or electronic. The participants next prioritize the ideas. Sixth, the top 5–10 topics are sent to idea generation software following a discussion. The process (idea generation, idea organization, prioritization) can be repeated or a final vote can be taken.

The major activities of a typical GSS session are listed in DSS in Focus 7.11. For examples of GSS use in practice, see DSS in Action 7.10 and the GroupSystems.com Web site (www.groupsystems.com).

DSS IN FOCUS 7.11

THE STANDARD GSS PROCESS

1. *Idea generation.* This exploratory step looks at the problem and attempts to develop creative ideas about its important features. The ideas can have anything to do with the problem, from potential solutions to criteria to mitigating factors. An electronic brainstorming tool is appropriate; its output is a list of ideas. Typical time is 30–45 minutes.

2. *Idea Organization.* An idea-organizing tool places the many ideas generated on a list of key issues. The output of this stage is a list of a few key ideas (about 1 for every 20 original ideas) with the supporting details. Typical time is 45–90 minutes.

3. *Prioritization.* At this stage, the key ideas are prioritized. A voting tool is appropriate; its output is a prioritized list of ideas and details. Typical time is 10–20 minutes.

4. *Idea generation.* New ideas are generated based on the prioritization of the key ideas. A brain-

storming tool that provides structure, such as Topic Commentator, is appropriate here. The ideas generated are typically focused on solutions. This stage's output may consist of about 20 ideas for each of the original key ideas.

The process continues until a final idea is selected as a solution to the problem that prompted the meeting, or a few solutions are identified to be investigated in more depth. Some meetings are decision making-oriented. Others are exploratory in nature and are focused simply on generating ideas to pursue in follow-up meetings or individual work. Often a GSS meeting takes longer than a nonsupported one, but participants are generally more thorough in their brainstorming and analysis, and they "feel" that they have made a better decision using the system.

See Nunamaker et al. (1991) for more details.

Anytime/any place meetings have become a standard approach because of the proliferation of Web-based GSS. Some differences are that participants want to know about the other participants (if they are not using videoconferencing concurrently or have never met the other participants), task completion times must be assigned (especially if the meeting spans multiple time zones), and the facilitator's task becomes more difficult, especially when the meeting runs around the clock (McQuaid et al., 2000). Deadlines are imposed so that the group can move on to the next phase of the meeting. The same issues affect distance learning environments.

According to Romano et al. (1997), it becomes increasingly important to remind participants of where they are in the process and to keep them focused on tasks that may take long periods of time. Other issues include security (to protect valuable information from theft), universal access (from home or other sites), folder invitations and information (participants must be invited to participate in meeting segments), information about the participants (on virtual business cards), indicating who is on the system (to alleviate feelings of loneliness), and facilitator controls (how to start and stop sessions, how to restrict access to different activities). *Planning the session* is the most critical recommendation. Facilitators should provide incentives and develop a vested interest in the outcome, communicate often and explicitly, assign roles and tasks with accountability, and be explicit in the communication of goals and activities.

GSS SUCCESS

The success of a GSS is based mostly on its effectiveness. When a system is used, cuts costs, supports participants in making better decisions, and/or increases productivity substantially, then it succeeds (see the Opening Vignette, the case applications, and DSS in Action 7.4 and 7.10). For a GSS to succeed, it needs many of the usual information system success factors: an organizational commitment, an executive sponsor, an operating sponsor, user involvement and training, a user-seductive interface, and so on.

Having a dedicated, well-trained, personable facilitator is critical. Finally, the GSS must have the correct tools to support the organization's groupwork and must include *parallelism* and *anonymity* to provide process and task gains. *Good planning* is the key to running successful meetings, and this also applies to electronic meetings (see DSS in Focus 7.5). If anything, bad planning might make a group believe that the GSS is to blame for its poor performance.

7.9 DISTANCE LEARNING

LEARNING, COLLABORATIVE COMPUTING AND GSS

The classroom is a natural setting in which to enhance learning by providing computerized support, either in a supplementary way or through complete courseware. Learning is the basic process of incorporating new knowledge into one's own. It typically involves the sequence of predetermined steps outlined in DSS in Focus 7.12. The learning process generally requires communication and collaboration. Collaborative computing (GSS) can improve the classroom experience. GSS features such as brainstorming (a form of discussion or chat), voting, and so on, can support class members performing groupwork. GSS use in the classroom increases observed learning, self-reported learning, on-task participation, and satisfaction (Reinig et al., 1997). On the other hand, anonymity and other GSS features can introduce some process losses into the education process, such as flaming and buffoonery, which must be planned for by the instructor and thoughtfully managed (Reinig et al., 1997) (see DSS in Focus 7.13).

The Web is an effective vehicle for distributing course materials, including lecture notes. Even with the availability of detailed course materials, class attendance does not seem to drop off. (Not attending class is ill-advised. Education research indicates that class attendance is the most significant factor impacting on course success.) Textbooks feature Web sites as well (e.g., ours). Even simple collaborative computing technologies like e-mail and listservs can enhance the educational experience (Warnock et al., 2000). A critical success factor is that class members and instructors be properly trained in use of the technology.

DSS IN FOCUS 7.12

WHAT IS LEARNING?

A learning process normally incorporates

1. Establishing the objectives of the learning process
2. Finding and revising (or creating) instructional material
3. Assessing students' levels of knowledge
4. Assigning appropriate material to students
5. Defining the form of access students have to components or modules

6. Revising and following up students' progress and intervening when necessary
7. Providing and managing communication between students and instructors and between students
8. Assessing the learning process
9. Preparing reports on the learning process results.

Source: Adapted from UCAID, "The Internet2 Project," www.internet2.edu, Apr. 9, 1999.

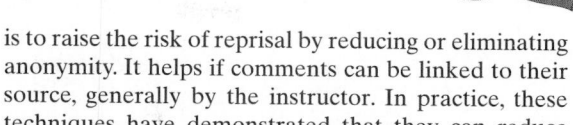

DSS IN FOCUS 7.13

IS THE ELECTRONIC CLASSROOM BURNING (FLAMING)?

Flaming is a verbal attack intended to offend either persons or organizations and is often characterized by profanity, obscenity, and insults. Not all disruptive communication is flaming; off-task jocularity or buffoonery may also occur, thus limiting the usefulness of online classroom interactions. The instructor is ultimately responsible if students engage in flaming (verbal attacks), which may offend other members of the class. Flaming usually indicates that something is wrong. Hostility increases flaming, and anonymity increases the likelihood of flaming because there is no way to identify the flamer.

Flaming can often be reduced by switching to a task with a clear vested interest or making greater efforts to convince students that they have a stake in the task at hand. Students need proper motivation. They must have a vested interest in the outcome of a task so that they will participate freely and stay focused. So the task must be appropriate for the class. This reduces hostility, which in turn reduces flaming. Another approach

is to raise the risk of reprisal by reducing or eliminating anonymity. It helps if comments can be linked to their source, generally by the instructor. In practice, these techniques have demonstrated that they can reduce flaming in the electronic classroom.

Unlike flaming, buffoonery may occur without any malicious intention or hostility. Some buffoonery allows students to relax a bit, but is acceptable only to a certain point. Learners may engage in some buffoonery as a reaction to the novelty of anonymous interaction at the start of the first session, or they may engage in buffoonery when they run out of useful ideas at the end of a session. This is similar to making a few joking comments as a class or meeting starts or ends, and most instructors find it acceptable. It is important for an instructor to expect flaming and buffoonery in electronic classroom discussions and to decide ahead of time how to respond when either arises.

Source: Adapted from Reinig et al. (1997).

WHY USE COLLABORATIVE COMPUTING IN LEARNING?

Tyran and Shepherd (2000) describe an interesting research framework for collaborative technology use (GSS) in the traditional classroom. There are factors related to the context of the group learning situation, the group learning process, and the outcomes of the learning process. Alavi et al. (1995) showed that students in a distant collaborative environment exhibited higher critical thinking and were found to be more committed to and cohesive with their teams. It seems to be a worthwhile effort to move courses online.

Collaborative computing technologies are directly applicable to distance learning environments. By the end of the 1990s, technology had advanced to the point where computer supported traditional classes could move to online, Web-based distance learning environments. There is a definite need to enhance existing classrooms with collaborative support and to make education available outside the confines of the classroom.

DISTANCE LEARNING

Distance learning (DL) takes place when learning involves tools or technologies designed to overcome the restrictions of same time/same place learning. The history of distance learning in the United States dates back to 1728, when an advertisement in *The Boston Globe* offered shorthand lessons through the mail. Bunker (1999) and Matthews (1999) provide the history of DL.

Distance learning is exciting and has unlimited potential to revolutionize learning at universities and colleges, at public and private schools, and in on-the-job training. But distance learning is not a new concept! When television was invented in the 1920s, it was heralded as a device that would revolutionize education. Radio was used in the 1920s and

1930s for distance learning programs (it is still used in the Australian Outback), and video distance learning systems have been in operation for decades (see DSS in Action 7.14 for the "early" experiences of one author). Now that technology has evolved, television, or rather videoconferencing and collaborative computing through the Internet, can finally fulfill its destiny by providing support tools to enabling distance learning.

Internet and videoconferencing and collaborative computing tools customized to the classroom environment allow inexpensive and widespread distance learning. Distance learning has developed into a substantive sector of higher education around the world over the last few decades. It is becoming an increasingly popular alternative to traditional degree programs and workshops. DL is a nontraditional way of delivering education and focuses on working professionals whose primary requirement is the element of convenience. Student profiles have changed dramatically over the last two decades. As the economics of education and socioeconomic trends evolve, students are completing their college educations in nontraditional ways (Matthews, 1999). More than 1,500 educational institutions worldwide offer courses through DL, not including the comparable if not larger number of independent companies offering remote education courses. These numbers are growing daily (Larsen, 1999).

DSS IN ACTION 7.14

DISTANCE LEARNING—DÉJÀ VU? AGAIN?

In 1980 I accepted a position as an assistant professor at Southern Methodist University (SMU). During my interview, I discovered that about half my teaching would be "education at a distance" through the TAGER Network (The Association of Graduate Education and Research Network—now the Green Education Network), a closed-circuit television system over which almost all of the masters level programs in engineering were offered (see www.seas.smu.edu/disted/). TAGER, operational since 1964, is a consortium of five colleges and universities and many companies in the Dallas–Fort Worth Metroplex. TAGER broadcasts courses from the colleges and universities to the firms. The video and audio signal is sent via closed-circuit microwave, while the talk back from students off campus is by way of leased phone lines (audio only). The firm is obligated to provide a media classroom for the course and to allow students to attend. On campus there are four classroom studios, each equipped with two cameras (one in the rear and one overhead).

Students saved driving time (up to 3 days per week—possibly 80 miles each way—and in many cases this was the *only* way they could pursue a graduate degree), while the universities were able to increase class sizes without requiring additional space and, more importantly, to attract high-level, highly motivated students who enriched the classroom experience for all. In 1978 the program was expanded to include videotape that could be mailed anywhere in the world. In the mid-

1980s, SMU joined the National Technological University (NTU) as a member school. NTU offers its own degree programs, but students attend classes from any member school, generally beamed by satellite to their workplace. This enhanced career portability for part-time students.

It did not take me long to figure out that telephone office hours would be necessary and that the class would require a lot of extra preparation time. Even so, the preparation paid off when the course was offered a second time. There were a few other benefits: If a faculty member had to miss class (rarely, of course), he or she could record the lecture in advance; I got really good at identifying students by their voices, to the point that when they came to my office I could recognize them as soon as they spoke; and the evidence of a very occasional academic honesty issue could be recorded on videotape.

Even though this technology seems quite passé now, it was remarkably robust and challenging then, and a good experience for the students and the faculty. Many of the lessons, tips, and research topics I now see in distance learning articles are the same ones that I experienced, learned, or developed on the fly in the early 1980s.

Source: Jay E. Aronson, Mar. 2000.

Most major colleges and universities utilize technology to offer a variety of sophisticated DL programs. In 1999 more than 300 fully accredited major colleges and universities in the United States offered DL-delivered degrees in more than 800 fields. Almost all offered bachelor's degrees, and most offered master's degrees. About 80 offered MBAs and doctorates. Programs ranged from those delivered by traditional institutions to those sponsored by Jones International University—a virtual campus only. See Petersons.com, ECollege.com, www-icdl.open.ac.uk/icdl/, and usdla.org for information about specific distance learning programs (Larsen, 1999).

For an example of an executive MBA program offered as a mix of on-campus experience and distance learning technology at The University of Georgia, see DSS in Action 7.15. For experiences involving moving courses and partial courses to online environments, see Berger (1999), Dollar (2000), Schell (2000) and Warnock et al. (2000). DL programs have many advantages, and unfortunately some disadvantages.

ADVANTAGES OF DL PROGRAMS[3]

- Learning can be as effective as by traditional means, or even more so.
- The flexible time frame provides education opportunities for many, including senior managers and executives.
- A student need not quit his or her job.
- A student can travel as part of an existing job.
- Access is available anywhere and anytime.
- New technology can be presented to a large audience cheaply.
- Online classes can teach specific skills.
- Online classes can cost less.

---

[3]Partly adapted from Larsen (1999), Jana (2000), and Schell (2000).

DSS IN ACTION 7.15

THE NEW SEMI-DISTANCE LEARNING MBA

The University of Georgia and PricewaterhouseCoopers (PWC) have partnered to pioneer a new kind of MBA program. The 2-year program combines distance, classroom, and team learning with technical and business courses.

The program begins with all enrolled students visiting the campus for 2 weeks to meet the faculty and to get to know each other. After the first week, students split into teams of about five people, and they work within these teams for the rest of the school year.

The teams write a contract to define their responsibilities and commitments, such as the amount of time to be spent on conference calls and how to handle collaborative research. The contract can also include consequences for people who don't live up to their responsibilities. After the 2-week stint, consultants return to work. Each week, they log on to Learning Space (a Lotus Notes distance learning application) via the Web to listen to prerecorded lectures and complete weekly reading assignments. The teams participate in conference calls as needed. Each semester students regroup at The University of Georgia for on-site learning for a week.

This program readily handles logistical and content problems with traditional full-time programs (difficult because of the 1- to 2-year commitment away from work) and typical part-time programs (the employees travel in their consulting). At the time that the PwC program began, pure distance learning MBA programs were still evolving.

This semi-distance learning program provides students with many of the benefits of both an on-campus experience and a distance learning environment.

Source: Adapted from J. Mateyaschuk, "An MBA on the Go," *InformationWeek,* No. 744, July 19, 1999; also see J. Reingold, and M. Schneider, "The Executive MBA Your Way," *BusinessWeek,* No. 3651, Oct. 18, 1999.

- More information can be made available to students, adding breadth and depth to a course.
- It is possible to have more one-on-one interaction with an instructor (through e-mail).
- Student/faculty contact time increases.
- DL meets the need for continuous learning.
- The course materials are consistent.
- Attendance is not required and can be handled flexibly (a plus and a minus).
- The technology can handle "discussion-style" courses as well as technical courses.
- Students' attitudes evolve and improve as familiarity with the technology increases.
- Students show positive gains in learning.
- Impacts (higher learning levels, higher test scores) have been observed to be greater in online courses (Dollar, 2000; Reid, 1999).

DISADVANTAGES OF DL PROGRAMS[4]

- There are fewer (or very different) social interactions (lack of face-to-face meetings).
- There is less or no on-campus interaction.
- There can be communication problems (especially with video).
- Students must be highly self-motivated and tightly focused.
- Students must be highly disciplined and organized.
- Students must have effective time management skills.
- Students must be extremely dedicated.
- Online classes require major administrative support.
- Online classes require major technical support.
- Faculty preparation and delivery time is significantly higher than that for a traditional course (up to three times the time and effort is needed).
- Courses must be redesigned to utilize the best presentation mechanisms for topic delivery.
- Extra rewards for faculty are recommended because of the extra effort (could be a plus).
- Faculty need special training in effective instruction methods and in the technology.
- Students need special training in the technology.
- The course requires a *very reliable* technological infrastructure including hardware, software, and a *trained* staff.
- The learner must assume much more responsibility.
- Mastery of the material establishes the grade, though collaborative methods allow an instructor to identify contributors.
- Students must work hard—these are real courses, not correspondence courses.

DISTANCE LEARNING COURSEWARE

There are hundreds of courseware packages that enable distance learning. These range from more general collaboration tools like Lotus Notes, Microsoft NetMeeting, Novell GroupWise (Chaffee, 1998), and GroupSystems to specialized tools like the popular Lotus Learning Space (Figure 7.4) and WebCT. Learning Space (written in Lotus

---

[4]Partly adapted from Larsen (1999), Jana (2000), and Schell (2000).

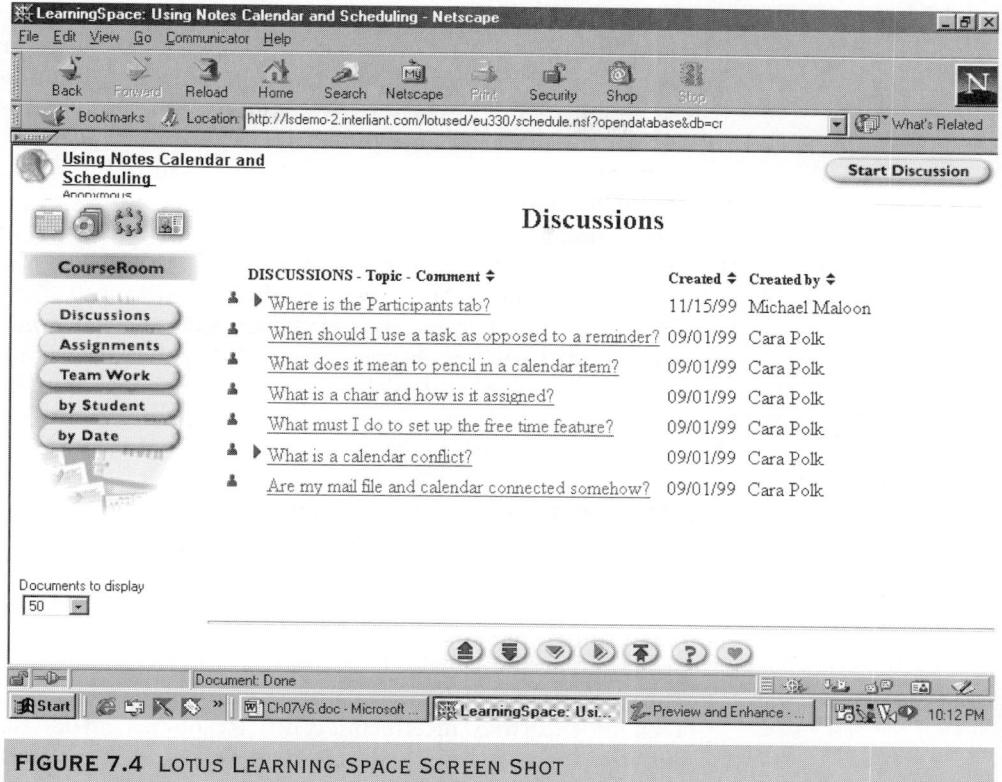

FIGURE 7.4 LOTUS LEARNING SPACE SCREEN SHOT

Source: Screen capture (©2000) Lotus Development Corporation. Used with permission of Lotus Development Corporation. Learning Space is a registered trademark of Lotus Development Corporation.

Notes/Domino Server) is a powerful collaborative support tool that handles most aspects of online learning in a Web environment. The University of Georgia program described in DSS in Action 7.15 uses Learning Space for student interaction through discussion lists, e-mail between students and between students and faculty, submission of assignments, and feedback. Also, lectures and lecture notes are enabled on Learning Space.

Mottl (1999) describes LearnLinc Virtual Classroom (LearnLinc Corporation), which lets online instructors control class presentations using synchronized multimedia and content over the Web. It also offers application sharing, electronic hand raising, and a "glimpse" feature that allows instructors to acquire a screen capture of any student's desktop. One-way streaming video and audio or prerecorded communications, as well as two-way audio in multicast audioconferencing, can be used. See *2000 Buyer's Guide of Tools for Conferences, Meetings, and Distance Learning* (Anonymous, 1999c) for a list of available tools.

ONLINE CORPORATE TRAINING

Because of the current IT labor shortage, more and more organizations are training their employees in the latest technologies. This shortage means that IT professionals are increasingly pressed for time. Web-based learning technologies allow IT organizations to keep their staff members up-to-date with the latest innovations in IT. In 1999 private industry spent $58 billion annually on employee training (Markel, 1999). Driven by the demand for cheaper, more interactive courses, online learning is fast becoming the standard operating procedure: Classroom use is projected to drop dramatically from its 77 percent share of the training market in 2000 to 51 percent by 2003. Conventional classroom instruction costs (in 2000) are about $75 per hour, with full-week programs costing $3,000 to $5,000. Computer-based training costs about half that and does not involve travel costs or have class size restrictions. Web-based or online courses will account for 50 percent or more of all training by 2002 (from 17 percent in 1998). Training via the Web can run 24 hours per day every day (24/7). Web-based training (WBT) can be faster and cheaper than classroom training. IBM estimates a savings of $500,000 for every 1,000 hours of training outside the traditional classroom. International Data Corporation (IDC) predicts revenue from Internet-based training program sales to grow at a compound annual rate of 64.5 percent through 2003. Advanced electronic learning requires real-time, two-way communication via either audio- or videoconferencing tools allowing students and instructors to interact and providing feedback. For most Web training, students view a live or recorded class and participation is limited to posting on bulletin boards and e-mail discussions. (See DSS in Focus 7.16, Boisvert, 2000; Kiser, 1999; Markel, 1999; and Mottl, 2000.)

DISTANCE LEARNING RESOURCES

The following organizations are involved in promoting and supporting distance learning:

- The Center for Distance Learning at Texas A&M University (www.cdlr.tamu.edu). This resource center has a model classroom that can be viewed on the Web.
- The Center for Excellence in Distance Learning (CEDL) at Lucent Technologies (www.lucent.com/cedl/). Resources include research abstracts, published articles, case studies, and brochures with tips on how to set up a distance learning course or program.
- The American Council on Education ACENET; www.acenet.edu. This organization stays current on many important issues in education. They publish a checklist on how to evaluate the quality of an organization's distance learning program: *Distance Learning Evaluation Guide,* (ACENET, 1999).

EVALUATION OF DISTANCE LEARNING

Distance learning is a form of collaboration and knowledge management and can be done in a 24/7 framework. It is critical to assess the impact of Web-based courses in terms of benefits and costs (Gaud, 1999). Most student experiences are positive (e.g.,

---

DSS IN FOCUS 7.16

CORPORATE TRAINING WISDOM

Here are some key lessons for online training:

1. Do involve technology-savvy employees when planning.
2. Don't dump data online and call it training.
3. Do use the Web to teach soft skills.
4. Don't expect people to train on their own time.
5. Do keep the lessons short.
6. Do keep traffic moving.

7. Don't use plug-ins.
8. Do ensure that everyone knows the basics.
9. Don't forget the human touch.
10. Do recognize that the Web will not put classroom trainers out of work.

Source: Adapted from Kiser (1999).

Dollar, 2000; Schell, 2000). Students tend to learn more using groupware, especially when learning spans a distance. Students in distance learning environments tend to perform better than those in traditional classrooms (Alavi et al., 1995; Reinig et al., 1997; Dollar, 2000). Several factors are important in distance learning situations. A high level of student motivation, a strong work ethic, and intensive student support measures typically result in success for distance learners (Reid, 1999). The most important factor for achieving success in distance learning is the degree to which instructors and support staff are able to encourage students to undertake responsibility for their own learning (Reid, 1999).

Both students and faculty must understand how collaborative technology impacts on how they perform course work (Berger, 1999). Some issues revolve around training, determining which technology to use and how, what to distribute and when, what standards to use for files that students submit, and so on.

Distance learning is radically changing education, and socioeconomic and technological changes should be examined as the learning behaviors and expectations of learners change. There is a sharply growing demand for flexible, adaptive, time- and geography-independent learning environments (Meso and Liegle, 2000). Despite its disadvantages, distance learning is growing dramatically because of the increased demand.

7.10 CREATIVITY AND IDEA GENERATION

CREATIVITY

Creativity is complex. It can be considered a fundamental human trait and a level of achievement (see DSS in Focus 7.17 for a formal description of creativity). Personality-related creativity traits (inventiveness, independence, individuality, enthusiasm, and flexibility) can be assessed through a 36-item scale called Personal Barriers to Creative Thought and Innovative Action (Hellriegel and Slocum, 1992, pp. 237–238), and the widely used Torrance Tests of Creative Thinking (TTCT) (Cramond, 1995; Torrance, 1988). However, researchers have established that creativity can be learned and improved and is not as strongly dependent on individual traits as originally thought. Innovative companies recognize that creativity may not necessarily be the result of genius as much as the result of being in an idea-nurturing work environment.

Once a problem is formulated, potential criteria and alternatives must be identified. Idea generation is an ideal approach. Creative ideas generally lead to better solutions. In brainstorming, there are some specific creativity measures: the quantitative (number of ideas) and qualitative (quality of ideas) components. Both can be positively impacted by the use of a **creativity support system (CSS)** (essentially a GSS) (Wierenga and van Bruggen, 1998; Massetti, 1996).

Many organizations recognize the value of creativity and innovation. They are aware of the collaborative nature of creativity and the kinds of environments that foster it (e.g., one critical aspect required for creativity is permission to fail: the Post-it notes adhesive from 3M Corporation was a dismal failure as a superglue but became remarkably successful once a purpose was discovered for a weak adhesive). Creativity and innovation go hand in hand. Quite often what seems like a bad idea becomes the source of a creative innovation many years in the future. For example, the limiting factor in building a mile-high skyscraper (designed in 1956 by Frank Lloyd Wright) was the fact that cabled elevators could not ascend that far. About 40 years later, Otis Elevator

DSS IN FOCUS 7.17

WHAT IS CREATIVITY?

Creativity is fairly complex to define formally but very easy to recognize when you see it. Formally, *creativity* can be defined as either a trait or an achievement (Eysenck, 1994). As a trait, creativity is a dispositional variable characteristic of a person leading to the production of acts, items, and instances of novelty. As an achievement, we refer to the creative product, for example, the output of a process such as the "quality" of the ideas generated in an electronic brainstorming session. Creative achievement may depend on the trait of creativity but also on much more. The following variables have been mentioned in formal research as affecting creativity as achievement: cognitive variables (intel-

ligence, knowledge, skills, and so on), environmental variables (cultural and socioeconomic factors), and personality variables (motivation, confidence, and creativity as a trait) (Eysenck, 1994, p. 209). In their study of factors affecting the creativity of marketing programs, three classes of influencing factors were described: problem-solving inputs, situational factors, and motivational factors (Andrews and Smith, 1996). These factors are very similar to Eysenck's variables. All in all, experts know when they see creative traits and achievements.

Source: Partly adapted from Wierenga and van Bruggen (1998).

Company unveiled a viable prototype (that could even transport people sideways). Fundamental innovations can take 15–25 years to reach fruition (Port and Carey, 1997).

Schrage and Peters (1999) believe that collaboration, serious play, and prototyping (serious trial and error—mostly error) are necessary to foster creativity. The workplace should be a fun place for the innovative knowledge worker. *Play* involves improvising with the unanticipated in ways that create new value. Creative processes cannot be managed the same way that conventional incremental improvements are. "Innovation can be nurtured and guided by setting soft goals, by evaluating progress with a shrewd eye toward long-range strategy and changes in the outside world, and by creating a climate that encourages bold thinking" (Port and Carey, 1997). A manager fostering creativity should "allow and enable" rather than structure and control, according to John Kao, founder and CEO of The Idea Factory (Silverstone, 1999). Vance and Deacon (1997, 1999) claim that to encourage creativity it is important to be "outrageous" in our attitudes and activities (also see Kaneshige, 2000). Thinking "outside the box" unleashes creative energy. It is important to develop many simulations (prototypes) that eventually (hopefully) will lead to a success (Thomas Edison had over 1,800 failures before he developed a sustainable light bulb). Some specific advice from Schrage and Peters (1999) is "Be willing to fail early and often; know when the costs outweigh the benefits; know who wins and who loses from an innovation; build a prototype that engages customers, vendors, and colleagues; create markets around prototypes; and simulate the customer experience." Once creativity is unleashed, in the long run it can dramatically enhance the bottom line. Creativity is important in problem solving, and thus it is critical to develop computerized support systems for it.

Creativity and innovation can be stimulated by a number of environmental factors. An environment that meets the "serious play" criterion is part of the process. Stimulation by other creative people in the environment can push a group forward. How? Some stimulation can come directly from exciting ideas that are developed as a consequence of association (or synergy) among creative people. This can be done formally by presenting a person with a string of related (even distantly related) concepts.

A number of association methods have been proposed and empirically proven to be effective in stimulating creativity. And viewing ideas in a different frame (again outside the box, from different angles, and so on) can stimulate creativity [see von Oech (1998) and Creative Think at www.creativethink.com]. Next we discuss creativity and innovation in the context of idea generation and electronic brainstorming.

IDEA GENERATION THROUGH ELECTRONIC BRAINSTORMING

Idea generation methods and techniques have been adopted to enhance the creativity of both individuals and groups. **Idea generation** software (**electronic brainstorming**) helps to stimulate a free flow of turbulent creative thinking: ideas, words, pictures, and concepts set loose with fearless enthusiasm, based on the principle of synergy (association). Some packages are designed to enhance the creative thought process of the human mind and can be used to create new product ideas, marketing strategies, promotional campaigns, names, titles, slogans, or stories, or just for brainstorming.

A key feature in idea-generating software is bombarding the user with many ideas. This is critical because it helps the user move away from an analytic mode and into a creative mode. Psychological research indicates that people tend to anchor their thoughts early on, using their first ideas as springboards for other ideas. Therefore, subsequent ideas may not be significantly new, but simply minor variations of the original idea. Because brainstorming software is free of human subjectivity, it can help broaden the thinking platform and encourage truly unique ideas to emerge. Recent studies have characterized creativity and how it can be enhanced by software tools.

By definition, idea generation in GSS is a collaborative effort. One person's idea triggers another's ideas, which trigger even more ideas (in *idea chains* developed by association). With collaborative computing support tools (e.g., GSS), the individuals do all the thinking while the software system encourages them to move along. The technology is an anonymous, safe way to encourage participants to voice opinions that they might be reluctant to express in a more conventional setting. By building on each other's ideas, people can obtain creative insights they did not have before based on associations with existing ideas and with their memories. There is a percolation effect as ideas work their way through the process. Associations trigger memories that can activate creativity. The exchange of information (learning) can lead to increases in output and creativity (Dennis, 1996; Dennis et al., 1997/1998; Rees and Koehler, 1999). There are many relatively inexpensive idea generation packages on the market. We list a sample on this book's Web site, www.prenhall.com/turban.

Under the right electronic brainstorming conditions, more ideas and more creative ideas overall can be generated. A number of different conditions have been explored. Aronson et al. (2000) investigated time pressure impacts on idea generation and quality. Time pressure does matter. Dennis et al. (1997) studied single versus multiple dialoges in brainstorming, and Dennis et al. (1999) examined the impact of decomposing a problem by time periods or by task. Massetti (1996) investigated the impact of different brainstorming tools on creativity, and Hilmer and Dennis (2000) studied categorization impacts.

Generally, if the right approach is used in electronic brainstorming, more ideas and more creative ideas are generated. But a word of caution is in order. This may not always be a good idea in that a group may experience a process gain in the number of ideas and the number of creative ideas but also experience a process loss resulting from *information overload*. The results of each idea generation session can be stored (GSS provides organizational memory) so that they can be carried over from one meeting to another to enhance the creativity of more people.

What if an individual needs to brainstorm alone? There are methods for enhancing individual brainstorming. Satzinger et al. (1999) developed simulated brainstorming to help individuals trigger more creative responses when brainstorming alone. They compared the impact of a simulator that randomly generates ideas to an individual decision maker, versus an individual decision maker not using a simulator in brainstorming. The participants using the simulator generated more ideas and more creative ideas than the others.

Research on how a group should organize itself to generate ideas shows that, in contrast to findings on non-computer-mediated idea generation, a single GSS-supported group generates more ideas of higher quality than the same number of participants working as individuals or in several smaller groups (Bostrom et al., 1993). Web-based systems for idea generation (e.g., TCBWorks) are readily available.

Loosely related to brainstorming, cognitive maps (e.g., Banxia Decision Explorer) can help an individual or group understand a *messy* (wicked) problem, develop a common frame, and enhance creativity. A cognitive map shows how concepts relate to each other, thus helping users organize their thoughts and ideas. In this way they can visualize the problem they are trying to solve. (Lipp and Carver, 2000; Sheetz et al., 2000.)

CREATIVITY-ENHANCING SOFTWARE

Though electronic brainstorming enhances creativity, human beings primarily produce the results. In the next two subsections we describe software and methods that enhance human creativity by actually performing some of the creative tasks of a human being. Some of these systems actually exhibit creative behavior.

COMPUTER PROGRAMS THAT EXHIBIT CREATIVE BEHAVIOR

For several decades people have attempted to write computer programs that exhibit intelligent behavior. A major characteristic of intelligent behavior is creativity. Can computers be creative?

Intelligent agents (smartbots) can function as facilitators in GSS. Chen et al. (1995) describe an experiment in which an intelligent agent assisted in idea convergence. The agent's performance was comparable to that of a human facilitator in identifying important meeting concepts but inferior in generating precise and relevant concepts. But the agent was able to complete its task faster than its human counterparts. This concept is in its infancy but has potential for supporting Web-based GSS, where the facilitator cannot be available on a 24/7 basis.

Rasmus (1995) describes three creativity tools. The first one is called Copycat, a program that seeks analogies in patterns of letters. Identifying patterns is the essence of intelligence. Copycat, consisting of several intelligent agents, can find analogies to strings of letters (e.g., find an analogy for transforming aabc to aabd). This ability can be generalized to other problems that require conceptual understanding and the manipulation of objects. The ability of the program to anticipate the meaning of the transformation and find analogous fits provides evidence that computers can mimic a human being's ability to create analogies. The second system, Tabletop, is also capable of finding analogies. A third system, AARON, is a sophisticated art drawing program and the result of 15 years of research. Its developer, Harold Cohen, created a comprehensive knowledge base to support AARON. Similar computer programs have been developed to write poems and music and create works in other media. The increased knowledge base, processing speed, and storage now available enable such programs to create artwork of good quality.

CREATIVITY SOFTWARE ALTERNATIVES TO IDEA GENERATION

CoBrain (Invention Machine Corporation, Cambridge, MA, www.invention-machine.com) is an intelligent partner that accelerates technical innovation. CoBrain's semantic processing technology reads, understands, and extracts key concepts from company databases, intranets, and the Internet. The software reads the content, creates a problem solution tree (knowledge index), and delivers an abstract listing the technical content in relevant documents. CoBrain uses scientific and engineering knowledge as the foundation for its semantic algorithms to accelerate new product and process design innovations (www.invention-machine.com). A demo version of the Web-based software is running at www.cobrain.com.

CoBrain is based on the theory of inventive problem solving (TRIZ—a Russian acronym). TRIZ was first developed by Genrich Altshuller and his colleagues in Russia in 1946. Over 2 million patents were examined, classified by level of inventiveness, and analyzed to look for the following innovation principles:

1. Problems and solutions repeated across industries and sciences.
2. Patterns of technical evolution repeated across industries and sciences.
3. Innovations used scientific effects outside the field where they were developed.

The TRIZ creative process is described on the Web sites of *The TRIZ Journal* (www.triz-journal.com) and Ideation International (www.ideationtriz.com).

SOFTWARE THAT FACILITATES HUMAN CREATIVITY

There are several good software packages that can help stimulate creativity. Some have very specific functions, and others use word associations or questions to prompt the user to take new, unexplored directions in their thought patterns. This activity can help users break cyclic thinking patterns, get past mental blocks, or overcome procrastination. Such software can use several different approaches to release the user's flow of ideas. Project KickStart, ThoughtPath, Creative WhackPack, and IdeaFisher are just a few of these packages.

Project KickStart (www.projectkickstart.com) supports the creative aspect of a very specific problem: organizing a project at its inception. It walks the user through a series of standard steps through which every project should progress. It helps the user organize his or her ideas to start the project quickly. It also makes information from other projects available to help work out the details every step of the way. A downloadable demo is available from the company's Web site.

ThoughtPath (Synectics Company, www.thoughtpath.com) enhances creativity by walking a user through a series of steps that have demonstrated success in practice. ThoughtPath guides the user through problems and opportunities toward a creative, workable solution. It helps users gain insights into their problems and issues. ThoughtPath is designed to promote "outside-the-box" thinking. A tour is available on the Web.

Creative Think (www.creativethink.com) provides the Creative WhackPack [based on von Oech (1998)], a deck of 64 cards that will "whack" you out of habitual thought patterns and let you look at your problem in a new way. The cards ("a physical package") are designed to stimulate the imagination. Fortunately, all 64 illustrated cards are up and running on the Web site (as software); you can select the Give Me Another Creative Whack button to select one at random.

DSS IN ACTION 7.18

FISHING FOR IDEAS WITH IDEAFISHER

IdeaFisher has three components: QBank, IdeaBank, and Notepad. QBank's questions are organized to assist in formulating an exact problem more accurately; a series of modification questions encourage the user to branch into different lines of thought, and a series of evaluation questions help the user to test and compare the quality of creative ideas to the original objective. This list of central ideas can then be used to decide what to pursue in IdeaBank.

IdeaBank is a massive database of idea words, concepts, and associations with the cross-referencing power of a huge number of direct idea associations and a very large number of secondary (linked) associations. The inclusion of polar opposites stimulates an even larger group of associations.

For example, using the word *car,* the set of Topical Categories includes

- Varieties/Examples (cars)
- Varieties/Examples (named automobiles)
- Varieties/Examples (trailers)
- Varieties/Examples (trucks/buses/vans).

Under the heading Varieties/Examples (car), we find a long list that includes

- Abandoned vehicle
- American muscle car
- Antique car
- Clown's funny car
- Gas guzzler
- Fleet of vehicles.

IdeaBank also lets the user add personal associations and phrases to Topical Categories or to create their own customized Topical Categories.

The third component of the system, Notepad, allows the two databases to work together efficiently. The user can then focus on productive efforts in selecting alternative lines of thought, maximizing the number of high-quality ideas, and selecting the best ones.

IdeaFisher, has an associative lexicon of the English language that cross-references words and phrases. The associative links make it easy for the computer to provide the user with words related to a given theme on some level, based on analogies and metaphors. Many such nonlinear associations can be outrageous, but as mentioned earlier, outrageousness can often trigger new, useful (and profitable) ideas. Personal associations can also be added to the database to broaden its creative application base. IdeaFisher has been described as "a thesaurus on steroids." In 2000 IdeaFisher had 15 add-on modules designed for specific creative problem-solving situations. The modules include Strategic Planning, Speech and Presentation, Public Relations, General Problem Solving, and more. Writers can use IdeaFisher's Creative Writing Module to help generate analogies to get past writer's block. In DSS in Action 7.18, we describe IdeaFisher's components and list of some of the Varieties/Examples IdeaFisher presents for the Topical Category *car.*

7.11 GSS AND COLLABORATIVE COMPUTING ISSUES AND RESEARCH

Groupware is still experiencing robust growth in industry, mainly because there is more and more need for groups to collaborate. According to International Data Corporation (IDC), in 1998 there were 84 million users of groupware who created a $2.1 billion market. By 2003 this market is expected to reach $2.6 billion annually (Dugan, 1999). By 2000 there were more than 50 million users of Lotus Notes alone. There are still many unanswered issues and questions concerning collaborative computing in theory and practice. One problem with these issues is that the technology advances so far so fast that before an issue can be explored sufficiently, new ones pop up. Initially the main question was whether GSS make groupwork more efficient and/or effective. At the time the question of efficiency and effectiveness was posed, the technology was new (and experimental, expensive, or both), and there was a lot of resistance to using it (this changed with its demonstrated success). In many cases, its effectiveness has been clear, but its efficiency sometimes is in question in that groups can sometimes take longer to do their work because of problems like information overload. For example, the volume of ideas generated in brainstorming can be huge; so the process gain of developing a larger set of solutions can introduce a process loss simultaneously. But as with DSS in general, it is not unusual for computerized support methods to require more time since a more detailed analysis can be performed, which can take longer.

Most early studies focused on the electronic meeting setting versus the traditional meeting setting. Researchers investigated important issues such as anonymity, parallelism, and especially group size (de Vreede et al., 2000). Many studies involve brainstorming (electronic versus traditional, electronic versus alternative electronic), for which one can readily measure the number of ideas generated and their originality. These measures are typically higher for GSS groups, and in a real-word field study (Dennis and Garfield, 1999), the proposals of the supported groups were of higher quality and deemed more acceptable than those of the unsupported groups. Many studies have compared GSS methods to determine which might be the better or the best way to utilize the technologies for better results or for more results. For example, Dennis et al. (1997) examined multiple dialogs versus single dialogs for electronic brainstorming, while in another study Dennis et al. (1999) investigated whether there was any impact on brainstorming when a problem was decomposed by task, by time, or by both. Other studies involved the impact of imposed structure on groupwork to stimulate thinking that would lead to more effective work [e.g., for brainstorming, time pressure impacts were examined by Aronson et al. (2000), and categorization impacts by Hilmer and Dennis (2000)]. Studies have investigated how group members learn as they work (Rees and Koehler, 1999) and how they can effectively exchange information (Dennis, 1996; Dennis et al., 1997/1998).

Web groupware (Catalano, 1999; Lipp and Carver, 2000) presents new opportunities and challenges. Establishing how IS and organizational behavior theories explain the effectiveness of groupware [e.g., task-technology fit by Shirani et al. (1999) and Murthy and Kerr (2000); and the interplay by Williams and Wilson (1999)] presents new issues. Other issues involve how the social behavior of groups (cohesiveness, and so on) is impacted on by groupware (Pendergast and Hayne, 1999; Chidambaram, 1997; Powell, 2000). Some facilitation issues such as how to run meetings and how to support facilitators are still open (Griffith et al., 1998), while others have clearly been settled (McQuaid et al., 2000).

Fjermestad and Hiltz (1998) describe the wealth of GSS research as the field moves forward to determine the best ways to run electronic meetings and approach many of these open issues. Also see the entire special issue of the *Journal of Management Information Systems,* Vol. 15, No. 3, Winter 1997/1998. See Downing and Clark (1999) for descriptions of how groupware is used in practice.

Now that groupware is readily available and running on the Web, many organizations are attempting to *virtualize* the way they operate (Warkentin et al., 1999; Greenhalgh, 1999). In essence, organizations are attempting to form a **virtual corporation**

(Fritz et al., 1998) where people work wherever and whenever it is appropriate. As we move toward this situation, more questions arise (how to manage such an organization is still an open question, just as it was when the workers involved were called telecommuters). Finally, research is being done to determine the best way to utilize groupware in the classroom.

❖ CHAPTER HIGHLIGHTS

- People collaborate in their work. Groupware (collaborative computing software) supports groupwork.
- Group members may be within the same organization or may span organizations; they may be in the same or in different locations; they may work at the same or at different times.
- When people work in teams, especially when the members are in different locations and may be working at different times, they need to communicate, collaborate, and access a diverse set of information sources in multiple formats.
- Collaborative computing is known by a number of terms, including groupware, group support systems (GSS), and computer-supported cooperative work (CSCW).
- The Internet (Web), intranets, and extranets support decision making through collaboration tools and access to data, information, and knowledge.
- Internet and Web technology has had a major impact on how we communicate and work.
- An intranet is an internal Internet.
- An extranet links a workgroup, such an intranet for group members from several different organizations. A common use is for groupware applied to a supply chain involving several organizations using Internet technology.
- Groups and groupwork (teams and teamwork) in organizations are proliferating. Consequently, groupware continues to evolve to support effective groupwork.
- Communication technologies are the foundation on which groupware rests.
- Collaboration is much deeper than communication; it conveys meaning or knowledge; material is actively worked on during collaboration.
- The time/place framework is a convenient way to describe the communication and collaboration patterns of groupwork. Different technologies can support different frameworks.
- People might work together at the same time or at different times, in the same place or in different places.
- The term *groupware* refers to software products that provide collaborative support to groups (including meetings).
- Though meetings can be inefficient and ineffective, most groupwork occurs in meetings.
- Groupware typically contains capabilities for electronic brainstorming, electronic conferencing or meeting, group scheduling, calendaring, planning, conflict resolution, model building, videoconferencing, electronic document sharing, voting, and so on.
- Groupware can support anytime/anyplace groupwork.
- Most groupware allows group members to communicate over the Internet with a Web browser interface.

- There are many benefits (process and task gains) to groupwork, but there are also many dysfunctions (process and task losses).
- A group support system (GSS) is any combination of hardware and software that enhances groupwork.
- Group support systems (GSS) are also known as electronic meeting systems (EMS), computer-supported cooperative work (CSCW) systems, collaborative computing, and groupware.
- GSS attempts to increase process and task gains and reduce process and task losses of groupwork.
- Parallelism and anonymity provide many GSS gains.
- GSS may be considered in terms of the common group activities of information retrieval, information sharing, and information use.
- GSS can be deployed in an electronic decision room environment, in a multipurpose computer lab, or over the Web.
- Web-based groupware is the norm for anytime/anyplace collaboration.
- GSS software may include modules for idea generation (via outlining or brainstorming), idea organization, stakeholder identification, topic commentator, voting, policy formulation, and enterprise analysis.
- The success of a GSS session depends largely on the quality, activities, and support of the facilitator.
- GSS same time/same place meetings generally follow a fixed pattern: (1) planning, (2) question posing, (3) brainstorming, (4) idea organization, (5) discussion and idea prioritization, and (6) more idea generation.
- There are many new GSS issues involving anytime/anyplace groupware.
- Good planning is the key to running a successful electronic meeting.
- The classroom is a natural setting in which to enhance learning by providing computerized support.
- Collaborative computing (GSS) can improve the classroom experience.
- Distance learning (DL) takes place when learning is performed with tools or technologies designed to overcome the restrictions of same time/same place learning.
- Videoconferencing and collaborative tools enable distance learning.
- As the economics of education and socioeconomic trends evolve, students are completing their college educations in nontraditional ways.
- There are many advantages and disadvantages of distance learning.
- Both students and faculty must understand how collaborative technology impacts on how they perform course work.
- Creativity is a complex concept.
- Creativity can be learned and fostered with good management techniques and a supportive environment.
- Idea generation (electronic brainstorming) allows participants to generate and share ideas simultaneously and anonymously.
- Creativity support systems (CSS), essentially GSS, can provide computer support to the creative process.
- Human creativity can be supported with idea generation (electronic brainstorming) systems.
- Creativity software programs use association and "thinking outside the box" to trigger new concepts.
- GSS and collaborative computing research continues to establish the best ways to perform groupwork, and the best tools to use.

❖ KEY WORDS

- anonymity
- asynchronous
- collaborative computing
- computer-supported cooperative work (CSCW)
- courseware
- creativity
- creativity support system (CSS)
- decision room
- Delphi method

- distance learning (DL)
- electronic brainstorming
- electronic meeting systems (EMS)
- electronic meeting (e-meeting)
- enterprise-wide collaboration systems
- extranet
- firewall
- group support systems (GSS)
- groupware

- groupwork
- idea generation
- Internet
- intranet
- nominal group technique (NGT)
- parallelism
- process gain
- process loss
- synchronous
- virtual corporation

❖ QUESTIONS FOR REVIEW

1. List the characteristics of groupwork.
2. List the activities of meetings.
3. What is the primary objective of groupware.
4. List the reasons why communication is so important for collaborative computing.
5. List the differences between collaboration and communication.
6. List the frames and collaborative technologies in the time/place framework of IT communication support.
7. List the reasons why meetings can be ineffective and inefficient. Also, list potential ways to solve the problems.
8. Define groupware. List its goals.
9. List the possible capabilities of groupware.
10. List the various groupware packages described in this chapter and indicate the capabilities of each one.
11. List the benefits (gains) of groupwork.
12. List the dysfunctions (losses) of groupwork.
13. Define a group support system (GSS). List its potential capabilities.
14. Define an electronic meeting system (EMS).
15. List the group tasks that are included in EMS.
16. List the common group activities supported by GSS.
17. What is parallelism? What is anonymity?
18. List the three options for deploying GSS technology.
19. List the advantages and disadvantages of special electronic decision rooms.
20. List the benefits and disadvantages of a multipurpose computer lab/electronic decision room.
21. List the benefits and disadvantages of Web-based groupware.
22. List the standard tools of GroupSystems.
23. List the important features of Lotus Notes.
24. List the important features of Microsoft NetMeeting.
25. List the factors that lead to GSS success.
26. List the important issues involving anytime/anyplace meetings.
27. What is learning?
28. List the features of collaborative computing that can enhance the traditional classroom environment.

29. List the reasons why distance learning is becoming more popular.
30. List the advantages and disadvantages of distance learning.
31. Define creativity.
32. List the ways that GSS (CSS) can enhance creativity.
33. List several tools that can enhance creativity.
34. List the major issues in GSS research.

❖ QUESTIONS FOR DISCUSSION

1. Explain the differences and similarities among features of the Internet, intranets, and extranets.
2. Explain how a group might be noncooperative but need to collaborate.
3. How does groupware attain its primary objective?
4. Why is communication a vital (foundation) element for group decision support?
5. Describe in detail why communication is so important for collaborative computing.
6. What is nonverbal communication? Explain why it is important in human-to-human interaction.
7. What methods are currently being used to incorporate nonverbal communication into collaborative computing?
8. Explain why collaboration is *deeper* than communication.
9. Explain why it is useful to describe groupwork in terms of the time/place framework.
10. Explain how anytime/anyplace meetings differ from same time/same place meetings.
11. Describe the kinds of support that groupware can provide.
12. Explain why most groupware is deployed over the Web.
13. Describe and compare each of the groupware packages mentioned in this chapter.
14. Explain how collaborative computing can be combined with videoconferencing for effective meeting support.
15. Describe the advantages of deploying groupware over the Web.
16. Compare GSS to noncomputerized group decision making.
17. Explain why meetings can be so inefficient?
18. Explain how effective meetings can be run.
19. Discuss the details of process gains (benefits) of groupwork.
20. Discuss the details of process losses (dysfunctions) of groupwork.
21. Explain how GSS can increase some of the benefits of collaboration and eliminate or reduce some of the losses.
22. Explain how some of the features of GSS have become embedded in computerized productivity tools.
23. The original term for group support system was *group decision support system (GDSS)*. Why was the word *decision* dropped? Does this make sense? Why or why not?
24. What is the goal of GSS?
25. Discuss how parallelism and anonymity can produce improvements in group processes.
26. Describe the three technologies through which GSS is deployed. What are the advantages and disadvantages of each?

27. Describe the steps in the GSS meeting process.
28. Why are deadlines important for anytime/anyplace meetings? What can happen if they are not set?
29. Explain what factors lead to GSS success.
30. Discuss the impact of good meeting planning on electronic meetings.
31. In electronic brainstorming in an anytime/anyplace system, how can the process gains be different from those achieved in a decision room GSS environment?
32. Describe in detail how the features of GSS collaborative computing can enhance learning.
33. In terms of the advantages and disadvantages of distance learning, explain why some students prefer a distance learning environment and others prefer a traditional learning environment.
34. How have the Web and videoconferencing enabled distance learning?
35. Explain in detail why companies are moving toward online training.
36. Explain in detail what creativity is.
37. Explain how GSS can support creativity.
38. Explain how idea generation (electronic brainstorming) works.
39. Describe which features of creativity enhancing software do the job.
40. Can computers be creative? Why or why not?
41. Describe the paradox that the use of GSS technologies sometimes does not yield gains in effectiveness or efficiency. What is going on?
42. List three areas of GSS research and explain why each is important.

❖ EXERCISES

1. Make a list of all the communications methods you use during your day (work and personal). Which are the most effective? Which are the least effective? What kind of work or activity does each communications method enable?
2. Investigate the impact of turning off every communication system in a firm (telephone, fax, television, radio, and all computer systems). How effective and efficient would the following types of firms be: airline, bank, insurance company, travel agency, department store, and grocery store? What would happen? Do customers expect 100 percent uptime? (When was the last time a major airline's reservation system was down?) How long would it be before each type of firm would not be functioning at all? Investigate what organizations are doing to prevent this situation from occurring.
3. In many nations telephone systems are inadequate, inefficient, or nonexistent, despite the widespread availability of computer systems. What do firms operating in countries under these conditions do to bypass these crippling effects on communication?
4. Investigate body language and report your findings. If possible, use this subject as a presentation topic. How does body language impact on the meaning of the message being conveyed? Include in your report how researchers are attempting to incorporate the nonverbal cues of body language into collaborative computing.
5. Investigate how researchers are trying to develop collaborative computer systems that portray or display nonverbal communication factors.
6. For each of the following software packages, check the trade literature and the Web for details and explain how computerized collaborative support system capabilities are included: Lotus Notes, GroupSystems, TCBWorks, NetMeeting, GroupWise, and WebEx.

7. Investigate methods for improving the effectiveness and efficiency of meetings.

8. From your own experience or from the vendor's information, list all the major capabilities of Lotus Notes and explain how they can be used to support decision making.

9. Compare Simon's four-phase decision-making model to the GSS use sequence described in DSS in Focus 7.11.

10. How would you feel about taking a distance learning course that uses the Internet or a package such as Lotus Notes to enhance group communication and communication with the instructor? Find three (or more) articles in the literature that describe the experiences of students and faculty in a distance learning course and compare your thoughts with their experiences. What advantages and disadvantages does such an approach have?

❖ GROUP EXERCISES

1. Access this book's Web site (www.prenhall.com/turban) and do the group brainstorming exercises.

2. Access the GSS TCBWorks on the Web (tcbworks.terry.uga.edu). Using the guest log-in procedure on the main screen, create a session folder for your group and brainstorm and vote on a specific problem or issue. When brainstorming, think broadly. Did you feel comfortable with the software? Why or why not?

3. Access the Web site of a for-lease, Web-based groupware service (e.g., WebEx). Describe what features it offers and how they could help a groupwork together. If the site offers a free trial, have your group try it out and report your experience to the class.

4. Identify colleges and universities that provide courses via distance learning (use both traditional library sources and Web sources). Find at least four articles on the topic. What types of groupware do these institutions use? Are the groupware tools effective when compared with standard teaching methods?

5. *Case Study.* As part of some recent fieldwork (Dennis and Garfield, 1999), several groups at a hospital met to discuss issues of and develop ideas for strategic planning. Some groups used GSS-supported electronic meetings (reluctantly), while other groups used the traditional meeting approach. Most of the members who started with the GSS discarded it, realized how much better off they were with it, and went back to it. When the central administration examined suggestions from both sets of groups (traditional meetings and GSS supported meetings), they pursued the ideas of the GSS-supported groups almost exclusively. Why do you think this happened? Explain.

❖ INTERNET EXERCISES

1. How are decisions supported by groupware? Identify software products on the Web that help groups work and make decisions. Download a package, install it, and try it (or if it runs on the Web, just run it). Report your findings to the class.

2. Search the Internet to identify sites that describe methods for improving meetings. Investigate ways that meetings can be made more effective and efficient.

3. Access the Web site of GroupSystems.com (www.groupsystems.com) and identify their current GSS products.

4. Access the Expert Choice Inc. Web site (www.expertchoice.com).
   a. Find information about their group support products.
   b. Team Expert Choice is related to the concept of the AHP described in Chapter 5. Evaluate this product in terms of decision support. Do you think that keypad use provides process gains or process losses? How and why?

5. Identify five real-world GSS success stories by searching vendor Web sites (use at least three different vendors). Describe them. How did GSS software and methods contribute to the success? What common features do they share? What different features do individual successes have?

6. Access the GSS TCBWorks on the Web (tcbworks.terry.uga.edu). Use the guest log-in procedure on the main screen and join the electronic brainstorming project (session) on how to improve this textbook. Add any ideas that you have, including suggestions for new software and new topics. Think broadly (it is an electronic brainstorming session). Did you feel comfortable with the software? Why or why not? If you have any comments later in the course or in the future, please access TCBWorks and add them.

7. Identify three distance learning tools available on the Web. Compare and contrast their features. If a "test drive" or demo is available, try it out. Which one do you prefer and why? Report your findings to the class.

8. Go the Creative Think Web site (www.creativethink.com) with a problem in mind that you are trying to solve (e.g., select a graduate school, an undergraduate school, a job). Use the Give Me Another Whack button to enhance your thinking. Try a few of their Whacks to see if they can help you. Did they?

9. For one of the creativity software packages described in the text, go to the company's Web site, download and try out a demo, and describe your experience in a report. Include what you liked and didn't like, and what you found useful and didn't find useful.

❖ **TERM PAPERS**

1. Describe the latest developments in collaborative computing / GSS in a term paper.

2. The activities and competence of a group facilitator are critical to the success of a GSS session. Identify recent articles and Web sites on GSS facilitation and write a term paper describing what makes a good facilitator for GSS and how GSS can support the facilitator.

3. Some GSS researchers are concerned with the cross-cultural effects of computer system use. This is especially important in GSS, where opinions are usually entered and synthesized by meeting participants at different places around the globe. Examine the literature and write a term paper on the major issues of how GSS provides either process gains or processes losses in a multicultural electronic meeting setting.

CASE APPLICATION 7.1

WELCOM WAY TO SHARE IDEAS IN A WORLD FORUM[5]

THE WORLD ECONOMIC FORUM

The World Economic Forum (WEF) is a consortium of top business, government, academic, and media leaders from virtually every country in the world. WEF's mission is to foster international understanding. Until 1998 the members conferred privately or debated global issues only at the forum's annual meeting in Davos, Switzerland, and at regional summits. Follow-up was difficult because of the members' geographic dispersion and conflicting schedules.

WELCOM COLLABORATION

Bruno Giussani heads up WEF online strategy and operations. He developed a collaborative computing system to allow secure communication among members, making the nonprofit group more effective in its mission. The system is the World Electronic Community (WELCOM), a groupware and videoconferencing system that gives members a secure channel through which to send e-mail, read reports in a WEF library, and communicate in point-to-point or multipoint videoconferences. Forum members now hold real-time discussions on pressing issues such as the 1998 Asian financial market crisis.

"The speed of information is increasingly rapid, (and) the scope of a global organization is much wider," Giussani says. "The basic idea behind WELCOM was to link the various members . . . to create an environment where members continue to share without physically being together. . . ." Members meet (electronically) more frequently, and they are more productive. Giussani believes the group is making faster progress toward solutions for the global problems it studies. According to him, if the system had been in place during the Mexican peso crisis of the early 1990s, for example, Mexican officials could have mitigated its effects by gaining immediate access to World Bank leaders and investors, many of whom are forum members.

THE WELCOM SYSTEM

USWeb Corporation worked with the WEF to develop a prototype system in October 1997, and the full system was implemented in February 1998, based heavily on a platform of Microsoft products. Members access WELCOM on a secure section of the forum's Web site.

The system runs on a single Windows NT server. Microsoft's Internet Information Server hosts the WEF Web page and the WELCOM discussions and library. Also on the server are a Microsoft Exchange Server with scheduling and e-mail, as well as NetMeeting and NetShow. An Intel videoconferencing system is accessed via a browser. The client software running on the desktop of each of the 2,500 forum members consists of Windows and Internet Explorer.

Among other functions, WELCOM provides online forums for real-time briefings on important issues and milestones, for example, when Hong Kong reverted to Chinese control.

The WELCOM system was designed with a graphical user interface (GUI) to be easily accessible to inexperienced computer users because many WEF members might not be computer-literate or proficient typists. The forum also set up a 24/5 "concierge service" for technical support, based in Boston, Singapore, and Geneva, to arrange videoconferences and meetings—a virtual same time/same place collaboration environment. To handle anytime/anyplace meetings, members can access recorded forum events and discussions that they may have missed, as well as an extensive library, one of the most heavily used features of the system.

COMMENTS AND THE FUTURE

"This kind of application is entering a new dimension as collaborative products such as Exchange continue to improve," says Eric Brown, an analyst with Forrester Research Inc. in Cambridge, MA. "The idea of creating virtual communities through collaboration technologies is not really a new idea." We're not reinventing this; we're just making it . . . a lot easier than it used to be. WELCOM weaves together physical meetings and e-mail communications. As a result, the online interactions are more intimate, and the face-to-face meetings are more productive. It's a convergence of real-time meetings and non-real-time meetings."

Enthusiasm among members for the system has grown. In the fall of 1998, the WEF held about 700 virtual conferences a year, compared with the dozen or so times that

---

[5]Adapted from J. Madden, "WELCOM Way to Share Ideas," *PC Week,* Aug. 17, 1998, pp. 53–54.

members meet in person annually. There have been some communications problems. "ISDN connections vary from continent to continent and can be free and clear one minute and completely clogged the next," Giussani observes.

The system will continue to improve. One possibility is that some external content like news feeds will be provided. As it evolves, system use continues to support groupwork and allows group members to focus on their global tasks instead of dealing with communications problems. Using WELCOM would ideally be seamless—like walking into a conference room with someone else. As hardware, software, and the network infrastructure improve, the system will move closer to the ideal.

CASE QUESTIONS

1. Comment on how WELCOM supports WEF members in meeting, discussing, and working through major international issues.

2. Comment on the groupware technology developed. Why was this software selected? Check the prices and see how this setup compares to a possible Lotus Notes implementation.
3. How does WELCOM handle same time/same place meetings? How does it handle anytime/anyplace meetings?
4. What kinds of communications problems do WELCOM users face? How can these be overcome?
5. Why do you think that the WEF needed a secure system for WELCOM?
6. Given the choice of using a system like WELCOM to collaborate versus traveling 2 days to and from a 1-day meeting, which would you rather do and why? If possible, compare results in class—how many made which choice and what were the major reasons?

PFIZER'S EFFECTIVE AND SAFE COLLABORATIVE COMPUTING PILL[6]

INTRODUCTION

In the United States the long, difficult research and development involved in getting a new drug to market often require an immense collaborative effort. Drug companies must conduct broad, expensive trials before their products even reach the Food and Drug Administration (FDA) for approval. Out of the tens of thousands of compounds discovered each year, only 7 percent make it to market. After an extensive development phase, pharmaceutical companies must back up their drug efficacy claims with mountains of paper (typically more than 1 million pages—equivalent to a tractor trailer full of paper) sent to the FDA, the federal agency that evaluates pharmaceutical products before they are placed on the market. The FDA's approval process is also a long, detailed one.

In addition, drug companies also face added pressure because of a congressionally mandated restructuring of the FDA's review process. The FDA is required to shorten its review process to 12 months from its typical 18–24 months to get drugs to market faster without compromising safety.

To move documentation more swiftly through the FDA's approval procedure, Pfizer developed an electronically-based drug submission process. Pfizer's Electronic Submission Navigator (ESUB) is a vast improvement over its old paper-based method of submitting documentation to the FDA. Pfizer's award-winning system cost $3.2 million to develop and has netted the company at least $142 million in revenues through the start of 2000 because of shorter cycle times. But Esub has also changed the way that research clinicians and the IT staff collaborate.

"Esub has had enormous impact in that it has transformed the way we do things internally," says George Milne, president of research and development for Pfizer's central research division in Groton, CT. "Our ability to execute new drug filings has been brought to an unprecedented scale," he claims. "It's much more than just an interesting computer system. The tools that Esub gives us will stimulate insight. We expect it to lead to a cascading effect of innovation." Esub has directly impacted the industry and serves as a benchmark for the FDA submission process.

---

[6]Adapted from M. Blodgett, "Prescription Strength," *CIO,* Feb. 1, 2000, pp. 94–98.

TRUCKLOADS OF PAPER

In mid-1995 Pfizer's researchers were developing Trovan, a new antibiotic drug being readied for FDA approval. The potential new product would be the largest anti-infective submission ever received by the FDA.

Typically, researchers and support staff produced separate sections of a paper document reporting the results of drug trials. Each section was eventually assembled into a master document called a *new drug application* (NDA). Once compiled, the NDA was edited, copied, and sent to the FDA to start the approval process.

The FDA distributed portions of the report to reviewers who wrote their own analyses. Document management, revision control, and cross-reference accuracy were a major challenge. Individual reviewers worked with 20,000-page sections, each a stack 5 or 6 feet high. Cross-referencing caused major headaches. If a reviewer needed to check something on a page outside his or her section, they had to wait for the FDA to send a runner to copy it from the master version in the library warehouse. The reviewers needed access to the latest version of every section of the document.

To solve this problem, Pfizer's staff used computer-aided NDAs (CANDAs) to build sections of the document electronically. Though they didn't provide all the data and performance was slow, it was the best that current technology could provide in 1995.

At that time the Web was beginning to take off, and Walter Hauck (an associate director in charge of clinical applications development and now director of clinical systems) suggested that it might be time to experiment with it. In April 1996 Hauck and his IT team showed a crude prototype to one of the Trovan clinicians, who in turn showed it to Scott Hopkins, executive director of anti-infectives. Hopkins instantly saw the benefit of the project and gave it the go-ahead.

Pfizer's IT team created about one Esub prototype per week, rewriting the code nearly 40 times until it became easier to manage. During Esub's development, the size of the NDA for Trovan was grossly underestimated. The submission grew to almost 50,000 documents, close to 180 gigabytes. As the project grew, the prototyping process created excitement among members of the IT team and the clinical team.

ESUB EMERGES

On December 28, 1996, nine months after its conception, Esub was delivered. Because Trovan was so complex in terms of its trials and use, the teams identified and solved tough problems first. In March 1997, Esub handled the submission of Viagra with ease. Now, the clinical team can collaborate on new drug applications with the FDA and its reviewers using Esub to coordinate their work.

ESUB BENEFITS

The benefits of Esub go far beyond a typical return on investment. Esub has become a company-wide collaborative data-sharing system that is also being considered by the FDA as a benchmark for other drug company submissions. Pfizer maintains a competitive advantage in building quality dossiers in real time. Esub has also created a heightened role for IT within the Pfizer organization.

By working collaboratively with its business partners, Pfizer's IT team constructed a system that

- Provides a global view of the status of a trial or application process.
- Enhances Pfizer's competitive advantage by linking drug researchers around the world; Esub has attracted business partners, including other drug manufacturers seeking to forge strategic alliances with Pfizer to help market and distribute their drugs.
- Enables Pfizer to penetrate world markets much more quickly by filing concurrent submissions in different countries.
- Gives the company the ability to deliver five new drugs every 12 months—the fastest rate in the industry.
- Features an electronic table of contents to negotiate the forms of an NDA.
- Allows portable review with a full-featured system—important because the FDA frequently uses outside consultants.

The number of users of the system had increased to 2,000 worldwide by 2000 at both Pfizer and government regulatory agencies. The Esub repository has grown to 5 terabytes, with roughly 1 terabyte of new data added each quarter. The most important Esub benefit is intangible: new, safe, effective drugs can be offered to patients quickly.

CASE QUESTIONS

1. What kind of collaboration does Pfizer's Esub support?
2. Who are the collaborators?
3. How does Esub support collaboration?
4. What are the benefits of Esub? What possible disadvantages might Esub have?
5. What specific benefits does the FDA obtain from collaborating with Pfizer through Esub?
6. How could Esub function as the heart of an extranet with Pfizer, its regulatory agency (FDA), salespersons, pharmacies, medical researchers, and doctors treating patients?

ENTERPRISE DECISION SUPPORT SYSTEMS

The support systems described in the previous chapters were designed to support individual decision makers making specific decisions (Chapters 3–6) and the processes of individuals collaborating from a distance, as well as group work (Chapter 7). In this chapter we shift our attention to systems that deal with enterprise-wide support. First, attention is given to top executives, especially for their role in discovering problems, or trends that may create problems, as well as in identifying opportunities. The work of these executives can be enhanced by computerized support. Second, attention is given to decisional situations involving many decision makers who may be in different locations. Finally, we describe enterprise resource planning (ERP) systems that integrate all the routine transaction processing in the organization. Lately, ERP is being integrated with decision support capabilities as well as being extended to business partners along the supply chains.

8.1 OPENING VIGNETTE: PIZZERIA UNO'S ENTERPRISE SYSTEM MAKES THE DIFFERENCE[1]

Pizzeria Uno (www.pizzeriauno.com) has expanded the concept of a casual dining, full-service restaurant into 150 eateries located throughout the United States, Puerto Rico, and Canada. Being in a very competitive industry, the company was looking for ways to boost its competitiveness and profitability.

Prior to 1995 Pizzeria Uno used a manual system for tracking and reporting restaurant performance, costs, and labor information. With this system, the reports were labor-intensive to produce and the information was not very timely. Reports were static and did not support ad hoc information needs, and critical business information was not readily available to field managements.

Each evening, restaurant managers left voice messages for their regional directors reporting the day's sales figures. It took the directors more than an hour and a half to pull the figures off the voice mail and compile the results.

In 1995 the company started to install an enterprise-wide information system using a Pilot Software (www.pilotsw.com) OLAP package. This system allows executives and store managers to interactively access and analyze information about store performance and staffing at both individual and corporate levels.

Each evening, daily sales and labor information is downloaded from each restaurant point-of-sale and back-office system onto a server located at the company's Boston headquarters. Marketing, operations, and finance executives at Uno headquarters access the server's database from their PCs. Regional managers dial into the server each day to download up-to-date data on to their laptop computers.

The system, which was integrated with the corporate intranets in 2000, has an intuitive, easy-to-use interface which is an important feature for Pizzeria Uno as well. Pilot's graphical user interface and its ability to easily perform complex multidimensional analyses make it an excellent tool for senior executives who don't have a lot of time to learn how to use new software tools but want to access in-depth information.

The system makes it possible for Pizzeria Uno executives to analyze data in ways that were unimaginable when the company used the manual system. Executives can drill through data hierarchies, manipulate data, view data from different dimensions, such as deep-dish pizza take-home sales versus retail sales, and create reports tailored to their specific informational needs. Exploiting the system's inherent time-intelligence capabilities, the company can quickly and accurately report business results on a daily, weekly, monthly, quarterly, or year-to-date basis.

The food service industry is fast-moving and is managed within a very small time frame; therefore, managers are interested in knowing about daily and weekly performance. With the new system, management can quickly react to dynamic business variables such as food and labor costs.

For example, if on a Sunday top management executives see that costs for some restaurants in a particular region are rising, they can immediately discuss the problem with the divisional vice president and determine an appropriate course of action. The more quickly Uno can respond to increasing costs, the greater its profits.

Uno's use of Pilot's OLAP technology has increased the productivity of its regional directors as well. Regional directors, who could handle only six restaurants prior to 1996, now handle nine restaurants each. This illustrates how information is the key to growth

---

[1]Condensed from "Customer Success Stories," www.pilotsw.com/synergy/profile/pizzeriauno.html, 1999.

and to reducing overhead. For example, marketing executives have also found the system to be a valuable tool for measuring results of test marketing a new menu or the success of a special lunch promotion and how it relates to labor and other costs. The use of the system is impacting the bottom line *across the board.* By making valuable business intelligence more readily available, the system has changed the corporate culture for the better because it can *give customers the quality menus* and *service* they demand.

❖ **QUESTIONS FOR THE OPENING VIGNETTE**

1. Why is timely reporting critical to success in the pizza business?
2. Identify EIS capabilities in Pizzeria Uno's system.
3. The old voice-based system was time consuming. Why not just use faxes, which are much cheaper than building an enterprise system?
4. Identify the various types of users of the system.
5. The vignette does not mention a data warehouse. In your opinion, is the system based on one? Why or why not?
6. Identify the supply chain activities in this case.

8.2 ENTERPRISE SYSTEMS: CONCEPTS AND DEFINITIONS

The Opening Vignette introduces us to a system that supports a variety of decisions by middle and top managers, marketing analysts, and other knowledge workers in many locations, even in different countries. What is unique about this system is that it can support diversified groups of users across a multinational corporation, including top executives whose information needs are very particular. In the 1980s and until the late 1990s, systems serving the needs of top executives were designed as independent (standalone) systems and were called **executive information systems (EIS).** This approach made such systems affordable mostly only to large corporations. Today, executives are supported by systems that support other employees as well. They are called **enterprise information systems** (also labeled **EIS**). These systems serve many other users, and therefore they are most cost-effective. Well-built enterprise systems, such as Pizzeria Uno's, provide executives with basically the same capabilities that the previous EIS used to provide and in addition serve many other users throughout the enterprise.

In this chapter we will cover several types of enterprise systems. We will start with a discussion of the information needs of executives and what IT capabilities are available to meet these needs across the enterprise. Then we will relate enterprise systems to the data warehousing concept presented in Chapter 4. Following that will be a discussion of organizational decision support systems, which will lead us to the concept of a supply chain and its management.

8.3 THE EVOLUTION OF EXECUTIVE AND ENTERPRISE INFORMATION SYSTEMS

During the 1980s it was felt that the then existing information technologies, including DSS, were not sufficient for executive use (Rockart and Delong, 1988). The published information about DSS showed that the majority of personal DSS supported the work of professionals and middle-level managers. Organizational DSS provided support primarily to planners, analysts, and researchers. Rarely did top executives directly use a DSS. This situation is in contrast to the fact that the most important job of top executives is to make decisions. What was needed was a tool that could handle executives' special needs for timely and accurate information in a meaningful format. Nord and Nord (1996) found in a study that the most popular uses of EIS were for decision support (50 percent) by providing data and information, for scheduling (50 percent), to set agendas and schedule meetings (43.8 percent), for electronic briefing (31.5 percent), and for browsing data and monitoring situations (31.3 percent).

Executive information systems (EIS), also known as **executive support systems (ESS)** (Watson et al., 1997), is a technology that emerged in response to the situation just described (see also DSS in Focus 8.1). In a survey conducted by the Center for Information Systems Research (CISR) at MIT, it was found that people with the title of chief executive officer (CEO), chief financial officer (CFO), or chief operations officer (COO) were the major users of EIS.

In the mid-1990s, with advances in data warehousing (Chapter 4) and in Web networks, the independent EIS concept was replaced by a more cost-effective enterprise system such as that used at Uno.

DEFINITIONS

The terms *executive information system* and *executive support system* mean different things to different people. Often the terms are used interchangeably. The

---

DSS IN FOCUS 8.1

WHY EIS?

The most common benefits of an EIS are improvement in the quality and quantity of information available to executives. The following factors were identified by Watson et al. (1996, 1997).

INFORMATION NEEDS (INTERNAL AND EXTERNAL)

- More timely information
- Greater access to operational data
- Greater access to corporate databases
- More concise, relevant information
- New or additional information
- More information about the external environment
- More-competitive information
- Faster access to external databases
- Faster access to information
- Reduced paper costs.

EIS IMPROVEMENTS IN EXECUTIVE JOB PERFORMANCE ABILITY

- Enhanced communications
- Greater ability to identify historic trends
- Improved executive effectiveness
- Improved executive efficiency
- Fewer meetings and less time spent in meetings
- Enhanced executive mental models
- Improved executive planning, organizing, and control
- More focused executive attention
- Greater support for executive decision making
- Increased span of control.

following definitions, based on Rockart and DeLong (1988), distinguish between EIS and ESS.

> - ***Executive information system (EIS).*** An EIS is a computer-based system that serves the information needs of top executives. It provides rapid access to timely information and direct access to management reports. EIS is very user-friendly, is supported by graphics, and provides exceptions reporting and drill-down capabilities. It is also connected to the Internet, intranets, and extranets.
> - ***Executive support system (ESS).*** An ESS is a comprehensive support system that goes beyond EIS to include communication, office automation, analysis support, and business intelligence.
> - ***Enterprise information system (EIS).*** This is a corporate-wide system that provides holistic information from a corporate point of view. Different users across the enterprise can use the system for different purposes. These systems serve the needs of top executives as well. Enterprise systems are an important part of the *enterprise resources management* (ERP) concept, which will be presented later in this chapter.

ENTERPRISE SUPPORT SYSTEMS

The most important goal of enterprise support systems (ESS) is providing a tool for *enterprise support.* For this reason, one can distinguish two types of EIS: one designed especially to support top executives and one intended to serve a wider community of users.

An executive-only EIS can be modified to be part of an enterprise-wide information system. As such, executive systems are becoming less strictly defined, and EIS applications are embracing a range of products targeted to support professional decision makers throughout the enterprise (see DSS in Action 8.2). EIS are already providing some of the needed capabilities. In addition, there are an increasing number of tools designed to help functional managers (finance, marketing); these tools are integrated with EIS.

DSS IN ACTION 8.2

BANC ONE SHIFTS TO ENTERPRISE SUPPORT SYSTEMS

For 25 years, Banc One, one of the most profitable U.S. banks, used a homegrown profit tracking and management information system. The system was accessed by about 200 managers and financial analysts to evaluate their unit's performance on a variety of profit indexes.

As of the end of 1994, the bank was using one of the largest client/server decision support networks in the banking industry. The profit monitoring system is from Treasury Services Corporation (Santa Monica, CA). It distributes financial information to more than 2,000 employees. The technology allows Banc One to disseminate information not only to the privileged few but also to anyone who needs it.

The new system, which can be regarded as a combination of EIS and ESS, gives employees more detailed financial information right down to the revenue, costs, and profits for an individual customer. It allows users to deliver much more detailed data to support decision making throughout the bank.

Source: Based on a story published in *InformationWeek,* Nov. 1, 1993, p. 14; and on information provided by Treasury Services Corporation.

Furthermore, EIS is diffusing into lower organizational levels. Nord and Nord (1995), in their study of all *Fortune* 500 companies using EIS, discovered that 50 percent of all CEOs, 31.3 percent of all presidents, 93.8 percent of all vice presidents, and 87.5 percent of all middle managers used EIS on a regular basis.

For this reason, the acronym *EIS* is now interpreted to mean enterprise information system or everybody's information system. As a matter of fact, most vendors do not use the term *executive information systems* at all in the names of their products. Instead, the term **business intelligence (BI)** or *enterprise systems* is used to describe the new role of EIS, especially now that data warehouses can provide data in easy-to-use, graphics-intensive query systems capable of slicing and dicing data and providing active multi-dimensional analysis.

8.4 EXECUTIVES' ROLES AND THEIR INFORMATION NEEDS

In Chapter 2 we discussed the roles of managers, including decision making. The executive decisional role is a major one, and so we divide it into two phases. Phase I involves the identification of problems and opportunities. Phase II involves decisions on what to do about them. Figure 8.1 provides a flowchart of this process. This division can be used to understand executives' information needs and consequently the capabilities of an EIS.

As shown in Figure 8.1, information flows to the system from the external and the internal environments. Internal information is generated from the functional units (finance, marketing, production, accounting, personnel, and so on). External information comes from sources such as the Internet and other online databases, newspapers, Internet news services, industry publications, government reports, and personal contacts. Clearly the combined information is extremely valuable; it is an important organizational resource needed for successful competition and survival. However, because of the large amount of information available, **environmental scanning** is needed to find the relevant items. Some scanning of news stories, internal reports, and Web information can be performed by intelligent software agents (Liu et al., 2000) (Chapter 17). The collected information is then evaluated and channeled to quantitative and qualitative analyses (carried out by experts when needed). Then, a decision by an executive or by a team is made on whether a problem or opportunity exists. If it is decided that there is a problem, this interpretation becomes an input to the next phase: making a decision on what to do about the problem. Not shown in the figure is the extensive communication that may take place among executives, managers, and staff. The basic purpose of EIS is to support phase I of the process as shown in Figure 8.1. Phase II can be supported by specific DSS applications.

METHODS FOR FINDING INFORMATION NEEDS

There are several methods for determining executives' information needs (Watson et al., 1997) (see the Minicase in Focus W8.1 on this book's Web site, www.prenhall.com/turban). For a discussion of information requirements in a global EIS, see Palvia et al. (1996).

One major complication in ascertaining the information needs of executives is that needs change as their tasks and responsibilities change. Because of this, in many organizations EIS is considered to evolve and is never considered completely finished.

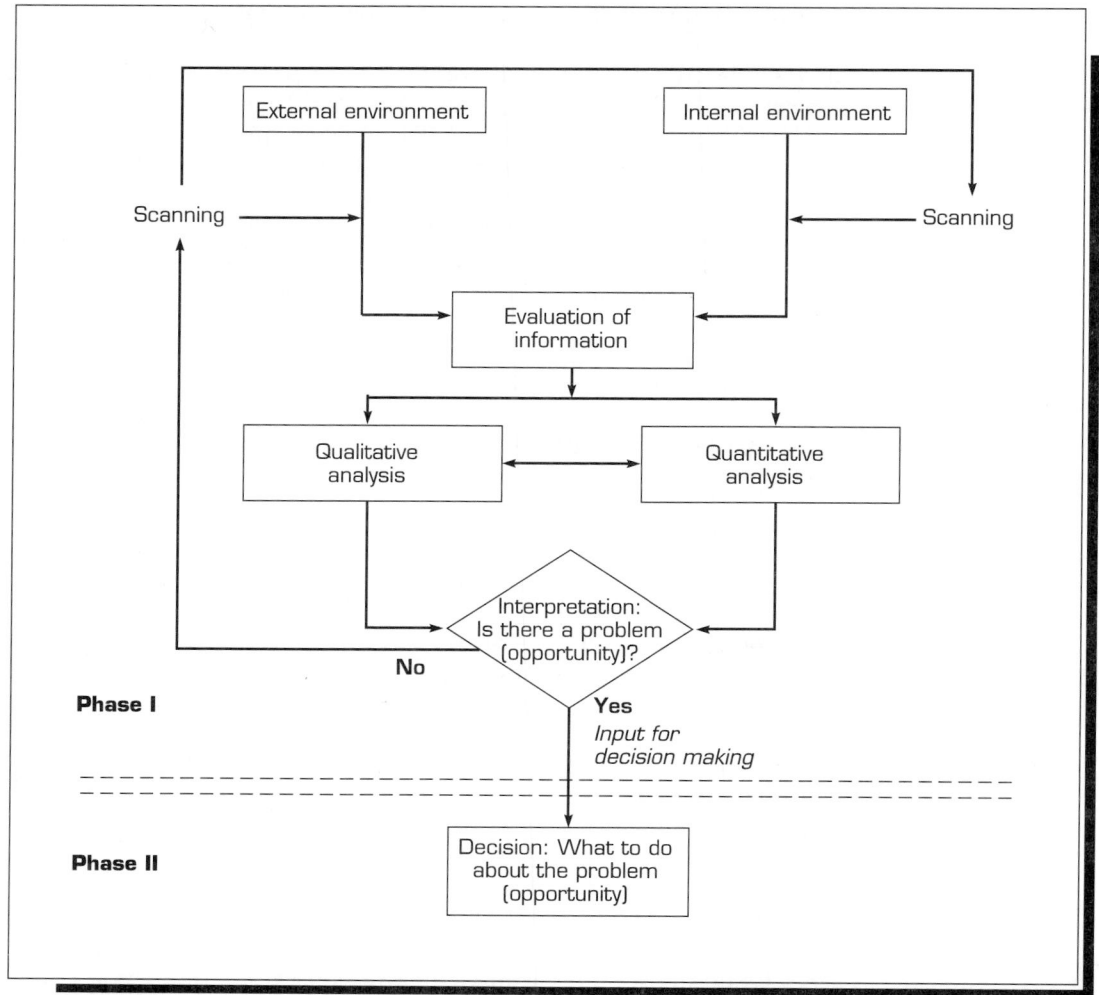

FIGURE 8.1 THE DECISION-MAKING PROCESS OF EXECUTIVES (DECISIONAL ROLE)

8.5 CHARACTERISTICS AND CAPABILITIES OF EXECUTIVE SUPPORT SYSTEMS

The desired characteristics of an EIS and some of its capabilities are presented in Table 8.1. Most vendors provide these capabilities in their business intelligence enterprise systems. The important ones are described next in some detail.

DRILL DOWN

One of the most useful capabilities of an EIS is to provide details of any summarized information. For example, an executive may notice a decline in corporate sales in a daily (or weekly) report. To discover the reason, he or she may want to see the sales for each region. If a problematic region is identified, the executive may want to see further de-

TABLE 8.1 The Characteristics and Benefits of EIS

Quality of information
- Is flexible
- Produces correct information
- Produces timely information
- Produces relevant information
- Produces complete information
- Produces validated information

User interface
- Includes a sophisticated graphical user interface (GUI)
- Includes a user-friendly interface
- Allows secure and confidential access to information
- Has a short response time (timely information)
- Is accessible from many places
- Includes a reliable access procedure
- Minimizes keyboard use by including infrared controllers, a mouse, touch pads, and a touch screen
- Provides quick retrieval of desired information
- Is tailored to the management styles of individual executives
- Contains a self-help menu

Technical capability provided
- Access to aggregate (global) information
- Access to electronic mail
- Extensive use of external data
- Written interpretations
- Highlighting of problem indicators
- Hypertext and hypermedia
- Ad hoc analysis
- Multidimensional presentation and analysis
- Information presented in hierarchical form
- Incorporation of graphics and text in the same display
- Management-by-exception reports are provided
- Trends, ratios, and deviations are shown
- Access to historical and most current data is provided
- Organization around critical success factors
- Provides forecasting
- Information produced at various levels of detail (drill down)
- Filtering, compressing, and tracking of critical data
- Support of open-ended problem explanation

Benefits
- Facilitates the attainment of organizational objectives
- Facilitates access to information
- Allows the user to be more productive
- Increases the quality of decision making
- Provides a competitive advantage
- Saves time for the user
- Increases communication capacity
- Increases communication quality
- Provides better control in the organization
- Allows the anticipation of problems and opportunities
- Allows planning
- Allows a search for the cause of a problem
- Meets the needs of executives

Source: Based on Bergeron et al. (1991).

tails (e.g., by product or by salesperson). In certain cases, this **drill-down** process may continue into several levels of detail.

Drill-down paths that are manually constructed and maintained typically use hypertext-style connections rather than menus in systems with a GUI (i.e., the button for requesting a drill-down path is typically defined as a hot spot directly over the high-level data to be explained). This frees up screen space for delivering information and can speed access to drill-down information by eliminating the additional mouse movements typically required by pull-down or pop-up menus. Similarly, Web tools and hyperlinks can be used for an intranet-based drill down.

Menu-driven drill down is generally a characteristic of ad hoc query applications, and the menus in these applications are almost always automatically generated by the software based on the user's logical position in the database and knowledge of the structure of the database. This knowledge of the database structure may have been specified in advance, or it may have been obtained dynamically by the application directly querying the database dictionary. Conceivably, a query application could generate several hundred menus and submenus covering all possible combinations of logical positions and valid drill-down paths.

In the not-so-distant future much of the task of drill down will be automated. An executive noticing a drop in sales, for example, will ask "Why did sales drop yesterday?" An intelligent agent will alert the executive, do the drill down and provide an answer.

CRITICAL SUCCESS FACTORS

Factors that *must* be considered in attaining an organization's goals are called **critical success factors (CSFs).** Such factors can be strategic, managerial, or operational and are derived mainly from three sources: organizational, industrial, and environmental. Success factors can be at the corporate level as well as at the division, plant, or department level. Sometimes it is necessary to consider the CSFs of individuals.

Once identified, critical success factors can be monitored according to five types of information: key problem narratives, highlight charts, top-level financials, key factors, and detailed responsibility reports (Kogan, 1986). The monitoring can be done by intelligent agents. A brief description of each of the five types follows:

- *Key problem narratives.* These reports highlight overall performance, key problems, and possible reasons for the problems within an organization. Explanations are often combined with tables, graphs, or tabular information.
- *Highlight charts.* These summary displays show high-level information based on the user's own judgment or preference. Because they are designed from the user's perspective, these displays quickly highlight areas of concern, visually signaling the state of organizational performance against CSFs.
- *Top-level financials.* These displays provide information on the overall financial health of the company in the form of absolute numbers and comparative performance ratios.
- *Key factors.* These factors provide specific measures of CSFs, called **key performance indicators (KPIs),** at the corporate level. The displays are often used on an exception basis to examine specific measures of CSFs flagged as problems on highlight charts (see DSS in Focus 8.3).
- *Detailed KPI responsibility reports.* These reports indicate the detailed performance of individuals or business units in areas critical to the success of the company.

STATUS ACCESS

In this mode, the *latest data* or reports on the status of key indicators can be accessed at any time via networks. The *relevance* of information is important, and emphasis is placed on current data. This may require daily (as in the Pizzeria Uno case) or even hourly operational tracking and reporting. In extreme cases, real-time reporting may be required.

DSS IN FOCUS 8.3

TYPICAL KEY PERFORMANCE INDICATORS

Profitability	Profitability measures for each department, product, region, and so on; comparisons among departments and products and with competitors
Financial	Financial ratios, balance sheet analysis, cash reserve position, rate of return on investment
Marketing	Market share, advertisement analysis, product pricing, weekly (daily) sales results, customer sales potential
Human resources	Turnover rate, level of job satisfaction
Planning	Corporate partnership ventures, sales growth and market share analysis
Economic analysis	Market trends, foreign trade and exchange rates, industry trends, labor cost trends
Consumer trends	Consumer confidence level, purchasing habits, demographic data

ANALYSIS

Analytic capabilities are available in executive support systems (ESS). Instead of merely having access to the data, executives can use the ESS to do analyses on their own. Analyses can be performed in the following ways:

- *Using built-in functions.* Several EIS products include built-in analytic functions similar to those available in DSS generators. For example, Comshare's DecisionWeb features ad hoc analysis capabilities that allow executives to easily compute trends and variances. Also, it is possible to perform multidimensional analyses on data and convert tables to graphics. Most recent software packages include an integrated analysis capability as part of their online analytical processing (OLAP) engine. These include Pilot Software's Decision Support Suite, Informix's MetaCube Product Suite, and Cognos's PowerPlay and Impromptu Data Access (Section 8.17).
- *Integration with DSS products.* Several EIS products have easy interfaces to DSS tools. For example, Comshare's DecisionWeb includes an open scripting language that allows it to integrate easily with many mainframe, server, or workstation DSS tools such as Excel. Others export multidimensional data cubes for further analysis by OLAP engines.
- *Analysis by intelligent agents.* Simple comparisons, trends, or ratios can be calculated automatically and an alert issued if there are significant deviations from standards.

An example of the use of intelligent agents for strategic management in the pulp and paper industry in Finland is provided by Liu et al. (2000). The agent scans the environment by monitoring certain Web sites, looking for relevant news and price information. Findings are customized for each executive and can be sent as e-mail alerts.

This is how an analysis can be done: First, executives identify information that they want to analyze in more depth. Then they either directly request the analysis action from an ESS menu (e.g., to compute a trend line) or export the data shown in the current display to a separate product that offers the desired analysis capability. Depending on the ESS, the process of exporting to and starting up another tool may simply be a menu choice within the ESS or can require the executive to save the display to a file, exit the ESS, launch the other tool, and read the file written by the ESS. Once the executive accesses the other tool (often a spreadsheet), analysis features are typically selected from menus. Whether the analysis is performed within the ESS or by an external tool, the results of the analysis are displayed in a default format, and the executive then has options to modify the display to improve its understandability.

EXCEPTION REPORTING

Exception reporting is based on the concept of *management by exception.* Accordingly, attention should be given by the executive to exceptions to standards. Thus, in exception reporting the executive's attention is called only to cases with a very bad (or a very good) performance. For example, the EIS can compute variances, and if these variances exceed a certain threshold, they are highlighted. This approach saves considerable time in sifting through data for exception conditions.

USE OF COLORS AND AUDIO

Typically, critical items are reported not only numerically but also in color: green for OK, yellow for a warning, and red for performance outside the preset boundaries of the plan (danger). The colors (or shading, for the color-blind) alert the executive user to potential problems requiring immediate attention. Some systems are equipped with audio signals to alert the user to arriving information.

NAVIGATION OF INFORMATION

Navigation of information is a capability that allows large amounts of data to be explored easily and quickly. To enhance this capability, one can use hypermedia tools (Frolick and Ramarapu, 1993), and intelligent agents (Murch and Johnson, 1999).

COMMUNICATION

Executives need to communicate with others. Communication can be by e-mail, a transfer of a report addressed to the attention of someone, a call for a meeting, or a comment made to a news group on the Internet. Additional communication can be provided through collaborative computing technologies such as those provided by GSS (such as Lotus Notes, Netscape Communicator, Microsoft's NetMeeting, and others; see Chapter 7). Executive chat rooms, bulletin boards, and other Web support tools are becoming popular, and as is video teleconferencing (Chapter 7).

8.6 COMPARING AND INTEGRATING EIS AND DSS

The above characteristics and capabilities are unique primarily because an EIS is designed to support top executives, helping them to discover problems and opportunities. A DSS, on the other hand, supports analyses that attempt to answer the question of what to do with a specific problem or opportunity. Tables 8.2 and 8.3 compare the two systems. Table 8.2 contains portions of typical DSS definitions related to EIS. Table 8.3 compares EIS and DSS along several dimensions derived from the characteristics and capabilities of EIS.

Examination of the two tables shows that in a general sense, EIS is really part of the decision support field. That is, EIS is designed to support some tasks of the top management decision-making process. However, in a functional sense EIS and DSS are two different but complementary applications. The differences are simple but profound. Fundamentally, EIS is a structured, automated tracking system that operates continuously to keep management abreast of what is happening in all important areas both in-

TABLE 8.2   Definitions of DSS as They Relate to EIS

Relevant Portion of DSS Definition	*Author*	*Comparison to EIS*
CBIS consisting of three subsystems: a problem-solving subsystem . . .	Bonczek et al. (1980)	No problem-solving subsystem exists in an EIS.
DSS can be developed only through an adaptive process . . .	Keen (1980)	EIS may or may not be developed through an adaptive process.
Model-based set of procedures . . .	Little (1970)	EIS is not model-based.
Extendible system supporting decision modeling used at irregular intervals	Moore and Chang (1980)	EIS is not extendible, might not have modeling capabilities, and is used at regular intervals.
Utilizes data and models . . .	Scott Morton (1971)	EIS does not use models.

side and outside the corporation. EIS has been described as being similar to a pilot's cockpit in an airplane. The gauges and indicators tell the pilot the current status and the direction in which the airplane is heading. The pilot can determine when there are problems if certain indicators are out of range, colored lights flash, or a siren sounds.

EIS delivers information that managers need in their day-to-day jobs. The information is typically presented in a structured, easy-to-access manner with only limited capability for direct ad hoc analysis. If there are analytic capabilities in EIS, they tend to be of a repetitive nature (such as trend analysis), as opposed to the unique ad hoc analysis of DSS. Although this is the usual case, both DSS and EIS may center on the investigation and understanding of problems that are not necessarily predictable, structured, or repetitive.

EIS is designed very differently from DSS. For example, a good EIS must offer a high-speed, nontechnical way for managers to investigate business dynamics (i.e., to understand where and why things are happening so that tactical changes and course corrections can be made). This is also a major area that distinguishes EIS from a standard MIS reporting system. Any summary appearing on an EIS screen must offer instant access to the supporting detail; otherwise, it is just a glorified briefing book (slide show). In addition, the supporting details must be meaningful (such as time-series orientation with graphical and numerical content, written narratives from knowledgeable staff, or AI-provided explanations—see Chapter 17).

INTEGRATING EIS AND DSS: AN EXECUTIVE SUPPORT SYSTEM

We have just concluded that EIS differs from DSS. Indeed, they are used as two independent system applications in many organizations. However, in some cases there are major benefits in integrating the two technologies. For example, at a large drug company product managers download the previous day's orders of their products from an EIS to their PCs. Then they run a spreadsheet DSS model with the data to predict their end-of-month status. The results of this model are then uploaded to the EIS. By 11:00 A.M. every day, senior managers can check their EIS to see each brand manager's end-of-month status prediction.

The integration of EIS and DSS can be accomplished in several ways. One alternative is to use the EIS output to launch the DSS application. For instance, if executives

TABLE 8.3   Comparison of EIS and DSS

Dimension	EIS	DSS
Focus	Status access, drill down	Analysis, decision support
Typical users	Senior executives	Analysts, professionals, managers (via intermediaries)
Impetus	Expediency	Effectiveness
Application	Environmental scanning, performance evaluation, identification of problems and opportunities	Diversified areas where managerial decisions are made
Decision support	Indirect support, mainly high-level and unstructured decisions and policies	Supports semistructured and unstructured decision making, ad hoc decisions, and some repetitive decisions
Type of information	News items, external information on customers, competitors, and the environment; scheduled and demand reports on internal operations	Information supporting specific situations
Principal use	Tracking and control, opportunity identification	Planning, organizing, staffing, and controlling
Adaptability to individual users	Tailored to the decision-making style of each individual executive, offers several options of outputs	Permits individual judgments, what-if capabilities, some choice of dialog style
Graphics	A must	Important part of many DSS
User-friendliness	A must	A must if no intermediaries are used
Processing of information	Filters and compresses information, tracks critical data and information	EIS triggers questions, answers worked out by using the DSS and fed back into the EIS
Supporting detailed information	Instant access to the supporting details of any summary (drill down)	Can be programmed into the DSS but usually is not
Model base	Limited built-in functions	The core of the DSS
Construction	By vendors or IS specialists	By users, either alone or with specialists from the information center or IS department
Hardware	Mainframe, RISC workstations, LANs, or distributed systems	Mainframe, RISC workstations, PCs, or distributed systems
Nature of software packages	Interactive, easy access to multiple databases, online access, sophisticated DBMS capabilities, complex linkages	Large computational capabilities, modeling languages and simulation, application and DSS generators
Nature of information	Displays pregenerated information about the past and present, creates new information about the past, present, and future	Creates new information about the past, present, and future

at General Electric's major appliance division decide that an immediate marketing response is needed to a competitor's action reported by the EIS, exactly what that response should be is determined by DSS models and simulation tools. The DSS is fed from the same reservoir of raw data that feeds the EIS (e.g., the data warehouse), but the DSS action is triggered by the EIS. More sophisticated systems include feedback from the DSS to the EIS, and even an explanation capability. If an intelligent module with explanation and interpretation capabilities is added, then the system can be defined as an intelligent ESS (Chapter 18).

Another dimension along which EIS and DSS can be integrated is users' roles. Executive roles differ substantially from the roles of typical DSS users, namely, middle-line and functional supervisory levels and functional analysts such as financial and marketing analysts. Although lower-level managers focus much of their time on pursuing predetermined strategies, executives are faced with developing these strategies. Ambiguity and uncertainty characterize an executive's environment, resulting in a need for what-if and goal-seeking analyses which are provided by most DSS. Yet studies have shown that many senior executives leave this technical analysis to lower-level functional managers and staff analysts.

Most business intelligence and enterprise software vendors (like Pilot, Microstrategy, and Business Objects) provide software products for EIS and DSS applications such as sales reporting and analysis, product profitability reporting, profit/loss analysis and reporting, enterprise budget reporting, critical success factor and key performance indicator reporting, and performance analysis and reporting. Such software transforms existing corporate data into usable performance information for management decision making. In addition, such products often include productivity tools (such as a personal calendar) and communication tools designed to meet the divergent information needs of executives.

In a study conducted on some major DSS and EIS vendors, Thiriez (1992) found a strong trend toward the integration of traditional DSS and EIS tools (see this book's Web site), which accelerated during 1996–2000. Furthermore, this integration is based on a distributed database, and the role of the spreadsheet is that of a front-end interface. This is currently the preferred viewing mode for multidimensional analyses (Chapter 4). Finally, both DSS and EIS capabilities are now added to ERP products, as will be shown later in this chapter.

INTEGRATING EIS AND GROUP SUPPORT

As shown in Figure 8.1, the information generated in Phase I flows to Phase II, where a decision is made on what to do about the problem. A DSS supports the quantitative analysis of Phase I and can support Phase II as well. In Phase II, however, the decision can be made by a group. Therefore, it is likely that the EIS will be integrated with some groupware applications. Several EIS vendors have developed easy interfaces with GSS. For example, IMRS has enhanced its On Track product with a Lotus Notes/Domino application called Executive Forum. Several enterprise software vendors have Lotus Notes–based enhancements and Web links in their major products.

8.7 EIS, DATA ACCESS, DATA WAREHOUSING, OLAP, MULTIDIMENSIONAL ANALYSIS, PRESENTATION, AND THE WEB

In Chapter 4 we discussed the data warehouse: a repository of cleansed and filtered enterprise-wide data for read-only access and use by executives, managers, and analysts. The issue of data access in an enterprise was also discussed in Chapter 4. Rather than designing and implementing an EIS to access several disparate databases in a variety of formats on different computing platforms, data warehouses are increasingly being used as data sources for EIS. When a data warehouse is front-ended by an SQL query code generator (such as PowerBuilder), natural language query system, or automatic form builder, it enhances the ability of any user (not just executives) to access needed data. In the mid-1990s, developers and researchers started to explore advanced data visualization methods (Chapter 4) and hypermedia use within EIS. Hypermedia is essentially multimedia data with hyperlinks and has been proposed by Frolick and Ramarapu (1993) as a means of providing useful data to executives. Hypermedia can be provided over an intranet via Web links with Web browser software within the EIS or via proprietary packages such as Lotus Notes. Most vendors have deployed Web-ready modules as part of their EIS development packages (e.g., the Internet Publishing module of Pilot's Decision Support Suite).

Once data are accessed and provided, analysis and display become important. **Multidimensional analysis** combined with online analytical processing (OLAP) tools allow the display of data in both spreadsheet and graphical formats, along with the ability to slice and dice the multidimensional data cube that the user requests from the data warehouse. OLAP methods provide analysis tools (see DSS in Action 8.4 and 8.5). Many of these tools are being developed to be Web-ready so that OLAP of the data from the data warehouse can be directly tapped into via the corporate intranet. Some representative packages include

- BrioQuery (Brio Technology Inc.)
- Business Objects (Business Objects Inc.)
- DecisionWeb (Comshare Inc.)
- DataFountain (Dimensional Insight Inc.)
- DSS Web (MicroStrategy Inc.)
- Focus Fusion (Information Builders Inc.)
- InfoBeaconWeb (Platinum Technology Inc.)
- Oracle Express Server (Oracle Corporation)
- Pilot Internet Publisher (Pilot Software Inc.).

DSS IN ACTION 8.4

WELLCOME PRESCRIBES EIS/OLAP FOR DECISION SUPPORT

Increasing global competition in the pharmaceutical industry prompted British drug giant Wellcome Foundation to install an EIS to help senior managers track product and sales information. Since its implementation a year ago, the system has provided a timely antidote for the firm's productivity problems. Despite its size (Wellcome is the world's top revenue-producing pharmaceutical firm), Wellcome had trouble distributing decision support data to end users. Senior executives wasted valuable time trying to access information that should have been available at their fingertips. The company had numerous information sources, but none were coordinated. With information coming from both internal and external sources and no structured guidelines for dealing with it, inconsistency and duplicated efforts were common. Managers needed a way to identify trends and easily manipulate data. For example, they wanted to be able to discover not only which Wellcome products were selling well in each country but how quickly sales of drugs were rising or falling and what portion of revenue could be attributed to each drug. Although the term *data warehousing* had not been coined at the start of the project, there was a strong view that all the information should be brought together in one place.

In its move to allow end users to perform online analytical processing (OLAP) tasks, Wellcome opted for a multidimensional database design based on Decision Support Suite from Pilot Software Inc. The system has enabled senior managers in various locales to access important data—from corporate sales and marketing statistics to industry news to prices and exchange rates—from their desktops.

The system has been enthusiastically received. Users are banging on the door asking, "When do I get it?" It has had a big impact on the way the company does business.

Source: Condensed from *Software Magazine,* Vol. 15, No. 13, Dec. 1995, pp. 94–95.

DSS IN ACTION 8.5

ALLIED SIGNAL SAYS YES TO EIS

Allied Signal is a $12 billion worldwide manufacturer of aerospace and automotive components and specialty materials such as fibers, chemicals, plastics, and circuit board laminates. Aerospace president Dan Burnham was the catalyst for the EIS. The project started in January 1993 because the president wanted to get reports faster, wanted the information organized more usefully, and wanted to get it all on his desktop. The biggest hurdle was distribution. Dozens of division executives at remote sites needed to contribute information that could be collated quickly into a single system. Comshare's Commander OLAP was used to develop a prototype of the information Burnham requested. In just 30 days, all sorts of drill-down capabilities with charts and graphs were demonstrated to financial executives. Then they ironed out what data they were going to collect.

Three months later, Dan Newsum, manager of distributed applications, installed the first EIS on Dan Burnham's desktop. Then, after a month of training sessions and fine-tuning based on user reactions, Newsum rolled out the system to the desktops of more than 150 people at 15 different sites. Commander's ability to accommodate rapid application updates made it possible to use rapid prototyping to provide updates to users in a couple of hours without involving the user.

In 18 months, system use has spread to 500 users, and when new applications are completed, it will reach 750. "People are working with information they never could access before in ways they had never thought possible," Newsum remarks. When the EIS was getting started, Newsum's group tracked 29 general metrics on the company performance. After months of user feedback, many of these abstract numbers have been fleshed out into full-blown applications using Comshare's Execu-View and Prism. Many of the applications are running on client/server platforms using Comshare's OLAP Server, which includes a multidimensional data store. This OLAP Server has greatly improved users' ability to analyze data. Now, Comshare's OLAP is being employed for new budgeting applications and a financial data warehouse. These applications have raised the level of knowledge in the company about how to work with information.

Source: Condensed from Comshare Brochure 718282, 1995, and from www.comshare.com, 2000.

BusinessQuery for Excel from Business Objects is an example of an OLAP tool that uses Excel as its front end. It lets Excel users easily define their queries in the spreadsheet and add information extracted from corporate databases directly to the spreadsheet for further analyses. This Excel interface enables users who are familiar with spreadsheets to instantly access and manipulate data from a variety of sources.

Of special interest is Pilot Software's Decision Support Suite. With Decision Support Suite, an end user can extract data from various sources and turn them into intuitive, screen-based information. The on-screen data view allows the user to drill down into deeper levels of information.

Pilot Decision Support Suite's interface is based on objects, such as documents, menus, images, charts, and text. These items can have data or actions (an SQL query, for example) associated with them. Building an interface includes selecting an object, pasting it in the workspace, sizing it, and then tying a desired action or predefined function to it. Generally, various objects combine to produce a particular result.

Note: A Decision Support Suite demo, a tutorial, and a limited development tool are available from the Web site of this book, courtesy of Pilot Software Inc. A similar product is Forest and Trees (from Platinum Software Corporation). Decision Support Suite is reviewed in *PCWeek,* Oct. 14, 1996.

We briefly describe the system developed at Sara Lee Corporation in DSS in Action 8.6. The Sara Lee system combines an integrated set of executive information and decision support applications to perform multidimensional OLAP dynamically with a data warehouse in an open environment. For further information, see Barquin and Edelstein (1997a), the five articles entitled "Data Warehousing: The Essential

---

DSS IN ACTION 8.6

SARA LEE UPGRADES SALES ANALYSIS WITH A DSS/EIS SUITE

As a consumer products manufacturer, Sara Lee Corporation depends on its ability to analyze the sales of the retailers it serves. In 1993, however, the meat division of Sara Lee, which represents about $4 billion of the company's $16 billion in annual sales, was having a tough time performing sales analyses for the brands it supports. The division's DSS was running in an older-generation proprietary IBM mainframe environment that could not be easily upgraded or expanded to accommodate a growing number of users. The solution, which began to be installed in late 1993 and went live in May 1994, was a three-tier client/server system now known as the IA Decision Support Suite from Information Advantage. The suite is an integrated set of executive information and decision support applications designed to perform multidimensional online analytical processing dynami-

cally against a data warehouse in an open environment. Users can drill down, drill up, skip multiple hierarchy levels, and create personal sets and calculations without having the IS department predefine drill paths or write stored procedures. In doing so, they can identify trends and exceptions, draw comparisons, perform calculations, and obtain fast answers. Users also benefit from the intuitivity and flexibility of a customizable GUI. The data warehouse is based on a high-speed relational database sorting and indexing engine from Red Brick Systems.

Source: Condensed from *Chain Store Age,* Vol. 71, No. 9 (Sec. 3), Sept. 1995, pp. 22B–22C. Also see "How Sara Lee Replaced a Mainframe Decision Support System with Client/Server-based Analysis Tools," *I/S Analyzer Case Studies,* Vol. 34, No. 4, Apr. 1995, pp. 7–11.

Guide," *CIO,* Oct. 1, 1998 (you can find current articles at www.cio.com), dmreview.com, and the Data Warehousing Institute Web site, www.dw-institute.org.

8.8 INCLUDING SOFT INFORMATION IN ENTERPRISE SYSTEMS

Watson et al. (1996) recognized that decision makers require *soft information,* often provided informally, for making decisions. The authors performed an in-depth study of how and to what extent soft information is included in EIS. **Soft information** is "fuzzy, unofficial, intuitive, subjective, nebulous, implied, and vague." They found that soft information was used in most EIS, broken down into the following categories:

- Predictions, speculations, forecasts, and estimates (78.1 percent)
- Explanations, justifications, assessments, and interpretations (65.6 percent)
- News reports, industry trends, and external survey data (62.5 percent)
- Schedules and formal plans (50.0 percent)
- Opinions, feelings, and ideas (15.6 percent)
- Rumors, gossip, and hearsay (9.4 percent).

The widespread use of soft information in the form of predictions, speculations, forecasts, and estimates is important for planning purposes. Other research documents the use of these types of soft information. Generally the EIS support staff can enter this information, but sometimes the EIS may generate the information automatically based on historical data (by data mining) or by **intelligent agents (IAs)** scanning news sources and internal reports. Explanations, justifications, assessments, and interpretations help executives make sense of what is happening inside and outside the firm. Many enter-

---

prise systems allow users to clip explanations onto screens or e-mail before providing the information to other users. News reports are gaining popularity as **news feeds,** both textual and video, and are becoming widely available, especially via the Web. As intelligent agents filter news (internal and external), we expect more news feeds to be provided through enterprise systems.

The inclusion of soft information enhances the value of enterprise systems for executive users (see DSS in Action 8.7). Most of the participants in the Watson et al. (1996) study indicate that with respect to soft information they plan to concentrate efforts on external news services, competitor information, and the ease of process entering soft information. A few firms are focusing on making it easier for users to add soft information themselves.

8.9 ORGANIZATIONAL DSS

Organizational decision support was first defined by Hackathorn and Keen (1981), who distinguished three types of decision support: individual, group, and organizational. They maintain that computer-based systems can be developed to provide decision support for each of these levels. They perceive an organizational decision support as one that focuses on an organizational task or activity involving a sequence of operations and actors (such as developing a divisional marketing plan or corporate capital budgeting). Furthermore, they believe that each individual's activities must mesh closely with other people's work. The computer support was seen primarily as a vehicle for improving communication, coordination, and problem solving. A visualization of an organizational decision support system from a research dimension is provided by Konsynski and Stohr (1992).

There are several definitions of **organizational decision support system (ODSS):**

- Watson (1990) defined an ODSS as "a combination of computer and communication technology designed to coordinate and disseminate decision-making across functional areas and hierarchical layers in order that decisions are congruent with organizational goals and management's shared interpretation of the competitive environment."

- Carter et al. (1992) defined ODSS as "a DSS that is used by individuals or groups at several workstations in more than one organizational unit who make varied (interrelated but autonomous) decisions using a common set of tools."
- Swanson (Swanson and Zmud, 1990) called ODSS a distributed decision support system (DDSS). He stated that an organizational DSS should not be thought of as a manager's DSS. Rather, it should be viewed as supporting the organization's division of labor in decision making. He defined a DDSS as a DSS that supports distributed decision making.
- King and Star (1990) provided a different perspective. They believe that the concept of ODSS in principle is simple: Apply the technologies of computers and communications to enhance the organizational decision-making process. In principle, ODSS takes the vision of technological support for group processes to the higher level of organizations in much the same way that group DSS extends the vision of technological support for individual action to the group process. This is done today on an intranet (see Ba et al., 1997).

Based on the above definitions, George (1991/1992) found the following common characteristics of ODSS:

- The focus of an ODSS is an organizational task, activity, or decision that affects several organizational units or corporate problems.
- An ODSS cuts across organizational functions or hierarchical layers.
- An ODSS almost necessarily involves computer-based technologies and may also involve communication technologies.

For implementation issues of ODSS see Kivijarvi (1997).

RELATIONSHIP OF ODSS TO GSS AND EIS

Because of its complexity, ODSS can be integrated with a GSS and/or an EIS. For example, the Egyptian cabinet ODSS (see DSS in Action 8.8) includes an EIS. Furthermore, since a GSS can be used to prioritize items and resolve conflicts, the structure of ODSS can be integrated with that of GSS.

RELATIONSHIP WITH ENTERPRISE SYSTEMS

ODSS are a type of enterprise system directly concerned with decision support. While such systems were constructed as independent systems in the past (e.g., Carter et al., 1992), today they are most likely to be part of an intranet support infrastructure. Both ODSS and EIS are closely related to ERP and lately are being deployed with it, as is described next.

8.10 SUPPLY AND VALUE CHAINS AND DECISION SUPPORT

A special class of enterprise systems are those that are related to the supply chain and its management. In this section we present some basic information on supply chains and their management.

DSS IN ACTION 8.8

ODSS IN THE EGYPTIAN CABINET

INTRODUCTION

The Egyptian cabinet is composed of 32 ministries, each responsible for one department (such as labor, energy, or education). The cabinet is headed by the Prime Minister and deals with countrywide policies and strategic issues. The cabinet also includes four sectored ministerial committees assisted by staff. The cabinet makes extremely important decisions in areas such as national socioeconomics and infrastructure. Many of the issues are complex and require considerable preparation and analysis. Furthermore, because of conflicting interests, there is considerable disagreement among the ministries.

The cabinet must work with the parliament and with many government agencies. In addition, there are many links between the cabinet and external agencies ranging from universities to international bodies. Information is essential for effective decision making. Decisions are made by many people (individually or in groups) at many locations and levels, and the composition of the decision makers changes frequently. All this makes the decision-making process very complex.

THE CABINET INFORMATION AND DECISION SUPPORT CENTER

To properly support the information needs of the cabinet, a special center was developed—the information and decision support center (IDSC). Dozens of specific DSS were developed, and since the center's inception in 1985, several of them have been highly interrelated and interconnected. Examples of specific DSS are the following:

- *Customs tariff policy formulation DSS.* This problem area involved six ministries, and so coordination was difficult and the diversity of opinions played a major role in decisions. The DSS helped to achieve a consistent tariff structure and increased government revenue (yet minimized the burden on low-income families).

- *Debt management DSS.* Egypt relies on foreign debt (about 5,000 loans amounting to more than $40 billion in the mid-1990s). The purpose of the DSS was to manage the debt (e.g., to schedule payments, decide on appropriate refinancing, and simulate projections of the debt structure).

CONCLUSION

The use of ODSS has significantly leveraged the strategic decision-making process in Egypt. However, the system supported by the ODSS was very complex. The system provided for ODSS analysis throughout a complex organization and was used by many people in several organizational units. This large-scale ODSS was highly integrated with an extensive data management system.

Source: Based on material from H. El Sherif, "Managing Institutionalization of Strategic Decision Making for the Egyptian Cabinet," *Interfaces,* Vol. 20, No. 1, 1990; and H. El Sherif and O. A. El Sawy, "Issue-based Decision Support Systems for the Egyptian Cabinet," *MIS Quarterly,* Vol. 12, No. 4, Dec. 1988.

DEFINITIONS AND BENEFITS

Initially the concept of a supply chain referred to the flow of materials from its sources (suppliers) to a company and then inside the company to areas where it was needed. At that time there was also recognition of a **demand chain** that described order generation, taking, and fulfillment. Soon it was realized that these two concepts are interrelated, and so they have been integrated under the name *supply chain.*

DEFINITIONS

A **supply chain** refers to the flow of materials, information, and services from raw material suppliers through factories and warehouses to the end customers. A supply chain also includes the *organizations* and *processes* that create and deliver these products, information, and services to the end customers. It involves many activities such as purchasing, materials handling, production planning and control, logistics and warehousing inventory control, and distribution and delivery.

The function of **supply chain management (SCM)** is to deliver an effective supply chain and do it in an effective manner, namely, to plan, organize, and coordinate the supply chain's activities. For an overview of SCM see Handfield and Nichols (1999).

BENEFITS

The goals of modern SCM are to reduce uncertainty and risks in the supply chain, thereby positively affecting inventory levels, cycle time, processes, and customer service. All these contribute to increased profitability and competitiveness.

The benefits of supply chain management were recognized long ago not only in business but also in the military. In today's competitive environment the efficiency and effectiveness of supply chains in most organizations are critical for their survival and are greatly dependent on the supporting information systems.

THE COMPONENTS OF THE SUPPLY CHAINS

The term *supply chain* comes from a picture of how partnering organizations in a specific supply chain are linked together. As shown in Figure 8.2, a simple supply chain links a company that manufactures or assembles a product (in the middle of the chain) with its suppliers (on the left) and distributors and customers (on the right). The upper part of the picture shows a generic supply chain, while the bottom part shows a specific example of making wine.

Note that the supply chain involves three parts:

1. *Upstream.* This part includes the suppliers (they can be manufacturers and/or assemblers) and their suppliers. Such relationships can be extended to the left in several tiers, all the way to the origin of the material (e.g., mining ores or growing crops).
2. *Internal supply chain.* This part includes all the processes used in transforming the inputs of suppliers to outputs, from the time materials enter an organization to the time the product(s) goes to distribution outside the organization.
3. Downstream. This part includes all the processes involved in delivering the product to the final customers. The supply chain actually ends when the product reaches its after-use disposal—presumably back to Mother Earth somewhere.

A supply chain involves activities that take place during a **product life cycle,** from "dirt to dust." However, a supply chain is more than that because we also deal with a movement of information and money and with procedures that support the movement of a product or a service. Finally, the organizations and individuals involved are part of the chain as well [e.g., see Poirier (1999)].

Supply chains come in all shapes and sizes and can be fairly complex, as shown in Figure 8.3. As can be seen in the figure, the supply chain for a car manufacturer includes hundreds of suppliers, dozens of manufacturing plants (parts) and assembly plants (cars), dealers, direct business customers (fleets), wholesalers (some of which are virtual, e.g., www.cardirect.com), customers, and support functions such as product engineering and purchasing.

Notice that in this case the chain is not strictly linear as in Figure 8.2. Here we see some loops in the process. Sometimes the flow of information and even of goods can be bidirectional. For example, not shown in this figure is the *return* of cars to dealers, known as **reverse logistics,** in the case of defects or a recall by the manufacturer.

Also notice that a supply chain is much more than physical. It includes both information and financial flows. As a matter of fact, a supply chain of a digitizable product or service may not include any physical material.

FIGURE 8.2 SUPPLY CHAINS OF WINE MAKING

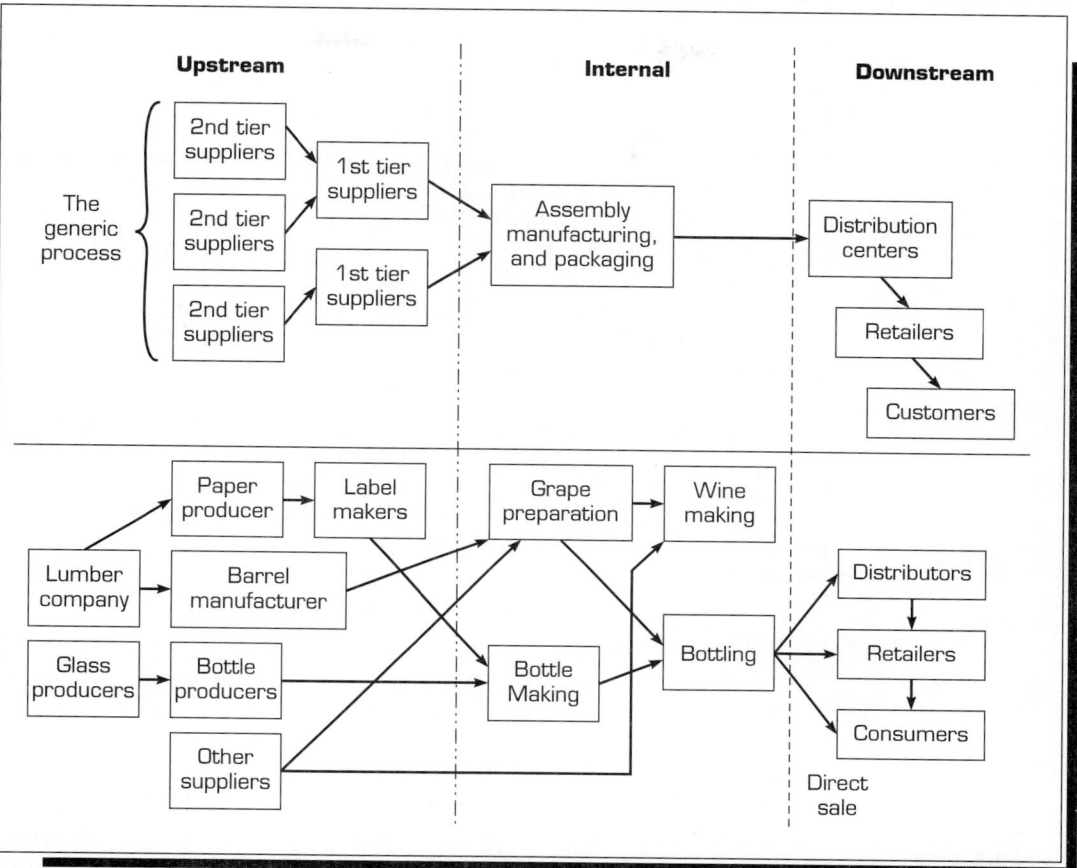

The flow of goods, services, information, and so on, is usually designed not only to effectively transform raw items to finished products and services but also to do it in an efficient manner. Specifically, the flow must end with the delivery of a product or service to the customer whenever it is needed, and it must also be followed with an increase in value that can be analyzed by the value chain.

THE SUPPLY CHAIN AND THE VALUE CHAIN

The concept of the supply chain is related to the concepts of **value chains** and value systems. According to the **value chain model** (Porter, 1985), the activities conducted in any organization can be divided into two parts: primary activities and support activities. The five *primary activities* are (1) inbound logistics (inputs), (2) operations (manufacturing and testing in a manufacturing firm), (3) outbound logistics (storage and distribution), (4) marketing and sales, and (5) service.

These activities are linked together. The output of the first is the input to the second, and so on. Each time an input changes to an output a value is added. The primary activities are sequenced and work progressively in the following manner while value is added at each activity.

Incoming materials are processed (in receiving, storage, and so on), and value is added to them in what is called inbound logistics. Then, the materials are used in operations,

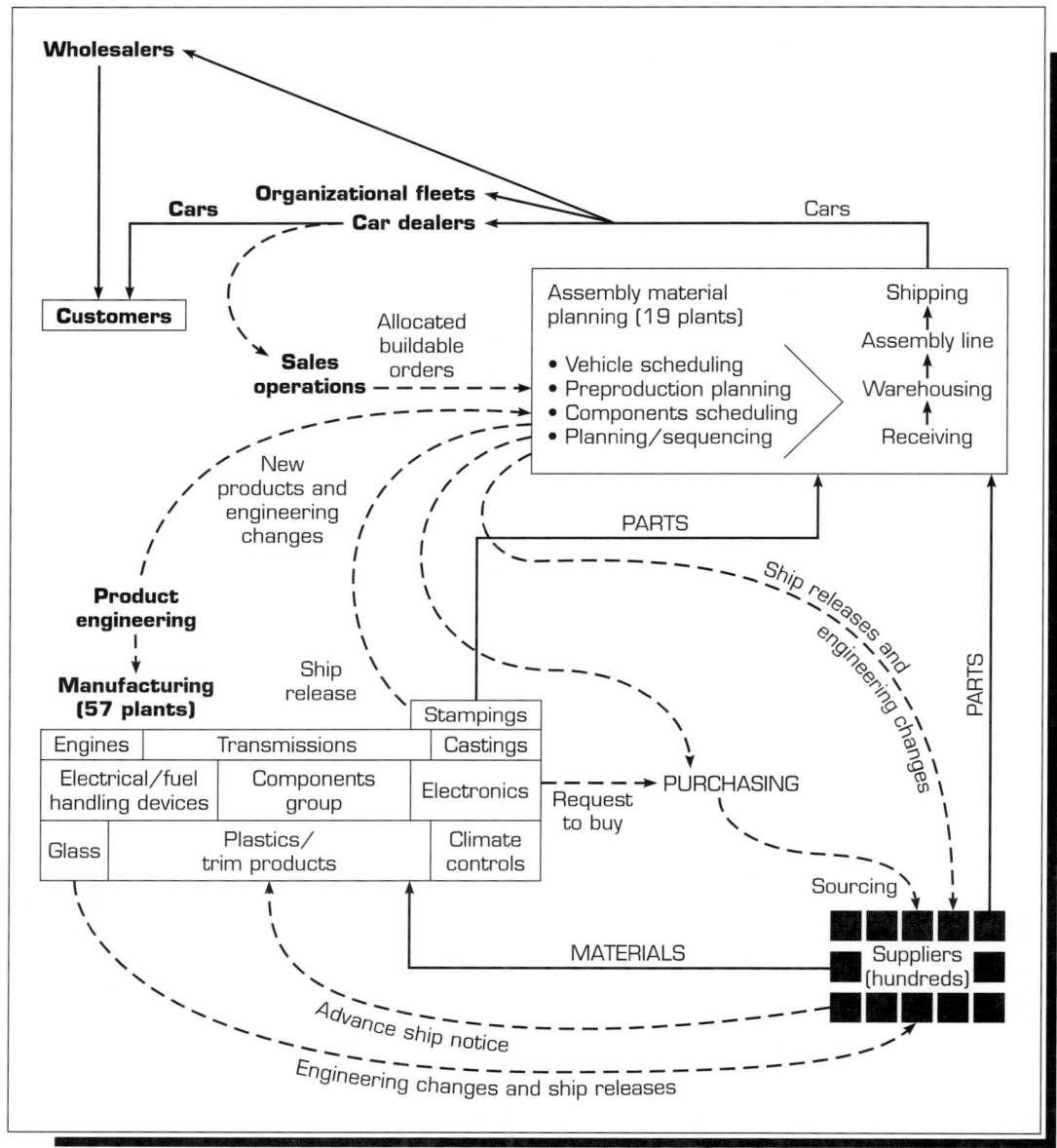

FIGURE 8.3 AN AUTOMOTIVE SUPPLY CHAIN

Source: Modified from INTRODUCTION TO SUPPLY CHAIN MANAGEMENT by Handfield/Nichols, ©1998. Reprinted by permission of Prentice-Hall, Inc., Upper Saddle River, NJ. Handfield, R.B., and E.L. Nichols, Jr. (1999). *Introduction to Supply Chain Management.* Upper Saddle River, NJ: Prentice Hall.

where more value is added in making products. The products need to be prepared for delivery packaging, storing, and shipping, and so more value is added. Then, marketing and sales deliver the products to customers. Finally, after-sales service is performed for the customer. All the value-adding activities result in profit (it is hoped). They are supported by the following *support activities:* (1) the firm infrastructure (accounting, finance, management), (2) human resources management, (3) technology development (R&D), and (4) procurement. Each support activity can support any or all of the primary activities, which can also support each other.

Firms try to optimize the total value along the entire chain. There are many ways to increase this value, and many decisions need to be made for this purpose.

A firm's value chain is part of a larger stream of activities, that Porter calls a value system. A **value system** includes both the suppliers that provide the inputs necessary to the firm and their value chains, which include suppliers to the suppliers (possibly in several tiers). Once the firm creates products, they pass through the value chains of distributors (who also have their own value chains), all the way to the buyers (customers), who also have their own value chains. Gaining and sustaining a competitive advantage and supporting this advantage by means of IT require an understanding of this entire value system. The value chain and value system concepts can be drawn for both products and services and for any organization, private or public.

A close examination of the value chain and value system concepts shows that they are closely related to the supply chain. The primary activities of the value chain correspond to the generic model in Figure 8.2. Some of the support activities of the value chains can be identified in Figure 8.3. Note also that the value system concept corresponds to the concept of an **extended supply chain,** which includes suppliers and other business partners. One of the major goals of SCM is to maximize the value added along the supply chain, and this is where computerized decision support enters the picture.

DECISION MAKING AND THE SUPPLY CHAIN

To maximize the value added along the supply chain it is necessary to make decisions and evaluate their potential impact. For example, in inbound logistics one must decide where, when, and how much to buy. Transporting inbound materials can be done in various ways; the question is which one to select. In each link of the chain, decisions must be made on how to move material, information, and money so that the value will increase the most.

Supply chain management software is available for decision support for both primary and secondary activities. These include, for example, optimization of manufacturing processes (see www.manugiotics.com), scheduling, inventory management, and procurement. These activities and others are described in Section 8.12.

Special DSS models can determine the cost benefit of investing in information technologies in an attempt to create value along the supply chain.

The implementation of DSS in the supply chain environment is complex because of the difficulties and uncertainties along the way. Let us explain.

8.11 SUPPLY CHAIN PROBLEMS AND SOLUTIONS

INTRODUCTION

Adding value along the supply chain is essential for competitiveness or even survival. Unfortunately, such additions are limited by many potential problems along the chain.

Supply chain problems have been recognized both in the military and in business operations for generations. Some of them have even caused armies to lose wars and companies to go out of business. These problems are most evident in a complex or long supply chain and in cases where many business partners are involved.

In the business world there are hundreds of examples of companies that were unable to meet demands or had inventories too large and too expensive to maintain. Several other problems are typical in a supply chain. For example, there is a lack of overall supply chain strategy and a failure to recognize the breadth of organizational implications. Furthermore, there is a misconception that good SCM can be attained solely through an ERP system.

Some companies that experienced such problems paid substantial penalties, while others went out of business. On the other hand, some world-class companies such as Wal-Mart, Federal Express, and Dell have superb supply chains with innovative applications.

A recent example of a supply chain decision-making problem involved the difficulty in fulfilling orders received electronically for toys during the holiday season preceding the year 2000. During the last months of 1999, online toy retailers, including eToys, Amazon.com, and Toys' Я 'Us, conducted a massive advertisement campaign for Internet orders featuring $20- to $30-discount vouchers. Customer response was overwhelming, and retailers that underestimated the demand made incorrect ordering, inventory, and shipment decisions. As a result they were unable to obtain the necessary toys from manufacturing plants and warehouses and deliver them to customers by Christmas Eve.

In the remaining portion of this section we will look closely at some of the specific problems in managing the supply chain and some of the proposed solutions, many of which are supported by information systems.

TYPICAL PROBLEMS ALONG THE SUPPLY CHAIN

The problems along the supply chain stem mainly from *uncertainties* and the need to coordinate several activities and/or internal units and business partners.

The major source of the uncertainties is the *demand forecast,* which can be influenced by several factors such as competition, prices, weather conditions, and technological developments. Other uncertainties exist in *delivery times,* which depend on many factors ranging from machine failures to road conditions. Quality problems with materials and parts can also create production time delays, and traffic jams can interfere with shipments.

Many other factors can cause supply chain problems [see Jacobs and Whybark (2000) for details]. A major symptom of poor SCM is poor customer service—meaning that people do not get the product or service when and where it is needed, or that they get poor-quality goods and services. Other symptoms are high inventory costs, loss of revenue, extra costs for special shipments and for expediting shipments, and more.

SOLUTIONS TO SUPPLY CHAIN PROBLEMS

Over the years organizations have developed many solutions to supply chain problems. One of the earliest was vertical integration. For example, Henry Ford purchased rubber plantations in South America in order to control tire production. Undoubtedly, the most common solution used by companies is building *inventories* as insurance against uncertainties. In this way, products and parts flow smoothly. The main problem with this approach is that it is very difficult to determine inventory levels correctly, which must be done for each product and part. When inventory levels are set too high, the cost of keeping the inventory is very large. When the inventory is too low, there is no insurance against high demand or slow delivery (lead) times, and revenues (and customers) may be lost. In either event the total penalty cost, including opportunities lost and bad reputations gained, can be very high. Thus, major attempts are made to properly control inventory, as shown in DSS in Action 8.9.

Proper SCM and inventory management require making decisions and coordinating the different activities and links of the supply chain so that goods can move smoothly and on time from suppliers to customers. This practice keeps inventories low

DSS IN ACTION 8.9

HOW LITTLEWOODS STORES IMPROVED ITS SCM

Littlewoods Stores is one of Britain's largest retailers of high-quality clothing, with 136 stores throughout the United Kingdom. The retail clothing business is very competitive, and so in the late 1990s the company embarked on an IT-supported initiative to improve its supply chain efficiency. A serious SCM problem was overstocking.

In order to get better SCM, the company first introduced a Web-based performance reporting system. Using DSS models, the system analyzes marketing and finance data, space planning, merchandizing, and purchasing data on a daily basis. For example, merchandizing can now perform sophisticated sales, stock, and supplier analyses to make key operational decisions on pricing and inventory.

Using the Web, analysts can view sales and stock data in veritably any grouping of levels and categories, even at SKU and day levels. Furthermore, users can easily drill down to detailed sales and other data. The system uses a data warehouse, DSS, and other end-user-oriented software to make better decisions. Here are some other examples of decisions made and their results:

- The ability to strategically price merchandise differently in different stores saved $1.2 millions in 1997 alone.
- Reducing the need for stock liquidations saved $1.4 million a year.
- Marketing distribution expenses were cut by $7 million a year.
- Reduction in logistic employees from 84 to 49 people saves about $1 million annually.
- Reducing backup inventory expenses by about $4 million a year. For example, because of quick replenishment, stock levels went down by 80 percent.

Within a year the number of Web-based users grew to 600 and the size of the data warehouse grew to over 1 gigabits.

Source: Condensed from "Customers' Success Stories," www.microstragy.com, Jan. 2000.

---

and costs down. Coordination is needed because companies depend on each other but do not always work together toward the same goal.

Effective SCM requires that suppliers and customers work together in a coordinated manner by sharing and communicating the information necessary for decision making. For example, Wal-Mart allows its major suppliers to enter its intranet and retrieve sales data on a daily basis. Thus, the suppliers can make better production scheduling decisions. A rapid flow of information along the supply chains makes suppliers very efficient. Therefore, both suppliers and buyers must participate together in the design of supply chains to achieve their shared goals.

To properly control the uncertainties mentioned earlier, it is necessary to identify and understand the causes of the uncertainties, determine how uncertainties will affect other activities up and down the supply chain, and formulate ways to reduce or eliminate these uncertainties. Combined with this issue is the need for an effective, efficient communication environment for all business partners. For example, computerized POS information can be transmitted once a day, or even in real time, to distribution centers, suppliers, and shippers. This enables optimal inventory levels.

The following are some other solutions to SCM problems:

- Use outsourcing rather than do it yourself during demand peaks.
- Similarly, "buy" rather than "make" whenever appropriate.
- Configure the optimal shipping plans.
- Optimize purchasing.
- Create strategic partnerships with suppliers.

- Use a just-in-time approach to purchasing so that suppliers quickly deliver small quantities whenever supplies, materials, and parts are needed.
- Reduce the number of intermediaries, which usually add to supply chain costs, by using electronic commerce for direct marketing.
- Reduce the lead time for buying and/or selling by automatic processing using EDI or extranets.
- Use fewer suppliers.
- Improve the supplier–buyer relationship.
- Manufacture only after orders are in, as Dell does with its custom-made computers.
- Achieve accurate demand by working closely with suppliers.

Most of the above solutions are enhanced by IT support, especially in the form of enterprise resource planning (ERP) systems.

8.12 COMPUTERIZED SYSTEMS: MRP, ERP, AND SCM

The concept of the supply chain is interrelated with the computerization of its activities, which has evolved over the last 50 years.

THE EVOLUTION OF COMPUTERIZED AIDS

Historically, many supply chain activities were managed with inefficient and ineffective paper transactions. Therefore, since the early business utilization of computers, attention has been given to the automation of processes along the supply chain. The first software programs appeared in the 1950s and the early 1960s and supported short segments along the supply chain. Typical examples are inventory management systems, scheduling, and billing. The major objective was to reduce cost, expedite processing, and decrease errors. Such applications were developed in the functional areas independently of each other.

In a short time it becomes clear that interdependencies exist among some supply chain activities. One of the earliest realizations was that the production schedule is related to inventory management and purchasing plans. As early as the 1960s, the material requirements planning (MRP) model was devised. It then became clear that in order to use this model, which may require daily updating, computer support was needed. This resulted in commercial MRP software packages.

While MRP packages were useful in many cases, helping to drive inventory levels down and streamlining portions of the supply chain, they failed in as many cases. One of the major reasons for failure was the realization that schedule/inventory/purchasing operations are closely related to both financial and labor resources. This realization resulted in an enhanced MRP methodology and software called manufacturing requirements planning or MRP II.

Notice that during this evolution more and more integration of information systems occurred. This evolution continued, leading to the enterprise resource planning (ERP) concept, which concentrated on integrating enterprise transaction processing activities. Later, ERP was expanded to include internal suppliers and customers and then external suppliers and customers, in what is known as extended ERP/SCM software.

WHY INTEGRATION

Creating a twenty-first-century enterprise cannot be done effectively with twentieth-century computer technology, which is functionally oriented. Functional systems may not let different departments communicate with each other in the same language. Worse yet, crucial sales, inventory, and production data often have to be painstakingly entered manually into separate computer systems each time a person who is not a member of a specific department needs ad hoc information related to the specific department. In many cases employees simply do not get the information they need, or they get it when it is too late.

Sandoe and Saharia (2001) list the following major benefits of integration (in order of importance).

- *Tangible benefits:* inventory reduction, personnel reduction, productivity improvement, order management improvement, financial close cycle improvements, IT cost reduction, procurement cost reduction, cash management improvements, revenue and profit increases, transportation logistics cost reduction, maintenance reduction, and on-time delivery improvement.
- *Intangible benefits:* information visibility, new and/or improved processes, customer responsiveness, standardization, flexibility, globalization, and business performance.

Note that in both types of benefits many items are directly related to improved SCM. For a further discussion of the improvements integration has provided to SCM, see the white paper, "Competition's New Battleground: The Integrated Value Chain," at www.combridgetechnology.com.

INTEGRATING THE SUPPLY CHAIN

For generations companies managed the various links of the supply chain independently of each other. However, since the 1950s, and thanks to the introduction of computer-based information systems, companies have started to integrate these links. Integration was facilitated by the need to streamline operations in order to meet customer demands in the areas of product and service costs, quality, delivery, technology, and cycle time brought about by increased global competition. Furthermore, the new forms of organizational relationships and the information revolution, especially the Internet and electronic commerce, brought SCM to the forefront of attention. This attention created a willingness to invest money in the hardware and software needed for seamless integration, as shown in the case of Warner Lambert Corporation (see DSS in Action 8.10).

ENTERPRISE RESOURCE PLANNING

With the advance of enterprise-wide client/server computing comes a new challenge: how to control all major business processes with a single software architecture in real time. The integration solution, known as **enterprise resource planning (ERP),** promises benefits from increased efficiency to improved quality, productivity, and profitability [see Appleton (1997) for details]. The name *ERP* is somewhat misleading because the software does not concentrate on either planning or resources. An ERP major objective is to integrate all departments and functions across a company into a single computer system that can serve the entire enterprise's needs. For example, improved order entry allows immediate access to inventory, product data, customer credit history, and prior order information. This raises productivity and increases customer satisfaction. One option is to self-develop an integrated system by using existing best-of-the-breed functional commercial packages or by programming your own systems. The other option is to use commercially available integrated software known as ERP. The leading software for ERP is SAP R/3. Oracle, J. D. Edwards, Computer Associates, PeopleSoft,

DSS IN ACTION 8.10

HOW WARNER LAMBERT APPLIES AN INTEGRATED SUPPLY CHAIN

It all begins on eucalyptus farms in Australia, where the fast-growing trees produce some of the materials used in Listerine antiseptic mouthwash, one of the major products of Warner Lambert (WL). The materials collected from eucalyptus trees are shipped from Australia to the WL manufacturing plant in the United States. The major problem there is to determine how much Listerine to produce. Listerine is purchased by thousands of retail stores, some of which are giants, such as WalMart, and many of which are small. The problem that the manufacturing plant faces is how to forecast the overall demand. A wrong forecast will result either in high inventories at WL or in shortages. Inventories are expensive to keep, and shortages may result in loss of business and reputation.

WL forecasts demand with the help of Manugistic's Demand Planning DSS. (Manugistic is a vendor of IT software for SCM.) Used with other products in Manugistics' Supply Chain Planning Suite, the system analyzes manufacturing, distribution, and sales data against expected demand and business climate information to help WL decide how much Listerine (and other products) to make and distribute and how much of each raw ingredient is needed. For example, the model can anticipate the impact of promotions or of a production line being down. The sales and marketing groups at WL meet monthly with WL employees in finance, procurement, and other departments. The groups enter the expected demand for Listerine into a Marcam Corporation Prism Capacity Planning DSS that schedules the production of Listerine in the amounts needed and generates electronic purchase orders for WL's suppliers.

WL's supply chain excellence stems from its innovative collaborative planning, forecasting, and replenishment (CPFR) program. WL launched CPFR a few years ago when it started sharing strategic plans, performance data, and market insight with Wal-Mart Inc. over private networks. The company realized that it could benefit from WL's market knowledge just as Wal-Mart could benefit from its product knowledge. During the CPFR pilot, WL increased its products' shelf-fill rate—the extent to which a store's shelves are fully stocked—from 87 percent to 98 percent, earning the company about $8 million a year in additional sales, or the equivalent of a new product launch. WL now uses the Internet to expand the CPFR program to all its suppliers and retail partners.

Source: Compiled from *Store,* June 15, 1998; *CIO,* Aug. 15, 1998; and *Logistics Management and Distribution Reports,* Nov. 1999.

---

and Baan Company make similar products, which include Web modules (see *Interactive Week,* Nov. 3, 1997).

ERP software crosses functional departments and can be extended along the supply chain to suppliers and customers. Companies have been successful in integrating several hundreds of applications using ERP software, saving millions of dollars and significantly increasing customer satisfaction. For example, Mobil Oil consolidated 300 different information systems by implementing SAP R/3 in U.S. petrochemical operations alone. ERP forces discipline and organization around business processes, making the alignment of IT and business goals more likely. Moreover, by using ERP a company discovers all the "dusty corners" of its business.

An ERP suite provides a single interface for managing all the routine activities performed in manufacturing—from entering sales orders to coordinating shipping, as well as after-sales customer service. More recently, ERP systems have begun to incorporate functionality for customer interaction and managing relationships with suppliers and vendors, making the system less inward-looking.

ERP has played a critical role in getting small- and medium-sized manufacturers to become focused, which facilitates business process changes across the enterprise. By tying multiple plants and distribution facilities together, ERP solutions have facilitated a change in thinking that has its ultimate expression in the extended enterprise and in better supply chain management. For a comprehensive treatment of ERP, its costs, implementation problems, and payback, see Koch et al. (1999).

But ERP was never meant to fully support supply chains. ERP solutions are transaction-centric. As such, they do not provide the computerized models needed to respond rapidly to real-time changes in supply, demand, labor, or capacity. This deficiency could be overcome by the second generation of ERP, which includes decision support capabilities.

SECOND-GENERATION ERP

First-generation ERP aimed at automating key business office processes. And indeed, ERP projects saved companies millions of dollars. By the late 1990s the major benefits of ERP had been exploited, but the ERP movement was far from over. A second more powerful generation of ERP development started with the objective of leveraging existing systems to increase efficiency in handling transactions, improve decision making, and further transform ways of doing business.

As you may recall, in Chapter 4 OLTP and OLAP were considered two different but complementary activities. First-generation ERP basically supported OLTP and other routine transactional activities. For example, an ERP system has the functionality of electronic ordering, or the best way to bill the customer—all it does is automate the transactions.

The reports generated by ERP systems provided planners with statistics about what happened in the company, costs, and financial performance. However, with ERP the planning systems were rudimentary. Reports from ERP systems provided a snapshot of time, but they did not support the continuous planning activities central to supply chain planning, one that continues to refine and enhance the plan as changes and events occur, up to the very last minute before the plan is executed.

This deficiency created a need for decision making-oriented systems, and this is what SCM and business intelligence software vendors provided. These products offer DSS capabilities in short segments of the supply chain. As an illustration, we look at the ERP and SCM approach to the planning problem. There is a fundamental difference— the question in SCM becomes, Should I take your order? instead of the ERP approach, How can I best take or fulfill your order?

Thus, SCM systems have emerged as a *complement* to ERP systems to provide intelligent decision support capabilities. An SCM system can be designed to overlay existing ERP systems and to extract data from every step of the supply chain, providing a clear global picture of where the enterprise is heading. Creating a plan from an SCM system allows companies to quickly assess the impact of their actions on the entire supply chain, including customer demand. Therefore, it makes sense to integrate ERP and SCM.

How Is Such Integration Done?

One approach to achieving such integration is to work with different software from different vendors, for example, using SAP as an ERP and adding Manugistics manufacturing-oriented software, as shown earlier in the Warner Lambert case. Such an approach requires integrating and fitting together different software, which may be a complex issue unless special interfaces exist. A suboption is to use **advanced planning and scheduling (APS)** packages, which are modules that can be integrated with ERP or total SCM. APS help in optimizing production and ensuring that the right materials are in the right warehouse at the right time to meet customers' demands.

The second approach is for ERP vendors to add decision support and business intelligence capabilities, which solves the integration problem. But, as in the integration of DBMS and spreadsheets in Excel or Lotus 1-2-3, you get a product with some weaker functionalities. Most ERP vendors add such functionalities for another reason, because it is cheaper for the customer. The added functionalities, which create the second-generation ERP, include not only decision support but also CRM, electronic commerce, and data warehousing and mining. Companies were eager to use post-ERP systems, as shown in DSS in Action 8.11.

The third option is to rent applications rather than build systems. When applications are rented, the ERP vendor (or other rentee) takes care of the functionalities and the integration problems. This relatively new approach is known as "the ASP alternative."

APPLICATION SERVICE PROVIDERS AND ERP OUTSOURCING

An **application service provider (ASP)** is a software vendor who leases ERP-based applications, including those with DSS capabilities, to organizations. The basic concept is the same as the old-fashioned time-sharing. The outsourcers set up the systems and run them for you. Use of ASP is considered a risk management strategy and it best fits small- to middle-sized companies.

The ASP concept is especially useful in ERP projects that are expensive to install, that take a long time to implement, and for which staffing is a major problem. However, an ASP offering is also evident in ERP added functions such as DSS, EC, CRM, data marts, desktop productivity, and other supply-chain-related applications.

The use of an ASP has some downsides. First, ERP vendors demand a 5-year commitment. In 5 years ERP software may change drastically and may even be bundled

---

DSS IN ACTION 8.11

HOW U.S. COMPANIES ARE USING POST-ERP

- Owens Corning, a maker of building materials, changed its business model and corporate thinking in 1999. For example, instead of selling shingles and roofing vents separately, it started to sell complete roofing systems that include parts, installation, delivery, and other services. To do this economically the company uses business intelligence (data warehouse and mining) to analyze the data generated by the ERP system (from SAP). The data warehouse provides valuable information on customer profitability, product line profitability, sales performance, and SCM activities. The ERP is also integrated with shop floor process control that uses SCM software.

- General Instruments, a telecom equipment maker, and SCM software vendor, pushes parts data into Metaphase's product management tool. From there data enter Oracle's ERP system. Previously product data were entered manually into each system, resulting in high costs and many errors. The company also uses product configuration tools that assist the sales force and manufacturing department to ensure that certain product

configurations are possible before orders are placed on the ERP. More than 3,000 component suppliers have direct access to product data over the Web using Metaphase's technology.

- At in-line skate maker Rollerblade Inc., an ERP (from J. D. Edward) is the platform for the company's forecasting, sales force automation, and data warehousing systems. With the ERP integrated platform decision support activities were ineffective. Now a profitability and sales analysis by product, region, and time is done regularly and effectively.

- Mott's North America installed ERP and found that it did not address its marketing and customer service problems properly. Using SAP's advanced features, the company added production planning and shipment scheduling optimization. Also, integration with electronic commerce was achieved. Now, for example, distributors can use the Web to check their order status by themselves with the R/3 system.

with a PC and given away free. Second, flexibility is lost. Rented systems are fairly standard and may not fit your needs. For a discussion of ASPs see several papers in *Datamation,* July 1999.

CORPORATE (ENTERPRISE) PORTALS AND EIS

As Web technologies come to dominate corporate networks, existing EIS or business intelligence systems will probably be replaced by *corporate enterprise portals.* Virtually every OLAP/DSS/BI vendor was promoting portals by the end of 1999.

A **corporate (enterprise) portal** integrates internal applications such as database management, document management, and e-mail with external applications such as news services and customer Web sites. It is a Web-based interface that gives users access to all these applications through their PCs. Corporate portals are basically on advanced or second-generation intranets. They bring both external and internal information to the manager's desk, similar to what an EIS does. Corporate portals can filter extraneous information throughout the enterprise.

Corporate portals have diversified capabilities and as such they employ several layers of multiple technologies such as the following:

- *Groupware technologies:* discussions, chat sessions, and library projects
- *Presentation:* data visualization tools such as Web OLAP, JavaScript, and HTML for Web display
- *Personalization and customization:* software agents that customize information for individual users using push technology
- *Publishing and distribution:* storehouses of documents in portable formats, as well as publish and subscribe engines
- *Search:* both full-text search engines and those that search descriptions of documents and other content
- *Categorization:* tools for creating and maintaining different categories of information for different audiences, such as multidimensionality tools
- *Integration:* tools for accessing disparate back-end data sources such as ERP packages, relational databases, and external data such as stock price quotations.

The first generation of most business portals is a slightly rehashed version of products once labeled *business intelligence tools* or *document management tools* because portals that perform all of the above tasks to their fullest are difficult and expensive to build. However, it is expected that by 2001 there will be products from specialized portal vendors such as Verity Inc., Dataware Technologies Inc., Viador Inc., Plumtree Software, and Digital Pilot Corporation. Companies reported that 70–80 percent of their employees use corporate portals. One problem is that the larger the number of users, the greater the cost, and that this cost is difficult to justify because almost all the benefits are intangible.

8.13 FRONTLINE DECISION SUPPORT SYSTEMS

Decisions at all levels in the organization contribute to the success of a business. But decisions that maximize a sales opportunity or minimize the cost of customer service requests are made on the front lines by those closest to situations that arise during the course of daily business. Whether it is an order exception, an upselling opportunity, or a contract that hangs on a decision, a decision maker must be able to make effective decisions rapidly based on context and according to strategies and guidelines set forth by senior management.

Frontline decision making is the process by which companies automate decision processes and push them down into the organization and sometimes out to partners. It includes **empowering employees** by letting them devise strategies, evaluate metrics, analyze impacts, and make operational changes.

Frontline decision making serves business users such as line managers, sales executives, and call center representatives by incorporating decision making into their daily work. These workers need applications to help them make good operational decisions that meet overall corporate objectives. Frontline decision making provides users with the right questions to ask, the location of needed data, and metrics (e.g., for customer and product profitability) that translate data into corporate objectives and suggest actions that can improve performance. Analytic application products are now emerging to support these actions.

Today's transactional applications and decision support tools by themselves do not readily enable frontline users to make better decisions. Systems like those from SAP AG and Siebel Systems Inc. do not implement simple decision processes or present data in a way that can be analyzed in complex situations. Executives may obtain context from reports and systems created from them (such as financial or executive information systems), but these don't provide frontline workers with guidance on daily problems. At the same time, traditional decision support from vendors like Pilot Software, Cognos Inc., and Business Objects SA is intended for experts—those who can access data, slice and dice it, and give it business meaning—who are unlikely to be at the front lines. So organizations need a new generation of enterprise analytic applications to implement frontline decision making.

FRONTLINE SYSTEMS

In frontline decision making, every operational process has a corresponding decision process for evaluating choices and improving execution. For example, order management has cross-selling suggestions, and a customer service representative can offer additional items to customers based on their specific needs.

Frontline decision making automates simple decisions—like freezing the account of a customer who has failed to make payments—by predefining business rules and events that trigger them. At more complex decision points, such as inventory allocation, frontline decision making gives managers the necessary context—available alternatives, business impacts, and success measurements—to make the right decision. In order for business users to take advantage of ordinary decision support, they have to know what questions to ask, where the information resides, and the components of any metric.

Frontline software that started to appear on the market in late 1999 can solve standard problems, such as what to do if a specific bank customer withdraws 100 percent more than the average withdrawal, by packaging in a single browser-based self-service solution that requires business logic (including rules, algorithms, intelligent systems, and so on). Also provided are metrics such as life cycle expectancy, decision workflow, and so on. Finally, to be successful, such systems must work hand in hand with transactional systems.

According to Forrester Research Inc., such systems are essential for the survival of many companies, but it will take 5 years for the technology to mature. The major current vendors are Heperion Solutions Corporation, NCR Corporation, SAS Institute Inc., and i2 Technology. However, almost all the SCM, ERP, and business intelligence vendors mentioned in this chapter may be involved in such systems. For further details see McCullough (1999) and Sheth and Sisodia (1999).

8.14 THE FUTURE OF EXECUTIVES AND ENTERPRISE SUPPORT SYSTEMS[2]

Executives and other managers place substantial requirements on computerized support. *First,* they often ask questions that require complex, real-time analyses for the answers. This is why many of today's EIS/ESS are being linked to data warehouses and are built using real-time OLAP in separate multidimensional databases along with organizational DSS, which provide the necessary analytical tools. But sometimes even these systems lack the ability to respond in real time. Delay in the delivery of information can mean loss of competitive position, loss of sales, and loss of profits. *Second,* like other infrequent, untrained, or uncooperative users, executives require systems that are easy to use, easy to learn, and easy to navigate. Current support systems generally possess these qualities. However, ease of use can also mean that the system has enough intelligence to automatically determine which tasks need to be performed and either performs these tasks directly or guides the user through them. Although current systems enable executives to monitor the present state of affairs, they typically cannot automate the processes of interpreting or explaining information. Automation of these tasks requires integration of current executive support systems capabilities with those of an intelligent system. *Third,* executives tend to have highly individualized work styles. Although the current generation of enterprise systems can be molded to the needs of an executive, it is very difficult to alter the look and feel of the system or to change the basic way in which the user interacts with it. *Finally,* any information system is essentially a social system. One of the key elements of an enterprise system is the communication capabilities it provides for members of the executive team. Therefore, visualization including multimedia documents is becoming critical.

Enterprise systems of the future will look substantially different from today's systems. Developers of decision support technology for executives must be alert to the needs of top executives. Like most other systems, enterprise and stand-alone EIS/ESS have migrated to the networked world of the technical workstation and intranets. Within 5 years, these will have at least 10 times the speed and memory of today's PCs, will have at least 4 to 8 times the disk capacity, will possess a very high-resolution bitmapped screen, will be multitasking, and will be connected with other workstations over an ultra-high-speed network. Finally, access to these systems will be available from cell phones and wireless devices. The advantages of such configurations are that data and programs can be distributed and easily shared as needed. Individual workstations and PCs will have the ability to house and run mainframe versions of most DSS and enterprise software. Because of their multitasking capabilities, these programs can run simultaneously (in separate windows). Furthermore, the impact of computer-aided software engineering (CASE) developments, rapid application development (RAD), object-oriented programming (OOP), and Java, Pearl, and other Internet-related programming languages will affect the structure, development, and deployment of enterprise systems.

The following list briefly describes some of the features that are emerging or are likely to appear in the next generation of enterprise systems that support executives

---

[2]This section was condensed in part from unpublished work of D. King, Comshare Inc., 2000. (Courtesy of D. King)

and other major users in the enterprise (to be referred to as enterprise support systems).

- *A toolbox for building customized systems.* To quickly configure a system for an executive, the builder of the system needs a toolbox of graphical and analytical objects that can be easily linked together to produce the system. In the future, enterprise support systems vendors are likely to provide toolkits for building visual and graphical front ends. Decision Web, Forest and Trees, and Pilot Decision Support Suite are examples of such tools.

- *Multimedia support.* The requirement that an enterprise support system be configurable also necessitates support of multiple input–output modes. The current generation provides text and graphics output with a touch screen, mouse, or keyboard input. The rapid proliferation of databases supporting image data and video as well as voice input–output, along with the multimedia PC, will no doubt mean that future enterprise support systems will be multimedia in nature. Video and audio news feeds (soft information) already flow from the Internet to users via intranets or other infrastructures. Even features of multimedia-oriented geographic information systems will be incorporated. In the next generation of systems, an executive may be able to sit in front of a high-resolution map of the company's sales regions. By touching one of these regions the executive might access an animated display of the region's revenue and expense figures over the past few years, along with a voice summary of results e-mailed daily by the regional sales directors. The Pizzeria Uno system described earlier has some of these capabilities. This means not only that PCs will support the storage and display of multimedia objects but also that the network will support the transfer of these objects.

- *Virtual reality and three-dimensional image displays.* The development of virtual reality standards (virtual reality mark-up language, VRML), the ability to examine megabytes of data in a map form or on a landscape (Chapter 4) via three-dimensional visualization, and higher-quality display units are beginning to affect enterprise systems. As these tools are deployed for general use, executives will adopt them to assist in data visualization for information evaluation and decision making.

- *Merging of analytic systems with desktop publishing.* Many of the reports prepared for executives contain tables, graphs, and text. To support the preparation of these reports, some software companies have merged desktop publishing capabilities with various analytic capabilities. In keeping with the multimedia features, enterprise systems have the capability to cut and paste data and graphs from various windows into a document and to ship this document via e-mail to other executives or to post it on a Web site. Some systems, such as Pilot Decision Support Suite, can publish multimedia Web documents directly.

- *Web-enabled support systems.* Web browser software is the simplest and cheapest client software for an enterprise system and is leading toward Web-enabled EIS. The current generation of software supports information delivery via the corporate intranet, which is evolving into the norm rather than the exception. For example, Comshare provides DecisionWeb, Pilot Decision Support Suite contains an Internet publishing module, the SAS Institute provides Internet support for its Enterprise Software Suite, and several of Microstrategy's products are Web-based.

- *Automated support and intelligent assistance.* Expert systems and other AI technologies (such as natural language) are currently being embedded in or integrated with existing enterprise and decision support systems. This clearly adds more automated support and assistance to the analytic engines underlying enterprise systems. However, we are also likely to see other forms of intelligent or automated assistance. One such form is the intelligent agent (Chapter 17). Another example of currently deployed agent technology is news filtering. Thus, instead of thinking of an executive support system as a single system, we can think of it as a society of cooperating agents whose actions need to be coordinated. For example, Comshare's Detect and Alert agent, which is embedded in Decision Web, provides automatic surveillance of large databases and external news sources, with delivery of immediate personal alerts to users' desktops. Comshare's Decision Web uses intelligent component expansion (ICE) to identify the drill-down paths of exceptions (see DSS in Focus 8.4).

  Another agent tracks users' actions, learns how they use the system, and adopts appropriate screens in the user's preferred order. Other agents can be deployed in Web-enabled EIS. For example, Chi and Turban (1995) proposed a framework for distributed intelligent EIS in which expert systems, neural networks, and intelligent agents play an active role in the executive decision-making process.

- *Integration of EIS and group support systems.* Much of the technology developed for group support systems (groupware, see Chapter 7) can be used effectively by executives for a number of managerial tasks. In this area, Haley and Watson (1996) document 10 cases in which Lotus Notes was specifically chosen for EIS development. Volonino et al. (1995) describe the case of a major Wall Street investment bank that developed a Lotus Notes—based system on a network of specialized workstations that enables bankers to access and share mission- and time-critical information on market conditions directly from the trading floor, along with specific business development data on the firm's clients and prospects.

- *Global support systems.* As organizations become more global in nature, providing information around the world is becoming critical to their success. The timeliness and accuracy of the information needed for decision making becomes critical. Palvia et al. (1996) investigated the kinds of data that global executives would require under two scenarios: introducing a new product or service into other countries, and distribution channel expansion into other countries. Most of the information that executives require includes market and demographic data from public sources and soft information from personal contacts. The authors believe that EIS can be used to provide the soft information.

- *Integration and deployment with ERP products.* The trend toward providing a business intelligence capability to supplement ERP will mature within 2–3 years, resulting in either fully integrated systems or systems that can easily accept add-on products. Various ERP vendors already provide what SAP calls "strategic enterprise management systems," which have EIS capabilities. Such integration will leverage the capabilities of existing ERPs and reduce their cost.

❖ CHAPTER HIGHLIGHTS

- Enterprise systems serve the whole organization and frequently business partners as well.
- The major enterprise systems are (1) for executive support, (2) for organizational decision support, and (3) for support along the supply chain.
- Executives' work can be divided into two major phases: finding problems (opportunities) and deciding what to do about them.
- EIS serves the information needs of top executives. It used to be an independent system, but today its capabilities are usually provided as part of a business intelligence/enterprise system.
- EIS provides rapid access to timely information at various levels of detail. It is very user-friendly.
- Drill down is an important capability of EIS. It allows an executive to look at details (and details of details).
- EIS uses a management-by-exception approach. It centers on CSFs, key performance indicators, and highlighted charts.
- Data warehouses and client/server front-end environments make an EIS a useful tool.
- Organizational DSS (ODSS) deals with decision making across functional areas and hierarchical organizational layers.
- ODSS is used by individuals and groups and operates in a distributed environment.
- The effectiveness and efficiency of the supply chain is critical to the survival of organizations.
- The major components of the supply chain are upstream (suppliers), internal, and downstream (customers).
- The value chain is a concept that attempts to maximize the value added when moving along the supply chain.
- Enterprise systems are becoming part of corporate portals for communication, collaboration, access, and dissimilation of information.
- Frontline systems automate or facilitate decisions at the place where customers interface with organizations.

❖ KEY WORDS

- advanced planning and scheduling (APS)
- application service provider (ASP)
- business intelligence (BI)
- critical success factor (CSF)
- corporate (enterprise) portal
- demand chain
- drill down
- empowering employees
- enterprise information systems (EIS)
- enterprise resource planning (ERP)
- environmental scanning
- exception reporting
- executive information system (EIS)
- executive support system (ESS)
- extended supply chain
- frontline decision making
- intelligent agent (IA)
- key performance indicators (KPI)
- multidimensional analysis
- navigation of information
- news feeds
- organizational decision support system (ODSS)
- product life cycle
- reverse logistics
- soft information (in EIS)
- supply chain
- supply chain management (SCM)
- value chain
- value chain model
- value system

❖ QUESTIONS FOR REVIEW

1. Define executive information system (EIS).
2. Define executive support system (ESS).
3. What are the key differences between an EIS and an ESS?
4. List the pressures for the creation of an EIS.
5. Define enterprise support system.
6. List the major benefits of an EIS.
7. Define drill down and list its advantages.
8. Define status access.
9. Define exception reporting.
10. List the major differences between EIS and DSS.
11. Describe how soft information can help an executive in decision making.
12. Define ODSS (give at least two definitions).
13. Define supply chain and list its major components.
14. Discuss supply chain management (SCM) and its benefits.
15. Define enterprise resource planning (ERP).
16. List the major characteristics of ERP.
17. List the major tangible and intangible benefits of system (and software) integration.
18. Describe an ASP.
19. Define a corporate portal.
20. Describe frontline decision making.

❖ QUESTIONS FOR DISCUSSION

1. If a DSS is used to find answers to management questions, what is an EIS used for?
2. Discuss how CSFs can be monitored and why they should be.
3. What are the major benefits of integrating EIS and DSS? What problems can occur?
4. It is said that drill down will be fully automated someday. What advantage will such automation give the executive? How can an intelligent agent be used to automate drill down in EIS?
5. What is soft information? Why is it important for an EIS to provide soft information?
6. Data mining (Chapter 4) is becoming critical for enterprise-wide EIS. Explain why.
7. Describe how multidimensional analysis and OLAP are influencing EIS design and use.
8. Compare and contrast value chain and a supply chain.
9. How can cooperation between a company and its suppliers reduce inventory costs?
10. Discuss the reasons for ERP's inability to directly support decision making.
11. Discuss the major problems that could develop along the supply chain.

12. A major trend is toward connecting ERP software to the Web. Discuss the possible benefits of such a connection.

13. Discuss why EIS is moving toward a corporate portal.

14. Business intelligence and ERP software as we know them today cannot support frontline decisions. Why not?

❖ **EXERCISES**

1. Prepare a diagram showing the supply chains of (a) a toy manufacturer, (b) a PC manufacturer, and (c) a university. Clearly show the major components.

2. A. Paller described an EIS as being like the displays in an airplane cockpit. Because most of us are not airplane pilots, we can use the analogy of the gauges and indicator lights on a car dashboard. Explain the analogy between an airplane cockpit or an automobile dashboard and EIS in terms of its use and effect on an organization.

3. Three surprising benefits of enterprise systems are that, as one is developed, an organization settles on common terminology for its information, a common format is used, and a common depository of data is developed (now called a data warehouse). How might this happen otherwise? Consider several organizations with which you are affiliated. How might common terminology and a data warehouse be helpful to you? What disadvantages might there be? Explain.

4. Choose a real-world information scanning and reporting problem for which Pilot Decision Support Suite might be appropriate. Implement a prototype EIS in Pilot Decision Support Suite.

5. There are documented cases in the literature of EIS development strictly in spreadsheet packages. Develop a small EIS in Excel (or another spreadsheet). Use the U.S. Census data described in the exercises in Chapter 4.

6. Compare and contrast the capabilities of Web servers and browsers to those of the data server and of an EIS client. Develop a screen in HTML that could be used in an EIS deployed over a corporate intranet. Develop a second screen that represents drill down from the first screen and use a hypertext link to do the drill down. Optionally, use Java.

7. Compare the benefits described in DSS in Focus 8.1 and the benefit categories shown in Table W8.1 on this book's Web site (www.prenhall.com/turban). Do the benefit groupings make sense? Why or why not? Do you think that "Greater responsiveness to changing customer needs" belongs under *Economy?* Should the category title *Economy* be changed to *Productivity?* If you replace *Economy* with the categories "Supports reengineering and strategic efforts," "Productivity," and "Decision making," how would you regroup the benefits within each category?

8. Why are EIS diffusing down to lower levels of management? How does this affect an organization's ability to provide the same level of support to all levels of management using an EIS? Explain.

9. Consider the supply chain for a textbook. Explain how ERP could help Prentice Hall, the publisher of this book. Identify some major decisions that need to be made with respect to textbook production and distribution and explain what type of DSS could be useful and how it could be integrated with an ERP.

❖ GROUP PROJECTS

1. Develop an EIS in a Windows-based database system (such as Access) to access critical census data (assume that it changes regularly). Highlight exceptional cases in color. Use regression and forecasting models. Link the data to a spreadsheet (such as Excel) containing the models. Describe the system in a report and highlight the difficulties encountered.

2. Divide the class into groups and assign each group to an ERP vendor (Oracle, SAP, Peoplesoft, and so on). Each group will investigate what business intelligence capabilities, including EIS, are incorporated into the core ERP (such as SAP R/3). Have the groups compare results and prepare a unified report.

❖ INTERNET EXERCISES

1. Access the Web sites of www.sap.com, www.oracle.com, and www.peoplesoft.com and find out how they incorporate business intelligence and EIS in their offerings.

2. EIS is related to data warehousing and OLAP. Find recent articles on this relationship (you can try www.cio.com for the search). Also, check vendor Web sites such as www.SAS.com. Contact the SAS Institute and identify their product strategy regarding EIS, data warehousing, and OLAP. Access Cognos's Web site, download a demo of one of their EIS products, and try it. Report your experience to the class.

3. Access the Data Warehousing Institute's Web site (www.dw-institute.org) and identify current database trends, data warehousing, data mining, multitiered architectures, client/server architecture, and OLAP specifically as they relate to EIS. Report your findings.

4. Access the Web sites of several EIS software vendors. Compare their products. What are their latest product offerings? What hardware platforms do they promote for their products? Which companies provide products that are Web-ready? Describe their capabilities. Which companies provide collaborative computing (GSS) capabilities?

5. Access the BusinessObjects Web site (www.businessobjects.com) and download and try BusinessQuery for Excel. Describe your experience. Do the same for the currently available downloadable demo version of BusinessObjects.

6. Access www.supply-chain.com, www.cio.com, and other sources and find the recent developments that relate to SCM and decision making.

7. Prepare a presentation of state-of-the-art corporate portals. Start with www.microstrategy.com and www.oracle.com and point out the capabilities and benefits.

8. Access www.acxiom.com, www.epiphay.com, www.ncr.com, www.hyperion.com, and www.ptc.com. Identify their frontline system initiatives.

KNOWLEDGE MANAGEMENT[1]

Knowledge management, while conceptually ancient, is a relatively new form of collaborative computing. The goal of knowledge management is to capture, store, maintain, and deliver useful knowledge in a meaningful form to anyone who needs it anyplace and anytime within an organization. Basically, knowledge management is collaboration at the organization level. Knowledge management has the potential to revolutionize the way we collaborate and use computing, as discussed in the following sections:

9.1 OPENING VIGNETTE: KNOWLEDGE MANAGEMENT GIVES MITRE A SHARPER EDGE[2]

INTRODUCTION

At the Mitre Corporation, a federally funded research and development center (in Bedford, MA, and McLean, VA), the Mitre information infrastructure (MII) has become a single information system that knows everything important at Mitre. MII is a

---

[1]Portions of this chapter were contributed by Babita Gupta, California State University—Monterey Bay; Lakshmi S. Iyer, University of North Carolina—Greensboro; Richard McCarthy, Central Connecticut State University; and Patrick Simpkins, NASA.
[2]Adapted from T. Field, "Common Knowledge," *CIO,* Feb. 1, 1999, pp. 50–52.

Web-based knowledge repository that stores information about every significant task performed and can make it available to any employee anywhere. MII is a *knowledge management system (KMS)*.

THE MITRE CORPORATION

In 1958 Mitre was incorporated to integrate the U.S. Air Force's Semi-Automatic Ground Environment (SAGE) air defense system. Mitre's mission is to *use leading-edge technology to develop innovative, practical improvements for its customers' systems and processes.* Mitre's four primary customers are the Department of Defense, the Federal Aviation Administration, the U.S. intelligence community, and the Internal Revenue Service. Though Mitre is at the cutting edge of technology solutions, in 1996, when Victor A. DeMarines took over its presidency, he believed that Mitre did not effectively leverage its expertise as well it could.

PROJECT INITIATION

In 1996 Mitre had a culture of silos, each with its own pocket of knowledge. These silos functioned like rivals, and they compromised Mitre's abilities. Expertise at Mitre was static, a commodity closely held within each of the company's three independent business units. No one even knew who Mitre's in-house experts were, or how to find them and share their knowledge. DeMarines intended to develop a *culture of sharing*. To create and sustain such a culture shift, Mitre needed an information architecture that would not just enable but would also *encourage* sharing. In February 1997 DeMarines approached Andrea Weiss, the company's CIO. Weiss knew that Mitre was structured in such a way that you needed to "know someone who knew someone who knew who was expert in what" to get answers to questions. DeMarines charged Weiss with developing an information system that would move away from this culture and allow Mitre executives to, as Weiss says, "know what we know, use what we know and bring it all to bear on all of our customers' jobs."

MII HISTORY AND INITIAL FEATURES

MII was conceived in 1993 when Mitre technologists were developing a wide area information system. Mitre engineers built a rudimentary corporate intranet in 1994. By 1995 all employees had access to an intranet that included the employee directory, administrative policies, and corporate information. In 1997 Weiss wanted to enrich this basic network with information essential to employees' everyday work, from the mundane to the creative. Weiss and her team met with senior managers and others to develop a set of business requirements (knowledge to incorporate) including the following:

- *A corporate directory:* includes personal profiles, contact information, resumes, and publications.
- *A lessons learned library:* the systems engineering process library (SEPL) captures the best practices of internal software systems; the risk assessment and management program (RAMP) collects lessons learned from *all* Mitre projects.
- *Improved efficiency reports:* MII handles *all* HR documents.
- *Facility-scheduling system:* allows users to locate, schedule, and set up meetings.

SELLING THE SYSTEM

One critical issue in deploying a knowledge management system is to determine how to motivate employees to contribute their knowledge and encourage them to use it. Two approaches were taken to convince users to buy into the system. DeMarines (by then the CEO) was the executive sponsor. He clearly indicated often that he expected people to use MII. Weiss made MII attractive to use. She initially put tedious paperwork and processes online (like the company phone book—eventually only the online version was available; the same was true for time cards, expense sheets, and technical information). As the prototyping development process was performed, real expertise eventually came online, and MII became a knowledge management system.

CULTURE SHIFT

As MII was phased in, more and more employees started to use it. People became more aware of other projects that they were not actively involved in but in which they had some expertise, and people started to collaborate more. Their approach to work changed. MII has transformed Mitre's culture. Globally, all 63 of Mitre's sites are connected to MII. More than 4,000 employees interact with the system daily. MII's primary Web servers record up to 10 million transactions per month.

CONCLUSIONS

Although Mitre's size and budget are government-restricted, MII allows Mitre to deliver more work faster to its customers. Since 1995 Mitre has invested $7.19 million in the system, netting an ROI of $54.91 million in reduced operating costs and improved productivity. As stated in Chapter 6, success breeds success. Internally, each of Mitre's business units has programs underway to further leverage MII company-wide. Experts can easily be identified, and their expertise is fluid, shared not only within the company but also with Mitre's customers. "MII is part of delivering the company," DeMarines says. "Before we had MII, we were very successful. Now we're still very successful, and we bring the rest of the company's resources to bear with every customer." Weiss, who met DeMarines' initial challenge, feels the system has embodied Mitre's mission statement, "Solutions that make a difference," which according to Weiss has become "the way of life for us."

❖ QUESTIONS FOR THE OPENING VIGNETTE

1. How did Mitre's goal of being "the organization that makes a difference" for their customers and their mission of using leading-edge technology to develop innovative, practical improvements for its customers' systems and processes lead to development of the MII?
2. How does Mitre view knowledge (intellectual) assets?
3. What does leveraging expertise mean? How did Mitre do this? Explain how this relates to the high return on investment.
4. Describe the benefits of the MII knowledge management system.
5. Explain the meaning of transformation of culture as occurred at Mitre.
6. Explain how the Internet and Web technology enabled MII.

9.2 INTRODUCTION TO KNOWLEDGE MANAGEMENT

Mitre Corporation developed the MII knowledge management system to leverage its **intellectual assets.** They were structured organizationally in a way that encouraged little knowledge sharing, and what little sharing there was generally took place in an unsystematic, informal way. The Mitre organizational culture changed as the knowledge management system was deployed. The MII system gathers, catalogs, stores, and maintains knowledge. It delivers appropriate solutions to anyone, anywhere in the world, who might need them.

All organizations use knowledge in many ways at every level. In this sense, knowledge management (KM) *is not* new. The formal acknowledgment of knowledge as an intellectual asset to be created, captured, and utilized deliberately to a company's advantage *is* new, as is the use of modern technology to do so. Successful managers have always recognized and used intellectual assets and recognized their value. But such efforts were not systematic, nor did they ensure that knowledge gained was shared and dispersed appropriately for maximum organizational benefit.

Knowledge management has been practiced since ancient times. Oral traditions were passed from generation to generation. When writing was invented, oral traditions were written down and codified into histories and laws. Libraries stored tablets, then scrolls, and then books, which contained the important knowledge of the times.

Early in the industrial era, organizations improved their efficiency, effectiveness, and hence their competitive edge, by automating manual labor and reducing redundancy. Now, in the *age of the knowledge worker,* many organizations have gone through massive restructuring to eliminate redundant workers and jobs. Sometimes these efforts are swept up into the ideas of business process reengineering. Downsizing resulted in major losses, sometimes irreplaceable, of core knowledge assets as employees walked out the door with their knowledge. (Often firms hire employees back as consultants at a significantly higher cost.) The effects of such knowledge dissipation are stunted innovation, teamwork, and productivity.

In the 1990s alone, the nature of competition changed radically because of increased global connectivity, distributed expertise, and shorter product development cycles. Organizations are streamlining their processes and exploring ways of working smarter through improved collaboration and communication. As we continue to migrate toward a knowledge-based economy, knowledge management has emerged as a methodology for capturing and managing the intellectual assets of an organization as a key to sustaining competitive advantage. Knowledge management is a new strategic initiative that is changing the paradigm of information systems from one of processing data and providing information to one of harvesting and capitalizing on the knowledge of an entire organization, ranging from expertise in individuals' heads to documented material.

Knowledge management is a process that helps organizations identify, select, organize, disseminate, and transfer important information and expertise that are part of the organizational memory that typically resides within the organization in an unstructured manner. This enables effective and efficient problem solving, dynamic learning, strategic planning, and decision making. Knowledge management focuses on identifying knowledge, explicating it in a way so that it can be shared in a formal manner, and thus reusing it.

Through a supportive organizational climate, ideally through good knowledge management, an organization can bring its entire organizational memory and knowledge to bear on any problem anywhere in the world and at anytime. *Knowledge, as a form of capital, must be exchangeable among persons, and it must be able to grow.* Knowledge about how problems are solved can be captured so that knowledge management can promote organizational learning, leading to further knowledge creation. Organizations are making major long-term investments in knowledge management. Worldwide spending on knowledge management services is expected to grow from about $1.8 trillion in 1999 to more than $8 trillion by 2003 (Dyer, 2000). Obviously, managing knowledge is important (see DSS in Focus 9.1).

Knowledge management requires a major transformation in organizational culture to create a desire to share (give and receive) (see DSS in Focus 9.2 and 9.3), the development of methods that ensure that knowledge bases are kept current and relevant, and

---

DSS IN FOCUS 9.1

THE IMPORTANCE OF MANAGING KNOWLEDGE

Knowledge or intellectual capital management is critically important because

- Intellectual capital is a firm's only appreciable asset. Most assets depreciate from the day of acquisition.
- Knowledge work is increasing, not decreasing. The service economy is growing, and so intellectual capital is growing in importance.
- Employees with the most intellectual capital have become volunteers because the best ones are relatively portable.

- Many managers ignore intellectual capital and lose out on the benefits of its capture and use.
- Employees with the most intellectual capital are often the least appreciated.
- Many current investments in intellectual capital are misfocused (e.g., knowledge is mismanaged).

Source: Adapted from Ulrich (1998).

DSS IN FOCUS 9.2

HOW TO ENCOURAGE KNOWLEDGE SHARING

Though knowledge sharing not difficult, many people do not understand what it is all about, do not see the value in it for their organization, or have been discouraged by organizational culture barriers. Here are some tips on how to convince people to share knowledge.

- Educate people on the value of knowledge.
- Revamp reward and recognition systems.
- Show people what knowledge sharing looks like.

- Let people know it's alright to make a mistake and not know something.
- Make knowledge sharing a requirement of the job.
- Educate people about the kinds of knowledge that are valuable and how they can be used.
- Make the technology work for people; don't expect the people to work for the technology.

Source: Adapted from Holloway (2000).

DSS IN FOCUS 9.3

WHY PEOPLE DON'T SHARE KNOWLEDGE

Even though it can cripple an organization, sometimes people refuse to share what they know. Usually organizational culture barriers create this situation. Here are some reasons of why people hoard their knowledge.

- People believe that knowledge is power and that hoarding it guarantees job security.
- People won't get credit for sharing knowledge or won't be able to *own* it anymore.
- People don't have time to share knowledge.

- People are afraid of making mistakes and looking bad or being reprimanded.
- The technology for sharing knowledge does not really meet their needs.
- People don't know how much they know.
- People don't realize that their knowledge is valuable to the organization.
- People don't know how to share their knowledge.

Source: Adapted from Holloway (2000).

a commitment at all levels of a firm for it to succeed. There are as many techniques for implementing knowledge management as there are definitions of knowledge management. We now explore knowledge management and its impact on organization.

9.3 KNOWLEDGE

KNOWLEDGE

Before we discuss knowledge management, we must first define knowledge and make a distinction among data, information, and knowledge in the IS context (Figure 9.1). Whereas data are a collection of facts, measurements, and statistics, information is defined as organized or processed data that are timely (i.e., inferences from the data are drawn within the time frame of applicability) and accurate (i.e., with reference to the original data) (McFadden et al., 1998; Watson, 1998). **Knowledge** is information that is *contextual, relevant,* and *actionable.* Therefore, the implication is that knowledge has strong experiential and reflective elements that distinguish it from information in a given context. Having knowledge implies that it can be exercised to solve a problem, whereas having information does not carry the same connotation. An ability to act is an integral part of being knowledgeable. For example, two people in the same context with the same information may not have the same ability to use the information to the same degree of success. Hence there is a difference in the human capability to add value through context. The differences in ability may be due to different experiences, different training, different perspectives, or other differences.

While data, information, and knowledge can all be viewed as assets of an organization, knowledge provides a higher level of meaning about data and information. It conveys *meaning,* and hence tends to be much more valuable, yet more ephemeral.

There is a vast amount of literature about what knowledge and knowing mean in terms of epistemology, social sciences, philosophy, and psychology. Although the business perspective is much more pragmatic, there is no uniform definition or consensus on what knowledge and knowledge management specifically mean. See Polanyi (1958, 1966) for the history of knowledge and epistemology.

FIGURE 9.1 DATA, INFORMATION, AND KNOWLEDGE

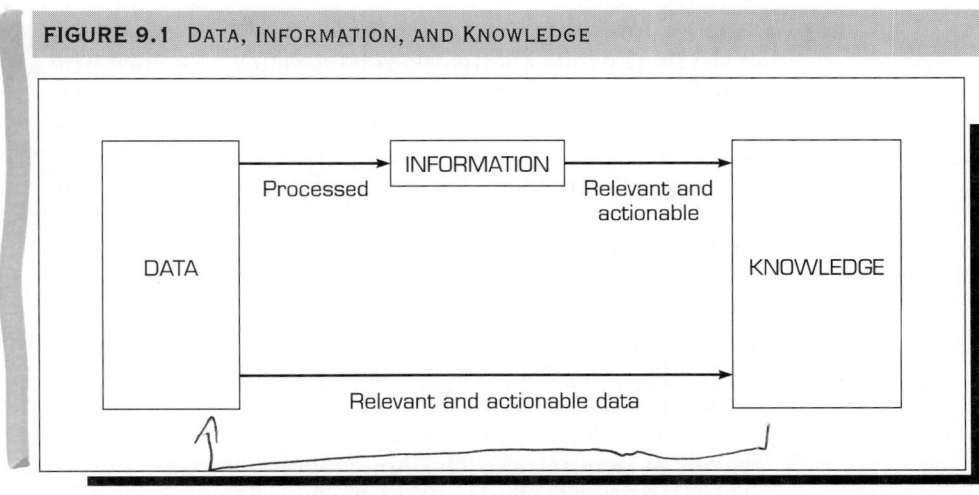

Whereas information is structured, knowledge is fuzzy and loosely coupled. Information is valuable only if it can be understood within a context which itself requires knowledge of the organizational practices and business environment. Information is valid in an isolated context, whereas knowledge is valid only if it has a shared context. Also, while information as a resource is not always valuable (i.e., information overload can distract from the important), knowledge as a resource is valuable because it focuses attention back toward what is important (McFadden et al., 1998). Information can be rendered useless or be misused if the user has a paucity of understanding, whereas knowledge implies implicit understanding and experience that can discriminate between its use and misuse. Knowledge is still valuable (or reusable) after a lapse of time and has historical relevance, while the value of information tends to decline with time without preservation of the context in which it was acquired. Over time, information accumulates, while knowledge evolves. Knowledge is *dynamic* in nature.

KNOWLEDGE TYPES AND COMPONENTS

Holsapple and Whinston (1996) define six types of knowledge that knowledge management applications can contain. These include descriptive, procedural, reasoning, linguistic, presentation, and assimilative knowledge. *Descriptive knowledge* is information about the past, present, future, or hypothetical states of relevance concerned with *knowing what. Procedural knowledge* is concerned with *knowing how* and specifies step-by-step procedures for how tasks are accomplished. *Reasoning knowledge* is concerned with *knowing why,* evaluating conclusions that are valid for a set of circumstances. *Presentation knowledge* facilitates communication. It is concerned with the method of delivery of knowledge. *Linguistic knowledge* interprets communication once it has been received. *Assimilative knowledge* helps to maintain the knowledge base by improving on existing knowledge. It is important to distinguish among knowledge types in order to understand how to act on knowledge. The first three types are the basic knowledge that an organization has in terms of performing its business processes. The latter three provide communicating, understanding, and learning of knowledge in order to use it. Different methods and means of storing each kind of knowledge are appropriate, as well as the use of each.

Knowledge includes a level of understanding that a human attributes to information. We focus on the aspects of knowledge that help us understand how it is used in an organization. Davenport and Prusak (1998) define knowledge as a fluid mix of framed experience, values, contextual information, and expert insight that provides a framework for evaluating and incorporating new experiences and information. Clarke (1998) defines knowledge as the understanding of why and how something works. Davenport et al. (1998) define knowledge as information combined with experience, context, interpretation, and reflection.

Knowledge has also been classified as *advantaged knowledge,* which can be described as the knowledge that can provide competitive advantage; *base knowledge* as knowledge that is integral to an organization, providing it with short-term advantages (e.g., best practices); and *trivial knowledge* as knowledge that has no major impact on the organization (Clarke, 1998). **Intellectual capital** is another term for knowledge. Ulrich (1998) defines intellectual capital as the competence of an individual and the commitment of the individual to contribute to the organization's goals (intellectual capital = competence × commitment). Alavi and Leidner (1999) believe that knowledge is a justified personal belief that increases an individual's capacity to take action. They use Churchman's idea that "knowledge resides in the user and not in the collection of information." Action refers to physical skills and competencies, cognitive or intellectual activity, or both (Gray, 1999). We adopt the elegant knowledge definition of O'Dell et al. (1998): **knowledge** is *information in action.*

Davenport and Prusak (1998) claim that knowledge is derived from information as information is derived from data. According to them, information is converted to knowledge through the process of comparison, connection (understanding relations), conversation (uncovering what others think about the same information), and consequences (how information affects decisions). We list the key components of knowledge in DSS in Focus 9.4.

Most organizations already have a massive reservoir of knowledge in a wide variety of organizational processes, best practices, know-how, policy manuals, customer trust, MIS, culture, and norms. However, this knowledge is usually diffused and mostly unrecognized. Often, organizational culture itself prevents people from sharing and disseminating their know-how in an effort to hold onto individual powerbases and viability, as was true at Mitre. Useful (or better) knowledge is a critical asset to an organization, as it is closer to action than data or information (Marshall, 1997; Davenport and Prusak, 1998).

TACIT AND EXPLICIT KNOWLEDGE

Polanyi (1958) first conceptualized and distinguished between an organization's tacit knowledge and explicit knowledge. **Tacit knowledge** is usually in the domain of subjective, cognitive, and experiential learning, whereas **explicit knowledge** deals more with objective, rational, and technical knowledge (data, policies, procedures, software, documents, and so on) and is highly personal and hard to formalize (Nonaka and Takeuchi, 1995).

Explicit knowledge is the policies, procedural guides, white papers, reports, designs, products, strategies, goals, mission, and core competencies of the enterprise and the information technology infrastructure—knowledge that has been codified (documented) in a form that can be distributed to others without requiring interpersonal interaction or transformed into a process or strategy. For example, a description of how to process a job application is documented in a firm's HR policy manual.

Tacit knowledge is the cumulative store of the experiences, mental maps, insights, acumen, expertise, know-how, trade secrets, skills set, understanding, and learning that an organization has, as well as the organizational culture that has embedded in it the past and present experiences of its people, processes, and values. Tacit knowledge, also referred to as embedded knowledge (Badaracco, 1991; Madhaven and Grover, 1998), is usually localized either within the brain of an individual or embedded in the group interactions within a department or branch office. Tacit knowledge typically involves expertise or high-level skills. It is diffused, unstructured, without tangible form, and

---

DSS IN FOCUS 9.4

THE KEY COMPONENTS OF KNOWLEDGE

Knowledge develops over time with experience, which makes connections among new situations and events in context. Knowledge can be characterized by

- *Ground truth:* This is the truth gained from experience, not theory; this is what works in practice.
- *Complexity:* Complex situations indicate complex approaches to solving them. Sometimes a lack of knowledge makes a problem complex.

- *Judgment:* Puts knowledge into an actionable context. Knowledge evolves and may no longer apply to the situation that it originally did.
- *Heuristics (rules of thumb) and intuition:* Guides to action, shortcuts, and simplifications for problem solving.
- *Values and beliefs:* Different people have different problem-solving frames.

Source: Adapted from Davenport and Prusak (1998).

therefore difficult to codify. Polanyi (1966) suggests that it is difficult to put tacit knowledge into words. For example, directions for how to ride a bicycle would be difficult to document explicitly, and thus are tacit. Successful transfer or sharing of tacit knowledge usually takes place through associations, internships, apprenticeships, conversations, other means of social and interpersonal interactions, or even through simulations (e.g., see Robin, 2000). Nonaka and Takeuchi (1995) claim that intangibles like insights, intuitions, hunches, gut feelings, values, images, metaphors, and analogies are the often overlooked assets of organizations. Harvesting this intangible asset can be critical to a firm's bottom line and its ability to meet its goals.

Historically, MIS has focused on capturing, storing, managing, and reporting explicit knowledge. Organizations now recognize the need to integrate both types of knowledge.

Leonard and Sensiper (1998) suggest that most knowledge falls between the extremes of tacit and explicit. Some elements (explicit) are objective/rational and others (tacit) are subjective/experiential and created in the "here and now." However, they go on to say that tacit does not mean that such knowledge cannot be codified.

Unlike other assets, knowledge has the following characteristics (Gray, 1999):

- *Extraordinary leverage and increasing returns.* Knowledge is not subject to diminishing returns. When it is used, it is not consumed. And its consumers can add to it, thus increasing its value. It can also improve over time.
- *Fragmentation, leakage, and the need to refresh.* As knowledge grows, it branches and fragments. Knowledge is dynamic; it is information in action. Thus, an organization must continually refresh its knowledge base to maintain it as a source of competitive advantage.
- *Uncertain value.* It is difficult to estimate the impact of an investment in knowledge.
- *Uncertain value of sharing.* Similarly, it is difficult to estimate the value of sharing knowledge, or even who will benefit most.

Organizations are just beginning to recognize, develop, and deploy specific methodologies and technologies to convert tacit knowledge to explicit knowledge. Knowledge can be codified: captured, stored, managed, disseminated, transmitted, used, and be acted on by others. This powerful concept has fueled the development of knowledge management methodologies, tools, and applications.

9.4 ORGANIZATIONAL LEARNING AND ORGANIZATIONAL MEMORY

Because knowledge management involves the intellectual assets and activities of an entire organization, it is important to define the concepts of organizational learning and organizational memory. In Chapter 7, we described the *group memory* concept as provided by a GSS. The basic idea is to capture what the group knows electronically and provide it on an as-needed basis. Knowledge management attempts to do this at an organizational level.

LEARNING

Lane and Lubatkin (1998) identified three methods of learning new external knowledge: passive, active, and interactive. *Passive learning* occurs when a firm acquires technical knowledge from sources such as training, seminars, and journals. *Active learning* occurs when a firm enhances its capabilities through benchmarking and competitor analysis. *Interactive learning* requires face-to-face interaction in order to assimilate tacit knowledge. They concluded that face-to-face interaction is necessary for interorganizational learning to take place. Knowledge repositories can overcome this deficit through their collaborative nature (see the Opening Vignette and the case applications).

Historically, organizations that do not adapt to changing business conditions (e.g., learn) fail. The average lifespan of a *Fortune* 500 firm is between 40 and 50 years (Hackbarth and Grover, 1999). So the cultivation of organizational memory is critical for a company to establish, grow, and nurture a learning organization, and to survive.

THE LEARNING ORGANIZATION

The term **learning organization** (DiBella, 1995) refers to an organization's capability for learning from past experience. Garvin (1993) describes the process of building a learning organization. Before a company can improve, it must first learn. And to learn, it must tackle three critical issues: (1) meaning (determining a vision of what the learning organization is to be); (2) management (determining how the firm is to work); and (3) measurement (assessing the rate and level of learning). He defines a learning organization as one that performs five main activities well: systematic problem solving, creative experimentation, learning from past experience, learning from the best practices of others, and transferring knowledge quickly and efficiently throughout the organization.

ORGANIZATIONAL MEMORY

A learning organization implies that there is an **organizational memory** and a means to save, represent, and share it. Estimates vary, but it is generally felt that only 10–20 percent of business data is actually used. Hackbarth and Grover (1999) divide organizational memory into six categories, which they called bins but we call wells because wells are water sources that are replenished in a very natural way and individuals can drink from them. They are

- *Individual wells.* These contain information about each individual in a meaningful form, including an individual's files and reports.
- *Information well.* These are formal information systems that contain data and information, for example, an MIS.
- *Culture well.* These are beliefs as described by Schein (1997, 1999); this information can be spread throughout the organization in either tacit or explicit form.
- *Transformation well.* This contains frequently occurring business processes.
- *Structural well.* This contains information about the organizational structure, both formal and informal.
- *Ecology well.* This is the physical structure of the organization.

Human intelligence can draw from these wells and add value by creating new knowledge. A knowledge management system can capture this new knowledge and make it available in its enhanced form by pouring it back into an appropriate well.

ORGANIZATIONAL LEARNING

Organizational learning is the development of new knowledge and insights that have the potential to influence behavior. It occurs when associations, cognitive systems, and memories are shared by members of an organization (Croasdell et al., 1997). Establishing a corporate memory is critical for success (e.g., Brooking, 1999; Hackbarth and Grover, 1999). Information technology must play a critical role in organizational learning, and management must place emphasis on this area to foster it (Andreu and Ciborra, 1996). (See DSS In Action 9.5.)

Since organizations are becoming more virtual in nature, it is important to determine how organizational learning can be performed effectively. Modern collaborative technologies can help in knowledge management initiatives, as is clear from the success of Xerox Corporation. Goodman and Darr (1998) describe how computer-aided systems can encourage individuals to contribute to learning systems and use contributions, thus accessing a knowledge repository in an effective manner. Nevis et al. (1995) characterize organizations as learning systems. They describe the organization learning process as three steps: (1) knowledge acquisition, (2) knowledge sharing, and (3) knowledge utilization. They describe seven learning orientations, one of which most firms tend to lean toward although they can often be characterized by several. Each orientation requires different methods and tools to enhance learning, and thus if a particular organization is not using one of them, it can enhance its organizational learning by focusing on that area. The orientations are as follows:

1. *Knowledge source.* The source of knowledge can be internal or external.
2. *Product-process focus.* Chrysler (see Case Application 9.1) was originally process-focused, specifically on functional areas, and switched to a process focus with the platform approach.
3. *Documentation mode.* Concerns how knowledge is stored and maintained: on paper, expert systems, databases, and so on, formally or informally.
4. *Dissemination mode.* Learning can evolve from a grass roots perspective or from a directive from the top. It can be structured or unstructured.

DSS IN ACTION 9.5

THE U.S. ARMY'S AFTER ACTION REVIEW (AAR)

The three hallmarks of an aggressively collaborative environment are the following:

- Users are encouraged to add to and take from the system.
- The quality of knowledge within the system is subject to ongoing review.
- The organization addresses individual compensation for participation in the system.

The U.S. Army is an aggressively collaborative culture. Soldiers need to communicate knowledge based on experience accurately in battle situations. Whenever the Army has a training event, it always conducts an after-action review (AAR). The AAR asks participants four basic questions: What was your plan? What happened? Why did that happen? What are you doing to fix it next time? This process works its way up to the top command. The AAR encourages participant buy-in and leadership involvement. In the 1980s the Army noticed that different units made the same mistakes during training. They formed the Center for Army Lessons Learned (CALL) to capture mistakes and solutions and make them available to the entire army. In this way, tacit knowledge can be distributed to those who did not experience the situation first-hand. The effectiveness of the AAR organizational learning approach was demonstrated by the Army in Haiti during a real deployment. While there, a CALL team incorporated lessons learned into 25 training vignettes that were shared with the next army division to go into action. The new division encountered 24 of the 25 situations described in the vignettes and was prepared to handle them. The AAR is a simple and very effective way to create a learning organization and an organizational memory in practice.

Source: Adapted from Robin (2000); and P. Glasser, "Armed with Intelligence," *CIO*, Aug. 1997, pp. 104–110.

5. *Learning focus.* Formal learning can be focused on what is currently being done or on how it is being done, thus creating general principles or methods.
6. *Value chain focus.* Concerns the specific core competencies and learning investments the firm has.
7. *Skill development focus.* The organization may focus on individuals or on groups.

Facilitating factors for organizational learning are a scanning imperative, a performance gap, concern for measurement, an experimental mind-set, a climate of openness, continuing education, operational variety, multiple advocates, involved leadership, and a systems perspective. Learning can be enhanced by focusing on the facilitating factors to enhance the environment and by recognizing and fostering the learning orientations that match the organizational culture. Organizational learning and memory depend less on technology than on the people issues we describe next.

ORGANIZATIONAL CULTURE

The ability of an organization to learn, develop memory, and share knowledge is dependent on its culture. *Culture* is a pattern of shared basic assumptions (Schein, 1997, 1999). Over time organizations learn what works and what doesn't work. As the lessons become second nature, they become part of the **organizational culture.** New employees learn the culture from their mentors along with know-how.

Generally when a technology project fails, it is because the technology does not match the organization's culture. This is especially true of knowledge management because it relies so heavily on individuals contributing knowledge to the repository (e.g., Sherif and Mandviwalla, 2000).

It is difficult to measure the impact of corporate culture on an organization. However, it has been established that a strong culture produces strong bottom-line results: net income, return on invested capital, and yearly increases in stock price (Hibbard, 1998). Buckman Laboratories measures culture impact by the sales of new products. Following Buckman's knowledge-sharing initiative in which knowledge sharing became part of the company's core values, sales of products less than 5 years old rose to 33 percent of total sales, up from 22 percent (Hibbard, 1998).

The key to success is to create an enterprise with a culture of continuous change where employees are not threatened by change but are encouraged by it because they believe it will improve their quality of life. This can be done with strong leadership on the part of executives and good internal marketing to future users (see the Opening Vignette). Generally, knowledge management success is dependent on cultural issues, which are addressed by managerial activities, not technology. For example, see DSS in Focus 9.6, which indicates that the reasons why people do not share knowledge are related to the organizational culture. During implementation of a knowledge management program, the organizational culture must shift to one of sharing (see the Opening Vignette). There are a number of different ways to do this, and most of them are directly related to the success and failure factors we discuss later. They include showing executive-level support and providing an incentive for employees to contribute their knowledge and use the system. For example, the system should be easy to use and provide usable knowledge. Employees who contribute knowledge should gain some recognition. Xerox provides recognition by attributing tips in its Eureka system to the author. The author is recognized for contributing and also as having expertise (which can be cataloged). Ideally, employees are rewarded financially for their contributions. Some firms simply indicate that contributing to the knowledge repository is part of the job description: no contribution implies a low raise. Another approach is to find strong champions willing to make

DSS IN FOCUS 9.6

WHY PEOPLE DON'T SHARE KNOWLEDGE

The main reasons why employees don't share knowledge include the following (note that only one is directly related to technology):

- Willing to share, but there is not enough time to do so
- No skill in knowledge management techniques
- Don't understand knowledge management and benefits

- Lack of appropriate technology
- No commitment from senior managers
- No funding for knowledge management
- Culture does not encourage knowledge sharing.

_____
Source: Adapted from Vaas (1999).

contributions and lead the way in getting others to join. This type of internal marketing is very effective; it can be contagious.

9.5 KNOWLEDGE MANAGEMENT

KNOWLEDGE MANAGEMENT

Knowledge management, through information, collaborative, and communication technologies, is the formalization of organizational memory and learning into an available resource, typically through a knowledge repository. Knowledge management is fundamentally the management of corporate knowledge and intellectual assets that can improve a range of organizational performance characteristics and add value by enabling an enterprise to act more intelligently (Wiig, 1993). Knowledge management enables the communication of knowledge from one person to another so that it can be used by the other person (Gray, 1999). The domains in which knowledge concepts are leveraged in organizations are listed in DSS in Focus 9.7. Alavi and Leidner (1999) determined that the most important knowledge domains concern customer service, business partners, internal operations, and marketing and sales. The least important one concerns knowledge about suppliers.

There is no one accepted definition of knowledge management (KM) because of the broad nature of knowledge. Essentially, knowledge management is a set of processes for transferring intellectual capital primarily residing as tacit knowledge in individuals, localized groups within the organization, and the geographically dispersed branch offices of an organization to value processes that lead to innovation, knowledge creation, and replenishment of the organization's core competency. (Figure 9.2 shows a model of how core competency is linked to explicit and tacit knowledge.) Knowledge management can be considered the art of transforming information and intellectual assets into enduring value for clients and people.

Primarily, knowledge management is a process of elicitation, transformation, and diffusion of knowledge throughout an enterprise so that it can be shared and thus reused. Knowledge management helps organizations find, select, organize, disseminate, and transfer important information and expertise necessary for activities such as problem solving, dynamic learning, strategic planning, and decision making (Gupta et al., 1999, 2000). Knowledge management transforms data and/or information into action-

DSS IN FOCUS 9.7

KNOWLEDGE CONCEPT DOMAINS

The top 10 domains in which knowledge concepts are leveraged in organizations through knowledge initiatives are

- Sharing knowledge and best practices
- Instilling responsibility for sharing knowledge
- Capturing and reusing best practices
- Embedding knowledge in products, services, and processes
- Producing knowledge as a product

- Driving knowledge generation for innovation
- Mapping networks of experts
- Building and mining customer knowledge bases
- Understanding and measuring the value of knowledge
- Leveraging intellectual assets.

Source: Xerox Corporation, *Top 10 Domains for Knowledge Management,* partly adapted from Barth (2000).

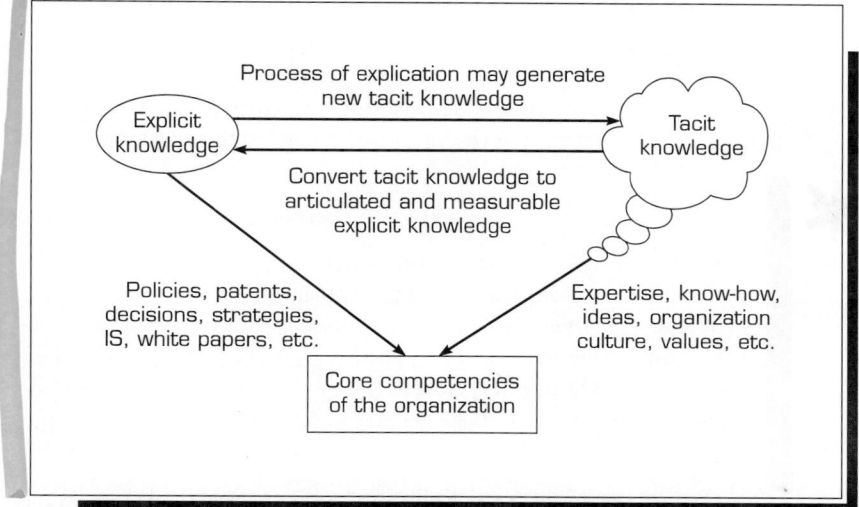

FIGURE 9.2 How Core Competency Is Linked to Explicit and Tacit Knowledge

able knowledge in a format that when it is made available can be utilized effectively and efficiently throughout an organization (Angus et al., 1998; Davis, 1998; Davenport et al., 1998; Leary, 1998; Skyrme, 1999).

Knowledge management is a set of processes for transferring the intellectual assets of the firm to value processes such as innovation and knowledge acquisition (Knapp, 1998); or, stated simply, knowledge management is making shared information useful (Bushko and Raynor, 1998).

THE GOALS AND OBJECTIVES OF KNOWLEDGE MANAGEMENT

Knowledge management involves a strategic commitment to improving the organization's effectiveness, as well as to improving its opportunity enhancement. Its goal is not cost control (Davis, 1998). The goal of knowledge management as a process is to improve the organization's ability to execute its core processes more efficiently.

Davenport et al. (1998) describe four broad objectives of knowledge management systems in practice:

1. Create knowledge repositories.
2. Improve knowledge access.
3. Enhance the knowledge environment.
4. Manage knowledge as an asset.

Most firms have one primary objective; for example, in the Opening Vignette Mitre attempted to enhance the knowledge environment. While doing so, it achieved the other three goals as well.

The key to knowledge management is capturing intellectual assets for the tangible benefit of the organization. As such, the imperatives of knowledge management are to

- Transform knowledge to add value to the processes and operations of the business
- Leverage knowledge strategic to business to accelerate growth and innovation
- Use knowledge to provide a competitive advantage for the business.

Finding the person with the knowledge one needs and then successfully transferring it from that person to another are difficult processes. The library metaphor is valuable for conceptualizing knowledge repository projects. The yellow pages metaphor helps in understanding the intent of knowledge access projects.

Knowledge management system processes are designed to manage

- Knowledge creation through learning
- Knowledge capture and explication
- Knowledge sharing and communication through collaboration
- Knowledge access
- Knowledge use and reuse
- Knowledge archiving.

THE CONCEPTUAL BASIS OF KNOWLEDGE MANAGEMENT

Essentially, knowledge management is rooted in the concepts of organizational learning and organizational memory. When members of an organization collaborate and communicate ideas, teach, and learn, knowledge is transformed and transferred from individual to individual. Managers realized that when organizational learning occurs, and when managers support this learning, it affects the bottom line in a positive way. Essentially, learning concepts have been modernized with technology. At this point in time, knowledge management's genuine success stories are demonstrating that with a supportive organizational culture, technology can be used to enhance organizational learning and knowledge management (O'Dell et al., 1998).

THE KNOWLEDGE REPOSITORY

Knowledge repositories are widely recognized as key components of most knowledge management systems. Once knowledge is captured, it must be stored in a knowledge repository. A **knowledge repository** is a collection of both internal and external knowledge. Informal knowledge repositories seek to capture tacit knowledge that resides in the minds of experts within the organization but has not been put in a structured format. Explicit knowledge has generally already been captured in some form, simply based on its definition. But sometimes explicit knowledge must be filtered, organized, and stored in a central knowledge repository (e.g., HR forms and instructions at the Mitre Corporation) to make them available efficiently and effectively. This is similar conceptually to the Arthur Andersen Subject Files created in the early 1960s. Recognized experts wrote white papers which were stored and indexed in the Subject Files for future reference. A word of caution is necessary here. A knowledge repository is neither a database, and nor a knowledge base in the strictest sense of the terms. A knowledge repository stores *knowledge,* which has very different characteristics (Section 9.3).

Capturing knowledge is the objective of a knowledge repository. The structure of the repository is highly dependent on the kinds of knowledge stored. The repository can range from simply a list of frequently asked (and obscure) questions and solutions to a listing of individuals with their expertise and contact information, to detailed best practices for a large organization.

The Chevron approach of recognizing four levels of best practices makes sense. They include (1) a good idea not yet proven but one that makes intuitive sense; (2) a good practice, an implemented technique, methodology, a procedure, or a process that has improved business results; (3) a local best practice, a best approach for all or a large part of the organization based on analyzing hard data; and (4) an industry best practice, similar to item 3 but using hard data from industry (O'Dell et al., 1998).

Davenport et al. (1998) describe three basic types of repositories found in practice:

- *External knowledge,* such as competitive intelligence, which generally needs explanations and interpretation.
- *Structured internal knowledge,* such as research reports, presentations, and marketing materials. These are mostly explicit knowledge with some tacit knowledge.
- *Informal internal knowledge,* such as discussion databases, help desk repositories, and shared information databases. This is tacit knowledge in the minds of people and can be exchanged via collaborative technologies, face-to-face meetings, or formal knowledge management systems.

KNOWLEDGE MANAGEMENT ACTIVITIES

Knowledge management consists of four basic functions: externalization, internalization, intermediation, and cognition (Frappaolo, 1998).

- *Externalization* is capturing knowledge in an external repository and organizing it by some framework in an effort to discover similar knowledge. Technologies that support externalization are imaging systems, databases, workflow technologies, document management systems using clustering techniques, and so on.
- *Internalization* is the process of identifying knowledge, usually explicit, relevant to a particular user's needs. It involves mapping a particular problem, situation, or point of interest against the body of knowledge already captured through externalization.
- *Intermediation* is similar to the brokering process for matching a knowledge seeker with the best source of knowledge (usually tacit) by tracking the experience and interest of individuals and groups of individuals. Some technologies that facilitate this process are groupware, intranets, workflow, and document management systems.
- *Cognition* applies the knowledge exchanged by the preceding three processes. This is probably the knowledge management component that is the most difficult to automate because it relies on human cognition to recognize where and how knowledge can be used. Few technologies can support cognition.

Figure 9.3 shows the integration of the elements of an organization through a knowledge management system. In terms of the framework the tenets of knowledge, a knowledge management system in an organization should encompass the following features (Allee, 1997):

1. *Creating a knowledge culture.* Knowledge management, at its core, has a strong human component. An organization's knowledge management strategy cannot be successful unless the organization has developed a trusting knowledge culture that emphasizes the role and value of knowledge in day-to-day business decisions and enterprises. The culture must be geared toward rewarding innovation, learning, experimentation, scrutiny, and reflection.

2. *Capturing knowledge.* All actions without exception culminate in knowledge (Bhagavad Gita, III:33). However, the problem is usually in its realization and capture. An organization is constantly involved in accomplishing something, right from its operational activities to its strategic missions. In the process, it generates data, information, inferences, decisions, policies, markets, and so on. Knowledge management must incorporate the process of sifting through this maze of activities to identify, isolate, and capture the core knowledge that drives and adds value to this activity. This core knowledge can reside in an individual, processes, policies, parameters, specifications, and/or interactions.

3. *Knowledge generation.* A decision maker rarely, if ever, makes a decision in isolation (Chapters 2 and 7). People rely on other people considered knowledgeable to aid in their decision-making process. The knowledge generation process is geared not just toward including people who are known to have the needed knowledge but also toward identifying and including people who are instrumental in creating new ideas and synthesizing disparate disciplines. Another key aspect is the ability to put to use the new creations, the knowledge and the innovations, for the business' advantage.

FIGURE 9.3 INTEGRATION OF ORGANIZATIONAL ELEMENTS THROUGH A KNOWLEDGE MANAGEMENT SYSTEM

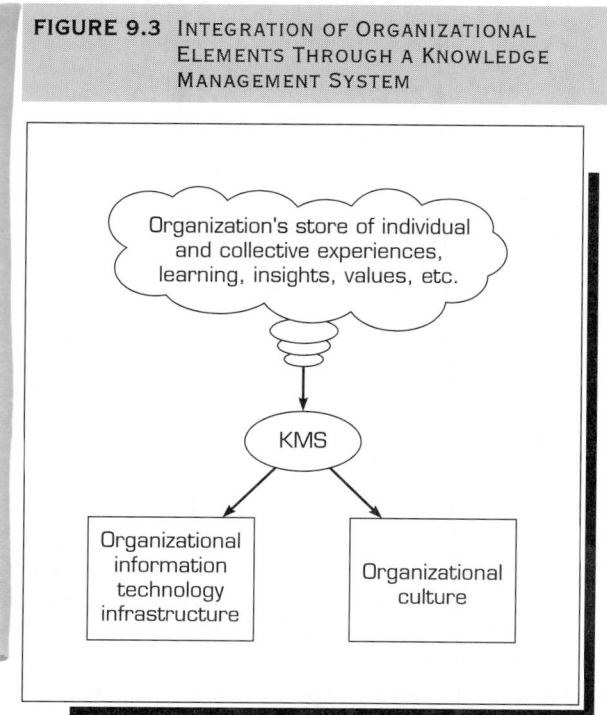

4. *Knowledge explication (and digitization).* The fuzzy nature of tacit knowledge suggests that most of it may never be explicated. However, much organizational tacit knowledge could be of tremendous benefit if it were in a form that facilitates convenient knowledge exchange. The knowledge explication process refers to the process of identifying who has the knowledge, who needs it, about what, in what form, when, and transforming it into a form that can be used by others. Explicated knowledge is knowledge that someone else can interpret and use in their own context. It is important for the process of explication to preserve the original context within which the knowledge was acquired or created, otherwise it will merely result in the duplication of a set of actions without the overarching meaning and interpretation that make them unique and valuable. Note that not all explicated knowledge can be digitized. For example, apprenticeships provide opportunities for individuals to gain knowledge by association through unstructured interactions.

5. *Knowledge sharing and reuse.* Access to knowledge and its seamless transfer to individuals is the key aspect of knowledge management. Explicated and digitized knowledge must have the right technology for it to be dispersed, as well as for the sharing of nondigitized knowledge. Sharing of knowledge can be facilitated through shared language and vocabulary and through the sharing of collective narratives (Nahapiet and Ghoshal, 1998). The emergence of shared narratives within a community allows the creation and transfer of new interpretations. (Chapter 2). This facilitates the combination of different forms of knowledge including that which is largely tacit. Knowledge reuse is similar to software reuse as discussed in Chapter 6. Hughes Space & Communications recognized the need to reuse knowledge in developing spacecraft, saving an estimated $7 million to $25 million per spacecraft (O'Dell et al., 1998) (see DSS in Action 9.8).

6. *Knowledge renewal.* One of the distinguishing features of knowledge is that it is actionable and dynamic. Like a living organism, it evolves with continual use. Decision makers should be able to adapt this evolved knowledge into new contexts to ease organizational stresses. If it is not treated as dynamic but as an object to be created and managed (and archived), knowledge cannot provide strategic benefits. Then it will be in danger of becoming a static entity with little or no relevance to organizational goals or renewal in the long-term. Fahey and Prusak (1998) discuss this in terms of the perspective of knowledge *flow* as opposed to knowledge *stock*.

The knowledge management process must have a methodology to determine if the explicated knowledge is to be free-flowing. In other words, is it to be shared with all, independent of the individual or group that contributed it? Or is there to be a selective sharing process primarily through involvement of the owner(s) with the sharing based on a unit of exchange (monetary, new knowledge, labor, and so on)? The former process is designed to promote knowledge reuse, while the latter promotes knowledge regeneration through an interactive knowledge exchange.

It may be imprudent to attempt a process that provides access to all knowledge to everyone in the organization because access to knowledge depends on the following factors:

1. The level of rarity determines the relevance of the knowledge to the receiver.
2. The level of complexity determines the process of transferring knowledge to the receiver.
3. The level of effort expended by the owner(s) in acquiring the knowledge in the first place determines their willingness to share it with the receivers.

DSS IN ACTION 9.8

KNOWLEDGE MANAGEMENT PREVENTS REPEATING THE ERRORS OF THE PAST

Knowledge management can keep us from repeating the errors of the past. By capturing best practices, and especially solutions to problems, similar situations can be dealt with efficiently and effectively anywhere in the world. In the past, Xerox Corporation shared stories with service technicians, but only in small groups; and their service manuals were very much out of date. Technicians generally improvised in the field, and there was no mechanism for sharing solutions until Eureka was deployed. Its effectiveness was demonstrated when Xerox had a situation involving a leading copier that developed intermittent failures all over the world. Xerox was unable to identify the source of the problem and had already replaced six of the machines. Another copier failure occurred in Rio de Janeiro, where a replacement would cost about $40,000, not to mention the loss of customer goodwill. Gilles Robert, a service technician at Xerox Canada in Montreal had traced the problem to a 50-cent fuse holder that had a tendency to oxidize and needed to be swabbed with alcohol every

so often. He had posted the tip on Eureka, the Xerox knowledge management system for copier service technicians. As the copier was failing in Rio, Eureka was just coming online in Brazil in Portuguese. The engineers there mentioned the problem, and Eureka provided the solution.

Technicians are motivated to submit tips to Eureka because they achieve personal recognition. Each tip has an author's name published with it. By early 2000, Eureka contained nearly 5,000 tips. Xerox has deployed this system to over 44,000 technicians worldwide. One of Eureka's guiding principles is, "We should never create the same solution twice. If a solution already exists, it should be used rather than recreating a new solution. In addition, we should focus on continuously improving existing solutions." Eureka works! For another example how to avoid repeating past mistakes, see Case Application 9.1.

Source: Partly adapted from Barth (2000) and Moore (1999).

All these factors affect the cost of knowledge sharing, in terms of both financial and social interactions and relationships.

CYCLIC MODEL OF KNOWLEDGE MANAGEMENT

Essentially, a deployed knowledge management system follows the six simple steps listed below in a cyclic fashion (Figure 9.4). The reason for the cycle is that knowledge is refined over time and is dynamic. A good knowledge management system is never finished because, over time, the environment changes and the knowledge must be updated to reflect the changes (see Case Application 9.1 for Chrysler's view on this).

1. *Create knowledge.* Knowledge is created as people determine new ways of doing things or develop know-how. Sometimes external knowledge is brought in.
2. *Capture knowledge.* New knowledge must be identified as valuable and be represented in a reasonable way.
3. *Refine knowledge.* New knowledge must be placed in context so that it is actionable. This is where human insights (tacit qualities) must be captured along with explicit facts.
4. *Store knowledge.* Useful knowledge must then be stored in a reasonable format in a knowledge repository so that others in the organization can access it.
5. *Manage knowledge.* Like a library, knowledge must be kept current. It must be reviewed to verify that it is relevant and accurate.
6. *Disseminate knowledge.* Knowledge must be made available in a useful format to anyone in the organization who needs it anywhere and anytime.

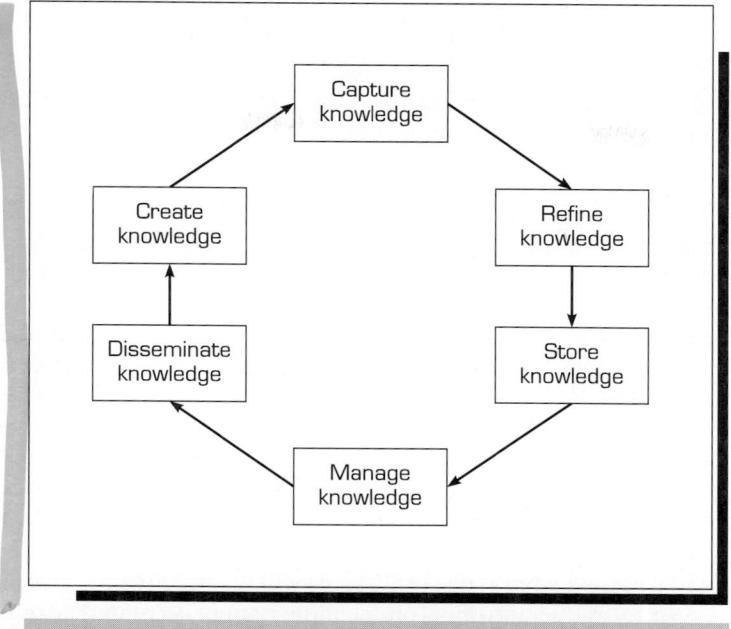

FIGURE 9.4 THE KNOWLEDGE MANAGEMENT CYCLE

As knowledge is disseminated, individuals develop, create, and identify new knowledge or update old knowledge which they return to the system.

Because knowledge is a resource that is not consumed when used, it can be used over and over again as needed. Knowledge is never depleted, though it can age (e.g., driving a car in 1900 is much different than driving one now, but many of the same basic principles still apply). Knowledge must be updated. Thus, the knowledge repository grows over time.

SOME KNOWLEDGE MANAGEMENT INITIATIVES

Dow Chemical Company defined its knowledge management strategy to use intellectual capital to improve its capacity to add value to the business. Dow uses a knowledge *value chain model* starting with ideas, know-how, and other intangible intellectual capital assets transformed into measurable, tangible **intellectual assets** through patents (Lloyd, 1996). Siemens linked their knowledge core competencies to organizational objectives and core products. They focused on developing knowledge through R&D using groupware to transform the knowledge into action (Lloyd, 1996). Companies often characterized as *agile companies* (Goldman et al., 1994) use a knowledge-based next-generation manufacturing model to develop products that can be easily customized to the individual requirements of customers.

Organizations can realize the full value of their knowledge assets only when they can be effectively transferred between individuals. Based on the work of Nonaka and Takeuchi (1995), Dataware Technologies identified in their executive briefing, the following four processes commonly used by organizations for knowledge conversion: socialization, capture, dissemination, and internalization.

- *Socialization:* sharing of experiences through observation, imitation, and practice; generally occurs through workshops, seminars, apprenticeships, and conferences, as well as at the water cooler.

- *Capture:* converting tacit knowledge (e.g., what one learned at a workshop) to an explicit form (e.g., a written report).
- *Dissemination:* copying and distribution of explicit knowledge.
- *Internalization:* experiencing knowledge through an explicit source; for example, one can combine the experience of reading a workshop report with previous experiences.

Companies are moving toward new organizational models, emphasizing radical decentralization coupled with advanced IT that allows an organization to tap into its intellectual assets. This approach is used by Monsanto Company in its knowledge management architecture (KMA) initiative, which allows it to harness its intellectual capital to have the advantages of a large global company combined with the flexibility of a small company, and addresses knowledge management from the perspective of creating value (Lloyd, 1996). The KMA adaptation of the Nonaka and Takeuchi (1995) three-step, three-spiral model features a learning map that identifies questions to be answered and decisions to be made, an information map that specifies the kind of information that users need, and a knowledge map that explains what users do with specific information. The knowledge map represents the conversion of information to insight or knowledge.

Once the three maps have been developed, a balanced scorecard evaluation is performed to assess what types of IT tools will be effective for leveraging the information repositories, and an information technology map is created. Monsanto's focus is on the *sense-making* capability of people.

WHY FIRMS ADOPT KNOWLEDGE MANAGEMENT

Knowledge management initiatives were initially begun because executives saw a need but did not have any hard cost/benefit estimates. Once these systems were in place (e.g., at Chrysler and at Xerox), the cost savings were documented and found to be dramatic. Returns on investment within 1–2 years were factors of 2 or more. For example, in the Opening Vignette, Mitre invested $7.9 million with a 4-year return of $54.91 million and an ROI of more than 7. By the end of the 1990s, collaborative and communication support technologies had led to many successes indicating how knowledge management has had a definite impact on the bottom line of many organizations *when done right.* Published stories about firms including Xerox, Monsanto, Chrysler, Chevron, Buckman Laboratories, KPMG, Ernst & Young, Arthur Andersen, Andersen Consulting, and others clearly outlined the methods, tools, managerial issues, and impressive returns on investment.

The growing consensus is that the fastest, most effective and powerful way to manage knowledge assets is through the *systematic transfer of best practices* (O'Dell et al., 1998). Clearly if best practices can be codified, stored, and made available, and if methods for problem solving (e.g., technical support or technicians) can be maintained and made available instantaneously, people won't have to spend time looking for answers. They will be able to move more quickly in their problem solving anywhere and anytime. These benefits are usually documented to establish the value of knowledge management systems. Though knowledge management systems can be expensive, they pay off relatively quickly by letting people work more effectively and more efficiently. The idea of leveraging expertise (see the Opening Vignette) is a very powerful one.

Because of the demonstrated success of knowledge management, researchers and computer market research firms have performed studies involving why systems are being developed, what factors hinder development, and what factors lead to success. Of the top five reasons why knowledge management systems are developed listed in DSS in Focus 9.9, the two most important ones are better decision making and reduced costs.

DSS IN FOCUS 9.9

WHY FIRMS IMPLEMENT KNOWLEDGE MANAGEMENT SYSTEMS

According to a survey for KPMG conducted by the Harris Research Center, the top five reasons that firms initiate knowledge management systems are

- Better decision making
- Reduced costs

- Faster response time to key issues
- Improved productivity
- Shared best practices.

Source: Adapted from Vaas (1999).

According to the IDC 1999 knowledge management survey described in Dyer (2000), the top three reasons for developing a knowledge management system were to (1) increase profits or revenues, (2) retain key talent and expertise, and (3) improve customer retention and/or satisfaction. Cost reduction was the seventh item on the list.

Alavi and Leidner (1999) suggest that the perceived benefits of existing knowledge management systems can be divided into process outcomes (communication improvements and overall efficiency) and organizational outcomes (financial, marketing, and general improvements). Knowledge availability leads to desirable organizational benefits, or as King (1993) indicates, knowledge should make a difference in some way.

Published success stories caution organizations not to implement knowledge management systems until they can move their organizational culture to where users are willing to both use the knowledge in the system and contribute new knowledge to it. The system should not be implemented until people are ready for it. Unlike business fads, knowledge management can succeed if an organization follows a careful, deliberate implementation path. Knowledge management success is discussed further in a later section.

9.6 THE CHIEF KNOWLEDGE OFFICER

Knowledge management projects that involve establishing a knowledge environment conducive to the transfer, creation, or use of knowledge attempt to build *cultural receptivity*. These attempts are centered on changing the behavior of the firm to embrace the use of knowledge management. Behavior-centric projects require a high degree of support and participation from the senior management of the organization to facilitate their implementation. Most firms developing knowledge management systems have created a knowledge management officer, a **chief knowledge officer (CKO),** at the senior level. The objectives of the CKO's role are to maximize the firm's knowledge assets, design and implement knowledge management strategies, effectively exchange knowledge assets internally and externally, and promote system use.

The CKO is responsible for defining the area of knowledge within the firm that will be the focal point, based on the mission and objectives of the firm (Davis, 1998). The CKO is responsible for standardizing the enterprise-wide vocabulary and for controlling the knowledge directory. This is critical in areas that must share knowledge across departments to ensure uniformity. CKOs must get a handle on the company's repositories of research, resources, and expertise, including where they are stored and who manages and accesses them. Then the CKO must encourage pollination among disparate work groups with complementary resources. The CKO is responsible for creating an

DSS IN FOCUS 9.10

THE CHALLENGES OF THE CHIEF KNOWLEDGE OFFICER

A chief knowledge officer must

- Set knowledge management strategic priorities
- Establish a knowledge repository of best practices
- Gain a commitment from senior executives to support a learning environment
- Teach information seekers how to ask better and smarter questions

- Establish a process for managing intellectual assets
- Obtain customer satisfaction information in near real time
- Globalize knowledge management.

Source: Adapted from Duffy (1998).

---

infrastructure and a cultural environment for knowledge sharing. He or she must assign or identify the _knowledge champions_ within the business units. Their job is to manage the content their group produces (e.g., the Chrysler Team Clubs), continually add to the knowledge base, and encourage their colleagues to do the same. A successful CKO should have the full and enthusiastic support of their manager and of top management. Ultimately, the CKO is responsible for the entire knowledge management project while it is under development, and then for management of the system and the knowledge once it is deployed.

Davenport and Prusak (1998) claim that the most important responsibilities of the CKO are building a knowledge culture, creating a knowledge management infrastructure, and making it all pay off economically. Davenport (1994) indicates that for a CKO to be successful, the following personal characteristics are deemed highly desirable:

- Extensive experience in some aspect of knowledge management, including its creation, dissemination, or application.
- Familiarity with knowledge-oriented companies and technologies, such as libraries and groupware.
- Ability to set a good example by displaying a high level of knowledgeability and success.

Most CKOs have most of these attributes, but they face many challenges, as outlined in DSS in Focus 9.10.

The CKO position is most often aligned with the IS function within an organization, but the CKO role should be separate from the chief information officer (CIO) role. Most progressive organizations place the position outside the IS organization and assign a high level of status and authority to it. See Herschel and Nemati (1999) and Duffy (1998) for details.

9.7 KNOWLEDGE MANAGEMENT DEVELOPMENT

Forming a _knowledge strategy_ is straightforward (Clarke, 1998). The first step is to develop sophisticated scenarios for current and future competitive environments. The next step is to describe ideal successful companies with respect to the future scenarios. A vital characteristic of this step is evaluation of the advantages and base knowledge required in these successful organizations (Clarke, 1998). Following identification of the knowledge needed at a successful firm, the next important step is to identify individuals within the firm who have the knowledge required or the capability to acquire that knowledge. It is important to identify external knowledge sources to help determine and understand current and future customers, suppliers, and markets. The source of intellectual capital may not reside within the organization but can be leveraged elsewhere. The next step for the organization is to model its efforts on those of a conceptually ideal company. The business strategy for such an ideal company would include a plan for acquiring and maintaining the necessary knowledge. Once the knowledge strategy is in place, the stage is set (see DSS in Focus 9.11). It is then time to develop the system.

Zack (1999) suggested that knowledge assets should be analyzed in relation to their support of business strategy by performing a SWOT (strengths, weaknesses, opportunities, and threats) analysis. This makes intuitive sense in that knowledge management has strategic value; it identifies critically important intellectual assets of an organization. In a 1999 survey of 200 IT managers, 94 percent considered knowledge management strategic (Stahl, 1999).

Generally, implementing a knowledge management methodology follows seven steps:

1. *Identify the problem.* Corporate knowledge is typically found in isolated systems or knowledge silos. The access and technological barriers protecting this knowledge lead users to perceive that there is a lack of knowledge. The knowledge segments should be identified (see the case applications).
2. *Prepare for change.* This refers to change in terms of business efforts, especially in how the business is operated.
3. *Create the team.* Most organizations that have successfully implemented knowledge management have created a corporate-level knowledge management team charged with and responsible for implementing a pilot project. At this point, a chief knowledge officer is appointed to lead the effort.
4. *Map out the knowledge.* Identify what the knowledge is, where it is, who has it, and who needs it. Once the knowledge map is clear, define and prioritize the key features and identify appropriate technologies that can be used to implement the knowledge management system.
5. *Create a feedback mechanism* indicating to management how the system is used and report any difficulties.
6. *Define the building blocks* for a knowledge management system. The base structures of a viable knowledge management system should consist of a

---

DSS IN FOCUS 9.11

SETTING THE STAGE FOR KNOWLEDGE MANAGEMENT

To set the stage for knowledge management implementation, organizations must create a culture of sharing, transfer, and change. This includes developing

- A process improvement orientation
- A common methodology for improvement and change

- The ability to work effectively in teams
- The ability to capture learning
- The technology to support cataloging and collaboration.

Source: Adapted from O'Dell et al. (1998).

knowledge repository, knowledge contribution and collection processes, knowledge retrieval systems, a knowledge directory, and content management.

7. *Integrate existing information systems* to contribute and capture knowledge in an appropriate format.

Usually a prototyping process is used, starting with a small group in a pilot program. Once it has demonstrated success, other members of the organization generally request access, and the system is expanded. For example, the Xerox Eureka system was initially deployed by a small group of researchers in France. Now, more than 40,000 technicians worldwide use Eureka (see DSS in Action 9.12). Of course, there are many challenges, mostly cultural, in implementing a knowledge management system. We outline these in DSS in Focus 9.13.

DSS IN ACTION 9.12

XEROX CORPORATION IS DOCUMENTS

Xerox Corporation has recognized that the bulk of the knowledge in an organization is contained in its documents and in how people interact with each other and with these documents. The document becomes a focal point, while human collaboration results in new knowledge because people are able to interpret and act on a document's content. According to Rick Thoman, president and CEO, "In the digital age, knowledge is our lifeblood. And documents are the DNA of knowledge." Xerox has transformed itself from a copy machine developer and manufacturer to a developer of knowledge management. As part of the Xerox knowledge work initiative, Xerox started by developing internal knowledge-sharing systems such as Eureka, a service technician system. The cultural infrastructure for sharing was in place when Xerox deployed AmberWeb, a community-of-practice Web site that started out as a solution for 500 researchers involved in the knowledge capture integra-

tion and access initiative. In early 2000, AmberWeb was used by 30,000 Xerox employees. Now that knowledge sharing has become a way of life at Xerox, the firm is attempting to not lose sight of innovations that can lead to viable products. Xerox developed DocuShare for in-house use. DocuShare is a knowledge management system that lets people share information, collaborate on documents, and stay connected with coworkers. It is a Web-based knowledge management system. Eighteen months after DocuShare was developed for use by a small internal group of researchers, more than 10,000 Xerox employees with no training, administration, or technical support were using the system. DocuShare is used at thousands of organizations worldwide.

Source: Partly adapted from Barth (2000), Moore (1999), and Anonymous (1999a).

DSS IN FOCUS 9.13

MAJOR IMPLEMENTATION CHALLENGES OF KNOWLEDGE MANAGEMENT

The major challenges to implementing knowledge management systems in practice are as follows:

- Lack of understanding of knowledge management and benefits (55 percent)
- Lack of time for knowledge management by employees (45 percent)
- Lack of skill in knowledge management techniques (40 percent)
- Culture does not encourage sharing (35 percent)

- Lack of incentives to share (30 percent)
- Lack of funding of knowledge management initiatives (24 percent)
- Lack of appropriate technology (18 percent)
- Lack of commitment from senior management (15 percent)

Source: Adapted from Dyer (2000).

Based on successful adoptions of knowledge management, Huang et al. (1999) identify the following 10 strategies for successful knowledge management implementation:

1. *Establishing a knowledge management methodology.* This can be based on the intellectual capital management (ICM) methodology adopted by IBM global services in 1994 (Huang, 1998a, b). The key components of the ICM method are a vision that values sharing and reusing knowledge; processes for efficiently gathering, evaluating, structuring, and distributing intellectual capital; a competency community of practice consisting of knowledge workers in a core competency area; technologies that enable company-wide knowledge sharing; and incentives to encourage intellectual capital contribution and reuse.

2. *Designate a pointperson.* Appoint a chief knowledge officer to promote and manage the knowledge management activities in the company.

3. *Empower knowledge workers.* In any organization knowledge originates from its knowledge workers. Thus, empowering and supporting knowledge workers by making them a key component of the knowledge management system is critical to the success of the company's knowledge management strategy. Rover in Britain and Levi in the United States use education and training policies to empower their knowledge workers (Huang et al., 1999, p. 119).

4. *Manage customer-centric knowledge.* A firm can strengthen its position in a competitive environment not only by emphasizing customer satisfaction but also by focusing on both learning about and learning from their customers. BMW has used this strategy effectively to increase both customer service and market share.

5. *Manage core competencies.* Core competencies can vary among firms based on the unique benefits they intend to provide to their customers by effectively combining human capital, intellectual and intangible assets, processes, and technologies in the firm. Thus, the core competency of one firm may not be easily replicated by other firms, as their capabilities may not essentially be the same. See Huang et al. (1999, p. 123) for examples of core competency-based businesses; also see Figure 9.2.

6. *Foster collaboration and innovation.* A firm can nurture collaboration by accentuating the importance of teamwork, learning, sharing, trust, and flexibility. Developing an appropriate reward structure for innovation also fosters high creative potential among individuals. Buckman Laboratories developed K'Netix, a knowledge network, to provide e-mail and seven forums (each consisting of a message board, a library, and a virtual conference room) (Huang et al., 1999, p. 126).

7. *Learn from best practices.* By recording and sharing best practices, firms can prevent reinvention and thus be more efficient and more effective by encouraging reuse of the best ideas and methods. In the past, firms shared and learned about best practices through symposiums, conferences, and seminars. Now, Web-based approaches such as the initiatives at Andersen Consulting (KnowledgeSpace) are becoming the norm.

8. *Extend knowledge sourcing.* Successful retrieval of information and dissemination of value-added knowledge are referred to as *knowledge sourcing.* Through different media such as the Internet, intranets, and extranets, firms can retrieve and deliver knowledge.

9. *Interconnect communities of expertise (communities of practice).* Firms create a link between internal and external communities by using formal virtual

communities or teams, and through electronic libraries such as white papers or knowledge banks. Internal experts aid in problem solving, while external experts are generally connected with senior management to advise on specific areas.

10. *Report the measured value of knowledge assets.* It is important that firms measure how knowledge management contributes to the business. It is a difficult but important task to validate the development and use of a knowledge management system, as is true for any information system. Skandia, a Stockholm-based insurance company, records its knowledge assets in its financial report by using a management tool navigator that combines financial and nonfinancial indicators of the company's assets (Huang et al., 1999, p. 129).

Holsapple and Joshi (2000) maintain that there is no consistent taxonomy of knowledge management methodologies but were able to characterize 10 consistent frameworks in the literature. Clearly, more work needs to be done to provide a better understanding of knowledge management for academicians and practitioners. We discuss the methods, technologies, and tools for knowledge management systems in the next section.

9.8 KNOWLEDGE MANAGEMENT METHODS, TECHNOLOGIES, AND TOOLS

Although knowledge management is primarily process-oriented with strategies determined by the organizational culture, motivation, and policies, knowledge management needs the right methods, technologies, and tools for a successful implementation. A **knowledge management system (KMS)** facilitates knowledge management by ensuring knowledge flow from the person(s) who know to the person(s) who need to know throughout the organization, while knowledge evolves and grows during the process. The next fundamental step in establishing a comprehensive and effective system is to decide which methods, tools, and technologies should be employed in implementing a knowledge management strategy.

Knowledge management is multidisciplinary and draws on aspects of science, interpersonal communication, organizational learning, cognitive science, motivation, training, and publishing and business process analysis. It is not solely about technology but does require the integration of existing information systems. Leveraging intellectual capital requires attention to structures and attributes that must be in place for a successful knowledge management program to exist. An organization must ensure that available knowledge provides value, a learning attitude is in place, there is a trusting culture, there is an effort to measure knowledge management effects, and the right tools are deployed (Knapp, 1998). The system objectives that support the knowledge management goal are knowledge gathering, organizing, refining, and distributing. Each of these objectives has a host of enabling functions. Knowledge organizing, for example, is performed by searching, filtering, cataloging, linking, and so on.

Knowledge management is more a methodology applied to business practices than a technology or product. So we find that the existing products do not always match the needs of the business practices. Typically an organization creates a knowledge architecture that allows collaboration with and access to one or more knowledge repositories via Web browser technology. There is no one product that provides a complete set of knowledge management capabilities.

Organizations building knowledge management systems use several tools, technologies, and systems to support the distribution of knowledge and aid in the decision-making process. Standard knowledge management initiatives involve the creation of knowledge bases, active process management, knowledge centers, collaborative technologies, and knowledge webs (Skyrme, 1997).

A variety of technologies can make up a knowledge management system: The Internet, intranets, data warehousing, decision support tools, and groupware are just a few among many (e.g., see DSS in Focus 9.14).

In their survey, Alavi and Leidner (1999) identify knowledge management systems development technologies currently being used. See DSS in Focus 9.15. Intranets seem to be the primary means of displaying and distributing knowledge in organizations, with 90 percent of organizations using browser tools. The other two most common tools are electronic mail and search/retrieval tools.

About half of the companies recently surveyed by Delphi Consulting are creating an intranet to improve their knowledge management, while 25 percent plan to do so soon. Similarly, one-third of those surveyed by Delphi are creating data warehouses, while nearly 25 percent plan to. Also, one-third are implementing decision support tools, while 20 percent plan to do so.

The following is a list of some of the key elements of a knowledge management infrastructure built over time:

- Communication networks, including the Internet, intranets, and extranets
- Collaboration tools (such as Lotus Notes, GroupSystems, and so on)
- Desktop videoconferencing
- Multimedia mail

DSS IN FOCUS 9.14

KNOWLEDGE MANAGEMENT SYSTEM TECHNOLOGIES

Dyer (2000) reports that the following technologies are important in developing a knowledge management system:

- E-mail or messaging (64 percent)
- Document management (53 percent)
- Search engines (51 percent)

- Enterprise information portal (41 percent)
- A data warehouse (41 percent)
- Groupware (39 percent)
- Workflow management (37 percent)
- Web-based training (37 percent)

DSS IN FOCUS 9.15

KNOWLEDGE MANAGEMENT SYSTEMS WITH VARIOUS TECHNOLOGIES OR TOOLS

- Browser (90 percent)
- Electronic mail (84 percent)
- Search/retrieval tools (73 percent)
- Information repositories (52 percent)
- WWW server (42 percent)
- Agents or filters (36 percent)

- External server services (31 percent)
- Videoconferencing (23 percent).

(Multiple items could be specified when applicable.)

Source: Adapted from Alavi and Leidner (1999).

- Electronic document management systems
- Artificial intelligence tools
- Information retrieval engines
- Help desk applications
- Data warehousing and data mining tools
- Knowledge creation analysis tools
- Enterprise-wide messaging
- Web content management tools (browsers and search engines)
- Push technologies and pull technologies
- Case-based retrieval
- Object databases
- Process management tools
- Open interoperable computing platforms
- External and internal content
- Intelligent agents
- Portable documents.

The issue that organizations face is how to combine these technologies to manage knowledge effectively, and this depends on the type of knowledge the organization wants to access and share. For example, e-mail and other collaborative tools are methods of sharing knowledge throughout an organization that may require engineers in laboratories around the world to communicate regularly.

Knowledge management and group support systems (collaborative computing) share the concepts of working, sharing, and facilitating in groups. Knowledge management and data mining are related, as knowledge management deals with knowledge creation that can be performed by identifying creative means to glean knowledge from existing data (in databases, data warehouses, text documents, and so on). The real essence of these approaches is the development of a *knowledge core,* an engine that knows what it takes to fashion information in disparate locations and differing databases into answers—knowledge that can be used anywhere and at anytime in the enterprise.

The level of complexity can range dramatically. Using a combination of e-mail, file transfer, and threaded bulletin boards, one can create a significant *starter* knowledge management environment. A more complex design could start with a browser-type user interface. The next layer would be the Web infrastructure or perhaps Lotus Notes. Below this layer would be a concept classification, which is a taxonomy for identifying the various bits of knowledge.

There are three tool categories needed to harvest knowledge. The first is an *information architecture,* which includes new languages, categories, and metaphors for identifying and accounting for skills and competencies. The second is a *technical architecture,* which is more social, such as the Internet. The third is an *application architecture* oriented toward problem solving and representation rather than output and transactions. Tools for capturing knowledge unobtrusively (with minimal effort and impact) are helpful. See DSS in Action 9.16.

The following applications could address an organization's knowledge management needs. First, eliciting the knowledge of experts is important. Implementing a methodology and tools to capture the knowledge of employees requires implementation of the concept of a browser. In addition, there should be an expert seeker application that identifies experts within the organization. Collaborative computing and workflow tools that will enhance collaboration within and across functional organizations are also important. Such tools enhance decision making by identifying previously encountered scenarios similar to current ones, adapt the previous experiences to the current problems, and thus provide a new solution.

DSS IN ACTION 9.16

CAPTURE KNOWLEDGE ORGANICALLY

There are several organic, relatively unobtrusive approaches to capturing knowledge about expertise. For example, Organik, a suite of software products (Orbital Software) uses statistical models of people based on their interests and expertise. As users of a system contribute, say, to a discussion forum, their profiles are automatically updated. One potentially powerful use of this type of software is to update online directories. Organik is embedded in PersonaServer, a component of an end-user application called KnowledgeWare, which provides an interface with the knowledge environment created by the technology (McKenna, 1999).

A common feature of successful knowledge management projects is the use of a common language (Skyrme, 1997). Typically the literature points to the use of knowledge databases where a common language is gathered. There are several steps that information professionals can take to move beyond basic knowledge databases to something more useful. These include adding contextual information, such as where the information is used. Giving details about the originator of the information is important. Allowing users of the information to contact contributors via e-mail hypertext links, offering an experts' database, or other means can aid in the effort. Database formats have the obvious advantages of transmittability, ease of access, and speed of dissemination (Skyrme, 1997).

The information is in data stores partitioned into sets of structured and unstructured data. Information in data warehouses is an example of structured data, whereas unstructured data are documents and text-based information. After the information is located, the knowledge management system needs a way to access it from various information stores. Once all the information is in place, a method must be devised to retrieve the knowledge and discover the relationships among its various pieces. The knowledge retrieval level is the highest level of the current set of knowledge management components; to obtain knowledge and not just information, a knowledge management system must integrate knowledge retrieval technologies.

KNOWLEDGE MANAGEMENT SOFTWARE

There are few general-purpose systems because each firm stores and uses knowledge differently. However, more and better tools are becoming available. Technology vendors are responding to the growing demand for knowledge management tools with intense innovation. Technology tools that support knowledge management are called *knowware*. They include DecisionSuite, Wincite, DataWare, KnowledgeX, KnowledgeShare, SolutionBuilder, Intraspect, DocuShare, GrapeVine, and others. Search/retrieval vendors Excalibur, Fulcrum, and Verity are transforming older products into what are called knowledge management platforms. Wincite, ChannelManager, and BackWeb help firms identify, organize, store, manage, and disseminate knowledge and information. Most rely on Web browser technology for access, and each tends to be strongest in one area. Even Lotus Development Corporation and Microsoft Corporation have repositioned their groupware products in light of the knowledge management trend.

Search/retrieval vendors have made knowledge management the cornerstone of their recent products. Dataware Technologies, Excalibur, Fulcrum, and Verity offer engines that can search hundreds of document formats across multiple repositories in one query. Users can create agents that perform specific searches regularly and deliver the results via personalized Web pages or push technology. AgentWare (Autonomy) within ActiveKnowledge provides a probability-based intelligent search agent in its Dynamic Reasoning Engine. It analyzes a document, performs categorization, and recommends real-time links to relevant documents including news feeds, Web sites, Lotus Notes files, e-mail messages, and text.

As search results grow more complex, the need for intuitive visualization increases. InfraRed (Context Media LLC) displays results in an interface based on the Doppler radar system. ThemeMedia (ThemeMedia Inc.) represents clusters of results as three-dimensional landscapes. PerspectaView (Perspecta Inc.) lets users seemingly fly past clustered files suspended in three-dimensional space. Inxight (a Xerox Corporation Enterprise Company) offers both semantic and visualization technology. Their fisheye interface is a unique way to map information (try it out at www.inxight.com).

GrapeVine contains a collaborative filtering product that can run as a Lotus Notes application or run directly on an intranet where it scans for information that matches the interest profile set by the user. Collaborative filtering is the leading advanced technology for knowledge retrieval versus information retrieval. Net Perceptions is another collaborative filtering vendor. GrapeVine lets users determine the importance of documents routed to them. Users can create profiles of their interests, and when matching documents are added to repositories on the network, they show up automatically in users' personalized views of available resources. Deploying GrapeVine requires a user to create and maintain a corporate taxonomy or hierarchy of subject categories.

Intraspect combines a database from Objectivity and a search engine from Verity to create a knowledge repository. As users create documents and collect documents from various sources, they drop them into folders on their desktops. All documents in public folders are indexed and made retrievable by others connected to the network. Other users can create a link in their own folders to a document stored in another user's folder.

KnowledgeX (KnowledgeX Inc.) acquires, discovers, publishes, and distributes knowledge obtained from various information sources such as databases and the Internet. KnowledgeX tries to provide context by automatically analyzing information in its repository, thus attempting to convert information to knowledge. It provides a visual representation of the relationships among knowledge chunks.

Wincite maps knowledge to markets, products, processes, and manager responsibilities, along with supporting the distribution of intelligence. Beehive's Abuzz links people with experts and answers instead of with documents. Abuzz is more of an FAQ repository.

Dataware Knowledge Management Suite provides a fairly comprehensive set of tools for a knowledge management initiative. It includes Knowledge Audit, which leads to Knowledge Map, Knowledge Warehouse which is accessible via standard Web browsers, Expert Identification, Knowledge Map Navigator for knowledge contributors, and e-mail integration.

Knowledge management methodologies based on collaboration use systems like Lotus Notes and DocuShare. DocuShare (Xerox Corporation) provides a simple and effective system for aggregating an organization's electronic documents into a natural repository. It makes these documents directly available to everyone in an organization.

LiveLink and Lotus Notes provide collaborative technologies for use over the Internet. For information on collaborative technologies, see Chapter 7.

Suppliers of more traditional applications are embracing knowledge management, too. Database vendors are positioning universal databases to play a central role in knowledge management architectures. IBM, Informix Software, Oracle, and Sybase all have introduced variants on the universal database. These systems manage multiple-format data, making them better knowledge management platforms. With each new release, each of these products gains more functionality.

CONSULTING FIRMS

All of the Big Five accounting firms (Arthur Andersen, Deloitte & Touche, Ernst & Young, KPMG, and PricewaterhouseCoopers) and the major consulting firms (Andersen Consulting, IBM, and so on) have massive internal knowledge management initiatives. Usually these become products as they succeed internally (e.g., KnowledgeSpace from Arthur Andersen; try it out at www.knowledgespace.com) and provide assistance in establishing knowledge management systems and measuring their effectiveness. They also provide some direct, out-of-the-box proprietary systems for vertical markets. For more on consulting activities and products, see Abramson (1999) and McDonald and Shand (2000).

THE COST OF DEVELOPING A KNOWLEDGE MANAGEMENT SYSTEM

Costs of implementing a knowledge management system can vary quite a bit. For example, Alavi and Leidner (1999) report that estimated average budgets associated with knowledge management systems development range from $25,000 to $50 million. The wide range may be attributed to the size of the organization, the current level of infrastructure, and the scope of the knowledge management initiative. Of course, the cost depends on whether or not there is an existing infrastructure. For example, if a firm already has a site license and a support team in place for Lotus Notes applications, a knowledge management initiative can be piggy-backed on it. McDonald and Shand (2000) report that a typical consultant-assisted knowledge management system costs between $1 million and $1.5 million to develop.

9.9 KNOWLEDGE MANAGEMENT SUCCESS

SUCCESS FACTORS

Organizations can gain several benefits from implementing a knowledge management strategy. Tactically, they can reduce loss of intellectual capital due to people leaving the company, reduce costs by decreasing and achieving economies of scale in obtaining information from external providers, reduce the redundancy of knowledge-based activities, increase productivity by making knowledge available more quickly and easily, and increase employee satisfaction by enabling greater personal development and empowerment. The best reason may be a strategic need to gain a competitive advantage in the marketplace (Knapp, 1998).

Knowledge management success factors may be links to economic performance or industry value; a technical and organizational infrastructure; a standard, flexible knowledge structure; a knowledge-friendly culture; a clear purpose and language; a change in motivational practices; multiple channels for knowledge transfer; and senior management support (Davenport et al., 1998). In their analysis of value creation, Moran and Ghoshal (1996) identify three conditions that must be satisfied for the exchange and combination of resources to actually take place. First, there must be an opportunity to make the combination or exchange. Recent developments in technology, such as Lotus Notes and the Internet, have considerably increased the opportunities for knowledge combination and exchange. Second, there must be an expectation that the exchange will create value. Third, there must be proper motivation encouraging exchange.

Success indicators with respect to knowledge management are similar to those for assessing the effectiveness of other business change projects. They include growth in the resources attached to the project, growth in the volume of knowledge content and usage (as at Mitre), the likelihood that the project will survive without the support of a particular individual or individuals, and some evidence of financial return either for the knowledge management activity itself or for the entire organization (Davenport et al., 1998). This might be perceptual rather than absolute. At Mitre and Chevron, the return on investment was documented explicitly. We list the major success factors in DSS in Focus 9.17.

Sherif and Mandviwalla (2000) found a consistent, deep skepticism toward knowledge codification when examining the role of an organizational memory information system (the knowledge management system in a sample of four firms). The stakeholders believed that it is hard to capture experts' knowledge because of the difficulty of expressing and capturing tacit knowledge.

Effective knowledge sharing and learning require cultural change within the organization, new management practices, senior management commitment, and technological support. All of these factors are necessary to overcome the known barriers to implementation.

DSS IN FOCUS 9.17

MAJOR FACTORS THAT LEAD TO KNOWLEDGE MANAGEMENT PROJECT SUCCESS

- A link to economic or industry value to demonstrate financial viability and maintain executive sponsorship.

- A technical and organizational infrastructure to build on.

- A standard, flexible knowledge structure to match the way the organization performs work and uses knowledge. Usually, the organizational culture must change to effectively create a knowledge-sharing environment.

- A knowledge-friendly culture leading directly to user support and use; Mitre developed this.

- A clear purpose and language to encourage users to buy into the system. Sometimes simple, useful knowledge applications need to be implemented first.

- A change in motivational practices to create a culture of sharing, as was done at Mitre, described in the Opening Vignette.

- Multiple channels for knowledge transfer — needed because individuals have different ways of working and expressing themselves. Also, different people can contribute the same knowledge to the system. The multiple channels should reinforce one another. Knowledge transfer should also be easily accomplished and be as nonobtrusive as possible.

- A level of process orientation to make it worthwhile

- Nontrivial motivational aides to encourage users to contribute and use knowledge.

- Senior management support: critical to initiate the project, to provide resources, to help identify important knowledge on which the success of the organization relies, and to "market" the project.

Source: Adapted from Davenport et al. (1998).

MEASURING SUCCESS

There are three main reasons why managers want to measure their intangible assets and knowledge assets, and their impacts:

1. It provides a basis for company valuation. Valuation is important in trading assets or in pricing the company in the marketplace and earning a proper return for shareholders. Skandia shows evidence of this asset approach with its focus on intellectual capital for survival, renewal, and growth.
2. It stimulates management to focus on what's important. By developing appropriate performance metrics and making managers accountable, the right things get their attention and action. This is the role of approaches such as the balanced scorecard.
3. It justifies investing in knowledge management activities. In many companies, the proponents of knowledge management agonize over what measures they can use to convince top management of its value.

There is no absolute means of measuring the success of a knowledge management effort, though various measures are used in practice. Besides the number of patents, trademarks, copyrights, trade secrets, new products and services, enhanced business processes, and wiser strategic decisions, there are other aspects of knowledge application: customer satisfaction; the financial bottom line (stock prices, dividends, net present value); effectiveness of business processes; ability to sustain innovation, change, and improvement through organizational learning; and quantifying critical success factors. Traditional ways of financial measurement fall short because *they do not consider intellectual capital an asset* (rather as the debit for salaries paid to employees for their skill and experience). There is a need to develop procedures for valuing the intangible assets of an organization, as well as incorporating models of intellectual capital that in some way quantify the speed of innovation and development of core competencies. See DSS in Focus 9.18 for a description of some new asset bases.

Alavi and Leidner (1999) report that although it is important to try to develop metrics to assess benefits of knowledge management systems, none of the organizations participating in their survey had conducted (or were planning to conduct) a formal cost/benefit analysis for their systems. The respondents felt that the development of meaningful metrics for measuring the value, quality, and quantity of knowledge is a key factor for long-term success and growth of KMS. To this end, knowledge management

---

DSS IN FOCUS 9.18

THE NEW ASSET BASES

When evaluating intangibles, there are a number of new ways to view capital. In the past, only customer goodwill was valued as an asset. Now the following are included:

- *External relationship capital:* how an organization links with its partners, suppliers, customers, regulators, and so on.
- *Structural capital:* systems and work processes that leverage competitiveness, such as information systems, and so on.

- *Human capital:* individual capabilities, knowledge, skills, and so on, that people have.
- *Social capital:* the quality and value of relationships with the larger society.
- *Environmental capital:* the value of relationships with the environment.

Source: Adapted from V. Allee, "Are You Getting Big Value from Knowledge?" *KMWorld,* Sept. 1999, pp. 16–17.

initiatives should be directly linked to explicit and important aspects of organizational performance (e.g., customer satisfaction, product or service innovations, time to market, cost savings, competitive positioning, and market shares). In other words, organizations need to find leverage points where enhanced "knowledge" can add value and then develop KMS to deliver the requisite knowledge.

Even though traditional accounting measures are incomplete, they are often used as quick justification for a knowledge management initiative (e.g., Mitre in the Opening Vignette). Returns on investment (ROIs) are reported to range from 20:1 for chemical firms to 4:1 for transportation firms, with an average of 12:1, based on the knowledge management projects one consulting firm assisted on. (Abramson, 1998).

One way to measure success is by peer evaluation. For example, Xerox, Ernst & Young, and Monsanto are considered leaders by their industry peers and regarded as most effective in their knowledge management efforts. See DSS in Action 9.19.

As more companies develop their knowledge management capabilities, some of the ground rules are becoming clearer. Success depends on a clear strategic logic for knowledge sharing, the choice of an appropriate infrastructure (technical or nontechnical), and an implementation approach that addresses the typical barriers: motivation to share knowledge, resources for capturing and synthesizing organizational learning, and the ability to navigate the knowledge network to find the right people and data.

In general, companies take either an asset-based approach to knowledge management or one that links knowledge to its applications and business benefits (Skyrme and Amidon, 1998). The former starts with the identification of intellectual assets and then focuses management's attention on increasing their value. The second uses variants of

---

DSS IN ACTION 9.19

WHO DOES KNOWLEDGE MANAGEMENT BEST?

How do companies manage knowledge to increase their success, and which ones do it best? As described in "The Most Admired Knowledge Enterprises," a 1999 report by Management Trends International, 1,500 CEOs, CFOs, and CTOs of *Fortune* 500 companies and 297 CKOs were asked to nominate the top three knowledge-based organizations within their companies' own business sector and across all sectors worldwide. Organizations were evaluated on a 1 to 10 scale for eight key knowledge performance criteria.

For the criterion of having an overall quality knowledge management program, Xerox, Ernst & Young, and Monsanto were the top three companies. Xerox had transformed itself from a manufacturer to a document company, reflecting its conscious conversion of individual implicit knowledge to explicit corporate knowledge. The three leading companies with top management support for knowledge management were Buckman Laboratories, Hewlett-Packard, and BP Amoco. The companies with the best contribution to knowledge approaches by innovation in all areas of the business were Lucent Technologies, 3M Corporation,

and Nokia. 3M Corporation was found to have the most effective employee-friendly practices in encouraging creativity, innovation, and renewal.

Intel, Lucent Technologies, and Monsanto were best at maximizing intellectual assets, that is, best at measuring and managing intellectual property, assets, and reuse of corporate knowledge. Ernst & Young, Xerox, and Intel were best at developing and managing the capture, categorization, and use of knowledge. Lucent, 3M, and Nokia had the best culture of continuous learning. Lucent, Arthur Andersen, and Ernst & Young were best at promoting customer value and loyalty. Microsoft, Intel, and Lucent had the best strategies for generating shareholder value through a broad understanding of how to create and manage intellectual capital, leading to long-term shareholder value.

These firms are clearly leading the way in knowledge management. They are identified as advancing and using knowledge management effectively.

Source: Adapted from O. Zundel, "Applying Knowledge to Profitability," *Intelligent Enterprise,* Mar. 1, 1999, p. 15.

the balanced scorecard, where financial measures are balanced against customer, process, and innovation measures. Among the best developed methods in use are the balanced scorecard approach, Skandia's Navigator, Stern Stewart's economic value added, and M'Pherson's inclusive valuation methodology, which we discuss next.

THE BALANCED SCORECARD

A *balanced scorecard* (Kaplan and Norton, 1992) adds other perspectives, those of customers, internal business processes, and innovation and learning, to financial measures. A balanced scorecard helps organizations move from being financially driven to being mission-driven. It encourages cross-organizational activities because it forces managers to understand the interdependencies. Developing a balanced scorecard is not without difficulties. It forces a manager to consider soft factors, a departure from the past. It also forces a manager to link knowledge management to strategy. Going through the process also helps managers sort out priorities.

THE SKANDIA NAVIGATOR

Skandia AFS, a Swedish financial services company, has taken a lead in developing measures of intellectual capital as a practical management tool. Skandia's *Navigator,* a variant of the balanced scorecard, incorporates measures in several dimensions. Additional details appear in Duffy (1999). Navigator is used as a model to drive sustained business development and to ensure that management actions and behaviors are consistent with renewal and development as well as financial performance. It provides what Skandia describes as a "taxonomy of intellectual capital reporting" in which intellectual capital represents the "hidden values of an organization." It is a management and reporting model that helps managers visualize and develop measures reflecting intangible assets.

ECONOMIC VALUE ADDED

A final perspective on the asset view is provided by *economic value added* (EVA), a method of evaluating corporate performance developed and trademarked by the Stern Stewart consulting firm. It provides a measure most directly linked to return on capital employed. EVA is related to the market value added (MVA) performance measure, which measures stock market capitalization against shareholders funds. By assessing a charge for using capital, managers are concerned with managing assets as well as income and with properly assessing the trade-offs between the two.

INCLUSIVE VALUATION METHODOLOGY

One of the more interesting frameworks for valuing intangibles is the inclusive valuation methodology of Philip M'Pherson (City University, London). M'Pherson believes that most methodologies tend to value intangibles from an asset perspective rather than in terms of their usefulness in running a business. M'Pherson's inclusive valuation methodology has two levels of valuation that combines financial and intangible measures. The first level involves applying attributes of value to the various intangibles in a business. The second level of valuation deals with combining monetary and intangible values in a coherent framework. This model has proved useful in getting executives to think about the links between information, knowledge, and bottom-line performance.

Knowledge management projects may not generate an immediate return on investment, however, they should plan to demonstrate future returns. Projects aimed at improving customer service and support, providing operational improvements for a particular process or function, or developing new products may take time to produce the expected payback.

CAUSES OF FAILURE: THE FLIP SIDE

One of the core tenets of a knowledge management project is the ability to detect and correct errors in an organization's knowledge (Fahey and Prusak, 1998). Organizations that have developed knowledge management systems have faced common problems that if left unchecked would lead to the building of a knowledge repository based on faulty knowledge. Fahey and Prusak (1998) identified 11 common causes of error associated with knowledge management. It is instructive to examine what can lead to failure (yet another piece of knowledge):

1. Not developing a working definition of knowledge. Many managers seem to be reluctant to distinguish among data, information, and knowledge.
2. Overemphasis on knowledge stock rather than on knowledge flow. This approach fails to recognize the importance of the need to transmit knowledge throughout the organization.
3. The view that knowledge exists predominately outside the heads of individuals. This idea results in too strong an emphasis on providing tools that assist in the transfer of explicit knowledge but ignores the importance of tacit knowledge.
4. Failure to recognize the importance of managing knowledge to create a shared context. Developing a shared context means creating a dynamic shared environment, taking into account that knowledge will change over time.
5. Failure to manage tacit knowledge. Managers in some organizations do not understand the importance of tacit knowledge or its consequences. This limits their understanding of the value of knowledge management systems.
6. Failure to disentangle knowledge from its uses. Knowledge should support information with decision- and action-relevant meaning. Knowledge management systems should not be centered on capturing knowledge without a purposeful use.
7. Downplaying reason and thinking. Organizations must pay attention to the underlying models and relationships that support organizational knowledge in order to understand why changes occur.
8. Focusing on the past and present instead of the future. Knowledge has no impact unless it is used in dealing with upcoming issues and problems.
9. Failure to recognize the importance of experimentation. Many organizations document their best practices but fail to seek to improve on them. Most experiments in the chemical and pharmaceutical industries fail to produce blockbuster final products, but lessons learned through failure can lead to later successes. Managers *must* understand that failure is to be expected (Chapter 2).
10. Substituting technological contact for the human interface. It is a misconception that a knowledge management system replaces the need for all human dialog.
11. Overemphasis on trying to measure knowledge directly instead of attempting to measure its outcomes or consequences.

9.10 KNOWLEDGE MANAGEMENT AND ARTIFICIAL INTELLIGENCE

RELATIONSHIP WITH ARTIFICIAL INTELLIGENCE

Knowledge management has a natural relationship with artificial intelligence (AI) methods and software. Much work is being done in the field of artificial intelligence relating to knowledge engineering, tacit-to-explicit knowledge transfer, knowledge identification, understanding and dissemination, and so on. Companies are attempting to realign these technologies and resultant products with knowledge management. Though, strictly speaking, knowledge management is not a form of AI, its software systems often have AI methods embedded in them.

AI METHODS IN KNOWLEDGE MANAGEMENT SYSTEMS

AI methods can be used in knowledge management systems to

- Assist in and enhance searching knowledge (e.g., intelligent agents in Web searches)
- Help establish profiles to determine what kinds of knowledge to scan for individuals and groups
- Help determine the relative importance of knowledge, both when knowledge is contributed to and accessed from the knowledge repository
- Scan e-mail, documents, and databases to perform knowledge discovery to determine meaningful relationships or to glean knowledge
- Scan e-mail, documents, and databases to perform knowledge discovery to induce rules for expert systems
- Identify patterns in data (usually neural networks)
- Forecast future results using existing knowledge
- Provide advice directly from knowledge, for example, use knowledge to construct an expert system for novices to use, perhaps for bank loan approvals (neural networks or expert systems)
- Provide a natural language or voice command-driven user interface for a knowledge management system.

The AI technologies most often used for the above are intelligent agents, expert systems, neural networks, and fuzzy logic.

REPRESENTATIVE PRODUCTS

Some knowledge management products that use embedded AI methodologies are the following:

- KnowledgeBridge (Molloy Group) is a help desk package that uses fuzzy logic to identify solutions to queries based on similar problems.
- Raven (Lotus Development Corporation) automates expertise profile creation and content categorization.
- KnowledgeMail (Tacit) scans e-mail and establishes public and private profiles of users based on their communications.

Automated help desk systems were among the first widely available commercial products to embed expert systems and other syntactic and semantic AI tools to determine the meaning of a natural language question and attempt to reach a conclusion about a diagnostic situation. Some even have embedded mechanisms for capturing knowledge about errors they make so that they can update their knowledge bases.

DATA MINING, DATA WAREHOUSING, AND KNOWLEDGE DISCOVERY IN DOCUMENTS AND DATABASES

Data mining, data warehousing, and knowledge discovery in documents and databases (KDD) were described in Chapters 4 and 5. Here we touch on how these concepts relate to knowledge management.

A data warehouse is sometimes used as a knowledge repository, depending on the application. Tags indicating the meaning of cleansed information can be used to express knowledge. Data mining, generally in text (electronic documents), **data warehouses**, and e-mail, can identify relationships among facts, identify patterns in data, and induce rules. These activities are powerful ways of identifying knowledge in data or documents. In a search for knowledge, data mining becomes a KDD methodology. KDD can be used to identify the meaning of data or text. For example, earlier we described Organik, which builds an expertise profile of a person based on the content of their e-mail messages. (Hopefully no personal messages are scanned. Someone might be identified as an expert on bees if they refer to their significant other as "honey.")

The Coca-Cola Company uses data mining methods to boost not only their sales but also those of their customers through analyses run on a SAS software development system. They target the identification of opportunities to grow the customer's business along with growing their own (Melymuika, 1999).

If a system stores the causes of failure of a new part, ZYX, installed in a device in the field, a KDD system can be used to identify the cause of failure. It might track the cause to a new technician who did not have proper training in the installation. Then, a rule could be induced: If the ZYX part needs to be replaced, do not assign the job to this particular technician; or better yet, it could indicate that the technician needs to be trained. See Becker (1999), Bigus (1996), and Groth (1998) for more on data mining and knowledge discovery.

9.11 ELECTRONIC DOCUMENT MANAGEMENT

In Chapter 4, we discussed **electronic document management (EDM)** systems. These systems center on the document in electronic form as the collaborative focus of work. EDM systems allow users to access needed documents, generally via a Web browser over a corporate intranet. EDM systems enable organizations to better manage documents and workflow for smoother operations. They also allow collaboration on document creation and revision.

Many knowledge management systems use an EDM system as their knowledge repository and access to it (see the use of EDM in the Chevron Case Application 9.1). There is a natural fit in terms of the purpose and benefits of the two. Strictly speaking, the only difference between a KMS and an EDM system is that the knowledge management system specifically stores knowledge. Knowledge can be and is stored in documents.

Most of the benefits of EDM are possible because the most recent versions of documents are readily available anytime to the appropriate people. Consequently, among other benefits, the document life cycle is automated (creation through distribution and update), productivity improves (with faster access and no more searching for documents or worrying about what version is being used), there is less paper to handle (fewer reports are generated and stored), and there is better security (access can be controlled).

The Pfizer Esub system described in Case Application 7.2 is a large-scale document management system that handled the equivalent of truckloads of paper documents passed between Pfizer and the FDA, its regulating agency. Because the system is used to handle FDA drug approval applications, the documents certainly contain knowledge about how to use medications, interpretations of the testing, and so on. This EDM system dramatically cut the time required for FDA submission and review, making Pfizer more competitive in getting new and effective drugs to market.

Other EDM system applications include

- Vendor software documentation
- Import–export license form maintenance
- ISO 9000 compliance documentation
- Automation of workflow through an insurance company.

Systems like DocuShare (Xerox Corporation) and Lotus Notes (Lotus Development Corporation) allow direct collaboration on a common document. Other EDM systems are EDMS (Documentum Inc.), Enterprise Work Management (Eastman Software Inc.), FYI (Identitech), The Discovery Suite (FileNet Corporation), Livelink (Open Text Corporation), PageKeeper Pro (Caere Corporation), Pagis Pro (ScanSoft Inc.), and CaseCentral.com for the legal profession (Document Repository Inc.).

9.12 KNOWLEDGE MANAGEMENT ISSUES AND THE FUTURE

Knowledge management is not just another expensive fad in the business arena. Knowledge management is a new paradigm for the way we work. We have known about the use of knowledge for millennia. Now modern organizations have found a way to use modern technology to perform true knowledge management. The leveraging of an entire organization's intellectual resources is a powerful concept that can become a reality. Firms that do not adopt it—those that do not evolve—will go the way that most firms established 100 years ago have gone.

We have discussed the key issues in knowledge management and summarize some of the more important ones here. They include research directions because many of these issues involve open questions.

- Determining the best way to approach and manage the necessary organizational culture shift needed for knowledge management to be effective, including motivating people to share knowledge and access it through the system
- Determining good metrics for evaluating the effectiveness of knowledge management
- Determining the right balance between technology and people processes
- Determining the best way to perform a knowledge audit
- Determining how people create, communicate, and use knowledge
- Developing effective ways to capture knowledge unobtrusively
- Determining the best ways to filter knowledge
- Determining the importance of knowledge

- Determining the best ways to identify knowledge effectively in information
- Determining how to store a newly mined actionable component with the information from which it is derived
- Determining how best to represent knowledge and match it to an application
- Determining a better taxonomy of organizations and knowledge management methods
- Determining the correct focus on knowledge creation—the individual, groups (communities of practice), or the entire organization
- Determining the appropriate focus for communities of practice
- Determining the best way for a knowledge management system to communicate knowledge, both when created and when accessed
- Matching the appropriate software to the knowledge management application
- Obtaining the appropriate level of resources to develop comprehensive KMS
- Developing more inclusive, integrated KMS software packages
- Determining more and better AI methods for knowledge management
- Determining how to use knowledge management to enhance learning.

For knowledge management, the definition is clear, the concepts are clear, the methodology is clear, the challenges are clear and surmountable, the benefits are clear and can be quite large, and the tools and technology, though not yet complete or inexpensive, are viable. The key issues are organizational culture, executive sponsorship, and measuring success. Once addressed properly, almost all the other issues involved in developing a knowledge management system fall into place.

The future should bring more comprehensive, standardized packages for knowledge management implementations. Hopefully these packages will take into consideration organizational culture fit.

Organizations need to be not just nimble but also intelligent. "The wise see knowledge and action as one" (Bhagavad Gita). Intelligent organizations recognize that knowledge is an asset, perhaps the only one that grows over time, and that when harnessed effectively it can sustain the ability to continuously compete and innovate.

❖ CHAPTER HIGHLIGHTS

- Knowledge management (KM) is an effective way for an organization to leverage its intellectual assets.
- Successful managers have always recognized and used intellectual assets and recognized their value.
- Knowledge is different from information and data. Knowledge is information that is contextual, relevant, and actionable. Knowledge provides a higher level of meaning about data and information. It conveys meaning.
- As a form of capital, knowledge, must be exchangeable among persons, and it must be able to grow.
- Knowledge is information in action. Knowledge is dynamic in nature.
- Tacit knowledge is usually in the domain of subjective, cognitive, and experiential learning.
- Explicit knowledge deals with more objective, rational, and technical knowledge (data, policies, procedures, software, documents, and so on) and is highly personal and hard to formalize.
- Historically, organizations that do not adapt to changing business conditions (e.g., learn) fail.
- A learning organization is one that is capable of learning from its past experience.

- In a learning organization there is an organizational memory and a means to save, represent, and share it.
- Organizational learning is the development of new knowledge and insights that have the potential to influence behavior.
- The ability of an organization to learn, to develop memory, and to share knowledge is dependent on its culture. Culture is a pattern of shared basic assumptions.
- Knowledge management is a process that helps organizations identify, select, organize, disseminate, and transfer important information and expertise that are part of the organizational memory and typically reside within the organization in an unstructured manner.
- Knowledge management requires a major transformation in organizational culture to create a desire to share (give and receive), the development of methods that ensure that knowledge bases are kept current and relevant, and a commitment at all levels of a firm for it to succeed.
- The goal of knowledge management as a process is to improve the organization's ability to perform its core processes more efficiently.
- The four broad objectives of knowledge management systems are to create knowledge repositories, improve knowledge access, enhance the knowledge environment, and manage knowledge as an asset.
- A knowledge repository is a collection of both internal and external knowledge.
- The cyclic model of knowledge management involves the following steps: create knowledge, capture knowledge, refine knowledge, store knowledge, manage knowledge, disseminate knowledge, and repeat.
- The fastest, most effective and powerful way to manage knowledge assets is through the systematic transfer of best practices.
- The chief knowledge office (CKO) is primarily responsible for changing the behavior of the firm to embrace the use of knowledge management and then managing the development operation of a knowledge management system.
- Implementing a knowledge management methodology follows these steps: identify the problem, prepare for change, create a team, map the knowledge, create a feedback mechanism, define the building blocks, integrate existing information systems.
- There are many strategic steps to be taken in the successful adoption of an knowledge management system.
- A knowledge management system (KMS) facilitates knowledge management by ensuring knowledge flow from person(s) who know to person(s) who need to know throughout the organization, while knowledge evolves and grows during the process.
- Knowledge management is more of a methodology applied to business practices than a technology or product.
- Organizations building knowledge management systems use several tools, technologies, and systems to support the distribution of knowledge and aid in the decision-making process.
- Standard knowledge management initiatives involve the creation of knowledge bases, active process management, knowledge centers, collaborative technologies, and knowledge webs.
- A variety of technologies can make up a knowledge management system: the Internet, intranets, data warehousing, decision support tools, groupware, and so on.

- Intranets are the primary means of displaying and distributing knowledge in organizations.
- Technology tools that support knowledge management are called *knowware*.
- Costs of implementing a knowledge management system have a wide range depending on the depth and breadth of the effort.
- The best reason for implementing a KMS may be a strategic need to gain a competitive advantage in the marketplace.
- Knowledge management success factors are economic, technical, and organizational.
- Indicators of success with respect to knowledge management are similar to those for assessing the effectiveness of other business change projects.
- It is difficult to measure the success of a KMS. Traditional methods of financial measurement fall short, as they do not consider intellectual capital an asset.
- New methods for measuring success include the balanced scorecard and Skandia Navigator.
- Knowledge management is not a form of AI, however, its software systems often have AI methods embedded in them.
- In searches for knowledge data mining becomes a KDD methodology. KDD can be performed to identify the meaning of data or text.
- EDM systems enable organizations to better manage documents and workflow for smoother operation. They also allow collaboration on document creation and revision.
- Knowledge management is not just another expensive fad in the business arena. It is a new paradigm for the way we work.

❖ KEY WORDS

- chief knowledge officer (CKO)
- data mining
- data warehousing
- electronic document management (EDM)
- explicit knowledge

- intellectual asset
- intellectual capital
- knowledge
- knowledge management (KM)
- knowledge management system (KMS)

- knowledge repository
- learning organization
- organizational culture
- organizational learning
- organizational memory
- tacit knowledge

❖ QUESTIONS FOR REVIEW

1. Define what is meant by an intellectual asset.
2. Define knowledge.
3. Define knowledge management.
4. Define explicit knowledge.
5. Define tacit knowledge.
6. How can tacit knowledge be transferred or shared?
7. Define organizational learning and relate it to knowledge management.
8. Define organizational memory and relate it to the idea of a knowledge repository.
9. Define organizational culture.
10. List the ways that organizational culture can impact on a knowledge management effort.

11. List the characteristics of knowledge management.
12. What is the primary goal of knowledge management?
13. List the four broad objectives of knowledge management.
14. List the benefits of knowledge management.
15. What is a CKO? List the responsibilities of a CKO.
16. List the desired personal characteristics of a CKO.
17. List the features of a knowledge management system.
18. List the steps in the cyclic model of knowledge management. Why is it a cycle?
19. How does knowledge management provide or support organizational learning and organizational memory?
20. List the steps in forming a knowledge management strategy.
21. List the steps in knowledge management implementation.
22. List the major challenges to implementing knowledge management in practice.
23. List the 10 strategies for successful knowledge management.
24. List the major knowledge management success factors.

❖ QUESTIONS FOR DISCUSSION

1. Explain why there are so many different definitions of knowledge.
2. Explain why knowledge is different from information and data.
3. Describe and relate the different characteristics of knowledge.
4. Explain why it is important to capture and manage knowledge.
5. Compare and contrast tacit knowledge and explicit knowledge.
6. Explain why organizational culture must sometimes change before knowledge management is introduced.
7. How does knowledge management attain its primary objective?
8. What methods are currently being used to incorporate knowledge management into organizational cultures?
9. How can employees be motivated to contribute to and use knowledge management systems?
10. Explain the common aspects of knowledge management and holy works.
11. Describe the conceptual basis of knowledge management.
12. What is the role of a knowledge repository in knowledge management?
13. Explain the differences and similarities between knowledge management and collaborative computing.
14. Explain the importance of communication and collaboration technologies to the processes of knowledge management.
15. Explain why firms adopt knowledge management initiatives.
16. Explain how knowledge management can transform an organization.
17. Explain how the wrong organizational culture can reduce the effectiveness of knowledge management.
18. Explain the role of the CKO in developing a knowledge management system. What major responsibilities does he or she have?
19. How can an organization motivate employees to share knowledge?
20. What is meant by a culture of knowledge sharing?
21. Describe the steps in forming a knowledge management strategy.
22. Describe the steps in knowledge management implementation.

23. Describe how each of the elements of a knowledge management infrastructure can contribute to the system.

24. Describe the knowledge management success factors.

25. Why is it so hard to evaluate the impacts of knowledge management?

26. Compare and contrast the four new methods for measuring KMS success: balanced scorecard, Skandia Navigator, EVA, and IVM.

27. Explain how the Internet and its related technologies (Web browsers, intranets, and so on) enable knowledge management.

28. List three top technologies that are most frequently used for implementing knowledge management systems and explain their importance.

29. Explain how a knowledge management initiative can fail.

30. List the reasons why managers want to measure their intangible assets and knowledge assets and how they are managed.

31. Compare computerized knowledge management to noncomputerized knowledge management.

32. Describe the most important responsibilities of the chief knowledge officer.

33. What are the major advantages of developing knowledge-sharing initiatives?

34. Explain how electronic document management (EDM) systems provide benefits to organizations.

35. Explain how data mining (KDD) can be done in a KMS.

36. How can AI methods be embedded in KMS?

37. List the three knowledge management issues you feel are the most important and explain why they are important.

38. Why is managing the organizational culture change the most important issue in deploying a knowledge management systems?

❖ Exercises

1. Make a list of all the knowledge management methods you use during your day (work and personal). Which are the most effective? Which are the least effective? What kinds of work or activities does each knowledge management method enable?

2. Investigate the literature for information on the position of CKO. Find out what percentage of firms with KM initiatives have them and what their responsibilities are.

3. Investigate the literature for new measures of success (metrics) for knowledge management and intellectual capital. Write a report on your findings.

4. Describe how each of the key elements of a knowledge management infrastructure can contribute to its success.

5. Based on your own experience or on the vendor's information, list all the major capabilities of a particular knowledge management product and explain how it can be used in practice.

6. Describe how to ride a bicycle, drive a car, or make a peanut butter and jelly sandwich. Now, have someone else try to do it based solely on your explanation. How can you best convert this knowledge from tacit to explicit (or can't you)?

❖ Group Exercises

1. Compare and contrast the capabilities and features of electronic document management with those of collaborative computing and those of knowledge management systems.

2. Search the Internet for knowledge management products and systems and create categories for them. For a sample of 25 products and services, describe the categories and justify them.

❖ GROUP PROJECTS

1. If you are working on a decision-making project in industry for this course (such as an expert choice-based or expert system decision-making problem) as part of the project (if not, use one from another class or from work), explain how you "extracted" knowledge and information from the decision maker and "learned" it. Describe the transfer process and the specific knowledge you gained. Can you use this knowledge in practice? Why or why not? (For examples see Case Application 2.3 about a key grip's decision making and Case Application 5.2 about Scott Homes' mobile home vendor selection.)

2. Look into ancient religious or cultural literature that has survived to this day (The Bible, The Koran, *The Art of War* by Sun Tzu, and so on). Identify five items of important knowledge in the chosen literature. Explain why they are important and how they have survived the ages.

3. Consider the epistemological debates surrounding what knowledge is. Each group should take a different perspective or position ranging from the rationalist perspective (Descartes, seventeenth century), to the empiricist perspective (Locke and others in the eighteenth century), and to the interactionist perspective (Kant and others in the nineteenth century) and describe and defend the point of view. Compare notes and contrast the different views.

❖ INTERNET EXERCISES

1. How does knowledge management support decision making? Identify products or systems on the Web that help organizations accomplish knowledge management. Try one out and report your findings to the class.

2. Search the Internet to identify sites dealing with knowledge management. How many did you find? Categorize the sites based on whether they are academic, consulting firms, vendors, and so on. Sample one of each and describe the main focus of the site.

3. Identify five real-world knowledge management success stories by searching vendor Web sites (use at least three different vendors). Describe them. How did knowledge management systems and methods contribute to their success? What features do they share? What different features do individual successes have?

4. Find a knowledge management product (such as KnowledgeSpace, which has a version running on the Web at www.knowledgespace.com), try out a demo, and write up your experience. Be sure to include a description of the features that make it a true knowledge management system.

5. Check out Inxight (www.inxight.com). Examine its capabilities and indicate how it could be used in a knowledge management system.

❖ TERM PAPERS

1. Describe the latest developments in knowledge management in a term paper.

2. Investigate organizational culture and how one manages change and write a term paper.

3. The CKO is critical to the success of a knowledge management initiative. Identify recent articles and Web sites on CKOs and write a term paper describing what makes a good CKO and what activities he or she must undertake to ensure the success of a knowledge management system.

CASE APPLICATION 9.1[3]

CHRYSLER'S NEW KNOW-MOBILES

CHRYSLER FROM THE 1980S TO THE YEAR 2000

In 1980 Chrysler Corporation came back from near bankruptcy with innovative designs and a view of a shared culture in design, development, and manufacturing. The company began new ways of looking at its business, its suppliers, and its workers (e.g., see the Chapter 7 Opening Vignette).

Chrysler bought American Motors Corporation (AMC) in 1987. Company executives saw the enormous potential for the dedicated *platform production* method that AMC was developing. After the acquisition, Chrysler developed and deployed advanced platform design and production ideas.

Jack Thompson worked closely with chairman Lee Iacocca on the development of a new, modern engineering and design facility. Thompson, who was technology center development director, designed the center around knowledge-sharing and productivity principles: open air, natural light, and escalators (people don't talk on elevators). In 1994 the tech center opened, providing a home for a transformed engineering culture at Chrysler. Two years later, the corporate headquarters was moved next to the tech center because executives wanted to be nearby. By 2000, more than 11,000 people were working at Chrysler's Auburn Hills, MI, campus.

In 1996 Chrysler Corporation made *knowledge management* a vital condition for design and engineering. This led to dramatic improvements in productivity for Chrysler.

In November 1998, Daimler-Benz became the majority owner of Chrysler Corporation, renaming the company Daimler Chrysler. Chrysler's fast, efficient, innovative nature, a result of the extremely successful platform approach to design and engineering, led to the buy in—the largest merger in manufacturing history.

PLATFORMS LEAD TO THE NEED FOR KNOWLEDGE MANAGEMENT

Platform production has teams of engineers focused on a single type of car platform (small car, minivan, and so on) working on new models as a system from concept to production. Cars are designed around customer needs and preferences, unlike the standard practice of organizing work around organizational functions, for example, stovepipes (see the Opening Vignette description of Mitre). Platform teams of employees work and learn together focused on the product, with a payoff in market responsiveness, reduced cost, and increased quality. The first model to use the platform approach,

the Chrysler LH, was produced in 39 months, while the typical time to market is more than 50 months.

While the benefits were clear, Chrysler executives noticed that unexplained errors were popping up in the new platforms (e.g., leaving a moisture barrier out of a car's door). *There was a memory problem.* When employees were moved to platforms, they were not interacting with their professional peers who were assigned to other platforms. Mentoring and peer support became limited in scope. *Informal and formal professional collaboration had stopped.* The same mistakes were being made, corrected, and repeated again; people were not learning about new developments in their core areas. The typical collaboration found among groups doing similar work was sharply reduced, and so the (sometimes) folklore of problems and solutions was not being documented or shared.

THE KNOWLEDGE AND KNOWLEDGE MANAGEMENT DEVELOPMENT EFFORT

Collaboration and communication needed to be reestablished within groups with common training, interests, and responsibilities (design, engineering, body, engine, manufacturing, and so on). The goal was to reestablish these links while becoming more competitive with even faster product cycle times. Chrysler needed to institutionalize knowledge sharing and collaboration.

First, engineers mapped out where the knowledge was within the organization. There were many "buckets of knowledge" ranging from product databases to CAD/CAM systems to manufacturing, procurement, and supply vehicle test data. Within each category, details were identified and codified.

Sharing knowledge meant integrating these knowledge buckets while resolving cultural issues that impeded sharing among platforms. The answer was to create informal cross-platform *Tech Clubs,* functionally organized communities of practice to reunite designers and engineers with peers from other platform groups. Each community would then codify its knowledge and provide mentoring and apprenticing opportunities for learning.

THE ENGINEERING BOOK OF KNOWLEDGE

Chrysler wanted to take advantage of lessons learned from prior programs, best practices, with whom to discuss spe-

[3]Partly adapted from W. Karlenzig, "Chrysler's New Know-Mobiles," *Knowledge Management,* May 1999, pp. 58–66; and other sources.

cific issues, and a list of who the knowledge experts in the company are. Most of this is not hard data but is based on opinions and on the intangible, tacit knowledge that can be learned only through experience, for example, through a mentor–apprentice or peer-to-peer relationship over time.

The *Engineering Book of Knowledge (EBOK)* is Chrysler's intranet supporting a knowledge repository of process best practices and technical know-how to be shared and maintained. It was initially developed by two engineering managers but continues through encouraged employee participation in grass roots (i.e., supported at the lower levels of the organization) Tech Clubs. EBOK is written in GraveVine (GrapeVine Technologies) running as a Lotus Notes application and is accessed with the Netscape browser, and NewsEdge.

The development process of Chrysler's EBOK is like the codification of oral and written traditions that some religious leaders undertook thousands of years ago. The *right way to do things* was argued over by experts until a conclusion was reached. Then, it was written into the movement's holy book(s), sometimes with supporting documentation (commentary).

Knowledge is explored and entered into the EBOK though an iterative team approach: the Tech Clubs. Best practices are identified, refined, confirmed, and finally entered into the EBOK. All this is done in a secure interactive electronic repository.

When an author proposes a best practice, users (in the Tech Club responsible for that area of knowledge) react by commenting on the knowledge through a discussion list. The book owner joins the conversation. The author can respond to the comments by either building a better case or going along with the discussion. Ultimately the Tech Club decides, and the book owner enters the new knowledge. The EBOK is Chrysler's official design review process.

The EBOK even contains best practice information about Chrysler's competitors. Chrysler has determined that EBOK is both a best practices tool and a collaboration tool. Chrysler officials recognize that because the environment changes and new methods are continually being developed, the EBOK will never be fully complete. EBOK is a *living book*.

The quality of the information in the EBOK is continually updated from real-world feedback based on experience and then synthesized into a system containing the important information discovered by everyone. This adds relevant breadth and depth to the entire process of creating better and better cars. The EBOK *leverages* technology.

Chrysler is looking into including suppliers in the EBOK because many knowledge experts work for their vendors. The issue of the location of knowledge is not important when a customer has a disabled vehicle and a vendor's part or its misuse, perhaps in the transmission, may have caused a major problem. The customer needs a solution, and fast. (See the Chapter 7 Opening Vignette describing how Chrysler created supply chain collaboration.)

KNOWLEDGE MANAGEMENT SUCCESS

The EBOK is central to Chrysler's new way of working. It functions like a bible, or at least the first book of one. The plan is to have more than 5,000 users with access to 3,800 chapters, of which just over half had been completed by early 1999.

With the use of the EBOK, Chrysler reconciled its platform problems and developed a technical memory while tracking competitive information, quality information, and outside standards.

Even though there is no central budget for books of knowledge and associated processes, Chrysler is deploying knowledge in other departments such as manufacturing, finance, and sales and marketing. Success breeds success! At the grass roots level, people recognize that these books of knowledge can enhance their work. So there are many grass roots knowledge initiatives under way.

CONCLUSIONS

Sales have been stronger than ever, with a record number of vehicles sold in 1998. Execution has been faster and cleaner, and Chrysler has won several market awards. The 1999 Chryslers were the first produced by a start-to-finish high-speed engineering process based on virtual and physical networks of knowledge.

Knowledge management with the EBOK played a critical role in Chrysler's success. The cultural and technical processes empowering knowledge workers resulted in successful real-world products: well-engineered automobiles.

CASE QUESTIONS

1. Platform design at Chrysler led directly a reduction in the time to market and in costs for new vehicles. Explain how it caused new problems.
2. What is meant by a community of practice? How did Chrysler leverage the knowledge within such a community?
3. Describe the Engineering Book of Knowledge (EBOK). Explain how it is updated by adding new knowledge of practice.
4. Explain how the EBOK is similar to the codification of an ancient religious work.
5. It has been said that the proper role for all knowledge management tools is to leverage technology in service to human thinking. Explain this statement.
6. How successful was the knowledge management initiative at Chrysler?
7. Consider how a book of knowledge could impact another organization, ideally one with which you are affiliated (e.g., your university, job, part-time job, family business). Describe the potential impacts and list the benefits. Would there be any organizational culture issues to deal with? Why or why not?

CASE APPLICATION 9.2[4]

KNOWLEDGE THE CHEVRON WAY

INTRODUCTION

Knowledge management has paid off dramatically at Chevron. In a speech at the Annual Knowledge Management World Summit in San Francisco (January 1999), Kenneth T. Derr, chairman and CEO of Chevron said, "Of all the initiatives we've undertaken at Chevron during the 1990s, few have been as important or as rewarding as our efforts to build a learning organization by sharing and managing knowledge throughout our company."

Improved management of knowledge was instrumental in reducing operating costs from $9.4 billion to $7.4 billion from 1992 to 1998 and in reducing energy costs by $200 million a year. During the 1990s, efforts like this were essential in reducing costs, in achieving productivity gains of more than 50 percent (in barrels of output per employee), and in improving employee safety performance more than 50 percent.

Chevron now calls itself a learning organization. Some gains made from knowledge management at Chevron are qualitative: Employees' work is more interesting and challenging when it involves finding and applying new knowledge. Jobs are potentially more fulfilling and personally more rewarding.

CHEVRON'S APPROACH

Like Mitre in the Opening Vignette, Chevron explored, developed, adapted, and adopted knowledge management methods to leverage its expertise throughout the enterprise. The improvements gained from identifying, sharing, and managing intellectual assets impact positively on drilling, office work, safety, and refineries. The improvements were generated by focusing on process, culture, best practices, and technology, including Internet technology.

DRILLING

Chevron adopted an *organizational learning system (OLS)* that improves drilling performance by sharing information globally. "In drilling, [the system] uses a simple software tool to capture lessons from the first wells in a new area, and then it helps to use that knowledge to drill the rest of the wells faster and cheaper," said Derr. "We've seen well cost drop by 12% to 20% and cycle time reduced as much as 40% in some cases—and that really adds up with big offshore drilling vessels that cost up to $250,000 a day." Oil &

Gas Consultants International developed the OLS for Amoco. Chevron found it through a best-practices survey.

REFINERIES

The company uses knowledge management to maintain six refineries. Sam Preckett, a reliability-focused maintenance system manager, is developing a process to improve information and knowledge sharing. Preckett and others realized that they were not effectively using the data and information already stored in Chevron's enterprise information systems. "We're trying to improve getting information out to our people," said Preckett. He recognizes that the first issue is to determine what information is needed. Preckett has been developing an informal best practices methodology for maintenance by "trying to learn how we do things." Getting knowledge to users is only part of the system; another part captures the tacit knowledge and experiences of workers. Chevron is trying to motivate workers to participate, especially those who are not enthusiastic about participating. Preckett said that at Chevron creative thinking is promoted from the executive level, which "allows him to do interesting things" to achieve efficiency gains through knowledge sharing.

ELECTRONIC DOCUMENT MANAGEMENT

Another specific need under the knowledge management umbrella was addressed by the DocMan system, which was initiated in December 1994 to improve the timeliness of document access, management and integration, and sharing of information among individual divisions in order to meet regulatory compliances. A longstanding application, DocMan works for the Warren Petroleum Limited Partnership Mont Belvieu complex in Texas (Chevron is a joint owner). Mont Belvieu has three fractionation trains for treatment and separation of liquefied petroleum gas components and 27 underground storage wells.

Most of the critical maintenance and operational information was on paper, and so it could not easily be updated or retrieved. Key areas were identified first, including safety management and safe operations. Safety data sheets were stored in five four-volume sets scattered around the facility for employees to use, but they were difficult to locate and keep updated. The engineering drawing books system—approximately 2,500 drawings—needed to

---

[4]Adapted from L. Velker, "Knowledge the Chevron Way," *KMWorld,* Vol. 8, No. 2, Feb. 1, 1999, pp. 20–21; and Anonymous (1999a).

be shared by personnel throughout the facility. Before DocMan, they too were outdated and difficult to locate. Other information that needed to be handled quickly included geologic and geographic records and OSHA compliance documentation.

System components include a Windows NT 4.0 server and workstations with a Microsoft SQL Server 6.5 database, as well as software from FileNet, Cimmetry Systems, and Green Pasture Software. It took about 9 months for a multidisciplinary team to deploy the system.

To address cultural resistance to the change, management emphasized the benefits of the new system: faster access to documents, elimination of wasted effort searching for documents, and assets protection. DocMan delivered a 95 percent return on investment over its 5-year project life. The investment payout period was 1.1 years based on an annual savings of $480,000. Employees can now focus on their real jobs instead of hunting down needed materials, which sometimes took half their time. Future plans call for including more process safety management documents, environmental records, and permits.

CAPITAL PROJECT MANAGEMENT

Though knowledge management, Chevron implemented a new standard methodology for capital project management. In one case, 60 companies shared data and practices, and so it was possible to compare performance to determine which companies were best and why. By doing this, Chevron developed its own effective capital project management process.

KNOWLEDGE MANAGEMENT BENEFITS

Chevron uses knowledge management in drilling, in refinery maintenance, and in safety management, capital project management, and other areas. The electronic document management system impacts on several different areas at Chevron.

Overall, the company has transformed itself into a learning organization. The innovative nature of the firm lets people approach problems in a creative manner. Chevron developed an approach based on the concept of systematically identifying and transferring best practices. Employees have more fulfilling and more interesting jobs. The knowledge is permanent. People save time and effort by not having to track down material. Instead, when it is needed, it is at their fingertips. Finally, Chevron has demonstrated cost savings with large returns on investments for its knowledge management systems.

CASE QUESTIONS

1. What is meant by a learning organization?
2. Describe the gains that Chevron achieved through its knowledge management programs.
3. To what different areas did Chevron apply knowledge management, and how successful was it?
4. Why is it important to document cost savings of knowledge management systems?
5. If dramatic payoffs can be achieved through knowledge management (as with the DocMan system), why don't more companies attempt to do so? (*Hint:* See the text.)

FUNDAMENTALS OF INTELLIGENT SYSTEMS

Artificial intelligence (AI) is a dynamic, varied, growing field. Its applied technologies range from expert systems to computer vision. In this part we first present an overview of expert systems (Chapter 10). These systems are constructed through knowledge engineering, which involves several tasks. First, knowledge is collected (from people or from documented sources) by a process called *knowledge acquisition* (Chapter 11). Knowledge acquisition can be accomplished manually and with some degree of automation. Then the acquired knowledge is organized into a knowledge base. In many systems knowledge representation (Chapter 12) involves IF-THEN rules, but there are other useful representations (such as frames).

Represented knowledge is used through reasoning, or inferencing, procedures (Chapter 13), which can be done under assumed certainty or uncertainty. Finally, the knowledge engineering development process is described in Chapter 14.

KNOWLEDGE-BASED DECISION SUPPORT: ARTIFICIAL INTELLIGENCE AND EXPERT SYSTEMS

Managerial decision makers are primarily knowledge workers. Thus, it is only natural that they incorporate knowledge in their decision making. It can take people many years to acquire knowledge, and access to knowledge is becoming more difficult as the number of knowledge sources increases. A knowledge-based decision support system can enhance the capabilities of decision support not only by supplying a tool that directly supports a decision maker but also by enhancing various computerized decision support systems. In addition, knowledge-based systems offer expertise in data management and modeling.

Knowledge-based decision support is provided by a variety of applied artificial intelligence tools—expert systems being the primary one. This chapter introduces the reader to the essentials of both artificial intelligence and expert systems in the following sections:

10.1 OPENING VIGNETTE: A KNOWLEDGE-BASED DSS IN A CHINESE CHEMICAL PLANT[1]

THE PROBLEM

Dalian Dyestuff plant is one of the largest chemical plants in China. It produces about 100 different kinds of dyes and other chemical products. As a result of the recent economic reforms in China, manufacturing decisions were decentralized, and plant managers were suddenly faced with the problem of making their own production plans. Because of the size of the plant and the number of products, it became very difficult to make and appropriately change production plans, which depend on market demand. The plant also had to make purchasing decisions and decisions regarding the disposal of environmentally damaging materials.

THE SOLUTION

An intelligent DSS equipped with expert systems (ES) was jointly constructed by decision makers and analysts. The DSS is composed of five subsystems: production planning, accounting and cost control, financing and budgeting, inventory and material management control, and information services.

The database is divided into six parts, corresponding to the five subsystems and a global integrating part. The model base includes a linear programming—based optimization model for production planning and product-mix determination, and many other models to support the various subsystems. An MBMS is used to handle optimization, conduct sensitivity analysis, store intermediate results, and maintain the model base.

The knowledge base component includes two expert systems that apply the knowledge of experienced managers to better plan monthly production and analyze working capital. The first system supports demand forecasts. Expertise is particularly required to make demand forecasts because traditional forecasting methods, based on historical data, were inappropriate because of the new economic environment. Accurate market demand forecasts are critical because production decisions are derived from them. The DSS generates a proposed plan, and the user can then use the ES to improve it. Four sets of rules are employed: for products produced regularly, for finished products, for relationships among products, and for adjusting production planning.

Another ES is used to model working capital. The purpose of this model is to provide sufficient working capital at the lowest possible cost.

Since its implementation, the system has proven to be a success, providing advantages such as the following:

- Allowing a combination of quantitative and qualitative analysis
- Providing flexibility and adaptability to changes
- Involving decision makers in all stages of the decision process
- Allowing better and more efficient decisions to be made

---

[1]Adapted from D. L. Yang and W. Mou, "An Integrated DSS in a Chinese Chemical Plant," *Interfaces,* Nov/Dec. 1993.

- Increasing profit by more than $1 million each year (about a 10 percent increase)
- Allowing users to express preferences and expertise
- Improving service to customers.

Overall, the system significantly improved the competitive position of the plant in the chemical dye industry.

❖ QUESTIONS FOR THE OPENING VIGNETTE

1. Justify the need for a DSS.
2. Describe the role of the ES. Why was such a component needed?
3. Review the role of the managers (users) in this situation.
4. What unique aspects are related to the Chinese environment?
5. Describe the benefits of the system.
6. What managerial lessons about DSS can be learned from this system?

10.2 CONCEPTS AND DEFINITIONS OF ARTIFICIAL INTELLIGENCE

The Opening Vignette illustrates that decision situations can be so complex that the support offered by data and model management alone may not be sufficient. Additional support at Dalian Dyestuff was provided by expert systems (ES) to substitute for human expertise by supplying the necessary knowledge. However, several other intelligent technologies can be used to support decision situations that require expertise. All these technologies use **knowledge** to provide the needed supports referred to as *knowledge-based systems*. All are considered applications of *artificial intelligence*.

ARTIFICIAL INTELLIGENCE DEFINITIONS[2]

Artificial intelligence (AI) is a term that encompasses many definitions (Jackson, 1999; and Raynor, 1996), and most experts agree that AI is concerned with two basic ideas. First, it involves studying the thought processes of humans (to understand what intelligence is); second, it deals with representing these processes via machines (such as computers and robots).

One well-publicized definition of AI is as follows: Artificial intelligence is behavior by a machine that, if performed by a human being, would be called intelligent. A thought-provoking definition is provided by Rich and Knight (1991): "Artificial intelligence is the study of how to make computers do things at which, at the moment, people are better."

Let us explore the meaning of the term *intelligent behavior*. Several abilities are considered signs of intelligence:

- Learning or understanding from experience
- Making sense out of ambiguous or contradictory messages
- Responding quickly and successfully to a new situation (different responses, flexibility)
- Using reasoning in solving problems and directing conduct effectively

---

[2]Part of the discussion in this chapter was adapted from Frenzel (1987).

- Dealing with perplexing situations
- Understanding and inferring in ordinary rational ways
- Applying knowledge to manipulate the environment
- Thinking and reasoning
- Recognizing the relative importance of different elements in a situation.

Although AI's ultimate goal is to build machines that mimic human intelligence, the capabilities of current commercial AI products are far from exhibiting any significant success in the abilities just listed. Nevertheless, AI programs are continually improving, and they increase productivity and quality by automating several tasks that require some human intelligence.

TESTING FOR INTELLIGENCE

An interesting test designed to determine whether a computer exhibits intelligent behavior was designed by Alan Turing and is called the **Turing test.** According to this test, a computer can be considered smart only when a human interviewer conversing with both an unseen human being and an unseen computer cannot determine which is which. The idea of the Turing test has been challenged by John Searle, (Bourbaki, 1990), and it contradicts the Rich and Knight (1991) definition.

The definitions of AI presented to this point concentrate on the notion of intelligence. The following definitions and characteristics of AI focus on decision making and problem solving.

SYMBOLIC PROCESSING

Symbolic processing is an essential characteristic of artificial intelligence, as reflected in the following definition: Artificial intelligence is the branch of computer science dealing primarily with *symbolic, nonalgorithmic* methods of problem solving. This definition focuses on two characteristics:

- *Numeric versus symbolic.* Computers were originally designed specifically to process numbers (**numeric processing**). However, people tend to think symbolically; our intelligence seems to be based in part on our mental ability to manipulate **symbols** rather than just numbers. Although symbolic processing is at the core of AI, this does not mean that AI does not involve math, rather, the *emphasis* in AI is on the manipulation of symbols.
- *Algorithmic versus nonalgorithmic.* An **algorithm** is a step-by-step procedure that has well-defined starting and ending points and is guaranteed to find a solution to a specific problem. Most computer architectures readily lend themselves to this step-by-step approach. Many human reasoning processes tend to be nonalgorithmic; in other words, our mental activities consist of more than just following logical, step-by-step procedures.

HEURISTICS

Heuristics are included as a key element of AI in the following definition: Artificial intelligence is the branch of computer science that deals with ways of representing knowledge using symbols with rules-of-thumb, or heuristics, methods for processing information (*Encyclopedia Britannia*). People often use heuristics, consciously or otherwise, to make decisions. By using heuristics, one does not have to rethink completely what to do every time a similar problem is encountered. Also, many AI methods employ some kind of search mechanism. Often heuristics are used to limit the search and focus on the most promising areas.

INFERENCING

Artificial intelligence involves an attempt by machines to exhibit *reasoning* capabilities. This reasoning consists of **inferencing** from facts and rules using heuristics or other search approaches. Artificial intelligence is unique in that it makes inferences by using a pattern-matching approach.

PATTERN MATCHING

The following definition of AI focuses on **pattern-matching** techniques: Artificial intelligence works with pattern-matching methods that attempt to describe objects, events, or processes in terms of their qualitative features and logical and computational relationships.

KNOWLEDGE PROCESSING

Although a computer cannot as yet have a diversity of experiences or study and learn as the human mind can, it can use knowledge given to it by human experts. Such knowledge consists of facts, concepts, theories, heuristic methods, procedures, and relationships. Knowledge is also information that has been organized and analyzed to make it understandable and applicable to problem solving or decision making.

KNOWLEDGE BASES

The collection of knowledge related to a problem (or an opportunity) used in an AI system is organized, and it is called a **knowledge base.** Most knowledge bases are limited in that they typically focus on some specific, usually narrow, subject area or **domain.** In fact, the narrow domain of knowledge and the fact that an AI system must involve some qualitative aspects of decision making are viewed as critical for AI application success. Once a knowledge base is built, AI techniques are used to give the computer an inferencing capability based on the facts and relationships contained in the knowledge base.

A distinction must be made between the knowledge base of a problem as defined here and an *organizational knowledge base,* which we introduced in Chapter 9.

USING THE KNOWLEDGE BASE IN AI PROGRAMS

With a knowledge base and the ability to draw inferences from it, a computer can be put to practical use as a problem solver and decision maker. Figure 10.1 illustrates the concept of a computer running an AI application. By searching the knowledge base for

FIGURE 10.1 APPLYING AI CONCEPTS WITH A COMPUTER

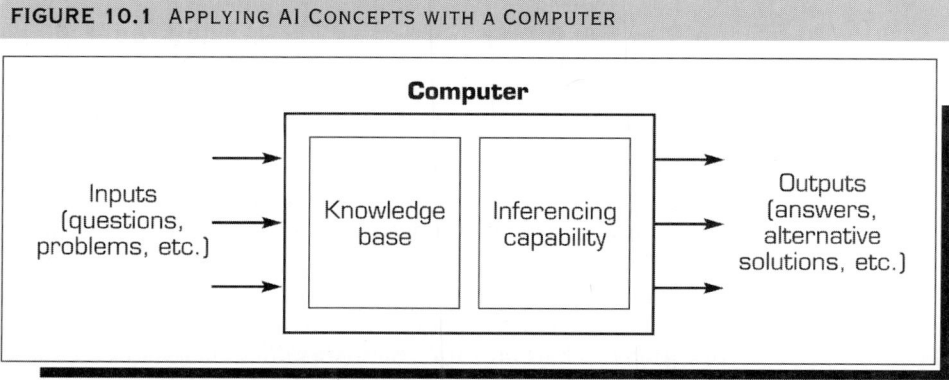

relevant facts and relationships, the computer can find one or more alternative solutions to a given problem. The computer's knowledge base and inferencing capability augment those of the user, who is typically a novice.

10.3 ARTIFICIAL INTELLIGENCE VERSUS NATURAL INTELLIGENCE

The potential value of artificial intelligence can be better understood by contrasting it with natural, or human, intelligence. AI has several important commercial advantages:

- *AI is more permanent.* Natural intelligence is perishable from a commercial standpoint in that workers can change their place of employment or forget information. However, AI is permanent as long as the computer systems and programs remain unchanged.
- *AI offers ease of duplication and dissemination.* Transferring a body of knowledge from one person to another usually requires a lengthy process of apprenticeship; even so, expertise can seldom be duplicated completely. However, when knowledge is embodied in a computer system, it can be easily transferred from that computer to any computer on the Internet or on an intranet.
- *AI can be less expensive than natural intelligence.* There are many circumstances in which buying computer services costs less than having corresponding human power carry out the same tasks. This is especially true when knowledge is disseminated over the Web.
- *AI, being a computer technology, is consistent and thorough.* Natural intelligence is erratic because people are erratic; they do not always perform consistently.
- *AI can be documented.* Decisions made by a computer can be easily documented by tracing the activities of the system. Natural intelligence is difficult to document. For example, a person may reach a conclusion but at some later date may be unable to recreate the reasoning process that led to that conclusion, or to even recall the assumptions that were part of the decision.
- *AI can execute certain tasks much faster than a human can.*
- *AI can perform certain tasks better than many or even most people.*

Natural intelligence does have several advantages over AI, such as:

- Natural intelligence is *creative,* whereas AI is rather uninspired. The ability to acquire knowledge is inherent in human beings, but with AI, tailored knowledge must be built into a carefully constructed system.
- Natural intelligence enables people to benefit from and use *sensory experience* directly, whereas most AI systems must work with symbolic input and representations.

Perhaps most importantly, human reasoning uses a *wide context of experience* at all times and brings it to bear on individual problems. In contrast, AI systems typically gain their power by having a very narrow focus.

The advantages of natural intelligence over AI show the many limitations of applied AI technologies. However, in many cases AI technologies provide significant improvement in productivity and quality.

10.4 THE ARTIFICIAL INTELLIGENCE FIELD

Artificial intelligence is not in itself a commercial field; it is a science and a technology. It is a collection of concepts and ideas that are appropriate for research but cannot be marketed. However, AI provides the scientific foundation for several commercial technologies, which are shown in Figure 10.2. The major areas are the following:

EXPERT SYSTEMS

The name **expert system** was derived from the term *knowledge-based expert system*. An expert system (ES)[3] is a system that uses human knowledge captured in a computer to solve problems that ordinarily require human expertise. Well-designed systems imitate the reasoning processes experts use to solve specific problems. Such systems can be used by experts as knowledgeable assistants. ES are used to propagate scarce knowledge resources for improved, consistent results. Ultimately, such systems could function better than any single human expert in making judgments in a specific, usually narrow, area of expertise (referred to as a domain). This possibility may have a significant impact on advisory professionals (financial analysts, lawyers, tax advisors, and so on). Expert systems are discussed in Sections 10.6–10.16 and in Chapters 11–14.

NATURAL LANGUAGE PROCESSING

Natural language technology gives computer users the ability to communicate with a computer in their native language. This technology allows for a conversational type of interface, in contrast to using a programming language consisting of computer jargon, syntax, and commands. Limited success in this area is typified by current systems that can recognize and interpret written sentences. The field of **natural language processing (NLP)** consists of two subfields: Natural language *understanding* investigates methods of enabling computers to comprehend instructions given in ordinary English so that they can understand people more easily. Natural language *generation* strives to have computers produce ordinary English language so that people can understand them more easily. Details on these topics are discussed in Appendix W10-B on our Web site and by Reiter and Dale (2000).

SPEECH (VOICE) UNDERSTANDING

Speech understanding is the recognition and understanding of spoken language by a computer. This topic is presented in detail in Appendix W10-C on our Web site and in Balentine et al. (1999).

ROBOTICS AND SENSORY SYSTEMS

Sensory systems, such as vision systems, tactile systems, and signal-processing systems, when combined with AI, define a broad category of systems generally called **robotics.** A *robot* is an electromechanical device that can be programmed to perform manual tasks. The Robotics Institute of America formally defines a robot as "a reprogrammable multifunctional manipulator designed to move materials, parts, tools, or specialized devices through variable programmed motions for the performance of a variety of tasks."

An "intelligent" robot has some kind of sensory apparatus, such as a camera, that collects information about the robot's operation and its environment. The intelligent

---

[3]ES is both a singular and plural abbreviation (*expert system* or *expert systems*).

FIGURE 10.2 THE DISCIPLINES OF AI (THE ROOTS) AND THE APPLICATIONS

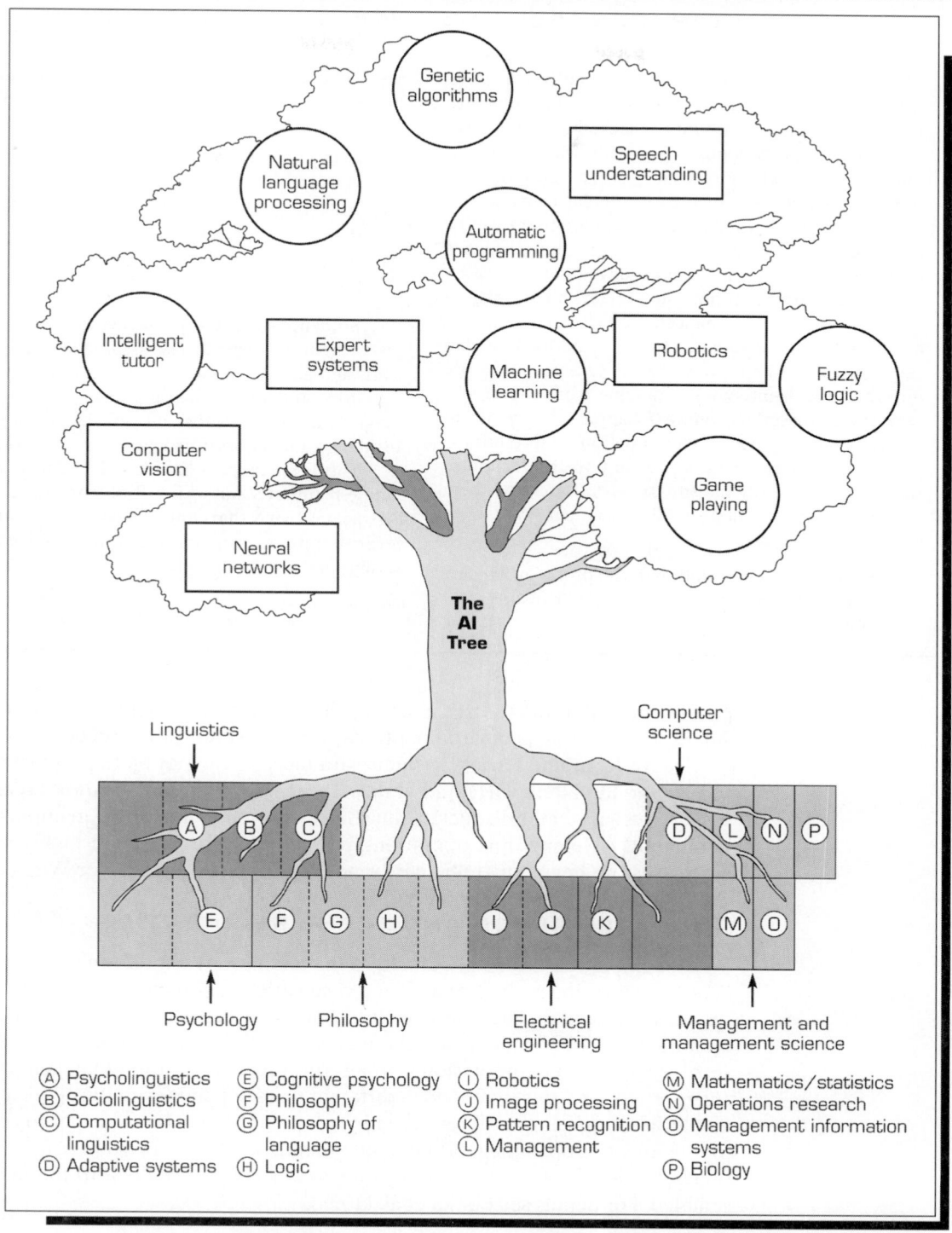

Genetic algorithms

Natural language processing

Speech understanding

Automatic programming

Intelligent tutor

Expert systems

Machine learning

Robotics

Fuzzy logic

Computer vision

Game playing

Neural networks

The AI Tree

Linguistics

Computer science

A B C

D L N P

E

F G H

I J K

M O

Psychology

Philosophy

Electrical engineering

Management and management science

Ⓐ Psycholinguistics
Ⓑ Sociolinguistics
Ⓒ Computational linguistics
Ⓓ Adaptive systems

Ⓔ Cognitive psychology
Ⓕ Philosophy
Ⓖ Philosophy of language
Ⓗ Logic

Ⓘ Robotics
Ⓙ Image processing
Ⓚ Pattern recognition
Ⓛ Management

Ⓜ Mathematics/statistics
Ⓝ Operations research
Ⓞ Management information systems
Ⓟ Biology

AN INTERNET-BASED INTELLIGENT TUTORING SYSTEM

Many companies are introducing Internet-based intelligent tutoring systems (ITS) as a cost-effective approach to deliver training to where trainees are. This is especially beneficial in complex domains where students must master a variety of concepts and apply them in unique situations. For such cases regular training over the Internet is not enough. With ITS, programs can be customized and instructors can monitor students' progress from a distance. Course developers can easily maintain and update training materials, and the instructor's productivity is enhanced by ITS. These systems also provide for customized training and for remediation, similar to one-to-one "private" tutoring. ITS use different intelligent systems, ranging from expert systems to case-based reasoning (Chapter 13), which contains realistic problem-solving situations and solutions.

The case base of examples and exercises capture realistic problem-solving situations and presents them to the student as virtual simulations. Each example or exercise includes the following:

- A multimedia description of the problem, which may evolve over time (such as in a tactical scenario)

- A description of the correct actions to take, including order-independent, optional, and alternative steps

- A multimedia explanation of why these steps are correct

- A list of methods for determining whether students have correctly performed the steps

- A list of principles that must be learned to take the correct action.

Students solve the problems interactively, which gives them an opportunity to practice the necessary skills and also reveals any knowledge deficiencies. ITS monitors students as they perform these simulations, diagnosing the strengths and weaknesses of their performance, and tailors instruction to correct weaknesses.

This is a new paradigm for ITS education. An example is the ITS Authoring Tool from Stottler Henke Associates (www.shai.com), which helps in building enterprise training programs that can be delivered on intranets and corporate portals.

Source: Condensed from *PC AI,* July/Aug. 1999.

---

part of the robot allows it to interpret the collected information and to *respond* and *adapt* to changes in its environment rather than just follow instructions.

Robots combine sensory systems with mechanical motion to produce machines of widely varying intelligence and ability. The research and application areas under the sensory systems umbrella include machines that sense, move, and manipulate their environment. Assembly line operations, particularly those that are highly repetitive or hazardous, are beginning to be performed by robots. For details see Wise (1999).

COMPUTER VISION AND SCENE RECOGNITION

Visual recognition has been defined as the addition of some form of computer intelligence and decision making to digitized visual information received from a machine sensor such as a camera. The combined information is then used to perform or control such operations as robotic movement, conveyor speed, and production line quality. The basic objective of computer vision is to interpret scenarios rather than generate pictures. *Interpreting scenarios* is defined in different ways depending on the application. For example, in interpreting pictures taken by a satellite, it may be sufficient to roughly identify regions of crop damage. On the other hand, robot vision systems can be designed to precisely identify assembly components to correctly affix them to the item being assembled. For details see Sonka et al. (1998).

INTELLIGENT COMPUTER-AIDED INSTRUCTION

Intelligent computer-aided instruction (ICAI) refers to machines that can tutor humans. To a certain extent, such a machine can be viewed as an expert system. However, the major objective of an expert system is to render advice, whereas the purpose of an ICAI is to teach.

Computer-assisted instruction, which has been in use for many years, brings the power of a computer to bear on the educational process. Now AI methods are being applied to the development of *intelligent* computer-assisted instruction systems in an attempt to create computerized tutors that shape their teaching techniques to fit the learning patterns of individual students. These are known as **intelligent tutoring systems (ITS),** and many more have been implemented on the Web (e.g., see AIS in Focus 10.1).

ICAI applications are not limited to schools; in fact, they have found a sizable niche in the military and corporate sectors. ICAI systems are used today for various tasks such as problem solving, simulation, discovery, learning, drill and practice, games, and testing. Such systems are also being used to support disabled people. For details see Goettl (1998).

Often these programs are databases structured to respond to specific inputs with specific answers within a predetermined structure. See the special issues of *Educational Technology* (Sept./Oct. 1999) and *Educational Media International* for details on ICAI and ITS including new Web-based technologies.

NEURAL COMPUTING

A **neural (computing) network** is a mathematical model of the way a human brain functions. Neural networks are starting to have a positive impact on many business disciplines. For examples, see Ainscough, et al. (1997), Trippi and Turban (1996c), and Haykin (1998). Such models have been implemented in flexible, easy-to-use PC-based neural network packages such as BrainMaker (California Scientific Software, Grass City, CA). We discuss neural computing in depth in Chapters 15 and 16.

OTHER APPLICATIONS

AI has been developed in several other commercial areas. Some interesting examples are presented next.

SUMMARIZING NEWS
Some computer programs "read" stories in newspapers or on the Web and make summaries in English or several other languages. This process helps in handling the information overload problem. It is also used to alert managers to news items that may need special attention. For example, see Wee et al. (1997), which shows how news is summarized and translated into several languages.

LANGUAGE TRANSLATION
Computer programs are able to translate words and sentences from one language to another. For example, the LOGOS Group (modena, italy, www. logos.it) has created a software package for multiple language translations. Globalink Inc. has a Language Assistant Series that runs under Windows. Several programs translate Web pages to foreign languages (e.g., see www.worldpoint.com, www.babelfish.altavista.com and www.free.translation.com).

Korea Telecom offers Koreans an opportunity to access Web sites in Japanese and read an abstract of their content (www.idetect.com). Once a Web site is selected for a detailed view, an automatic translation is provided.

FUZZY LOGIC
Fuzzy logic (fuzzy sets) extends the notions of logic beyond a simple true/false to allow for partial (or even continuous) truths. Inexact knowledge and imprecise reasoning are important aspects of expertise in applying common sense to decision-making situations. In fuzzy logic, degrees of set membership are important. For example, in the traditional boolean logic framework, a car can be said to be skidding or not skidding when the

brakes are applied. However, an expert driver can recognize the degree to which the car is skidding and can apply control according to a variable amount of skidding. One of the first commercial applications of fuzzy logic was in producing superior antilock brakes. See Chapter 16, and Nguyen and Walker (1999) for fuzzy logic details.

GENETIC ALGORITHMS

Genetic algorithms are intelligent heuristic search methods that follow a process that simulates evolution in a computer. For a specific problem, the solution is represented as a "chromosome," which generally contains a sequence of 0s and 1s indicating values of decision variables. For each string of chromosomes, an objective value can be computed. A genetic method starts with a randomly generated population of solutions and randomly combines portions of chromosomes to form new solutions with an occasional mutation. The new solutions are tested for feasibility, and the best feasible ones from the previous and current generations are selected to survive to reproduce. After several combination iterations, the best solution is typically a near-optimal solution to the decision-making problem. Genetic algorithms have been applied to many large-scale combinatorial (difficult) mathematical programming problems, such as large-scale scheduling problems, and even in producing police sketches of criminals. See Chapter 16 and Goldberg (1994) for details.

INTELLIGENT AGENTS

Intelligent agents can be best explained by presenting an example. Suppose that early every week you type a note into your computerized appointment book reminding you that you have a lunch date with Stephanie at 12:15 on Thursday at The Grill. An intelligent agent runs in the background and learns your behavior patterns. After the third week, your appointment agent notices the pattern and, when you click on a Thursday, it inserts "Lunch with Stephanie at 12:15 at The Grill" for you. It might even call the restaurant to make reservations if you always did that next. Like any other agent working for you (such as a real estate agent), to serve you well, it must learn your needs in an unobtrusive way. Intelligent agents are finding applications in personal assistant devices, electronic mail and news filtering and distribution, appointment handling, and Web applets for electronic commerce and information gathering (Chapter 17).

10.5 TYPES OF KNOWLEDGE-BASED DECISION SUPPORT SYSTEMS

As noted in Chapter 3, there are several modes of knowledge-based decision support. The Opening Vignette illustrates a situation in which expert systems provided expertise not included in the DSS database or model base. This expertise helped the inexperienced managers to better plan the production resources and analyze the needed working capital. The activities supported by the expert systems in this case were different from (although related to) the activities supported by the data and model components of the DSS. Thus, the knowledge component enabled a wider range of decisions; it extended the capabilities of computers well beyond data-based and model-based DSS (Goul et al., 1992).

Other areas of possible support are as follows:

- Support for the steps in the decision process not addressed by mathematics. For example, selection of the appropriate input data requires expertise as well as assessment of the impact of proposed solutions on people.
- Support for the building, storing, and managing of models in a multiple-model DSS. This use enhances the capability the MBMS, making it intelligent. This topic is discussed in Chapter 18.

- Support for the analysis of uncertainty, where expertise in applying tools ranging from fuzzy logic to neural computing is needed. Uncertainty is one of the major characteristics of the modern business environment, and so many decision situations involve uncertainty (also see Chapter 14).
- Support for the user interface. The user interface plays a major role in DSS implementation. Knowledge-based systems can greatly improve the user interface. For example, natural language processors and voice technologies can make the interface very easy and natural.
- Other types of support. Knowledge-based decision support can have several other configurations, as described in Chapters 15–18.

10.6 BASIC CONCEPTS OF EXPERT SYSTEMS

In order to describe the major concepts of ES we will review one of its pioneering commercial applications as shown in AIS in Action 10.2.

AIS IN ACTION 10.2

CATS-1 AT GENERAL ELECTRIC

THE PROBLEM

As the top locomotive field service engineer at General Electric (GE), David I. Smith, had been with the company for more than 40 years. He was the top expert in troubleshooting diesel electric locomotive engines. Smith traveled throughout the country to places where locomotives were in need of a major repair to determine what was wrong and to advise young engineers about what to do. The company was very dependent on Smith. The problem was that he was nearing retirement.

TRADITIONAL SOLUTION: APPRENTICESHIP

GE's traditional approach in such a situation was to create teams that paired senior and junior engineers. These pairs worked together for several months or years, and by the time the older engineers retired, the younger engineers had absorbed enough of the seniors' expertise in performing troubleshooting and other tasks. This practice proved to be a good short-term solution. In the 1980s employees were more inclined to change their jobs, and so GE could have been left without experts if the junior engineers decided to change jobs after experts such as Smith retired. Therefore, GE wanted a more effective, dependable way to disseminate expertise among its engineers. Furthermore, having railroad service shops throughout the country requires extensive travel by an expert or moving the locomotives to an expert because it is not economically feasible to have an expert in each train shop.

THE EXPERT SYSTEM SOLUTION

In 1980 GE built one of the pioneering expert systems (ES) to model the way a human troubleshooter works. The system builders spent several months interviewing Smith and transferring his knowledge to a computer. The computer program was prototyped over a 3-year period, its knowledge slowly increasing as expressed in terms of decision rules stored in a computer. The result was a new diagnostic technology that enables a novice engineer or a technician to uncover a fault by spending only a few minutes at the computer. The system, named CATS-1, was also able to explain the logic of its advice to the user, thus serving as a teacher. Furthermore, the system was able to lead users through the required repair procedures by presenting a detailed, computer-aided drawing of parts and subsystems and providing specific how-to instructional demonstrations.

The system is based on a flexible, humanlike thought process rather than on rigid procedures expressed in flowcharts or decision trees.

The system, originally developed on a minicomputer, now operates on a personal computer at every railroad repair shop served by GE. Thousands of similar diagnostic systems are in operation all over the world. For further information about the original version, see Bonissone and Johnson (1985).

Expert systems are used today by most large- and medium-sized organizations as a major tool for improving productivity and quality (Durkin, 1996). They are also an important tool for supporting strategic decisions and Business Process Reengineering (BPR) (Turban et al., 2000) (see AIS in Action 10.3).

AIS in Action 10.2 introduces the basic concepts of expert systems: expertise, experts, transferring expertise, inferencing rules, and explanation capability. These concepts are defined in this section, and the remainder of the chapter is devoted to a more detailed description and discussion of them and their role in ES.

EXPERTISE

Expertise is the extensive, task-specific knowledge acquired from training, reading, and experience. It includes the following types of knowledge:

- Theories about the problem area
- Rules and procedures regarding the general problem area
- Rules (heuristics) about what to do in a given problem situation
- Global strategies for solving these types of problems
- Metaknowledge (knowledge about knowledge)
- Facts about the problem area.

These types of knowledge enable experts to make better and faster decisions than nonexperts in solving complex problems. It takes a long time (usually several years) to become an expert, and novices become experts only incrementally.

SOME FACTS ABOUT EXPERTISE

- Expertise is usually associated with a high degree of intelligence, but it is not always associated with the smartest person.
- Expertise is usually associated with a vast quantity of knowledge.

AIS IN ACTION 10.3

STRATEGIC APPLICATIONS OF EXPERT SYSTEMS

Expert systems can be used to support strategic decision making. Here are some examples:

Merger and acquisition ES provide expert guidance to complex merger and acquisition decisions. They provide an appropriate framework and ensure systematic and detailed evaluation of the merger or acquisition. They assess the management strengths, the organization's current strategic focus, the most suitable acquisition partner, the price range with which to begin negotiations, and the current merger and acquisition climate (Beerel, 1993).

SMARTPlan is a strategic market planning expert system. It assists in understanding planning techniques, providing suitable market planning frameworks, providing the necessary environment background (such as industry comparisons and competitors' statistics), evaluating the inhibiting factors (such as customer resistance and cost analysis), and providing the appropriate marketing mix required to achieve economic success (Beerel, 1993).

A family of 10 expert systems assists the port of Singapore in competing successfully against neighboring ports (in Malaysia and Indonesia) where the costs of labor and services are much lower. The system plans the optimal use of the port's resources, which serve 800 vessels daily, and reduces the stay in the port from days to hours (Tung and Turban, 1996).

Online Advisory Solution facilitates self-management of the welfare program as it transitions administering responsibility from the states of Arizona, New Mexico, and Utah to the Navajo Nation. The program provides financial and human services to approximately 28,000 Navajo clients. The interactive solution Case Worker Advisor (from MultiLogic Inc.) integrates the tribe's unique cultural heritage while following complex federal, state, and tribal guidelines (www.exsys.com, Oct. 1999).

- Experts learn from past successes and mistakes.
- Expert knowledge is well-stored, organized, and quickly retrievable from an expert.
- Experts can call up patterns from their experience (excellent recall).

EXPERTS

It is difficult to define what an expert is because we actually talk about degrees or levels of expertise. (The real question is how much expertise a person should possess before qualifying as an expert.) Nevertheless, it has been said that nonexperts outnumber established experts in many fields by a ratio of 100:1. The distribution of expertise appears to follow the same shape regardless of the type of knowledge being considered. In general, experts in the top tenth in any given area are believed to perform 3 times as well as average experts and 30 times as well as those in the lowest tenth. This distribution suggests that the overall effectiveness of human expertise could be significantly increased (up to 200 percent) if we could somehow make top-level expertise available to less knowledgeable decision makers.

Typically, human expertise includes a constellation of behavior that involves the following activities:

- Recognizing and formulating the problem
- Solving the problem quickly and correctly
- Explaining the solution
- Learning from experience
- Restructuring knowledge
- Breaking rules if necessary
- Determining relevance
- Degrading gracefully (being aware of one's limitations).

To mimic a human expert, it is necessary to build a computer system that exhibits all these characteristics. To date, work in ES has primarily explored the second and third of these activities (solving problems and explaining the solutions). In addition, ES can generally give a measure of how confident it is in its solutions as it reaches the boundaries of its knowledge (see the examples in Section 10.10).

TRANSFERRING EXPERTISE

The objective of an expert system is to transfer expertise from an expert to a computer system and then on to other humans (nonexperts). This process involves four activities: knowledge acquisition (from experts or other sources; see Chapter 11), knowledge representation (in the computer; see Chapter 12), knowledge inferencing (Chapter 13), and knowledge transfer to the user. The knowledge is stored in the computer in a component called a *knowledge base*. Two types of **knowledge** are generally distinguished:

1. Facts
2. Procedures (usually rules) regarding the problem domain.

INFERENCING

A unique feature of an expert system is its ability to reason ("think"). Given that all the expertise is stored in the knowledge base and that the program can access relevant databases, the computer is programmed so that it can make inferences. Inferencing is performed in a component called the **inference engine** which includes procedures regarding problem solving.

TABLE 10.1 Comparison of Conventional Systems and Expert Systems

Conventional Systems	Expert Systems
Information and its processing are usually combined in one sequential program.	Knowledge base is clearly separated from the processing (inference) mechanism (i.e., knowledge rules are separated from the control).
Program does not make mistakes (programmers or users do).	Program may make mistakes.
Do not (usually) explain why input data are needed or how conclusions are drawn.	Explanation is a part of most ES.
Require *all* input data. May not function properly with missing data unless planned for.	Do not require all initial facts. Typically can arrive at reasonable conclusions with missing facts.
Changes in the program are tedious (except in DSS).	Changes in the rules are easy to make.
The system operates only when it is completed.	The system can operate with only a few rules (as the first prototype).
Execution is done on a step-by-step (algorithmic) basis.	Execution is done by using heuristics and logic.
Effective manipulation of large databases.	Effective manipulation of large knowledge bases.
Representation and use of data.	Representation and use of knowledge.
Efficiency is usually a major goal.	Effectiveness is the major goal.
Effectiveness is important only for DSS.	
Easily deal with quantitative data.	Easily deal with qualitative data.
Use numerical data representations.	Use symbolic and numerical knowledge representations.
Capture, magnify, and distribute access to numeric data or information.	Capture, magnify, and distribute access to judgment and knowledge.

RULES

Many commercial ES tools and ready-made systems are **rule-based systems;** that is, knowledge is stored mainly in the form of rules, as are problem-solving procedures. A rule in the CATS-1 example may look like this: "IF the engine is idle, and the fuel pressure is less than 38 psi, AND the gauge is accurate, THEN there is a fuel system fault." There are about 600 such rules in the CATS-1 system. Other knowledge representation schema, such as frame (object-oriented) representation, sometimes complement or substitute for rule representation. (See Chapter 12 for details.)

EXPLANATION CAPABILITY

Another unique feature of an ES is its ability to explain its advice or recommendations. The explanation and justification is done in a subsystem called the **justifier,** or the **explanation subsystem.** It enables the system to examine its own reasoning and explain its operation.

The above characteristics and capabilities of ES make them different from conventional systems. For a comparison, see Table 10.1.

10.7 STRUCTURE OF EXPERT SYSTEMS

Expert systems can be viewed as having two environments: the development environment and the consultation (runtime) environment (Figure 10.3). The **development environment** is used by an ES builder to build the components and put knowledge into

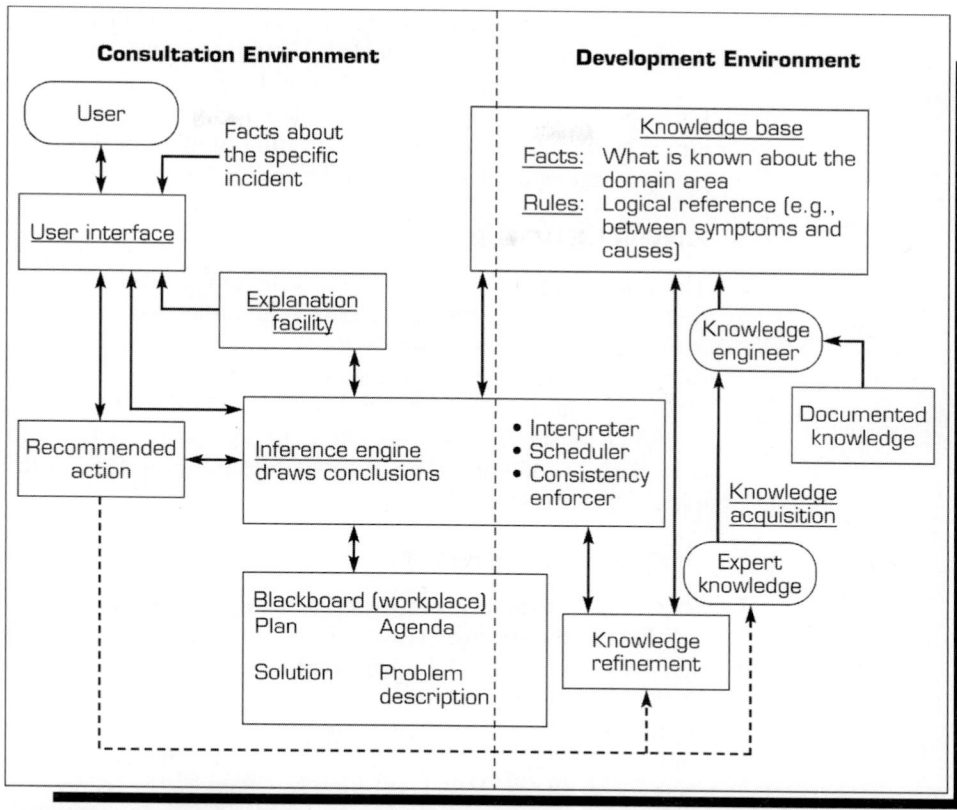

FIGURE 10.3 STRUCTURE OF AN EXPERT SYSTEM

the knowledge base. The **consultation environment** is used by a nonexpert to obtain expert knowledge and advice. These environments can be separated once a system is completed.

The three major components that appear in virtually every expert system are the knowledge base, inference engine, and user interface. In general, though, an expert system can contain the following additional components:

- Knowledge acquisition subsystem
- Blackboard (workplace)
- Explanation subsystem (justifier)
- Knowledge refining system
- User(s).

Currently, most expert systems do not contain the knowledge refinement component. A brief description of each component follows.

KNOWLEDGE ACQUISITION SUBSYSTEM

Knowledge acquisition is the accumulation, transfer, and transformation of problem-solving expertise from experts or documented knowledge sources to a computer program for constructing or expanding the knowledge base. Potential sources of knowledge include human experts, textbooks, multimedia documents, databases (public and private), special research reports, and information available on the Web.

Acquiring knowledge from experts is a complex task that often creates a bottleneck in ES construction. In building large systems one needs a knowledge engineer or knowledge elicitation expert to interact with one or more human experts in building the knowledge base. Typically the knowledge engineer helps the expert structure the problem area by interpreting and integrating human answers to questions, drawing analogies, posing counterexamples, and bringing conceptual difficulties to light.

KNOWLEDGE BASE

The **knowledge base** contains the relevant knowledge necessary for understanding, formulating, and solving problems. It includes two basic elements: (1) facts such as the problem situation and the theory of the problem area, and (2) special heuristics or rules that direct the use of knowledge to solve specific problems in a particular domain. (In addition, the inference engine can include general-purpose problem-solving and decision-making rules.) The heuristics express the informal judgmental knowledge in an application area. Knowledge, not mere facts, is the primary raw material of expert systems.

INFERENCE ENGINE

The "brain" of the ES is the **inference engine,** also known as the *control structure* or the *rule interpreter* (in rule-based ES). This component is essentially a computer program that provides a methodology for reasoning about information in the knowledge base and on the blackboard, and for formulating conclusions. This component provides directions about how to use the system's knowledge by developing the agenda that organizes and controls the steps taken to solve problems whenever consultation takes place.

USER INTERFACE

Expert systems contain a language processor for friendly, problem-oriented communication between the user and the computer. This communication can best be carried out in a natural language. Sometimes it is supplemented by menus, electronic forms, and graphics.

BLACKBOARD (WORKPLACE)

The **blackboard** is an area of working memory set aside as a *database* for the description of a current problem as specified by the input data; it is also used for recording intermediate hypotheses and decisions. Three types of decisions can be recorded on the blackboard: a *plan* (how to attack the problem), an *agenda* (potential actions awaiting execution), and a *solution* (candidate hypotheses and alternative courses of action that the system has generated thus far).

Consider an example. When your car fails, you enter the symptoms of the failure into the computer for storage in the blackboard. As the result of an intermediate hypothesis developed in the blackboard, the computer may then suggest that you do some additional checks (e.g., see whether your battery is connected properly) and ask you to report the results. This information is recorded in the blackboard.

EXPLANATION SUBSYSTEM (JUSTIFIER)

The ability to trace responsibility for conclusions to their sources is crucial both in the transfer of expertise and in problem solving. The **explanation subsystem** can trace such responsibility and explain the ES behavior by interactively answering questions such as the following:

- Why was a certain question asked by the expert system?
- How was a certain conclusion reached?
- Why was a certain alternative rejected?
- What is the plan to reach the solution? For example, what remains to be established before a final diagnosis can be determined?

In simple ES, the explanation shows the rules that were used to derive the specific recommendations.

KNOWLEDGE REFINING SYSTEM

Human experts have a **knowledge-refining system;** that is, they can analyze their own knowledge and its use, learn from it, and improve on it for future consultations. Similarly, such evaluation is necessary in computerized learning so that the program can analyze the reasons for its success or failure. This could lead to improvements that result in a more accurate knowledge base and more effective reasoning. Such a component is not available in commercial expert systems at the moment but is being developed in experimental ES at several universities and research institutions.

THE USER

The user of an expert system is usually a nonexpert human who needs advice or training. However, robots and other automatic systems that use ES output as an input to some action can use expert systems results. The user is considered part of the ES while other people are involved in its construction.

10.8 THE HUMAN ELEMENT IN EXPERT SYSTEMS

At least two humans, and possibly more, participate in the development and use of an expert system. At a minimum, there is a builder and a user. Often, there is also an expert and a knowledge engineer.

THE EXPERT

An **expert** is a person who has the special knowledge, judgment, experience, and methods, along with the ability to apply these talents to give advice and solve problems. It is the expert's job to provide knowledge about how he or she performs the task that the knowledge-based system will perform. The expert knows which facts are important and understands the meaning of the relationships among facts. In diagnosing a problem with an automobile's electrical system, for example, an expert mechanic knows that fan belts can break and cause the battery to discharge. Directing a novice to check the fan belts and interpreting the meaning of a loose or missing belt are examples of expertise. When more than one expert is used, a situation can become difficult if the experts disagree (Chapter 11).

THE KNOWLEDGE ENGINEER

The **knowledge engineer** helps the expert structure the problem area by interpreting and integrating human answers to questions, drawing analogies, posing counterexamples, and bringing conceptual difficulties to light. He or she is usually also the system builder. The shortage of experienced knowledge engineers has been a major bottleneck in ES construction. To overcome this problem, ES designers use productivity tools (such as special editors and logic debuggers), and research is being conducted on building machine learning systems that will minimize the need for knowledge engineers.

THE USER

Most computer-based systems have evolved into a single-user mode. In contrast, an ES has several possible classes of users:

- *A nonexpert client seeking direct advice.* In such a case, the ES acts as a *consultant* or *advisor.*
- *A student who wants to learn.* Here, the ES acts as an *instructor.*
- *An ES builder who wants to improve or increase the knowledge base.* Here, the ES acts as a *partner.*
- *An expert.* The ES acts as a *colleague* or *assistant.* For example, an ES can provide a second opinion so that the expert can validate his or her judgment. An expert can also use the system as an assistant to carry out routine analyses or computations or to search for and classify information.

OTHER PARTICIPANTS

Several other participants may be involved in ES. For example, a *system builder* or *system analyst* may help integrate the expert system with other computerized systems. A *tool builder* may provide or build specific tools. *Vendors* may supply tools and advice, and *support staff* may offer clerical and technical help. In addition, a *network expert* may be needed for distributed and Internet-based systems. Note that one person can have several roles. For example, some systems include only an expert and a user; while others include a system builder, an expert, and a user.

10.9 HOW EXPERT SYSTEMS WORK

ES construction and use consist of three major activities: *development, consultation,* and *improvement.*

DEVELOPMENT

The *development* of an expert system involves the construction of a problem-specific knowledge base by acquiring knowledge from experts or documented sources. The knowledge is then separated into *declarative* (factual) and *procedural* aspects. Development activity also includes the construction (or acquisition) of an inference engine, a blackboard, an explanation facility, and any other required software, such as interfaces. The knowledge is represented in the knowledge base in such a way that the system can draw conclusions by emulating the reasoning process of human experts. Determining appropriate knowledge representations takes place during development.

The process of developing ES can be lengthy (Chapter 14). The **ES shell** is a tool often used to expedite development. ES shells include all the major components of an ES, but they do *not* include the knowledge. The pioneering EMYCIN is a shell constructed by taking the MYCIN (an early ES described on the book's Web site) and deleting its specific knowledge. (The letter *E* in EMYCIN stands for *empty*; that is, MYCIN without its knowledge.) Exsys from Exsys Corporation, for which a current demo version is available on the Web (www.exsys.com), is a Windows-based ES shell.

CONSULTATION

Once the system has been developed and validated, it can be deployed to users. The ES conducts a bidirectional dialog with the user, asking for facts about a specific incident. While accepting the user's answers, the ES attempts to reach a conclusion. This effort is made by the inference engine, which chooses heuristic search techniques to be used to determine how the rules in the knowledge base are to be applied to each specific problem. The user can ask for explanations. The quality of the inference capability is determined by the quality and completeness of the rules (or appropriateness and depth of the knowledge representation), by the knowledge representation method used, and by the power of the inference engine.

Because the user is usually a computer novice, the ES must be very easy to use. At the present state of ES technology, the user must sit at a PC or computer terminal and type in a description of the problem (although some ES can use voice input). The ES asks questions, and the user answers them; additional questions can be asked and answered; and, finally, a conclusion is reached. The consultation environment is also used by the builder during the development phase to test the system. At that time, the interface and the explanation facility can be tested.

IMPROVEMENT

Expert systems are improved several times through a process called **rapid prototyping** during their development (Chapter 14).

10.10 EXAMPLE OF AN EXPERT SYSTEM CONSULTATION

Let's look at a simple rule-based expert system programmed in Exsys. A typical consultation is illustrated by *Select Auto,* an advisory system for car purchasing. The opening statement is

> Select Auto is an expert system designed to help a user make a right decision when buying a new car. It will review prospective cars that match the user's needs and preferences.

Now the consultation begins. The system's questions are *italicized,* and the user's answers are in **boldface**. In this menu-driven consultation, the user selected answer number 1 for both sample questions.

Q. #1. *The car is made in*
1. the United States
2. foreign countries
3. don't know
1

Q. #2. *Quality is*
1. the highest concern
2. of high concern
3. of moderate concern
4. don't know
1

The computer keeps asking questions based on the answers provided earlier. The user may want to know why specific information is needed by the computer. WHY is typed as a response to the next menu question on the left. In reply to the user question, the computer displays the rules in which price is a factor on the right. This is part of its explanation capability. Rules can be presented either in plain English or as they are programmed. For example, Exsys shows rule 5 as follows:

Q. #3. *Price of the car is*	Rule 5
	(response to WHY)
1. important	IF: (1) Price of the car is unimportant
2. unimportant	And
3. don't know	(2) The payment is in installments
WHY	THEN: The monthly payment is determined.

Now the user is able to answer the price question (e.g., with a 1).

The computer asks more questions. Later we will explain why and when questions are being asked. Here are some typical questions with a user's answers shown in **boldface.**

Q. #4. *The monthly payment is no more than*
1. $100
2. $150
3. $200
4. $250
5. $300
4

Q. #6. *Acceleration is*
1. strong
2. moderate
3. don't know
2

Q. #5. *The front seat is*
1. important
2. unimportant
1

Q. #7. *The engine size is*
1. 1,000–1,500
2. 1,501–2,000
3. over 2,000
4. don't know
2

Notice that "don't know" is an option. Expert systems can work with fuzzy or incomplete information just as human experts do. The computer asks some more questions.

Q. #8. *Reliability of a car is*

1. of high concern
2. of concern
3. of less concern
4. not sure
4

Q. #9. *The most considered factor in making a decision to buy a car is*
1. price
2. fuel economy
3. comfort and convenience
4. performance of a car
5. safety
6. reliability
7. quality
8. don't know
1, 7

Note that in the answer to Question 9, the user stated that both price (1) and quality (7) are most important. Most ES allow for this.

Once all the questions are answered, the computer displays a statement such as

The following are the automobiles most likely to suit your stated needs. If no selection has been made, it is probably because an automobile does not exist with all the attributes you desire. Should this occur, readjust your criteria and try again.

This is exactly what happened. Therefore, the computer displays the questions and answers to allow the user to change some answers:

1. The car is made in the United States.
2. Quality is the highest concern.
3. The price of the car is important.
4. The monthly payment is no more than $250.
5. The front seat is important.
6. Acceleration is moderate.
7. Engine size is 1,501–2,000 cc.
8. Reliability is not sure.
9. The most considered factors are price and quality.

The user changed the first answer from a car made in the United States to a car made in a foreign country. This time we were advised that two cars are recommended:

Value based on a system of −100 to +100	Value
1. Toyota Corolla	51
2. Renault Alliance	23

Because 100 points is the highest possible recommendation (a measure of certainty), neither car is really highly recommended, and so we may want to change our criteria again.

The user can ask *how* a certain recommendation has been derived. The computer then displays all the rules that were used in deriving the recommendation.

Now it is your turn to use an ES by yourself. Visit www.diadex.com and try to use the free demo for diagnosing a problem with your car and/or your computer.

In Chapters 11–14 we will explain how expert systems are built and how recommendations are derived.

10.11 PROBLEM AREAS ADDRESSED BY EXPERT SYSTEMS

Expert systems can be classified in several ways. One way is by the general problem areas they address. For example, *diagnosis* can be defined as "inferring system malfunctions from observations." Diagnosis is a generic activity performed in medicine, organizational studies, computer operations, and so on. The generic categories of expert systems are listed in Table 10.2. Some ES belong to two or more of these categories. A brief description of each category follows:

Interpretation systems infer situation descriptions from observations. This category includes surveillance, speech understanding, image analysis, signal interpretation, and many kinds of intelligence analyses. An interpretation system explains observed data by assigning them symbolic meanings describing the situation.

TABLE 10.2   Generic Categories of Expert Systems

Category	Problem Addressed
Interpretation	Inferring situation descriptions from observations
Prediction	Inferring likely consequences of given situations
Diagnosis	Inferring system malfunctions from observations
Design	Configuring objects under constraints
Planning	Developing plans to achieve goals
Monitoring	Comparing observations to plans, flagging exceptions
Debugging	Prescribing remedies for malfunctions
Repair	Executing a plan to administer a prescribed remedy
Instruction	Diagnosing, debugging, and correcting student performance
Control	Interpreting, predicting, repairing, and monitoring system behaviors

Prediction systems include weather forecasting, demographic predictions, economic forecasting, traffic predictions, crop estimates, and military, marketing, and financial forecasting.

Diagnostic systems include medical, electronic, mechanical, and software diagnoses. Diagnostic systems typically relate observed behavioral irregularities to underlying causes.

Design systems develop configurations of objects that satisfy the constraints of the design problem. Such problems include circuit layout, building design, and plant layout. Design systems construct descriptions of objects in various relationships with one another and verify that these configurations conform to stated constraints.

Planning systems specialize in planning problems, such as automatic programming. They also deal with short- and long-term planning in areas such as project management, routing, communications, product development, military applications, and financial planning.

Monitoring systems compare observations of system behavior with standards that seem crucial for successful goal attainment. These crucial features correspond to potential flaws in the plan. There are many computer-aided monitoring systems for topics ranging from air traffic control to fiscal management tasks.

Debugging systems rely on planning, design, and prediction capabilities for creating specifications or recommendations to correct a diagnosed problem.

Repair systems develop and execute plans to administer a remedy for certain diagnosed problems. Such systems incorporate debugging, planning, and execution capabilities.

Instruction systems incorporate diagnosis and debugging subsystems that specifically address the student's needs. Typically, these systems begin by constructing a hypothetical description of the student's knowledge that interprets her or his behavior. They then diagnose weaknesses in the student's knowledge and identify appropriate remedies to overcome the deficiencies. Finally, they plan a tutorial interaction intended to deliver remedial knowledge to the student.

Control systems adaptively govern the overall behavior of a system. To do this, the control system must repeatedly interpret the current situation, predict the future, diagnose the causes of anticipated problems, formulate a remedial plan, and monitor its execution to ensure success.

Not all the tasks usually found in each of these categories are suitable for expert systems. However, there are thousands of decisions that do fit into these categories. As an example, we selected the area of human resource management, as shown in Table 10.3.

TABLE 10.3 Expert Systems in Human Resource Management

Category	Description	ES and Its Functionality	Applications
Planning	Employment requirement Existing employment inventory Strategic planning	Planning ES Eliminate any gaps that may exist between supply and demand Intelligent agents match job and applicants on the Web	Recruitment Layoff Overtime Retirement Dismissal
Interpretation, design	Organization and process chart Characteristics of the job Required behaviors Employee characteristics	Job analysis ES Fit each job into the total fabric of the organization	Job description Job specification
Design, planning, prediction	Employer's requirements Candidates' performance Recruitment goals State of labor market Status of possible inside recruits	Recruitment ES Distinguish between qualifications of potential applicants and desirable ones Find appropriate resumes on the Web	Methods of recruitment Sources of recruits Recruitment policies
Planning, design, interpretation, diagnosis	Application blank Personality and performance test Physical examination Selection criteria	Selection ES Most likely meet organization's standards of performance and increase the proportion of successful employees selected Interpretation of online tests	Selection ratio Acceptance or rejection
Design, planning, monitoring, control	Individual difference Profit amount of organization Contributions to meeting organizational goals	Compensation ES Meet all the criteria, are equitable to employer and employee, provide incentives, and are acceptable to the employee	Methods of payment Incentive form Pay level Pay structure Rate ranges
Monitoring, interpretation, instruction, control	Quality and quantity of work Job knowledge Personal qualities Performance standards Evaluation policies	Performance evaluation ES Evaluate employee performance to meet standards	Salary adjustment Promotion Improvement in performance Layoff Transferral
Debugging, instruction, control	Organization's needs Knowledge, skill, and ability needed to perform the job Employee's needs, performance, and characteristics	Training ES Match the organization's objectives with the firm's human talent, structure, climate, and efficiency	Determining training needs Developing training criteria Choosing trainers and trainees Determining training type Assignment, placement, and orientation follow-up
Monitoring, design, planning	State of the economy Goals of the bargaining parties Public sentiment Issues being discussed Labor laws and regulation Precedents in bargaining	Labor–management relations ES Support management negotiation with unions on contracts	Contract Lockout Arbitration

Source: Compiled from D. H. Byum, and E. H. Soh, "Human Resource Management Expert Systems Technology," *Expert Systems,* May 1994; and M. G. Martinsons, "Human Resource Management Applications of Knowledge Based Systems," *International Journal of Information Management,* Vol. 17 No. 1, 1997.

10.12 BENEFITS OF EXPERT SYSTEMS

Thousands of ES are in use today in almost every industry and in every functional area. For example, Wong and Monaco (1995) provided a comprehensive review and literature analysis of expert systems in business. Eom (1996) also prepared a comprehensive survey of about 440 operational expert systems in business. His survey revealed that many ES have a profound impact, shrinking the time for tasks from days to hours, minutes, or seconds, and that nonquantifiable benefits include improved customer satisfaction, improved quality of products and services, and accurate and consistent decision making. For many firms, ES have become indispensable tools for effective management. See Krovvidy (1999). The major *potential* ES benefits are discussed next.

INCREASED OUTPUT AND PRODUCTIVITY

ES can work faster than humans. For example, XCON (see this book's Web site) has enabled DEC to increase the throughput of VAX configuring orders fourfold.

DECREASED DECISION-MAKING TIME

Using the system's recommendations, a human can make decisions much faster. For example, American Express authorities make charge approval decisions in less than 5 seconds, compared to about 3 minutes before implementation of an ES. This property is important in supporting frontline decision makers (Chapter 8) who must make quick decisions while interacting with customers.

INCREASED PROCESS AND PRODUCT QUALITY

ES can increase quality by providing consistent advice and reducing the size and rate of errors. For example, XCON reduced the error rate of configuring computer orders from 35 percent to 2 percent (initially—to even less in later releases), thus improving the quality of the minicomputers.

REDUCED DOWNTIME

Many operational ES (such as the CATS-1 system described earlier) are used for diagnosing malfunctions and prescribing repairs. By using ES it is possible to reduce machine downtime significantly. For example, on an oil rig one day of lost time can cost as much as $250,000. A system called Drilling Advisor was developed to detect malfunctions in oil rigs. This system saved a considerable amount of money for the company by significantly reducing downtime.

CAPTURE OF SCARCE EXPERTISE

The scarcity of expertise becomes evident in situations where there are not enough experts for a task, the expert is about to retire or leave the job, or expertise is required over a broad geographic area. Examples of systems that capture scarce expertise are CATS-1 (see AIS in Action 10.2) and TARA (see AIS in Action 10.4).

FLEXIBILITY

ES can offer flexibility in both the service and manufacturing industries.

AIS IN ACTION 10.4

INNOVATIVE EXPERT SYSTEMS: A SAMPLE

Of the many innovative expert systems on the market, the following are of particular interest.

TARA: An intelligent assistant for foreign traders. Foreign exchange currency traders cannot afford to think over multimillion dollar situations for long. In real time, they must examine large quantities of data, consider historical trends, determine what is relevant, and, many times in the course of a day, make the critical decision to buy or sell. It is a high-risk, high-reward job of prediction where even the best traders are pleased with being right 60 percent of the time. At Manufacturers Hanover Trust, an expert system called the Technical Analysis and Reasoning Assistant (TARA) was built to assist foreign currency traders. (*Source:* A. Schorr and A. Rappaport, *Innovative Applications of Artificial Intelligence,* Menlo Park, CA: AAAI Press, 1989.)

Managing toxicological studies. This system helps in identifying computing resources (and their costs) that support toxicological research programs for assessing the risks posed by toxic chemicals in an effort to reduce human health hazards. (*Source:* H. Berghel et al., "An Expert System for Managing Toxicological Studies," *Expert Systems: Planning, Implementation, Integration,* Spring 1991.)

Combating fraud. Medlife, a large U.S. life insurance company is using an expert system to detect fraud. One area of potential fraud involved suspicious death claims. The company is looking for patterns in death claims occurring at the end of—or shortly after—the 2-year contestability period. The rules for the expert system can be used to provide explanations. The anom-

alies detected by the systems are forwarded to an auditing group for special investigation. An interesting finding, for example, was a case in which the death occurred in a state other than the state of issuance or the state where the descendent lived during the effect of the policy. Such cases are associated with high levels of fraud. (*Source:* Condensed from *PC AI,* Jan./Feb. 1998.)

Forecasting short-term regional gas demand. Forecasting of future events is a major factor in planning. Forecasting accuracy is important because mistakes can be very costly. Regional gas companies have difficulties in forecasting demand because there are many influencing factors. Using an expert system, it is possible to obtain substantial improvement over traditional forecasting techniques. For details see Smith et al. (1996).

United Nations payroll automation system. The United Nations (U.N.) employs 15,000 people doing thousands of jobs in more than 100 locations worldwide in dozens of currencies. The U.N. decided to translate the paper-based rules and complex calculations that determine pay plus entitlements into an online knowledge base. The ES determines and applies entitlements automatically and reassesses the entitlements whenever an employee changes status. For details see Baum, (1996).

China's freight train system. An expert system was developed in China to allocate freight cars and determine what and how much to load on each car. The ES is integrated with the existing MIS, and the system is distributed to many users. For details see Geng et al. (1999).

EASIER EQUIPMENT OPERATION

ES makes complex equipment easier to operate. For example, STEAMER is an early ES intended to train inexperienced workers to operate complex ship engines. Another example is an ES developed for Shell Oil Company to train people to use complex computer program routines.

ELIMINATION OF THE NEED FOR EXPENSIVE EQUIPMENT

Often a human must rely on expensive instruments for monitoring and control. ES can perform the same tasks with lower-cost instruments because of their ability to investigate the information provided by instruments more thoroughly and quickly.

OPERATION IN HAZARDOUS ENVIRONMENTS

Many tasks require humans to operate in hazardous environments. An ES can allow humans to avoid such environments. It enables workers to avoid hot, humid, or toxic environments such as a nuclear power plant that has malfunctioned. This feature is extremely important in military conflicts.

ACCESSIBILITY TO KNOWLEDGE AND HELP DESKS

Expert systems make knowledge accessible, thus freeing experts from routine work. People can query systems and receive useful advice. One area of applicability is the support of help desks (Dryden, 1996). See the Exsys Corporation (www.exsys.com), www.inference.com, and Ginesys Corporation (www.ginesys.com) Web sites. Another is the support of call centers which now use Web-based intelligent systems (Thomas et al., 1997; Orzech, 1998) (see www.clarify.com).

ABILITY TO WORK WITH INCOMPLETE OR UNCERTAIN INFORMATION

In contrast to conventional computer systems, ES can, like human experts, work with incomplete, imprecise, uncertain data, information, or knowledge. The user can respond with "don't know" or "not sure" to one or more of the system's questions during a consultation, and the expert system will still be able to produce an answer although it may not be a certain one.

PROVIDE TRAINING

ES can provide training. Novices who work with ES become more and more experienced. The explanation facility can also serve as a teaching device, and so can notes and explanations that can be inserted into the knowledge base.

ENHANCEMENT OF PROBLEM SOLVING AND DECISION MAKING

ES enhance problem solving by allowing the integration of top experts' judgment into the analysis. For example, an ES called Statistical Navigator was developed to help novices use complex statistical computer packages.

IMPROVED DECISION-MAKING PROCESSES

ES provide rapid feedback on decision consequences, facilitate communication among decision makers on a team, and allow rapid response to unforeseen changes in the environment, thus providing a better understanding of the decision-making situation.

IMPROVED DECISION QUALITY

ES are reliable. They do not become tired or bored, call in sick, or go on strike, and they do not talk back to the boss. ES also consistently pay attention to all details and do not overlook relevant information and potential solutions, thereby making fewer errors. Also, ES provide the same recommendations to repeated problems.

ABILITY TO SOLVE COMPLEX PROBLEMS

One day ES may explain complex problems whose solution is beyond human ability. Some ES are already able to solve problems in which the required scope of knowledge exceeds that of any one individual. This allows decision makers to gain control over complicated situations and improve the operation of complex systems. (For a discussion, see Benders and Manders, 1993.)

KNOWLEDGE TRANSFER TO REMOTE LOCATIONS

One of the greatest potential benefits of ES is its ease of transfer across international boundaries. An example of such a transfer is an eye care ES (for diagnosis and recommended treatment) developed at Rutgers University in conjunction with the World Health Organization. The program has been implemented in Egypt and Algeria, where serious eye diseases are prevalent but eye specialists are rare. The PC program is rule-based and can be operated by a nurse, a physician's assistant, or a general practitioner. The Web is used extensively to disseminate information to users in remote locations. The U.S. government, for example, places advisory systems on safety and other topics on its Web sites (www.osha-slc.gov/dts/osta/oshasoft).

ENHANCEMENT OF OTHER INFORMATION SYSTEMS

Expert systems can often be found providing intelligent capabilities to other information systems. (Examples are presented in Chapter 16.) (Also see Klahr and Byrnes, 1993.)

Many of these benefits lead to improved decision making, improved products and customer service, and a sustainable strategic advantage. Some may even enhance the organization's image. See Tsai et al. (1994a) for details on industry practices. Basden (1994) provides a model of three levels of benefits from ES: *feature benefits, task benefits,* and *role benefits.* This model can be used to predict ES success (Section 10.4).

10.13 PROBLEMS AND LIMITATIONS OF EXPERT SYSTEMS

Available ES methodologies may not be straightforward and effective, even for many applications in the generic categories. The following problems have slowed down the commercial spread of ES:

- Knowledge is not always readily available.
- It can be difficult to extract expertise from humans.
- The approach of each expert to a situation assessment may be different yet correct.
- It is hard, even for a highly skilled expert, to abstract good situational assessments when he or she is under time pressure.
- Users of expert systems have natural cognitive limits.
- ES work well only within a narrow domain of knowledge.
- Most experts have no independent means of checking whether their conclusions are reasonable.
- The vocabulary, or jargon, that experts use to express facts and relations is often limited and not understood by others.
- Help is often required from knowledge engineers who are rare and expensive, a fact that could make ES construction costly.
- Lack of trust on the part of end users may be a barrier to ES use.
- Knowledge transfer is subject to a host of perceptual and judgmental biases.

Last, but not least, is the fact that expert systems may not be able to arrive at conclusions. For example, the initial fully developed XCON could not fulfill about 2 percent of the orders presented to it. Finally, expert systems, like human experts, sometimes produce incorrect recommendations.

The Web is the major facilitator of ES that overcomes several of these limitations. The ability to disseminate ES to the masses makes them more cost-effective. Consequently, more money can be spent on better systems.

Gill (1995) studied the longevity of commercial expert systems. He discovered that only about one-third of all commercial ES studied survived over a 5-year period. The short-lived nature of so many systems was generally not attributable to failure to meet technical performance or economic objectives. Instead, managerial issues such as lack of system acceptance by users, inability to retain developers, problems in transitioning from development to maintenance, and shifts in organizational priorities appeared to be the most significant factors resulting in long-term ES disuse. Proper management of ES development and deployment can resolve most of these issues in practice.

These limitations clearly indicate that today's ES fall short of generally intelligent human behavior. However, several of these limitations will diminish or disappear with technological improvements over time.

10.14 EXPERT SYSTEM SUCCESS FACTORS

Several researchers have investigated the reasons why ES succeed and fail in practice. This work includes studies by Eom (1996), Guimaraes et al. (1996), Kunnathur et al. (1996), Tsai et al. (1994a), and Yoon et al. (1995). As with many MIS, two of the most critical factors are *a champion in management, user involvement,* and *training.* Management must support the project, and users must feel ownership. Many studies have shown that the level of managerial and user involvement directly affects the success level of MIS, specifically ES. However, these factors alone are not sufficient to guarantee success, and the following issues should also be considered:

- The level of knowledge must be sufficiently high.
- Expertise must be available from at least one cooperative expert.
- The problem to be solved must be mostly qualitative (fuzzy), not purely quantitative (otherwise, a numerical approach should be used).
- The problem must be sufficiently narrow in scope.
- ES shell characteristics are important. The shell must be of high quality and naturally store and manipulate the knowledge.
- The user interface must be friendly for novice users.
- The problem must be important and difficult enough to warrant development of an ES (but it need not be a core function).
- Knowledgeable system developers with good people skills are needed.
- The impact of ES as a source of end-user job improvement must be considered. The impact should be favorable. End-user attitudes and expectations must be considered.
- Management support must be cultivated.

Managers attempting to introduce ES technology should establish end-user training programs, thus demonstrating its potential as a business tool (Guimaraes et al., 1996). As part of the managerial support effort, the organizational environment should favor new technology adoption (Kunnathur et al., 1996). Finally, Tsai et al. (1994a) present the following conclusions:

- Business applications for expert systems are often justified by their strategic impact in terms of gaining a competitive advantage rather than their cost-effectiveness. The major value of expert systems stems from capturing and disseminating expert-type skills and knowledge to improve the quality and consistency of business operations.
- The most popular and successful expert systems are those that deal with well-defined, structured applications, or where no more than several hundred rules are needed, such as those in the production area. Expert systems have been less successful when applications require instincts and experienced judgments, as in the human resource management area, or where there are thousands of rules and their exceptions.

Gill (1996b) conducted a survey of 52 successful ES and found that ES that persist over time change the nature of the users' tasks and jobs in a manner that motivates continued use of the expert system. These tools offer users a greater sense of control, increase work-related variety or decrease work-related drudgery, enable users to perform tasks at much higher proficiency levels or to assess their own task performance, and so on. Gill cautioned expert systems developers and their managers to recognize that design features providing such intrinsic motivation must be built into the technology. As soon as the idea for an expert system (or, in fact, an IT based application) has been conceived, it is time to start assessing its impact on user motivation. And if the outcome of such assessments is that motivational impacts will most likely be negative, the viability of the development effort should be reconsidered—expert systems whose "motivation for use" is negative just do not last very long. An interesting study on a failing system at a large consumer product company is reported by Vedder et al. (1999).

10.15 TYPES OF EXPERT SYSTEMS

Expert systems appear in many varieties. The following classifications of ES are not exclusive; that is, one ES can appear in several categories.

EXPERT SYSTEMS VERSUS KNOWLEDGE-BASED SYSTEMS

According to this classification, an ES is a system whose behavior is so sophisticated that we would call a person who performed in a similar manner an expert. MYCIN and XCON are good examples. (See the descriptions on this book's Web site.) Highly trained professionals diagnose blood diseases (MYCIN) and configure complex computing equipment (XCON). These systems truly attempt to emulate the best human experts.

In the commercial world, however, there are systems that can effectively and efficiently perform tasks that do not really need an expert. Such systems are called **knowledge-based systems**[4] (also known as advisory systems, knowledge systems, intelligent job aid systems, or operational systems). As an example, let us look at a system that gives advice on the immunizations recommended for travel abroad. This advice depends on many attributes such as the age, gender, and health of the traveler and the country of destination. One needs to be knowledgeable to give such advice, but one need not be an expert. In this case, practically all the knowledge that relates to this advice is documented in a manual available from most public health departments (in only 1 or 2 percent of the cases it

---

[4]This terminology is not widely accepted as yet. Therefore, the terms *expert systems* and *knowledge-based systems* are often used interchangeably.

is necessary to consult a physician). Another example is automated help desks (see AIS in Action 10.5).

The distinction between the two types of ES systems may not be so sharp in reality. Many systems involve both documented knowledge and undocumented expertise. Basically it is a matter of *how much* expertise is included in systems that classifies them in one category or the other. Knowledge systems can be constructed more quickly and cheaply than expert systems.

RULE-BASED EXPERT SYSTEMS

Many commercial ES are **rule-based systems** because the technology of rule-based systems is well developed and the development tools can be used by end users. In such systems knowledge is represented as a series of rules.

FRAME-BASED SYSTEMS

In **frame-based systems,** knowledge is represented as frames, a representation of the object-oriented programming approach (Chapter 12).

HYBRID SYSTEMS

Hybrid systems include several knowledge representation approaches, typically, at a minimum they involve frames and rules.

MODEL-BASED SYSTEMS

Model-based systems are structured around a model that simulates the structure and function of the system under study. The model is used to compute values, which are compared to observed values. The comparison triggers action (if needed) or further diagnosis (Chapter 12).

READY-MADE (OFF-THE-SHELF) SYSTEMS

ES can be developed to meet the particular needs of a user (custom-made), or they can be purchased as ready-made packages for general use. **Ready-made systems** are similar to application packages such as an accounting general ledger or project management in

---

AIS IN ACTION 10.5

AUTOMATING THE HELP DESK

Millions of employees work in organizations as providers of information and are in direct contact with customers. Often customers are frustrated because all the lines are busy when they call an information center. ("All agents are busy. You are important to us; please stay on the line. Someone will be with you as soon as possible."). Also, the information provided may not be accurate. The solution is to automate the help desk by using expert systems. An example is Color Tile Company, which uses Expert Advisor (from Software Artistry Inc.) to support queries from its own employees. Formerly, operators had to search through numerous manuals to provide advice on how to fix problems in the point-of-sale terminals at the many Color Tile stores. Using the ES, operators can now determine the solution to the problem much faster and more accurately. For more details on the system, see Kulik (1992). Such systems are now available for employees on intranets and for customers on extranets. For example, Peppers et al. (1999) provide the example of Canadian Tire Acceptance Ltd., which serves 4 million credit card holders. By employing Web technology the intelligent center integrated all incoming inquiries (fax, telephone, Web). Using an ES, the system analyzes customers' profiles and recognizes needs so that better service can be provided.

operations management. Ready-made systems enjoy the economy of mass production and therefore are considerably less expensive than customized systems. They also can be used as soon as they are purchased (several are available on the Web, as shown in AIS in Action 10.4). Unfortunately, ready-made systems are very general in nature and the advice they render may not be of value to a user involved in a complex situation. However, their popularity increases as their prices decrease and their capabilities increase. We distinguish between two types: those for general use, and those that are industry-, country-, or product-specific (see AIS in Action 10.6 for both types).

AIS IN ACTION 10.6

READY-MADE SYSTEMS: A SAMPLER

There are hundreds of commercial ready-made off-the-shelf ES. Here are a few interesting examples:

Plan Write Expert Edition acts as a consultant that helps you write a business plan. As you write the plan, the ES examines your assumptions and provides you with feedback. It is a comprehensive system that provides charts, text, and so on. The system can be used for a start-up company or for expanding an existing one. For details, see www.brs-inc.com and *Information Week*, Nov. 8, 1999.

The *FS* system (from Athena Group) advises on foreign exchange trading activity. It supports a number of different analysis techniques and provides probabilistic decision support. Thus, it can be considered a DSS/ES combination. The system contains several trading, hedging, and risk-control strategies.

Paint Advisor advises customers in Europe about do-it-yourself paint jobs and appropriate products. It tells the user how to prepare for painting, clean up, and do the job under different conditions. The program, which includes about 300 rules, is available at a chain of department stores in Europe for free use by potential buyers of paint products.

Negotiator Pro provides advice on how to negotiate and can be used to improve negotiating skills. The system builds personality profiles of the participants (self-assessments) and then helps in building a negotiation.

Expert Labor Scheduler (from Software Artistry) is designed to meet the labor scheduling needs of retail organizations with multiple departments and locations. The system enables users to keep overhead low while making sure everyone is at the right place at the right time.

Fair-Cost (from DM Data Inc.) provides an interactive planning aid for strategic planning, system costing, engineering, and purchasing involved in obtaining custom very-large-scale integrated (VLSI) circuits for electronic systems.

Cotton++ is an expert system developed by the U.S. Department of Agriculture to advise farmers on how to manage cotton farms. By making appropriate decisions supported by the system regarding irrigation, fertilization, and harvesting, farmers have increased the yield of cotton by 10 percent. For details see Lemmon and Chuk (1995).

The Interviewer (from Park City Group Inc.) is an ES that guides an applicant in filling out an electronic questionnaire. Based on the answers, more questions are asked. At the end, the system summarizes the interview and prepares a list of questions for an oral interview by retail store managers to check on areas of concern.

The Operations Experts (from Park City Group Inc.) identifies the most efficient stores in a large chain of retail stores. The ranking is based on comparisons of utility costs, labor costs, and other factors. An analysis of each store is also generated.

Origin Basic (from Nifco Synergy Ltd.) is a NAFTA expert system that helps a company take best advantage of cross-border trading opportunities. Origin Basic determines whether a finished product qualifies for preferential tariff treatment, produces an audit trail that documents the reasons for categorizing a specific product the way a company did, and helps companies better set their own buying policies. For details see McCarthy (1996).

Internal Operations Risk Analysis (from Business Foundations) helps a CPA acquire in-depth knowledge about a business by analyzing functional business areas. The program assigns a risk rating to each of 27 categories and identifies the individual questionnaire responses that contributed to medium and high ratings. For details see Smith and Smith (1996).

Business Analyst, (from Redflag, www.redflag.com) is a consultant ES that keeps tabs on a company's health. The program analyzes financial information and provides management reports. A companion program is Inventory Analyst (introduced in 2000). For details see Internet Exercise 10.

Resumix 5 (www.resumix.com) matches resumes and job openings and supports several other recruiting activities.

REAL-TIME EXPERT SYSTEMS

Real-time ES have a strict limit on the system's response time, which must be fast enough to control the process being computerized. In other words, the system *always* produces a response by the time it is needed.

10.16 EXPERT SYSTEMS AND THE INTERNET/INTRANETS/WEB

The relationship between ES and the Internet (the Net) and intranets can be divided into two categories. The first is the use of ES on the Net. In this case the Net supports ES (and other AI) applications. The second is the support ES (and other AI methods) give to the Net.

USING ES ON THE NET

One of the early reasons for ES development was its potential to provide knowledge and advice to large numbers of users. Because knowledge is disseminated to many people, the cost per user becomes small, making ES very attractive. However, according to Eriksson (1996), attaining this goal has proven to be very difficult. Because advisory systems are used infrequently, they need a large number of users to justify their construction. As a result, very few ES disseminate knowledge to many users.

The widespread availability and use of the Internet and intranets provide the opportunity to disseminate expertise and knowledge to mass audiences. By implementing expert systems (and other intelligent systems) as knowledge servers, it becomes economically feasible and profitable to publish expertise on the Net. ES running on servers can support a large group of users who communicate with the system over the Net. In this way user interfaces based on Web protocols and the use of browsers provide access to the knowledge servers. This implementation approach is described in Eriksson (1996). For an example, see the Exsys Web Runtime Engine WREN at OSHA (see AIS in Action 10.7).

ES can be transferred over the Net not only to human users but also to other computerized systems, including DSS, robotics, and databases. Other ES Net support possi-

---

AIS IN ACTION 10.7

CHECK OUT OSHA'S WEB-BASED EXPERT SYSTEMS

Want to see the latest ES developments at the U.S. Department of Labor Occupational Safety and Health Administration (OSHA)? Access the OSHA Web site, www.osha.gov. OSHA has several up-and-running Web-based ES developed and deployed in the Exsys Web Runtime Engine—WREN. Try the Confined Spaces Advisor (CSA, version 1.1 released in December 1997), which provides guidance to help employers protect workers from the hazards of entry into permit-required confined spaces. The system helps de-

termine if a space is covered by OSHA's Permit-required Confined Spaces Regulation. The software follows the structure of the example in Section 10.10, is rich in detail, and uses a Web browser as an interface. Run it to see if you need a special government permit for your workplace or apartment. The ES can be downloaded from www.osha-slc.gov/dts/osta/oshasoft along with several other safety advice ES. Keep your browser pointed to the OSHA Web site. More applications are coming soon!

bilities include system construction. Here, collaboration between builders, experts, and knowledge engineers can be facilitated by Internet-based groupware. This can reduce the cost of building ES. Knowledge acquisition costs can be reduced, for example, in cases where there are several experts or where the expert is in a different location from the knowledge engineer. Knowledge maintenance can also facilitate the use of the Net, which is also helpful to users.

Finally, the Web can greatly support the spread of multimedia-based expert systems. Such systems, called **intelimedia systems,** support the integration of extensive multimedia applications and ES. Such systems can be very helpful for remote users, such as those in the tourism industry, and in remote equipment failure diagnosis [for details see Fuerst et al. (1995)].

The other aspect of the ES–Internet relationship is the support ES and other AI technologies can provide to the Internet and intranets. The major contributions of AI to the Internet and intranets are summarized in Table 10.4 [for details see O'Leary (1996) and Chapter 14].

Information about the relationship among expert systems, intelligent agents, and other AI and the Internet is readily available on the Internet itself. For example, Hengl (1995) provides a list of more than 1,600 AI-related Web sites. Also see the Web sites of *PC AI* (a magazine) (www.pcai.com) and the American Association for Artificial Intelligence (www.aaai.org).

❖ CHAPTER HIGHLIGHTS

- The primary objective of AI is to build computer systems that perform tasks that can be characterized as intelligent.
- The major characteristics of AI are symbolic processing, the use of heuristics instead of algorithms, and the application of inference techniques.
- AI has several major advantages over people: It is permanent, it can be easily duplicated and disseminated, it can be less expensive than human intelligence, it is consistent and thorough, and it can be documented.
- Natural (human) intelligence has advantages over AI: It is creative, it uses sensory experiences directly, and it reasons from a wide context of experiences.

TABLE 10.4   Artificial Intelligence Contributions to the Internet

Technology and Applications

Intelligent agents
  Assist Web browsing
  Assist in finding information
  Assist in matching items
  Filter e-mail
  Access databases, summarize information
  Improve Internet security
  Conduct information retrieval and discovery, smart search engines (metasearch)
  Browse large documents (knowledge decomposition)
  Monitor data and alert for actions (e.g., looking for Web site changes), monitor users and usage

Expert systems
  Match queries to users with canned answers to frequently asked questions (FAQs)
  Intelligent browsing of qualitative databases
  Browse large documents (knowledge decomposition)

Web robots (spiders)
  Conduct informational retrieval and discovery, smart search engines (metasearch)

- Knowledge rather than data or information is the key concept of AI.
- In conventional computing we tell the computer how to solve the problem. In AI, we tell the computer what the problem is and give it the knowledge needed to solve similar problems and the necessary procedures to use the knowledge.
- Major application areas of AI include expert systems, natural language processing, speech understanding, intelligent robotics, computer vision, fuzzy logic, intelligent agents, intelligent computer-aided instruction, and neural computing.
- Expert systems, the most applied AI technology, attempt to imitate the work of experts. They apply expertise to problem solving.
- For an expert system to be effective, it must be applied to a narrow domain of knowledge and include qualitative factors.
- Natural language processing is an attempt to allow users to communicate with computers in a natural language. Currently, conversation takes place via the keyboard and monitor; in the future, it will be carried out by voice.
- An intelligent robot is one that can respond to changes in its environment. Most of today's robots do not have this capability.
- Computers can be used as tutors. If they are supported by AI, they can dramatically improve training and teaching.
- The various AI technologies can be integrated among themselves and with other computer-based technologies.
- Expert systems imitate the reasoning process of experts in solving difficult problems.
- The power of an ES is derived from the specific knowledge it possesses, not from the particular knowledge representation and inference schemes it uses.
- Expertise is task-specific knowledge acquired from training, reading, and experience.
- Experts can make fast and good decisions regarding complex situations.
- Most of the knowledge in organizations is possessed by a few experts.
- Expert system technology attempts to transfer knowledge from experts and documented sources to the computer and make it available for use by nonexperts.
- Expert systems involve knowledge processing, whereas other CBIS process data or information.
- The reasoning capability in expert systems is provided by an inference engine.
- A distinction is made between a development environment (building an ES) and a consultation environment (using an ES).
- The major components of an ES are the knowledge acquisition subsystem, knowledge base, inference engine, blackboard, user interface, and explanation subsystem.
- The knowledge engineer captures the knowledge from the expert and programs it into the computer.
- Although the major user of ES is a nonexpert, other users (such as students, ES builders, and even experts) can use ES.
- Knowledge can be declarative (facts) or procedural.
- When expert systems are constructed, they are improved repeatedly in an iterative manner using a process called rapid prototyping.
- The 10 generic categories of ES are interpretation, prediction, diagnosis, design, planning, monitoring, debugging, repair, instruction, and control.
- Expert systems can provide many benefits. The most important are improvement in productivity or quality, preservation of scarce expertise, en-

hancing other systems, coping with incomplete information, and providing training.
- Many ES failures are caused by nontechnical problems such as lack of managerial support and poor end-user training.
- Although there are several technical limitations to the use of expert systems, some of them will disappear with improved technology.
- Expert systems, like human experts, can make mistakes.
- Some make a distinction between expert systems, where most of the knowledge comes from experts, and knowledge systems, where the majority of the knowledge comes from documented sources.
- Some ES are available as ready-made systems; they render advice for standard situations. A trend is developing toward disseminating such advice on the Internet, intranets, and extranets.
- Some expert systems provide advice in a real-time mode.
- ES and AI provide support to the Internet and intranets as well.

❖ KEY WORDS

- algorithm
- artificial intelligence (AI)
- blackboard
- consultation environment
- development environment
- domain
- expert
- expert system (ES)
- expert system shell
- expertise
- explanation subsystem
- frame-based system
- fuzzy logic
- genetic algorithms
- heuristics

- inference engine
- inferencing
- intelimedia systems
- intelligent agent (IA)
- intelligent computer-aided instruction (ICAI)
- intelligent tutoring system (ITS)
- justifier
- knowledge
- knowledge acquisition
- knowledge base
- knowledge engineer
- knowledge-refining system
- knowledge-based system
- model-based system

- natural language processing (NLP)
- neural computing (networks)
- numeric processing
- pattern matching
- rapid prototyping
- ready-made system
- real-time ES
- real-time system
- robotics
- rule-based system
- speech understanding
- symbol
- symbolic processing
- Turing test
- visual recognition

❖ QUESTIONS FOR REVIEW

1. Define artificial intelligence.
2. What is the Turing test?
3. What do we mean by inferencing?
4. List the major advantages of artificial intelligence over natural intelligence.
5. List the major disadvantages of artificial as compared to natural intelligence.
6. Define a knowledge base for an application and organizational knowledge base.
7. How does a computer use a knowledge base?
8. List the major AI technologies.
9. Define an expert system.
10. Define natural language processing.
11. Define speech recognition and understanding.
12. Define fuzzy logic. Why is it useful?
13. Define an intelligent agent. Why is it useful?
14. What is a robot? How is it related to AI?
15. Define visual recognition as it applies to computer technology.

16. List the major benefits of intelligent computer-aided instruction.

17. Distinguish between an organizational knowledge base and a specific problem knowledge base.

18. Explain how ES can distribute (or redistribute) the available knowledge in an organization.

19. List the types of knowledge included in expertise.

20. List and describe the eight activities that human experts perform (Section 10.6). Which activities are performed well by current expert systems?

21. Define the ES development environment and contrast it with the consultation environment.

22. List and define the major components of an ES.

23. What is the difference between knowledge acquisition and knowledge representation?

24. What is the role of a knowledge engineer?

25. A knowledge base includes facts and rules. Explain the difference between the two.

26. Which component of ES is mostly responsible for the reasoning capability?

27. What are the major activities performed in the ES blackboard (workplace)?

28. What is the function of the justifier?

29. List four types of potential users of ES.

30. List the 10 generic categories of ES.

31. Describe some of the limitations of ES.

32. Describe some success factors of ES.

33. What is a ready-made (off-the-shelf) ES?

34. What is a real-time ES?

35. What benefits are there in deploying an ES on the Web?

36. How can an ES help a decision maker in Web use?

37. List five major benefits of ES.

❖ QUESTIONS FOR DISCUSSION

1. Compare numeric and symbolic processing techniques.

2. Speech understanding or even recognition could increase the number of managers using a computer directly 10-fold. Do you agree with this statement? Why or why not?

3. Explain why an expert system user is typically a novice, whereas a DSS user is typically an expert decision maker.

4. It is said that reasoning ability, powerful computers, inference capabilities, and heuristics are necessary but not sufficient for solving real problems. Why?

5. A major difference between a conventional decision support system and ES is that the former can answer a "how" question, whereas the latter can also answer a "why" question. Discuss.

6. Explain how the Web improves the benefit/cost ratio of ES and enables systems that otherwise are not justifiable.

7. Why is it so difficult to build a component that can automatically refine knowledge?

8. Explain the relationship between the development environment and the consultation (run-time) environment.

9. What kind of mistakes might ES make and why? Why is it easier to correct mistakes in ES than in conventional programs?

10. Table 10.2 provides a list of 10 categories of ES. Compile a list of 20 examples, 2 in each category, from the various functional areas in an organization (accounting, finance, production, marketing, and HR).

11. Review the limitations of ES discussed in this chapter. From what you know, which of these limitations are the most likely to still be limitations in the year 2100? Why?

12. A ready-made ES is selling for $5,000. Developing one will cost you $50,000. A ready-made suit will cost you $100, and a tailored one will cost you $500. Develop an analogy between the two situations and describe the markets for the ready-made and customized products. Why is it that a ready-made ES costs only 1 percent of the cost of developing one, while a ready-made suit costs 20 percent of the cost of a tailored one?

13. Given the current status of the Web, discuss how it is changing the availability of ES and how it is being used to embed expertise in other systems.

❖ EXERCISES

1. Interview an information system manager. Determine the extent to which the company is using AI-based technologies. Also, ask what the company plans for the next 3–5 years. Are there any problems? (List and discuss.) Prepare a two-page report on your visit.

2. Explore the literature to identify the major problems in getting AI applications accepted. What is required on the part of management?

3. Search for references on computerized chess (e.g., IBM's Deep Blue) and write a paper on the latest developments. Are these developments simply algorithmic advances, hardware advances, or advances in artificial intelligence?

4. Read the article, "How Campbell Soup Company Uses Expert Systems to Cut Equipment Downtimes from Days to Hours," I/S Analyzer Case Studies, March 1995. Describe the basic ES developed. What problem area (Section 10.11) did it address? Which of the benefits described in Section 10.12 were obtained? What problems and limitations (Section 10.9) were encountered? Which factors (from those listed in Section 10.14) were instrumental in the success of the ES? Were there others? What type (Section 10.15) of ES is this?

5. Refer to Wong and Monaco (1995) which reviews expert systems in business. What major problem domains are described? What domains are growing? Which ones are shrinking? What are the generic problem areas? What levels of management do expert systems attempt to address? What development methods are used?

6. Find five applied expert systems in the recent literature (within 1 year) in one or several business functional areas in which you have a strong interest. Compare their purpose, complexity, knowledge representation, and the tools with which they were constructed (shells or programming languages).

❖ GROUP EXERCISES

1. *In-class knowledge exercise:* Make a peanut butter and jelly sandwich. Describe all the details of what you do as you make it and have someone in the class write down all the steps. How long is the list? Did you leave anything out? Next, have a classmate attempt to make a sandwich by following the instructions explicitly as written (someone else should read the instructions aloud). Did it work? Add the missing steps to the original list. How much longer is the new list than the old one? Would you follow the same sequence of steps if you were making 100 sandwiches instead of one? Explain why or why not. If you were selling sandwiches, what would you do differently?

2. Consider the decision-making situation defined by the following rules:
- If it is a nice day and it is summer, then I go to the golf course.
- If it is a nice day and it is winter, then I go to the ski resort.
- If it is not a nice day and it is summer, then I go to work.
- If it is not a nice day and it is winter, then I go to class.
- If I go to the golf course, then I play golf.
- If I go to the ski resort, then I go skiing.
- If I go skiing or I play golf, then I have fun.
- If I go to work, then I make money.
- If I go to class, then I learn something.
  a. Follow the rules for the following situations (what do you conclude for each one?):
     - It is a nice day and it is summer.
     - It is not a nice day and it is winter.
     - It is a nice day and it is winter.
     - It is not a nice day and it is summer.
  b. Are there any other combinations that are valid? Explain.
  c. What needs to happen for you to "learn something" in this knowledge universe? Start with the conclusion "learn something" and identify the rules used (backward) to get to the needed facts.
  d. Encode the knowledge into a graphical diagram (like an influence diagram). Use a circle to represent a fact such as
     The day is nice
     or
     The day is not nice
     and an arrow to indicate influence.
  e. Write a BASIC (or other third-generation language) program to execute this knowledge. Use IF-THEN-(ELSE) statements in your implementation. How many lines long is it? How hard would it be to modify the program to insert new facts and a rule such as
     - If it is cloudy and it is warm
     - and it is not raining
     - and it is summer
     - then I go play golf.
  f. Implement the knowledge in a spreadsheet or database package on a PC.
  g. *Advanced exercise.* In an implementation similar to the one in part (d), write a new implementation but store the knowledge in variables. Let the program search the arrays to make decisions.

❖ INTERNET EXERCISES

1. In 1995 there were about 2,000 Web sites related to AI (Hengl, 1995). Today there are substantially more. Do a search and describe how many Web sites you find. Categorize the first 20 into groups, or if you used a search engine that grouped them, what groups did you find?

2. Identify some news groups that have an interest in applied AI. Post a question regarding the use of AI technologies for decision support.

3. Link yourself to several demonstrations from www.zdwebopedia.com/artificial-intelligence/expert-system.html. Go over the tutorials and the "try me" samples. The Web site www.pcia.com/pcai, Feb. 26, 1999, lists all major AI–expert systems vendors, including links to several demos. Try them.

4. Access the Web site of *PC AI* magazine (www.pcai.com/pcai and www.abnet.org/lmp/catdiv/es/html). Investigate the current state of the art for ES. Write up your findings in report form.

5. Access the Web site of the American Association for Artificial Intelligence (www. aaai.org). Examine the workshops they have offered over the last year. What major topics of expert systems are the focuses of current research? Why?

6. Access the Web site of Ginesys Corporation (www.ginesys.com). Try the online loan prequalification demo developed in KnowledgeWave. Describe your experience. Why might having access to an ES provide better service than waiting for a loan officer? Examine their success stories.

7. Access the Web Site of Exsys Corporation (www.exsys.com). Evaluate the underlying structure of Exsys RuleBook. Does it seem to be a natural way to represent knowledge? What kinds of problems fit this knowledge representation type? Exsys WREN (Web Runtime Engine) allows the Exsys ES shell to provide expertise over a Web server. Describe its capabilities. What advantages and disadvantages are there? Run a WREN application and describe how it worked. Examine the commercial loan approval predictor example ES application. What features made this problem ideal for solution with an ES? Examine at least one other application and compare its problem features with those of the loan approval predictor.

8. Access the Web site of Acquire Intelligence Inc., Victoria, BC, Canada (www. vvv.com/ai/acquire/acquire.html). Run the graduate school admissions demo live over the Web. Did you feel comfortable using it? Did you get into graduate school? Compare its use to the process of filling out an application and waiting for results from the school or talking to an admissions director.

9. Search the Web for vendors of help desk software. Try a demo if one is available. What is used to give the software intelligence? What communication means are used in a typical installation? Are they designed for customer access or for help desk personnel access?

10. Visit www.redflag.com and view the Inventory Analyst demo. Write an evaluation of its usefulness. Then go through the interactive presentation of Business Analyst. Explain what it does for you. Also look at customers' success stories.

11. Enter www.gensym.com/successstories/nabisco.html and read the Nabisco Biscuit Company case. Then play the video clip. Prepare a report that will indicate the role of knowledge bases and ES in direct and indirect support of the POG and other programs. Summarize the benefits.

❖ DEBATES

1. Computers are programmed to play chess, scrabble and even crossword puzzles (*American Scientist,* Sept./Oct. 1999). They are getting better and better, and one such system beat the world's number-one Grand Master Garry Kasparov in May 1997. Do such computer systems exhibit intelligence? Why or why not?

2. Prepare a table showing all the arrangements you can think of that justify the position that computers cannot think. Then prepare arguments that show the opposite.

3. Bourbaki (1990) describes Searle's argument against use of the Turing test. Summarize all the important issues in this debate.

4. Proponents of AI claim that we will never have machines that truly think because they cannot, by definition, have a soul. Supporters claim a soul is unnecessary. They cite the fact that originally humanity set out to create an artificial bird for flight. An airplane is not a bird, but it functionally acts as one. Debate the issue.

❖ GROUP TERM PROJECT

1. *Development of a prototype expert system.* Identify an organization with which at least one member of your group has a good contact who has a decision-making problem that requires some expertise (but is not too complicated). Some examples include selection of suppliers, selection of a new employee, job assignment, computer

selection, market contact method selection, and determining admission into graduate school. Try to state the problem that will be implemented in an expert system. Later on, as you move to Chapter 11–14 and learn new material, interview an expert and develop and implement an expert system. Keep your rule base limited to 50 rules and use Exsys or another demo ES shell available over the Web.

CASE APPLICATION 10.1

GATE ASSIGNMENT DISPLAY SYSTEM[5]

PROBLEM

Gate assignment, the responsibility of gate controllers and their assistants, is a complex and demanding task at any airport. At O'Hare airport in Chicago, for example, two gate controllers typically plan berthing for about 500 flights a day at about 50 gates. Flights arrive in clusters for the convenience of customers who must transfer to connecting flights, and so controllers must sometimes accommodate a cluster of 30 or 40 planes in 20 to 30 minutes. To complicate the matter, each flight is scheduled to remain at its gate a different length of time, depending on the schedules of connecting flights and the amount of servicing needed. Mix these problems with the need to juggle gates constantly because of flight delays caused by weather and other factors and you get some idea of the challenges. The problem is even more complex because of its interrelationship with remote parking and constraints related to ground equipment availability and customs requirements.

SOLUTION

Many airports are introducing expert systems to solve these problems. The pioneering work was done at Chicago O'Hare in 1987–1988. The Korean Air system at Kimpo Airport, Korea, won the 1999 innovative application award from the American Association of Artificial Intelligence (www.aaai.org). The two systems have several common features and similar architectures.

SYSTEM CAPABILITIES

An intelligent gate assignment system can be set up and quickly rescheduled and contains far more information than a manual system. Its superb graphical display shows times and gate numbers. The aircraft are symbolized as colored bars; each bar's position indicates the gate assigned, and its length indicates the length of time the plane is expected to occupy the gate. Bars with pointed ends identify arrival–departure flights; square ends are used for originator–terminator flights. The system also shows, in words and

numbers near each bar, the flight number, arrival and departure times, plane number, present fuel load, flight status, ground status, and more.

Each participating aircraft carries a small radio transmitter that automatically reports to the mainframe system when the nose wheel touches down on the field. The system immediately changes that plane's bar from "off", meaning off the field, to "on", meaning on the field. When the plane is stopped at its gate, the code changes to "in". So gate controllers have access to an up-to-the-second ground status for every flight in their display.

The system also has a number of built-in reminders. For instance, it won't permit an aircraft to be assigned to the wrong kind of gate and explains why it can't. The controller can manually override such a decision to meet an unusual situation. The system also keeps its eye on the clock—when an incoming plane is on the field and its gate hasn't been assigned yet, flashing red lines bracket the time to alert the controller.

BENEFITS OF THE SYSTEM

Three major benefits have been identified. First, the assistant gate controller can start scheduling the next day's operations 4 or 5 hours earlier than was possible before. The Korean system, for example, produces a schedule in 20 seconds instead of in 5 manually worked hours. Second, the ES is also used by zone controllers and other ground operations, (towing, cleaning, resupply). At O'Hare, for example, each of the 10 zone controllers is responsible for all activities at a number of gates (funneling, baggage handling, catering service, crew assignment, and the rest). Third, superreliability is built into these systems.

CASE QUESTIONS

1. Why is the gate assignment task so complex?
2. Why is the system considered a real-time ES?
3. What are the major benefits of the ES compared to the manual system? (Prepare a detailed list.)

[5]Based on press releases from the American Association of Artificial Intelligence (1999) and Texas Instruments Data System Group (1988).

CHAPTER

11

KNOWLEDGE ACQUISITION AND VALIDATION[1]

Knowledge acquisition is the process of extracting, structuring, and organizing knowledge from one or more sources. This process has been identified by many researchers and practitioners as a (or even as *the*) bottleneck that constrains the development of expert systems and other AI systems. This chapter, which attempts to present the most important issues and topics in knowledge acquisition, is divided into the following sections:

11.1	Opening Vignette: American Express Improves Approval Selection with Machine Learning
11.2	Knowledge Engineering
11.3	Scope of Knowledge
11.4	Difficulties in Knowledge Acquisition
11.5	Methods of Knowledge Acquisition: An Overview
11.6	Interviews
11.7	Tracking Methods
11.8	Observations and Other Manual Methods
11.9	Expert-Driven Methods
11.10	Repertory Grid Analysis
11.11	Supporting the Knowledge Engineer
11.12	Machine Learning: Rule Induction, Case-Based Reasoning, Neural Computing, and Intelligent Agents
11.13	Selecting an Appropriate Knowledge Acquisition Method
11.14	Knowledge Acquisition from Multiple Experts
11.15	Validation and Verification of the Knowledge Base
11.16	Analyzing, Coding, Documenting, and Diagramming
11.17	Numeric and Documented Knowledge Acquisition
11.18	Knowledge Acquisition and the Internet/Intranets
11.19	Induction Table Example

---

[1]This chapter was updated with help from in part by Stephen Ives of Hong Kong.

11.1 OPENING VIGNETTE: AMERICAN EXPRESS IMPROVES APPROVAL SELECTION WITH MACHINE LEARNING[2]

For years, American Express UK loan officers used an automated statistical method based on discriminant analysis to support their decisions regarding whether a loan should be made. The statistical method was automated and provided decisions for 85–90 percent of all loan applications. The remaining 10–15 percent had to be handled manually. Loan officers were required to make decisions about the latter loan applications but were at most only 50 percent accurate in predicting whether these gray-area applicants would default. This cost the company too much money. To solve the problem American Express developed a supporting intelligent system. The knowledge for this system was acquired by an automated approach called *machine learning*. The computer "learned" by examining 1,014 historical loan applications. A method called *rule induction* was used to create a decision tree that described the problem. For the gray-area loan applications, the induced decision tree correctly predicted the answer 70 percent of the time compared with the 50 percent achieved by the loan officers. Furthermore, the induced rules explain to applicants why they are being rejected. The knowledge base was deployed even though the project was an exploratory one that took less than 1 week of effort to produce.

❖ QUESTIONS FOR THE OPENING VIGNETTE

1. Why was the system's accuracy so much better than that of the human loan officers?
2. Why was an explanation facility so important in this expert system?
3. Why do you think the expert system predicted defaults much more accurately than the loan officers did?
4. What are the implications for the expert system when there are changes in the economic climate? Explain.
5. Why do you think so many test cases were needed?
6. Could the expert system be used to train loan officers? Explain.
7. Given that the rule-induced decision tree is much more accurate than the loan officers, comb the literature and try to estimate how much money can be saved by denying predicted loan defaults.

11.2 KNOWLEDGE ENGINEERING

The Opening Vignette illustrates the idea that acquiring knowledge and deploying it is a powerful and valuable way to assist decision makers (also see AIS in Action 11.1). It also illustrates an exciting kind of knowledge acquisition, one that involves a computer that can learn from historical cases (which we return to in Section 11.12). Furthermore, it illustrates an AI situation in which the computer software system increases the productivity of decision making and the accuracy of the predication. Although machine learning may look like an ideal tool for knowledge acquisition because many cases can be examined quickly, most knowledge-based systems rely on knowledge acquired directly from human experts.

---

[2]Condensed from P. Langley and H. A. Simon, "Applications of Machine Learning and Rule Induction," *Communications of the ACM,* Vol. 38, No. 11, Nov. 1995.

AIS IN ACTION 11.1

INVENTION MACHINE'S SOFTWARE PICKS INVENTORS' BRAINS

Invention Machine Corporation (Cambridge, MA) has developed a software program that is being snapped up by a growing number of America's biggest companies to provide inventing partners for their engineers. The program, Invention Machine Lab, codifies the invention principles behind about 2 million international patents and the inventive techniques of some of the world's greatest inventors.

The software inventor, Valery Tsourikov, says the product grew out of his early studies in the former Soviet Union under a Russian scholar, Genrich Altshuller, who posited that invention is not a random process but has a certain method or algorithm that drives it. Tsourikov captured the knowledge from many sources and deployed it in the software.

Source: Condensed from A. Choi, "Invention Machine's Software Wins Orders for Picking Brains of Inventors," *The Wall Street Journal,* Feb. 12, 1996, p. B19E.

The activity of **knowledge engineering (KE)** has been defined by Feigenbaum and McCorduck (1983) as

> the art of bringing the principles and tools of AI research to bear on difficult applications problems requiring experts' knowledge for their solutions. The technical issues of acquiring this knowledge, representing it and using it appropriately to construct and explain lines of reasoning are important problems in the design of knowledge-based systems. The art of constructing intelligent agents is both part of and an extension of the programming art. It is the art of building complex computer programs that represent and reason with knowledge of the world.

Knowledge engineering can be viewed from two perspectives: narrow and wide. According to the narrow perspective, knowledge engineering deals with knowledge acquisition, representation, validation, inferencing, explanation, and maintenance. Alternatively, according to the wide perspective, the term describes the entire process of developing and maintaining AI systems. In this book, we use the narrow definition.

Knowledge engineering involves the cooperation of human experts in the domain who work with the knowledge engineer to codify and make explicit the rules (or other procedures) that a human expert uses to solve real problems.

Knowledge engineering usually has a synergistic effect. The knowledge possessed by human experts is often unstructured and not explicitly expressed. The construction of a knowledge base helps the expert to articulate what he or she knows. It can also pinpoint variances from one expert to another (if several experts are involved).

A major goal in knowledge engineering is to construct programs that are modular in nature so that additions and changes can be made in one module without affecting the workings of other modules. An object-oriented design and implementation approach can be applied.

THE KNOWLEDGE ENGINEERING PROCESS

The knowledge engineering process [see Bebenham (1998)] includes five major activities:

- **Knowledge acquisition.** Knowledge acquisition involves the acquisition of knowledge from human experts, books, documents, sensors, or computer files. The knowledge may be specific to the problem domain or to the problem-solving procedures, it may be general knowledge (such as knowledge about business), or it may be **metaknowledge** (knowledge about knowledge). By the latter, we mean information about how experts use their knowledge to solve problems and problem-solving procedures in general. Byrd (1995) formally verified that knowledge acquisition is the bottleneck in expert system development. Thus, much theoretical and applied research is still being conducted in this area. Shadbolt et al. (1999) further evaluated knowledge acquisition techniques and methods, identifying problems and possible solutions.

- **Knowledge validation.** The knowledge is validated and verified (e.g., by using test cases) until its quality is acceptable. Test case results are usually shown to the expert to verify the accuracy of the ES.
- **Knowledge representation.** The acquired knowledge is organized in an activity called knowledge representation. This activity involves preparation of a **knowledge map** and encoding the knowledge in the knowledge base.
- **Inferencing.** This activity involves the design of software to enable the computer to make inferences based on the knowledge and the specifics of a problem. Then the system can provide advice to a nonexpert user.
- **Explanation and justification.** This involves the design and programming of an explanation capability, for example, programming the ability to answer questions such as *why* a specific piece of information is needed by the computer or *how* a certain conclusion was derived by the computer.

The process of knowledge engineering and the relationships among these activities are shown in Figure 11.1. We discuss the topics of knowledge acquisition and validation in this chapter and present the other activities in subsequent chapters.

FIGURE 11.1 Process of Knowledge Engineering

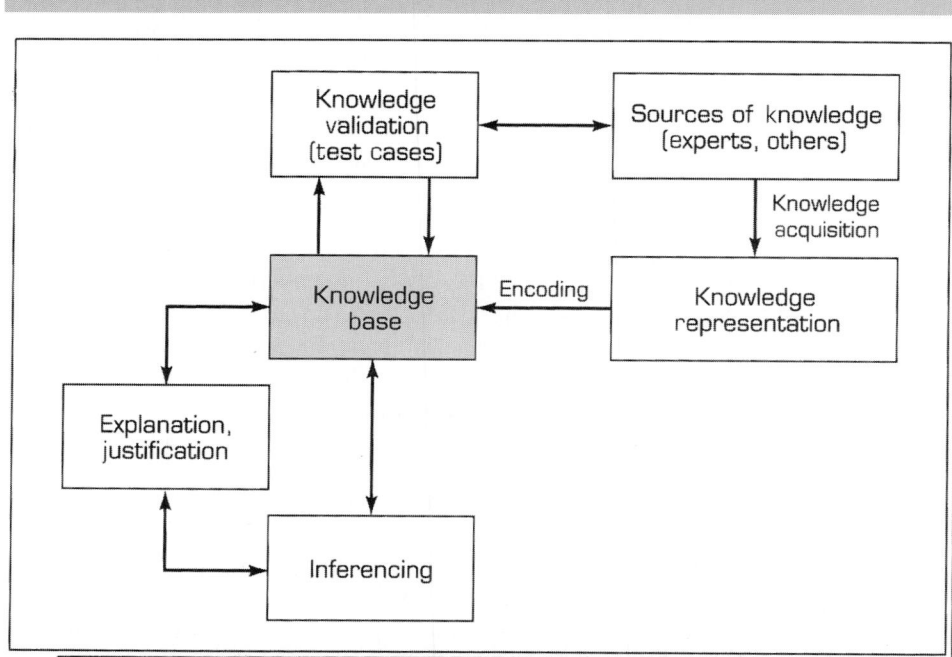

11.3 SCOPE OF KNOWLEDGE

Knowledge acquisition is the extraction of knowledge from sources of expertise and its transfer to the knowledge base and sometimes to the inference engine. Acquisition is actually done throughout the entire development process.

Knowledge is a collection of specialized facts, procedures, and judgment rules. Some types of knowledge used in AI are shown in Figure 11.2. These types of knowledge may come from one source or from several sources.

SOURCES OF KNOWLEDGE

Knowledge can be collected from many sources such as books, films, computer databases, pictures, maps, flow diagrams, stories, sensors, songs, or even observed behavior. These sources can be divided into two types: **documented** and **undocumented.** The latter resides in people's minds. Knowledge can be identified and collected by using one or several of the human senses. It can also be identified and collected by machines (sensors, scanners, pattern matchers, intelligent agents, and so on).

FIGURE 11.2 TYPES OF KNOWLEDGE TO BE REPRESENTED IN THE KNOWLEDGE BASE

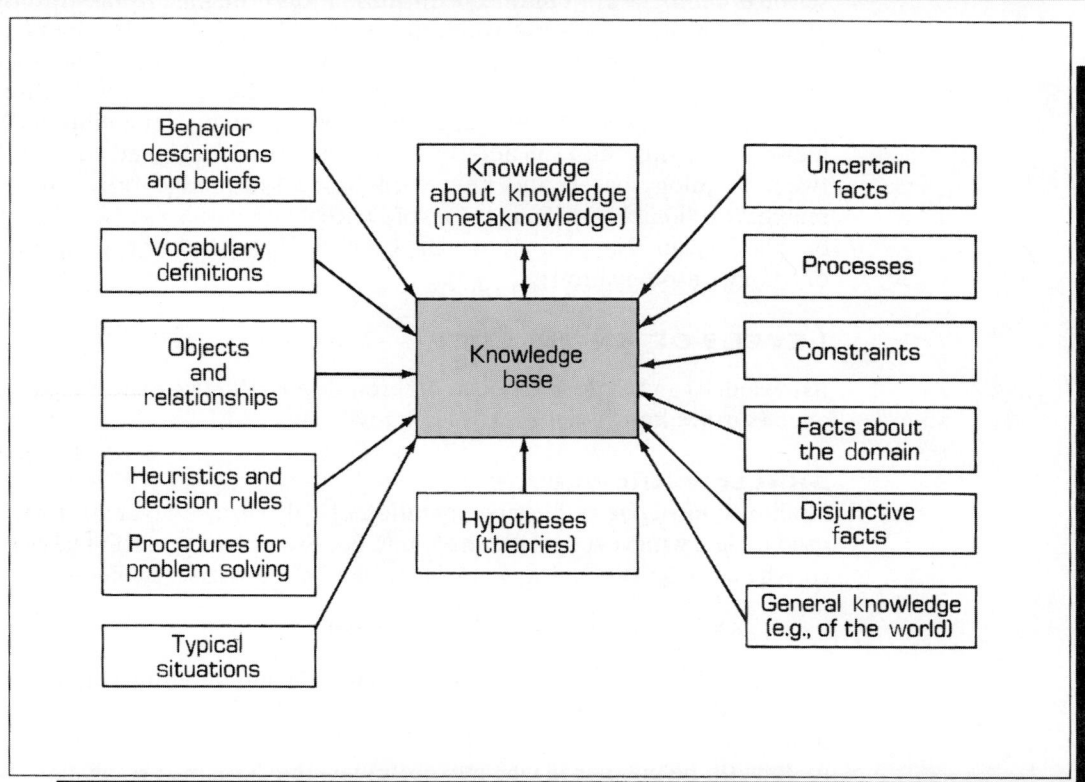

Source: Adapted from R. Fikes and T. Kehler, "The Role of Frame-based Representation in Reasoning," *Communications of ACM,* Sept. 1985. Copyright 1985, Association for Computing Machinery Inc. Reprinted by permission.

The multiplicity of sources and types of knowledge contributes to the complexity of knowledge acquisition. This complexity is only one reason why it is difficult to acquire knowledge. Other reasons are discussed in Section 11.4.

ACQUISITION FROM DATABASES

Many ES are being constructed from knowledge that is extracted in full or in part from databases. With the increased amount of knowledge stored in databases, the acquisition of such knowledge becomes more difficult. For discussion and methods, see the *Data Mining and Knowledge Discovery Journal* (www.research.microsoft.com/datamine/), Cupit and Shadbolt (1996), and Wu (1995). Lavington et al. (1999) give practical descriptions regarding the interfacing of knowledge discovery algorithms with respect to large database management systems.

ACQUISITION VIA THE INTERNET

With the increased use of the Internet, it is possible to access vast amounts of knowledge. The acquisition, availability, and management of knowledge via the Internet are becoming critical issues for the construction and maintenance of knowledge-based systems, particularly because they allow the acquisition and dissemination of large quantities of knowledge in a short time across organizational and physical boundaries. Methods and standards were first established in 1996. For details, see Stewart (1996). The Internet community provides an "expert system" with a scope far greater than that possible with standard computer-based systems. Benjamins et al. (1999) describe *ontologies* for building acquisition tools utilizing intranet/Internet tools available within organizations. Adopting tools such as HTML browsers allows users to quickly become familiar with acquisition systems. Additions to standard HTML can be applied to include metadata information, allowing explicit information to be stored and retrieved. Detailed case studies are given by Benjamins et al. (1999), which highlight the difficulties in adopting this type of approach and address differences between ontology-based and key word–based knowledge retrieval. Also worth researching is "Ontological Foundations of Conceptual Modeling and Knowledge Engineering" on the Italian National Research Council Web site (www.ladseb.pd.cnr.it/infor/ontology/ontology.html).

LEVELS OF KNOWLEDGE

Knowledge can be represented at different levels. The two extremes are shallow knowledge (surface knowledge) and deep knowledge.

SHALLOW KNOWLEDGE

Shallow knowledge is the representation of only surface-level information that can be used to deal with very specific situations. For example, if you don't have gasoline in your car, the car won't start. This knowledge can be shown as a rule:

If gasoline tank is empty, then car will not start.

The shallow version basically represents the input–output relationship of a system. As such, it can be ideally presented in terms of IF-THEN rules. Shallow representation is limited. A set of rules by itself may have little meaning for the user. It may have little to do with the manner in which experts view the domain and solve problems. This may limit the ability of the system to provide appropriate explanations to the user. Shallow knowledge may also be insufficient in describing complex situations. Therefore, a deeper presentation is often required.

DEEP KNOWLEDGE

Human problem solving is based on deep knowledge of a situation. **Deep knowledge** is the internal and causal structure of a system and involves the interactions among the system's components. Deep knowledge can be applied to different tasks and different situations. It is based on a completely integrated, cohesive body of human consciousness that includes emotions, common sense, intuition, and so on. This type of knowledge is difficult to computerize. The system builder must have a perfect understanding of the basic elements and their interactions as produced by nature. To date, such a task has been found to be impossible. However, it is possible to implement a computerized representation that is deeper than shallow knowledge. To explain how this is done, let us return to the gasoline example. If we want to investigate at a deeper level the relationship between lack of gasoline and a car that won't start, we need to know the various components of the gas system (e.g., pipes, pump, filters, and a starter). Such a system is shown schematically in Figure 11.3.

To represent this system and knowledge of its operation, we use special knowledge representation methods such as *semantic networks* and *frames* (Chapter 12). They allow the implementation of deeper-level reasoning such as abstraction and analogy, an important expert activity. We can also represent the objects and processes of the domain of expertise at this level; the relationships among objects are important.

One important type of expertise that has been represented with a deep-level approach is tutoring. The goal of tutoring is to convey to students a domain knowledge that is best represented at the deep level: concepts, abstractions, analogies, and problem-solving strategies.

Deep knowledge is much more difficult to collect and validate. For a discussion, see Maniezzo et al. (1993) and DeFanti et al. (1997).

MAJOR CATEGORIES OF KNOWLEDGE

Knowledge can be categorized as declarative knowledge, procedural knowledge, or metaknowledge.

DECLARATIVE KNOWLEDGE

Declarative knowledge is a descriptive representation of knowledge. It tells us facts: what things are. It is expressed in a factual statement "There is a positive association between

FIGURE 11.3 SCHEMATIC REPRESENTATION OF DEEP KNOWLEDGE:
AUTOMOBILE GAS SYSTEM

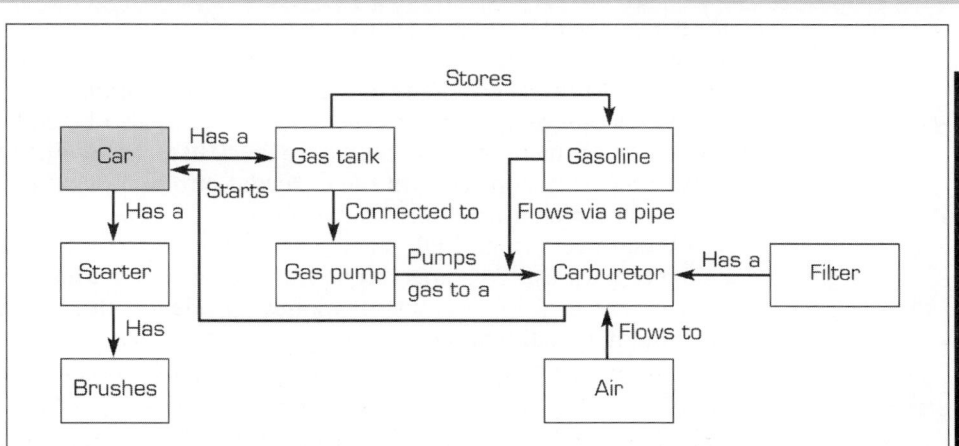

smoking and cancer." Domain experts tell us about truths and associations. This type of knowledge is considered shallow or surface-level information that experts can verbalize. Declarative knowledge is especially important in the initial stage of knowledge acquisition.

PROCEDURAL KNOWLEDGE

Procedural knowledge considers the manner in which things work under different sets of circumstances. The following is an example: "Compute the ratio between the price of a share and the earnings per share. If this ratio is larger than 12, stop your investigation. Your investment is too risky. If the ratio is less than 12, check the balance sheet." Thus, procedural knowledge includes step-by-step sequences and how-to types of instructions; it may also include explanations. Procedural knowledge involves automatic response to stimuli. It may also tell us how to use declarative knowledge and how to make inferences.

Declarative knowledge relates to a specific object. It includes information about the meaning, roles, environment, resources, activities, associations, and outcomes of the object. Procedural knowledge relates to the procedures used in the problem-solving process (such as information about problem definition, data gathering, the solution process, and evaluation criteria).

METAKNOWLEDGE

Metaknowledge is knowledge about knowledge. In ES, metaknowledge is knowledge about the operation of knowledge-based systems, that is, about its reasoning capabilities.

11.4 DIFFICULTIES IN KNOWLEDGE ACQUISITION

In general, transferring information from one person to another is difficult. Several mechanisms can be used to conduct such a transfer—written words, voice, pictures, music—and not one of them is perfect. There are also problems in transferring any knowledge, even simple messages. Transferring knowledge in ES is even more difficult. Now, we'll see why.

PROBLEMS IN TRANSFERRING KNOWLEDGE

EXPRESSING THE KNOWLEDGE

To solve a problem, a human expert performs a two-step process. First, the expert inputs information about the external world into the brain. This information is transmitted by people, computers, or other media. It can also be collected via sensors or retrieved from memory. Second, the expert uses an inductive, deductive, or other problem-solving approach on the collected information. The result (output) is a recommendation on how to solve the problem.

This process is internal. When collecting knowledge from an expert, a knowledge engineer must ask the expert to be introspective about his or her (the expert's) decision-making process and about the inner experiences that are involved in it. An expert may find it very difficult to express his or her experiences about this process, especially when these experiences are made up of sensations, thoughts, sense memories, and feelings. The expert is often unaware of the detailed process he or she uses to arrive at a conclusion. Therefore, the rules used by the expert to solve real-life problems may actually be different than those stated in a knowledge acquisition interview.

TRANSFER TO A MACHINE

Knowledge is transferred to a machine, where it must be organized in a particular manner. The machine requires the knowledge to be expressed explicitly, at a lower, more detailed level than humans use. Human knowledge exists in a compiled format. A human being simply does not remember all the intermediate steps used by his or her brain in transferring or processing knowledge. Thus, there is a mismatch between computers and experts.

NUMBER OF PARTICIPANTS

In a normal transfer of knowledge process, there are two participants (a sender and a receiver). In ES, there can be as many as four participants (plus a computer): the expert, the knowledge engineer, the system designer (builder), and the user. Sometimes there are even more participants (such as programmers and vendors). These participants have different backgrounds, use different terminology, and possess different skills and knowledge. The experts, for example, may know very little about computers, and the knowledge engineer may know very little about the problem area.

STRUCTURING THE KNOWLEDGE

In ES it is necessary to elicit not only the knowledge but also its structure. We must represent the knowledge in a structured way (e.g., as rules).

OTHER ISSUES

Several other factors add to the complexity of transferring knowledge:

- Experts may lack time or may be unwilling to cooperate.
- Testing and refining knowledge is complicated.
- Methods for knowledge elicitation may be poorly defined.
- System builders tend to collect knowledge from one source, but the relevant knowledge may be scattered across several sources.
- Builders may attempt to collect documented knowledge rather than use experts. The knowledge collected may be incomplete.
- It is difficult to recognize specific knowledge when it is mixed up with irrelevant data.
- Experts may change their behavior when they are being observed or interviewed.
- Problematic interpersonal communication factors may affect the knowledge engineer and the expert.

OVERCOMING THE DIFFICULTIES

Many efforts have been made to overcome some of these problems [for a comprehensive survey, see Boose (1989), Eriksson (1992), and Lightfoot (1999)]. For example, research on knowledge acquisition tools has begun to focus on ways to decrease the representation mismatch between the human expert and the program under development. One form of this research might be characterized as research on "learning by being told." The attempt here is to develop programs capable of accepting advice as it would often be given to a human novice. Several ES development software packages, such as Exsys, Level5, Acquire, and VP-Expert, greatly simplify the syntax of the rules (in a rule-based system) to make them easier for an ES builder to create and understand without special training. Also, a natural language processor can be used to translate knowledge to a specific knowledge representation structure.

The process of knowledge acquisition can be greatly influenced by the roles of the three major participants: the knowledge engineer, the expert, and the end user.

A unique approach to the relationships among these participants is offered by Sandahl (1994). Sandahl indicates that experts should take a very active role in the creation of the knowledge base. The knowledge engineer should act more like a teacher of knowledge structuring, a tool designer, and a catalyst at the interface between the expert and end users. This approach could minimize problems such as interhuman conflicts, knowledge engineering filtering, and end-user acceptance of the system. Also, knowledge maintenance problems can be reduced. Wagner and Holsapple (1997) have analyzed the roles the participants play in knowledge acquisition. They suggest that it is more appropriate to think of the participants as playing one or more roles, including acting as knowledge sources, agents, and targets for knowledge acquisition processes. They further develop a participant model to explain participant interactions in a metaview of knowledge acquisition. This view allows for a more flexible consideration of the many possible combinations that can and do occur in reality.

The ability and personality of the knowledge engineer directly influence the expert. Part of successful knowledge acquisition involves developing a positive relationship with the expert. The knowledge engineer is responsible for creating the right impression, positively communicating information about the project, understanding the expert's style, preparing the sessions, and so on (Awad, 1996).

Finally, some of the difficulties may be lessened or eliminated with computer-aided knowledge acquisition tools and with extensive integration of the acquisition efforts (see "Evaluation Methods for Knowledge Engineering" on the University of New South Wales Web site, www.cse.unsw.edu.au.~timm/pub/eval/). For further details, also see the Internet mailing list service VAVTALK which specifically addresses the validation and verification of intelligent systems (www.csd.abdn.ac.uk/~apreece/vavtalk.html).

REQUIRED SKILLS OF KNOWLEDGE ENGINEERS

The use of computers and special methods to overcome difficulties requires qualified knowledge engineers. Listed here are some of the skills and characteristics that are desirable in knowledge engineers:

- Computer skills (hardware, programming, software)
- Tolerance and ambivalence
- Effective communication abilities (sensitivity, tact, and diplomacy)
- Broad educational background
- Advanced, socially sophisticated verbal skills
- Fast-learning capabilities (of different domains)
- Understanding of organizations and individuals
- Wide experience in knowledge engineering
- Intelligence
- Empathy and patience
- Persistence
- Logical thinking
- Versatility and inventiveness
- Self-confidence.

These requirements make knowledge engineers in *short supply* (and costly because of high salaries). Some of the automation developments described later attempt to overcome the short-supply problem.

11.5 METHODS OF KNOWLEDGE ACQUISITION: AN OVERVIEW

The basic model of knowledge engineering portrays teamwork in which a knowledge engineer mediates between the expert and the knowledge base. The knowledge engineer elicits knowledge from the expert, refines it with the expert, and represents it in the knowledge base. The **elicitation of knowledge** from the expert can be done manually or with the aid of computers. Most manual elicitation techniques have been borrowed (but often modified) from psychology or from system analysis. These elicitation methods are classified in different ways and appear under different names [for a discussion, see Awad (1996) and Moody et al. (1999)].

The methods described in this book are classified in three categories: manual, semiautomatic, and automatic.

Manual methods are basically structured around some kind of interview. The knowledge engineer elicits knowledge from the expert or other sources and then codes it in the knowledge base. The process is shown in Figure 11.4. The three major manual methods are *interviewing* (structured, semistructured, unstructured), *tracking the reasoning process,* and *observing.* Manual methods are slow, expensive, and sometimes inaccurate. Therefore, there is a trend toward automating the process as much as possible.

Semiautomatic methods are divided into two categories: those intended to support the experts by allowing them to build knowledge bases with little or no help from knowledge engineers (Figure 11.5) and those intended to help knowledge engineers by allowing them to execute the necessary tasks in a more efficient or effective manner (sometimes with only minimal participation by an expert).

In *automatic methods,* the roles of both the expert and the knowledge engineer are minimized or even eliminated. For example, the *induction method* shown in Figure 11.6 (see Section 11.12 for details) can be administered by any builder (such as a system analyst). The role of the expert is minimal, and there is no need for a knowledge engineer. The term *automatic* may be misleading. There will always be a human builder, but there may be little or no need for a knowledge engineer and an expert.

KNOWLEDGE MODELING

During the 1980s, several key contributions shaped our current perception of the knowledge acquisition problem: Allen Newell's notion of knowledge level, William Clancey's critical analyses, and the broader wave of second-generation expert system

FIGURE 11.4 MANUAL METHODS OF KNOWLEDGE ACQUISITION

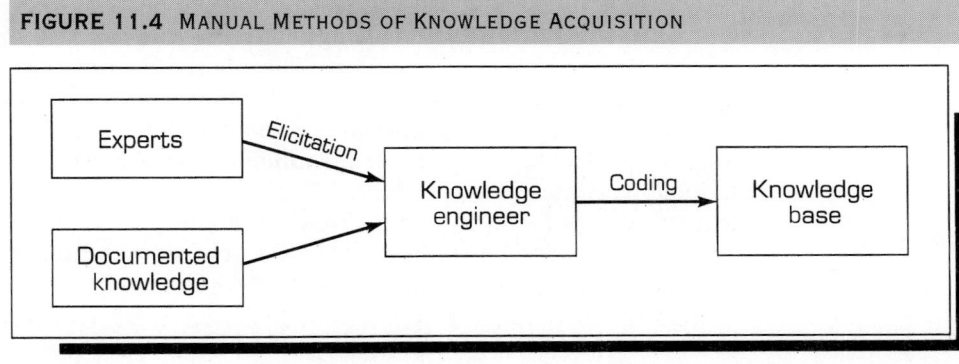

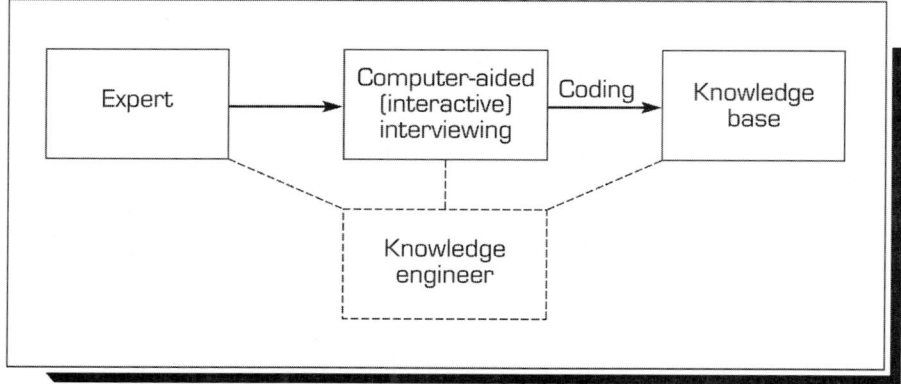

FIGURE 11.5 EXPERT-DRIVEN KNOWLEDGE ACQUISITION

Broken lines designate optional interactions.

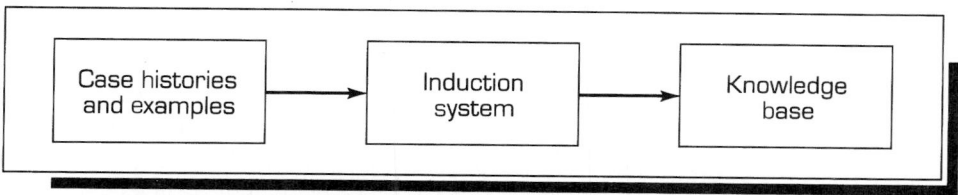

FIGURE 11.6 INDUCTION-DRIVEN KNOWLEDGE ACQUISITION

research. Central to this perception is the *knowledge model,* which views knowledge acquisition as the construction of a model of problem-solving behavior—that is, a model in terms of knowledge instead of representations.

The concept of knowledge-level modeling has matured considerably. Practical knowledge-level models incorporated in today's methodologies not only reflect the knowledge content of a system but also make explicit the structures within which the knowledge operates in solving particular classes of problems. This enables the *reuse of models* across applications.

The structures provide a framework for knowledge acquisition and a decomposition of the overall acquisition task. Identified parts of knowledge-level models—domain models or problem-solving methods—can serve in different systems or in different roles in the same system. The main advantage remains: The knowledge level focuses attention on the knowledge that makes systems work rather than on the symbol-level, computational design decisions that provide the operational framework. The topic of knowledge modeling and its current state of the art are described in a series of articles in *IEEE Expert* (Feb.–Aug., 1996). Musen et al. (1999) report the use of a domain model to drive an interactive knowledge-editing tool, allowing expertise to be entered regardless of representation requirements of the target expert system.

11.6 INTERVIEWS

The most commonly used form of knowledge acquisition is face-to-face **interview analysis.** It is an explicit technique and appears in several variations. It involves a direct dialog between the expert and the knowledge engineer. Information is collected with the aid of conventional instruments (such as tape recorders or questionnaires) and is subsequently transcribed, analyzed, and coded.

In the interview, the expert is presented with a simulated case or, if possible, with an actual problem of the type that the ES will be expected to solve. The expert is asked to "talk" the knowledge engineer through the solution. Sometimes this method is called the **walkthrough** method. One variant of the interview approach begins with no information at all being given to the expert. Any facts the expert requires must be asked for explicitly. When this is done, the expert's path through the domain can be made more evident, especially in terms of defining the input an ES would require.

The interview process can be tedious. It places great demands on the domain expert, who must be able not only to demonstrate expertise but also to express it. On the other hand, it requires little equipment, it is highly flexible and portable, and it can yield a considerable amount of information. There are two basic types of interviews: unstructured (informal) interviews and structured interviews.

UNSTRUCTURED INTERVIEWS

Many knowledge acquisition interview sessions are conducted informally, usually as a starting point. Starting informally saves time; it helps to move quickly to the basic structure of the domain. Usually it is followed by a formal technique. Contrary to what many people believe, **unstructured interviews** are not simple. In fact, they may present the knowledge engineer with some very problematic aftereffects.

Unstructured interviewing, according to McGraw and Harbison-Briggs (1989), seldom provides complete or well-organized descriptions of cognitive processes, for the following reasons: The domains are generally complex; the experts usually find it very difficult to express some of the more important elements of their knowledge; domain experts may interpret the lack of structure as requiring little preparation on their part; data acquired from an unstructured interview are often unrelated, exist at varying levels of complexity, and are difficult for the knowledge engineer to review, interpret, and integrate; and because of a lack of training and experience, few knowledge engineers can conduct an efficient unstructured interview.

EXAMPLE

Here is a simple, hypothetical example of acquisition of knowledge about site selection for a hospital extension clinic. The dialog between the expert (E) and the knowledge engineer (KE) might look like the following:

E: I understand that you are somehow going to try to capture my knowledge about site selection of clinics so that hospital administrators in our system in other cities can use it. . . .

KE: Yes, indeed! And thank you for spending time with me, Kathleen. We've noticed that you have a special knack for identifying the right locations. So far, you've picked very successful operations.

E: Well, thanks.

> KE: So, tell me, what's the most important factor in determining where to put a new facility?
>
> E: Really, it's demographics. We need to locate it close to our potential customers.
>
> KE: So, is it also important that it not be too close to another agency's operation?
>
> E: Not necessarily. It is important that it not be located too close to our main hospital or our other facilities, but if the population density is high enough, we can locate it close to a competitor.
>
> KE: Tell me then, what kind of demographics are you looking for?
>
> E: Well, in a large city, if there are at least 2,000 people per square mile over about 4 square miles, generally they can support a profitable clinic.
>
> KE: What about competitors' locations?
>
> E: If a competitor is within 2 miles, the density has to exceed 3,500 people per square mile. And if there are two competitors within 2 miles of each other already, there's no point in even trying to break into the market, except for certain special services.
>
> KE: What about income? Is that important?
>
> E: We *must* limit our indigent cases to no more than 2 percent of our clients, and so we generally look for an average family income greater than $30,000 per year.
>
> KE: Is being near public transportation important?
>
> and so on.

By interviewing the expert, the knowledge engineer slowly learns what is going on. Then he or she builds a representation of the knowledge in the expert's terms.

The process of knowledge acquisition involves uncovering the attributes of the problem and making explicit the thought process (usually expressed as rules) that the expert uses to interpret these attributes.

The unstructured interview is most common and appears in several variations. In addition to the talkthrough, one can ask the expert to teach through or read through. In a teachthrough the expert acts as an instructor and the knowledge engineer as a student. The expert not only tells *what* he or she does but also explains *why* and instructs the knowledge engineer in the skills and strategies needed to perform the task. In a readthrough approach the expert is asked to instruct the knowledge engineer *how* to read and interpret the documents used for the task.

STRUCTURED INTERVIEWS

A **structured interview** is a systematic goal-oriented process. It forces organized communication between the knowledge engineer and the expert. The structure reduces the interpretation problems inherent in unstructured interviews, and it allows the knowledge engineer to prevent the distortion caused by the subjectivity of the domain expert. Structuring an interview requires attention to a number of procedural issues, which are summarized in Table 11.1.

Because of the specific nature of each interview, it is difficult to provide good guidelines for the entire interview process. Therefore, interpersonal communication and analytic skills are important. However, there are several guidelines, checklists, and instruments that are fairly generic in nature (McGraw and Harbison-Briggs, 1989).

There are many structured interview methods. Some are based on psychology (Awad, 1996). Others are based on disciplines such as anthropology. A good online resource is the Multi-Health Systems Inc. (MHS) Web site (at www.mhs.com). MHS is a knowledge-

TABLE 11.1   Procedures for Structured Interviews
• The knowledge engineer studies available material on the domain to identify major demarcations of the relevant knowledge.
• The knowledge engineer reviews the planned expert system capabilities. He or she identifies targets for the questions to be asked during the knowledge acquisition session.
• The knowledge engineer formally schedules and plans the structured interviews (using a form). Planning includes attending to physical arrangements, defining knowledge acquisition session goals and agendas, and identifying or refining major areas of questioning.
• The knowledge engineer may write sample questions, focusing on question type, level, and questioning techniques.
• The knowledge engineer ensures that the domain expert understands the purpose and goals of the session and encourages the expert to prepare before the interview.
• During the interview the knowledge engineer follows guidelines for conducting interviews.
• During the interview the knowledge engineer uses directional control to retain the interview's structure.

Source: Condensed from K. L. McGraw and B. K. Harbison-Briggs, *Knowledge Acquisition, Principles and Guidelines.* Englewood Cliffs, NJ: Prentice Hall, 1989.

based company engaged in the development and delivery of integrated assessment and diagnostic products and aimed at mental health and counseling professionals. Knowledge is gathered by the company via standard psychologically based interview sheets (either pencil-and-paper or computer tests). In addition the Web site is used to gather information through opportunities to ask the experts questions (used by professionals in the field)—these questions and answers enhancing the knowledge base of the site.

Interviewing techniques, though very popular, have many disadvantages. They range from inaccuracy in collecting information to bias introduced by the interviewers (Kuhn and Zohar, 1995; Liang, 2000).

In summary, interviews are important techniques, but they must be planned carefully, and the interview results must be subjected to thorough verification and validation methodologies. Interviews are sometimes replaced by tracking methods. Alternatively, they can be used to supplement tracking or other knowledge acquisition methods.

A RECOMMENDATION

We recommend that before a knowledge engineer interviews the main experts, he or she interviews a less knowledgeable or minor expert using the interviewing approaches outlined above. This may help the knowledge engineer learn about the problem, its significance, the experts, and the users. The interviewer will also be able to better understand the basic terminology and (for a novice in the area) identify archived sources about the problem first. The knowledge engineer should next read about the problem. Then, the main experts can be interviewed much more effectively.

11.7 TRACKING METHODS

Process tracking is a set of techniques that attempt to track the reasoning process of an expert. It is a popular approach among cognitive psychologists who are interested in discovering the expert's train of thought as he or she reaches a conclusion. The knowledge engineer can use the tracking process to find what information is being used and how it is being used. Tracking methods can be informal or formal. The most common formal method is *protocol analysis.*

Protocol analysis, particularly a set of techniques known as *verbal protocol analysis,* is a common method by which the knowledge engineer acquires detailed knowledge from the expert. A *protocol* is a record or documentation of the expert's step-by-step information-processing and decision-making behavior. In this method, which is similar to interviewing but more formal and systematic, the expert is asked to perform a real task and to verbalize his or her thought processes. The expert is asked by the knowledge engineer to think aloud while performing the task or solving the problem under observation. Usually, a recording is made as the expert thinks aloud; it describes every aspect of the information-processing and decision-making behavior. This recording then becomes a record, or protocol, of the expert's ongoing behavior. Later, the recording is transcribed for further analysis (e.g., to deduce the decision process) and coded by the knowledge engineer. [For further details, see Ericsson and Simon (1984) and Wolfgram et al. (1987).]

In contrast with interactive interview methods, a protocol analysis involves mainly a one-way communication. The knowledge engineer prepares the scenario and plans the process. During the session the expert does most of the talking as he or she interacts with data to solve the problem. Concurrently, the knowledge engineer listens and records the process. Later, he or she must be able to analyze, interpret, and structure the protocol into knowledge representation for review by the expert.

The process of protocol analysis is summarized in Table 11.2, and its advantages and limitations are presented in Table 11.3.

TABLE 11.2   Procedure of Protocol Analysis

- Provide the expert with a full range of information normally associated with a task.
- Ask the expert to verbalize the task in the same manner as would be done normally while verbalizing his or her decision process and record the verbalization on tape.
- Make statements by transcribing the verbal protocols.
- Gather the statements that seem to have high information content.
- Simplify and rewrite the collected statements and construct a table of production rules from the collected statements.
- Produce a series of models by using the production rules.

Source: Organized from J. Kim and J. F. Courtney, "A Survey of Knowledge Acquisition Techniques and Their Relevance to Managerial Problem Domains," *Decision Support Systems,* Vol. 4, Oct. 1988, p. 273.

TABLE 11.3   Advantages and Limitations of Protocol Analysis

Advantages
    The expert consciously considers decision-making heuristics.
    The expert consciously considers decision alternatives, attributes, values.
    The knowledge engineer can observe and analyze decision-making behavior.
    The knowledge engineer can record, and later analyze with the expert, key decision points.

Limitations
    The expert must be aware of why he or she makes a decision.
    The expert must be able to categorize major decision alternatives.
    The expert must be able to verbalize the attributes and values of a decision alternative.
    The expert must be able to reason about the selection of a given alternative.
    View of decision making is subjective. Explanations may not track with reasoning.

Source: K. L. McGraw and B. K. Harbison-Briggs, *Knowledge Acquisition, Principles and Guidelines,* Englewood Cliffs, NJ: Prentice Hall, 1989, p. 217. © 1989. Reprinted by permission of Prentice-Hall, Inc., Upper Saddle River, NJ.

11.8 OBSERVATIONS AND OTHER MANUAL METHODS

OBSERVATIONS

Sometimes it is possible to observe an expert at work. In many ways, this is the most obvious and straightforward approach to knowledge acquisition. However, the difficulties involved should not be underestimated. For example, most experts advise several people and possibly work in several domains simultaneously. The observations being made thus cover all the other activities as well. Therefore, large quantities of knowledge are being collected of which only a little is useful. In particular, if recordings or videotapes are made, the cost of transcribing large amounts of knowledge should be carefully considered.

Observations, which can be viewed as a special case of protocols, are of two types: motor and eye movement. In the first type the expert's physical performance of the task (such as walking, reaching, and talking) is documented. In the second type, a record of where the expert fixes his or her gaze is made. Observations are used primarily as a way of supporting verbal protocols. They are generally expensive and time-consuming.

OTHER MANUAL METHODS

Many other manual methods can be used to elicit knowledge from experts. A representative list is given here; for a complete discussion, see Hart (1992) and Scott et al. (1991).

- *Case analysis.* Experts are asked how they handled specific cases in the past. Usually this method involves analyzing documentation. In addition to the experts, other people (such as managers and users) may be questioned.
- *Critical incident analysis.* In this approach only selected cases are investigated, usually those that are memorable, difficult, or of special interest. Both experts and nonexperts may be questioned.
- *Discussions with the users.* Even though users are not experts, they can be quite knowledgeable about some aspects of the problem. They can also indicate areas where they need help. The expert may be unaware of some of their needs.
- *Commentaries.* With this method, the knowledge engineer asks experts to give a running commentary on what they are doing. This method can be supported by videotaping the experts in action or by asking an observer to do the commentary.
- *Conceptual graphs and models.* Diagrams and other graphical methods can be instrumental in supporting other acquisition methods. A conceptual model can be used to describe how and when the expert's knowledge will come into play as the expert system performs its task.
- *Brainstorming.* These methods can be used to solicit the opinions of multiple experts and can help generate ideas. Electronic brainstorming can also be used (Chapter 10), including blackboarding (Awad, 1996), which has been implemented as electronic whiteboards.
- *Prototyping.* Working with a prototype of the system is a powerful approach to induce experts to contribute their knowledge. Experts like to criticize systems, and changes can be made instantly.
- *Multidimensional scaling.* The complex technique of **multidimensional scaling** identifies various dimensions of knowledge and then places the knowledge in a form of a distance matrix. With the use of least-squares fitting regression, the various dimensions are analyzed, interpreted, and integrated.

- *Johnson's hierarchical clustering.* This is another scaling method, but it is much simpler to implement and therefore is used more often. It combines related knowledge elements into clusters (two elements at a time).
- *Performance review.* Because expert system development is an ongoing process, all of the above can be applied iteratively as the system evolves.

11.9 EXPERT-DRIVEN METHODS

In the previous methods, the major responsibility and task of knowledge acquisition belongs to the knowledge engineer. However, knowledge engineers typically lack knowledge about the domain, their services are expensive, and they may have problems communicating with experts. As a result, knowledge acquisition can be a slow process with many iterations (for verification and learning purposes). The procedure is expensive and even unreliable because the experts may find it difficult to contribute their knowledge via the knowledge engineer (Sleeman and Mitchell, 1996).

Perhaps experts should be their own knowledge engineers, encoding their own expertise into computers. Such expert-driven arrangements could solve some of the difficulties described earlier and result in less "noise" being introduced into the knowledge base. The role of knowledge engineers would be reduced, and the acquisition process drastically expedited. There are two approaches to expert-driven systems available: *manual* and *computer-aided (semiautomatic).*

MANUAL METHOD: EXPERT'S SELF-REPORTS

Sometimes it is possible to elicit knowledge from experts manually by using a self-administered questionnaire or an organized report. Open-ended questionnaires are appropriate for **knowledge discovery,** in which high-level concepts are usually the result. Close-ended (or forced-answer) questionnaires are more structured and easy to fill in, but the knowledge collected is limited. In addition to filling out questionnaires, experts may be asked to log their activities, prepare an introductory lecture, or produce reports about their problem-solving activities.

Experts' reports and questionnaires present a number of problems according to Wolfgram et al. (1987), Hart (1992), and Scott et al. (1991).

- They essentially require the expert to act as a knowledge engineer without having a knowledge engineer's training.
- The reports tend to have a high degree of bias; they typically reflect the expert's opinion concerning how the task should be done rather than how it is really done.
- Experts often describe new and untested ideas and strategies they have been contemplating but still have not included in their decision-making behavior. Thus, there is a mixture of past experience, actual behavior, and ideal future behavior.
- Experts' reports are time-consuming efforts, and the experts lose interest rapidly. The quality of information attained rapidly decreases as the report progresses.
- Experts must be proficient in flowcharting or other process-documenting techniques.

- Experts may forget to specify certain pieces of knowledge (which may result in ambiguity).
- Experts are likely to be fairly vague about the nature of associations among events (which may result in an indeterminate bias).

Given these caveats, under certain conditions such as the inaccessibility of an expert to the knowledge engineer, expert reports and self-questionnaires may provide useful preliminary knowledge discovery and acquisition (Hamilton, 1996a). Some of the limitations of the manual approach can be eliminated with proper computer support.

COMPUTER-AIDED APPROACHES

The purpose of computerized support for the expert is to reduce or eliminate the potential problems discussed, especially those of indeterminate bias and ambiguity. These problems dominate the gathering of information for the initial knowledge base and the interactive refinements of this knowledge. A smart knowledge acquisition tool must be able to add knowledge to the knowledge base incrementally and refine or even correct existing knowledge.

Sleeman and Mitchell (1996) describe two systems, REFINER+ and TIGON, that allow a domain expert to perform knowledge acquisition directly. These systems have been used for patient management and for the diagnosis of turbine errors, respectively. REFINER is a case-based system that infers a prototypical description for each class, which is labeled by the domain expert. REFINER+ uses existing cases directly from databases. It then allows the expert to work with proposed modifications that would remove particular inconsistencies. TIGON was developed to detect and diagnose faults in a gas turbine engine. It incorporates background material from which it produces analogous rule bases automatically. See Sleeman and Mitchell (1996) for details. The KAVAS-2 project (see Medical Informatics Laboratory ApS, www.ehto.be/aim/volume2/kavas.html) is a knowledge acquisition, visualization, and assessment system that addresses the requirement to manage data and information flow in medicine. Protocols and procedures are provided to increase data and information generation, improve the quality of patient management, and reduce costs in health care service. As a result, a toolbox (KAVIAR) is provided to define modeling process goals, identify suitable tools to address these goals, apply selected tools to the problem, measure the quality of the proposed solution, and validate the results.

Visual modeling techniques are often used to construct the initial domain model. The objective of the visual modeling approach is to give the user the ability to visualize real-world problems and to manipulate elements of them through the use of graphics (Lee et al., 1995; Humphrey, 1999; Demetriads et al., 1999). Kearney (1990) indicates that diagrams and drawings are useful in representing problems; they serve as a set of external memory aids and can reveal inconsistencies in an individual's knowledge (Lockwood and Chen, 1994). Machine learning methods can induce decision trees and rules (Section 11.12) (Eriksson, 1992; Sheetz et al., 1994). A tool available for download via the Internet is XpertRule from Attar Software (www.attar.com). It provides a graphical development environment, allowing specification of decision trees based on business process logic. Deployment of developed applications can be via stand-alone machines, networks, or Internet/intranets via the XpertRun run-time environment.

Experts can use several other tools [for a survey, see Boose and Gaines (1990)]. Of special interest are methods based on repertory grid analysis, presented next.

11.10 REPERTORY GRID ANALYSIS

Experience is often based on perception, insight, and intuition. Therefore, many experts have difficulty in expressing their line of reasoning. Experts may also be confused between facts and factors that actually influence decision making. To overcome these and other limitations of knowledge acquisition by gaining insight into the expert's mental model of the problem domain, a number of elicitation techniques have been developed. These techniques, derived from psychology, use an approach called the *classification interview*. Because they are fairly structured when applied, these methods are usually aided by a computer. The primary method is **repertory grid analysis (RGA).**

BASIS FOR THE GRID

RGA is based on Kelly's model of human thinking called **personal construct theory** (Hart, 1992; Stewart and Mayes, 2000) (also see the BizTech archives at www.brint. com). According to this theory, each person is viewed as a personal scientist who seeks to predict and control events by forming theories, testing hypotheses, and analyzing results of experiments. Knowledge and perceptions about the world (or about a domain or a problem) are classified and categorized by each individual as a personal, perceptual model. Based on the model developed, each individual is able to anticipate and then act on the basis of these anticipations.

This personal model matches our view of an expert at work; it is a description of the development and use of the expert's knowledge, and so it is suitable for expert systems as suggested by Hart (1992). RGA is a method of investigating such a model.

HOW RGA WORKS

RGA uses several processes. First, the expert identifies the important objects in the domain of expertise. For example, computer languages (LISP, C++, COBOL) are objects in the situation of needing to select a computer language. This identification is done in an interview.

Second, the expert identifies the important attributes considered in making decisions in the domain. For example, the availability of commercial packages and ease of programming are important factors in selecting a computer language.

Third, for each attribute, the expert is asked to establish a bipolar scale with distinguishable characteristics (traits) and their opposites. For example, in selecting a computer language, the information shown in Table 11.4 can be included.

Fourth, the interviewer picks any three of the objects and asks, "What attributes and traits distinguish any two of these objects from the third?" For example, if a set includes LISP, PROLOG, and COBOL, the expert may point to orientation. Then the expert will say that LISP and PROLOG are symbolic in nature, whereas COBOL is numeric. These answers are translated to points on a scale of 1 to 3 (or 1 to 5). This step

TABLE 11.4   RGA Input for Selecting a Computer Language

Attribute	Trait	Opposite
Availability	Widely available	Not available
Ease of programming	High	Low
Training time	Low	High
Orientation	Symbolic	Numeric

TABLE 11.5   Example of a Grid

Attribute	Orientation	Ease of Programming	Training Time	Availability
Trait Opposite	Symbolic (3) Numeric (1)	High (3) Low (1)	High(1) Low (3)	High (3) Low (1)
LISP	3	3	1	1
PROLOG	3	2	2	2
C++	3	2	2	3
COBOL	1	2	1	3

continues for several triplets of objects. The answers are recorded in a grid, as shown in Table 11.5. The numbers in the grid designate the points assigned to each attribute for each object.

Once the grid is completed, the expert may change the ratings in the boxes. The grid can be used afterward to make recommendations in situations where the importance of the attributes is known. For example, in a simplistic sense, it can be said that if numeric orientation is very important, then COBOL will be the recommended language. For an interesting application see Hunter and Becker (2000).

USE OF RGA IN EXPERT SYSTEMS

A number of knowledge acquisition tools have been developed based on RGA. These tools are aimed at helping in the conceptualization of the domain. Three representative tools are ETS, AQUINAS, and KRITON.

Expertise transfer system (ETS) is a computer program that interviews experts and helps them build expert systems. ETS interviews experts to uncover vocabulary conclusions, problem-solving traits, trait structures, trait weights, and inconsistencies. It has been used to construct prototypes rapidly (often in less than 2 hours for very small ES), to aid the expert in determining whether there is sufficient knowledge to solve a problem, and to create knowledge bases for a variety of different ES shells from its own internal representation. An improved version of ETS, called NeoETS, has been developed to expand the capabilities of ETS. The method is limited to classification-type problems [for details, see Boose and Gaines (1990)]. ETS is now part of AQUINAS.

AQUINAS is a very complex tool (Boose and Bradshaw, 1993, 1999) that extends the problem-solving and knowledge representation of ETS by allowing experts to structure knowledge in hierarchies. A set of heuristics has been defined and incorporated in Dialog Manager, a subsystem of AQUINAS, to provide guidance in the knowledge acquisition process to domain experts and knowledge engineers.

Enquire Within (www.EnquireWithin.co.nz) is an online interactive software tool that charts and clarifies thoughts and perceptions based on Repertory Grid interview techniques. Users are taken through compare and contrast processes, resulting in a graphical representation indicating how one has evaluated and described the subject matter for a particular session. Uses can involve analyzing personal relationships or opportunities, decision-making support, and development of expert systems, and as a computer-based school study aid.

A few PC-based repertory grid analysis tools are available (such as PCGRID from April Metzler at Lehigh University). One of the first Web-based tools for knowledge acquisition, WebGrid (Section 11.18) enhances collaborative knowledge acquisition (see also tiger.cpsc.ucalgary.ca/WebGrid). Also there are software packages such as

Circumgrids (W. Chambers, University of South Florida) for analyzing repertory grids via methods such as cluster analysis and factor analysis or principal component analysis. In addition there is an open-source code program called WinGrid and its successor Ingrid99 (available for download via ingrid.netpedia.net/wingrid.html).

11.11 SUPPORTING THE KNOWLEDGE ENGINEER

A number of acquisition and encoding tools can greatly reduce the required time (or skill level) of the knowledge engineer. Nevertheless, the knowledge engineer still plays an important role in the process, as shown in Figure 11.7, which depicts the major tasks of the knowledge engineer:

- Advise the expert on the process of interactive knowledge elicitation.
- Set up and manage the interactive knowledge acquisition tools appropriately.
- Edit the unencoded and coded knowledge base in collaboration with the expert.
- Set up and manage the knowledge-encoding tools appropriately.
- Validate application of the knowledge base in collaboration with the expert.
- Train clients in effective use of the knowledge base in collaboration with the expert by developing operational and training procedures.

This use of interactive elicitation can be combined with manual elicitation and with the use of the interactive tools by the knowledge engineer. The knowledge engineer can directly elicit knowledge from the expert and use interactive elicitation tools to enter knowledge into the knowledge base. For example, see AIS in Action 11.2.

AIS IN ACTION 11.2

A CLONED DIGITAL TWIN OF CHRISTINE DOWNTON'S
BRAIN MANAGES MILLIONS

In 1993 Christine Downton, a star analyst at the British investment house Pareto Partners Ltd., visited Hughes Research Laboratories (Malibu, CA) to upload her knowledge of the world's bond markets into a machine. That knowledge now manages funds worth $200 million from inside a computer at Pareto's London offices. Another clone of Christine will join it shortly, choosing the best markets in which to invest. Pareto and Hughes have decided that in the war for the world's markets, the mechanized divisions are going to win.

Christine Downton says, "Emotions distort people's rational judgments. There's a fear factor: People tend to make mistakes when they're losing money. They also make mistakes when they've made money." There are other cognitive biases. The captured expertise, which includes her intuition, filters out emotional impacts on the judgments.

At Hughes, Charles Dolan developed a system called Modular Knowledge Acquisition Toolkit (M-KAT), software tools for extracting and encoding human expertise. M-KAT allows a knowledge engineer to extract knowledge at 3 to 10 times the benchmark rate. Even so, and combined with the fact that Christine was a capable expert with an above-average access to her internal thought processes, it took 18 months to perform knowledge acquisition and develop the expert system with 2,000 rules that require access to 800 economic data indicators via electronic market feeds. The system makes purchase recommendations to traders, who make the deals.

Source: Condensed from C. Davidson, "Christine Downton's Brain," *Wired,* Dec. 1996, pp. 170–176.

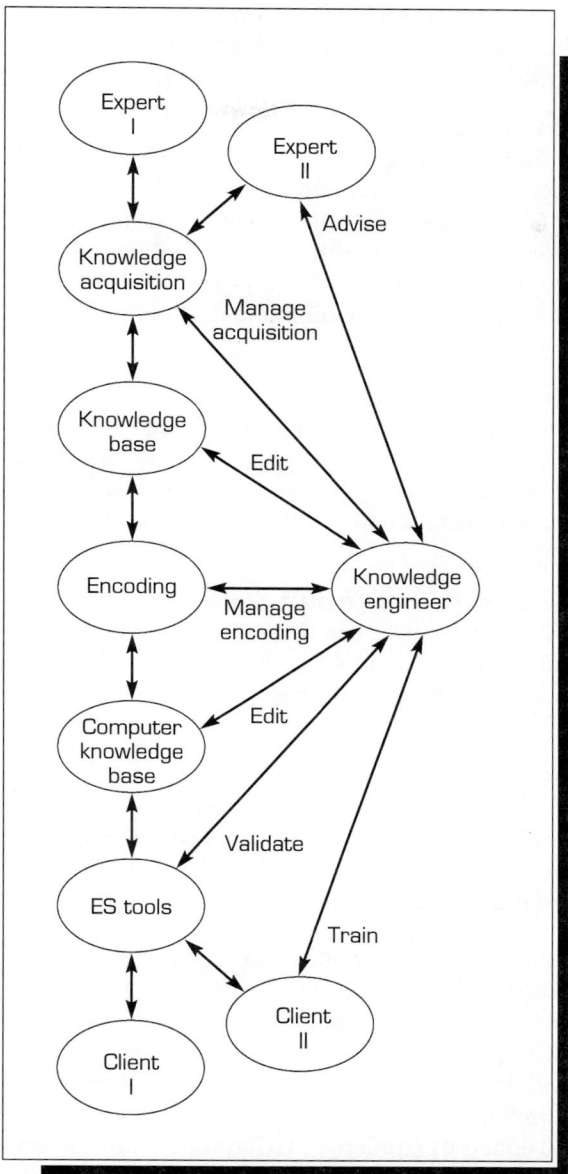

FIGURE 11.7 KNOWLEDGE ENGINEERS' ROLES IN
INTERACTIVE KNOWLEDGE ACQUISITION

Source: Adapted from B. R. Gaines, University of Calgary,
with permission.

KNOWLEDGE ACQUISITION AIDS

Several types of tools have been developed for supporting knowledge acquisition.
Some representative examples follow.

SPECIAL LANGUAGES

Several special knowledge acquisition (and sometimes representation) languages have
recently been developed. One such language is KARL [see Fensel (1996) for a discussion]

and the extension New KARL (see "Modeling Problem-Solving Methods in New KARL," on the University of Calgary's Knowledge Science Institute Internet site, ksi.cpsc.ucalgary.ca/kaw/kaw96/angele/angele.html).

EDITORS AND INTERFACES

Use of a text editor or a special knowledge base editor can facilitate the task of entering knowledge into the system and decrease the chance of errors. A good editor provides smooth user interfaces that facilitate instruction and display information conveniently. For example, the editor checks syntax and semantics for completeness and consistency. The rule editor of Exsys simplifies rule input and testing. It also checks for redundant rules. A spelling and grammar checker can also be used to detect errors.

EXPLANATION FACILITY

The explanation subsystem serves not only the user but also the knowledge engineer and the expert in refining and improving the knowledge base. In addition to general-purpose devices (such as debugging and trace mechanisms), there are specially constructed explanation facilities that can trace the chain of reasoning after it has been completed.

REVISION OF THE KNOWLEDGE BASE

Changes in the knowledge base can be made by selecting an appropriate revision from a set of possibilities. To avoid introducing new bugs or inconsistencies with the existing knowledge base, aids such as a semantic consistency checker or automated testing can be used.

PICTORIAL KNOWLEDGE ACQUISITION

Pictorial Knowledge Acquisition (PIKA) is a graphics editor whose output is a collection of structured graphic objects that can be combined to support a multilevel interface (Freiling et al., 1985). ACQUIRE, described later, produces network objects that are incorporated into expert systems.

EXAMPLE OF A KNOWLEDGE ACQUISITION AID

TEIRESIAS (Davis, 1993) is a classic program that was developed to assist knowledge engineers in the creation (or revision) of rules for a specific ES while working with the EMYCIN shell. The program uses a natural language interface to help the knowledge engineer test and debug new knowledge, and it provides an expanded explanation capability. For example, if system builders find that a set of knowledge rules lead to an inadequate conclusion, they can have TEIRESIAS show all the rules used to reach that conclusion. With the rule editor, adjustments can easily be made. To expedite the process, TEIRESIAS translates each new rule, which is entered in natural language, into LISP. Then it retranslates the rule into natural language. The program thus can point out inconsistencies, rule conflicts, and inadequacies (For acquisition aids from databases, see the *International Journal of Intelligent Systems,* Sept. 1992.). A more recent use of TEIRESIAS has been in assisting in the tracking of computer system hackers. TEIRESIAS is used to monitor systems during normal operation and analyzes the information flow, looking for repeating strings of information; these strings represent an individual computer system. An attempt to break into the computer system would modify these string patterns, allowing a computer to monitor its own operation (see *Wired,* Oct. 29, 1998, www.wired.com/news/technology/story/0,1282,15905,00.html). For further information and actual applied use, refer to the IBM Web site, www.research.ibm.com/topics/serious/bio.

INTEGRATED KNOWLEDGE ACQUISITION AIDS

Most of the preceding tools and many others were designed as stand-alone tools based on the assumption that they would be used by a specific ES participant (such as an expert) for the execution of a specific task. In reality, however, participants can play multiple roles or even exchange roles. Therefore, there is a trend toward integrating the acquisition aids. For an overview of such integration tools, see Boose and Gaines (1990) and Diamantidis and Giakoumakis (1999). Examples of such tools are PROTÉGÉ-II (Musen et al., 1995), KSM (Cuena and Molina, 1996), ACQUIRE (described in Section 11.18), and KADS, which we describe next.

KNOWLEDGE ACQUISITION AND DOCUMENTATION SYSTEM

The purpose of the Knowledge Acquisition and Documentation System (KADS), which was developed at the University of Amsterdam, is to aid the knowledge engineer in acquiring, structuring, analyzing, and documenting expert knowledge. KADS is known to be very successful in increasing the knowledge engineer's productivity.

Formal modeling languages such as KADS and its variation, CommonKADS, can improve the development of knowledge-based systems. It is now viewed as the leading methodology for supporting structured knowledge engineering and is the European de facto standard for knowledge analysis and knowledge-intensive system development. The usability of CommonKADS has been greatly improved by (ML), a formal language based on knowledge models. For details, see www.commonkads.uva.nl and van Harmelen (1996).

FRONT-END TOOLS

Knowledge must be coded in a specific manner in various knowledge-based tools. In an attempt to automate the coding, various tools have been developed. For example, Knowledge Analysis Tool (KAT) from DMSO (www.dmso.mil), converts knowledge to a specific rule format for a tool called Level5 (see www.rulmachines.com/object/docs/ugo.htm for detailed information). NEXTRA (from Neuron Data) is a similar tool that helps the knowledge engineer code rules in Nexpert Object.

11.12 MACHINE LEARNING: RULE INDUCTION, CASE-BASED REASONING, NEURAL COMPUTING, AND INTELLIGENT AGENTS

The elicitation methods presented so far are labor-intensive. The two major participants are the knowledge engineer, who is highly paid and difficult to get, and the domain expert, who is usually busy and sometimes uncooperative. Therefore, manual and even semiautomatic elicitation methods are both slow and expensive. In addition, they have some other deficiencies:

- There is often weak correlation between verbal reports and mental behavior.
- In certain situations, experts are unable to provide an overall account of how their decisions are made.
- The quality of the system depends too much on the quality of the expert and the knowledge engineer.

- The expert does not understand the ES technology.
- The knowledge engineer does not understand, in many cases, the nature of the business problem.
- It is difficult to validate the acquired knowledge.

Thus, it makes sense to develop knowledge acquisition methods that will reduce or even eliminate the need for these two participants. These methods, which are described as *computer-aided* knowledge acquisition, or automated knowledge acquisition, vary in their objectives, some of which are the following:

- Increase the productivity of knowledge engineering (reduce the cost).
- Reduce the skill level required from the knowledge engineer.
- Eliminate (or drastically reduce) the need for an expert.
- Eliminate (or drastically reduce) the need for a knowledge engineer.
- Increase the quality of the acquired knowledge.

Four topics are often considered automated knowledge acquisition, also known as **machine learning,** namely, **rule induction,** case-based reasoning, neural computing, and intelligent agents.

MACHINE LEARNING

A recent successful development in knowledge acquisition is the development of successful methods and tools for machine learning. These methods sometimes fall under the headings *knowledge discovery* and *data mining* and include methods for reading documents (sometimes in a natural language, sometimes as forms) and inducing knowledge, often in the form of rules. For an example, see Hahn et al. (1996). Other knowledge sources include databases. See Wu (1995) for a description of how to mine databases for knowledge. XpertRule from Attar Software (www.attar.com) is a software tool that extracts information from graphical decision trees. PolyAnalyst from Megaputer Intelligence Ltd. (www.megaputer.com) is a set of tools that automate knowledge discovery from databases. For more information on machine learning, see Fayyad et al. (1996b) and the following Web sites:

- Austrian Research Institute for AI–Machine Learning Group, www.ai.univie.ac.at/oefai/ml/ml.html
- Machine Learning Network at UCI, www.ics.uci.edu/ai/ml/machine-learning.html
- MINEit Software Limited, www.kdnuggets.com/software.html
- Machine Learning Network–Online Information Service, www.mlnet.org
- Machine Learning Applied to Information Retrieval, National Research Council, Canada, www.iit.nrc.ca/bibliographies/ml-applied-to-ir.html.

Also see Chen (1996) for a summary of automated knowledge acquisition and a description of role-limiting methods for enhancing automatic learning.

AUTOMATED RULE INDUCTION

Induction is a process of reasoning from the specific to the general. In ES terminology it is the process by which rules are generated from example cases by a computer program.

A rule induction system is given examples of a problem (called a *training set*) for which the outcome is known. After it has been given enough examples, the rule induction system can create rules that fit the example cases. The rules can then be used to assess new cases for which the outcome is not known. The heart of a rule induction system is an algorithm used to induce the rules from the examples (see AIS in Focus 11.3).

An example of a simplified rule induction can be seen in the work of a loan officer in a bank. Requests for loans include information about the applicants such as income level, assets, age, and number of dependents. These are the attributes, or characteristics, of the applicants. If we log several example cases, each with its final decision, we will find a situation that resembles the data in Table 11.6.

From these cases, it is easy to infer the following three rules:

- If income is $70,000 or more, approve the loan.
- If income is $30,000 or more, age is at least 40, assets are above $249,000, and there are no dependents, approve the loan.
- If income is between $30,000 and $50,000 and assets are at least $100,000, approve the loan.

TABLE 11.6 Case for Induction: A Knowledge Map (Induction Table)

Applicant	Annual Income ($)	Assets ($)	Age (years)	Number of Dependents	Decision
Mr. White	50,000	100,000	30	3	Yes
Ms. Green	70,000	None	35	1	Yes
Mr. Smith	40,000	None	33	2	No
Ms. Rich	30,000	250,000	42	0	Yes

AIS IN FOCUS 11.3

INDUCTION ALGORITHMS

Induction methods use a variety of algorithms to convert a knowledge matrix of attributes, values, and selections to rules. Such algorithms vary from statistical methods to neural computing.

A popular induction algorithm is ID3. ID3 first converts the knowledge matrix into a decision tree. ID3 eliminates irrelevant attributes and organizes the relevant attributes in an efficient manner. For more information on ID3, see P. R. Cohen and E. A. Feigenbaum, *The Handbook of Artificial Intelligence,* Vol. 3, Reading, MA: Addison-Wesley, 1982, pp. 406–410; and A. Colin, "Building Decision Trees with the ID3 Algorithm," *Dr. Dobb's Journal Software Tools Professional Program,* Vol. 21, No. 6, 1996. Also refer to the Haley Enterprises Inc. Web site (www.haley.com) for details on their ClassIE induction algorithms.

Extensions to include uncertain reasoning (probabilistic knowledge) in ID3 are due to P. E. Maher and D. St. Clair, "Uncertain Reasoning in an ID3 Machine Learning Framework," *Second IEEE International Conference on Fuzzy Systems,* IEEE, Piscataway, NJ, 1993. Inclusion of fuzzy logic (another type of probabilistic knowledge) in the decision trees and further applications are given by M. Umano et al., "Fuzzy Decision Trees by Fuzzy ID3 Algorithm and Its Application to Diagnosis Systems," *IEEE International Conference on Fuzzy Systems,* Vol. 3, 1994.

An inductive learning algorithm, as defined by M. R. Tolun and S. M. Abu-Soud ("ILA: An Inductive Learning Algorithm for Rule Extraction," *Expert Systems with Applications,* Vol. 14, No. 3, Apr. 1998), further addresses problems with symbolic learning algorithms such as ID3 when working on unseen training examples (small-junctions problem). In this instance the ID3 is unable to classify unknown examples because the decision tree is too specific. ILA selects features after considering all the examples for a given decision, therefore providing more general rules which do not contain unnecessary and irrelevant conditions.

ADVANTAGES OF RULE INDUCTION

One of the leading researchers in the field, Donald Michie, has pointed out that only certain types of knowledge can be properly acquired using manual knowledge acquisition methods such as interviews and observations. These are cases in which the domain of knowledge is certain, small, loosely coupled, or modular. As the domain gets larger or uncertain, and more complex, experts become unable to explain how they perform. However, they can still supply the knowledge engineer with suitable examples of problems and their solutions. Using rule induction allows ES to be used in more complicated and more commercially rewarding fields.

Another advantage is that the builder does not have to be a knowledge engineer. He or she can be the expert or a system analyst. This not only saves time and money but also solves the difficulties in dealing with the knowledge engineer who may be an outsider unfamiliar with the business.

Machine induction also offers the possibility of deducing *new knowledge.* Once rules are generated, they are reviewed by an expert and modified if necessary. A big advantage of rule induction is that it enhances the thinking process of the reviewing expert.

Cercone (1999) indicates the advantages of utilizing rule induction and case-based reasoning with respect to traditional one-representation architectures (also available on the IEEE Computer Society Web site, www.computer.org).

DIFFICULTIES IN IMPLEMENTATION

Despite the advantages, there are several difficulties with the implementation of rule induction:

- Some induction programs may generate rules that are not easy for a human to understand because the way the program classifies a problem's attributes and properties may not be the way a human would do it.
- Rule induction programs do not select the attributes. An expert still must be available to specify which attributes are significant (e.g., important factors in approving a loan).
- The search process in rule induction is based on special algorithms that generate efficient decision trees, which reduce the number of questions that must be asked before a conclusion is reached. Several alternative algorithms are available. They vary in their processes and capabilities.
- The method is good only for rule-based classification problems, especially of the yes/no type. (However, many problems can be rephrased or split so that they fall into the classification category.)
- The number of attributes must be fairly small. The upper limit on the number of attributes is approached very quickly.
- The number of examples necessary can be very large.
- The set of examples must be "sanitized"; for example, cases that are exceptions to rules must be removed. (Such exceptions can be determined by observing inconsistent rules.)
- The method is limited to situations under certainty.
- A major problem with the method is that the builder does not know in advance whether the number of examples is sufficient and whether the algorithm is good enough. To be sure of this would presuppose that the builder had some idea of the solution; the reason for using induction in the first instance is that the builder does not know the solution but wants to discover it by using the rules.

Because of these limitations, the induction method is usually used to provide a first prototype; then it is translated into something more robust and crafted into an improved system through an evolutionary design and development method.

SOFTWARE PACKAGES

There are several induction software packages on the market, both for personal computers and for larger computers. Most are included in ES shells to enhance their usefulness. The following is a list of some representative packages:

- ACQUIRE (personal computer), vvv.com/ai/
- EZ-Xpert (personal computer), www.ez-xpert.com
- XpertRule (personal computer), www.attar.com
- Nexpert Object/Smart Elements (personal computer and larger), www.rimatech.com
- Level5 (personal computer), www.rulmachines.com/object/docs/ugo.htm.

Most of these programs not only generate rules but also check them for possible logical conflict. Furthermore, all of them are ES shells; that is, they can be used to generate the rules and then to construct an ES that uses this knowledge. K-Vision even allows incorporation of an entire induction table into a set of rules represented as a single node. For further details see Reynolds and Zannon (2000).

INTERACTIVE INDUCTION

The combination consisting of an expert supported by a computer is called **interactive induction.** One interesting tool that combines induction and interactive acquisition is ACQUIRE (Acquired Intelligence Inc., www.aiinc.ca).

ACQUIRE captures the knowledge of an expert through interactive interviews, distills the knowledge, and automatically generates a rule-based knowledge base. ACQUIRE provides a variety of ways of capturing human knowledge, all of which are focused on a qualitative representation of knowledge, and uses specific patterns of information to describe the situations experts can observe or contemplate. Thus, ACQUIRE can capture both explicit and implicit knowledge.

ACQUIRE guides an expert through successive steps of knowledge structuring, yielding models of domain knowledge at varying levels of generality. The most general of these models is the Object Network. An object is anything that occurs, is considered, or is concluded by the expert. The domain expert attributes a set of values or meanings to each object and organizes them into a network. The details of the individual rules are completed by a number of methods, including action tables (induction tables) and IF-THEN-ELSE rules. Finally, the reasoning path is created, and conflicts among reasoning paths are resolved. Contexts in which a rule is applied are also specified.

ACQUIRE interacts with experts (without knowledge engineers); it helps them bypass their cognitive defenses and biases and identify the important criteria and constructs used in decision making. For details, see http://www.aiinc.ca/products/acquire.html.

CASE-BASED REASONING

Case-based reasoning is an approach for building ES by accessing problem-solving experiences (called *cases*) for inferring solutions for solving future problems. Thus, a collection of the historical cases and their resolutions constitutes a knowledge base. The decision maker recalls previous cases, which may be identical to the new ones but usually are not. They may exhibit only slight hints of similarity with a new case, but even such a hint may be useful. Knowledge acquisition is very simple because the historical data are on file, and only minor verifications with experts may be needed. The AC-QUIRE system mentioned above has a case-oriented reasoning facility. For details, see Chapter 13. Also check out the University of Kaiserslautern's case-based reasoning Web site (www.cbr-web.org).

NEURAL COMPUTING

Neural computing is another problem-solving approach in which historical cases are used for deriving solutions to new problems. In contrast to case-based reasoning, neural computing works in fairly narrow domains using a pattern recognition approach. Therefore, a large volume of historical cases is needed (Chapter 14). Knowledge acquisition becomes simple because historical cases and their resolutions are usually available in corporate databases. Again, experts can be consulted during the validation and verification, but their role is greatly reduced and so are the efforts and expenses of knowledge acquisition.

INTELLIGENT AGENTS FOR KNOWLEDGE ACQUISITION

Another mechanism for automated knowledge acquisition involves the use of intelligent agents (Chapter 17). Intelligent agents (software robots) for finding or accessing knowledge have led to the development of the Knowledge Query and Manipulation Language (KQML). KQML is a language and protocol for exchanging information and knowledge. It allows an application program to interact with an intelligent system, or for two or more intelligent systems to share knowledge in support of cooperative problem solving. The development of KQML was part of the Knowledge Sharing Effort sponsored by ARPA for the development of methodologies and software for the sharing and reuse of knowledge. Another development is the Knowledge Interchange Format (KIF), a computer-oriented language for the interchange of knowledge among disparate programs. Intelligent agents can work within a document or search the Web and return with knowledge in a predesignated format. See Dieng (1995) for an example of agent-based knowledge acquisition. For an example of an intelligent agent approach for knowledge sharing, see AIS in Action 11.4. (For more information on KQML, access the University of Maryland Baltimore County Web site, www.cs.umbc.edu/kqml/.)

AIS IN ACTION 11.4

INTELLIGENT AGENTS SHARE KNOWLEDGE AMONG COMPLEX, INTERDEPENDENT APPLICATIONS AREAS

The Advanced Technological Operations System (ATOS) is a project of the European Space Agency for integrating advanced applications, especially knowledge-based applications, with ground systems for spacecraft mission operations. The Spacecraft Missions Operations System (SMOS) is a set of facilities divided into mission preparation, mission planning, and mission operations.

In general, independently developed applications, possibly running on different platforms, support each of these areas. However, the areas are highly interdependent. ATOS, an agent-based knowledge-sharing system, was designed to handle the complex interrela-

tionships coordinating the three groups. There is an infrastructure that links the objects from each area to each application system. The links are the agents. Each one is defined by the application program and the needed link. It then knows what to do and how to do it. Knowledge is stored in the KQML format, and messages are handled in KIF. The first prototype system has proved successful, and a full deployment is under way.

Source: Modified from M. Jones et al., "An Agent Based Approach to Spacecraft Mission Operations," in Mars, N. J. I. (ed.) (1995) *Towards Very Large Knowledge Bases,* Amsterdam: 105 Press.

A good online reference for on Internet intelligent agents is the BotSpot Web site (www.botspot.com). Information of agents addressing areas such as search tools, news gathering, and automatic Web site fine-tuning is available along with software downloads.

Klush (1999) gives a detailed survey of intelligent information agents with respect to corporate information systems and agents, rational information agents, electronic commerce, mobile agents, and security.

Tecuci (1998) provides a theory and a supportive tool set to enable the construct of agents. In addition, case studies are outlined covering areas such as educational assessment, statistical analysis, and engineering design assistance.

11.13 SELECTING AN APPROPRIATE KNOWLEDGE ACQUISITION METHOD

The objectives of an ideal knowledge acquisition system were outlined by Hill et al. (1986):

- Direct interaction with the expert without intervention by a knowledge engineer
- Applicability to unlimited, or at least a broad class of, problem domains
- Tutorial capabilities to eliminate the need for prior training of the expert
- Ability to analyze work in progress to detect inconsistencies and gaps in knowledge
- Ability to incorporate multiple sources of knowledge
- A human interface (i.e., natural conversation) that will make use of the system enjoyable and attractive
- Ability to interface easily with different expert system tools as appropriate to the problem domain.

To attain these objectives it is necessary to automate the process. However, automatic knowledge acquisition methods, also known as machine learning, are limited in their capabilities. Nevertheless, diligent efforts on the part of researchers, vendors, and system builders are helping to slowly approach these objectives. One difficult task is to select which machine learning approach to use. As with model selection in DSS, special ES can be developed to help. The best results can be achieved in knowledge acquisition that is difficult to acquire manually (such as large databases). In the interim, acquisition will continue to be done manually in most cases, but it will be supported by productivity improvement aids.

HYBRID ACQUISITION

Because both manual methods and induction have their own limitations, it makes sense to combine the two approaches. Jeng et al. (1996) developed a system in which an inductive learning algorithm is responsible for reasoning and consistency checking, whereas human experts are responsible for problem solving. Le Roux (1996) describes another hybrid approach for knowledge acquisition derived from both KADS and ACKnowledge's Generalized Directive Model. A prototype software environment is used to produce a knowledge model and perform elicitation.

11.14 KNOWLEDGE ACQUISITION FROM MULTIPLE EXPERTS

An important element in the development of an ES is the identification of experts. This is a complicated task, perhaps because often so many support mechanisms are used by practitioners for certain tasks (such as questionnaires, informal and formal consultations, and texts). Together, these support mechanisms contribute to the high quality of professional output. However, they may also tend to make it difficult to identify a knowledge "czar," whose estimates, processes, or knowledge are clearly superior to what the system and mix of staff, support tools, and consulting skills produce in the rendering of normal client service. See Byrd (1995) and Stein (1992) for details of identifying experts and their opinions concerning the knowledge acquisition process. Further information is available on the ACACIA Web site (www.inria.fr/acacia/), which provide models, methods, and tools to assist knowledge engineers in acquiring knowledge from multiple sources (experts and documents). This site particularly addresses knowledge capitalization, knowledge servers and knowledge-based systems. Also worth checking are the online journals available at the Defense Systems Management College (www.dsmc.dsm.mil).

The usual approach to this problem is to build ES for a very narrow domain in which expertise is clearly defined. Then it is easy to find one expert. However, even though many ES have been constructed with one expert—an approach advocated as a good strategy for ES construction—there could be a need for **multiple experts,** especially when more serious ES are being constructed or when expertise is not particularly well defined.

The major purposes of using multiple experts (Medsker et al., 1995) are

- To better understand the knowledge domain
- To improve knowledge base validity, consistency, completeness, accuracy, and relevancy
- To provide better productivity
- To identify incorrect results more easily
- To address broader domains
- To be able to handle more complex problems and combine the strengths of different reasoning approaches.

Table 11.7 lists benefits and problems of multiple experts.

When multiple experts are used, there are often differences of opinion and conflicts that must be resolved. This is especially true when knowledge bases are being developed from multiple sources, where these systems address problems that involve the use of subjective reasoning and heuristics.

Other related issues are identifying different aspects of the problem and matching them to different experts, integrating knowledge from various experts, assimilating conflicting strategies, personalizing community knowledge bases, and developing programming technologies to support these issues.

MULTIPLE EXPERT SCENARIOS

There are four possible scenarios, or configurations, of using multiple experts (McGraw and Harbison-Briggs, 1989; O'Leary, 1993; Scott et al., 1991; Rayham and Fairhurst, 1999): individual experts, primary and secondary experts, small groups, and panels.

TABLE 11.7   Benefits of and Problems with Participation of Multiple Experts

Benefits	*Problems*
On the average, fewer mistakes by a group of experts than by a single expert	Groupthink phenomena
Several experts in a group eliminate the need for using a world-class expert (who is difficult to get and expensive)	Fear on the part of some domain experts of senior experts or a supervisor (lack of confidentiality)
Wider domain than a single expert's	Compromising solutions generated by a group with conflicting opinions
Synthesis of expertise	Wasted time in group meetings
Enhanced quality from synergy among experts	Difficulties in scheduling the experts
	Dominating experts (controlling, not letting others speak)

INDIVIDUAL EXPERTS

In this case, several experts contribute knowledge individually. Using multiple experts in this manner relieves the knowledge engineer of the stress associated with multiple-expert teams. However, this approach requires that the knowledge engineer have a means of resolving conflicts and handling multiple lines of reasoning. An example of a Delphi process performed with questionnaires for acquiring knowledge about hospital operating room scheduling is provided by Hamilton (1996a). Once acquired, the knowledge was deployed in an expert system at multiple sites.

PRIMARY AND SECONDARY EXPERTS

In this case, a primary expert is responsible for validating information retrieved from other domain experts. Knowledge engineers may initially consult the primary expert for guidance in domain familiarization, refinement of knowledge acquisition plans, and identification of potential secondary experts.

SMALL GROUPS

In this case, several experts are consulted together and asked to provide agreed-upon information. Working with small groups of experts allows the knowledge engineer to observe alternate approaches to the solution of a problem and the key points made in solution-oriented discussions among experts.

PANELS

To meet goals for verification and validation of ongoing development efforts, some programs choose to establish a council of experts. These individuals typically meet together at times scheduled by the developer for the purpose of reviewing knowledge base development efforts, content, and plans. In many cases, the functionality of the expert system itself is tested against the expertise of such a panel.

   These scenarios determines in part the method to be used for handling multiple experts.

METHODS OF HANDLING MULTIPLE EXPERTISE

Several major approaches to the issue of integrating experts' opinions have been defined by Medsker et al. (1995), O'Leary (1993), and Scott et al. (1991).

- Blend several lines of reasoning through *consensus methods* such as Delphi, NGT, and GSS, which were described in Chapter 7 (Barrett and Edwards, 1994; Awad, 1996).
- Use an analytic approach such as group probability (O'Leary, 1993).
- Keep the lines of reasoning distinct and select a specific line of reasoning based on the situation (Scott et al., 1991).
- Automate the process, using software (ACACIA web site: www.sop.inria.fr/acacia/) or a blackboard approach (Englemore and Morgan, 1989) (see AIS in Action 11.5).
- Decompose the knowledge acquired into specialized knowledge sources (blackboard systems) (*PC AI,* 1997).

AIS IN ACTION 11.5

INVEX: INVESTMENT ADVISORY EXPERT SYSTEM

Large-scale capital investment is a critical business decision because it is largely irreversible and usually long term. Such a decision can be very complex because of the many variables and uncertainties involved. Considerable expertise is needed to make such decisions, and so an expert system can be a useful decision aid. Such ES can be used interactively by an investor. The INVEX system is based on an ES architecture that allows the combination of knowledge from several experts, each stored in a different knowledge base. It can also use different methods to capture this knowledge. Judgmental investment ranking and selection collected from expert economists are embedded in such rule-based knowledge bases. Economists' knowledge is then combined with decisions for operations research methods (embedded in a knowledge source that fully respects multicriteria optimization, MCDM) and from risk analysis methods (embedded in a conventional procedural knowledge source). When the decisions from different types of knowledge sources are combined, redundancy is likely to be reduced and the combined decision becomes more effective. A flow diagram of the system is shown in Figure 11.8. As described, this system can be viewed as an expert support system that integrates ES, DSS, and optimization.

11.15 VALIDATION AND VERIFICATION OF THE KNOWLEDGE BASE

Knowledge acquisition involves quality control aspects that appear under the terms *evaluation, validation,* and *verification.* These terms are often confused or used interchangeably. We use the definitions provided by O'Keefe et al. (1987).

- **Evaluation** is a broad concept. Its objective is to assess an expert system's overall value. In addition to assessing acceptable performance levels, it analyzes whether the system would be usable, efficient, and cost-effective.
- **Validation** is the part of evaluation that deals with the *performance* of the system (e.g., as it compares to the expert's). Simply stated, validation is building the right system, that is, substantiating that a system performs with an acceptable level of accuracy.

- **Verification** is building the system right or substantiating that the system is correctly implemented to its specifications.

In the realm of ES, these activities are dynamic because they must be repeated each time the prototype is changed.

In terms of the knowledge base, it is necessary to ensure that we have the *right* knowledge base (i.e., that the knowledge is valid). It is also essential to ensure that the knowledge base was constructed properly (verification).

In performing these quality control tasks, we deal with several activities and concepts, as listed in Table 11.8. The process can be very difficult if one considers the many sociotechnical issues involved (Sharma and Conrath, 1992).

A method for validating ES, based on validation approaches from psychology, was developed by Sturman and Milkovich (1995). The approach tests the extent to which the system and the expert decisions agree, the inputs and processes used by an expert compare to the machine, and the difference between expert and novice decisions. Validation and verification techniques on specific ES are described by Ram and Ram (1996) for innovative management. Avritzer et al. (1996) provide an algorithm for reliability testing of expert systems designed to operate in industrial settings, particularly to monitor and control large real-time systems.

TABLE 11.8 Measures of Validation

Measure or Criterion	Description
Accuracy	How well the system reflects reality, how correct the knowledge is in the knowledge base
Adaptability	Possibilities for future development, changes
Adequacy (or completeness)	Portion of the necessary knowledge included in the knowledge base
Appeal	How well the knowledge base matches intuition and stimulates thought and practicability
Breadth	How well the domain is covered
Depth	Degree of detailed knowledge
Face validity	Credibility of knowledge
Generality	Capability of a knowledge base to be used with a broad range of similar problems
Precision	Capability of the system to replicate particular system parameters, consistency of advice, coverage of variables in knowledge base
Realism	Accounting for relevant variables and relations, similarity to reality
Reliability	Fraction of the ES predictions that are empirically correct
Robustness	Sensitivity of conclusions to model structure
Sensitivity	Impact of changes in the knowledge base on quality of outputs
Technical and operational validity	Quality of the assumed assumptions, context, constraints, and conditions, and their impact on other measures
Turing test	Ability of a human evaluator to identify whether a given conclusion is made by an ES or by a human expert
Usefulness	How adequate the knowledge is (in terms of parameters and relationships) for solving correctly
Validity	Knowledge base's capability of producing empirically correct predictions

Source: Adapted from B. Marcot, "Testing Your Knowledge Base," *AI Expert,* Aug. 1987.

Automated verification of knowledge is offered in the ACQUIRE product described earlier. Verification is conducted by measuring the system's performance and is limited to classification cases with probabilities. It works as follows: When an ES is presented with a new case to classify, it assigns a confidence factor to each selection. By comparing these confidence factors with those provided by an expert, one can measure the accuracy of the ES for each case. By performing comparisons on many cases, one can derive an overall measure of ES performance (O'Keefe and O'Leary, 1993).

Rosenwald and Liu (1997) have developed a validation procedure that uses the rule base's knowledge and structure to generate test cases that efficiently cover the entire input space of the rule base. Thus, the entire set of cases need not be examined. A symbolic execution of a model of the ES is used to determine all conditions under which the fundamental knowledge can be used. For an extensive bibliography on validation and verification, see Grogono et al. (1991) and Juan et al. (1999).

11.16 ANALYZING, CODING, DOCUMENTING, AND DIAGRAMMING

The collected knowledge must be analyzed, coded, and documented. The manner in which these activities take place depends on the methods of acquisition and representation. The following example, based on Wolfgram et al. (1987), illustrates some of the steps in this process. It deals with knowledge acquired with the use of verbal protocols and includes four steps.

TRANSCRIPTION

First, a complete transcription of the verbal report is made, including not only the expert's utterances but also those of the knowledge engineer and any other distractions or interferences that may have occurred during the session.

PHRASE INDEXING

Second, a phrase index is compiled by breaking up the transcription into short phrases, each identified by an index number. Each phrase should correspond to the knowledge engineer's assessment of what constitutes a piece of knowledge, that is, a single task, assertion, or data collection process by the expert.

KNOWLEDGE CODING

Third, knowledge is coded. This activity attempts to classify the knowledge. One useful classification is to distinguish between descriptive and procedural knowledge.

DOCUMENTATION

Fourth, the knowledge should be properly organized and documented. One way of organizing the documentation is to divide it into four parts: comprehensive domain listing, descriptive knowledge, procedural knowledge, and a glossary.

KNOWLEDGE DIAGRAMMING

Knowledge diagramming is a graphical approach to improving the process of knowledge acquisition. It consists of hierarchical top-down descriptions of the major types of knowledge used to describe facts and reasoning strategies for problem solving in expert systems. These types are objects, events, performance, and metaknowledge. Diagramming also describes the linkages and interactions among the various types of knowledge. As knowledge is acquired, the diagrams support the analysis and planning of subsequent acquisitions. The process is similar to diagramming in system analysis; with a high-level representation of knowledge, the *productivity* of the builders and the *quality* of the system can be increased. Such **conceptual graphs (CG)** are useful in analyzing the knowledge acquired. One tool for handling these is CGKAT (Martin, 1996), a tool that integrates a CG workbench with a structured document editor to provide an advanced technique for organizing, accessing, and handling knowledge and information.

Hierarchical diagramming ends with a primitive level that cannot be decomposed. The decomposition at all levels is diagrammed to provide a partitioned view of events and objects. The process uses a special Knowledge Representation Language (KRL). Graphical techniques augment the scope, understanding, and modularity of knowledge. In addition, some knowledge is best expressed in diagrammatic form by the domain experts. Such representations are natural. It would be prudent to be able to analyze the diagrams to codify the knowledge. See Cheng (1996) for details.

Knowledge diagramming can be used to manage acquisition very effectively when it is tied to the five-stage model of knowledge acquisition (Hart, 1992). A special expert system called INQUEST has been developed using this approach. For information about this system and knowledge diagramming in general, see Cheng (1996).

11.17 NUMERIC AND DOCUMENTED KNOWLEDGE ACQUISITION

ACQUISITION OF NUMERIC KNOWLEDGE

Traditional knowledge acquisition methods are designed to deal mainly with symbolic representation of knowledge. Drake and Hess (1990) claim that a special approach is needed to capture numeric knowledge. They suggest complementing symbolic knowledge acquisition with a numeric one. Drake and Hess present a methodology called *abduction,* which handles numeric, complex, and uncertain relationships.

ACQUISITION OF DOCUMENTED KNOWLEDGE

Often, knowledge can be acquired from other sources in addition to, or instead of, human experts. The major advantage of this approach is that there is no need to use an expert. This approach is employed in knowledge-based systems where the concern is to handle a large or complex amount of information rather than world-class expertise. Searching through corporate policy manuals or catalogs is an example of such a situation.

At present, very few methodologies deal with knowledge acquisition from documented sources. It may be difficult to find the necessary knowledge in a database. One approach to improve such searches is the use of domain knowledge to guide the search (Owrang and Groupe, 1996). Another approach is to use intelligent agents (Chapter 17). However, acquisition from documented sources has a great potential for automation. Documented knowledge of almost any type can be easily and inexpensively scanned and transferred to a computer's database. Analysis of the knowledge can then be done manually, but it can also be done with the use of AI technologies (a combination of natural language processing, intelligent agents, and expert systems). Thus, expert systems can be used to build other expert systems. Hahn et al. (1996) are developing a methodology for knowledge acquisition and concept learning from texts (in German). The method relies on a quality-based model of terminological reasoning (using concepts from natural language processing). The goal is to be able to scan two kinds of documents: test reports on information technology products (about 100 documents with 100,000 words) and medical findings reports (about 120,000 documents with 10 million words). Another approach, based on explicit relation markers, is proposed by Bowden et al. (1996). Initial tests with their implementation, KEP, are encouraging.

It is possible to construct an ES that can scan databases and digitized books, journals, and magazines, and this capability is increasing. Data stored in another computer system can be retrieved electronically to create or update the knowledge base of the expert system, all without the intervention of a knowledge engineer or an expert. For discussion, see the articles on text and Web mining on the About.Com Web site (ai.about.com/compute/ai/library/weekly/aa102899.htm). The field is basically at the stage of developing new methods that interpret meaning to determine rules and other forms of knowledge, such as frames for case-based reasoning. A number of new methods are being developed and implemented. For details, see several chapters in Shadbolt et al. (1996).

11.18 KNOWLEDGE ACQUISITION AND THE INTERNET/INTRANETS

There are many reasons for the poor productivity of manual knowledge acquisition methods, which were addressed earlier in this chapter. Tochtermann and Fathi (1994) further indicate that interviewing methods attempt to map the unstructured, nonlinear knowledge of an expert into a linear structure (rules) by which knowledge losses occur. Furthermore, the linear structure is mapped back onto a nonlinear structure when implemented, leading to more inconsistencies. Hypermedia (such as the Web) can be used to represent the expertise in a more natural way. Natural links can be created in the knowledge (Tochtermann and Zink, 1995; Tung et al., 1999). HypEs (Tung et al., 1999) is a proposed architecture for the development of media-rich expert systems. It is designed to employ multiple media (text, sound, image, graphics, animation, and video) for knowledge acquisition, storage, and user interface activities.

The Internet or an intranet can be used to facilitate knowledge acquisition. For example, electronic interviewing can be conducted if the knowledge engineer and the experts are in different locations. Also, experts can validate and maintain knowledge bases from a distance. Documented knowledge can be reached via the Internet. The problem is to identify the relevant knowledge, a task that can be facilitated by intelligent agents.

Ralha (1996) addresses issues pertaining to the problem of automatically structuring informal knowledge available on the Internet through a distributed hypermedia system: the Web. Hypermedia technology via the Web provides an ideal approach to the development of knowledge-based systems by enlarging the human–machine communication channel. This new approach to integrating hypermedia technology with knowledge acquisition deals with knowledge before formalizing it. A twofold qualitative spatial reasoning approach is taken: First, dynamic linking takes place; second, the topology of the hyperspace, with qualitative spatial relations based on a primitive concept of connections between spatial regions (called a *hypermap*), is developed.

Many Web search engines are incorporating intelligent agents to identify and deliver the intended information an individual wants. Smeaton and Crimmins (1996) have developed a data fusion agent to conduct multiple Web searches and organize them for the user. Yahoo provides recommended Web sites from a search using automated collaborative filtering (ACF) technology. ACF is a technique that provides recommendations based on statistical matches of peoples' evaluations of a set of objects in some given domain (movies, books, Web pages, and so on). The agent contacts other people's agents to determine the likelihood that a given object will match your needs. Descriptions of these and other Web-related intelligent agents are provided at www.agents.umbc.edu and in Chapter 17. AnswerChase from MODiCO Inc. (www.answerchase.com) provides an internet search robot that provides search results based on query strings entered in the form of paragraphs. An example of this type of robot in action can be seen on the Ask Jeeves Web site (www.askjeeves.com).

The tools described above provide intelligent search capabilities through documents or the Web. One key to using the Web is to provide a method for eliciting knowledge from experts via an anyplace/anytime collaborative computing environment. WebGrid-II is one of the first Web-based knowledge elicitation approaches. Shaw and Gaines (1996) describe the features of WebGrid-II, an Internet implementation grounded in personal construct theory (Gaines and Shaw, 1993). WebGrid-II allows a group of people to collaborate through the Internet to develop knowledge in a different place/different time environment while adhering to the constructs from the repertory grid techniques to elicit personal constructs about a set of elements relevant to the domain of interest. It is available for use at tiger.cpsc.ucalgary.ca/WebGrid/. See Shaw and Gaines (1996) for WebGrid examples and instructions. See also Figure 11.8.

Finally, because the amount of information provided over the Web is growing exponentially, scientists are developing methods for structuring information in distributed hypermedia systems. Such integration between hypermedia technology (such as the Web) and knowledge acquisition can provide a powerful tool in knowledge acquisition. See Ralha (1996) for details.

FIGURE 11.8 DISPLAY OF AN ANALYSIS OF ADVANCED INFORMATION SYSTEMS (WEB GRID)

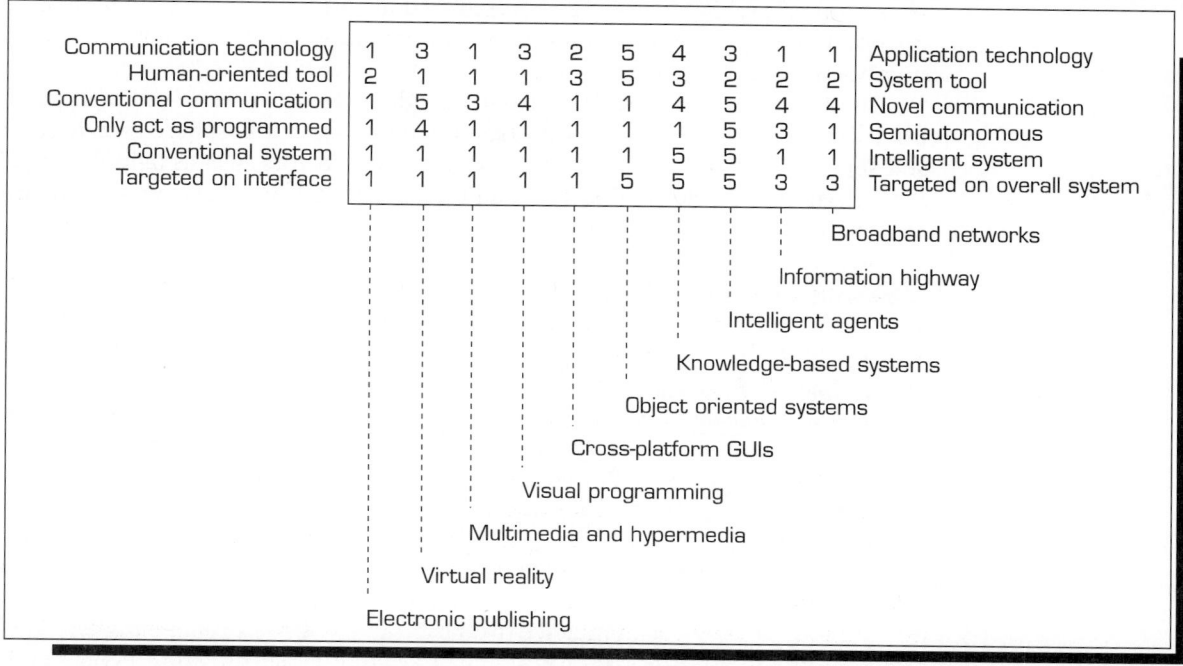

11.19 INDUCTION TABLE EXAMPLE

Induction tables or knowledge maps were mentioned earlier in the chapter. They provide a means of focusing the knowledge acquisition process by providing a convenient and easy way to understand means of mapping rule-based logic. Consider the case of choosing a site for a hospital clinic facility described in Section 11.6. While interviewing the expert, the knowledge engineer can fill in a table in which the rightmost column represents the decision being made and the other columns represent the important factors (attributes, traits) used in the decision-making problem (Table 11.9). The names of these factors are written in the first row. In the second row, we establish valid values of these factors and the valid choices (in the last column) during the interview. For example, the knowledge engineer may initially ask for some potential choices and write them down in the second row of the last column (in this case, yes or no; in others, they may be choices to be made, such as where to have lunch). Then the KE picks one and asks "What factors would lead you to make this choice?" (The KE might even ask, "Are there any factors that would direct you to making a unique choice?") When the expert indicates the factors, the KE asks for potential values for the factor, given other choices. There is no need to fill in the table completely. Experts often use partial information in their judgments. Also, over time and over multiple sessions, the knowledge in the map becomes refined. During knowledge acquisition, columns are added and deleted as needed. For example, in the unstructured interview, it was first stated that a competitor within 2 miles was important, and then the number of competitors was mentioned as important. The latter factor can supersede the first one, compactifying the knowledge.

This table then becomes the basis of the prototype ES. Each row becomes a potential IF-THEN-ELSE rule. For example, IF the population density is greater than or equal to 2,000 AND the density is greater than or equal to 4 AND the number of near competitors is 0, THEN the site is acceptable. Usually, most factors are qualitative in nature (small, medium, or large; near or far; low, medium, or high; and so on). However, some numeric variables may be required, and most ES shells can handle them. The induction table can take into consideration *or* conditions within the column (as in "if the number of near competitors is 0 or 1").

Induction tables can also be used to encode *chains of knowledge*. For example, suppose that in choosing a restaurant (see the exercises), atmosphere (romantic, casual, self-serve, and so on) is an important factor. Other factors such as lighting (candle and dim), cloth menus, cloth tablecloths, and slow but attentive service might determine a

TABLE 11.9   Induction Table (Knowledge Map) Example

Population Density	Density over How Many Square Miles?	Number of Near Competitors (within 2 miles)	Average Family Income	Near Public Transportation?	Decision
Number of people per square mile	Numeric, Region Size	0, 1, 2, 3, . . .	Numeric, dollars per year	Yes or No	Yes or No
≥2,000	≥4	0			Yes
≥3,500	≥4	1			Yes
		≥2			No
			<30,000		No

romantic atmosphere. These factors would appear in a separate table, concluding with the choice of atmosphere (which of course is a factor immediately affecting the real decision). When multiple tables are used, factors may appear in several tables (e.g., service type might determine atmosphere as well as cuisine type). These knowledge chains are used by inference engines in their backward chaining and forward chaining as they work to determine the decision to be made (Chapter 13).

❖ CHAPTER HIGHLIGHTS

- Knowledge engineering involves acquisition, representation, reasoning (inference), and explanation of knowledge.
- Knowledge is available from many sources, some of which are documented, and others undocumented (experts).
- Knowledge can be shallow, describing a narrow input–output relationship, or deep, describing complex interactions and a system's operation.
- Knowledge acquisition, especially from human experts, is difficult because of several communication and information-processing problems.
- The methods of knowledge acquisition can be divided into manual, semiautomated, and automated.
- The primary manual approach is interviewing. Interviewing methods range from completely unstructured to highly structured.
- The reasoning process of experts can be tracked by several methods. Protocol analysis is the primary method used in AI.
- Although it is possible to observe experts in action, such observations are usually limited in scope.
- Attempts are being made to reduce or even eliminate the role of the knowledge engineer by providing experts with manual or computerized tools for self-knowledge acquisition.
- Repertory grid analysis (RGA) is the most common technique for semiautomated interviews used in AI. Several software packages that use RGA improve the knowledge acquisition process.
- Many productivity tools are available for knowledge acquisition (such as editors, interfaces, and diagramming).
- Rule induction examines historical cases and generates the rules that were used to arrive at certain recommendations.
- There are benefits as well as limitations and problems in using several experts to build a knowledge base.
- The major methods of dealing with multiple experts are consensus methods, analytic approaches, selection of an appropriate line of reasoning, automation of the process, and a blackboard system.
- Validation and verification of the knowledge base are critical success factors in ES implementation.
- More than a dozen specific measures are available to determine the validity of knowledge.
- Automated knowledge acquisition methods are easier to validate and verify.
- Knowledge collected must be analyzed and coded before its representation in the computer.
- Case-based reasoning, neural computing, intelligent agents, and other machine learning tools can enhance the task of knowledge acquisition.
- The Internet and intranets are expanding on the methods for performing knowledge acquisition.

❖ KEY WORDS

- conceptual graph (CG)
- declarative knowledge
- deep knowledge
- documented knowledge
- elicitation of knowledge
- evaluation
- expertise transfer system (ETS)
- explanation and justification
- induction table
- inferencing
- interactive induction
- interview analysis

- knowledge acquisition
- knowledge diagramming
- knowledge discovery
- knowledge engineering (KE)
- knowledge map
- knowledge representation
- knowledge validation
- machine learning
- metaknowledge
- multidimensional scaling
- multiple experts
- personal construct theory

- procedural knowledge
- protocol analysis
- repertory grid analysis (RGA)
- rule induction
- shallow knowledge
- structured interview
- undocumented knowledge
- unstructured (informal) interview
- validation
- verification
- walkthrough

❖ QUESTIONS FOR REVIEW

1. Define knowledge engineering.
2. What are the steps in the knowledge engineering process?
3. What is metaknowledge?
4. Define knowledge acquisition and contrast it with knowledge representation.
5. List several sources of knowledge.
6. What is the difference between documented knowledge and undocumented knowledge?
7. Compare declarative knowledge and procedural knowledge.
8. Give four reasons why knowledge acquisition is difficult.
9. What are the desired major skills of a knowledge engineer?
10. Name three techniques of automated knowledge acquisition.
11. Describe the process of protocol analysis.
12. What is repertory grid analysis?
13. Describe some activities involved in observing an expert at work.
14. What is the major advantage of using documented knowledge?
15. Briefly discuss three deficiencies of manual knowledge acquisition.
16. What is machine learning?
17. What are the current strategies and applications for performing machine learning?
18. Describe the process of automated rule induction.
19. List the major difficulties of knowledge acquisition from multiple experts.
20. Briefly discuss the five major approaches to knowledge acquisition from multiple experts.
21. Describe the four possible scenarios of multiple experts.
22. Define evaluation, validation, and verification of knowledge.
23. Describe how the Internet and intranets can be used to enhance or perform knowledge acquisition.

❖ QUESTIONS FOR DISCUSSION

1. Discuss the major tasks performed by knowledge engineers.
2. Define and contrast shallow knowledge and deep knowledge.

3. Assume that you are to collect knowledge for one of the following systems:
   a. An advisory system on equal opportunity hiring situations in your organization
   b. An advisory system on investment in residential real estate
   c. An advisory system on how to prepare your federal tax return (form 1040).
   What sources of knowledge would you consider? (Consult Figure 11.2.)

4. Why is knowledge acquisition often considered the most difficult step in knowledge engineering?

5. Discuss the major advantages of rule induction. Give an example that illustrates the method and indicate a situation where you think it would be most appropriate.

6. Discuss the difficulties of knowledge acquisition from several experts. Describe a situation with which you are familiar in which there could be a need for several experts.

7. Transfer of knowledge from a human to a machine to a human is said to be a more difficult task than transfer from a human to a human. Why?

8. Explain the importance of observation and compare it to interviewing.

9. What are the major advantages and disadvantages of interviews based on example problems?

10. Compare and contrast protocol analysis with interviews based on example cases.

11. What are the major advantages and disadvantages of working with a prototype system for knowledge acquisition?

12. Why is repertory grid analysis so popular? What are its major weaknesses?

13. What are the major advantages and disadvantages of the observation method?

14. Discuss some of the problems of knowledge acquisition through the use of expert reports.

15. What are the present and future benefits of knowledge acquisition through analysis of documented knowledge? What are its limitations?

16. Why are manual elicitation methods so slow and expensive?

17. Why can the case analysis method be used as a basis for knowledge acquisition?

18. What are the advantages of rule induction as an approach to knowledge acquisition?

19. What are the major benefits of ACQUIRE (or similar products) compared to a conventional rule induction package?

20. How can productivity improvement tools expedite the work of a knowledge engineer?

21. Give an example for which an automated approach to knowledge acquisition from multiple experts would be feasible.

22. Explain why it is necessary to both verify and validate the content of a knowledge base. Who should do it?

23. Why is it important to have knowledge analyzed, coded, and documented in a systematic way?

24. What are the major advantages of acquiring knowledge through a knowledge engineer?

25. Compare and contrast acquisition of documented knowledge and nondocumented knowledge.

26. Knowledge engineers are compared to system analysts. Why?

27. Discuss the conditions that are necessary to ensure success when an expert is his or her own knowledge engineer.

28. Explain why machine learning techniques such as rule induction and neural computing can enhance knowledge acquisition.

29. Explain how hypermedia (as on the Web) can be used to store and retrieve knowledge.

30. Explain why the Internet and intranets can be effective means of gathering knowledge from multiple experts.

❖ EXERCISES

1. Fill in Table 11.10 with regard to the type of communication between the expert and the knowledge engineer. Use the following symbols: Y, yes; N, no; H, high; M, medium; L, low.

2. Evaluate the current success of automated rule induction and interactive methods in knowledge acquisition using Table 11.11. Then comment on the major limitations of each method.

3. Read the accompanying knowledge acquisition session involving a knowledge engineer (KE) and an expert (E) and complete the following:
   a. List the heuristics cited in this interview.
   b. List the algorithms mentioned.

> KE: Michael, you have the reputation for finding the best real estate properties for your clients. How do you do it?
>
> E: Well, Marla, first I learn about the clients' objectives.
>
> KE: What do you mean by that?
>
> E: Some people are interested in income, others in price appreciation. There are some speculators, too.
>
> KE: Assume that somebody is interested in price appreciation. What would your advice be?
>
> E: Well, I first find out how much money the investor can put down and to what degree he or she can subsidize the property.
>
> KE: Why?

TABLE 11.10   Communication between Expert and Knowledge Engineer

Method	Type of Communication				
	Face-to-Face Contact	Written Communication	Continuing for a Long Time	Time Spent by Expert	Time Spent by Knowledge Engineer
Interview analysis					
Observations of experts					
Questionnaires and expert report					
Analysis of documented knowledge					

TABLE 11.11   Comparisons of Automated Rule Induction and Interactive Methods

Method or Tool	Time of Expert	Time of Knowledge Engineer	Skill of Knowledge Engineer
Rule induction			
Autointelligence			
Smart editors			
ETS			

> E: The more cash you use as a down payment, the less subsidy you will need. Properties with high potential for price appreciation need to be subsidized for about 2 years.
>
> KE: What else?
>
> E: Location is very important. As a general rule, I recommend looking for the lowest-price property in an expensive area.
>
> KE: What else?
>
> E: I compute the cash flow and consider the tax impact by using built-in formulas in my calculator.

4. Examination of the admission records of Pacifica University showed the admission cases listed in Table 11.12.
   a. Assume that admission decisions are based only on GMAT scores and GPAs. Find, by induction, the rules used. Subject all five cases to the rules generated; make sure they are consistent with the rules.
   b. Assume that only two rules were used. Can you identify these rules?

5. Give examples of shallow knowledge and deep knowledge in an area of interest to you.

6. What do experts do? How? Choose something you are good at doing (such as mathematics, computer programming, investing, rock climbing, knitting, or baseball). Describe it in detail to a novice in the class while he or she takes notes. Then, you be the novice and extract expertise from a classmate. How hard was each activity?

7. In many ways, knowledge acquisition is a translation process. Consider the machine translation of natural languages. How is this similar? How is it different?

8. The authors of this book are coming to town and would like to know where to go for lunch. Unfortunately, you will be out of town, and you don't know specifically what they like to eat or the kind of atmosphere they like. But you do know how to encode your knowledge in an induction table like the one shown in Table 11.9. Using specific restaurants as the decisions (not yes/no but the restaurants themselves), construct an induction table reflecting your knowledge about local restaurants. To make this problem a good learning experience, work with a classmate; each of you should play the part of the knowledge engineer and the expert. For a second advisory problem (when you switch roles), recommend a local hotel. (Note that because these are not yes/no decision problems, the advice can conclude with more than one choice.)

9. In the 1970s a small knowledge acquisition demonstration program called ANIMALS.BAS was widely available on Digital Equipment Corporation's PDP-8 minicomputers. It was a guessing game, and it worked like this: The computer would tell you to think of an animal. Then it would ask you initially if it were a giraffe, to which you would respond either yes or no. If you responded yes, then you were finished and it would ask you to think of another animal (and repeat the process). If you responded no, it would prompt you for the name of the animal (say, dog) with a question that would distinguish between a giraffe and a

TABLE 11.12 Admission Cases

Case	GMAT	GPA	Decision
1	510	3.5	Yes
2	620	3.0	Yes
3	580	3.0	No
4	450	3.5	No
5	660	2.5	Yes

dog (Does the animal have a long neck?) and a correct response for the new animal (no). Then, the program again would ask you to think of an animal and ask if it had a long neck. If you typed yes, it guessed giraffe; if no, it guessed dog. If its guess was wrong, it would again prompt you for the animal name, differentiating feature (factor) by way of a question, and an answer. In this way, the program quickly learned about animals. Form a group with the leader running the session and encode this kind of knowledge in an induction table. *Extra credit:* Write a program to implement this knowledge in a procedural language (recommended approach: store the questions, answers, and animals in an array or a file but not in the logic of the program).

10. Read the paper by C. W. Holsapple and W. P. Wagner entitled "Process Factors in Knowledge Acquisition," *Expert Systems,* Vol. 13, No. 1, Feb. 1996, pp. 55–61. Describe their ideas about the knowledge acquisition process and compare them to the material described in this chapter.

❖ **GROUP EXERCISE**

The group should visit a personal contact in a business or organization and interview a decision maker. Try to identify one problem that he or she is currently working on and capture knowledge about the problem and decisions through one or more interviewing technique described in the chapter. Then answer the following:

1. Which interviewing technique did you use, and why?
2. What problems did you encounter in interviewing the decision maker?
3. What problems occurred because this was a group interview instead of a dialog? Did one person function as a spokesperson for the group? Why or why not? Do you think the process would work better if one person had acted as a spokesperson? Why or why not?
4. What personality traits helped and hindered the group and the decision maker? Why?
5. If the decision maker actually makes a decision while you are interviewing him or her (or makes a decision shortly after), ask him or her how she reached the conclusion being implemented.
6. Describe your findings in a report. If possible, present the report in class and compare your results to those of other groups in the class.

❖ **INTERNET EXERCISES**

1. Access the Web site of the University of Calgary's Knowledge Science Institute (KSI) (ksi.cpsc.ucalgary.ca/KSI/). What are their latest developments in knowledge acquisition (check out the articles available at ksi.cpsc.ucalgary.ca/articles/). What are the important issues? At KSI, try the demo of WebGrid, a system for eliciting, modeling, and comparing personal construct systems. Describe its capabilities and operation in a report.
2. Search the Internet for Web sites that deal with case-based reasoning (CBR) (try www.inference.com). Examine the latest research and demo software for knowledge acquisition in CBR. Try some and write up your experience in a report.
3. Access the *PC AI* Web site (www.pcai.com/pcai/) to identify existing knowledge acquisition tools. Find them, evaluate them, and describe them in a report. Access the Acquire Intelligence Inc. Web site (www.aiinc.ca) and investigate the latest developments in knowledge acquisition. Examine Application Stories. To what kinds of problems was ACQUIRE applied? For a sample of five stories, state what knowledge acquisition methods were used in each one.

4. Search the Web for additional developments on using the Internet and intranets for knowledge acquisition.

5. Examine the latest developments on using intelligent agents for knowledge acquisition. Search the Web for these developments and report your findings. If you find a demo, run it. Be sure to visit the University of Maryland Baltimore County Web site at www.agents.umbc.edu to investigate the many uses of intelligent software agents. Also, be sure to visit the Infinite Ink Web site for resources on robots and mail filtering at www.ii.com/internet/robots/.

KNOWLEDGE REPRESENTATION

Once knowledge is acquired, it must be organized in an applications knowledge base for later use. A knowledge base can be managed like a database. It can be organized in several different configurations to facilitate fast inferencing (or reasoning) from the knowledge. The topics in this chapter are divided into the following sections:

12.1 OPENING VIGNETTE: AN INTELLIGENT SYSTEM MANAGES FORD'S ASSEMBLY PLANTS[1]

Ford Motor Company assembles about 7 million cars in a typical year in dozens of plants worldwide. In an effort to improve the operation of its automated assembly lines, Ford introduced the direct labor management system (DLMS). The DLMS uses several AI technologies including expert systems and natural language processing. In addition, automatic machine translation to foreign languages is used, thus allowing deployment of DLMS in countries that do not use English as their main language.

The heart of DLMS is a knowledge base that uses a *semantic network model* to represent all the automobile assembly planning information. The semantic network is part of knowledge representation and will be described later in this chapter. A special variation of semantic networks is called KL-ONE. Ford Motor Company had earlier considered the more common method of knowledge representation, a strictly rule-based

---

[1]Compiled from www.aaai.org, 1999.

approach because of its simplicity; however, the complexity of the dynamic domain (vehicle assembly) and uncertainty about the future maintainability of the system resulted in this approach being ruled out. Semantic network representation permits frequent and complex changes to be made in one component of the knowledge base without affecting other components. The project started in one assembly plant and within 10 years was fully deployed at all Ford assembly plants worldwide.

❖ QUESTIONS FOR THE OPENING VIGNETTE

1. Identify all AI technologies used and relate them to those described in Chapter 10.
2. What are some of the major criteria one should use in deciding what method of knowledge representation to use?
3. What are the benefits of the system?

12.2 INTRODUCTION

The Opening Vignette illustrates that a knowledge base can be organized in different ways. One important aspect of a good knowledge representation is that it should naturally represent the problem domain at hand. Furthermore, although much academic research is concerned with fairly high-level advances in the field, the important thing to remember as a knowledge-based system developer is that if a new knowledge representation is unintelligible to you or to a user, then it is wrong (Stein, 1996). Knowledge can be represented in different ways; see Bonissone (1993) and Jackson (1999) for an overview. Also refer to the University of Manchester Department of Computer Science Web site (www.cs.man.ac.uk/~franconi/kr/htme/) and the KR Inc. Web site (www.kr.org/kr/). In this chapter we describe knowledge representation methods that have proved useful in practice.

Knowledge can be organized in a knowledge base in one or more configurations. Furthermore, the knowledge in the knowledge base can be organized differently from that in the inference engine.

A variety of **knowledge representation** schemas have been developed over the years. They share two common characteristics. First, they can be programmed with existing computer languages and stored in memory. Second, they are designed so that the facts and other knowledge contained within them can be used in reasoning. That is, the knowledge base contains a data structure that can be manipulated by an inference system using search and pattern-matching techniques on the knowledge base to answer questions, draw conclusions, or otherwise perform an intelligent function.

The major knowledge representation schemas are production rules and frames and are described in detail in this chapter. Other methods are mentioned briefly.

12.3 REPRESENTATION IN LOGIC AND OTHER SCHEMAS

The general form of any logical process is illustrated in Figure 12.1. First, information is given, statements are made, or observations are noted. These form the inputs to the logical process and are called *premises*. The premises are used by the logical process to create

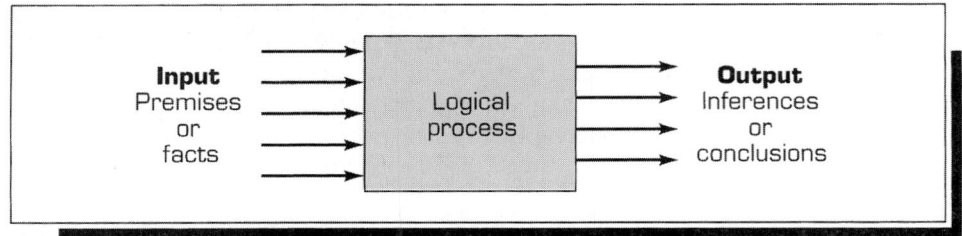

FIGURE 12.1 USING LOGIC TO REASON

the output, which consists of conclusions called *inferences*. With this process, facts that are known to be true can be used to derive new facts that also must be true.

For a computer to perform reasoning using logic, some method must be used to convert statements and the reasoning process into a form suitable for manipulation by a computer. The result is what is known as *symbolic logic*. It is a system of rules and procedures that permit the drawing of inferences from various premises using a variety of logical techniques.

The two basic forms of computational logic are **propositional logic** (or propositional calculus) and **predicate logic** (or **predicate calculus**). The term *calculus* here does not refer to the differential and integral calculus that we ordinarily associate with the term. Instead, *calculus* refers simply to a system for computing.

PROPOSITIONAL LOGIC

A proposition is nothing more than a statement that is either true or false. Once we know what it is, it becomes a premise that can be used to derive new propositions or inferences. Rules are used to determine the truth (T) or falsity (F) of the new proposition.

In **propositional logic** we use symbols such as letters of the alphabet to represent various propositions, premises, or conclusions. For example, consider the propositions used in this simple deductive process:

Statement: A—The mail carrier comes Monday through Friday.
Statement: B—Today is Sunday.
Conclusion: C—The mail carrier will not come today.

Single, simple propositions such as these are not very interesting or useful. Real-world problems involve many interrelated propositions. To form more complex premises, two or more propositions can be combined using logical connectives. These connectives or operators are designated as AND, OR, NOT, IMPLIES, and EQUIVALENT. The resulting symbolic expression looks very much like a math formula. It can then be manipulated using the rules of propositional logic to infer new conclusions.

PREDICATE CALCULUS

Because propositional logic deals primarily with complete statements and whether they are true or false, its ability to represent real-world knowledge is limited. Consequently, AI uses predicate logic instead.

Predicate logic permits you to break a statement down into component parts, namely, an object, a characteristic of the object, or some assertion about the object. In addition, predicate calculus lets you use variables and functions of variables in a symbolic logic statement. Predicate logic (calculus) is the basis for the AI language called

PROLOG (programming in logic). (*Note: Predicate* refers to the verb part of a sentence. In PROLOG, the action or relationship among objects is stated first.) For example, in PROLOG we represent the fact that the mail carrier comes on Monday as

comes_on(mail_carrier,monday).

Facts such as this one, along with rules expressed within the language, form the basis for inferencing. For further details, refer to Covington, et al. (1997).

SCRIPTS

A **script** is a knowledge representation scheme describing a *sequence of events*. Some of the elements of a typical script include entry conditions, props, roles, tracks, and scenes. The entry conditions describe situations that must be satisfied before events in the script can occur or be valid. *Props* are objects used in the sequence of events that occur. *Roles* are the people involved in the script. The result is conditions that exist after the events in the script have occurred. *Track* refers to variations that might occur in a particular script. Finally, *scenes* describe the actual sequence of events that occur.

Scripts are a particularly useful form of knowledge representation because there are so many stereotypical situations and events that people use every day. Scripts are used in case-based reasoning (Chapter 13).

LISTS

A **list** is a written series of related items. A list can consist of names of people you know, things to buy at the grocery store, things to do this week, or products in a catalog.

Lists are normally used to represent hierarchical knowledge where objects are grouped, categorized, or graded according to rank or relationship. Another way to look at related lists is as an outline. An outline is nothing more than a hierarchical summary of some subject. The various segments of the outline are lists.

DECISION TABLES

In a **decision table** (or induction table; see Chapter 11), knowledge is organized in a spreadsheet format using columns and rows. The table is divided into two parts. First, a list of attributes is developed, and for each attribute all possible values are listed. Then, a list of conclusions is developed. Finally, the different configurations of attributes are matched against the conclusion.

Knowledge for the table is collected in knowledge acquisition sessions. Once constructed, the knowledge in the table can be used as input to other knowledge representation methods. It is not possible to make inferences with the domain tables by themselves except when rule induction is used. Some ES shells can incorporate an entire decision table into a single rule (such as K-Vision from Ginesys Corporation, www.ginesys.com).

Decision tables are easy to understand and program. For further discussion, see Awad (1996).

DECISION TREES

Decision trees are related to tables and are often used in system analysis [in non-AI systems; see Carrico et al. (1989)]. These trees are similar to the decision trees used in decision theory. They are composed of nodes representing goals and links representing decisions.

The major advantage of decision trees is that they can simplify the knowledge acquisition process. *Knowledge diagramming* is often more natural to experts than formal representation methods (such as rules or frames). For further discussion, see Gruber and Cohen (1987) and Jackson (1999). Decision trees can easily be converted to rules. The conversion can be performed automatically by a computer program. In fact, machine learning methods are capable of extracting decision trees automatically from textual sources and converting the decision trees to rule bases (Chapter 11).

A simple approach in the implementation of decision trees is in the use of HTML Web pages. A good example on the Web is given on the Salford University site (www.surveying.salford.ac.uk/kbe/dtree.htm). In this example, a simple decision tree is designed to help diagnose the reasons behind an automobile not starting (Figure 12.2). A number of HTML Web pages are provided that enable navigation through the tree

FIGURE 12.2 A DECISION TREE FOR A DIAGNOSIS OF CAR MALFUNCTION

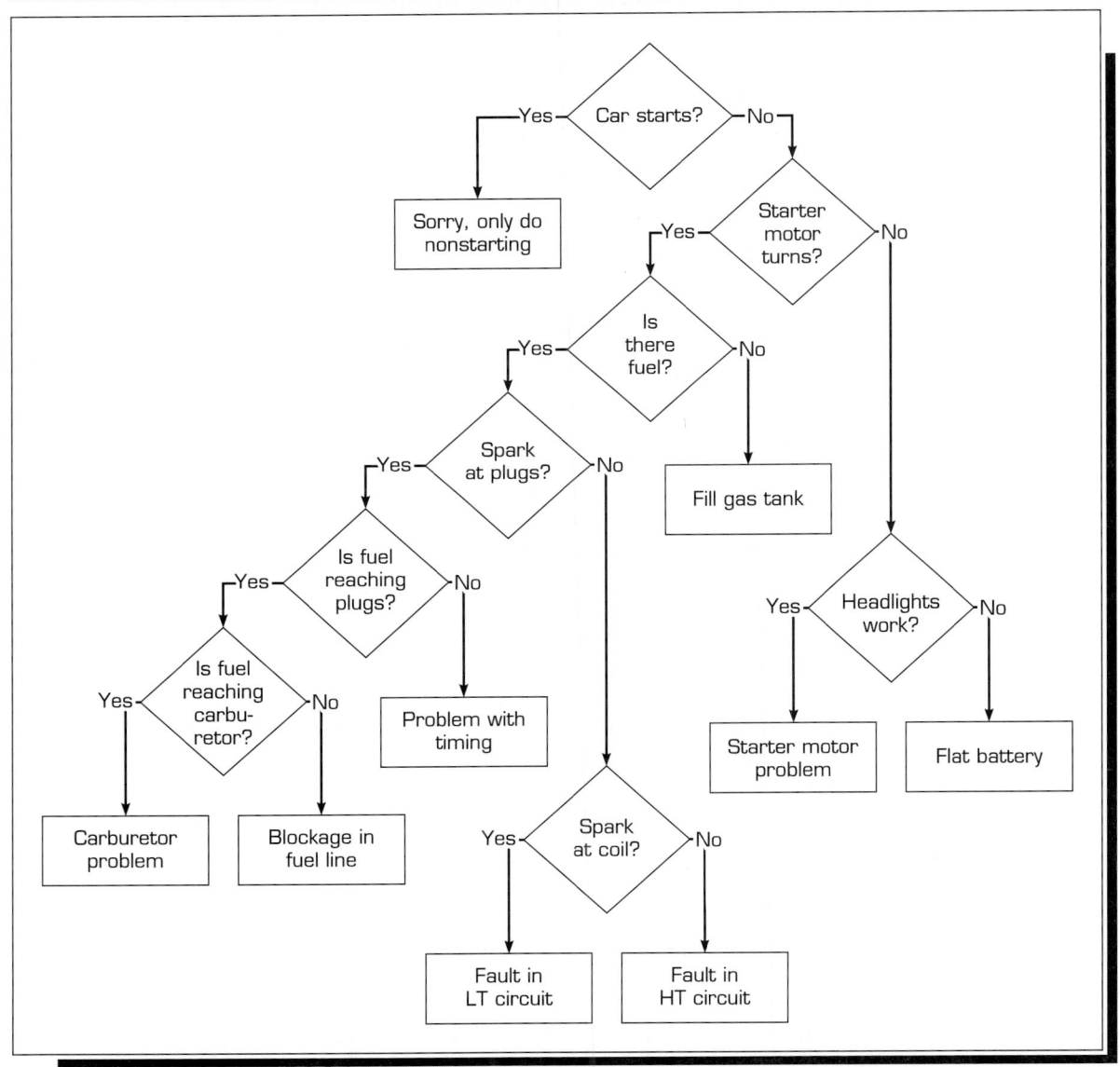

(see www.surveying.salford.ac.uk/kbe/node1.htm). This problem can be described as a number of knowledge rules, for example:

- RULE 1: IF the car does not start
  THEN check that the motor turns
- RULE 2: IF the motor turns
  THEN check if there is fuel in the tank
  ELSE check that the headlights work
- RULE 3: IF headlights do not work
  THEN battery is flat
  ELSE there is a starter motor problem

O-A-V TRIPLET

Another way to represent knowledge is to use objects, attributes, and values—the **O-A-V triplet.** *Objects* can be physical or conceptual. *Attributes* are the characteristics of the objects. *Values* are the specific measures of the attributes in a given situation. Table 12.1 presents several O-A-V triplets. An object can have several attributes, and an attribute itself can be considered a new object with its own attributes. For example, in Table 12.1 a bedroom is an attribute of a house but also an object of O-A-V triplets are used in both frame and semantic network representations.

DEFAULT LOGIC

This is a special form of knowledge representation addressing uncertainties and reasoning based on incomplete information (Reiter, 1980). Recent research has investigated evolving default logic from purely declarative representation formalism into a practical high-level computational environment. This has led to implementation of the default reasoning system (DeRes); see Cholewinski et al. (1999) and the University of Kentucky Web site (www.cs.engr.uky.edu/~mirek/computing-with-dl.html and www.cs.engr.uky.edu/~mirek/computing-with-dl.html).

KNOWLEDGE MAPS

Knowledge maps consist of a visual representation, including circles or images connected by lines, each labeled, giving a hierarchical view of the knowledge and drawing attention to conceptual (as opposed to specific) knowledge. These maps attempt to represent experiences, methods, processes, and judgements used by a person or group regarding a specific intent. A map is constructed using initial thoughts about the problem to be solved; once these have been identified, lower-level thoughts for specific parts of the map and relationships between these parts are investigated and entered onto the map. For further information see Beck et al. (1999), Hall et al. (1999), and the University of Toronto Web site at www.clr.utoronto.ca:1080/papers/kmap.html).

TABLE 12.1   Representative O-A-V Items

Object	Attributes	Values
House	Bedrooms	2, 3, 4, and so on
House	Color	Green, white, brown, and so on
Admission to a university	Grade-point average	3.0, 3.5, 3.7, and so on
Inventory control	Level of inventory	14, 20, 30, so on
Bedroom	Size	9 10, 10 12, so on

12.4 SEMANTIC NETWORKS

Semantic networks are basically graphical depictions of knowledge composed of *nodes* and *links* that show hierarchical relationships between objects; see Sowa (1997) and the Duke University Web site (www.duke.edu/~mccann/mwb/15semnet.htm).

A simple semantic network is shown in Figure 12.3. It is made up of a number of circles or nodes, which represent objects and descriptive information about these objects. Objects can be any physical item such as a book, a car, a desk, or even a person. Nodes can also be concepts, events, or actions. A concept might be the relationship between supply and demand in economics, an event such as a picnic or an election, or an action such as building a house or writing a book. Attributes of an object can also be used as nodes. These might represent size, color, class, age, origin, or other characteristics. In this way, detailed information about objects can be presented.

FIGURE 12.3 REPRESENTATION OF KNOWLEDGE IN A SEMANTIC NETWORK

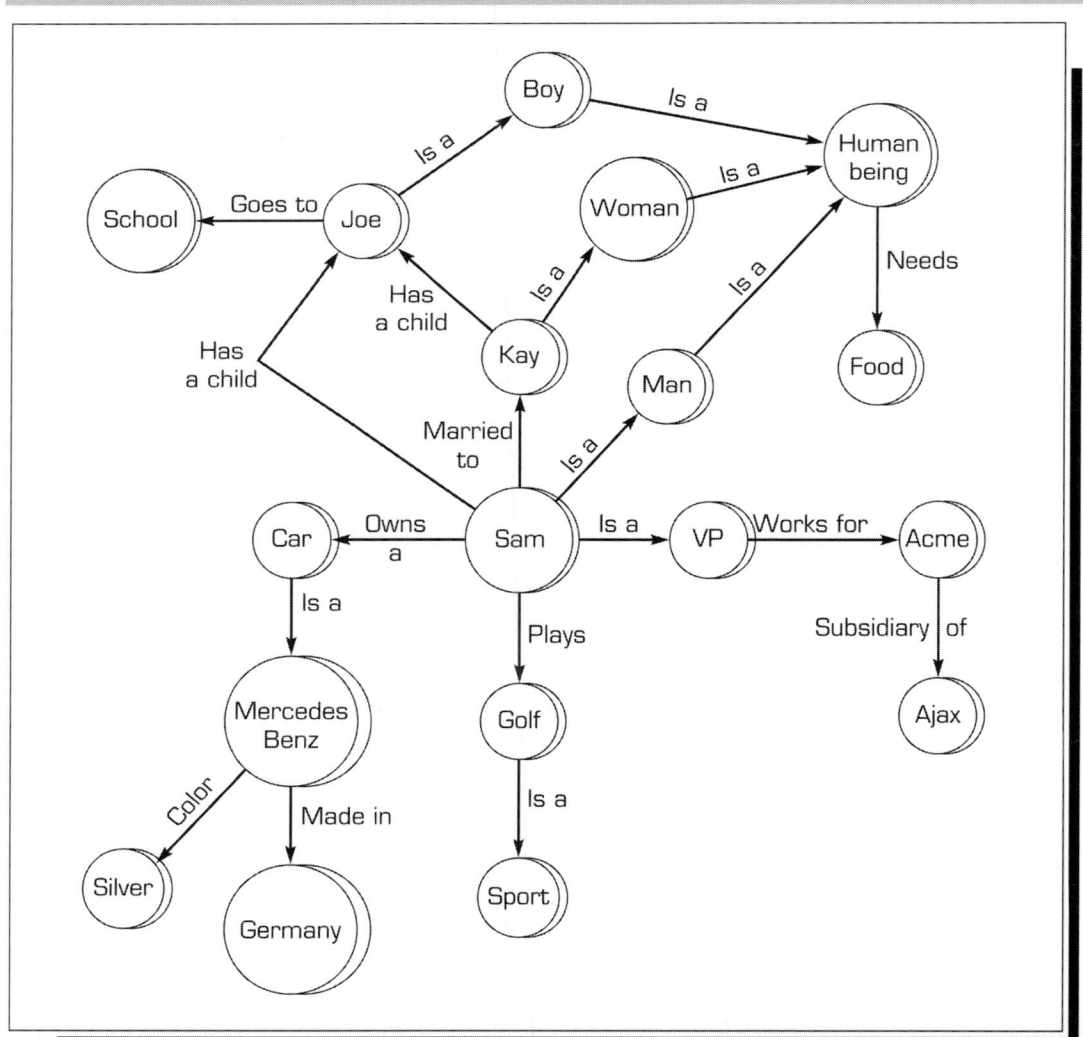

Nodes are interconnected by links or arcs. These arcs show the relationships between the various objects and descriptive factors. Some of the most common arcs are of the *is-a* or *has-a* type. *Is-a* is used to show a class relationship, that is, that an object belongs to a larger class or category of objects. *Has-a* links are used to identify characteristics or attributes of object nodes. Other arcs are used for definitional purposes.

Now refer to the example in Figure 12.3. As you can see, the central figure in the domain of knowledge is a person called Sam. One link shows that Sam is a man and that a man is a human being or is part of a class called humans. Another arc from Sam shows that he is married to Kay. Additional arcs show that Kay is a woman and that a woman is in turn a human being. Other links show that Sam and Kay have a child, Joe, who is a boy and goes to school.

Some nodes and arcs show other characteristics about Sam. For example, he is a vice president for Acme, a company that is a subsidiary of Ajax. We also see that Sam plays golf, which is a sport. Furthermore, Sam owns a Mercedes Benz whose color is silver. We also see that Mercedes Benz is a type of car that is made in Germany.

One of the most interesting and useful facts about a semantic network is that it can show **inheritance.** Because a semantic network is basically a hierarchy, the various characteristics of some nodes actually inherit the characteristics of others. As an example, consider the links showing that Sam is a man and that a man is in turn a human being. Here, Sam inherits all the properties of human being. We can ask the question, Does Sam need food? Because of the inheritance links, we can say that he needs food if human beings need food. See Mili and Pachet (1995) for details on a hierarchical semantic network concept called *regularity* that subsumes inheritance. They present novel ways in which semantic networks can support hypertext functionality with a specific interest in generating argumentative documents (documents that develop a thesis or prove an assertion).

Semantic nets are used basically as a visual representation of relationships and can be combined with other representation methods.

12.5 PRODUCTION RULES

The basic idea of this discussion is that knowledge is presented as **production rules** in the form of condition–action pairs: IF this *condition* (or premise or antecedent) occurs, THEN some action (or result or conclusion or consequence) will (or should) occur. Consider these two examples:

- If the stop light is red AND you have stopped, THEN a right turn is okay.[2]
- If the client uses purchase requisition forms AND the purchase orders are approved and purchasing is separate from receiving AND accounts payable AND inventory records, THEN there is strongly suggestive evidence (90 percent probability) that controls to prevent unauthorized purchases are adequate. (This example from an internal control procedure includes a probability.)

Each production rule in a knowledge base implements an autonomous chunk of expertise that can be developed and modified independently of other rules. When combined and fed to the inference engine, the set of rules behaves synergistically, yielding better results than the sum of the results of the individual rules. In reality, knowledge-based rules are not independent. They quickly become highly interdependent. For example, adding a new rule may conflict with an existing rule, or it may require a revision of attributes or rules.

[2]But don't turn left from a one-way street onto another one-way street in North Carolina.

Rules can be viewed, in some sense, as a simulation of the cognitive behavior of human experts. According to this view, rules are not just a neat formalism to represent knowledge in a computer, rather, they represent a model of actual human behavior.

Rules can appear in different forms. Some examples follow:

- *IF premise, THEN conclusion.* If your income is high, THEN your chance of being audited by the IRS is high.
- *Conclusion, IF premise.* Your chance of being audited is high, IF your income is high.
- *Inclusion of ELSE.* If your income is high OR your deductions are unusual, THEN your chance of being audited by the IRS is high, OR ELSE your chance of being audited is low.
- *More complex rules.* IF the credit rating is high AND the salary is more than $30,000 OR assets are more than $75,000 AND pay history is not "poor," THEN approve a loan up to $10,000 and list the loan in category B. The action part may include additional information: THEN approve the loan and refer the applicant to an agent.

The IF side of a rule can include dozens of IFs. The THEN side can include several parts as well.

For further discussions about the use of production rules within active and deductive databases, see Palopoli and Torlone (1997). For an example of the use of production rules in an expert system used in production environments, see Stack (1997) and Guth (1999).

KNOWLEDGE AND INFERENCE RULES

Two types of rules are common in AI: knowledge and inference. Knowledge rules, or **declarative rules,** state all the facts and relationships about a problem. Inference rules, or **procedural rules,** on the other hand, advise on how to solve a problem given that certain facts are known.

For example, assume you are in the business of buying and selling gold. Knowledge rules may look like the following:

- RULE 1: IF an international conflict begins
  THEN the price of gold goes up.
- RULE 2: IF the inflation rate declines
  THEN the price of gold goes down.
- RULE 3: IF the international conflict lasts more than 7 days and IF it is in the Middle East
  THEN buy gold.

Inference (procedural) rules may look like the following:

- RULE 1: IF the data needed are not in the system
  THEN request them from the user.
- RULE 2: IF more than one rule applies
  THEN deactivate any rules that add no new data.

Inference rules contain rules about rules. These types of rules are also called **metarules.** They pertain to other rules (or even to themselves).

The knowledge engineer separates the two types of rules: Knowledge rules go to the knowledge base, whereas inference rules become part of the inference engine.

ADVANTAGES AND LIMITATIONS OF RULES

Rule representation is especially applicable when there is a need to recommend a course of action based on observable events (see AIS in Action 12.1). It has several major advantages:

- Rules are easy to understand. They are communicable because they are a natural form of knowledge.
- Inference and explanations are easily derived.
- Modifications and maintenance are relatively easy.
- Uncertainty is easily combined with rules.
- Each rule is often independent of all others.

The major limitations of rule representation are as follows:

- Complex knowledge requires thousands of rules, which may create difficulties in both using the system and in maintaining it.
- Builders like rules; therefore, they try to force all knowledge into rules rather than looking for more appropriate representations.
- Systems with many rules may have a search limitation in the control program. Some programs have difficulty in evaluating rule-based systems and making inferences.

The major characteristics of rules are summarized in Table 12.2.

AIS IN ACTION 12.1

RULE-BASED SYSTEM TACKLES EMPLOYEE SHRINK

Innovative computer-based technologies are taking the battle against employee-related shrink (theft) to a higher level. Several new applications are aimed at identifying dishonest personnel, who account for an estimated 38 percent of retail shrink, as well as those who may simply be making errors at the point of sale.

PLATINUM Solutions offers a rule-based system that targets employee theft at the retailer's point of sale. "The rules are interrelated statements or business policies governing what is allowed and what is not allowed," explains Carl Fijat, a management consultant with PLATINUM Solutions.

Rule-based software can help retailers find fraud patterns by collecting and storing information about incidents occurring at the point of sale and classifying them according to the policies expressed as knowledge in the program. For example, it can be programmed to post "self-ringing employee" alerts when employees ring up returns for themselves. "Excessive credit to purchases" is posted when a staff member processes purchases whose value exceeds a certain limit and the account being credited is labeled "in-house."

One of the products of PLATINUM Technologies (the parent company) is AionDS, which models and encapsulates retailers' business policy logic into rules, Fijat explains. Each rule defines a premise and one or more resulting actions. Rules can be expressed in an easy-to-understand, English-like language; this makes it easier for loss prevention executives to communicate system requirements to those developing rule-based software, thus leading to more effective knowledge representation and acquisition.

AionDS, and rule-based software in general, is particularly valuable in isolating patterns not discernible from reading exception reports. For example, if an employee authorizes a legitimate cash sale, signs off, then signs on under someone else's identification number to refund the immediate sale, and then signs back on again as himself or herself, the system can use a rule to track such fraudulent activity.

Source: Modified and condensed from J. R. Ross, "New Rule-based Systems Tackle Employee Shrink," *Stores,* Vol. 78, No. 8, Aug. 1996, pp. 71–72.

TABLE 12.2   Characteristics of Rule Representation

	First Part	*Second Part*
Names	Premise Antecedent Situation IF	Conclusion Consequence Action THEN
Nature	Conditions, similar to declarative knowledge.	Resolutions, similar to procedural knowledge.
Size	Can have many IFs.	Usually has one conclusion.
Statements	AND statements	All conditions must be true for a conclusion to be true.
	OR statements	If any of the OR statement conditions are true, the conclusion is true.

12.6 FRAMES

DEFINITIONS AND OVERVIEW

A **frame** is a data structure that includes all the knowledge about a particular object. This knowledge is organized in a special hierarchical structure that permits a diagnosis of knowledge independence. Frames are basically an application of **object-oriented programming** for AI and ES. They are used extensively in ES (see AIS in Action 12.2). See Fensel et al. (1998) for a discussion of the frame-based Knowledge Acquisition and Representation Language (KARL), Jackson (1999) for a more detailed description of frames and their uses, and Chaudhri and Lowrance (1998) for details of the frame representation system and the graphical browsing tool GKB-Editor.

Each frame describes one *object*. To describe what frames are and how the knowledge is organized in a frame we need to use special terminology, which is presented in Table 12.3. These terms will be defined as we encounter them.

Frames, as in *frames of reference,* provide a concise structural representation of knowledge in a natural manner. In contrast to other representation methods, the values that describe one object are grouped together into a single unit called a *frame.* Thus, a frame encompasses complex objects, entire situations, or a management problem as a single entity. The knowledge in a frame is partitioned into slots. A **slot** can describe declarative knowledge (such as the color of a car) or procedural knowledge (such as "activate a certain rule if a value exceeds a given level"). The major capabilities of frames are summarized in Table 12.4.

A frame provides a means of organizing knowledge in slots that contain characteristics and attributes. In physical form, a frame is somewhat like an outline with categories and subcategories. A typical frame describing an automobile is shown in Figure 12.4. Note that the slots describe attributes such as name of manufacturer, model, origin of manufacturer, type of car, number of doors, engine, and other characteristics.

CONTENT OF A FRAME

A frame includes two basic elements: slots and facets. A slot is a set of attributes that describe the object represented by the frame. For example, in the automobile frame, there are weight and engine slots. Each slot contains one or more **facets.** The facets

AIS IN ACTION 12.2

PACE: AN ES PLANNING ADVISOR ON CURRICULUM AND ENROLLMENT

The National University of Singapore is developing an advising system for students studying for the BBA degree. The system uses a combination object-oriented knowledge-based paradigm, which provides efficient and flexible knowledge representation, improved performance, and ease of software development and maintenance. The idea of the ES is not to provide wise and sympathetic counsel but to focus students more clearly on issues to consider and let them simulate different scenarios before seeking advice, cutting down the effort required from the advising staff. The planning advisor on curriculum and enrollment (PACE) simplifies the process of ensuring consistency and schedulability by combining object-oriented and knowledge-based system methodologies. Object hierarchies (trees) represent data and knowledge structures (such as courses and curriculum requirements). Localized knowledge is embedded as methods within objects, and global knowledge is stored in a rule base.

The inference engine uses both forward and backward chaining on global and relevant local rules to generate advice and guide students in course selection and scheduling.

Production rules are stored as methods within objects. Separate concepts are stored as separate objects and linked dynamically (such as relationships among curriculum, courses, and staff). By embedding the rules within objects, performance improves because the search time is less. Curriculum objects have properties (much like a frame) and are structured in a curriculum tree. A student chooses courses from the course tree. Then a long-term schedule is generated. There are also links to the university's databases.

Source: Adapted from H. Gunadhi, K. -H. Lim, and W. -Y. Yeong, "PACE: A Planning Advisor on Curriculum and Enrollment," *Proceedings of the 28th Annual Hawaii International Conference on Systems Sciences,* Hawaii, 1995.

TABLE 12.3   Terminology for Frames

Default	Instantiation
Demon	Master frame
Facet	Object
Hierarchy of frames	Range
If added	Slot
If needed	Value (entry)
Instance of	

TABLE 12.4   Capabilities of Frames

- Ability to clearly document information about a domain model (e.g., a plant's machines and their associated attributes)
- Related ability to constrain the allowable values that an attribute can take on
- Modularity of information, permitting ease of system expansion and maintenance
- More readable and consistent
- Syntax for referencing domain objects in the rules
- Platform for building a graphic interface with object graphics
- Mechanism that allows the scope of facts considered during forward or backward chaining to be restricted
- Access to a mechanism that supports the inheritance of information down a class hierarchy

Automobile Frame

Class of: Transportation
Name of manufacturer: Audi
Origin of manufacturer: Germany
Model: 5000 Turbo
Type of car: Sedan
Weight: 3300 lb.
Wheelbase: 105.8 inches
Number of doors: 4 (default)
Transmission: 3-speed automatic
Number of wheels: 4 (default)
Engine: (Reference Engine Frame)
  • Type: In-line, overhead cam
  • Number of cylinders: 5
Acceleration (procedural attachment)
  • 0–60: 10.4 seconds
  • Quarter mile: 17.1 seconds, 85 mph
Gas mileage: 22 mpg average (procedural attachment)

Engine Frame

Cylinder bore: 3.19 inches
Cylinder stroke: 3.4 inches
Compression ratio: 7.8 to 1
Fuel system: Injection with turbocharger
Horsepower: 140 hp
Torque: 160 ft/LB

FIGURE 12.4 FRAME DESCRIBING AN AUTOMOBILE

(sometimes called *subslots*) describe some knowledge or procedural information about the attribute in the slot. Facets can take many forms:

- *Values.* These describe attributes such as blue, red, and yellow for a color slot.
- *Default.* This facet is used if the slot is empty, that is, without any description. For example, in the care frame one default value is that the number of wheels on the car is 4. It means that we can assume the car has four wheels unless otherwise indicated.
- *Range.* Range indicates what kind of information can appear in a slot (such as integer numbers only, two decimal points, 0 to 100).
- *If added.* This facet contains procedural information or attachments. It specifies an action to be taken when a value in the slot is *added* (or modified). Such procedural attachments are called **demons.**
- *If needed.* This facet is used in a case when no slot value is given. Much like the if-added situation, it triggers a procedure that goes out and gets or computes a value.
- *Other.* Slots can contain frames, rules, semantic networks, or any type of information.

Certain procedures can be attached to slots and used to derive slot values. For example, slot-specific heuristics are procedures for deriving slot values in a particular context. An important aspect of such procedures is that they can be used to direct the reasoning process. In addition to filling slots, they can be triggered when a slot is filled.

In Figure 12.4, both acceleration and gas mileage are procedural attachments. They refer to a step-by-step procedure that defines how to acquire this information. For example, to determine acceleration, time needed to go from 0 to 60 mph and quarter-mile elapsed time would be described. A procedural attachment to determine gas mileage would state a procedure for filling the gas tank, driving a certain number of miles, determining the amount of gasoline used, and computing the gas mileage in terms of miles per gallon.

HIERARCHY OF FRAMES

Most AI systems use a collection of frames linked together in a certain manner. For example, Figure 12.5 illustrates five frames. Frame A is connected to frame B in a slot named *is-a*. The same frame also has a capacity slot that refers to a mixer (frame E) and

FIGURE 12.5 HIERARCHY OF FRAMES

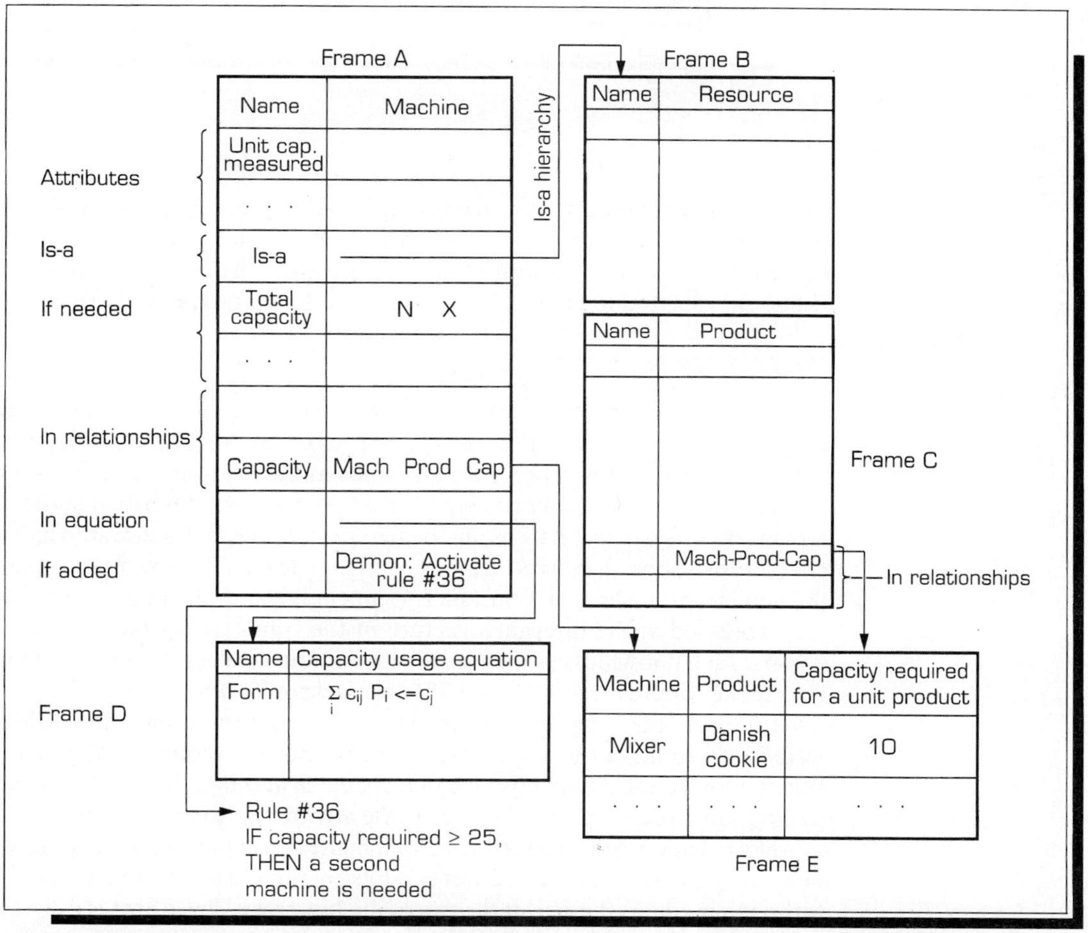

Source: R. W. Blanning, "The Application of AI to Model Management," Working Paper, Owen Graduate School of Management, Vanderbilt University, 1988.

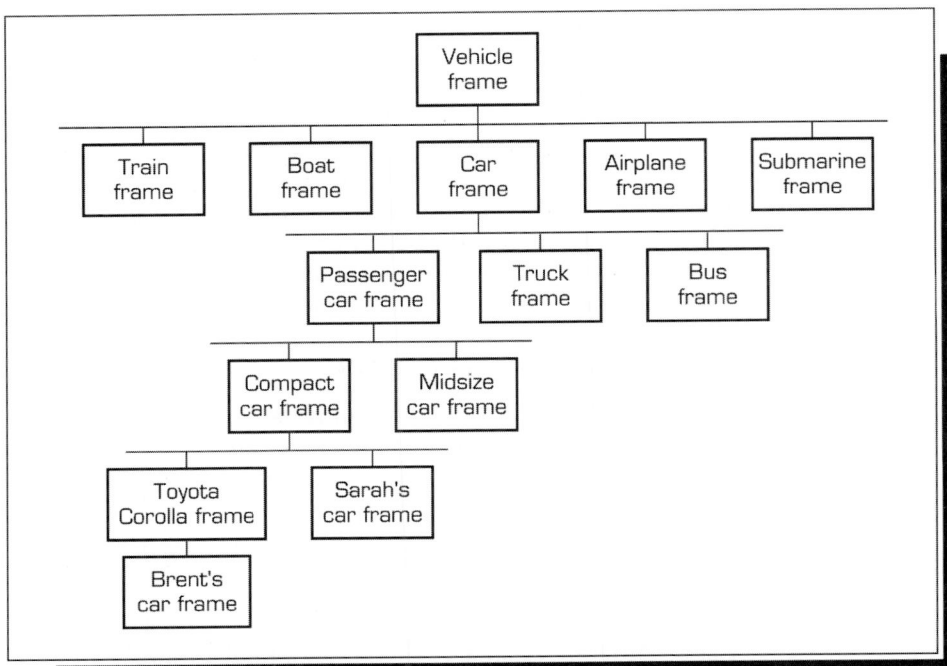

FIGURE 12.6 HIERARCHY OF FRAMES DESCRIBING VEHICLES

a procedure (demon) that activates rule 36 when a second machine is added. Notice that these relationships create a hierarchy of frames. This hierarchy is not necessarily on a one-to-one basis. For example, frame A is formed from slots in frames A and C. Also, frame A is related to frames B, D, and E and to an independent rule.

INHERITANCE

The hierarchical arrangement of frames permits inheritance frames. Figure 12.6 shows a set of vehicles organized in a tree. The root of the tree is at the top, where the highest level of abstraction is represented. Frames at the bottom are called leaves of the tree. The hierarchy permits inheritance of characteristics (as described in the object-oriented approach for systems analysis and design in Chapter 4). Each frame usually inherits the characteristics of all related frames of higher levels. For example, a passenger car has the general properties of a car (such as an engine and carburetor). These characteristics are expressed in the internal structure of the frame. **Inheritance** is the mechanism for passing such knowledge, which is provided in the value of the slots, from frame to frame. For further details see Tanier (1997) and Jackson (1998).

Parent frames provide a more general description of the entities. More general descriptions are higher in the hierarchy. Parent frames contain the attribute definitions. When we describe actual physical objects, we **instantiate** the child's frame. The instances (child frames) contain actual values of the attributes. An example is shown in Figure 12.7.

Note that every parent is a child of a higher-level parent. In building a frame it is possible to have a frame in which different slots are related to different parents. The only frame without a parent is the one at the top of the hierarchy. This frame is called a master frame. It is the *root frame,* and it has the most general characteristics. The use of frame-based tools to build expert systems is demonstrated in tools such as Exsys, Level5 Object (Chapter 14).

```
┌─────────────────────────────────────────┬─────────────────────────────────────────┐
│ Name: Toyota Corolla                      │ Name: Brent's car                         │
│                                           │        Instance of: Toyota Corolla frame  │
│                                           │                                           │
│ Slots          Facets                     │ Slots          Facets                     │
│                                           │                                           │
│ Owner          Check registration list    │ Owner          Brent                      │
│ Color          List, per manufacturer     │                                           │
│ No. of cylinders                          │ Color          Blue                       │
│    Range       4 or 6                      │                                           │
│    If needed   Ask owner                  │ No. of cylinders  6                        │
│                                           │                                           │
│                                           │                                           │
│ Model          Sedan sport                │ Model          4D sedan                   │
│    Range       2–4 doors                   │                                           │
│    If needed   Ask owner                  │                                           │
│ Vintage (year)                            │ Vintage (year)  1994                      │
│    Range       1970–1995                   │                                           │
│    If needed   Ask owner                  │                                           │
│                                           │                                           │
│ (a) Parent frame                          │ (b) Child frame                           │
└─────────────────────────────────────────┴─────────────────────────────────────────┘
```

FIGURE 12.7 PARENT AND CHILD FRAMES

12.7 MULTIPLE KNOWLEDGE REPRESENTATION

Knowledge representation should support the tasks of acquiring and retrieving knowledge as well as subsequent reasoning. Several factors must be taken into account in evaluating knowledge representation for the above three tasks:

- Naturalness, uniformity, and understandability of the representation
- Degree to which knowledge is explicit (declarative) or embedded in procedural code [for further information on implicit/explicit knowledge, see Dienes and Perner (1999) and O'Brien and Opie (1999)].
- Modularity and flexibility of the knowledge base
- Efficiency of knowledge retrieval and the heuristic power of the inference procedure. (*Heuristic power* is the reduction of the search space achieved by a heuristic mechanism.)

No single knowledge representation method is by itself ideally suited for all tasks (Table 12.5). When several sources of knowledge are used simultaneously, the goal of uniformity may have to be sacrificed in favor of exploiting the benefits of **multiple knowledge representations,** each tailored to a different subtask. The necessity of translating among knowledge representations becomes a problem in these cases. Nevertheless, some recent ES shells use two or more knowledge representation schemes (e.g., Exsys).

OBJECT-ORIENTED KNOWLEDGE REPRESENTATIONS

The object-oriented approach to systems analysis, design, and programming is directly affecting hybrid approaches to knowledge representation. Clearly, hypermedia, especially over the Web, can exploit the object-oriented approach. In this approach,

TABLE 12.5   Advantages and Disadvantages of Different Knowledge Representations

Scheme	Advantages	Disadvantages
Production rules	Simple syntax, easy to understand, simple interpreter, highly modular, flexible (easy to add to or modify).	Hard to follow hierarchies, inefficient for large systems, not all knowledge can be expressed as rules, poor at representing structured descriptive knowledge.
Semantic networks	Easy to follow hierarchy, easy to trace associations, flexible.	Meaning attached to nodes might be ambiguous, exception handling is difficult, difficult to program.
Frames	Expressive power, easy to set up slots for new properties and relations, easy to create specialized procedures, easy to include default information and detect missing values.	Difficult to program, difficult for inference, lack of inexpensive software.
Formal logic	Facts asserted independently of use, assurance that only valid consequences are asserted (precision), completeness.	Separation of representation and processing, inefficient with large data sets, very slow with large knowledge bases.

different kinds of knowledge can be encapsulated in objects, and these objects can communicate actions directly. Devedzic et al. (1996) describe how knowledge can be represented as objects in ES, along with the reasoning process. Their model, Reasoning Objects for Building Inference Engines (ROBBIE), is based on a hierarchy in which each level is more detailed. At the highest level is a blackboard and agents for interaction (Chapter 17). As we move down the hierarchy, first the system is defined, then its blocks, then its components, and finally the primitives that form the pattern matching, conflict resolution, and so on. Also see Kuechler et al. (1995) for an example that uses a variety of knowledge representations and reasoning strategies in one object-oriented system.

A rather successful combination of knowledge representation methods is that of production rules and frames. By themselves, production rules do not provide a totally effective representation facility for many ES applications. In particular, their expressive power is inadequate for defining terms and for describing domain objects and static relationships among objects. In essence, frames are objects and fit the paradigm of an object-oriented approach to ES development rather well. Objects encapsulate properties and actions, just as frames store knowledge. Furthermore, frames are organized into classes, which are organized into hierarchies. Each frame inherits its properties from its parent frame, just as an object inherits properties. Rules can either guide the frames' behaviors or be embedded in the frame (some accounting applications using frames and rules adopt the latter approach). The object-oriented paradigm fits the hybrid ES structure well in working with frames and rules. Bogarin and Ebecken (1996) describe an object-oriented approach of combining objects and rules for flexible pipe evaluation and design in the petroleum industry. The objects select which sets of rules to apply to a given situation. The ES runs numerical heuristics as well. For a detailed overview of frames and rule integration, see Thuraisingham (1989). For a related application, see AIS in Action 12.2. Also check out the Object Data Management Group Web site (www.odmg.org) for the latest information on object-relational mapping products and object database management systems.

12.8 EXPERIMENTAL KNOWLEDGE REPRESENTATIONS

A number of experimental knowledge representations are just starting to be commercialized. Usually they are developed by university AI faculty members, sometimes as parts of large-scale, government-sponsored programs. Three such experimental knowledge representations are Cyc, NKRL, and the Spec-Charts Language, described next. Another knowledge management system, based on scalable ontology, is Parka-DB (Hendler and Stoffel, 1999) which builds on experience gained from systems such as Cyc when dealing with large relational database techniques in the management of large medical data systems.

Other knowledge representation research involves the Internet and fuzzy logic (Chapter 16) (see Carnegie Mellon University School of Computer Science, www.cs.cmu.edu, and check the fuzzy logic development tool TILShell3 produced by Ortech Engineering Inc., along with a good repository of useful fuzzy logic information at www.ortech-engr.com).

Fuzzy logic can be seen as an approach for managing uncertainty (Section 12.9); recent research has also involved approximating functional mappings (Yen, 1999; Jackson 1999).

CYC

The Cyc system (Lenat and Guha, 1990; Mili and Pachet, 1996) (see Cycorp, www.cyc.com) is an ambitious attempt to represent a substantial amount of common-sense knowledge. Some bold assumptions are made on the nature of intelligence, the main one being that intelligence needs a large amount of knowledge. Thus, the only way to exhibit artificial intelligence is to build a large support base for the intelligence. Over time Cyc is developing as a repository of a consensus reality (the background knowledge possessed by a typical U.S. resident). Initially Cyc was based on a frame-oriented view of knowledge representation. Since then it has evolved and now comprises a multicontextual knowledge base, a set of interface tools, and a number of special-purpose application modules running on UNIX, Windows NT, and other platforms. The user interface operates primarily with logical expressions in a reified first-order logic (a form of predicate calculus). Assertions on a frame appear as predicates. In 2000 Cyc was estimated to contain more than 1 million hand-entered assertions (or rules) (such as "when someone owns something, he or she also owns all the parts of the owned object"), along with thousands of constants (such as *JamesJoyce, France,* and *WorldWarII*), collections (such as car lists), and predicates (such as *isa* and *partOf* relationships (Mili and Pachet, 1995). As Cyc further evolves, it is believed that it will be able to provide more general advice and be a good base for the development of other knowledge-based systems. For more details, see Lenat and Guha (1990), Mili and Pachet (1995), Pinto et al. (1995), and the Cycorp Web site (www.cyc.com). Current applications of this tool set have been regarding WWW information retrieval, distributed AI, integration of heterogeneous databases, and online brokering services.

NARRATIVE KNOWLEDGE REPRESENTATIONAL LANGUAGE

Narrative Knowledge Representational Language (NKRL) is similar to the hybrid, canonical hybrid, and terminological languages KL-ONE (see the Opening Vignette) and CLASSIC (Brachman et al., 1999). NKRL was designed to be a standard, language-independent

AIS IN ACTION 12.3

E-CYC: BRINGING CYC TO THE WEB

e-Cyc (a division of Cycorp) is now offering the Cyc knowledge base to the Internet and to corporate intranets. The e-Cyc portal toolkit delivers much more than "knowledge management" as it is built atop the world's largest general-purpose knowledge base containing more than 1 million facts and rules about the world.

Typing a word with multiple meanings (such as Java, chips, china, and so on), results in e-Cyc separating out the different meanings: computer chips, french fries, potato chips, and so on. Clicking on one will result in related follow-up links or topics being displayed. E-Cyc has common sense and therefore knows how to classify related information based on your query. The knowledge in the Cyc knowledge base consists of things we all know already; what is new is that now your computer can know these things as well. Therefore, when "china" is entered in an e-Cyc based search engine for "your wedding", it will not return results for "Chairman Mao". This built-in common sense saves time when looking for information via the Web.

A demo of the beta version of this search engine is available at the HotBot site (beta.hotbot.com). Also available is the e-Cyc Portal Toolkit, which allows Internet and intranet Web sites to add common-sense intelligence to their environments.

Source: Cycorp Inc. Web site, www.e-cyc.com.

description of the content of narrative textual documents. It is one of several official knowledge representation tools of the EuroKnowledge consortium. In a nutshell, NKRL can translate natural language expressions directly into a meaningful set of templates that represent the knowledge. See Zarri (1995) for details. Also see Zarri and Jacqmin (1999) for research on CONCERTO, which incorporates a Resource Description Format eXtensible Markup Language (RDF/XML)-compliant version of NKRL to address processing of World Wide Web metadata.

A special knowledge interchange format (KIF) has been developed to allow knowledge-based systems to share knowledge and interact. This KIF has proven helpful not only with ES but also with intelligent agents (Chapter 19). For more information about KIF, see Genesereth and Fikes (1992) and the Stanford University Web site metastanford.edu/kif/kif.html.

SPEC-CHARTS LANGUAGE

Spec-Charts Language (Vahid et al., 1991; Cyre, 1997) is based on conceptual graphs, which are used to define objects and relationships. **Conceptual graphs** are a restricted form of semantic networks, described earlier. Spec-Charts Language has evolved into a commercial product called STATEMATE, which uses three embedded languages—State-Charts, Module-Charts, and Activity-Charts—to represent the control, structural, and functional aspects of a system. See Cyre (1997) and Harel and Politi (1998) for details. Another knowledge modeling language, based on conceptual graphs, is described by Lukose (1996). Also check out the Conceptual Graph Knowledge Acquisition Tool available from the ACACIA Web site (www-sop.inria.fr/acacia/).

Current research is identifying the advantages of adopting conceptual graph techniques for indexing Web documents (Martin and Eklund, 1999). The retrieval of precise information is better supported by languages designed to represent semantic content and logical inference than by metadata languages based on Extensible Mark-up Language.

KNOWLEDGE REPRESENTATION AND THE INTERNET

With the rapid growth of the Internet, a number of AI researchers have been experimenting with ways of creating hypermedia documents that encode knowledge directly, in which relationships among hypermedia express relationships. Model-based and Incremental Knowledge Engineering (MIKE) (Tochtermann and Zink, 1995) represents expertise as a set of typed nodes and typed links and is easily structured to run on the Web. The formal model of expertise is described in the specification language KARL (Angele et al., 1993; Fensel et al., 1998) (see "Modeling Problem-Solving Methods in New KARL" on the University of Calgary Knowledge Science Institute Internet site, ksi.cpsc.ucalgary.ca/kawkaw96/angele/angele.html). Semantic networks are also ideally suited for hypermedia representation.

Essentially, Web-based documents are ideally suited for knowledge representation. Another aspect of using the Web is how to present knowledge in a meaningful way with an appropriate level of multimedia presentation. Ralha (1996) deals with the problem of automatically structuring informal knowledge available on the Internet through a distributed hypermedia system such as the Web. This is a new approach to the integration of hypertext and hypermedia technology with knowledge acquisition, which deals with knowledge before the process of formalization; also see Edman and Hamfelt (1999), for a further analysis of merged intelligent hypermedia and knowledge systems. Lechner et al. (1998) adopts an encyclopedic approach to organizing and structuring Internet-based scientific information.

Finally, Far and Koono (1996) describe a Web-based distributed expert system (Ex-W-Pert System) for sharing knowledge-based systems and groupware development activities. This novel form of groupware illustrates the ability of AI methods to capitalize on the potential process and task gains that occur in electronic meetings (Chapter 8). A number of expert systems use hypermedia (such as Exsys WREN from Exsys Corporation) over the Web.

12.9 REPRESENTING UNCERTAINTY: AN OVERVIEW

One of the basic assumptions previously made was that any rule must have only one of two truth values (i.e., it is either true or false). In this sense, our previous discussion forced us to be exact about the truth of statements.

However, human knowledge is often inexact. Sometimes we are only partly sure about the truth of a statement and still have to make educated guesses to solve problems. Some concepts or words are inherently inexact. For instance, how can we determine exactly whether someone is tall? The concept *tall* has a built-in form of inexactness. Moreover, we sometimes have to make decisions based on partial or incomplete data.

The term *uncertainty* has several meanings. According to *Webster's New World Dictionary of the American Language,* it can mean doubtful, dubious, questionable, not sure, or problematical. Uncertainty can imply anything from a mere lack of absolute sureness to such vagueness as to preclude anything more than guesswork.

One source of uncertainty occurs when a user cannot provide a definite answer when prompted for a response. For example, when asked to make a choice between responses B and C, the user may respond that he or she is 30 percent sure of B and 70 percent sure of C.

Another source of uncertainty stems from imprecise knowledge. In many situations, a set of symptoms can help indicate a particular diagnosis without being conclusive.

Yet another source of uncertainty is incomplete information. The information (or some parts of it) is simply not available or is too expensive or time-consuming to obtain.

In dealing with inexact knowledge in knowledge-based systems, it is necessary to understand how people process uncertain knowledge. In addition, in AI there is a need for inexact inference methods because we often have many inexact pieces of data and knowledge that must be combined. [See Day and Sarkar (2000).]

Most ES (and also DSS) applications are poorly equipped to deal with uncertainty. There are several approaches that deal with uncertainty; none is clearly superior to all others in all cases. Most of the approaches are related to mathematical and statistical theories such as Bayesian statistics, Dempster and Shafer's belief functions (Chapter 13), and fuzzy sets (Chapter 16). A framework for dealing with uncertainty in decision support is proposed by Ribeiro et al. (1995). The proposed framework includes a user-friendly dialog case base, a knowledge base, approximate reasoning, and a fuzzy logic component. For further details on fuzzy logic, see Yen (1999) and Jackson (1999) and www.aaai.org/Resources/Eductiona/Repository-Mirror/fuzzy-resources.html.

UNCERTAINTY IN AI

In AI, the term **uncertainty** (also called *approximate reasoning* or *inexact reasoning*) refers to a wide range of situations in which the relevant information is deficient in one or more of the following ways:

- Information is partial.
- Information is not fully reliable (e.g., observation of evidence is unreliable).
- Representation language is inherently imprecise.
- Information comes from multiple sources, and it is conflicting.
- Information is approximate.
- Nonabsolute cause–effect relationships exist.

In representing knowledge, it is often necessary to address uncertainty. One can include probability in the rules. For example, "IF the interest rate is increasing, THEN the price of stocks will decline (80 percent probability)."

In a numeric context, uncertainty can be viewed as a value with a known error margin. When the possible range of values for a variable is *symbolic* rather than *numeric*, uncertainty can be represented in terms of qualitative expressions or by using fuzzy sets with a corresponding membership function. For further discussion see Chapters 13 and 16 and *International Journal of Uncertainty, Fuzziness and Knowledge-Based Systems* (www.wspc.com.sg/journals/ijufks/ijufks.html).

❖ CHAPTER HIGHLIGHTS

- To build a knowledge base, a variety of knowledge representation schemes are used including logic, lists, semantic networks, frames, scripts, and production rules.
- Propositional logic is a system of using symbols to represent and manipulate premises, prove or disprove propositions, and draw conclusions.
- Predicate calculus is a type of logic used to represent knowledge in the form of statements that assert information about objects or events and apply them in reasoning.
- Semantic networks are graphical depictions of knowledge that show relationships (arcs) between objects (nodes); common relationships are *is-a, has-a, owns,* and *made from.*

- A major property of networks is the inheritance of properties through the hierarchy.
- Scripts describe an anticipated sequence of events (like a story); they indicate the participants, actions, and setting.
- Decision trees and tables are often used in conjunction with other representation methods. They help organize the knowledge acquired before it is coded.
- Production rules take the form of an IF-THEN statement such as, "IF you drink too much, THEN you should not drive."
- There are two types of rules: declarative (describing facts) and procedural (inference).
- Rules are easy to understand, and inferences can be easily derived from them.
- Complex knowledge may require thousands of rules, which may create problems in both search and maintenance. Also, some knowledge cannot be represented by rules.
- A frame is a holistic data structure based on object-oriented programming technology.
- Frames are composed of slots that may contain different types of knowledge representation (such as rules, scripts, and formulas).
- Frames can show complex relationships, graphical information, and inheritance in a concise manner. Their modular structure helps in inference and maintenance.
- Integrating several knowledge representation methods is gaining popularity because of decreasing software costs and increasing capabilities.
- Experimental knowledge representations focus on expressing general knowledge about the world and specialized languages that incorporate graphs and logic.
- Knowledge may be inexact, and experts may be uncertain at a given time.
- Uncertainty can be caused by several factors ranging from incomplete to unreliable information.

❖ KEY WORDS

- conceptual graph (CG)
- decision table
- decision tree
- declarative rules
- demon
- facet
- frame
- inheritance

- instantiation
- knowledge representation
- list
- metarules
- multiple knowledge representation
- O-A-V triplet
- object-oriented programming
- predicate logic (calculus)

- procedural rules
- production rules
- propositional logic
- script
- semantic network
- slot
- uncertainty

❖ QUESTIONS FOR REVIEW

1. What is knowledge representation?
2. What are some benefits of diagramming knowledge?
3. List the major knowledge representation methods.
4. What is propositional logic? Give an example.
5. Describe the sources of uncertainty and provide examples.
6. Define a semantic network.

7. List two advantages and two limitations of semantic networks.
8. Define O-A-V.
9. What is a list? Give an example.
10. What is a production rule? Give an example.
11. What are the basic parts of a production rule? List several names for each part.
12. Define and contrast declarative and procedural knowledge.
13. What is an inference rule?
14. List two advantages and two disadvantages of rule representation.
15. Describe a frame. Give an example of a frame for *sailboat* or *kitchen*.
16. What is an instantiation of a frame?
17. List three types of facets of a frame and explain their meaning.
18. What is a demon and what is its role in frames?
19. What is a slot in a frame?
20. Describe inheritance by using an example.
21. What is unique about Cyc versus other knowledge representations?

❖ QUESTIONS FOR DISCUSSION

1. Give an example that illustrates the difference between propositional logic and predicate calculus.
2. Give examples of production rules in three different functional areas (such as marketing and accounting).
3. Why is the frame representation considered more complex than the production rule representation? What are the advantages of the former over the latter?
4. It is said that multiple knowledge representation can be very advantageous. Why?
5. Compare knowledge representation to data representation in a database.
6. Provide an example that shows how a semantic network can depict inheritance.
7. Give an example that shows inheritance in a banking system or hospital.
8. Compare a knowledge rule with a procedural rule.
9. Review the benefits of frames over rules. In what cases would you use frames? (Give two examples.)
10. Explain this statement: Every parent is a child of a higher-level parent.
11. What are the major advantages of combining rules and frames?
12. Explain why a standardized knowledge interchange format could be important.
13. Explain what is meant by uncertainty in ES.

❖ EXERCISES

1. Construct a semantic network for the following situation: Mini is a robin; it lives in a nest, which is on a pine tree in Ms. Wang's backyard. Robins are birds; they can fly and they have wings. They are an endangered species, and they are protected by government regulations.
2. Create a rule base to determine whether a particular job–city combination would be acceptable to you after graduation. What factors did you use? What do the rules tend to indicate? Were there any holes in your knowledge?
3. Write a frame describing the object *robin,* in Exercise 1.
4. Prepare a set of frames of an organization given the following information:
   • Company: 1,050 employees, $130 million annual sales, Mary Sunny is the president

- Departments: accounting, finance, marketing, production, personnel
- Production department: five lines of production
- Product: computers
- Annual budget: $50,000 + $12,000 × number of computers produced
- Materials: $6,000 per unit produced
- Working days: 250 per year
- Number of supervisors: 1 for every 12 employees
- Range of number of employees: 400–500 per shift (two shifts per day). Overtime or part-time on a third shift is possible.

5. Write a narrative of Figure 12.3.

6. List attributes and values in the following objects: a lake, a stock market, a bridge, a car's engine. Use the O-A-V representation.

7. Prepare a frame of a university that you are familiar with. Show at least two levels of hierarchies. Fill some slots, use a demon, and show at least one rule as it relates to a slot.

8. The following is a typical instruction set found in the manuals in most car shops (this one is based on Nissan's shop manual):
- *Topic:* starter system troubles.
- *Procedures:* Try to crank the starter. If it is dead or cranks slowly, turn on the headlights. If the headlights are bright (or dim only slightly), the trouble is in the starter itself, the solenoid, or the wiring. To find the trouble, short the two large solenoid terminals together (not to ground). If the starter cranks normally, the problem is in the wiring or in the solenoid; check them up to the ignition switch. If the starter does not work normally, check the bushings. If the bushings are good, send the starter to a test station or replace it. If the headlights are out or are very dim, check the battery. If the battery is okay, check the wiring for breaks, shorts, and dirty connections. If the battery and connecting wires are not at fault, turn the headlights on and try to crank the starter. If the lights dim drastically, it is probably because the starter is shorted to ground. Have the starter tested or replace it. (Based on Carrico et al., 1989.) Now translate the information into rules. (Can you do it in only six rules?)

9. Prepare an O-A-V diagram of this rule: IF animal lays eggs and animal has feathers THEN animal is bird. *Hint:* It is necessary to add an assumption to solve this problem.

10. Prepare a script about shopping in a supermarket.

❖ GROUP EXERCISES

1. Have everyone in the group consider the fairly easy task of doing laundry. Individually, write down all the motions you use in sorting clothes, loading the washer and dryer, and folding the clothes. Compare notes. Are any members of the group better at the task than others? For simplicity, leave out details such as "go to the laundromat." Code the doing laundry facts in a rule base. How many exceptions to the rules did you find?

2. As a group, consider the task of selecting a spring break vacation site. Using a frame representation, codify all the facts relating to the group problem. How well did it work? Now try a rule-based approach.

3. Describe the characteristics of your group and the members' relationships in a semantic net representation. Consider factors such as whether you live near each other, whether you have common classes or interests, and so on. What difficulties did you encounter? Were there any ambiguities?

❖ GROUP TERM PROJECT

With a contact in a real-world organization, identify a small decision-making problem (such as vendor selection, computer or software selection, hiring candidates, or site selection) and determine the best way to represent the knowledge. Was there more than one representation that would have worked? Why or why not? (*To be continued.*)

❖ INTERNET EXERCISES

1. Use the Internet to find information that will enable you to expand Table 12.5 which lists the advantages and disadvantages of the various knowledge representation methods.
2. Search the Internet to find knowledge representation support tools (look for ES shells). Examine three tools and report on the representation methods they use.
3. Visit the American Association for Artificial Intelligence Web site (www.aaai.org) and examine papers and workshop descriptions that involve knowledge representation. What are the latest developments?
4. Explore research and vendor Web sites about managing large knowledge bases, and the tools for mining them.
5. Visit the Cycorp Inc. Web site at www.cyc.com and investigate applications that are being built on the Cyc knowledge base.
6. Visit the Hotbot beta search engine site at www.beta.hotbot.com and experiment with various search queries. Compare the results and follow-up suggestions with other Web-based search engines (Yahoo, Excite, and so on).

CHAPTER

13

INFERENCE TECHNIQUES[1]

In Chapters 11 and 12 we saw how knowledge is acquired and organized in a knowledge base. In this chapter we consider the specific reasoning strategies that can be used to draw inferences. We also discuss the central strategies that can be employed to guide a knowledge-based system in using the stored knowledge and communicating with the user. Finally, we show how to make inferences in an uncertain environment. The following topics are addressed in this chapter:

13.1 OPENING VIGNETTE: KONICA AUTOMATES A HELP DESK WITH CASE-BASED REASONING[2]

Konica Business Machines (Windsor, CT) wanted to fully automate its help desk for internal and external support (both for its commercial products and for in-house applications and systems). This need arose from its desire to be a $1 billion operation by the

---

[1]This chapter was updated by Narasimha Bolloju of The City University of Hong Kong.
[2]Based on L. The, "AI Automates a Help Desk," *Datamation,* Vol. 42, No. 2, Jan. 15, 1996, pp. 54–64. Also see L. The, "Morph Your Help Desk in Customer Support," *Datamation,* Vol. 42, No. 2, Jan. 15, 1996, pp. 52–54 and the accompanying "Feature Summary on Help Desk Software, pp. 56–57.

next millennium and because the company had received past awards for superior tech support for office products.

Case-based reasoning (CBR) was chosen as the most promising approach. After Konica evaluated several case-based reasoning tools, Ty Butler, the director of domestic tech support, selected Software Artistry's Expert Advisor. The most unusual feature of Expert Advisor is its multiple problem resolution modes. It also uses decision trees and has adaptive learning, tech search, and other useful features.

The case-based reasoning approach has been demonstrated to be an effective means of automating help desks. In CBR, the situation to be diagnosed is entered into the system verbatim. Then, the text is analyzed by a natural language processor to interpret the situation and make a first attempt at structuring the information to compare it to existing cases stored in a (knowledge) case base. Once the cases are examined, the most likely situations are presented and the user can either go with the recommended course of action or refine the wording to tighten up the description of the problem. Clearly, the cases must be written very carefully so that the system can apply AI technology in solving real problems. In the early prototypes, Konica knowledge engineers started building cases for five products using technical documentation as a source document. At a certain point, actual calls to the help desk were used to generate cases. Moving to real cases brought the hit rate up.

Konica's implementation, Expert Advisor, runs on IBM Pentium servers. It is used by both the internal tech support people and by customers directly. Konica's 750 technicians and 6,000 dealer technicians generate 90 percent of the support calls for copiers, 20 percent of those for fax machines, and 30 percent of those for multifunction products. The rest of the calls come from end users. There are 20 help desk technicians plus 6 knowledge engineers. Knowledge engineers build decision trees rather than case bases and focus on clearing the bulk of the calls instead of developing highly specialized structures. The tech support people still handle unusual cases, but the system is also incorporating digitized photos of components and procedures, which are especially useful to the help desk agents.

At the early stages of development, Expert Advisor produced a 65 percent hit rate for problem resolution. The adaptive learning features will be incorporated next to improve the hit rate.

❖ QUESTIONS FOR THE OPENING VIGNETTE

1. Why did Konica want to automate its help desk?
2. Why was CBR selected as the technology of choice?
3. Who are the Expert Advisor end users? Does this present any challenges for the implementation team?
4. Why did the hit rate go up when the knowledge engineers dropped the technical manuals in favor of real cases?
5. What will the adaptive learning feature of Expert Advisor do to the effectiveness of the system?

13.2 REASONING IN ARTIFICIAL INTELLIGENCE

The Opening Vignette illustrates the fact that once knowledge is acquired, it must be stored and processed (reasoned with) to provide effective results for its users. Expert Advisor works with knowledge acquired from experts and users, employing the case-based reasoning approach.

Once knowledge representation in the knowledge base is completed, or is at least at a sufficiently high level of accuracy, it is ready to be used. A computer program is needed to access the knowledge for making inferences. This program is an algorithm that controls a reasoning process and is usually called the **inference engine** or the *control program.* In rule-based systems, it is also called the **rule interpreter.**

The inference engine directs the search through the knowledge base, a process that may involve the application of inference rules in what is called *pattern matching.* The control program decides which rule to investigate, which alternative to eliminate, and which attribute to match. The most popular control programs for rule-based systems, forward and backward chaining, are described in the next section.

Before we investigate the specific inferencing techniques used in AI, it is interesting to examine how people reason, which is what AI attempts to mimic. There are several ways people reason and solve problems. An interesting view of the problem-solving process is one in which they draw on "sources of power." Lenat (1982) identified nine such sources:

- Formal reasoning methods (such as logical deduction)
- Heuristic reasoning, or IF-THEN rules
- Focus, or common sense applied to specific goals
- Divide and conquer, or dividing complex problems into subproblems (sometimes called *chunking*)
- Parallelism—neural processors (perhaps a million) operating in parallel
- Representation, or ways of organizing pieces of information
- Analogy, or the ability to associate and relate concepts
- Synergy, in which the whole is greater than the sum of its parts
- Serendipity, or fortuitous accidents.

These sources of power range from the purely deductive reasoning best handled by computer systems to inductive reasoning, which is more difficult to computerize. Lenat believes that the future of AI lies in finding ways to tap sources that have only begun to be exploited. These sources of power are translated to specific reasoning or inference methods as summarized in Table 13.1.

TABLE 13.1   Reasoning Methods

Method	*Description*
Deductive reasoning	Move from a general principle to a specific inference. A general principle is composed of two or more premises.
Inductive reasoning	Move from some established facts to draw general conclusions.
Analogical reasoning	Derive an answer to a question by known analogy. It is a verbalization of internalized learning process (Owen, 1990). Use of similar past experiences.
Formal reasoning	Syntactic manipulation of a data structure to deduce new facts following prescribed rules of inferences (such as predicate calculus).
Procedural (numeric) reasoning	Use of mathematical models or simulation (such as model-based reasoning, qualitative reasoning, and **temporal reasoning,** or the ability to reason about the time relationships between events).
Metalevel reasoning	Knowledge about what is known (e.g., about the importance and relevance of certain facts and rules).

REASONING WITH LOGIC

In performing either **deductive** or **inductive reasoning,** several basic reasoning procedures allow the manipulation of logical expressions to create new expressions. The most
important method is called **modus ponens.** In this method, given the rule "If A, then B"
and the fact that A is true, then it is valid to conclude that B is also true. In the terminology of logic, we express this as

$$[A \text{ AND } (A \to B)] \to B$$

A and $(A \to B)$ are *propositions* in a knowledge base. Given this expression, we can
replace both propositions with proposition B. In other words, we can use modus ponens
to draw the conclusion that B is true if the first two expressions are true. The following
is an example:

A: It is sunny.
B: We will go to the beach.
$A \to B$: If it is sunny, then we will go to the beach.

The first premise simply states that it is a sunny day. The second says we will go to
the beach. Furthermore, A IMPLIES B. So if both A and A IMPLIES B are true, then
B is true. Using modus ponens, you can then deduce that we will go to the beach.

A different situation is inferring that A is false when B is known to be false. This is
called **modus tollens. Resolution** (which combines substitution, modus ponens, and
other logical syllogisms) is yet another approach. For details on these and other reasoning approaches, see Bonissone (1993) and Awad (1996).

13.3 INFERENCING WITH RULES:
FORWARD AND BACKWARD CHAINING

Inferencing with rules involves the implementation of modus ponens, which is reflected
in the search mechanism. Consider the following example:

Rule 1:   IF an international conflict begins,
          THEN the price of gold will go up.

Let us assume that the ES knows that an international conflict has just started. This
information is stored as a fact in the database (or assertion base), which means that the
premise (the IF part) of the rule is true. With modus ponens, the conclusion is then accepted as true. We say that rule 1 fires. **Firing a rule** occurs only when all the rule's hypotheses (conditions in the IF part) are satisfied (evaluated to be true). Then, the conclusion drawn is stored in the assertion base. In our case, the conclusion (the price of
gold will go up) is added to the assertion base and can be used to satisfy the premise of
other rules. The true (or false) values for either portion of the rules can be obtained by
querying the user or by checking other rules. Testing a rule premise or conclusion can
be as simple as matching a symbolic pattern in the rule to a similar pattern in the assertion base. This activity is called **pattern matching.**

Every rule in the knowledge base can be checked to see whether its premise or conclusion can be satisfied by previously made assertions. This process can be done in one
of two directions, forward or backward, and continues until no more rules can fire or
until a goal is achieved.

FORWARD AND BACKWARD CHAINING: AN OVERVIEW

There are two methods for controlling inference in rule-based ES: *forward chaining* and *backward chaining* (each of which has several variations). First, we provide an intuitive description of the two methods; then we discuss them in detail.

EXAMPLE 1

Suppose you want to fly from Denver to Tokyo and there are no direct fights between the two cities. Therefore, you try to find a chain of connecting flights starting from Denver and ending in Tokyo. There are two basic ways you can search for this chain of flights:

- Start with all the flights that arrive in Tokyo and find the city where each flight originated. Then look up all the flights arriving at these cities and determine where they originated. Continue the process until you find Denver. Because you are working backward from your goal (Tokyo), this search process is called **backward chaining** (or goal-driven). Or,
- List all the flights leaving Denver and note their destination cities. Then look up all the flights leaving these cities and find where they land; continue this process until you find Tokyo. In this case, you are working forward from Denver toward your goal, and so this search process is called **forward chaining** (or data-driven).

This example also demonstrates the importance of heuristics in expediting the search process. Going either backward or forward, you can use heuristics to make the search more efficient. For example, in the backward approach you can look only at flights that go westward. Depending on the goals of your trip (e.g., minimize cost, minimize travel time, or maximize stopovers), you can develop additional rules to expedite the search even further.

EXAMPLE 2

Suppose your car does not start. Is it because you are out of gas? Or is it because the starter is broken? Or is it because of some other reason? Your task is to find out why the car won't start. From what you already know (the *consequence*—the car won't start), you go backward and try to find the *condition* that caused it. This is a typical application of ES in the area of diagnosis (i.e., the conclusion is known and one or more of the causes are sought).

A good example of forward chaining is a situation in which a water system is overheating. Here the goal is to predict the most likely reason. After reviewing the rules and checking additional evidence, you can finally find the answer. In forward chaining, you start with a condition or a symptom that is given as a fact.

As we show later, the search process in both cases involves a set of knowledge rules. After determining which rules are true and which are false, the search ends with a finding. The word *chaining* signifies the linking of a set of pertinent rules.

The search process is directed by what is sometimes called a **rule interpreter,** which works as follows:

- In forward chaining, if the premise clauses match the situation, then the process attempts to assert the conclusion.
- In backward chaining, if the current goal is to determine the correct conclusion, then the process attempts to determine whether the premise clauses (facts) match the situation.

BACKWARD CHAINING

Backward chaining is a *goal-driven* approach in which you start from an expectation of what is going to happen (hypothesis) and then seek evidence that supports (or contradicts) your expectation. Often this entails formulating and testing intermediate hypotheses (or subhypotheses).

On a computer the program starts with a goal to be verified as either true or false. Then it looks for a rule that has this goal in its *conclusion*. It then checks the *premise* of the rule in an attempt to satisfy the rule. It examines the assertion base first. If the search fails there, the program looks for another rule whose conclusion is the same as that of the first rule. An attempt is then made to satisfy the second rule. The process continues until all the possibilities that apply are checked or until the rule initially checked (with the goal) is satisfied. If the goal is proven false, then the next goal is tried. (In some inferencing, even if the goal is proven true, the rest of the goals can be tried in succession.)

EXAMPLE 3

Here is an example involving an investment decision: whether to invest in IBM stock. The following variables are used:

> A = Have $10,000
> B = Younger than 30
> C = Education at college level
> D = Annual income of at least $40,000
> E = Invest in securities
> F = Invest in growth stocks
> G = Invest in IBM stock (the potential goal)

Each of these variables can be answered as true (yes) or false (no).

The facts: We assume that an investor has $10,000 (that A is true) and that she is 25 years old (B is true). She would like advice on investing in IBM stock (yes or no for the goal).

The rules: Our knowledge base includes these five rules:

> R1:   IF a person has $10,000 to invest and she has a college degree
> THEN she should invest in securities.
> R2:   IF a person's annual income is at least $40,000 and she has a college degree
> THEN she should invest in growth stocks.
> R3:   IF a person is younger than 30 and she is investing in securities
> THEN she should invest in growth stocks.
> R4:   IF a person is younger than 30 and older than 22
> THEN she has a college degree.
> R5:   IF a person wants to invest in a growth stock
> THEN the stock should be IBM.
>
> These rules can be written as:
> R1:   IF A and C, THEN E.   R4:   IF B, THEN C.
> R2:   IF D and C, THEN F.   R5:   IF F, THEN G.
> R3:   IF B and E, THEN F.

Our goal is to determine whether to invest in IBM stock.

Start. In backward chaining we start by looking for a rule that includes the goal (G) in its conclusion (THEN) part. Because rule R5 is the only one that qualifies, we start with it. If several rules contain G, then the inference engine will dictate a procedure for handling the situation.

Step 1: Try to accept or reject G. The ES goes to the assertion base to see whether G is there. At present, all we have in the assertion base is

A is true.   B is true.

Therefore, the ES proceeds to step 2.

Step 2: R5 says that if it is true that we invest in growth stocks (F), then we should invest in IBM (G). If we can conclude that the premise of R5 is either true or false, then we have solved the problem. However, we do not know whether F is true. What shall we do now? Note that F, which is the premise of R5, is also the conclusion of R2 and R3. Therefore, to find out whether F is true, we must check either of these two rules.

Step 3: We try R2 first (arbitrarily); if both D and C are true, then F is true. Now we have a problem. D is not a conclusion of any rule, nor is it a fact. The computer can then either move to another rule or try to find out whether D is true by asking the investor for whom the consultation is given if her annual income is above $40,000.

What the ES does depends on the search procedures used by the inference engine. Usually a user is asked for additional information only if the information is not available or cannot be deduced. We abandon R2 and return to the other rule, R3. This action is called **backtracking** (i.e., knowing that we are at a dead end, we try something else. The computer must be preprogrammed to handle backtracking).

Step 4: Go to R3; test B and E. We know that B is true because it is a given fact. To prove E, we go to R1, where E is the conclusion.

Step 5: Examine R1. It is necessary to determine whether A and C are true.

Step 6: A is true because it is a given fact. To test C, it is necessary to test R4 (where C is the conclusion).

Step 7: R4 tells us that C is true (because B is true). Therefore, C becomes a fact (and is added to the assertion base). Now, E is true, which validates F, which validates our goal (i.e., the advice is to invest in IBM).

A negative response to any of the preceding statements would result in a "Do not invest in IBM stock" response. Then, another investment decision (conclusion) would have to be considered, but this time all the facts derived from the previous tries would be used.

Notice that during the search the ES moved from the THEN part to the IF part to the THEN part and so on (Figure 13.1). This is a typical search pattern in back-

FIGURE 13.1 BACKWARD CHAINING

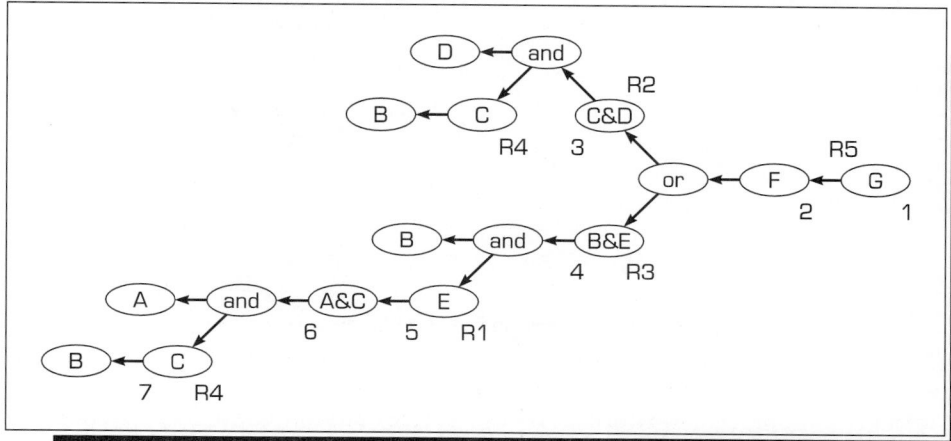

ward chaining. As we show next, forward chaining starts with the IF part, moves to the THEN part, then to another IF part, and so on. Some systems allow a change in the direction of the search midstream; that is, they can go from THEN to THEN (or from IF to IF) as needed.

FORWARD CHAINING

Forward chaining is a *data-driven* approach. We start from available information as it becomes available or from a basic idea, and then we try to draw conclusions.

The ES analyzes the problem by looking for the facts that match the IF part of its IF-THEN rules. For example, if a certain machine is not working, the computer checks the electricity flow to the machine. As each rule is tested, the program works its way toward one or more conclusions.

EXAMPLE 4

Let us use the same example we introduced in backward chaining. Here we reproduce the rules:

R1:   IF A and C, THEN E.   R4:   IF B, THEN C.
R2:   IF D and C, THEN F.   R5:   IF F, THEN G.
R3:   IF B and E, THEN F.

and the facts:

A is true (the investor has $10,000). B is true (the investor is younger than 30).

Start: In forward chaining (Figure 13.2), we start with known facts and derive new facts using rules having known facts on the IF side.

Step 1: Because it is known that A and B are true, the ES starts deriving new facts using rules having A and B on the IF side. Using R4, the ES derives a new fact C and adds it to the assertion base as true.

Step 2: Now R1 fires (because A and C are true) and asserts E as true in the assertion base.

Step 3: Because B and E are both known to be true (they are in the assertion base), R3 fires and establishes F as true in the assertion base.

Step 4: Now R5 fires (because F is on its IF side), which establishes G as true. So the expert system recommends an investment in IBM stock. If there is more than one conclusion, more rules may fire, depending on the inferencing procedure.

FIGURE 13.2 FORWARD CHAINING

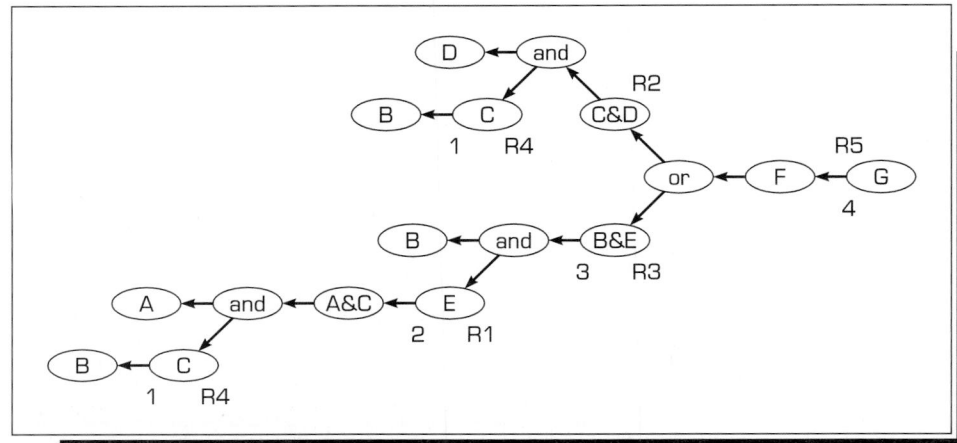

AIS IN FOCUS 13.1

THE FUNCTIONS OF THE INFERENCE ENGINE

1. Fire the rules.

2. Present the user with questions.

3. Add the answer to the ES blackboard (assertion base).

4. Infer a new fact from a rule.

5. Add the inference fact to the blackboard.

6. Match the blackboard to the rules.

7. If there are any matches, fire the rules.

8. If there are two further matches, check to see whether a goal is reached.

9. Fire the lowest-numbered unfired rule.

This program works through the knowledge base until it can post a fact (or a partial fact if certainty factors are being used) to the blackboard.

Once a fact has been posted, the system goes back to the knowledge base to infer more facts. This process continues until the present goal is achieved or until all rules have been fired.

We have seen that an antecedent–consequence rule system can run forward or backward, but which direction is better? The answer depends on the purpose of the reasoning and the shape of the search space. For example, if the goal is to discover all that can be deduced from a given set of facts, the system should run forward, as in accounting audit applications, because most facts are initially available in documents and forms. In some cases, the two strategies can be mixed (the process is bidirectional).

The execution of forward or backward chaining is accomplished with the aid of a rule interpreter. Its function is to examine production rules to determine which are capable of being fired and then to fire these rules. The control strategy of the rule interpreter (e.g., backward chaining) determines how the appropriate rules are found and when to apply them (see AIS in Focus 13.1).

Inferencing with rules (as well as with logic) can be very effective, but there are some obvious limitations to these techniques. One reason for this is summarized by the familiar axiom that there is an exception to every rule. For example, consider the following argument:

> Proposition 1: Birds can fly.
> Proposition 2: An ostrich is a bird.
> Conclusion: An ostrich can fly.

The conclusion is perfectly valid but is false for this limited knowledge universe; ostriches simply do not cooperate with the facts. For this reason, as well as for increased efficiency of the search, we sometimes use other inferencing methods.

13.4 THE INFERENCE TREE

An **inference tree** (also called a *goal tree* or *logical tree*) provides a schematic view of the inference process. It is similar to a decision tree and an influence diagram (Russell and Norvig, 1995). Note that each rule is composed of a premise and a conclusion. In building an inference tree, the premises and conclusions are shown as nodes. The branches connect the premises and the conclusions. The operators AND and OR are used to reflect the structures of the rules. There is no deep significance to the construction of such trees—they just provide better insight into the structure of the rules. Inference trees map the knowledge in a convenient manner. In fact, the current generation of Windows-based ES shells use a kind of inference tree to display the knowledge base on the screen (such as G2, and Exsys Professional).

Figure 13.3 presents on inference tree for Example 3. Using the tree, we can visualize the process of inference and movement along its branches. This is called *tree traversal.* To traverse an AND node, we must traverse all the nodes below it. To traverse an OR node, it is sufficient to traverse just one of the nodes below. The inference tree is constructed upside-down: The root is at the top (end), and the branches point downward. The tree starts with "leaves" at the bottom. (It can also be constructed from left to the right, much like a decision tree.) Inference trees are composed basically of clusters of goals. Each goal can have subgoals (children) and a supergoal (parent).

FIGURE 13.3 INFERENCE TREE

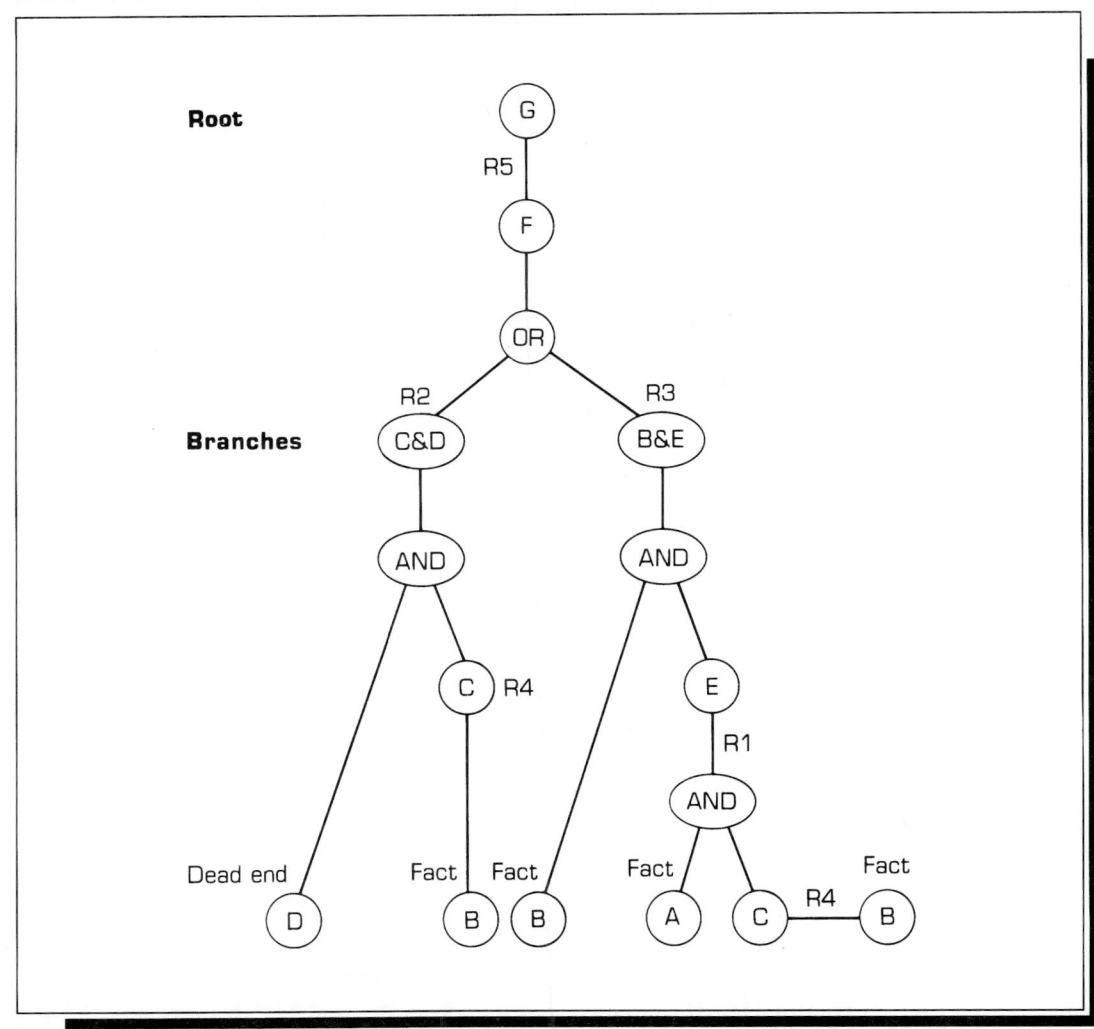

Single inference trees are always a mixture of AND nodes and OR nodes; they are often called AND/OR trees (note that the NOT operation is allowed). The AND node signifies a situation in which a goal is satisfied only when *all* its immediate subgoals are satisfied. The OR node signifies a situation in which a goal is satisfied when *any* of its immediate goals are satisfied. When enough subgoals are satisfied to achieve the primary goal, the tree is said to be satisfied. The inference engine contains procedures for expressing this process as backward or forward chaining. These procedures are organized as a set of instructions involving inference rules. They aim at satisfying the inference tree and collectively contribute to the process of goal (problem) reduction. For further discussion, see Russell and Norvig (1995).

The inference tree has another big advantage: It provides a guide for answering the *why* and *how* questions in the explanation process. The *how* question is asked by users when they want to know how a certain conclusion has been reached. The computer follows the logic in the inference tree, identifies the goal (conclusion) involved in it and the AND/OR branches, and reports the immediate subgoals. The *why* question is asked by users when they want to know why the computer requests certain information as input (in backward chaining). To deal with *why* questions, the computer identifies the goal involved with the computer-generated query and reports the immediate subgoals.

13.5 INFERENCING WITH FRAMES

Reasoning with frames is much more complicated than reasoning with rules. The slot provides a mechanism for a kind of reasoning called **expectation-driven processing.** Empty slots can be filled, subject to certain conditioning, with data that confirm expectations. Thus, frame-based reasoning looks for confirmation of expectations and often just involves filling in slot values.

Perhaps the simplest way to specify slot values is by default. The default value is attached loosely to the slot so as to be easily displaced by a value that meets the assignment condition. In the absence of information, however, the default value remains attached and expressed.

The frame-based reasoning process is essentially the seeking of confirmation of various expectations. This amounts to filling in the slots and verifying that they match the current situation. With frames, it is easy to make inferences about new objects, events, or situations because the frames provide a knowledge base drawn from previous experience.

Frames can be classified, by their application, as situational frames, action frames, and causal frames (Giarratano and Riley, 1994). Knowledge about what to expect in a given situation is represented by situational frames. Actions to be performed under specific conditions (e.g., triggers and procedures) are represented by action frames. Causal frames represent a combination of situational and action frames in describing cause-and-effect relationships.

A rule can reason about the characteristics of a frame by referring to its slot values, which can also be frames. Reasoning in frames can be implemented in a number of different ways. The two most common are using rules similar to production rules (e.g., rule 1 in the example below) and using rules with **hierarchical reasoning** (e.g., rule 2). Many frame-based systems combine rules with these two types of reasoning.

Consider the customer profiling process in a Web-based sales application. The application represents knowledge about customers using frames. A typical customer frame, in addition to customer details, includes procedural knowledge (rule 1) in the form of an *if-needed* rule attached to slots such as PURCHASE-POTENTIAL.

> Rule 1:   if VISIT-NUMBER of ?CUSTOMER > 6
> and PURCHASES-SO-FAR of ?CUSTOMER > 2
> then set PURCHASE-POTENTIAL of ?CUSTOMER to very high.

This rule infers a purchase potential slot value for a given customer depending on the total number of visits and purchase made so far.

Rules can also be used to process the structural knowledge contained in a taxonomy. The following rule determines the class of a given insurance product.

> Rule 2:   if ?PRODUCT is-a INSURANCE-PRODUCT
> and ?PRODUCT has-a ?FAMILY-COVER
> and ?PRODUCT is-a FAMILY-INSURANCE-PRODUCT.

This rule classifies a product as a family insurance product if the product *is-an* insurance product and it *has-a* family cover component associated with it.

Reasoning with knowledge taxonomy is not the exclusive province of rules, although many frame-based systems use rule-based knowledge extensively. For further details on frame-based systems and their applications, see Hendler and Stoffel (1999), Karimi and Zand (1998), and Nault and Storey (1998).

13.6 MODEL-BASED REASONING

Model-based reasoning is based on knowledge of the structure and behavior of the devices a system is designed to understand. Model-based systems are especially useful in diagnosing difficult equipment problems. Model-based ES can overcome some of the difficulties of rule-based ES (see AIS in Action 13.2). These systems include a (deep-knowledge) model of the device to be diagnosed which is then used to identify the causes of the equipment's failure. Because they draw conclusions directly from knowledge of a device's structure and behavior, model-based expert systems are said to reason from "first principles" (common sense). In many cases model-based reasoning is combined with other representation and inferencing methods.

The hardware troubleshooting group in MIT's AI lab assessed the use of model-based ES to diagnose malfunctioning computers. The group used a computer repair scenario to contrast the rule-based and model-based approaches. First, the rule-based approach:

AIS IN ACTION 13.2

MODEL-BASED ES HELPS THE ENVIRONMENT

At the Westinghouse Savannah River Company, a project is under way to develop a representation schema for engineering and commonsense knowledge about the environmental and biological impacts of a nuclear weapons processing facility. There are often difficulties in representing and using commonsense knowledge, such as "Smoke travels downwind and dissipates with distance." The process consists of a learn-by-doing approach. As new concepts are identified, they are compared to the knowledge in Cyc, a set of general knowledge about the world. New concepts are added to the qualitative model as they are found. Dynamic events such as a leak can be described via models developed through the large knowledge base. Furthermore, relevant portions of the knowledge can be shared or reused by other ES on an as-needed basis. Model-based ES can overcome some of the difficulties of rule-based ES.

Source: Adapted from Pinto et al. (1995).

Consider the likely behavior of an engineer with a great deal of repair experience. He or she simply stares briefly at the console, noting the pattern of lights and error messages, and then goes over to one of the cabinets, opens it, raps sharply on one of the circuit boards inside, and restarts the machine.

The diagnostic process involved in this episode represents the approach that is incorporated in a rule-based expert system. A knowledge engineer formalizes the reasoning process that an expert uses to discover the source of the problem and encodes this procedure in a series of production rules.

A model-based approach, on the other hand, is represented by a scenario such as the following:

Consider a new engineer who has just completed training. He or she carefully notes the symptoms, opens a thick book of schematics, and spends the next half-hour poring over them. At last, he or she looks up, goes over to one of the cabinets, opens it, raps sharply on one of the circuit boards inside, and restarts the machine.

Although in this example the rule-based and model-based approaches resulted in the same actions, the procedures used to arrive at the conclusions were very different. Because the novice engineer in the latter scenario could not rely on his or her expertise to diagnose and repair the computer, they had to refer to documentation that explained how the computer worked. Similarly, a model-based system depends on knowledge of the structure and behavior of a device rather than relying on production rules that represent expertise.

One especially attractive feature of a model-based ES is its transportability. A rule-based ES that incorporates an expert's knowledge of troubleshooting problems with a particular computer might be of no value in repairing a different kind of computer. On the other hand, if a model-based ES includes a thorough working knowledge of digital electronic computer circuits, it theoretically could be used to diagnose the problem of any computer.

EXAMPLE 5

An example of model-based reasoning is given by Fulton and Pepe (1990). Their systems are implemented for troubleshooting by NASA at the Kennedy Space Center. Rule-based systems are not effective in situations where there is a mass of sensor information. Such systems cannot make the necessary association between the set of sensor data and the fault.

The model-based system includes a model that simulates the structure and function of the machinery under diagnosis. Instead of reasoning only from observable values, these systems reason from first principles; that is, they know the machinery's internal processes. These systems can compute the machine state rather than attempt to match such a state against complex symptoms (which a rule-based system does).

Once signals are received from the sensors, the expert system activates a simulation program that generates predicted values. These values are compared to information provided by the sensors. As long as the actual data are within the range of the predicted values (the tolerance), nothing is done. If the actual data are outside the tolerance, a diagnosis is automatically performed. The result of the diagnosis may activate control commands to prevent the system from entering a dangerous state. This mode of reasoning is very important in intelligent robots.

The models used in this type of reasoning can be either **mathematical models** or **component models.** For example, a mathematical model can simulate the function of a grandfather clock, taking into account the oscillator length, gear size, and so forth. The model can predict the position of the hands after a specific time interval and, with more complexity, can diagnose why the clock runs too fast (or too slowly). In contrast, a component model contains a functional description of all components and their interactions. As the clock ticks, each component alters itself, propagates its final position to the relevant components, and then allows them to alter their positions.

Special model-based tools are available (usually involving frames) that are helpful in inferencing that involves monitoring production processes (and taking appropriate actions) and diagnosing malfunctions. A necessary condition for model-based reasoning is the creation of a complete and accurate model of the system under study. This approach is especially useful in real-time systems. For further details see Awad (1996), Pinto et al. (1995), and Russell and Norvig (1995).

13.7 CASE-BASED REASONING

BASICS

The basic idea of **case-based reasoning (CBR)** is to adapt solutions that have been used to solve old problems for use in solving new problems. One variation of this approach is the rule induction method described in Chapter 11. In rule induction, the computer examines historical cases and generates rules, which then can be chained (forward or backward) to solve problems. Case-based reasoning, on the other hand [according to Kolonder (1993)], follows a different process:

- It finds cases in memory that contain solved problems similar to the current problem.
- It adapts the previous solution or solutions to fit the current problem, taking into account any differences between the current and previous situations.

The process of finding relevant cases involves the following:

- Characterizing the input problem by assigning appropriate features to it
- Retrieving cases from memory with these features
- Picking the case or cases that match the input best.

Case-based reasoning has proved to be an extremely effective approach in complex cases (Kolonder, 1993). According to Riesbeck and Schank (1989), the basic justification for the use of this approach is that human thinking does not use logic (or reasoning from first principles). It is basically a processing of the right information retrieved at the right time. So the central problem is the identification of pertinent information whenever needed. This is done in case-based reasoning with the aid of scripts.

CASE DEFINITION[3]

A case is the primary knowledge-base element in a case-based reasoning application. It defines a situation or problem in terms of natural language descriptions and answers to questions and associates with each situation a proper business action. For example, in a customer support application, a case might be as follows:

Description: Customer requests price adjustment for merchandise purchased the day before a sale.

---

[3]Per G. Vrooman, "Commercialization Case-based Reasoning Technology," *AI Review,* Summer 1991.

Question: What was the method of payment?
Answer: Revolving charge.
Action: Credit the difference between the purchase price and the discounted sale price to the customer's charge account.

SCRIPTS

As you may recall from Chapter 12, **scripts** describe a well-known sequence of events. If a restaurant script is available, then you don't have to think much in an attempt to infer the intentions of a waitress. These intentions are either documented in the script or can be easily inferred. Therefore, in many cases, it is possible to say that reasoning is no more than applying scripts. The more scripts available to us, the less thinking we need to do. All that is necessary is to find the right script to use. Riesbeck and Schank (1989) postulate that given a choice between thinking hard (reworking the problem) and applying an old script, people choose the script every time. Scripts can be constructed from historical cases that reflect human experience. The experience can be that of the decision makers or of others. Case-based reasoning is the essence of how people reason from experience.

Case-based reasoning has been proposed as a more psychologically plausible model of the reasoning of an expert than a rule-based model. A theoretical comparison of the two was made by Riesbeck and Schank (1989), and a summary is provided in Table 13.2.

TABLE 13.2   Comparison of Case-based and Rule-based Reasoning

Criterion	*Rule-based Reasoning*	*Case-based Reasoning*
Knowledge unit	Rule	Case
Granularity	Fine	Coarse
Knowledge acquisition units	Rules, hierarchies	Cases, hierarchies
Explanation mechanism	Backtrack of rule firings	Precedent cases
Characteristic output	Answer and confidence measure	Answer and precedent cases
Knowledge transfer across problems	High if backtracking; low if deterministic	Low
Speed as a function of knowledge base size	Exponential if backtracking; linear if deterministic	Logarithmic if index tree is balanced
Domain requirements	Domain vocabulary	Domain vocabulary
	Good set of inference rules	Database of example cases
	Either few rules or rules apply sequentially	Stability (a modified good solution is probably still good)
	Domain mostly obeys rules	
		Many exceptions to rules
Advantages	Flexible use of knowledge	Rapid response
	Potentially optimal answers	Rapid knowledge acquisition
		Explanation by examples
Disadvantages	Computationally expensive	Suboptimal solutions
	Long development time	Redundant knowledge base
	Black-box answers	

Source: Based on M. Goodman, "PRISM: A Case-based Telex Classifier," in A. Rappaport and R. Smith (eds.), *Innovative Applications of Artificial Intelligence,* Vol. 2. Cambridge, MA: MIT Press, 1990. Courtesy of Marc Goodman, Cognitive Systems Inc.

EXAMPLE 6: PAY-TV HELP DESK APPLICATION

This example of a pay-TV help desk application describes a demonstration of CaseAdvisor in Action! (available from Sententia Software Inc., www.cs.sfu.ca/~isa/isaresearch.html#systems). This CBR application assists help desk operators in solving pay-TV reception problems reported by customers. The processes of case authoring (performed by experts) and problem solving (performed by help desk operators) are illustrated below.

Authoring new cases: A new case is added to the **case library** with the following details.

Case name:	Pay-TV channels are scrambled
Description:	Scrambled picture due to faulty converter or descrambler box
Solution:	Reauthorize the box

As part of the case definition, a set of questions (e.g., Is there a sound or a picture problem?) can be added with possible answers (e.g., sound problem, picture problem, both). Such questions are associated with one or more cases, and weights are assigned to each possible answer (e.g., 89 percent weight to the picture problem in the scrambled pay-TV channels case).

The case description can also include a reference to existing documents, links to solution pages (e.g., starting point in a decision tree), and a list of key words with synonym definitions.

Possible solutions to each problem are described as a series of steps with associated decision tree(s) for each step. For example, a solution to the pay-TV picture problem has the following steps:

1. Reauthorize the converter box.
2. Ask the customer to tune to Channel 54.
3. Ask whether all the channels work after tuning to Channel 54.

Thus, case descriptions include all the necessary information and/or links to the procedure for solving problems associated with the cases.

Problem resolution: Help desk operators use the problem resolution mode to solve problems reported by customers. The resolution process requires operators to enter a problem description (e.g., snow on Channel 14) as reported by customers. In response, the system displays a set of questions and case names related to the specific problem:

QUESTIONS:

Is the problem on all or on only some channels?
Is the problem affecting more than one outlet?
Are channels 29 through 36 working?

CASES:

30	No picture above channel 13
17	No reception on all channels
12	Poor reception

The number associated with each case name identifies the score of relevance (0 least relevant and 100 most relevant) of the case to the reported problem. Answers provided to one or more of these questions revise the scores of relevance. For example, answering "all channels above 13" to the first question revises the relevance scores for the three cases:

96	No picture above Channel 13
12	Poor reception
9	No reception on all channels

> **TABLE 13.3**   Advantages of Case-based Reasoning
>
> - Knowledge acquisition is improved: easier to build, simpler to maintain, less expensive to develop and support.
> - System development time is faster.
> - Existing data and knowledge are leveraged.
> - Complete formalized domain knowledge (as is required with rules) is not required.
> - Experts feel better discussing concrete cases (not general rules).
> - Explanation becomes easier. Rather than showing many rules, a logical sequence can be shown.
> - Acquisition of new cases is easy [can be automated; for an example of knowledge acquisition of cases, see diPiazza and Helsabeck (1990)].
> - Learning can occur from both successes and failures.

The help desk operator then requests the solution procedure for the most relevant case (the first one in the above list), which has detailed steps and documentation required for solving the specific problem.

ADVANTAGES

Although in the above example case authoring and problem resolution are performed separately, it is possible for new cases corresponding to newly reported problems to be added to the case library immediately after the problem is resolved. Such ability to learn from experience is a major advantage of CBR over other knowledge-based systems development methods (Mahapatra, 1997/1998). Case-based reasoning has several potential benefits, which are summarized in Table 13.3.

PROCESS OF CASE-BASED REASONING

The process of case-based reasoning is shown graphically in Figure 13.4. Boxes represent processes, and ovals represent knowledge structure. The major steps in the process are described in the following list [reprinted from Slade (1991)].

1. *Assign indexes.* Features of the new event are assigned as indexes characterizing the event. For example, our first air shuttle flight might be characterized as an airplane flight.
2. *Retrieve.* The indexes are used to retrieve a similar past case from memory. The past case contains the prior solution. In our example, we might be reminded of a previous airplane trip.
3. *Modify.* The old solution is modified to conform to the new situation, resulting in a proposed solution. For our airplane case, we would make appropriate modifications to account for changes in various features such as destination, price, purpose of the trip, departure and arrival times, weather, and so on.
4. *Test.* The proposed solution is tried out. It either succeeds or fails. Our airplane reminder generates certain expectations.
5. *Assign and store.* If the solution succeeds, then assign indexes and store a working solution. The successful plan is then incorporated into the case memory. For a typical airplane trip there will be few expectation failures and, therefore, little to make this new trip memorable. It will be just one more instance of the airplane script.
6. *Explain, repair, and test.* If the solution fails, then explain the failure, repair the working solution, and test again. The explanation process identifies the source

of the problem. The predictive features of the problem are incorporated into the indexing rules to anticipate this problem in the future. The failed plan is repaired to fix the problem and the revised solution is then tested. For our air shuttle example, we realize that certain expectations fail. We learn that we do not get an assigned seat and that we do not have to pay ahead of time. We might decide that taking the air shuttle is more like riding on a train. We can then create a new case in memory to handle this new situation and identify predictive features so that we will be reminded of this episode the next time we take the shuttle. In support of this process are the following types of knowledge structures, represented by ovals in this figure:

- *Indexing rules.* Indexing rules identify the predictive features in the input that provide appropriate indexes in the case memory. Determining the significant input features is a persistent problem.
- *Case memory.* Case memory is the epsisodic memory, which comprises the database of experience.
- *Similarity metrics.* If more than one case is retrieved from episodic memory, the similarity metrics can be used to decide which case is more like the current situation. For example, in the air shuttle case, we might be reminded of both airplane rides and train rides. The similarity rules might initially suggest that we rely on the airplane case.
- *Modification rules.* No old case is going to be an exact match for a new situation. The old case must be modified to fit. We require knowledge about what kinds of factors can be changed and how to change them. For the airplane ride, it is acceptable to ride in a different seat, but it is usually not advisable to change roles from passenger to pilot.
- *Repair rules.* Once we identify and explain an expectation failure, we must try to alter our plan to fit the new situation. Again, we have rules for what kinds of changes are permissible. For the air shuttle, we recognize that paying for the ticket on the plane is an acceptable change. We can generate an explanation that recognizes an airplane ride as a type of commercial transaction and suggests that there are alternative, acceptable means of paying for services.

See Allen (1994) for a related description of the process.

USES, ISSUES, AND APPLICATIONS

Case-based reasoning can be used on its own or it can be combined with other reasoning paradigms. Several implementations of CBR systems combine rule-based reasoning (RBR) in order to address limitations such as accuracy in case indexing and adaptation (Golding and Rosenboom, 1996). Table 13.4 provides some guidelines for the selection of CBR applications.

Demonstrations of sample CBR applications can be found on CBR-Works demo pages (www.tecinno.de/english/products/demos/). Table 13.5 provides CBR applications in different fields (see www.cbr-web.org for more details).

Case-based reasoning is a new field (it started in the late 1980s) with little, but growing, practical experience. Therefore, issues and problems can be anticipated. The following issues and questions regarding case-based implementation have been raised:

- What makes up a case? How can we represent case memory?
- Automatic case adaptation rules can be very complex.

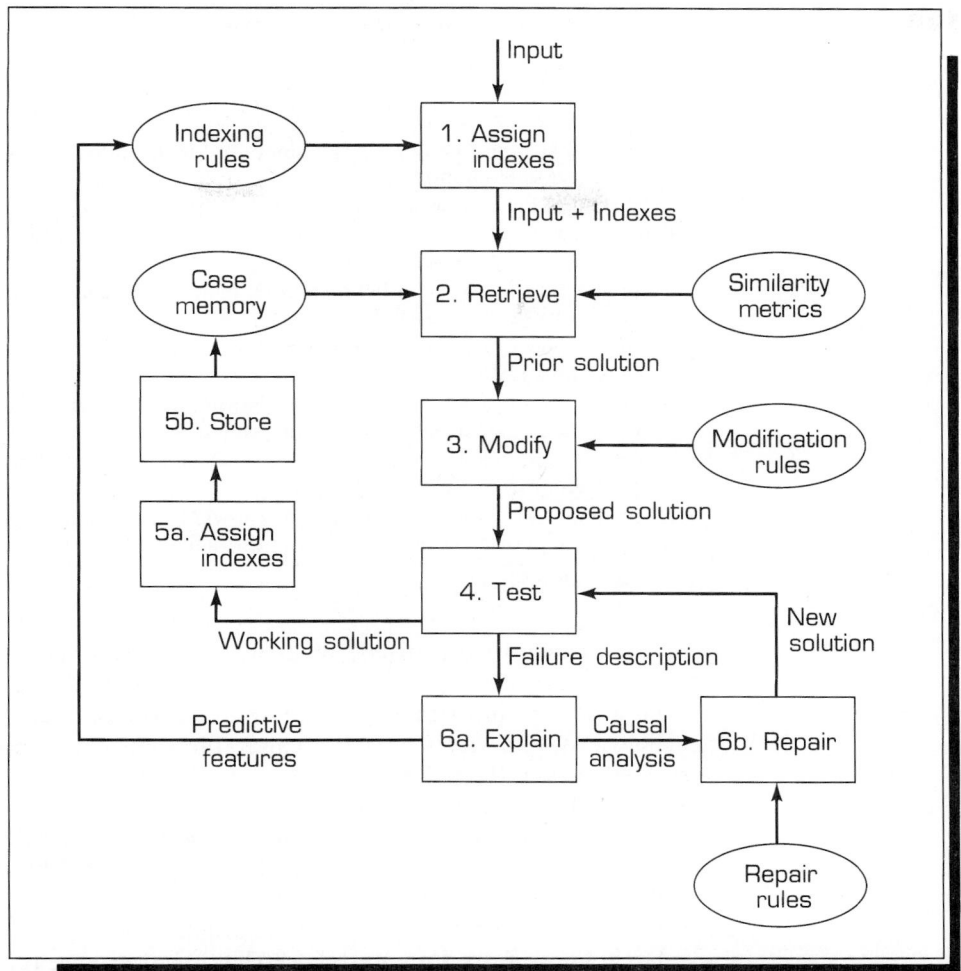

FIGURE 13.4 CASE-BASED REASONING FLOWCHART

Source: AI Magazine, Spring 1991, p. 46; based on C.K. Riesback and R.L. Schank, I*nside Case-based Reasoning,* Hillsdale, NJ: Lawrence Erlbaum Associates, 1989, p. 32. Copyright © 1989, American Association for Artificial Intelligence. All rights reserved.

TABLE 13.4 When to Use Case-based Reasoning

Domain cannot be formalized with rules because

- Domain has a weak or unknown causal model.
- Domain has undefined terms.
- Contradictory rules apply in different situations.

Application requires complex output (such as battle plans).

Domain is already precedent-based (e.g., in fields such as law, medical diagnosis, and claim settlement).

Domain formalization requires too many rules.

Domain is dynamic, requiring rapid generation of solutions to new problem types.

Domain task benefits from records of past solutions to reuse successful ones and avoid bad ones.

Source: Based on M. Goodman, "PRISM: A Case-based Telex Classifier," in Rappaport and Smith (1990). Courtesy of Marc Goodman, Cognitive Systems Inc.

TABLE 13.5 Case-based Reasoning Application Categories and Examples

- CBR in electronic commerce—intelligent product catalog search, intelligent customer support and sales support.
- WWW and information search—browsing advisor, retrieving tour packages from travel catalog, case-based information retrieval in construction, and skill profiling in electronic recruitment.
- Planning and control – conflict resolution in air traffic control and planning of bioprocess recipes in brewing industry.
- Design—conceptual building design aid, conceptual design aid for electromechanical devices, and VLSI design.
- Reuse—reuse of structural design calculation documents, reuse of object-oriented software, and reuse assistant for engineering designs.
- Diagnosis—predicting blood alcohol content, online troubleshooting and customer support, and medical diagnosis.
- Reasoning—heuristic retrieval of legal knowledge, reasoning in legal domains, and computer-supported conflict resolution through negotiation or mediation.

Source: www.cbr-web.org.

- How is memory organized? What are the indexing rules?
- The quality of the results is heavily dependent on the indexes used.
- How does memory function in relevant information retrieval?
- How can we perform efficient search (knowledge navigation) of the cases?
- How can we organize (cluster) the cases?
- How can we design the distributed storage of cases?
- How can we adapt old solutions to new problems? Can we simply adapt the memory for efficient query, depending on context? What are the similarity metrics and the modification rules?
- How can we factor errors out of the original cases?
- How can we learn from mistakes? That is, how can we repair and update the case base?
- The case base may need to be expanded as the domain model evolves, yet much analysis of the domain may be postponed.
- How can we integrate CBR with other knowledge representations and inferencing mechanisms?
- Are there better pattern-matching methods than the ones we currently use?
- Are there alternative retrieval systems that match the CBR schema?

See Lenz et al. (1996), Hunt (1997), and Slade (1991) for details. Since 1995, increasing evidence has shown positive results for the use of case-based reasoning in solving practical problems (Althoff, 1995; Azuaje et al., 1999; Cercone et al., 1999; Grupe et al., 1998; Lawton, 1999; Leake, 1996; Lenz et al., 1996; Liang and Turban, 1993; Pal and Palmer, 2000; Williams and Clayton, 1994 (see AIS in Action 13.3).

SUCCESS FACTORS FOR A CASE-BASED REASONING SYSTEM

Case-based reasoning systems exhibit some unique properties that, if properly managed and implemented, can lead to very successful systems. Klahr (1997) describes seven principles for a successful CBR strategy. They are as follows:

- *Determine specific business objectives.* Every software project should have a business focus. Call center and help desk environments have great potential for CBR methods.

AIS IN ACTION 13.3

CASE-BASED REASONING IMPROVES JET ENGINE MAINTENANCE, REDUCES COSTS

Snecma is the leading French manufacturer of aircraft engines, ranking fourth in the world. One of Snecma's goals is to improve engine maintenance technology to reduce the cost of ownership for its customers. The CASSIOPÉE project was designed to perform engine troubleshooting using CBR. It performs technical maintenance of the Cfm 56-3 aircraft engines on all Boeing 737s.

Troubleshooting accounts for 50 percent of the average engine downtime. The 16,000 cases were culled from an 8-year history of all Cfm 56-3 engines sold. Error cases were removed from the set, and the model was supplemented with technical parameters of the engines. A decision tree is used to organize the cases and drive the questioning. On average, a case is described by 40 attributes out of a total of 80 (not all are used simultaneously).

The demonstrated benefits of CASSIOPÉE are the following:

- Reduced downtime for the engines, avoiding delays for the airlines
- Minimized diagnosis costs
- Reduced diagnostic errors
- Development of a record and documentation of the expertise of the most skilled maintenance specialists to build a corporate memory and help transfer know-how to the novice.

The CASSIOPÉE system is in use in the aftersale division at Cfm-International, a subsidiary of Snecma and General Electric. It is fully integrated in the end-user environment. CASSIOPÉE assists Cfm engineers in offering quicker and better advice to airline maintenance crews when airplanes are at the departure gate.

Source: Abstracted and modified from Lenz et al. (1996). Also see Manago and Auriol (1995).

- *Understand your end users and customers.* A successful case base directly supports the end user. The case base (knowledge) must be at the level of expertise of the end users. For more knowledgeable end users, shortcuts should be provided.
- *Design the system appropriately.* This includes understanding the problem domain and types of information the case base will provide and recognizing system and integration requirements.
- *Plan an ongoing knowledge management process.* The knowledge in the case base must be updated as new cases arise (to avoid gaps in the case base) or new products or services are delivered (new content is added).
- *Establish achievable returns on investment (ROI) and measurable metrics.* Develop a level of acceptable ROI (5–13 percent is being achieved in the field) and a means to measure it (20 fewer phone calls with a 13 percent larger customer base handled; or the ability to handle 4 times the number of questions than under the manual system).
- *Plan and execute customer access strategy.* The strength of CBR is that it can be put into the hands of customers, even over the Web, thus providing service 24 hours every day (e.g., Broderbund Software's Gizmo Trapper). This empowers customers to obtain the assistance they need when they need it. It also further broadens the use of the system, which helps in identifying exceptions and updating the case base. This is a key success component (Klahr, 1997).
- *Expand knowledge generation and access across the enterprise.* Just as knowledge is made available to customers, internal customers, who are in direct contact with external customers, may be able to provide helpful feedback and knowledge.

TABLE 13.6   Case-based Reasoning Tools

Vendor and Product(s)	URL
AcknoSoft—KATE	www.acknosoft.com
Atlantis Aerospace Corporation—SpotLight	www.atlantis.com
Brightware Inc.—ART*Enterprise	www.brightware.com
Case Bank Support Systems Inc.—Spotlight	www.casebank.com
Continuum Software Inc.—PV/FutureView	www.continuumsi.com
Inductive Solutions Inc.—CasePower	www.inductive.com
Inference Corporation—k-commerce (formerly called CBR3 or CBR Express, CasePoint, Generator, and WebServer)	www.inference.com
IET-Intelligent Electronics—TechMate	www.ietusa.com
Intellix—KnowMan	www.intellix.com
Sententia Software Inc.—CASE Advisor and Case Advisor Webserver	www.cs.sfu.ca/~isa/ isaresearch.html#systems
ServiceSoft—Knowledge Builder and Web Adviser	www.servicesoft.com
TecInno GmbH—CBR-Works and Inference's k-commerce	www.tecinno.com
TreeTools—HELPDESK-3	www.treetools.com.br
The Haley Enterprise Inc.—Easy Reasoner, CPR, and Help!CPR	www.haley.com

Source: AI-CBR, www.ai-cbr.org.

See Klahr (1997) for further details and examples of successfully deployed CBR systems.

CONSTRUCTION
Case-based reasoning systems are usually built with the help of special tools. Representative tools are listed in Table 13.6. The home page of AI-CBR (www.ai-cbr.org) and the University of Kaiserslautern's case-based reasoning Web site (www.cbr-web.org) provide details and pointers to numerous CBR tools and applications.

13.8 EXPLANATION AND METAKNOWLEDGE

EXPLANATION

Human experts are often asked to explain their views, recommendations, or decisions. If ES are to mimic humans in performing highly specialized tasks, they need to justify and explain their actions as well. An explanation is an attempt by an ES to clarify its reasoning, recommendations, or other actions (such as asking a question). The part of an ES that provides explanations is called an **explanation facility** (or **justifier**). The explanation facility has several purposes:

- Make the system more intelligible to the user.
- Uncover the shortcomings of the rules and knowledge base (debugging of the systems by the knowledge engineer).
- Explain situations that were unanticipated by the user.

- Satisfy psychological and social needs by helping a user feel more assured about the actions of the ES.
- Clarify the assumptions underlying the system's operations to both the user and the builder.
- Conduct sensitivity analyses (using the explanation facility as a guide, the user can predict and test the effects of changes on the system).

Explanation in rule-based ES is usually associated with a way of tracing the rules that are fired during the course of a problem-solving session. This is about the closest to a real explanation that today's systems come, given that their knowledge is usually represented almost exclusively as rules that do not include basic principles necessary for a human-type explanation.

Programs such as MYCIN replay the exact rule used when asked for an explanation. DIGITAL ADVISOR is a slight improvement over this. Instead of feeding back the rule verbatim, ADVISOR determines the generic principle on which the rule is based (at that point in the consultation) and displays this general principle. Exsys provides the rules in the chain of reasoning leading to the conclusion that is hypothesized as the current goal.

In developing large ES, a good explanation facility is essential. Large ES always include more facts and rules than one can easily remember. Often, a new rule added during ES development interacts with other rules and data in unanticipated ways and can make the ES display strange explanations.

Explanation is an extremely important function because understanding depends on explanation, thus making implementation of proposed solutions easier. For example, an experiment conducted with auditors by Ye and Johnson (1995) indicated that ES explanation facilities can make a system's advice more acceptable to users. They also found that justification is the most effective type of ES explanation for bringing about a change in users' attitudes toward the system. Also, explanation is essential in ES used for training purposes.

To understand an event or a situation, you have to explain to yourself exactly what is going on, the role of every participant, and their actions. You need to know the goals of the participants, their intentions, and their potential behavior. Thus, constructing explanations can become a very complex task, especially when it is done by machines. For this reason, many of the explanation facilities available in development tools provide only two basic types of explanation: the *why* and the *how*.

WHY EXPLANATIONS

A typical *why* question is posed by the user to the computer after the computer asks the user to provide some information. For example, in an investment example (Section 13.3), we might have the following dialog:

> COMPUTER: What is your annual income?
> CLIENT: Why? (Why do you need to know?)

The computer displays rule 2 as a response. However, ideally we would like to see a reply like this:

> COMPUTER: In checking R2, I need to know whether your income is above $40,000. If this is true, I will conclude that because you have a college degree, you should invest in growth stocks.

The ES asks for this input when it is unable to find income information in the conclusion part of any rule. In the example cited, the computer actually backtracked to R3 and successfully arrived at a final conclusion.

HOW EXPLANATIONS

A typical *how* question is posed by users when they would like to know how a certain conclusion or recommendation was reached. Simple systems are limited to the final conclusion. More complex systems can handle intermediate conclusions as well. The system can explain why a certain rule was fired; that is, it shows the chain of rules used to reach the conclusion. In the investment problem, the *how* explanation might look like this:

COMPUTER:	Invest in IBM stocks.
CLIENT:	How? (How was the conclusion reached?)
COMPUTER:	(Displays the rules R5-R3-R7-R4 in the sequence that they were fired.)
IDEAL COMPUTER:	Given that you have $10,000 to invest and you are younger than 30, then according to R4 you have a college degree. If this is the case, then according to R1 you should invest in securities. For a young investor such as you, according to R3, you should invest in growth stocks if you are going to invest at all. Finally, according to R5, if you need to invest in growth stocks, then IBM is your best bet.

The *why* and *how* explanations often show the rules as they were programmed and not in a natural language. However, some systems have the ability to present these rules in a natural language.

OTHER EXPLANATIONS

Wick and Slagle (1989) expanded on the two basic questions by proposing a "journalistic" explanation facility. They view the user–system interaction as an event to be reported, much like a news story, which ideally includes the six elements *who, what, where, when, why,* and *how.* When an explanation facility is designed along these lines, all bases are covered.

Some sophisticated ES do supply other explanations. For example, some systems provide a limited *why not* capability. Let us assume that the system selects IBM as a growth stock. The user may ask, "Why not GE?" and the system may answer, "Because the annual growth rate of GE is only 7 percent, whereas that of IBM is 11 percent, using rule 78." Then, rule 78 might be displayed. This example illustrates a possible connection between the ES and a regular database. The computer may need to access a database to provide explanations.

There are special problems in explaining the reasoning process when rules are (automatically) induced. Such systems generally can display only the rules and leave the real explanation up to the user. Kim and Park (1996) developed a system that produces detailed explanations (see AIS in Action 13.4).

Explanation in non-rule-based systems is much more difficult than in rule-based ones because the inference procedures are more complex. For an overview of the topic of explanation, see Cawsey (1995). For recent advances, see *Expert Systems with Applications* and the special issue of *Explanation: The Way Forward,* Vol. 8., No. 4, 1995.

METAKNOWLEDGE

A system's knowledge about how it reasons is called **metaknowledge,** or *knowledge about knowledge.* The inference rules presented earlier are a special case of metaknowledge. Metaknowledge allows the system to examine the operation of the declarative and procedural knowledge in the knowledge base.

Explanation can be viewed as another aspect of metaknowledge. Over time, metaknowledge will allow ES to do even more. They will be able to create the rationale behind individual rules by reasoning from first principles. They will tailor their explana-

A NEW APPROACH FOR AUTOMATICALLY GENERATING MEANINGFUL ES EXPLANATIONS

Many commercial ES shells produce explanations by simply restating rules in the chain of inference. Researchers Sung Kun Kim and Jeong II Park developed a system that creates detailed explanations directly from the problem domain of which rules are automatically induced. The rules are based on important factors provided by an expert, instead of all the rules being acquired directly from an expert. Once the rules are acquired (in an object-oriented framework constructed as a decision tree that outlines the causalities), Kim and Park apply a (statistically based) structured equation modeling approach to the data that was originally used in the rule induction.

They used Korean Stock Market data to verify that the explanations were plausible, and 85 percent of the time they were. Now the scientists are working on refining the system to increase its accuracy, because "unless users are given an appropriate explanation of the system conclusion, the users' acceptance of the system would be severely degraded."

Enhancements of this induced explanation method should prove quite effective for ES for which the rules are obtained by mining large databases or sets of documents.

Source: Condensed and modified from Kim and Park (1996).

tions to fit the requirements of their audience. And they will be able to change their own internal structure through rule correction, reorganization of the knowledge base, and system reconfiguration.

There are different methods for generating explanations. One easy way is to preinsert pieces of English text (scripts) into the system. For example, each question that can be asked by the user can have an answer text associated with it. This is called a **static explanation.** Several problems are associated with static explanations. For example, all questions and answers must be anticipated in advance, and for large systems this is very difficult. Also, the system essentially has no idea about what it is saying. In the long run, the program might be modified without changing the text, thus causing inconsistency.

A better form of explanation is a **dynamic explanation,** which is reconstructed according to the execution pattern of the rules. With this method, the system reconstructs the reasons for its actions as it evaluates rules.

Most current explanation facilities fail to meet some of the objectives and requirements listed earlier. The following are some thoughts on this topic [based on Kidd and Cooper (1985) and communicated by A. Kidd to the authors].

Most ES explanation facilities consist of printing out a trace of the rules being used. Explanation is not treated as a task that requires intelligence in itself. If ES are to provide satisfactory explanations, future systems must include not only knowledge of how to solve problems in their respective domains but also knowledge of how to effectively communicate to users their understanding of this problem-solving process. Obviously, the balance between these two types of knowledge varies according to the primary function of the system. Constructing such knowledge bases involves formalizing the heuristics used in providing good explanations.

With current ES, much of the knowledge vital to providing a good explanation (such as knowledge about the system's problem-solving strategy) is not expressed explicitly in the rules. Therefore, the purely rule-based representation may be difficult to grasp, especially when the relationships between the rules are not made explicit in the explanation. Kidd and Cooper (1985) have developed an explanation facility that can show the inference tree and the parts of it that are relevant to specific queries, thus overcoming some of the deficiencies cited earlier.

In keeping with Kidd's concepts of explanation, Ye and Johnson (1995) provide a categorization of the explanation methods. They provide a *typology of ES explanations* which include the following:

- *Trace* or *line of reasoning,* which refers to a record of the inferential steps taken by an ES to reach a conclusion
- *Justification,* which is an explicit description of the causal argument or rationale behind each inferential step taken by the ES (based on the empirical associations involving the encoding of large chunks of knowledge)
- *Strategy,* which is a high-level goal structure that determines how the ES uses its domain knowledge to accomplish a task (or metaknowledge).

Justification requires a deeper understanding of the domain than the trace method does because by demonstrating that the conclusions developed by the system are based on sound reasoning, it increases the confidence of ES users in the problem-solving ability of the system and hence the acceptability of the conclusions. Because ES can achieve high performance levels only within narrow problem areas, justification enables users to make more informed decisions on whether the advice is to be followed. Strategy involves knowledge about the problem-solving procedure. Generally, the last two explanation types are more difficult to incorporate in an ES because strategic knowledge tends to be buried implicitly in the knowledge base and an ES does not need an explicit representation of justification knowledge to execute (Ye and Johnson, 1995). Future ES may provide these advanced explanation capabilities.

13.9 INFERENCING WITH UNCERTAINTY

Uncertainty in AI can be treated as a three-step process [according to Parsaye and Chignell (1988)], as shown in Figure 13.5. In step 1 an expert provides inexact knowledge in terms of rules with likelihood values. These rules can be numeric (such as a probability value), graphical, or symbolic ("It is most likely that").

FIGURE 13.5 THREE-STEP PROCESS FOR DEALING WITH UNCERTAINTY IN AI

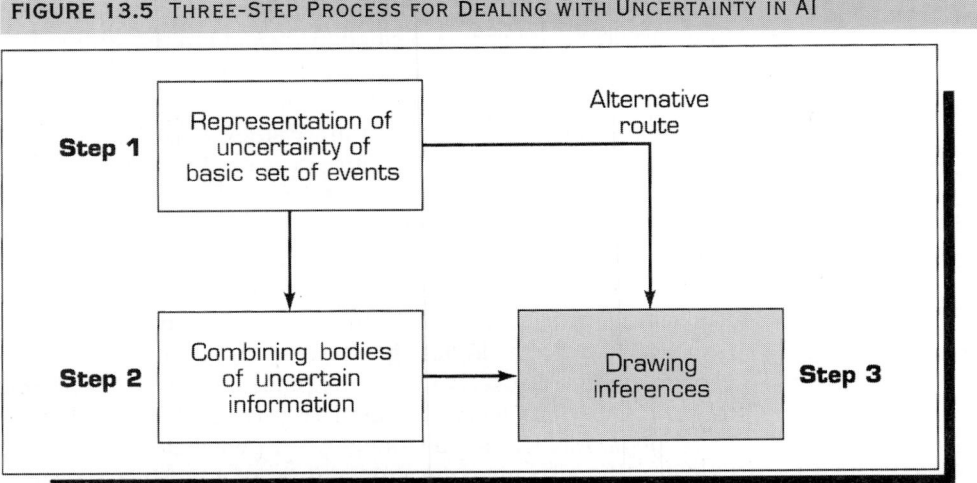

In step 2, the inexact knowledge of the basic set of events can be directly used to draw inferences in simple cases (step 3). However, in many cases the various events are interrelated. Therefore, it is necessary to combine the information provided in step 1 into a global value for the system. Several methods can be used for such integration. The major methods are Bayesian probabilities, theory of evidence, certainty factors, and fuzzy sets.

In step 3, the purpose of the knowledge-based system is to draw inferences. These are derived from the inexact knowledge of steps 1 and 2, and usually they are implemented with the inference engine. Working with the inference engine, experts can adjust the input they give in step 1 after viewing the results in steps 2 and 3.

THE IMPORTANCE OF UNCERTAINTY

Although uncertainty is widespread in the real world, its treatment in the practical world of AI is very limited. As a matter of fact, many real-world knowledge-based systems completely avoid the issue of uncertainty. People feel that it is not necessary to represent uncertainty in dealing with uncertain knowledge. Why is this so?

The answer given by practitioners is very simple. Even though they recognize the problem of uncertainty, they feel that none of the methods available are accurate or consistent enough to handle the situation. In fact, some knowledge engineers have experimented with several proposed methods for dealing with uncertainty and have either found no significant difference from treating the situation as being under assumed certainty or found large differences among the results when they used different methods. Does this mean that **uncertainty avoidance** is the best approach and that this material should be deleted from this book? Certainly not!

Uncertainty is a serious problem. Avoiding it may not be the best strategy. Instead, we need to improve the methods for dealing with uncertainty. Theoreticians must realize that many of the concepts presented in this chapter are foreign to many practitioners. Even structured methods, such as the Bayesian formula, seem extremely strange and complex to many people.

13.10 REPRESENTING UNCERTAINTY

The three basic methods of representing uncertainty are numeric, graphical, and symbolic.

NUMERIC

The most common method of representing uncertainty is numeric, using a scale with two extreme numbers. For example, 0 can be used to represent complete uncertainty, while 1 or 100 represents complete certainty. Although such representation seems trivial to some people (maybe because it is similar to the representation of probabilities), it is very difficult for others.

In addition to the difficulties of using numbers, there are problems with cognitive bias. For example, experts figure the numbers based on their own experience and are influenced by their own perceptions. For a discussion of these biases, see Parsaye and Chignell (1988). Finally, people may be inconsistent in providing numeric values at different times.

GRAPHICAL AND INFLUENCE DIAGRAMS

Although many experts can describe uncertainty in terms of numbers, such as "It is 85 percent certain that," some have difficulties in doing so. By using horizontal bars, for example, it is possible to help experts express their confidence in certain events. Such a bar is shown in Figure 13.6. Experts are asked to place markers somewhere on the scale. Thus, expert A expresses very little confidence in the likelihood of inflation, whereas expert B is more confident that inflation is coming.

Even though graphical presentation is preferred by some experts, graphs are not as accurate as numbers. Another problem is that most experts do not have experience in marking graphical scales (or setting numbers on the scale). Many experts, especially managers, prefer *ranking* (which is symbolic) over either graphical or numeric methods.

One form of graphical presentation is influence diagrams, which were presented in Chapter 5. Gottinger and Weimann (1995) describe influence diagram inference techniques for logical probabilistic and decision theoretic reasoning. In an alternative but similar graphical representation of knowledge, Shafer (1996) describes the propagation of probabilities in join trees.

SYMBOLIC

There are several ways to represent uncertainty by using symbols. Many experts use a Likert scale to express their opinion. For example, an expert may be asked to assess the likelihood of inflation on a five-point scale: very unlikely, unlikely, neutral, likely, and very likely. Ranking is a very popular approach among experts with nonquantitative preferences. Ranking can be either ordinal (i.e., listing of items in order of importance) or cardinal (ranking complemented by numeric values). Managers are especially comfortable with ordinal ranking. When the number of items to be ranked is large, people may have a problem with ranking and also tend to be inconsistent. One method that can be used to alleviate this problem is a pairwise comparison combined with a consistency checker; that is, rank the items two at a time and check for consistencies. One methodology for such ranking, the *Analytical Hierarchy Process,* was described in Chapter 5. For further discussion of ranking, see Parsaye and Chignell (1988).

The method of fuzzy logic, presented in Chapter 18, includes a special symbolic representation combined with numbers.

Symbolic representation methods are often combined with numbers or converted to numeric values. For example, it is customary to give a weight of 1 to 5 to the five options on a Likert-like scale.

FIGURE 13.6 CONFIDENCE SCALE ABOUT THE OCCURRENCE OF INFLATION

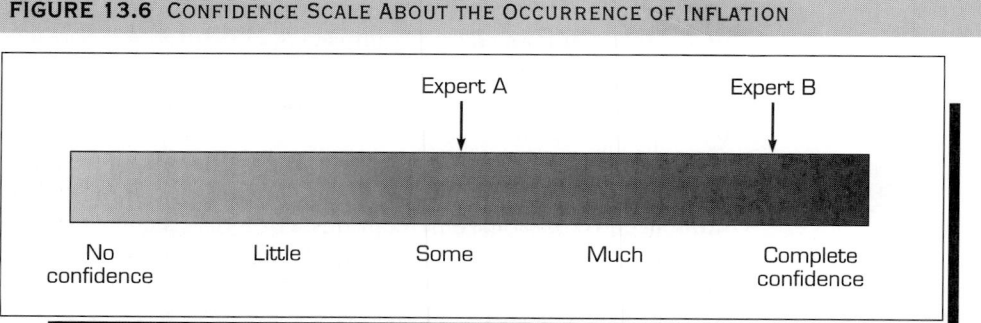

13.11 PROBABILITIES AND RELATED APPROACHES

THE PROBABILITY RATIO

The degree of confidence in a premise or a conclusion can be expressed as a probability. *Probability* is the chance that a particular event will occur (or not occur). It is a ratio computed as follows:

$$P(X) = \frac{\text{Number of outcomes favoring the occurrence of X}}{\text{Total number of outcomes}}$$

The probability of X occurring, stated as $P(X)$, is the ratio of the number of times X occurs to the total number of events that take place.

Multiple probability values occur in many systems. For example, a rule can have an antecedent with three parts, each with a probability value. The overall probability of the rule can be computed as the product of the individual probabilities if the parts of the antecedent are independent of one another. In a three-part antecedent, the probabilities may be .9, .7, and .65, and the overall probability is

$$P = (.9)(.7)(.65) = .4095$$

The combined probability is about 41 percent. But this is true only if the individual parts of the antecedent do not affect or interrelate with one another.

Sometimes one rule references another. Here, the individual rule probabilities can propagate from one to another, and so we must evaluate the total probability of a sequence of rules or a path through the search tree to determine whether a specific rule fires. Or we may be able to use the combined probabilities to predict the best path through the search tree.

In knowledge-based systems, there are several methods for combining probabilities. For example, they can be multiplied (i.e., joint probabilities) or averaged (using a simple or a weighted average); in other instances, only the highest or lowest values are considered. In all such cases, rules and events are considered independent of each other. If there are dependencies in the system, the Bayes extension theorem can be used.

THE BAYESIAN EXTENSION

Bayes' theorem is a mechanism for combining new and existent evidence, usually given as subjective probabilities. It is used to revise existing *prior probabilities* based on new information.

The Bayesian approach is based on **subjective probabilities;** a subjective probability is provided for each proposition. If E is the evidence (sum of all information available to the system), then each proposition P has associated with it a value representing the probability that P holds in light of all the evidence $E,$ derived by using Bayesian inference. Bayes' theorem provides a way of computing the probability of a particular event given some set of observations we have already made. The main point here is not how this value is derived but that what we know or have inferred about a proposition is represented by a single value for its likelihood.

This approach has two major deficiencies. The first is that the single value does not tell us much about its precision, which may be very low when the value is derived from uncertain evidence. To say that the probability of a proposition being true in a given situation is .5 (in a range of 0–1) usually refers to an *average* figure that is true within a given range. For example, .5 plus or minus .001 is completely different from .5 plus or minus .3, yet both can be reported as .5. The second deficiency is that the single value combines the evidence for and against a proposition without indicating the individual value of each.

The subjective probability expresses the degree of belief, or how strongly a value or a situation is believed to be true. The Bayesian approach, with or without new evidence, can be diagrammed as a network.

DEMPSTER–SHAFER THEORY OF EVIDENCE

The Dempster–Shafer theory of evidence is a well-known procedure for reasoning with uncertainty in artificial intelligence. [For details see Shafer (1976) and Yager et al. (1994).] It can be considered an extension of the Bayesian approach.

The Dempster–Shafer approach distinguishes between uncertainty and ignorance by creating **belief functions.** Belief functions allow us to use our knowledge to bound the assignment of probabilities when these boundaries are unavailable.

The Dempster–Shafer approach is especially appropriate for combining expert opinions because experts differ in their opinions with a certain degree of ignorance and, in many situations, at least some *epistemic information* (i.e., information constructed from vague perceptions). The Dempster–Shafer theory can be used to handle epistemic information as well as ignorance or lack of information. Unfortunately, it assumes that the sources of information to be combined are statistically independent of each other. In reality, there are many situations in which the knowledge of experts overlaps; that is, there are dependencies among sources of information. For such cases, extensions such as those proposed by Ling and Rudd (1989) are necessary.

13.12 THEORY OF CERTAINTY (CERTAINTY FACTORS)

CERTAINTY FACTORS AND BELIEFS

Standard statistical methods are based on the assumption that an uncertainty is the probability that an event (or fact) is true or false. In **certainty theory,** as well as in fuzzy logic, uncertainty is represented as a *degree of belief.* There are two steps in using every nonprobabilistic method of uncertainty. First, it is necessary to be able to express the degree of belief. Second, it is necessary to manipulate (combine, for example) degrees of belief when using knowledge-based systems.

Certainty theory relies on the use of certainty factors. **Certainty factors (CFs)** express belief in an event (or fact or hypothesis) based on evidence (or on the expert's assessment). There are several methods of using certainty factors in handling uncertainty in knowledge-based systems. One way is to use 1.0 or 100 for absolute truth (complete confidence) and 0 for certain falsehood. These certainty factors are not probabilities. For example, when we say there is a 90 percent chance of rain, then there is either rain (90 percent) or no rain (10 percent). In a nonprobabilistic approach, we can say that a certainty factor of 90 for rain means that it is very likely to rain. It does not necessarily mean that we express any opinion about our argument of no rain (which is not necessarily 10). Thus, certainty factors *do not* have to sum up to 100.

Certainty theory introduces the concepts of belief and **disbelief.** These concepts are independent of each other and so cannot be combined in the same way as probabilities, but they can be combined according to the following formula:

$$CF(P,E) = MB(P,E) - MD(P,E)$$

where

$$CF = \text{certainty factor}$$
$$MB = \text{measure of belief}$$
$$MD = \text{measure of disbelief}$$
$$P = \text{probability}$$
$$E = \text{evidence or event}$$

Another assumption of certainty theory is that the knowledge content of rules is much more important than the algebra of confidences that holds the system together. Confidence measures correspond to the information evaluations that human experts attach to their conclusions, for example, "It is probably true" or "It is highly unlikely."

COMBINING CERTAINTY FACTORS

Certainty factors can be used to combine different estimates of experts in several ways. Before using any ES shell, make sure that you understand how certainty factors are combined [for an overview see Kopcso et al. (1988)]. The most acceptable way of combining them in rule-based systems is the method used in EMYCIN. In this approach, we distinguish between two cases, described next.

COMBINING SEVERAL CERTAINTY FACTORS IN ONE RULE
Consider this rule with an AND operator:

IF inflation is high, CF = 50 percent (A) AND
 unemployment rate is above 7 percent, CF = 70 percent (B)
AND
 bond prices decline, CF = 100 percent (C)
THEN stock prices decline.

For this type of rule, for the conclusion to be true, *all IFs must be true,* but in some cases there is uncertainty as to what is happening. Then, the CF of the conclusion is the minimum CF on the IF side:

$$CF(A, B, C) = \text{minimum}[CF(A), CF(B), CF(C)]$$

Thus, in our case, the CF for stock prices to decline is 50 percent. In other words, the chain is as strong as its weakest link.

Now look at this rule with an OR operator:

IF inflation is low, CF = 70 percent; OR
 bond prices are high, CF = 85 percent;
THEN stock prices will be high.

In this case it is sufficient that only one of the IFs is true for the conclusion to be true. Thus, if *both* IFs are believed to be true (at their certainty factor), then the conclusion will have a CF with the maximum of the two:

$$CF (A \text{ or } B) = \text{maximum } [CF (A), CF (B)]$$

In our case, CF = 85 percent for stock prices to be high. Note that both cases hold for any number of IFs.

COMBINING TWO OR MORE RULES
Why might rules be combined? There may be several ways to reach the same goal, each with different CFs for a given set of facts. When we have a knowledge-based system with several interrelated rules, each of which makes the same conclusion but with a different

certainty factor, then each rule can be viewed as a piece of evidence that supports the joint conclusion. To calculate the certainty factor (or the confidence) of the conclusion, it is necessary to combine the evidence, which is done as follows:

Let's assume there are two rules:

R1:   IF the inflation rate is less than 5 percent
      THEN stock market prices go up (CF = 0.7)

R2:   IF the unemployment level is less than 7 percent
      THEN stock market prices go up (CF = 0.6).

Now, let's assume it is predicted that during the next year the inflation rate will be 4 percent and the unemployment level will be 6.5 percent (i.e., we assume that the premises of the two rules are true). The combined effect is computed as

$$
\begin{aligned}
CF(R1,R2) &= CF(R1) + [CF(R2)] \times [1 - CF(R1)] \\
&= CF(R1) + CF(R2) - [CF(R1)] \times [CF(R2)]
\end{aligned}
$$

In probabilistic terms, when we combine two dependent probabilities (joint probabilities), we get

$$
CF(R1,R2) = [CF(R1)] \times [CF(R2)]
$$

Here, we have deleted this value from the sum of the two certainty factors, assuming an independent relationship between the rules. For example,

$$
\text{Given } CF(R1) = 0.7 \text{ AND } CF(R2) = 0.6,
$$

$$
CF(R1,R2) = 0.7 + 0.6 - (0.7)(0.6) = 0.88
$$

That is, the ES tells us that there is an 88 percent chance that stock prices will increase.

Note: If we just added the CFs of R1 and R2, their combined certainty would be larger than 1. We modify the amount of certainty added by the second certainty factor by multiplying it by (1 minus the first certainty factor). Thus, the greater the first CF, the less the certainty added by the second. But additional factors always add some certainty.

For a third rule to be added, the following formula can be used:

$$
\begin{aligned}
CF(R1,R2,R3) &= CF(R1,R2) + [CF(R3)] [1 - CF(R1,R2)] \\
&= CF(R1,R2) + CF(R3) - [CF(R1,R2)][CF(R3)]
\end{aligned}
$$

Assume a third rule is added:

R3:   IF bond price increases,
      THEN stock prices go up (CF = 0.85).

Now, assuming all the rules are true in their IF part, the chance that stock prices will go up is

$$
CF(R1,R2,R3) = 0.88 + 0.85 - (0.88)(0.85) = 0.982
$$

That is, there is a 98.2 percent chance that stock prices will go up. Note that CF(R1,R2) was computed earlier as 0.88. For a situation with more rules, we can apply the same formula incrementally.

See Russell and Norvig (1995) for more information on uncertainty and probabilistic ES.

13.13 APPROXIMATE REASONING USING FUZZY LOGIC

Fuzzy logic offers a theory of uncertainty for dealing with quantifying and reasoning using imprecise and uncertain values. **Fuzzy logic,** in a narrow sense, is a logical system that aims at formalizing **approximate reasoning** process. In a broader sense, it also includes fuzzy set theory and its various branches (e.g., fuzzy arithmetic, fuzzy mathematical programming, fuzzy topology) (Zadeh, 1994).

As a knowledge representation technique, fuzzy rules define the mapping of input variables with precise or imprecise values to output variables with precise values. The partial set of rules listed below define a mapping of input variables SYSTEM-SIZE and COMPLEXITY to the output variable EFFORT-REQUIRED for building an information system of a given system size and complexity. Linguistic values (e.g., *LARGE*, *HIGH*, *MEDIUM*) of the variables are defined using membership functions to capture imprecision (Figure 13.7).

Rule 1:   if SYSTEM-SIZE is *LARGE* and COMPLEXITY is *HIGH*
          then EFFORT-REQUIRED is very HIGH.

Rule 2:   if SYSTEM-SIZE is *LARGE* and COMPLEXITY is *MEDIUM*
          then EFFORT-REQUIRED is *HIGH*.

Fuzzy reasoning is the process of making logical inferences based on a given set of fuzzy rules and a set of inputs corresponding to the variables on the IF side of the rules. The input variable values (e.g., SYSTEM-SIZE = 750 KLOC, COMPLEXITY = 7) determine a set of applicable fuzzy rules. Each applicable rule in this set, with its level of

FIGURE 13.7 FUZZY MEMBERSHIP FUNCTIONS REPRESENTING LINGUISTIC VALUES

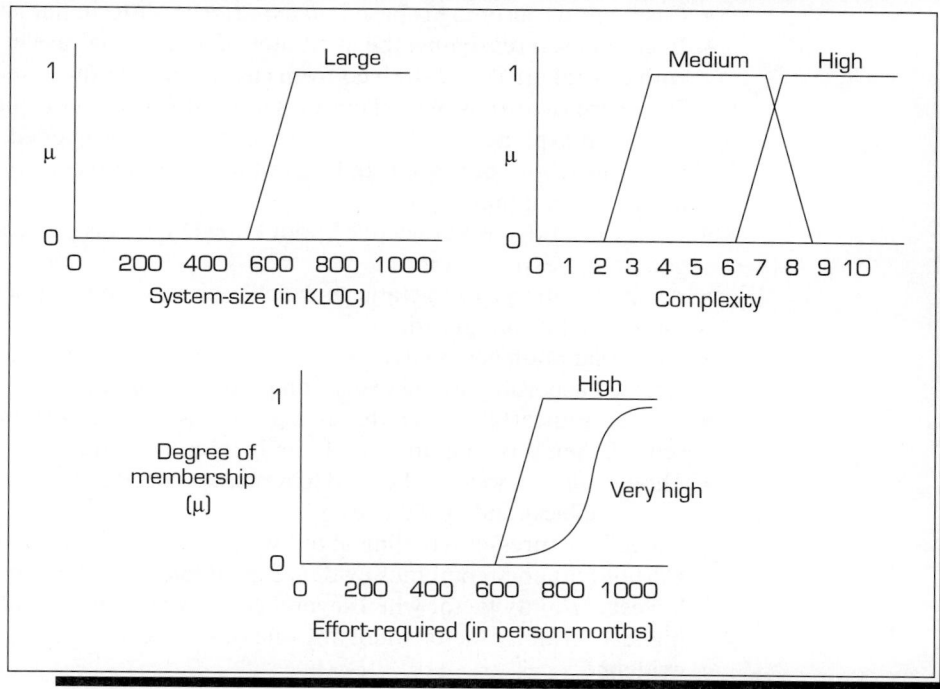

applicability, will result in a temporary fuzzy set that corresponds to the linguistic value of the variable in the consequence part of the rule. All the resulting temporary fuzzy sets will determine the final shape of a fuzzy set that represents the output variable value. A precise value for the output variable (e.g., EFFORT = 565 person-months) is obtained using a **defuzzification** process.

Chapter 17 presents further details on fuzzy logic–based systems. For more details on approximate reasoning using fuzzy logic and its applications, see Munakata and Jani (1994), Zadeh (1994), Harmon (1993), Dubois and Prade (1995), Cox and Terlaga (1992), Machacha and Bhattacharya (2000), and Li (2000).

❖ CHAPTER HIGHLIGHTS

- Several methods can direct searching and reasoning. The major ones are chaining (backward and forward), model-based reasoning, and case-based reasoning.
- Analogical reasoning relates past experiences to a current case.
- Modus ponens is a reasoning procedure that says that in an IF-THEN rule, if one part is true, so is the other.
- Testing rules to find whether they are true or false is based on a pattern-matching approach.
- In backward chaining, the search starts from a specific goal. You seek evidence that supports (or contradicts) the acceptance of your goal. Then, depending on your application of the rules, whether your goal is contradicted or accepted, you can try another goal.
- In forward chaining, the search starts from the facts (evidence) and you try to arrive at one or more conclusions.
- The chaining process can be described graphically by an inference tree.
- Inferencing with frames often involves the use of rules.
- In model-based reasoning, a model describes the system. Experimentations are conducted using a what-if approach to solve the problem.
- Case-based reasoning is based on experience with similar situations.
- In case-based reasoning, the attributes of an existing case are compared with critical attributes derived from cases stored in the case library.
- There are two types of explanations in most ES: the *why* question, which requests an explanation of why certain information is needed; and the *how* question, whose purpose is to find out how a certain conclusion was arrived at by the computer.
- Metaknowledge is knowledge about knowledge. It is especially useful in generating explanations.
- An explanation can be static, in which case a canned response is available for a specific configuration.
- An explanation can be dynamic, in which case the explanation is reconstructed according to the execution pattern of the rules.
- AI treats uncertainty as a three-step process: First uncertainty is represented, then it is combined, and finally inferences are drawn.
- Three basic methods can be used to represent uncertainty: numeric (probability-like), graphical, and qualitative.
- Disbelief expresses a feeling about what is *not* going to occur.
- Certainty theory combines evidence available in one rule by seeking the lowest certainty factor when several certainty factors are added, and the highest certainty factor when any one of several factors is used to establish evidence.

- Certainty theory uses a special formula to combine evidence available in two or more rules.
- Fuzzy logic provides a theory of uncertainty concerned with quantifying and reasoning with imprecise and uncertain values.

❖ KEY WORDS

- analogical reasoning
- approximate reasoning
- backtracking
- backward chaining
- belief function
- case-based reasoning (CBR)
- case library
- certainty factor (CF)
- certainty theory
- component model
- deductive reasoning
- defuzzification
- disbelief

- dynamic explanation
- expectation-driven processing
- explanation facility
- firing a rule
- forward chaining
- fuzzy logic
- hierarchical reasoning
- inductive reasoning
- inference engine
- inference tree
- justifier
- mathematical model
- metaknowledge

- model-based reasoning
- modus ponens
- modus tollens
- pattern matching
- procedural (numeric) reasoning
- resolution
- rule interpreter
- script
- static explanation
- subjective probability
- temporal reasoning
- uncertainty
- uncertainty avoidance

❖ QUESTIONS FOR REVIEW

1. List the nine sources of power. How are they related to problem solving?
2. Define deductive reasoning and contrast it with inductive reasoning.
3. What is meant when we say that a rule fires?
4. Define pattern matching. Explain how it is used in rule chaining.
5. Explain why backward chaining is considered goal-driven.
6. Explain why forward chaining is considered data-driven.
7. Explain the difference between an AND and an OR operation in a rule.
8. Define backward chaining and contrast it with forward chaining.
9. What is an inference tree? What is its major purpose?
10. Explain this statement: Reasoning with frames may involve hierarchical reasoning.
11. Define model-based reasoning.
12. Define case-based reasoning.
13. List five advantages of case-based reasoning.
14. Review the case-based reasoning process. Briefly discuss each step.
15. List some of the purposes of the explanation capability.
16. In current expert systems explanation is accomplished by tracing the rules. Discuss how it is executed.
17. What is the *why* question? What is a typical computer reply to this type of question?
18. What is the *how* question? What is a typical computer reply to this type of question?
19. What is the journalistic view of an explanation system?
20. What is metaknowledge? How is it related to the explanation facility?
21. Define static explanation.
22. Why can knowledge be inexact?
23. Describe the general process of dealing with uncertainty.
24. Describe how approximate reasoning is performed using fuzzy rules.

❖ QUESTIONS FOR DISCUSSION

1. Describe analogical reasoning. How is it related to case-based reasoning?

2. What are some of the potential problems with the qualitative method of representing uncertainty?

3. It is said that chaining (backward or forward) is an implementation of modus ponens. Why?

4. Certainty factors are popular in rule-based systems. Why? What unique features does the theory of uncertainty provide?

5. Discuss the major deficiencies of existing explanation facilities. Organize your discussion as a comparison with a potential explanation given by a human.

6. The explanation facility serves the user as well as the developer. Discuss the benefits derived by each.

7. If you had a dialog with a human expert, what questions besides "Why?" and "How?" would you be likely to ask? Give examples.

8. It is said that reasoning with frames almost always involves rules. Explain why.

9. What is meant by reasoning from first principles? Give an example. Give an example of *not* reasoning from a first principle.

10. Summarize the major advantages of model-based reasoning. When would you use it?

11. Comment on this statement: An understander of the world is an explainer of the world.

12. Describe the relationship between metaknowledge and explanations.

13. List and discuss some of the potential problems of using case-based reasoning.

14. Explain the basic premise of case-based reasoning.

15. Explain the relationship between scripts and case-based reasoning.

16. Compare rule-based and case-based reasoning.

17. Which applications are most suitable for case-based reasoning? Why?

18. Explain why the six elements *who, what, when, where, why,* and *how* produce a much better explanation capability than that present in most ES.

19. Provide an example that shows why numeric presentation of uncertainty is difficult or even impossible.

20. What are the advantages of the graphical representation of uncertainty? What are the disadvantages?

21. What is the role of belief functions in the theory of evidence?

22. What is degree of disbelief? Give an example.

23. Why does one select a minimum value when using an AND operator and a maximum value when using an OR operator in combining certainty factors?

❖ EXERCISES

1. You are given a set of rules for this question: Should we buy a house or not?
   R1: IF inflation is low,
        THEN interest rates are low,
        ELSE interest rates are high.
   R2: IF interest rates are high,
        THEN housing prices are high.
   R3: IF housing prices are high,
        THEN do not buy a house,
        ELSE buy a house.
       a. Run backward chaining with a high inflation rate as given.
       b. Run forward chaining with a low inflation rate as given.
       c. Prepare an inference tree for the backward chaining case.

2. You are given an ES with the following rules:

R1: IF interest rates fall,
THEN bond prices will increase.

R2: IF interest rates increase,
THEN bond prices will decline.

R3: IF interest rates are unchanged,
THEN bond prices will remain unchanged.

R4: IF the dollar rises (against other currencies),
THEN interest rates will decline.

R5: IF the dollar falls,
THEN interest rates will increase.

R6: IF bond prices decline,
THEN buy bonds.

    a. A client has just observed that the dollar exchange rate is falling. He wants to know whether to buy bonds. Run a forward and a backward chaining and submit a report to him.

    b. Prepare an inference tree for the backward chaining you did.

    c. A second client observed that interest rates are unchanged. She asks for advice on investing in bonds. What will the ES tell her? Use forward chaining.

3. Assume you plan to drive from New York to Los Angeles to arrive mid-afternoon for an appointment. You want to drive no more than 2 hours the day you arrive, but on other days you're willing to drive 8–10 hours. One logical way to approach this problem is to start at Los Angeles, your goal, and work backward. First you find a place about 2 hours from Los Angeles for your final stopover before arrival and then plan the rest of your trip by working backward on a map until your route is completely planned. You have a limited number of days to complete the trip. Analyze and solve this problem using a road map of the United States.

    How would you analyze the problem starting from New York? What are the major differences? Which approach would you use? Why? Solve this problem using a road map of the United States.

4. You are given an expert system with seven rules pertaining to the interpersonal skills of a job applicant:

R1: IF the applicant answers questions in a straightforward manner,
THEN she is easy to converse with.

R2: IF the applicant seems honest,
THEN she answers in a straightforward manner.

R3: IF the applicant has items on her resume that are found to be untrue,
THEN she does not seem honest,
ELSE she seems honest.

R4: IF the applicant is able to arrange an appointment with the executive assistant,
THEN she is able to strike up a conversation with the executive assistant.

R5: IF the applicant strikes up a conversation with the executive assistant and the applicant is easy to converse with,
THEN she is amiable.

R6: IF the applicant is amiable,
THEN she has adequate interpersonal skills.

R7: IF the applicant has adequate interpersonal skills,
THEN we will offer her the job.

Solve the following three *independent* cases:

    a. Assume that the applicant does not have any items on her resume that are found to be untrue and that she is able to arrange an appointment with the executive assistant. Run a forward chaining analysis to find out whether we will offer her the job.

      b. It is known that the applicant answers questions in a straightforward manner. Run a backward chaining analysis to find out whether we will offer the applicant the job.

      c. We have just discovered that the applicant was able to arrange an appointment with the executive assistant. It is also known that she is honest. Does she have interpersonal skills?

5. Given the following two sets of statements and conclusions, what type of reasoning was used to arrive at the conclusions?

Case **a:** Students who do not study do not pass exams. Nancy is a student.

Nancy did not study.

Conclusion: Nancy will not pass her exam.

Case **b:** Jack did not study for the exam. Jack is a student. Jack did not pass the exam.

Conclusion: Students who do not study do not pass exams.

6. Review the message classification example in the case-based Section 13.7. Compare the steps to Figure 13.4 and discuss.

7. You are given the following rules:

R1: IF inflation is high,
     THEN unemployment is high.

R2: IF inflation is high and interest rates are high,
     THEN stock prices are low.

R3: IF the price of gold is high or the dollar exchange rate is low,
     THEN stock prices are low.

R4: IF the price of gold is high,
     THEN unemployment is high.

Conduct the following computations and list the rules used:

      a. The certainty factor for high inflation is 0.8, and for high interest rates it is 0.6. Find the certainty factor for stock prices.

      b. The certainty factor for a high gold price is 0.5, and that for a low dollar exchange rate is 0.7. Find the certainty factor for stock prices.

      c. Given all the information in parts (a) and (b), compute the certainty factor for low stock prices and for high stock prices.

      d. Figure the certainty factor for a high unemployment rate given that the inflation rate is high and the price of gold is high. Use the data in parts (a) and (b).

8. You are given the following three rules:

R1: IF blood test results yes,
     THEN there is 0.8 evidence that the disease is malaria.

R2: IF in malaria zone yes,
     THEN there is 0.5 evidence that the disease is malaria.

R3: IF bit by flying bug is true,
     THEN there is 0.3 evidence that the disease is malaria.

What certainty factors for having malaria will be computed by the expert system if

      a. The first two rules are considered to be true.

      b. All three rules are considered to be true.

9. You are given the following rules:

R1: IF you study hard, THEN you will receive an A in the course. CF 0.82.

R2: IF you understand the material, THEN you will receive an A in the course. CF 0.82.

R3: IF you are very smart, THEN you will receive an A in the course. CF 0.90.

      a. What is the certainty of getting an A in the course if you study hard and understand the material?

      b. What is the certainty of getting an A in the course if all the premises of the rules are true?

10. Uncertainty avoidance is a strategy used by many builders of knowledge-based systems. Review the literature or conduct an interview with a builder. Prepare statements for and against uncertainty avoidance.

11. You are given the following information (problem provided by E. Rivers):
    - Brenda is younger than the dancer, who lives directly west of Ginny.
    - The dancer lives directly north of Ms. Quinn, who lives exactly 5 miles from Helen, who lives exactly 2 miles from the singer.
    - The pianist is older than Ms. Chadwick, and Cindy is older than the actress.
    - Helen is older than Ms. Howell, who lives exactly 3 miles from Ginny, who lives directly south of Ms. Bien.

    The fact that all four women are delightful people has nothing to do with the solution to the following questions.
    a. Represent this knowledge using two of the methods described in this chapter.
    b. Explain your rationale for selecting the two methods you chose.
    c. What inferencing method would need to be used with each of the two representation methods you selected to answer the following questions?
    - How far does Cindy live from Brenda?
    - Which woman is the oldest?
    d. What are your answers to the question in part (c)?
    e. Of the two methods you selected, which do you prefer (based on your answers to parts (c) and (d))? Explain your rationale.

❖ GROUP EXERCISES

1. Produce a group report on the merits of the different inferencing schemes found in the literature and on the Internet. Identify emerging methods and describe how they work and what the future holds for them.

2. For the real-world decision-making problem in the Group Term Project in Chapter 14, consider representing the knowledge in a semantic network and in a case-based framework. Which method seems to be the easiest to encode and why?

❖ INTERNET EXERCISES

1. Explore the Web to find ES shell vendors. Identify two that have downloadable demos. Download, install, and run the demos. How do they compare in terms of capabilities? What uncertainty method do they use (if any)?

2. Access the Ginesys Corporation Web site (www.ginesys.com). Examine its help desk software and determine how it represents knowledge and performs inferencing. How does it compare to the material in this chapter?

3. Access the Web sites of Inference Corporation or Cognitive Systems and find information about their case-based reasoning products. Try a demo, if available, and compare it to standard, rule-based ES methods.

4. Access the University of Kaiserslauten's case-based reasoning Web site (www.agr.informatik.uni-kl.de/~Isa/cbr/cbr-homepage.html). Examine the latest CBR research and demo software. How is CBR different from rule-based concepts? Try some reasoning software, compare the method to rule-based inferencing, and write up your experience in a report.

5. Case-based reasoning has been used lately for data mining. Explore the Web to find vendors and research literature about this topic.

6. Identify a news group that is interested in case-based reasoning. Post a question regarding recent successful applications. What are the latest concerns and questions?

7. Search the Web to find out what is new in model-based reasoning.
8. Visit the Web site www.surveying.salford.ac.uk/kbe/ hosting a "My Car Won't Start" expert system. Discuss the differences among decision trees, production rules, and case-based reasoning approaches used for reasoning in this expert system.

CASE APPLICATION 13.1

COMPAQ QUICKSOURCE: USING CASE-BASED REASONING FOR PROBLEM DETERMINATION[4]

Compaq Inc. is one of the largest manufacturers of PCs. To help its customers, the company developed an electronic problem solver and information system for Compaq's line of network printers. This expert system was built with case-based reasoning technology. The system's main purpose is to allow customers to solve advanced network printer problems entirely on their own. The product is called QuickSource, and the case-based reasoning module is called QuickSolve. The product is used to assist Compaq's customer support representatives and is given to customers as well.

QuickSource contains five modules:

- *Quick Tour* provides a guided tour of printer capabilities and features.
- *Quick Config* provides online support for printer installation and configuration.
- *QuickHelp* provides online documentation on maintenance procedures and general information.
- *QuickSolve* provides intelligent troubleshooting analysis and advice.
- *Quick Tutorial* provides an online tutorial on how to use QuickSolve.

QUICKSOLVE ARCHITECTURE

- QuickSolve was case-based–developed using Inference Corporation's CBR Express tool. It contains 500 cases.

- Each case consists of a title, a description field that describes the case's symptoms in a natural language, a question area, and a solution section.
- Compaq's customers can either key in a problem description or select a problem category, drill down to a subcategory, and drill down further until the detailed problem is found.
- QuickSolve provides solutions to printer problems in both text and graphical formats.
- QuickSolve asks the user a series of questions. When sufficient information has been acquired by QuickSolve, it recommends specific actions to resolve the problem.

A screen shot from QuickSolve is shown in Figure 13.8.

BENEFITS OF QUICKSOURCE

- Calls to Compaq's customer service center have, by conservative estimates, been reduced by 20 percent (a possible savings of $10 million to $20 million per year).
- QuickSource has increased customer satisfaction. Customers now obtain answers to their problems more quickly.
- QuickSource has been a good training tool for Compaq's new customer support representatives.
- QuickSource provides Compaq with a market differentiator. It has become an extremely effective competitive tool.

---

[4]Based on T. Nguyen et al., "Compaq QuickSource," *Proceedings: 1993, Fifth Annual Conference on Innovative Applications of Artificial Intelligence,* American Association of Artificial Intelligence, Menlo Park, CA, 1993.

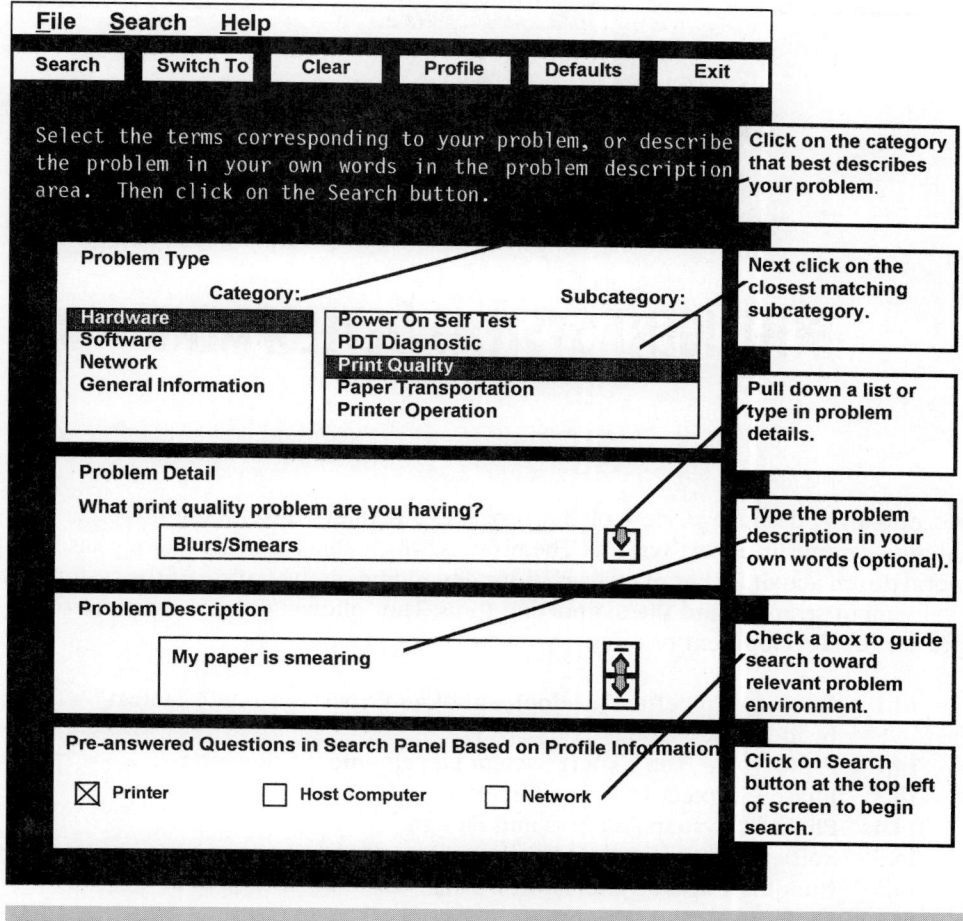

FIGURE 13.8 SCREEN EXAMPLE FROM A QUICKSOLVE PANEL

Source: Inference Corp., Novato, CA.

CASE QUESTIONS

1. How can QuickSource empower Compaq's customers?
2. How is the system matching the problem description to the case base?
3. What are the benefits of the system to the customers? To Compaq?

4. How can QuickSolve provide a competitive advantage to Compaq?
5. When problems are really hard or QuickSolve cannot determine a recommendation, what should be done (e.g., what can the software do)?

Intelligent Systems Development

We now provide an overview of the process of actually developing intelligent systems—primarily expert systems. The process, which consists of six major phases and several dozen activities, has many variations depending on the nature of the system, the development strategy, and the supporting tools. The following topics form the framework for the development process:

14.1 OPENING VIGNETTE: DEVELOPMENT OF AN EXPERT SYSTEM TO DETECT INSIDER STOCK TRADES[1]

PHASE I: PROJECT INITIALIZATION

A major responsibility of the American Stock Exchange (AMEX, now part of the NASDAQ-AMEX Market Group) is to monitor trading to ensure that securities rules are not violated. The equities surveillance department (ESD) developed an ex-

---

[1]Adapted from H. C. Lucas, Jr., "Market Expert Surveillance System," *Communications of the ACM,* Vol. 36, No. 12, Dec. 1993, pp. 27–34; and other sources.

pert system to detect possible insider trading rules violations to recommend for further investigation.

Detecting insider trading applies logic to evaluate qualitative factors (news reports, price and volume movement interpretation, and other judgmental factors). Insider trading generally occurs around a meaningful company announcement. For example, when Greyhound announced the release of its new, highly advanced reservation system, its CEO and CFO sold their stock just before its value dropped by 90 percent (the CIO had insisted that the system was not ready for release). At AMEX, an automated system was necessary because of the high volume of stock trading.

The stock watch department (SWD at AMEX) identifies allegedly suspicious trades with a statistical model, collects data, and refers the case to the ESD. At this point, an expert system could ideally recommend whether to file the case without action or to begin an initial investigation. The initial investigation involves gathering more data and, with a supervisor, an analyst decides whether to pursue a full investigation.

The ESD manager, an AMEX systems analyst, and a consultant met to discuss using an expert system (ES) approach. The consultant and the analyst were to develop a demonstration ES prototype to present to the manager to observe immediate progress and determine if the approach was viable. Rapid prototyping led the development team quickly though the analysis and design development phases to identify the key concepts in a formal structure. Within 2 weeks, the manager saw a rough, 15-rule prototype in the Exsys backward chaining, rule-based expert system shell (development software). After a few meetings, two senior staff members from ESD joined the project with the manager, forming a team of three experts.

PROTOTYPING

The team met weekly for about 6 months. The experts brought completed cases, which were run through the market expert surveillance system (MESS) prototype. The MESS recommendations were compared to the actual decisions, and rules were either modified or added to the knowledge base to improve its accuracy. Early in the process, the systems analyst developed a more appropriate, user-friendly interface to gather necessary data in the framework that AMEX generally used.

After several months, an interfacing system was developed to retrieve some data directly from a database, run them through some calculations in a spreadsheet, and send them to MESS instead of manually keying them in. Because this could be done (almost) automatically, 53 days worth of data would be investigated instead of the usual 33 days when manual analysis was used. At this point, a special user interface was developed so that users could enter data on one form and pass it to Exsys instead of entering each item one screen at a time.

MULTIPLE EXPERTS AND RECOMMENDED SOLUTIONS

An interesting phenomenon occurred in that when marginal cases were presented, the experts disagreed. The manager had a tendency to recommend opening cases, while the staff members recommended the opposite (they knew how much work each case would involve, and they were quite busy at the time).

Essentially there are two possible recommendations, either open an investigation or do not. Using different sets of rules with the same facts, Exsys is capable of concluding both, but with different weights. For example, one set of rules might indicate to open an investigation with a weight of 0.75 and not open it with a weight of 0.65. Reasonable cutoffs were established.

EVALUATION

As the system neared completion, the three experts were independently given a set of eight cases to review. Their decisions were compared with the recommendations of MESS. In six of the eight cases, MESS and the experts agreed. For one of the other two cases only two experts evaluated the situation and even they disagreed; in the remaining case, the experts indicated not to open it, while MESS recommended *both* opening and not opening it. One thing that was noticed at the evaluation meeting was how the experts focused on only a few facts, while MESS utilized *all* necessary information to establish a recommendation. MESS also provided an explanation of its reasoning.

CONCLUSION

Based on the evaluation, the ESD manager required analysts to use MESS for all new insider trading cases when it was decided not to open a case. In this way, MESS could provide additional analysis in case some facts were overlooked in making the recommendation (all cases were not evaluated because it was a bit tedious to download database data and enter other pertinent information). The SEC audits surveillance files, and so AMEX must be able to defend its decision not to conduct an investigation. MESS provides consistency in the decisions and is also used to train novice analysts.

❖ Questions for the Opening Vignette

1. Describe the need for the system.
2. Explain why the system was developed even though no formal cost–benefit analysis was performed.
3. List the steps taken in developing the system and compare them to the traditional system development life cycle (SDLC) and prototyping approaches described in Chapter 6.
4. Describe the problems that occurred because there were multiple experts.
5. Does it make sense that MESS can recommend both opening a case and not opening a case? Why or why not? (*Hint:* What if there were a committee of 11 who had to decide and the vote went 5 for, 4 against, and 2 abstentions?)
6. The Exsys shell was used to develop the system. What features does a shell like Exsys provide that makes it possible to deploy a system like MESS so quickly?
7. Should a forward-chaining ES approach have been used? Why or why not?
8. Why did the manager of EDS deploy the system the way he did? Is it possible today to automate the whole process, even the statistical evaluation performed by the SWD? Should this be done? Why or why not?

14.2 PROTOTYPING: THE EXPERT SYSTEM DEVELOPMENT LIFE CYCLE

Rapid prototyping (Chapter 6) was the method followed for development of the expert system described in the Opening Vignette. The demonstration prototype that took 2 weeks to complete was critical in gaining the department manager's support (and no doubt, funding). Though unusual, most of the systems analysis and design phase took place concurrently with development of a demonstration prototype; and most of the implementation phase took place concurrently with development of the rule base. The evaluation, though involving only a small number of cases, indicated that the system was capable of making expert-level decisions. Hopefully, the system was evaluated after deployment. Finally, the system was deployed and the ESD analysts were required to use it under very specific conditions, essentially dictated by the Securities and Exchange Commission (SEC), to prevent errors of omission.

The Opening Vignette illustrates how an extremely successful ES project can start, evolve, and be deployed. In this chapter we focus on the phases and issues relating to the development of ES in practice.

An expert system is basically computer software—an information system; so its development follows a software development process. The goal of a development process is to maximize the probability of developing viable, sustainable software within cost limitations and on schedule, while managing change (because introducing a new, computerized approach or even implementing software to perform an existing method of working involves change).

In Chapter 6, we introduced the traditional system development life cycle (SDLC), which consists of four fundamental phases: *planning, analysis, design,* and *implementation* (Figure 6.1). We also introduced *prototyping,* which involves performing the analysis, design, and implementation phases concurrently and repeatedly in short cycles, ultimately leading to deployment of the system (Figure 6.3). Prototyping is also known as *iterative design* or *evolutionary development.* Prototyping is the most commonly used DSS development methodology. One of its advantages is that decision maker(s) and user(s) learn more about the problem they are trying to solve while performing the prototyping process, as occurred in the Opening Vignette and in the case applications.

Prototyping is the generally accepted approach to developing ES. We defer to the literature on ES development and describe it in six phases that effectively map into the prototyping process described succinctly in Chapter 6 (Figure 14.1):

- Phase I: project initialization
- Phase II: system analysis and design
- Phase III: rapid prototyping and a demonstration prototype
- Phase IV: system development
- Phase V: implementation
- Phase VI: postimplementation.

The *project initialization* phase is sometimes called *initiation* (which precedes the SDLC and prototyping processes described in Chapter 6). Here the stage is set for the development of a new system. It includes the *planning* phase from the traditional SDLC. The *analysis* and *design* phases of the SDLC are combined in ES development into one phase. Because this is a prototyping process, the analysis and design phases are repeated as the system undergoes development and ultimately implementation. Typically in ES development, the prototype evolves into the deployed system as the implementation phase progresses.

When expert systems are constructed, most of the six development phases are included. The process is not linear; rather, some tasks are performed simultaneously and a return to previous tasks or even phases happens often. The nature of the specific application determines the depth to which each phase is performed, and the order might perturbate a bit. For example, a large-scale ES could be developed according to a complex life-cycle process, generally in systems analysis and design, based more on the traditional SDLC (large-scale accounting and finance ES are known to follow this approach until the time of knowledge acquisition), whereas a small-scale system developed by and for end users could follow the six phases in minimal depth (Appendix 14-A). We describe these

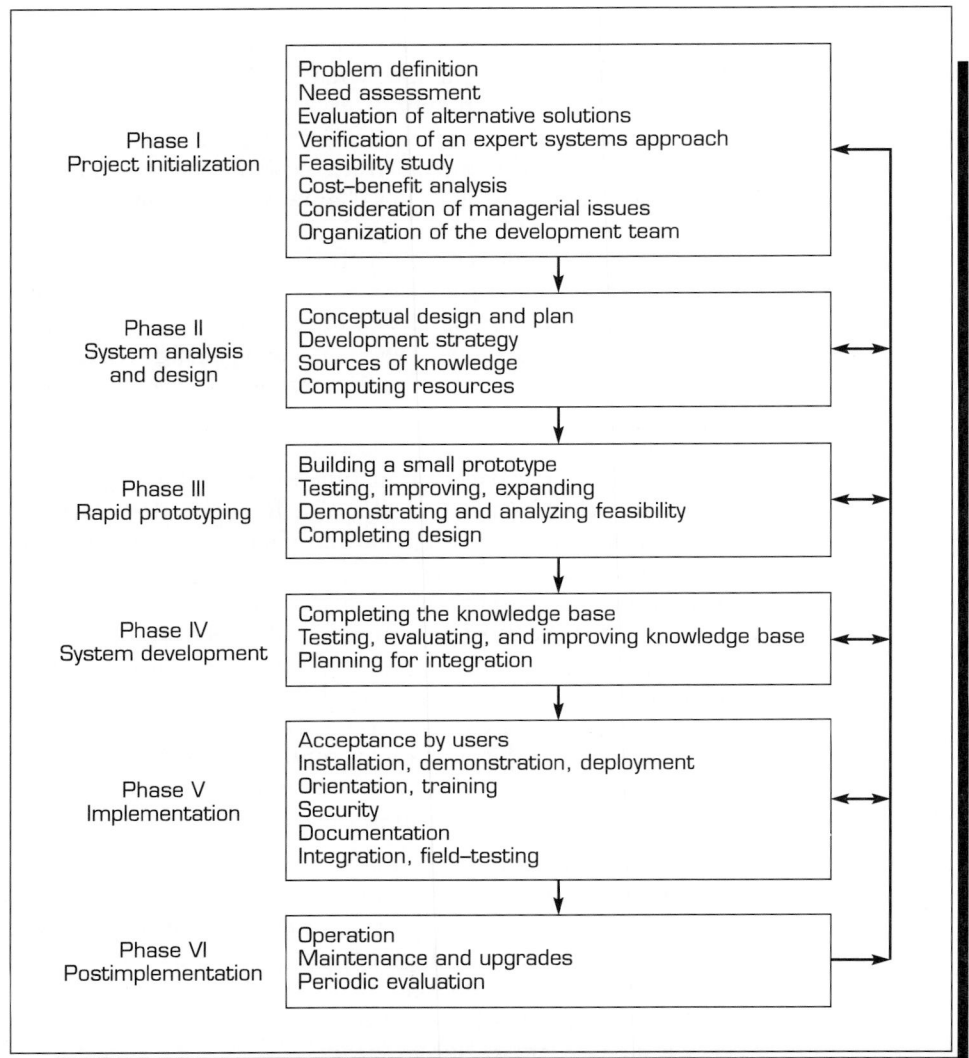

FIGURE 14.1 SCHEMATIC VIEW OF THE ES DEVELOPMENT LIFE CYCLE

phases and some of the important tasks in the remaining sections of this chapter. To illustrate the phases, along with the brief Opening Vignette, we have provided Case Application 14.1 and a running case described in a series of AIS in Action boxes. This running case[2] describes the development of Picker International Inc.'s Questor expert system to assist field engineers in the diagnosis and repair of medical diagnostic systems. Case Application 14.2 contains a summary of the running case and its case questions.

---

[2]This running case spans the chapter. It was adapted from S. Wallace, "Experts in the Field," *Byte*, Vol. 19, No. 10, Oct. 1994, pp. 86–96 (www.byte.com); and other sources.

14.3 PHASE I: PROJECT INITIALIZATION

See the project initialization of the running case in AIS in Action 14.1 and 14.2. Starting an ES project can be tricky, and determining that ES is a viable approach to solving a particular problem is not trivial. Many factors must be considered, and many ES projects fail because of poor problem selection (e.g., ES may be an inappropriate technology to utilize). There are methodologies and checklists for determining the fit between a problem and the ES approach (Awad, 1996; Hartman, 1993; Prerau, 1990; Medsker and Liebowitz, 1994). The main factors are that the problem must have a sufficiently *narrow domain* and that some aspects of the problem must be *qualitative,* so that conventional computing approaches do not apply.

The major tasks of phase I are shown in Table 14.1. The tasks are interrelated and might not follow any specific sequence. We discuss details next.

PROBLEM DEFINITION AND NEED ASSESSMENT

A clear problem definition simplifies the remaining tasks significantly. (The analysis paralysis suffered at Picker International may have been due to not understanding the

---

AIS IN ACTION 14.1

PICKER INTERNATIONAL RUNNING CASE

PHASE I: PROJECT INITIALIZATION

Just a few years ago, each of Picker International's more than 900 field engineers carried a carload's worth of hard-copy reference documents, a pager, and test gear on service calls. There were about 100 products, each of which had as many as nine three-ring binders of technical documentation, most of which was typically out of date. The cost of a documentation set was about $500. Each engineer supported up to six products (up to 54 binders, valued at about $3,000).

Picker, in Cleveland, OH (a billion-dollar-a-year medical diagnostic systems provider), had an excellent reputation in field service. There were major limitations on leveraging the company's experience and growing knowledge base with a paper-based system. Picker executives wanted *more effective capture, management,* and *use of product and service information.* Essentially, they targeted development of an electronic document management (EDM) system to be used to leverage knowledge throughout the organization (essentially a knowledge management system).

Because of the nature of the diagnostic work, the solution was to include an *expert system* at its heart. The expert system would capture and synthesize critical knowledge from the company's field engineers and make it available throughout the entire organization. *Problem*

definition requires diagnosing problems in medical hardware in the field and recommending solutions. Part of this process involves capturing information in the field and establishing how the new knowledge can be synthesized into the existing system. Since this is a diagnostic-type problem with some qualitative factors (such as "Does the part sound like it is squeaking or whirring?"), an expert system is suitable. Top management and the field engineers supported the approach. Five years earlier a *feasibility study* had indicated that an expert system was indeed an appropriate approach. Both groups recognized that it would improve the performance of the field engineers and keep their customers satisfied. But *analysis paralysis* stalled the project.

When Picker decided to move forward with the Questor expert system initiative, it had already identified the significant benefits of serving customers better and faster, and better and more accurate capturing of field knowledge, even though a formal *cost–benefit analysis* had not been performed. The magnitude and value of the benefits was unknown. But, strong intuition on the part of top management about potential improvements in productivity lead to the development of Questor. Early testing revealed that significant benefits in serving customers could be achieved (a competitive advantage).

AIS IN ACTION 14.2

PICKER INTERNATIONAL RUNNING CASE

SETTING THE STAGE: THE ELECTRONIC DOCUMENT MANAGEMENT SYSTEM

Picker recognized that the first issue was to move away from their paper and telephone-based system to a nation-wide PC-based system to be designed and developed. Hardware and software were selected. Each engineer received a laptop computer along with access to the information they needed to be more productive. When paged for a service call, information about equipment, service history, and inventory and billing for the customer is downloaded to the engineer's laptop by a dispatching system to better prepare him or her to resolve the problem. The dial-up capability of the faulty medical equipment even allows engineers to call the equipment directly and run diagnostics remotely. When the engineer finishes a service call, his or her report is uploaded back into the system, capturing information about defective parts, creative solutions, billing, and so on. In the home office, the service call information is used to measure characteristics about the products, design better products, and update the set of solutions. This knowledge capture paved the way for the expert system.

This effort reduced the number of personnel performing dispatching and the number of errors made in transcribing phone calls into the information system. Other savings came directly from migrating from the mainframe to the PC system. Overall, $2.5 million was invested for an annual savings of $1 million.

TABLE 14.1   Project Initialization Tasks

- Problem definition
- Need assessment
- Evaluation of alternative solutions (availability of experts, education and training, packaged knowledge, conventional software)
- Verification of an expert system approach (requirements, justification, appropriateness)
- Feasilibity study (evaluate whether the project is technologically feasible, managerially feasible, and change can be initiated and sustained)
- Cost–benefit analysis (this last part of the feasibility study involves determining economic feasibility: formally identifying and estimating the potential costs and benefits of the system)
- Consideration of managerial issues (project initiator, financing, resources, legal and other constraints, selling the project, identifying a champion, potential of gaining access to users and user support)
- Organizing the development team (the team must be assembled and commitment established before starting formal development because of the nature of the prototyping process)
- Ending milestone: approval of the project in principle

---

problem sufficiently to apply an ES to it.) Defining the problem accurately is a matter of answering some basic questions. What exactly is the problem? What are the real needs? Typical business problems can be low productivity, lack of sufficient expert knowledge throughout the organization, information overload, time problems, or people problems. Write a clear statement of the problem or need and provide as much supporting information (e.g., about the proposed ES solution, the estimated resource requirements for its development, and the potential benefits) as possible (ideally as a one-page design).

The best way to understand a problem or need is to conduct a formal **need assessment.** Assessing the need to solve the problem is related to several other activities, such as cost–benefit analysis and justification, and to determining the system requirements.

Usually the manager responsible for solving the problem is aware of the need and will support its solution if the solution's benefits appear to outweigh the costs (as in the Opening Vignette, Case Application 14.1, and the running case).

EVALUATION OF ALTERNATIVE SOLUTIONS

Before starting a major ES development program, consider alternative solution approaches to the problem. Applying expert systems is not the only way to capture and deploy knowledge. Here are some alternatives:

Use experts. If the problem is knowledge-related, then usually someone has the needed knowledge. One approach may simply be to make an existing or new expert accessible to those who need the expertise. This is a viable approach when the need for expertise is infrequent.

Provide education and training. Providing education and training to those who need it in the form of courses, seminars, and related materials may be cheaper and just as effective as developing an expert system. This can be done through distance learning courses.

Package the knowledge. Another alternative is to package the knowledge and related information into documents, either printed or electronic. This can be less expensive than developing an ES.

Develop or use conventional software. If an ES is inappropriate because algorithmic methods exist, use them. Conventional computing approaches may work.

Purchase knowledge. Much knowledge can be obtained for a fee, for example, by purchasing books or hiring consultants, or through knowledge management systems such as KnowledgeSpace over the Web. Even existing, ready-made ES can sometimes be purchased. For example, Ask.Me Web (Ask.Me Online, www.amol.com) is a plug-and-play support ES for deploying help desk–type knowledge about computer software from KnowledgeBroker Inc.

VERIFICATION OF AN EXPERT SYSTEM APPROACH: PROBLEM SELECTION

The fact that other alternatives are not appropriate for solving a problem does not mean that an expert system is necessary. Waterman (1985) proposed a framework for determining problem fit with an ES approach (modified here). It consists of a three-part study: requirements, justification, and appropriateness.

REQUIREMENTS FOR ES DEVELOPMENT

The following 12 requirements are *all* necessary to make ES development successful:

- The task does not require common sense.
- The task requires only cognitive, not physical, skills.
- There is at least one genuine expert who is willing to cooperate (he or she can be skeptical but must be cooperative).
- Experts involved can articulate their methods of problem solving.
- Experts involved can (mostly) agree on the knowledge and the solution approach to the problem.
- The task is not too difficult.
- The task is well understood and is defined clearly.
- The task definition is fairly stable.
- Conventional (algorithmic) computer solution techniques are not satisfactory.

- Incorrect or nonoptimal results generated by the ES can be tolerated.
- Data and test cases are available.
- The task's vocabulary has no more than a few hundred concepts.

JUSTIFICATION FOR ES DEVELOPMENT

Like any other information system, an expert system must be justified. Of the following eight factors, *at least one* must be present to justify developing an ES:

- The solution to the problem has a high payoff.
- The ES can preserve scarce human expertise so that it will not be lost.
- Expertise is needed in many locations.
- Expertise is needed in hostile or hazardous environments.
- The expertise improves performance or quality.
- The system can be used for training.
- The ES solution can be derived faster than one provided by a human.
- The ES is more consistent or accurate than a human.

The derived benefits in one or more of these areas must be compared to the costs of developing the system. A preliminary justification is conducted in this phase, whereas a detailed analysis is performed in later phases.

APPROPRIATENESS OF THE ES

Three factors should be considered in determining when it is appropriate to develop an ES:

- *Nature of the problem.* The problem should have a symbolic structure, and heuristics should be available for its solution; in addition, it is desirable that the task be decomposable.
- *Complexity of the task.* The task should be neither too easy nor too difficult for a human expert.
- *Scope of the problem.* The problem should be of a manageable size; it also should have some practical value.

Problem selection should also take into consideration the generic areas where ES have proved successful in practice. Finding appropriate problems for an ES solution is a critical factor in implementing ES. An alternate view is to determine if a problem can be solved by an ES. For example, the problems described in the Opening Vignette, the running case, and Case Application 14.1 are all good fits.

FEASIBILITY STUDY

The **feasibility study** for an ES is essentially the same as for any information system (e.g., Dennis and Wixom, 2000). It involves considering the economic feasibility, technical feasibility, and organizational feasibility; see Table 14.2. The technical feasibility question involves whether the technology exists to construct the system. Less familiarity with the technology or application implies more risk of failure. In the running case, we shall later see that the knowledge engineers were required to obtain domain knowledge so that they could accurately characterize the knowledge, thus increasing the likelihood of success. Also, the larger a problem, the greater the likelihood of failure (Chapter 6). Organizational feasibility involves many of the success factors of general information systems, plus a few more. Critical aspects include obtaining a champion in upper management, getting the support of managers and users, and providing user

TABLE 14.2 Elements of a Feasibility Study

Economic (financial) feasibility: Should we build it?	Estimated development costs Estimated operating costs Anticipated benefits (cost savings and revenues) Intangible benefits Intangible costs Cash flow analysis Risk analysis
Technical feasibility: Can we build it?	Familiarity with application: more implies less risk Familiarity with technology: more implies less risk Project size: larger implies more risk Interface requirements Networking issues Availability of knowledge and data Security of confidential knowledge Knowledge representation scheme Hardware and software availability and compatibility
Organizational feasibility: If we build it, will they come?	Project champion(s) Senior management support Management support Experts' support and availability Knowledge engineers' support and availability User support, training, and environment Other stakeholders Other resources Organizational and implementation issues Priority Need assessment justification Legal and other constraints Corporate culture

training. In addition, the experts must be cooperative and made available. Finally the issue of economic feasibility must be addressed in some kind of cost–benefit analysis.

COST–BENEFIT ANALYSIS

Each ES project requires an investment of resources in exchange for expected benefits. Once we have selected a problem for which an ES is to be developed, some estimate of benefits and costs must be performed in a **cost–benefit analysis.** As is true for DSS, often only a *feeling* on the part of the manager responsible for the problem is enough to justify its development (see the Opening Vignette, the running case, and Case Application 14.1). This feeling is based on knowledge of the business and a sense that the ES will contribute to the bottom line, either directly or indirectly through a more competitive position. In the running case, there was a sense that the ES would make the field engineers more productive, but it was not known at the inception that there would be a 40 percent improvement. As the system evolves through the prototyping process, estimates of costs and benefits are refined to justify its continued development. A certain percentage of ES projects will fail. In fact, one factor leading to ES success is "permission to fail," indicating the high level of risk associated with these systems and the potentially high benefits that can be obtained.

The viability of a project is determined by comparing the expected costs with the anticipated benefits in a cost–benefit analysis. What can complicate the analysis is that many benefits are intangible and that there are unknown risk factors leading to system success. It is often difficult to estimate the exact value of making better decisions or to estimate an increase in productivity (see the running case). The iterative nature of building ES makes it difficult to predict costs and benefits because the systems evolve constantly. Actually, most ES are considered *never* to be finished because after the system is deployed the knowledge must be updated to keep it current (see the running case).

DEVELOPMENT COSTS

System development costs include those of the tools (e.g., languages and shells), additional software and hardware, the experts' time (whether internal or external to the organization), the knowledge engineers' time, and the time of any other personnel associated with the project (programmers, systems analysts, consultants, managers, users, and others). Development includes system specification, coding, writing documentation, knowledge acquisition and representation, system construction, testing, debugging, and maintenance before it is deployed. Realistic estimates of the scope of the project and the time required of all the stakeholders can lead to fairly accurate predictions of system development cost and time. Experience, though, is the best teacher.

Depending on the expected size of a proposed ES, a small system with fewer than 100 rules may take only several weeks and require two or three people. It could cost as little as $2,000 or as much as $75,000 depending on the availability of in-house tools and hardware and the level of in-house expertise. A large expert system could easily cost more than $100,000 at the low end and millions of dollars at the high end.

Du Pont, recognizing that it was a knowledge-intensive organization, decided to purchase a worldwide site license for the Exsys expert system development shell and let *all* its employees determine their own needs for expert systems. By making the tools available to everyone, they lowered system development costs substantially. See AIS In Action 14.3.

TRAINING AND MAINTENANCE COSTS

Other costs include training and maintenance. The initial users must be trained, as well as new users. The system must be maintained, and the knowledge updated periodically as part of this maintenance (see the running case). Experts must be paid. Hardware must be replaced. Software improves, and modifications might be necessary as new versions of the development platform are released or as the system is ported to other hardware (see Case Application 14.1). Finally, corrections and improvements to the system may need to be made.

BENEFITS

The assessment of benefits is usually more difficult because (1) most benefits are intangible (e.g., better service as in the running case), (2) often benefits cannot be precisely related to a single cause, and (3) some benefits occur over time. Intangible benefits are extremely difficult to measure. For example, for a calciner control ES at Aughinish Alumina Ltd. (Limerick, Ireland), the intangible operator benefits include reduced workload and reduced stress, along with the estimated tangible benefits of an increased throughput of 5.5 percent and savings of between 500,000 and 750,000 annually (Gensym, 2000).

Initially, it is important to produce a list of potential benefits (such as an increase in productivity of 40 percent from the field engineers), along with an estimate of their value. Like costs, most benefits may be very hard to estimate or even be unknown at the project's onset. For example, in Case Application 14.1, an ES developed for internal use became an IBM product that generated revenue.

TIMING OF COST–BENEFIT ANALYSES

A cost–benefit analysis is actually a continuous process throughout the development and use of an ES. Benefits, costs, and the system's scope must be reexamined to keep the project on track during every phase of the development process and typically are formally evaluated

- At the end of phase I, when the project is initially approved
- At the end of phase II, when the complete design is ready
- After the initial prototype is completed
- Once the full prototype is running
- Once field testing is completed (before deployment)
- Periodically after the system is deployed (e.g., every 6 or 12 months, depending on the volatility of the environment[3]).

ES SYSTEM JUSTIFICATION

Costs, benefits, and an assessment of project risk are used in a variety of system justification methods. Because the resources of an organization are limited, the ES project must be compared to other projects in what can sometimes become a lengthy, complex decision-making process (perhaps a DSS could help!). Common approaches are based on simple cash flow evaluations such as determining the return on investment (ROI), internal rate of return, net present value, and payback period. Each method has some advantages and disadvantages, as outlined in Table 14.3 for five common methods.

More-advanced methods take the estimated risk into consideration. Methods from finance that view systems developments as a set of investments can be analyzed like a stock portfolio. Finally, methods like the Analytical Hierarchy Process (using Expert Choice software; see Chapter 5), can take into consideration both qualitative and quantitative factors.

ORGANIZING THE DEVELOPMENT TEAM

Most expert systems are developed by a team. Some members of the team (the core) participate in the initial steps (phases I–V); others are added only after the development strategy has been finalized (phase VI).

---

[3]This is why stock prediction ES (and neural networks) are so unreliable. Economic and market conditions change frequently, and these ES are typically not upgraded fast enough.

TABLE 14.3   Commonly Used Methods of Evaluating ES Proposals

Method	Advantages	Disadvantages
Internal rate of return (IRR)	Brings all projects to common footing Conceptually familiar No assumed discount rate	Assumes reinvestment at same rate Can have multiple solutions
Net present value (NPV)	Very common Maximizes value for unconstrained project or selection	Difficult to compare projects of unequal lives or sizes
Equivalent annuity (EA)	Brings all project NPVs to common footing Convenient annual figure	Assumes projects repeat to least multiple of lives, or imputes salvage value
Payback period	Can be discounted or nondiscounted Measure of exposure Indicates when a project is completely paid off	Ignores flows after payback is reached Assumes standard project cash-flow profile
Benefit/cost ratio	Conceptually familiar Brings all projects to common footing	May be difficult to classify outlays as expense or investment

Source: Based partly on Smith A., and C. Dagli, "An Analysis of Worth: Justifying Funding for Development and Implementation," in E. Turban and J. Liebowitz (eds.), *Managing Expert Systems,* Harrisburg, PA: Idea Group Publishers, 1992.

TABLE 14.4   Potential Functions and Roles in an Expert System Team

Documentation writer	Legal advisor	System analyst
End users	Network expert	System integrator
Expert	Programmer	System operator
Hardware (software) specialist	Project champion	System tester (evaluator)
Internet/intranet expert	Project manager	Trainer
Knowledge engineer	Security specialist	Vendor or consultant
	Special tool developer	

Source: Based on D. S. Prerau, *Developing and Managing Expert Systems,* Reading, MA: Addison-Wesley, 1990, p. 57.

A typical development team consists of an expert, a knowledge engineer, and an IS systems analyst/programmer. A vendor or system integrator may also be included. The knowledge engineer extracts the expert's knowledge and represents it in a suitable manner. The knowledge engineer or a programmer writes code for storing and manipulating the knowledge and creates and/or links the inference engine, interfaces, and other components as required.

Although the team approach is probably the best development arrangement, it requires a great deal of cooperation and communication among the team members. Table 14.4 lists some of the possible functions and roles that can be found in an ES team.

Many teams include two important players: the project champion and the project leader. The *project champion* is a top management person with power and influence who has a major interest in facilitating the project's successful completion. The project champion provides the project with the resources needed for success. He or she is usually a senior vice president or a high-level manager. In practice, the level of top management involvement is a leading indicator of ES project quality and success. Also, top management involvement tends to impact on the project leader in requiring him or her to formulate a high-quality, complete overall development plan (Wong, 1996). The *project leader* is the specialist who manages the project daily. The leader is familiar with the application, is user-oriented, and understands the technology. Managing an ES development team is comparable to managing any IS project, with some additional, specialty roles. Good project management skills are critical for the project leader (Chapter 6).

Users are often *not* represented on ES development teams, which is a *big mistake*. There is a subtle, important difference between a DSS and an ES. A DSS user is an expert decision maker, while an ES user is generally, but not always, a novice. For example, consider a loan approval ES for a bank. There is no need for an expert to use the system because he or she can look at an application and arrive at a valid solution (though perhaps not as quickly as an ES can; see the Running Case), while an inexperienced loan officer would use it. This mismatch between expertise and user leads to an interesting problem in that normally one wants users involved in system development, but for ES the users usually do not understand the knowledge to be captured and implemented. Even so, *the potential system users must be involved in the ES development.* Otherwise major problems may occur. For example, even though users may be satisfied with the recommendations made by an ES and they become more productive, they might not feel a sense of accomplishment (Klein and Jiang, 1999). For example, at the Aughinish Alumina Limited calciner, where an expert system control system was deployed, the users did not accept the system at first. They were quite skeptical until they realized how it could benefit them (Gensym, 2000). Had they been involved, their buy-in could have been attained before deployment.

MANAGERIAL ISSUES

ES projects are initiated for a number of reasons. Sometimes there is an acute need. Often someone in the organization believes that an ES is an appropriate approach to solving a problem and will support a project (see the Opening Vignette, Case Application 14.1, and the running case). Sometimes the ES technology and/or knowledge are already in-house and there is a search for an appropriate project (as at Du Pont). Sometimes a competitor may already have one (the New York Stock Exchange was already using expert systems like the ES in the Opening Vignette).

Once the decision to consider developing an ES is made, there are several other managerial issues that must be considered:

- *Selling the project.* All interested parties and especially top management must be convinced of the project's value.
- *Identifying a champion.* Someone in top management must be a *strong* sponsor of the project.
- *Level of top management support.* This can directly influence the level of success of the system. This is critical.
- *End-user involvement, support, and training.* End users must be involved early in the project. Their proper support and training are critical.
- *Availability of financing and other resources.* Resources are generally made available because of the champion.
- *Access to a cooperative expert.* Without an expert, no expertise is available.
- *Legal and other potential constraints.* As with any IS, the environment can influence the development and use of the system (e.g., in the Opening Vignette, SEC rules forced the development of some kind of system and ultimately dictated the ES use pattern).

14.4 PHASE II: SYSTEM ANALYSIS AND DESIGN

Once the concept of the project has been approved, a detailed system analysis must be conducted to estimate system functionality. See AIS in Action 14.4. This phase is cycled through as part of the prototyping process. We list the tasks in Table 14.5 and describe them in the following discussion.

CONCEPTUAL DESIGN

A conceptual design of an ES is similar to an architectural sketch of a house. It provides a general idea of what the system will look like and how it will solve the problem. The design shows the general capabilities of the system, the interfaces with other computer-based information systems, the areas of risk, the required resources, the anticipated cash flow, the final composition of the team including identification of the expert(s) and an estimate of their commitment, and any other information that will be necessary for detailed design later. Once the conceptual design is completed, it is necessary to determine the development strategy.

TABLE 14.5   Project Conceptualization and System Analysis Tasks

- Conceptual design and plan
- Development strategy
- Sources of knowledge
- Computing resources
- Ending milestone: approved complete project plan

AIS IN ACTION 14.4

PICKER INTERNATIONAL RUNNING CASE

PHASE II: SYSTEM ANALYSIS AND DESIGN

With field-service laptops deployed and dispatching enhanced, Picker had the hardware and support necessary to provide field engineers with Questor, its yet-to-be-developed expert system diagnostic support tool. Now it was time to analyze and design the system. The TestBench (Carnegie Group, Pittsburgh, PA) expert system shell was selected, and knowledge engineers planned to obtain knowledge from in-house experts. From working with experts, they concluded that an induction tree knowledge representation approach would work well. Explanation could be provided at each node to inform an engineer *why* a particular line

of reasoning was being followed. A *prototyping* approach would be used. New knowledge would be developed, entered, and tested in an iterative fashion, one product line at a time. Ultimately, part of the system design would have field engineers log their results directly into the system so that their knowledge, once approved, could lead to new rules to update the system, keeping its accuracy level as high as possible. So *all* field service engineers could have access to the new expertise, the expert system was to be deployed on the field engineers' PCs.

At this point, the experts have been selected, the software (shell) has been selected, and the hardware is in place. The conceptual design is finished.

DEVELOPMENT STRATEGY AND METHODOLOGY

There are two AI **development strategies:** develop in-house or outsource. There is a blended approach in which external consultants (possibly even from software vendors) join in-house teams. The needs of the particular project and expected development costs and benefits or the organization's policies dictate which approach should be chosen.

IN-HOUSE DEVELOPMENT

In-house development is attractive for organizations that already have the needed skills and resources. It is also appropriate if the AI applications will contain proprietary or sensitive knowledge. One way to enable in-house development is to provide the tools and training to existing employees or to hire new, experienced AI system developers. Regardless of how the expertise is brought in-house, there are several options, including the following:

- *End-user computing.* The principal benefit of this strategy is that it can provide a low-cost, low-risk entry into using AI technology. It is an attractive option for organizations that are highly decentralized. Du Pont Inc. (see AIS in Action 14.3) adopted this policy by obtaining a worldwide site license for an expert system shell. By 1997 it had over 1,000 ES in use, saving about $30 million annually.
- *Centralized computing.* All AI projects are developed by a special unit or department, typically in organizations that are heavily involved with AI or when an organization develops its first AI project.
- *End-user computing with centralized control.* Systems are developed using the Du Pont strategy, but they are registered and licensed in a central unit. This unit ensures that appropriate development methodologies are followed and that the proper maintenance, security, documentation, standardization of technologies, and interfacing with other computer-based information systems are performed.
- *High-technology islands.* Some companies have several specialized units for AI development, each operating independently of the others.
- *Information centers:* Organizations use the existing information (or help) centers as vehicles for creating and disseminating ES.

OUTSOURCING

There are a number of different ways to perform outsourcing, including the following:

- *Hire a consulting firm:* Contract with a consulting firm or a consultant and outsource the entire effort. The consulting firm can be an expert system software vendor. This is attractive for firms that do not have (or cannot afford) knowledge engineers in-house.
- *Become a test site:* Become the test site for a new, industry-wide ES product so that the consulting firm can develop a product for sale and the firm gets the software relatively inexpensively.
- *Partner with a university:* Partner with a university by sponsoring the development as research. This is how the XCON ES was constructed; Digital Equipment Corporation joined forces with a team at Carnegie Mellon University. Sponsoring student projects is a variation of this strategy.
- *Join an industry consortium:* Join an industry-wide consortium of companies to develop or acquire a system for all the firms. For example, the

Underwriting Advisor ES was developed by several insurance companies (Harmon et al., 1988).

- *Buy into an AI firm:* Purchase all or part of, or merge with, an AI company. For example, General Magic Corporation, which develops intelligent agents for the Internet, is partially owned by Apple, IBM, Sony, and other large corporations.

BLENDED APPROACH

It is possible to assemble a team, consisting partly of in-house members and partly of members external to the firm, from vendors, consulting firms, consortium members, universities, and so on. Essentially, the effort is divided between the two groups. This is how MESS in the Opening Vignette was developed; there was one external consultant. One advantage is that the organization can bring development, tool and knowledge expertise in-house. The disadvantages are that when the consultants leave, their expertise leaves and proprietary information may leave with them, along with system maintenance and update capabilities.

EXPERTS

Human experts possess knowledge that is much more complex than that in documented sources. It is based on experience and is usually qualitative and expressed via heuristics (see AIS in Focus 14.5).

SELECTING EXPERT(S)

Expert systems use both human experts and documented sources for knowledge. The more human expertise needed, the longer and more complicated the acquisition process becomes. Several issues may surface in selecting experts.

- Who selects the experts?
- Who is an expert (possessing what characteristics)?
- How can several experts be managed if need be?
- How can the expert be motivated to cooperate?

Experts are relatively easy to identify, especially when recommended by others. They solve problems quickly, find high-quality appropriate solutions, and focus on what is important. The issue of managing several experts can be difficult, mainly if the experts disagree. Generally it is wise to use a single expert (especially if dealing with economics-based systems), if their point of view has been helpful in problem solving in the past. Other experts' knowledge can be incorporated into the system later.

Expert cooperation was not an issue in most early expert systems. The experts were researchers, professors, or specialists nearing retirement. The whole idea of ES was challenging and new, and so experts tended to cooperate (though sometimes they were skeptical). Several experts contributed a small portion of a large knowledge base in some systems.

This cooperative situation can change when different types of experts are involved. Experts ask questions such as, "What's in it for me?" "Why should I contribute my wisdom and risk my job?" and so on. Before building an ES that requires the cooperation of experts, management should ask questions such as the following:

- Should experts be compensated for their contributions (royalties, special rewards, payment)?
- Are experts truthful in describing how they solve problems?

AIS IN FOCUS 14.5

THE IDEAL ATTRIBUTES OF AN EXPERT

Ideally, experts

- Have highly developed, specialized content knowledge (experts know a lot and keep up with the latest developments)
- Are thoroughly familiar with the domain, including task expertise built up over a long period of task performance, knowledge of the organizations that will be developing and using the ES, knowledge of the user community, and knowledge of technical and technological alternatives
- Have a solid knowledge base and reputation so that the ES recommendations will be credible and authoritative
- Are more creative than most people (experts are better able to find novel solutions to problems)
- Are aware of the difference between relevant and irrelevant information (experts concentrate on what is important)
- Are able to simplify complexities (experts make sense out of chaos)
- Are selective about which problems to solve (experts recognize significance)
- Have strong communication skills (experts demonstrate and can articulate their expertise); can easily communicate knowledge, judgment, and experience (experts often cannot do this well)
- Have highly developed perceptual attention (experts can see what others cannot)

- Know when to make exceptions (experts know when to break rules)
- Have a strong sense of responsibility toward their choices (experts stand behind their decisions)
- Have outward confidence in their decisions (experts believe in themselves and their abilities)
- Are able to adapt to changing task environments (experts are flexible)
- Have greater automaticity of cognitive processes (experts habitually do what others have to work hard at doing and do so quickly)
- Are able to tolerate stress (experts can work effectively and efficiently under adverse conditions)
- Can commit a substantial amount of time to development of the system, including temporary work if necessary
- Are cooperative, easy to work with, and eager to work on a project (this is another ideal trait that is often not the case in practice)
- Are interested in computer systems, even if not a computer specialist.

Source: Adapted from S. K. Goyal et al., "COMPASS: An Expert System for Telephone Switch Maintenance," *Expert Systems,* July 1985; J. Shanteua, "Psychological Characteristics of Expert Decision Makers," *Proceedings, of a Symposium on Expert Systems and Audit Judgment,* University of Southern California, Los Angeles, Feb. 16–18, 1986.

- How can experts be assured that they will not lose their jobs or that their jobs will not be deemphasized once the ES is fully operational?
- What about the other people in the organization whose jobs may change or be eliminated because of the ES?

In general, management should use incentives to motivate experts so that they will cooperate fully with the knowledge engineer. Once the experts are identified, the builder can turn to software considerations.

14.5 SOFTWARE CLASSIFICATION: ES TECHNOLOGY LEVELS

ES software can be classified in five technology levels: languages, support tools, shells, hybrid systems, and ES applications (specific ES). The boundaries between the levels are fairly fuzzy, and our classification is mainly for an understanding of ES software. Figure 14.2 illustrates the levels.

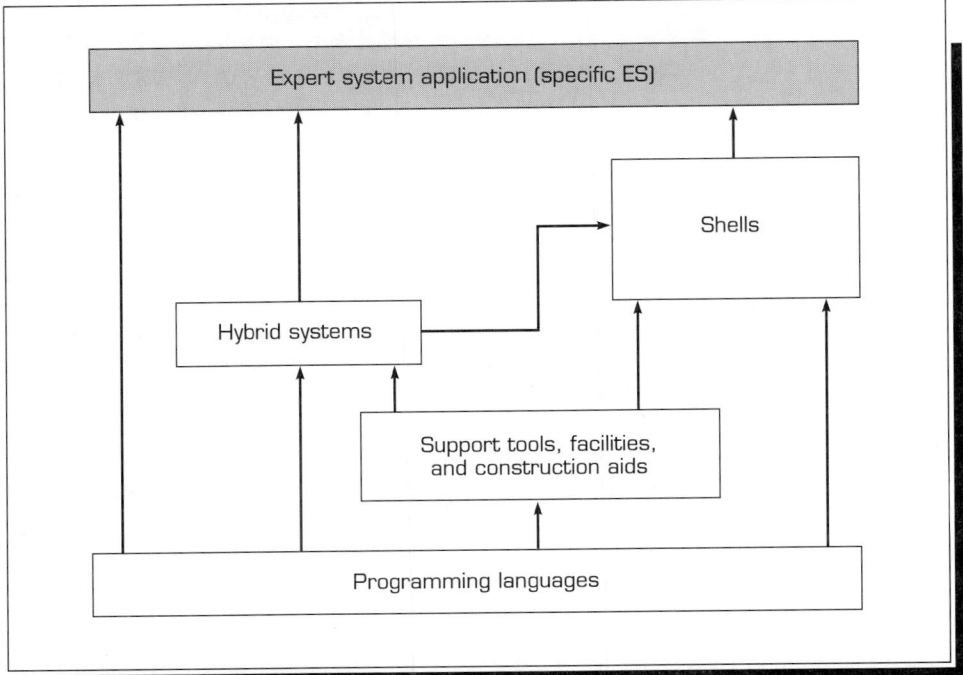

FIGURE 14.2 TECHNOLOGY LEVELS OF EXPERT SYSTEM SOFTWARE

Roughly speaking, the specific application (at the top) can be constructed with one or more shells, support tools, hybrid systems, or languages. Shells and hybrid systems can be constructed with languages or support tools, and support tools are constructed with languages.

The higher the level of the software in Figure 14.2, the less programming is required. The trade-off is that the higher the level, the less flexible the software. Generally speaking, the use of higher levels of software enables faster programming (even by end users). On the other hand, complex and nonstandard applications must be built with lower levels of software.

DESCRIPTION OF ES TECHNOLOGY LEVELS

SPECIFIC EXPERT SYSTEMS
Specific ES are the application products that advise users on a specific issue, such as a consultation system that diagnoses a malfunction in a locomotive, or systems that advise on tax shelters or on buying software or selecting wine. Currently most of these can be accessed directly through consistent Web–browser interfaces.

SHELLS
Instead of building a specific ES from scratch, it is often possible to borrow extensively from a previously built specific ES. This strategy has resulted in several integrated software tools described as shell (skeletal) systems. Initially, expert systems, like MYCIN, were stripped of their knowledge component, which left an empty shell: the explanation and inference mechanisms, and knowledge acquisition and representation aids. Even the name of the shell EMYCIN was derived from the name Empty MYCIN. The first generation of shells were designed and developed this way.

Shells are now integrated packages in which the major components of the expert systems (except for the knowledge base) are preprogrammed. These include the user interface, inferencing, and interfaces with other software. The trade-off is that specific shells generally support only one or two knowledge representations, inference methods, and means of handling uncertainty. On the other hand, the programmer needs only to insert the knowledge to build a specific expert system. Exsys, used in the ES in the Opening Vignette, is a popular, fully functional ES shell.

SUPPORT TOOLS

With shells, the system builder needs only to construct the knowledge base, usually in small systems. In contrast, many other types of tools help in building the various parts of complex systems. They are aids for knowledge acquisition, knowledge validation and verification, and construction of interfaces to other software packages. For example, ACQUIRE (Acquired Intelligence Inc., www.aiinc.ca) is a tool that assists in knowledge acquisition. Its SDK derivative allows it to integrate with other applications. EZ-Xpert (AI Developers Inc., www.ez-xpert.com) is a rapid application development (RAD) tool. Once the knowledge is encoded in it, EZ-XPERT is capable of generating 26 different format expert system knowledge-base files, including 8 language shells (in 2000).

HYBRID SYSTEMS (ENVIRONMENTS)

Hybrid systems (environments) consist of several support tools and programming languages. They enable complex, multiple-knowledge representation systems to be built faster than they would be built if only programming languages were used. Hybrid systems provide skilled programmers with a rapid prototyping environment in which they can build shells or specific ES. These hybrid systems are also called **toolkits,** from which the knowledge engineer can select appropriate tools for appropriate tasks. ART (Brightware Inc.), for example, contains modules from which an inference engine can be assembled. One module provides a procedure for handling measures of uncertainty, and another provides a Bayesian procedure for handling probabilities. The Common KADS Workbench and TestBench (see the Running Case) are other toolkits.

PROGRAMMING LANGUAGES

Expert systems can be developed in a programming language, ranging from AI languages to object-oriented languages and environments such as the cT programming language environment (available free from Carnegie Mellon University, www.andrew.cmu.edu). cT is an enhanced algorithmic language that includes the ability to manipulate multimedia objects. Some can even be programmed directly in a spreadsheet like Excel. On this book's Web site (www.prenhall.com/turban), we provide a brief description of **fifth-generation languages (5GL), LISP,** and **PROLOG,** in which many ES tools, toolkits, shells, and deployed systems have been developed (e.g., SMECI from ILOG Inc. is written in LISP). As a variation, one could consider using KnowledgePro (KPWin from Knowledge Garden, www.kgarden.com), which can generate C++ code directly from an entered rule base. Also see Covington et al. (1997), Slade (1997), Spivey (1996), and AIS in Action 14.6.

OBJECT-ORIENTED PROGRAMMING

With the increased complexity of problems for which ES are developed, there is a trend toward using more frames and other object-oriented methods. As CASE tools for managing the development of object-oriented systems improve, specialized CASE methods are evolving to handle object-oriented ES. Object-oriented programming (OOP) tools are especially appropriate for applications that include multimedia and for delivering

AIS IN ACTION 14.6

TEMPLE UNIVERSITY DENTAL SCHOOL USES A PROLOG-BASED EXPERT SYSTEM TO SCHEDULE STUDENTS' CLINICAL ROTATIONS

Each semester, the Temple University School of Dentistry must develop a complex schedule for students' clinical rotations in seven clinics. The problem is constrained in that all clinics must be adequately staffed, students need time off for lectures and treating patients, and each student must serve about the same number of rotations over 2 years. When a manual process was used, it required 5 days to develop schedules. In 1988 a 2,500-line BASIC program was developed in 250 hours. The parameters of the scheduling problem were hard-coded, and given the answer, the (human) scheduler had to schedule specific rotations because the code could not handle that level of complexity. It still took the scheduler 3–5 days to work out schedules, totaling up to 20 days per year.

A PROLOG implementation was designed and developed in 1990. The knowledge is stored in *predicates* that *relate* the objects (students, clinics, times, days, and so on) of the scheduling problem. The sched-

uling program contains only about 16 predicates, consisting of 45 clauses. The entire PROLOG program (really a collection of facts and rules) is about 200 lines long and took 40 hours to develop. In the first 4 years of its operation, the developer was called in once to update the program to reflect changes in the assignment rules. Updating the program took a few minutes. The input and output routines took 98 hours to develop. The time required to enter data and generate a usable schedule is about 1 hour (a savings of up to 19 days per year). All the clinics now use the PROLOG scheduler (the expertise was transferred across the organization). The schedules are consistent and complete, and the students are more satisfied with them because they even out the work.

Source: Condensed and modified from T. K. L. Schleyer, "Temple Dental School Uses an Expert System to Schedule Students' Clinical Rotations," *Interfaces,* Vol. 24, No. 5.

ES capabilities to Internet Web servers (e.g., Exsys, InstantTea, K-Vision, and KPWin). Some powerful OOP development tools are ART*Enterprise (Brightware Inc.) and Advisor Solutions Suite and Blaze Expert (Blaze Software). An interesting Active-X language-enhancing tool is ActiveAgentX (The Haley Enterprise Inc.). ActiveAgentX for business rule automation is based on the Eclipse inference engine. It fully supports Microsoft's component object model (COM) and integrates into Windows application software.

WEB/INTERNET/INTRANET-BASED TOOLS

Based on the desire to disseminate expertise organization-wide or to customers, anyplace and anytime, most vendors have expanded their ES shells, toolkits, and languages to provide an ES interface directly through Web browsers. This feature provides a consistent interface style. For example, ES developed in Exsys (www.multilogic.com) and InstantTea (www.instanttea.com) can be accessed directly through a Web browser. This is a very powerful approach to providing automated help desk capabilities to employees and customers. The consistent interface the Web browsers provide can make expertise widely available.

AUTOMATED KNOWLEDGE ACQUISITION SOFTWARE

The concepts that underlie knowledge discovery in databases (KDD) and text apply to knowledge acquisition for expert systems. It is possible to induce rules or create an induction tree based on information or data storage in databases and textual material. There are a number of software tools that have been developed especially for this purpose. For example, CBR: The Easy Reasoner (The Haley Enterprise Inc.) uses associative memory to learn in the process of mining data into decision trees.

14.6 BUILDING EXPERT SYSTEMS WITH TOOLS

Building an ES with knowledge engineering tools involves the following steps:

1. The builder uses the development engine to load the knowledge base.
2. The knowledge base is tested on sample problems using the inference engine. The results may suggest additions and changes that could result in an improved knowledge base. This activity might even reveal the appropriateness of the knowledge representation or tool. This is basically a prototyping step performed with the aid of the editor and debugging tools.
3. The process is repeated until the system is operational.
4. The development engine is removed, and the specific expert system is ready for its users (using a separate run-time—(executable)—component of the tool).

14.7 SHELLS AND ENVIRONMENTS

SHELLS

Expert systems consist of six basic components: knowledge acquisition subsystems, an inference engine, an explanation facility, an interface subsystem (for conducting consultation), a knowledge-base management facility, and knowledge base(s). The first five subsystems are usually part of an expert system **shell.** The knowledge base is the content inside the shell. There is no need to program the first five subsystems of the shell for every application. On the contrary, once a shell is constructed, it can be used for many applications; all one needs to do is insert new knowledge. With the shell approach, expert systems can be built much faster. Consequently, the programming skill level required is much lower. These factors together contribute to cost reduction. Reusability is a powerful concept in systems development. The shell concept, illustrated in Figure 14.3, is extremely useful in developing rule-based systems. Generally a shell can represent knowledge in only one or two forms (e.g., rules and cases) and manipulate them in a limited number of ways (e.g., backward or forward chaining). A good shell allows the knowledge engineer to focus on the knowledge because the shell automatically manages the knowledge, the interface, the inferencing method(s), and the inferencing rules. Examples of some rule-based shells are Exsys, InstantTea, XpertRule KBS, G2, Guru, K-Vision, CLIPS, and JESS. See this book's Web site and Durkin (1994) for more. For additional information on many types of specific shells, see the current "*PC AI* Buyer's Guide" (www.pcai.com/pcai) and the *AI Expert* "Expert Systems Resource Guide."

Shells can be categorized as *general* or *domain-specific.* In selecting a shell, make sure that it can handle the specific nature of the application properly, including explanation and interfacing with databases and other systems. In the Opening Vignette, the shell could not interface easily with data from a mainframe database, which negatively influenced its usefulness. Also, financial applications typically use forward chaining because all the facts are generally known in advance, while Exsys has the ability to perform only backward chaining.

Shells do have limitations and disadvantages. Because they are inflexible, it can be difficult to fit them to nonstandard problems and tasks. As a result, a builder may use several shells, as well as environments and other tools, in a single application. This may

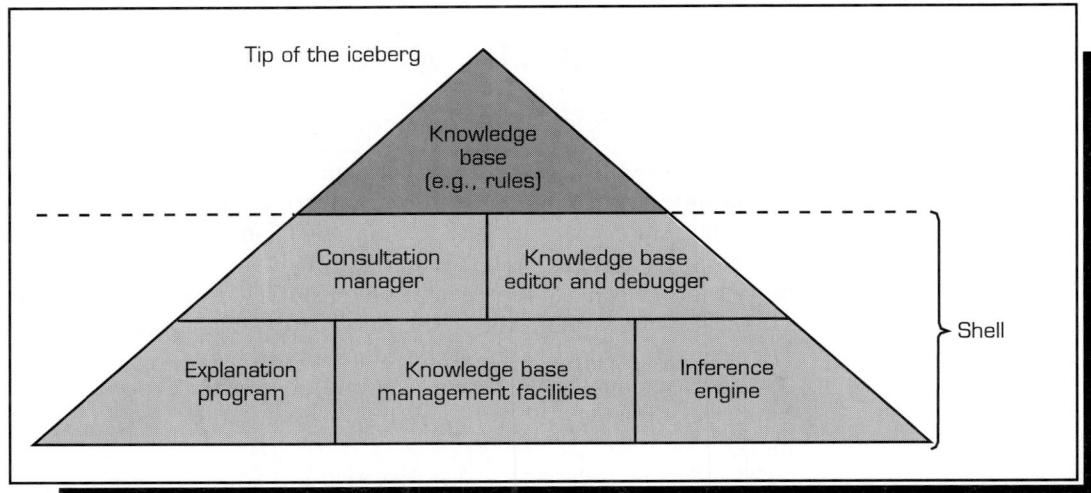

FIGURE 14.3 SHELL CONCEPT FOR BUILDING EXPERT SYSTEMS

Source: B. G. Buchanan, in Texas Instruments' first satellite program.

cause problems as each software package is upgraded and in training and maintenance. Shells are end-user tools (similar to DSS generators), and their use is subject to all the problems of end-user computing (poor documentation, security, development of inappropriate methods, use of stale data or knowledge, improper maintenance, and so on).

Despite their limitations, shells are extremely useful and are used extensively by many organizations. In some cases, they are employed primarily in training or as the initial tool in the prototyping cycle (which makes a shell that can produce code quite useful).

Domain-specific tools are designed to be used only in the development of an ES for a specific application area. For example, there are shells for diagnostic systems, configuration, financial applications, help desks (Knowledge Library at Ask.Me OnLine for computer software support, www.amol.com, and PlanWrite for developing a business plan, www.brs-inc.com), and scheduling. Domain-specific tools may include some rule-based tools, an inductive mechanism, or a knowledge verification component. Domain-specific tools enhance the use of more standard tools by providing special development support and a user interface. These features permit faster application development. Some include embedded knowledge (e.g., Knowledge Library at Ask.Me OnLine, www.amol.com; the Australian legal expert system Shyster, cs.anu.edu.au/software/shyster; and Joseph, a medical expert system that helps interpret EKGs). There are only a few commercial domain-specific shells and tools.

ENVIRONMENTS

Development environments are development systems that support several different ways to represent knowledge and handle inferences. They can use frames, object-oriented programming, semantic networks, rules and metarules, different types of chaining (forward, backward, and bidirectional), nonmonotonic reasoning, a rich variety of inheritance techniques, and more (Table 14.6). Hybrid systems (environments) create a programming environment that enhances the building of complex specific systems or complex tools. Initially, hybrid tools were developed for large computers and AI workstations, but now they are available for personal computers. Some representa-

---

TABLE 14.6   Features of Hybrid Systems

- Backward, forward, and bidirectional chaining
- Object-oriented programming, frames
- Metarules
- Semantic networks
- Other graphical representations such as inference trees and decision trees
- Hypothetical reasoning
- Case-based reasoning
- Complete pattern-matching or variable rules
- Automatic rule identification
- Nonmonotonic reasoning or truth maintenance
- Dynamic graphics, icons, visual interactive simulations
- High-quality browsing utilities
- CASE library facilities
- Debugger to set break points or interrupt consultation
- Interfaces to databases, spreadsheets and hypermedia, neural networks, the Web, and other packages
- Ability to import and export knowledge, data, and results
- Real-time capabilities
- Graphical user interface
- Knowledge editor
- Rule verifier
- Command language
- Blackboard
- Ability to generate computer code (usually C)
- Explanation subsystem
- Additional modeling and solution routines such as optimization, neural networks, fuzzy logic, and genetic algorithms

Source: Modified from *Expert Systems Strategies 4,* Harmon Associates, No. 2, 1988.

---

tive packages are ART-IM, Level5 Object, and KAPPA PC. See this book's Web site for other packages.

Environments are more specialized than languages. They can increase the productivity of system developers. Although environments require more programming skills than shells, they are more flexible. Several hybrid systems are based on Smalltalk and OPS.

14.8 SOFTWARE SELECTION

Software packages of languages, aids, environments, and shells are plentiful [see Stylianou et al. (1995), the latest "*PC AI* Buyer's Guide," the "Expert Systems Resource Guide" in *AI Expert,* and the FAQs of ES news groups]. There are several hundred commercial packages for knowledge acquisition, representation, browsing, debugging, editing, explaining, and so on. Selecting software can be complicated because of the frequent changes in technology and the many criteria against which the alternative packages are compared (Anderson, 1990).

Tool selection should be based on a match between the knowledge to be represented and the tool features. In practice, selection is complex because

- It is difficult to make the transition from problems to tools.
- Tool selection is affected by whatever tool the company already has and its familiarity with ES tools.
- Many of the tools on the market are more similar than different.

The major issues involved in the selection of ES development software are summarized in Table 14.7 (also see Stylianou et al., 1995). For complex systems a developer might use several software development packages.

SOFTWARE EVALUATION PROCEDURES

Several methods have been proposed for the evaluation of ES software. Generally, these methods use a set of attributes against which packages are compared. In addition, in-depth evaluations of popular packages appear periodically in AI magazines. One problem is that most of these evaluations are subjective. Also, the package capabilities change rapidly with new releases. See Harmon et al. (1988) and Stylianou et al. (1992, 1995). All other things being equal, cost-effectiveness can be the determining factor in software selection. The best approach is to try the software and evaluate it directly. Then develop and/or use a selection model, perhaps in Expert Choice (Chapter 5), to assist in selecting the appropriate software for your application.

SHELLS VERSUS LANGUAGES

Choosing which software tool to use is a major decision in the development process and depends on several important factors. For example, is programming capability available in-house, and if so, which languages are used? What type of computer system will be used to develop the software and what is the user's host computer? The selection of a tool is also affected by the amount of time and the funds available to create the software. Should a shell, an AI language, a conventional programming language, or some combination of these be used?

The fastest and easiest approach is to use a shell. But does the shell format fit the domain of interest? Is the shell capable of handling the proposed project? If this is a first expert system development project, try to use a shell. Start by identifying the shells available for the available hardware. Most shells run on PC-compatible computers and/or Unix workstations. Dozens of packages are available for IBM personal computers and various compatibles; fewer programs are available for the Apple Macintosh series. Several shells run directly on networks or on Web servers as Java applets. Most vendors provide demo versions of their shells on the Web. These are generally close to fully functional and can be downloaded and tested. Some run directly on the Web. There are also a number of free shells available from AI repositories on the Web.

If a shell is available for your computers and is within budget, determine whether its capabilities can deal with the problem. If necessary, perform some initial knowledge engineering to verify whether the domain can be expressed properly in the shell's knowledge representations. Build a demonstration prototype in this phase. Match the specifications of the tool to other aspects of the problem, and if there is a fit, by all means make the investment. If a shell does not match the requirements of the project, or if it requires extensive interfaces with conventional software, you should probably use conventional programming. Expert systems have been programmed in COBOL, Pascal, C, C+, and C++, and in the AI languages PROLOG and LISP.

Lists of software, shells, tools, languages, and so on, for ES development are available on many Web sites and in Durkin (1994).

TABLE 14.7 Representative Issues in Software Selection for Expert System Development

- Can the tool be easily obtained and installed? (This includes cost factors, legal arrangements, and compatibility with existing hardware.)
- How well is the tool supported by the vendor? Is the current version of the system fairly stable?
- How responsive is the vendor to the market (in terms of upgrading features and fixing bugs)?
- What are the vendor's plans for improvement? Will backward compatibility be maintained (or a conversion subsystem made available)?
- Can the vendor provide training and consulting if needed? How well is this supported?
- How easy is it for a developer to learn to use the tool? For a user?
- What training programs and materials are there?
- What training is necessary for the builder and for the users? Are there online tutorials?
- How easy is it for the developer and the user to use the interface?
- How difficult will it be to expand, modify, or ad a front end or back end to the tool? Is the source code available or is the system sold only as a black box?
- Is it simple to incorporate PROLOG (or other language) functions to compensate for necessary features that are not built in?
- What existing programming languages, databases, other knowledge bases, and other systems are likely to interface with the proposed application? Which ones will it support?
- What kind of knowledge representation schemes does the tool provide? (Rules? Networks? Frames? Others?) How well do these match the intended application?
- Can knowledge be easily imported and exported? If so, what formats does it support?
- Can the tool handle the expected form of the application knowledge (continuous, error-filled, inconsistent, uncertain, time-varying, and so on)?
- Do the inference mechanisms provided match the problem?
- How does the inference mechanism handle uncertainty? Is it appropriate for the problem?
- Does the allowable granularity of knowledge match what is required by the problem?
- Does the expected speed of the developed system match the problem if real-time use is required?
- Is there a delivery (consultation) vehicle available if many copies of the application will be needed (such as a run-time executable module)?
- What is the track record of success of the package?
- Have there been any failures? If so, why?
- What are the in-house software capabilities? Are programmers available and qualified?
- What are the future plans and strategy regarding AI dissemination and the use of languages and tools? Can the software generate HTML or KQML? Is there a Web server version?
- Is this the organization's first ES application? Or have systems been developed before? What software was used in the past?
- What is the anticipated maintenance plan? Who will be responsible for it?
- Where is the product going to be used and by whom?
- How easy is it to port applications to different hardware environments?
- Does the software have a good knowledge verifier and logic debugger?
- What platforms will the software run on? Are the versions on the multiple platforms compatible?
- What hardware and networks are present in the organization?
- Can multiple knowledge representations be used if needed?
- What knowledge acquisition aids does it provide, and what methods does it support?
- Is the software capable of automatic learning from documents and databases?
- What kind of explanation facilities does it support?
- Do we have software in-house already? Will it work?

Source: Modified from S. K. Goyal et al., "COMPASS: An Expert System for Telephone Switch Maintenance," *Expert Systems,* July 1985. Reprinted from *Expert Systems* with permission of Learned Information Inc., Medford, NJ.

14.9 HARDWARE

The choice of software packages is often determined by the hardware and its processing and memory power.

Initially, ES were programmed in special languages, such as LISP and PROLOG, that required specialized hardware (AI workstations). Today many commercial vendors have moved away from LISP and PROLOG and toward conventional languages such as C++ and toward shells and other tools that run on standard hardware. This ensures widespread distribution and compatibility.

The first ES developments were mainframe-based. As computer technology advanced, capable workstations and PCs were developed. ES software migrated to the smaller machines. Now, workstations and PCs are the ES development and deployment platforms of choice because

- There are many more personal computers and users.
- ES development tools for the personal computer are usually superior and cheaper.
- It is easy to buy a low-cost shell and experiment with the technology.
- PCs provide consistent, user-friendly interfaces.
- Many AI researchers have computer science backgrounds and tend to be biased toward working in a Unix environment. Unix runs on most RISC workstations and on the current generation of PCs and is inexpensive.

Some systems are still developed and deployed on mainframes (e.g., servers) to exploit the advantages of fast computation or large storage capacity.

14.10 PHASE III: RAPID PROTOTYPING AND A DEMONSTRATION PROTOTYPE

The prototyping process is actually less a phase and more a cycle of phases. Because of the way that knowledge is acquired and incorporated into an ES, we describe it as a phase. Prototyping has been crucial to the development and success of many ES. (See AIS in Action 14.7.) A prototype in ES starts as a small-scale system. It includes representation of the knowledge captured in a manner that enables quick inferencing and creation of the major components of an ES on a rudimentary basis. For example, in a rule-based system the first prototype, the **demonstration prototype,** may include only 10–50 rules and be built with a shell. A small number of rules is sufficient to produce limited consultations and test the proof of concept of the ES.

A prototype helps the builder decide on the structure of the knowledge base before spending time on acquiring and implementing more rules. Developing a prototype has other advantages, as shown in Table 14.8. Rapid prototyping is essential in developing large systems because the cost of a poorly structured and/or discarded ES can be quite high.

The process of rapid prototyping is shown in Figure 14.4. We start with the design of a small system. The designer determines what aspect (or segment) to prototype, how many rules to use in the first iteration, and so on. The knowledge is acquired for the first iteration and represented in the ES. Next, a test is conducted. The test can be done using historical or hypothetical cases, and the expert is asked to judge the re-

PICKER INTERNATIONAL RUNNING CASE

PHASE III: RAPID PROTOTYPING AND A DEMONSTRATION PROTOTYPE

Service-engineering specialists, offering both engineering and manufacturing expertise, as well as regional and district specialists, collaborated with knowledge engineers to articulate diagnostic and repair strategies. However, developing tactics and tools to support these strategies was slow going. It had taken more than 5 years to reach this point. Even though the firm recognized that expert systems was the way to go, they were hit by a bad case of analysis paralysis.

They started with a flowchart approach, a diagnostic tree that represented IF/THEN/ELSE rules. This mapping helped the developers focus on the knowledge because ultimately there was a one-to-one correspondence between the knowledge in the flowchart and the rules developed in Questor. Ultimately, the flowchart was the demonstration prototype. It identified how to represent the knowledge and how the system would function.

As the system evolved, the flowchart was used less and less because the knowledge was transferred directly to the system and updated only there as prototypes were checked and double-checked.

TABLE 14.8 Advantages of Rapid Prototyping

- It allows project developers to determine whether ES technology is feasible.
- It provides a vehicle through which to study the effectiveness of the knowledge acquisition and representation.
- It provides information about the initial definition of the problem domain, the need for the ES, and so on.
- It can predict important gaps or important problems in the proposed final system.
- It provides an opportunity to impress project champions with the system capabilities, helping to retain or increase support for the project.
- It makes selling the system to skeptics easier.
- It helps sustain the expert's and the manager's interest.
- It can help build user support.
- It makes it easier for experts to criticize existing programs or provide exceptions to the rules (to be incorporated).
- It accelerates the process of knowledge acquisition.
- It allows the possibility of early and midcourse corrections of the project direction based on feedback from management, consulting experts, and potential users.
- It yields a tangible, functional version of the project at an early stage.
- In early development stages, it provides a system that can be field-tested, yielding experience in using and testing the system and, if the tests are successful, credibility that the final system will perform well.
- Early prototypes might provide enough utility to be deployed in the field. This yields benefits, such as giving experience to system deployers, operators, and maintainers, and can provide early feedback to the system developers.
- It helps in estimating the benefits of the system and the degree of the expert's cooperation.

Source: Based in part on D. S. Prerau, *Developing and Managing Expert Systems,* Reading, MA: Addison-Wesley, 1990, p. 39.

sults. The knowledge representation methods and the software and hardware effectiveness are also examined. A potential user should also test the system. The results are then analyzed by the knowledge engineer, and if improvement is needed, the system is redesigned. Usually the system goes through several iterations with refinements, and the process continues until it is ready for a formal demonstration. Once

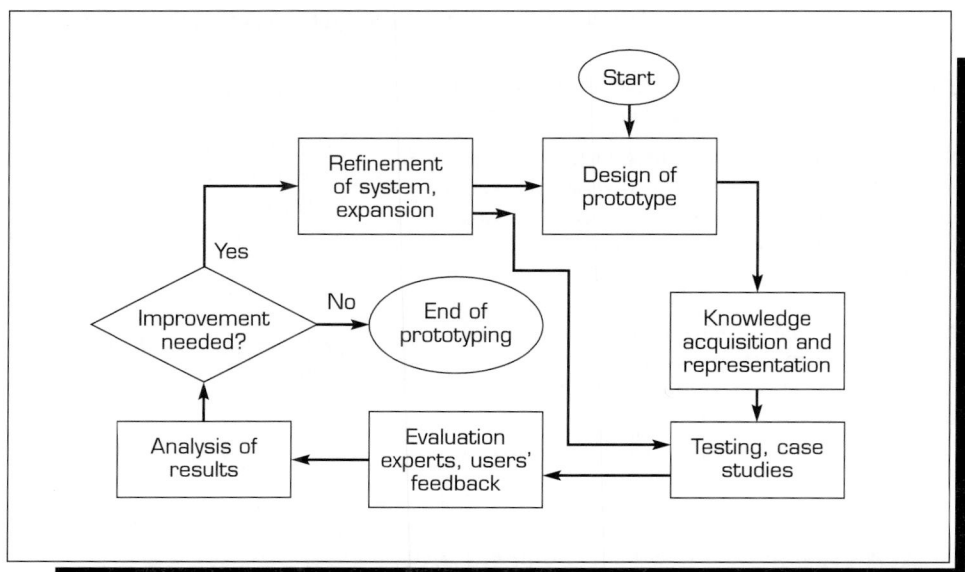

FIGURE 14.4 Rapid Prototyping

the system has been demonstrated, it is tested again and improved. This process continues until the final (complete) prototype is ready. For details, see Studt (1994) and Chapter 6.

One advantage of rule-based systems, especially when combined with frames, is that they are modular. It is possible to construct small chunks of knowledge and test them one at a time. They can be added to the system in a piecemeal fashion gradually leading to the final system. If each chunk is tested and validated separately, the final system should work the first time. In fact, some inferencing systems such as Algernon (Kuipers and Crawford, 1994) use a hierarchical representation of rules and limit the inferencing to chunks of knowledge (frames) that will most likely lead to conclusions, thus speeding up their search.

The prototyping phase can be short and simple, or it can take several months and be fairly complex. Some early ES such as the famous Campbell Soup Company Soup Cooker diagnostic ES took a little more than a year to develop. The lessons learned during rapid prototyping are automatically incorporated into the final design as the process iterates. After the demonstration prototype is shown, another go/no-go decision is made.

14.11 PHASE IV: SYSTEM DEVELOPMENT

Once the initial prototype is ready and management is satisfied, system development begins (see AIS in Action 14.8 and 14.9). Plans must be made for how to continue. At this stage, the development strategy may be changed (e.g., a consultant may be hired). The detailed design is also likely to be changed, and so are other elements of the plan.

PICKER INTERNATIONAL RUNNING CASE

PHASE IV: SYSTEM DEVELOPMENT

Building the Knowledge Base
Picker knowledge engineers familiar with its products and skilled in the construction of knowledge bases used technical service notes and online documentation to supplement the flowcharts and interviews with domain experts. For example, it took 3 months to develop the knowledge base for the computed tomography (CT) product line. This involved one experienced knowledge engineer working 300 hours researching and preparing the CT knowledge base in TestBench. TestBench's object-oriented approach kept the development time short. TestBench includes an object-oriented, diagnostic-specific development system with proven problem-solving strategies and a diagnostic methodology. These approaches include decision tree reasoning for structured but simple problems; fault hierarchy reasoning for

highly structured and complex problems; case-based reasoning for shallow, simple lookup types of problems; and rule-based reasoning for exception-oriented problems. TestBench is designed to help field engineers, novices and experts, diagnose and repair problems faster. TestBench helps them through the diagnostic process. *It augments their intuition.* TestBench is an ideal tool for developing the Questor expert system.

Picker's experience recommended that the knowledge engineers learn about the domain as they constructed the system. Questor includes *Electronic Documents* to support the diagnostic processes, linked through TestBench. These include documentation, repair procedures, parts lists, block and schematic diagrams, and so on. Other tools are used to convert the knowledge and inferencing mechanisms to the deployed system.

PICKER INTERNATIONAL RUNNING CASE

PHASE IV: SYSTEM DEVELOPMENT (CONTINUED)

Testing, Validating, Verifying, and Improving
As the knowledge base evolved, the system was tested, validated, verified, and improved. Faulty knowledge was corrected, and updates were incorporated. Knowledge about additional products was phased into the system over time.

The initial version of Questor was tested once the knowledge about its MTX product family was encoded.

Two separate classes (about 36 engineers) had just been trained on Questor. As a baseline, the firm had just measured the mean time to diagnose problems for its manual diagnostic methods for a set of six system faults. In both classes, five of the six repairs were performed faster with Questor. More testing was done. The new metrics allowed Picker to determine where people spent most of their time so that these areas could be targeted for support.

Depending on the nature of the system—its size, the amount and type of required interfaces with other systems, the dynamics of the knowledge, and the development strategy—one or both of the following approaches is used for system development:

- Continue with prototyping (common)
- Use the traditional SDLC (rare).

System development can be a lengthy and complex process. In this phase, the knowledge base is developed, and continuous testing, reviews, and improvements are performed. Other activities include the creation of interfaces (e.g., with databases, documents, multimedia objects, hypermedia, and the Web), creating and testing the user's interface, and so on. In the Opening Vignette, a user interface was created so that facts could be entered at once rather than screen by screen, and another interface was developed for database interaction. In this phase, prototyping continues, but needs are handled as they arise. The two major tasks are to develop the knowledge base and to evaluate and improve the system.

DEVELOPING THE KNOWLEDGE BASE

Developing the knowledge base means acquiring and representing knowledge in an appropriate form in the computer and involves a number of activities. See AIS in Action 14.8.

DEFINE THE POTENTIAL SOLUTIONS

The first step in organizing the domain knowledge is to list all the possible solutions, outcomes, answers, choices, or recommendations that the system can yield. (At least all that are known now—more can be added throughout the prototyping process.) In a rule-based system, each potential solution is in a THEN portion of at least one rule.

DEFINE THE INPUT FACTS

The next step is to identify and list all the facts and data that will be required by the system. These are the facts and data that the developer may hard-code or obtain from a database or other source or that the user may enter into the system. (This list also evolves with prototyping.) An expert system asks questions to obtain such inputs (in backward chaining and CBR). For example, the system may ask how old you are if there is a rule saying that if you are 18 or older you can vote in a federal election. (In forward chaining and other methods, all the facts are available upfront.)

DEVELOP AN OUTLINE

This process helps in preparing to write the rules. Large, complex knowledge domains usually require some additional organization that an outline can provide.

DRAW A DECISION TREE

The elements of knowledge (or portions of it) may be such that they organize themselves quickly into a tree format. If so, you may be able to proceed directly to the development of a decision or search tree. This fits well with newer ES shells.

CREATE A KNOWLEDGE MAP (MATRIX)

Some knowledge organizes itself neatly into a matrix showing the various attributes that produce a particular conclusion. Induction shells use this knowledge-formatting technique. If you have selected such a shell, you can proceed immediately to organizing your knowledge as examples via an induction table.

CREATE THE KNOWLEDGE BASE

Once the rules are written, you can enter them directly into the shell. Your first objective should be to build a small prototype as described above. Select one small subset of the knowledge base and enter its rules into the shell. This can usually be done quickly. The result will be a prototype that can be tested to check ideas and verify their implementation quickly. When this prototype is demonstrated to the users, their reactions can be used in designing the user interface and initial logic. If the prototype works, proceed with confidence to develop the remainder of the rules.

TESTING, VALIDATING, VERIFYING, AND IMPROVING

The prototype, and later improved versions of the system, are tested and evaluated for performance both in the lab and in the field (see AIS in Action 14.9). Initially, evaluation is done in a simulated environment. Test problems (like historical cases or sample cases provided by experts and users) are fed into the system.

The process of evaluating the knowledge and the knowledge base was discussed in an earlier chapter. However, in addition to testing the knowledge, it is necessary to test the entire system both before and after it has been fielded (Adelman, 1992; Touchton and Rausch, 1993). Grogono et al. (1991) provide an extensive bibliography on both evaluation techniques and the way they are applied. The expert system may be only one component in a decision support system and, as a result, the evaluation may be complex (Adelman, 1992). Several evaluation techniques were surveyed by Sharma and Conrath (1993), who described the scope and limitations of each and divided them into three categories: quantitative, qualitative, and hybrid.

Evaluation also deals with the issue of the quality of the advice rendered. Determining quality can be a very difficult activity if we lack standards for comparison (see AIS in Focus 14.10). Expert systems often give advice in areas for which there are no standards, and so simple comparisons are impossible (see the Opening Vignette).

A common method used to evaluate an ES is to compare its performance with an accepted criterion, such as a human expert's decision. In this approach, called the **modified Turing test,** experts are given two solutions to a problem. One is the result of human judgment and the other is that from an ES. Without knowing which is which, they are asked to compare and evaluate the solutions. There are several problems with this approach. First, the open-endedness of many management problems may make it difficult

---

AIS IN FOCUS 14.10

DIFFICULTIES IN EVALUATING AN EXPERT SYSTEM

The following questions indicate the difficulties that hinder ES evaluation studies:

- What characteristics should be evaluated? The performance of the system has been the main factor. However, the system's interface or ease of use may also be key to its acceptance.

- How should performance be evaluated? Because of the nature of expert system applications, it is sometimes hard to define a standard against which to compare the system's performance. For example, a match between the conclusions of the system and those of the expert may be hard to obtain. Indeed, different experts may disagree on certain details, or both the problem and one or more of the experts may be wrong. In evaluating performance, should one look only at the conclusion or should the program's line of reasoning be evaluated as well? What form should the evaluation take when the system provides multiple (as opposed to unique) answers?

- How should the test problems be selected? The fact that the realism of real-world exceptions and irrelevancies can seriously affect the performance of an expert system is well known. However, in certain areas the supply of realistic studies may be very limited. In geologic ES, for instance, there are only a small number of known ore deposits to draw on. Similar problems occur with ES that diagnose rare diseases.

- How should one evaluate the program's mistakes? In judgmental areas, it is interesting to observe the type of mistakes an expert system can make. A search for error patterns takes place in intelligent tutoring systems, but the implications for evaluation studies appear to be unexplored. Clearly, this issue also relates to the requirement that expert systems degrade gracefully.

Source: A. A. Assad and B. L. Golden, "Expert Systems, Microcomputers, and Operations Research," *Computers and Operations Research,* Vol. 13, Nos. 2 and 3, 1986. Reprinted with permission.

to describe them to an independent evaluator. The problems may be so complex that even experienced decision makers may disagree on their proper interpretation and solution. Second, expert systems used by teams of managers should probably be evaluated by teams of managers; hence they may be more difficult to evaluate because of possible disagreements (see the Opening Vignette). Despite this, an ES might be useful even if it only reduces task time while maintaining high-quality recommendations. Task time reduction may be a good initial criterion for the evaluation of an ES (as in the Opening Vignette).

In business settings, ES can often be evaluated by experimentation. Suppose that preventive maintenance is to be performed on several identical machines. An expert system's advice about the frequency of maintenance could be implemented in some of the machines, whereas the rest could be scheduled according to the vendor's or expert's recommendations. The breakdown rates and repair and maintenance costs under the two methods could then be compared to determine which one is superior. This has been done in farming situations in which an ES advised farmers when, how, and how much to plant, when to irrigate, when to fertilize, and so on.

AN ITERATIVE PROCESS OF EVALUATION

Each time an ES is presented with a new case, or whenever there are changes in the environment, the system must be refined (new capabilities are often added at this time). In a rule-based system, such a refinement is likely to produce more rules. XCON, for example, grew from a few hundred to about 20,000 rules over 10 years. Each time a substantial refinement is made, an evaluation should follow.

Evaluation also takes place during and after each development iteration. Performance is recorded as the system improves its use in either a simulated or a real-life environment. Development and evaluation continue as long as improvements are necessary. Once a system is deployed in the field, it is wise to attempt to capture knowledge from users to help refine it. (see the running case). Evaluation ensures that the system will make reasonable recommendations (see AIS in Focus 14.11). It involves both validation and verification. **Validation** is determining whether the right system was built or whether the system does what it was meant to do and at an acceptable level of accuracy. **Verification** confirms that the ES has been built correctly according to specifications. See Sturman and Milkovich (1995).

AIS IN FOCUS 14.11

SOME REQUIREMENTS OF A GOOD EXPERT SYSTEM

- The ES should be developed to fulfill a recognized and important need.
- The processing speed of the system should be very fast.
- The ES should be able to increase the users' expertise level and/or speed.
- Error correction should be easily accomplished.
- The program should be able to respond to simple questions from users.
- The system should be capable of asking questions to gain additional information.

- Knowledge should be easily modified (add, delete, and modify rules).
- The user should feel that he or she is in control.
- The novices' degree of effort (physical and mental) should be reasonable.
- Input requirements (facts and data) should be clear and simple.

Source: Based on D. C. Berry and A. E. Hart, "Evaluating Expert Systems," *Expert Systems*, Nov. 1990.

14.12 PHASE V: IMPLEMENTATION

The process of implementing an ES can be long and complex, like the implementation of any software project. See AIS in Action 14.12. Here, we briefly touch on several issues; in a later chapter, implementation problems and strategies are revisited.

ACCEPTANCE BY THE USER

Acceptance depends on behavioral and psychological considerations, as well as on quality and ease of use. It is important that the development of specific ES be discussed as widely as possible to foster a climate of acceptance among the people who will use it. Behavioral aspects play a major role in dealing with the user (Suh and Suh, 1993). Some users must be involved in the ES development effort because user satisfaction is positively related to user satisfaction in systems development (McKeen and Guirmaraes, 1997). In AIS in Focus 14.13 we show a list of important, empirically

---

AIS IN ACTION 14.12

PICKER INTERNATIONAL RUNNING CASE

PHASE V: IMPLEMENTATION

The system was implemented as soon as the knowledge base was developed. The prototypes evolved into the system as it was expanded and refined. Field engineers were trained in the use of Questor. Questor guides field engineers through the diagnosis

and repair of Picker products. Because it provides links to online documentation and because it presents a diagnostic approach developed and refined by Picker subject matter experts, the system makes diagnostic procedures in the field more uniform and more successful.

AIS IN ACTION 14.13

WAYS THAT USERS SHOULD BE INVOLVED IN ES DEVELOPMENT

The core activities of user involvement in ES development include

- Performing the feasibility study
- Meeting information or knowledge requirements
- Approving information or knowledge requirements
- Defining input–output forms, screens, and reports
- Installing the system.

When low participation is necessary, users should also be involved in

- Approving the project's cost justification
- Functioning as a liaison between the user community and the development team.

When there is high task and/or system complexity, users should be involved in

- Taking responsibility for project definition
- Defining physical controls and security measures
- Defining input–output forms, screens, and reports
- Conducting system tests
- Initiating the project
- Developing and approving management schedules and progress reports
- Ensuring that managers properly assess user participation
- Leading the project team

Source: Based on J. D. McKeen and T. Guimaraes, "Successful Strategies for User Participation in Systems Development," *Journal of MIS,* Vol. 14, No. 2, pp. 133–151, Fall 1997.

proven ways that users can be involved in ES development. These are important aspects of how change management is performed and how it applies to all IS.

ORIENTATION AND TRAINING

Sufficient and high-quality user training is an important factor in user acceptance of ES. Depending on the mode of deployment, the builders must plan appropriate orientation and training. If the users are assigned maintenance responsibilities, the training can be fairly extensive. This is *critical* to ES success.

DEMONSTRATION

Demonstrating the early prototypes and the fully operational system to the user community is important. This is part of user involvement. *Viewers can become believers.*

INSTALLATION APPROACHES AND TIMING

The expert system is ready for field-testing when it reaches a certain level of stability and quality. In rule-based systems, this may be when it can handle 75 percent of the cases and exhibit less than a 5 percent error rate. In some cases, the accuracy must be higher, especially if dictated by law (e.g., medical diagnosis). In some cases, once a specific set of products is incorporated, the system can be pilot-tested in the field just for these products (see the running case). The system can be installed in parallel with a human expert for a test period. When to deploy the system is a key issue in ES development.

MODE OF DEPLOYMENT

Several deployment modes for ES can be considered. The final system can be delivered to users as a turnkey, stand-alone system, it can be operated as a separate entity but integrated into the users' environment, it can be *embedded* into another system, or it can run as a service, with the users' requests and data accessed remotely and results delivered to the users. The Web is a convenient way to integrate an ES into the users' environment.

EMBEDDED ES

Embedding an ES into another system or consumer product is fairly common. Many people are still afraid of artificial intelligence but are perfectly happy to use computer-generated recommendations to improve their quality of life. ES have been embedded in intelligent database systems for years. The best help desk software has embedded ES in it (e.g., Knowledge Library at Ask.Me OnLine, www.amol.com, and K-Vision at www.ginesys.com). Some knowledge management software uses expert systems in cataloging knowledge and in determining how it can be stored, how it can be managed, and where it might be best used.

SECURITY

Security is a heightened concern in ES that may contain proprietary knowledge of a firm, which is considered intellectual property and has value. Communicating and distributing the end product, protecting the software, and at the same time providing an environment that does not constrain authorized users are substantial practical problems.

DOCUMENTATION

As is true for most IS projects, the 10 percent of the budgeted time and resources allocated for writing documentation generally disappears as the effort runs over schedule and budget. Consequently, there is a tendency either to skip writing the documentation or to do it minimally at the end. This is dangerous. Rules and other knowledge can be documented as they are entered into the knowledge base.

The planned documentation accompanying the system might consist of printed manuals, online documentation, or both. There may be different sets of documentation for system maintainers, operators, and users. Beerel (1993) specifically recommends the following maintenance documentation: a system overview, a technical description, a high-level map of the whole problem, maps of the individual tasks, an index of all the items within a knowledge base that depend on actions outside that knowledge base, a record of all computer files used, and printed versions and backups of all computer files used. For user documentation, she recommends including an introductory brochure, the system overview, a brief user guide, and a means of encouraging users to provide feedback on the system.

INTEGRATION AND FIELD TESTING

If the expert system stands alone, it can be field-tested. Otherwise, it must be integrated with or embedded in another information system before field-testing can commence. Field-testing is extremely important because conditions in the field may differ from those in cases provided by experts (see the Opening Vignette).

14.13 PHASE VI: POSTIMPLEMENTATION

Several activities are performed once the system is deployed to users. See AIS in Action 14.14. The most important of the activities are system operation, maintenance, upgrading and expansion, and evaluation.

OPERATION

According to Prerau (1990),

> If the expert system is to be delivered as a service, a system operations group (or several groups if there are several sites) should be formed and trained. If the system is to be a product run by users, an operator training

---

AIS IN ACTION 14.14

PICKER INTERNATIONAL RUNNING CASE

PHASE VI: POSTIMPLEMENTATION

In the field, the online documents embedded in Questor increase the productivity of field engineers by 40 percent. The time required to solve problems in the field has diminished, providing better customer support.

The system is updated as new products come online. The existing knowledge base must be updated as new problems arise and are solved. Questor also in-

cludes a notepad for field engineers to record observations and capture errors or improvements. Once reviewed, if appropriate, the new knowledge is incorporated in the next release. This feedback loop between Questor users and developers provides for improvements in the product itself and collects information about diagnostic and repair processes and procedures. These observations can drive process improvements throughout the entire field-service organization.

group may need to be formed, and consideration should be given to providing help for user-operators with problems. If the system is embedded into another system, the operators of the other system should be trained in any new operating procedures required.

MAINTENANCE

Because an expert system evolves over time, it is never really finished. Thus, it is important to plan maintenance. It must be revised on a regular basis with regard to the applicability of the rules, the integrity and quality of the data feeds, the use of the interlinked databases, and so on (Beerel, 1993). Because experts are constantly training themselves on new situations or reorganizing their knowledge in accounting for unencountered situations, an ES must be adjusted for these cases. In addition, software and hardware bugs must be fixed as found and the system must be upgraded to run on new software releases and hardware platforms. Just as in the traditional system development life cycle, there is a maintenance cycle, and a long-term maintenance team must be formed and trained to perform these tasks. See Beerel (1993) and Prerau (1990) for details. See AIS in Action 14.15 for an example of an ES in which the users maintain the knowledge base.

If the expert system is embedded in another system, some thought should be given to whether one maintenance group will serve the overall system or whether the expert system will be maintained separately. For separate maintenance, procedures for coordinating the two maintenance groups must be developed. For further discussions of maintenance and upgrading, see McCaffrey (1992) and Karimi and Briggs (1996).

AIS IN ACTION 14.15

DELIVERING MARKETING EXPERTISE TO THE FRONT LINES

The needs of customers and business often coincide but never so readily as when customer service representatives have knowledge about products and services at their fingertips and never so effectively as when this knowledge is tailored to the needs of each client. This is the idea behind CSR-Advisor, an expert system application at AGT, a Canadian telecommunications company. The program integrates marketing expertise into the order entry process, putting it on the front lines with customer service representatives (CSRs).

To be effective, marketing strategies must be fine-tuned regularly in response to changing market conditions and feedback from previous marketing initiatives. The task of mapping a diverse, constantly changing set of products and services to an individual customer's needs is very knowledge-intensive. To be most effective, it must be possible for marketing personnel to make the changes themselves and for the changes to take effect immediately. This worked for some representatives but not for others, who required a knowledge engineer's assistance. An external task-specific knowledge base for marketing knowledge was structured for the system.

CSR-Advisor was designed for serviceability as well. The knowledge base is partitioned into packets of standard types for easy understanding and debugging. The client/server architecture also helped in that most of the development team's effort is on the PC side. In initial trials, CSR-Advisor focused on residential installation orders (20 percent of service orders), which have the greatest potential payoff. In addition to reducing CSR training time and error, CSR-Advisor increased revenue by 71 percent per order.

Source: Condensed from C. D. Stafford and J. de Haan, *IEEE Expert,* Apr. 1994, pp. 23–32.

EXPANSION (UPGRADING)

Expert systems evolve continuously and therefore expand continuously. All new knowledge must be added, and new features and capabilities must be included as they become available. Upgrading tasks generally falls under the jurisdiction of the maintenance team. However, some expansion can also be performed by the original developer(s) or even by a vendor. Some systems can automatically capture problem areas to be addressed in the next version (see the running case).

EVALUATION

Expert systems need to be evaluated periodically (e.g., every 6 or 12 months, depending on the volatility of their environment). When evaluating an ES, questions like the following should be answered:

- What is the actual cost of maintaining the system as compared to the actual benefits?
- Is the maintenance provided sufficient to keep the knowledge up to date so that system accuracy remains high?
- Is the system accessible to all users?
- Is acceptance of the system by users increasing?

If the users have been encouraged to comment on the ES and the feedback process is easy, it is much easier to maintain a system under continuous feedback. This also reduces the effort of the periodic evaluation.

WHY EXPERT SYSTEMS FAIL

There are a number of reasons why expert systems fail. If they are never deployed, then there usually have been some major complications in one or more of the earlier phases of development. Usually, these problems are based on managerial or economic issues. Rarely are failures due to technological problems. For a deployed system, organizational issues are usually the problem. Often, system maintenance or economic issues arise. For example, if the environment changes, making the ES recommendations infeasible, or the nature of the task simply changes, then the ES should be updated to reflect the changes. In AIS in Focus 14.16 we list the 10 explanations reported by Gill (1996b) for a set of 38 ES of which two-thirds were permanently discontinued or abandoned over a 5-year period. The first two relate to performance and economics, while the remainder are organizational in nature. Related to this is a study by Tsai et al. (1994a), who identified which tasks were considered the most difficult in ES development (in order: knowledge acquisition, validation and verification, encoding, and maintenance) and identified the major problems associated with ES (the top three are integration, resistance to change, and finding experienced knowledge engineers). The key to ES success then is to develop a high-quality system, keep it current, and involve the users in every step of system development.

RUNNING CASE

In AIS in Action 14.17 we conclude the Picker International running case with a set of lessons learned. A summary appears in Case Application 14.2, along with case questions.

AIS IN ACTION 14.16

WHY EXPERT SYSTEMS FAIL

Here are 10 reasons why expert systems have failed in practice either during the development process or after deployment:

- *Change in task.* The expert system no longer solved a meaningful problem or could not provide meaningful solutions.
- *Maintenance costs became too expensive.* In some cases, external funding stopped.
- *System became misaligned with the computing environment.* Interfaces needed to be updated because of changes in the field.
- *Change in company focus or industry outlook.* The business environment changed or the company no longer had to deal with the problem that the ES solved.
- *Failure to recognize task domain size.* As the system was developed, the true size of the task domain was identified and the budget did not increase accordingly (e.g., in product support, too many products were released in a short time frame).

- *Users did not perceive the problem as critical.* There was no demand to solve the problem or it was easy to solve.
- *Subjected developer to potential liability.* A system that provides legal advice can cause problems if the advice is faulty.
- *User resistance.* Sometimes users don't want systems imposed on them from outside, especially if they were not involved in their development.
- *Unwillingness to take on development responsibilities.* No one was willing to provide maintenance to some of the systems. Top management obviously did not demand that this be done.
- *Loss of key development personnel.* Turnover prevented system completion or maintenance. (This was a problem in one-half of the cases examined.)

Source: Adapted from T. G. Gill "Expert Systems Usage: Task Change and Intrinsic Motivation." *MIS Quarterly,* Vol. 20, No. 3, pp. 301–330, Sept. 1996b.

AIS IN ACTION 14.17

PICKER INTERNATIONAL RUNNING CASE

LESSONS LEARNED IN DEVELOPING THE QUESTOR DIAGNOSTIC EXPERT SYSTEM

The Picker experience demonstrates that when applying expert systems in practice, the following advice might be of use:

- Expert systems should be built incrementally. Don't wait to develop the complete design before starting and making some progress.
- The knowledge engineer needs to have some domain knowledge.
- The object-oriented approach provides flexibility.

- Capturing equipment and repair statistics not only provides support and repair process improvements but also provides product improvements.
- Empirical information about product failures and repairs doesn't provide all of the necessary information. More may need to be obtained with a special accounting approach.
- Making information available more broadly and flexibly leverages this information by enabling its use when and where it will do the most good (a fundamental goal of knowledge management; see Chapter 9).

14.14 THE FUTURE OF EXPERT SYSTEM DEVELOPMENT PROCESSES

New, more capable ES shells, toolkits, and language capabilities are being developed and made commercially available on a continuous basis. In keeping with this tradition, we expect to see advances in the following areas:

- Further advances in flexible toolkit capabilities, especially to include hybrids of inferencing such as combinations of ES, neural computing, fuzzy logic, and genetic algorithms
- Improved languages and development systems
- Better front ends to help the expert provide knowledge
- Improved interfaces via Windows-based environments (which are especially critical for software developed under Unix)
- Further use of intelligent agents in toolkits
- Better ways to handle multiple knowledge representations such as rules and frames
- Use of intelligent agents to assist developers
- Use of blackboard architectures and intelligent agents in ES itself
- Advances in the object-oriented approach, both as a means of representing knowledge (such as frames or semantic network nodes) and for ES programming
- Improved and customized CASE tools to manage ES development
- Increased hypermedia use and development, especially via the World Wide Web
- Improvements in automated machine learning of databases and text to induce rules and explanations immediately in deployed systems (knowledge discovery in databases, KDD).

❖ CHAPTER HIGHLIGHTS

- Building an expert system is a complex process with six major phases: system initialization, system analysis and design, rapid prototyping, system development, implementation, and postimplementation.
- The main indications that ES is an appropriate technology are that the problem has a sufficiently narrow domain and that some aspects of the problem are qualitative, so that conventional computing approaches do not apply.
- Many ES projects fail because of poor problem selection.
- Defining the problem properly can simplify the remaining development tasks.
- Choosing the correct knowledge representation of the problem domain and the appropriate ES shell or tool is important.
- Sometimes conventional technologies, such as training, are better than expert systems at capturing and deploying knowledge.
- Justification is made several times during the development process.
- Expert systems are difficult to justify because of the many intangible factors.
- There are detailed checklists indicating the requirements, justification, and appropriateness of ES for a problem.

- A feasibility study and a cost–benefit analysis help to justify the development of an ES.
- A feasibility study is essential for the success of any medium- to large-sized ES.
- As is true for DSS, often only a feeling on the part of the manager responsible for the problem is enough to justify development of an ES.
- One factor leading to ES success is permission to fail. ES projects have a high level of risk and potentially high benefits.
- Without the proper level of resource commitment, an ES will fail.
- Like costs, most benefits can be very hard to estimate or even be unknown at the start of an ES project.
- Top management support is essential from the inception of the project.
- Developing a proper team for ES development can be challenging; size, composition, leadership, and project management are some of the important factors to consider.
- A large ES needs a high-level champion as a sponsor.
- The potential system users must be involved in the ES development.
- The conceptual design of an ES contains a general idea of what the system will look like and how it will solve the problem.
- Expert systems can be developed in-house, by outsourcing, or through a blend of the two. There are several variations of each approach.
- Expert systems developed by end users can be successful. One system may save a little in costs and many small savings accumulate.
- Human experts possess knowledge that is much more complex than that in documented sources. It is based on experience and is usually qualitative and expressed via heuristics.
- Selecting and managing experts is challenging.
- Management should use incentives to motivate experts so that they will cooperate fully with the knowledge engineer.
- ES software can be classified into five technology levels: languages, support tools, shells, hybrid systems, and ES applications (specific ES).
- Specific ES are the application products that advise users on a specific issue.
- Shells are now integrated packages in which the major components of expert systems (except for the knowledge base) are preprogrammed.
- The Internet/Web is changing the way we provide expertise in organizations adopting ES technology.
- Expert systems consist of six basic components: knowledge acquisition subsystems, an inference engine, an explanation facility, an interface subsystem (for conducting consultation), a knowledge base management facility, and a knowledge base(s). The first five subsystems are usually part of an expert system shell.
- Despite their limitations, shells are extremely useful and are used extensively by many organizations.
- Several methods have been proposed for the evaluation of ES software. Generally, these methods utilize a set of attributes.
- Although ES can be developed with several tools, the trend is toward developing the initial prototype with a simple (and inexpensive) integrated tool (either a shell or a hybrid environment).
- New, potentially powerful ES development methods include the object-oriented approach toward ES design and development and ES Web server engines.

- Workstations and PCs are the ES development and deployment platforms of choice.
- Prototyping has been crucial to the development and success of many ES.
- Many ES are built by creating a small-scale demonstration prototype, testing it, and improving and expanding it. This process, which is repeated many times, has many advantages.
- The lessons learned during rapid prototyping are automatically incorporated into the final design as the process iterates.
- The major aspects of system development are developing the knowledge base and evaluating and improving the system.
- In a modified Turing test, experts are given a human and an ES solution to a problem. If the solutions are indistinguishable in quality, the ES is considered functional.
- Evaluation of expert systems is difficult because of the many attributes that must be considered and the difficulties in measuring some of them.
- Validation is determining whether the right system was built or whether the system does what it was meant to do and at an acceptable level of accuracy. Verification confirms that an ES has been built correctly according to specifications.
- Implementing an ES is similar to implementing any other computer-based information system. Change management is an important aspect of deployment.
- As is true for most IS projects, the 10 percent of the budgeted time and resources allocated for writing documentation generally disappears as the effort runs over the schedule and budget.
- Once the system is distributed to users, it is necessary to perform several tasks: operation, maintenance, upgrading, expansion, and postimplementation evaluation.
- There are many reasons why expert systems can fail in practice. Most are related to organizational issues.
- New, more capable ES shells, toolkits, and language capabilities are being developed and made commercially available on a continuous basis.

❖ KEY WORDS

- cost–benefit analysis
- demonstration prototype
- development environments
- development strategies
- domain-specific tools
- feasibility study

- fifth-generation languages (5GL)
- hybrid systems (environments)
- LISP (list processor)
- modified Turing test
- need assessment
- PROLOG

- shell
- toolkit
- validation
- verification

❖ QUESTIONS FOR REVIEW

1. List the phases in the ES development life cycle.
2. Describe the criteria that can be used to justify ES.
3. Give some guidelines for selecting a task suitable for an ES.
4. What can happen if ES technology is inappropriately applied to a problem?
5. What can happen if the wrong knowledge representation of the problem domain or an inappropriate ES shell or tool is selected?
6. Why is top management support crucial from the inception of an ES project?

7. Describe the activities of project initialization.
8. What is included in a conceptual design of ES?
9. Why is it important to estimate benefits and costs before developing a new ES?
10. Why is it difficult to estimate benefits and costs?
11. List the alternatives for ES development.
12. How can end users go about developing their own ES?
13. Who should be on the ES development team and why?
14. Describe the difficulties in finding a good expert.
15. What are the major guidelines for selecting experts?
16. What is a feasibility study? Why is it done?
17. What is a *champion?*
18. How should users be involved in ES development?
19. What is the difference between a shell and a programming environment?
20. How can an ES project start based just on a feeling on the part of a manager?
21. List the technology levels of ES.
22. What is a specific ES?
23. Define an ES shell.
24. What are the major components of a shell?
25. Describe the major advantages of a shell; also list the major limitations.
26. What are the differences between domain-specific tools and general-purpose tools?
27. Define programming environments and discuss their use.
28. Explain the difficulties in selecting ES software packages.
29. What is the purpose of rapid prototyping?
30. What is a demonstration prototype?
31. List all the activities conducted in implementation.
32. What is a modified Turing test?
33. Define validation.
34. Define verification.
35. Define postimplementation.
36. Why is evaluating ES performance difficult?
37. Describe the ES documentation task.
38. How is the Internet/Web changing the way we provide expertise in organizations adopting ES technology?
39. List the reasons why ES fail.
40. List the three most important advances expected in ES and explain why they are important.

❖ QUESTIONS FOR DISCUSSION

1. List and describe the phases of ES development.
2. The selection of an appropriate ES project is considered one of the most important tasks in ES development. Why? Why is it difficult?
3. Training is an alternative to using an expert system. Under what circumstances would you train rather than develop and use an ES (and vice versa)?

4. Review the elements that go into a feasibility study. Why is it difficult to conduct one?

5. Describe three intangible benefits of expert systems in detail and explain why they are important.

6. Explain how experts as users can benefit from an ES.

7. Why is it necessary to conduct cost–benefit analyses several times during the development process?

8. Explain why users are often not, but should be, represented as members of an ES development team.

9. Describe the roles of the key people in ES development in detail.

10. Describe the importance of having a top management champion in ES development.

11. Why is permission to fail so important in developing ES projects?

12. Describe what is meant by a conceptual design.

13. Discuss the general classes of ES development strategies.

14. Describe the different software technology levels of ES and compare them to those of DSS.

15. Why is it hard to evaluate expert systems?

16. Since it is so hard to evaluate expert systems, how do companies decide whether to develop one or not?

17. Why is the security issue so important to expert systems?

18. Review the attributes of experts listed in AIS in Focus 14.5. Which of them, in your opinion, are the five most important ones and why?

19. Choosing between a shell and a language is an ongoing debate. Find some material on the topic and prepare a table showing the advantages and disadvantages of each.

20. How do ES shells enable the quick development of ES?

21. Prototyping has many benefits. List and explain any disadvantages.

22. Review the elements that go into an ES. Relate these elements to the components of ES shells. Describe differences in terminology.

23. Why are so many domain-specific ES shells geared to dealing with diagnosis and prescribing a treatment?

24. Comment on the following statement: Constraints in software development tools may be very helpful.

25. Review the process of building a specific ES with knowledge engineering tools. Compare it with building any information system with tools (e.g., a spreadsheet).

26. Some say it is much easier to program with a simple ES shell (such as Exsys) than to program in a language like C++ or Visual Basic. Why?

27. Explain the difference between a domain-specific shell and a general shell. Why is the former more expensive?

28. Why is it difficult to match a problem with ES development tools?

29. Explain some advantages of the object-oriented approach to ES design and development.

30. Explain why prototyping is important.

31. Explain the importance of the demonstration prototype.

32. How is a modified Turing test used?

33. Why is it so difficult to obtain good documentation for a specific ES?

34. Explain why so many ES fail.

❖ EXERCISES

1. *Feasibility study for expert systems.* Assume that the president of a company or the commander of a military base asks you to do a feasibility study on the introduction of an expert system into the organization. Prepare a report that includes the following information:
   a. Identification of a problem area (go through the process in this chapter)
   b. Description of the experts to be involved, their capabilities, and their willingness to participate
   c. Software and hardware to be used in the project and reasons for your choice
   d. Development team and why each member is necessary
   e. Timetable for development and implementation
   f. List of potential difficulties during construction
   g. List of managerial problems (related to use of the system) that could appear if the expert system is introduced
   h. Construction and operating budgets
   i. List of interfaces (if needed) with other computer-based information systems.

2. *How to buy a used car.* Develop an expert system for advising a person on buying a used car. If you don't know much about buying a car but you have to buy one soon, you might consult with someone knowledgeable in this area. If an expert is unavailable, an expert system could provide advice.

   First, outline the activities in the development life-cycle steps required for such a system. Determine who the users of such a system might be. (Consider possible Web deployment to help users of new online buying services.) Identify experts and work with them iteratively to obtain knowledge about the process. While doing so, identify a few potential ES shells and the knowledge representation you think you'll need. Normally, you might use a rule-based approach, but frames or CASE-based reasoning might be appropriate. Consider them and decide whether they are appropriate ways to represent knowledge.

   Follow the phases of the development life cycle as outlined in the chapter. Make sure you validate the system with cases and let the expert judge the quality of the results. Then answer the following:
   a. Who are the potential users of your system?
   b. Who was your expert?
   c. What factors are important in choosing a car according to your expert? Why?
   d. Which knowledge representation method did you use and why? How did you decide this?
   e. What method of inferencing did you use and why? How did you decide this?
   f. What factors did you consider in choosing the ES shell? Was the ES shell appropriate? Would another one have been better? How about a language or a toolkit?
   g. Describe any problems you had in working with the expert.
   h. How many pieces of knowledge (rules, frames, cases) does your system have? Does it seem excessive? How many more do you think you would need to make your system operational and why?
   i. When you validated your system, how many cases did your ES get right out of the total? How much time or money would it take to expand the system to improve the results significantly?
   j. Were there any significant deviations from the development life cycle? If so, why? What was their effect on the development process and finished product?
   k. Did you ever have to repeat a step in the cycle? If so, why?
   l. What must be done to move from a prototype ES to a truly usable one?

3. Choose a real-world decision making problem for which ES is appropriate (recommending a restaurant, hotel, car, vacation spot, and so on). Describe the advantages and disadvantages of each software technology level for implementation

of the ES. Which one do you recommend and why? Then, use Expert Choice (Chapter 5) to choose the best one. Compare the two approaches.

4. Review the literature to determine the potential that the Internet/Web/intranets have to change the way expertise is distributed in organizations. Search the literature to identify information about Du Pont's AI strategy. Describe some of their recent projects.

5. Compare the ES development life-cycle phases to the Simon four-phase decision-making model. How do the phases overlap?

6. Explain how the object-oriented approach to systems can be applied to ES. (Check the relevant literature.)

7. Examine the literature and vendor information (possibly via the Web) to establish which of the advances mentioned in Section 14.14 are occurring in ES development systems.

8. We have observed in our classes that for team-developed ES, a team of five students can typically produce about one rule per day (using Exsys). Though this number sounds pretty low, it includes all system analysis and design time, meetings with experts and users, all the way through final report writing and presentations. Explain how this estimate can impact on the scope and time frame of an ES development project.

9. For the Opening Vignette, Case Application 14.1, and the running case, examine the requirements, justification, and appropriateness of the problem in terms of the Waterman (1985) framework for determining problem fit with an ES approach.

❖ Group Exercises

1. Get the most recent "*PC AI* Buyer's Guide" (in the magazine or on the Web) and examine ES development tools. Categorize them. What headings did you use? If demos are available on the Web, download at least three, try them, compare them, and write up your results in a report.

2. Find a salesperson who is willing to spend time with you to perform knowledge acquisition to build an ES that could help a novice in approaching a variety of potential customers. Then develop an ES with his or her advice in a shell.

❖ Group Projects

1. Complete the development of the real-world ES that your group started in Chapter 10. Present a demo of the system and then make a report to the class.

2. If you are in the process of developing an ES for a real-world organization as part of your course, describe the ES development process you are following and relate it to the phases and major activities described in this chapter.

3. For the group ES project, determine how it could provide benefits for the company for which you built it. Formally estimate potential benefits and costs. Are there any disadvantages? How serious are they? Demonstrate the project to the client and gauge his or her reaction. Will he or she be likely to adopt ES technology in the near future? Why or why not? Include with your final report a letter from your contact in the company.

❖ Internet Exercises

1. Search the Internet for ES shell vendors. Find information about new ES shells. Pick two and compare their structure and capabilities. Download at least one free demo and one commercial demo and compare them directly. Use Expert Choice (Chapter 5) to select the best one for the ES projects you are doing in this class.

2. Learn about CLIPS (or JESS, the Java version), a tool for building expert systems. Obtain a demo of CLIPS or the nongovernmental version, install it, and try it. What features make CLIPS useful? What could potentially hinder it?

3. Access an ES shell vendor's Web site (e.g., MultiLogic, Gensym, Knowledge Garden) and examine case studies of applications of their software. Produce a list of their clients and the types of problems being solved.

4. Access the Web site of MultiLogic (Exsys at www.multilogic.com) to evaluate their current generation of expert systems and their approach toward Web integration in their products. Run the online demos and compare the way they work. Write up your results in a report.

5. Repeat Question 4 for InstantTea (www.instanttea.com).

6. Search the Web for AI toolkits. Select five and compare and contrast their capabilities (and prices) in a report.

7. On the Web, investigate domain-specific ES development systems and software packages. Report your findings of the current status of these systems.

8. On the Web, search for and explore help desk systems and software and determine to what extent an ES is embedded in it. Also, search and explore vendors of ES shells and determine to what extent they are capable of supporting help desks.

APPENDIX
14-A

DEVELOPING A SMALL (RULE-BASED) EXPERT SYSTEM FOR WINE SELECTION[4]

Building a small knowledge base with an expert system shell is fairly easy. Here is an example. Selecting an appropriate wine for a certain type of food is not so simple. There are many qualitative factors influencing the choice. Delegating the decision to a waiter can be risky in some restaurants and even riskier at home if you are trying to impress someone. So, it may be useful to develop an expert system and bring your laptop computer with you to dinner. Here are the steps that were followed in developing an ES for wine selection. (The expert system shell Exsys was chosen in advance for this student project. Exsys walks you through most of the steps.):

1. Specify the problem (pairing wine and food at a restaurant).
2. Name the system (Sommelier).
3. Write the starting text ("Sommelier will help you select a wine...").
4. Decide on an appropriate coding for an uncertainty situation (such as 0/1, 0 to 10, or −100 to 100: we will use 0 to 10).
5. Decide on any other inferencing parameters as required by the shell (e.g., use all the rules or only some of the rules; set the threshold levels).
6. Prepare any concluding note that you want the user to see at the end of the consultation ("Thank you for using Sommelier. Bon appetit!").
7. Work with an expert to list the potential choices. There are 12 possible wines, including aged cabernet sauvignon blanc, crisp chardonnay, gerwürztraminer, merlot, pinot noir, zinfandel, and so on.
8. Develop a working knowledge of food and wine (this is the best part for the knowledge engineers who must gain some familiarity with the problem domain).
9. Develop a knowledge map with an expert (OK, maybe we did some testing on our own) in tabular form. This helps us focus on the knowledge.

10. Build the initial set of rules, the knowledge base, in the shell and debug them. In Exsys, this involves developing qualifiers, which are the questions to be posed to derive facts, and the answer set of possible fact values for each one. Qualifiers are explained below.
11. Demonstrate the system to the expert, refine the rules, and collect additional cases and rules.
    Repeat steps 9–11 until the recommendation given by the expert(s) and the system are the same.
12. Deploy the system (Bon appetit!).

Write the rules in the standard format required by the shell. Exsys uses the concept of qualifiers. For example, it is known that the wine depends on the menu selection: You might have meat, fish, poultry, or pasta, and you may have an appetizer as well. Each fact-gathering statement is called a *qualifier*. For example, qualifier 1 is the meat menu selection. Literally its text is the phrase "The meat menu selection is". Qualifier text generally ends in a verb. The qualifier can assume the following values: (1) prime rib, (2) grilled steak, and (3) filet mignon. These are called the *values* of the qualifier.

Now the first rule might be constructed as

> IF the meat menu selection is prime rib
> THEN pinot noir, confidence 9/10
> AND merlot, confidence 8/10
> AND aged cabernet sauvignon, confidence 6/10.

This means that each of the three choices is appropriate, but pinot noir is the best choice (9), followed by merlot (8), and then by aged cabernet sauvignon (6).

To build this rule, create a new qualifier and then select the number of the qualifier (1) and the appropriate value (1 for prime rib). This forms the IF part of the rule. Click to the THEN part of the rule and call up the choices (step 7) and select the appropriate values for the THEN

---

[4]Lisa Sandoval, a graduate student at California State University, Long Beach, developed this ES student project: "Your Sommelier."

part with the appropriate confidence level (don't forget the confidence level or the system will recommend no wine, leading to a rather dour evening). In this case the three wines are appropriate, but pinot noir is the best recommendation.

When all the rules are applied to the particular meal, the system might not recommend pinot noir overall. As other rules are consulted, the certainty in the choice may decrease. For example, the appetizer and the cost of the wine may influence the recommendation. Another consideration is the universe of the system's knowledge. If your menu selection is not on the considered list, the system will not know what to recommend because the main course is not part of its knowledge universe.

The first prototype's knowledge base included 14 rules. Each rule can include *notes* and *references*. Try developing an ES like this on your own. It's worth the time to attempt to become an expert as well.

CASE APPLICATION 14.1

THE DEVELOPMENT OF THE LOGISTICS MANAGEMENT SYSTEM (LMS) AT IBM

INITIATION

In June 1985, at IBM's Burlington, VT, plant, the industrial engineering group (IEG) manager proposed development of the logistics management system (LMS), an expert system to improve line flow and use and reduce cycle time in semiconductor manufacturing. IBM wanted to increase throughput with no further capital investment, improve product delivery, and enhance awareness of emerging opportunities in the fast-changing semiconductor wafer-manufacturing lines. IBM's advanced engineering and manufacturing group (which supports corporate-wide projects) funded the proposed project initially for only 1 year because of doubts that the IEG could develop LMS (they basically funded the development of a prototype).

INITIAL SYSTEM: GATEWAY

With top management's full support, a development team that included IEG's manager, several IEG building representatives, LMS building representatives, two industrial engineers, and an internal software development consultant was assembled. No end users were included, nor were IS group members, although they did assist with the technical aspects of the existing shop-floor control system.

After 6 months, the team built the GATEWAY and management access technique (MAT) prototypes, running under the VM operating system on an IBM Model 390 (mainframe). GATEWAY organized all the shop-floor data from individual systems in real time. MAT provided real-time access to all manufacturing information. By May 1986 (the end of the initial funding period) few changes had been recommended and the two systems were deemed stable. Once deployed, they quickly became embedded in IBM's business processes. In June 1986 Burlington's top management continued the project and picked up most of the bill.

SECOND SYSTEM: ALERT

The development team wrote rules for the ALERT subsystem prototype, an expert system that monitors the shop-floor transaction stream, generates alerts, and routes mail messages about alerts to the right person. The team created the prototype of ALERT using knowledge obtained in developing GATEWAY and MAT, along with discussions with experts. In December 1986 the ALERT prototype was delivered. It was stabilized by June 1987. Using ALERT, managers could increase throughput because the ES could detect conditions indicating that potential bottlenecks would occur in the future. The conditions, once identified, could be corrected. In June 1987 Burlington's top management elevated the status of LMS from exploratory to tactical and increased the funding levels, and IEG responded by expanding the staff and equipment.

Adapted from P. Duchessi and R. M. O'Keefe, "Evolutionary Steps in Expert Systems Projects," *Interfaces,* Vol. 25, No. 5, Sept.–Oct. 1995, pp. 194–208.

THIRD SYSTEM: DDM

In June 1987 a demand surge led the IEG to develop a dispatch decision maker (DDM) module of LMS, another ES that automatically responds to shop-floor problems and performs dispatching. The prototype helped avert a scheduling disaster by boosting throughput, thus allowing the organization to meet the demand. By September DDM was stabilized. Almost immediately, it identified major bottlenecks in the production line and through its corrective action saved tens of millions of dollars.

ENHANCEMENTS

From June 1988 to June 1990 the development team enhanced LMS with better interfaces to other systems and portability features. For maintenance purposes, it was reprogrammed in an object-oriented framework and ported to a PC. Simultaneously, IBM recognized the value of providing LMS to its customers, and so LMS became a *product*. In 1994 Burlington's top management elevated LMS to a strategic application. Royalties from non-IBM sales and consulting provided a revenue stream.

THE PROTOTYPING STEPS

LMS is an example of a successful long-term ES. The factors involved in its development were as follows:

- Willingness to take on a risky project (for 1 year)
- Establishment of a funded project
- Establishment of a multidisciplinary development team
- Understanding and control of data
- Broad user involvement (later in the project)

- Internal development of new expertise
- Expansion of the user base
- Personnel shifts and reassignment of tasks and responsibilities
- Emergence of new business opportunities (in a broader market).

Top management support, business benefits, and a talented multidisciplinary team were deemed critical to LMS implementation success.

CASE QUESTIONS

1. How did the LMS project get started? Is it common in organizations for initial funding of a project such as this to be made in the manner described? Why or why not?
2. Comment on the fact that IBM kept elevating the formal status of LMS. Is this important? Why or why not?
3. What could be different about developing and maintaining LMS as a commercial product rather than an internally used system?
4. Explain the evolutionary phases of LMS development and compare them to the phases and tasks outlined in this chapter. Why are they described as evolutionary instead of simply as phases or steps?
5. Could the traditional system development life cycle have been used for the development of LMS? Why or why not?
6. Why were the three items mentioned at the end of the case application critical to LMS implementation success? (*Hint:* Use the material in this chapter.)

CASE APPLICATION 14.2

PICKER INTERNATIONAL'S QUESTOR EXPERT SYSTEM RUNNING CASE

SUMMARY AND CONCLUSION

Picker International implemented the Questor expert system to assist field engineers in their service work. It took about 5 years before the firm was able to get past the analysis paralysis and start implementation of the Questor ES. Questor uses an induction tree to represent its knowledge, and each node in the tree includes an explanation of why that particular line of logic is being followed.

Questor, along with an electronic document management (EDM) system, was extremely effective in improving the productivity of field engineers, leading to higher levels of customer and field service engineer satisfaction. Here is a summary of the running case.

THE CHALLENGE

Picker International wanted to maximize return on field-service investment by

- Decreasing response time
- Lessening reliance on costly maintenance methods (paper documentation)
- Increasing the efficiency of field engineers (faster access to information)
- Capturing dissemination expert knowledge
- Leveraging expert knowledge.

THE SOLUTION

These goals moved Picker to restructure its field-service operation by

- Moving field engineers to a portable computing platform
- Restructuring dispatching to get information to engineers more quickly
- Moving from a static, bulky paper-based documentation system to an EDM system
- Providing diagnostic and repair expertise through an expert system.

THE FOCUS

Expert system technology let Picker tie its field-service infrastructure together by

- Providing engineers access to the experience of the experts in the home office and in the field
- Providing on-site engineers access to *all* needed documentation
- Capturing site knowledge for updating the knowledge base
- Providing practical knowledge and information for product design and manufacturing.

CASE QUESTIONS

1. Explain how development of the EDM set the stage for development of the Questor ES.
2. Describe how the Picker International approach to the development of Questor matched the phases of expert system development as described in the body of this text.
3. What features of TestBench made it extremely useful in developing a diagnostic-type expert system?
4. How was development of the Questor system justified in lieu of a formal cost–benefit analysis?
5. Why did it take 5 years to get started?
6. Describe the benefits of the Questor system.
7. Investigate how two other diagnostic expert systems (e.g., the one in the Opening Vignette and another one) were developed and compare and contrast the approaches with the development of the Questor system.

ADVANCED INTELLIGENT SYSTEMS

The decision-making technologies described up until now are relatively new but have solidly established themselves commercially. In Part V, we describe several cutting-edge technologies that are just proving themselves viable in the commercial world: neural computing, genetic algorithms, and fuzzy logic. Chapter 15 provides an introduction to neural computing from the theoretical point of view. Chapter 16 describes applications of neural computing, genetic algorithms, and fuzzy logic, and their integration.

Neural Computing: The Basics[1]

Neural computing is a problem solving methodology that attempts to mimic how our brains function. It is one of several successful approaches to machine learning. Machine learning refers to computer technologies that learn (refine their knowledge capabilities and accuracy) from experience (historical cases). This chapter describes the basic foundations of neural computing in the following sections:

---

[1]Some material on neural computing in this chapter was written by Larry Medsker, American University, Washington, DC.

15.1 OPENING VIGNETTE: HOUSEHOLD FINANCIAL'S VISION SPEEDS LOAN APPROVALS WITH NEURAL NETWORKS[2]

INTRODUCTION

Household Financial Corporation (HFC) sells and services auto loans and credit cards, including private label cards. In mid-1998, Household acquired Beneficial Corporation, creating the HFC and Beneficial divisions with 1,400 branch offices in 46 states. Its largest revenue-generating business unit is the consumer finance division that underwrites equity loans. The keys to competitiveness are *efficiency* and *customer intimacy*.

A problem experienced by consumer finance companies investing in technology is that loan products are complicated and subject to heavy regulatory restrictions. Laws vary by state and sometimes by county. The loan approval decision process uses many variables (consumer's income, employment history, credit history, outstanding debts, and so on). Capturing them in a software application is difficult.

Around 1994 the head of consumer finance, Bob Elliot, determined that Household should offer faster underwriting decisions than its rivals to compete effectively. Household could use technology to obtain central loan approval while a customer was still in the office, rather than ship the hard copy of the application and wait for days. This vision was the start of the Vision system.

SYSTEM DEVELOPMENT

System development began in late 1994. An object-oriented approach was taken so that multiple versions (more than 59) could be easily maintained and quickly updated. Test piloting began in mid-1996, and the entire system was completely deployed in early 1997. At the heart of Vision is a *neural network*. The network has been trained to recognize patterns of successful and unsuccessful loans based on past company history. Given a set of data representing an online loan application, the neural network can quickly recommend approval or denial of a loan. It can quickly be rerun with new information, dramatically speeding up the approval process, and creating a competitive advantage.

THE VISION SYSTEM

Household's Vision system integrates all phases of the process from lead to loan and connects to an *intelligent* underwriting engine. Vision contains seven integrated modules: (1) *Training* for account executives (AE), (2) *Lead Management Actions and Inquiries* to better manage customers, (3) *Solicitation* to handle contact management and create loan proposals, (4) *Underwriting* to model financial solutions using the customer's financial information, (5) *Closing* to generate all the necessary documents; (6) *Perfected Product* to bar-code documents to be sent to a central loan processing facility for scanning, and (7) *Service* to handle all aspects of customer service.

THE NEURAL NETWORK

In the Underwriting module, a neural network is fed risk, the interest rate, and other variables along with customer data for evaluation to determine loan terms. Typical underwriting requests are performed in minutes rather than in hours or days, the standard

---

[2]Adapted partly from D. Slater, "Loan Star," *CIO,* Vol. 13, No. 8, Feb. 1, 2000, p. 100–106, www.cio.com.

for the industry. The neural network engine for underwriting decisions is based on technology from HNC Software Inc. and Fair, Isaacs & Company. The HNC neural network performs fraud detection. Strategyware (Fair, Isaacs & Company) is at the heart of the system's suggestive selling component. The networks are trained with data patterns for good and bad customers so that they can identify these cases when deployed. Once the neural networks have been trained, they can estimate creditworthiness and potential fraud, even for cases unlike those they have seen before.

BENEFITS AND COSTS

The cost of the entire system over 3 years came to $83 million. Two key benefits of Vision are the reduced training time for new AEs and the reduced AE administrative overhead. The AEs spend almost all their time servicing customers, directly leading to increased sales. When this was demonstrated in pilot testing, minimal resistance among the AEs disappeared, thus ensuring their cooperation. By mid-1999, Vision was handling an average of 11,000 new loan applications per day, totaling 3 million transactions per day.

Household's branches now sell at least 10 percent more loans than before, and branches added to Household's network through acquisition show gains as high as 18 percent. Another key measure of corporate performance in consumer finance is the managed basis efficiency ratio, expenses divided by revenue, minus policyholders' benefits. Household has lowered this ratio from more than 40 percent to less than 35 percent (lower is better). Household achieved a 40 percent total return on investment over Vision's first few years and expects a 5-year return on investment of 129 percent. Household continues to tweak the system as regulations change and as AEs generate ideas for new functionality (leading to regular retraining of the neural networks).

UNEXPECTED BENEFITS

The Vision system's neural network has already produced several unexpected benefits. As Vision learns, it helps the company make smarter decisions about customers by recognizing patterns and how they can be successfully used, a data mining approach. Suppose an irate credit card holder calls about a late fee. He is not yet a profitable customer for the company. He has a single card with little or no balance and has rejected Household offers for credit insurance products and equity loans. Vision considers the potential lifetime value of the customer and cancels the late fee.

Vision recognizes patterns in the customer's history, including the fact that this is the first late payment and that the customer fits the profile of a person who will most likely be in the market for significant new loans the following year. Vision authorizes waiving the fee. Then the system can prompt the rep with *suggestive selling* for this now-happy customer.

CONCLUSION

The system ties the company more closely to existing and prospective customers. Loan approvals are faster, sales proposals more targeted, and customer service more responsive. The Vision system dramatically cuts down the approval waiting time and creates more opportunities. Household has developed a customer intimacy that translates to higher profits.

❖ QUESTIONS FOR THE OPENING VIGNETTE

1. Describe why neural networks were used in Vision.
2. Describe how neural networks were used in Vision.

3. Explain how neural networks use historical patterns.
4. Describe some benefits of integrating the neural network systems into the Vision system. Explain what could have happened otherwise.
5. What is the benefit of retraining the system regularly?
6. Describe the benefits of using an object-oriented approach in Vision?
7. Explain how the top management champion supported the development of Vision and how the users ultimately bought into the system (refer to Chapters 6 and 14).
8. Consider and then describe some additional unexpected benefits that Vision might conceivably provide in the future.

15.2 MACHINE LEARNING

Many organizations use neural networks to automate complex decision making. These networks can readily identify patterns from which they generate a recommended course of action. Neural networks learn from past experience to improve their own performance levels. They are members of a technology family called **machine learning.** Machine learning is different from conventional problem-solving methods in several ways. Attempts at automated problem solving have been made for generations, long before the computer age. Consider the following: statistical models such as regression or forecasting, management science models such as inventory level determination and resource allocation, and financial models such as make-versus-buy decisions and equipment replacement methods. Unfortunately, such methods work with *shallow knowledge,* or **knowledge-poor procedures.** When problems are complex, standard models cannot solve them; additional, deeper, richer knowledge is needed. This knowledge can sometimes be provided by expert systems either by themselves or when integrated with other CBIS. However, ES use a reasoning approach, and so their use is limited to narrow and usually shallow domains. For more complex situations, or when knowledge acquisition is difficult or expensive, we employ an alternative approach called *machine learning,* of which neural computing is the most commonly utilized technology. Machine learning is a family of methods that attempt to teach machines to solve problems, or to support problem solving, by showing them historical cases.

Machine learning is nontrivial. One problem is that there are many models of learning. Sometimes it is difficult to match the learning model with the problem type (e.g., scheduling). Machine learning is considered an artificial intelligence method even though some of its technologies do not formally exhibit intelligence. However, it is definitely categorized as a type of decision support system.

LEARNING

Until recently, machine learning had not been a major concern for decision support. Most decision support researchers initially felt that it was necessary to concentrate on how to make a computer program exhibit intelligence before developing methods for teaching the program to learn to improve its performance. Early examples of machine learning are checkers- and chess-playing programs. These programs can improve their performance with experience.

Learning is accomplished by analogy, discovery, and special procedures; by observing; or by analyzing examples. Learning can directly improve the performance of AI technologies such as expert systems and robotics.

Learning is a support area of AI because it is an investigation into the basic principles that underlie intelligence rather than being an application itself. The following are relevant observations of how learning relates to AI:

- Learning systems demonstrate interesting learning behaviors, some of which (like chess- and checkers-playing programs) actually challenge the performance of humans (in May 1997 Gary Kasparov, the reigning grand master lost a six-game match to Deep Blue, an IBM chess-playing computer).
- Although human-level learning capabilities are sometimes matched, no claims have been made about being able to learn as well as humans or in the same way that humans do (e.g. checkers-playing programs learn quite differently from humans).
- There is no claim that machine learning can be applied in a creative way, though such systems can handle cases to which they have never been exposed. Simulated creativity is an intensely studied AI topic (see the Imagination Engines Inc. Web site at www.imagination-engines.com).
- Learning systems are not anchored in any formal bedrock; thus, their implications are not well understood. Many systems have been exhaustively tested, but exactly why they succeed or fail is not precisely clear.
- A common thread running through most AI approaches to learning (distinguishing them from non-AI approaches to learning) is the manipulation of symbols rather than numeric information.

MACHINE LEARNING METHODS

Following are several examples of machine learning methods and algorithms:

- *Neural computing.* This approach can be used for knowledge acquisition; thus, it can be used for decision support.
- **Inductive learning.** This method is used in knowledge acquisition, as in rule induction.
- *Case-based reasoning and* **analogical reasoning.** This approach is employed in knowledge acquisition and inferencing.
- *Genetic algorithms.* These algorithms attempt to follow the evolutionary processes of biological systems in which the fittest survive and so are excellent learners.
- *Statistical methods.* Although more suitable to knowledge-poor situations, some of these methods have been applied to knowledge acquisition, forecasting, and problem solving.
- *Explanation-based learning.* This approach assumes that there is enough existing theory to explain why one instance is or is not a prototypical member of a class (Mitchell et al., 1986).

For further discussion of methods see Adeli and Hung (1995), Quiroga and Rabelo (1995), Ramsay (1996), Saitta (1996), and Weiss and Sen (1995).

15.3 NEURAL COMPUTING

For decades, the field of artificial intelligence has made swift progress toward automating human reasoning. Nevertheless, the tools of AI have been mostly restricted to sequential processing and only certain representations of knowledge and logic. A different approach to intelligent systems involves developing computers with architectures and processing capabilities that mimic the processing capabilities of the human brain. The results are knowledge representations based on massive parallel processing, fast retrieval of large amounts of information, and the ability to recognize patterns based on historical cases. **Neural computing,** or **artificial neural networks (ANNs),** is the technology that attempts to simulate the thought processes of the human brain.

Artificial neural networks are an information-processing technology inspired by studies of the brain and the nervous system. After falling into disfavor in the 1970s (because of a mathematical roadblock), the field of ANNs experienced a dramatic resurgence in the late 1980s (once the roadblock was removed). This renewed interest developed because of the need for brainlike information processing, advances in computer technology, and progress in neuroscience toward better understanding of the mechanisms of the brain. Potential commercial and military applications with large payoffs also motivated (and funded) this research.

15.4 THE BIOLOGY ANALOGY

BIOLOGICAL NEURAL NETWORKS

The human brain is composed of special cells called **neurons.** These cells do not die when a human is injured (all other cells reproduce to replace themselves and then die). This phenomenon may explain why we retain information. Information storage spans sets of neurons. The estimated number of neurons in a human brain is 50 billion to 150 billion, of which there are more than 100 different kinds. Neurons are partitioned into groups called *networks*. Each network contains several thousand neurons that are highly interconnected. Thus, the brain can be viewed as a collection of neural networks.

The ability to learn and react to changes in our environment requires intelligence. Thinking and intelligent behavior are controlled by the brain and the central nervous system. For example, people who suffer brain damage have difficulty learning and reacting to changing environments. Even so, undamaged parts of the brain can often compensate with new learning.

A portion of a network composed of two cells is shown in Figure 15.1. The cell itself includes a **nucleus** (at the center). To the left of cell 1, the **dendrites** provide input signals to the cell. To the right, the axon sends output signals to cell 2 via the axon terminals. These **axon** terminals merge with the dendrites of cell 2. Signals can be transmitted unchanged, or they can be altered by synapses. A **synapse** is able to increase or decrease the strength of the connection from neuron to neuron and cause excitation or inhibition of a subsequent neuron. This is where information is stored.

ARTIFICIAL NEURAL NETWORKS

An artificial neural network model emulates a biological neural network. Neural computing actually uses a very limited set of concepts from biological neural systems (see AIS in Focus 15.1). It is more of an analogy to the human brain than an accurate model of it. Neural concepts are usually implemented as software simulations of the massively parallel processes that involve processing elements (also called *artificial neurons* or *neurodes*) interconnected in a network architecture. The artificial neuron receives inputs analogous to the electrochemical impulses the dendrites of biological neurons receive from other neurons. The output of the artificial neuron corresponds to signals sent out from a biological neuron over its axon. These artificial signals can be changed by weights in a manner similar to the physical changes that occur in the synapses (Figure 15.2).

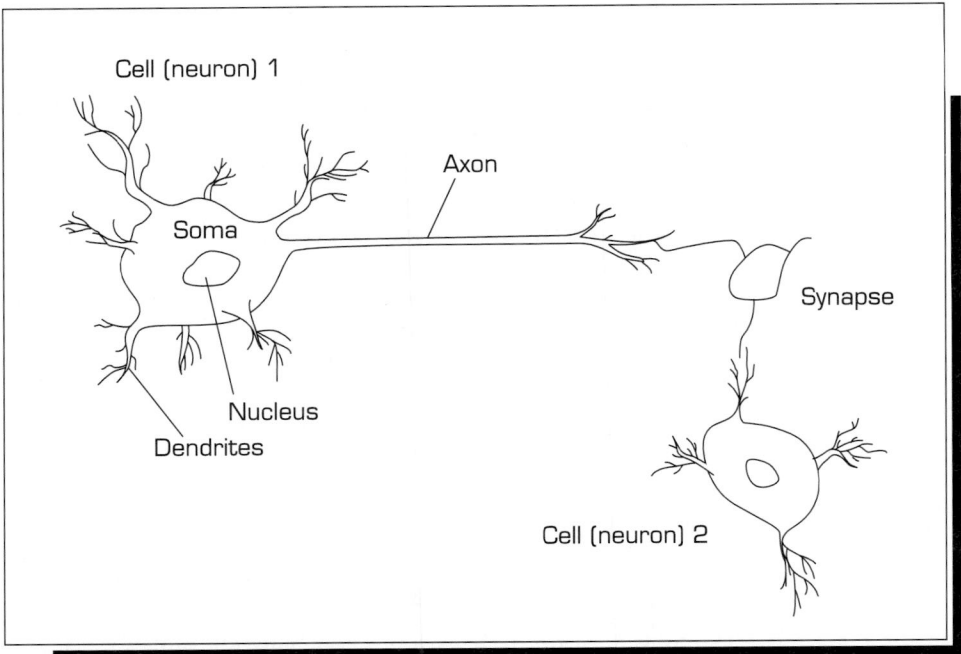

FIGURE 15.1 PORTION OF A NETWORK: TWO INTERCONNECTED BIOLOGICAL CELLS

AIS IN FOCUS 15.1

THE RELATIONSHIP BETWEEN BIOLOGICAL AND ARTIFICIAL NEURAL NETWORKS

The list below (Medsker and Liebowitz, 1994, p. 163) shows some of the relationships between biological and artificial networks.

Biological	*Artificial*
Soma	Node
Dendrites	Input
Axon	Output
Synapse	Weight
Slow speed	Fast speed
Many neurons (10^9)	Few neurons (a dozen to hundreds of thousands)

Zahedi (1993) sees a dual role for artificial neural networks (ANNs). We borrow concepts from the biological world to improve the design of computers. ANN technology is used for complex information processing and machine intelligence. And it can also be used as simple biological models to test hypotheses about biological neuronal information processing.

It is important to recognize that artificial neural networks were originally proposed to model the human brain's activities. The human brain has much more complexity than the model can capture. So, neural computing models are not very accurate representations of real biological systems. Despite extensive research in neurobiology and psychology, important questions remain about how the brain and the mind work. Research and development on ANNs continue to produce interesting and useful results that inspire systems that borrow features from biological systems.

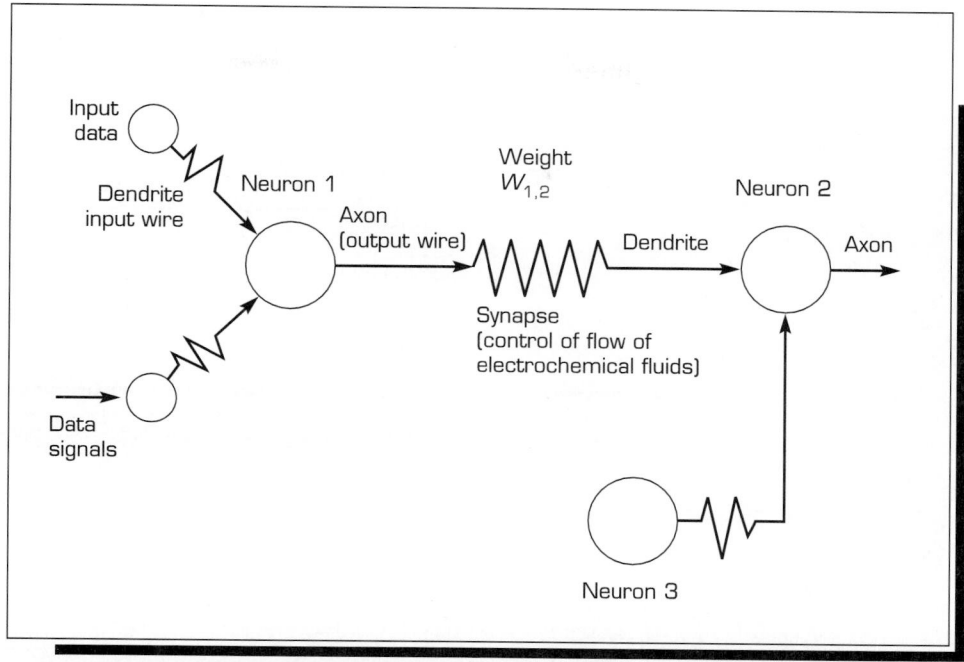

FIGURE 15.2 THREE INTERCONNECTED ARTIFICIAL NEURONS

15.5 NEURAL NETWORK FUNDAMENTALS

COMPONENTS AND STRUCTURE

A network is composed of processing elements organized in different ways to form the network's structure.

PROCESSING ELEMENTS

An ANN is composed of artificial neurons; these are the **processing elements (PEs).** Each of the neurons receives inputs, processes the inputs, and delivers a single output, as shown in Figure 15.3. The input can be raw input data or the output of other processing elements. The output can be the final result (e.g., 1 means yes, 0 means no) or it can be inputs to other neurons.

THE NETWORK[3]

Each ANN is composed of a collection of neurons grouped in layers. A typical structure is shown in Figure 15.4. Note the three layers: input, intermediate (called the **hidden layer**), and output. Several hidden layers can be placed between the input and output layers.

---

[3]Our initial focus is on multilayer feedforward neural networks, the most common ones used in decision making. See Haykin (1999, p. 21).

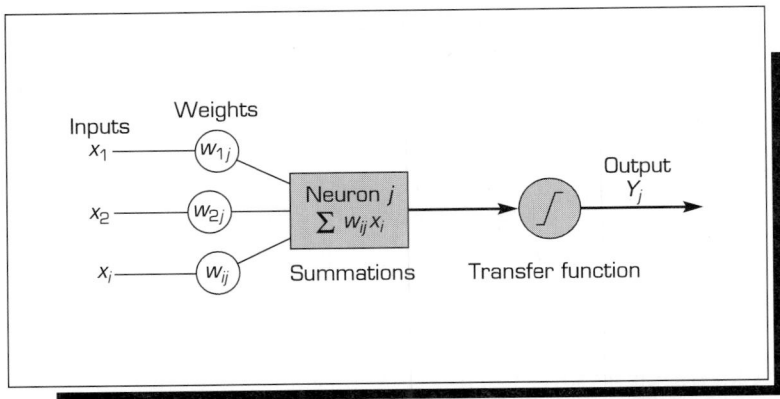

FIGURE 15.3 PROCESSING INFORMATION IN AN ARTIFICIAL NEURON

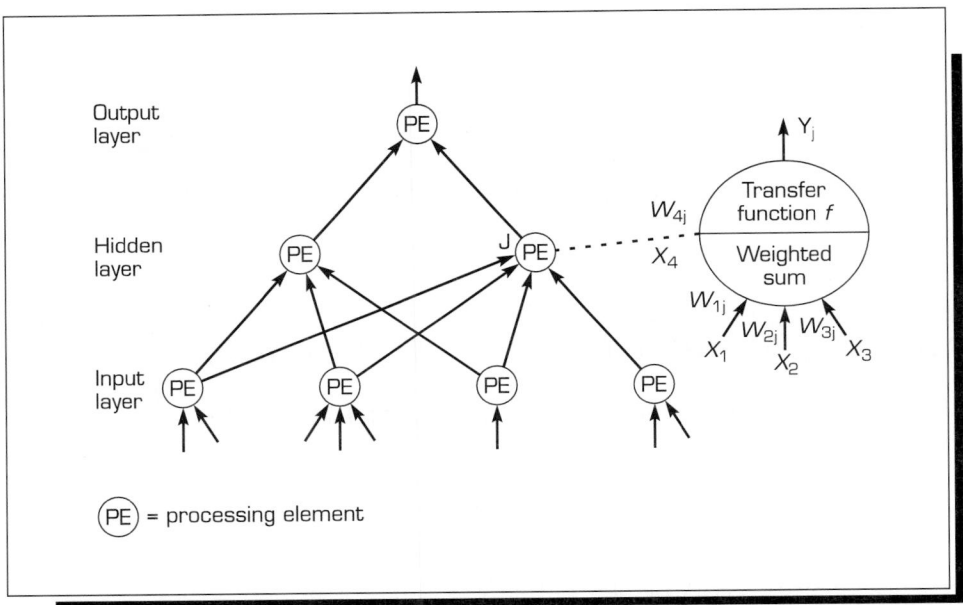

FIGURE 15.4 NEURAL NETWORK WITH ONE HIDDEN LAYER

NETWORK STRUCTURE

Like a biological network, an ANN can be organized in several different ways (topologies or architectures); that is, the neurons can be interconnected in different ways. Therefore, ANNs appear in many configurations called *architectures*. In processing information, many of the processing elements perform their computations at the same time. This **parallel processing** resembles the way the brain works, and it differs from the serial processing of conventional computing.

NETWORK INFORMATION PROCESSING

Once the structure of a network is determined, information can be processed. We now present the major concepts related to the processing.

AIS IN FOCUS 15.2

INPUT TO NEURAL NETWORKS

Neural computing can process only numbers, either integer or continuous. If a problem involves qualitative attributes or pictures, they must be preprocessed to numeric equivalents before being input into the artificial neural network (most packages can do this automatically).

Examples of inputs to neural networks are pixel values of characters and other graphics, digitized images and voice patterns, digitized signals from monitoring equipment, and coded data from loan applications. In all cases, an important initial step is the design of a suitable coding system so that the data can be fed into the neural network, often as sets of 1s and 0s. For example, the letter *A* is expressed as

```
00●00        0 0 1 0 0
0●0●0        0 1 0 1 0
●000●        1 0 0 0 1
●000●        1 0 0 0 1
●●●●●        1 1 1 1 1
●000●        1 0 0 0 1
●000●        1 0 0 0 1       0100 0001
```

Pixel diagram   Input code   ASCII code

INPUTS

Each input corresponds to a single attribute. For example, if the problem is to decide on approval or disapproval of a loan, some attributes could be the applicant's income level, age, and home ownership. The numeric value, or representation of an attribute, is the input to the network. Several types of data, such as text, pictures, and voice, can be used as inputs (see AIS in Focus 15.2). Preprocessing may be needed to convert the data to meaningful inputs from symbolic data or to scale the data.

OUTPUTS

The outputs of the network contain the solution to a problem. For example, in the case of a loan application it can be yes or no. The ANN assigns numeric values, like 1 for yes and 0 for no. The purpose of the network is to compute the values of the output. Often, *postprocessing* of the outputs is required. (Why? Some networks use two outputs, one for yes and another for no. What does it mean to have an answer of 0.8 for yes and 0.4 for no?)

WEIGHTS

Key elements in an ANN are the **weights.** Weights express the *relative strength* (or mathematical value) of the input data or the many connections that transfer data from layer to layer. In other words, weights express the *relative importance* of each input to a processing element and ultimately the outputs. Weights are crucial in that they store learned patterns of information. It is through repeated adjustments of weights that the network learns.

SUMMATION FUNCTION

The **summation function** computes the weighted sum of all the input elements entering each processing element. A summation function multiplies each input value by its weight and totals the values for a weighted sum Y. The formula for n inputs in one processing element (Figure 15.5a) is

$$Y = \sum_{i=1}^{n} X_i W_i$$

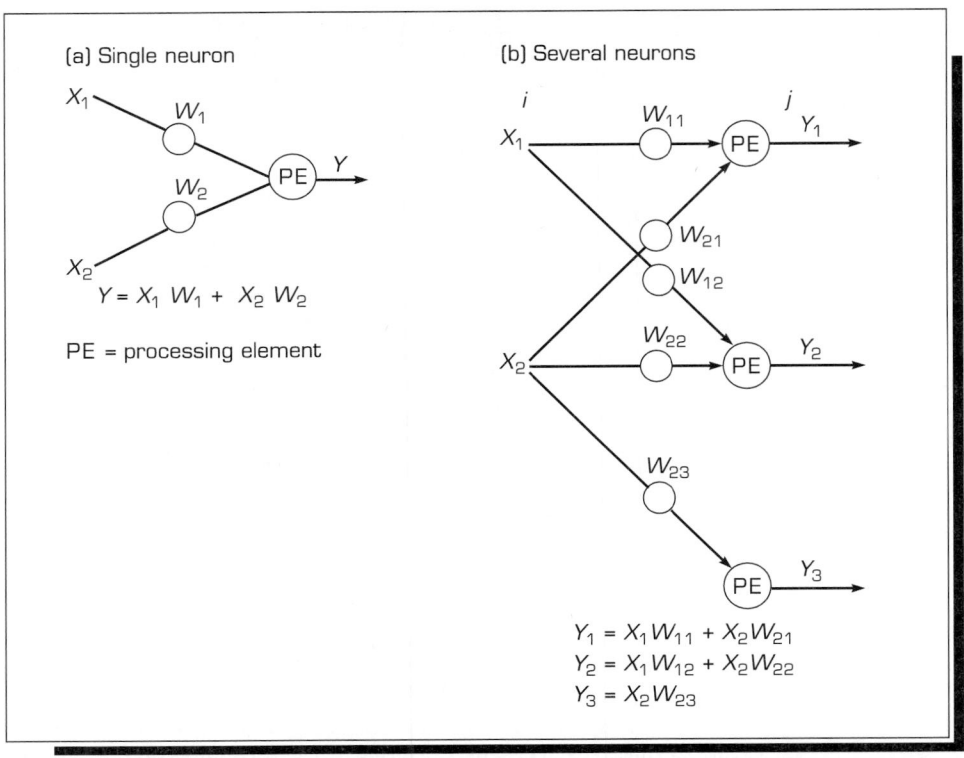

(a) Single neuron

X_1
W_1
W_2
PE Y
X_2

$$Y = X_1 W_1 + X_2 W_2$$

PE = processing element

(b) Several neurons

i
W_{11}
j Y_1
X_1 PE
W_{21}
W_{12}
W_{22} Y_2
X_2 PE
W_{23}
PE Y_3

$$Y_1 = X_1 W_{11} + X_2 W_{21}$$
$$Y_2 = X_1 W_{12} + X_2 W_{22}$$
$$Y_3 = X_2 W_{23}$$

FIGURE 15.5 SUMMATION FUNCTION FOR SINGLE NEURON (A) AND SEVERAL NEURONS (B)

For the jth neuron of several processing neurons in a layer (Figure 15.5b), the formula is

$$Y_j = \sum_{i=1}^{n} X_i W_{ij}$$

TRANSFORMATION (TRANSFER) FUNCTION

The summation function computes the internal stimulation, or activation level, of the neuron. Based on this level, the neuron may or may not produce an output. The relationship between the internal activation level and the output can be linear or nonlinear. The relationship is expressed by one of several types of **transformation (transfer) functions.** Selection of the specific function impacts the network's operation. The **sigmoid (logical activation) function** (or *transfer function*) is a popular and useful nonlinear transfer function:

$$Y_T = 1/(1 + e^{-Y})$$

where Y_T is the transformed (normalized) value of Y (see AIS in Focus 15.3).

The transformation modifies the output levels to be within reasonable values (typically between 0 and 1). This transformation is performed before the output reaches the next level. Without such a transformation, the value of the output becomes very large, especially when there are several layers of neurons. Sometimes, instead of a transformation function, a *threshold value* is used. For example, any value of 0.5 or less becomes 0, and any value above 0.5 becomes 1.

A transformation can occur at the output of each processing element, or it can be performed only at the final output nodes.

AIS IN FOCUS 15.3

EXAMPLE OF ANN FUNCTIONS

Summation function: $Y = 3(0.2) + 1(0.4) + 2(0.1) = 1.2$

Transformation (transfer) function: $Y_T = 1/(1 + e^{-1.2}) = 0.77$

$X_1 = 3$ $W_1 = 0.2$
$X_2 = 1$ $W_2 = 0.4$ Processing element $Y = 1.2$
$X_3 = 2$ $W_3 = 0.1$

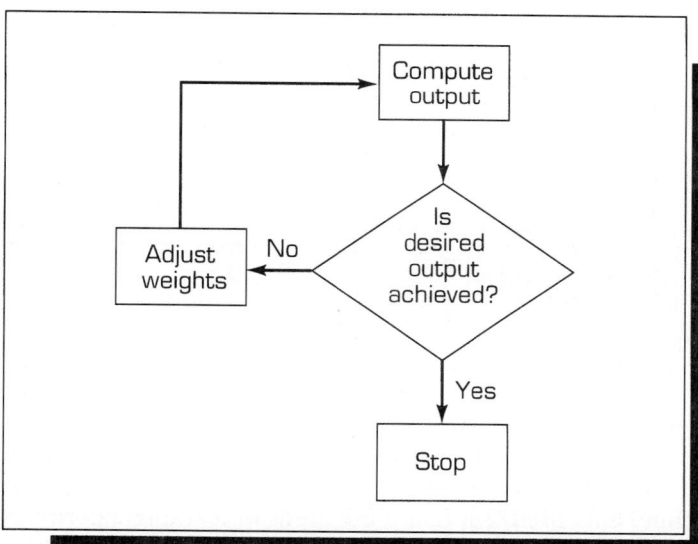

FIGURE 15.6 LEARNING PROCESS OF AN ARTIFICIAL NEURAL NETWORK

LEARNING

An ANN learns from experience. The usual process of learning involves three tasks (Figure 15.6):

1. Compute outputs.
2. Compare outputs with desired targets.
3. Adjust the weights and repeat the process.

When existing outputs for comparison are available, we call the learning *supervised*. The learning process starts by setting the weights, either by some rules or randomly. The difference between the actual output (Y or Y_T) and the desired output (Z) for a given set of inputs is an error called *delta* (in calculus, the Greek symbol delta means "difference").

AIS IN FOCUS 15.4

HOW PATTERNS ARE PRESENTED AND RECOGNIZED

Here we show seven ideal desired outputs (upper part). Actual cases can be exactly the same, or they can differ. The problem is to place each case pattern in a class (the interpretation).

The historical cases show how interpretation decisions were made. These cases are divided into two categories: training cases and testing cases.

Notice that the historical cases may deviate from the desired output. The ANN will try to minimize the difference and give an interpretation as close as possible to the desired pattern.

Desired Outputs

Pattern										Class
0	0	0	0	0	0	0	0	0	0	Down
1	1	1	1	0	0	0	0	0	0	Left
1	1	1	0	0	0	0	1	1	1	Valley
0	1	0	1	0	1	0	1	0	1	Alternating
0	0	0	0	0	0	1	1	1	1	Right
0	0	0	1	1	1	1	0	0	0	Hill
1	1	1	1	1	1	1	1	1	1	Up

Historical Cases

Pattern											Historical Interpretation
Test case											
1	1	1	0	0	1	1	0	0	1	1	Alternating
2	0	0	0	0	0	1	0	0	0	1	Right
3	1	1	0	1	1	1	0	0	0	0	Left
4	0	0	1	1	0	1	0	1	0	1	Alternating
5	0	0	0	1	1	0	1	1	0	0	Alternating
Test case											
6	1	1	1	0	1	1	1	0	1	1	Alternating
7	0	0	1	0	0	0	1	1	1	1	Right
8	0	1	0	1	1	0	1	1	0	0	Alternating
9	1	1	1	0	0	0	0	0	0	0	Left
10	1	1	1	1	0	0	1	1	1	1	Valley

Source: C. W. Engel and M. Cran, "Pattern Classifications: A Neural Network Competes with Humans," *PC AI,* May/June 1991. Used with permission.

The objective is to minimize the delta (reduce it to 0 if possible), and this is done by adjusting the network's weights. The key is to change the weights in the right direction, making changes that reduce the delta (error). We will show how this is done later.

Information processing with an ANN consists of an attempt to recognize patterns of activities (**pattern recognition**) (see AIS in Focus 15.4). During the learning stages, the interconnection weights change in response to training data presented to the system.

Different ANNs compute the delta in different ways, depending on the **learning algorithm** being used. There are hundreds of learning algorithms for various situations and configurations, some of which are discussed later.

15.6 NEURAL NETWORK APPLICATION DEVELOPMENT

Although the development process of ANNs is similar to the structured design methodologies of traditional computer-based information systems, some phases are unique or have some unique aspects. In the process described here, we assume that the preliminary steps of system development, such as determining information requirements, conducting a feasibility analysis, and gaining a champion in top management for the project, have been completed successfully. Such steps are generic to any information system.

As shown in Figure 15.7, the development process for an ANN application has nine steps. In step 1, the data to be used for training and testing of the network are collected. Important considerations are that the particular problem is amenable to neural network solution and that adequate data exist and can be obtained. In step 2 training data must be identified, and a plan must be made for testing the performance of the network.

FIGURE 15.7 FLOW DIAGRAM OF THE DEVELOPMENT PROCESS OF AN ARTIFICIAL NEURAL NETWORK

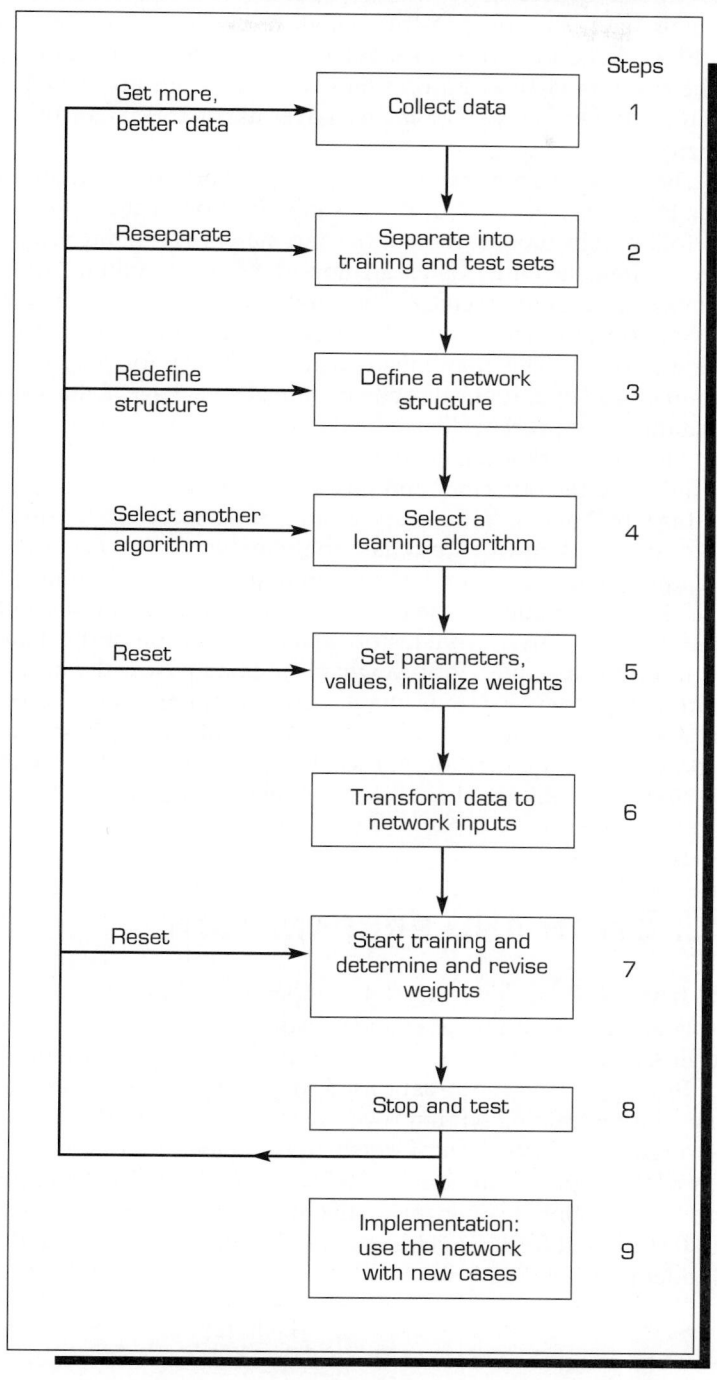

In steps 3 and 4, a network architecture and a learning method are selected. The availability of a particular development tool or the capabilities of the development personnel may determine the type of neural network to be constructed. Also, certain problem types have demonstrated high success rates with certain configurations (e.g., multilayer feedforward neural networks for loan application and fraud detection as in the opening vignette). Important considerations are the exact number of neurons and the number of layers (some packages use genetic algorithms to select the network design).

There are parameters for tuning the network to the desired learning performance level. Part of the process in step 5 is initialization of the network weights and parameters, followed by modification of the parameters as training performance feedback is received. Often, the initial values are important in determining the efficiency and length of training. Some methods change the parameters during training to enhance performance.

Step 6 transforms the application data into the type and format required by the neural network. This may mean writing software for *preprocessing* the data or performing these operations directly in an ANN package. Data storage and manipulation techniques and processes must be designed for conveniently and efficiently retraining the neural network when needed. The application data representation and ordering often influence the efficiency and possibly the accuracy of the results.

In steps 7 and 8, training and testing are conducted iteratively by presenting input and desired or known output data to the network. The network computes the outputs and adjusts the weights until the computed outputs are within an acceptable tolerance of the known outputs for the input cases. The desired outputs and their relationships to input data are *derived* from historical data (a portion of the data collected in step 1).

In step 9, a stable set of weights is obtained. Now the network can reproduce the desired outputs given inputs like those in the training set. The network is ready for use as a stand-alone system or as part of another software system where new input data will be presented to it and its output will be a recommended decision.

Now, let's examine these nine steps in some detail.

15.7 DATA COLLECTION AND PREPARATION

The first two steps in the ANN development process involve collecting data and separating them into a training set and a testing set. The training cases are used to adjust the weights, and the testing cases are used for network validation.

In general, the more data used, the better. Larger data sets increase processing times during training but improve the accuracy of the training and often lead to faster convergence to a good set of weights. For a moderately sized data set, typically 80 percent of the data are randomly selected for training, 10 percent for testing, and 10 percent for secondary testing; for small data sets, typically all the data are used for training and testing; and for large data sets, a sufficiently large sample is taken and treated like a moderately sized data set.

15.8 NEURAL NETWORK ARCHITECTURE

There are several effective neural network models and algorithms (Haykin, 1999). Representative architectures are shown in Figures 15.8 and 15.9.

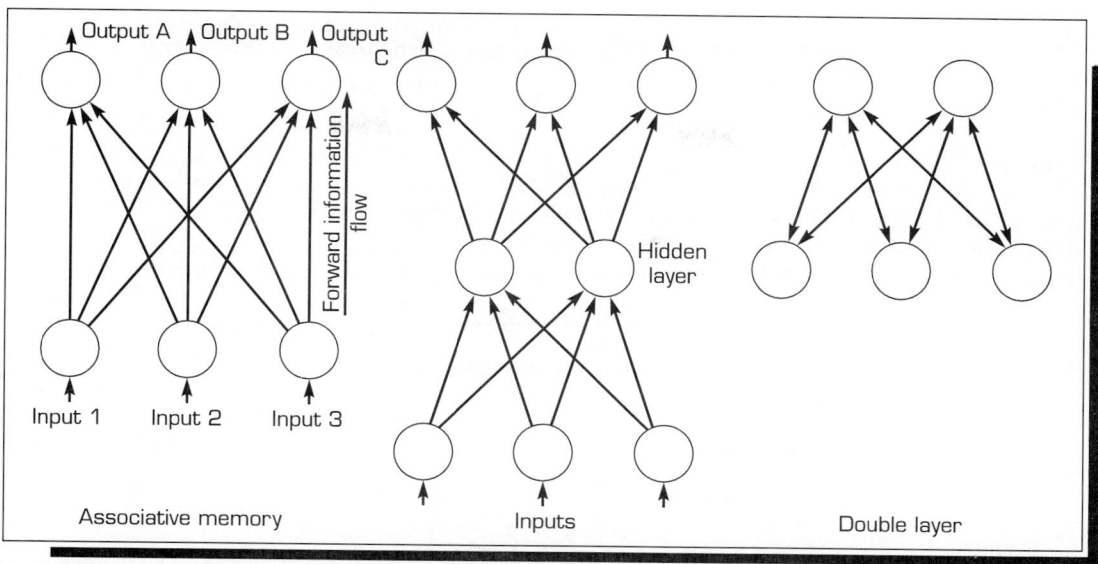

FIGURE 15.8 NEURAL NETWORK STRUCTURES: FEEDFORWARD FLOW

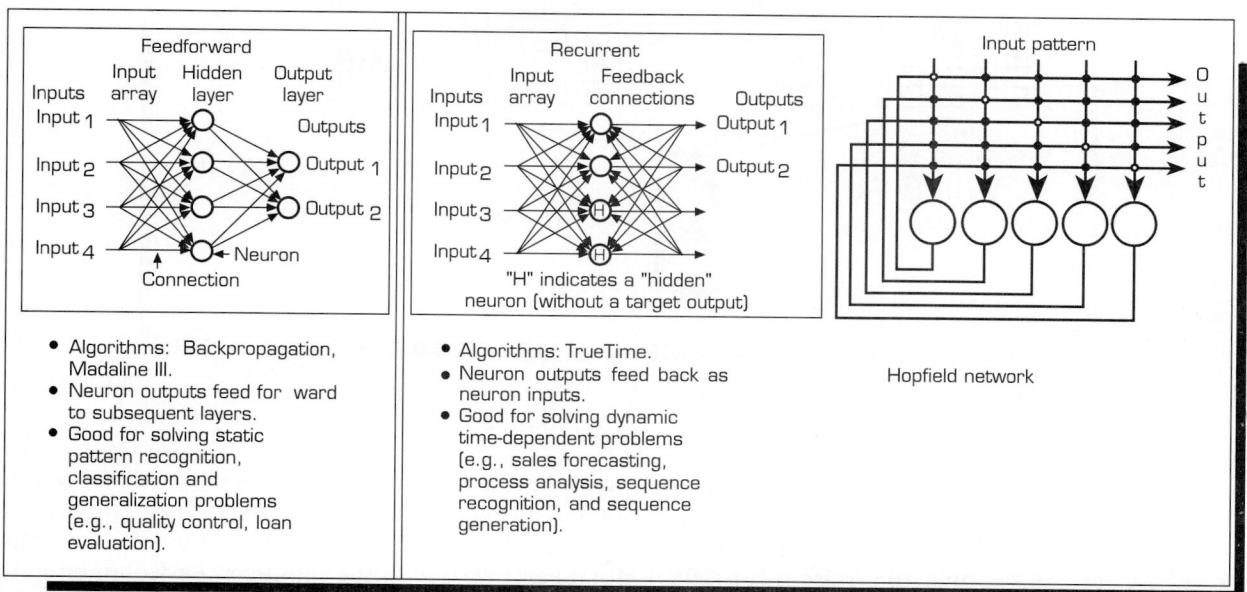

FIGURE 15.9 RECURRENT STRUCTURE COMPARED WITH FEEDFORWARD SOURCE

Source: Based on *PC AI,* May/June 1992, p. 35.

ASSOCIATIVE MEMORY SYSTEMS

Associative memory is the ability to recall complete situations from partial information. These systems correlate input data with information stored in memory. Information can be recalled from even incomplete or *noisy* input. Associative memory systems can detect similarities between new input and stored patterns (see AIS in Focus 15.5) (Haykin, 1999; Zurada, 1995).

OCR NEURAL NETWORK

This figure shows how a neural network can recognize characters better than template matching. Sets of neurons extract features from the input image. (Here neurons extract the locations of vertical, horizontal, and diagonal strokes.) The locations of these features indicate possible choices of the character class. Most of the evidence shows that 6 is the best choice. For details see Schantz (1991).

Source: AT&T Technology Magazine, Vol. 6, No. 4, © 1991.

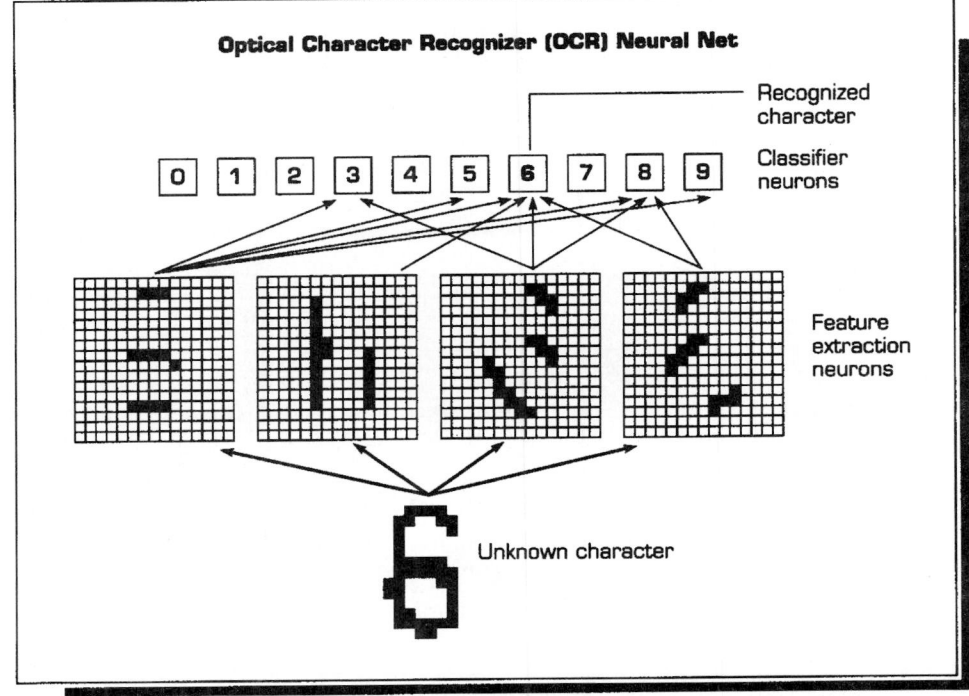

One type of unsupervised learning, competitive filter associative memory, can learn by changing its weights in recognition of categories of input data without being given examples in advance. A leading example of such a single-layer, self-organizing system for a fixed number of classes in the inputs is the Kohonen network (Haykin, 1999).

HIDDEN LAYER

Complex practical applications require one or more (hidden) layers between the input and output neurons and a correspondingly large number of weights. Many commercial ANNs include three, and sometimes up to five layers, with each containing 10–1,000 processing elements. Some experimental ANNs employ millions of processing elements. The use of more than three hidden layers is rare in most commercial systems because of the amount of computation required as each layer increases the training effort exponentially.

RECURRENT STRUCTURE

A recurrent network (double layer) is one in which an activity must go through the network more than once before the output response is produced. A recurrent structure does not require the knowledge of a precise number of classes in the training data. Instead, it uses a *feedforward* and *feedbackward* approach to adjust parameters as data are analyzed to establish arbitrary numbers of categories that represent the data presented to the system.

A well-known simple recurrent network is that of Hopfield, shown in Figure 15.9. Also shown in the figure is a recurrent network that includes neurons without output and a comparison of recurrent and feedforward systems.

15.9 NEURAL NETWORK PREPARATION

When the input data include text, pictures, and any other nonnumeric input, preparation may involve not only binary and continuous data representations but also simplification or decomposition (see AIS in Focus 15.5).

In preparation for the training, it is necessary to choose the learning algorithm (step 4 in Figure 15.7). This decision is related to the software development tools that are going to be used. A decision must be made at this stage because the structure and data preparation may have to be adjusted to fit the learning algorithm (especially if a software development tool is used).

Several training parameters must be determined in step 5. One parameter determines the learning rate (Section 15.11) and can be set high or low. Another parameter is the threshold value that determines the form of the output (an example is given in Section 15.11). Finally, the initial values of the weights need to be set, usually randomly. Several other parameters for validation and testing may also need to be set during preparation.

The choice of network structure (e.g., the number of nodes and layers) and the initial conditions determine the length of training time. These choices are important and require careful consideration. Unfortunately, the best way to learn how to set these values is through trial and error. Most neural network packages provide guidance by presetting values that generally work well. For example, the number of nodes in a single hidden layer should be somewhere between 1/2 and 1 1/2 times the total number of input and output nodes (1 1/2 is probably better). Error tolerances of 5 percent and a learning rate of 0.1 with randomized weights are good starting points.

The last preparation task is to transform the training and testing data to the format required by the network and its algorithm (step 6). This step is especially important when a software development tool is used. Most neural network packages perform a number of transformations automatically.

15.10 TRAINING THE NETWORK

The training phase (step 7) consists of presenting the training data set to the network so that the weights can be adjusted to produce the desired output for each of the inputs. Weights are adjusted after a number of input and output vectors are presented. Several iterations of the complete training set are required until a consistent set of weights that works for all the training data is derived (Caudill, 1991; Haykin, 1999; Principe et al., 2000).

15.11 LEARNING ALGORITHMS

An important consideration in an ANN is the use of an appropriate **learning algorithm** (or training algorithm). There are hundreds of them. Learning algorithms can be classified as *supervised learning* and *unsupervised learning* (Figure 15.10).

Supervised learning uses a set of inputs for which the appropriate (desired) outputs are known. For example, a historical set of loan applications with the success or failure of the individual to repay the loan has a set of input parameters and presumed known outputs. In one type, the difference between the desired and the actual output is used to calculate corrections to the weights of the neural network. A variation of this approach simply acknowledges for each input trial whether the output is correct as the network adjusts weights in an attempt to achieve correct results. Examples of this type of learning are backpropagation and the Hopfield network.

In **unsupervised learning,** only input stimuli are shown to the network. The network is **self-organizing**; that is, it organizes itself internally so that each hidden processing element responds strategically to a different set of input stimuli (or groups of stimuli). No knowledge is supplied about which classifications (outputs) are correct, and those that the network derives may or may not be meaningful to the network developer (this is useful for cluster analysis).

FIGURE 15.10 TAXONOMY OF ANN ARCHITECTURES AND LEARNING ALGORITHMS

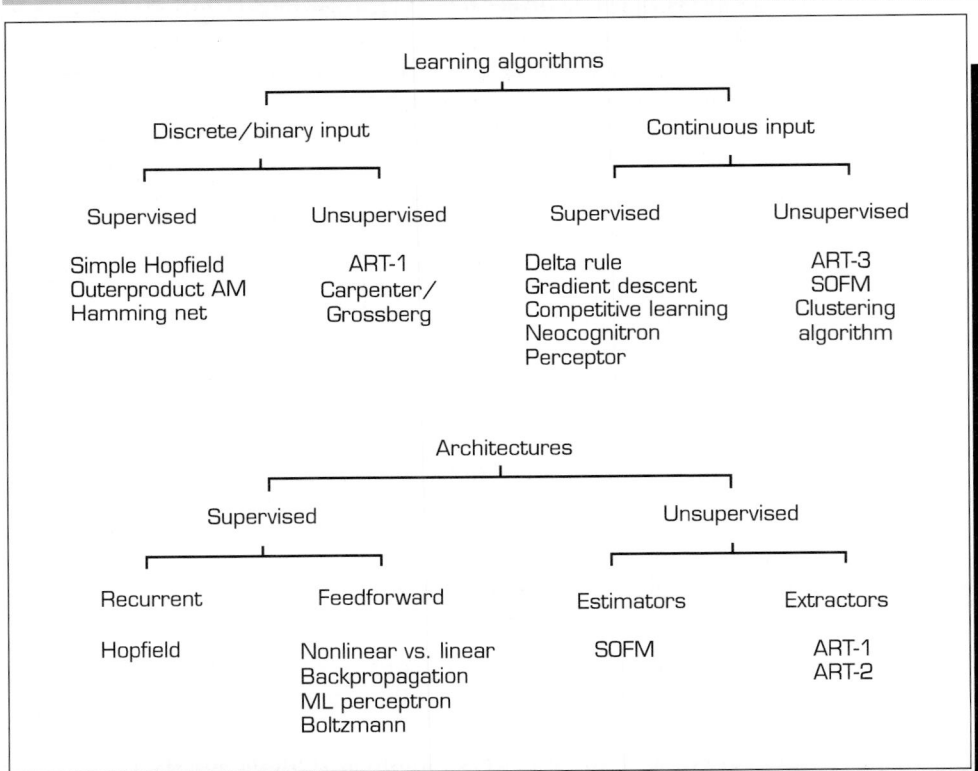

Source: Based on L. Medsker and J. Liebowitz, *Design and Development of Expert Systems and Neural Computing,* New York: Macmillan, 1994, p. 166.

However, setting model parameters can control the number of categories into which the network classifies the inputs. Regardless, a human must examine the final categories to assign meaning and determine the usefulness of the results. Examples of this type of learning are adaptive resonance theory (ART) and Kohonen self-organizing feature maps.

HOW A NETWORK LEARNS

Consider a single neuron that learns the inclusive OR operation—a classic problem in symbolic logic. There are two input elements, X_1 and X_2. If either or both of them have a positive value, then the result is also positive. This can be shown as

	Inputs		
Case	X_1	X_2	Desired Results
1	0	0	0
2	0	1	1 (positive)
3	1	0	1 (positive)
4	1	1	1 (positive)

The neuron must be trained to recognize the input patterns and classify them to give the corresponding outputs. The procedure is to present to the neuron the sequence of the four input patterns so that the weights are adjusted after each iteration (using feedback of the error found by comparing the estimate to the desired result). This step is repeated until the weights converge to a uniform set of values that allow the neuron to classify each of the four inputs correctly. The results shown in Table 15.1 were produced in Excel. In this simple example a threshold function is used to evaluate the summation of input values. After calculating outputs, a measure of the error (delta) between the output and the desired values is used to update the weights, subsequently reinforcing correct results. At any step in the process for a neuron j we have

$$\text{Delta} = Z_j - Y_j$$

TABLE 15.1   Example of Supervised Learning

Step	X_1	X_2	Z	Initial W_1	Initial W_2	Y	Delta	Final W_1	Final W_2
1	0	0	0	0.1	0.3	0	0.0	0.1	0.3
	0	1	1	0.1	0.3	0	1.0	0.1	0.3
	1	0	1	0.1	0.5	0	1.0	0.1	0.5
	1	1	1	0.3	0.5	1	0.0	0.3	0.5
2	0	0	0	0.3	0.5	0	0.0	0.3	0.5
	0	1	1	0.3	0.5	0	0.0	0.3	0.5
	1	0	1	0.3	0.7	0	1.0	0.5	0.7
	1	1	1	0.5	0.7	1	0.0	0.5	0.7
3	0	0	0	0.5	0.7	0	0.0	0.5	0.7
	0	1	1	0.5	0.7	1	0.0	0.5	0.7
	1	0	1	0.5	0.7	0	1.0	0.7	0.7
	1	1	1	0.7	0.7	1	0.0	0.7	0.7
4	0	0	0	0.7	0.7	0	0.0	0.7	0.7
	0	1	1	0.7	0.7	1	0.0	0.7	0.7
	1	0	1	0.7	0.7	1	0.0	0.7	0.7
	1	1	1	0.7	0.7	1	0.0	0.7	0.7

Parameters: alpha = 0.2; threshold = 0.5.

where Z and Y are the desired and actual outputs, respectively. Then, the updated weights are

$$W_i(\text{final}) = W_i(\text{initial}) + \text{alpha} \times \text{delta} \times X_1$$

where alpha is a parameter that controls how fast the learning takes place.

As shown in Table 15.1, each calculation uses one of the X_1 and X_2 pairs and the corresponding value for the OR operation along with initial values W_1 and W_2 of the neuron's weights. Initially, the weights are assigned random values and the *learning rate,* alpha, is set low. Delta is used to derive the final weights, which then become the initial weights in the next iteration (row).

The initial values of weights for each input are transformed using the above equation to assign values that are used with the next input (row). The threshold value (0.5) sets the output Y to 1 in the next row if the weighted sum of inputs is greater than 0.5; otherwise, Y is set to 0. In the first step, two of the four outputs are incorrect (delta = 1) and a consistent set of weights has not been found. In subsequent steps, the learning algorithm improves the results until finally producing a set of weights that give the correct results ($W_1 = W_2 = 0.7$ in step 4 of Table 15.1). Once determined, a neuron with these weight values can quickly perform the OR operation.

In developing an ANN, an attempt is made to fit the problem characteristic to one of the known learning algorithms. There are software programs for all the different algorithms, but it is best to use a well-known and well-characterized one, such as backpropagation, which we describe next.

15.12 BACKPROPAGATION

Backpropagation (short for *back error propagation*) is the most widely used learning algorithm (Haykin, 1999; Principe et al., 2000). It is a very popular technique that is easy to implement. It does require a set of training data before the network can be used with other data. A backpropagation network includes one or more hidden layers. This type of network is considered *feedforward* because there are no interconnections between the output of a processing element and the input of a node in the same layer or in a preceding layer. Externally provided correct patterns are compared with the neural network output during (supervised) training, and feedback is used to adjust the weights until all the training patterns are as correctly categorized as is possible by the network (the error tolerance is set in advance).

Starting with the output layer, errors between the actual and desired outputs are used to correct the weights for the connections to the previous layer (Figure 15.11). For any output neuron j, the error (delta) $= (Z_j - Y_j) (df/dx)$, where Z and Y are the desired and actual outputs, respectively. The sigmoid function, $f = [1 + \exp(-x)]^{-1}$, is an effective way to compute the output of a neuron in practice, where x is proportional to the sum of the weighted inputs to the neuron. With this function, the derivative of the sigmoid function $df/dx = f(1 - f)$ and the error is a simple function of the desired and actual outputs. The factor $f(1 - f)$ is the *logistic function,* which serves to keep the error correction well bounded. The weights of each input to the jth neuron are then changed in proportion to this calculated error. A more complicated expression can be derived to work backward in a similar way from the output neurons through the hidden layers to calculate the corrections to the associated weights of the inner neurons.[4]

---

[4]This complicated method is an iterative approach to solving a nonlinear optimization problem that is very similar in meaning to the one characterizing multiple linear regression.

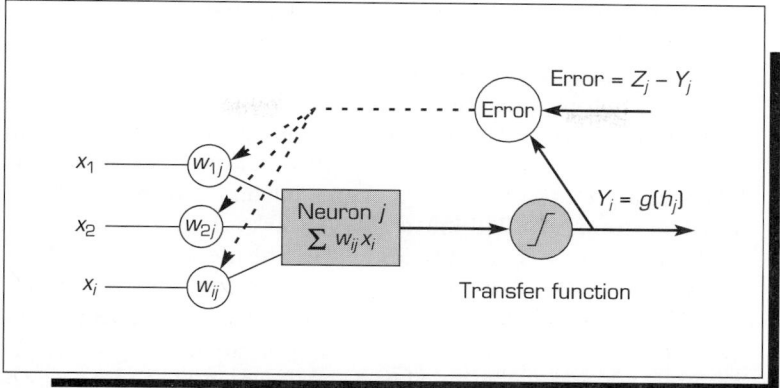

FIGURE 15.11   BACKPROPAGATION OF ERRORS FOR A SINGLE NEURON

The learning algorithm procedure is as follows:

1. Initialize weights with random values and set other parameters.
2. Read in the input vector and the desired output.
3. Compute the actual output via the calculations working forward through the layers.
4. Compute the error.
5. Change the weights by working backward from the output layer through the hidden layers.

The procedure is repeated for the entire set of input vectors until the desired and the actual outputs agree within some predetermined tolerance. Given the calculation requirements for one iteration, a large network can take a very long time to train (so, in one variation, a set of cases are run through and an aggregated error is fed backward to speed up learning). Sometimes, depending on the initial random weights and network parameters, the network does not converge to a satisfactory performance level. If so, new random weights must be generated, and the network parameters or even its structure possibly must be modified before another attempt is made. Current research is aimed at developing algorithms and using parallel computers to improve this process. For example, genetic algorithms (Chapter 16) can be used to guide the selection of the network structure.

15.13 TESTING

Recall that in step 2 of the development process (Figure 15.7) the available data are divided into training and testing data sets. Once the training has been completed, it is necessary to test the network. The testing (step 8) examines the performance of the network using the derived weights by measuring the ability of the network to classify the testing data correctly. Black-box testing (comparing test results to historical results) is the primary approach for verifying that inputs produce the appropriate outputs. Error terms can be used to compare results against known benchmark methods.

The network is generally not expected to perform perfectly (zero error is difficult, if not impossible, to attain), and only a certain level of accuracy is really required. For example, if 1 means grant a loan and 0 means do not grant a loan, then anytime the output is between 0.9 and 1 might indicate a loan approval. The neural network application is usually an alternative to another method that can be used as a benchmark with which to compare accuracy. For example, a statistical technique such as multiple regression or another quantitative method may be known to classify inputs correctly 50 percent of the time. The neural network implementation often improves on this. For example, Ainscough and Aronson (1999) investigated the application of neural network models in predicting retail sales given a set of several inputs (regular price, various promotions, and so on). They compared their results to those of multiple regression and improved the adjusted R^2 (correlation coefficient) from .5 to .7. If the neural network is replacing manual operations, performance levels and speed of human processing can be the standard for deciding whether the testing phase is successful. See the Opening Vignette and Case Application 15.1.

The test plan should include routine cases as well as potentially problematic situations. If the testing reveals large deviations, the training set must be reexamined and the training process may have to be repeated (some "bad" data may have to be omitted from the input set; see Group Exercise 3). (Note that one cannot equate neural network results exactly with those found by statistical methods. For example, in stepwise linear regression, input variables are sometimes determined to be insignificant, but because of the nature of neural computing, a neural network uses them to attain higher levels of accuracy. When they are omitted from a neural network model, its performance typically suffers.)

In some cases, other methods can supplement black-box testing. For example, the weights can be analyzed to look for unusually large values that indicate overtraining, or unusually small weights that indicate unnecessary nodes. Also, certain weights that represent major factors in the input vector can be selectively activated to make sure that corresponding outputs respond properly.

Even at a performance level comparable to that of a traditional method, the ANN may have other advantages. For example, the network can be easily modified (and performance improved) by retraining with new data. Other techniques may require extensive reprogramming when changes are needed.

15.14 IMPLEMENTATION

Implementation of an ANN (step 9) often requires interfaces with other computer-based information systems and user training. Ongoing monitoring and feedback to the developers are recommended for system improvements and long-term success. An important consideration is to gain the confidence of users and management early in the deployment to ensure that the system is accepted and used properly (see the Opening Vignette).

NEURAL COMPUTING PARADIGMS

In building an artificial neural network, the development team must make many decisions including the following:

- Size of training and testing data
- Learning algorithms
- Topology—number of processing elements and their configurations (inputs, layers, outputs)
- Transformation (transfer) function to be used
- Learning rates
- Diagnostic and validation tools.

A specific configuration determined by these decisions is called the network's *paradigm*. Again, we mention that experience is the best teacher.

15.15 NEURAL NETWORK SOFTWARE

Artificial neural networks are basically software applications that must be programmed. Like any other application, an ANN can be programmed with a programming language, a programming tool (neural network package or shell), or both.

A major portion of the programming effort involves the training algorithms and the transfer and summation functions. It makes sense, therefore, to use development tools in which these standard computations are preprogrammed. There are many neural network development tools (see this book's Web site; periodic resource lists in *PC AI*, www.pcai.com; Network of Excellence in Neural Networks, NEuroNet, www.kcl.ac.uk/neuronet/products; Akio Utsugi's "Artificial Neural Network Lab on the Web," National Institute of Bioscience and Human Technology, Japan, www.aist.go.jp/NIBH/~b0616/Lab/index-e.html; and CERN, www1.cern.ch/NeuralNets. Some of these tools function like expert system shells. They provide a set of standard architectures, learning algorithms, and parameters along with the ability to manipulate the data (e.g., the Trajan Neural Network Simulator, www.trajan-software.demon.co.uk). Even with the help of tools, however, developing a neural network may not be easy. Specifically, it may be necessary to program the layout of the database, partition the data (testing data, training data), and transfer the data to correctly formatted input files.

Some development tools can support up to several dozen network paradigms and learning algorithms. In addition to the standard products, there are many specialized products (e.g., Database Mining Marksman, HNC Software Inc.; NeuroShell DayTrader Professional, Ward Systems Group; and PRISM eFraud, Nestor Inc.) (Fisher, 1999). Like specific ES, these can be called specific ANNs.

Some ANN development tools are spreadsheet add-ins (Braincel, Promised Land Technologies, www.promland.com; and Pathfinder, ZSolutions, www.zsolutions.com). Most can read spreadsheet, database, and text files. Some are freeware or shareware. Some ANN systems have been developed in Java to run directly on the Web, accessible through a Web browser interface. These include Neural Bench Software (www.neural-bench.ru) and the demos of the Neural Network Group at Lebedev Physics Institute (canopus.lpi.msk.su/neurolab/). Other ANN products are designed to interface with expert systems as hybrid development products.

The use of ANN tools is constrained by their configuration. Developers may instead prefer to use more general programming languages such as C++ or a spreadsheet to program the model and perform the calculations. A variation on this is to use a library of ANN routines. hav.Software (www.hav.com) provides a library of C++ classes for implementing stand-alone or embedded feedforward, simple recurrent, and random-order recurrent neural networks. A number of neural network shells can generate code, usually C++, that can be embedded in another system that can access source data or called directly by a GUI for deployment independent of the development system. Or, after training an ANN in a development tool, given the weights, network structure, and transfer function, one can easily develop one's own implementation in a third-generation programming language such as C++. Some of the more popular or useful ANN development packages include BrainMaker, Braincel, Trajan Neural Network Simulator, NeuroShell Easy, SPSS Neural Connection, NeuroSolutions, and NeuralWare.

DATA SOURCES

Some interesting free data sets for learning about and testing neural networks can be reached on www.research.ed.asu.edu. Some data sets are available at ftp://psych.

colorado.edu/pub/stat/. The U.S. Census Bureau has data readily available at www.census.gov. Most ANN systems include several real and artificial data sets for their tutorials. For example, BrainMaker (California Scientific Software) includes a real estate appraisal data set, a financial forecasting data set, and a medical prediction data set.[5]

15.16 NEURAL NETWORK HARDWARE

Most neural network applications are software simulations that run on conventional sequential processors (called simulated artificial neural networks, or SANN). Simulating a neural network means mathematically defining the nodes and weights assigned to it. So instead of using one CPU for each neuron, one CPU is used for all the neurons in sequence. This simulation may take long processing times. Advances in hardware technology have greatly enhanced the performance of neural network system training and execution by exploiting the inherent advantage of **massive parallel processing.** In essence, the neural network training occurs in the manner that the neural network design was originally intended. Hardware improvements can meet the higher requirements for memory and processing speed and thus allow shorter training times for larger networks.

Each processing element (node) computes its output from the weights and input signals from other processors. Together, the network of neurons can store information that can be recalled to interpret and classify future inputs to the network.

The computational work in training an ANN can involve millions of repetitive mathematical instructions. To increase the computational speed of training and execution, the following hardware approaches have been developed:

- *Faster general-purpose computers.* Use a high-end PC with a fast processor or a RISC workstation such as an IBM RS/6000. As this text went to press, the 1-gigahertz Pentium processors and new midrange RS/6000 copper chip technology workstations had just entered the market.
- *General-purpose parallel processors.* There are a number of general-purpose parallel processors, ranging from the large-grained IBM RISC/6000 SP workstations to small-grained transcomputers such as the SGS-Thomson Microelectronics (formerly INMOS) transputer (many tiny computers hardwired together). Neural computing is inherently parallel in nature. There are a number of parallel neural network codes (such as NNET from NASA, www.nasa.gov).
- *Neural chips.* Neural chips are expensive, which has led to their limited use. A neural chip is a hardware implementation of many neural network nodes on a digital computer chip, several of which can be placed on a computer card, several of which can be installed in a PC or RISC workstation. IBM has developed a zero instruction set computer (ZISC) (see www.fr.ibm.com/france/cdlab/zisc.htm) on a chip. The ZISC036 neural chip contains 36 neurons. Sixteen of these chips have been put on the IBM ZISC/ISA576 ISA (PC) bus card for a total of 576 parallel neurons. PCs with up to five boards (2,880 neurons) have been tested. Another example is the pRAM-256 neurocomputer with on-chip learning from UCLi Ltd. Technically it is a specialized parallel RAM unit (memory) which has inherent neural processing capabilities (see crg.eee.kcl.ac.uk/clarkson). Other chips and boards are the NM64xx chips and

---

[5]Incidentally, in the technical support appendix of *BrainMaker User's Guide and Reference Manual* is a recipe for bittersweet chocolate truffles in case you really get stuck.

NMx boards by NeuroMatrix (www.module.vympel.msk.ru/products/neuromatrix.html) and the NNP chips from Accurate Automation Corporation (www.accurate-automation.com). Though the first ANNs were developed as analog circuits and some electronics firms manufactured analog ICs in the 1990s, these circuits are rare. Custom-made neural network chips have been used by the military for special-purpose, time-critical decision making (such as quickly identifying aircraft moving at high speeds).

- *Acceleration boards.* These are powerful, dedicated parallel/array processors that can be installed in computers (PCs, RISC workstations, and mainframes), similar to a math coprocessor. They can be specially designed for an ANN or they can perform mathematical calculations in parallel, extremely fast. These processors can be thousands of times faster than the host computer. Because they are general purpose (and lower priced than neural chips), acceleration boards are the best approach to speeding up neural network training. An example is the Mosaic (www.mosaic-industries.com) QED Board.

- *Parallel graphic array processors.* It is possible to use the parallel computer technology in PC processor chips as an acceleration board. The graphical parallel computer architecture MMX array in the Pentium III performs numerical computations that are spread across several internal processors. In addition, each processor is pipelined so that a series of different consecutive operations can be performed simultaneously in a single processor. Graphics acceleration cards can be used similarly. BrainMaker uses the Pentium MMX technology to obtain a substantial training and execution speed-up.

Experimental systems are continuously being developed and tested (e.g., Anguita et al., 2000). Further information on ANN hardware is available from the Network of Excellence in Neural Networks (NEuroNet, www.kcl.ac.uk/neuronet/products), CERN (www1.cern.ch/NeuralNets/), and in Lindsey (1998).

15.17 NEURAL NETWORK DEVELOPMENT EXAMPLES

Since neural network design and implementation is somewhat different from most DSS, it is useful to examine two neural network development examples, each in a different, well-known ANN package. Both use real-world data and illustrate how one develops a neural network model. The files are on this book's Web site.

EXAMPLE 1: ELECTRICITY DEMAND PREDICTION IN BRAINCEL

Electricity demand varies over time with many factors, including time of day, day of the week, television viewing (yes—popular programs and sporting events influence demand dramatically), and especially the weather. Low temperatures (heating) and high temperatures (air conditioning) result in higher electricity demands than moderate ones. A plot of the data looks like a bowl. They are definitely nonlinear (linear regression yields extremely poor results). Our model is to be simple: we want to predict electricity use as a function of temperature. Then, we can use temperature forecasts to determine electricity use. This is an important problem in practice, as electricity cannot be inventoried easily (see AIS in Action 15.6). Data are readily available (we use the data in the table in Group Exercise 2).

We use Braincel (Version 3.5), an ANN Excel add-in. A limited size but functional demo version of Braincel is available on Promised Land Technologies' Web site (www.promland.com). We install the software in its own folder and, of course, read the documentation and work through the excellent tutorial. We next type the temperature and electricity usage data in two columns in an Excel worksheet, Elec.xls (allowing us to plot them), and copy the columns beneath the originals twice so that we can manipulate them. On the third set, we move the actual electricity use over to the right by one column to make room for the predictions. This is easier than using a split range. We next name the range (Insert Name Define) of the numeric data in the two columns of the second set *TRAIN,* and we name the third set range containing the temperature column with the blank column between the temperature and electricity use column *TEST.* Because there are so few data points, we will train the network and test it on the same set of data. These ranges are highlighted in color in the worksheet.

We then activate Braincel by opening the Braincel.xll file. (Enable the macros.) This adds Braincel to the Excel menu bar. We click on Braincel | Braincel Menu to activate Braincel. We select File | New Expert, give it the name Elec, set the number of inputs and outputs to 1, and the system recommends a neural network design with a single hidden layer of two nodes. We select a linear function for modeling the output node and are ready to train the network.

To train the network, we select Expert | New Train. The worksheet we choose is Elec.xls, we add the *TRAIN* range for training, and we use the defaults of Train error = 0.5%, Learning rate = 0.3, Initial weight range = +/− 0.4, and so on. We check the box to show the error chart during training so that we can watch the training progress as the error decreases. After the network (quickly) trains, we save it as Elec.net. We show the progression of the training (error) in Figure 15.12a (saved as ElecErrTrain.xls).

To run the network on existing data, we click on Expert | Ask Expert, select Worksheet Elec.xls, select the range Test, and select a standard display; Braincel automatically loads the predictions into the blank column. We show our results in the Excel worksheet in Figure 15.12.b, and a bar chart of actual versus predicted generated by Braincel in Figure 1512.c (saved as OutputVar1KWH.xls). It is possible now to substitute any value for temperature and predict electricity use.

In addition to training the neural network, we ran a linear regression and took the results of a quadratic function regression from the original data source. In analyzing the sum of the errors squared for each of these analyses, the neural network obtained 5,348,315.1, the linear regression obtained 45,415,491.5, and the quadratic regression obtained 8,672,975.6. The neural network prediction's sum of squares error was less than 12 percent of that of the linear regression, and 62 percent of that of the quadratic regression. For the three runs, the worst errors were 10.44, 31.25, and 11.79 percent, respectively, with the neural network having only one result out of 12 input cases worse than 10 percent, while the other two had 8 and 4, respectively. Overall, the neural network model was much more accurate than the other two.

Another example of a neural network performing nonlinear curve fitting ("flexible" regression) like this can be found on the SPSS Web site (www.spss.com/software/Neural/).

EXAMPLE 2: GPA PREDICTION IN BRAINMAKER

BrainMaker Professional is much more powerful than Braincel but as a consequence is a bit more complicated to use and explain. It requires running two separate codes, NetMaker Professional to construct data and network files, and BrainMaker to perform the neural network runs, save the network, and run test cases. Our example was done on a Pentium III computer running Windows 98, and we followed the BrainMaker installation instructions.

The problem we are modeling is one of predicting the end of freshman year grade point average (GPA) for an engineering school, based on the student's high school ranking (HSRANK) and verbal (SATV) and math (SATM) SAT scores. The

FIGURE 15.12 DEMONSTRATION EXAMPLE OF NEURAL NETWORK SOFTWARE BRAINCEL

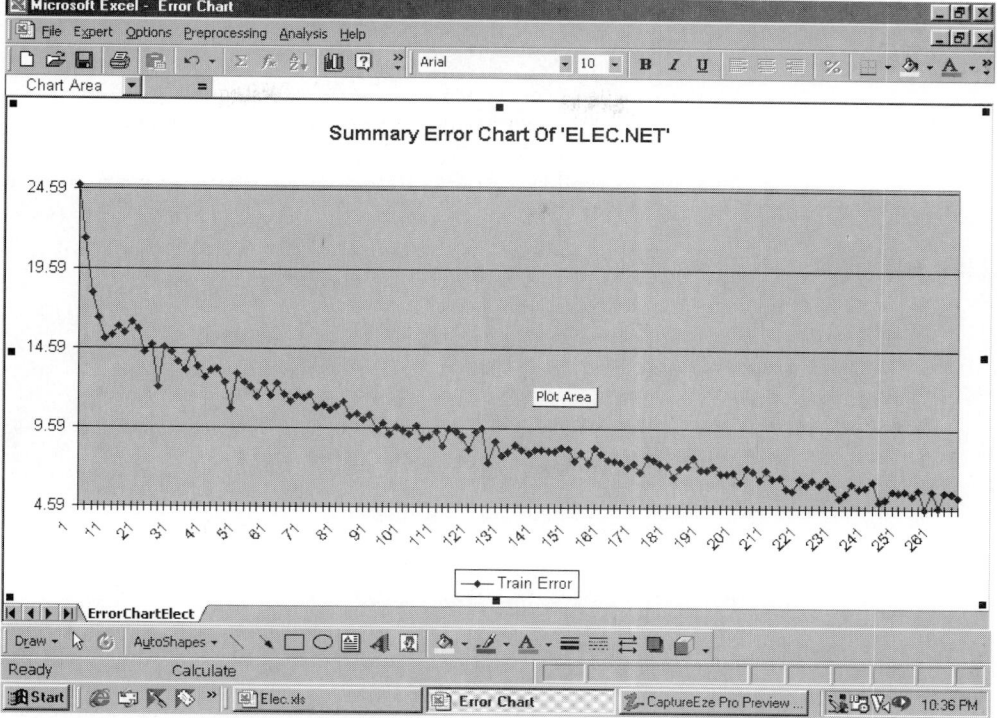

a. Progression of the training (error)

	A	B	C	D	E	F	G	H	I	J	K	L
49			83.40	18860								
50												
51												
52			Test Range:							Linear Regression		
53			NN			Pred-Actl					Pred-Actl	
54			Predicted	Actual				Percent		Predicted		
55			Temperature	Kilowatts	Kilowatts	Error	Err^2	Error		Kilowatts	Error	Err^2
56			46.90	11051.71	11330	-278.3	77444.8	-2.46%		9021.6	-2308.4	5328
57			52.00	10840.83	11260	-419.2	175700.1	-3.72%		9949.7	-1310.3	1716
58			54.90	10730.61	11530	-799.4	639019.1	-6.93%		10477.4	-1052.6	1107
59			59.30	10576.05	10160	416.0	173095.0	4.09%		11278.2	1118.2	1250
60			62.00	10510.85	9900	610.9	373140.8	6.17%		11769.5	1869.5	3495
61			66.10	10524.31	10090	434.3	188624.0	4.30%		12515.6	2425.6	5883
62			70.10	10817.09	10090	727.1	528659.6	7.21%		13243.6	3153.6	9945
63			76.90	12887.39	12540	347.4	120682.3	2.77%		14481.1	1941.1	3767
64			79.10	14356.26	16030	-1673.7	2801403.1	-10.44%		14881.4	-1148.6	1319
65			80.10	15215.55	15440	-224.4	50377.0	-1.45%		15063.4	-376.6	141
66			81.70	16881.15	16470	411.2	169044.6	2.50%		15354.6	-1115.4	1244
67			83.40	19086.11	18860	226.1	51124.6	1.20%		15664.0	-3196.0	10214
68						SUM:	5348315.1				Sum	4541549
69			Linear Regression Results:				11.776%		of SumErr^2 Linear			
70			Intercept	486.5391			61.666%		of SumErr^2 Quadratic			
71			X Variable 1	181.9834								
72												

b. Results in the Excel worksheet

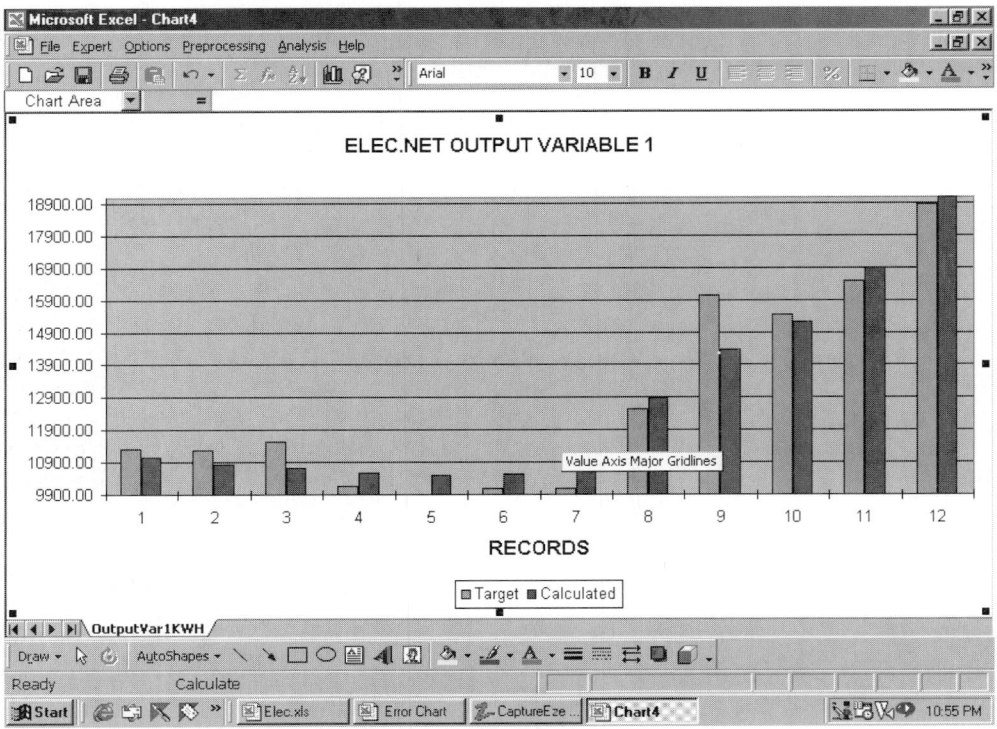

c. Bar chart of the actual versus predicted

FIGURE 15.12 (CONTINUED)

original data file gpa.txt was obtained from ftp://psych.colorado.edu/pub/stat/. A second text file, gpa2.txt, is created by eliminating all the heading information from the file except for the column names. The combined SAT score can be eliminated now or in NetMaker. We delete a few data rows corresponding to 0 GPA. (In our initial testing, these confounded the network because they looked like good candidates who had apparently flunked out for other reasons. Since these reasons are not available, the network need not be confused by inputs that it cannot know.)

There are a total of 411 valid data points. We activate NetMaker, Read Data File gpa2.txt, select Manipulate data, and define the columns by selecting each one in turn, and Label | Mark Column each one. The GPA is labeled Pattern, while the HSRANK, SATV, and SATM columns are labeled Input. We then File | Save NetMaker file as gpa2.dat and create our BrainMaker files as gpa2.def (definition file of the network), gpa2.fct (fact file), and gpa2.tst (test file). By default, 80 percent of the facts are in the definition file, and 10 percent each (41) in the other two. We want to see how well the network will perform on all 411 data points and so we recreate the test file in NetMaker, read in gpa2.txt, and create a new test file.

We exit (or Minimize) NetMaker and start BrainMaker. We select File | Read Network gpa2.def. Using the defaults, Learning rate = 1, Tolerance = .1, 3 inputs, 1 output, a single hidden layer with 10 neurons, and other factors, we select Operate | Train Network, which performed 942 runs on 336 facts for a total of 348,506. In Figure 15.13a we show the results of the network progress at the end of the run. Once the network was trained, we saved it; then, we selected File | Open Output Files (use the default names) to write the results of running the fact file to gpa2.out. We next select Operate | Run Facts File, which writes the predictions into gpa2.out.

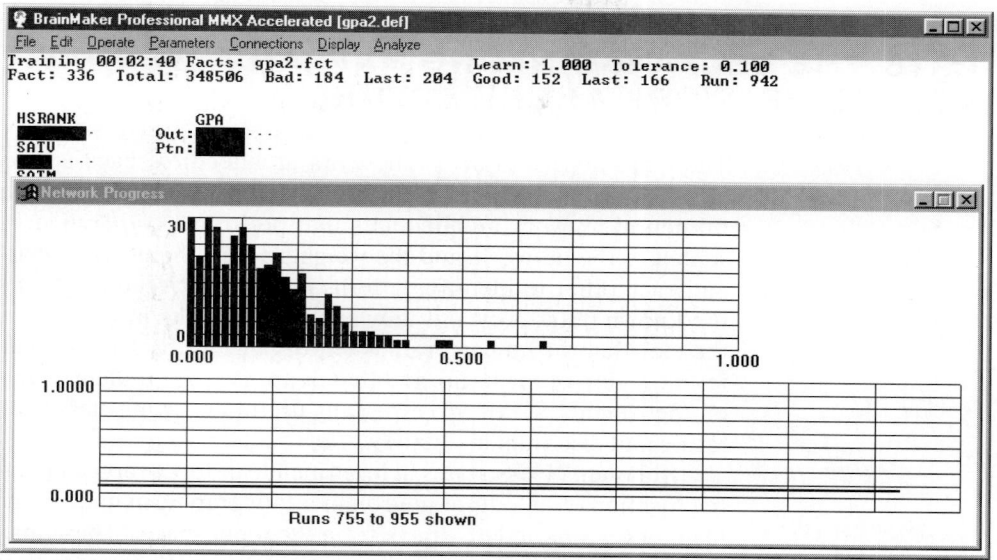

a. Results of the network progress at the end of the run

b. Results copied into an Excel worksheet and compared to multiple linear regression

FIGURE 15.13 DEMONSTRATION EXAMPLE OF NEURAL NETWORK SOFTWARE BRAINMAKER

We exit BrainMaker and edit the file to put the results into tabular form, which
   we later analyze in an Excel spreadsheet. The accuracy of the GPA predictions
   was a bit better than those of a multiple linear regression analysis that we
   performed (Figure 15.13b) (see the worksheet, gpatest2.xls, on this book's
   Web site).

15.18 THE SELF-ORGANIZING MAP: AN ALTERNATIVE NEURAL NETWORK ARCHITECTURE

There are dozens of neural network architectures, each applicable to solving specific classes of problems. The self-organizing map (SOM) is one of the more popular and useful neural network architectures that perform *unsupervised learning.* Inputs are presented to the network, and the weights adjust themselves relative to the input pattern and each other to identify patterns in the input vectors. The neural network does not use known outputs even if they are available. The mapping architectures are based on the idea that the human brain is self-organizing, each sensory input mapping into a different region of the brain, and that neurons can stimulate or inhibit nearby ones, based on the weights. SOMs are especially useful in solving classification problems like clustering and discriminant analysis.

Kohonen (1990) states in his principle of topographic map formation that "the spatial location of an output neuron in a topographic map corresponds to a particular domain or feature of data drawn from the input space." These maps can be two- or three-dimensional (or higher). We discuss the former. We show an example of the topology of the Kohonen SOM model in Figure 15.14a as a lattice in a plane. We show the lattice of neurons in Figure 15.14b.

Though this model is not an accurate representation of the brain, it captures the essential features of computational maps in the brain and is computationally tractable, unlike other, more accurate SOM models (Haykin, 1999). When an input pattern is presented to the SOM, the network's outputs configure into a topological representation of the pattern (Deboeck, 1999). To use the SOM, small weights are initially distributed through the network. The learning algorithm is unsupervised and competitive; that is, the neuron with the largest output "wins" and identifies the pattern in the data corresponding to its definition. Some network training algorithms are so competitive that only one neuron can have an output of 1, while the rest are inhibited strongly and after training are equal to 0. When cooperative learning is used, the winning neuron indicates a spatial location of the neighborhood of excited neurons. See Kohonen (1997), Haykin (1999), Deboeck (1999), and Principe at al. (2000) for explicit details on how to structure and apply Kohonen SOM ANN models. See Kaski et al. (1997) and liinwww.ira.uka.de for bibliographies on self-organizing maps.

EXAMPLES

There is an example of a Kohonen SOM solving the famous Fisher's iris classification problem on the SPSS Web site (www.spss.com). There are 50 flowers to be classified into three species. This example includes a description of how to structure the problem and run it in SPSS Neural Connection, along with screen shots. DemoGNG is a set of competitive learning neural networks written in a Java applet and running on the Web at www.neuroinformatik.ruhr-uni-bochum.de/ini/VDM/research/gsn/DemoGNG/GNG.html (by H. S. Loos and B. Frizke, Institut für Neuroinformatik, Ruhr-Universität, Bochum, Germany). DemoGNG includes an example of an SOM that can be manipulated by using the mouse to pull on the nodes. Many faculty and neural network vendors have SOM Kohonen neural network tutorials on the Web, some with running demos. For example, see K. N. Gurney's at www.shef.ac.uk/psychology/gurney/notes/content.html (Department of Psychology, University of Sheffield, Sheffield, UK). A good six-node SOM example is described in the tutorial.

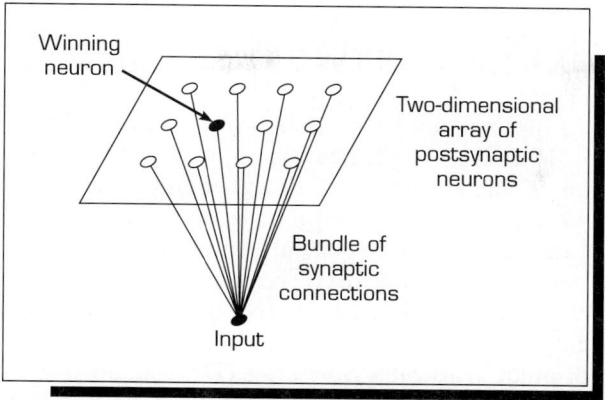

(a) Topology of the Kohonen SOM model as a lattice in a plane

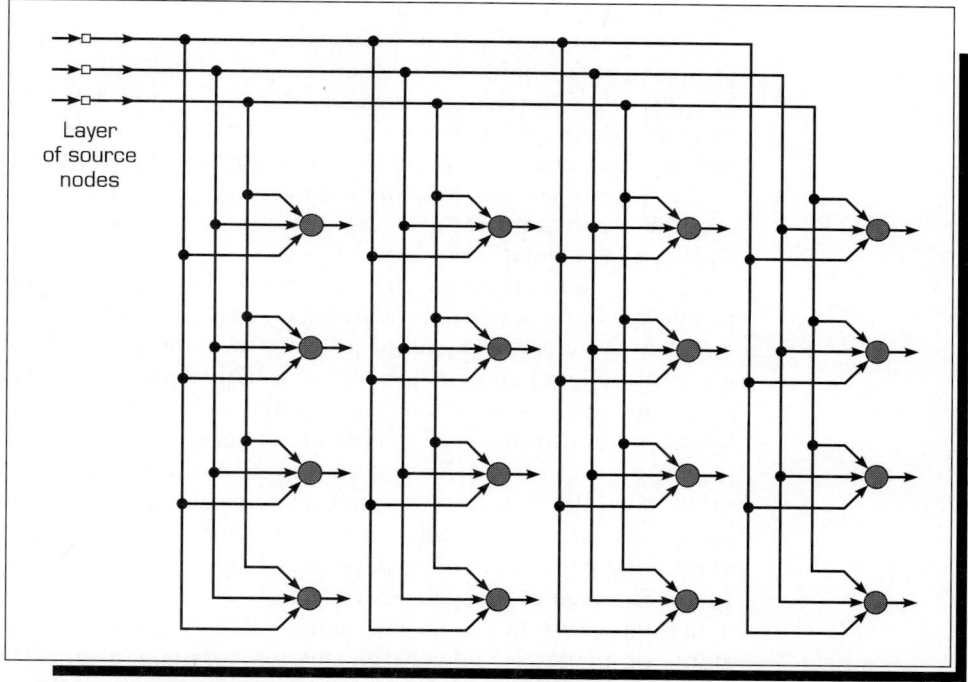

(b) The lattice of neurons

FIGURE 15.14 EXAMPLE OF KOHONEN MODEL

Source: NEURAL NETWORKING by Haykin © 1999. Reprinted by permission of Prentice-Hall, Inc., Upper Saddle River, NJ.

ANN TOOLS

Deboeck (1999) describes both public domain and commercial tools for creating and applying SOM. Many of the ANN tools mentioned earlier have SOM as a one of the standard neural network architectures (Trajan, NeuroSolutions, SPSS Neural Connection, and others).

15.19 BENEFITS OF NEURAL NETWORKS

The value of neural network technology includes its usefulness for pattern recognition, learning, classification, generalization and abstraction, and interpretation of incomplete and *noisy* inputs. There is a natural overlap with traditional AI applications in pattern recognition. Several important commercial applications and research areas of pattern recognition include, but are not limited to, handwriting (and typed text) recognition (Plamonden and Srihari, 2000; Schantz, 1991), image recognition (Nagy, 2000) (important for military and operations management), and voice and speech recognition (Russell and Kumar, 2000). The popular Naturally Speaking (Dragon Software) and ViaVoice (IBM) voice and speech recognition systems utilize neural networks. They must be trained for each user and are retrained as new words are misrecognized. The Palm Pilot Operating System (Palm, Inc., www.palm.com) Graffiti handwriting recognition system utilizes neural networks.[6]

Another type of pattern recognition is used in weather forecasting. Patterns indicate weather conditions to occur. Kroening (1999) discusses several weather ANN-based weather forecasting systems, and McCann (1999) describes how two ANNs were used to predict extremes of weather conditions that cause aircraft icing, a dangerous situation (see www.awc-kc.noaa.gov/awc/Neural_Net_Icing.html).

Systems that learn are more natural interfaces to the real world than systems that must be programmed. Speed considerations indicate the need to exploit parallel processing implementations.

Neural networks have the potential to provide some human characteristics to problem solving that are difficult to simulate using the logical, analytical techniques of expert systems and standard software technologies. For example, neural networks can analyze large amounts of data to establish patterns and characteristics in situations where rules are not known (as when an incomplete rule set must be developed by induction through KDD). Neural networks have successfully been applied to financial applications such as measuring stock fluctuations for determining an appropriate portfolio mix. Likewise, neural networks can provide the human characteristic of making sense of incomplete or noisy data and can perform data mining, identifying patterns in large databases (Bigus, 1996; Deck, 1999a; Fu, 1999; Larson, 1999). For example, Cognos Corporation provides a neural network in its 4Thought data mining system for business intelligence (www.cognos.com). We describe an example of an electric power transmission company using 4Thought to predict electricity use in AIS in Action 15.6. These applications have thus far proven too difficult for the symbolic, logical approach of traditional AI and less successful analytical techniques.

---

[6]Accurate and commercially viable automatic handwriting recognition was fairly difficult to accomplish until the mid to late 1990s. The user must learn a new way of writing for more accurate recognition. The Graffiti system simplifies the handwriting strokes (e.g., an *A* looks like an upside down *V* and must be started in the lower left corner) and separates numbers from letters (otherwise the letter *O* and the number 0 would be indistinguishable), thus enforcing consistency and improving the accuracy dramatically. This writing method takes about 2 minutes to learn, and in the Palm Pilot, when we compared it to the miniature keyboard, gave us a 60 percent boost in the speed at which we could enter text. Try Graffiti at www.palm.com.

AIS IN ACTION 15.6

NGC HALVES FORECASTING ERROR WITH NEURAL NETWORKS

National Grid Company (NGC) is the world's largest privately owned independent electricity transmission company and one of the UK's top 100 companies. It owns and operates the high-voltage transmission network in England and Wales, carrying electricity in bulk from the power stations to those who supply more than 23 million domestic and business customers.

NGC is responsible for meeting electricity demand. Electricity cannot be stored but must be generated as needed, a complex process. To produce a daily generating schedule, it is necessary to forecast the likely demand for electricity. Demand fluctuates widely, not only with the season, time of day, and weather but also with other factors such as "television pickup," when the turning on of lights and kettles at the end of popular television shows leads to a large surge in demand.

The National Grid Company has implemented Cognos' 4Thought business intelligence tool as a pilot project alongside its in-house multiple regression forecasting system.

4Thought forecasts a day's worth of electricity usage with about 10,000 input variables, stored in a mainframe database system, for 48 one-half hour intervals, leading to a typical schedule that involves bringing plants online or taking them offline, or adjusting their output on the order of 1,700 times. 4Thought's forecasts halve the error of the multiple regression model. It is leading to an increase in profitability by reducing under- and overcapacity and should lead to substantial costs savings.

One key feature is that, unlike the multiple regression approach, the neural network technology used by 4Thought can readily model nonlinear relationships. One example is the effect of temperature: Demand rises as temperatures fall in winter and also as they rise in summer (because of air conditioner use) but is relatively insensitive at intermediate temperatures. When both systems are given the same data on weather conditions, 4Thought explains more of the observed variation in demand than the in-house system does.

Source: Adapted from Cognos Corporation, Apr. 2000 www.cognos.com.

Neural networks can provide several other benefits:

- *Ability to solve new kinds of problems.* Neural computers are particularly effective at solving problems whose solutions are difficult, if not impossible, to define. This has opened up a new range of decision support applications formerly either difficult or impossible to computerize.
- *Robustness.* Neural networks tend to be more robust than their conventional counterparts. They have the ability to cope well with incomplete or fuzzy data and can deal with previously unspecified or unencountered situations (as a human brain does). Neural networks can be very tolerant of faults if properly implemented. This contrasts with conventional computer systems, in which failure of one component usually means failure of the entire system. This results in a higher level of accuracy compared to conventional methods.
- *Fast processing speed.* Because they consist of a large number of massively interconnected processing units, all operating in parallel on the same problem, neural networks can potentially operate at considerable speed (when implemented on parallel processors). This contrasts to the serial, one-step-at-a-time processing used by most methods in conventional computers.
- *Flexibility and ease of maintenance.* Neural computers are very flexible in adapting their behavior to new and changing environments. They are also easier to maintain, with some having the ability to learn from experience to improve their own performance (the operational system can retrain with new cases like the voice and speech recognition systems Naturally Speaking and ViaVoice).

Thus, neural computing differs from traditional computing methods in many ways, and application developers can exploit these differences. Neural networks can be applied in areas where data are multivariate, there is a high degree of interdependence among attributes, data are noisy or incomplete, or many hypotheses are to be pursued in parallel and high computational rates are required.

Beyond its role as an alternative, neural computing can be combined with conventional software to produce powerful *hybrid systems*. Such integrated systems can include database, expert system, neural network, and other technologies to produce computerized solutions to complex problems (see AIS in Action 15.6) (for examples, see Chin, 1999; Back et al., 1996; Quah et al., 1996). Moon et al. (1998) describe the integration of two expert systems, a neural network and a database, into an automatic early warning system (AEWS) for accurately predicting product reliability at United Technologies Carrier. The new AEWS replaced a statistically based system and resulted in a significant boost in productivity by at least 8 times in terms of process time. ANNs are especially suitable for complex decision support (Wang, 1994; Schocken and Ariav, 1994).

15.20 LIMITATIONS OF NEURAL NETWORKS

In general, ANNs do not perform well on tasks that people do not perform well. For example, arithmetic and data processing tasks are not suitable for ANNs and are best accomplished by conventional computing methods. ANNs excel at classification and pattern recognition.

Neural networks do not produce an explicit model even though new cases can be fed into it and new results obtained. It is difficult to explain to researchers and practitioners who normally use statistical methods that there is no measure of input variable significance. Yet despite this, neural networks can make more accurate predictions empirically, which explains their commercial success.

Most neural network systems lack explanation capabilities. Justification for results is difficult to obtain because the connection weights usually do not have obvious interpretations. This is particularly true in pattern recognition, where it is very difficult or even impossible to explain the logic behind specific decisions. However, some ANN tools offer some explanations based on analyzing the importance of the input data in relationship to the output. But when seemingly insignificant inputs (statistically speaking) are removed from a network and it is retrained, the richness provided by the nonlinearities created by these inputs disappears and the prediction accuracy degrades. The limitations and expense of current parallel hardware technology restrict most applications to software simulations. With current technologies, training times can be excessive and tedious. Thus, the need for frequent retraining may make a particular application impractical. Finally, neural computing usually requires extensive training and testing of data.

15.21 NEURAL NETWORKS AND EXPERT SYSTEMS

When ANNs were revived, they were sometimes called sixth-generation computing. This labeling gave the erroneous impression that fifth-generation computing, which includes expert systems, had been replaced. Although ANNs can sometimes perform tasks better (or faster) than ES, in most instances the two technologies are not applicable to the same problem types. The characteristics of the technologies are so different that they complement each other rather well in some cases.

In principle, expert systems represent a logical symbolic problem-solving approach, whereas neural networks are model-based and use numeric and associative processing. The main features of each approach are summarized in Table 15.2

TABLE 15.2 Comparing Expert Systems and Artificial Neural Networks

Expert Systems	*Artificial Neural Networks*
Have user development facilities, but systems should preferably be developed by skilled developers because of knowledge acquisition complexities.	Have user development facilities and can be easily developed by users with minimal training.
Take longer to develop. Experts must be available and willing to articulate their problem-solving process.	Can be developed in a short time. Experts only need to identify the inputs, outputs, and a wide range of sample cases.
Rules must be clearly identified. Difficult to develop for intuitively made decisions.	Does not need rules to be identified. Well suited for decisions made intuitively.
Weak in pattern recognition and data analysis such as forecasting.	Well suited for such applications but need a wide range of sample data.
Not fault-tolerant.	Highly fault-tolerant.
Changes in problem environment warrant maintenance.	Highly adaptable to changing problem environments.
Applications must fit into specific knowledge representation schemes (an explicit form of knowledge).	Can be tried if the application does not fit into one of ES's knowledge representation schemes.
The performance of the human expert who helped create the ES places a theoretical performance limit for the ES.	May outperform human experts in certain applications such as forecasting.
Have explanation systems to explain why and how a decision was reached. Required when the decision needs an explanation to inspire user confidence. Recommended when the problem-solving process is clearly known.	Have no explanation system and act like black boxes.
Useful when a series of decisions can be represented by a decision tree and when, in such cases, user interaction is required.	Useful for one-shot decisions.
Useful when high-level human functions such as reasoning and deduction need to be emulated.	Useful when low-level human functions such as pattern recognition need to be emulated.
Are not useful in validating the correctness of ANN system development.	Are sometimes useful in validating the correctness of ES development.
Use a symbolic approach (people-oriented).	Use a numeric approach (data-oriented).
Are driven by knowledge.	Are driven by data.
Use logical (deductive) reasoning.	Use associative (inductive) reasoning.
Use sequential processing.	Use parallel processing (in theory).
Are closed systems.	Are self-organizing.
Learning takes place outside the system and is structured and placed in the system by human effort.	Learning takes place automatically within the system; a human structures the network.
Are developed through knowledge extraction.	Are developed through training, using examples.

Source: Partly adapted from J. R. Slater et al., "On Selecting Appropriate Technology for Knowledge Systems," *Journal of Systems Management,* Oct. 1993, p. 15.

EXPERT SYSTEMS

Expert systems are especially good for closed-system applications for which inputs are literal and precise and lead to logical outputs. They are particularly useful for interacting with the client/user to define a specific problem and bring in facts unique to the problem being solved. Expert systems reason by using established facts and established rules.

A major limitation of the expert system approach arises from the fact that experts do not always think in terms of rules. Also, experts may not be able to explain their line of reasoning and/or they may explain it inaccurately. Thus, in many instances it is difficult or even impossible to build the knowledge base. To overcome this and other limitations, development of an ANN can be attempted instead.

NEURAL NETWORKS IN KNOWLEDGE ACQUISITION

An ANN can be useful for fast identification of implicit knowledge by automatically analyzing cases of historical data. The ANN analyzes the data sets to identify patterns and relationships that may subsequently lead to rules for expert systems. The network may be the sole technique for knowledge acquisition, or it may supplement explicit rules derived by other techniques (such as interviews or rule induction).

Another possible contribution of ANNs to knowledge acquisition occurs when the interface with an expert can best be accomplished with an expert system module that asks questions and directs data gathering from the expert efficiently and comprehensively. A trained neural network can then rapidly process information to produce associated facts and consequences. Next, an expert system module can perform further analysis and report results. Thus, fewer explicit rules may be necessary because the neural network embeds general knowledge in its connection weights and produces specific knowledge relevant to the user's specific problem. See Coleman and Watenpool (1992) and Medsker and Turban (1994) for more information.

15.22 NEURAL NETWORKS FOR DECISION SUPPORT

The Opening Vignette and Case Application 15.1 illustrate how neural networks can provide direct support to a decision maker: The neural networks in the Opening Vignette determined creditworthiness and recommended loan approvals. In Case Application 15.1, the ANN identified stocks with the highest predicted yield to be considered for inclusion in an investment portfolio. Schocken and Ariav (1994) showed how neural computing can provide inductive means of gathering, storing, and using experiential knowledge. They carried out an analysis of the potential contribution of neural networks to decision support in the context of a general-purpose DSS framework that examines all the key factors that come into play in the design of any DSS. Neural networks have a direct impact on key aspects of decision support such as classification, pattern recognition, multiattribute scoring, and prediction. However, Schocken and Ariav argue that neural networks do not provide a sweeping alternative to standard computing. In terms of use, ANNs are marked by low face validity and a lack of explicit explainability. Effective explanation capabilities and mechanisms of explicit accountability must be developed to transform neural networks into a widely used DSS tool. On the other hand, commercial successes abound (check out the literature and the vendors' Web sites). In AIS in Action 15.7, we provide an example of a successful neural network application for real estate appraisal. Another area of decision support is forecasting, especially when uncertainty is involved. We provide an example in AIS in Action 15.8. Also see Ainscough et al. (1997).

NEURAL NETWORKS QUICKLY AND ACCURATELY APPRAISE REAL ESTATE

Richard Borst, a senior vice president at Day & Zimmerman Inc., the nation's leading provider of mass appraisal services to state and local governments, developed a neural network–based DSS to appraise real estate in New York. The network has 18 inputs, including number of dwelling units, fireplaces, plumbing fixtures, square feet of living area, age, months since last sale, and air conditioning. The system also takes into consideration a qualitative measure of neighborhood rating. Using 217 sales records, he trained the network using BrainMaker Professional (California Scientific Software). The neural network is able to predict the actual sale price of properties within 10 percent, much closer than multivariate analysis can.

Source: Adapted from California Scientific Software, "BrainMaker Real Estate Appraisal," www.calsci.com; and R. A. Borst, "Artificial Neural Networks: The Next Modeling/Calibration Technology for the Assessment Community?" *Property Tax Journal,* Vol. 10, No. 1, 1991, pp. 69–94.

NEURAL NETWORKS SUPPORT REENGINEERING AT WRANGLER

Wrangler, a manufacturer of blue jeans, like most consumer goods manufacturers has historically planned production based on forecasts of order demand. The problem was that order demand was inconsistent with sales. To improve production planning and forecasting, Wrangler uses neural network forecasting technology. It generates forecasts based on consumer demand data, rather than retail buyers' orders, to drive production planning.

This information is combined with consumer sales information and fed into a neural network–based forecasting model. Forecasts are created for each retail chain. The aggregate of these chain forecasts drives Wrangler's production planning. The manufacturing and sourcing are better matched with consumer demand. This application is part of Wrangler's reengineering effort to increase sales volumes, lower inventory investments, and improve inventory turnover for retail customers and for Wrangler. An important part of the supply chain reengineering has been revamping product forecasting and production planning. By forecasting production needs more accurately, Wrangler is able to maintain a high level of in-stock customer service, carrying less finished goods inventories.

Source: Adapted from *Expert Systems,* Feb. 1996, p. 73.

Another advantage of an ANN is pointed out by Poh (1994), who studied the use of ANNs in strategic management and other unstructured problems. He believes that the ease with which neural computing can conduct sensitivity analysis and partial analysis of the input factors is a big advantage of ANNs in decision support. Sensitivity analysis allows the user to understand the effect of changes in input variables (like competitive factors), which help in implementation. A new input set (case) can be quickly generated from an old one and run through the ANN. An ANN can help in decision making by increasing the number of alternatives examined and by providing new insights and learning. For example, if an ANN denies a loan, the down payment can be increased, decreasing the monthly payments, which the ANN might recognize as leading to approving the loan. The relationship between a combined expert system, an ANN, and a DSS is shown in Figure 15.15. Notice that each technology performs different tasks in the decision-making process. Examples of applications of this type of system are provided in the next chapter.

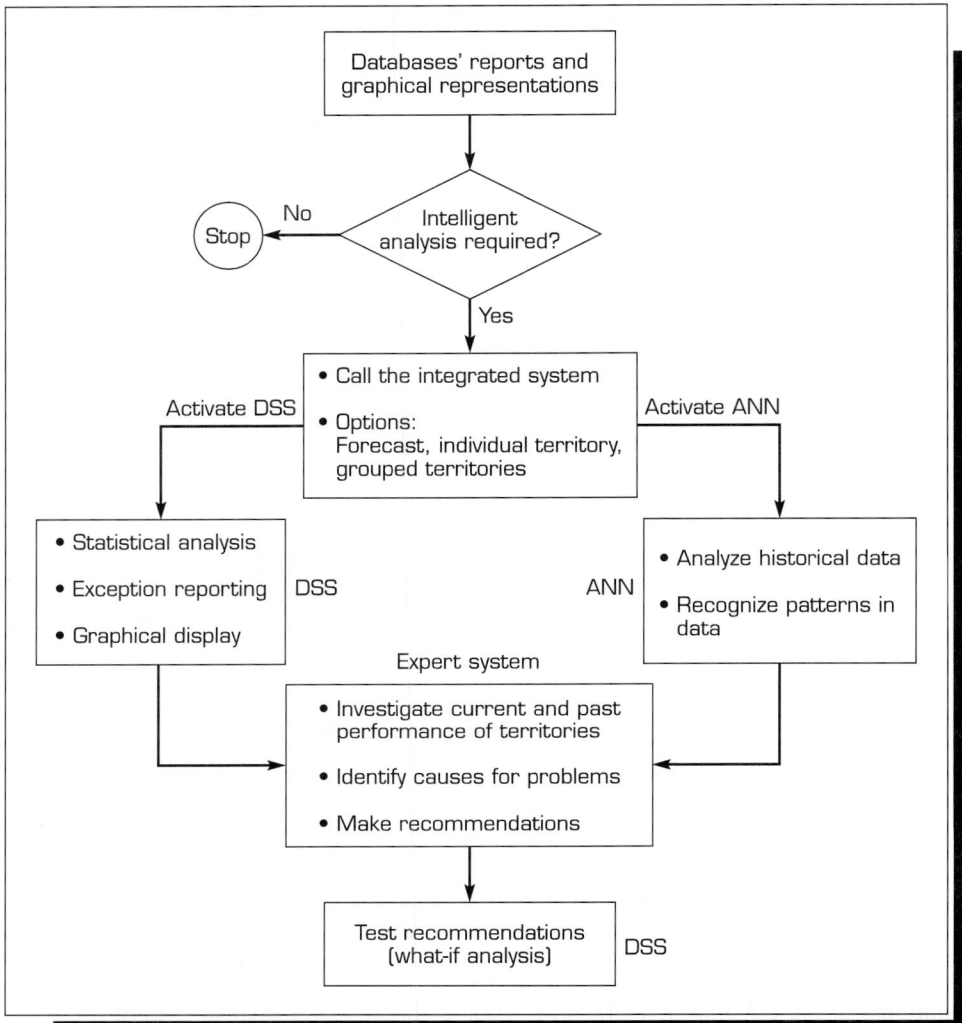

FIGURE 15.15 CONCEPTUAL FLOWCHART FOR THE INTEGRATED SYSTEM

Source: Benjamin and Bannis, 1991.

Finally, because of the proliferation of e-commerce, vendors have released neural network applications that determine credit fraud quickly online. Credit card fraud is a $1.5 billion per year problem worldwide. Web-related e-commerce soared sixfold from 1997 to 1998 (Lach, 1999). HNC Software's neural network service, eFalcon, analyzes volumes of transaction-level data for patterns of fraud and provides a rank-ordered scoring system that users can adjust to set their own fraud parameters (Deck, 1999b).

The above examples show that an ANN can expand the boundaries of DSS. In the next chapter we provide specific examples of ANNs in decision support and show how they can be integrated with other intelligent systems to improve their functionality in enabling a computerized approach to solving fairly complex problems.

❖ CHAPTER HIGHLIGHTS

- Machine learning involves techniques that describe how computer systems learn from experience.
- Machine learning is used in knowledge acquisition as well as in inferencing and problem solving.
- Machines learn differently from the way people learn and usually do not learn as well, nor can they (yet) replace human creativity.
- Neural computing uses procedures conceptually similar to those of biological systems.
- The human brain is composed of billions of cells called neurons, grouped in interconnected clusters.
- Neural systems are composed of processing elements called artificial neurons. They are interconnected and receive, process, and deliver information. A group of connected neurons forms an artificial neural network.
- An artificial neural network can be organized in many different ways. The major elements are the processing elements, connections among the processing elements, inputs, outputs, and weights.
- Weights express the relative strength (or importance) given to specific input data.
- Each neuron has an activation value that is expressed by summing the input values multiplied by their weights.
- An activation value is translated to an output by going through a transformation (transfer) function. The output can be related in a linear or a nonlinear manner or via a threshold value.
- Artificial neural networks learn from historical cases. The learning (training) produces the values of the weights that make the computed outputs close in value to the desired outputs.
- The neural network learning process is performed with training algorithms. There are hundreds, and they are relatively easy to computerize.
- Supervised learning is a neural network training approach in which computed outputs are compared to known outputs produced from the known inputs. The weights are adjusted, based on the error in an attempt to minimize the error. In unsupervised learning, the network is self-organized to produce categories (patterns) into which a series of inputs fall.
- Testing is done with additional historical data to see whether the computed outputs match the known values.
- A typical approach to training, testing, and deploying a neural network is to use 80 percent of the data for training and 10 percent for initial testing. If the network is accurate enough, then it can be deployed, otherwise, it is retrained with the 90 percent of the data used thus far and tested again with the remaining 10 percent.
- Neural computing is often integrated with traditional computer-based information systems and with expert systems in effective DSS.
- Many ANNs are built with tools that include learning algorithms and other computational procedures.
- There are several different neural network architectures with features that make them useful in solving specific classes of problems.
- ANNs lend themselves naturally to parallel processing. Even so, most ANNs are solved on standard computers where multiprocessing is simulated on a single processor (such as simulated artificial neural networks, SANN).

- There are many ANN packages that run on PCs and Unix systems. There are even spreadsheet add-in packages. Many can generate C++ source code to incorporate into other systems.
- Parallel processors can improve the training and running of neural networks.
- Parallel processing hardware, including neural chips, acceleration boards, and MMX technology, can speed up the computational work of neural computers, especially the training.
- Neural computing excels in pattern recognition, learning, classification, generalization and abstraction, and interpretation of fuzzy and incomplete input data.
- Artificial neural networks do not perform well on tasks that people do not perform well, nor are they good at performing tasks that traditional computer systems perform well (such as transaction processing and nonrepetitive scientific computing).
- Neural networks are useful in data mining.
- Neural networks have the potential to enhance DSS.

❖ KEY WORDS

- analogical reasoning
- artificial neural networks (ANNs)
- associative memory
- axon
- backpropagation
- case-based reasoning (CBR)
- dendrites
- explanation-based learning
- genetic algorithms
- hidden layer
- inductive learning
- knowledge-poor procedures
- learning algorithm
- machine learning
- massive parallel processing
- neural computing (networks)
- neurons
- nucleus
- parallel processing
- pattern recognition
- processing elements (PEs)
- self-organizing
- sigmoid (logical activation) function
- statistical methods
- summation function
- supervised learning
- synapse
- transformation (transfer) function
- unsupervised learning
- weights

❖ QUESTIONS FOR REVIEW

1. What is machine learning? List its major technologies.
2. What are the major objectives of machine learning? Why is there such interest in the topic?
3. What is an artificial neural network?
4. Explain the following terms: *neuron, axon, dendrite,* and *synapse.*
5. Describe biological and artificial neural networks.
6. What is a hidden layer?
7. How do weights function in an artificial neural network?
8. Describe the role of the summation function.
9. Describe the role of the transformation function.
10. What is a threshold value?
11. Why are learning algorithms important to ANN?
12. Define associative memory.
13. Briefly describe backpropagation.
14. Explain the potential use of acceleration boards.
15. List the major benefits of neural computing.
16. List the major limitations of neural computing.
17. What capabilities of neural networks make them good candidates for performing data mining?

❖ QUESTIONS FOR DISCUSSION

1. Compare artificial and biological neural networks. What aspects of biological networks are not mimicked by artificial ones? What aspects are similar?

2. Draw a picture of two connected biological neurons and explain the flow of information.

3. Compare neural computing and conventional computing.

4. How is parallelism related to ANNs? How can an ANN be developed and run on a single processor?

5. Discuss the role of weights in ANNs.

6. Explain the combined effects of the summation and transformation functions.

7. Discuss the relationship between a transformation function and a threshold value.

8. Explain how ANNs learn in a supervised and in an unsupervised mode.

9. Why is an ANN so closely related to pattern recognition?

10. Describe several pattern recognition problems in practice.

11. Explain how learning (training) is performed and why there are so many different learning algorithms.

12. Review the development process of ANNs. Compare it to the development process of expert systems.

13. What is meant by initialization of the parameters of the network?

14. Explain what is meant by a neural network architecture.

15. Describe how a self-organizing neural network works and give an example of a problem that can be readily solved by one.

16. Discuss the major advantages of ANNs. Discuss the disadvantages.

17. Explain the difference between a training set and a testing set. Can the same set be used for both purposes? Why or why not?

18. *Real-world scenario:* A neural network has been constructed to predict the creditworthiness of applicants. There are two output nodes, one for yes (1, yes; 0, no) and one for no (1, no; 0, yes). An applicant received a score of 0.83 for the "yes" output node and a 0.44 for the "no" output node. Discuss what may have happened and whether the applicant is a good credit risk.

19. What features of an ANN make it much easier to maintain than an expert system?

20. Compare a neural chip with an acceleration board.

21. What deficiencies of expert systems can be overcome by artificial neural networks?

22. Explain how ANNs can perform knowledge acquisition.

23. Expert systems and ANNs can complement each other very well. Explain how and be specific.

❖ EXERCISES

1. For the following applications, would it be better to use neural networks or expert systems? Explain your answers, including possible exceptions or special conditions.
   a. Diagnosis of a well-established but complex disease
   b. Price lookup subsystem for a high-volume merchandise sale
   c. Automated voice inquiry processing system
   d. Training new employees
   e. Handwriting recognition

2. Give possible applications of neural networks for the following:
   a. Character recognition
   b. Financial index forecasting
   c. Stock selection

3. Several companies are flooded by hundreds and even thousands of job applications. Prepare a conceptual design of an integrated ANN and ES that will help in the screening process of a company for which security considerations are important. Explain which tasks will be supported by which technology.

4. Check the literature (and use the Web if you can) on chess- and checkers-playing programs. Describe their machine learning aspects in a report. Include an explanation of why game playing is so important in AI research.

5. Review this neural network and compute Z.

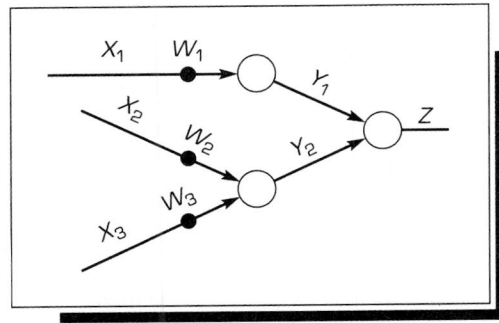

where $X_1 = 15, X_2 = 8, X_3 = 14, W_1 = 0.6, W_2 = 0.3, W_3 = 0.1$,
        weight for $Y_1 = 0.6$, weight for $Y_2 = 0.45$.

   a. Compute the value of Z without a transfer function.
   b. Compute the value of Z with a threshold function. If the value is 5 or less, call it 0; otherwise call it 1.
   c. Compute the value of Z with the sigmoid transfer function used at all neurons.

6. Using the Braincel neural network package (download a demo from the Web, www.promland.com) or another, build, train, and test a neural network to solve the following simple regression formula that predicts Y as a function of X (for this simple case, train the network on the entire set of data):

X	Y
0	0
.1	.05
.2	.11
.3	.25
.4	.4
.5	.66
.6	.89
.7	1.0

In a spreadsheet, plot the data, and solve the simple linear regression formula $Y = a + bX$. Compare the estimates made by the neural network and by the regression. Calculate the sum-of-the-squares error and R^2 for each. Which one is better?

7. Investigate how neural networks are applied to forecasting. Check the literature and vendors' Web sites. Discuss your findings in a five-page report.

❖ **GROUP EXERCISES**

1. *Self-organizing neural network class exercises.*
   a. Everyone in the class stands in the front of the room, away from the desks and chairs (a room free of furniture or an open field is even better). Without speak-

ing, everyone lines up in order by height, tallest to shortest. Then, at a signal lines up alphabetically. Notice that only minimal information is really needed by each person to identify his or her position. Discuss how this relates to how self-organizing neural networks learn.

b. An alternative is to blindfold everyone except the instructor. The instructor whispers to each student a unique number from 1 to the number of students in the class. Without assigning a leader and instructing everyone in the class not to speak, they are asked to line up in numerical order.

2. Consider the set of data that relates daily electricity usage as a function of outside high temperature (for the day).

Temperature, X	Kilowatts, Y
46.8	12,530
52.1	10,800
55.1	10,180
59.2	9,730
61.9	9,750
66.2	10,230
69.9	11,160
76.8	13,910
79.7	15,110
79.3	15,690
80.2	17,020
83.3	17,880

a. Plot the raw data. What pattern do you see? What do you think is really affecting electricity usage?

b. Solve this problem with linear regression $Y = a + bX$ (in a spreadsheet). How well did this work? Plot your results. What is wrong? Calculate a sum-of-the-squares error and R^2.

c. Solve this problem with nonlinear regression. We recommend a quadratic function, $Y = a + b_1X + b_2X^2$. Again, how well did this work? Plot your results. Is anything wrong? Calculate a sum of the squares error and R^2.

d. Break up the problem into three sections (look at the plot) and solve it with three linear regression models, one for each section. How well did this work? Plot your results. Calculate a sum of the squares error and R^2. Is this modeling approach appropriate? Why or why not?

e. Build a neural network to solve the original problem. (You may have to scale the X and Y values to be between 0 and 1.) Train it (on the entire set of data) and solve the problem (make predictions for each of the original data items). How well did this work? Plot your results. Calculate a sum of the squares error and R^2.

f. Which method worked best and why?

3. Build a real-world neural network. Using demo software downloaded from the Web (Braincel at www.promland.com or another), identify real-world data (e.g., start searching on the Web at www.research.ed.asu.edu or use data from an organization with which someone in your group has a contact) and build a neural network to make predictions. Topics might include sales forecasts, predicting success in an academic program (predict GPA from high school rating and SAT scores—see ftp://psych.colorado.edu/pub/stat/gpa.txt, being careful to look out for "bad" data, e.g., GPAs of 0.0), housing prices, or even survey the class for weight, gender, and height and try to predict height based on the other two. (*Hint:* Use U.S. Census data, on this book's Web site or at www.census.gov, by state to identify a relationship between education level and income.) How good are your predictions? Compare the results to predictions generated by standard statistical methods (regression). Which method was better? How could your system be embedded in a DSS for real decision making?

❖ INTERNET EXERCISES

1. Explore the Web sites of several neural network vendors, such as California Scientific Software (www.calsci.com), NeuralWare Inc. (www.neuralware.com), Trajan Neural Network Simulator (www.trajan-software.demon.co.uk), Promised Land Technologies Inc. (www.promland.com), Ward Systems Group (www.wardsystems.com), NeuroDimension Inc. (www.nd.com), Neural Bench Development (www.neuralbench.ru), and review some of their products. Download at least two demos and install, run, and compare them.

2. Search the Web to find recent information about John Deere & Company's pension fund (see Case Application 15.1) and about other institutions that use neural networks (try Fidelity Investments).

3. Explore the Web to find information about neural network hardware. Write a report that describes the current offerings and capabilities.

4. Explore the Web to identify the use of neural networks in pattern recognition, handwriting recognition, and speech recognition.

5. Explore the Web to identify the current status of neural network research.

CASE APPLICATION 15.1

MAXIMIZING THE VALUE OF THE JOHN DEERE & COMPANY PENSION FUND

Managing the pension fund of John Deere & Company, a large manufacturer of earthmoving machines, agricultural machines, and other heavy equipment, is not simple. About $1 billion of the more than $5 billion is managed internally by the corporate finance department. To achieve a better return on the investment, this department has been using neural computing since 1993. Initially, the company allocated $100 million on an experimental basis to be invested in high-technology, large capitalization stocks (such as IBM). Later, another $100 million was allocated to mid-sized stocks.

Using historical data, an individual artificial neural network has been built for each of the 1,000 largest U.S. corporations. The data include 40 input fundamental and technical variables, such as growth rate, financial ratios, historical price movements, market share, and earning per share. Once a week, the current data of each company are fed into a neural network model that predicts the future performance of each stock (Figure 15.16). The model then ranks the 1,000 stocks based on their anticipated performance in the stock market. From this list, a portfolio of the top 100 stocks is selected and the fund is allocated proportionally to the predicted return. The neural network models are frequently retrained because of changing conditions in the marketplace.

Although the internal structure of the model and its performance level (success) are trade secrets of the company, the returns are well ahead of industry benchmarks.

Based on M. G. Star, "Deere Pension Fund Uses Neural Network." *Pensions and Investments,* Vol. 22, No. 22, Oct. 31, 1994, pp. 1, 42.

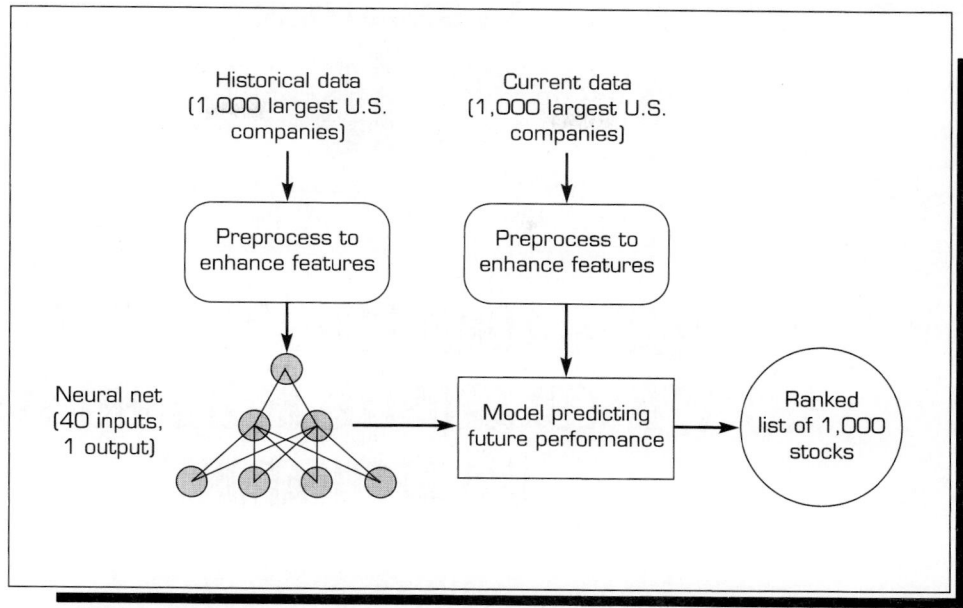

FIGURE 15.16 SCHEMATIC REPRESENTATION OF THE PROCESS USED IN THE JOHN DEERE & COMPANY STYLE ROTATION PORTFOLIO

Courtesy of John Deere & Company.

CASE QUESTIONS

1. Explain why neural networks are used.
2. Why is historical data used?
3. Is the neural network really learning? Why or why not?

4. How could the neural network possibly outperform a human?
5. Describe at least two related applications of neural computing.

CHAPTER
16

NEURAL COMPUTING APPLICATIONS, AND ADVANCED ARTIFICIAL INTELLIGENT SYSTEMS AND APPLICATIONS

In the last chapter, we introduced neural computing. In this chapter, we provide several real-world applications. We also introduce the three decision support technologies: genetic algorithms, fuzzy logic, and qualitative reasoning. Since these advanced technologies are often integrated among themselves and with expert systems, we provide methods and examples.

16.1 OPENING VIGNETTE: NEW YORK CITY'S PUBLIC HOUSING AUTHORITY GETS WARM AND FUZZY[1]

FUZZY LOGIC

Temperature is a *fuzzy* quantity. Though it can be accurately measured, the human-based concepts of ice cold, cold, mild, lukewarm, warm, and hot have vague connotations and can have somewhat different meanings for different people. Though people are vague in their language use (completely disabling Boolean logic–based systems), the context and meaning of situations involving concepts such as temperature and weather are generally clear. Fuzzy logic is based on the vagueness properties in human expressed logic. There are gradations of truth and falseness in logic statements which have been theoretically developed into a consistent system called *fuzzy logic.* Fuzzy logic can be directly applied or combined with other technologies into very *accurate* (often termed *concise*), automated decision-making systems.

THE REAL WORLD

Losses associated with poor operation and maintenance cost industry and government billions of dollars each year. Organizations that automate the process of diagnosing faults and performance degradation in equipment can lower costs and increase profits by increasing the life cycle of critical components.

NEW YORK CITY HOUSING AUTHORITY SYSTEM

Hoping to reduce complaints about heating problems in cold weather, the New York City Housing Authority has installed new artificial intelligence (AI)–based controls in the boilers at Smith Houses, a public housing project on Manhattan's Lower East Side.

The AI component is a fuzzy expert system for optimizing performance, combined with a neural network that can recognize patterns in data on a boiler's performance. The neural network can spot signs of trouble before operations are affected, giving the control system time to correct the problem through the fuzzy expert system controls, or time to call for help. The diagnostics package uses existing instrumentation to determine the system's state and its relation to proper operating conditions. Using the combination of neural networks and fuzzy logic principles, the diagnostician predicts, identifies, and diagnoses degradation and faults. The basic system can also be applied to valves, heat exchangers, compressors, filters, generators, and electric equipment to provide integrated degradation and fault diagnoses in real time.

THE GOOD NEWS AND THE BETTER NEWS

If the technology succeeds, the $1.4 million system will more than pay for itself. Otherwise, the developer, Battelle Memorial Institute, will *not* be paid. Battelle expects the cumulative operating savings for one building to be at least $2 million over 10 years, plus a $1.5 million savings in overhaul costs because of better maintenance.

---

[1]Partly adapted from O. Port and P. Raeburn, "AI in the Air Conditioning," *Business Week,* No. 3658, Dec. 6, 1999, p. 83; and Battelle Memorial Institute, "Operation and Maintenance Decision Support," *Energy Products Case Study,* 1999, www.battelle.org.

If the system were installed in the housing authority's 2,990 buildings, the savings could be huge. And, Battelle's technology has been demonstrated in practice to work.

❖ **QUESTIONS FOR THE OPENING VIGNETTE**

1. Describe the problem facing the New York City Housing Authority.
2. What is meant by fuzzy logic?
3. Explain how a fact can simultaneously be partially true and/or partially false.
4. How can AI-based technology help in this situation?
5. What is the benefit of combining fuzzy logic with neural networks?
6. Once the fuzzy logic research required for the system is paid for, do you think there is a possibility of developing a system like this for commercial office buildings and homes? Why or why not?

16.2 OVERVIEW OF ANN APPLICATION AREAS

The Opening Vignette illustrates an application of fuzzy logic combined with neural networks integrated with an expert system. The neural network identifies potential problems for the fuzzy logic with which to deal. Artificial neural networks can solve difficult problems that are not solvable by standard quantitative models either on their own or in combination with other intelligent systems. Some representative business applications are the following:

Accounting	Identifying tax fraud
	Enhancing auditing by finding irregularities
Finance	Signature and bank note verification
	Mortgage underwriting
	Foreign exchange rate forecasting
	Country risk rating
	Predicting stock initial public offerings (IPOs)
	Bankruptcy prediction
	Customer credit scoring
	Credit card approval and fraud detection
	Stock and commodity selection and trading
	Forecasting economic turning points
	Bond rating and trading
	Loan approvals
	Economic and financial forecasting
	Risk management
Human resources	Predicting employees' performance and behavior
	Determining personnel resource requirements
Management	Corporate merger and takeover predictions
	Country risk rating
Marketing	Classification of consumer spending patterns
	New product analysis
	Identification of customer characteristics

	Sales forecasts
	Data mining
	Airfare management
	Direct mail optimization
	Targeted marketing (telephone, mailers, other)
Operations	Airline crew scheduling
	Predicting airline seat demand
	Vehicle routing
	Assembly and packaged goods inspection
	Quality control
	Matching jobs to candidates
	Production and job scheduling
	Factory process control

Many financial applications of artificial neural networks have been and are currently under development (Ainscough et al., 1997; Trippi and Turban, 1996b). We next describe a number of specific neural network applications.

16.3 CREDIT APPROVAL WITH NEURAL NETWORKS[2]

CREDIT APPROVAL

Millions of people around the world seek loans daily for many reasons, ranging from buying a car to financing a college education. Financial institutions require them to fill out an application that includes contact information, employment information, and complete financial information. The information on the form is then compared to information purchased from credit bureaus. Application processing can be lengthy because some information may be missing or incomplete. Fortunately neural networks can make accurate predictions even when some information is missing. Neural computing has successfully been used in credit application processing, increasing the productivity of the processors by 25–35 percent compared to processing done with other computerized tools.

FRAUD

There is a related application of ANN in fraudulent credit card use. Credit card losses cost banks several billion dollars per year worldwide. Almost all credit card fraud involves counterfeit cards, use of stolen cards, use of stolen numbers, and fraudulent credit card applications. ANN applications are making major inroads in fraud detection. Because of the speed of e-commerce, immediate fraud detection has become a critical business problem. Neural network vendors have responded with a number of services and products customized for Web-based fraud detection. These include PRISM eFraud (Nestor Inc.), Decider eCommerce (Neural Technologies), and eFalcon (a service of HNC Software Corporation). For details

---

[2]This section has been partly compiled from two articles written by C. C. Kilmasauskas, published in *PC AI*, Jan./Feb. 1991, pp. 30–33, and Mar./Apr. 1991, pp. 27–34. Reproduced with permission of *PC AI*.

on how ANN can be used for fraud detection, see Anonymous (1999b), Deck (1999b), Fisher (1999), Green (1999), Lais (1999), Slater (2000), Wareham (1999), and ANN vendor Web sites. See AIS in Action 16.1 for a description of how ANNs detect insurance fraud.

NEURAL NETWORK APPROACH TO CREDIT APPLICATION

Either the application is filled out online or data are entered online from the paper application and transferred to a database. Basically, the format of the data in the database matches that of the form. Some items are calculated, such as debt to equity ratios or total monthly expenses set equal to monthly credit card payments plus mortgage payments. Some *preprocessing* is done manually, and some automatically, depending on the system.

Before the network can be used to recommend credit for new potential customers, the neural network has to be trained with many good and bad risk cases so that when it is fed a particular set of input data, it can predict whether the applicant will be a good-paying or poor-paying (good risk or poor risk) customer.

The process used to build this neural network credit authorizer is as follows:

1. *Collect data.* Gather all the pertinent data. For this case, all the data were readily available in a single database.

NEURAL NETWORKS DETECT INSURANCE CLAIM FRAUD AND IDENTIFY BEST MEDICAL PRACTICES

The Workers' Compensation Board (WBC) of British Columbia (Canada) has implemented an impartial new claimant tracking system to reduce fraud losses and identify best medical practice guidelines.

The WBC has deployed VeriComp Claimant and ProviderCompare from HNC Software Inc. VeriComp Claimant monitors ongoing claim activity and recognizes patterns showing fraud and abuse as they appear. Its neural network quickly processes hundreds of variables to produce scores indicating the likelihood of abuse. ProviderCompare is a physician profiling system that measures claim cost and treatment pattern differences on a case-adjusted basis.

"Estimates show that 10 to 20 per cent of the dollars spent for workers' compensation are for unwarranted claims," says Anu Pathria, executive director of modeling at HNC, "Only 20 per cent of the abuse is ever detected and if it is, it is often too late. The money has already been paid out."

Although privacy issues have been a concern for the WCB, the organization ensures that the information and databases are secure. The software acts impartially in determining whether to investigate each claim or not.

Claimant fraud and abuse were the initial motivation for adopting the systems. The WBC now uses the software to monitor expenses like prescription costs and medical service fees. Prescription drug monitoring could save on the order of $1.8 to $2.4 million (U.S.) per year initially.

The Worker's Compensation Fund of Utah has also been working with HNC to detect fraudulent claims. According to senior vice-president Robert Short, VeriComp Claimant saved them more than $2 million in its first year. "Sixty-two per cent of our fraud savings last year came from claims that scored high on the VeriComp Claimant system," he says, "We can trace back $3.8 million of our $7 million savings last year to VeriComp's scoring."

HNC estimates that workers' compensation fraud costs the insurance industry more than $6 billion annually in the United States and Canada.

Source: Adapted from E. Wareham, "Fraud-buster App Raises Concerns," *Computing Canada,* Vol. 25, No. 27, July 9, 1999, p. 6.

2. *Separate data into training and test sets* by partitioning the available data into two groups (sometimes three are used).
3. *Transform data into network-appropriate inputs.* Some neural networks accept only numeric inputs. Entries such as *Occupation* must be converted to a number. This transformation from numeric or symbolic inputs to purely numeric inputs is part of the preprocessing. Some neural network tools perform the transformation automatically. If the network cannot be trained, the method may be suspect.
4. *Select, train, and test the network.* Picking the right network configuration can have a substantial impact on the performance of the training and the quality of the resulting system. Once selected, the system is trained and tested repeatedly until it reaches a satisfactory accuracy level. Some neural network packages either recommend configurations or use genetic algorithms to obtain a good configuration.
5. *Deploy the network.* The trained neural network must be integrated into the credit approval system so that users see a user-friendly interface with the credit approval system, not the analysis system.

COLLECT DATA

The process of training a neural network entails looking at all the possible or potentially useful information about the problem and using it to predict a certain behavior or characteristic. For purposes of generating training and test sets, all this information must be gathered.

In many applications where the objective is to predict the behavior of a specific individual, zip code or block code overlays are used to provide additional information about the individual. Block code overlays are available from U.S. Census Bureau data. The Census Bureau has divided the entire United States into blocks, each consisting of approximately 30 families. When census data are collected every 10 years, they are summarized by block. These data are available directly from the Census Bureau, libraries, and various third-party companies that merge other information into it.

Credit bureaus often match customers in their database to block groups and incorporate specific fields from census data into the customer record for purposes of developing creditworthiness or bankruptcy likelihood. In a large company, different groups within the company may manage various components of the customer database. In developing a neural network model, selected fields from various databases might need to be combined.

SEPARATE THE DATA INTO TRAINING AND TEST SETS

Why not use all the data available to train and test a neural network? First, doing so prevents determining whether the neural network has memorized the data or learned the relationships between the inputs and the predicted output(s). Memorizing the relationships between inputs and outputs generally results in a poor or erratic response to new situations. (Memorization is different than learning. When a neural network memorizes, there is an almost direct link from the inputs to the outputs through a set of fairly unique neurons. Only these neurons activate when the input for this set is presented. Learning distributes the knowledge in the weight patterns throughout the network.) Setting aside a certain number of examples increases our confidence in the performance of the trained neural network.

Second, depending on the particular problem, certain neural networks may not learn well if the data are not properly distributed among the possible outcomes. Thus, it is important to select the training cases carefully. For testing purposes, an *n*th item or a randomly selected subset of cases provides the best picture of how the network will perform overall.

Why is it so important to have about the same numbers of training items in each output category? Part of the answer is that many neural networks are basically lazy. They attempt to find the easiest way to solve a particular problem. If 95 percent of the examples are good and 5 percent bad, the network may adjust itself so that it is right most of the time by classifying everything as good. This kind of swamping effect is even more pronounced when the boundaries between good and bad are fuzzy. This presents problems because one would hope when approving credit that most cases on file are good cases and most not on file are bad cases (which unfortunately have unknown results because the credit was not approved).

What is the ideal training set? For the most popular class of neural networks, back-propagation of the error is used: The ideal training set is equally distributed among the possible outcomes. The ideal test set is one that is representative of the data as a whole. In particular terms, it is often easier to extract a test set first and then select a training set from the remaining examples.

For example, suppose that the database has about 31,000 examples in it. Each of the examples has been categorized as one of the possible outcomes: good risk, poor risk, and indeterminate risk. An analysis of the frequency of each of these is shown in the second column of Figure 16.1.

We first extract a test set. For our purposes, 10 percent is sufficient. The test set is extracted by going through the data sequentially and picking out every tenth case.

The second step is to select the training set. The smallest single outcome is poor risk. After choosing the test set, there are 6,179 (6,851 − 672) poor risk cases left. Of the remaining elements, we randomly pick cases until 6,179 in each category are selected. When a particular category is full, no new cases are selected for it. All the cases for the poor risk category are included. The results are shown in the fourth column of Figure 16.1. Training cases are picked randomly to remove any bias in the natural ordering of the data.

As a general rule, the more training examples available, the better the network will ultimately perform. For a variety of neural network implementations, 30,000–40,000 training cases have been adequate. There is minimal improvement with more cases. For simple problems with few inputs and well-defined boundaries, as few as 50 or 100 cases may be adequate.

FIGURE 16.1 POSSIBLE OUTCOMES AND THEIR FREQUENCY

Category	Initial Data	Test Dataset	Training Dataset	Unused Cases
Good risk	17,284	1,739	6,179	9,366
Indeterminate risk	7,523	755	6,179	589
Poor risk	6,851	672	6,179	0
Total:	31,658	3,166	18,537	9,955

TRANSFORM DATA INTO NETWORK-APPROPRIATE INPUTS

Neural networks typically work with inputs in the range 0 to 1 or -1 to $+1$. Each of the fields in our database must be mapped into one or more network inputs, each in the appropriate range.

SELECT A NETWORK ARCHITECTURE

A multilayer feedforward network using backpropagation has almost universally become the standard network paradigm for modeling, forecasting, and classifying when outputs are known. Selecting an optimal architecture is tricky, but with a bit of experimentation can be readily determined. Key structural parameters include the number of hidden units, the transfer function, the learning rule, the learning rate, and others.

TRAIN AND TEST THE NETWORK

Depending on the data set, the training process may be very slow. The basic training process consists of showing the network a set of inputs and its actual output. The network uses the current inputs to compute an output. The computed output is compared to the actual output to determine the error used to modify the weights to move the computed output closer to the actual output next time. During training, several diagnostic tools (as in BrainMaker) show the progress of the mean square error of the entire output layer, a histogram of all the weights in the network, and Pearson's R coefficient for each of the outputs every few iterations for the test set. These diagnostics facilitate understanding the system status while training.

DEPLOY THE NETWORK

Once the network is trained to be sufficiently accurate, the final step is to convert it to a form that can be deployed with the application. Most ANN tools can generate a runtime module. Some ANN tools are capable of generating C++ code, while others only report the weights. Given the weights, the transfer functions, and input transformations, it is a straightforward task to create a deployed ANN code (but if retraining the ANN is required, recoding could be painful).

RESULTS

Figure 16.2 shows a network that has been trained for 16,000 iterations. (The problem actually requires about 50,000 iterations for best performance.) This training takes a few seconds on a Pentium PC. The root mean square (RMS) error (a measure of the quality of the system's results) has not dropped very much and is quite jagged. For each output, there is a confusion matrix. The *confusion matrix* is a graphical way to represent the network's performance. Along the x axis is the desired output—what the network should actually be producing, for example, the real system's result. Along the y axis is the computed output of the network. Both the actual output and the computed outputs have been discretized into bins. The bars in one column of the interior of the confusion matrix show the distribution of computed network outputs for a particular desired output. If the network were performing perfectly, the only interior quadrants would be in the lower left and upper right of the interior area. From this, the network is starting to learn to distinguish good from nongood cases (confusion matrix 3).

The number along the y axis is Pearson's R coefficient, a correlation coefficient that measures how well the actual outputs and computed outputs are correlated. A perfect correlation results in a score of 1.0. The scores shown are poor $= .3372$, indeterminate

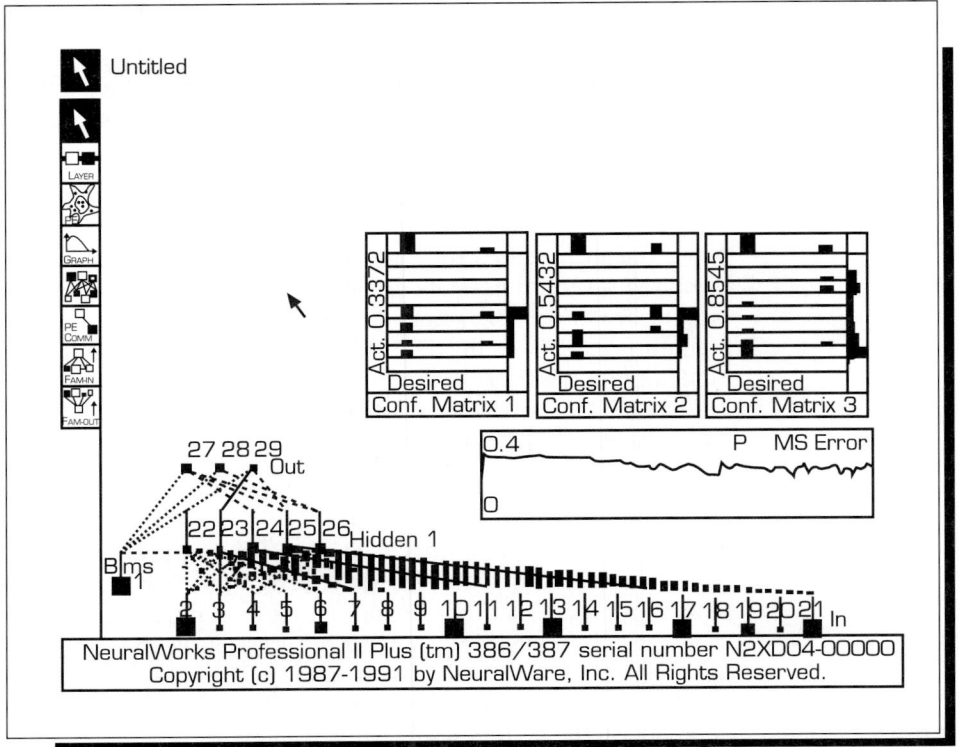

FIGURE 16.2 A Trained Network for Credit Approval

This network has run through 50,000 training iterations. The RMS error graph shows how well the network is performing.

Reproduced with permission of *PC AI*.

= .5432, and good = .8545 (e.g., if the score is less than .4, conclude no credit; if it is greater than .8, conclude credit; anything else is indeterminate). This is a concise numeric representation of the graphical representation. The decision maker can use this result to decide whether to approve credit for the applicant, and given the weights and the transfer functions, the trained solution can be embedded in a user-friendly system.

16.4 BANKRUPTCY PREDICTION WITH NEURAL NETWORKS[3]

CONCEPT PHASE

There has been a lot of work on developing neural networks to predict bankruptcy using financial ratios and discriminant analysis accurately. For example, see Zhang (1999). The ANN paradigm selected in the design phase for this problem was a three-layer

---

[3]Based on R. L. Wilson and R. Sharda, "Bankruptcy Prediction Using Neural Networks," *Decision Support Systems,* Vol. 11, No. 5, June 1994, pp. 545–557.

feedforward ANN using backpropagation. The data for training the network consisted of a small set of numbers for well-known financial ratios, and data were available on the bankruptcy outcomes corresponding to known data sets. Thus, a supervised network was appropriate, and training time was not a problem.

APPLICATION DESIGN

There are five input nodes, corresponding to five financial ratios:

X1:   Working capital/total assets
X2:   Retained earnings/total assets
X3:   Earnings before interest and taxes/total assets
X4:   Market value of equity/total debt
X5:   Sales/total assets.

A single output node gives the final classification showing whether the input data for a given firm indicated a potential bankruptcy (0) or nonbankruptcy (1). The data source consists of financial ratios for firms that did or did not go bankrupt between 1975 and 1982, as given in Moody's industrial manuals. Financial ratios were calculated for each of the five aspects shown above, each of which became the input for one of the five input nodes. For each set of data, the actual result, whether or not bankruptcy occurred, can be compared to the neural network's output to measure the performance of the network and monitor the training. The NeuroShell ANN tool (Ward Systems Group Inc., www.wardsystems.com) was used.

DEVELOPMENT

The architecture of the ANN is shown in Figure 16.3. The set of ratios for the case data was stored in a file of continuous values that NeuroShell could read directly.

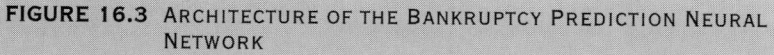

FIGURE 16.3 ARCHITECTURE OF THE BANKRUPTCY PREDICTION NEURAL NETWORK

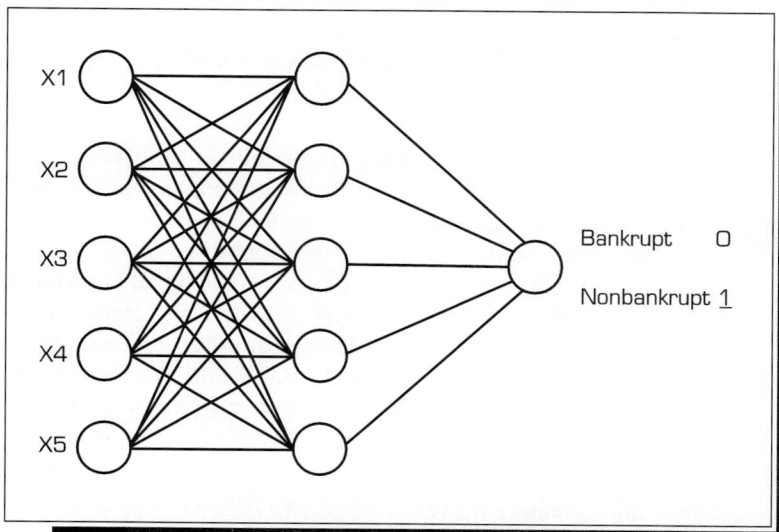

TRAINING

The data set, consisting of 129 firms, was partitioned into a training set and a test set. The training set of 74 firms consisted of 38 that went bankrupt and 36 that did not. The needed ratios were computed and stored in the input file to the neural network and in a file for a conventional discriminant analysis program for comparison of the two techniques.

NeuroShell has three important parameters to be set: learning threshold, learning rate, and momentum. The learning threshold allows the developer to vary the acceptable overall error for the training case. The learning rate and momentum allow the developer to control the step sizes the network uses to adjust the weights as the errors between computed and actual outputs are fed back.

TESTING

The neural network was tested in two ways: by using the test data set and by comparison with discriminant analysis. The test data set consisted of 27 bankrupt and 28 nonbankrupt firms. The neural network was able to correctly predict 81.5 percent of the bankrupt cases and 82.1 percent of the nonbankrupt cases. Overall, the ANN did much better predicting 22 out of the 27 actual cases (the discriminant analysis predicted only 16 correctly). An analysis of the errors showed that five of the bankrupt firms classified as nonbankrupt were also misclassified by the discriminant analysis method. A similar situation occurred for the nonbankrupt cases. Although not done, retraining could have been done with the test data set, and even a modified network with different numbers of hidden layers and nodes could have been developed. The parameters could also have been varied in an attempt to improve the performance.

The result of the testing showed that neural network implementation is at least as good as the conventional approach. An accuracy of about 80 percent is usually acceptable for neural network applications. (But, of course, the accuracy of the neural network must be compared to the accuracy of alternative methods and the impact of an error.) At this level, a system is useful because it automatically identifies problem situations for further analysis by a human expert.

Additional applications of neural networks to bankruptcy are described by Luther (1998), Yang et al. (1999), and Zhang et al. (1999).

16.5 STOCK MARKET PREDICTION SYSTEM WITH MODULAR NEURAL NETWORKS[4]

Accurate stock market prediction is a complex problem. Several mathematical models have been developed, but the results have been disappointing. We chose this application to confirm that neural networks can produce a successful stock market prediction model.

Fujitsu and Nikko Securities developed a buying and selling prediction system called TOPIX. The inputs consist of several technical and economic indexes. In this system, several modular neural networks learned the relationships between past technical and economic indexes and the timing for when to buy and sell. A prediction system made up of modular neural networks was found to be very accurate. Simulation of buying and selling stocks using the prediction system showed an excellent profit.

---

[4]Condensed from a paper by T. Kimoto, K. Asakawa, M. Yoda, and M. Takeoka. Portions have been reprinted with permission from *Proceedings of the IEEE International Joint Conference on Neural Networks,* pp. 11–16, San Diego, CA. Copyright 1990, IEEE.

ARCHITECTURE

SYSTEM OVERVIEW

The prediction system is made up of several neural networks that have learned the relationships between various technical and economic indexes and the timing for when to buy and sell stocks. The goal is to predict the best time to buy and sell during the entire next month.

TOPIX is a weighted average of the market prices of all stocks listed on the first section of the Tokyo Stock Exchange. It is weighted by the number of stocks issued for each company, and its use is similar to that of the Dow–Jones average. Figure 16.4 shows the basic architecture of the TOPIX prediction system. It converts the technical and economic indexes into a space pattern to input to the neural networks. The timing for when to buy and sell is a weighted sum of the weekly returns.

NETWORK ARCHITECTURE

Network Model   The basic network architecture used for the prediction system was the same as the one shown in Figure 16.3. A standard sigmoid function is used as the output function. The output is continuous in the [0, 1] range. The builders developed a new high-speed learning method called *supplementary learning.*

TRAINING DATA

Data Selection   The development team assumed that stock prices were determined by time–space patterns of economic indexes such as foreign exchange rates and interest rates and of technical indexes such as vector curves and turnover. The prediction system uses a moving average of weekly average data for each index to minimize influence due to random walk. Some of the technical and economic indexes used are vector curve, turnover, interest rate, foreign exchange rate, Dow–Jones average, and so on.

Training Data   The timing for when to buy and sell is indicated in one output unit as a continuous value in the [0, 1] range. For training, the timing for when to buy and sell was based on the weighted sum of weekly returns.

PREPROCESSING

Input indexes converted to space patterns and training data are often remarkably irregular. The data are preprocessed by log or error functions to make them as regular as

FIGURE 16.4 BASIC ARCHITECTURE OF THE TOPIX PREDICTION SYSTEM

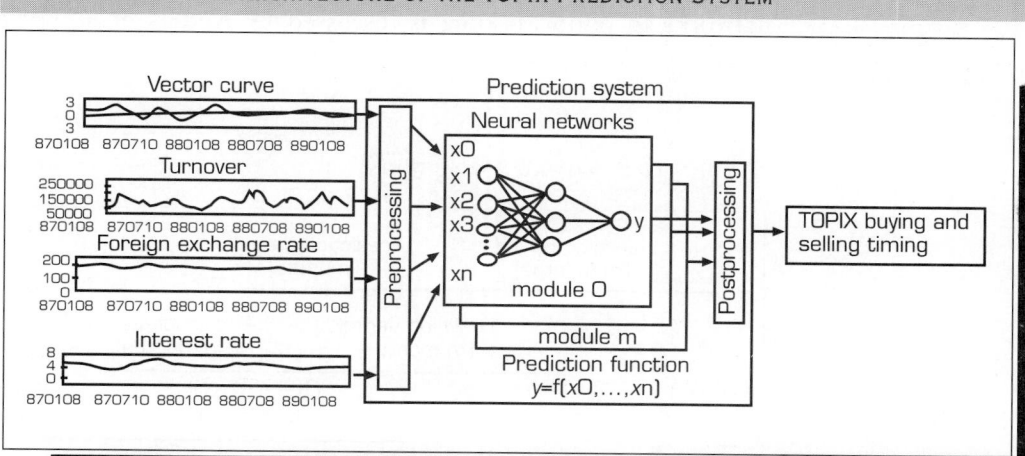

Source: Portions reprinted, with permission, from T. Kimoto, K. Asakawa, M. Yoda, and M. Takeoka, *Proceedings of the IEEE International Joint Conference on Neural Networks,* pp. 11–16, San Diego, CA © 1990 IEEE.

possible. They are then processed by a normalization function to correct for the irregular data distribution.

MOVING SIMULATION

To predict variables in an economic system (such as stock prices) in which the prediction rules change continuously, learning and prediction must track the changes.

A prediction method called *moving simulation* was used. Prediction is done by simulation while moving the objective learning and prediction periods (a rolling horizon method). The moving simulation predictions are as shown in Figure 16.5. The system learns data from the past m months and then makes a prediction for the next l months. [A similar method was developed by Seiler and Aronson (1995) for predicting spot currency exchange rates with neural networks.]

RESULT OF SIMULATIONS

SIMULATION FOR BUYING AND SELLING STOCKS

To verify the effectiveness of the TOPIX prediction system, a simulation of buying and selling of stocks was done.

Buying and selling were simulated by a one-point buying and selling strategy so that performance could be clearly evaluated. One-point buying and selling means all available money is used to buy stocks and all stocks held are sold at the same time. In the prediction system, an output of 0.5 or more indicates buy, and an output less than 0.5 indicates sell. Signals are intensified as they approach 0 or 1.

The buying and selling simulation considered "buy" to be an output above some threshold, and "sell" to be an output below some threshold. Figure 16.6 shows an example of the simulation results. In the upper part of the diagram, the buy-and-hold performance (i.e., the actual TOPIX) is shown as a dotted line, and the prediction system's performance is shown as a solid line. The TOPIX index for January 1987 was considered to be 1.00; it was 1.67 for the buy-and-hold strategy at the end of September 1989. It was 1.98 for the buying and selling operation according to the prediction system. Use of the system's recommendations showed an excellent profit as compared to just buying at the beginning of the test period and holding until the end.

The addition of neural network applications to stock price forecasting and trading are described by Chandra and Reeb (1999), Qi (1999), Qi and Maddala (1999), McGuire (1999), Rublin (1999), and Beltratti et al. (1996). Work on applying neural networks to option trading is discussed by Anders et al. (1998) and Geigle and Aronson (1999).

FIGURE 16.5 MOVING SIMULATION

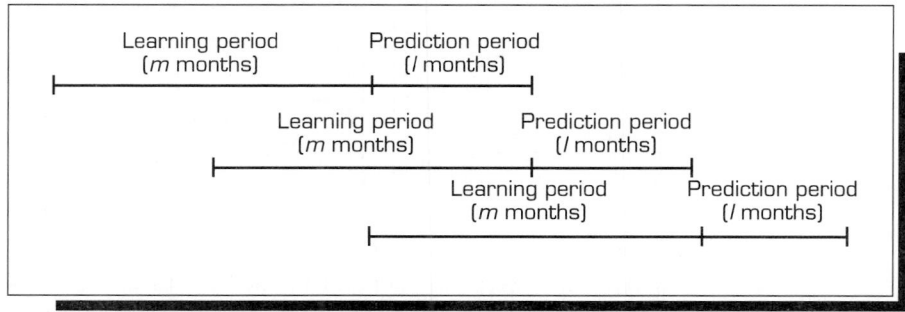

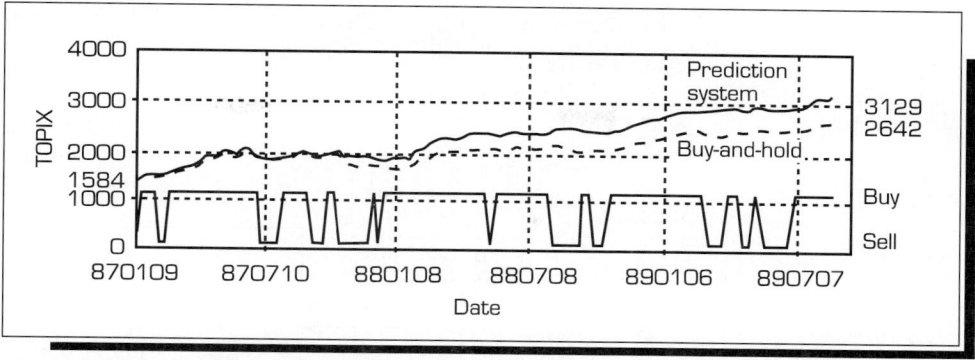

FIGURE 16.6 PERFORMANCE OF THE TOPIX PREDICTION SYSTEM

Source: Portions reprinted, with permission, from T. Kimoto, K. Asakawa, M. Yoda, and M. Takeoka, Proceedings of the IEEE International Joint Conference on Neural Networks, pp. 11–16, San Diego, CA © 1990 IEEE.

16.6 INTEGRATED ANNS AND EXPERT SYSTEMS

As discussed in the last chapter, there are complementary aspects of ES and ANNs that make them ideal partners. In this section we provide examples of integrated ANNs and ES.

RESOURCE REQUIREMENT ADVISOR

A prototype system using the expert system shell AUBREY and the neural network tool NeuroShell advises on resource requirements for developing database systems (Hillman, 1990). The neural network analyzes experiential data on the time and effort required to finish previous database projects. The ES supports the data collection, the ANN performs data evaluation, and the ES is applied to the final analysis. This method provides the flexibility of presenting new data files to supply information to the system without having to enter new rules or information extracted from separate data analyses.

PERSONNEL RESOURCE REQUIREMENT ADVISOR

Hanson and Brekke (1988) developed a system that projects personnel resource requirements for maintaining networks or workstations at NASA. A rule-based expert system determines the final resource projections, and an ANN provides project completion times for the services requested. The projections are based on historical cases and the current service request activity list. The neural network is easily retrained via new data sets on completion times for recent services (Figure 16.7).

DIAGNOSTIC SYSTEM FOR AN AIRLINE

A diagnostic system was developed for Singapore Airlines to help technicians diagnose a critical piece of avionics equipment. The system, known as the inertial navigation system interactive diagnostic expert (INSIDE), reduces diagnosis time. For details, see Lui et al. (1991). A flow diagram of the system is shown in Figure 16.8.

The diagnostic software consists of an ANN example module that captures the knowledge of technicians based on past diagnoses (cases) and an ES flowchart module that performs troubleshooting flowcharts faithfully. These two modules complement each other to

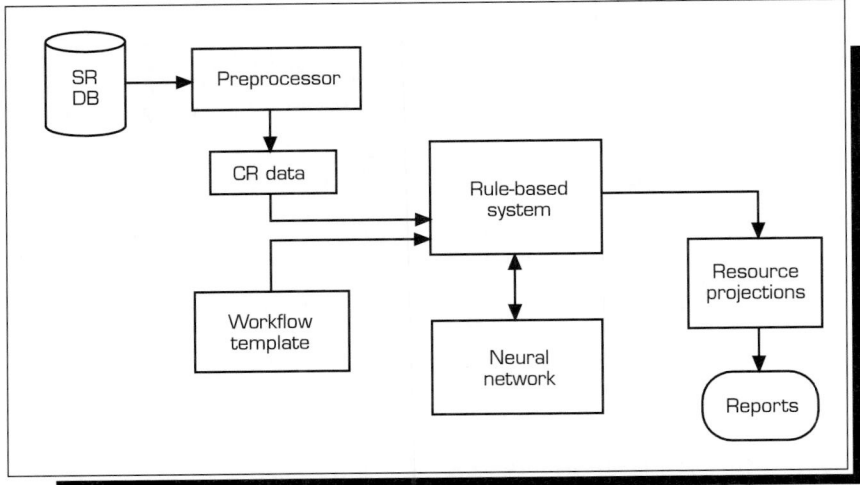

Drawn by L. Medsker, American University. Reproduced with permission.

FIGURE 16.8 INSIDE BLOCK DIAGRAM

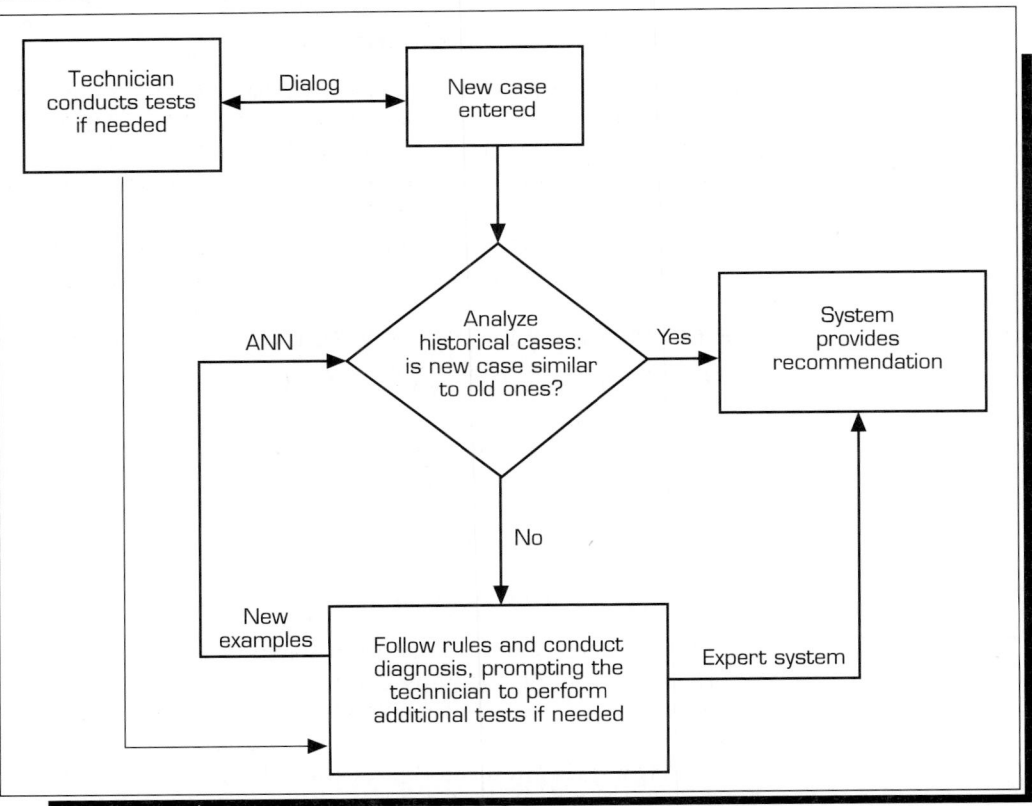

Drawn by L. Medsker, American University. Reproduced with permission.

achieve fast diagnosis and extensive coverage of all cases. During consultation, the system first activates the example module to check whether the set of symptoms observed in newly checked equipment is similar to any of those shown by previous defective equipment. If so, the system quickly reports its finding and pinpoints the defective part. Otherwise, the system passes control to the flowchart module which prompts a technician to perform a sequence of tests as recommended by the manufacturer's flowcharts. A unique feature of this system is that after the flowchart module finds the fault, it formulates the result as a new case for the example module to learn. With this kind of incremental learning capability, the knowledge base of the example module expands as the system is used.

MANUFACTURING PRODUCT RELIABILITY

Manufacturing firms continually search for more accurate ways to predict product reliability. United Technologies Carrier developed a system based on a statistical distribution. But predicting accurate reliability requires a specialist's expertise. So United Technologies Carrier developed two expert systems to capture and store the knowledge. The statistical plots were a critical aspect of interpreting failure rates. Once understood, the patterns resulting from the interpretation process were fed into multilayer feedforward neural networks which were later deployed. Both the expert systems and the neural networks are integrated into an existing early warning system (EWS) and standard databases. The resulting automatic early warning system (AEWS) at United Technologies Carrier has led to a significant productivity boost of at least eightfold in terms of process time. See Moon et al. (1998) for details.

OIL REFINERY PRODUCTION SCHEDULING AND ENVIRONMENTAL CONTROL

Citgo Petroleum Corporation's refinery in Corpus Christi, TX, achieves lower operating costs, improves safety, and enhances product quality and yields through innovative use of AI technology, notably ANN and ES. The Corpus Christi facility refines heavy sour crude oil into high-quality finished petroleum products (the plant's capacity is 4.2 million gallons per day) and secondary feedstocks to manufacture consumer goods.

Citgo's Corpus Christi refinery has implemented expert systems technology to improve plant safety and to optimize the production process to achieve greater economies of scale. Expert systems assist in process unit control throughout the refinery. An operator advisor expert system handles the plant's emergency shutdown system. The real-time, online standard operating procedures enable better communication of knowledge between different operators and shifts and yield a substantial return on investment. Operations are more consistent, which leads to swift responses to the market, consistent product quality, and a more efficient plant. Refinery utilization is at record highs. Also, knowledge is captured from the best people, so that if they retire, Citgo does not lose this knowledge.

The Corpus Christi facility is also committed to protecting the environment. The refinery has reduced waste disposal and is working to reduce its emissions further by being able to predict them and adjust plant operations. ANN are replacing error-prone instrumentation for continuous emission monitoring. By installing predictive emissions monitoring, the Corpus Christi refinery will be able to coordinate the relative efficiencies of the separate units while maintaining accepted lower levels of emissions.

These technologies allow the Corpus Christi plant to have one central control room instead of the six separate facilities originally used. The technology has been so successful that Citgo is implementing advanced automation projects at another refinery in Lake Charles, LA. This facility has a much larger production capacity than the Texas one. See Weber (1996) and www.gensym.com for details.

For further discussion and examples of ANN and ES integration, see Huang and Zhang (1995), Osyk and Vijayaraman (1995), Quah et al. (1996), Yoon et al. (1994), Nilson (1998), Li and Love (1999), and Rublin (1999).

16.7 GENETIC ALGORITHMS

An *algorithm* is a set of instructions that is repeated to solve a problem. A *genetic algorithm* conceptually follows steps inspired by the biological processes of evolution. Better and better solutions evolve from previous generations until an optimal or near-optimal solution is obtained.

Genetic algorithms (also known as *evolutionary algorithms*) demonstrate *self-organization* and *adaptation* similar to the way that the fittest biological organisms survive and reproduce. The method *learns* by producing offspring that are better and better as measured by a fitness (to survive) function.

EXAMPLE 1: THE VECTOR GAME

To illustrate how genetic algorithms work, we describe the game Vector (Walbridge, 1989). This game is similar to the game MasterMind. As your opponent gives you clues about how good your guess is (a fitness function), you create a new solution using knowledge of the current solutions and their quality.

DESCRIPTION

This game is played against an opponent who secretly writes down a string of six digits (in a genetic algorithm, this string consists of chromosomes). Each digit can be either 0 or 1. For this example, the secret number is 001010. You must try to guess this number as quickly as possible. You present a number (a guess) to your opponent, and he or she tells you how many of the digits (but not which ones) you guessed are correct (the fitness function or quality of your guess). For example, the guess 110101 has no correct digits (score = 0). The guess 111101 has only one correct digit (the third one). Thus, the score (the fitness, or the value of the solution) = 1.

RANDOM TRIAL AND ERROR

There are 64 possible six-digit strings of numbers. If you pick numbers at random, on average, it will take 32 guesses to obtain the right answer. Can you do it faster? Yes, if you can interpret the feedback provided to you by your opponent (a measure of the goodness or fitness of your guess). This is how a genetic algorithm works.

GENETIC ALGORITHM SOLUTION

Step 1. Present to your opponent four strings selected at random. (Select four arbitrarily. Through experimentation, you may find that five or six would be better.) Assume that you have selected these four:

    (A)   110100; for a score = 1 (one digit correctly guessed)
    (B)   111101; score = 1
    (C)   011011; score = 4
    (D)   101100; score = 3

Because none of the strings is entirely correct, continue.

Step 2. Delete (A) and (B) because of their low scores. Call (C) and (D) parents.
Step 3. "Mate" the parents by splitting each number as shown between the second and third digits (the position of the split is randomly selected):

(C)   01:1011
(D)   10:1100

Now, combine the first two digits of (C) with the last four of (D) (this is called *crossover*). The result is (E), the first offspring:

(E)   011100; score = 3

Similarly, combine the first two digits of (D) with the last four of (C). The result is (F), the second offspring:

(F)   101011; score = 4

It looks as though the offspring are not doing much better than the parents.

Step 4. Now copy the original (C) and (D).

Step 5. Mate and crossover the new parents but use a different split. Now you have two new offspring, (G) and (H):

(C)   0110:11
(D)   1011:00
(G)   0110:00; score = 4
(H)   1011:11; score = 3

Next, repeat step 2: Select the best "couple" from all the previous solutions to reproduce. You have several options—such as (G) and (C). Select (G) and (F). Now duplicate and crossover. Here are the results:

(F)   1:01011
(G)   0:11000
(I)   111000; score = 3
(J)   001011; score = 5

Also, you can generate more offspring:

(F)   101:011
(G)   011:000
(K)   101000; score = 4
(L)   011011; score = 4

Now repeat the processes with (J) and (K) as parents and duplicate the crossover:

(J)   00101:1
(K)   10100:0
(M)   001010; score = 6

This is it! You have reached the solution after 13 guesses. Not bad when compared to the average of 32 for a random guess out of 64 possibilities.

Note: Using common sense and logic, this problem can be solved faster. However, this example is easy to follow; if the problem is complex, the logical solution is not as obvious. We outline the general genetic algorithm process in Figure 16.9.

GENETIC ALGORITHM DEFINITION AND PROCESS

A genetic algorithm is an iterative procedure that represents its candidate solutions as strings of genes called **chromosomes** and measures their viability with a fitness function. The *fitness function* is a measure of the objective to be obtained (maximum or minimum). As in biological systems, candidate solutions combine to produce offspring in each algorithmic iteration called a *generation*. The offspring themselves can become candidate

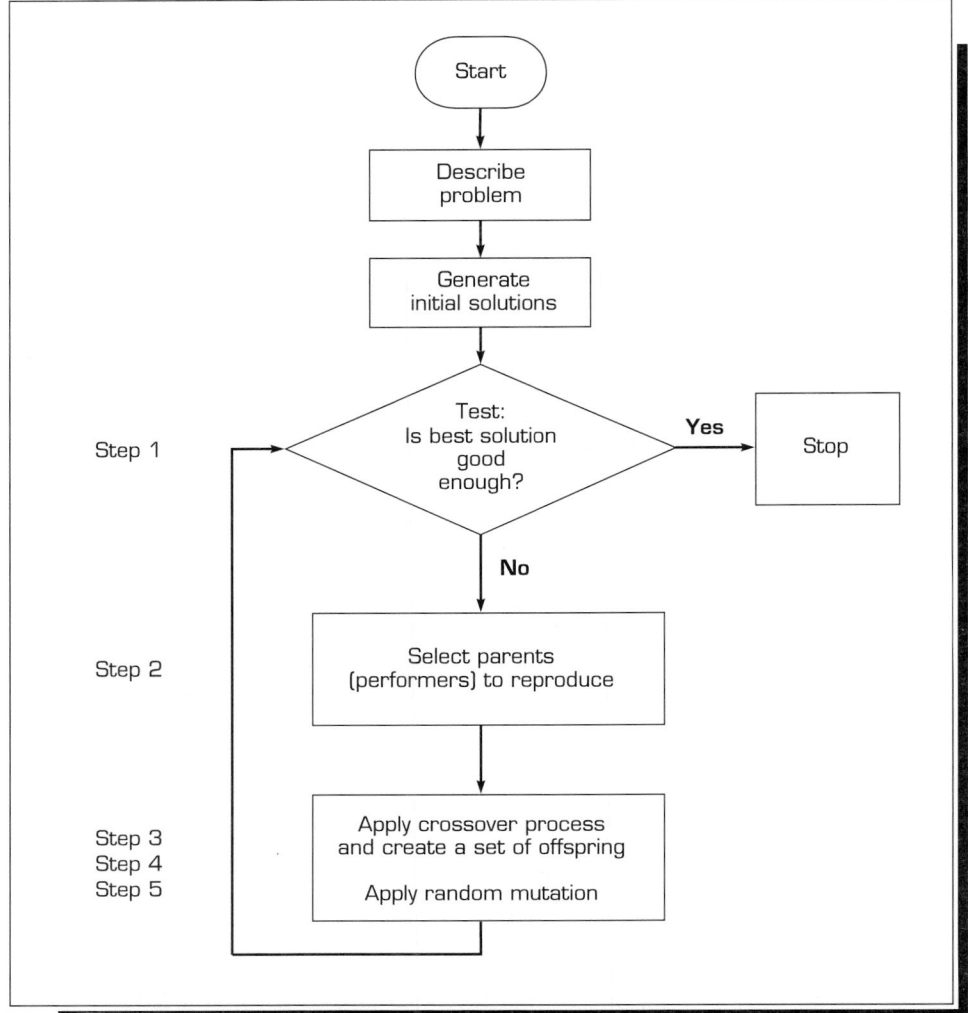

FIGURE 16.9 FLOW DIAGRAM OF THE GENETIC ALGORITHM PROCESS

solutions. From the generation of parents and children, a set of the fittest survive to become parents that produce offspring in the next generation. Offspring are produced by specific *genetic operators* that include reproduction, crossover, and mutation:

- *Reproduction.* Through **reproduction,** genetic algorithms produce new generations of improved solutions by selecting parents with higher fitness ratings or by giving such parents a greater probability of being contributors and by using random selection.
- *Crossover.* Many genetic algorithms use strings of binary symbols for chromosomes, as in our Vector game, to represent solutions. **Crossover** means choosing a random position in the string (e.g., after two digits) and exchanging the segments either to the right or to the left of this point with another string partitioned similarly to produce two new offspring.

- *Mutation.* This genetic operator was not shown in the game. **Mutation** is an arbitrary change in a situation. Sometimes it is used to prevent the algorithm from getting stuck. The procedure changes a 1 to a 0 or a 0 to a 1 instead of duplicating them. This change occurs with a very low probability (say, 1 in 1000).

HOW A GENETIC ALGORITHM WORKS

Figure 16.9 is a flow diagram of a typical genetic algorithm process. In describing a problem, it must be represented in a manner that is amenable to solution by a genetic algorithm. Typically, this means that a string of 1s and 0s can represent a solution and that an easily computed fitness function, which we assume is to be maximized, can be established. (In the general case, integer or continuous variables can be used; minimization presents no conceptual problem.) An initial set of solutions is generated, and their fitness functions are computed. The sum of the fitness functions is computed, and each solution's probability of being selected to generate a pair of offspring is equal to its fitness function divided by the sum.

A set of new offspring is generated through crossover and a small random amount of mutation. Parents are selected based on the probability distribution described above. The next generation consists of a set of the best new offspring and parents. The process continues until a good enough solution is obtained, an optimum is guaranteed, or no improvement occurs over several generations.

There are only a few parameters that must be set. They depend on the problem being solved and are usually determined by trial and error. These are the

- Number of initial solutions to generate
- Number of offspring to generate
- Number of parents and offspring to keep for the next generation
- Mutation probability (very low)
- Probability distribution of crossover point occurrence (generally equally weighted).

Sometimes these parameters can be varied for better performance as the algorithm is running. For more information on the methodology, see Goldberg (1989, 1994), Dhar and Stein (1997), Mitchell (1999), Niettinen (1999), and Reed and Marks (1999).

EXAMPLE 2: THE KNAPSACK PROBLEM

The knapsack problem is a conceptually simple optimization problem that can be solved directly with analytical methods. Even so, it is ideal for illustrating a genetic algorithm approach. You are going on an overnight hike and have a number of items that you could take along. Each item has a weight (in pounds) and a benefit or value to you on the hike (say, in U.S. dollars), and you can take one of each item at most (sorry, no partial items allowed—it's all or nothing). There is a capacity limit on the weight that you can carry (only one constraint, though there can be several measures and capacities including volume, time, and so on). The knapsack problem has many important applications including determining what items to carry on a space shuttle mission. For our example, there are seven items, numbered 1 through 7, with respective benefits and weights as follows:

Item	1	2	3	4	5	6	7
Benefit	5	8	3	2	7	9	4
Weight	7	8	4	10	4	6	4

The knapsack holds a maximum of 22 pounds. The string 1010100, with a total benefit or fitness of $7 + 4 + 4 = 15$, can represent a solution of items 1, 3, and 5.

We set up the problem in an Excel worksheet, where we represent a solution as a string of seven 1s and 0s, and the fitness function as the total benefit, which is the sum of the gene values in a string solution times their respective benefit coefficients. The method generates a set of random solutions (initial parents), uses the objective functions (total benefit) for the fitness function, and selects parents randomly to create generations of offspring by crossover and mutation operations. Selection is statistically based on the parents' fitness values. Higher values are more likely to be selected than lower ones. In Figure 16.10, we show the best solution found by Evolver an easy-to-use, Excel add-in genetic algorithm package (Palisade Software, www.palisade.com; demo available online).

GENETIC ALGORITHM APPLICATIONS

Genetic algorithms are a type of machine learning for representing and solving complex problems. They provide a set of efficient, domain-independent search heuristics for a broad spectrum of applications that include

- Dynamic process control
- Induction of optimization of rules
- Discovering new connectivity topologies (such as neural computing connections, i.e., neural network design)
- Simulating biological models of behavior and evolution

FIGURE 16.10 EVOLVER SOLUTION TO THE KNAPSACK PROBLEM EXAMPLE

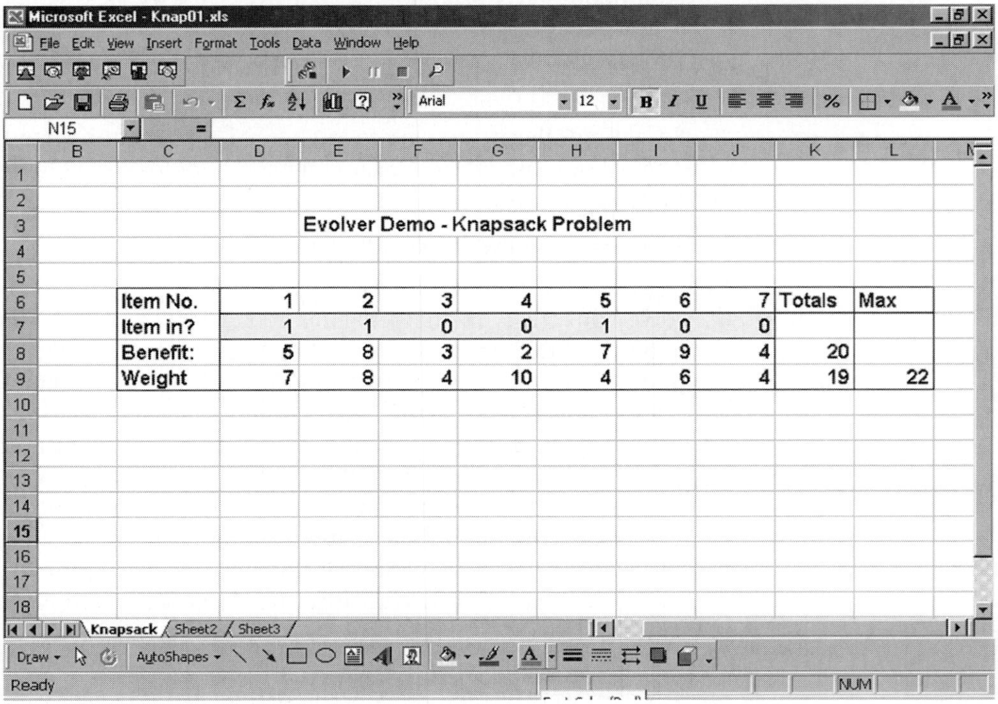

	B	C	D	E	F	G	H	I	J	K	L	M
3					Evolver Demo - Knapsack Problem							
6		Item No.	1	2	3	4	5	6	7	Totals	Max	
7		Item in?	1	1	0	0	1	0	0			
8		Benefit:	5	8	3	2	7	9	4	20		
9		Weight	7	8	4	10	4	6	4	19	22	

- Complex design of engineering structures
- Pattern recognition
- Scheduling
- Transportation and routing
- Layout and circuit design
- Telecommunication
- Graph-based problems

A genetic algorithm interprets information that enables it to reject inferior solutions and accumulate good ones, and thus it learns about its universe. Genetic algorithms are also suitable for parallel processing (Mitchell, 1999).

Over the last decade, the number of successful business applications of genetic algorithms has been increasing. For example, since 1993 Channel 4 television (England) has been using a genetic algorithm (embedded in an ES) to schedule its commercials to maximize revenues (see Attar Software Limited's Web site, www.attar.com, and *ComputerWorld,* Dec. 20, 1993). And a team of researchers at the Electrotechnical Laboratory (ETL) in Japan has developed a hardware-implemented genetic algorithm on a central processing unit (CPU) chip that minimizes the impact of imperfect clock cycles in integrated-circuit fabrication variations. They have demonstrated that increasing the chip yield rate from 2.9 percent to 51.1 percent, clearing the path toward an inexpensive gigahertz clock rate CPUs for PCs (Johnson, 1999).

Examples of genetic algorithms applied to real problems include assembly line balancing (Kim et al., 1998; Rao, 1998) (see AIS In Action 16.2), facility layout (Tavakkoli-Moghaddain and Shayan, 1998), machine and job shop scheduling (Cheng et al., 1999; Liu and Tang, 1999; Norman and Bean, 2000), production planning (Hung et al., 1999), industrial packing and cutting (Hopper and Turton, 1999), assigning tasks to earth-observing satellites (Wolfe and Sorensen, 2000), construction scheduling with limited resources (Leu and Chung, 1999), utility pricing (Wu, 1999), personnel planning (Easton and Nashat, 1999), sawmill board cut selection (Ferrar and King, 1999), scheduling ship maintenance for a large fleet (Deris et al., 1999), solving routing problems based on the traveling salesperson problem (Schmitt and Amini, 1998; Hwang et al., 1999), design and improvement of water distribution systems and similar networks (Roe, 1998; Castillo and Gonzalez, 1998), and determining creditworthiness and aircraft design (Rao, 1998). Several applications are listed in Kumar and Gupta (1995), Koza (1992), and Goldberg (1994). These include driver scheduling for a public transportation system, job shop scheduling, and assignment of destinations to sources. Genetic algorithms can support stock trading (see *AI Expert,* May 1995), and whisky production (see AIS in Action 16.3). Also see Grunther (1996). Genetic algorithms are often used to improve the performance of other AI methods such as expert systems or neural networks.

GENETIC ALGORITHM SOFTWARE

Many free genetic algorithm codes are available (search the Web for research and commercial sites), as well as a number of commercial packages with online demos. Representative commercial packages include Evolver, an Excel spreadsheet add-in (Palisade Software, www.palisade.com); Generator, another Excel add-in (New Light Industries Ltd., www.iea.com/~nli/); Genetic Algorithm User Interface (GAUI, Adaptive Software, www.gaui.com); Sugal Genetic Algorithms Simulator (Trajan Software Ltd., www.trajan-software.demon.co.uk/sugal.htm); and XpertRule GenAsys, an ES shell with an embedded genetic algorithm (Attar Software, www.attar.com). See this book's Web site (www.prenhall.com/turban/) for others. Genetic algorithms are

---

AIS IN ACTION 16.2

GENETIC ALGORITHMS SCHEDULE ASSEMBLY LINES AT VOLVO TRUCKS NORTH AMERICA

The buyer of a Volvo 770 trailer cab has dozens of choices: engine size, paint color, fabric, wood grain finish, stereo, type of suspension, axles, bumpers, pneumatic systems, transmissions, and so on. When the cost is more than $100,000 and the time to be spent in it is about 2,000 hours a year, he or she should have plenty of options. This leads to millions of configurations in which Volvo can build a truck. When a specific truck is to be built, all the tools and parts must be available, which is difficult to schedule with so many possible combinations.

Gus N. Riley is responsible for scheduling the assembly line in Volvo's million-square-foot factory in Dublin, VA. He must cope with hundreds of constraints. Until 1995 Riley solved this operations research problem by eyeballing the production requirements for each week (average output is 550 trucks) and sorted color-coded punch cards, each representing one truck and its characteristics that might affect scheduling. It took 4 days to construct a week's schedule, and there were always bottlenecks as conditions changed on the factory floor.

In August 1996 Volvo installed OptiFlex (I2 Technologies), which uses *genetic algorithms* to evolve a good schedule from a sequence of so-so schedules. Jeffrey Herrmann, a vice president at I2 Technologies, explains, "You tell it what the production at the end of a period should be and then you go have a cup of cof-

fee." The program randomly devises 100 feasible solutions and ranks them according to costs, labor constraints, material availability, and productivity. Then the program connects parts of good schedules to parts of other ones in an effort to find even better solutions. The process is similar to cattle breeding (but much faster).

The offspring of these genetic pairings are thrown into the pool, which is evaluated and ranked again. The pool is always kept at 100 by deleting poorer solutions. Running through roughly five iterations a second, it comes up with maybe not the best possible schedule, but a good one, in minutes.

Each Wednesday Riley feeds in data to make the weekly schedule 5 weeks out. He eyeballs it and tinkers with it by tightening some constraints and loosening others. He catches errors in data entry. OptiFlex, running on a Pentium PC connected to the factory network, accepts corrections and quickly generates new solutions. Creating a schedule takes only one day instead of four. And, reworking the schedule because of unforeseen events such as customers changing their minds about features or broken equipment takes only minutes.

Source: Adapted from S. S. Rao, "Evolution at Warp Speed," *Forbes,* Vol. 161, No. 1, Jan. 12, 1998, pp. 82–83.

---

also related to artificial life scenarios, such as John Conway's Game of Life (e.g., Stephen Stuart's Java implementation at www.tech.org/~stuart/life/). Genetic algorithms that generate music can exhibit aspects of human creativity (e.g., Al Biles' GenJam, Genetic Jammer, is an interactive genetic algorithm that learns to play jazz solos at www.it.rit.edu/~jab/GenJam.html).

For additional examples of interesting genetic algorithm codes and demos, see "Introduction to Genetic Algorithms" (Marek Obitko, Department of Computer Science and Engineering, Czech Technical University, Prague, Czech Republic, cs.felk.cvut.cz/~xobitko/ga/), which includes Java applets running online; the "Fortran Genetic Algorithm (GA) Driver" (David L. Carroll, Department of Aeronautical and Astronautical Engineering, University of Illinois at Urbana–Champaign, Urbana, IL, www.staff.uiuc.edu/~carroll/ga.html); the "Traveling Salesman Problem Using Genetic Algorithms" (Michael LaLena, www.lalena.com/ai/tsp/); "GAlib, A C++

AIS IN ACTION 16.3

GENETIC ALGORITHMS INCREASE PRODUCTIVITY AT UNITED DISTILLERS CORPORATION

The genetic algorithm–based XpertRule system from Attar Software minimizes the movement of whisky casks required to produce high-quality blends. United Distillers uses a large Digital VAX computer for its warehouse administration system and an associated bar-coding scheme that provide details about the site and the exact position of the whisky stock within each warehouse. The firm uses XpertRule as part of a client/server solution to optimize the blend and cask selection process.

Information on the VAX about recipes, site constraints, and the blending program is given to XpertRule, which works out the best combinations of stocks to produce the blends. This information is then supplemented with positional information about the casks. The system then optimizes the selection of required casks, keeping to a minimum the number of "doors" (i.e., warehouse sections) from which the casks must be taken and the number of casks to be moved to clear the way. Other constraints must be satisfied, such

as the current working capacity of each warehouse and the maintenance and restocking work that may be in progress.

Nonproductive cask movement has plummeted from a high of around 50 percent to a negligible level of around 4 percent, and the cask handling rates have almost doubled.

Warehouse staff provide weekly information about the maximum number of casks they are able to move at any site, and about warehouses that can only receive or only dispatch casks, as well as details of other restrictions that might apply, such as upgrading warehouse facilities or constraints resulting from inclement weather. These constraints are added to the variables assessed by the XpertRule system and help guide the selection process.

Source: Adapted from *Expert Systems,* Feb. 1996, pp. 75–76.

Library of Genetic Algorithm Components" (lancet.mit.edu/ga/); and "Genetic MasterMind" (J. J. Merelo, Universidad de Granada, Granada, Spain, kal-el.ugr.es/mastermind.html).

16.8 OPTIMIZATION ALGORITHMS

The traditional management science techniques discussed in Chapter 2 may yield optimal solutions, but they are confined to structured problems. DSS and expert system technologies might not obtain optimal solutions. Neural computing can sometimes derive optimal (or nearly optimal) solutions, but only genetic algorithms and their derivatives provide powerful methods for optimizing (or nearly optimizing) complex problems. One such technique is dynamic hill climbing (De La Maza and Yuret, 1994). This method combines genetic algorithms and traditional optimization methods to form an extremely powerful tool. For example, the new tool is used in a medical imaging system that helps brain surgeons plan and perform operations. Several other algorithms can be used to solve difficult problems, such as scheduling complex operations (see AIS in Action 16.4).

AIS IN ACTION 16.4

SCHEDULING A ROTATION OF LOCOMOTIVES IN PARIS, AND IN AIRPORTS IN THE UNITED KINGDOM

Scheduling a rotation of locomotives for the Paris-based French National Railway Company (SNCF) is subject to many constraints: Locomotives must be maintained weekly, diesel engines must refuel every 900 kilometers, engines must sit idle for a minimum amount of time before a run, and "deadheads" (engines not pulling cars) must be scheduled with the fewest number of runs. SNCF's planning team once took up to 2 weeks to work out a schedule for a single 30-station network, but SNCF has built an automated system, CARAIBE, based on ILOG Inc.'s (Mountain View, CA) ILOG Solver, an object-oriented development tool that has a C++ library for building constraint-based reasoning applications.

CARAIBE output schedules keep a minimum number of locomotives running and reduce the mileage covered by deadheads. ILOG Solver helps implement two scheduling algorithms: One uses backtracking to generate a schedule that satisfies all constraints, and the second helps make the schedule cost-effective via a permutation search. It also provides a two-dimensional graphical library to display trip and train information. In about 20 minutes, a scheduler can generate a new rotation schedule. Often, the schedule must be modified to take into account the user's preferences and expert-

ise, and this is where CARAIBE's graphical interface becomes extremely useful. For instance, the scheduler might need to assign the same locomotive to pull two different trains. To add these constraints, all the scheduler has to do is point and click.

Flexibility is another key to the system. Because ILOG Solver separates constraints from algorithms, different algorithms can be used with the same constraint model.

The added bonus of ILOG Solver is its ability to assist SNCF in other resource management areas, including loading of containers onto freight cars, maintenance scheduling, and personnel planning, thus giving SNCF more bang for its buck.

In the United Kingdom, a similar system is used to manage airports. Scheduling runways is also a constrained optimization problem. The simulation study predicts complex aircraft movements, permitting the investigation of proposed solutions so that the airport can obtain an optimal capacity level. A similar system is used by British Airways to optimize the allocation of gangways connecting terminals to airplanes.

Source: Adapted from P. Anrado, "Application Watch," *AI Expert,* Mar. 1994, p. 48; and *Expert Systems,* Feb. 1996, p. 78.

16.9 FUZZY LOGIC

Fuzzy logic deals with the kind of uncertainty that is inherently human in nature. This technique, which uses the mathematical theory of **fuzzy sets** (Jamshidi et al., 1997; Klir and Yuan, 1995; McNeill and Freiberger, 1993; Nguyen and Walker, 1999), simulates the process of normal human reasoning by allowing the computer to behave less precisely and logically than conventional computer methods require.

The thinking behind this approach is that decision making is not always a matter of black and white or true or false; it often involves gray areas, that is, *maybe.* In fact, creative decision-making processes are unstructured, playful, contentious, and rambling.

Fuzzy logic can be useful because it is an effective and accurate way to describe human perceptions of decision-making problems. Most situations are not 100 percent true or false. There are many control and decision-making problems that do not easily fit into the strict true–false situation required by mathematical models; or if they can be described this way, it is not the best way to do so (see the Opening Vignette).

Let's look at an example of a fuzzy set that describes a tall person. If we survey people to define the minimum height that a person must attain before being considered tall, the answers could range from 5 to 7 feet (1 foot is about 30 cm., 1 inch is 2.54 cm.). The distribution of answers may look like the following:

Height	Proportion Voted for
5'10"	0.05
5'11"	0.10
6'	0.60
6'1"	0.15
6'2"	0.10

Suppose that Jack is 6 feet tall. From probability theory, we can use the cumulative probability distribution and say that there is a 75 percent chance that Jack is tall.

In fuzzy logic, we say that Jack's *degree of membership* within the set of tall people is 0.75. The difference is that in probability terms Jack is *perceived* to be either tall or not tall and we are *not completely sure* whether he is tall. In contrast, in fuzzy logic we *agree* that Jack is more or less tall. Then, we can assign a membership function to show the relationship of Jack to the set of tall people (the fuzzy logic set):

<Jack, 0.75 ≡ Tall>

This can be expressed in a knowledge-based system as *Jack is tall* (CF = 0.75). An important difference from probability theory is that related memberships do not have to total 1. For example, the statement *Jack is short* (CF = 0.15) indicates that the combination is only 0.90. In probability theory if the probability that Jack is tall is .75, then the probability that he is not tall (i.e., he is short, assuming only two events) must be .25.

In contrast to certainty factors that include two values (such as the degrees of belief and disbelief), fuzzy sets use a spectrum of possible values called *belief functions*. We express our belief that a particular item belongs to a set through a membership function, as shown in Figure 16.11. At a height of 69 inches, a person starts to be considered tall, and at 74 inches he or she is definitely tall. Between 69 and 74 inches, his or her membership function value varies from 0 to 1. Likewise, a person has a membership function value in the set of short people and medium-height people, depending on his or her height. The medium range spans both the short and tall ranges, and so a person has a belief of potentially being a member of more than one fuzzy set at a time. This is a critical strength of fuzzy sets; they lack crispness, yet they are *consistent* in their logic.

FIGURE 16.11 MEMBERSHIP FUNCTIONS IN FUZZY SETS

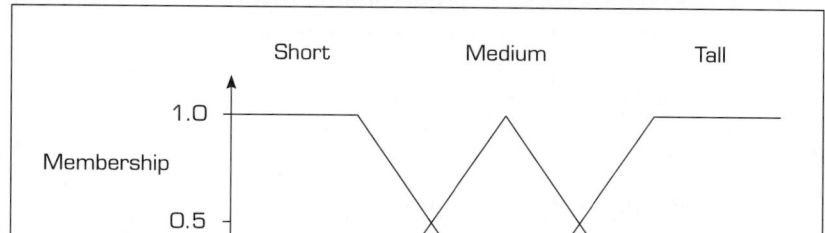

Fuzzy logic has recently gained momentum in its application in managerial decision support despite the fact that it is complex to develop, requires considerable computing power, and is difficult to explain to users. However, with increasing computational power and software, this situation has been changing since the 1990s.

FUZZY LOGIC IN RULE-BASED SYSTEMS

In a standard rule-based system, a production rule has no concrete effect at all unless the data completely satisfy the antecedent of the rule. The operation of the system proceeds sequentially, with one rule firing at a time; if two rules are simultaneously satisfied, a conflict resolution policy is needed to determine which one takes precedence.

In a fuzzy rule-based system, in contrast, *all* rules are executed during each pass through the system, but with strengths ranging from "not at all" to "completely," depending on the relative degree to which their fuzzy antecedent propositions are satisfied by the data.

FUZZY LOGIC APPLICATIONS

Fuzzy logic is difficult to apply when people supply the membership information. The problems stem from linguistic vagueness to difficulties in supplying the definitions needed. One area in which fuzzy logic is being used extensively is in consumer products where the input is provided by sensors rather than by people. Some examples are air conditioners, antilock brakes, toasters, video camcorders, dishwashers, and microwaves (see AIS in Focus 16.5 and 16.6). Fuzzy logic in consumer products is sometimes called *continuous logic* (after all, who wants a fuzzy camcorder?). Fuzzy logic provides smooth motion in consumer products. This is appropriate for subway control systems and for other motor controls and navigation (e.g., Bartos, 1999; McFetridge and Ibrahim, 1998; McNeill and Freiberger, 1993).

Most fuzzy logic applications are in the area of controls. See James (2000) for details on applying fuzzy logic to paper mill automation. Machacha and Bhattacharya (2000) apply fuzzy logic to project selection. Fuzzy logic has proven accurate in predicting accident risk (Anonymous, 2000). Other business applications involve integration with other information systems (Section 16.11). We next describe three fuzzy logic applications.

EXAMPLE 3: FUZZY STRATEGIC PLANNING[5]

Hall (1987) developed STRATASSIST, a fuzzy expert system that helps small- to medium-sized firms plan strategically for a single product. During a consultation, STRATASSIST asks questions in five areas that a firm should consider in evaluating its own strengths and weaknesses:

- Threat of substitutes
- Threat of new entries
- Buyer group power
- Supplier group power
- Rivalry within the industry.

Each question asks the user to rate his or her firm along these dimensions. STRATASSIST feeds the answers into its fuzzy knowledge base, which consists of rules such as

IF the importance of personal service in the distribution of your product is at least more or less high,

---

[5]From *PC AI,* Mar./Apr. 1993, p. 28.

AIS IN FOCUS 16.5

FUZZY LOGIC APPLICATIONS

- Selecting stocks to purchase (e.g., the Japanese Nikkei stock exchange)
- Retrieving data (fuzzy logic can find data quickly)
- Regulating antilock braking systems in cars
- Autofocusing in cameras
- Automating the operation of laundry machines
- Building environmental controls
- Controlling the image position in video cameras
- Controlling the motion of trains
- Identifying the dialect of orca whales

- Inspecting beverage cans for printing defects
- Keeping space shuttle vehicles in steady orbit
- Matching golf clubs to customers' swings
- Regulating water temperature in shower heads
- Controlling the amount of oxygen in cement kilns
- Increasing accuracy and speed in industrial quality control applications
- Sorting problems in multidimensional spaces
- Enhancing models involving queuing (waiting lines)
- Decision making

AIS IN FOCUS 16.6

HOW FUZZY LOGIC WORKS

There are many consumer products that use *fuzzy (continuous) logic*. Their control systems are very different from traditional control systems that attempt to keep a working system strictly on target. Video camcorders monitor the image they record and compare the current frame to previous ones. When the device is recording, and being wiggled, it can determine that the photographer's intention is *probably* not that he/she wants to blur the image but to home in on the object(s) being recorded. The central object stays centered a little longer because the fuzzy logic circuitry aims back at it, assuming its membership in the set of desired objects is relatively high. The image remains stable because of a delay in moving the image across to the new position since the camcorder "expects" to come back to its original position. Sanyo first produced these camcorders in 1989.

Antilock brakes on automobiles determine when a wheel is about to lock up by sensing about 18 factors. When the state of the wheel's motion (its membership function) approaches that of being locked, the brake attempts to maximize pressure but eases up a bit to pre-

vent locking. This prevents the odd on/off pumping action of traditional antilock braking systems.

Fuzzy logic appliances have sensors that detect the state of the items on which they are acting. If a toaster senses that the toast is 10 percent burnt, that might be all right (after all, toast is *burnt bread*), but as it approaches 50 percent, it turns down the heat "somewhat" and eventually turns the heat off. Fuzzy logic air conditioners not only detect ambient room conditions such as temperature and humidity but also detect the presence and absence of people in a room, saving up to 24 percent in energy costs. Fuzzy logic vacuum cleaners monitor the surface being vacuumed and the condition of the material being pulled in and adjust themselves automatically. Washing machines use a fuzzy expert system to merge information from three inputs: the amount of dirt, the type of dirt, and the load size. Sensors detect these conditions and adjust the load parameters and time to wash and rinse. Tens of thousands of fuzzy logic washing machines are sold monthly in Japan. See Babyak (1999) and McNeill and Freiberger (1993) for more on smart, fuzzy logic–enhanced appliances.

THEN strategic action should be to distribute the firm's product or service through small, flexible, local units.

Hall used uncommonly rigorous experimental design procedures to test STRATASSIST's effectiveness. He asked MBA students to develop strategic plans for a fictional company. One-third of the students used STRATASSIST output in their planning, one-third used answers to the questions in the five strength/weakness areas, and one-third worked without STRATASSIST. Twelve expert judges from academia and industry rated the students' plans. Results indicated that the students who used STRATASSIST were judged to have formulated significantly better strategies than the others. See Hutchinson (1998) for additional applications of fuzzy logic in decision making.

EXAMPLE 4: FUZZINESS IN REAL ESTATE[6]

In conducting property appraisals it is necessary to use judgment to generate estimates. Experience and intuition are essential factors. Some of the needed estimates are land value, value of buildings, building replacement costs, and the amount the building has appreciated. Then it is necessary to review sales of comparable property, decide what is relevant, and finally estimate the net income.

Most of the above data are fuzzy. Using a program called FuziCalc, a spreadsheet program modeled on Excel, Dilmore facilitated the appraisal process, making it faster and more accurate. See Bagnoli and Smith (1998) for additional fuzzy logic applications in real estate.

EXAMPLE 5: A FUZZY BOND EVALUATION SYSTEM

The value of bonds depends on factors such as company profitability, assets and liability, market volatility, and even foreign exchange risk (for foreign bonds). In factors such as foreign exchange risk, there is considerable fuzziness. Chorafas (1994) constructed a fuzzy logic system that helps in making decisions about investing in bonds. The results indicate superior values over an average noncomputerized bond evaluation.

New applications of fuzzy logic are continually being developed because of its effectiveness. For examples, see Derra (1999), Gungor and Arikan (2000), Gupta (1995), Jamshidi et al. (1997), Lin and Lee (1996), Ptyra (1996), Von Altrock (1996), and Yen and Langari (1998).

FUZZY LOGIC SOFTWARE

There are a number of fuzzy logic software packages on the market. Fuzzy Inference Development Enviroment (FIDE, Aptronix Inc., www.aptronix.com) is a complete integrated tool set environment for the development of fuzzy logic–based systems. Aptronix Inc. also provides Z Search, a fuzzy query language (FQL) intelligent search engine for databases. Check out the live Java demos, especially the fuzzy pendulum controller, on the Aptronix Web site. HyperLogic Corporation has a fuzzy logic truck "backer-upper" and CubiCalc demos (www.hyperlogic.com), and Timothy J. Ross at the University of New Mexico has some downloadable academic fuzzy logic software. See Kandel (1996) and this book's Web site for other examples.

16.10 QUALITATIVE REASONING

Qualitative reasoning (QR) is a means of representing and making inferences using general physical knowledge about the world. QR is a model-based procedure that consequently incorporates deep knowledge about a problem domain. Typically, QR in-

---

[6]Condensed from G. Dilmore "Fuzziness in Real Estate," *PC AI,* Mar./Apr. 1995.

volves logic such as "If you touch a kettle full of boiling water on a stove, you will burn yourself" and "If you throw an object off a building, it will go down." The first situation does not require specific knowledge that water boils at 100 degrees Celsius, and it varies slightly depending on altitude. It only matters to the decision maker that the water is very hot. Likewise, in the second situation, the height of the building and the properties of the object are not issues unless you happen to be the object or you are trying to catch the object.

The main goal of QR is to represent commonsense knowledge about the physical world and the underlying abstractions used by engineers and scientists when they create quantitative models (you don't have to know the actual value of the gravitational constant to know that objects fall). Given such knowledge and appropriate reasoning methods, an ES with QR can make predictions and diagnoses and explain the behavior of physical systems qualitatively, even when exact quantitative descriptions are unavailable or intractable. QR exploits the fact that programs can accept and derive useful inferences from problem statements having much less information than is usually known in traditional mathematical formulations (Hamscher et al., 1995). The important point about qualitative representations is not that they are symbolic and use discrete quantity spaces but that relevant behavior is modeled (e.g., throwing a kettle off a building has nothing to do with its "behavior" on the stove). Temporal and spatial qualities in decision making are represented effectively by qualitative reasoning methods. Some scientists call QR a dynamic method because the problems to which it is usually applied concern the passage of time (Cohn, 1995; Kuipers, 1994). QR is particularly useful in application domains where inferences are to be made using imprecise data (Iwasaki, 1997).

The way QR works without explicitly solving mathematical models is by applying commonsense mathematical rules to the values of variables and functions in the model (observed) and the interconnections among these elements, such as constraints.

Certain relationships among variables hold, and certain valid intervals can be specified for variables (such as 3–15, or simply negative, zero, or positive). There are structure rules and behavior rules. When variables are out of bounds (e.g., an infeasible condition occurs), a decision is made to correct the error through the relationships among the variables. Despite the name *qualitative reasoning,* typical applications involve the solution of an algorithm or running a simulation to converge on a solution to a problem (Raghunathan, 1994). QR offers several advantages (e.g., coping with imprecise information, resulting in imprecise but reasonably correct predictions, and facilitating easy exploration of alternatives and interpretation) over conventional numeric simulation (Iwasaki, 1997).

A major difference between inferencing with production rules and with QR can be explained in terms of the imprecise values of variables and imprecise relationships between variables. For example, a rule such as "If demand for an item is over 20,000 units, then set the item price as demand times 0.004" requires a precise numeric value for the variable demand (e.g., 18,000 or 22,500) for evaluation. A similar rule with QR can handle imprecisely known values for demand (e.g., between 18,000 and 20,000 units). QR provides techniques such as qualitative arithmetic (using variables taking imprecise values such as positive, negative, 0, or a range) and qualitative functional relations (e.g., monotonically increasing or decreasing relationships between variables) for the reasoning process (Iwasaki, 1997).

Though more than 25 years old, QR is still in its infancy in terms of real-world ES development. Special QR workshops and conferences have been held, and there are a number of real-world cases in which qualitative reasoning has had an impact. QR is used in a number of applications involving tasks such as real-time monitoring, diagnosis, design, education, and so on [see Iwasaki (1997) for details]. Kitamura et al. (1996) applied QR to nuclear plant fault diagnoses. Their system, KCIII, is a model-based diagnostic shell designed to diagnose mechanical systems by reasoning about their qualitative behavior. Given a model of a target system and a symptom, KCIII generates faults explaining the symptom (an abnormal value of an observable parameter obtained by sensors or testers). They have applied their model to the heat transportation system of a nuclear power plant. When an anomalous observation occurs, the reasoning engine determines which values the other parameters take when the system achieves the heat-balanced state. Their results for a real plant matched those provided by an expert.

A QR application involving steam production in a marine propulsion system is illustrated on MONET's Web site (monet.aber.ac.uk/technology_docs/example_qr.html). This Web site also provides links to material that illustrates differences between quantitative modeling and qualitative modeling.

Business processes, financial markets, and economic systems can be modeled mathematically; because we assume they follow laws like physical laws (the laws sometimes vary by philosophical modeling assumptions, however), it is possible to reason about such systems with QR. Some notable QR examples are those discussed by Berndsen and Daniels (1994), who describe a QR method for describing economic systems; Alpar and Dilger (1995), who present a QR approach to predicting the effect of marketing activities on market share (using influence diagrams as the modeling base); and Benaroch and Dhar (1995), who describe an approach to investment portfolio selection. Ferguson and Forbus (1999) and Donlon and Forbus (1999) describe QR tools and methods for use in geographic information systems. Also see Hamscher et al. (1995) and Lang et al. (1995) for others.

QSIM is a well-known software package for performing QR. There is also a compositional compiler for qualitative models, QPC, written in Algernon (which uses access-limited logic; see Kuipers and Crawford (1994)).

16.11 INTELLIGENT SYSTEMS INTEGRATION

Neural computing, expert systems, genetic algorithms, and fuzzy logic are effective ways to deal with complex problems efficiently. Each method handles uncertainty and ambiguity differently, and these technologies can often be blended to utilize the best features of each, achieving impressive results. A combination of neural computing and fuzzy logic can result in synergy that improves speed, fault tolerance, and adaptiveness. For example, in the Opening Vignette we showed how ES, fuzzy logic, and ANNs could be effectively integrated to control boiler units in a housing project.

There are many real-world applications of intelligent systems integration. These include the United Technologies Carrier product reliability system [expert system and neural network (Moon et al., 1998)], plastic molding control [neural networks and fuzzy logic (Mapleston, 1999)], construction price estimation [expert system and neural network (Li and Love, 1999)], forecasting [genetic algorithms and fuzzy logic (Cox, 1999)], motor control [neural networks, expert systems, and fuzzy logic (Bartos, 1999)], and the prediction and optimization of a ceramic casting process (neural networks and fuzzy logic (Lam et al., 2000)], among others.

Each intelligent system can be a valuable component in a management support system in which each technology can be used in series or in parallel. For instance, the neural network can identify classes of membership for the fuzzy system. The genetic learning method can perform rule discovery in large databases, with the rules fed into the conventional expert system. The machine learning component can perform rule discovery or confidence function generation and be called by the conventional expert system. The output of the "defuzzified" fuzzy system can become the input to a model-based expert system, and the output can be rendered in a decision-making process such as speech recognition. We describe an example of combining fuzzy logic with ANNs next.

EXAMPLE 6: INTERNATIONAL STOCK SELECTION[7]

An international investment company uses a combination of fuzzy logic and ANNs (called FuzzyNet) to forecast the expected returns from stocks, cash, bonds, and other assets to determine the optimal allocation of assets. Because the company invests in global markets, it is first necessary to determine the creditworthiness of various countries, based on past and estimated performances of key socioeconomic ratios, and then select specific stocks based on

---

[7]Adapted from Wong et al. (1992).

FIGURE 16.12 FUZZYNET ARCHITECTURE

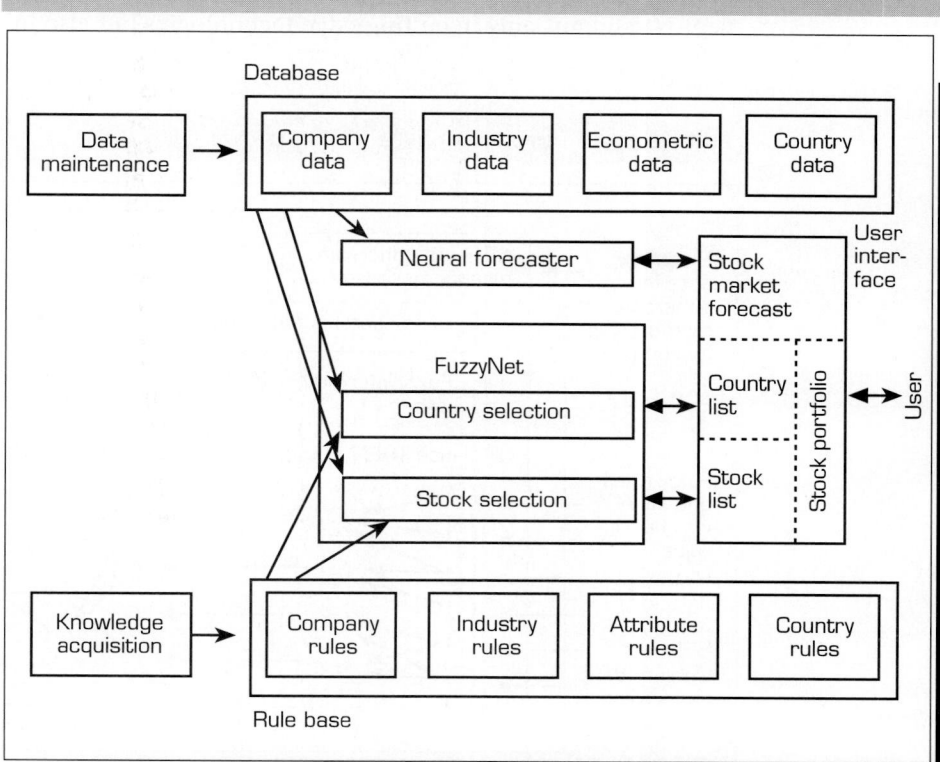

Source: F. Wong et al., "Neural Networks, Genetic Algorithms, and Fuzzy Logic for Forecasting," *Proceedings, International Conference on Advanced Trading Technologies,* New York, July 1992, p. 48. Adapted, with permission, from *Financial Analysts Journal,* Jan./Feb. 1992. Copyright 1992, Association for Investment Management and Research, Charlottesville, VA. All rights reserved.

company, industry, and economic data. The final stock portfolio must be adjusted according to the forecast of foreign exchange rates, interest rates, and so forth, which are handled by a currency exposure analysis. The integrated network architecture of the system is shown in Figure 16.12. The integrated system includes the following technologies:

- *Expert system.* The system provides the necessary knowledge for both country and stock selection (rule-based system).
- *Neural network.* The neural network conducts forecasting based on the data included in the database.
- *Fuzzy logic.* The fuzzy logic component supports the assessment of factors for which there are no reliable data. For example, the *credibility* of rules in the rule base is given only as a probability. Therefore, the conclusion of the rule can be expressed either as a probability or as a fuzzy membership degree.

The rule base feeds into FuzzyNet (Figure 16.13) along with data from the database. FuzzyNet is composed of three modules: membership function generator (MFG), fuzzy information processor (FIP), and backpropagation neural network (BPN). The modules are interconnected, and each performs a different task in the decision process.

By using several advanced technologies it is possible to handle a broader range of information and solve more complex problems (see AIS in Action 16.7). This concept is valid not only in cutting-edge technologies but also in any MSS integration.

FIGURE 16.13   Information Flow in FuzzyNet

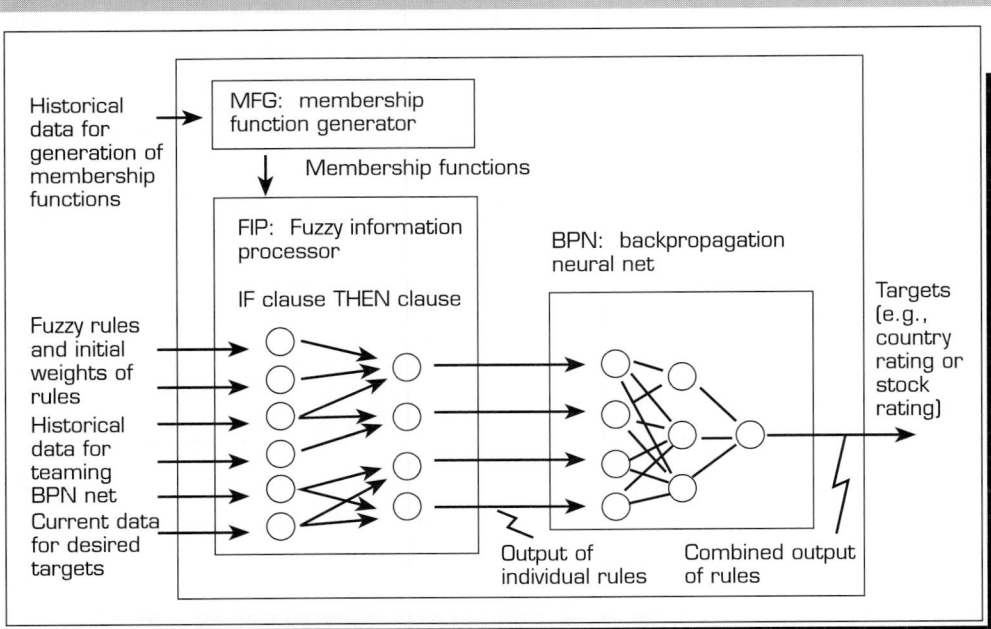

AIS IN ACTION 16.7

HYBRID EXPERT AND FUZZY LOGIC SYSTEM DISPATCHES TRAINS

The Carajás line is one of the busiest railway routes and leading carriers of iron ore in the world. The 892-kilometer-long single-track line connects São Luís Harbor with the Carajás iron ore mine in the state of Pará in the Amazon (Brazil). The line has become even busier because a unique real-time knowledge-based system is increasing its productivity and reducing its operating costs, without compromising safety.

Train dispatchers try to keep the trains running safely all day and all night while attempting to maximize the amount of iron ore transported per day, economize on fuel consumption, and minimize train delays. For over 10 years, paper and pencil were used to solve this difficult task.

An innovative, rule-based expert system that uses fuzzy logic has transformed the culture of train operations. Operational rules are directly used in the ES. Fuzzy logic techniques analyze train movement and help the operators make the best possible decisions (priorities of trains, and so on). The module that generates the initial train movement plans has helped increase the volume of iron ore transported by about 15 percent while saving about 1.6 liters of fuel per 1,000 metric tons of ore transported. With system improvements, further gains are expected.

Source: Modified from Vieira and Gomide (1996), pp. 51–53.

16.12 DATA MINING AND KNOWLEDGE DISCOVERY IN DATABASES

In Chapters 4 and 5, we introduced and described the importance and use of data mining. The data mining methods used with a data warehouse are insufficient when data are fuzzy, complex, or poorly organized. This situation often occurs with external data and even with internal data that are not cleansed and stored in a data warehouse. Even clean data must often be refined and processed before they undergo data mining (Bigus, 1996). In most situations, neural networks and other intelligent data mining tools are extremely valuable in identifying relationships in data (Cox, 1999; Deck, 1999a; Fu, 1999; Lach, 1999).

HIDDEN VALUE IN DATA

Data mining (also known as *knowledge discovery*) is the efficient discovery of valuable, nonobvious information from a large collection of data (Bigus, 1996). The value of the discovery must exceed the cost of obtaining it for a method to be useful.

KNOWLEDGE DISCOVERY IN DATABASES

Fayyad et al. (1996a) describe the knowledge discovery in databases (KDD) process as one of starting with raw data and performing the following activities:

1. Selection to target the appropriate data
2. Preprocessing to filter the data
3. Transformation
4. Data mining to identify patterns
5. Interpretation and evaluation, resulting in knowledge.

THEORETICAL ADVANCES

There have been many theoretical advances in knowledge discovery, machine learning, and data mining, some of which are becoming practical methods for data mining [e.g., Feldman and Dagan (1995) describe an interesting method for knowledge discovery in textual databases; also see Fayyad et al. (1995, 1996b) and Shadbolt et al. (1996)]. Real-world problems are currently being attacked with methods based on statistics, cluster analysis, discriminant analysis, fuzzy logic, genetic algorithms, and neural networks, which are quite good at identifying patterns in data, ideal for data mining.

AI METHODS AND DATA MINING

In many cases, artificial intelligence and statistical methods (clustering, factor analysis, and so on) are applied to data in a search mode. A database or data from a data warehouse are presented to a set of techniques (neural network, rule induction, and so on), and the methods attempt to identify nuggets of useful relationships from the data. In many ways this is similar to real mining, where one digs through or sluices tons of soil to find an occasional gold nugget. Sometimes this data mining process is automated, as in DataX, an intelligent data mining software suite from Zaptron Systems Inc. (www.zaptron.com); sometimes it is manually driven. Even the best automated methods generally require user interaction for better performance.

For example, for a large data table containing advertising and multiple product sales information, along with census data, a data mining package might attempt to build a neural network predictor of the various sales and other outputs as a function of everything else automatically. But, an analyst with a good sense of the relationships can guide the process by suggesting relationships and techniques to try.

Finally, rule induction methods can use semantic and syntactic clues in the language to identify facts and relationships among facts in either databases or textual sources. Automatic tools for identifying knowledge sources in knowledge management systems were just reaching the marketplace in early 2000 (Chapter 9).

APPLICATIONS

Fayyad mentions several applications in the areas of marketing, investment, fraud detection, and manufacturing. American Express reports a 10–15 percent increase in its card use because of database marketing efforts. LBS Capital Management uses expert systems, neural networks, and genetic algorithms to manage portfolios totaling $600 million. Their methods have outperformed the stock market since 1993 (Hall et al., 1996). Major credit card companies custom-print color inserts with sale offers to individual customers based on profiles and data mining analyses that run simultaneously with bill computation, printing, and envelope stuffing. Techniques for identifying the *market of one* are quite valuable. For a survey of applications, see Piatetsky-Shapiro et al. (1996).

Bigus (1996) describes applications in marketing using customer relationship management, a way to exploit customer-related information and use it to enhance revenue flow from existing customers. This technique includes database marketing, which can improve the customer retention rate by identifying customers who are likely to switch to another provider. It also includes targeting specific promotions to customers who are more likely to buy. Direct mail marketers employ such methods. In retailing, data mining is used to identify relationships between seemingly unrelated products (such as disposable diapers and beer) that can be located near each other to boost sales. There are many examples in the finance, manufacturing, health and medical, and energy and utilities sectors.

Neural networks are a major tool of data mining. HNC, a neural network vendor, produces the DataBase Mining Workstation (DMW). It provides customized applications for customers and works through value-added resellers who tailor the DMW to specific applications.

INFORMATION OVERLOAD

Information overload grows exponentially over time. The amount of information on the Internet doubles in less than every 9 months, and this rate is accelerating. This growth has triggered a commercial need for methods to perform discovery in information-rich environments, mainly the Web. Data mining methods can deal with information overload to sift through soft information and identify relationships automatically (machine learning of induced rules). These include intelligent agents that search the Web, databases, or even e-mail for important information for a decision maker. Some existing intelligent agents include Create Your Own Newspaper (CRAYON, crayon.net), CNN.com (customnews.cnn.com/cnews/), and Digimedia. com, L.P. (www.headliner.com) which can be used to create an ad-supported newspaper that searches a wide variety of sources for relevant documents; see Internet.com Corporation (www.botspot.com) for more news bots, a kind of intelligent agent (also see bots.internet.com/search/s-news.htm). Several of these bots can be used to greatly reduce the amount of time and effort spent in searching for bits of information.

❖ CHAPTER HIGHLIGHTS

- ANNs have many real-world applications.
- ANNs can be applied to difficult problems in finance. Credit authorization, fraud detection, and stock market prediction are three important applications.
- ANNs can help interpret information in large databases.
- Genetic and similar algorithms can be used to solve complex optimization problems.
- Genetic algorithms are evolutionary in nature.
- Genetic algorithms use a three-step iterative process: Test the best solution to see how good it is, select the best parents, and generate offspring. The results improve as knowledge accumulates.
- Fuzzy logic represents uncertainty by using fuzzy sets.
- Fuzzy logic is based on two premises: First, people reason using vague terms (such as *tall, young,* and *beautiful*). Boundaries between classes are vague and are subject to interpretation. Second, human quantification is often fuzzy.
- Fuzzy sets have boundaries that are well defined. Items have membership values to define the imprecise nature of belonging to a set.
- Membership functions determine at what level an item belongs to a fuzzy set.
- Qualitative reasoning is a means of representing and reasoning with knowledge about the physical world in general terms.
- The following hybrid integrations have many benefits: expert systems and ANNs, fuzzy logic and genetic algorithms, and fuzzy logic and ANNs.
- Data mining methods identify hidden relationships in databases.
- Data mining can boost an organization's performance by targeting appropriate customers and in other useful ways.
- Intelligent systems, especially intelligent agents and neural computing, can help overcome information overload.

❖ KEY WORDS

- chromosome
- crossover
- data mining

- fuzzy logic
- fuzzy sets
- genetic algorithms

- mutation
- qualitative reasoning (QR)
- reproduction

❖ QUESTIONS FOR REVIEW

1. Give some examples of ANN applications in pattern recognition.
2. List three ANN applications in the area of data interpretation.
3. List three ANN applications in finance.
4. Describe the learning process in genetic algorithms. Why is it similar to a biological process?
5. Describe the major genetic algorithm operators.
6. List three applications of genetic algorithms.
7. What are the basic premises on which the fuzzy logic approach is based?
8. What are the major advantages of fuzzy logic? What are the major disadvantages?
9. Define *qualitative reasoning*.
10. Explain the basic idea underlying qualitative reasoning.
11. Describe the benefits of integrating cutting-edge technologies.
12. Define data mining.
13. Describe how neural networks can perform data mining.
14. What other methods can be used in data mining?

❖ QUESTIONS FOR DISCUSSION

1. Explain how neural computing can alleviate some of the limitations of expert systems.
2. Why is an ANN so effective in the interpretation of data?
3. Why is credit card approval a difficult management issue and how can an ANN support decisions in this area? (Section 16.3.)
4. Why is bankruptcy prediction such an important task for lending institutions? What information can be provided by an ANN and how can it be used?
5. Everyone would like to make a great deal of money in the stock market. Only a few are very successful. Why is an ANN a promising approach? What can it do that other decision support technologies cannot do? How could it fail?
6. You are playing a game in which your opponent thinks about an object and you ask questions. Your opponent's answers guide you to identify the object. To what AI technology is this game similar and why?
7. Explain the analogy between genetic algorithms and evolution.
8. Describe three advantages of fuzzy reasoning and provide an example to support each. If you disagree in any of the three cases, explain why.
9. Explain, in detail, how qualitative reasoning can be applied to a real decision-making problem.
10. Qualitative methods such as multiple choice (the Likert scale) and ranking are popular among experts. Why do they like these methods?
11. Compare quantitative reasoning with qualitative reasoning.
12. Describe the differences between qualitative reasoning and approximate reasoning using fuzzy logic.

13. Identify the benefits of fuzzy logic and neural network integration.
14. Why are intelligent systems so important for data mining?
15. Explain the analogy between gold mining and data mining.
16. Explain the relationship between data mining and customer relationship management (CRM)?
17. Describe knowledge discovery in data (KDD).
18. Explain why information overload has become a critical problem and how MSS can help solve this problem.

❖ **EXERCISES**

1. Investigate the phenomenon of memorization in neural network training and the methods used to prevent it from occurring.
2. Develop a deployable neural network code for a credit approval system. There are three neurons in the input layer, four in the hidden layer, and one in the output layer. Three input factors were considered for a potential client: credit rating, debt to income ratio, and net income. They have already been scaled so that the lowest value for any potential customer is 0 and the highest value is 1. These are the inputs. The output represents credit approval. If the output is 1, then credit is approved. If the output is 0, then credit is denied. The transfer function is a threshold function. If the total flow arriving in a hidden layer neuron is 0.5 (one-half) or greater, then, the *flow out* is set to 1, otherwise it is set to 0. The weights from the three inputs to the hidden layer are (rows = from inputs, columns = to hidden nodes)

		Hidden Node			
	from to	1	2	3	4
Input	1	0.1,	0.3,	0.4,	0.6
Node	2	0.2,	0.1,	0.6,	0.3
	3	0.1,	0.6,	0.4,	0.15

The weights from the hidden layer neurons to the output node are 0.3, 0.4, 0.2, 0.2.

3. Draw the membership function for tall as described in Section 16.9. Compare this to results from a class survey.
4. Express the following statements in terms of fuzzy sets:
   a. The chance for rain today is 80 percent. (Rain? No rain?)
   b. Mr. Smith is 60 years old. (Young?)
   c. The salary of the President of the United States is $250,000 per year. (Low? High? Very high?)
   d. The latest survey of economists indicates that they believe that the recession will bottom out in April (20 percent), in May (30 percent), or in June (22 percent).
5. You are trying to identify a specific number in the set of 1–16. You can ask questions such as, "Is this number in the set 1–8?" The answer can be only yes or no. In either case, you continue to ask more questions until you identify the number.
   a. How many questions are needed, in the worst and the best possible cases, to identify such a number?
   b. Is the problem suitable for parallel processing? Why or why not?
   c. Relate this problem to solution with a genetic algorithm.
6. Identify the role that ANNs and ES play in supporting each other or in supporting solution of the tasks under consideration. Prepare a brief report on the support identified in each case.

7. Some people believe that computers may get so smart that they will be able to drive a car by themselves in 3–5 years. Others say that this will never happen. Explain the positions of the two contradicting opinions. Identify relevant literature to support both of these views.

8. Compare the effectiveness of genetic algorithms versus standard methods for problem solving as described in the literature. How effective are genetic algorithms?

9. Look for hybrids of neural networks, expert systems, genetic algorithms, and fuzzy logic in the literature and report on their effectiveness. Which ones seem more common? Why do you think this is the case?

10. Solve the knapsack problem in Section 16.7, first manually, then use Evolver. Try another code (find one on the Web). Develop your own genetic algorithm code in Visual Basic, C++, or FORTRAN.

11. Investigate vendors of data mining products. Identify and categorize the methods they use. Which ones use artificial intelligence methods? Evaluate any case studies you find in the corporate or mainstream literature. Write up at least one success story along with your survey report.

12. Look up data mining and customer relationship management (CRM). How are these related? Which techniques are most commonly used in practice? Why?

❖ GROUP EXERCISES

1. *Fuzzy logic.* Survey your class by having everyone write down a height representing tall, medium, and short for men and for women. Tally the results and determine what is meant by tall, medium, and short in a fuzzy way. Create the membership functions in these sets and examine the results.

2. Examine the marketplace for consumer products that incorporate fuzzy logic. Note that sometimes this feature is called *continuous logic*. Try some of the products out if they are available in your area. Determine the advantages and disadvantages (if any) of these products over their nonfuzzy counterparts.

3. Have the members of your group play the manual version of MasterMind for about 30 minutes to 1 hour (or use one of the many online versions running on the Web). How do the better players in your group win? Write down the game concepts in terms of genetic algorithms and express winning strategies. Do you ever have to try random solutions to converge on a solution? Explain.

❖ INTERNET EXERCISES

1. Examine genetic algorithm vendor Web sites and investigate their business applications. What kinds of applications are most prevalent?

2. Search the Web for genetic algorithm–based games and simulations. Be sure to try out J. J. Merelo's MasterMind (kal-el.ugr.es/mastermind.html), M. S. Miller's Manna Mouse (www.caplet.com/mannamouse.html), and the Artificial Painter (AP) program demo (www.daimi.aau.dk/~hhl/ap.html) by L. Pagliarini, H. H. Lund, and O. Miglino.

3. Access the Web site of a genetic algorithm lab (try the Illinois Genetics Algorithms Laboratory). Find current research and relationships to neural computing.

4. Access *PC AI* magazine's Web site. Search for fuzzy logic, genetic algorithms, neural networks, and hybrid intelligent systems used in business. Examine definitions and vendors. What is new in these areas?

5. Examine fuzzy logic vendor Web sites and identify the kinds of problems to which fuzzy logic is currently being applied. Find a demo version of a system and try it out. Report your findings to the class.

6. Use the Internet to find information about neurofuzzy logic systems.

7. Access the MIT qualitative reasoning Web site (www.context.mit.edu). Try the online COIN demo and describe its capabilities and limitations. Also explore other developments on this site and on the QR Web sites of The University of Texas at Austin (www.cs.utexas.edu/users/qr/) and Northwestern University (multivac.ils.nwu.edu). What kinds of problems are the researchers generally trying to solve (both theoretical and applied)?

8. Search the Internet to find out and report on what is new in qualitative reasoning.

9. Investigate custom online newspaper systems on the Web (e.g., CRAYON) and evaluate how effective they are at filtering the news so that you get only the material you really want. Which ones worked best?

10. Examine the tools that DataX (or another data mining system) uses. Which ones are automated? Manual? Which ones seem like they would be most successful and why?

11. Investigate vendor software for credit card and fraud detection. Describe their effectiveness.

12. Investigate at least two Web sites of computer systems that exhibit creative behavior (e.g., GenJam, www.it.rit.edu/~jab/genjam.html). What types of creative behavior do they exhibit? Explain how they work.

17

INTELLIGENT SOFTWARE AGENTS[1]

In the previous chapters we presented various types of intelligent systems that can be used to support decision making. Some of these systems, especially expert systems and artificial neural computing systems, can be used in autonomous software programs that accomplish many tasks, some of which require decision making. These software programs, called *intelligent agents,* are the subject of this chapter, which includes the following specific sections:

17.1 OPENING VIGNETTES: EXAMPLES OF INTELLIGENT AGENTS

VIGNETTE 1. EMPOWERING EMPLOYEES BY USING SOFTWARE AGENTS AT NIKE AND AT SIGNET BANK[2]

Organizations offer a large variety of fringe benefits to their employees. Employees have several options in deciding which benefits to use and in what ways. Fringe benefits are often equated with a cafeteria: People mix and match what they like within the

---

[1]Contributions to this chapter were made by Debbie McElroy, Bob Morrison, and Brad Nye, MBA students at California State University, Long Beach, 1996.
[2]Information provided by Edify Corporation, Santa Clara, CA.

constraints of what is available and how much they can use. The management of fringe benefits is a very resource-intensive process, especially when thousands of employees are involved. Nike, the athletic footwear maker, and Signet Bank have installed special software that empowers employees to access, by telephone or computer, the human resources (HR) databases and conduct activities such as selecting and changing benefits or making charity contributions.

The software that supports these activities is called Electronic Workforce (Edify Corporation, a subsidiary of S1 Corporation). It enables employers such as Nike to delegate some time-consuming, repetitive tasks previously performed by human resources employees to any employee supported by a computer. The software enables employees to enter and delete data, command the computer, and interpret information. It also cuts down on errors. If employees make mistakes or request benefits they are not eligible for, the system automatically alerts them to the problem. Previously, paperwork had to be routed to an employee for corrections and then back to the HR department. The use of the software enables companies to increase benefits options, making employees more satisfied, with the same number of or even fewer human resources employees. The enabling software is an example of an intelligent agent.

VIGNETTE 2: SOFTWARE AGENTS COOPERATING TO PROVIDE THE BEST TRAVEL PLANS[3]

Several months ago, one of the authors of this book took a trip to Bali. He had been dreaming about the trip for years and was willing to pay the high price quoted by the travel agent. However, on arriving on the island, he discovered not only that had he paid too much for the accommodations but also that the hotel was on a rocky beach unsuitable for swimming. When he complained to the travel agent, he received the following reply: "I've never been in this hotel. I contacted a travel agency in Bali and this is what they provided me with." Fairly soon such incidents will not be able to occur. Consider the following futuristic scenario: You plan to take a trip to Hawaii. You could try to do the planning yourself, using a physical or a virtual travel agent. In most cases, however, you find that this may not be the most effective or efficient solution. Tomorrow's alternative is to use intelligent agents.

This is how intelligent agents will work.

Step 1. You turn on your PC and enter your destination, dates, budget, special requirements, and desired entertainment.

Step 2. Your computer dispatches an agent that shops around, entering sellers' Web sites and communicating with the electronic agents of airlines, hotels, and other vendors.

Step 3. Your agent attempts to match your requirements to what is available, negotiating with the vendors' agents. These agents may activate other agents to make special arrangements, cooperate with each other, activate multimedia presentations, or make special inquiries.

Step 4. Your agent returns to you within minutes with one or more recommendations. You have a few questions; you want modifications. No problem. Within a few minutes, it's a done deal. No waiting on the telephone; no mistakes made by people. Once you approve the deal, the agent makes the reservations, arranges for payments, and reports any changes to you.

How do you communicate with your agent? By voice, of course.

---

[3]Condensed from *Fortune,* June 24, 1994.

❖ **QUESTIONS FOR THE OPENING VIGNETTES**

1. List the benefits of intelligent agents at Signet Bank.
2. List the benefits of intelligent agents at Nike.
3. How can employees save time by working with intelligent agents? How would you feel about interacting with an intelligent agent instead of a human being? What if the cost of the service is 25 percent lower? What if the service cannot reasonably be offered otherwise?
4. How would you feel about making travel arrangements with a machine instead of a human travel agent?

17.2 INTELLIGENT AGENTS: AN OVERVIEW

The Opening Vignettes illustrate two situations involving software and intelligent agents. An **intelligent agent** (**IA**) is a computer program that helps a user with routine computer tasks. The first vignette describes an example of a first-generation individually operated software agent. The second represents a futuristic scenario involving a group of cooperative intelligent agents.

Intelligent agents are relatively new technology, and as such they have several definitions and fluctuating capabilities. Yet they have the potential to become one of the most important tools of information technology in the twenty-first century. They can overcome the most critical limitation of the Internet—information overflow—and make electronic commerce a viable organizational tool. For a tutorial, "Agents 101: Start To Learn About Intelligent Agents," see agents.umbc.edu. In this section we provide definitions and discuss the capabilities of such agents. In subsequent sections we describe what agents are, how they act, and what limitations and issues surround their use. Then, we discuss Internet and electronic commerce applications. Finally, we present multiple-agent systems.

NAMES

Several names are used to describe intelligent agents, including **software agents,** (see Brenner et al., 1998) wizards, knowbots, and **softbots (intelligent software robots)**. These terms sometimes refer to different types of agents or agents with different intelligence levels.

The term **bot** has become a common substitute for the term *agent*. *Bot* is an abbreviation for *robot*. Bots have been given specific prefixes, according to their use. Typical bots are chatterbots, docbots, hotbots, jobbots, knowbots, mailbots, musicbots, shopbots, spiderbots, spambots, and sexbots (of course—it had to be).

DEFINITIONS

The term **agent** is derived from the concept of agency, referring to employing someone to act on your behalf. A human agent represents a person and interacts with others to accomplish a predefined task.

INTELLIGENT AGENTS

There are several definitions of what an intelligent agent is. It seems that each definition is attempting to explicate the definer's perspective. Here are some examples:

- Intelligent agents are software entities that carry out some set of operations on behalf of a user or another program, with some degree of independence or autonomy, and in so doing, employ some knowledge or representation of the user's goals or desires. (IBM, www.ibm.com.)

- Autonomous agents are computational systems that inhabit some complex dynamic environment, sense and act autonomously in this environment, and by doing so realize a set of goals or tasks for which they are designed. (Maes, 1995, p. 108.)

- Intelligent agents continuously perform three functions: perception of dynamic conditions in the environment, action to affect conditions in the environment, and reasoning to interpret perceptions, solve problems, draw inferences, and determine actions.

- A software implementation of a task in a specified domain, on behalf or in lieu of an individual or other agent. The implementation will contain homeostatic goal(s), persistence, and reactivity, to the degree that the implementation (1) will persist long enough to carry out the goal(s), and (2) will reach sufficiently within its domain to allow the goal(s) to be met and to know that fact (Hess et al., 2000).

These definitions points out the capabilities of agents that will be described later. For more definitions and sources see Murch and Johnson (1999) and Brenner (1998).

INTELLIGENCE LEVELS

Definitions of agents are greatly dependent on the agents' levels of intelligence, which are described by Lee et al. (1997) as follows:

- *Level 0 (the lowest).* These agents retrieve documents for a user under straight orders. Popular Web browsers fall into this category. The user must specify the URLs where the documents are. These agents help in navigating the Web.

- *Level 1.* These agents provide a user-initiated searching facility for finding relevant Web pages. Internet search agents such as Google, Alta Vista, and Infoseek are examples. Information about pages, titles, and word frequency is stored and indexed. When the user provides key words, the search engine matches them against the indexed information. These agents are referred to as **search engines.**

- *Level 2.* These agents maintain user's profiles. Then they monitor Internet information and notify the users whenever relevant information is found. Examples of such agents are WebWatcher (www.cs.cmu.edu). Agents at this level are frequently referred to as semi-intelligent or **software agents.**

- *Level 3.* Agents at this level have a learning and deductive component of user profiles to help a user who cannot formalize a query or specify a target for a search. DiffAgent (CMU) and Letizia (MIT) are examples of such agents. Agents at this level are referred to as *learning* or *truly intelligent* agents.

- More information about agents at each level is provided later in this chapter.

Throughout this chapter and this book we use the terms *intelligent agents* and *software agents* interchangeably. This is the manner in which agents are presented in the not so technical literature.

Similar to the concept of levels is the concept of "agent generation." For a description of these generations today and in the future, see Murch and Johnson (1999).

COMPONENTS OF AN AGENT

Intelligent agents can contain the following components:

- *Owner.* User name, parent process name, or master agent name. Intelligent agents can have several owners. Humans can spawn agents, processes can spawn agents (such as stock brokerage processes using agents to monitor prices), or other intelligent agents can spawn their own supporting agents.
- *Author.* Development owner, service, or master agent name. Intelligent agents can be created by people or processes and then supplied as templates for users to personalize.
- *Account.* Intelligent agents must have an anchor to an owner's account and an electronic address for billing purposes or as a pointer to their origin.
- *Goal.* Clear statements of successful agent task completion are necessary, as well as metrics for determining the task's point of completion and the value of the results. Measures of success can include simple completion of a transaction within the boundaries of the stated goal or a more complex measure.
- *Subject description.* The subject description details the goal's attributes. These attributes provide the boundaries of the agent, task, possible resources to call on, and class of need (such as stock purchase or airline ticket price).
- *Creation and duration.* The request and response dates requested.
- *Background.* Supporting information.
- *Intelligent subsystem.* An intelligent subsystem, such as a rule-based expert system or a neural computing system, provides several of the characteristics described above.

BRIEF HISTORY OF AGENTS

The concept of agents goes surprisingly far back. More than 50 years ago, Vannevar Bush envisioned a machine called a *memex.* In his mind he could see the memex assisting humans through huge fields of data and information. In the 1950s, John McCarthy developed Advice Taker, a software robot that would navigate the networks of information that would develop in time. Advice Taker's similarity to today's agents is amazing. Given a task by a human user, the robot takes the necessary steps or asks for advice from the user when it gets stuck. The futuristic prototypes of intelligent personal agents, such as Apple's Phil and Microsoft's Bob, perform complicated tasks for their users following the same functions laid out by McCarthy in Advice Taker. The modern approach to intelligent agents moved to mobile and multiple agents in the mid-1980s under research topics such as distributed artificial intelligence (Bond and Gasser, 1988) and agency theory.

17.3 CHARACTERISTICS OF AGENTS

Although there is no single commonly accepted definition for the term *intelligent agent,* there are several traits or abilities that many people think of when they discuss intelligent agents.

AUTONOMY OR EMPOWERMENT

An agent is autonomous; that is, it is capable of acting on its own or of being *empowered.* An agent must be able to make some decisions on its own as a result of being goal-oriented, collaborative, and flexible. It must be able to alter its course or behavior when it meets an obstacle and find ways around the impediment. Maes (1995) points out that regular computers respond only to direct manipulation, but with the advent of agents, users are able to give open-ended commands to their electronic agents to get work done. For example, an agent should be able to accept high-level requests and decide on its own where and how to carry out the request. In the process, the agent should be able to ask clarification questions and modify requests instead of blindly obeying commands.

Autonomy implies that an agent takes initiative and exercises control over its own actions in the following ways:

- *Goal-oriented.* Accepts high-level requests indicating what a human wants and is responsible for deciding how and where to satisfy the requests. These are referred to by Hess et al. (2000) as *homeostatic goal(s).*
- *Collaborative.* Does not blindly obey commands but can modify requests, ask clarification questions, or even refuse to satisfy certain requests.
- *Flexible.* Actions are not scripted; able to dynamically choose which actions to invoke, and in what sequence, in response to the state of its external environment.
- *Self-starting.* Unlike standard programs directly invoked by a user, an agent can sense changes in its environment and decide when to act.

The autonomy capability is also created by the agents' *intelligence, mobility,* and *interactivity* attributes which will be described later.

17.4 SINGLE TASK

In most cases an agent is designed to accomplish a single task. A single task could be searching the Internet to find where and when certain items are auctioned. Another might be filtering electronic mail. Although the more advanced agents are capable of doing multiple tasks, it is more likely that many future agent systems will really be **multiagents,** collections of different agents each handling a simple task.

COMMUNICATION (INTERACTIVITY)

Many agents are designed to interact with other agents, humans, or software programs (see the second Opening Vignette). This is a critical ability in view of the narrow repertoire of any given agent. Instead of making a single agent conducting several tasks, additional agents can be created to handle undelegated tasks. Thus, there is need for communication. Agents communicate by following certain communication languages and standards such as ACL and KQML (Bradshaw, 1997; Jennings et al., 1998).

AUTOMATES REPETITIVE TASKS

An agent is designed to perform narrowly defined tasks, which it can do over and over without getting bored or sick or going on strike.

REACTIVITY

Agents perceive their environment (which may be the physical world, a user via a graphical user interface, a collection of other agents, the Internet, or perhaps all of these combined) and respond in a timely fashion to changes that occur in it. That means that agents can recognize changes in their environment.

PROACTIVENESS (OR PERSISTENCE)

Agents do not simply act in response to their environment. They are able to exhibit goal-directed behavior by taking an initiative.

TEMPORAL CONTINUITY

The agent should be a continuously running process, not a one-shot deal that terminates after completing a series of commands. The program can also be temporarily inactive, waiting for something to occur.

PERSONALITY

For an agent to be effective, it must be believable and be able to interact with human users.

OPERATING IN THE BACKGROUND: MOBILITY

An agent must be able to work out of sight, within the realm of cyberspace or other computer systems, without the constant attention of its user (or "master"). Some developers use the term *remote execution* or mobile agents in referring to this attribute.

MOBILE AGENTS

An mobile agent can transport itself across different system architectures and platforms, and it is far superior to those that cannot. However, some agents are not designed to be mobile. For instance, many of the wizards in software programs are designed to carry out a very specific purpose while you are using your computer. In contrast, electronic commerce agents are mobile (Section 17.7).

INTELLIGENCE AND LEARNING

Currently, the majority of agents are not truly intelligent because they cannot learn; only some agents can learn. This goes beyond mere rule-based reasoning because the agent is expected to use learning to behave autonomously. Although many in the AI community argue that few people want agents who learn by "spying" on their users, the ability to learn often begins with the ability to observe users and predict their behavior. One of the most common examples of learning agents is the wizards found in many commercial software programs (e.g., in Microsoft Office applications). These wizards offer hints to the user, based on patterns the program detects in the user's activities. Some of the newer Internet search engines boast intelligent agents that can learn from previous requests the user has made.

For a comprehensive discussion of the above and additional characteristics, see Hess et al. (2000).

17.5 WHY INTELLIGENT AGENTS?

Alvin Toffler, in *Future Shock* (1970) warned of an impending flood, not of water, but of information. He predicted that people would become so inundated with data that they would become paralyzed and unable to choose between options. His prediction is becoming a reality.

Information overload is one of the unintended by-products of the information age. Managers and other decision makers cannot be expected to read every document that crosses their desks, every relevant datum available in databases, every article in the magazines and journals to which they subscribe, or even all the e-mail that hits their computer mailboxes. The Gartner Group believes that

- The amount of data collected by large enterprises doubles every year.
- Knowledge workers can analyze only about 5 percent of this data.
- Most of their efforts are spent in trying to discover important patterns in the data (60 percent or more), a much smaller percentage is spent determining what these patterns mean (20 percent or more), and very little time (10 percent or less) is spent actually doing something about the patterns.
- Information overload reduces our decision-making capabilities by 50 percent.

However, the real crisis started to develop with the emergence of the Internet. The Internet contains a collection of information-generating and -replicating machines. Thousands of new systems and even more new users bring new sources of data onto the Net every minute. It can be an overwhelming experience to log onto the Net for the first time because so many resources are immediately available. Experienced users look for ways to filter the data so that they can make sense out of the streams of information found online. Search engines and directories help with the winnowing process, but even they bring up volumes of data, much of which is only loosely tied to the immediate concerns of the decision maker. In addition, search engines rarely discriminate between copies of the same information offered through different sources, and so replication adds to the pile of useless information.

In spite of all of this, managers are expected to take into account key business information and make good decisions.

A major value of intelligent agents is that they are able to assist in searching through all the data. They save time by making decisions about what is relevant to the user. With these agents at work, the competent user's decision-making ability is enhanced with information rather than paralyzed by too much input. Agents are artificial intelligence's answer to a need created by computers (e.g., Nwana and Ndumu, 1999).

Information access and navigation are today's major applications of intelligent agents, but there are several other reasons why this technology is expected to grow rapidly. For example, intelligent agents can improve computer network security, support electronic commerce, empower employees (see the first Opening Vignette), and increase productivity and quality. The advantage of agents can be even greater when a wireless computing environment is involved. The cost of nonagent wireless systems for information discovery is very high. The reasons for the success of agents are as follows:

- *Decision support.* There is a need for increased support for tasks performed by knowledge workers, especially in the decision-making area. Timely and knowledgeable decisions made by these professionals greatly increase their effectiveness and the success of their businesses in the marketplace.
- *Frontline decision support.* As indicated in Chapter 8, there is a need to empower employees interacting with customers at the frontline. Such empowerment can be achieved by using intelligent agents.
- *Repetitive office activities.* There is a pressing need to automate tasks performed by administrative and clerical personnel in functions such as sales or customer support, to reduce labor costs and increase office productivity.

- *Mundane personal activity.* In a fast-paced society, time-strapped people need new ways to minimize the time spent on routine personal tasks such as booking airline tickets so that they can devote more time to professional activities.
- *Search and retrieval.* It is not possible to directly manipulate a distributed database system in an electronic commerce setting with millions of data objects. Users will have to relegate the tasks of searching, costing, and other comparisons to agents. These agents perform the tedious, time-consuming, repetitive tasks of searching databases, retrieving and filtering information, and delivering it to users.
- *Domain experts.* It is advisable to model costly expertise and make it widely available. Examples of expert software agents could be models of real-world agents such as translators, lawyers, diplomats, union negotiators, stockbrokers, and even clergy.

Here are some management-oriented tasks that an agent can perform: advise, alert, broadcast, browse, critique, distribute, enlist, empower, explain, filter, guide, identify, match, monitor, navigate, negotiate, organize, present, query, remind, report, retrieve, schedule, search, secure, solicit, sort, store, suggest, summarize, teach, translate, and watch.

In short, software agents can improve the productivity of the end user by performing a variety of tasks. The most important of these are gathering information, filtering it, and using it for decision support, as shown in Sections 17.6–17.10, but first we classify the agents into meaningful groupings.

17.6 CLASSIFICATION AND TYPES OF AGENTS

Agents can be classified in different ways. Franklin and Graesser (1996) use a taxonomic tree to classify autonomous agents (Figure 17.1). Relevant to managerial decision making are *computational* agents, *software* agents, and *task-specific* agents.

APPLICATION TYPES

Other classifications are according to control structure, computational environment, programming language, and application type. Here, we basically look at applications. For a comprehensive coverage see Chapter 8 in Murch and Johnson (1999).

FIGURE 17.1 CLASSIFICATION OF INTELLIGENT AGENTS

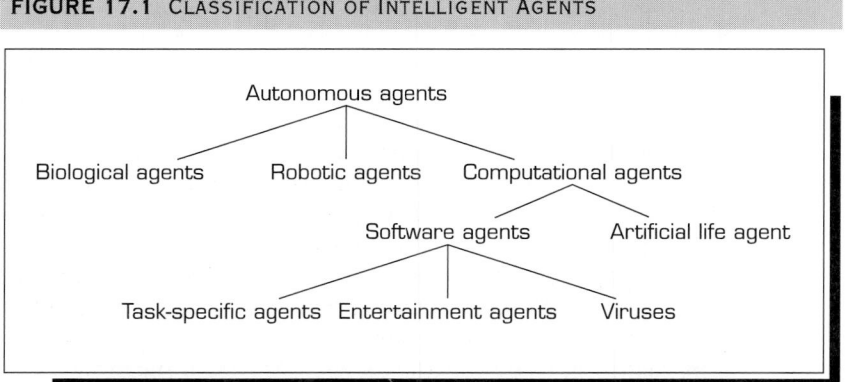

Source: S. Franklin and A. Graesser, Institute for Intelligent Systems, University of Memphis, TN.

ORGANIZATIONAL AND PERSONAL AGENTS

Organizational agents execute tasks on behalf of a business process or computer application. **Personal agents** perform tasks on the behalf of individual users.

For example, corporate use of agent monitoring software is becoming a key component in the drive to cut support costs and increase computer productivity. Intelligent agents can search through e-mail messages for certain **key words.** Depending on what key words are contained in a message, the agent automatically sends out answers based on frequently asked questions (FAQs) files. A company can use such an agent to help customers obtain answers to their questions quickly (e.g., www.egain.com and www.brightware.com).

Another example of an organizational intelligent agent is an automatic e-mail sorting system. When a new message comes in, it is automatically routed to the right file and folder.

Personal agents are very powerful. They allow users to go directly to the information they want on the Internet. Busy people do not have the time or desire to browse for a long time through the Internet, and so the agent can help in browsing. For more information on these two types of agents, see www.stac.com.

PRIVATE AGENTS VERSUS PUBLIC AGENTS

A **private agent** (personal) works for only one user who creates it. **Public agents** are created by a designer for the use of anybody who has access to the application, network, or database.

SOFTWARE AGENTS AND INTELLIGENT AGENTS

According to Lee et al. (1997), truly intelligent agents (level 3 of intelligence) must be able to learn and exhibit autonomy. However, most Internet and electronic commerce agents do not exhibit these characteristics yet. Therefore, they are often called *software agents* (level 2 of intelligence). The second generation of Internet and electronic commerce being developed includes some learning capabilities. (see www.media.mit.edu/research/softwareagents/projects).

CLASSIFICATION BY CHARACTERISTICS

Of the various characteristics of agents, three are of special importance: *agency, intelligence,* and *mobility.* According to IBM (1995), agents can be classified in terms of a space defined by these three dimensions. The definitions of these dimensions are as follows:

Agency is the degree of autonomy and authority vested in the agent and can be measured, at least qualitatively, by the nature of the interaction between the agent and other entities in the system. At a minimum, an agent must run asynchronously. The degree of agency is enhanced if an agent represents a user in some way. A more advanced agent can interact with other entities, such as data, applications, or services. Even more advanced agents collaborate and negotiate with other agents.

Intelligence is the degree of reasoning and learned behavior: the agent's ability to accept the user's statement of goals and carry out the tasks delegated to it. At a minimum, there can be some statements of preferences, perhaps in the form of rules, with an inference engine or some other reasoning mechanism to act on these preferences. Higher levels of intelligence include a user model or some other form of understanding and reasoning about what a user wants done and planning the means to achieve this goal. Farther out on the intelligence scale are systems that *learn* and *adapt* to their environment, both in terms of the user's objectives and in terms of the resources available to the agent. Such a system, like a human assistant, might discover new relationships, connections, or concepts independently of the human user and exploit these in anticipating and satisfying user needs.

Mobility is the degree to which the agents themselves travel through the network. Some agents may be static, either residing on the client machine (to manage a user interface, for instance) or initiated at the server. *Mobile scripts* can be composed on one machine and shipped to another for execution in a suitably secure environment; in this case, the program travels before execution, and so no state data need be attached. Finally, agents can be mobile with state, transporting from machine to machine in the middle of execution and carrying accumulated state data with them. Such agents can be viewed as mobile objects, which travel to agencies where they can present their credentials and obtain access to services and data managed by the agencies. Agencies can also serve as brokers or matchmakers, bringing together agents with similar interests and compatible goals and providing a meeting point at which they can interact safely.

Mobile agents can move from one Internet site to another and send data to and retrieve data from the user, who can focus on other work in the meantime. This can be very helpful to a user. For example, if users want to continuously monitor an electronic auction that takes a few days (such as at www.onsale.com), they essentially would have to be online continuously for days. Software applications that automatically watch auctions and stocks are readily available. For example, a mobile agent travels from site to site, looking for information on a certain stock as instructed by the user. If the stock price hits a certain level, or if there is news about the stock, the agent alerts the user. What is unique about a mobile agent is that it is a software application that moves on its own to different computers to execute (Murch and Johnson, 1999).

Nonmobile agents can be defined by two dimensions (Figure 17.2a), and mobile agents are defined in a three-dimensional space (Figure 17.2b). For example, in Figure 17.2a we see that expert systems, which are not agents, may fall below the threshold line and so are regular software agents. True intelligent agents are listed above the threshold line.

OTHER CLASSIFICATIONS

King (1995) classifies agents into interface, tutors, scheduling assistants, search agents, report agents, presentation agents, navigation agents, and role-playing agents.

FIGURE 17.2 INTELLIGENT AGENTS SCOPE IN TWO DIMENSIONS (A) AND (B) IN THREE DIMENSIONS

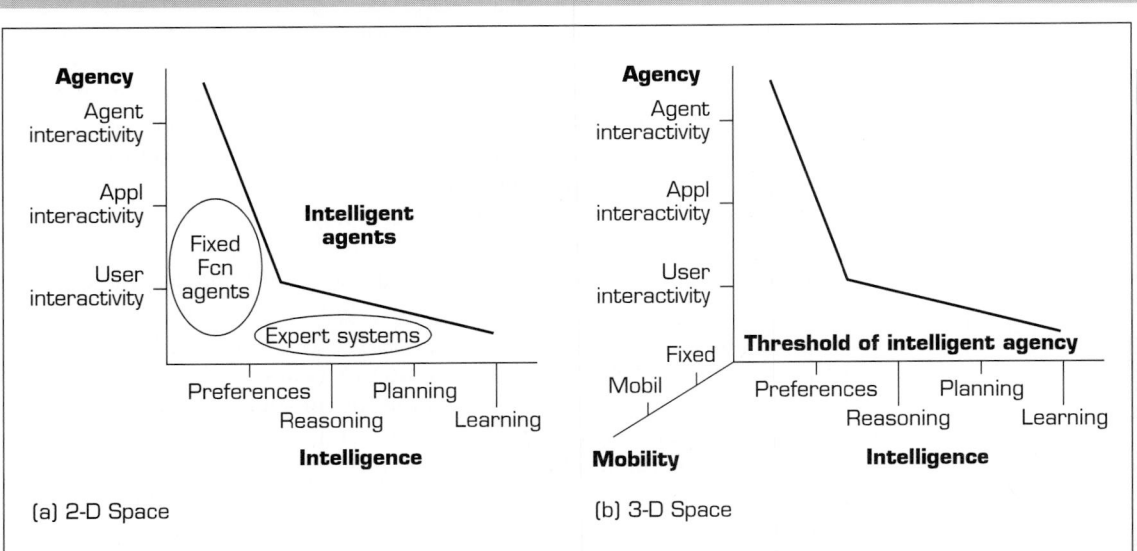

Source: Based on IBM (1995) and Gilbert and Janca (1997).

Murch and Johnson (1999) use the following categories: personal use, network management, information and Internet access, mobility management, e-commerce, user interface, application development, and military applications. Gilbert and Janca (1997) classify Internet agents into nine categories based on the area of application. These will be presented in the next section.

In the final part of this chapter agents are classified as Internet-based agents, electronic commerce agents, and others. They are discussed with representative examples in the three following sections.

17.7 INTERNET-BASED SOFTWARE AGENTS

The use of network- and Internet-based software agents is growing rapidly. New and improved applications seem to appear almost every week (see agents.umbc.edu).

According to IBM's white paper (Gilbert and Janca, 1997), there are nine major application areas that relate to Internet agents:

- Assistance in workflow and administrative management
- Collaboration with other agents and people
- Support of electronic commerce
- Support of desktop applications
- Assisting in information access and management, including searching and FAQs
- Processing e-mail and messages
- Controlling and managing network access
- Managing systems and networks
- Creating user interfaces, including navigation (browsing).

Gilbert and Janca have predicted that by the year 2000 all could be in mainstream use. And, indeed, several of these agents became part of the mainstream in 2000. Gilbert and Janca also provide many examples of agents in each of the nine categories. Examples of applications in the network- and Internet-related areas are presented in the following sections.

E-MAIL AGENTS (MAILBOTS)

These agents assist the user with e-mail (Figure 17.3). For example, Maxims (Maes, 1994) monitors what the user does routinely with e-mail and memorizes the user's situation–action pairs. These pairs are stored in a memory of examples. The situations are described in terms of a set of features, including the names of those who send or receive messages to or from the user. When a new situation occurs, the agent analyzes the features of the situation and suggests an action to the user (such as read, delete, forward, or archive). The process is similar to case-based reasoning. The agent communicates with Eudora, a Windows-based e-mail software system.

The agent measures the confidence (or fit) of a suggested action to a situation. If the confidence is high, the agent executes the suggestion with the approval of the user. Otherwise, the agent waits for instructions on what to do. The agent's performance improves with time as the memory of examples increases. Several commercial e-mail agents are available (such as Beyond Mail for intelligent messaging from Banyan Inc. www.banyan.com).

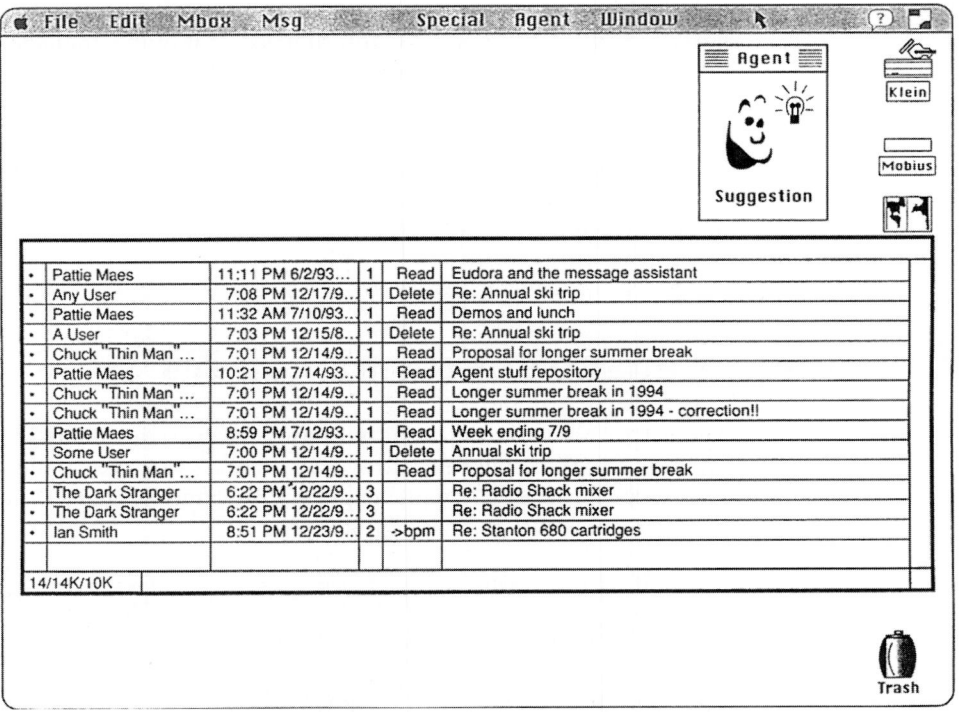

•	Pattie Maes	11:11 PM 6/2/93...	1	Read	Eudora and the message assistant
•	Any User	7:08 PM 12/17/9...	1	Delete	Re: Annual ski trip
•	Pattie Maes	11:32 AM 7/10/93...	1	Read	Demos and lunch
•	A User	7:03 PM 12/15/8...	1	Delete	Re: Annual ski trip
•	Chuck "Thin Man"...	7:01 PM 12/14/9...	1	Read	Proposal for longer summer break
•	Pattie Maes	10:21 PM 7/14/93...	1	Read	Agent stuff repository
•	Chuck "Thin Man"...	7:01 PM 12/14/9...	1	Read	Longer summer break in 1994
•	Chuck "Thin Man"...	7:01 PM 12/14/9...	1	Read	Longer summer break in 1994 - correction!!
•	Pattie Maes	8:59 PM 7/12/93...	1	Read	Week ending 7/9
•	Some User	7:00 PM 12/14/9...	1	Delete	Annual ski trip
•	Chuck "Thin Man"...	7:01 PM 12/14/9...	1	Read	Proposal for longer summer break
•	The Dark Stranger	6:22 PM 12/22/9...	3		Re: Radio Shack mixer
•	The Dark Stranger	6:22 PM 12/22/9...	3		Re: Radio Shack mixer
•	Ian Smith	8:51 PM 12/23/9...	2	->bpm	Re: Stanton 680 cartridges

14/14K/10K

FIGURE 17.3 E-MAIL AGENT

The e-mail agent makes recommendations to the user (middle column). It predicts what actions the user will take on messages, such as which messages will be read and in which order and which messages will be deleted, forwarded, archived, and so on.

Source: Maes (1994), p. 34. Maes, P. (1994, July). "Agents That Reduce Work and Information Overload." *Communication of the ACM,* Vol. 37, No. 7.

Several other e-mail agents help the user to handle large numbers of messages. For example, Motiwalla (1995) developed an intelligent agent for prioritizing e-mail messages based on the user's preferences or knowledge.

According to Murch and Johnson (1999), e-mail agents can

- Control any unwanted, unsolicited e-mail.
- Alert users by voice if a certain designated message arrives.
- Automatically forward mail messages to designated destinations.
- Consolidate mail from several sources, the way the user wants it.
- Search the Internet for certain sources and deliver them to the user by e-mail.
- Distinguish business-related e-mail from private or personal mail. Automatically answer mail and respond according to conditions, for example, "I am on vacation until.... My agent will automatically make an appointment for you."
- Perform regular administrative tasks involving desktop e-mail (e.g., backing up files, archiving, indexing).

WEB BROWSING ASSISTING AGENTS

Some agents can facilitate browsing by offering the user a tour of the Internet. Such an agent, known as a *tour guide,* works while the user browses. For example, WebWatcher (www.cmu.edu) helps in finding pages related to the current page, adding hyperlinks to meet the user's search goal and giving advice on the basis of user preference.

Another example is Letizia (www.media.mit.edu/research/softwareagents). This agent monitors the user's activities with a browser and collects information about the user's behavior. Using various heuristics, the agent tries to anticipate additional items that might be of interest to the user. A similar agent is Netcomber Activist from IBM (activist.gpl.ibm.com). This agent monitors a user surfing through the Yahoo catalog. Then the user can build an interest profile, customize newspapers for daily reading, and so on.

For further details see O'Leary (1996), Etzioni and Weld (1995), and www.botspot.com, and agents.umbc.edu.

FREQUENTLY ASKED QUESTIONS AGENTS

These agents guide people to the answers to FAQs. People tend to ask the same or similar questions, and in response newsgroups, support staffs, and vendors have developed files of FAQs and the most appropriate answer to each. The problem is that people use natural language, thus asking the same question in several different ways. The agent addresses the problem by indexing large numbers of FAQ files and providing an interface at which people can pose their questions in a natural language. The agent uses the text of a question to locate the answer. Because of the limited number of FAQs and the semistucturedness of the questions, the reliability of FAQ agents is very high. GTE Laboratories has developed a FAQ agent that accepts questions from users of Usenet news groups in natural language and answers them by matching question–answer pairs (Whitehead, 1995). FAQFinder can deal with complex FAQs that change over time. The agent can also deal with multiple FAQs in the same domain. For details see O'Leary (1996). Also, www.askjeeves.com and www.nefdesk.com are available to the public (see Internet Exercise 10).

INTELLIGENT SEARCH (OR INDEXING) AGENTS

Web robots, spiders, wanderers, and similar names describe agents that traverse the Web and perform tasks such as information retrieval and discovery, validating links or HTML, and generating statistics. These **search engines** (or *indexing agents*) are very popular, and thousand of them, many of which are very specialized, are available (www.serachengineguide.com). Representative names are InfoSeek, Lycos, Excite, and Hotbot. To achieve better results there are **metasearch engines** that combine several search engines and other methods of search. Metasearch engines (such as Spider, Savvy Search, Metacrawler, All-in-One, and Web Compass) integrate the findings of the various search engines to answer queries posted by the user.

Indexing agents carry out a massive autonomous search of the Web. First, they scan millions of documents and store an index of key words and words from document titles and texts. The user can then query the agent by asking it to find documents containing certain key words. For details, see Etzioni and Weld (1995).

Indexing agents were developed for knowledge sharing and acquisition in large databases and documents. For example, see Jones et al. (1995).

INTERNET SOFTBOT FOR FINDING INFORMATION

The previously described search agents suggest locations on the Web to the user. Such suggestions are based on a weak model of what the user wants and what information is available at the suggested location. An **Internet Softbot** [for pioneering work at the University of Washington, see cs.washington.edu/research/projects and Etzioni and Weld (1994)] attempts to determine what the user wants and understand the contents of information services. Early softbot agents were able to work only with structured information, such as stock quotes and weather maps or the Federal Express package tracking service. Therefore, early agents relied on a simple model of the information service for the precise semantics associated with information provided by the service, increasing the reliability of the search. Also see Chen et al. (1997). By the year 2000, Internet softbots such as google.com and www.askjeeves.com had become more powerful.

NETWORK MANAGEMENT AND MONITORING

A slew of intelligent agents were developed to monitor, diagnose problems, conduct security, or manage Internet (or other network) resources. Representative agents are as follows:

- *Patrol Application Management.* This is a family of products that uses intelligent agents to perform tasks such as monitoring and managing applications, databases, middleware, and underlying network resources. It also automates administrative action by pinpointing and correcting potential problems before they affect user productivity. Similar software is AgentWorks (Legent Corporation), which also has the ability to work with other intelligent agents (see AIS in Action 17.1), and Optivity Planning network monitoring (Nortel Networks Inc.).
- *WatchGuard.* (Seattle Software Labs, www.watchguard.com) is an intelligent Internet and intranet firewall which includes a built-in intelligent agent designed to simplify the configuration, management, and security of networks. The intelligence of the system provides automatic alerts to system administrators whenever questionable configurations or outside attacks are detected.
- *AlertView.* (Intel Corporation) uses agents to monitor network resources, databases, and e-mail systems for threshold violations. It has about 100 predefined threshold templates to make programming these responses easier.
- *InterAp.* InterAp (California Software) is a suite of Internet applications for Windows that uses agent technology to search the Web and automate file transfer.

AIS IN ACTION 17.1

SALLIE MAE USES INTELLIGENT AGENTS

Sallie Mae, the government-sponsored loan services company, is known for its student loan programs. To manage $35 billion in insured student loans, the company relies on an enterprise-wide computer network spanning several states and on large databases. This large information system must operate continuously and must be secured. The networks, servers, and other resources must be monitored around the clock, and any irregularities detected must be reported and fixed quickly. To perform these tasks manually would not only cost a fortune but would also result in major interruptions to the system and poor service to loan customers. The solution is AgentsWorks, which monitors the system's databases, networks, and applications, working with intelligent agents. The agents are programmed to oversee network management tasks, send alerts, and restore failed procedures.

AgentWorks manages remote resources from a central location. The intelligent agent executes several tasks such as monitoring thresholds at remote locations and taking action when the thresholds are exceeded. The agents are controlled by a command center that can run on its own or be incorporated with other network management systems.

More than 100 critical processes are managed by agents. These agents are also used to identify the sources of problems they cannot fix in kind of a problem determination drill down. Overall, a significant improvement in response time has occurred, and the numbers of agents and tasks are expanding. By using multiple agents, a wide-spectrum solution is provided.

Source: Condensed from K. B. Sullivan, "Sallie Mae Takes on Intelligent Agents," *PC Week*, Mar. 6, 1995.

- *Mercury Center's NewsHound* (www.sjmercury.com/hound.html) is a watcher agent that enables information to automatically come back to you based on your query. It can save a lot of time and effort if you structure your query correctly, thus allowing you to automatically scan a variety of national newspapers without having to look at each of them. You just have to construct a good query. Newshound allows you to create a mini Nexis eclipse or a mini Dialog alert. For a small businessperson or investor, it is great. Granted, you are not searching the megavolume of data that you can on Dialog, Nexis, Newsnet, or Datatimes, but you can't beat the price.
- *Infosage* (www.infosage.ibm.com) allows users to set up their own simple topical trees as alerts. The user sends IBM an interest profile, and IBM uses the profile to filter various news feeds and then sends the filtered information back to the user via e-mail. Related to this is the concept of **Webcasting,** a form of customized broadcasting in which information appears on the user's screen in a ticker-tape format as it becomes available (push technology).

17.8 ELECTRONIC COMMERCE AGENTS

Intelligent agents play an increasing role in EC. See Wang (1999), Jacso (1999), and Murch and John (1999). Hundreds of commercial agents perform several major EC activities on the Web. Here we classify these agents by major type of activity, based on Maes et al. (1999). The six classes parallel a customer's six steps in purchasing decision making and are shown in Figure 17.4 together with a brief explanation. Note that the process is cyclic and that the steps may overlap each other.

The classification in Figure 17.4 can help in identifying where agent technologies can be of assistance. [e.g., see the CASBA system in Kraff et al., (2000)]. The characteristics of agents described earlier make them well-suited for mediating consumer behaviors involving information filtering and retrieval, personalized evaluations, complex coordinations, and time-based interactions. Here are some details and examples.

NEED IDENTIFICATION

Agents can assist the buyer with need identification by providing product information and stimuli. For example, Amazon.com provides its customers with an agent that continuously monitors a set of data (like the arrival of new books) and notifies customers when a book in their area of interest arrives. Similar agents watch for stocks to go below or above a certain level, sending out an e-mail when that level is reached. Expedia.com notifies customers about low-priced airline tickets for a desired destination whenever they become available. AuctionRover.com watches auctions for you. Need identification is frequently combined with product brokering because some agents that find products compare prices as well.

Several commercial agents can facilitate need recognition directly or indirectly. The following are several examples:

- Salesmountain.com helps people who are looking for certain items when they are put "on sale." If you specify what you want, you receive notification. But general browsing is also available to boost your need recognition.
- Likemind.com helps people decide what to look at, what to sample, what to try, and what to buy.

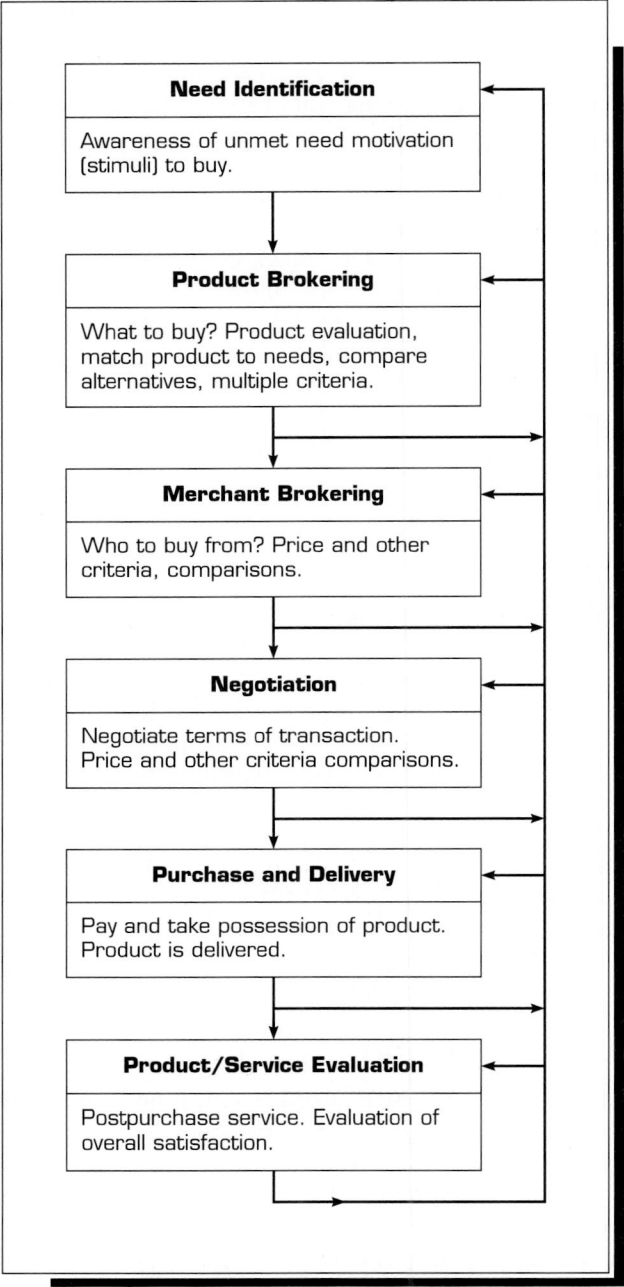

FIGURE 17.4 THE PURCHASING DECISION-MAKING PROCESS

- Giftfinder.com asks you to tell it something about the person you are buying a gift for and helps you hunt down the perfect present.
- Eboodlebar.com not only looks for deals but also finds related information such as a news group discussion about the type of product for which you are searching.

PRODUCT BROKERING

Once a need is established, customers search for a product (or service) that will satisfy this need. Several agents are available to assist customers with this task.

The pioneering agent in this category was *Firefly*. This agent, which was purchased by Microsoft and is no longer available, initially helped users find music they were likely to enjoy. Firefly built profiles of people who visited its Web site. Users received a "passport" that identified them when they visited sites participating in the Firefly program, and products and services were recommended to them. Based on people's likes (favorite movies, music, interests), Firefly helped marketers predict what customers were likely to want next, and the means to reach them with a customized pitch could be much cheaper yet more effective than mass advertising. A similar agent is AOL's *Personalogic* (www.personalogic.com), which makes product recommendations to users based on prioritization of attributes such as price and delivery time (see Internet Exercise 2). For a commercial application of another agent, see AIS in Action 17.2. Personalogic and similar agents can provide benefits to individuals who are not sure what to buy. For example, they can listen to recommended CD sound samples and then buy albums while they are online. Furthermore, some agents can even match people with similar profiles of interest.

Even more ambitious agents try to predict which brands of computers, cars, and other goods will appeal to customers, based on preferences in entirely different product categories such as wine, music, or breakfast cereal.

Webdoggie (MIT Media Lab) recommends Web documents, and NewsWeeder (www.cs.cmu.edu) finds news articles based on monitored users' reading interests. Both are examples of product brokering agents.

MERCHANT BROKERING

Once a customer knows what product he or she wants, it is necessary to find out *where* to buy it. Bargain Finder (Andersen Consulting, bf.cstar.ac.com/bf) was the pioneering agent in this category. This agent, used in online CD shopping, queried the price of a

---

FUJITSU (JAPAN) USES AGENTS FOR TARGETED ADVERTISING

Since 1996 Fujitsu has been using an agent-based technology called Interactive Marketing Interface (iMi) that allows advertisers to interact directly with targeted customers, providing valuable services and information. The system enhances the customers' Internet experience.

The iMi service provides advertisers with the ability to interact directly with specific segments of the consumer market through the use of software agents, while ensuring that consumers remain anonymous to advertisers. Consumers submit a profile to iMi indicating personal characteristics, such as product categories of interest, hobbies, travel habits, and the maximum number of e-mail messages per week they want to receive from the iMi service. In turn customers electronically receive

product announcements, advertisements, and marketing surveys from advertisers based on their personal profile information. By answering marketing surveys or acknowledging the receipt of advertisements, consumers earn iMi points redeemable for gift certificates and telephone cards.

The system demonstrates practical commercial applications of agent technology and closely maps the concept of mobile, active agents. The system is based on Telescript (General Magic Inc.).

Source: Condensed from a news release from General Magic Corporation, Sept. 1996.

specific CD at a number of online vendors and returned a list of prices. However, this system encountered problems because vendors who did not want to compete on price only managed to block out the agent's requests.

The blocking problem has been solved by Jango (jango.excite.com) and other new agents. Jango originates the requests from the user's site instead of from Jango's. This way vendors have no way of determining whether the request is from a real customer or from the agent. Jango is also more complete than Bargainfinder because it includes more categories of products. Furthermore, Jango provides product reviews in addition to price comparisons. Several other agents compete with Jango, including Inktomi Shopping Agent, My Simon, and Junglee (Amazon.com).

PRODUCT (SERVICES) COMPARISON AGENTS

Large numbers of agents enable consumers to perform all kinds of comparisons. The following are some examples:

- Allbookstores.com and bestbookbuys.com are two of several agents that help you find the lowest prices of books available online.
- Bottomdollar.com, compare.net, pricewonders.com, shopper.com, smarts.com, and fido.com are examples (out of several dozen) of agents that suggest brands and compare prices once you specify what you want to buy.
- Buyerzone.com is a business-to-business portal at which businesses can find the best prices for many products and services.
- Pricescan.com is your guide to finding the best prices for thousands of computer hardware and software products.

A special agent-based mediator worth mentioning is Kasbah (MIT media lab). With Kasbah, users wanting to buy or sell a product assign the task to an agent who is then sent out to proactively seek buyers or sellers. In creating the agent, users must specify constraints including desired price, highest (or lowest) acceptable price, and a date by which the transaction must be completed. The agent's goal is to complete an acceptable transaction based on these parameters. This agent can also negotiate on the part of the buyers, as will be discussed next.

NEGOTIATION

The concept of "market" implies negotiation, mostly about prices. While many retail stores use fixed-price selling, many small retail stores and most markets (especially in developing countries) use negotiations extensively. In business-to-business transactions negotiation is very common. The benefit of dynamically negotiating a price is that the decision is shifted from the seller to the marketplace. In a fixed-price situation, if the seller fixes the price and it is too high, sales will suffer. If the price is set too low, profits will be lower.

Negotiations, however, consume time and frequently are disliked by individual customers who cannot negotiate properly because they lack information about the marketplace and prices. Many vendors do not like to negotiate either. Therefore, electronic support of negotiation can be extremely useful (e.g., Beer et al., 1999). One type of negotiating agent is used in electronic auctions that last several hours or days (e.g., www.onsale.com and www.ebay.com). Here, buyers have to manage their own negotiation strategies, which is a time-consuming task.

Almost all auctions require users to personally execute the bidding. This is not the case with AuctionBot, in which users create intelligent agents that will take care of the bidding process. With AuctionBot (www.auction.eesc.umich.edu), users create auction agents by specifying a number of parameters that vary depending on the type of auction selected. Then it is up to the agent to manage the auction until a final price is met or the deadline for the offer is reached.

Kasbah is another environment in which intelligent agents are involved in the negotiation process. Kasbah agents (www.media.mit.edu/kasbah) are capable of negotiating with each other following specific strategies assigned by their creators. However, this agent's usefulness is limited by the fact that price is the only parameter considered. A more capable agent called Tete-@-tete has been developed by the creators of Kasbah and is described next.

Tete-@-tete is unique compared to other online negotiation systems because the agents negotiate a number of different parameters: price, warranty, delivery time, service contracts, return policy, loan options, and other value-added services. Another innovative feature of this system is that, unlike the situation in Kasbah, where negotiation is conducted along the lines of simple increase or decrease functions, negotiation of Tete-@-tete agents is argumentative. This, de facto, integrates three stages of the decision purchasing model shown in Figure 17.4. This integrating approach makes Tete-@-tete the most advanced agent-based environment currently available (2000).

Agents can negotiate in pairs, or one agent can negotiate for a buyer with several sellers' agents. In such a case the contact is made with each seller's agent individually, but the buyer's agent can conduct comparisons (Yan et al., 2000) (see Section 17.9 and the second Opening Vignette).

PURCHASE AND DELIVERY

Agents are used extensively during the actual purchase, including arranging payment and delivery with the customer. For example, if you make a mistake while filling an electronic order form, an agent will point it out immediately. In buying stocks, for example, the agent tells you when a stock you want to buy on margin is not marginable or when you do not have sufficient funds. Delivery options at Amazon.com, for example, are posted by agents, and the total cost is calculated in real time.

AFTERSALE SERVICE AND EVALUATION

Agents can be used to facilitate aftersale service. For example, the automatic answering agents for e-mail cited earlier are usually productive in answering customer queries. Agents can monitor usage and notify you that it is time to take your car in for periodic maintenance. Agents that facilitate feedback from customers are also useful.

Some agents support several of the decision steps shown in Figure 17.4. For example, Answer Agent and Advice Agent (www.brightsare.com) deal with e-mail from customers, providing replies to queries and advice. Other EC agents are described next.

OTHER EC AGENTS

A large number of agents support many EC activities ranging from advertisement to payment support [see Turban et al. (2000) for a description]. Also see the lists provided periodically by www.botspot.com and by www.agents.umbc.edu (see the Agents 101 tutorial). For a comprehensive guide to EC agents, see Peter Finger's article, "A CEO's Guide to EC Using Intelligent Agents" (home1.gte.net/pfingar/eda). The following are just a few examples:

- *BullsEye2* (www.intelliseek.com) is an intelligent desktop portal. Intelligent agents offer you a productive way to find and manage products, news, and even research. This is a free service that delivers personalized content to users. A similar agent is Portico (see the demo at www.genmagic.com).

- *VReps* (www.neuromedia.com) provides tools for companies to create virtual online sales, customer service representatives who dynamically interact with customers via real time, natural language dialog for EC support (try to converse with their demo agent, Red).
- *Opennating.com* offers a service designed to dramatically increase the level of trust, reliability, and brand recognition for buyers and sellers.
- *Mysimon.com* tries to imitate human navigational behavior on the Net. Simon shops in *real time,* and so you find the product at the right place and at the best price.
- *Salesmountain.com* surfs the Net to find items that are part of promotions or on sale. If an item is "put on sale," you will get an e-mail notification.
- *Resumix.com* is an application that wanders the Web looking for Web pages containing resume information. If it identifies a page as being a resume, it attempts to extract pertinent information from the page, such as the e-mail address, phone number, skill descriptions, and location. The resulting database is used to connect job seekers with recruiters.

AUCTION SUPPORT AGENTS

Several agents support auction buyers. The most common support is provided by *auction aggregators,* such as auctionrover.com, rubylane.com, auctionwatch.com (which also monitors offline auctions), auctionwatchers, and auctionoctopus. These sites tell you when certain items will be auctioned online and where. Some aggregators provide real-time access to auctions.

FRAUD PROTECTION AGENTS

Fraud is a big problem in EC because buyers cannot see the products or the sellers. Several vendors offer agent-based fraud-detecting systems. One such system is eFalcon (www.ehnc.com), which is based on pattern recognition driven by neural computing.

LEARNING AGENTS

Several learning agents are used in EC. For example, Learn Sesame (Open Sesame) uses learning theory in monitoring customers' interactions and preferences. Then the agent delivers customized advertisements. Netperceptions Corporation uses a similar approach to personalize content and to create customer loyalty programs. Finally, Plangent (Toshiba) "moves around and thinks." It performs tasks relying on a knowledge base of auctions. For more on learning agents, see Huang (1999).

17.9 OTHER AGENTS, INCLUDING DATA MINING, USER INTERFACE, AND INTERACTIVE, BELIEVABLE AGENTS

For many users, it was difficult to learn and use a graphical user interface, especially its nonroutine functions. As capabilities and applications of computers improve, the user interface must accommodate the increase in complexity. As user populations grow and diversify, computer interfaces will need to learn user habits and preferences and adapt to individuals. Intelligent agents can help with both these problems. Intelligent agent technology allows systems to monitor the user's actions, develop models of user abilities, and automatically help out when problems arise (Conway and Koehler, 2000).

Some interface agents use GUI methods in interacting with users. However, as more natural interaction techniques emerge, more human-centered methods of interaction are becoming appropriate for interfaces with agents. Speech recognition, speech synthesis, natural language processing, and animated facial images work together to represent agents' states and activities anthropomorphically. As these agents grow in accuracy and sophistication, they promise to greatly enhance the human–computer interface in general, and intelligent agent applications and services in particular. These agents provide a personalized user interface with applications by integrating a variety of human–computer interaction techniques into a single, user-friendly interface. Specifically, these agents employ a variety of animated forms that respond to user input with text, synthesized voice, and visual expressions.

This type of agent has animation, or perhaps personalities, that make them *believable*. They are not really intelligent, rather they are versatile and employ friendly front ends to communicate with users. They are referred to as **avatars,** which are computer representations of users in a computer-generated three-dimensional world. An avatar shows where a user is in the virtual world and where other users are. Advanced avatars can "speak" and act like robots. Their purpose is to introduce believable emotions so that agents can gain credibility. They are considered part of **social computing,** an approach that aims to make human–computer interfaces more natural. Studies conducted at www.extempo.com showed that interactive characters can improve customer attraction, satisfaction, and retention by offering personalized one-to-one service. They can also help companies to get to know their customers.

An interesting subcategory of such agents is "virtual pets." Children are required to feed, nourish, and clean up after virtual pets. Tamagotchi, the "cute little egg," a handheld computer toy, is probably the most well-known of these products. "Dogz and Catz" (PF Magic Inc.), which resides in your PC, is another example.

Many Web sites use characters for interacting with customers, including the following:

- *Personal Job Search Agent* (www.monster.com) helps find jobs for free.
- *Digit* (www.bankone.com) is an interactive agent that can speak and move around at Bank One online services. Digit interacts with site visitors, assisting them in exploring the site.
- *Max* (www.extempo.com) guides visitors who wish to learn more about products and tools available from a vendor specializing in avatars.
- *Merlin* (www.extempo.com) guides visitors who want to visit the Web sites of shops, restaurants, and other enterprises on San Francisco's Haight Street.

For further information on interactive characters see Hayes-Roth (1998, 1999).

OPERATING SYSTEMS AGENTS

Agents can assist in the use of operating systems. For example, Microsoft Corporation has several agents (called **wizards**) in its NT operating systems. Some reside on the NT server, others on the workstations. These agents assist in the following tasks: adding user accounts, group management, managing file and folder access, adding printers, adding or removing programs, network client administration, managing licenses, and installing new modems. For details, consult www.microsoft.com.

SUPPLY CHAIN MANAGEMENT AGENTS

Several companies develop agents that support different activities along the supply chain. An example of such an application is reported in *Intelligent Systems Report,* January 1999. Lockheed Martin Aircraft uses several agents to monitor the entire supply chain to provide comprehensive decision support information.

SPREADSHEET AGENTS

Spreadsheet agents make software more friendly. An example of an intelligent agent is the wizard feature found in Microsoft's Excel. The wizard is a built-in package capability that watches users and offers suggestions as they attempt to perform tasks by themselves. For example, suppose you are trying to format a group of spreadsheet cells or locations in a particular manner. If you are not adept at using the spreadsheet package, you might try to format each cell individually. A much faster method is to select the entire group of designated cells and then conduct the formatting once for all the selected locations.

Suppose a friend of yours is watching you format spreadsheet cells and notes that you are working on an individual cell basis. Suppose further that your friend is more of an expert on the software package than you are. Presumably, your friend will tell you that you are formatting unproductively. In a similar sense, the wizard can detect your laborious, repetitive attempts and tell you that there is a better way, or even take the next step and offer to complete the remainder of the formatting task for you.

WORKFLOW AND ADMINISTRATIVE MANAGEMENT AGENTS

Administrative management includes both workflow management and areas such as computer–telephone integration, where processes are defined and then automated. In these areas, users need not only to make processes more efficient but also to reduce the cost of human agents. Intelligent agents can be used to ascertain and then automate user wishes or business processes. An example is FlowMark (IBM Corporation, www.software.ibm.com/ad/flowmark) which provides an environment for direct manipulation of graphical objects that define and capture the activity steps of any business process (such as handling a claim, approving a line of credit, or registering a patent). An activity can be automated (carried out by the execution of a program) or performed by a person. The user defines the process by drawing connectors between the activities and specifying the rules for when each is to be carried out. FlowMark supports both parallel and sequential activities, where the output of one activity step is the input to the next activity step. Once defined, the model can be verified for completeness and correctness. For a more complex system, see Fakes and Karakostas (1999).

COMPETITIVE INTELLIGENCE

Large numbers of agents were developed to help in conducting a competitive intelligence. For a comprehensive coverage of this topic, see Murch and Johnson (1999, Chapter 8) and www.scip.org.

SOFTWARE DEVELOPMENT

Software development includes many routine tasks that can be carried out or supported by agents. For example, Neural Network Utility (NNU, www.research.ibm.com) is an intelligent assistant for software developers that offers the pattern recognition and learning so necessary for information access. With NNU, the developer can define and graphically connect neural networks, fuzzy rule systems, and data filtering or translation and then embed them in applications. NNU supports online learning controlled by scripts or application programs. It can be extended by adding custom neural network models and custom data filters.

DATA MINING

Data mining is one of the most important capabilities of information technology. Appropriate data mining tools can give users an edge when sifting through large amounts of information. For example, it can generate sales leads, as does ProspectMiner (www.intarka.com). Data mining is the engine that propels intelligent agents to sift and properly sort information. Intelligent agents are most useful in discovering previously unknown relationships.

Web mining is an important part of data mining and, according to Etzioni (1996), can be organized into the following subsets:

- *Resource discovery:* locating unfamiliar documents and services on the Web
- *Information extraction:* automatically extracting specific information from newly discovered Web resources
- *Generalization:* uncovering general patterns at individual Web sites and across multiple sites.

The information discovered and extracted from Web sites must be generalized based on users' experience. Several intelligent agents can learn about their user's interests, but this is a more difficult task (Etzioni, 1996).

IBM (www.ibm.com—look for intelligent agents) offers an intelligent data mining family, including Intelligent Decision Server (IDS), for finding and analyzing massive amounts of data in an enterprise.

ProdeBeacon (www.prode.com) includes programmable agents designed to simplify the process of database access in data warehouses where data mining is frequently done. This software can help in fetching specific information. The agents are triggered by events (such as a specific query) and significantly cut down the time required, for example, to create reports for sales forces.

For example, Gentia (Planning Sciences International, www.gentia.com) is a DSS/EIS tool that uses intelligent agents to facilitate data mining with Web access and data warehouse facilities. It increases productivity by automatically performing repetitive, manually intensive tasks involving complex database queries, such as monitoring trends and exceptions against SQL and OLAP databases.

Another example is Convectis (HNC Software Inc., www.ehnc.com), which uses neural networks to search text data and images for words and relationships between words to discern the meaning of documents. This tool is used by InfoSeek, an Internet search engine, to speed up the creation of hierarchical directories of Web topics.

Related to data mining is data warehousing. Liu (1998) developed an agent that can assist in the creation and maintenance of data warehouses.

MONITORING AND ALERTING

An interesting example of a monitoring and alerting agent is NewsAlert, developed by King and Jones (1995). NewsAlert ensures that the data that reaches the manager's desktop is of paramount importance. It does this by

- Putting software agents to work to routinely monitor data according to individual, personalized rules
- Immediately delivering alerts produced by these agents to the user's desktop (users see their alerts in a personalized newspaper, which they can easily navigate, understand, and customize)
- Organizing alerts by user-specified subject areas

- Providing a set of smart tools to allow users to investigate the context of an alert and to communicate their findings to other managers.

The key components of NewsAlert and similar agents include software agents, alert objects, and a newspaper client.

Liu et al. (2000) implemented a similar agent in the pulp and paper industry in Finland. The agent monitors a few dozen Web sites and provides the user with news on specific topics, prices, and any other needed information. The information is delivered as an electronic newsletter customized for the user.

Hundreds of other Web agents provide specialized information in many areas, mostly free (e.g., myyahoo.com). News agents work like this: First, the end user specifies the data sources to which the detection rule is to be applied. Here the user can choose from selected Web sites, accumulated e-mail received, or even news groups. The user then creates detection rules. At this point, the user is provided with a simple form for entering key words or phrases. Once the user has specified a detection rule, the rule is shipped to the server where the agent is located. The agent runs on a scheduled basis, for example, once a day for a morning edition of the user newspaper.

On a given run, the agent loops through the rules, applying the search criteria against news in the Web sources, messages in the specified news groups, and e-mail messages. When a match occurs, the message is extracted and converted to a news item.

News items produced by the same rule from different sources are grouped into a single alert (metafile), which itself has a title and a priority (set when the user defined the rule). Once a run has been made, all the alert files generated during that run are shipped to the PC where they are alerted and their accompanying news items are extracted and added to the database. Any item tagged as a personal edition of the electronic newspaper is then generated.

An electronic newspaper can combine the features of a paper newspaper: Stories come from multiple sources, and stories are prioritized [e.g., front-page stories (Figure 17.5) are more important than back-page stories]. Thus, the format is familiar to the intended audience. Because it is an electronic paper, it is easily navigated, its contents can be personalized, and stories can be augmented with other tools for understanding and communication.

COLLABORATION

Lotus Notes/Domino (Chapter 7) is a comprehensive collaborative software product. It includes Notes Agents, which allows automation of many tasks within Notes. Agents operate in the background to automatically perform routine tasks for the user, such as filing documents, sending e-mail, looking for particular topics, or archiving older documents. These agents can be created by designers as part of an application for automating routine tasks such as progress tracking or serving as reminders of overdue items, or for performing more powerful functions such as manipulating field values and bringing data in from other applications. Agents can be either private, created by the user and used only by the user, or shared, created by a designer and used by anyone who has access to the application or database.

Because an agent typically represents an individual user's interests, collaboration is a natural area for agent-to-agent interaction and communication. IBM, for example, is exploring multiagent interaction through several research efforts. Multiagent interaction is the subject of the next section.

OTHER AGENTS

Hundreds of other agents are used in all functional areas and in all industries. For an example of how an agent can help an HR department, see AIS in Action 17.3.

FIGURE 17.5 FRONT PAGE FOR THE NEWSALERT AGENT

Courtesy of Comshare Inc.

AIS IN ACTION 17.3

INTELLIGENT AGENTS IN HUMAN RESOURCES WORK AT HEWLETT-PACKARD

The Atlanta-based U.S. field services operations (USFO) group at Hewlett-Packard (HP) has developed a paperless wage review (PWR) system. The PWR system uses intelligent agents to deal with quarterly reviews of HP's 11,000 employees. The agent software resides on a PC server on the HP network and lets USFO managers and personnel access employee data from both personnel and e-mail databases, drive e-mail communications, and initiate phone and fax transactions through the telecommunications network.

Via software agents, the PWR system tracks employee review dates and automatically initiates the wage review process. It sends wage review forms to first-level managers by e-mail or fax every quarter on the appropriate date. PWR speeds up all the administrative tasks, eliminates paperwork, and improves accuracy throughout the entire process.

Source: Condensed from D. Blanchard, "Agents Infiltrate the Business World," *PC AI,* July/Aug. 1996, pp. 39–42.

17.10 DISTRIBUTED AI, MULTIAGENTS, AND COMMUNITIES OF AGENTS

Agents can *communicate, cooperate,* and *negotiate* with other agents. The basic idea is that it is easy to build agents with a small amount of specialized knowledge. However, in executing complex tasks that require much knowledge, it is necessary to employ several software agents in one application. These agents need to *share* their knowledge, or the results of applying this knowledge together may fail (Bradshaw, 1997).

In today's business environment, machines are providing more and more decisions that are not made in isolation but in concert with other machines. An example is routing among telecommunication networks. Information can pass through a network controlled by one company into another network controlled by another company. Computers that control a telecommunications network might find it beneficial to enter into agreements with other computers that control other networks about routing packets more efficiently from source to destination.

We are also seeing the emergence of tools such as **personal digital assistants (PDAs),** small, hand-held computers (such as Palm VII in 2000). These personal assistants are assuming the roles of a number of machines involved in managing our daily lives, such as notebooks, communicators, fax machines, telephones, and automated schedulers. We will soon have some kind of agent software on the personal assistant that will ultimately perform part of its work by interacting with other agents on other personal assistants.

Wireless telephones and pagers are continuously increasing their functionality. With the WAP protocol and Bluetooth systems, cell telephones not only allow Internet access and electronic commerce transactions but also enable device-to-device communication. You can take a photograph with your digital camera in one location and transmit it in seconds to your home or office computer. Intelligent agents embedded in such devices facilitate this interaction.

Each of these situations is an instance in which computers control certain resources and might be able to help themselves by strategically sharing this resource with other computers. With personal digital assistants, the resource might be a person's time, whereas with a telecommunications network, the resource might be communication lines, switching nodes, or short- and long-term storage. In each situation, the computers that control these resources can do their own job better by reaching agreements with other computers.

EXAMPLE: THE CIG SEARCHBOTS (UNIVERSITY OF MASSACHUSETTS)

CIG Searchbots are an example of cooperative information gathering, a multiagent approach to information retrieval. CIG Searchbots are not a database search engine tool. To satisfy your query, multiple agents actually perform live searches at heterogeneous remote sites via the Web. Domain experts determine what sites to search and the path to the best solution quality with the lowest search cost. Multiple agents work together cooperatively to locate information relevant to your query (see mas.cs.umass.edu/research).

DISTRIBUTED ARTIFICIAL INTELLIGENCE VERSUS INTELLIGENT AGENTS

The theoretical basis for multiple agents started with research in a field called **distributed artificial intelligence (DAI),** which basically represents the intelligent part of distributed problem solving. DAI is the study of distributed but centrally designed AI systems (Avouris and Gasser, 1992) and involves the design of a multiple-agent distributed system with a problem to solve or a task to accomplish. The issue is how to perform in an effective and efficient manner. The DAI approach decomposes the task into subtasks, each of which is addressed by an agent. Therefore, in distributed problem solving it is assumed that there is a single body that is able, at design time, to influence the preferences of all the agents in the system directly (O'Hare and Jennings, 1996). The infrastructure of DAI can be constructed with an architecture known as a *blackboard* (Avouris and Gasser, 1992). Nute et al. (1995) provide an example of how to perform forest management with a blackboard architecture written in PROLOG. Shih and Srihari (1995) describe DAI in manufacturing system control.

However, DAI systems contrast with **multiagent systems.** In multiagent systems, there is no single designer who stands behind all the agents. Each of these agents can be working toward different goals, even contradictory goals, and sometimes in parallel. Either competition or cooperation is possible among the agents (Decker et al., 1999). In a DAI system an agent acting in a particular way is good for the system as a whole, which is not necessarily the case in a multiagent system. However, by using incentives, it is possible to influence the agents in a multiagent system. For example, Chi and Turban (1995) proposed a DAI system for an EIS. The conceptual framework is shown in Figure 17.6. Also see AIS in Action 17.4. Wang et al. (1996) define a model of an autonomous agent in a multiagent environment, focusing on the belief state models of agents and the changes that communication forces on their belief states. This should lead to better communication so that they can solve a problem cooperatively in a distributed open system. The agent environment is called a multiagent processing environment (MAPE).

In a multiagent system, for example, a customer may want to place a long-distance call. Once this information is known, agents representing the carriers submit bids simultaneously. The bids are collected, and the best bid wins. In a complex system, the customer's agent may take the process one step further by showing all bidders the offers,

FIGURE 17.6 THE CONCEPTUAL FRAMEWORK OF DIEIS

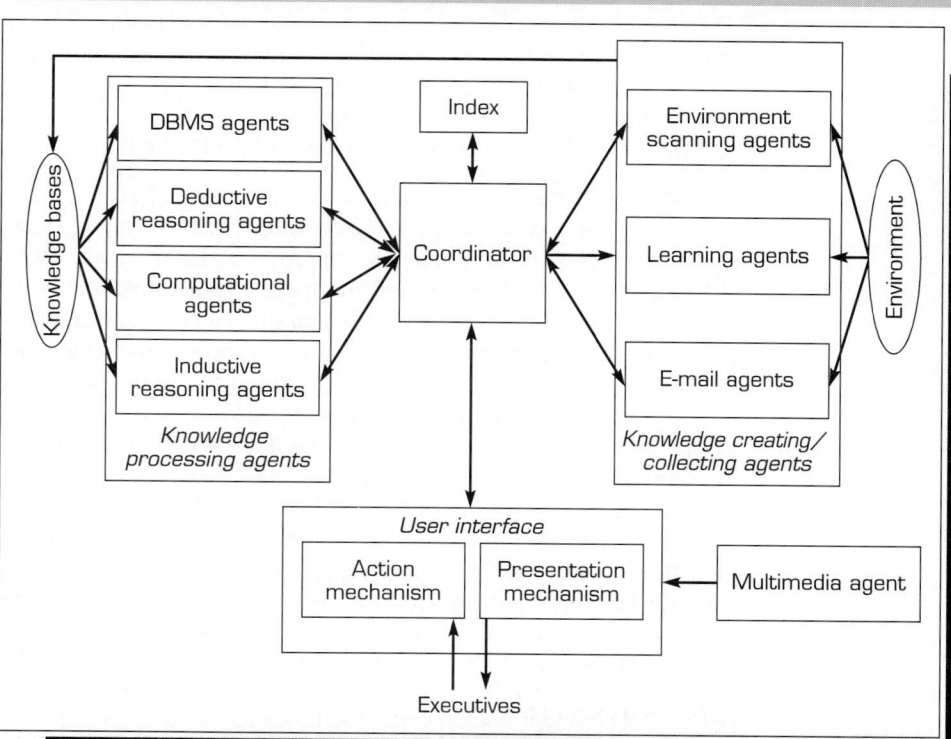

Source: R. Chi and E. Turban, Working Paper, CSULB, 1995.

AIS IN ACTION 17.4

DISTRIBUTED ARTIFICIAL INTELLIGENCE (DAI) IN EIS

The framework of the distributed intelligent EIS (DIEIS) is a decentralized group of agents cooperatively attempting to provide a solution to a complex problem through a coordinator (Figure 17.6). The agents, perhaps at different geographic locations, running on different systems, work independently and are supported by specific knowledge bases. There are seven independent but closely related subsystems: knowledge-processing agents, knowledge bases, knowledge creation and collecting agents, user interface, multimedia agent, the environment, and a coordinator. The knowledge-processing agents automate the process of obtaining information from both internal and external databases. Clearly, the intent is to provide executives with infor-

mation in a format they want in a timely manner, but the interactions among system components are agent interactions. When an executive makes a query, multiple knowledge processing agents may be triggered to access data from databases and process them into properly formatted information. If no data are available, knowledge creation and collecting agents are activated. These consist of three types: inductive or deductive learning agents, environmental scanning agents, and deductive learning agents. Information processing is classified as knowledge processing and knowledge creating or collecting.

Source: R. Chi and E. Turban, Working Paper, CSULB, 1995.

---

allowing them to rebid or negotiate. This process is currently accomplished manually by increasing the number of companies that place projects and subassemblies up for bids in business-to-business electronic commerce (Turban et al., 2000).

A complex solution is decomposed into subproblems, each of which is assigned to an agent that works on the problem independently of others and is supported by a knowledge base. Acquiring and interpreting information is done by knowledge processing agents that use deductive and inductive methods as well as computations. The data are refined, interpreted, and sent to the coordinator, who transfers to the user interface whatever is relevant to a specific user's inquiry or need. Multimedia agents can organize the presentation to fit individual executives. If no existing knowledge is available to answer an inquiry, knowledge creating and collecting agents of various types are triggered.

SOME TOPICS IN MULTIAGENT SYSTEMS

NEGOTIATION IN ELECTRONIC COMMERCE

A considerable amount of research and development is being done on multiagent negotiation systems in electronic commerce (Beer et al., 1999). Consider the second Opening Vignette. There, agents cooperate to arrange for a vacation. However, the scenario can be extended to one in which the user's agents negotiate the best price for the car, hotel, and airfare. Such a situation is shown for human agents in Figure 17.7. The user's agent notifies the seller's agent about the user's needs, and the seller's agent submits a bid. The user's agent reports the lowest bid and tries to get lower rebids. The seller's agent can use rules for the negotiations. For an application of agent negotiation in banking, see Sadaranda and Acharya (1993).

The process of negotiation and its relationship to bidding processes are being investigated. For example, Oliver (1996) examines two issues: Can automated agents learn strategies that enable them to effectively participate in typical, semistructured, multi-issue business negotiations? What is required and how does it work? Other issues of negotiations were also investigated by Rosenschein and Zlotkin (1994), Yan et al. (2000), Robinson (1997), and Beer et al. (1999).

COORDINATION

Coordination is a key factor in the success of multiagent systems. The purpose of the coordination mechanism is to manage problem solving so that cooperating agents work together

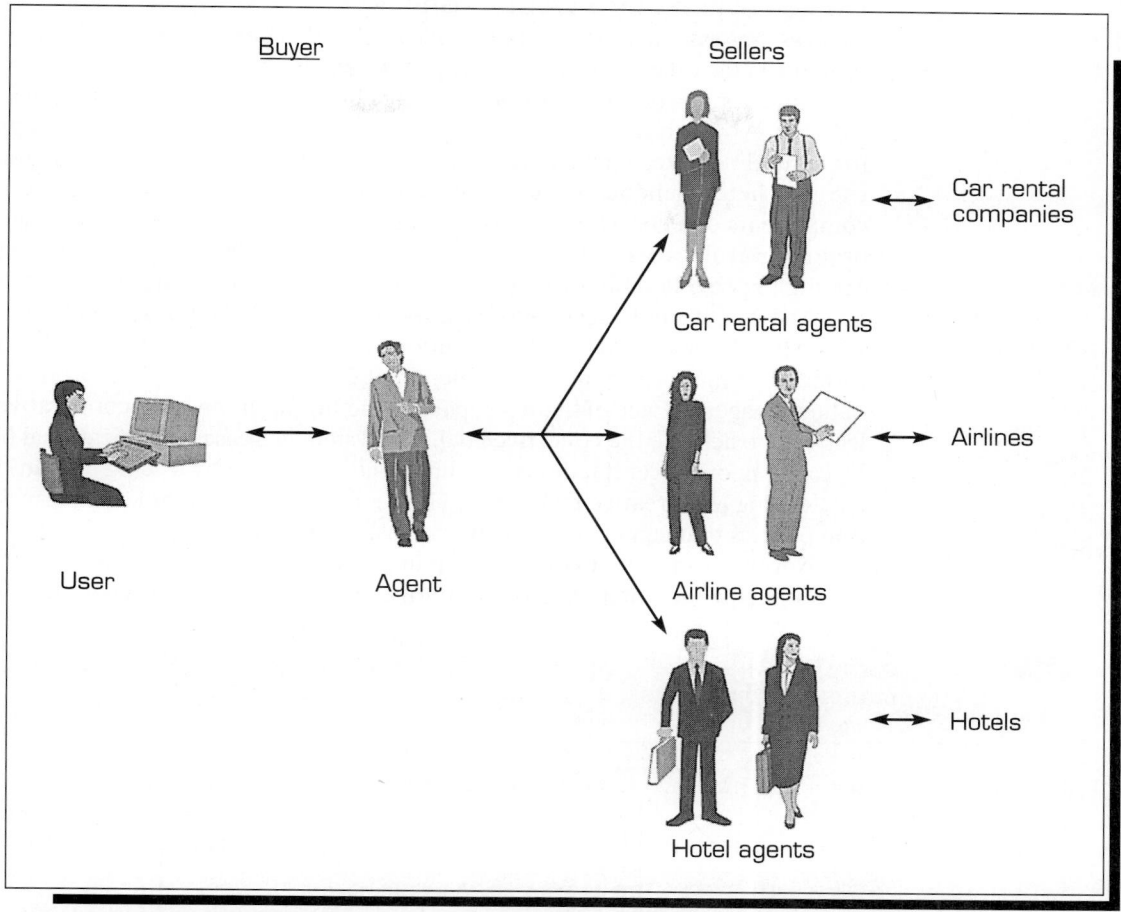

FIGURE 17.7 A MULTIAGENT SYSTEM FOR TRAVEL ARRANGEMENTS

as a coherent team. Coordination is achieved by exchanging data, providing partial solution plans, and constraints among agents. Coordination can be done by reversing actions, synchronization, structured group mediation, and information sharing. See Jamali et al. (1999).

THE NATURE OF THE AGENTS

Multiagent systems are usually assumed to have heterogeneous, self-motivated agents (Rosenschein and Zlotkin, 1994). However, the systems are not assumed to be centrally designed. For example, if you have a personal digital assistant, you might have a Palm VII from 3Com, but the next person might have one that was built by IBM. These devices don't necessarily have a notion of global utility. Each agent operating from your machine is interested in what your idea of utility is and in how to further your notion of goodness. They are dynamic. For example, agents might enter and leave the system in an unpredictable way. The system as a whole is flexible. An example of coordinating the completion of components in a multistage production system is reported by Brun and Portioli (1999).

LEARNING AGENTS

Being self-motivated requires some agents to have learning capabilities. Although not all agents in a multiagent system need to have this ability, some must be able to learn. Aiba and Terano (1996) developed a model for incorporating distributed software agents with learning mechanisms.

COOPERATION AND COLLABORATION

DAI systems assume a central control mechanism that ensures cooperation throughout the system. On the other hand, in a multiagent system, there is a need to induce cooperation.

An example of **collaborating multiagents** in a non-Internet environment is provided by Alwast and Miliszewska (1995). Their agents are designed to support a DSS for natural resource management. The DAI architecture permits the integration of distributed heterogeneous systems for DSS application. The agents enable the various components of a complex DSS to work together. A system consisting of agents collaborating over networks was created by Arisha et al. (1999). A system with agents cooperating to provide replies to queries was developed by Berg and Wong (2000).

Another example of collaborating agents is provided by Bose (1996), who proposed a framework for automating the execution of collaborative organizational processes performed by multiple organizational members. The agents emulate the work and behavior of human agents. Each of them is capable of acting autonomously, cooperatively, and collectively to achieve the collective goal. The system increases organizational productivity by carrying out several tedious watchdog activities, thereby freeing humans to work on challenging and creative tasks. Bose (1996) describes an example of a travel authorization process that can be divided into subtasks delegated to agents (Figure 17.8).

Another example involves scheduling a meeting. Several agents can cooperate in proposing meeting times and places until a mutually acceptable schedule is found. Note

FIGURE 17.8 COORDINATION AND COLLABORATION IN COOPERATIVE DISTRIBUTED PROBLEM SOLVING: TRAVEL AUTHORIZATION PROCESS

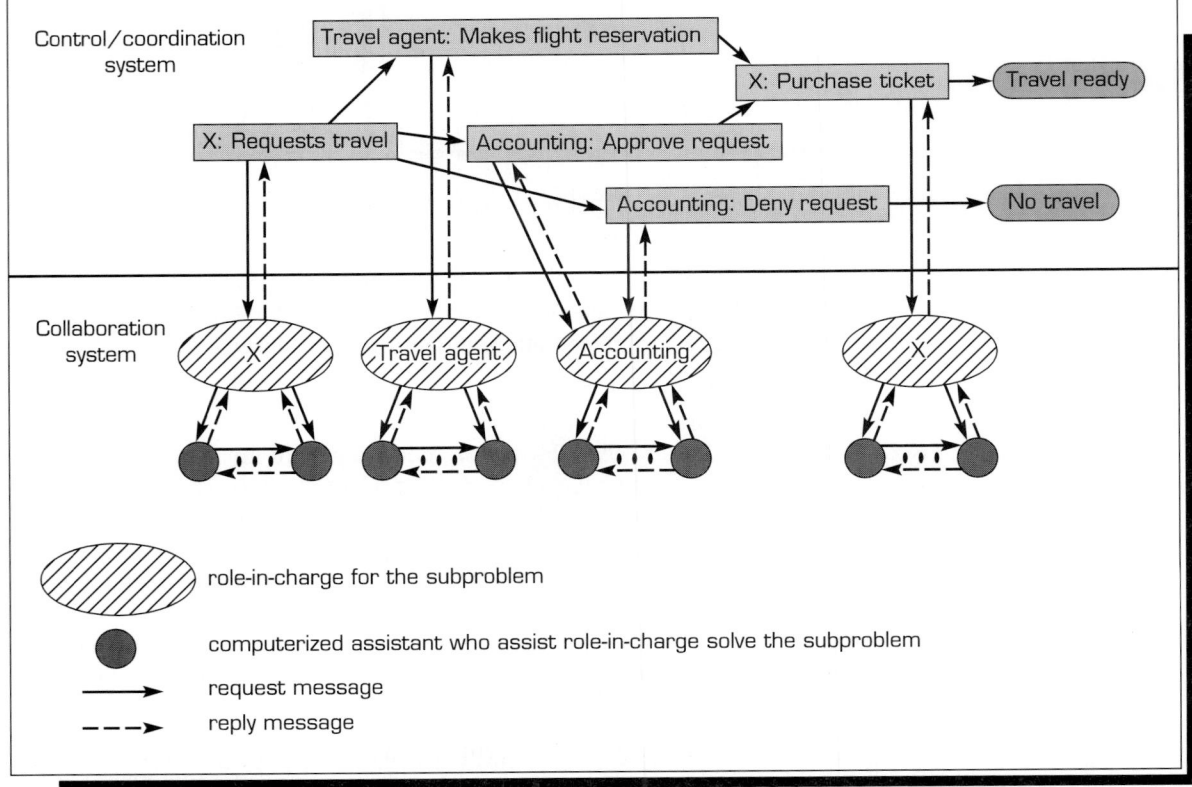

Source: Bose, R. (1996). "Intelligent Agents Framework for Developing Knowledge-Based DSS for Collaborative Organizational Processes." *Expert Systems with Applications,* Vol. 11, No. 3, p. 249.

AIS IN ACTION 17.5

INTELLIGENT AGENTS TRIM PAPERMAKING COSTS

Medison Paper Industries, a 282-employee Maine company was struggling to compete against larger papermaking companies. Costs of transportation from suppliers and to customers seemed to be high, paper loss during production was cutting into profits, and scheduling work was difficult and lengthy.

A cooperative multiagent system, initially developed at Carnegie Mellon University (www.cs.cmu/afs/cs/project/edrc-22) and commercialized by IBM cooperative decision support group (www.research.ibm.com/coopds) was implemented in an attempt to solve the problem.

The knowledge for the system was solicited from human schedulers whose experience over the years created a pool of candidate scheduling solutions.

The agent-based system evaluates each of the solutions in light of multiple business objectives (cost, speed of delivery, and so on). The human schedulers now work with the system interactively, posting "what-if" questions to help find a solution that best fits a set of multiple business objectives that frequently conflict with each other. Working as an intelligent assistant, the system frees the schedulers of real-time computational tasks, giving them time to concentrate on more important tasks.

The system is structured around the concept of an A team, a cyclic network of shared memories and agents in which multiple solution methods cooperate by evolving a shared population of solutions. The agents can modify solutions created by other agents, which leads to better, more diverse solutions.

Traditional approaches to scheduling in the paper industry have involved scheduling each process independently, often using different software packages for each step. Because of the lack of interaction between applications, the combined schedules have been less than satisfactory in the past. They might, for instance, minimize trim waste at the expense of an inefficient, costly vehicle-loading schedule. In contrast, IBM's approach simultaneously considers numerous scheduling objectives and multiple manufacturing and distribution stages in a global multicriteria optimizing framework.

The system cuts paper trim losses by about 6 tons per day at Madison Paper, as well as 10 percent of freight costs, for annual savings of more than $5 million.

Source: Compiled from *IEEE Intelligent Systems,* Mar./Apr. 1999, and from the Carnegie Mellon University and IBM Web sites (Mar. 2000).

---

that a simpler case is that of a single agent that checks the calendars of the participants to determine when all of them are free and then books a free meeting room and notifies the participants.

A multiagent system for assigning air cargo to airline flights in creative ways is presented by Zhu et al. (2000), and the collaboration issue has been researched by Nardi et al. (1998).

A successful commercial system was developed by IBM for improved planning and scheduling operations for certain papermaking plants. The details are provided in AIS in Action 17.5.

COMMUNITIES OF AGENTS

Elofson et al., (1997) introduce the concept of *communities of agents* behaving in believable ways, in the entertainment industry. There is great scope for more sophisticated agents of this form to be used in movies and games, possibly even in generating a new genre of interactive movies. (See Cliff et al. 1999).

17.11 DSS AGENTS

Some of the agents described earlier can be classified as problem solving or DSS agents. (See Kvarroov.com.) A framework for DSS agents has been proposed by Hess et al. (2000), who distinguishes five types: data monitoring, data gathering, modeling, domain managing, and preference learning. Table 17.1 maps these categories against three major characteristics and against three reference points. This table, based on the prior work of Holsapple and Whinston (1996), presents examples from a manufacturing firm DSS.

TABLE 17.1 Example Agents Utilized in the Extension of the Holsapple and Whinston (1996) Manufacturing Firm DSS.

Autonomous Agent	Agent Agent Essential Characteristics			Reference Point		
	Homeostatic Goal	Persistence	Reactivity	Employer/Client	Task	Domain
Data monitoring	Report when any price change crosses threshold values	Stay at supplier's site "forever" or as long as the vendor supplies parts	Capable of detecting vendor price changes	User	Monitor the current rates of the three types of resources and report on them	Vendor site on an extranet
Data gathering	Report discovery of potential suppliers of manufactured parts at reasonable prices	Lifetime of the DSS	Capable of examining directory sites and understanding language used there	User	Look for alternate vendors of specific part; if found, send message back with name and location of source	Travel to directory sites
Modeling	Maintain "optimal" price and resource policies; report significant dollar consequences	Lifetime of the DSS	Capable of receiving inputs from the domain manager agent (DMA) and passing results back to the DMA	Domain manager agent (DMA)	When notified by DMA, formulate an LP model, solve it using Excel's solver, and report solution to DMA	Model base management system (MBMS) of DSS
Domain managing (say, in the DBMS)	Monitor location and tasks of both local and remote agents functioning on behalf of domain activities; respond to all messages.	Lifetime of the DSS	Capable of communicating with agents (even at a distance) and keeping track of their whereabouts	User	Monitor all other agents (both local and remote) acting on behalf of the domain; trigger appropriate actions on hearing from them	Data base management system (DBMS) of DSS (similar agents exist in the MBMS and DGMS)
Preference learning	Learn a specific user's preferences based on the actual history of user/DSS interactions	"Lifetime" of a user of the DSS, even across different sessions	Capable of observing user actions and storing them	User	Record whether specific user takes modeling agent's advice or proceeds on own	Dialog generation and management system (DGMS) of DSS

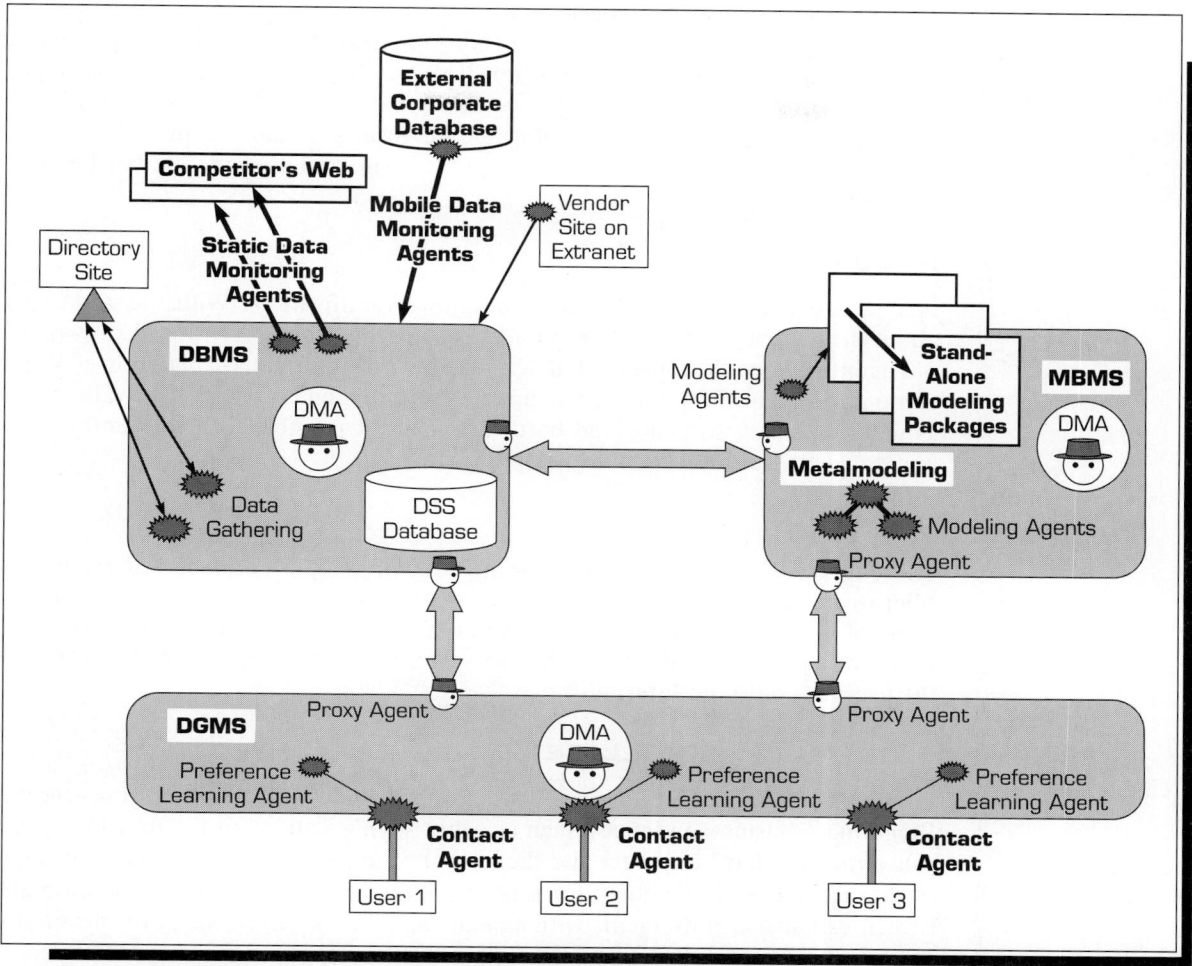

FIGURE 17.9 THE AGENT-ENHANCED GENERAL DSS FRAMEWORK

Furthermore, Hess et al. have proposed a general framework in which they map the five types of agents against the three major components of DSS (data, modeling, user interface). This framework is shown in Figure 17.9, and it can be used as a guide in agent development and research.

17.12 MANAGERIAL ISSUES

The following sections describe some representative managerial issues.

COST JUSTIFICATION

With technology rapidly changing and with intelligent agents still evolving, it may be hard to justify spending lots of money on something that may be obsolete tomorrow. Simple software agents such as wizards found in software products are fairly easy to justify because they are usually included as one of the features of the software product (e.g., in Excel)

Stand-alone agents that perform complex tasks, on the other hand, can be quite expensive. Most of the cost of these agents derives from the tremendous amount of R&D that goes into creating them. In addition, they may be custom programs that require extensive programming time. Justifying agents is like justifying other decision support systems. The benefits are often intangible and the results are hard to quantify, but if you do not invest in the technology, your competitor will, and you may be left behind. (See Hendler, 1999.)

SECURITY

Agents are a technology with many unknown ramifications. With the great concerns about the security of systems, does it make sense that a company would knowingly send out agents that could come back laden with a virus or hiding a Trojan horse? Will other companies even allow unfamiliar agents to visit their systems? Firewalls and other available security software and hardware make it possible to forbid entry to an unknown agent, but it is difficult to stop imposers.

PRIVACY

There are cases in which agents have intruded on people's privacy. For example, some Microsoft users have been informed that the software giant has built "cookies" into some of its packages that capture information about new owners and Web users. This information is delivered back (if the users do not object) to Microsoft by its agent when the user logs onto the Internet.

INDUSTRIAL INTELLIGENCE AND ETHICS

Legitimate industrial intelligence gathering is usually expensive and time-consuming. Illegitimate business practices, such as cyber spying, can be all the more tempting because they are hard to detect and there are no clear-cut rules or laws governing many of these activities. If a competitor is not satisfied with just getting information about a firm, it can also arm its agents with assault capabilities. Given the borderless nature of the Internet, the risk that an unethical firm will compete unfairly by stealing another's costly research and development becomes even more frightening. What is to keep seemingly friendly programs from doing untold damage? Perhaps it will be possible to build an intelligent agent that can discriminate friendly or neutral agents from belligerent outside agents and take appropriate defensive action (Mandry et al. 1999).

OTHER ETHICAL ISSUES

Agents represent a significant new way of interacting with the world. Just as a unique etiquette (netiquette) has evolved on the Internet, there will need to be new definitions of acceptable and unacceptable uses for agents. Who will establish the definitions and the ethical philosophy for how agents are to be used?

New technology is accompanied by new opportunities for those who have access to it. Who will have access to agents? Will all companies have agents? Will those with early access to agents be able to build insurmountable barriers to competition? Will agents displace people from jobs in research and strategic planning?

AGENT LEARNING

The theory behind these agents is that the more you use them, the more they learn and, therefore, the more effective they are. Agents can learn from one of three sources. The first is defined rules established in the programming of the agent. The second is the user interface; in other words, the agent learns the net activities and the preferences of the user. The third source is exterior databases or a knowledge base. The managerial issue is one of justifying the cost (determining which method is most cost-effective) and making sure the agent learns what you want it to learn.

AGENT ACCURACY

Along with agent learning comes agent accuracy. Assuming that the agent develops the ability to learn, the next issue facing managers is the accuracy of the data submitted to and returned by the agent. The inherent desire is to blindly accept recommendations from an agent that has cost so much, both in time and money. But is this wise? Managers must be comfortable with the source from which agents draw data. There must be some control over the quality of this information, or the agent's results will not be believable. Even worse is the possibility that strategic decisions will be made using incorrect information.

HEIGHTENED EXPECTATIONS

With any new technology or product come high expectations. This is especially true when it comes to intelligent agents. The concept of having an agent carry out tasks in only a few minutes that would normally take hours or days to accomplish sounds wonderful. But the reality today is that many agents are not yet a cure-all in the expanding world of information. Because the development of intelligent agents is far from complete, their cost-effectiveness may be small. This will result in disappointment and rejection by people who are not prepared for what they get. Managers pushing for the use of intelligent agents must communicate with all those involved to ensure that expectations are realistic.

SYSTEM ACCEPTANCE

Like the introduction of any new technology, the addition of intelligent agents to an existing system can sometimes create problems. Systems have different architectures and operating systems. This, along with the presence of a whole host of different software packages that maintain databases, can make agents less effective or even nonfunctional. Methods are being developed to provide standards for interagent and agent-to-system interoperability (Finin et al., 1997; Genesereth, 1997).

SYSTEM TECHNOLOGY

As intelligent agents become more powerful, the systems required to run them also must be more powerful. Many companies have obsolete computer systems that are only a few years old. Managers must ensure that before investing in agent technology, their system can provide the resources required by the agents. In addition, agent technology is rapidly expanding, and so system technology flexibility is a must.

STRATEGIC INFORMATION SYSTEMS

Management has a great need to survey the environment for opportunities and for threats to the long-term survival and success of the company. Intelligent agents are an excellent long-term strategic asset a company can develop for gathering data from a variety of sources around the world. Firms that invest in building strategic information systems can create a barrier to entry by being able to anticipate and counter the moves of competitors. Motorola, for example, is often said to be unsurprisable because it keeps seeking information about opportunities as well as potential obstacles and threats.

Clearly companies like Motorola that rely heavily on information gathering will be at the forefront of developing software allowing them to access and process as much data as possible. For an application of intelligent agents to strategic management, see Liu et al. (2000).

❖ CHAPTER HIGHLIGHTS

- There are several definitions of intelligent agents (IA). Basically, they are software entities that execute tasks with some degree of autonomy.
- IA can save time and are consistent.
- Some agents have a considerable amount of autonomy. Others have very little.
- The major characteristics of IA are autonomy, background operation, communication capabilities, and reactivity. Some are mobile, mainly if they are Web-related.
- More autonomous agents must be able to learn and improve their actions.
- The major purpose of IA is to deal with information overload. However, agents can improve productivity, quality, and speed.
- Agents can be classified in several ways, depending on their mission.
- Mobile agents can perform tasks in different locations. Other agents work in one place (such as a server or a workstation).
- Agents can be classified into three major applications types: Internet, EC, and others.
- Multiagent systems can be used to perform tasks more complex than those performed by single agents, but they have not yet matured.
- Intelligent agents play a major role in data mining, helping to find unnoticeable relationships, and quickly providing answers to queries.

❖ KEY WORDS

- agency
- agent
- avatars
- bots
- collaborating multiagents
- data mining
- distributed artificial intelligence (DAI)
- intelligence
- intelligent agent (IA)

- Internet softbot
- key words
- metasearch engines
- mobile agents
- mobility
- multiagent systems
- multiagents
- organizational agents
- personal agent
- personal digital assistants (PDAs)

- private agent
- public agents
- search engines
- social computing
- softbots (intelligent software robots)
- software agents
- Webcasting
- Web mining
- wizards

❖ QUESTIONS FOR REVIEW

1. Define intelligent agent (IA).
2. List the major components of IA.
3. Define the autonomy of IA.
4. List the major characteristics of IA.
5. Define mobile agents.
6. List the major advantages of IA.
7. List and describe the nine types of agents according to IBM.
8. Describe the work of an FAQ agent.

9. Describe how agents that compare prices, and so on, work.
10. Define data mining.
11. Define distributed artificial intelligence (DAI).
12. List the six steps in electronic shopping.
13. Define avatars and explain their role in EC.

❖ QUESTIONS FOR DISCUSSION

1. What are the major characteristics of the information overload problem?
2. Relate the Internet to the information overload problem.
3. How can IA solve the information overload problem?
4. Distinguish between personal and private agents.
5. Discuss the tasks carried out by an e-mail agent.
6. Distinguish between a search engine and a metasearch engine.
7. What is the difference between a browsing agent and a search (indexing) agent?
8. Personalogic and similar agents attempt to learn about people's preferences. Explain how such information can be used in marketing and advertising.
9. What role can IA play in electronic communities?
10. Explain the role of IA in data mining. What is the difference between IA and other methods of data mining?
11. Explain the benefits of NewsAlert and similar agents in reducing information overload.
12. Distinguish between DAI and multiagents.
13. Why is negotiation so important in electronic commerce? What is the advantage of IA negotiation?
14. Review the four levels of IA intelligence. Relate them to software and intelligent agents.
15. Review IBM's IA model: agency, intelligence, mobility. Can you compare a search engine to Personalogic in this model?
16. Explain how interactive characters can increase people's trust in electronic shopping.

❖ EXERCISES

1. Read the paper by Maes et al. (1999) regarding the use of IA in electronic commerce. Examine the categories of applications and find commercial examples of each.
2. Find the relationship between fuzzy logic and DAI (or intelligent agents). Prepare a report. Explain the importance of fuzzy logic systems in this situation.
3. How are IA actually constructed? Investigate the literature and write a report. Visit www.robocup.org and examine their annual competition. Explain how IA are used there.
4. What mundane tasks would you like an intelligent agent to perform for you? List them (you may want to include some tasks that people are handling for you) and describe how an IA could help. Compare your results to those of other class members.
5. Interactive characters play an important role on the Web (Hayes Roth et al., 1998,1999). Visit www.extempo.com and find information on these characters. Also view chevronacr.com. Is there a value to these characters? Prepare a report.

❖ GROUP EXERCISES

1. Contact Microsoft or their resellers. Find out what IA wizards do to improve the use of operating systems, spreadsheets, and other software products. Prepare a report on recent developments.

2. Investigate the use of intelligent agents in electronic commerce. Begin with www.botspot.com. Search recent work described at www.media.mit.edu, www.agents.umbc.edu, and other universities. Prepare a report.

❖ INTERNET EXERCISES

1. Access www.compare.net. Ask the agent to price a specific CD for you. Do you think that you can get the CD cheaper at a local store?

2. Access www.personalogic.com. Use the service to obtain suggestions for music and movies that you may like. Also, access the Web site of Entertainment Connection (www.econnection.com). Watch the recommended movie and listen to the music. How good was the agent's advice? Prepare a report on the relationship between Entertainment Connection and Personalogic.

3. Access Autonomy Inc.'s Web site (www.autonomy.com). Examine the various products and services they provide. Identify where intelligent systems and agents might be used. Examine products for KM, EC, i-WAP, and new media.

4. Access the IBM Corporation agents Web site (www.almaden.ibm.com/cs/wbi.html). Download the current version of Web Browsing Intelligence (WBI, or Webby), install it, and try it. Also, while at this Web site, investigate the white papers on intelligent agents. What is IBM's strategy with regard to agents?

5. Examine Botspot of the Week (www.botspot.com/dailybot/archive.htm). Evaluate the progress of intelligent agents based on Botspot of the Week archive. Then, access Pete Edwards's agent Web site (University of Aberdeen, www.csd.ac.uk/~pedwards/agents.html and www.agents.umbc.edu) and describe the most recent advances found there (alternatively go to www.media.mit.edu; go to "research" and to "software agents").

6. Visit www.firstlook.com and examine the use they make of EC agents.

7. Investigate the latest research on DAI systems and multiagent systems (start with www.dis.cs.umas.edu/dis.html and www.agentlink.org).

8. Access the Computer Science Department at the University of Maryland Baltimore County (www.cs.umbc.edu/agents/). Identify and describe the latest developments on intelligent software agents and agents on, by, and for the Web. Also look at botspot.com's list of shopping agents.

9. Post several queries in a natural language to www.askjeeves.com and to www.nefdesk.com. Compare the top 10 answers provided. What is the major difference between the two sites? Now enter www.botspot.com and look for Eliza and for Shallow Red. Prepare a report.

PART

VI

IMPLEMENTATION, INTEGRATION, AND IMPACTS

The management support systems described in this book and Web site (www.prenhall.com/turban) can be implemented as stand-alone systems, but they also can be integrated with other computer-based information systems. Certain integrations occur when the systems are being developed; others occur only during implementation. Part VI begins in Chapter 18 with coverage of the Implementation and Integration of Management Support Systems. MSS technologies continue to have sweeping impacts on organizations and society. Development of learning organizations, the Internet/World Wide Web, easy to use, inexpensive graphical user interfaces, and other developments are reshaping the way we work and live. Chapter 19 introduces the reader to some major issues in organizational and societal impacts of Management Support Systems.

IMPLEMENTING AND INTEGRATING MANAGEMENT SUPPORT SYSTEMS[1]

Building MSS is the first phase of supporting decision making and problem solving. Perhaps it is more important to introduce these systems into organizations and use them for their intended purpose. In this chapter, we introduce two main topics. First, we discuss the issue of implementation and follow with a special issue of implementation: the integration of MSS technologies among themselves and with other information systems. The specific sections of this chapter are as follows:

18.1 OPENING VIGNETTE: INCA EXPERT SYSTEMS FOR THE SWIFT NETWORK[2]

The Society for Worldwide Interbank Financial Telecommunication (SWIFT) network provides automated international message-processing and message transmission services between financial institutions on all continents, with banks in more than

---

[1]This chapter was updated by Narasimha Bolloju of The City University of Hong Kong.
[2]Adapted from R. Phelps et al., "INCA—An Innovative Approach to Constructing Large-scale, Real-time Expert Systems," in A. Rappaport and R. Smith, (eds.), *Innovative Applications of Artificial Intelligence*, Menlo Park, CA: AAAI Press/MIT Press, 1991.

60 countries, totaling more than 3,000 users (mostly banks). The SWIFT network handled more than 1 million messages per day in the early 1990s. Originally, day-to-day control of the network, running over telephone lines or dedicated links, was done by teams of operators working 24 hours a day at each of eight active systems called switches. The switches coordinate the network communications. There are four switches located at each of two control centers, one in the United States and another in The Netherlands. A number of "events" (node failures, open communication links, and so on) that affect the network can occur, and dealing with these events required expertise.

A real-time decision-making system was necessary for network control. *The system could not fail* (a backup ES running on a separate workstation was also deployed). The Intelligent Network Controller Assistant (INCA) was designed specifically to filter incoming events, determine which combinations indicate problems, and display problems requiring attention. It was a core business application. Developing working prototypes that eventually converged on a final version was not possible. INCA had to run when deployed.

A special software development methodology was developed and followed to ensure tight quality control. Simultaneously, the development process attempted to allow the flexibility required for AI development where incremental extraction of knowledge from the experts was not possible. The system could not degrade or fail, and a traditional development approach could not be taken. INCA could be introduced online only once. Thus, rapid prototyping refinements could not be done with the working system. However, a modular prototyping approach was taken.

Schedules were set. The hardware and software were standard workstations running LISP with an ES shell (Dantes). The future users and experts were involved in every implementation phase, including quality control sign-off and installation approval. User training plans were created and implemented simultaneously with system development, along with documentation.

An object-oriented paradigm was used for automated event handling. Events, identified by online monitoring of the network, trigger rules to fire, thus avoiding complicated and time-consuming searches through the knowledge base.

A core team of five people developed INCA: three from SWIFT's corporate research group and two from operations. During the first half of the development project, there were also two knowledge engineers from Texas Instruments.

After a brief prototyping exercise, the INCA project started in April 1989. In October 1989 the first deployment was performed at one control center. Its processing functions were introduced in modular phases to minimize risks. In February 1990 INCA became fully operational at the Netherlands control center, and in May 1990 at the United States center. Minor bugs were fixed over the next several months, and maintenance was gradually turned over to the internal system support group.

INCA can automatically handle 97 percent of all events. There are now only two INCA teams, each of which can do the work of the original eight teams. The estimated staff reduction is 50. The quick, on-schedule development of this complex system prompted a series of requests for additional features and functions to handle other network aspects.

❖ QUESTIONS FOR THE OPENING VIGNETTE

1. Why was INCA not allowed to fail? That is, what would the consequences of failure be?

2. Why couldn't rapid prototyping be used as an implementation method?

3. Describe some of the unique aspects of INCA that required a modified development approach.
4. Describe some difficulties in developing a system design methodology while developing the system.
5. Why did the object-oriented approach make sense here? Do you think that INCA used a variant of forward chaining or backward chaining for its inference engine? Why?

18.2 IMPLEMENTATION: AN OVERVIEW

The Opening Vignette illustrates several major points about system implementation. The most important one is that there may be situations where standard methods do not work and custom implementation methods must be designed, tested, and implemented along with the system development. It also clearly shows that users must be involved in every phase of the development (Barki and Hartwick, 1994), management support is crucial (though not explicitly mentioned, INCA was being designed as a core business system), and the experts must be cooperative. The criteria for success were clearly defined (which is not always true in the initial phases of ES development). INCA is an expert system that communicates directly with other systems. Finally, the Opening Vignette demonstrates that a large-scale, real-time ES can be developed on schedule and with the same reliability expected of conventional MIS.

INTRODUCTION

As with any other computer-based information system, implementation of MSS is not always successful. For example, there is increasing evidence that AI technologies, and especially expert systems, fail at an extremely high rate (Gill, 1995; Keyes, 1989; and Yorman, 1988). Several instances of failure of expert systems are not entirely due to technical reasons. AIS in Focus 18.1 illustrates failure of an expert system due to nontechnical problems in implementation. Implementation is an ongoing process of preparing an organization for the new system and introducing the system in such a way as to help ensure its success. For a detailed description of a nine-phase implementation process, see the Northfield Company case study at www.eye-ris.com/casestudies/index.htm.

MSS technology implementation is complex because these systems are not merely information systems that collect, manipulate, and distribute information. Rather, they are linked to tasks that may significantly change the manner in which organizations operate. Nevertheless, many of the implementation factors are common to any information system. For an overview, see Swanson (1988), Ballantine et al. (1996), DeLeon and McLean (1992), Guimaraes et al. (1992, 1996), and Kappelman and McLean (1991, 1994). Hence, the discussion in the following sections is limited to some factors directly related to MSS.

WHAT IS IMPLEMENTATION?

Machiavelli astutely noted more than 450 years ago that there is "nothing more difficult to carry out, nor more doubtful of success, nor more dangerous to handle, than to initiate a new order of things." The implementation of MSS is in effect the initiation of a new order of things or, in contemporary language, the *introduction of change*.[3]

---

[3]It has been said that the only people who really like *change* are babies with dirty diapers.

AIS IN FOCUS 18.1

AN EXPERT SYSTEM THAT WAS

In the production of cosmetics Mary Kay used a team of executives to market its products. This process attempted to iron out potential weaknesses before production, however, costly errors were resulting from such problems as product-container incompatibility, interaction of chemical compositions, and marketing requirements with regard to type of dispenser and packaging.

An eclectic group of people representing various areas of formulation would meet over a period of 6 weeks to make decisions based on a loosely structured process. The marketing team, constrained by costs, would give their requirements to the product formulator and the package engineer at the same time. Often asking for designs that proved beyond the allocated budget or technical possibilities or without knowing the ultimate product formulation, resulted in more meetings and redesigning.

Mary Kay decided to implement an expert system to help. In an effort to keep costs to a minimum, it engaged the services of a research university that developed a system using a product from Neuron Data involving 40 rules and consisting of a mathematical tool plus two ES components. The first component was able to select compatible packages for a given cosmetic product and test product and package suitability; the second ES component used this information to guide users through design and to determine associated production costs.

At first this was a tremendous success; there was a clear match between the abilities of the system technology and the nature of the problem. The director of package design enthusiastically embraced the system solution. The entire decision process could be made in 2 weeks with no inherent redesign. By formulating what was previously largely intuitive, the ES improved understanding of the decision process itself, increasing the team's confidence. By reducing the time required for new product development, executives were freed for other tasks, hence the team met only rarely to ratify the recommendations of the ES.

However, without support staff to maintain the ES or to update the Neuron Data software, no one knew how to add new rules. Even the firm's IT unit was unable to help, and so the system fell into disuse.

More importantly, when the director of package design left the firm, so did his enthusiasm. No one else was willing to make the effort necessary to maintain the ES or sustain the project. Without firm managerial direction about the importance of the system to the firm's success, the whole project floundered.

Source: Condensed from R. G. Vedder et al., "An Expert System That Was," *Proceedings,* DSI International, Athens, Greece, July 1999.

The definition of implementation is complicated because implementation is a long, involved process with vague boundaries. *Implementation* can be defined simplistically as getting a newly developed or significantly changed system to be used by those for whom it was intended.

MSS implementation is an ongoing process that occurs during the entire development of the system, from the original suggestion through the feasibility study, system analysis and design, programming, training, conversion, and installation. IS professionals often call implementation the final stage in the system's life cycle. The definition of implementation for MSS is more complicated because of the iterative nature of their development.

If the MSS is intended for repetitive use, then implementation means a commitment to routine and frequent use of the system, or **institutionalization.** For ad hoc decisions, implementation means a one-time use of the system.

PARTIAL IMPLEMENTATION

Feasibility decisions are often made on the assumption of a payoff to be realized if total implementation is achieved. In reality, a 90 percent or even 70 percent implementation is likely. One reason for less than 100 percent implementation is that a change introduced at one place in the system may precipitate compensatory and possibly negative impacts elsewhere. Management may then drop the parts of the project that created the negative impacts. Thus, less than 100 percent of the original project is implemented. Other reasons for partial implementation are budget reductions or cost overruns.

MEASURING IMPLEMENTATION SUCCESS

The definition of implementation includes the concept of success. A number of possible indicators for a successful information system have been suggested in various implementation studies. Unless a set of success measures is agreed on, it will be difficult to evaluate the success of a system. Dickson and Powers (1973) suggest five independent criteria for success:

- Ratio of actual project execution time to estimated time
- Ratio of actual cost to develop the project to the budgeted cost for the project
- Managerial attitudes toward the system
- How well managers' information needs are satisfied
- Impact of the project on the computer operations of the firm.

Other measures for judging the success of MSS include the following:

- Use of the system, as measured by the intended or actual use (e.g., the number of inquiries made of an online system)
- User satisfaction (measured with a questionnaire or by an interview; see Swanson [1988] and Chapter 4)
- Favorable attitudes (either as an objective by itself or as a predictor of the use of a system)
- Degree to which a system accomplishes its original objectives (e.g., for an ES, whether it provides reasonable advice)
- Payoff to the organization (through cost reductions, increased sales, and so on)
- Benefit/cost ratios
- Degree of institutionalization of MSS in the organization.

In evaluating DSS, one can use a methodology such as the one offered by Athappilly (1985). Because of the diversity of DSS, measuring its success can be difficult. [Typical success measures are given by Guimaraes et al. (1992) and Sprague and Watson (1996a).] In evaluating the success of expert systems in particular, additional measures of success can be used:

- Degree to which the system agrees with a human expert when both of them are presented with the same cases
- Adequacy of the explanations provided by the system
- Percentage of cases submitted to the system for which advice was not given
- Improvement of the ES on the learning curve, or how fast the system reaches maturity.

Some contributing factors to DSS success include user involvement, user training, top management support, information sources, level of managerial activity being supported, and the characteristics of the tasks involved (structure, uncertainty, difficulty, and interdependence) (Guimaraes et al., 1992).

For an overview of expert system evaluation, see Grogono et al. (1991), Guimaraes et al. (1996), and Yoon et al. (1995). For a detailed technical approach to MSS evaluation, see Adelman (1992).

DSS IN FOCUS 18.2

THE SUCCESS OF DSS

In a survey conducted by Meador et al. (1984a), respondents were asked to rate their agreement with several statements indicating the success of their DSS. These statements included the following:

- The DSS fits in well with our planning methods.
- It fits in well with our reporting methods.
- It fits in well with our way of thinking about problems.
- It has improved our way of thinking about problems.

- It fits in well with the politics of how decisions are made around here.
- Decisions reached with the aid of the DSS are usually implemented.
- It has resulted in substantial time savings.
- It has been cost-effective.
- It has been valuable relative to its cost.
- It will continue to be useful to our organization for a number of years.
- It has so far been a success.

IMPLEMENTATION FAILURES

The implementation of information systems involves several problems that have been subjected to extensive research (Lucas, 1995; Beckley and Gaines, 1990). However, very little evidence is available to substantiate the true extent and magnitude of these problems. Actual information about implementation failures is a closely held secret in many organizations, especially when millions of dollars have been spent on uncompleted or incorrect systems (Kimball and Strehlo, 1994).

The expected synergy of human and machine in interactive DSS simply has not developed, and the number of actual instances of managers sitting at a computer solving problems is growing very slowly.

Although not many formal data are available on MSS failures, there are many informal reports on unsuccessful implementation. A series of events that led to the failure of an expert system are illustrated in AIS in Focus 18.1. For an example of a major operation support system deemed a technical success but an organizational failure, see Coe (1996). For failures and successes of ES, see Duchessi and O'Keefe (1992). Why such systems fail and the necessary conditions for minimizing failures are discussed in the following sections.

18.3 THE MAJOR ISSUES OF IMPLEMENTATION

MODELS OF IMPLEMENTATION

The importance of the implementation problem has led to extensive research on the determinants of successful implementation (Alavi and Joachimsthaler, 1992). Research began several decades ago with studies conducted by behavioral scientists to examine resistance to change. The management science field has been preoccupied with this issue since the late 1950s, and MIS researchers have been studying implementation issues for more than two decades. Considerable numbers of ideas and theories have accumulated, and several early models of implementation have been proposed for information systems (Lucas, 1981; Meredith, 1981; Swanson, 1988). Because of the large failure rate of ES, several papers have appeared that have attempted to analyze the problems and prescribe remedies. For example, see Barsanti (1990), Gill (1995), and Medsker and Liebowitz (1994). Managerial issues in ES implementation are explored by Hauser and Hebert (1992) and Kunnathur et al. (1996).

In a study conducted by Sviokla (1996) on the introduction of expert systems, it was found that managers need to assemble constellations of actions, consider political ramifications, manage the momentum of the project, and work to achieve economies of scale. Thus, it can be seen that many factors could determine the degree of success of any information system. The term *factor* or *success factor* refers to a condition present in the organization (such as the support of top management) or to the specific application (such as the use of appropriate software). Success factors can be divided into two categories: generic factors that relate to any information system and factors related specifically to MSS technologies. A methodology for overcoming organizational and behavioral implementation barriers can be found in Dologite and Mockler (1989).

The success factors of implementation discussed in this section are grouped in nine categories (Figure 18.1). These categories are often interrelated, and some factors can be classified in two or more categories. Thus, this classification is a rough attempt to organize the many factors involved.

TECHNICAL FACTORS

Technical factors relate to the mechanics of the implementation procedure. Several of major importance are listed in Table 18.1.

Technical issues can be classified in two categories: technical constraints, which result mainly from the limitations of available technology, and technical problems, which are not the result of the technology but are caused by other factors such as scarcity of resources. The first category may disappear when new technologies are developed. The second category can be solved by increasing the available resources.

FIGURE 18.1   DETERMINANTS OF SUCCESSFUL MSS IMPLEMENTATION

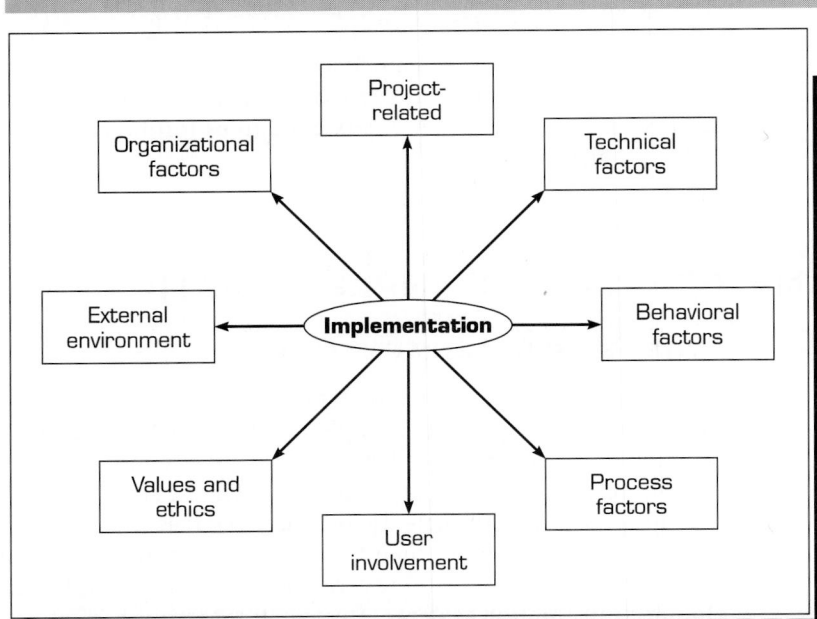

TABLE 18.1   Technical Implementation Issues

- Level of complexity (must be low)
- System response time and reliability (must be high)
- Inadequate functions (functions are needed)
- Lack of equipment (hardware and software can help)
- Lack of standardization (standards help integration and dissemination)
- Problems with the networks (such as connectivity); distributed MSS are on the rise
- Mismatch of hardware or software
- Low level of the technical capacity of the project team

TABLE 18.2   Behavioral Factors

Factors	Description
Decision styles	Symbolic processing of AI is heuristic; DSS and ANN are analytic.
Need for explanation	ES provides explanation, ANN does not. DSS may provide partial explanation. Explanation can reduce resistance to change.
Organizational climate	Some organizations lead and support innovations and new technologies, whereas others wait and lag behind in making changes.
Organizational expectations	Overexpectation can result in disappointments and termination of innovation. Overexpectation was observed in most early intelligent systems.
Resistance to change	Can be strong in MSS because the impacts may be significant. Many can resist (Alter, 1980; Guimaraes et al. 1992) (see AIS in Focus 18.3).

BEHAVIORAL FACTORS

The implementation of computer-based information systems in general, and MSS in particular, is affected by the way people perceive these systems and by how they behave in accepting them. For a discussion of behavioral factors in ES, see Suh and Suh (1993) and Berry and Hart (1990). The major behavioral factors are summarized in Table 18.2. AIS in Focus 18.3 presents different resisters in organizations to the use of expert systems.

User resistance is a major behavioral factor associated with the adoption of new systems. Jiang et al. (2000) have compiled, from a number of sources, the following reasons that employees resist new systems:

- Change in job content
- Loss of status
- Change in interpersonal relationships
- Loss of power
- Change in decision-making approach
- Uncertainty or unfamiliarity or misinformation
- Job security.

The most significant reason, among the above, for resisting DSS compared to transaction-processing systems is change in the decision-making approach. Jiang et al.

AIS IN FOCUS 18.3

THE RESISTERS TO EXPERT SYSTEMS

- *Managers.* Some fear their jobs will be automated or become less important.
- *Experts.* Some fear undue exposure or a reduction in importance; others are afraid of losing their jobs.
- *Nonexperts.* Some fear lack of recognition and less opportunity to prove themselves. Others are afraid of becoming unimportant.
- *CIO.* Some see consultants and vendors and fear a decline in their empires.
- *The generally insecure.* Some in every organization are routinely insecure and afraid of any change.

- *Technologists.* Some may fear that if the technology is outside their IS department, they will lose power and control.
- *Users.* Some resist computerization in general and experience problems with the human–machine interface.
- *Training staff and management.* Some may fear that self-instruction by interacting with the expert system will diminish their role.
- *Unions.* Some see resistance as an opportunity to gain membership.

Source: Based on Beerel (1993).

(2000), based on the findings of their study involving 66 managers from a wide variety of industries, suggest the following strategies for dealing with user resistance to DSS:

- Participative strategies such as user involvement were most desired by the subjects.
- Direct management methods such as arranging a job transfer, giving separation pay, and reassignment were viewed negatively by the subjects.
- User training–related strategies such as conducting orientation sessions, pacing conversion to allow for adjustment, and retraining employees were perceived to be more critical in the context of TPS than of DSS.

The technology acceptance model (TAM) developed by Davis (1989) explains user behavior across a broad range of end-user computing technologies and user populations in accepting information technology. User acceptance of new technology and systems is often determined by the perceived usefulness and perceived ease of use. For details on the acceptance of new information systems, see Davis (1989) and Liao and Landry (2000).

User acceptance and adoption of MSS are also linked to the awareness of users and their attitude toward use of a particular system. From a survey of attitudes toward expert system provision, Sangster (1994) found that more than 50 percent of users check its response and only about 17 percent of users follow its advice without question. It was suggested that a major educational initiative is required to enhance user awareness and understanding of the nature of expert systems.

PROCESS FACTORS

The way in which the process of developing and implementing MSS is managed can greatly influence the success of implementation. The following topics are important.

TOP MANAGEMENT SUPPORT

Top management support has long been recognized as one of the most important ingredients in the introduction of any organizational change (Meredith, 1981), and this has also been found to be true for expert systems (Kunnathur et al., 1996; Tyran and

George, 1993). For ES, the level of top management support directly influences the level of success.

An important aspect in MSS and especially ES is the need for continuous financial support to maintain the systems. Without a commitment for such support, projects are doomed. An example is the famous XCON ES, whose maintenance costs became so large that management had to completely reprogram the system at a large one-time charge to reduce the costs and avoid a failure (Barker and O'Connor, 1989).

There are only a few studies dealing with methods for increasing top management support for MSS. For example, Rockart and Crescenzi (1984) have proposed a three-phase process to encourage more meaningful involvement of senior managers in EIS projects: (1) linking management needs of the business to the proposed information system, (2) developing system priorities and gaining confidence in the recommended system, and (3) rapid development of low-risk managerially useful systems. The third phase is easily attainable for expert systems by using shells and rapid prototyping. Another model, proposed by Young (1987), recommends five activities: receiving executive guidance, forming a steering committee, educating senior management, developing functional budgets, and explaining tactical information system processes to senior managers.

MANAGEMENT AND USER COMMITMENT

Support, as described above, means understanding issues, participating, and making contributions. It is significantly different, however, from **user commitment.** Ginzberg (1981) has shown that two kinds of commitment are required for successful implementation. The first is a commitment to the project itself, and the second is a commitment to change. In expert systems, it is important to secure the experts' commitment (Tyran and George, 1993; Wong and Chong, 1992; Yoon et al., 1995).

INSTITUTIONALIZATION

Institutionalization is a process through which an MSS becomes incorporated as an ongoing part of organizational activities. Institutionalization clearly points to successful implementation. It also helps to create a supportive organizational culture for future applications.

LENGTH OF TIME USERS HAVE BEEN USING COMPUTERS AND MSS

The length of time that a user has been using computers has been shown to be a critical factor contributing to satisfaction with a decision support system (Sanders and Courtney, 1985; Sprague and Watson, 1996a). In general, research showed that the longer people use a DSS, the more satisfied they become. We can assume that the same is true for other MSS technologies because both support managerial processes.

USER INVOLVEMENT

User involvement is participation in the system development process by users or representatives of the user group. It is almost an axiom in the MIS literature that user involvement is a necessary condition for successful development of a CBIS (Ives and Olson, 1984; Sprague and Watson, 1996a). For user involvement in DSS and ES, see Barki and Hartwick (1994), Despres and Rosenthal-Sabroux (1992), Tyran and George (1993), Yoon et al. (1995), and Jiang et al. (2000). In expert systems, user involvement is less important than in DSS because the builder may not know who the users are going to be. It is only in the phases of testing and improving systems that user involvement becomes important. In building EIS, user involvement is a *must* because the system is tailored to the users (Rainer and Watson, 1995a, b; Watson et al., 1997).

Although there is agreement that user involvement is important, determining when it should occur and how much is appropriate are questions that have received inadequate research attention. In user-developed systems, the user obviously is very much involved. When teams are used, the involvement issue becomes fairly complex.

User involvement takes on a slightly different meaning with regard to a DSS than with traditional computer applications. In the latter, users are primarily involved in the planning stage and in testing and evaluation. In regard to DSS development, heavy user involvement is advocated throughout the developmental process, with a considerable amount of direct management participation. This joint application development (JAD) procedure is strongly recommended.

Table 18.3 depicts the results of a study (Sprague and Watson, 1996a) on management involvement in six phases of the DSS system development life cycle. The results reveal that there is substantial involvement in all phases of DSS development. Also evident from the data is that top management had almost no involvement in the building and testing phase of the decision support system and played only a small role in its demonstration. Middle management was deeply involved in all phases of the development process. The generally low levels of involvement by lower management can be explained by the fact that the systems studied were almost exclusively designed to support middle- or top-management decision making.

GOALS, PLANS, AND COMMUNICATIONS

The mission of the project, the responsibilities, the constraints, and the plans must all be clear. Plans and schedules for the project must be available, and sufficient information must be accessible to all participants. Formal lines of communication must be established among all concerned parties. In ES, the knowledge engineer is responsible for the communication among management, users, and experts. Much of ES success depends on his or her communication ability.

ORGANIZATIONAL FACTORS

Several organizational factors that are particularly important for MSS are discussed briefly in this section.

COMPETENCE (SKILLS) AND ORGANIZATION OF THE MSS TEAM

The participants' skills, especially those of the DSS builder and the technical support, were found to be critical for the success of DSS by Meador et al. (1984a) and of ES by Tyran and George (1993). The responsibility for the development and implementation of DSS is also an important factor. Studies show that most DSS development is controlled by users.

TABLE 18.3 Management Involvement in DSS Development: Percentage of Companies with Management Involvement at Each Management Level and Development Stage

Phase in Life Cycle	Lower	Middle	Top	Any Level
Conceptualization	0	61	61	100
Information requirements	0	78	61	100
System building	11	72	6	78
System testing	11	72	6	83
System demonstration	11	78	28	89
System acceptance	0	72	67	100

Source: Adapted from Sprague and Watson (1996a).

ADEQUACY OF RESOURCES

The success of any MSS project depends on the degree to which organizational arrangements facilitate access to the required computer system and other resources. Success depends on factors such as availability of personal computers and workstations, quality of the local area network, accessibility of databases, and user fees. Other factors include support and help facilities (such as the availability of a help center), maintenance of software (Swanson, 1988), and availability of hardware. [For ES see Wong and Chong (1992).]

RELATIONSHIP WITH THE INFORMATION SYSTEM DEPARTMENT

Many MSS applications may need to be connected to the organization's database. The existing information system must be capable of providing current and historical data. Distributed MSS requires the use of corporate networks and the Internet. Therefore, the user's relationship with the information system department may be crucial to the success of MSS.

ORGANIZATIONAL POLITICS

As an organization's growth slows, internal relationships tend to stabilize, division of authority and power is negotiated, and a sense of security and well-being sets in. Implementation of a large-scale MSS project may threaten this equilibrium and arouse opposition to the project. This is where politics often enters the picture. The prevalence of politics in organizations, especially large ones, is often underestimated or ignored. However, the successful implementation of a project may well depend on politics. The MSS team leader should be advised not to remain neutral but to become involved, learn the rules, and determine the power centers and cliques in the organization. For further discussion see Markus (1983), Carlsson and Walden (1995), and Gaskin (1997).

OTHER ORGANIZATIONAL FACTORS

Other organizational factors important in MSS implementation are the role of the **system advocate** (sponsor) who initiated the project and the compatibility of the system with the organizational and personal goals of the participants.

VALUES AND ETHICS

Management is responsible for considering the ethics and values involved in implementing an MSS project. Three points are important:

- *Goals of the project.* Because the process of implementation is based on an attempt to attain organizational or departmental goals, the development team should decide whether the ultimate goals are ethical. The team should also determine whether the goals are ethical for the people who are crucial to the implementation process.
- *Implementation process.* Another question the builders should ask is whether the implementation process is ethical or even legal. Although the goals are ethical, the implementation process itself may not be; for example, consider an attempt to attain a sales goal through violation of a government antitrust law.
- *Possible impact on other systems.* The goals and processes may both be ethical, but the impact of the implemented project on another system may not be.

EXTERNAL ENVIRONMENT

MSS implementation may be affected by factors outside the immediate area of the development team. The external environment includes legal, social, economic, political, and other factors that could impact the project implementation either positively or negatively.

For example, government regulations regarding telecommunications across international borders may restrict EDI or the use of an otherwise successful EIS to a single country. Legal considerations may limit the use of an ES because developers may be afraid of legal action if the advice rendered by the ES leads to damages. One example of restricting electronic commerce occurred in early 1997 when the French government required that all Web sites based in France be in French. (Some legal issues are discussed in the next chapter.) Other issues relate to cross-cultural impacts of information systems in global organizations [see Ishman (1996) for a recent study on measuring success in cross-cultural environments]. Vendors, research institutions, venture capital organizations, and universities can all play an important role in MSS implementation. Finally, Internet regulations may limit advertisements and some electronic commerce.

PROJECT-RELATED FACTORS

Most of the factors discussed in the previous sections can be considered elements in the implementation climate. The climate consists of the general conditions surrounding any application implementation; that is, climate is independent of any particular project. A favorable climate is helpful but not sufficient (Kunnathur et al., 1996). Each project must be evaluated on its own merits, such as its importance to the organization and its members. It must also satisfy certain cost–benefit criteria. Evaluation of a project involves several dimensions and requires the consideration of several factors. For information systems in general, these factors, according to Meredith (1981), can be described as follows:

- An important or major problem that needs to be resolved
- An opportunity that needs to be evaluated
- Urgency of solving the problem
- High-profit contribution of the problem area
- Contribution of the problem area to growth
- Substantial resources tied to the problem area
- Demonstrable payoff if the problem is solved.

Several of these factors are highlighted in the discussion that follows.

EXPECTATIONS FOR A SPECIFIC SYSTEM

Expectations on the part of users as to how a system will contribute to their performance and the resultant rewards can greatly affect which system is used (Robey, 1979). Furthermore, as systems are developed, the actual contribution may be scaled down or even changed dramatically. **Overexpectations** were observed for AI technologies, which sometimes are presented as being magical (Chapter 17). Shim (1999) examined the benefits of expert systems as perceived by IS professionals who have used ES in their operations and presented the following findings:

- Organizations had relatively high expectations regarding the benefits that would arise from ES use.
- Organizations had expected greater benefits in the value-added and productivity areas as compared to the managerial area.
- Actual benefits met the expectations related to consistency of decisions and managerial control.
- Actual benefits from ES use were only moderate or small and did not meet the expectations in all other areas.

COST–BENEFIT ANALYSIS

Any CBIS application can be viewed as an alternative investment. As such, the application should show not only a payoff but also an advantage over other investment alternatives, including the option of doing nothing. Since the mid-1980s, pressures to justify information systems, including MSS systems, have increased. Effective implementation depends to a great extent on the ability to make such justifications.

The issue of **cost–benefit analysis** was discussed in Chapter 6 for DSS, and in Chapter 14 for ES. Note that empirical studies indicate that very few companies conduct cost–benefit analyses on their DSS (Sprague and Watson, 1996a; Money et al., 1988), EIS (Watson et al., 1996), or ES (Turban and Liebowitz, 1992). Instead, they use a value analysis that includes nonmonetary benefits (Tsai et al., 1994a). Rosenstein (1999) describes a methodology for measuring the costs and benefits from DSS in a health care system environment. However, Sviokla (1996) argues that successful implementation of systems and technology for use by knowledge workers requires significant motivation beyond short-term individual economic benefits.

SELECTION OF PROJECTS
For a project to be implemented successfully, it must be compatible with the particular organization. This fit must occur at three levels: individual, small group, and organizational. For a comprehensive discussion of selecting projects for expert systems, see Medsker and Liebowitz (1994) and Awad (1996).

PROJECT MANAGEMENT
Several practical **project management** questions should be answered before implementation of the MSS project:

- Who will be responsible for executing each portion of the project?
- When must each part be completed?
- What resources (in addition to money) will be required?
- What information is needed?

For a discussion of project management for ES development, see Turban and Liebowitz (1992).

AVAILABILITY OF FINANCING AND OTHER RESOURCES
All required financing, cash flows, identification of sources, and assurances of funds should be planned in advance. Commitments should be secured so that money will be available when needed. Lack of appropriate financing is often cited as a major obstacle to implementation or continuous use of large-scale systems. The technical expertise of the builders is especially important in EIS and intelligent systems (Tyran and George, 1993).

TIMING AND PRIORITY
Two interrelated factors in project implementation are timing and priority. For example, an MSS builder may find that an issue considered very important at the time of the feasibility study is not as important at implementation time. Usually, timing and priority are uncontrollable factors as far as the MSS team is concerned.

18.4 IMPLEMENTATION STRATEGIES

During the last 25 years, many implementation strategies have been suggested for management science and information systems. Cule et al. (2000) recommend strategies to prevent IS project failures that center around the processes of risk identification and selection of appropriate managerial behavior to mitigate each risk. Many of these suggestions can also be used as guidelines in implementing DSS and ES. The purpose of this section is to summarize strategies developed specifically for DSS and ES.

IMPLEMENTATION STRATEGIES FOR DSS

Implementation strategies for DSS can be divided into four major categories:

- Divide the project into manageable pieces.
- Keep the solution simple.
- Develop a satisfactory support base.
- Meet user needs and institutionalize the system.

In general terms, each of these categories may seem obvious. Given a choice, who would want to provide a system that does not meet user needs or does not have a satisfactory support base? However, there are a number of distinct strategies under each heading. And as outlined in Table 18.4, each one of these strategies has a certain purpose and certain pitfalls.

EXPERT SYSTEM IMPLEMENTATION

The following topics are especially important in ES implementation:

- Quality of the system
- Cooperation of the experts
- Conditions that justify the need for a particular ES.

A brief discussion of these topics follows.

QUALITY OF THE SYSTEM

The success of ES depends on the quality of the system. Buchanan and Shortliffe (1984) believe that the following seven features should be present in a good ES:

- The ES should be developed to fulfill a recognized need.
- The ES should be easy to use even by a novice.
- The ES should be able to increase the expertise of the user.
- The ES should have exploration capabilities.
- The program should be able to respond to simple questions.
- The system should be capable of learning new knowledge (i.e., the system should be able to ask questions to gain additional information).
- The program knowledge should be easily modified (that is, add, delete, and changed).

These features are necessary but far from sufficient for a successful ES.

THE COOPERATION OF EXPERTS

For an ES to be successfully implemented it must give good advice. Such advice depends, most of all, on the cooperation of the domain expert. The following are some questions about experts' cooperation that must be discussed before building an ES:

- Should the experts be compensated for their contribution (e.g., in the form of royalties, a special reward, or payment)?
- How can one tell whether the experts are telling the truth about the way they solve problems?
- How can the experts be assured that they will not lose their jobs, or that their jobs will not be deemphasized, once the ES is fully operational?
- Are the experts concerned about other people in the organization whose jobs may suffer because of the introduction of ES, and what can management do in such cases?

In general, management should use incentives to influence the experts so that they will cooperate fully with the knowledge engineer. The experts have considerable power,

TABLE 18.4   DSS Implementation Strategies

Implementation Strategy	Typical Situation or Purpose	Pitfalls Encountered
Divide project into manageable pieces.	Minimize the risk of developing a large, failing system.	It may be difficult to integrate the pieces if they are too small.
Use Prototypes.	Success depends on novel concepts. Test the concepts before committing to the complete system.	Reactions to the prototype usually differ from reactions to a final deployed system.
Evolutionary approach.	Attempts to reduce feedback loops between implementer and clients and between intentions and products.	Users must live with continuous change.
Develop a series of tools.	Meets ad hoc analysis needs with databases and small models to be created, modified, and discarded.	Applicability is limited. Maintenance costs for infrequently used data.
Keep the solution simple.	Encourage use so as not to frighten users.	Usually beneficial but can lead to misrepresentation, misunderstanding, and misuse.
Be simple.	For naturally simple systems, this is not an issue. For complex systems or situations, select simple approaches if possible.	Some business problems are just not simple. Requiring simple solutions may lead to ineffective systems.
Hide complexity (encapsulation).	The system is viewed in its simplest fashion, as a black box that answers questions using procedures hidden from the user.	Black boxes can result in inappropriate system or results use.
Avoid change.	Automate existing processes if possible, instead of developing new ones. Stability.	New systems may have minimal impact. Not a viable policy when desiring process changes.
Develop a cooperative support base.	Some components of user-management support base are not present.	Danger that one support-gaining strategy will be applied without adequate attention to others.
Get user participation.	When the system effort is not initiated by users or the usage pattern is not obvious before development.	Multiple users imply multiple objectives to be balanced. Not all users are involved in every component and at every development phase. There can be coordination difficulties. Some sophisticated models are hard for users to understand.

Source: Compiled partly from S. L. Alter, *Decision Support Systems: Current Practice and Continuing Challenges.* Reading, MA: Addison-Wesley, 1980.

which they can even use to sabotage a system; this power must be recognized and respected.

CONDITIONS THAT JUSTIFY AN ES

Expert systems are more likely to succeed when one or more of the following conditions has prompted the need for the system (based on Van Horn [1986]):

- An expert is not always available or is expensive.
- Decisions must be made under pressure, or missing even a single factor could be disastrous.

- There is rapid employee turnover, resulting in a constant need to train new workers. Such training is costly and time-consuming.
- A huge amount of data must be sifted through.
- A shortage of experts is holding back development and profitability.
- Expertise is needed to augment the knowledge of junior personnel.
- There are too many factors—or possible solutions—for a human to keep in mind at once even when the problem is broken into smaller pieces.
- The problem requires a knowledge-based approach and cannot be handled by a conventional computational approach.
- Consistency and reliability, not creativity, are paramount.
- Factors are constantly changing, and it is very hard for a person to keep on top of them all and find what is needed at just the right time.
- Specialized expertise (such as statistics) must be made available to people in different fields (such as accounting or marketing) so that they can make better decisions.

Other factors mentioned earlier include commitment on the part of management, user involvement, and the characteristics of the knowledge engineer. For further discussion of successful ES implementation, see Wong and Chong (1992), Beerel (1993), Medsker and Liebowitz (1994), and Yoon et al. (1995).

18.5 WHAT IS SYSTEM INTEGRATION AND WHY INTEGRATE?

Integration of computer-based systems means that the systems are merged into one facility rather than having separate hardware, software, and communications for each independent system. Integration can be at the development tools level or at the application system level. There are two general types of integration: *functional* and *physical*.

Functional integration implies that different support functions are provided as a single system. For example, working with electronic mail, using a spreadsheet, communicating with external databases, creating graphical representations, and storing and manipulating data can all be accomplished at the same workstation. A user can access the appropriate facilities through a single, consistent interface and can switch from one task to another and back again.

Physical integration refers to packaging of the hardware, software, and communication features required to accomplish functional integration. Software integration is determined to a large extent by the hardware integration. The discussion in this chapter deals primarily with functional integration.

WHY INTEGRATE?

There are two major objectives for MSS software integration:

- *Enhancements of basic tools.* The purpose of such integration is to enhance other tools. For example, ES can enhance neural computing, or ANN can enhance the knowledge acquisition of an expert system. ES are often used as intelligent agents to enhance other tools or applications.
- *Increasing the capabilities of the applications.* In this case the tools complement each other. Each tool performs the subtasks at which it is the best. For example, in Chapter 16 we showed several examples of ES and ANN, each performing a different task in one application (also see Quah et al., 1996).

A major reason for integrating DSS and expert systems is the benefits that each technology provides to the other. These are organized in Table 18.5, which shows benefits by major component, as well as the overall benefits.

Empirical evidence of integrated DSS, ES, and EIS in the health care industry has been reported by Forgionne and Kohl (1995). Improvements were found in both the process and the outcome. Taboada et al. (1996) describe an integration of medical expert systems, patient databases, and user interfaces using conventional tools. See Evans (1997) for an in-depth discussion of PACE, a successful, comprehensive expert consulting system for nursing.

Integration of different MSS technologies results in combining the strengths of each individual technique. Li and Love (1999) present an integration of ES and ANN for estimating a contractor's mark-up percentage in the construction industry. Li (2000) describes a hybrid intelligent system for developing market strategy by combining the strengths of ES, fuzzy logic, and ANN.

TABLE 18.5   Summary of Integrating Expert Systems and Decision Support Systems

	ES Contribution	*DSS Contribution*
Database and database management systems	Improves construction, operation, and maintenance of DBMS Improves accessibility to large databases Improves DBMS capabilities Permits symbolic representation of data Advises on data warehouse	A database is provided to the ES Provides numeric representation of data
Models and model base management systems	Improves model management Helps in selecting models Provides judgmental elements to models Improves sensitivity analysis Generates alternative solutions Provides heuristics Simplifies building simulation models Makes the problem structure incrementally modifiable Speeds up trial-and-error simulation	Provides initial problem structure Provides standard model computations Provides facts (data) to models Stores specialized models constructed by experts in the model base
Interface	Enables friendlier interface Provides explanations Provides terms familiar to user Acts as a tutor Provides interactive, dynamic, visual problem-solving capability	Provides presentations to match individual cognitive and decision styles
System capabilities (synergy)	Provides intelligent advice (faster and cheaper than human) to the DSS or its user Adds explanation capability Expands computerization of the decision-making process	Provides effectiveness in data collection Provides effective implementation Provides individualized advice to users to match their decision styles

There are two general types of integration. The first is integration of different systems, such as ES and DSS. The second is integration of systems of the same type (such as multiple expert systems). For example, Kaula (1994) developed a framework that integrates several personal and organizational DSS using a knowledge-based approach for implementing the proposed framework.

18.6 GENERIC MODELS FOR MSS INTEGRATION

Functional integration, discussed above, can be considered at two different levels: across different MSS and within MSS (Figure 18.2). Integration of MSS at these levels is appropriate for systems that can be used to solve repetitive and/or dependent decision problems. MSS can also be used to facilitate integration by assisting in the transformation of the outputs of one system to the inputs to another system.

Combining several MSS, each addressing a specific class of decision problems, is an example of the first level of integration. For example, a system for the support marketing campaign decisions can be combined with a production planning decision support system with certain outputs of the first system as the inputs to the second system. Atanackovic et al. (1997) present an integrated knowledge-based model to support various activities associated with the planning and design of electric power systems integrating several major expert systems, supporting expert systems, and simulation tools.

FIGURE 18.2 MSS INTEGRATION AT DIFFERENT LEVELS

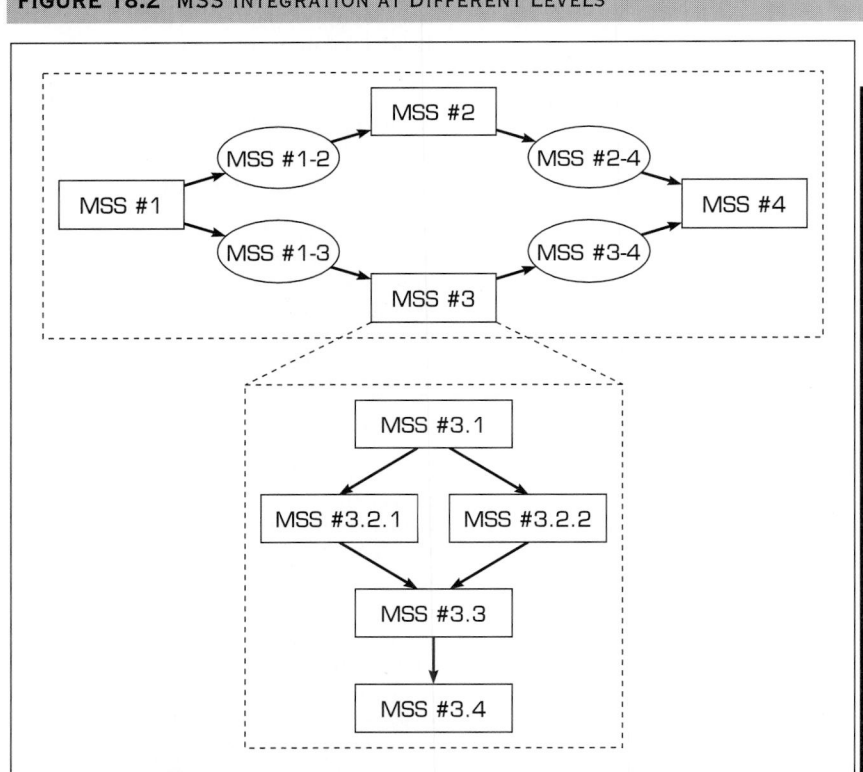

The integrative framework proposed by Dutta et al. (1997) can be helpful in understanding the extended role of MSS with an emphasis on learning to improve the decision and the decision process and with a focus on the process of decision-making in addition to traditional emphasis on the final decision. Their framework also guides the design of integrated MSS that facilitate different modes of decision support. An integrated approach to synthesizing an organization's computing infrastructure to support various tasks performed by users is presented by Nezlek et al. (1999). Different models of integration of DSS and ES are described later in Section 18.7.

The second level of integration refers to the integration of appropriate MSS technologies in building a specific MSS especially to take advantage of the strengths of specific MSS technologies. For example, artificial neural networks can be used for pattern recognition as part of the intelligence phase of the decision-making process, and an ES can be used to provide a solution to the problem. This type of integration can be either in the form of hybrids of different technologies [e.g., fuzzy logic and AHP in Kuo et al. (1999)], or in the form of supporting different phases or activities in decision making (e.g., ANN for pattern recognition in the intelligence phase and ES for the design and choice phases). Several examples of MSS integration at this level are described in Section 18.12.

Other forms of integration not discussed in this chapter include integration of MSS with other technologies and information systems such as the following:

- Computer telephony integration at "intelligent" call centers to select and assign an agent for a specific customer call in real-time (Marlin, 1999)
- Real-time decision making built around online transaction-processing systems (e.g., collaborative planning, forecasting, and replenishment in supply chain management (MMH, 2000), and real-time scheduling decision support system (Bistline et al., 1998)
- Incorporating intelligent DSS for process enhancements and management to support group decision making (Pervan, 1999).

Many of the issues presented in AIS in Focus 18.4 are equally applicable to the integration of MSS.

ENTERPRISE APPLICATION INTEGRATION—"THE DEVIL IS IN THE DETAILS"

Biggs (1999) suggests examining the following before deciding on enterprise application integration (EAI):

- Business and IT strategies must be joined at the hip.
- IT requires a deep understanding of business processes and their data.
- Plan your EAI architecture.
- Justify EAI now and later.
- Examine EAI vendor offerings, middle-tier adoption, and the changing market place.

- Evaluate the impact of EAI technology on your organization.
- Make sure you have the skills to drive EAI.
- Determine who will lead your EAI efforts.
- Prioritize what to do first and where to go from there.
- Determine how you will manage EAI.

Source: Based on Biggs (1999).

18.7 MODELS OF ES AND DSS INTEGRATION

Several models have been proposed for integrating expert systems and decision support systems (Goldbogen and Howe, 1993; Van Weelderen and Sol, 1993; Watkins et al., 1992). Such an integration appears under several names, ranging from expert support systems to **intelligent DSS** (discussed later in this chapter). The following models are described in this chapter: expert systems attached to DSS components, ES as a separate DSS component sharing in the decision-making process, ES generating alternative solutions for DSS, and a unified approach. Watkins et al. (1992) take the view that one should investigate where one should use a particular AI or other problem-addressing technology with DSS. Their model is problem-driven and suggests that AI (and other advanced technology) integration is a process of matching problems with appropriate methods, which can then be integrated to provide enhanced decision support.

EXPERT SYSTEMS ATTACHED TO DSS COMPONENTS

Expert systems can be integrated into any or all DSS components. This arrangement (according to Turban and Watkins, 1986) is shown in Figure 18.3. It includes five expert systems:

FIGURE 18.3 INTEGRATION OF ES INTO ALL DSS COMPONENTS

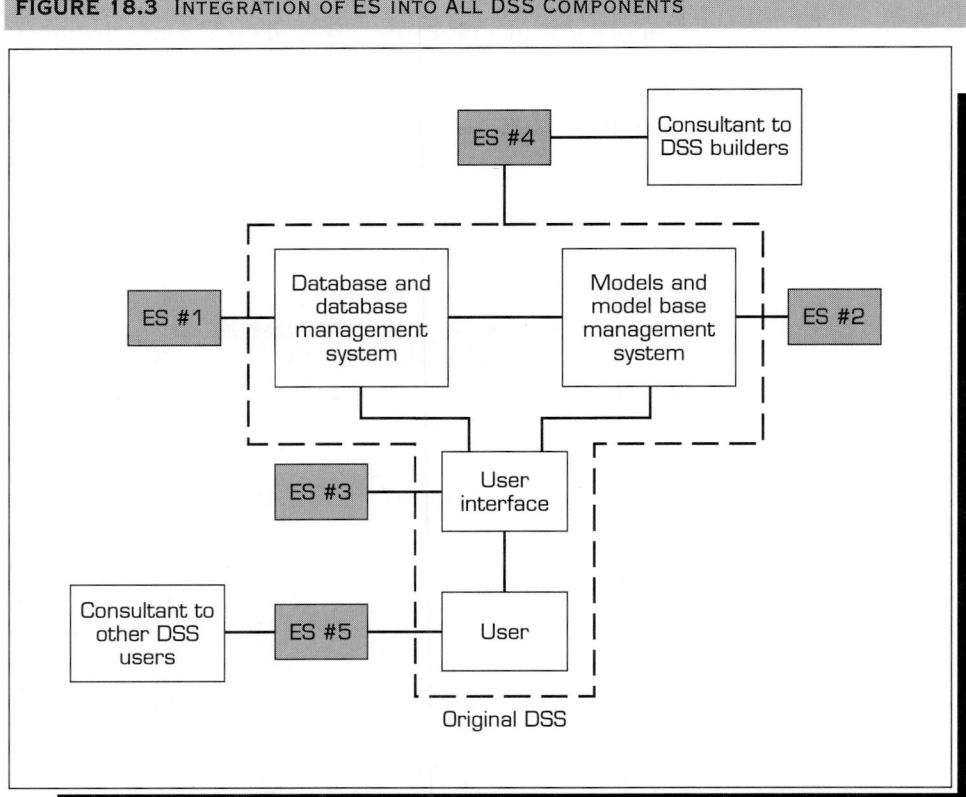

- ES 1: Database intelligent component
- ES 2: Intelligent agent for the model base and its management
- ES 3: System for improving the user interface
- ES 4: Consultant to DSS builders. In addition to giving advice on construct-ing the various components of the DSS, this ES gives advice on how to structure a DSS, how to join the various parts together, how to conduct a feasibility study, and how to execute the many activities involved in the con-struction of a DSS.
- ES 5: Consultant to users. The user of a DSS may need the advice of an ex-pert for complex issues such as the nature of the problem, the environmen-tal conditions, or possible implementation problems. A user also may want an ES that will guide them in how to use the DSS and its output.

In many cases not all five systems are operational. Often it is beneficial to attach only one or two expert systems.

ES AS A SEPARATE DSS COMPONENT

Teng et al. (1988) have proposed an architecture for ES and DSS integration, as shown in Figure 18.4. According to this proposal, the ES is placed between the data and the models. Its basic function is to integrate the two components in an intelligent manner. Another unified approach is proposed by Despres and Rosenthal-Sabroux (1992), who tie integrated systems to end-user computing.

FIGURE 18.4 UNIFIED ARCHITECTURE FOR AN INTELLIGENT DECISION SUPPORT SYSTEM

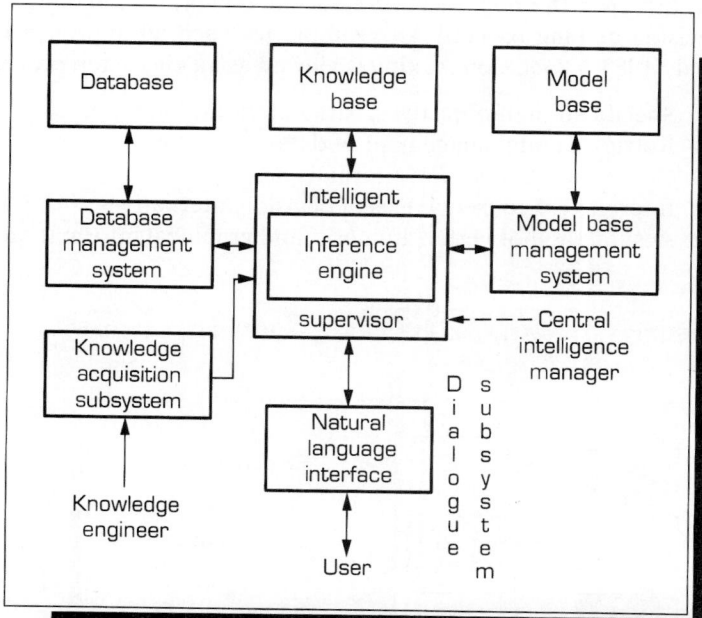

Source: J. T. C. Teng et al. "A Unified Architecture for Intelligent DSS," in *Proceedings of the Twenty-first Hawaii International Conference on Systems Science,* Hawaii, Jan. 1988. ©1988 IEEE.

According to Turban and Watkins (1986), an ES is added as a separate component. The ES shares the interface as well as other resources, and so the integration is tight. However, as indicated by King (1990), such an integration is also available via a communication link such as the Internet or a corporate intranet. Three possible configurations for such an integration follow.

ES OUTPUT AS INPUT TO A DSS

The ES output is used as input to the DSS. For example, the ES is used during the initial phase of problem solving to determine the importance of the problem or to classify the problem. Then the problem is transferred to a DSS for possible solution. For an example, see Courtney et al. (1987).

DSS OUTPUT AS INPUT TO ES

Often the results of computerized quantitative analysis provided by a DSS are forwarded to an individual or a group of experts for the purpose of interpretation. Therefore, it would make sense to direct the output of a DSS to an ES that would perform the same function as an expert whenever it is cheaper or faster to do so (especially if the quality of the advice is also superior). An example is postoptimality analysis of results provided by optimization models (Lee and Lee, 1987).

FEEDBACK

According to this configuration, the output from the ES goes to a DSS, and then the output from the DSS goes back to the original ES.

The three possibilities are illustrated in Figure 18.5.

SHARING IN THE DECISION-MAKING PROCESS

According to this approach, ES can complement DSS in one or more of the steps in the decision-making process. An example for such an approach is proposed by Meador et al. (1984a). Decision making is viewed as an eight-step process consisting of

1. Specification of objectives, parameters, probabilities
2. Retrieval and management of data
3. Generation of decision alternatives
4. Inference of consequences of decision alternatives
5. Assimilation of verbal, numeric, and graphical information

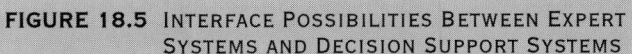

FIGURE 18.5 INTERFACE POSSIBILITIES BETWEEN EXPERT SYSTEMS AND DECISION SUPPORT SYSTEMS

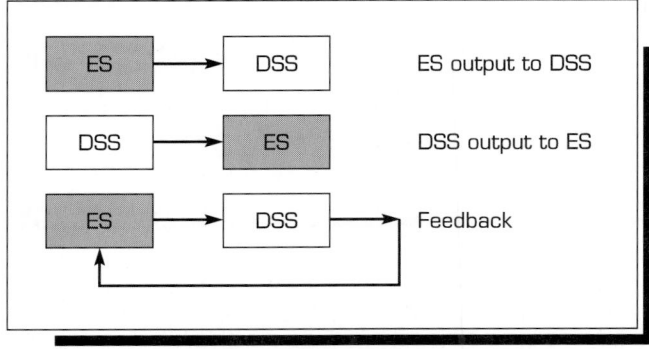

6. Evaluation of sets of consequences
7. Explanation and implementation of decisions
8. Strategy formulation.

The first seven are typical DSS functions, whereas the last one, which requires judgment and creativity, can be completed by an ES. The purpose of the ES is to supplement the DSS by using a built-in associative memory with knowledge of business and inferential rules.

Such integration can be visualized as follows: The user works with the DSS following the first seven DSS steps. On reaching the strategy formulation phase, he or she calls on the ES, which will be a completely separate system (loose integration) although it may share the database and perhaps use some of the capabilities of the model base. To better understand this type of integration, we assume that the ES plays the role of a human expert whom the user can call on when in need of expertise in strategy formulation. The expert may give an answer immediately or may conduct some analysis (such as forecasting). Such analysis can be accomplished by using the DSS database and its forecasting model.

The ES/DSS integration can be expanded to include other intelligent systems such as neural computing, case-based reasoning, and simulation. These can substitute or supplement the ES. For an example of case-based integrated systems, see Gan and Yang (1994). An example of an expanded system is provided by Liberatore and Stylianou (1995), who proposed a DSS/ES system that includes management science models for deciding on new product development. Lane et al. (1999) present an expert simulation system integrating ES and a simulation system for supporting local area network configuration decisions.

18.8 INTEGRATING EIS, DSS, AND ES, AND GLOBAL INTEGRATION

As indicated in Chapter 9, an EIS can be integrated with a DSS. Recall the example of the large drug company (Section 9.6) whose brand managers downloaded EIS data to a spreadsheet DSS forecasting model to predict monthly sales and uploaded them back to the EIS. EIS is commonly used as a data source for PC-based modeling.

The integration of EIS and DSS can be done in several ways. Most likely, the information generated by the EIS is used as an input to the DSS. More sophisticated systems include a DSS feedback to the EIS and a possible interpretation (see AIS in Action 18.5) and explanation capability performed by an ES.

GLOBAL INTEGRATION

Integration can include several MSS technologies, CBIS, and even crossovers to other organizations to form interorganizational systems. A comprehensive system is proposed by Forgionne and Kohl (1995). The conceptual architecture of the system is shown in Figure 18.6. It includes inputs, processing, and outputs.

INPUTS

The system has a database that captures and stores organizational data. A model base captures and stores economic and accounting models for describing and simulating organizational dynamics, statistical methodologies for forecasting model parameters, and

AIS IN ACTION 18.5

INTELLIGENT INTERPRETATION
AND DATA MANIPULATION

Several vendors are developing intelligent capabilities in their EIS. For example, the Information Discovery System (IntelligenceWare Corporation) suggests to the user what trends and relationships the user should ask the database about. To do this, the system scrutinizes the raw data and uses statistical analysis to generate rules about it. For example, while looking at a supermarket's national sales, the system generates a rule like this:

- IF the supermarket's size is between 25,000 and 50,000 square feet and IF it sells between 2,500 and 3,000 boxes of cereal per week in February,
- THEN the supermarket will sell 4,000–5,000 cases of milk in July (92 percent confidence).

The system allows you to conduct a graphical what-if analysis as well.

PowerPlay (Cognos Corporation) uses statistical analysis to automatically suggest how data should be summarized and structured. For example, it lets you determine whether a particular sample of time-series data would be more meaningful if it were displayed as a monthly or as year-to-year sampling. You can also determine how best to deploy the data (to minimize variability).

Source: Condensed from R. D. Cronk, "EISes Mine Your Data," *Byte,* June 1993.

management science models for optimizing organizational performance. In addition, there is a knowledge base that captures and stores linked organization data, policy issues, and historical management actions, all expressed in terms of rules.

PROCESSING

The EIS component is used to filter data, focus the filtered information, and communicate problems and opportunities among affected organization personnel. Intelligent agents can be used to filter information from a variety of sources (Chapter 17). ESS guide decision makers through the intelligent modeling and model base (MBMS), database (DBMS), and knowledge base (KBMS) management needed for EIS and DSS analyses and evaluations.

OUTPUTS

By controlling processing tasks in the desired way, the user can generate

- Visually attractive tabular graphical status reports describing the decision environment, track meaningful trends, and display important patterns
- Uncontrollable event and policy simulation forecasts
- Recommended decision actions and policies.

The system also depicts, graphically, the reasoning explanations and supporting knowledge that lead to the suggested actions.

FEEDBACK LOOPS

Feedback from the processing provides additional data, knowledge, and enhanced decision models that may be useful in future decision making. Output feedback (often in the form of sensitivity analyses) is used to extend or modify the original analyses and evaluations. A special case of intelligent EIS/DSS is a case of multiple expert systems or intelligent agents; for details see Chi and Turban (1995). For further information on EIS/DSS/ES integration, see King (1996).

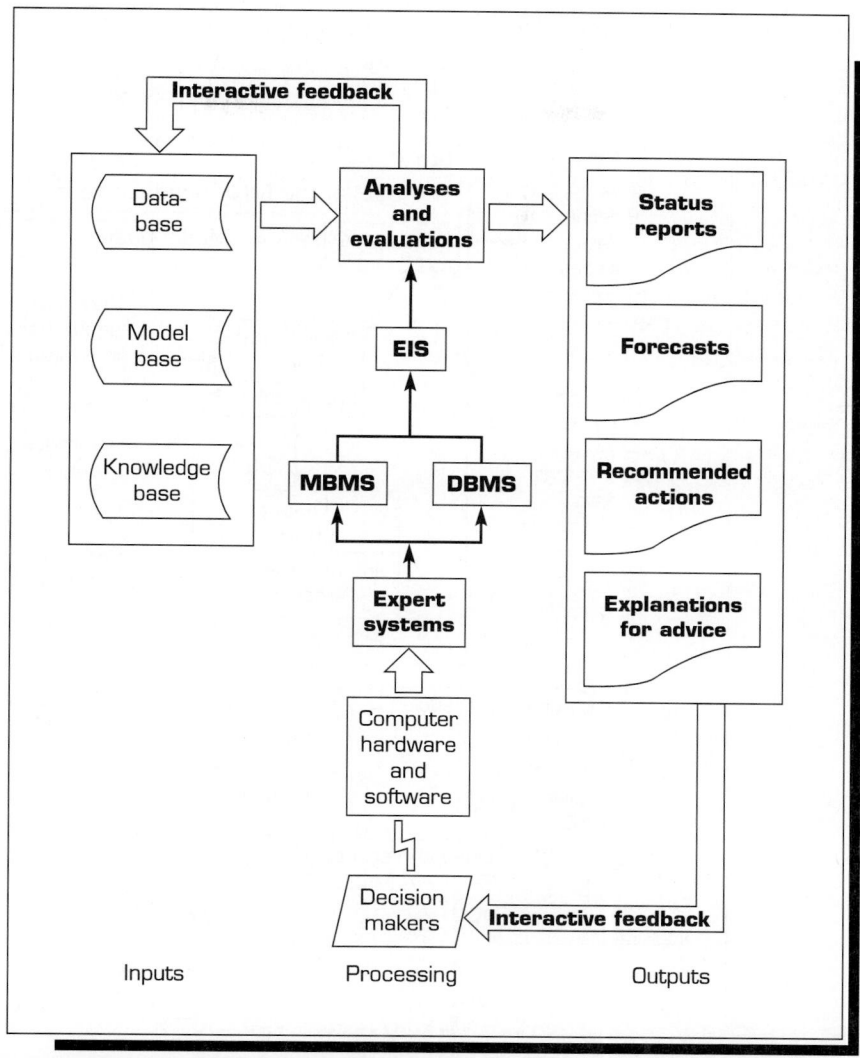

FIGURE 18.6 AN INTEGRATED EIS/DSS/ES SYSTEM

Source: Forgionne and Kohl (1995), p. 214. Forgionne, G. A., and R. Kohl. (1995, Nov.).
"Integrated MSS Effects: An Empirical Health Care Investigation." *Information Processing and Management,* Vol. 31, No. 6.

An example of a global integrated system is proposed by Min and Eom (1994). To connect the MSS to other organizations, EDI and the Internet are used (Figure 18.7). The corporate MSS includes DSS and ES, an Internet-based video conferencing system for group work, and EDI for transaction processing. For details on an architectural framework for integrating various systems to provide access through information portals, see the articles at www.intelligententerprise.com/000301/feat3.shtml and www.intelligententerprise.com/991611/feat1.shtml.

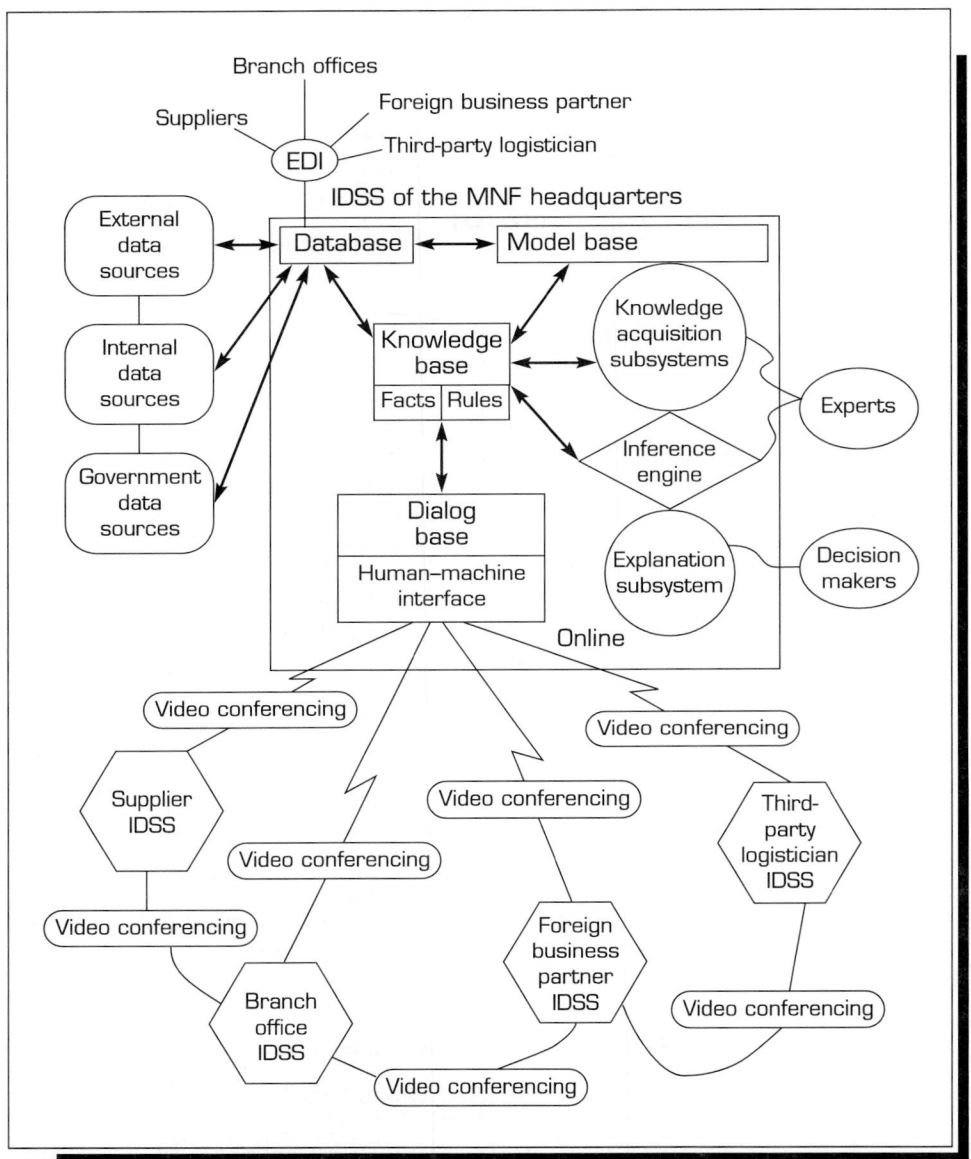

FIGURE 18.7 A Globally Integrated MSS

Source: Min and Eom (1994, p. 3).

18.9 INTELLIGENT DSS

Several models of intelligent DSS have been developed over the years. Representative examples are described in this section.

ACTIVE (SYMBIOTIC) DSS

Regular DSS play a passive role in human–computer interactions. The DSS executes computations, presents data, and responds to standard commands. But it cannot play the role of an intelligent assistant to the decision maker. This restricts the use of some DSS to well-defined, unambiguous tasks.

However, certain tasks in problem solving are ambiguous and complex, and then an active DSS is needed. For example, the DSS should be able to take the initiative or to respond to nonstandard requests and commands. This type of DSS is called **active** or **symbiotic DSS** (Manheim, 1989).

According to Mili (1990), an active DSS is an application that follows the tasks of

- *Understanding the domain* (terminology, parameters, interactions). Here the active DSS can provide explanations.
- *Formulating problems.* Here an active DSS can help in determining assumptions, abstracting reality, deciding what is relevant, and so on.
- *Relating a problem to a solver.* The active DSS can assist with proper problem–solver interaction, advise what procedures to use and what solution techniques to follow, and so on.
- *Interpreting results.*
- *Explaining results and decisions.*

For these tasks, one needs an intelligent component(s) in the DSS (see AIS in Action 18.6).

Critique and augmentation of candidate decisions are provided by another form of active DSS. For details on an intelligent DSS capable of assisting decision makers in substantiating their decisions, see Vahidov and Elrod (1999).

AIS IN ACTION 18.6

SIMPSON IS AN INTELLIGENT ASSISTANT FOR SHORT-TERM MANUFACTURING SCHEDULING

An intelligent decision support system was developed to assist in the day-to-day scheduling decisions at a manufacturing facility. The system has been fielded, has proved effective, and is in daily use.

The short-term intelligent manufacturing planning support for nuclear (SIMPSON) fuel tubes system is part of a larger effort, called MULTEX, still under development. MULTEX will test whether a combined operations research/artificial intelligence (OR/AI) ap-

proach to system design can provide more robust decision support than either method can individually. Integration of the two differing methodologies requires a separate expert system called the Moderator.

Source: Condensed from J. H. May and L. G. Vargas, "SIMPSON: An Intelligent Assistant for Short-term Manufacturing Scheduling," *European Journal of Operational Research,* Vol. 88, No. 2, Jan. 20, 1996, pp. 269–286.

SELF-EVOLVING DSS

A **self-evolving DSS** is a DSS design approach (Liang and Jones, 1987) whose basic premise is that a DSS should be "aware" of how it is being used and that it should then automatically adapt to the evolution of its users. To do so one needs capabilities such as the following:

- A dynamic menu that provides different hierarchies to fulfill different user requirements
- A dynamic user interface that provides different output representations for different users
- An intelligent model base management system that can select appropriate models to satisfy different preferences.

The purposes of a self-evolving DSS are increasing the flexibility of the DSS, reducing the effort required to use the system, enhancing control over the organization's information resource, and encouraging system sharing.

PROBLEM MANAGEMENT

Most DSS revolve around the design and choice phases of decision making. The intelligence phase, which includes problem finding, problem representation, and information surveillance, is neglected by most DSS. Furthermore, several activities in the design and choice phases, such as model management, are executed manually. To make DSS more effective, it is necessary to automate as many tasks as possible. Weber and Konsynski (1987) suggested dividing the decision-making process into five steps and proposed architecture to support the functional requirements of these steps. They called their approach **problem management.** As can be seen in Table 18.6, the suggested support involves several intelligent agents. For further discussion see Courtney and Paradice (1993).

TABLE 18.6   Problem Management, Functional Requirements, and Architectural Support

Problem Management Stage	Functional Requirements	Architectural Support
Problem finding	Perceptual filters, knowledge management	Flexible knowledge management, intelligent filters
Problem representation	Model and pattern management, suspension of judgment	Flexible dialog and knowledge management, reason maintenance system, pattern search strategies
Information surveillance	Knowledge and model management	Demons, intelligent lenses, scanners, evaluators, interpreters
Solution generation	Knowledge management, idea generation	Idea and solution model management, heuristic and analytical drivers
Solution evaluation	Meta-level dialog and knowledge management	Flexible knowledge management, analytical and symbolic processors

Source: Compiled from Weber and Konsynski (1987).

For more details on intelligent DSS in different types of decision-making environments see Walden et al. (1999), Palma-dos-Reis and Zahedi (1999), Matasatsinis and Siskos (1999), Hashemi et al. (1998), Borenstein (1998), Proudlove et al. (1998), and DePold and Gass (1999).

Some examples of intelligent decision support systems (IDSS) accessible on the Internet are listed below:

- Assessing the severity of an illness in the management of health care resources (www.bgsm.edu/bgsmneonatal/test/project_summary.html)
- Assisting help desk personnel at a consumer loan company by answering customers' queries (www.shai.com/projects/help_desk.htm)
- Assisting a space crew on a deep space mission in diagnosing problems with, and maintaining their life-support systems (www.shai/com/projects/ spacecraft_health.htm).

18.10 INTELLIGENT MODELING AND MODEL MANAGEMENT

Adding intelligence to the process of modeling (building models or using existing models) and to their management makes lots of sense because some of the tasks involved (such as modeling and selecting models) require considerable expertise. The topics of intelligent modeling and intelligent model management have attracted significant academic attention in recent years (Blanning, 1993; Chang et al., 1993) because the potential benefits could be substantial. However, it seems that the implementation of such integration is fairly difficult and slow. For a survey of approaches, see Suh et al. (1995). For a detailed study on computer-based modeling environments from the perspectives of modelers (analysts) and model users (decision makers), see Wright et al. (1998).

ISSUES IN MODEL MANAGEMENT

We discuss four interrelated subtopics of model management: problem diagnosis and selection of models, construction of models (formulation), use of models (analysis), and interpretation of the output of models.

PROBLEM DIAGNOSIS AND SELECTION OF MODELS

Several commercial ES are now helping to select appropriate statistical models (such as Statistical Navigator). Goul et al. (1984) have developed a selection of ES for mathematical programming, and Courtney et al. (1987) have produced an expert system for problem diagnosis. Zahedi (1987) has created a system for model selection. Liang and Konsynski (1993) have suggested using analogy as a source of knowledge for modeling. Dutta (1996) claims that model selection is a major area of AI and optimization integration. Venkatachalam and Sohl (1999) have presented an application of ANN for forecasting model selection. Lu et al. (2000) have proposed a guidance framework for designing intelligent systems to help a typical decision maker in selecting the most appropriate method for solving various multiobjective decision-making problems.

CONSTRUCTION OF MODELS

The construction of models for decision making involves the simplification of a real-world situation so that a less complex representation of reality can be made. Models can be normative or descriptive, and they can be used in various types of computer-based information systems (especially DSS). Finding an appropriate balance between simplification and representation in modeling requires expertise. The definition of the problem to be modeled, the attempt to select a prototype model (e.g., linear programming), the data collection, the model validation, and the estimation of certain parameters and relationships are not simple tasks either. For instance, data can be tested for suitability for a certain statistical distribution (e.g., does the arrival rate in queuing follow a Poisson distribution?). The ES could guide the user in selecting an appropriate test and interpreting its results, which in turn can help in appropriate modeling of the situation. For a discussion, see Bhargava and Krishnan (1993) and Dutta (1996).

Knowledge discovery techniques such as decision rule discovery offer intelligent support in decision modeling using input and output attribute values of past decisions. Such an approach can minimize the effort required for model builders (or analysts) to model decision-making processes of decision makers. For details see Hill and Remus (1994) and Bolloju (1999).

USE OF MODELS
Once models are constructed, they can be put to use. The application of models may require some judgmental values (such as setting an alpha value in exponential smoothing). Experience is also needed to conduct a sensitivity analysis as well as to determine what constitutes a significant difference (Is project A really superior to project B?). Expert systems can be used to provide the user with the necessary guidelines for the use of models.

INTERPRETATION OF RESULTS
Expert systems are able to provide explanation of the models used and interpretation of the derived results. For example, an ES can trace anomalies in the data. Furthermore, sensitivity analysis may be needed, or the translation of information to a certain format may be the desired result. An ES can advise in all of the above cases.

QUANTITATIVE MODELS
Most experimental ES are not developed according to the four model management issues just discussed. Instead, they are based on the type of quantitative model used. Then, some portion of one or more of the four issues may be considered. For a proposed architecture for a quantitative intelligent model management, see Figure 18.8.

Human experts often use quantitative models to support their experience and expertise. For example, an expert may need to forecast the sales of a certain product or to estimate future cash flow using a corporate planning model. Similarly, many models are used by experts in almost all aspects of engineering.

ES contributions in the area of quantitative models and model management can be demonstrated by examining the work of a consultant. A consultant is involved in the following steps:

1. Discussing the nature of the problem with the client
2. Identifying and classifying the problem
3. Constructing a mathematical model of the problem
4. Solving the model
5. Conducting sensitivity analyses with the model
6. Recommending a specific solution
7. Assisting in implementing the solution.

The system involves a decision maker (client), a consultant, and a computer.

If we can codify the knowledge of the consultant in an ES, we can build an intelligent computer-based information system capable of the same process. Unfortunately, little is known about the nature of the cognitive skills that consultants use. However, re-

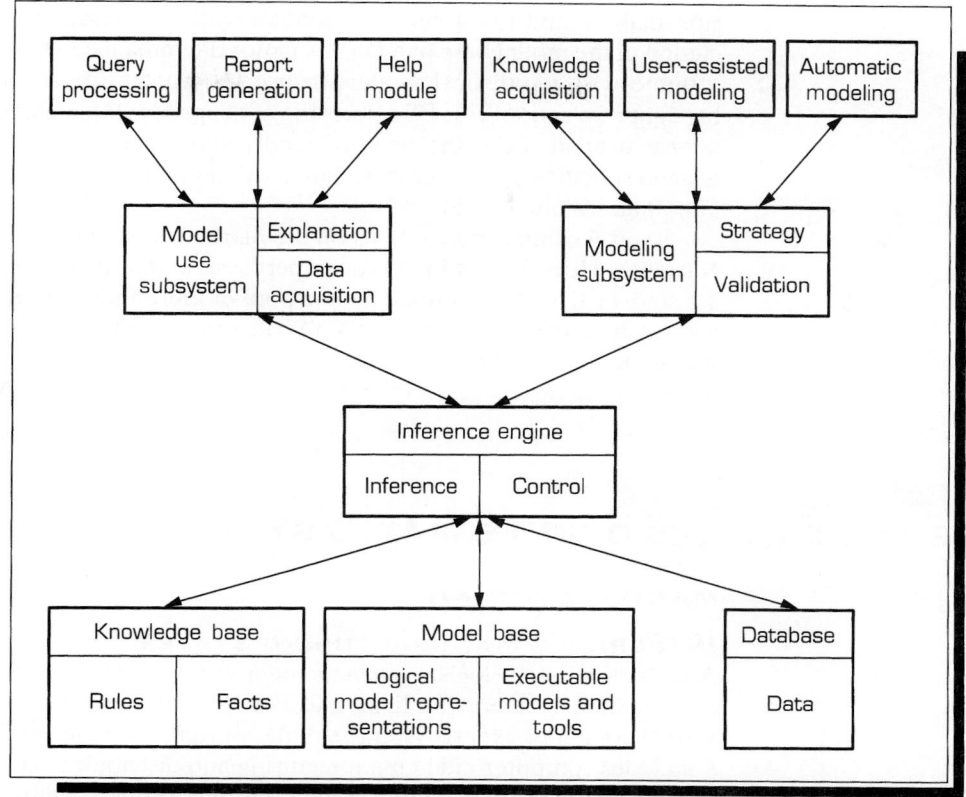

FIGURE 18.8 SOFTWARE ARCHITECTURE FOR MODEL MANAGEMENT SYSTEM

The module use subsystem (left) directs the effective use of the model. The modeling subsystem (right) helps in increasing the productivity of model building. The inference engine drives the model selection and integration, and the integration of the model base, database, and knowledge base.

Source: T. Liang, "Development of a Knowledge-based Model Management System." Reprinted with permission from *Operations Research,* Vol. 36, No. 6, Nov./Dec. 1988, pp. 849–863, Operations Research Society of America. No further reproduction permitted without the consent of the copyright owner.

lated research has been done by Goul et al. (1984), who have developed a system that attempts to replicate a manager–consultant–computer combination. In their system, the computer queries the manager to determine the general category of the managerial problem (e.g., an allocation problem versus inventory management). Next the computer queries the manager to determine the exact nature of the problem (e.g., what kind of allocation problem). Then the computer suggests which quantitative model to use (e.g., dynamic programming versus linear programming). The manager can ask the system to define terminology to justify the recommendation made by the machine and to explain the model used. The decision maker can then formulate the problem using the model, conduct a what-if analysis, or use an alternative model. The ES in this case helps to identify and classify the managerial problem, acts as a tutor, provides illustrative examples, and selects the set of models to be used.

Expert systems can be used as an **intelligent interface** between the user and quantitative models. Such an integration is demonstrated by BUMP, a statistical ES (Hand,

1984). Large numbers of statistical packages are available to support managerial decision making and research. They contain statistical tests and models that may be included in the model base of a DSS. A major dilemma faced by a nonexpert user is to determine which statistical models to use for what purposes. This is where BUMP is brought into action. This ES selects the appropriate statistical procedure and guides the novice user in using the not-so-friendly statistical packages that usually require a trained statistician for operation. For another application see Lyczak and Weber-Russel (1992) and White (1995).

Several commercial systems on the market assist with statistical analysis. Statistical Navigator (Idea Works Inc.) is an expert system that helps the user select an appropriate statistical analysis routine from a pool of more than 130 routines available in packages such as SPSS, SAS, and SYSTAT. The program does not perform the analysis, but it supplements many of the existing statistical packages. If several routines can do the job, Statistical Navigator ranks them by suitability. The program is built with an Exsys shell.

18.11 EXAMPLES OF INTEGRATED SYSTEMS

MANUFACTURING

INTEGRATED MANUFACTURING SYSTEM

A system called the logistics management system (LMS) was developed by IBM for operations management (Sullivan and Fordyce, 1990) (see Case Application 14.1). The system combines expert systems, simulation, and decision support systems. In addition, it includes computer-aided manufacturing and distributed data-processing subsystems. It provides plant manufacturing management a tool to help in resolving crises and in planning. A similar system is used at IBM by financial analysts to simulate long-range financial planning. As part of this system an ES supplies judgmental information and other pertinent factors, and the DSS conducts a forecast and generates plans.

Belz and Mertens (1996) describe a combination of several complex expert systems (which are implemented as intelligent agents) with a scheduling system and a simulation-based DSS for rescheduling production lines when problems occur. The problem schedule is used as input, and the user is queried for facts not supplied by the schedule. Another ES sets up and performs simulation runs. The simulation results are imported by a third ES, which determines how rescheduling can be accomplished. The new, desired schedule is applied through the scheduling system, and new scheduling problems, if they occur, are fed back into the first ES. For another example of intelligence integrated with scheduling, see May and Vargas (1996).

EMBEDDED INTELLIGENT SYSTEMS

There is an increased trend toward including intelligent systems in other CBIS. One example is the intelligent software agents discussed in the previous chapter. Such integration sometimes involves embedded systems. Embedded AI systems are an integral part of a larger system that provides a wide range of functions that support the system's mission and define its architecture. For details, see the special issue of *IEEE Expert,* June 1994. Furthermore, data mining systems typically embed neural networks, intelligent agents, and expert systems to perform effective knowledge discovery in large databases and documents. In embedded systems, the users see a single application with which they work, and the intelligent system is invisible to them.

Embedded systems, which are usually more efficient than systems with access approaches, could be the most important information technologies of the future. Although embedded systems seem to be desirable, they are more difficult and more expensive to construct. On the other hand, there are many standard components on the market that can support the access approaches and can result in savings of time or money. Selecting an appropriate integration mode is outside the scope of this chapter; however, it certainly should be considered in the design phase of an integrated project. For further discussion see King (1990, 1996).

DSS/DECISION SIMULATION

Decision simulation (DSIM) (IBM) is the outcome of combining decision support systems, statistics, operations research, database management, query languages, and artificial intelligence (Sullivan and Fordyce, 1990). AI, especially natural language interfaces and expert systems, provides three capabilities to DSIM:

- Ease of communication of pertinent information to the computational algorithm or display unit
- Assistance in finding the appropriate model, computational algorithm, or data set
- A solution to a problem in which the computational algorithm alone is not sufficient to solve the problem, a computational algorithm is not appropriate or applicable, or the AI creates the computational algorithm.

For details see Piramuthu et al. (1993).

INTELLIGENT COMPUTER-INTEGRATED MANUFACTURING

Important integration occurs in computer-integrated manufacturing (CIM). CIM involves several computer programs used to plan and control different machines, material handling facilities, robots, and other components. An expert system, for example, can be employed to perform production planning in conjunction with some DSS. The planning attempts to coordinate all the activities of the plant, to achieve efficiency in the use of resources, to maximize productivity, to meet delivery dates, and so forth.

Another application of ES is in the area of error recovery (e.g., see the Opening Vignette). An automated factory is monitored by several sensors and other detecting devices. Any interruption can be detected and interpreted.

Various MSS have been connected to computer-aided design/computer-aided manufacturing (CAD/CAM) systems, sensory systems, material handling, maintenance, quality control, assembly, and several manufacturing applications. For further information, see Kusiak (1988) and Siegel (1990). A comprehensive CIM system is explained in Table 18.7.

MARKETING

PROMOTER

The ES Promoter analyzes the effects of promotions and advertisements on sales in the packaged goods industry. It was developed by Management Decision Systems Inc., and it must be used together with the company's DSS development tools for data preprocessing to the ES.

TELESTREAM

TeleStream, an ES developed by Texas Instruments, supports distribution center salespeople who sell thousands of products. The system has two modules: Sales Advisor and

TABLE 18.7 Role of the MSS in Computer-Integrated Manufacturing: The Factory of the Future

Function Aided by Computers	Description	Supported by				
		ANN	ES	NP	Robots	DSS
Assembly and packaging	Uses robots to put together parts fabricated on site and purchased from outside. Packages ready for shipment.		X	X	X	X
Design (CAD) engineering	Creates the design for a product. Designs the tools, molds, and other facilities needed for manufacturing.		X X			X
Factory management	Runs the entire production process, coordinates incoming orders, requests components and material, plans and schedules, controls overseas costs, arranges deliveries.	X	X	X		X
Headquarters	Decides what products to make and when and how much (based on market research, available resources, and strategic planning).	X	X	X		X
Logistics and storage	Purchases and distributes materials, handles inventory control, removes materials, manages supplies. Shuttles incoming materials and parts, work in process, and final products.		X		X	X
Maintenance	Monitors equipment and processes, makes adjustments when needed, takes care of emergency breakdowns, diagnoses faults, does preventive and corrective maintenance.	X	X	X	X	X
Manufacturing (CAM)	Fabricates metals, plastics, and other materials by molding, machining, and welding.		X		X	
Quality control	Tests incoming materials and outgoing products, tests processes in progress, ensures quality.	X	X	X		X

Sales Assistant. The Sales Advisor ES tells the salesperson what to offer to the customer. It also describes accessories and supplies. The DSS part attempts to maximize management goals (such as profits and low inventories). Sales Assistant is an ES-based interface that determines the content of the information to be presented to the user and the method of presentation. For further details, see *AI Letter* (1988, 1989).

ENGINEERING

An integrated system was designed to boost engineers' productivity at Boeing. The DSS portion, called STRUDL (structured design language), is essentially a passive tool whose effectiveness depends on the user's abilities. By inserting the proper data into the formula or the graphical modeling application, a design engineer can gain insight into the potential of his or her design prototype. Unfortunately, STRUDL cannot help the engineer decide what questions to ask or what data to key in, nor can it give any hints about further actions to take based on the results of analysis. However, an expert system that assumes the role of teacher or partner was added for this purpose.

SOFTWARE ENGINEERING

Far et al. (1996) have developed several knowledge-based software engineering tools that integrate CASE tools with ES. The intention is to automate software design. One version, called CREATOR2, represents software design knowledge as design product knowledge and design process knowledge in frames. An extension, CREATOR3, incorporates graphics and designer comments in the frames. The intention is to provide a uniform modeling and advance reasoning environment for software design. The ES, for which knowledge was acquired by documentation from previous designs (of switching software for telecommunications networks, the domain of interest), determines the specifications needed, and the CASE software automatically generates C code. See Far et al. (1996) for further details.

FINANCIAL SERVICES

A large financial services company (Scott Morton, 1984) uses an integrated system to match its various services with individual customers' needs (e.g., placing a customer's assets in optimal investment packages). Similar applications are being actively developed by large international accounting firms for combining analytical methods and judgment in auditing, and by other business entities for credit evaluation, strategic planning, and related applications. General Dynamics Corporation, for example, uses expert systems to support project management financial analysis.

FINEXPERT[4] is an intelligent system designed to produce financial reports and analyses of corporations. Linked to a company's standard accounting system, a DSS produces all the standard financial reports and 50 different charts. Then an ES performs a financial analysis that includes financial activity, ratio analysis, risk analysis, profitability, and financial equilibrium. Its report satisfies the U.S. Securities and Exchange Commission's requirements for publically held corporations. The system can run simulations and forecasting models, and a sophisticated explanation facility is available. It is marketed worldwide as a ready-made system. For further details see *AI Letter* (1989).

AMERICAN EXPRESS

The 300 American Express employees who authorize credit card purchases may need to access as many as 13 different databases in making one decision. Now, they are being assisted by an expert system.[5]

Inference Corporation (El Segundo, CA) personnel worked with credit authorizers from American Express's Fort Lauderdale office, the credit authorization manager, and details from case histories to create the expert system. Figure 18.9 illustrates the credit authorization process with the authorization expert system assistant.

It took 1 year to build rules, check them, and fix them as necessary. A prototype was unveiled in April 1986 and tested for 5 months. The expert system became operational in January 1987 with 800 rules.

The only problem experienced with the system involved connecting the human credit authorizer's local area networks of IBM PCs with the IBM mainframe in Phoenix. The benefits of the expert system include a 20–30 percent increase in correctly authorized cases, a reduced number of cases of fraud and unpaid charges, and the ability to keep up with the growing number of transactions without increasing the staff.

---

[4]Based on information provided by Neuron Data Inc.
[5]Condensed from D. B. Davis, "Artificial Intelligence Goes to Work," *High Technology,* April 1987; and from J. M. Dzierzanowski et al., in H. Schorr and A. Rappaport (eds.), *Innovative Applications of Expert Systems.* Menlo Park, CA: AAAI Press, 1989.

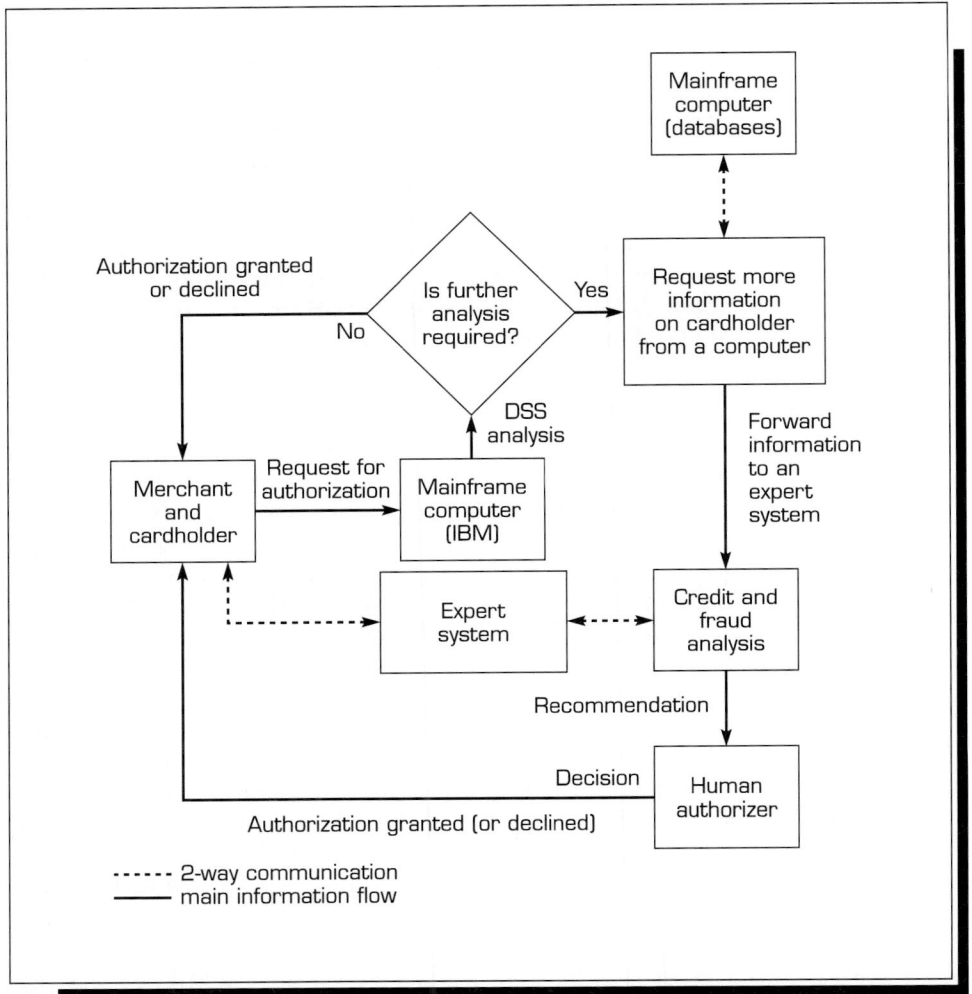

FIGURE 18.9 AMERICAN EXPRESS AUTHORIZER'S ASSISTANT

The merchant requests authorization from the mainframe computer. The computer checks the credit availability and performs a DSS analysis (e.g., checking the cardholder's normal charging pattern). If no further analysis is needed, the authorization is either granted or declined. If further analysis is necessary, the computer collects more information about the cardholder from another mainframe computer. The initial and the new information are forwarded to a rule-based expert system, which was developed in ART (Inference Corporation). The expert system may request more information from the cardholder if necessary; then it provides a recommendation to the human authorizer.

Source: Based on information provided by Inference Corporation and American Express.

RETAILING

BUYER'S WORKBENCH

In retailing, especially in the supermarket industry with its typically small profit margins, the ability to draw on the experience of senior buyers is a key factor in a company's success. Because of the thousands of items that must be tracked for pricing and inventory, buying is often a reactive process. The implementation of an expert system running in tandem with corporate databases can be an effective tool in changing the process into a proactive one.

A system called Buyer's Workbench[6] was developed by Deloitte and Touche for Associated Grocers (a supermarket chain in the Northwest). A buyer interacts with the knowledge base via an SQL interface. The interface is used to select items that are candidates for action; it also retrieves data from corporate databases and analyzes them with an expert system. The expert system contains a large rule base consumer preferences, vendor characteristics, seasonality, and a variety of other factors (Figure 18.10). The expert system then communicates the results of the analysis to the user.

Buyer's Workbench takes advantage of the division of functionality inherent in a client/server architecture. The user interface runs on the client machine, and the server contains the knowledge base, which is then linked to the mainframe database. The client/server model allows flexibility on the client's side by permitting new applications to be integrated via the user interface. Also, the portable nature of the expert system allows it to be scaled or redeployed to a remote server. In this way, the knowledge base can be expanded without sacrificing connectivity.

---

[6]Based on material provided by Neuron Data Inc. and in *AI Topics,* Aug. 1989.

FIGURE 18.10   CATEGORIES OF KNOWLEDGE IN AN EXPERT SYSTEM THAT IS PART OF BUYER'S WORKBENCH

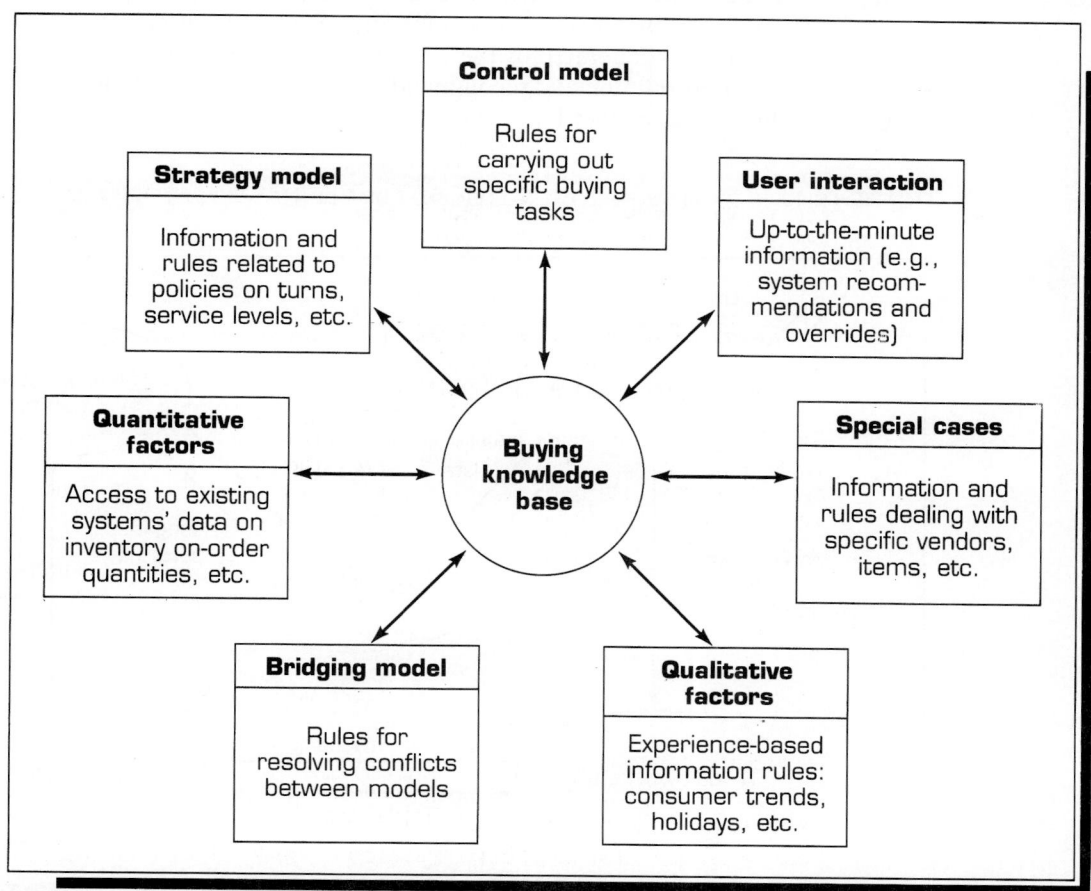

Source: AI Topics, Aug. 1989 (Deloitte and Touche).

COMMODITIES TRADING

The Intelligent Commodities Trading System (ICTS), developed by Fusion Group, integrates the capabilities of expert systems, neural networks, and relational databases in a distributed environment. After examining a set of broad market indicators, the system can make trading recommendations or optionally execute trades based on its own findings. The indicators watched include rising and falling volume, price movements, and market trends. The rule base applies analytics appropriate to the market situation and include DSS models such as moving averages, regression analysis, and risk analysis. The neural network is used to perform pattern recognition to forecast price velocity and direction. The process is shown schematically in Figure 18.11.

PROPERTY CASUALTY INSURANCE INDUSTRY DECISION MAKING

Decision making for the insurance industry is based on forecasting. Some of the major decisions involve determining what products to offer, pricing products, selecting territories in which to operate, and deciding how to invest the money collected as premiums. Benjamin and Bannis (1990) developed an integrated ES/ANN system that is combined with a DSS. A schematic view of the system is shown in Figure 18.12.

The flowchart shows the roles of each major component:

- The DSS provides statistical analysis and graphical display.
- The ANN analyzes historical data and recognizes patterns in the data.
- The results generated by the DSS and by the ANN are passed on to an ES for interpretation and recommendation. The recommendations are tested by the DSS using its what-if capabilities.

FIGURE 18.11 DATA FLOW FOR THE INTELLIGENT COMMODITIES TRADING SYSTEM (ICTS)

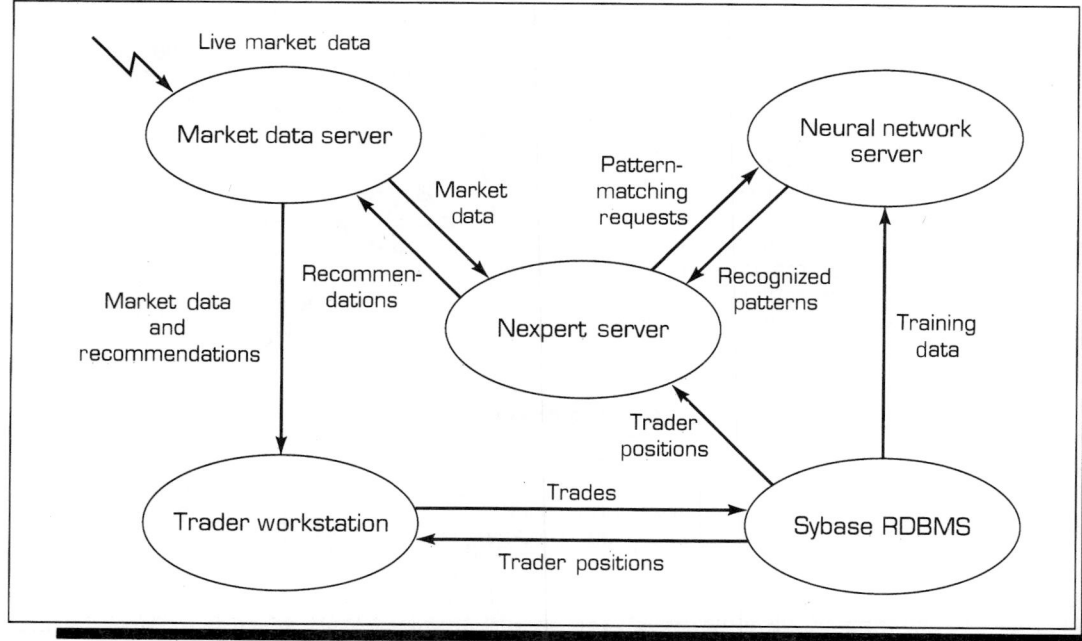

Courtesy of Neuon Data, Inc.

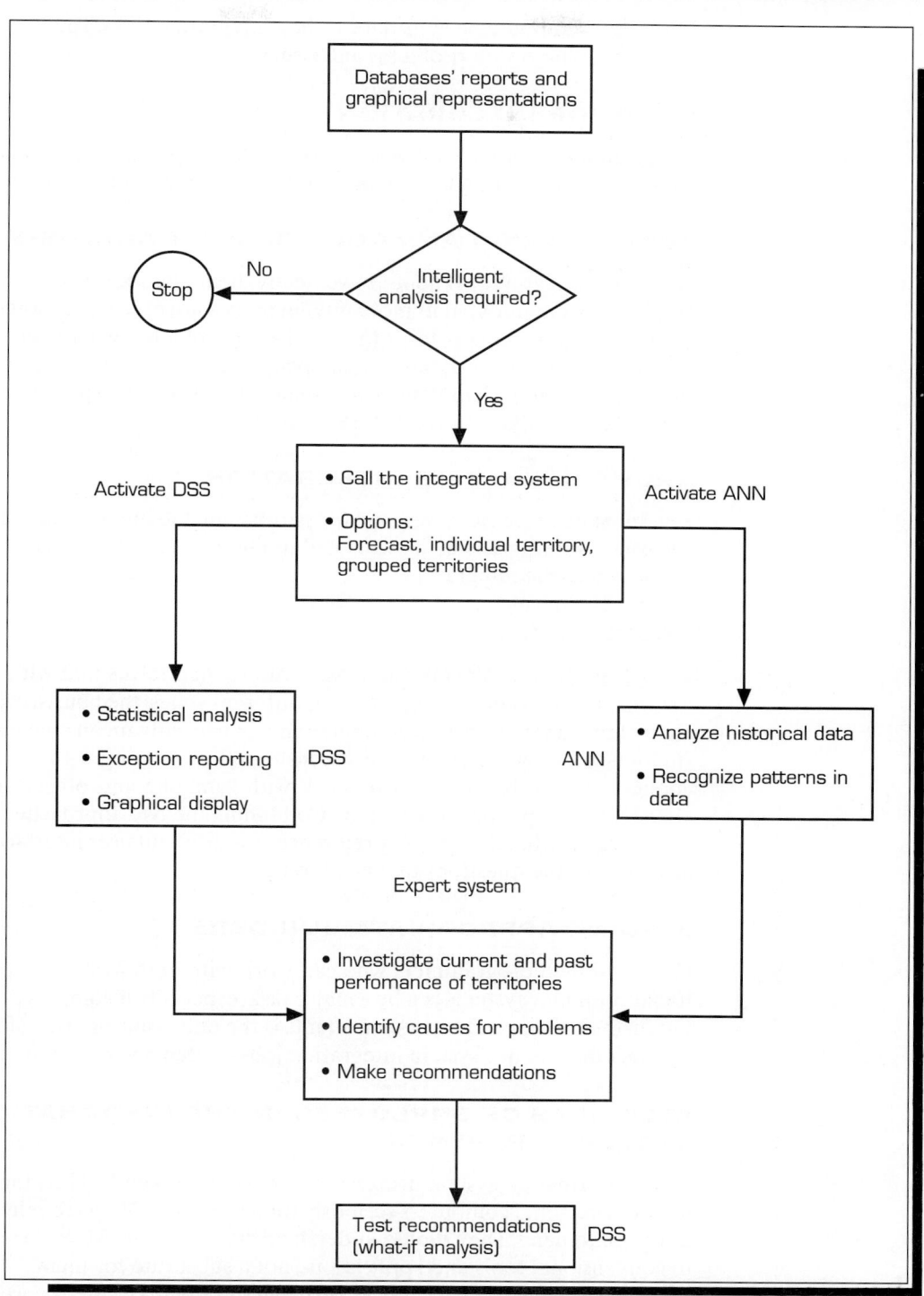

Source: Drawn by L. Medsker, American University. Reproduced with permission.

18.12 PROBLEMS AND ISSUES IN INTEGRATION

Many factors should be considered when integrating MSS. This section describes some of the most important problems and issues.

NEED FOR INTEGRATION

Integration may or may not be desirable. A comprehensive feasibility study is essential. Technological, economical, organizational, and behavioral aspects need to be analyzed.

JUSTIFICATION AND COST–BENEFIT ANALYSIS

Although integrated systems have many benefits, they also obviously have costs. Making a computer system more intelligent is a novel idea, but someone must take the responsibility for paying for it (generally the problem owner is involved). This issue is very important today because many people question the economics of computerized systems and their alignment with organizational goals (Sprague and Watson, 1996a; Watson et al., 1996, 1997; and Rosenstein, 1999).

ARCHITECTURE OF INTEGRATION

Several alternatives are available for performing the integration. Each of these options has some benefits as well as costs and limitations. A careful analysis should be undertaken before the integration.

PEOPLE PROBLEMS

The integration of MSS technologies among themselves and with conventional computerized systems brings together two different styles: the heuristic-judgmental and the algorithmic-analytical. This combination will certainly mean a change to many people. Builders and other users who are accustomed to working with conventional tools and applications are being asked to work with symbolic and object-oriented processing. How will these people be affected? Combining the two approaches may not be simple. For example, what if there are preferences for different user interface modes? These are just some of the questions that need to be answered.

FINDING APPROPRIATE BUILDERS

Finding skilled programmers who can work with both MSS technologies and conventional computer systems can be a major task, especially if complex systems are involved. Often, the use of vendors or consultants is the only solution. Therefore, companies subcontract most major system integration jobs—often a very expensive solution.

ATTITUDES OF EMPLOYEES IN THE INFORMATION SYSTEM DEPARTMENT

Some information system professionals have not taken MSS seriously, just as they did not take personal computers seriously for a long time. They are reluctant to learn about new technologies. They should understand, however, that MSS is a valuable supplement to conventional tools and applications, not a substitute for them.

Part of the problem is cultural. The analysis, design, knowledge acquisition, testing, and debugging of MSS and especially ES are much more difficult and time-consuming than the coding itself. Professionals can learn coding rather fast, but sometimes they do not have the desire or energy to learn all the other activities. Therefore, they depend on MSS experts and thus may reject opportunities to use MSS. New information technology paradigms require new approaches, which must be introduced properly, managed, and learned.

DEVELOPMENT PROCESS

The development process of many CBIS projects follows a sequential life-cycle approach. In contrast, most MSS are prototyped. When the two are combined, a problem of being out of phase may be created; that is, the CBIS project may not be ready for the MSS for a long time, and then, when it is ready, the MSS process may slow down the CBIS project because additional prototyping is needed. This coordination problem must be planned for, especially when developing large-scale institutional systems.

ORGANIZATIONAL IMPACTS

One of the biggest impacts of MSS could be on the director of information systems or chief information officer (CIO). This individual needs MSS to better manage conventional CBIS applications, and MSS could enhance his or her productivity. The manner in which the director reacts to such an opportunity, and the implications for structure, job description, and power distribution within the information system organization, as well as within the entire corporation, must be considered and researched. We discuss organizational impacts in Chapter 19.

DATA STRUCTURE ISSUES

AI applications are centered on symbolic processing, whereas DSS, EIS, ANN, and CBIS projects are built around numeric processing. When these systems are integrated, data must flow from one environment to a different one. Databases are structured quite differently from knowledge bases. In a knowledge base, procedural information and declarative information are separated, whereas in a database everything is combined. It is easy to develop a conceptual system with a database and a knowledge base and show that the two are interconnected. But somewhere a translation is needed. Who will do it and how?

DATA ISSUES

Several MSS applications, especially expert systems and neural computing, can absorb heterogeneous, partially inconsistent, and incomplete data of different dimensions and accuracy. DSS, EIS, and traditional CBIS applications cannot operate with this kind of input data. For example, when an ES is used as a front end to a DSS, the incomplete data must be organized and prepared according to the input requirements of the database. The same is true when DSS output is inputted into an ES.

CONNECTIVITY

AI applications, as we have seen, can be programmed in LISP, PROLOG, ES shells, C, C++, special knowledge engineering tools, or in a combination of these. Shells can be written in C, C++, or Pascal, but not necessarily in the same language that was used to write the DSS, EIS, or ANN being integrated with the AI part. Another problem is that although many AI tool vendors provide interfaces to DBMS, spreadsheets, and so on, these interfaces may not be easy to work with. Furthermore, they may be expensive and must be updated constantly. Some relief has been provided by the Windows environments; more is expected as applications are deployed on the Web and other client/server architectures (Tung et al., 1999; Bisby, 1999).

❖ Chapter Highlights

- Many MSS projects either fail or are not completed.
- Successful implementation is determined by many factors.
- Implementation is an ongoing process.
- Implementation means introducing change.
- The success of implementation can be partial, and it is usually measured by several criteria (such as user satisfaction, degree of use, and payoff to the organization).
- Technical success is related to the system's complexity, reliability, and responsiveness; hardware, network, and software compatibility; and the technical skills of the builders.
- Organizational climate and politics can be detrimental to the success of any application.
- There are many dimensions to change and to its resistance; overcoming resistance is a complex process.
- Top management support is crucial; it can be increased through guidance, education, participation, communication, and appropriate budget procedures.
- Involvement of users at the various stages of system development varies in importance depending on the MSS technology, but it is an important factor.
- Several organizational factors are important to successful implementation; they range from the profile of the team (organization, size, composition, skill levels) to the relationship with the information system department.
- Lack of adequate resources means failure.
- Medium-sized and large MSS projects must go through a rigorous cost–benefit analysis. Assessing benefits may be very difficult because many of them are intangible.
- When MSS technology is integrated with conventional computer-based information systems, the functionality of the latter is increased.
- Functional integration differs from the physical integration required to accomplish it.
- The major area of integration is databases (and database management systems) with expert systems and natural language processors. The result is intelligent databases.
- Expert systems can be used to improve accessibility to databases, either corporate or commercial (online).
- The second major area of integration is the use of expert systems to interpret results of data generated by models, particularly quantitative models.
- Expert systems can be used to enhance knowledge management, database management, and model management.
- Expert systems are being successfully integrated with decision support systems; the result is many useful applications.
- Several conceptual models of integration are applicable to expert systems and decision support systems.
- MSS technologies are being integrated with many computer-based information systems, ranging from CAD/CAM to office automation.
- There are many problems with respect to the integration of AI technology, including technical, behavioral, and managerial factors.

❖ KEY WORDS

- active (symbiotic) DSS
- cost–benefit analysis
- functional integration
- institutionalization
- intelligent DSS
- intelligent interface

- overexpectations
- physical integration
- problem management
- project management
- self-evolving DSS
- symbiotic DSS

- system advocate
- top management support
- user commitment
- user resistance

❖ QUESTIONS FOR REVIEW

1. Define implementation in a broad sense.
2. Define implementation in a narrow sense.
3. What is institutionalization?
4. Describe the various criteria for measuring the success of an implemented information system.
5. List several measures for evaluating the success of expert systems.
6. Describe the technical factors related to successful implementation.
7. What is meant by system response time?
8. What is a decision style?
9. List some of the potential resisters to ES.
10. List some strategies employed to deal with user resistance to DSS.
11. Why is the support of top management vital to system implementation?
12. Describe some of the organizational factors that can affect the success of implementation.
13. What is the difference between functional and physical integration?
14. Describe the two levels of functional integration.
15. DSS and ES integration may result in benefits along what three dimensions?
16. It is said that an ES is an intelligent DSS. Describe their common characteristics. Do you agree with this statement? Why or why not?
17. How can synergy result when decision support systems and expert systems are integrated?
18. Summarize the benefits a DSS can gain in terms of its database when it is integrated with an ES.
19. Discuss the importance of knowledge management.
20. How can the knowledge base of an ES help a DSS?
21. What is a model base management system?
22. Summarize the benefits an ES can provide to a DSS in the area of models and their management.
23. What is the major capability of BUMP?
24. Summarize the benefits that an ES can provide to a human–machine interface.
25. List the possibilities of integrating decision support systems and expert systems.
26. Give an example of an ES output that can be used as an input to a DSS. Also give an example of the reverse relationship.
27. List some technical issues of integration.
28. List some behavioral issues of integration.
29. List some design issues that may arise during MSS integration.

❖ QUESTIONS FOR DISCUSSION

1. Why is implementing MSS technologies more complex than implementing MIS technologies?

2. How can an organizational climate influence implementation?

3. What actions can be taken by top management to support MSS application?

4. Why is the issue of expectation so important in ES implementation?

5. The question of why so many expert systems fail is important. Find an article on this subject and discuss it. For example, see Chapter 1 in Turban and Liebowitz (1992).

6. Review the XCON case of Chapter 10 on this book's Web site. Identify factors that may have contributed to the success of this system.

7. Why may it be difficult to integrate an expert system with an existing information system? Comment on data, people, hardware, and software.

8. Explain the following statement and give an example of both cases: Integration of a DSS and an ES can result in benefits during the construction (development) of the systems and during their operation.

9. How can model management be made intelligent?

10. One expert system can be used to consult several decision support systems. What is the logic of such an arrangement? What problems may result when two or more decision support systems share one expert system?

11. Review the work of Goul et al. (1984). Assume that they are successful in developing an ES that will perform as well as a management science consultant. What could be the major implications of such a system? Why is such a system difficult to build?

12. Compare the work of Goul et al. (1984) with that of Hand (1984). Specifically, what is the major similarity between BUMP and Goul's system?

13. Why is visual modeling (Chapter 5) considered an integration of decision support systems and expert systems?

14. Explain how the addition of an ES capability can improve the chances of successful implementation of a DSS.

15. Review current journals and identify a system that you believe is an MSS integration. Analyze the system according to the models suggested in this chapter.

16. There are many potential problems in MSS integration. Find an example of such a problem in a real-life situation (check the journals if you cannot find one in a workplace) and report your findings.

17. In some of our models we suggested that several ES are included in one CBIS. What is the logic of such an arrangement?

18. Modeling involves three activities: construction, use, and interpretation. Give an example of modeling from an area with which you are familiar and explain how an ES could help the process.

❖ EXERCISES

1. Given below is a DSS success factor questionnaire developed by Sanders and Courtney (1985). Administer the following questionnaire to 10 users of DSS in your organization. Assign a 5 to strongly agree, a 4 to agree, a 3 to neutral, a 2 to disagree, and a 1 to strongly disagree. Compute the average results and rank the factors in order of their importance.

Overall Satisfaction

_____ I have become dependent on DSS.

_____ As a result of DSS, I am seen as being more valuable to this organization.

_____ I have personally benefited from the existence of DSS in this organization.

_____ I have come to rely on DSS in performing my job.
_____ All in all, I think that DSS is an important system for this organization.
_____ DSS is extremely useful.

Decision-making Satisfaction

_____ The use of DSS has enabled me to make better decisions.
_____ As a result of DSS, I am better able to set priorities in decision making.
_____ The use of data generated by DSS has enabled me to present arguments more convincingly.
_____ DSS has improved the quality of the decisions I make in this organization.
_____ As a result of DSS, the speed with which I analyze decisions has increased.
_____ As a result of DSS, more relevant information has been available to me for decision making.
_____ DSS has led me to greater use of analytical aids in my decision making.

Comment on the results.

2. Certain key factors strongly influence the success level of a DSS or ES. The IS/IT/ES literature abounds with cases of failure because key success factors were missing. Likewise, many more studies indicate what is actually meant by success (user satisfaction, level of use, money saved, payback period, and so on). Interview someone who was involved in either sponsoring or using (or both) a real-world DSS or ES. If possible, interview several people, including the system developers or maintainers. Guide your interviews to determine the following:
   a. What is the nature of the system? What problem is it intended to solve? Who is using it and why? Is its use mandatory or optional? Why?
   b. How was the system implemented. Did the implementation procedure contribute to its success in any way? If so, how? If not, why not?
   c. What measures are being used to determine the value of the system to the organization?
   d. What success measures are being used?
   e. Was the system deemed a success? Why?
   f. What are the future plans for the system?

3. Identify a failed DSS or ES (or one that is slated for replacement or a major upgrade because of problems) in an organization and evaluate why the system failed.

❖ GROUP EXERCISES

1. With the software identified in Internet Exercise 5, run several demos and compare their capabilities.

2. Compare the MSS literature on change management and technology adoption to literature describing political revolution and social change. Identify similarities and differences.

3. Meet and discuss ways in which intelligence could be integrated into your university's advising and registration system. Are there any concrete ways in which it could be accomplished quickly and at low cost? Explain.

❖ INTERNET EXERCISES

1. The topic of intelligent model management has challenged researchers for a long time. Search the Internet to identify some recent work in this area and prepare a report.

2. In an attempt to achieve efficiency, there is a trend toward producing expert systems and other intelligent systems on a chip. These chips can be embedded in other CBIS. Visit the Web site of Motorola and other chip manufacturers and find the newest chips on the market.

3. Resistance to change is an important factor in implementation. Write a report on how to handle resistance to change, based on what you find on the Internet.

4. The issue of justifying new technologies, especially intelligent systems, is of utmost importance. Join some news groups interested in AI and intelligent systems and conduct a discussion on this topic. Prepare a report.

5. Several EIS, ES, and other vendors have development tools that support the construction of integrated systems. Identify vendors that make such tools, prepare a representative list, and download and try some available demos.

6. Find a few examples of intelligent decision support systems on the Internet and list specific characteristics or functions that make these systems intelligent.

7. Search the Internet to identify failures of management support systems during implementation and prepare a report describing how such failures can be prevented.

CASE APPLICATION 18.1

URBAN TRAFFIC MANAGEMENT

Traffic management in a city is a complex task involving traffic signals, work on roads, accidents, parking, cars crossing railroad tracks, and pedestrians. The objective is to enable a reasonable flow of traffic, especially during rush hours and at accident sites. Many decisions are involved in traffic management, and many models have been created to support these decisions. GIS have been used to support such decisions. The situation becomes even more complex when a large number of conflicting goals are postulated by various groups ranging from environmentalists to law enforcement agencies. For this reason, it seems logical to use an intelligent DSS as proposed by Bielli (1992). Figure 18.13 shows the proposed DSS architecture. The main modules include resource optimization, modeling and simulation, and evaluation, each with

its separate database and model base. In addition, there are separate knowledge bases. The interaction between the user and the global database takes place through a decision-making process using models whose task is to refine the decision context, scenarios, objectives, main actors, and projects under consideration.

CASE QUESTIONS

1. Why is it necessary to use a DSS in this case?
2. Why is it necessary to include knowledge bases?
3. Why are there different databases, knowledge bases, and model bases?
4. How can GIS be incorporated into such a system?

Source: M. Bielli, "A DSS Approach to Urban Traffic Management," *European Journal of Operational Research,* Vol. 61, Nos. 1 and 2, Aug. 25, 1992.

FIGURE 18.13 A DSS ARCHITECTURE FOR URBAN TRAFFIC MANAGEMENT

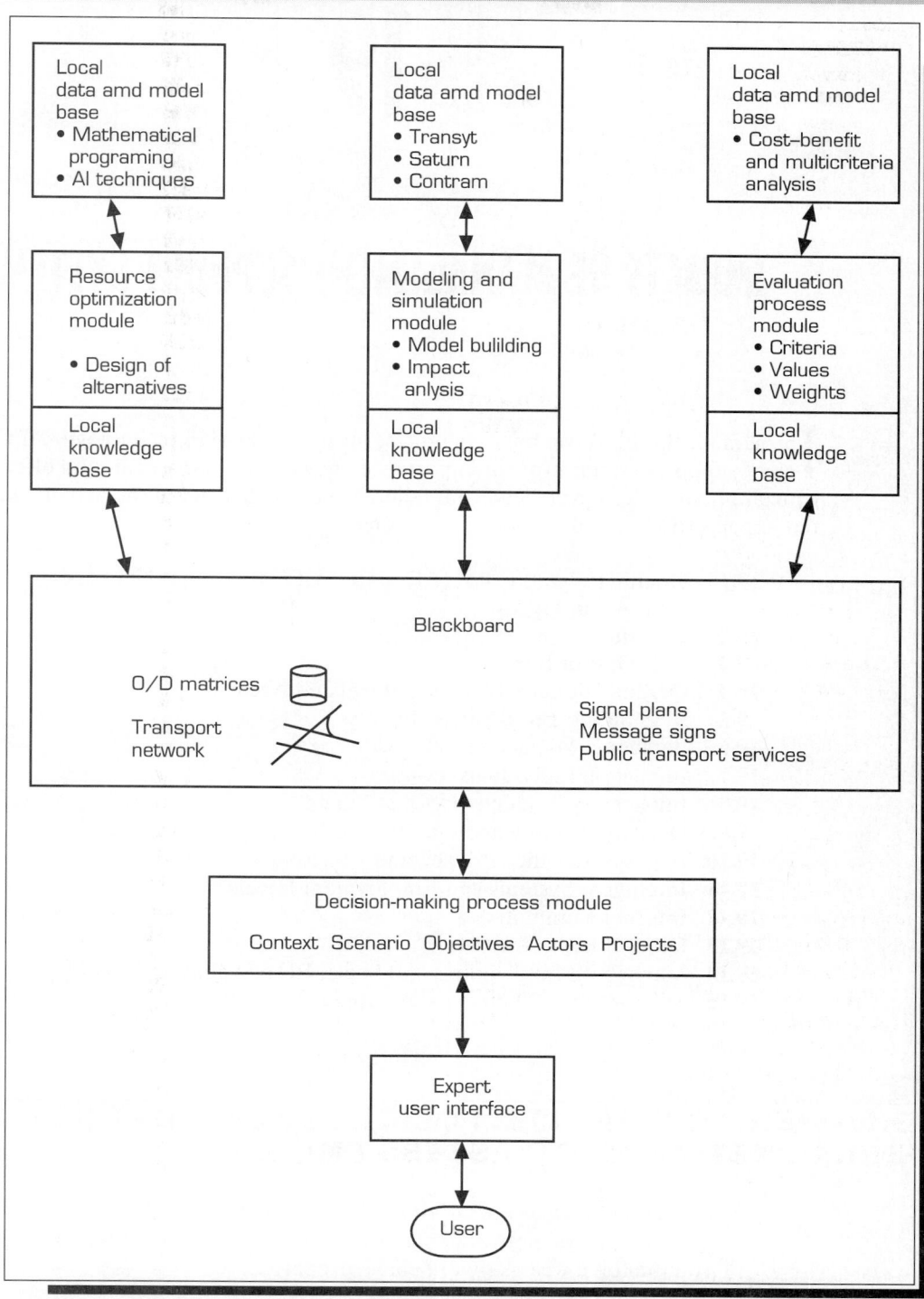

Source: Bielli (1992), p. 107. Bielli, M. (1992. Aug. 25). "A DSS Approach to Urban Traffic Management." *European Journal of Operational Research,* Vol. 61, Nos. 1 and 2.

IMPACTS OF MANAGEMENT SUPPORT SYSTEMS

Throughout this book, we have covered several applied MSS technologies. If management support systems grow in importance, they could have a profound effect on organizations, people, and society. This chapter deals with some of the actual and potential impacts of MSS in the following sections:

19.1 OPENING VIGNETTE: POLICE DEPARTMENT USES NEURAL NETWORKS TO ASSESS EMPLOYEES[1]

Several years ago, the internal affairs division of the Chicago Police Department started to use a neural network software model to predict whether each of the 12,500 officers on the force was likely to behave properly.

---

[1]Condensed from J. Holand, "Bad Apple Picker: Can a Neural Network Help Find Problem Cops?" *Scientific American,* Dec. 1994.

776

The system uses a model that was trained by comparing certain characteristics of all officers to a profile of about 200 officers who were dismissed or resigned under investigation for actions ranging from insubordination to misconduct. Those who match are classified as headed for trouble.

This application was found to be fairly accurate. About half of the 91 people identified by the program as having potential misconduct problems had already been manually identified and placed in an improvement program. The computer software created a major debate. The Chicago Police Department maintains that it is impossible to check so many officers manually to identify potential misconduct. If early detection of potential offenders is accomplished, a counseling program can rectify the situation. A computer program can screen many people periodically and cannot be biased one way or another as a supervisor can. Furthermore, neural networks have already proven to be helpful in similar tasks such as predicting recidivism by criminals on probation.

The labor union was unhappy, saying that the system was unethical. They claimed that it was merely a tactic by management to avoid managing the officers: "You got a guy slacking off? Supervise him, correct him." Other critics' main objection was that neural networks are a form of black box: They do not indicate how they arrived at a conclusion, and it is not fair to use a technology that you do not understand. The software developer said, "Users don't need to know what the software is doing—they only need to know whether it works." The Chicago Police Department believes that the computer program works very well.

❖ QUESTIONS FOR THE OPENING VIGNETTE

1. Is this another example, in which needs of the society are in conflict with the rights of the individual?
2. Is using the neural network computer program ethical? What if a standard statistical approach were used? Would that be ethical?
3. If you were an officer being evaluated, would you object to such a program? Why?
4. Is it fair for police departments to use a neural network program to screen new applicants? If so, what is wrong with using such a program retroactively?
5. As a citizen, would you want your police department to use the program? Why or why not?
6. Robert Jordan took an exam to become a New London (CT) police officer but scored too high and was rejected. He filed a federal lawsuit in early June 1997 alleging discrimination based on intelligence (B. Greenberg, "How Smart Is Too Smart to Be a Police Officer?" Associated Press news story, June 6, 1997). Debate the legal and ethical issues involved in this case.

19.2 INTRODUCTION

The Opening Vignette demonstrates that

- A MSS can radically change the decision-making process by using neural computing to increase the productivity and accuracy of decisions made by supervisors.

- There is a resistance to the introduction of new technology that is difficult for individuals and organized labor to understand.
- The value of a technology can be debatable.
- The introduction of one MSS application may have multiple impacts, including impacts external to the organization (such as a reduction in crime and a better police force).

MSS are important enablers of the **information and knowledge revolution,** a cultural transformation with which most people are only now coming to terms. Unlike slower revolutions of the past, such as the industrial revolution, the information revolution is taking place very quickly and affecting every facet of our lives. Inherent in this rapid transformation is a host of managerial and social problems: impact on organizational structure, resistance to change, rapidly increasing unemployment levels, and so on. The MSS share of the computer industry could reach 30 percent by the year 2005, and so its impact can be substantial.

Separating the impact of MSS from that of other computerized systems is a difficult task, especially because of the trend toward integrating, or even embedding, MSS with other computer-based information systems. There is very little published information about the impact of pure MSS technologies because the techniques are so new. Sometimes, by the time we understand the impact of a new information technology (such as the Internet), a new one is already on the near horizon that will revolutionize it (such as intranets and extranets). Thus, some of our discussion must relate to computer systems in general. We recognize, however, that MSS technologies do have some unique implications, which are highlighted throughout this chapter.

MSS can have both micro and macro implications. It can affect particular individuals and jobs, the work structure of departments, and units within an organization. It can also have significant long-term effects on total organizational structures, entire industries, communities, and society as a whole.

Figure 19.1 presents a framework that shows a complete management system. Such a system stays in equilibrium as long as all of its parts are unchanged. If there is a major change in one of the components, or in the relevant environment, the change will probably affect some of the other components. The major change stimuli (relevant to MSS) are strategy and technology, especially when computerized systems such as a DSS or ES are introduced. For further discussion, see Scott Morton (1991), Gill (1996), and Grudin and Wellman (1999).

One of the major changes that is occurring is the emergence of the Web and its impact (Wycoff et al., 2000) and knowledge management. Both are related to the organizational transformation of **business process reengineering (BPR).** Information technology, especially some intelligent systems, play a major role in supporting this change. According to Brancheau et al. (1996), using IT to support BPR, for example, was voted the most important issue of information management in 1994–1995. Hammer and Champy (1993) describe information technology as the major enabler of BPR.

The purpose of this chapter is to foster a basic understanding of the major impacts of widespread use of MSS.

19.3 OVERVIEW OF IMPACTS

The impacts of computers and MSS technology can be divided into three general categories: *organizational, individual,* and *societal.* Computers have had an impact on organizations in many ways. We cannot possibly consider all of them in this chapter, and so we

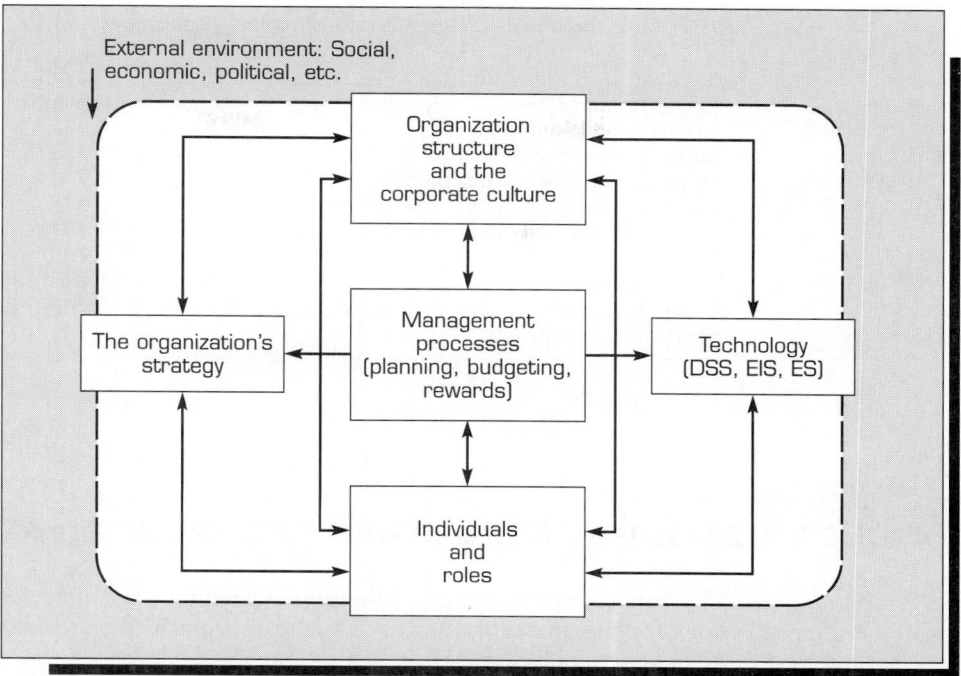

External environment: Social, economic, political, etc.

Organization structure and the corporate culture

The organization's strategy

Management processes (planning, budgeting, rewards)

Technology (DSS, EIS, ES)

Individuals and roles

FIGURE 19.1 FRAMEWORK FOR ORGANIZATIONAL AND SOCIETAL IMPACTS OF AI TECHNOLOGY

Source: M. Scott Morton, "DSS Revisited for the 1990s," paper presented at DSS 1986, Washington, DC, April 1986. Used with permission.

TABLE 19.1   Organizational Impacts of Computer Technology

Area of Impact	*Section in This Chapter*
Reengineering and restructuring	19.4
Span of control	19.4
Centralization versus decentralization	19.4
Authority, power, and status	19.4
New organizational units	19.4
Organizational culture	19.4
Job content and roles	19.6
Career ladder	19.6
Supervision	19.6
Individuals	19.7
Productivity and competitiveness	19.8
Decision making and the manager's job	19.9
Issues of legality, ethics, and privacy	19.10

have selected the topics we feel are most relevant to MSS. They are listed in Table 19.1 along with the sections in which they are discussed.

Computer technology has already changed our world, and much more change is anticipated. In addition to impacts on individuals, there are significant societal impacts. Table 19.2 summarizes some of the major areas of social impact and lists the sections in which they are discussed.

TABLE 19.2   Social Impacts of Computer Technology

Area of Impact	Section in This Chapter
Employment levels	19.11
Electronic communities	19.12
Work in hazardous environments	19.13
Opportunities for the disabled	19.13
Changing role of women	19.13
Telecommuting (working at home)	19.13
Consumers	19.13
Quality of life	19.13
Computer crime	19.13
Social responsibility	19.13

19.4 ORGANIZATIONAL STRUCTURE AND RELATED AREAS

The organizational impacts of computer technology can be felt along several dimensions, ranging from structure and degree of centralization to distribution of power. Here we deal with only some of the major issues.

STRUCTURE

Computer-based systems have already created changes in organizational structures. MSS could further enhance these changes in several ways.

FLATTER ORGANIZATIONAL HIERARCHIES
MSS allows increased productivity of managers, an increased span of control (less need for supervision), and a decreased number of experts (because of the availability of expert systems and other knowledge management systems that provide information directly via the Internet or intranets). It is reasonable to assume, then, that there will be fewer managerial levels in many organizations. There will also be fewer staff and line managers. This trend is already evidenced by the continuing phenomenon of the shrinking size of middle management (Pinsonneault and Kraemer, 1993).

Flatter organizational hierarchies will also result from a reduction in the total number of employees as a result of increased productivity and because of the ability of lower-level employees to perform higher-level jobs (e.g., by using ES and IA). For example, consider Bank of America's reorganization and Citicorp's reorganization, each of which resulted in a smaller corporation and a much flatter structure. The main reason for the downsizing of many organizations is the increased use of IT in general and intelligent support systems in particular.

STAFF-TO-LINE RATIO
The ratio of staff to line workers in most organizations has increased with clerical jobs being replaced by computer systems and with an increased need for information system specialists. The expansion of MSS, and especially ES, may reverse this trend. Specifically, the number of professionals and specialists could decline in relation to the total number of employees in an organization.

CENTRALIZATION OF AUTHORITY

The relationship between computerized systems and the degree of centralization of authority (and power) in organizations has been debated extensively, especially since the introduction of personal computers. However, it is still difficult to establish a clear pattern. For example, the introduction of ES in General Electric's maintenance area increased the power of the decentralized units because they became less dependent on the company's headquarters. On the other hand, ES can be used as a means of increasing control and centralization.

Computer-based information systems can support either centralization or decentralization of electronic information processing within an organization. For further discussion, see Huber (1990) and DSS in Focus 19.1. Although information systems are usually established after an organizational structure is completed, it is quite possible that a new or modified information system can change the organizational structure or the degree of decentralization.

Because of the trend toward smaller and flatter organizations, centralization may become more popular. However, this trend could be offset by a need for specialization in decentralized units.

POWER AND STATUS

Knowledge is power—this fact has been recognized for generations (Toffler, 1991). The latest developments in computerized systems are changing the power structure within organizations. The struggle over who will control the computers, information resources, and intranets has become one of the most visible conflicts in many organizations, both private and public. Expert systems, for example, may reduce the power of certain professional groups because their knowledge will be in the public domain (Ryan, 1988). On the other hand, people who control AI and KM application teams may gain consider-

---

DSS IN FOCUS 19.1

HUBER'S PROPOSITIONS ABOUT COMPUTERS' IMPACTS ON ORGANIZATIONS

The use of MSS and other computer-assisted communication technologies leads to the following organizational changes:

- A large number and variety of people participating as decision sources

- A decrease in the number and variety of people participating in traditional face-to-face communication

- Less time spent in meetings

- A better chance that a particular organizational level will make a particular decision

- Greater variation across the organization at the levels at which a particular type of decision is made

- Fewer organizational levels involved in authorizing actions

- Fewer intermediate information nodes within the organizational information processing network

- Fewer levels involved in processing messages

- More frequent development and use of databases

- More rapid and more accurate identification of problems and opportunities

- Less time required to authorize actions and/or make decisions

- Higher-quality decisions will be made.

Source: Condensed and compiled from Huber (1990).

able knowledge, power, and status. In contrast to the situation with a regular CBIS, the issues at stake for MSS could be much more important and visible because complex decision situations and upper management may be involved. An intelligent information system may control some of the major decisions in an organization, including long-range strategic ones.

NEW ORGANIZATIONAL UNITS

Another change in organizational structure is the possibility of creating a DSS department, management support department, AI department, or *knowledge management* department in which MSS plays a major role. These additional units can be an extension of the information center, can replace a management science unit, or can be a completely new entity.

There are DSS departments in several large corporations. For example, many major banks have a DSS department in their financial services division. Mead Corporation has a special corporate DSS applications department (see DSS in Action 19.2). Many companies have a small DSS unit. Several large corporations have already created AI departments. For example, FMC Corporation created one of the earliest and largest AI departments (see AIS in Action 19.3); Boeing Company operates a large AI department. In both cases, the departments are involved in extensive training in addition to research, consulting, and application activities. For details on how several corporations structure their AI units, see Turban, (1992). A number of firms have created knowledge management departments headed by a CKO (Chapter 9).

ORGANIZATIONAL CULTURE AND VIRTUAL TEAMS

Organizational culture can affect the diffusion rate of technology and can be influenced by it (Chapter 18). For example, the use of Lotus Notes changed the organizational climate of a large CPA firm by making employees more cooperative and willing to share information and to use computers. There is also some dissolution of organizational structure. Virtual teams can meet anytime and anyplace. People can join a virtual team for as long as the project lasts, or whenever their expertise is needed. When the project is completed, the team can disband.

VIRTUAL CORPORATIONS

A major structural change is the creation of **virtual corporations**, which appear in several forms (Magid, 1999). Virtual companies (or enterprises) enable companies to exploit their core competency. MSS facilitate decision-making processes in virtual corporations as shown by O'Leary et al. (1997).

19.5 MSS SUPPORT TO BUSINESS PROCESS REENGINEERING

BUSINESS REENGINEERING

Business process reengineering (BPR) is a major innovation changing the way organizations conduct their business. Such changes are often necessary for profitability or even survival. BPR is employed when major IT projects, such as ERP or EC, are undertaken. Reengineering involves changes in structure, organizational culture, and processes (Hammer and Stanton, 1995).

DECISION SUPPORT AT MEAD CORPORATION

Mead Corporation created a DSS department in the mid-1980s, which included an interactive help center, office systems, decision analysis, and financial modeling. In the 1990s, a new function was added: local area experts. These are people who report directly to users' departments and indirectly (broken lines in figure) to the director of the DSS department. They assist users in developing and maintaining DSS applications.

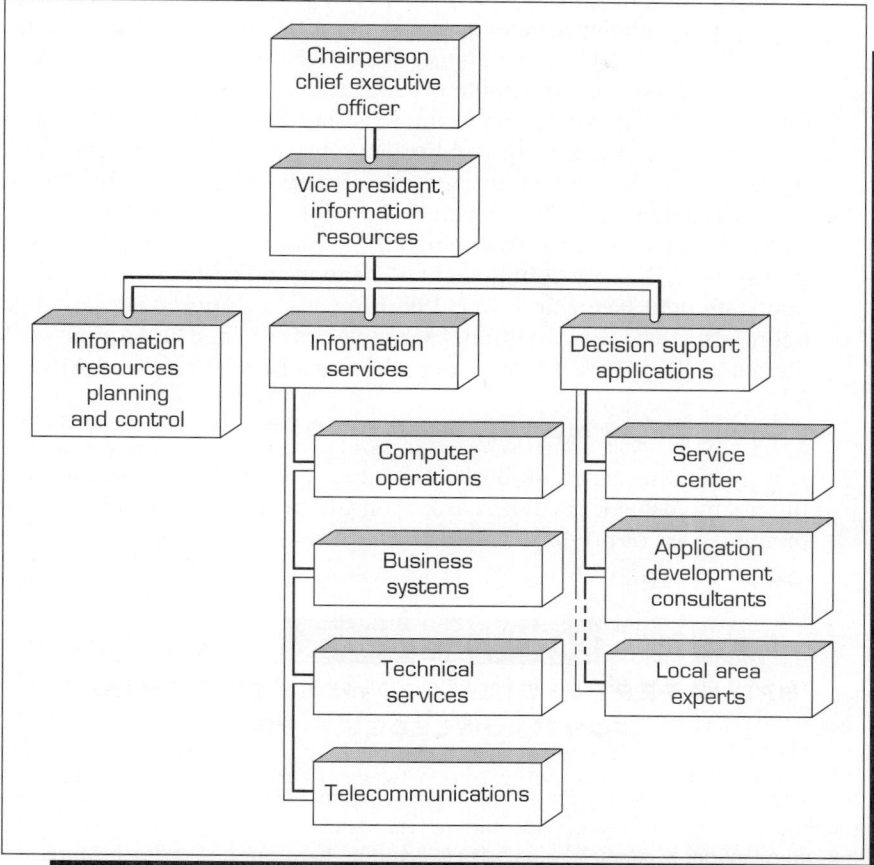

Source: R. H. Sprague, Jr., and B. C. McNurlin, *Information Systems in Practice,* 3rd ed. Englewood Cliffs, NJ: Prentice Hall, 1993, p. 28.

ARTIFICIAL INTELLIGENCE AT FMC CORPORATION

FMC Corporation (Santa Clara, CA) has made a major commitment to AI. In the mid-1980s the company built a 90-person AI center. Major applications started in the defense area and moved to the industrial machinery (manufacturing and maintenance) area. Initial expert systems were used in oil pumping operations, automotive engine design, and tool design. Applications now range from the operations of chemical plants to machinery manufacturing. Robotics and machine vision technology are being transferred from defense to the manufacturing plants.

To build up the necessary personnel, the company has designed an in-house training program equivalent to a master of science program for the AI specialists. With a rich application environment and strong corporate commitment, the company has become an industrial center of excellence in applied AI. By the mid-1990s the center had grown to include neural computing and other cutting-edge AI technologies.

Several concepts of BPR greatly change organizational structure: team-based organization, mass customization, empowerment, and telecommuting. In these cases, MSS are used extensively as an enabler (Turban et al., 2001).

MSS plays a major role in BPR (Currid et al., 1994). MSS (especially ES, DSS, AI, and EIS) allows business to be conducted in different locations, provides flexibility in manufacturing, permits quicker delivery to customers, and supports rapid, paperless transactions among suppliers, manufacturers, and retailers. In Chapter 7 we provided an example of GSS use, in which the impact of Lotus Notes at Price Waterhouse was explored.

Expert systems can enable organizational changes by providing expertise to non-experts (Yu et al., 1996). An example is shown in Figure 19.2. The upper part shows a bank before reengineering. A customer who needs several services must go to several departments. The bank keeps multiple records and provides the customer with several monthly statements. The reengineered bank is shown in the lower part. A customer makes contacts with only one person, an account manager, who is supported by an expert system. The new arrangement is cheaper, and customers save time and receive only one statement [see Min et al. (1996) for a description of an intelligent bank reengineering system). For additional examples of ES in BPR in real-world situations, see Strischeck and Cross (1996), Sugumaran and Bose (1996), and AIS in Action 19.4.

SIMULATION MODELING AND BPR

It is difficult to carry out business process reengineering calculations on a basic computer spreadsheet. For this reason, consultants and IT specialists are turning to an expanding class of products called *business simulation tools.* Many of these programs let

---

AIS IN ACTION 19.4

BPR EXPERT SYSTEM PROVIDES EXPERTISE FOR KNOWLEDGE FIRM

ALX Development Corporation was formed in 1983 to exploit the combination of artificial intelligence and proprietary methodology in bank financial analysis. The company has evolved into a personal service organization that uses the original technology as a productivity tool.

ALX Development Corporation, founded by John R. Segerstrom, serves mainly banks, banking consultants, and regulatory agencies in risk management and problem anticipation.

Although ALX Development Corporation provided excellent customer service and was recognized for its technical expertise, it failed to achieve significant market penetration. Management wanted help in allocating newly available financial resources. Because they were familiar with expert systems, they turned to Business Insight.

They answered Business Insight's questions regarding products, prospects, and resources and then reviewed the recommended strategies. Segerstrom says, "We simply would not have been able to perform this analysis ourselves, it isn't our area of expertise." Using

the Business Insight analyses, ALX embarked on a focused marketing program. Today, revenue growth is beginning to strain its service resources, a problem welcomed by ALX. The marketing effort has been supplemented by professionals in areas where it was weak, and Business Insight has dramatically reduced risk by providing standards that allow ALX to direct and measure its efforts. The program is run by ALX Development Corporation staff and was culturally integrated into the company at the start. An important fact is that very little of the company's recent expenditure for marketing has been wasted on mistakes or failures, as in the past.

According to Segerstrom, "Our experience has been that our expert system could say things about a bank that no one in the bank itself dared say, and get away with it! Business Insight has performed this function for ALX Development Corp."

Source: Adapted from "Case Studies in Business Strategy," Business Resource Software Inc., Austin, TX, Feb. 1997, www.brs-inc.com.

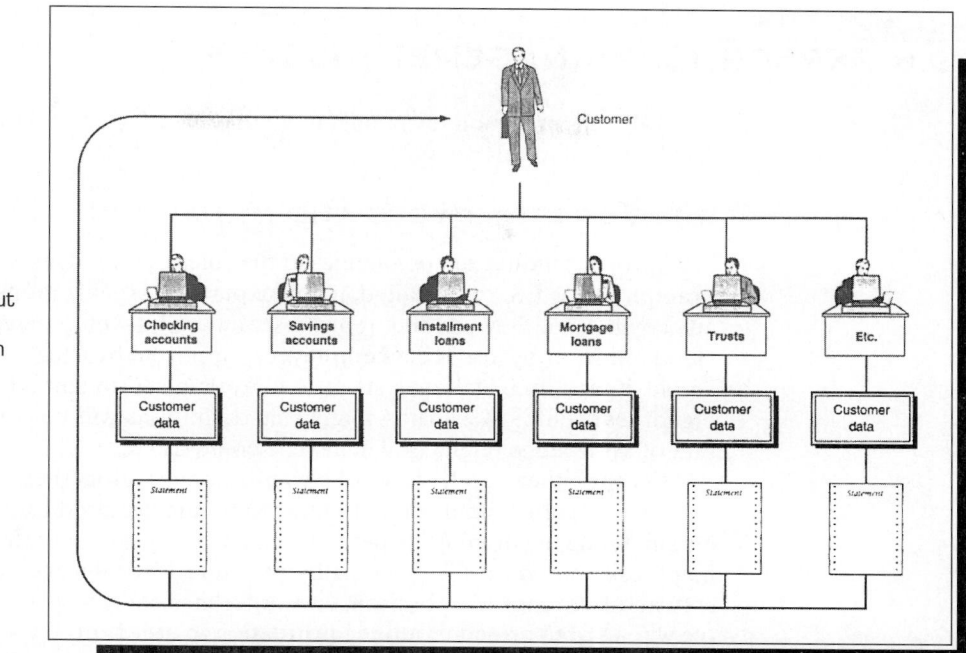

Without expert system

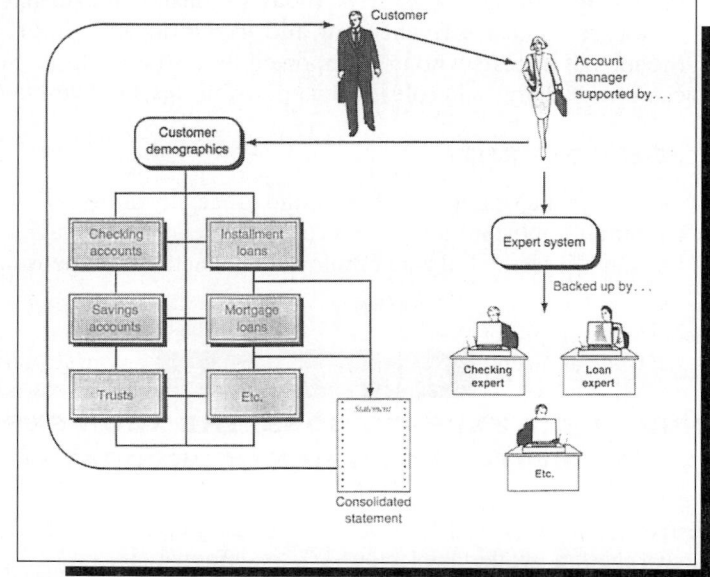

With expert system

FIGURE 19.2 THE ROLE OF ES IN A BANK'S BPR

Source: Turban et al. (2001), p. 113. Turban, E. et. al. (2001). *Information Technology Management,* 3rd ed. New York: Wiley.

users set up flowcharts to diagram the movement of resources through manufacturing or other business processes (El Sawy, 1998; Francis and Capon, 1996). Warren et al. (1995) provide a comprehensive description of how to use simulation modeling for BPR. See Case Application 19.1 for an example of how simulation can be used in BPR.

19.6 PERSONNEL MANAGEMENT ISSUES

Several areas in personnel management may be affected by MSS. Representative issues are described in this section.

ROLE OF EMPLOYEES AND MANAGERS

MSS projects induce major changes in the roles that managers and employees play. For example, once ES are installed, many experts in organizations stop providing routine advice; instead, they conduct more research and development. Routine advice is provided online or by less skilled employees supported by ES. At Bank of America, for example, junior financial analysts at low levels perform some tasks previously done by higher-level employees. Thus, many role definitions will be changed. New jobs such as that of knowledge engineer will also be created.

On the other hand, some jobs will disappear altogether. For example, an ES that can advise people about what immunizations are required when traveling abroad could eliminate the position of the person who currently gives out this information. Similarly, help desks based on ES (such as those offered by Ginesys Corporation, www.ginesy. com and Inference Corporation, www.inference.com) have eliminated the jobs of people who used to provide routine information to other employees and even to customers. Such software even captures mistakes, which are then reviewed by an expert.

The support staff for top management will generally consist of information and knowledge specialists, whereas today's typical manager has specialists mainly in functional areas (such as finance, law, and accounting). An interesting change could occur in the jobs of experts who are supported by ES (see AIS in Action 19.5). For further discussion of changes in roles and responsibilities, see Sviokla (1990).

JOB CONTENT

One of the major impacts of MSS, and especially of ES, is on the content of many jobs. **Job content** is important not only because it is related to organizational structure but also because it is interrelated with employee satisfaction, compensation, status, and productivity.

AIS IN ACTION 19.5

CHANGE IN THE EXPERTS' JOBS: THE XCON EXPERIENCE  AT DIGITAL EQUIPMENT CORPORATION

Before the expert system XCON was available, even experts had to do manual checking, undertake tedious jobs, and handle repetitive, boring tasks. They made mistakes that had to be corrected, and their jobs were considered to have low status.

After XCON became available, the experts' jobs changed. Here is what the experts do:

- They check what XCON does.
- They do the 2 percent of work that XCON cannot do (the challenging problems).

- They update XCON's knowledge base with new information.

Now the experts are considered custodians of XCON's pool of configuration knowledge, and they are accorded high status.

Source: Condensed from Sviokla (1990).

ROLE AMBIGUITY AND CONFLICT

Changes in job content will result in opportunities for promotion and employee development. But these changes could create problems of role conflict and **role ambiguity,** especially in the short run. In addition, there may be considerable resistance to changes in roles, primarily on the part of managers who favor a noncomputerized information system.

EMPLOYEE CAREER LADDERS

The increased use of MSS in organizations could have a significant and somewhat unexpected impact on **career ladders.** Today, many highly skilled professionals have developed their abilities through years of experience. This experience is gained by holding a series of positions that expose the person to progressively more difficult and complex situations. The use of MSS, and especially intelligent systems, may block out a portion of this learning curve. However, several questions remain unaddressed: How will high-level human expertise be acquired with minimal experience in lower-level tasks? What will be the effect on compensation at all levels of employment? How will human resource development programs be structured? What career plans will be offered to employees?

CHANGES IN SUPERVISION

The fact that an employee's work is performed online and stored electronically introduces the possibility for greater electronic supervision, especially when enhanced by AI technologies. For professional employees whose work is often measured by the completion of projects, remote supervision implies greater emphasis on completed work and less on personal contacts. This emphasis is especially true if employees work in geographically dispersed locations away from their supervisors.

OTHER CONSIDERATIONS

Several other personnel-related issues could surface as a result of using MSS. For example, what will be the impact of MSS on job qualifications, training requirements, and worker satisfaction? How can jobs involving the use of MSS tools be designed so they present an acceptable level of challenge to users? How might MSS be used to personalize or enrich jobs? What can be done to make sure that the introduction of MSS does not demean jobs or have other negative impacts from the workers' point of view? What principles should be used to allocate functions to people and machines, especially functions that can be performed equally well by either one? Should cost or efficiency be the sole or major criterion for such allocation? What is the role of the human resources department in a virtual organization?

19.7 IMPACT ON INDIVIDUALS

MSS systems may affect individuals in various ways. What is a benefit to one individual may be a curse to another. What is an added stress today can be a relief tomorrow. Some of the areas where MSS systems may affect individuals, their perceptions, and behaviors are described next.

JOB SATISFACTION

Although many jobs may become substantially enriched by MSS, other jobs may become more routine and less satisfying. For example, Argyris (1971) predicted that computer-based information systems would reduce managerial discretion in decision making and thus create dissatisfied managers. A study by Ryker and Ravinder (1995) showed that IT has had a positive effect on four of the five core job dimensions: identity, significance, autonomy, and feedback. No significant effect was found on skill variety.

INFLEXIBILITY AND DEHUMANIZATION

A common criticism of traditional data processing systems is their negative effect on people's individuality. Such systems are criticized as being impersonal: They dehumanize and depersonalize activities that have been computerized because they reduce or eliminate the human element that was present in noncomputerized systems. Many people feel a loss of identity; they feel like just another number. On the bright side, one of the major objectives of MSS is to create flexible systems and interfaces (Chapter 17) that will allow individuals to share their opinions and knowledge. Despite all the efforts, some people are simply afraid of computers.

COOPERATION OF EXPERTS

Human experts who are about to give their knowledge to an organizational or problem-specific knowledge base may have reservations. Consider these examples of thoughts that might enter an expert's mind:

- The computer may replace me.
- The computer may make me less important.
- Why should I tell the computer my secrets? What will I gain?
- The computer may reveal that I am not as great an expert as people think.

This kind of thinking may cause the expert not to cooperate, or even to give incorrect knowledge to the computer. To deal with such situations, management should motivate (and possibly compensate) the experts.

19.8 IMPACTS ON PRODUCTIVITY, QUALITY, AND COMPETITIVENESS

The major benefits of MSS, which can result in a competitive advantage, are as follows:

- *Increased productivity.* Productivity is increased when workers can accomplish their tasks faster or with fewer interruptions (Sviokla, 1990). Large increases are evidenced with intelligent agents (Murch and Johnson, 1999).
- *Increase in quality.* Quality is increased by reduction of errors, production of more consistent products and services, and improvements in inspection and quality control (all at a reasonable cost).
- *Cost reduction.* Producing a product or providing a service at a lower cost than competitors (yet with the same quality) provides a competitive edge.
- *Timely production.* Producing products (and providing services) whenever needed results in a competitive advantage.
- *Faster time to market.* Smaller, specialized batches of (even new) products can be manufactured to meet specific market niches. Software releases can take place via the Internet.
- *Fast training of employees.* The costs of training can be very high, especially if turnover is high or when there is rapid technical change. Training time

(and cost) can be dramatically reduced with intelligent computer-aided instruction through AI (Senker, 1989).
- *Increased production (service) capacity.* Because they allow improved planning, ES can increase production or service capacity.
- *Unique services.* Voice technology, for example, enables banks and telephone companies to offer new and unique services.
- *Enable BPR and organizational transformation.* MSS by its very nature enables BPR, which may lead to organizational transformation.

In addition to these benefits, MSS can enhance other computer systems that contribute to increased productivity and competitiveness. For an overview of information technology as a competitive weapon, see Neumann (1994) and Turban et al. (2001). For actual examples see Neo (1996). For specific ways that ES can be used to attain and sustain a competitive advantage, see the benefits described in Chapter 10.

19.9 DECISION MAKING AND THE MANAGER'S JOB

Computer-based information systems have had an impact on the manager's job for over three decades. However, this impact was felt mainly at the lower- and middle-managerial levels. Now MSS are affecting the top manager's job as well.

The most important task of managers is making decisions. MSS technologies can change the manner in which many decisions are being made and consequently change managers' jobs. The impacts of MSS on decision making can be many; the most probable areas are the following:

- Automation of routine decisions or phases in the decision-making process (e.g., for frontline decision making)
- Less expertise (experience) required for many decisions
- Faster decision making because of the availability of information and the automation of some phases
- Less reliance on experts and analysts to provide support to top executives; managers can do it by themselves with the help of intelligent systems
- Power redistribution among managers
- Support for complex decisions, making them faster and of better quality
- Information for high-level decision making.

Many managers have reported that the computer has finally given them time to get out of the office and into the field. (EIS can save an hour a day for every user.) They also have found that they can spend more time planning activities instead of putting out fires because they can be alerted to potential problems well in advance (via EIS with intelligent agents, expert systems, OLAP, and other analytical tools). Another aspect of the management challenge lies in the ability of MSS to support the decision process in general and strategic planning and control decisions in particular. MSS could change the decision-making process and even decision-making styles. For example, information gathering for decision making is completed much more quickly. Enterprise information systems are extremely useful in supporting strategic management (Liu et al., 2000; Wang and Turban, 1993). AI technologies are now used to improve environmental scanning of information (Elofson and Konsynski, 1990). As a result, managers can change their approach to problem solving. Research indicates that most managers tend to work on a large number of problems simultaneously, moving from one to another as they wait for more information on their current problem (Mintzberg, 1989). MSS tend to reduce the time required to complete tasks in the decision-making process and eliminate some of the nonproductive waiting time by providing knowledge and information. Therefore, managers will work on fewer tasks during each day but will complete more of them. The reduction in start-up time associated with moving from task to task could be the most important source of increased managerial productivity.

Another possible impact on the manager's job could be a change in leadership requirements. What are generally considered good leadership qualities may be significantly altered with the use of MSS. For example, as face-to-face communication is replaced by electronic mail and computerized conferencing, leadership qualities attributed to physical appearance could become less important.

Even if managers' jobs do not change dramatically, the methods that managers use to do their jobs will. For example, an increasing number of CEOs no longer use intermediaries; instead, they work directly with computers and the Web. Once voice understanding is economically feasible, we may see a real revolution in the manner in which managers use computers.

19.10 ISSUES OF LEGALITY, PRIVACY, AND ETHICS

LEGALITY

The introduction of MSS, and especially ES, may compound a host of legal issues already relevant to computer systems. The expensive, prolonged litigation of the IBM and Microsoft antitrust cases and the restructuring of AT&T are prominent examples. Questions concerning liability for the actions of intelligent machines are just beginning to be considered. The issue of computers as a form of unfair competition in business has already been raised in the well-known dispute over the practices of airline reservation systems.

In addition to resolving disputes about the unexpected and possibly damaging results of some MSS systems, other complex issues may surface. For example, who is liable if an enterprise finds itself bankrupt as a result of using the advice of MSS? Will the enterprise itself be held responsible for not testing such systems adequately before entrusting them with sensitive issues? Will auditing and accounting firms share the liability for failing to apply adequate auditing tests? Will the manufacturers of intelligent systems be jointly liable? Consider the following specific legal issues:

- What is the value of an expert opinion in court when the expertise is encoded in a computer?
- Who is liable for wrong advice (or information) provided by an ES? For example, what happens if a physician accepts an incorrect diagnosis made by a computer and performs an act that results in the death of a patient?
- What happens if a manager enters an incorrect judgment value into an MSS and the result is damage or a disaster?
- Who owns the knowledge in a knowledge base?
- Should royalties be paid to experts who provide knowledge to an ES or a knowledge base, and if so how much?
- Can management force experts to contribute their expertise?

For a discussion of these and other issues, consult Mykytyn et al. (1990), Warkentin et al. (1994), and Charles (1995).

ETHICS

Ethical issues for MSS are similar to those for other information systems (Table 19.3). Representative issues that could be of interest in MSS implementations are the following:

- Computer abuse and misuse
- Electronic surveillance (Diffie and Landau, 1998)
- Software piracy (Smith and Parr, 1998)
- Invasion of individuals' privacy (Mizell, 1998)
- Use of proprietary databases
- Use of intellectual property [Harris (1998), Yueng (1998)]
- Exposure of employees to unsafe environments related to computers
- Computer accessibility for workers with disabilities
- Accuracy of data, information, and knowledge
- Protecting the right of users [Karat (1998)]
- Accessibility to information
- Use of corporate computers for private purposes
- How much decision making to delegate to computers.

TABLE 19.3 A Framework for Ethical Issues

Privacy	*Accuracy*
<ul><li>What information about oneself should a person be required to reveal to others?</li><li>What kind of surveillance can an employer use on its employees?</li><li>What things can people keep to themselves and not be forced to reveal to others?</li><li>What information about individuals should be kept in databases and how secure is the information there?</li></ul>	<ul><li>Who is responsible for the authenticity, fidelity, and accuracy of information collected?</li><li>How can we ensure that information will be processed properly and presented accurately to users?</li><li>How can we ensure that errors in databases, data transmissions, and data processing are accidental and not intentional?</li><li>Who is to be held accountable for errors in information, and how is an injured party compensated?</li></ul>
Property	*Accessibility*
<ul><li>Who owns the information?</li><li>What are the just and fair prices for its exchange?</li><li>Who owns the channels of information?</li><li>How should one handle software piracy (copying copyrighted software)?</li><li>Under what circumstances can one use proprietary databases?</li><li>Can corporate computers be used for private purposes?</li><li>How should experts who contribute their knowledge to create expert systems be compensated?</li><li>How should access to information channels be allocated?</li></ul>	<ul><li>Who is allowed to access information?</li><li>How much should be charged for permitting access to information?</li><li>How can accessibility to computers be provided for employees with disabilities?</li><li>Who will be provided with equipment needed for accessing information?</li><li>What information does a person or an organization have a right or a privilege to obtain, under what conditions, and with what safeguards?</li></ul>

Source: Turban et al. (2001); compiled from Mason et al. (1995).

A major factor in the ethical decision-making issue is personal values. For a comprehensive study, see Fritzsche (1995). The study of ethical issues in MSS is complex because of its multidimensionality. Therefore, it makes sense to develop models to describe ethics processes and systems. Mason et al. (1995) explain how technology and innovation expand the size of the domain of ethics and discuss a model for ethical reasoning that involves four fundamental focusing questions: Who is the agent? What action was actually taken or is being contemplated? What are the results or consequences of the act? Is the result fair or just for all stakeholders (Figure 19.3)? They also describe a hierarchy of ethical reasoning in which a particular ethical judgment or action is based on rules and codes of ethics, which are based on principles, which in turn are grounded in ethical theories.

Loch and Conger (1996) describe a study evaluating ethical decision making and computer use based on the theory of reasoned action (TRA) and its extensions. The TRA relates an individual's attitudes and social norms to intentions to act. Attitudes and norms are expected to differ from situation to situation. Their results indicate that **deindividuation** (a feeling of being separated from others that can lead to behavior violating established norms of appropriateness), self-image, ethical attitude, computer literacy, and social norms impact ethical decision making and computer use. Other interesting information on MSS and ethics can be found in Conger et al. (1995) and in "Ethics and Computer Use," *Communications of the ACM,* December 1995.

For further discussion of ethical issues, see Dejoie et al. (1995) and Kallman and Grillo (1996).

PRIVACY

Modern computer systems can economically collect, store, integrate, exchange, and retrieve information and knowledge. This ability can affect every individual's right to privacy. Confidential information contained in information bases could be misused and re-

FIGURE 19.3 A MODEL FOR ETHICAL REASONING PROCESS

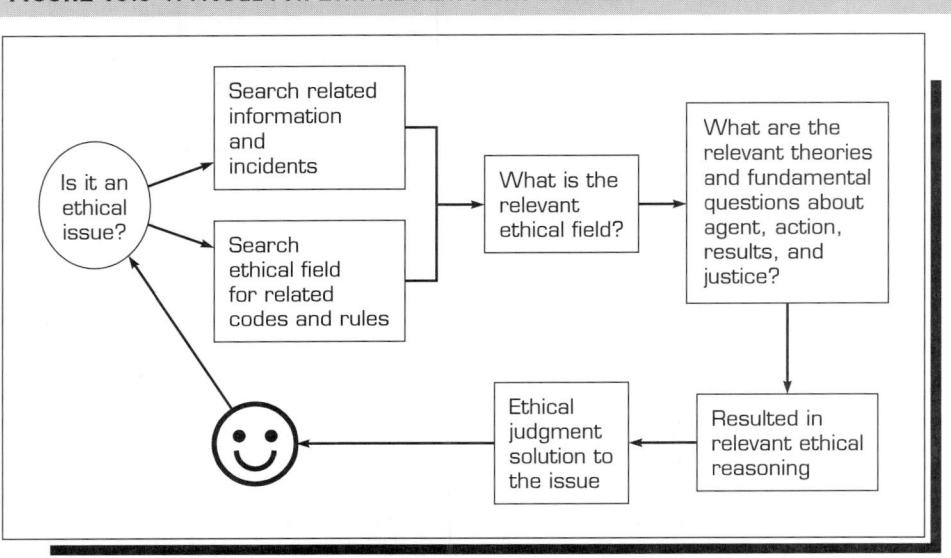

Source: Based in part on Mason et al. (1995), © Sage Publications Inc., with permission.

DSS IN FOCUS 19.6

OUTSMARTING THE COOKIE MONSTER

The cookie controversy is about privacy and the way that a technology is being used—or abused—by Web site developers. **Cookies** are simply strings of text stored on hard drive files to record the history of a particular user's actions at a particular Web site, including what links are followed, what sections of the site are visited, and what ads are clicked. The problem—and the controversy—is how they get on the hard drive and how they are used. The cookie can record actions, and when the user returns, the cookie may tell the server where the user has been before, what areas were accessed, and what links he or she has followed.

Cookies are viewed by some as a helpful way of narrowcasting, or providing specific information to a particular audience, based on past browsing (a form of directed marketing). Then, the Web server can direct a user to material or products of interest. The cookie problem is twofold: Most users do not know that a cookie has been written to their hard disk (when active, they can be detected and the user warned by some browsers), and cookies can be used to target both content and advertising.

Source: Modified and condensed from J. Piven, *Computer Technology Review,* Vol. 16, No. 11, Nov. 1996, p. 4.

---

sult in invasion of privacy and other injustices, especially in the Web environment. See DSS in Focus 19.6 for a discussion of "cookies."

The use of AI technologies in the administration and enforcement of laws and regulations may increase public concern regarding privacy of information. These fears, generated by the perceived abilities of AI, will have to be addressed at the outset of almost any AI development effort. For further discussion, see Exercise 4 at the end of this chapter. Also see O'Leary (1995), Mizell (1998), Cavoukian and Tapscott (1997), Denning (1998), Rainone et al. (1998), Cranor (1999), and Berghel (2000).

19.11 INTELLIGENT SYSTEMS AND EMPLOYMENT LEVELS

There is very little information on the relationship of MSS to employment levels. However, MSS and especially intelligent systems have the potential to significantly affect the productivity and employment of many types of employees. The material in this section summarizes the positions of some of the country's top experts with regard to the potential impact of intelligent systems on productivity and unemployment.

Although the impact of AI may take decades to materialize, there is agreement among researchers that AI in general, and ES, IA, and ANN in particular, will increase the productivity of **knowledge workers.** Technology will be inexpensive and thus create substantial shifts in jobs and job contents. Researchers disagree about the potential impact of intelligent systems on the aggregate employment level. The two extreme positions are massive unemployment and increased employment (or no change in the employment level). These positions have been supported by two Nobel prize winners: Wassily Leontief (1986), who supports the massive unemployment argument, and Herbert Simon, who takes the opposite position. Table 19.4 summarizes the major arguments of each side.

The following is a list of newly created MSS-related jobs: AI computer lawyer, AI headhunter, AI project manager, AI hardware architecture specialist, AI venture capitalist, AI user training specialist, expert system shell developer and vendor, industrial robotics supervisor/manager, knowledge acquisition and maintenance specialist, robotics

TABLE 19.4   Is Mass Unemployment Coming?

Massive Unemployment Will Come	No Massive Unemployment
• Benefit/cost advantage of computers increases with time.	• New occupations and jobs have always been created by automation.
• Less skillful employees are needed.	• There is much less unemployment in countries that use more automation.
• Shifting displaced employees to services is getting difficult.	• Work can be expanded to accommodate everyone.
• Many employees lost their jobs in the 1990s.	• Conversion to automation is slow, and the economy can adjust.
• Hidden unemployment exists in many organizations.	• Many tasks cannot be fully automated.
• Millions of help desk employees will be replaced by intelligent agents.	• There will always be some areas where people are better than machines.
• Electronic commerce will cause millions of intermediaries and agents to lose their jobs.	• People will work less but will have more money.
• Unemployment levels in certain countries is high and is increasing.	• Electronic commerce reduces the cost of many goods and services; thus their consumption will increase, resulting in more buying and more jobs.
• There is an upper limit to customer consumption.	

AIS IN ACTION 19.7

ROBOTS CLEAN TRAIN STATIONS IN JAPAN

With growing amounts of rubbish to deal with at Japanese train stations and fewer people willing to work as cleaners, officials have started turning the dirty work over to robots. Since May 1993, the central Japan Railway Company and Sizuko Company, a Japanese machinery maker, have been using robots programmed to vacuum rubbish. A railway official said that the robots, which are capable of doing the work of 10 people, have been operating 2 or 3 days a week at the Sizuko station in central Japan. The robots are about 1.5 meters wide and 1.2 meters long. The railway and Sizuko spent 200 million yen ($2 million) to develop the machines and are planning to program them for other tasks, such as sweeping and scrubbing.

More than any other country, Japan has made extensive use of robots in industry. It also uses them to assist the blind and the elderly, as well as to diagnose some illnesses.

---

maintenance engineer, system integrator, ANN software developer, software agent developer and vendor, chief knowledge officer (CKO), Web master, knowledge maintainer, and intelligent agent builder.

The debate about how intelligent systems will affect employment raises a few other questions: Is some unemployment really socially desirable? (People could have more leisure time.) Should the government intervene more in the distribution of income and in determination of the employment level? Can the "invisible hand" in the economy, which has worked so well in the past, continue to be successful in the future? Will AI make most of us idle but wealthy? (Robots will do the work; people will enjoy life. See AIS in Action 19.7.) Should the issue of income be completely separated from that of employment? The issue of how to handle unemployment both at the organizational and national levels is beyond the scope of this book.

19.12 INTERNET COMMUNITIES

Rheingold (1993) believes that the Web is being transformed into a social Web of communities. He thinks that every Web site should incorporate a place for people to chat. His popular Web site, www.minds.com, is an interesting place to visit, a kind of virtual community center. It is a place where discussions cover many controversial topics but mostly the impact of technology on life.

Electronic (virtual) communities are also related to electronic commerce. For example, Champy et al. (1996) describe online consumer-driven markets where most of the consumers' needs, ranging from finding a mortgage to job hunting, can be arranged from home. Electronic communities will eventually have a massive impact on almost every company that produces consumer goods and services. These electronic communities will change the nature of corporate strategy and the manner in which business is done.

Electronic communities are spreading quickly over the Internet. Hagel and Armstrong (1997) recognize the following four types of electronic communities.

COMMUNITIES OF TRANSACTIONS

These communities facilitate buying and selling. Members include buyers, sellers, intermediaries, and so on. An example is Virtual Vineyards (www.vine.com), which in addition to selling wines provides expert information on wines and a place for wine lovers to chat with each other. The GE/TPN network (www.tpn.geis.com) has created an infrastructure for communities of traders to conduct bids or simply to buy and sell (TPN-mart). Another example can be found at www.e-steel.com, which acts as a steel industry community center.

COMMUNITIES OF INTEREST

Here people have the chance to interact with each other on a specific topic. For example, if you are interested in gardening, try www.gardenweb.com. The Motley Fool (www.fool.com) is a forum for individual investors. City411 provides comprehensive information about local communities, and many topics such as entertainment, traffic, and weather reports are displayed. The community for IT professionals can be found at www.planetit.com.

Geocities' (www.geocities.com) several million members are organized into dozens of communities such as MotorCity (car lovers) and Nashville (country music). Members have a marketplace for buying and selling goods and services. One of the largest communities is the Web Chat Broadcasting System (www.wbs.net), which has several million members, mostly between 12 and 35 years of age, sharing Web-related interests.

Most of the successful communities were purchased by portals or other companies.

COMMUNITIES OF RELATIONS

These communities are organized around certain life experiences. For example, the cancer forum on CompuServe contains information and exchange of opinions regarding cancer. Parent Soup is a favorite gathering spot for parents, seniors like to visit SeniorNet, and Women's Wire is a well-known online community aimed at women, with regular celebrity chats and discussions.

Many communities are organized according to professional business interests. For example, plasticsnet.com is used by thousands of engineers in the plastics industry. A related extranet, www.comerx.com, provides a cybermarket for the industry.

COMMUNITIES OF FANTASY

Here, participants create imaginary environments. For example, AOL subscribers can pretend to be medieval barons at the Red Dragon Inn. On ESPNet, (www.go.espn.com)

participants can create competing teams and "play" with Michael Jordan. Related to this is a large number of games that thousands of people play simultaneously.

THE BUSINESS SIDE OF THE COMMUNITY
Interactive Week (May 11, 1998) provides the following suggestions on how to transform a community site into a commerce site:

1. Understand a particular niche industry, its information needs, and the step-by-step process by which it does the research needed to do business.
2. Build a site that provides this information, either through partnerships with existing publishers and information providers or by gathering it independently.
3. Set up the site to mirror the steps a user goes through in the information-gathering and decision-making processes, for example, how a chip designer whittles down the list of possible chips that will fit a particular product.
4. Build a community that relies on the site for decision support.
5. Start selling products and services, such as sample chips to engineers, that fit into the decision support process.

Forrester Research conducted a survey in 1998 that found the following expected paybacks in order of importance:

- Customer loyalty increases.
- Sales increase.
- Customer participation and feedback increase.
- Repeat traffic to site increases.
- New traffic to site increases.

For further discussion see Turban (2001) and Wellman (1999).

19.13 OTHER SOCIETAL IMPACTS

Several positive and negative social implications of MSS, and especially AI, systems could be far-reaching. [For an overview see Garson (1995), Kosko (2000), and Grudin and Wellman (1999).] MSS have already had many direct beneficial effects on society, being used for complicated human and social problems such as medical diagnosis, computer-assisted instruction, government program planning, environmental quality control, and law enforcement. Problems in these areas could not have been solved economically (or solved at all) by other types of computer systems. Furthermore, the spread and benefits of electronic commerce are greatly enhanced with the help of intelligent agents (Wyckoff et al., 2000). Specific examples of potential impact are described next.

POSITIVE EFFECTS

WORK IN HAZARDOUS ENVIRONMENTS
Expert systems, especially when combined with sensors and robots, can reduce or even eliminate the need for a human presence in dangerous or uncomfortable environments [see Oxman's (1991) work on cleaning up chemical spills].

OPPORTUNITIES FOR THE DISABLED
The integration of some AI technologies (speech recognition, vision recognition) into a CBIS could create new employment opportunities for disabled people. For example,

those who cannot type would be able to use a voice-operated keyboard, and those who cannot travel could work at home. Boeing Company is developing several ES to help disabled employees perform useful tasks. Adaptive equipment permits disabled people to do ordinary tasks by using computers. Lazzaro (1993) describes AI support for deaf, blind, and motor-disabled people. For further discussion see Turban et al. (2001).

CHANGING ROLE OF WOMEN

MSS could change the traditional role of women in the workplace. For example, the opportunity to work at home and the need for less travel (because of the Internet and computer teleconferencing) could help parents and especially women with young children assume more responsible (and demanding) managerial positions in organizations. It is interesting to note that males and females view ethical issues differently (Kreie and Cronan, 1998).

WORKING AT HOME (TELECOMMUTING)

Another trend gaining momentum is working at home via **telecommuting** (Niles, 1998) and Kalifa and Davidson [2000]). This phenomenon was discussed in depth in Chapter 7. The advantages are flexible hours, reduced travel time, less office and parking space needed, and employment for the housebound. There are some disadvantages, however, including supervision difficulties, lack of human interaction, and increased isolation. Despite these promising benefits, the spread of telecommuting has been slow.

IMPROVEMENTS IN HEALTH

Several early expert systems (such as MYCIN) were designed to improve the delivery of health care. Since they were first developed, we have seen an increased role for AI technologies in supporting various tasks carried out by physicians and other health care workers. Of special interest are expert systems that support the diagnosis of diseases and systems involving the use of machine vision in radiology.

AIDS FOR THE CONSUMER

Several AI products are already on the market, and many more are being developed, to help the layperson perform skilled or undesirable tasks. For example, Taxcut is an ES that assists in tax preparation, Willmaster is an ES that helps a layperson draft a simple will, and Wines on Disk provides advice to the consumer on how to select wines. Intelligent robots could clean the house and mow the lawn (see the lawnmower at www.friendlyrobotics.com and run the simulator; also see AIS in Action 19.7). Fuzzy logic has already provided blur-free video cameras, improved antilock brakes, and toasters that do not burn toast. Other advances include more realistic video games and virtual reality systems. Large numbers of intelligent agents provide comparisons and evaluations for consumers (Chapter 17) (see www.deja.com). These and many other improvements will contribute to an improved quality of life (Hanson and Stork, 1999).

QUALITY OF LIFE

On a broader scale, MSS have implications for the **quality of life** in general (Wycoff et al., 2000). Improved organizational efficiency may result in more leisure time. The workplace can be expanded from the traditional 9 to 5 at a central location to 24 hours a day at *any* location. This expansion provides flexibility that can significantly improve the quality of leisure time even if the total amount of leisure time is not increased.

LAW ENFORCEMENT

Computers and especially some AI technologies excel in supporting law enforcement agencies (Quarantiello, 1996) (see the Opening Vignette).

NEGATIVE EFFECTS

The introduction of MSS technologies may be accompanied by some negative effects (Williams, 1991; Baatz, 1996). In addition to unemployment and the creation of large economic gaps among people, MSS technologies may result in other problems, some of which are common to other computer systems.

COMPUTER CRIME

Computer fraud and embezzlement are increasing. The American Bar Association estimates that losses from the theft of tangible and intangible assets (including software), destruction of data, embezzlement of funds, and fraud total over $100 billion annually (1998). With ES, there is a possibility of deliberately providing bad advice (e.g., to advise employees to opt for early retirement when they should not). On the other hand, DSS, ES, and neural computing are being used to detect and prevent computer crimes (see examples in Chapter 10). Neural computing systems can detect stolen credit cards and cellular phones almost instantaneously upon their illegal use. Fraud on the Web is becoming a major problem (see www.ftc.gov).

TOO MUCH POWER

Distributed MSS may allow greater centralization in decision making and control of an organization. This may give some individuals or government agencies too much power over other people. Power may be used in an unethical manner (Dejoie et al., 1995).

THE DANGERS OF THE WEB

Extensive use of the Web has caused people to neglect their families and friends, resulting in some divorces. Also, a Web game addict in Korea died in February 2000 because he was too busy to break a nonstop playing record in order to eat. In Japan, two people died in 1999 after purchasing over the Web poison and advice on how to kill themselves.

BLAMING THE COMPUTER PHENOMENON

Many people tend to blame computers to cover up human errors or wrongdoing. You may hear someone say, "But the expert system told us to do it," to justify some action that otherwise would be unjustifiable.

SOCIAL RESPONSIBILITY

Organizations need to be motivated to use MSS to improve the quality of life in general. They should design their MSS to minimize negative working conditions. This challenge should be met not only by companies that produce MSS hardware and software but also by companies that use these technologies. Properly designed systems can be implemented and used in ways that are either positive or negative (Garson, 1995).

19.14 MANAGERIAL IMPLICATIONS AND SOCIAL RESPONSIBILITIES

The potential societal and organizational impacts of MSS discussed in this chapter raise the issue of what management can do about all these impacts. How can we anticipate the broad societal effects of MSS and the things it makes possible? What can we do to ensure that people's attitudes toward MSS are well founded and that their expectations about what these systems can and cannot do are accurate? How do we determine the potential positive and negative effects of MSS before they become realities?

PUBLIC PRESSURE

Increased exposure to the concepts and actual use of MSS will pressure public agencies and corporations to use the latest capabilities for solving social problems. At the same time, conflicting public pressures may rise to suppress the use of MSS because of concerns about privacy and "big brother" government. An example is the government's proposed use of intelligent agents to detect financial fraud on the Internet, which was proposed in the spring of 2000 and is opposed by free speech advocates.

COMPUTER AND STAFF RESOURCES

Obvious implications of the introduction of MSS involve the increased need for computer resources and people with computer skills. MSS may not be the dominant factor in the expected future growth of computer resources, but it will be a significant one. Depending on the level of involvement in MSS, significant impacts can be expected on the recruitment of personnel and training.

PLANNING

Management must be ready for all the potential impacts of MSS, especially that of intelligent systems. They may come faster than most of us think. Managers should plan the introduction of these emerging technologies after analyzing their potential impacts (Weitz, 1990). Smart machines can change our world (Gill, 1996). Let's be ready to make the most of them.

19.15 THE FUTURE OF MANAGEMENT SUPPORT SYSTEMS

Where is MSS in general and DSS in particular going? Is it matured enough to be classified as a mainstream IT? Is it still evolving? Is it taking new directions? Experts answer these questions differently, but most of them agree that MSS is migrating toward mainstream IT while it is still evolving in certain areas [see the papers in Carlsson and Turban (2001)]. The following is a summary of the major developments:

- As described in Chapters 3 and 8, MSS is certainly becoming a Web-based technology. This can be seen not only in the dissemination possibilities but also in the increasing use of the Web for MSS development.
- The trend toward making MSS systems more intelligent will continue. The major technologies that will make it happen are intelligent agents, expert systems, case-based reasoning, neural networks, and fuzzy logic (Carlsson and Walden, 2001).
- Management support systems will be available for dissemination via application service providers (ASPs). For a reasonable fee, specifically constructed centers will provide solutions to a large number of potential users (Wagner, 2001).
- Natural language–based search engines, such as about.com and askjeeves.com will populate the Internet, frequently specialized in a certain domain. This feature will facilitate MSS construction by reducing costs.
- Frontline decision support technologies that support mostly CRM will become an integral part of IT in most medium-sized and large organizations.
- MSS will be integrated with ERP to provide better supply chain management, including manufacturing planning and control.

- Large numbers of experts will offer expertise on the Internet. Web sites such as www.guru.com and www.xxx.com (which allow experts to bid on requests for expertise) will become an important part of knowledge dissemination.
- An increased number of companies will initiate formal knowledge management programs. Some will sell knowledge accumulated in their knowledge bases to others.
- With increased usage of wireless technologies and the ability to access the Web with various wireless devices, PalmPilot, hybrid cell phones, and other devices, employees will be able to access MSS and knowledge bases anytime and from anywhere. Therefore, the usage of MSS will increase considerably.
- The use of voice technologies and natural language processing will further facilitate the usage of MSS.
- Intelligent agents will roam the Internet and intranets, assisting decision making in the monitoring and interpretation of information. These agents will alert decision makers and provide alternative courses of action.
- Groupware technologies for collaboration and communication will become easier to use, more powerful, and less expensive. They will make electronic group support a viable initiative even in small organizations.
- Decision support tools for electronic commerce that are currently limited to recommendations of certain products and brands, and to providing comparing agents, will expand to include more and better applications.

SUMMARY AND CONCLUSIONS

MSS are clearly having far-reaching and dramatic impacts on society and organizations. These impacts range from providing rapid information access, to instantaneous communication around the world, to artificial intelligence assisting and even replacing human effort. Today we consider not the evolution of technology but the revolution of technology because of the nature and far reach of the impact. Often, MSS effects can be predicted, planned for, and used to benefit us all.

❖ Chapter Highlights

- MSS can affect organizations in many ways, as stand-alone systems or integrated with other computer-based information systems.
- Flatter organizational hierarchies are expected, but the ratio of staff to line workers may decrease.
- The impact of MSS on the degree of centralization of power and authority is inconclusive. Distributed MSS may increase decentralization.
- MSS could cause a power redistribution. Advisory professionals may be the losers as power shifts to administrators and managers who use online advisors.
- Special intelligent system units and departments are appearing in many organizations.
- MSS supports business process reengineering as an enabler.
- Many jobs will require fewer skills when supported by MSS.
- The job of the surviving expert will become more important as it becomes one of maintaining the expert systems and the knowledge base.
- MSS could reduce the need for supervision by providing more guidelines to employees through electronic means.
- The impact of MSS on individuals is unclear; it can be either positive or negative.

- Management should motivate experts to contribute their knowledge to knowledge bases.
- MSS can provide a competitive advantage through gains in productivity and quality.
- MSS improve a manager's decision-making ability.
- Organizational data and knowledge bases will be critical issues as MSS become more available.
- Serious legal issues may develop with the introduction of AI; liability and privacy are the dominant problem areas.
- There are many open ethical questions pertaining to MSS.
- Major factors in ethical decision making are personal values and deindividuation.
- In one view, intelligent systems will cause massive unemployment because of increased productivity, reduced required skill levels, and impacts on all sectors of the economy.
- In another view, intelligent systems will increase employment levels because automation makes products and services more affordable and so demand increases; the process of disseminating automation is slow enough to allow the economy to adjust to intelligent technologies.
- Many positive social implications can be expected from MSS. They range from providing opportunities to disabled people to reducing the exposure of people to hazardous work situations.
- Quality of life, both at work and at home, is likely to improve as a result of MSS.
- Electronic (virtual) communities are evolving and changing the way we live and work.
- Managers need to plan for the MSS of the future to be ready to make the most of them.

❖ KEY WORDS

- business process reengineering (BPR)
- career ladders
- cookies
- deindividuation
- electronic (virtual) communities
- information revolution
- Internet communities
- job content
- knowledge workers
- quality of life
- role ambiguity
- telecommuting
- virtual corporations (enterprises)

❖ QUESTIONS FOR REVIEW

1. Explain why organizations might have fewer managerial layers (or levels) because of MSS. Give at least two reasons.
2. Why might the ratio of staff to line workers decrease in the future?
3. How can MSS increase the trend toward decentralization?
4. Describe the impact of personal computers on the degree of organizational decentralization.
5. Describe the potential power shift in organizations when expert systems are used.
6. Describe some potential changes in jobs and job descriptions in organizations that use MSS extensively.
7. What are some of the issues related to human–computer interactions?
8. List some reasons why an expert may not be able or willing to contribute his or her expertise to an ES.

9. Why will managers in the future work on fewer problems simultaneously?

10. List the major ethical issues related to MSS.

11. Describe some of the legal implications of ES.

12. List three reasons why intelligent systems could result in massive unemployment.

13. Give three arguments to counter the arguments in no. 12.

14. List the four types of Internet communities.

15. Define the Internet or electronic community.

16. List some potential social benefits of MSS.

17. How can work done at home be increased through MSS?

18. How can telecommuting improve the quality of life?

19. List some possible negative effects of MSS technologies.

20. Could MSS provide more managerial opportunities for disabled people and minorities? Why or why not?

❖ QUESTIONS FOR DISCUSSION

1. Some say MSS in general, and ES in particular, dehumanize managerial activities and others say they do not. Discuss arguments for both points of view.

2. Explain why you agree or disagree with the following statement: Technologies will increase organizational productivity.

3. Describe the manager of the future in a workplace that uses MSS extensively.

4. Should top managers who use ES instead of a human assistant be paid more or less for their jobs? Why?

5. How can an ES increase the span of control of a manager?

6. The following excerpt is from the November 1974 issue of *InfoSystems*:

   I've seen the ablest executives insist on increased productivity by a plant manager, lean on accounting for improved performance, and lay it on purchasing in no uncertain terms to cut its staff. But when these same executives turn to EDP they stumble to an uncertain halt, baffled by the blizzard of computer jargon. They accept the presumed sophistication and differences that are said to make EDP activities somehow immune from normal management demands. They are stopped by all this nonsense, uncertainty about what's reasonable to expect, and what they can insist upon. They become confused and then retreat, muttering about how to get a handle on this blasted situation.

   Can MSS technologies change a situation that existed almost 30 years ago? Why or why not?

7. The Department of Transportation in a large metropolitan area has an expert system that advises an investigator about whether to open an investigation of a reported car accident. (This system, which includes 300 rules, was developed by T. J. Nagy at George Washington University.) Discuss the following questions:
   a. Should the people involved in an accident be informed that a machine is deciding the future of an investigation?
   b. What are some of the potential legal implications?
   c. In general, what do you think of such a system?

8. In all *Star Trek* television series and movies, the ship's main computer understands natural speech and replies orally. Discuss the impact of voice technology advances that could provide such capabilities to computers in a business enterprise.

9. Diagnosing infections and prescribing pharmaceuticals are the weak points of many practicing physicians (according to E. H. Shortliffe, one of the developers of

MYCIN). It seems, therefore, that society would be better served if MYCIN (and other expert systems) were used extensively, but few physicians use expert systems. Answer the following questions:

a. Why do you think ES are little used by physicians?

b. Assume that you are a hospital administrator whose physicians are salaried and report to you. What would you do to persuade these individuals to use ES?

c. If the potential benefits to society are so great, can society do something that will increase the use of ES by doctors?

❖ EXERCISES

1. Several hospitals are considering the introduction of an intelligent bedside assistant that will provide physicians and staff with a patient record database for diagnosis and prognosis. The system will supply any information required from the patient's medical records, make diagnoses based on symptoms, and prescribe medications and other treatments. The system includes an expert system as well as a DSS. The system is expected to eliminate some human error and improve patient care.

   You are a hospital administrator and you are very excited about the benefits for the patients. However, when you called a staff meeting, the following questions were raised: What if the system malfunctions? What if there is an undetected error in the program or the rules? The system, once implemented, will take full responsibility for patient care because physicians will rely on it. A loss of data or an error in the program may result in disaster. For example, suppose there is a bug in the database program and as a result a critical piece of information is missing from the patient's record. A physician who relies on the system could prescribe a drug on the basis of incomplete data. The consequence of this mistake may be life-threatening. Another possibility is that some of the rules in the knowledge base may not be accurate for all patients.

   Would you implement such a system? Why or why not?

2. One of the major complaints in the Olympic Games is that the judges are biased. We see this especially in figure skating. Would it be possible to use a computerized judge to do the job or at least to supplement the human judges? (Disregard the cost issue.)

   a. Is it possible to delegate such a task to a Robo-Judge? If your answer is no, please explain in detail why not.

   b. If your answer to part (a) is yes, explain how this could be done. Specifically, what tools and techniques could be used and how?

   c. There are two possible options: supporting the judges with a computer or replacing them with a computer. Explain what could be done in each case and how (list the tools and techniques as well).

3. According to D. E. Denning, a leading researcher on data security, personal privacy must be balanced against our collective interest in law and order. Denning supports proposed U.S. legislation that would require providers of electronic communications services and PBX operators to ensure that the communication signals of people named in a court order could be monitored and transferred, in real time, to a remote government monitoring facility. This would be done without detection by the subject and without degradation of service (Denning, 1998; Diffie and Landau, 1998) (see "Forum," *Communications of the ACM,* June 1993, pp. 11–14). The opponents of the proposed legislation raise the following concerns:

   • The proposal would hold back technology and stymie innovation.

   • This type of interception would jeopardize security and privacy, first because the remote monitoring capability would make the system vulnerable to attack, and second, because the intercept capability itself would introduce a new vulnerability into the systems.

- Implementing the intercept could harm the competitiveness of the United States.
- The cost of implementing the intercept might not be justified by the benefits.
- It is not clear who would have to comply with the proposed legislation and what compliance means.

What do you think? Should the government be allowed to intercept calls? (See *InformationWeek,* Feb. 14, 1994.)

4. Comment on the cookie controversy (see DSS in Focus 19.6). How do you feel about a Web server being able to attach an ID number to you, track your visits on its site, and later learn more about you? How do you feel about directed advertising sent to you using such information on the Web? How do you feel about such information being sold to other organizations? Could an intelligent agent use cookie information? Explain.

5. Perform a literature search on electronic voting, including allowing the general public voting via the Internet (see polls at www.cnn.com and www.cnnfn.com). Write a report describing the advantages and disadvantages of electronic voting.

6. Investigate developments in robotic vacuum cleaners and lawn mowers. Are these devices practical? Why or why not? Would you like to have one? Why or why not?

❖ GROUP EXERCISE

Intelligent advisory systems of all kinds are now available on the Web. Experts are selling services, and corporations are selling access to their knowledge bases (e.g., www.knowledgespace.com and www.guru.com). Each group member is assigned to one area of knowledge dissemination online (include training and education). Prepare a report on the legal issues involved in such a venture.

❖ INTERNET EXERCISES (USE WWW.GOOGLE.COM, WWW.ABOUT.COM, AND WWW.REFDESK.COM FOR YOUR SEARCHES)

1. Your mission is to identify ethical issues related to managerial decision making. Search the Internet, join news groups, and read articles from the Internet. Prepare a report.

2. There is considerable talk about the impact of the Internet on society. Concepts such as global village, Internet community, Internet society, and the like, are getting much attention (*Harvard Business Review,* May/June 1996; *Business Week,* May 5, 1997; Hanon and Stork, 1999; Magid, 1999; Kozko 2000). Search the Internet and prepare a short report on the topic. How does this concept relate to managerial decision making?

3. Search the Internet to find examples of how intelligent systems (especially expert systems and intelligent agents) facilitate activities such as empowerment, mass customization, and teamwork.

4. Access the Business Resource Software Inc.'s Web site (www.brs-inc.com). Read the case studies and their product information. How are their products helping businesses in reengineering? Download the demo of Business Insight, install it, and try it. What does it do and how effective do you think it could be in practice?

5. Access scout.cs.wisc.edu. Find the Scout Report. Look for information on social sciences, business, and economics. Find the issues discussed in the last 6 months that are related to the topics considered in this chapter.

6. Visit the Web sites www.minds.com, www.geocities.com, www.sino.net, and others to find the latest developments on electronic communities and virtual teams. Write a short report relating this subject to corporate decision making.

7. Investigate the American Bar Association's artificial intelligence Web site. What are the major legal and societal concerns and advances addressed there? How are they being dealt with?

8. The value of telecommuting and its slow adoption are the subject of extensive research (Kalifa and Davidson, 2000). Surf the Internet to find out what is happening. Join a relevant news group (or access postings via an archive on the Web) and identify some frequently asked questions (FAQs). Write up your results in a report.

9. Access the Agility Forum at Lehigh University (absu.amef.lehigh.edu) and the Computer-Aided Education Training Initiative (CAETI) at the University of North Carolina (www.cs.unc.edu/caeti). Identify and describe the latest trends in virtual organizations (also called virtual enterprises) and the virtual classroom.

❖ EFFECTIVENESS OF INFORMATION SYSTEMS AND ETHICAL ISSUES: DEBATES

Milberg et al. (1995) and Johnson and Mulvey (1995) pointed out some interesting issues relating to IT and decision making. Specifically, Milberg et al. believe that personal information privacy, the ability to personally control information about oneself, is fast becoming one of the most important ethical issues of the information age. Information technology developments—coupled with the increasing value of information to decision makers—are causing a rising tide of concern about personal information privacy management practices. As such concerns grow, the ability of businesses to use personal information may be threatened, and decision makers will have to make trade-offs between the efficient, effective operation of businesses and the protection of personal information privacy.

Johnson and Mulvey claim that computer decision systems have become an integral part of the decision-making apparatus of many public and private organizations. In the United States, decisions made by Congress and the executive branch are increasingly based on computer models that simulate the effects of public policy decisions. Congress has even passed legislation requiring the development of comprehensive plans and management strategies, which in effect mandates the use of computer decision systems. Computer decision systems provide a variety of benefits leading to more informed decision making: assistance in coping with complexity, the ability to manage uncertainty in a rational way, efficiency, and consistency. At the same time, they raise a variety of ethical issues. These issues center on the values and trade-offs made within the systems (e.g., How are risks to human life managed? Is it fair to put dollar amounts on human life?). System designers should articulate standards of behavior as part of a process of professionalization that will create accountability in the field of computer decision systems.

Other issues involved relate directly to the Internet, such as flooding of the Internet with pornography, hate material, and junk mail versus the right to free speech, or the electronic surveillance of potential criminals versus privacy.

Identify all the debatable issues and prepare a list of the major pro and con arguments for each point of view.

2. Are we relying too much on computers? Are we becoming too dependent on intelligent computers that do much thinking for us?

3. Many jobs will require fewer skills when supported by AI. Debate the positive and negative implications of such an impact.

4. The skill requirements for many jobs performed with AI support will be reduced. For example, a technician will be able to do the job of an engineer. Should we pay the technician more than he or she is making today, the same, or less (refer to Senker, 1989)?

XEROX REENGINEERS ITS $3 BILLION PURCHASING PROCESS WITH GRAPHICAL MODELING AND SIMULATION

Xerox Corporation is using Gensym's ReThink software to reengineer and validate its $3 billion process for purchasing all non-production-related goods and services such as furniture and computer leases. ReThink has helped Xerox identify a number of steps in its process that could be changed to achieve a purchase order life-cycle time savings of 10–15 percent and an overall cost savings of 5 percent, or $150 million per year.

"Our goal was to reengineer Xerox's semimanual 'non-production' procurement process into a comprehensive automated process beginning with the requisitioner and including the entire purchase order life cycle," says Robert Bowman, manager of major projects at Xerox. "Our goal was to decrease the purchase process time from 2 or more weeks to 2 days or less and to reduce the cost per transaction. We also wanted to be able to view the status of each purchase order over the life of the order."

Before using ReThink, Xerox's business process reengineering (BPR) team mapped their existing purchasing process with a simple flow diagramming tool. They then employed a paper-based methodology to propose a revised procurement process. After identifying a new 42-step procurement process, the BPR team turned to Gensym's ReThink. "Using ReThink, we were able to rapidly analyze and test the proposed revised system to see if it would really work when implemented," continues Bowman. "ReThink helped us validate and refine the proposed purchasing process and quickly evaluate different scenarios. This included identifying bottlenecks and areas where automation was essential."

Xerox's team took the process flows created with the flow diagramming tool and added them to ReThink along with transition volumes and staffing requirements at each process point. ReThink enabled the reengineering team to represent more refined flows and more detailed data points than the flow diagramming tool had. Using its simulation capabilities, ReThink graphically tracked individual items through each step of the proposed process and offered feedback to the reengineering team and business analysts. The team simulated daily, weekly, and annual volume cases to understand constraints and throughput performance. "As a result of our intensive modeling, ReThink was able to identify six steps that could benefit from being either combined or divided. It helped us fine-tune our plan," continued Bowman. "Moreover, it provided concrete evidence to management that our new procurement process could be successful when implemented."

Xerox is currently distributing the redesigned procurement process and ReThink to many of its offices worldwide. "We intend to keep the model 'evergreen' to assist in evaluating what-if? cases relating to fluctuations in purchase order volume caused by business changes such as new product launches or increases or decreases in personnel," says Bowman.

"Reengineering is too critical and complex to attempt without tools," says Tom Foley, ReThink's architect and product manager at Gensym. "Only powerful software tools can assist management in redesigning processes and understanding the performance implications of the new designs. ReThink allows managers to propose process changes and immediately see the financial and business impact these changes might have. It unifies process design, analysis, and implementation."

CASE QUESTIONS

1. Why is it so important to reduce cycle time in organizational processes?
2. What were the benefits of using simulation to model and test the proposed plan?
3. How did the visual nature of the simulation help the decision makers?
4. What other MSS tools could be combined with the simulator to make the decision making more effective?
5. Investigate the activities of the FedEx center for cycle time research at the University of Memphis Web site (www.people.memphis.edu/~cctr/). What basic ideas apply to this case? How?

Source: Condensed from Gensym Corporation, "Customer Stories: Gensym's ReThink Software Helps Xerox Re-engineer its $3 Billion Purchasing Process," www.gensym.com, Feb. 1997.

GLOSSARY

active (symbiotic) DSS A special type of intelligent DSS that can respond to changes and is viewed as proactive rather than reactive.

ad hoc DSS DSS that deals with specific problems that are usually neither anticipated nor recurring.

advanced planning and scheduling (APS) A software package that can be integrated with ERP or SCM software to help optimize software integration.

agency The degree of autonomy vested in a software agent.

agent Someone employed to act on behalf of another.

AI workstations *See* LISP machines.

algorithm A step-by-step search in which improvement is made at every step until the best solution is found.

analog model An abstract, symbolic model of a system that behaves like the system but appears different.

analogical reasoning Determining the outcome of a problem with the use of analogies. A procedure for drawing conclusions about a problem by using past experience.

analytical techniques Methods that use mathematical formulas to derive an optimal solution directly, or to predict a certain result, mainly in solving structured problems.

anonymity Being able to remain anonymous while contributing at a meeting.

application service provider (ASP) A software vendor who offers leased software applications to organizations.

approximate reasoning A computational modeling of processes (or parts of processes) used by humans to reason about natural phenomena.

artificial intelligence (AI) The subfield of computer science concerned with symbolic reasoning and problem solving.

artificial neural networks (ANN) Computer technology that attempts to build computers that will operate like a human brain. The machines possess simultaneous memory storage and work with ambiguous information. *See* neural computing.

associative memory The ability to recall complete situations from partial information.

asynchronous Occurring at different times.

autonomous agent A software agent with learning capability.

avatars Computer representations of users in an animated, three-dimensional format; also known as computer characters.

axon An outgoing connection (terminal) from a biological neuron.

backbone Long distance, high-capacity, high-speed networks that link the major Internet computer centers.

backpropagation The best-known learning algorithm in neural computing. Learning is done by comparing computed outputs to desired outputs of historical cases.

backtracking A technique used in tree searches. The process of working backward from a failed objective or an incorrect result to examine unexplored alternatives.

backward chaining A search technique (employing IF-THEN rules) used in production systems that begins with the action clause of a rule and works backward through a chain of rules in an attempt to find a verifiable set of condition clauses.

belief function The representation of uncertainty without the need to specify exact probabilities.

blackboard An area of working memory set aside for the description of a current problem and for recording intermediate results in an expert system.

blind search A search approach that makes use of no knowledge or heuristics to help speed up the search process. A time-consuming, arbitrary search process that attempts to exhaust all possibilities.

bots Intelligent software agents; an abbreviation of robots. Usually used as part of another term as in knowbots or shopbots.

brainstorming (electronic) A methodology of idea generation by association. This group process uses analogy and synergy. In GSS, it is computer-supported.

breadth-first search A search technique that evaluates every item at a given level of the search space before proceeding to the next level.

business (system) analyst An individual whose job is to analyze business processes and the support they receive (or need) from information technology.

business intelligence (BI) An information system that allows users to view data in databases and interpret them easily and quickly. It is usually related to an EIS.

business intelligence tools An information system that allows users to view data in databases and interpret them easily and quickly. It is usually related to an EIS.

business process reengineering (BPR) A methodology for introducing a fundamental change in specific business processes. It is usually supported by an information system.

career ladders   Different career paths that individuals may take in an organization. For example, there are management paths and technical paths.

case-based reasoning (CBR)   A methodology in which knowledge and/or inferences are derived from historical cases.

case library   The knowledge base of a case-based reasoning system.

case management system (CMS)   A system for managing the large volume of cases in an organizational decision support system.

certainty   A condition under which it is assumed that future values are known for sure and only one result is associated with an action.

certainty factor (CF)   A percentage supplied by an expert system that indicates the probability that the conclusion reached by the system is correct. Also, the degree of belief an expert has that a certain conclusion will occur if a certain premise is true.

certainty theory   A framework for representing and working with degrees of belief of true and false in knowledge-based systems.

chief knowledge officer (CKO)   The person in charge of a knowledge management effort in an organization.

choice phase   The third phase in decision making in which an alternative is selected.

chromosome   A candidate solution for a genetic algorithm.

class   A term used in object-oriented programming to designate a group of items with the same characteristics. (For example, the FIAT car is in a class of transportation.)

classification model   For ES, a model employed in building expert systems that uses production rules and covers a highly bounded problem with few known possible solutions.

client/server architecture   A network system in which several PCs (clients) share the memory and other capabilities of a larger computer or those of printers, databases, and so on (servers).

cognitive limits   The limits of the ability of the human mind to process, store, and recall information.

cognitive style (cognition)   The subjective process through which individuals organize and change information during the decision-making process.

collaborating multiagents   Multiple agents working on the same task.

collaborative computing   The shared computerized work when two or more people work together (e.g., by using screen sharing). *See* groupware and group support systems.

complete enumeration   The process of checking *every* feasible solution to a problem.

complexity   A measure of how difficult a problem is in terms of its formulation for optimization, its required optimization effort, or its stochastic nature.

component model   A model that contains a functional description of all components and their interactions.

computer-aided instruction (CAI)   In general, the use of computers as teaching tools. Synonymous with computer-based instruction, computer-assisted learning, and computer-based training.

computer-based information system (CBIS)   An information system specifically designed to run on computers.

computer-supported cooperative work (CSCW)   *See* collaborative computing.

conceptual graph (CG)   A diagram that describes how and when an expert's knowledge will come into play as an expert system operates.

conflict resolution (of rules)   Selecting a procedure from a conflicting set of applicable competing procedures or rules.

consistency enforcer   The component of the inference engine in an expert system that attempts to maintain a consistent representation of the emerging solution.

consultation environment   The part of an expert system that is used by a nonexpert to obtain expert knowledge and advice. It includes the workplace, inference engine, explanation facility, recommended action, and user interface.

control structure   *See* inference engine.

controllable variables   Decision variables such as quantity to produce, amounts of resources to be allocated, and so on, that can be changed and manipulated by the decision maker.

cookies   Text strings stored on a particular user's hard drive files to record the history of his or her actions at particular Web sites.

corporate portal   A system that integrates internal applications such as database management, document management, and e-mail with external applications such as news services and customer Web sites. It is a Web-based interface that gives users access to such applications.

cost–benefit analysis   A method of determining the viability of a project by comparing estimated costs with anticipated benefits.

courseware   A software system that supports learning.

creativity   The human trait that leads to the production of acts, items and instances of novelty; and the achievement of creative products.

creativity support system (CSS)   A group support system that helps users develop creative solutions to problems.

critical success factors (CSFs)   The factors that are most critical to the success of an organization.

crossover   The combining of parts of two superior solutions by a genetic algorithm in an attempt to produce even better solutions.

customer relationship management (CRM)   An organizational initiative whose objective is to properly deliver various services to customers, ranging from Web-based call centers to loyalty programs, such as rewarding frequent fliers.

data Raw facts that are meaningless by themselves (such as names or numbers).

data integrity The accuracy and accessibility of data. It is a part of data quality.

data marts Departmental data warehouses where only relevant data are kept.

data mining The activity of looking for very specific, detailed, but unknown, information in databases. A search for valuable, yet difficult to find, data. Previously called data dipping.

data quality The quality of data, including their accuracy, precision, completeness, and relevance.

data visualization A graphical animation or video presentation of data and the results of data analysis.

data warehouse The physical repository where relational data are specially organized to provide enterprise-wide, cleaned data in a standardized format.

data warehousing A relational database specially organized to provide data for easy access.

database The organizing of files into related units which are then viewed as a single storage concept. The data are then made available to a wide range of users.

database management systems (DBMS) Software for establishing, updating, and querying (e.g., managing) a database.

decision analysis Methods for determining the solution to a problem, typically when it is inappropriate to utilize iterative algorithms.

decision making The action of selecting among alternatives.

decision room An arrangement for a GSS in which PCs are available to some or all participants. The objective is to enhance groupwork.

decision style The manner in which a decision maker thinks and reacts to problems. It includes perceptions, cognitive responses, values, and beliefs.

decision support systems (DSS) Computer-based information systems that combine models and data in an attempt to solve nonstructured problems with extensive user involvement through a friendly user interface.

decision table A table used to represent knowledge and prepare it for analysis.

decision tree A graphical presentation of a sequence of interrelated decisions to be made under assumed risk.

decision variables *See* controllable variables.

declarative knowledge The representation of facts and assertions.

declarative rules Rules that state all the facts and relationships involved in a problem.

deductive reasoning In logic, reasoning from the general to the specific. Consequent reasoning in which conclusions follow premises.

deep knowledge A representation of information about the internal and causal structure of a system that considers the interactions among the system's components.

deep representation A model that captures all the forms of knowledge used by experts in their reasoning.

defuzzification Creating a crisp solution from a fuzzy logic solution.

deindividuation A feeling of being separated from others that can lead to behavior violating established norms of appropriateness.

Delphi Method A qualitative forecasting methodology using anonymous questionnaires. Effective for technological forecasting and for forecasting involving sensitive issues.

demand chain The flow of materials from an operation to the final demand. It includes order generation, taking, and fulfillment and has been integrated into the supply chain.

demon (or daemon) A procedure that runs if a specific predefined state is recognized.

demonstration prototype A small-scale prototype of a (usually expert) system that demonstrates some major capabilities of the final system on a rudimentary basis. It is used to gain support among users and managers.

dendrite The part of a biological neuron that provides inputs to the cell.

dependent variables A system's measure of effectiveness.

depth-first search A search procedure that explores each branch of a search tree to its full vertical length. Each branch is searched for a solution, and if none is found, a new vertical branch is searched to its depth, and so on.

descriptive models Models that describe things as they are.

design phase The second decision-making phase, finding possible alternatives in decision making and assessing their contribution.

deterministic models Models constructed under assumed certainty, namely, there is only one possible (and known) result of each alternative course of action.

development environments Parts of expert systems that are used by builders. They include the knowledge base, the inference engine, knowledge acquisition, and improving reasoning capability. The knowledge engineer and the expert are considered part of these environments.

development strategies Methods used to analyze, design, and implement computer systems.

directory A catalog of all the data in a database or all the models in a model base.

disbelief The degree of belief that something is *not* going to happen.

distance learning (DL) The process of learning when it involves tools or technologies designed to overcome the restrictions of either same time or same place learning. Students are not in a classroom but use telecommunication networks, groupware, telephones, faxes, and television to learn.

distributed artificial intelligence (DAI) A multiple-agent system for problem solving. Splitting of a problem into multiple cooperating systems in deriving a solution.

document management The automated management and control of digitized documents throughout their life cycle.

document management systems Information systems (hardware, software, and so on) that allow the flow, storage, retrieval, and use of digitized documents.

documented knowledge For ES, stored knowledge sources not based directly on human expertise.

domain An area of expertise.

domain-specific tools Software shells designed to be used only in the development of a specific area, for example, a diagnostic system.

drill down The investigation of information in detail, for example, finding not only total sales but also sales by region, by product, or by salesperson.

DSS application A DSS program built for a specific purpose, for example, a scheduling system for a specific company. *See* specific DSS.

DSS generator (engine) Computer software that provides a set of capabilities for quickly building a specific DSS.

DSS integrated tool A toolkit for DSS development. It includes a spreadsheet, a database management system, graphics, and other features.

DSS primary tools Features that facilitate the development of either a DSS generator or a specific DSS. They include programming languages, graphics, editors, query systems, and random-number generators.

DSS technology levels A framework for understanding DSS development: specific DSS, DSS generators, and DSS tools.

DSS tools Software elements (such as languages) that facilitate the development of a DSS or a DSS generator.

dynamic explanation In ES, an explanation facility that reconstructs the reasons for its actions as it evaluates rules.

dynamic models Models whose input data are being changed over time, for example, a 5-year profit (or loss) projection.

effectiveness The degree of goal attainment. Doing the right things.

efficiency The ratio of output to input. Appropriate use of resources. Doing the things right.

electronic brainstorming *See* Brainstorming (electronic).

electronic commerce (EC) Buying and selling products and services using computers and networks.

electronic (virtual) communities Groups of people with similar interests who use the Internet to communicate, collaborate, discuss issues of mutual concern, or conduct business.

electronic document management (EDM) A method for processing documents electronically, including capture, storage, retrieval, manipulation, and presentation.

electronic Internet communities *See* electronic (virtual) communities.

electronic meeting (Emeeting) A meeting that is enhanced by a group support system.

electronic meeting systems (EMS) An information technology–based environment that supports group meetings (groupware), which may be distributed geographically and temporally.

elicitation of knowledge *See* knowledge elicitation.

empowering employees Providing employees with access to information needed for decision making and with computer programs that generate recommended decisions for specific scenarios.

EMYCIN (Empty MYCIN) The nonspecific part (called the shell) of MYCIN consisting of what is left after the knowledge is removed. EMYCIN becomes a new problem solver when the knowledge (using rules) for a different problem domain is added.

encapsulation In object-oriented programming, the coupling of data and procedures and embedding them in an object.

end user–computing Developing one's own information system.

end-user development *See* end-user computing.

enhanced product realization (EPR) An Internet-based, state-of-the-art distributed system that allows manufacturers to make fast product modifications anywhere and accelerates the time to market for new products and services. EPR integrates and leverages the Internet with other existing and emerging information technologies to enable a host of collaborative manufacturing and electronic commerce applications. It is a kind of extranet.

enterprise computing An organization-wide system that enables people to communicate with each other and access data throughout an enterprise.

enterprise information systems *See* enterprise computing.

enterprise portal A corporate internal Web site (on its intranet) that integrates many internal applications with external ones. Users access them via standard Web browsers.

enterprise resource planning (ERP) A process that integrates the information processing of all routine activities inside an organization (e.g., ordering, billing, production scheduling, budgeting, and staffing) and among business partners.

enterprise systems *See* enterprise computing.

enterprise-wide collaboration systems Group support systems that support entire enterprises.

enterprise-wide computing *See* enterprise computing.

enumeration (complete) A listing of *all* possible solutions and a comparison of their results in order to find the best solution.

environmental scanning and analysis Conducting a search for and an analysis of information in external databases and flows of information.

evaluation The activity of assessing the overall value of an expert system in terms of acceptable performance levels, usefulness, flexibility, efficiency, and cost-effectiveness.

evolutionary development A systematic process for system development that is used in DSS. A portion of the system is quickly constructed and then tested, improved, and enlarged in steps. Similar to prototyping.

exception reporting Calling attention to a deviation larger than an agreed on threshold (e.g., 10 percent or $200,000).

executive information system (EIS) A computerized system specifically designed to support executive work.

executive support system (ESS) An executive information system that includes some analytical and communication capabilities.

expectation-driven processing A reasoning method, used with frames, that attempts to identify data to confirm expectations.

expert A human being who has developed a high level of proficiency in making judgments in a specific, usually narrow, domain.

expert-driven knowledge acquisition A situation in which an expert captures her or his own knowledge without the help of a knowledge engineer.

expert support system An expert system whose primary mission is to support problem solving and decision making.

expert system (ES) A computer system that applies reasoning methodologies to knowledge in a specific domain to render advice or recommendations, much like a human expert. A computer system that achieves a high level of performance in task areas that, for human beings, requires years of special education and training.

expert system shell A computer program that facilitates relatively easy implementation of a specific expert system. Similar to a DSS generator.

expert tool user A person who is skilled in the application of one or more types of specialized problem-solving tools.

expertise The set of capabilities that underlines the performance of human experts, including extensive domain knowledge, heuristic rules that simplify and improve approaches to problem solving, metaknowledge and metacognition, and compiled forms of behavior that afford great economy in a skilled performance.

expertise transfer system (ETS) A computer program that interviews experts and helps them build expert systems.

explanation and justification The design and programming of an explanation capability.

explanation-based learning A machine learning approach that assumes that there is enough existing theory to rationalize why one instance is or is not a prototypical member of a class.

explanation facility The component of an expert system that can explain the system's reasoning and justify its conclusions.

explanation subsystem *See* explanation facility.

explicit knowledge Knowledge that deals with objective, rational, and technical material (data, policies, procedures, software, documents, and so on).

extended supply chain A supply chain that includes business partners, such as customers and suppliers.

extract To capture data from several sources, synthesize them, summarize them, determine which of them are relevant, and organize them.

extranet A combination of corporate intranets and the Internet, specifically used in enhanced product realization (EPR).

facet An attribute or a feature that describes the content of a slot in a frame.

facilitator (in GSS) A person who plans, organizes, and electronically controls a group in a collaborative computing decision-making environment (such as a decision room).

facts Declarative knowledge: the true and false statements in an artificial intelligence system.

feasibility study A preliminary investigation for developing plans to construct a new information system. The major aspects of the study are cost versus benefit, technological, human, organizational, and financial.

fifth-generation languages (5GL) Artificial intelligence computer programming languages. The best known are PROLOG and LISP.

firewall A method for protecting an organization's computers from outsiders.

firing a rule Obtaining information on either the IF or the THEN part of a rule that makes the rule an assertion (true or false).

forecasting Predicting the future.

forward chaining A data-driven search in a rule-based system.

fourth-generation languages (4GLs) Nonprocedural, user-oriented languages that enable quick programming by specifying only the desired results.

frame-based system An expert system whose knowledge is represented as frames (object-oriented) in the knowledge base.

frame A knowledge representation scheme that associates one or more features with an object in terms of slots and particular slot values.

frontline decision making A process of automating decision processes and pushing them down the organization to empower employees who are in contact with customers. It includes evaluation matrices and ready-made DSS.

functional integration Providing different support functions as a single system through a single, consistent interface.

fuzzy logic Logically consistent ways of reasoning that can cope with uncertain or partial information; characteristic of human thinking and many expert systems.

fuzzy sets A set theory approach in which set membership is less precise than having objects strictly in or out of the set.

general-purpose problem solver (GPS) A procedure developed by Alan Newell and Herb Simon in an attempt to create an intelligent computer. Although unsuccessful, the concept itself made a valuable contribution to the AI field.

genetic algorithms Software programs that learn in an evolutionary manner, similarly to the way biological systems evolve.

geographic information system (GIS) An information system that uses spatial data such as digitized maps. A combination of text, graphics, icons, and symbols on maps.

goal-seeking analysis Asking a computer what values certain variables must have in order to attain desired goals.

graphical user interface (GUI) An interactive user-friendly interface in which, by using icons and similar objects, the user can control communication with a computer.

group DSS *See* group support systems.

group support systems (GSS) Information systems that support the work of groups (communication, decision making) generally working on unstructured or semistructured problems.

groupthink In a meeting, continual reinforcement of an idea by group members.

groupware Several computerized technologies and methods that aim to support the work of people working in groups.

groupwork Any work being performed by more than one person.

heuristic programming The use of heuristics in problem solving.

heuristics Informal, judgmental knowledge of an application area that constitutes the "rules of good judgment" in the field. Heuristics also encompasses the knowledge of how to solve problems efficiently and effectively, how to plan steps in solving a complex problem, how to improve performance, and so forth.

hidden layer The middle layer of an artificial neural network with three or more layers.

hidden unemployment A situation in which people are considered employed but work only part of the time. Thus, in such cases the same amount of work could be performed by fewer people.

hierarchical reasoning A reasoning method, based on a tree search, in which certain alternatives, objects, or events can be eliminated at various levels of the search hierarchy.

human–machine interface *See* user interface.

hybrid (integrated) computer systems Different computer programs or tools that are integrated to perform a complex task.

hybrid systems (environments) Software packages for expediting the construction of expert systems that include several knowledge representation schemas.

iconic model A scaled physical replica.

idea generation The process by which people generate ideas, usually supported by software, for example, developing alternative solutions to a problem. *See* brainstorming.

IF-THEN A conditional rule according to which a certain action is taken only if a particular condition is satisfied.

implementation phase The fourth decision-making phase, involving actually putting a recommended solution to work.

independent variables Variables in a model that are controlled by the decision maker and/or the environment and which determine the result of a decision (also called input variables).

induction table A table that facilitates rule induction for expert systems.

inductive learning A machine learning approach in which rules are inferred from facts or data.

inductive reasoning In logic, reasoning from the specific to the general. Conditional or antecedent reasoning.

inexact (approximate) reasoning A type of reasoning used when an expert system must make decisions based on partial or incomplete information.

inference The process of drawing a conclusion from given evidence. To reach a decision by reasoning.

inference engine The part of an expert system that actually performs the reasoning function.

inference tree A schematic view of the inference process showing the order in which rules are being tested.

inferencing Performing the inference function.

inferencing rules In ES, rules that direct the inference engine.

influence diagram A diagram that shows the various types of variables (decision, independent, result) in a problem and how they are related to each other.

information Data that are organized in a meaningful way.

information revolution The changes created by computers that have revolutionized our life. A concept similar to the industrial revolution, which changed the world when machines were introduced.

inheritance The process by which one object takes on or is assigned the characteristics of another object higher up in a hierarchy.

inputs The resources introduced into a system for transformation into outputs.

instantiation The process of assigning (or substituting) a specific value or name to a variable in a frame (or in a logic expression), making it a particular "instance" of that variable.

institutionalization The process through which an MSS system becomes incorporated as an ongoing part of organizational procedures.

institutionalized DSS (or MSS) A system that is a permanent fixture in an organization with continuing financial support. It deals with decisions of a recurring nature.

intelimedia systems Intelligent multimedia systems.

intellectual asset A specific part of the know-how of an organization. Intellectual assets often include the knowledge that employees possess.

intellectual capital The know-how of an organization. Intellectual capital often includes the knowledge that employees possess.

intelligence A degree of reasoning and learned behavior, usually task- or problem-solving–oriented.

intelligence phase The initial phase of problem definition in decision making.

intelligent agent (IA) An expert or knowledge-based system embedded in computer-based information systems (or their components) to make them smarter.

intelligent software agent *See* intelligent agent.

intelligent computer-aided instruction (ICAI) The use of AI techniques for training or teaching with a computer.

intelligent database A database management system exhibiting artificial intelligence features that assist the user or designer; often includes ES and intelligent agents.

intelligent DSS A DSS that includes one or more components of an expert system or other AI technology. With this component, the DSS behaves in a better (more "intelligent") manner.

intelligent interface A user interface exhibiting artificial intelligence features that assist the user; often includes ES and intelligent agents. It may learn the usage style of the decision maker.

intelligent tutoring system (ITS) Self-tutoring systems that can guide learners in how best to proceed with the learning process.

interactive induction A computer-based means of knowledge acquisition that supports an expert in performing knowledge acquisition directly by guiding the expert through knowledge structuring.

interfaces The parts of computer systems that interact with users, accepting commands from the computer keyboard and displaying the results generated by other parts of the systems.

intermediary A person who uses a computer to fulfill requests made by other people, for example, a financial analyst who uses a computer to answer questions for top management.

Internet A global network of hundreds of thousands of local networks.

internet communities *See* electronic (virtual) communities.

Internet softbot A software agent that can learn and be used on the Internet.

interpreter (rule interpreter) *See* inference engine.

interview analysis An explicit, face-to-face knowledge acquisition technique involving a direct dialog between the expert and the knowledge engineer.

intranet An internal network that uses Internet capabilities, such as browsing, search engines, and e-mail.

iterative design *See* evolutionary prototyping process; prototyping.

iterative process *See* evolutionary prototyping process; prototyping.

job content The specific tasks and responsibilities involved in a job.

justification facility (or justifier) *See* explanation facility.

justifier *See* explanation facility.

key performance indicators (KPIs) Specific measures of the critical success factors in an executive information system.

key words Important terms in a document-based (or Web-based) system. Used for searching.

key word search A method of looking for important terms in document- or Web-based systems.

knowledge Understanding, awareness, or familiarity acquired through education or experience. Anything that has been learned, perceived, discovered, inferred, or understood. The ability to use information. In a knowledge management system, knowledge is information in action.

knowledge acquisition The extraction and formulation of knowledge derived from various sources, especially from experts.

knowledge base A collection of facts, rules, and procedures organized into schemas. The assembly of all the information and knowledge about a specific field of interest.

knowledge-based system A typically rule-based system for providing expertise. Identical to ES, except that the source of expertise may include documented knowledge.

knowledge diagram A graphical representation of knowledge.

knowledge discovery A machine learning process that performs rule induction, or a related procedure for establishing knowledge from large databases or textual sources.

knowledge elicitation The act of extracting knowledge, generally automatically, from nonhuman sources; machine learning.

knowledge engineer An AI specialist responsible for the technical side of developing an expert system. The knowledge engineer works closely with the domain expert to capture the expert's knowledge in a knowledge base.

knowledge engineering (KE) The engineering discipline in which knowledge is integrated into computer systems to solve complex problems normally requiring a high level of human expertise.

knowledge inferencing *See* inferencing.

knowledge interchange format (KIF) A computer-oriented language used in the interchange of knowledge among disparate programs.

knowledge management The active management of the expertise in an organization. It involves collecting, categorizing, and disseminating knowledge.

knowledge management system (KMS) A system that facilitates knowledge management by ensuring knowledge flow from the person(s) who know to the person(s) who need to know throughout the organization; knowledge evolves and grows during the process.

knowledge map *See* induction table.

knowledge-poor procedures Standard methods for dealing with shallow knowledge domains.

knowledge query and manipulation language (KQML) A language and protocol for exchanging information and knowledge.

knowledge refining system A system that has the ability to analyze its own performance, learn, and improve itself for future consultations.

knowledge repository The actual storage location of knowledge in a knowledge management system. Similar in nature to a database.

knowledge representation A formalism for representing facts and rules in a computer about a subject or specialty.

knowledge validation Testing to determine if the knowledge in an AI system is correct and if the system performs with an acceptable level of accuracy.

knowledge warehouse A repository for an organization's expertise.

knowledge workers Employees who use knowledge as a significant input to their work.

knowledgeware Artificial intelligence software.

learning algorithm The training procedure used by an artificial neural network.

learning organization An organization capable of learning from its past experience, implying the existence of an organizational memory and a means to save, represent, and share it through its personnel.

life cycle In system development, a structured approach to the development of information systems in several distinct steps.

linear programming (LP) A mathematical model for the optimal solution of resource allocation problems. All relationships among the variables are linear.

LISP (list processor) An AI programming language, created by AI pioneer John McCarthy, that is especially popular in the United States. It is based on manipulating lists of symbols.

LISP machines (or AI workstations) A single-user computer designed primarily to expedite the development of AI programs.

list A written series of related items. Used to represent knowledge.

machine learning The process by which a computer learns from experience (e.g., using programs that can learn from historical cases).

management information system (MIS) A business information system designed to provide past, present, and future information appropriate for planning, organizing, and controlling the operations of an organization.

management science (MS) The application of the scientific approach and mathematical models to the analysis and solution of managerial decision problems.

management support system (MSS) The application of any type of decision support technology to decision making.

manufacturing requirements planning (MRP) A computerized integrated plan for purchasing and/or buying parts and subassemblies used for several items so that inventories are minimized but product deliveries are met on schedule.

massive parallel processing A fine-grained, parallel computing environment in which many small, limited-capability processing elements are used; describes artificial neural networks.

mathematical (quantitative) model A system of symbols and expressions representing a real situation.

mathematical programming An optimization technique for the allocation of resources subject to constraints.

metadata Data about data. In a data warehouse these describe the contents of the data warehouse and the manner of its use.

metaknowledge In an expert system, knowledge about how the system operates or reasons. More generally, knowledge about knowledge.

metarule A rule that describes how other rules should be used or modified.

metasearch engines Search engines that combine results from several different search engines.

microelectronics Miniaturization of electronic circuits and components.

mobile agents Intelligent software agents that move from one Internet site to another, retrieving and sending information.

mobility The degree to which agents travel through a computer network.

model base A collection of preprogrammed quantitative models (e.g., statistical, financial, optimization) organized as a single unit.

model base management system (MBMS) Software for establishing, updating, combining, and so on (e.g., managing), a DSS model base.

model-based reasoning *See* model-based system.

model-based system (or reasoning) An application whose knowledge is derived by a mathematical (or other type of) model.

model building blocks Preprogrammed software elements that can be used to build computerized models. For example, a random-number generator can be employed in the construction of a simulation model.

modeling tools Software programs that enable the building of mathematical models quickly. A spreadsheet and a planning language are modeling tools.

modified Turing test A test in which a manager is shown two solutions, one derived by a computer and one by a human, and is asked to compare them.

modus ponens An inference rule type which the rule "A implies B" justifies B by the existence of A.

modus tollens An inference rule type in which the rule "A implies B" may be true, but B is known to be false, implying that A is false.

Monte Carlo simulation A mechanism that uses random numbers to predict the behavior of an event whose probability is known.

multiagent system A system with multiple cooperating software agents.

multiagents *See* multiagent system.

multicriteria modeling *See* multiple goals.

multidimensional analysis An analysis of data by three or more dimensions. *See* multidimensionality.

multidimensional modeling A modeling method that involves data analysis in several dimensions. *See* multidimensional analysis.

multidimensional scaling A method that identifies various dimensions of knowledge and then arranges it in the form of a distance matrix. It uses least-squares fitting regression to analyze, interpret, and integrate the data.

multidimensional spreadsheets Spreadsheet software systems that manipulate spreadsheets in more than two dimensions. Multidimensional spreadsheets work with data cubes.

multidimensionality Organizing, presenting, and analyzing data by several dimensions, such as sales by region, by product, by salesperson, and by time (four dimensions).

multiple criteria problem (multicriteria problem) *See* multiple goals.

multiple experts Two or more experts used as the source of knowledge for an expert system.

multiple goals Refers to a decision situation in which alternatives are evaluated with several, sometimes conflicting, goals.

multiple knowledge representation The use of two or more representations of knowledge in an expert system, for example, frames and rules.

multiple-objective problem (multiobjective problem) *See* multiple goals.

mutation A genetic operator that causes a random change in a potential solution.

MYCIN An early rule-based expert system, developed by Edward H. Shortliffe, that helps to determine types of blood infections and to prescribe appropriate antibiotics.

natural language A language spoken by humans on a daily basis, such as English, French, Japanese, or German.

natural language interface A user interface that uses a natural (human) language for interaction.

natural language processing (NLP) Using a natural language processor to interface with a computer-based system.

natural language processor An AI-based user interface that allows the user to interact with a computer-based system in much the same way that he or she would converse with another human.

need assessment An analysis to determine if an MSS is worth developing.

neural computing (networks) An experimental computer design aimed at building intelligent computers that operate in a manner modeled on the functioning of the human brain. *See* artificial neural networks (CANN).

neural network *See* artificial neural networks (ANN).

neurons Cells (processing elements) of a biological or an artificial neural network.

nominal group technique (NGT) A simple brainstorming process for nonelectronic meetings.

nonprogrammed problem *See* unstructured decisions.

normative models Models that prescribe how a system should operate.

nucleus The central, processing portion of a neuron.

numeric processing The traditional use of computers to manipulate numbers.

O-A-V triplet A knowledge representation using objects, attributes, and values.

object A person, place, or thing about which information is collected, processed, or stored.

object-oriented database management system (OODBMS) A database that is designed and manipulated using the object-oriented approach.

object-oriented model base management system (OOMBMS) An MBMS constructed in an object-oriented environment.

object-oriented programming A language for representing objects and processing these representations by sending messages and activating methods.

online analytical processing (OLAP) An information system that enables the user to query the system, conduct an analysis, and so on, while the user is at his or her PC. The result is generated in seconds.

online (commercial) databases External databases provided to organizations and individuals for a fee.

open systems Computer systems on a network that permit the software and hardware of any vendor to be used by any user.

operational models Models that represent problems for the operational level of management.

operations research (OR) *See* management science.

optimal solution A best possible solution to a modeled problem.

optimization The process of identifying a best possible solution to a problem.

organizational agent *See* public agent.

organizational computing Organization-wide information systems and knowledge management.

organizational culture The aggregate attitudes in an organization concerning a certain issue (such as technology, computers, and DSS).

organizational decision support system (ODSS) A networked DSS that serves people at several locations, usually dealing with several decisions.

organizational intelligence *See* knowledge warehouse.

organizational knowledge base An organization's knowledge repository.

organizational learning The process of capturing knowledge and making it available enterprise-wide.

organizational memory That which an organization "knows."

outcome variable *See* result variable.

overexpectations Assumptions that a system can deliver more than it actually can; especially common in regard to early AI systems.

parallel processing An advanced computer processing technique that allows a computer to perform multiple processes at once—in parallel.

parallelism In a group support system, a process gain in which everyone in a group can work simultaneously (in brainstorming, voting, ranking, and so on).

parameters Fixed factors, not under the control of the decision maker, that affect the result variables in a decision situation.

pattern matching *See* pattern recognition. Sometimes this term refers specifically to matching the IF and THEN parts in rule-based systems. In this case, pattern matching can be considered one area of pattern recognition.

pattern recognition The technique of matching an external pattern to one stored in a computer's memory; used in inference engines, image processing, neural computing, and speech recognition (in other words, the process of classifying data into predetermined categories).

personal agent *See* private agent.

personal construct theory An approach in which each person is viewed as a "personal scientist" who seeks to predict and control events by forming theories, testing hypotheses, and analyzing results of experiments.

personal digital assistant (PDA) A (usually) handheld device that employs agent technology to help handle the day-to-day activities (appointments, and so on) of an individual.

personality (temperament) type The general attitude that a person has. It influences the general orientation toward goal attainment, selection of alternatives, treatment of risk, and reactions under stress.

phased development A methodology that involves breaking a system up into a series of versions that are developed sequentially. Each version has more functionality than the previous one, and they evolve into a final system.

physical integration The seamless integration of several systems into one functioning system.

predicate logic (calculus) A logical system of reasoning used in AI programs to indicate relationships among data items. The basis of the computer language PROLOG.

principle of choice The criterion for making a choice among alternatives.

private agent An agent that works for only one person.

problem management Dividing a decision-making process into steps and supporting the functional requirements of these steps.

problem ownership The jurisdiction (authority) to solve a problem.

problem solving A process in which one starts from an initial state and proceeds to search through a problem space to identify a desired goal.

procedural knowledge Information about courses of action; contrasts with declarative knowledge.

procedural (numeric) reasoning A reasoning method that utilizes a numeric rather than a symbolic approach.

procedural rules Rules that advise on how to solve a problem, given that certain facts are known.

process gain In GSS, improvements in the effectiveness of the activities of a meeting.

process loss In GSS, degradation in the effectiveness of the activities of a meeting.

processing elements (PEs) The neurons in a neural network.

product life cycle The process that starts with the creation of a product and ends with its disposal.

production rules A knowledge representation method in which knowledge is formalized into rules containing an IF part and a THEN part (also called a condition and an action, respectively).

productivity The ratio of outputs (results) to inputs (resources).

programmed problem Well-structured problems that are repetitive and routine and for which there are standard models.

project management The activity and methods of directing and controlling a project.

PROLOG A high-level computer language based on the concepts of predicate calculus.

propositional logic A formal logical system of reasoning in which conclusions are drawn from a series of statements according to a strict set of rules.

protocol analysis A set of instructions governing the format and control of data in moving from one medium to another.

prototyping In system development, a strategy in which a scaled-down system or portion of a system is constructed in a short time, tested, and improved in several iterations.

public agent An agent that serves any user.

qualitative reasoning (QR) A means of representing and making inferences using general physical knowledge about the world.

quality of life A usually descriptive measure of how well life is treating people in the workplace and the home; often used to describe the impact of MSS.

quantitative software packages Preprogrammed (sometimes called ready-made) models and optimization systems; sometimes they serve as building blocks for other quantitative models.

query facility The mechanism that accepts requests for data, accesses them, manipulates them, and queries them.

query language A language provided as part of a DBMS for easy access to data in the database.

query tools A DBMS subsystem that provides easy access to data in the database.

rapid application development (RAD) A development methodology that adjusts a system development life cycle so that parts of a system can be developed quickly so that users can obtain some functionality as soon as possible. It includes methods of phased development, prototyping, and throwaway prototyping.

rapid prototype In expert systems development, an initial version of an expert system (usually one with 25 to 200 rules) that is quickly developed to test the effectiveness of the proposed knowledge representation and inference mechanisms in solving a particular problem.

ready-made expert systems Mass-produced expert system packages that can be purchased from software companies. They are fairly general in nature.

ready-made quantitative models Mass-produced quantitative analysis models for specific vertical markets such as vehicle routing and product mixing.

ready-made systems Mass-produced system packages that can be purchased from software companies. They are fairly general in nature.

real time The actual occurrence of events; refers to results given rapidly enough to be useful in directly controlling a physical process or guiding a human user.

real-time system A system that is synchronized to run in real time. *See* real-time.

regression analysis A trend analysis method based on a statistical forecasting model.

relational database A database whose records are organized into tables that can be processed by either relational algebra or relational calculus.

relational model base management system (RMBMS) The relational approach (as in relational databases) to the design and development of a model base management system.

repertory grid analysis A tool used by psychologists to represent a person's view of a problem in terms of its elements and constructs.

reproduction The creation of new generations of improved solutions with the use of a genetic algorithm.

resolution A reasoning approach in artificial intelligence.

result (outcome) variable A variable that expresses the result of a decision (such as one concerning profit), usually one of the goals of a decision-making problem.

reverse logistics A flow of material or finished goods back to the source, for example, the return of defective products by customers.

risk A probabilistic or stochastic decision situation.

risk analysis A decision-making method that analyzes the risk (based on assumed known probabilities) associated with different alternatives. Also known as calculated risk.

robotics The science of using a machine (a robot) to perform manual functions without human intervention.

role ambiguity A situation in which the role to be performed by an employee is not clear. Lack of a job description and changing conditions often result in role ambiguity.

rule A formal way of specifying a recommendation, directive, or strategy, expressed as an IF premise and a THEN conclusion and possibly an ELSE conclusion.

rule-based system A system in which knowledge is represented completely in terms of rules (e.g., a system based on production rules).

rule induction The creation of rules by a computer from examples of problems for which the outcome is known. These rules are then generalized to other cases.

rule interpreter The inference mechanism in a rule-based system.

SAP R/3 The most widely used ERP product, from SAP A.G. (Germany). It is a highly integrated package.

satisficing A process during which one seeks a solution that will satisfy a set of constraints. In contrast to optimization, which seeks the best possible solution, satisficing simply seeks a solution that will work (well enough).

scenario A statement of assumptions and configurations concerning the operating environment of a particular system at a particular time.

script A framelike structure representing a stereotyped sequence of events (such as eating at a restaurant).

search engine A software agent that searches for information on the Internet (e.g., by key words).

self-evolving DSS A special type of intelligent DSS.

self-organizing Refers to a neural network architecture that uses unsupervised learning.

semantic network A knowledge representation method consisting of a network of nodes, representing concepts or objects, connected by arcs describing the relations between the nodes.

semistructured decisions Decisions in which some aspects of the problem are structured and others are unstructured.

sensitivity analysis A study of the effect of a change in one or more input variables on a proposed solution.

shallow knowledge A representation of only surface-level information that can be used to deal with very specific situations.

shallow (surface) representation A model that does not capture all the forms of knowledge used by experts in their reasoning. Contrasts with deep representation.

shell Software for systems development that consists of the basic structure of the system without the details related to a specific problem. A complete expert system stripped of its specific knowledge. In rule-based systems, it is a kind of expert system development tool consisting of two stand-alone pieces of software—a rule set manager and an inference engine capable of reasoning with the rule set built with the rule set manager.

sigmoid (logical activation) function An S-shaped transfer function in the range of zero to one.

simulation An imitation of reality.

slot A subelement of a frame of an object. A particular characteristic, specification, or definition used in forming a knowledge base.

social computing The use of computing and telecommunications for socialization, discussion, etc., instead of face-to-face interaction.

soft information Fuzzy, unofficial, intuitive, subjective, nebulous, implied, or vague information.

softbots (intelligent software robots) Software agents with learning capabilities.

software agents *See* softbots and intelligent agent (IA).

software intelligent agent (IA) *See* softbots and intelligent agent.

specific DSS (application) A system that actually accomplishes a specific task. It is similar to application software in conventional MIS.

specific expert systems An expert system that advises users on a specific issue.

speech recognition Translation of the human voice into individual words and sentences understandable by a computer.

speech understanding An area of AI research that attempts to allow computers to recognize words or phrases of human speech.

spreadsheet add-in Software programs designed to work with spreadsheets, such as optimization or decision trees.

staff assistant An individual who acts as an assistant to a manager.

static explanation In an ES, associating a fixed explanation text with a rule to explain the rule's meaning.

static models Models that describe a single interval of a situation.

statistical methods Mathematical methodologies based on probability and statistical theory.

status access A rapid access to current information, provided by a computer.

strategic models Models that represent problems for the strategic level (executive level) of management.

structured decisions Standard or repetitive decision situations for which solution techniques are already available.

structured interview A systematic goal-oriented interviewing process that forces organized communication between the knowledge engineer and the expert.

structured problem *See* structured decisions.

structured query language (SQL) A data definition and management language of relational databases. It front-ends most relational DBMS.

subjective probability An probability estimated by a manager without the benefit of a formal model.

suboptimization An optimization-based procedure that does not consider all the alternatives for or impacts on an organization.

summation function *See* transformation function.

supervised learning A method of training artificial neural networks in which sample cases are shown to the network as input and the weights are adjusted to minimize the error in its outputs.

supply chain The flow of material, information, and money from the creation of raw materials to their final processing into a product (or service) and the delivery of the product to end users. In addition, it includes all the necessary organizational units, people, and procedures that support the flow.

supply chain management (SCM) The activities involved in managing supply chains: planning, organizing, staffing, and control.

symbiotic DSS *See* Active DSS.

symbol A string of characters that represents a real-world concept.

symbol structures The meaningful relationships represented in an AI program.

symbolic processing The use of symbols, rather than numbers, combined with rules of thumb (or heuristics) to process information and solve problems.

synapse The connection (where the weights are) between processing elements in a neural network.

synchronous Occurring at the same time.

system A set of elements considered to act as a single goal-oriented entity.

system advocate The sponsor who initiates a project.

system analysis The investigation and recording of existing systems and the conceptual design and feasibility study of new systems.

system builder A person responsible for the implementation of a system.

system design The specification of appropriate hardware and software components required to implement an information system.

system development life cycle (SDLC) A systematic process for constructing large information systems in an effective manner.

tabu search A memory- and intelligence-based search procedure for computer problem solving.

tacit knowledge Knowledge that is usually in the domain of subjective, cognitive, and experiential learning. It is highly personal and hard to formalize.

tactical models Models that represent problems for the tactical level (midlevel) of management.

team-developed DSS A team assembled to build a large, usually interdisciplinary DSS.

technology levels of DSS (or ES) A classification of software as basic development tools, integrated development tools, and completed applications (DSS or ES).

telecommuting An arrangement whereby employees work at home, usually using a computer or a terminal linked to their place of employment.

teleconferencing The use of telecommunication in a meeting held at different locations.

temporal reasoning The ability to reason about the time relationships between events.

throwaway prototyping A development methodology that involves creating design prototypes to assist in understanding more about a system that may not clearly be understood. These help the user learn about requirements and the final system to be deployed.

time-series analysis A technique that analyzes historical data over several time periods and then makes a forecast.

toolkit A collection of related software that assists a system developer.

top management support The presence of a top-level manager as a system advocate; one of *the* most important factors necessary for the introduction of any organizational change.

transaction processing system (TPS) The system that processes an organization's routine, repetitive, basic transactions such as ordering, billing, or paying.

transformation (transfer) function In a neural network, the function that sums and transforms inputs before a neuron fires. The relationship between the internal activation level and the output of a neuron.

Turing test A test designed to measure the "intelligence" of a computer.

uncertainty In expert systems, a value that cannot be determined during a consultation. Many expert systems can accommodate uncertainty; that is, they allow the user to indicate if he or she does not know the answer.

uncertainty avoidance The omission of uncertainty from a stochastic model.

uncontrollable variables Factors that affect the result of a decision but are not under the control of the decision maker. They can be internal (e.g., related to technology or to policies) or external (e.g., related to legal issues or to climate).

undocumented knowledge Knowledge that comes from nondocumented sources, such as human experts.

unstructured decisions Complex decisions for which no standard solutions exist.

unstructured (informal) interview An informal interview that acquaints a knowledge engineer with an expert's problem-solving domain.

unstructured problems *See* unstructured decisions.

unsupervised learning A method of training artificial neural networks in which only input stimuli are shown to the network, which is self-organizing.

user commitment The extent to which a user buys into an MSS. A critical success factor in developing MSS.

user-developed DSS A DSS developed by one user or by a few users in one department.

user interface (or human–machine interface) The component of a computer system that allows bidirectional communication between the system and its user.

user interface management system (UIMS) *See* dialog generation and management system.

user interface objects In a Windows or other object-oriented environment, menus, hot keys, buttons, and other icons used by the user interface.

user resistance The behavioral aspects of the refusal of users to use new technology or even of their attempts to sabotage it.

validation Determination of whether the right system was built.

value chain The actual steps an item follows as it moves along the supply chain. *See* value chain model.

value chain model A model developed by Michael Porter that describes how value is added when a product moves along the supply chain. There are primary activities that add value directly (e.g., manufacturing, testing, storage) and secondary activities that support the primary activities (e.g., accounting, personnel, engineering).

value system In a firm's value chain, the suppliers and other business partners and their supply chains.

verification Confirmation that a system was built to specifications (correctly).

virtual corporation (enterprises) An organization in which people work wherever and whenever it is appropriate.

virtual learning *See* distance learning.

virtual organization A partnership of several organizations created for a specific accomplishment (usually short term). Each partner stays with a permanent organization and communicates and collaborates electronically.

virtual reality (VR) A three-dimensional interactive technology that gives the user a sense of being physically present in a real world.

virtual reality markup language (VRML) An Internet language for the Web that enables coding of three-dimensional graphics.

virtual workspace (or virtual workplace) The "place" where virtual meetings occur.

visual interactive modeling (VIM) Graphical animation in which systems and processes are presented dynamically to the decision maker. It enables visualization of the results of different potential actions.

visual interactive simulation (VIS) A special case of VIM in which a simulation approach is used in the decision-making process.

visual recognition The addition of some form of computer intelligence and decision making to digitized visual information, received from a machine sensor such as a camera.

visual simulation *See* Visual Interactive Simulation.

walkthrough (or talkthrough) In knowledge engineering, a process whereby the expert walks (or talks) the knowledge engineer through the solution to a problem.

Web An abbreviation for World Wide Web.

Web mining Data mining on the Internet via intelligent agents. It involves information discovery, extraction, summarization, and generalization.

Webcasting Customized broadcasting over the Web where the information appears as it becomes available on the user's screen in a ticker-tape format (push technology).

weights Values assigned to each connection at the input to a neuron. Analogous to a synapse in the brain. Weights control the inflow to the processing elements in neural networks.

what-if analysis Asking a computer what the effect of changing some of the input data or parameters will be.

wizards Software agents that conduct routine tasks for users.

World Wide Web (the Web) A set of standard protocols for organizing, storing, and retrieving information on the Internet.

REFERENCES

Abramson, G. (1999, May 15). "On the KM Midway," *CIO* (Enterprise Section 2).

Ackermann, F., C. Eden, and S. Cropper. (1996). "Cognitive Mapping: Getting Started with Cognitive Mapping," http://www.banxia.co.uk/depaper.html.

Adeli, H., and S. Hung. (1995). *Machine Learning: Neural Networks, Genetic Algorithms and Fuzzy Systems.* New York: Wiley.

Adelman, L. (1992). *Evaluating Decision Support and Expert Systems.* New York: Wiley.

Agatstein, K., and J. B. Rieley. (1998, Winter). "Using Simulation to Improve the Decision-making Process." *National Productivity Review,* Vol. 18, No. 1.

AI Letter. (1988, June; 1989, Apr.). Dallas: Texas Instruments.

Aiba, H., and T. Terano. (1996). "A Computational Model for Distributed Knowledge Systems with Learning Mechanisms." *Expert Systems with Applications,* Vol. 10, Nos. 3 and 4.

Ainscough, T. L., and J. E. Aronson. (1999). "A Neural Networks Approach for the Analysis of Scanner Data." *Journal of Retailing and Consumer Services,* Vol. 6.

Ainscough. T. L., J. E. Aronson, and T. M. Seiler. (1997, June). "Neural Network Applications in Business." *The Journal of Applied Management and Entrepreneurship* Vol. 3, No. 2.

Alavi, M., and D. Leidner. (1999, Feb.). "Knowledge Management Systems: Issues, Challenges, and Benefits." *Communications of the Association for Information Systems,* Vol. 1, Art. 7.

Alavi, M., and E. A. Joachimsthaler. (1992, Mar.). "Revisiting DSS Implementation Research: A Meta-analysis of the Literature and Suggestions for Researchers." *MIS Quarterly,* Vol. 16, No. 1.

Alavi, M., et al. (1995, Sept.). "Using IT to Re-engineer Business Education: An Exploratory Investigation of Collaborative Telelearning." *MIS Quarterly.*

Allee, V. (1997, Nov.). "12 Principles of Knowledge Management." *Training and Development,* Vol. 51, No. 11.

Allen, B. P. (1994, Mar.). "Case-based Reasoning: Business Applications." *Communications of the ACM,* Vol. 37, No. 3.

Alpar, P., and W. Dilger. (1995, Oct.). "Market Share Analysis and Prognosis Using Qualitative Reasoning." *Decision Support Systems,* Vol. 15, No. 2.

Alter, S. L. (1980). *Decision Support Systems: Current Practices and Continuing Challenges.* Reading, MA: Addison-Wesley.

Althoff, K. D., et al. (1995). *A Review of Industrial Case-based Reasoning Tools.* San Francisco: AI Intelligence Publishing.

Altier, W. J. (1999). *The Thinking Manager's Toolbox.* Oxford, UK: Oxford University Press.

Alwast, T., and I. Miliszewska. (1995). "An Agent-based Architecture for Intelligent DSS for Natural Resource Management." *The New Review of Expert Systems.*

Al-Zobaidie, A., and J. B. Grimson. (1987, Feb.). "Expert Systems and Database Systems: How Can They Serve Each Other?" *Expert Systems.*

Anders, U., O. Korn, and C. Schmitt. (1998, Sept./Nov.). "Improving the Pricing of Options: A Neural Network Approach." *Journal of Forecasting,* Vol. 17, Nos. 5 and 6.

Anderson, E. E. (1990, Spring). "Choice Models for the Evaluation and Selection of Software Packages," *Journal of MIS.*

Andreu, R., and C. Ciborra. (1996, June). "Organisational Learning and Core Capabilities Development: The Role of IT." *Strategic Information Systems,* Vol. 5, No. 2.

Andrews, J., and D. C. Smith. (1996, May). "In Search of the Marketing Imagination: Factors Affecting the Creativity of Marketing Programs for Mature Products." *Journal of Marketing Research,* Vol. 33.

Angele, J., D. Fensel, and R. Studer. (1993). "Formalizing and Operationalizing Models of Expertise with KARL," Research Report. Karlsruhe, Germany: Institute für Angewandte Informatik und Formale Beschreibungsverfahren, University of Karlsruhe.

Anguita, D., A. Boni, and G. Parodi. (2000, Mar.). "A Case Study of a Distributed High-performance Computing System for Neurocomputing." *Journal of Systems Architecture,* Vol. 46, No. 5.

Angus, J., J. Patel, and J. Harty. (1998, Mar. 16). "Knowledge Management: Great Concept . . . But What Is It?" *InformationWeek.*

Anonymous. (1999a, Sept. 15). "The Means to an Edge: Knowledge Management: Key to Innovation," Special Supplement, *CIO.*

Anonymous. (1999b, Nov.). "Credit Risk Analysis Software Makes E-commerce Safer," *ABA Banking Journal,* Vol. 91, No. 11.

Anonymous. (1999c, Dec.). "Tools for Conferences, Meetings, and Distance Learning. *Presentations,* Vol. 13, No. 12.

Anonymous. (2000, Mar.). "Fuzzy Logic Predicts Accident Risk." *Civil Engineering,* Vol. 70, No. 3.

Anthony, R. N. (1965). *Planning and Control Systems: A Framework for Analysis.* Cambridge, MA: Harvard University Graduate School of Business.

Aparico, G. (1995). "The Role of Intelligent Agents in the Information Infrastructure." *IBM's White Paper,* activist.gpl.com:81/WhitePaper/ptc2.htm.

Appleton, E. L., (1997, March). "How to Survive ERP," *Datamation.*

Argyris, C. (1971, Feb.). "Management Information Systems: The Challenge to Rationality and Emotionality." *Management Science,* Vol. 17, No. 6.

Arinze, B., and S. Banerjee. (1992, May). "A Framework for Effective Data Collection, Usage, and Maintenance of DSS." *Information and Management.*

Arisha K.A., et al. (1999, Mar./Apr.). "Impact: A Platform for Collaborating Agents." *IEEE Intelligent Systems.*

Aronson, J. E. (1989). "A Survey of Dynamic Network Flows." *Annals of Operations Research,* Vol. 20.

Aronson, J. E., R. M. Myers, and R. B. Wharton, (2000, June). "Time Pressure Impacts on Electronic Brainstorming in a Group Support System Environment." *Informatica,* Vol. 24, No. 2.

Atanackovic, D., D. T. McGillis, F. D. Galiana, J. Cheng, and L. Loud. (1997, July/Aug.). "An Integrated Knowledge-Based Model for Power System Planning." *IEEE Expert.*

Athappilly, K. (1985, Feb.). "Successful Decision Making Starts with DSS Evaluation." *Data Management,* Vol. 23, No. 2.

Austin, M., et al. (1997). "Security Market Timing Using Neural Network Models." *The Review of Applied Expert Systems.*

Avouris, M., and L. Gasser. (1992). *Distributed Artificial Intelligence: Theory and Praxis.* Boston: Kluwer Academic.

Avritzer, A., J. P. Ros, and E. J. Weyuker. (1996). "Reliability Testing of Rule-based Systems." *IEEE Software,* Vol. 13, No. 5.

Awad, E. M. (1996). *Building Expert Systems: Principles, Procedures, and Applications.* Minneapolis/St. Paul, MN: West Publishing.

Azuaje, F., W. Dubitzky, N. Black, and K. Adamson (1999, Oct.). "Improving Clinical Decision Support through Case-based Data Fusion." *IEEE Transactions on Biomedical Engineering,* Vol. 46, No. 10.

Ba, S., et al. (1997). "Enterprise Decision Support Using Intranet Technology." *Decision Support Systems,* Vol. 20, No. 2.

Baatz, E. B. (1996, May/June). "Will the Web Eat Your Job?" *Webmaster,* Vol. 1, No. 1.

Babyak, R. J. (1999, Feb.). "Brainstorming." *Appliance Manufacturer,* Vol. 47, No. 2.

Back, B., T. Laitinen, and K. Sere. (1996). "Neural Networks and Genetic Algorithms for Bankruptcy Predictions." *Expert Systems with Applications,* Vol. 11, No. 4.

Badaracco, J. L. (1991). *The Knowledge Link.* Boston: Harvard Business School Press.

Baer, T. (1998, Sept.). "The Culture of Components." *Application Development Trends.*

Bagnoli, C., and H. C. Smith. (1998). "The Theory of Fuzzy Logic and Its Application to Real Estate Valuation." *Journal of Real Estate Research,* Vol. 16, No. 2.

Baker, T. K., and D. A. Collier. (1999, Winter). "A Comparative Revenue Analysis of Hotel Yield Management Heuristics." *Decision Sciences,* Vol. 30, No. 1.

Balentine B., et al., (1999). *How to Build a Speech Recognition Application.* San Francisco: Enterprise Integration Group.

Ballantine, J., et al. (1996, Fall). "The 3-D Model of Information Success: The Search for the Dependent Variable Continues." *Information Resources Management Journal,* Vol. 9, No. 4.

Barker, V., and D. O'Connor. (1989, Mar.). "Expert Systems for Configuration at Digital, XCON and Beyond." *Communications of the ACM,* Vol. 32, No. 3.

Barki, H., and J. Hartwick. (1994, Mar.). "Measuring User Participation, User Involvement, and User Attitude." *MIS Quarterly,* Vol. 18, No. 1.

Barquin, R., and H. Edelstein. (1997a). *Building, Using and Managing the Data Warehouse.* Upper Saddle River, NJ: Prentice Hall.

Barquin, R., and H. Edelstein. (1997b). *Data Mining Techniques For Marketing, Sales and Customer Support.* New York: J Wiley.

Barrett, A. R., and J. S. Edwards. (1994). "Knowledge Elicitation and Knowledge Representation in a Large Domain with Multiple Experts." *Expert Systems with Applications,* Vol. 8.

Barsanti, J. B. (1990, Winter). "Expert Systems: Critical Success Factors for Their Implementation." *Information Executive,* Vol. 3, No. 1.

Barth, S. (2000, Feb.). "Knowledge as a Function of X." *Knowledge Management.*

Bartos, F. J. (1999, May). "Motion Control Tunes into AI Methods." *Control Engineering,* Vol. 46, No. 5.

Basden, A. (1994, May). "Three Levels of Benefits in Expert Systems." *Expert Systems,* Vol. 11, No. 2.

Baum, D. (1996, Nov.). "U.N. Automates Payroll with AI System," *Datamation,* Vol. 42, No. 17.

Bayles, D. (1996). *Intranets: Planning and Implementing the Enterprise.* Upper Saddle River, NJ: Prentice Hall.

Bazerman, M. (1998). *Judgment in Managerial Decision Making,* 4th ed. New York: Wiley.

Beach, L. R. (1997). *The Psychology of Decision Making: People in Organizations.* Thousand Oaks, CA: Sage Publications.

Bebenham, J., (1998). *Knowledge Engineering.* Berlin: Springer-Verlag.

Beck, D. F., et al. (1999, June). "Landscapes, Games, and Maps for Technology Planning." *Chemtech.*

Becker, G. (1999). "Knowledge Discovery," in Liebowitz, J. (ed.), *Knowledge Management Handbook.* Boca Raton, FL: CRC Press.

Beckley, G. B., and M. Gaines. (1990, Aug. 6). "12 Tips for Better Systems Implementation." *ComputerWorld,* Vol. 24, No. 32.

Beer M., et al. (1999). "Negotiation in Multi-agents Systems." *Knowledge Engineering Review,* Vol. 14, No. 3.

Beerel, A. (1993). *Expert Systems in Business: Real World Applications.* New York: Ellis Horwood.

Bell, P. C., C. K., Anderson, D. S. Staples, and M. Elder. (1999, Apr.). "Decision-makers' Perceptions of the Value and Impact of Visual Interactive Modeling." *Omega,* Vol. 27, No. 2.

Bell, D. E., and A. Schleifer, Jr. (1996). *Decision Making Under Uncertainty.* Cambridge, MA: Course Technology.

Beltratti, A., S. Margarita, and P. Terna. (1996). *Neural Networks for Economic and Financial Modeling.* London: International Thomson Computer Press.

Belz, R., and P. Mertens. (1996, May 21). "Combining Knowledge-based Systems and Simulation to Solve Rescheduling Problems." *Decision Support Systems,* Vol. 17, No. 2.

Benaroch, M., and V. Dhar. (1995, Oct.). "Controlling the Complexity of Investment Decisions Using Qualitative Reasoning Techniques." *Decision Support Systems,* Vol. 15, No. 2.

Benders, J., and F. Manders. (1993, Oct.). "Expert Systems and Organizational Decision Making." *Information and Management,* Vol. 25, No. 4.

Benjamin, C. O., and J. Bannis. (1990, May). "A Hybrid Neural Network/Expert System for the Property Casualty Insurance Industry." *Proceedings of the Fourth International Conference on Expert Systems in POM.* Chapel Hill, NC: University of North Carolina.

Benjamin, C. O., and J. Bannis. (1991). "A Hybrid Neural Network/Expert System for the Property Casualty Insurance Industry." *Proceedings of the IJCNN,* Seattle, WA.

Benjamins, V. R., D. Fensel, S. Decker, and A. G. Perez. (1999). "Building Onthologies for the Internet: A Mid-term Report." *International Journal of Human–Computer Studies.*

Berens, L. V., and D. Nardi. (1999). *The 16 Personality Types, Descriptions for Self-Discovery.* Huntington Beach, CA: Telos Publications.

Berg, M., and R. K. Wong. (2000, Jan.). "A Multi-agent Architecture for Cooperative Query Answering", *Proceedings of the Thirty-third Hawaii International Conference on Systems Sciences HICSS–33,* Los Alamitos, CA: IEEE Computer Society.

Berger, N. S. (1999, Dec.). "Pioneering Experiences in Distance Learning: Lessons Learned." *Journal of Management Education,* Vol. 23, No. 6.

Bergeron, F., et al. (1991). "Top Managers Evaluate the attributes of EIS," *DSS-91 Transactions,* Providence, RI: The Institute of Management Sciences.

Berghel, H. (2000, Feb.). "Identify Theft, Social Security Numbers, and the Web." *Communications of the ACM,* Vol. 43, No. 2.

Berglas, A., and P. Hoare. (1999, July/Aug.). Spreadsheet Errors: Risks and Techniques." *Management Accounting,* Vol. 77, No. 7.

Berndsen, R., and H. Daniels. (1994, Jan.). "Causal Reasoning and Explanation in Dynamic Economic Systems." *Journal of Economic Dynamics and Control,* Vol. 18, No. 1.

Berry, D., and A. Hart (eds.). (1990). *Expert Systems: Human Issues.* New York: Chapman and Hall.

Berry, M. J. A., and G. Linoff. (1997). *Data Mining Techniques: For Marketing, Sales and Customer Support.* New York: Wiley.

Berson, A., and S. J. Smith. (1997). *Data Warehousing Data Mining and OLAP.* New York: McGraw Hill.

Bhargava, H. K., and R. Krishnan. (1993, Jan.). "Computer-aided Model Construction." *Decision Support Systems,* Vol. 9, No. 1.

Bidgoli, H. (1995, May/June). "Geographic Information Systems: A New Strategic Tool for the 90's and Beyond." *Journal of Systems Management.*

Bieber, M. (1992). "Automating Hypermedia for Decision Support." *Hypermedia,* Vol. 4, No. 2.

Bieber, M. (1995, July). "On Integrating Hypermedia into Decision Support and Other Information Systems." *Decision Support Systems,* Vol. 14, No. 3.

Bielli, M. (1992, Aug. 25). "A DSS Approach to Urban Traffic Management." *European Journal of Operational Research,* Vol. 61, Nos. 1 and 2.

Biggs, M. (1999, July 26). "Enterprise Application Integration Offers Great Benefits After Careful Consideration." *InfoWorld,* Vol. 21, No. 30.

Bigus, J. P. (1996). *Data Mining with Neural Networks.* New York: McGraw-Hill.

Birkman, R. (1995). *True Colors.* Nashville, TN: Thomas Nelson.

Bisby, A. (1999, Oct. 1). "Microsoft Examines Digital Dashboard." *Computer Dealer News,* Vol. 15, No. 37.

Bishopp, F. T., Jr. (1991). *Automated Airline Control Systems: Existing Methodology, Technology Review, and a Suggested Solution Method.* Unpublished master's thesis, Terry College of Business, The University of Georgia, Athens, GA.

Bistline, W. G., Sr., S. Banerjee, and A. Banerjee. (1998, Nov.). "RTSS: An Interactive Decision Support System for Solving Real Time Scheduling Problems Considering Customer and Job Priorities with Schedule Interruptions." *Computers & Operations Research,* Vol. 25, No. 11.

Blanning, R. W. (1993, Jan.). "Model Management Systems: An Overview." *Decision Support Systems,* Vol. 9, No. 1.

Bloom, C. P., and R. B. Loftin. (1998). *Facilitating the Development and Use of Interactive Learning Environments.* New York: Erlbaum Associates.

Bodily, S. E. (1985). *Modern Decision Making.* New York: McGraw-Hill.

Bogarin, J. A. G., and N. F. F. Ebecken. (1996). "Integration of Knowledge Sources for Flexible Pipe Evaluation and Design." *Expert Systems with Applications,* Vol. 10, No. 1.

Boisvert, L. (2000, Winter). "Web-based Learning: The Anytime Anywhere Classroom." *Information Systems Management,* Vol. 17, No. 1.

Bolloju, N. (1999, Aug.). "Decision Model Formulation of Subjective Classification Problem-Solving Knowledge Using a Neuro-Fuzzy Classifier and its Effectiveness," *International Journal of Approximate Reasoning,* Vol. 21.

Bonczek, R. H., C. W. Holsapple, and A. B. Whinston. (1980). "The Evolving Roles of Models in Decision Support Systems." *Decision Sciences,* Vol. 11, No. 2.

Bond, A. H., and L. Gasser (eds.). (1988). *Readings in Distributed AI.* San Mateo, CA: Morgan Kaufman.

Bonissone, P. P. (1993). "Knowledge Representation and Inference in First-generation Knowledge-based Systems," in M. Grabowski and W. A. Wallace (eds.) *Advances in Expert Systems for Management,* Vol. 1. Greenwich, CT: JAI Press.

Bonissone, P. P., and H. E. Johnson, Jr. (1985). "Expert System for Diesel Electric Locomotive Repair." *Human Systems Management,* Vol. 4.

Boose, J. H. (1989, Mar.). "A Survey of Knowledge Acquisition Techniques and Tools." *Knowledge Acquisition,* Vol. 1.

Boose, J. H., and J. M. Bradshaw. (1993). "Expertise Transfer and Complex Problems: Using AQUINAS as a Knowledge-acquisition Workbench for Knowledge-based Systems," in B. G. Buchanan and D. Wilkins, (eds.). *Readings in Knowledge Acquisition and Learning: Automating the Construction and Improvement of Expert Systems.* San Mateo, CA: Morgan Kaufmann.

Boose, J. H., and J. M. Bradshaw. (1999, Aug.). "Expertise Transfer and Complex Problems: Using AQUINAS as a Knowledge-acquisition Workbench for Knowledge-based Systems." *International Journal of Human–Computer Studies.*

Boose, J. H., and B. R. Gaines (eds.). (1990). *The Foundations of Knowledge Acquisition.* New York: Academic Press.

Borenstein, D. (1998, July). "IDSSFLEX: An Intelligent DSS for the Design and Evaluation of Flexible Manufacturing Systems," *The Journal of the Operational Research Society,* Vol. 49, No. 7.

Bort, J. (1996, Apr. 29). "Data Mining's Midas Touch." *InfoWorld,* Vol. 18, No. 18.

Bose, R. (1996). "Intelligent Agents Framework for Developing Knowledge-based DSS for Collaborative Organizational Processes." *Expert Systems with Applications,* Vol. 11, No. 3.

Bostrom, R. P., R. Watson, and S. T. Kinney (eds.). (1993). *Computer Augmented Teamwork: A Guided Tour.* Florence, KY: Van Nostrand Reinhold.

Boswell, C. (1999, Sept. 27). "Process Simulation Software Offers Efficiency and Savings." *Chemical Market Reporter,* Vol. 256, No. 13.

Bourbaki, N. (1990, July). "Turing, Searle and Thought." *AI Expert.*

Bowden, P. R., P. Halstead, and T. G. Rose. (1996). "Extracting Conceptual Knowledge from Text Using Explicit Relation Markers," in N. Shadbolt, K. O'Hara, and G. Schreiber (eds.). *Advances in Knowledge Acquisition.* Berlin: Springer-Verlag.

Boyd, A. (1998, Oct.). "Airline Alliances." *OR/MS Today.*

Brachman, R. J., et al. (1999, Oct.). "Reducing CLASSIC to Practice: Knowledge Representation Theory Meets Reality." *Artificial Intelligence.*

Bradshaw, J. (ed.). (1997). *Software Agents,* Menlo Park, CA: AAAI Press/MIT Press.

Brancheau, J. C., et al. (1996, June). "Key Issues in Information Systems Management: 1994–95 SIM Delphi Results." *MIS Quarterly,* Vol. 20, No. 2.

Brenner, W., et al. (1998). *Intelligent Software Agents.* New York: Spring-Verlag.

Brezillon P., and J. C. Pomeral. (1997, Feb.). "Lessons Learned on Success and Failures of KBSs." *Failures and Lessons Learned in IT Management.*

Briccarello, P., G. Bruno, and E. Ronco. (1995). "REBUS: An Object-oriented Simulator for Business Processes." *Proceedings of the IEEE Annual Simulation Symposium, Los Alamitos, CA.*

Brooking, A. (1999). *Corporate Memory: Strategies for Knowledge Management.* London: International Thomson Business Press.

Brun A., and A. Portioli. (1999, Oct.). "Agent-based Shopfloor Scheduling of Multi Stage Systems." *Computers and Industrial Engineering.*

Buchanan, B. G., and E. H. Shortliffe. (1984). *Rule-based Expert Systems: The MYCIN Experiments of the Stanford Heuristic Programming Project.* Reading, MA: Addison-Wesley.

Buchanan, B. G., and D. Wilkins (eds.). (1993). *Readings in Knowledge Acquisition and Learning: Automating the Construction and Improvement of Expert Systems.* San Mateo, CA: Morgan Kaufmann.

Buede, D. (1998, Aug.). "Decision Analysis Software Survey: Aiding Insight IV," *OR/MS Today.*

Bui, T., and J. Lee. (1999, Apr.). "An Agent-based Framework for Building Decision Support Systems." *Decision Support Systems,* Vol. 25, No. 3.

Bunker, E. (1999). "History of Distance Education." Center for Excellence in Distance Learning (CEDL), Lucent Technologies, www.lucent.com/cedl/ .

Burden, K. (1999, Jan. 11). "Coming into Focus." *Computerworld*, 91–94.

Burger, J. (1995). *Multimedia for Decision Makers: A Business Primer.* Reading, MA: Addison-Wesley.

Burke, R. R. (1996, Mar./Apr.). "Virtual Shopping." *Harvard Business Review.*

Burrough, P., et al. (1998). *Principles of GIS.* London: Oxford University Press.

Bushko, D., and M. Raynor. (1998, Nov.). "Knowledge Management: New Directions for IT (and Other) Consultants." *Journal of Management Consulting,* Vol. 10, No. 2.

Bustamente, G. G., and K. Sorenson. (1994). *Decision Support at Land's End—An Evolution,* Vol. 33, No. 2.

Byrd, T. A. (1995). "Expert Systems Implementation: Interviews with Knowledge Engineers." *Industrial Management and Data Systems,* Vol. 95, No. 10.

Cabena, P., et al. (1997). *Discovering Data Mining from Concept to Implementation.* Upper Saddle River, NJ: Prentice Hall.

Caldwell, B. (1995, May 8). "CEOs Click on IT." *InformationWeek.*

Camm, J. D., and J. R. Evans. (1996). *Management Science: Modeling, Analysis and Interpretation.* Cincinnati, OH: South-Western.

Carlsson, C., and E. Turban (eds.). (2001, Feb.). "Decision Support Systems in the First Decade of the 21st Century," Special Issue. *Decision Support Systems.*

Carlsson, C., and P. Walden. (1995, July/Aug.). "AHP in Political Group Decision: A Study in the Art of Possibilities." *Interfaces,* Vol. 25, No. 4.

Carlsson, C., and P. Walden. (2001, Feb.). "Soft Computing and Decision Support." *Decision Support Systems.*

Carrico, M. A., et al. (1989). *Building Knowledge Systems: Developing and Managing Rule-based Applications.* New York: McGraw-Hill.

Carter, G. M., et al. (1992). *Building Organizational Decision Support Systems.* Cambridge, MA: Academic Press.

Castillo, L., and A. Gonzalez. (1998, Aug. 1). "Distribution Network Optimization: Finding the Most Economic Solution by Using Genetic Algorithms." *European Journal of Operational Research,* Vol. 108, No. 3.

Catalano, C. (1999, June 7). "Web-based Groupware." *Computerworld,* Vol. 33, No. 23.

Caudill, M. (1991, Jan.). "Neural Network Training Tips and Techniques." *AI Expert.*

Cavoukian, A., and D. Tapscott. (1997). *Who Knows: Safeguarding Your Privacy in a Networked World.* New York: McGraw-Hill.

Cawsey, A. (1995). "Developing an Explanation Component for a Knowledge-based System: Discussion." *Expert Systems with Applications,* Vol. 8, No. 4.

Cercone, N. (1999, Jan./Feb.). "Rule-Induction and Case-Based Reasoning: Hybrid Architectures Appear Advantageous." *IEEE Transactions on Knowledge and Data Engineering,* Vol. 11, No. 1.

Cercone, N., A. An, and C. Chan. (1999). "Rule-induction and Case-based Reasoning: Hybrid Architectures Appear Advantageous." *IEEE Transactions on Knowledge and Data Engineering,* Vol. 11, No. 1.

Cerpa, N. (1995). "Pre-physical Data Base Design Heuristics." *Information Management,* Vol. 28, No. 6.

Chaffee, D. (1998). *Groupware, Workflow and Intranets: Reengineering the Enterprise with Collaborative Software.* Boston: Digital Press.

Champy, J., et al. (1996, June 10), "Creating the Electronic Community," *Information Week.*

Chandra, A., et al. (eds.). (Forthcoming). "Business Applications of Data Mining." special issue: *International Journal of Intelligent Systems in Accounting, Finance, and Management.*

Chandra, N., and D. M. Reeb. (1999, Jan.). "Neural Networks in a Market Efficiency Context." *American Business Review,* Vol. 17, No. 1.

Chang, A. M., et al. (1993, Jan.). "Model Management Issues and Directions." *Decision Support Systems,* Vol. 9, No. 1.

Chang, Y. L. (1997). *QSB+ for Windows.* New York: Wiley.

Charles, R. B. (1995, Jan. 23). "Online Libel: A $200 Million Bug." *ComputerWorld,* Vol. 29, No. 4.

Chau, P. Y. K., and P. C. Bell. (1994, Nov.). "Decision Support for the Design of a New Production Plant using Visual Interactive Simulation," *Journal of the Operational Research Society,* Vol. 45, No. 11.

Chau, P. Y. K., and P. C. Bell. (1996, May). "A Visual Interactive Decision Support System to Assist the Design of a New Production Unit." *INFOR,* Vol. 34, No. 2.

Chaudhri, A. B., and M. Loomis (eds.). (1998). *Object Databases in Practice.* Upper Saddle River, NJ: Prentice Hall.

Chaudhri, V. K., and J. D. Lowrance, (1998). "Generic Knowledge-Base Editor," www.ai.sri.com/~gkb/welcome.shtml.

Chen, H. (1996). "An Inventory Decision Support System Using the Object-oriented Approach." *Computers & Operational Research,* Vol. 23, No. 2.

Chen, H., et al. (1995). "Intelligent Meeting Facilitation Agents: An Experiment on GroupSystems." Tucson: University of Arizona, ai.bpa.arizona.edu/papers/agent95/agent95.html.

Chen, H., et al. (1997, Jan.). "Intelligent Spider for Internet Searching." *Proceedings of the Thirtieth Hawaii International Conference on Systems Sciences.* Wailea, HI. Los Alamitos, CA: IEEE Computer Society Press.

Chen, Z. (1996). "Role-limiting Methods for Automated Knowledge Acquisition: A Problem-solving Perspective." *Information Processing & Management,* Vol. 32, No. 2.

Cheng, P. C-H. (1996). "Diagrammatic Knowledge Acquisition: Elicitation, Analysis and Issues," in N. Shadbolt, K. O'Hara, and G. Schreiber (eds.). *Advances in Knowledge Acquisition.* Berlin: Springer-Verlag.

Cheng, R., M. Gen, and Y. Tsujimura. (1999, Oct.). "A Tutorial Survey of Job-shop Scheduling Problems Using Genetic Algorithms: Part II. Hybrid Genetic Search Strategies." *Computers & Industrial Engineering,* Vol. 37, Nos. 1 and 2.

Chi, R. J., and E. Turban. (1995, June). "Distributed Intelligent Executive Information Systems." *Decision Support Systems,* Vol. 14, No. 2.

Chidambaram, L. (1996, June). "Relational Development in Computer-Supported Groups." *MIS Quarterly.*

Chin, K. (1999, Apr.). "Capturing The Power of the Human Mind." *Chemical Engineering,* Vol. 106, No. 4.

Cholewinski, P., V. W. Marek, and A. Mikitiuk. (1999, Aug.). "Computing with Default Logic." *Artificial Intelligence.*

Chorafas, D. N. (1994). *Chaos Theory in the Financial Markets.* Chicago: Probus Publishing.

Churchman, C. W. (1975). *The Systems Approach,* rev. ed. New York: Delacorte.

CiO.com. (1999, Nov. 1). "Supply Chain Integration: The Name of the Game Is Collaboration," Special Advertising Supplement. *CIO.*

Clarke, K. C. (1997). *Getting Started with Geographical Information Systems.* Upper Saddle River, NJ: Prentice Hall.

Clarke, P. (1998 Mar./Apr.). "Implementing a Knowledge Strategy for Your Firm." *Research Technology Management.*

Clemen, R. T. (1996). *Making Hard Decisions,* 2nd ed. Belmont, MA: Duxbury Press.

Cliff D., et al. (1999) "Making Money from Agents." *Knowledge Engineering Review,* Vol. 14, No. 3.

Coddington, P. D., et al. (1999). "Web-based Access to Distributed High Performance GIS for Decision Support." *Proceedings of the Thirty-Second Annual Hawaii International Conference on System Sciences HICSS-32.* Maui, HI. Los Alamitos, CA: IEEE Computer Society.

Coe, L. R. (1996, Fall). "Five Small Secrets to Success." *Information Resources Management Journal,* Vol. 9, No. 4.

Cognos Inc. (2000). "OLAP Reporting for the Enterprise." Cognos, Inc., www.cognos.com.

Cohn, A. G. (1995, Sept.). "The Challenge of Qualitative Spatial Reasoning." *ACM Computing Surveys,* Vol. 27, No. 3.

Cole, B. (1996, Nov. 4). "Oracle and Powersoft Ease Move to Web Applications." *NetworkWorld.*

Coleman, K. G., and S. Watenpool. (1992, Jan.). "Neural Networks in Knowledge Acquisition." *AI Expert.*

Conger, S., et al. (1995). "Ethics and Information Technology Use: A Factor Analysis of Attitudes Toward Computer Use." *Information Systems Journal,* Vol. 5.

Conway, D. G., and G. J. Koehler. (2000, Jan.). "Interface Agents: Caveat Mercater in Electronic Commerce." *Decision Support Systems.*

Cook, M. A. (1996). *Building Enterprise Information Architectures: Reengineering Information Systems.* Upper Saddle River, NJ: Prentice Hall.

Cougar, J. D. (1995). *Creative Problem Solving and Opportunity Finding.* Danvers, MA: boyd & fraser.

Cougar, J. D. (1996). *Creativity & Innovation in Information Systems Organizations.* Danvers, MA: boyd & fraser.

Courtney, J. F., and D. B. Paradice. (1993, June). "Studies on Managerial Problem Formulation Systems." *Decision Support Systems.* Vol. 3, No. 4.

Courtney, J. F., Jr., et al. (1987, Summer). "A Knowledge-based DSS for Managerial Problem Diagnosis." *Decision Sciences,* Vol. 18, No. 3.

Covington, M. A., D. Nute, and A. Vellino. (1997). *Prolog Programming in Depth,* 2nd ed. Upper Saddle River, NJ: Prentice Hall.

Cox, E. (1999, Sept./Oct.). "A Data Mining and Rule Discovery Approach to Business Forecasting with Adaptive, Genetically-Tuned Fuzzy System Models." *PC AI.*

Cox, E., and R. Terlaga. (1992, Fall). "A Clear Approach to Fuzzy Logic." *Chief Information Officer Journal,* Vol. 5, No. 2.

Craig, R. (1998, Dec.)."Analyzing the OLIVE branches." *Entonline.*

Cramond, B. (1995). "The Torrance Tests of Creative Thinking: From Design Through Establishment of Predictive Validity," in *Beyond Terman: Contemporary Studies of Giftedness and Talent,* R. F. Subotnik and K. D. Arnold (eds.), Norwood, NJ: Ablex Publishing Company, pp. 229–254.

Cranor, L. F. (Feb. 1999). "Internet Privacy," Special Issue. *Communications of the ACM.*

Croasdell, D., D. Paradice, and J. Courtney. (1997, Jan.). "Using Adaptive Hypermedia to Support Organizational Memory and Learning." *Proceedings of the Thirtieth Annual Hawaii International Conference on Systems Sciences HICSS-30,* Wailea, HI. Los Alamitos, CA: IEEE Computer Society Press.

Cuena, J., and M. Molina. (1996). "KSM: An Environment for Design of Structured Knowledge Models," in S. G. Tzafestas (ed.), *Knowledge-based Systems: Advanced Concepts, Techniques and Applications.* Singapore: World Scientific Publishing.

Cule, P., R. Schmidt, K. Lyytinen, and M. Keil. (2000, Spring). "Strategies for Heading Off IS Project Failure." *Information Systems Management.* Vol. 17, No. 2.

Cupit, J., and N. Shadbolt. (1996). "Knowledge Discovery in Databases: Exploiting Knowledge-Level Redescription," in N. Shadbolt, K. O'Hara, and G. Schreiber *Advances in Knowledge Acquisition.* Berlin: Springer-Verlag.

Currid, C. et al. (1994). *Computer Strategies for Reengineering Your Business.* Rocklin, CA: Prima.

Cyre, W. R. (1997). "Capture, Integration, and Analysis of Digital System Requirements with Conceptual Graphs." *IEEE Transactions on Knowledge and Data Engineering,* Vol. 9, No. 1.

Davenport, T. H. (1994, Mar./Apr.). "Saving IT's Soul: Human-centered Information Management." *Harvard Business Review.*

Davenport, T. (1998, July/Aug.). "Putting the Enterprise in the Enterprise System." *Harvard Business Review,* Vol. 76, No. 4.

Davenport, T., D. W. DeLong, and M. C. Beers. (1998, Winter). "Successful Knowledge Management Projects." *Sloan Management Review,* Vol. 39, No. 2.

Davenport, T. H., and L. Prusak. (1998). *Working Knowledge: How Organizations Manage What They Know.* Boston: Harvard Business School Press.

Davids, M. (1999, May/June). "Smiling for the Camera." *Journal of Business Strategy,* Vol. 20, No. 3.

Davis, F. D. (1989, Sept.). "Perceived Usefulness, Perceived Ease of Use, and User Acceptance of Information Systems." *MIS Quarterly.*

Davis, M. (1998, Fall). "Knowledge Management." *Information Strategy: The Executive's Journal.*

Davis, R. (1993). "Interactive Transfer of Expertise: Acquisition of New Inference Rules," in B. G. Buchanan and D. Wilkins (eds.). *Readings in Knowledge Acquisition and Learning: Automating the Construction and Improvement of Expert Systems.* San Mateo, CA: Morgan Kaufmann.

De La Maza, M., and D. Yuret. (1994, Mar.). "Dynamic Hill Climbing." *AI Expert.*

De Vreede, G. J., R. O. Briggs, R. van Duin, and B. Enserink. (2000). "Athletics in Electronic Brainstorming: Asynchronous Electronic Brainstorming in Very Large Groups." *Proceedings of the Thirty-Third Annual Hawaii International Conference on System Sciences HICSS-33.* Los Alamitos, CA: IEEE Computer Society Press.

Dearden, J. (1983, Fall). "SMR Forum: Will the Computer Change the Job of Top Management?" *Sloan Management Review.* Vol. 25, No. 1.

Deboeck, G. (1999, Jan./Feb.). "Public Domain vs. Commercial Tools for Creating Neural Self-organizing Maps." *PC AI.*

Deboeck, G., and T. Kohonen. (1997). *Visual Explorations in Finance with Self-Organizing Maps.* Berlin: Springer-Verlag.

Deck, S. (1999a, May 17). "Mining Your Business." *ComputerWorld,* Vol. 33, No. 20.

Deck, S. (1999b, May 24). "A Service to Combat Fraud." *ComputerWorld,* Vol. 33, No. 21.

Decker K., et al. (1999, Mar.). "Continuing Research in Multi-agent System." *Knowledge Engineering Review.*

DeFanti, T. A. (1997). "Deep Learning and Visualization Technologies." National Science Foundation, www.her.nsf.gov/lis/defanti.htm.

Dejoie, R. M. et al. (1995). *Ethical Issues in Information Systems,* 2nd ed. Cincinnati: boyd & fraser.

DeLeon, W. H., and E. R. McLean. (1992, Mar.). "Information System Success: The Quest for the Dependent Variable." *Information Systems Research,* Vol. 3, No. 1.

Demetriadis, S. et al. (1999, May). "Graphical Jog Through: Expert-Based Methodology for User Interface Evaluation, Applied in the Case of an Educational Simulation Interface." *Computers and Education.*

Denning, D. E. (1998). *Information Warfare and Security.* Reading, Mass: Addison Wesley.

Dennis, A., et al. (1988, Dec.). "Information Technology to Support Electronic Meetings." *MIS Quarterly.*

Dennis, A. R. (1996). "Information Exchange and Use in Group Decision Making: You Can Lead a Group to Information But You Can't Make It Think." *MIS Quarterly,* Vol. 20, No. 4.

Dennis, A. R., J. E. Aronson, W. G. Heninger, and E. D. Walker, II. (1999, Mar.). "Structuring Time and Task Decomposition in Electronic Brainstorming." *Management Information Systems Quarterly,* Vol. 23, No. 1.

Dennis, A. R., and M. J. Garfield. (1999, Nov. 12). "Breaking Structures: The Adoption and Use of GSS in Project Teams." Department of MIS Working Paper, Terry College of Business, The University of Georgia, Athens, GA.

Dennis, A. R., and T. A. Carte. (1998, June). "Using GIS for Decision Making." *Information Systems Research.*

Dennis, A. R., K. M. Hilmer, and N. J. Taylor. (1997/1998). "Information Exchange and Use in GSS and Verbal Group Decision Making: Effects of Minority Influence." *Journal of Management Information Systems,* Vol. 14, No. 3.

Dennis, A. R., S. K. Pootheri, and V. L. Natarajan. (1998, Spring). "Lessons from the Early Adopters of Web Groupware." *Journal of Management Information Systems,* Vol. 14, No. 4.

Dennis, A. R., J. S. Valacich, T. C., M. Garfield, B. Haley, and J. E. Aronson. (1997, Jun.). "The Effectiveness of Multiple Dialogues in Electronic Brainstorms." *Information Systems Research,* Vol. 8, No. 2.

Dennis, A., and B. H. Wixom. (2000). *Systems Analysis and Design: An Applied Approach.* New York: Wiley.

DePold, H. R., and F. D. Gass. (1999, Oct.). "The Application of Expert Systems and Neural Networks to Gas Turbine Prognostics and Diagnostics." *Journal of Engineering for Gas Turbines and Power,* Vol. 121, No. 4.

Deris, S., et al. (1999, Feb. 1). "Ship Maintenance Scheduling by Genetic Algorithm and Constraint-based Reasoning." *European Journal of Operational Research,* Vol. 112, No. 3.

Derra, S. (1999, Apr.). "Refocusing AI Research on Real-world Applications." *Research & Development,* Vol. 41, No. 5.

DeSanctis, G., and R. B. Gallupe. (1987). "A Foundation for the Study of Group Decision Support Systems." *Management Science,* Vol. 33, No. 5.

DeSanctis, G., and R. B. Gallupe. (1985, Winter). "Group Decision Support Systems: A New Frontier." *Data Base.*

Despres, S., and C. Rosenthal-Sabroux. (1992, Aug. 25). "Designing DSS and Expert Systems with Better End-user Involvement: A Promising Approach." *European Journal of Operational Research,* Vol. 61, Nos. 1 and 2.

Devedzic, V., J. Debenham, and D. Radovic. (1996, Oct.). "Object-oriented Modelling of Expert System Reasoning Process." *Proceedings, IEEE Conference on Systems, Man, and Cybernetics,* Beijing, China, 2716–2721.

Dhar, V., and R. Stein. (1997). *Intelligent Decision Support Methods.* Upper Saddle River, NJ: Prentice Hall.

Diamantidis, N. A., and E. A. Giakoumakis. (1999, Feb.). "An Interactive Tool for Knowledge Base Refinement." *Expert Systems.*

DiBella, A. J. (1995). "Developing Learning Organizations: A Matter of Perspective." *Academy of Management Journal.* Best Papers Proceedings 1995.

Dickson, G., and R. Powers. (1973). "MIS Project Management: Myths, Opinions, and Realities," in F. W. McFarlan, et al. (eds.), *Information Systems Administration.* New York: Holt, Rinehart & Winston.

Dienes, Z., and J. Perner. (1999, Oct.). "A Theory of Implicit and Explicit Knowledge." *Behavioral and Brain Sciences.*

Dieng, R. (1995). "Agent-based Method for Building a Cooperative Knowledge-based System." *Proceedings of the FGSC 1994 Workshop on Heterogeneous Cooperative Knowledge Bases: Lecture Notes in Computer Science.* Berlin: Springer-Verlag.

Diffie, W., and S. Landau (1998). *Privacy on the Line: The Politics of Wiretapping and Encryption.* Boston: MIT Press.

diPiazza, J. S., and F. A. Helsabeck. (1990, Fall). "Laps: Cases to Models to Complete Expert Systems." *AI Magazine.*

Dollar, G. (2000, Aug.). "Web-based Course Delivery: An Empirical Assessment of Student Learning Outcomes." *Proceedings of the Americas Conference of the Association for Information Systems,* Milwaukee, WI.

Dologite, D. G., and R. J. Mockler. (1989, Winter). "Developing Effective Knowledge-based Systems: Overcoming Organizational and Individual Behavioral Barriers." *Information Resource Management Journal.*

Donlon, J. J., and K. D. Forbus. (1999). "Using a Geographic Information System for Qualitative Spatial Reasoning about Trafficability." *Proceedings of the Qualitative Reasoning Workshop,* Loch Awe, Scotland.

Donovan, J. J., and S. E. Madnick. (1977). "Institutional and Ad Hoc DSS and Their Effective Use." *Data Base,* Vol. 8, No. 3.

Downing, C. E., and A. S. Clark. (1999, Spring). "Groupware in Practice." *Information Systems Management,* Vol. 16, No. 2.

Drake, K. C., and P. Hess. (1990, Sept./Oct.). "Abduction: A Numeric Knowledge Acquisition Approach." *PC AI.*

Dresner, H. (1993, June 3). *Multidimensionality: Ready or Not, Here It Comes,* Research Note. Boston: The Gartner Group.

Dryden, P. (1996, July 29). "Help for Harried Help Desk." *ComputerWorld,* Vol. 30, No. 31.

Dubois, D., and H. Prade. (1995, Sept.). "What Does Fuzzy Logic Bring to AI?" *ACM Computing Surveys,* Vol. 27, No. 3.

Duchessi, P., and R. H. O'Keefe. (1992, Aug. 25). "Constructing Successful and Unsuccessful Expert Systems." *European Journal of Operational Research,* Vol. 61, Nos. 1 and 2.

Duffy, D. (1998, Nov.). "Knowledge Champions." *CIO* (Enterprise-Section 2).

Duffy, D. (1999, Nov. 15). "A Capital Idea," *CIO* (Enterprise-Section 2).

Dugan, S. M. (1999, July 5). "Groupware Still Going Strong." *InfoWorld,* Vol. 21, No. 27.

Durkin, J. (1994). *Expert Systems: Design and Development.* New York: Macmillan.

Durkin, J. (1996, Apr.). "Expert Systems: A View of the Field." *IEEE Expert.*

Dutta, A. (1996, Nov.). "Integrating AI and Optimization for Decision Support." *Decision Support Systems,* Vol. 18, Nos. 3 and 4.

Dutta, S., B. Wierenga, and A. Dalebout. (1997, June). "Designing Management Support Systems Using an Integrative Perspective." *Communications of the ACM.* Vol. 40, No. 6.

Dyche, J. (1999, Feb. 1). "The Big Bang of Business Intelligence." *Telephony.*

Dyer, G. (2000, Mar.). "Knowledge Management Crosses the Chasm." *Knowledge Management.*

Dzida, W., and R. Freitag. (1998, Dec.). "Making Use of Scenarios for Validating Analysis and Design." *IEEE Transactions on Software Engineering,* Vol. 24, No. 12.

Easton, F. F., and M. Nashat. (1999, Nov.). "A Distributed Genetic Algorithm for Deterministic and Stochastic Labor Scheduling Problems." *European Journal of Operational Research,* Vol. 118, No. 3.

Edelstein, H. (1996, Jan. 8). "Mining Data Warehouses." *InformationWeek.*

Eden, C., and F. Ackermann. (1998). *Making Strategy: The Journey of Strategic Management.* Thousand Oaks, CA: Sage Publications.

Edman, A., and Hamfelt, A. (1999, Nov.) "A System Architecture for Knowledge-based Hypermedia." *International Journal of Human–Computer Studies.*

El Sawy, O. (1998). *The Business Process Reengineering Workbook.* New York: McGraw-Hill.

Eldabi, T., R. J. Paul, and S. J. Taylor. (1999, Oct.). "Computer Simulation in Healthcare Decision Making." *Computers & Industrial Engineering,* Vol. 37, Nos. 1 and 2.

Elofson, G., et al. (1997, May). "An Intelligent Agent Community Approach to Knowledge Sharing." *Decision Support Systems,* Vol. 20, No. 1.

Elofson, G. S., and B. R. Konsynski. (1990, Jan.). "Supporting Knowledge Sharing in Environment Scanning," in *Proceedings of the Twenty-third Annual Hawaii International Conference on System Sciences HICSS-23,* Wailea, HI. Los Alamitos, CA: IEEE Computer Society Press.

Englemore, R., and T. Morgan (eds.). (1989). *Blackboard Systems.* Reading, MA: Addison-Wesley.

Eom, S. B. (1996, Sept./Oct.). "A Survey of Operational Expert Systems in Business (1980–1993)." *Interfaces,* Vol. 26, No. 5.

Ericsson, K. A., and H. A. Simon. (1984). *Protocol Analysis, Verbal Reports and Data.* Cambridge, MA: MIT Press.

Eriksson, H. (1992, Sept.). "A Survey of Knowledge Acquisition Techniques and Tools and their Relationship to Software Engineering." *Journal of Systems & Software.*

Eriksson, H. (1996, June). "Expert Systems as Knowledge Servers." *IEEE Expert.*

Etzioni, O. (1996, Nov.). "The WWW: Quagmire or Gold Mine." *Communications of the ACM,* Vol. 39, No. 11.

Etzioni, O., and D. S. Weld. (1994, July). "A Softbot-based Interface to the Internet." *Communications of the ACM,* Vol. 37, No. 7.

Etzioni, O., and D. S. Weld. (1995, Aug.). "Intelligent Agents on the Internet: Fact, Fiction, and Forecast." *IEEE Expert,* Vol. 10, No. 4.

Evans, S. (1997). *The PACE System: An Expert Consulting System for Nursing.* New York: Springer-Verlag.

Eysenck, H. J. (1994). "The Measurement of Creativity," in *Dimensions of Creativity,* M. A. Boden (ed.). Cambridge, MA: MIT Press, pp. 199–242.

Fahey, L., and L. Prusak (1998, Spring). "The Eleven Deadliest Sins of Knowledge Management." *California Management Review,* Vol. 40, No. 3.

Fakas, G., and B. Karakotas. (1999). "A Workflow Management System based on Intelligent Collaborative Objects." *Information and Software Technology,* Vol. 41.

Far, B. H., and Z. Koono. (1996). "Ex-W-Pert System: A Web-based Distributed Expert System for Groupware Design." *Expert Systems with Applications,* Vol. 11, No. 4.

Far, B. H., et al. (1996, Sept.). "Merging CASE Tools with Knowledge-based Technology for Automatic Software Design." *Decision Support Systems,* Vol. 18, No. 1.

Fayyad, U., et al. (1996a). "From Knowledge Discovery in Databases." *AI Magazine,* Vol. 17, No. 3.

Fayyad, U. M., and R. Uthurusamy (eds.). (1995). *KDD-95: Proceedings of the First International Conference on Knowledge Discovery and Data Mining.* Menlo Park, CA: AAAI Press.

Fayyad, U. M., G. Piatetsky-Shapiro, P. Smyth, and R. Uthurusamy. (1996b). *Advances in Knowledge Discovery and Data Mining.* Menlo Park, CA: AAAI Press/MIT Press.

Fedorowicz, J., and A. O. Villeneuve. (1999, June). "Surveying Object Technology Usage and Benefits: A Test of Conventional Wisdom." *Information & Management,* Vol. 35, No. 6.

Feigenbaum, E., and P. McCorduck. (1983). *The Fifth Generation.* Reading, MA: Addison-Wesley.

Feldman, R., and I. Dagan (1995). "Knowledge Discovery in Textual Databases (KDT)," in U. M. Fayyad and R. Uthurusamy (eds.). (1995). *KDD-95: Proceedings of the First International Conference on Knowledge Discovery and Data Mining.* Menlo Park, CA: AAAI Press.

Fensel, D. (1996). *The Knowledge Acquisition and Representation Language KARL.* Amsterdam: Kluwer Academic.

Fensel, D., J. Angele, and R. Struder. (1998, July/Aug.). "The Knowledge Acquisition and Representation Language KARL." *IEEE Transactions on Knowledge and Data Engineering,* Vol. 10, No. 4.

Ferguson, R. W., and K. D. Forbus. (1999). "GeoRep: A Flexible Tool for Spatial Representation of Line Drawings." *Proceedings of the Qualitative Reasoning Workshop,* Loch Awe, Scotland.

Ferrar, R., and W. King. (1999, Aug.). "Rip First or Cut First? Use 'Evolution' to Choose." *Wood Technology,* Vol. 126, No. 7.

Finin, T., et al. (1997). "KQML as an Agent Communication Language," in J. Bradshaw (ed.), *Software Agents.* Menlo Park, CA: AAAI Press/MIT Press.

Fisher, B. (1999, Spring). "Mellon Creates Fraudwatch to Predict and Manage Risk Using Neural Technology." *Journal of Retail Banking Services,* Vol. 21, No. 1.

Fjermestad, J., and S. R. Hiltz. (1998, Winter). "An Assessment of Group Support Systems Experimental Research: Methodology and Results." *Journal of Management Information Systems,* Vol. 15, No. 3.

Forgionne, G. A., and R. Kohl. (1995, Nov.). "Integrated MSS Effects: An Empirical Health Care Investigation." *Information Processing and Management,* Vol. 31, No. 6.

Francis, P., and N. Capon. (1996, May). "BPR Software for Financial Services Industry." *Management Services,* Vol. 40, No. 5.

Franklin, S., and A. Graesser. (1996). "Is It an Agent, or Just a Program? A Taxonomy for Autonomous Agents." *Proceedings of the Third International Workshop on Agent Theories, Architecture and Languages.* Berlin: Springer-Verlag.

Frappaolo, C. (1998). "Defining Knowledge Management: Four Basic Functions." *ComputerWorld,* Vol. 32, No. 8.

Freeman, D. (1996, May). "How to Make Spreadsheets Error-proof." *Journal of Accountancy,* Vol. 181, No. 5.

Freiling, M. et al. (1985, Fall). "Starting a Knowledge Engineering Project: A Step by Step Approach." *AI Magazine.*

Frenzel, L. (1987). *Crash Course in Artificial Intelligence and Expert Systems.* New York: Howard W. Sams.

Fritz, M. B. W., S. Narasimhan, and H-S. Rhee. (1998, Spring). "Communication and Coordination in the Virtual Office." *Journal of Management Information Systems,* Vol. 14, No. 4.

Fritzsche, D. (1995, Nov.). "Personal Values: Potential Keys to Ethical Decision Making." *Journal of Business Ethics,* Vol. 14, No. 11.

Frolick, M. N., and N. K. Ramarapu. (1993, July). "Hypermedia: The Future of EIS." *Journal of Systems Management,* Vol. 44, No. 7.

Frolick, M. N., and B. P. Robichaux. (1995, June). "EIS Information Requirements Determination: Using a Group Support System to Enhance the Strategic Business Objectives Method." *Decision Support Systems,* Vol. 14, No. 2.

Fryer, B. (1997, Oct. 15). "Home Field Advantages." *CIO.*

Fu, L-M. (1999, Nov.). "Knowledge Discovery Based on Neural Networks." *Communications of the ACM,* Vol. 42, No. 11.

Fuerst, W., et al. (1994/1995, Winter). "Expert Systems and Multimedia: Examining the Potential for Integration." *Journal of Management Information Systems,* Vol. 11, No. 3.

Fulton, S. L., and C. O. Pepe. (1990, Jan.). "An Introduction to Model-based Reasoning." *AI Expert.*

Gaines, B. R., and M. L. G. Shaw. (1993). "Basing Knowledge Acquisition Tools in Personal Construct Psychology." *Knowledge Engineering Review,* Vol. 8, No. 1.

Gan, R., and D. Yang. (1994, Sept.). "Case-based DSS with Artificial Neural Networks." *Computers and Industrial Engineering,* Vol. 27, Nos. 1–4.

Garson, G. P. (1995). *Computer Technology and Societal Issues.* Harrisburg, PA: Idea Group.

Garvin, D. A. (1993, July/Aug.). "Building a Learning Organization." *Harvard Business Review.*

Gaskin, J. E. (1997). *Corporate Politics and the Internet: Connection Without Controversy.* Upper Saddle River, NJ: Prentice Hall.

Gaud, W. S. (1999, Nov./Dec.). "Assessing the Impact of Web Courses," *Syllabus.*

Geigle, D. S., and J. E. Aronson. (1999, Nov./Dec.). "An Artificial Neural Network Approach to the Valuation of Options and Forecasting of Volatility." *Journal of Computational Intelligence in Finance,* Vol. 7, No. 6.

Gendreau, M., G. Laporte, C. Musaraganyi, and E. D. Taillard. (1999, Oct.). "A Tabu Search Heuristic for the Heterogeneous Fleet Vehicle Routing Problem." *Computers & Operations Research,* Vol. 26, No. 12.

Genesereth, M. R. (1997). "An Agent-Based Framework for Interoperability," in J. Bradshaw (ed.), *Software Agents.* Menlo Park, CA: AAAI Press/MIT Press.

Genesereth, M. R., and R. E. Fikes. (1992, June). "Knowledge Interchange Format: Version 3.0 Reference Manual." Stanford, CA: Computer Science Department, Stanford University.

Geng, G., et al. (1999, Jan.). "Applying A1 to Railway Freight Loading." *Expert Systems with Applications.*

Gensym. (2000). "Gensym's Intelligent G2 Software Optimizes Calciner Throughput at Aughinish Alumina," Success Stories, Gensym Corporation, www.gensym.com.

George, J. F. (1991/1992). "The Conceptualizations and Development of Organizational Decision Support Systems." *Journal of MIS,* Vol. 8, No. 3.

Ghafoor, A. (1995). "Multimedia Database Management Decision Systems." *ACM Computing Surveys,* Vol. 27, No. 4.

Giarratano, J., and G. Riley. (1998). *Expert Systems: Principles and Programming,* 3rd ed. Pacific Grove, CA: PWS Publishing Co.

Gilbert, D., and P. Janca. (1997, Feb.). *IBM Intelligent Agents.* IBM White Paper. Raleigh, NC: IBM Corporation, www.networking.ibm.com/iag/iagwp1.html.

Gill, K. S. (ed.). (1996). *Information Society.* London: Springer Publishing.

Gill, T. G. (1995, Mar.). "Early Expert Systems: Where Are They Now?" *MIS Quarterly,* Vol. 19, No. 1.

Gill, P. J. (1996a, June 3). "Retooling for the Web." *InformationWeek,* 1A–8A.

Gill, T. G. (1996b, Sept.). "Expert Systems Usage: Task Change and Intrinsic Motivation." MIS Quarterly, Vol. 20, No. 3.

Ginzberg, M. J. (1981). "Key Recurrent Issues in the MIS Implementation Process." *MIS Quarterly,* Vol. 5, No. 2.

Glover, F., and M. Laguna. (1997). *Tabu Search.* Norwell, MA: Kluwer.

Goettl, B. (ed.). (1998 Aug.). *Proceedings of Intelligent Tutoring Systems Fourth International Conference,* San Antonio, TX.

Goldberg, D. E. (1989). *Genetic Algorithms in Search Optimization and Machine Learning.* Reading, MA: Addison-Wesley.

Goldberg, D. E. (1994, Mar.). "Genetic and Evolutionary Algorithms Come of Age." *Communications of the ACM,* Vol. 37, No. 3.

Goldbogen, G., and G. A. Howe. (1993). "Integrating Artificial Intelligence into Existing Software Applications," in M. Grabowksi and W. A. Wallace (eds.), *Advances in Expert Systems for Management.* Greenwich, CT: JAI Press.

Golding, A. R., and P. S. Rosenbloom. (1996, Nov.). "Improving Accuracy by Combining Rule-based and Case-based Reasoning." *Artificial Intelligence,* Vol. 87.

Goldman, J., R. Nagel, and K. Preiss. (1994). *Agile Competitors and Virtual Organizations: Strategies for Enriching the Customer.* New York: Van Nostrand Reinhold.

Golub, A. L. (1997). *Decision Analysis: An Integrated Approach.* New York: Wiley.

Goodhue, D. L. (1998, Winter). "Development and Measurement Validity of a Task-Technology Fit Instrument for User Evaluations of Information Systems." *Decision Sciences,* Vol. 29, No. 1.

Goodman, P. S., and E. D. Darr. (1998). "Computer-aided Systems and Communities: Mechanisms for Organizational Learning in Distributed Environments." *MIS Quarterly,* Vol. 22, No. 4.

Goralski, W. M., et. al. (1997). *VRML: Exploring Virtual World on the Internet,* Upper Saddle River, NJ: Prentice Hall.

Gorry, G. A., and M. S. Scott Morton. (1971). "A Framework for Management Information Systems." *Sloan Management Review,* Vol. 13, No. 1.

Gorry, G. A., and M. S. Scott Morton. (1989, Spring). "A Framework for Management Information Systems-Revisited." *Sloan Management Review.*

Gottinger, H. W., and H. P. Weimann. (1995, Sept.). "Intelligent Inference Systems Based on Influence Diagrams." *Decision Support Systems,* Vol. 15, No. 1.

Goul, M., B. Shane, and F. Tong. (1984, May). "Designing the Expert Component of a Decision Support System." ORSA/TIMS Joint National Meeting, San Francisco.

Goul, M., et al. (1992, Nov./Dec.). "The Emergence of AI as a Reference Discipline for Decision Support Systems Research." *Decision Sciences.*

Grabowski, M. and W. W. Wallace. (1993). *Advances in Expert Systems for Management.* Vol. 1. Greenwich, CT: JAI Press.

Grady, S. M. (1998). *Virtual Reality.* New York: Facts on File.

Gray, P. (1999). "Tutorial on Knowledge Management." *Proceedings of the Americas Conference of the Association for Information Systems,* Milwaukee, WI.

Gray, P., and H. J. Watson, (1998). *Decision Support in the Data Warehouse.* Upper Saddle River, NJ: Prentice Hall.

Green, J. (1999, Mar.). "Deluxe Beefs Up Its Debit Bureau." *Credit Card Management,* Vol. 11, No. 12.

Greenhalgh, C. (1999). *Large Scale Collaborative Virtual Environments.* Berlin: Springer Verlag.

Gregg, D. G., and Goul, M. (1999, Nov.). "A Proposal for an Open DSS Protocol." *Communications of the ACM,* Vol. 42, No. 11.

Griffith, T. L., M. A. Fuller, and G. B. Northcraft. (1998, Mar.). "Facilitator Influence in Group Support Systems: Intended and Unintended Effects." *Information Systems Research,* Vol. 9, No. 1.

Grimshaw, D. J. (1999). *Bringing Geographical Information Systems into Business.* New York: Wiley.

Grogono, P., et al. (1991, Nov.). "Expert System Evaluation Techniques: A Selected Bibliography." *Expert Systems,* Vol. 8, No. 4.

Groth, R. (1998). *Data Mining.* Upper Saddle River, NJ: Prentice Hall PTR.

Gruber, T. R., and P. R. Cohen. (1987). "Design for Acquisition Principles of Knowledge System Design to Facilitate Knowledge Acquisitions." *International Journal of Man-Machine Studies,* No. 2.

Grudin J., and B. Wellman. (1999, Feb.). "The Changing Relationship Between Information Technology and Society." *IEEM Intelligent Systems.*

Grunther, H. O. (1996). *Evolutionary Search and the Job Shop: Investigations on Genetic Algorithms for Production Scheduling.* New York: Springer-Verlag.

Grupe, F. H., R. Urwiler, and N. K. Ramarapu. (1998). "The Application of Case-based Reasoning to the Software Development Process." *Information and Software Technology,* Vol. 40, No. 9.

Guha, R. V., and D. B. Lenat. (1994, July). "Enabling Agents to Work Together." *Communications of the ACM,* Vol. 37, No. 7.

Guimaraes, T., et al. (1992, Mar./Apr.). "The Determinants of DSS Success: An Integrated Model." *Decision Sciences,* Vol. 23, No. 2.

Guimaraes, T., Y. Yoon, and A. Clevenson. (1996, June). "Factors Important to Expert Systems Success: A Field Test." *Information & Management,* Vol. 30, No. 3.

Gungor, Z., and F. Arikan. (2000, Jan. 15). "Application of Fuzzy Decision Making in Part-machine Grouping." *International Journal of Production Economics,* Vol. 63, No. 2.

Gupta, A., and R. Jain. (1997, May). "Visual Information Retrieval," *Communications of the ACM.*

Gupta, B., L. Iyer, and J. E. Aronson. (1999, Aug.). "An Exploration of Knowledge Management Techniques." *Proceedings of the Americas Conference of the Association for Information Systems,* Milwaukee, WI.

Gupta, B., L. Iyer, and J. E. Aronson. (2000). "Knowledge Management: A Taxonomy, Practices and Challenges." *Industrial Management and Data Systems,* Vol. 100, Nos. 1 and 2.

Gupta, M. (1995). *Fuzzy Logic and Intelligent Systems.* Norwell, MA: Kluwer.

Guth, M. (1999). "An Expert System for Curtailing Electric Power," www.wvjolt.wvu.edu.

Hackathorn, R. D., and P. G. W. Keen. (1981, Sept.). "Organizational Strategies for Personal Computing in Decision Support Systems." *MIS Quarterly,* Vol. 5, No. 3.

Hackbarth, G., and V. Grover. (1999, Summer). "The Knowledge Repository: Organizational Memory Information Systems." *Information Systems Management.*

Hagel, J. III, and A. G. Armstrong. (1997). *Net Gain: Expanding Markets through Virtual Communities.* Boston: Harvard Business School Press.

Hahn, U., M. Klenner, and K. Schnattinger. (1996). "A Quality-based Terminological Reasoning Model for Text Knowledge Acquisition," in N. Shadbolt, K. O'Hara, and G. Schreiber (eds.). *Advances in Knowledge Acquisition.* Berlin: Springer-Verlag.

Haley, B. J., and H. J. Watson. (1996, Winter). "Using Lotus Notes in EISs." *Information Systems Management.*

Hall, J., G. Mani, and D. Barr. (1996). "Applying Computational Intelligence to the Investment Process." *Proceedings of CIFER-96: Computational Intelligence in Financial Engineering.* Washington, DC: IEEE Computer Society.

Hall, N. (1987). "A Fuzzy Decision Support System for Strategic Planning," in E. Sanchez and L. Zadeh (eds.). *Approximate Reasoning in Intelligent Systems, Decision and Control.* Oxford: Pergamon Press.

Hall, R. H., et. al. (1999, Winter). "The Effects of Graphical Post-organization Strategies on Learning from Knowledge Maps." *The Journal of Experimental Education.*

Halpern, J. J., and R. N. Stern. (1998). *Debating Rationality: Nonrational Aspects of Organizational Decision Making.* Ithaca, NY: Cornell University Press.

Hamilton, D. M. (1996a). "Knowledge Acquisition for Multiple Site, Related Domain Expert Systems: Delphi Process and Applications." *Expert Systems with Applications,* Vol. 11, No. 3.

Hamilton, J. M. (1996b, Mar. 15). "A Mapping Feast." *CIO.*

Hammer, M., and J. Champy. (1993). *Reengineering the Corporation.* New York: Harper Business.

Hammer, M., and S. Stanton. (1995). *The Reengineering Revolution: A Handbook.* New York: HarperCollins.

Hammond, J. S., R. L. Kenney, and H. Raiffa. (1998). *Smart Choices: A Practical Guide to Making Better Decisions.* Boston: Harvard Business School Press.

Hamscher, W., M. Y. Kiang, and R. Lang. (1995). "Qualitative Reasoning in Business, Finance, and Economics: Introduction." *Decision Support Systems,* Vol. 15, No. 2.

Hand, D. J. (1984, Oct.). "Statistical Expert Systems Design." *Statistician,* Vol. 33, No. 4.

Handfield, R. B., and E. L. Nichols, Jr. (1999). *Introduction to Supply Chain Management.* Upper Saddle River, NJ: Prentice Hall.

Hanson, M. A., and R. L. Brekke. (1988). "Workload Management Expert System Combining Neural Networks and Rule-based Programming in an Operational Application," Special Report. Triangle Park, NC: Instrument Society of America.

Hanson R. D., and D. G. Stork. (1999, May/June). "Building Intelligent Systems: One E-Citizen at a Time." *IEEM Intelligent Systems.*

Harel, D., and M. Politi. (1998). *Modeling Reactive Systems with Statecharts: The STATEMATE Approach.* New York: McGraw-Hill.

Harmon, P. (ed.). (1993, Mar.) "Precisely Fuzzy Part I." *Intelligent Software Strategies,* Vol. 9, No. 4.

Harmon, P., et al. (1988). *Expert Systems Tools and Applications.* New York: Wiley.

Harris, L. E. (1998). *Digital Property.* New York: McGraw-Hall.

Harrison, E. F. (1999). *The Managerial Decision-Making Process.* 5th ed., Boston: Houghton Mifflin.

Hart, A. (1992). *Knowledge Acquisition for Expert Systems.* New York: McGraw-Hill.

Hartman, P. J. (1993, Mar.). "Finding Cost-effective Applications for Expert Systems." *Transactions of the ASME,* Vol. 115.

Hashemi, R. R., L. A. Le Blanc, C. T. Rucks, and A. Rajaratnam. (1998, Sept. 1). "A Hybrid Intelligent System for Predicting Bank Holding Structures." *European Journal of Operational Research,* Vol. 109, No. 2.

Haskin D. (1998, Feb). "Leveraging Your Knowledge Base" (Web-based document management systems), *Internet World.*

Hauser, R. D., Jr., and F. J. Hebert. (1992, Winter). "Managerial Issues in Expert System Implementation." *SAM Advanced Management Journal,* Vol. 57, No. 1.

Hayes-Roth, B., et al. (1998, Mar.). "Staffing the Web with Interactive Characters." *Communications of the ACM.*

Hayes-Roth, B., et al. (1999, Mar./Apr.). "Web Guides" *IEEE Intelligent Systems.* (Animated agents).

Haykin, S. S. (1999). *Neural Networks: A Comprehensive Foundation,* 2nd ed. Upper Saddle River, NJ: Prentice Hall.

Hellriegel, D., and J. W. Slocum, Jr. (1992). *Management,* 6th ed. Reading, MA: Addison-Wesley.

Hendler, J., and K. Stoffel. (1999, May/June). "Back-end Technology for High-Performance Knowledge Representation Systems." *IEEE Intelligent Systems and Their Applications,* Vol. 14, No. 3.

Hengl, T. (1995). *AI on the Internet.* Phoenix, AZ: Knowledge Technology.

Herschel R. T., and H. R. Nemati. (1999). "Knowledge Management: The Role of the CKO." *Proceedings of the Americas Conference of the Association for Information Systems,* Milwaukee, WI.

Hess T. J., et al. (2000, July). "Using Autonomous Software Agents to Create the Next Generation DSS." *Decision Sciences.*

Hibbard, J. (1998, Sept. 21). "Cultural Breakthrough." *InformationWeek.*

Hill, T. R., and W. E. Remus, (1994, June). "Neural Network Models for Intelligent Support of Managerial Decision Making." *Decision Support Systems,* Vol. 11, No. 5.

Hill, R. B., D. C. Wolfram, and D. E. Broadbent. (1986, Oct.). "Expert Systems and the Man–Machine Interface." *Expert Systems.*

Hillman, D. V. (1990, June). "Integrating Neural Networks and Expert Systems." *AI Expert.*

Hilmer, K. M., and A. R. Dennis. (2000). "Stimulating Thinking in Group Decision Making," *Proceedings of the Thirty-Third Annual Hawaii International Conference on System Sciences HICSS-33.* Los Alamitos, CA: IEEE Computer Society Press.

Holloway, P. (2000, Jan.). "Sharing Knowledge and Other Unnatural Acts." *Knowledge Management* (white paper).

Holsapple, C. W., and K. D. Joshi (1999). "Description and Analysis of Existing Knowledge Management Frameworks." *Proceedings of the Thirty-Second Annual Hawaii International Conference on System Sciences HICSS-32,* Los Alamitos, CA: IEEE Computer Society.

Holsapple, C. W., and A. B. Whinston. (1996). *Decision Support Systems: A Knowledge-Based Approach.* St. Paul, MN: West Publishing.

Hopper, E., and B. Turton, B. (1999, Oct.). "A Genetic Algorithm for a 2D Industrial Packing Problem." *Computers & Industrial Engineering,* Vol. 37, Nos. 1 and 2.

Huang, H. J. (1999, Fall). "Intelligent Diagnose Learning Agents for Intelligent Tutoring Systems." *Journal of Computer Information System.*

Huang, K. T. (1998a). "Knowledge is Power: So Use It or Lose It," (www.ibm.com/services/articles/), IBM Corporation.

Huang, K. T. (1998b). "Capitalizing on Intellectual Assets, Not Infrastructure." *IBM Systems Journal,* Vol. 37, No. 4.

Huang, K. T., Y. W. Lee, and R. Y. Wang, (1999). *Quality Information and Knowledge.* Upper Saddle River, NJ: Prentice Hall.

Huang, S. H., and H. C. Zhang. (1995, May). "Neural–Expert Hybrid Approaches for Intelligent Manufacturing: A Survey." *Computers in Industry,* Vol. 26, No. 2.

Huber, G. P. (1990). "A Theory of the Effects of Advanced Information Technologies on Organizational Design, Intelligence, and Decision Making." *Academy of Management Review,* Vol. 15, No. 1.

Humphrey, M. C. (1999, Feb.). "A Graphical Notation for the Design of Information Visualisations." *International Journal of Human–Computer Studies.*

Hung, Y-F., C-C. Shih, and C-P. Chen. (1999, Aug.). "Evolutionary Algorithms for Production Planning Problems with Setup Decisions." *The Journal of the Operational Research Society,* Vol. 50, No. 8.

Hunt, J. (1997, Feb.). "Case-based Diagnosis and Repair of Software Faults." *Expert Systems,* Vol. 14, No. 1.

Hunter, G., and J. E. Beck. (2000, Mar.). "Using Repertory Grids to Conduct Across Cultural Information Systems Research." *Information Systems Research.*

Huntington, D. (1997, Mar./Apr.). "Web-based AI: Expert Systems on the WWW." *PC AI.*

Hutchinson, M. O. (1998, Summer). "The Use of Fuzzy Logic in Business Decision-making." *Derivatives Quarterly,* Vol. 4, No. 4.

Hwang, C-P., B. Alidaee, and J. D. Johnson. (1999, Aug.). "A Tour Construction Heuristic for the Travelling Salesman Problem." *The Journal of the Operational Research Society,* Vol. 50, No. 8.

IBM Corporation. (1995). *Intelligent Agent Strategy.* IBM Corporation White Paper.

Information Advantage. (1997). "Putting the Data Warehouse on the Internet," white paper, www.inforadvan.com/1f.4_int.html.

Inmon, W. H. (1996). *Building the Data Warehouse,* 2nd ed. New York: Wiley.

Inmon, W. H. (1998, May). "Data Mart Does Not Equal Data Warehouse." *DM Review.*

Ishman, M. D. (1996, Fall). "Measuring Information Success at the Individual Level in Cross-cultural Environments." *Information Resources Management Journal,* Vol. 9, No. 4.

Ives, B., and M. H. Olson. (1984, May). "User Involvement in Information System Development: A Review of Research." *Management Science,* Vol. 30, No. 5.

Iwasaki, Y. (1997, May/June). "Real-World Applications of Qualitative Reasoning." *IEEE Expert,* Vol. 12, No. 3.

Jackson, P. (1998). *Introduction to Expert Systems,* 3rd ed. Reading, MA: Addison Wesley.

Jacobs, A. (1996, Aug. 5). "Mapping Software Finds the Net." *Computerworld,* Vol. 20, No. 32, p. 44.

Jacobs, F. R., and D. C. Whybark. (2000). *Why ERP?* Boston: McGraw-Hill.

Jacso, P. (1999, Dec.). "New Web Technology: Shopping Agents." *Information Today.* Vol. 16, No. 11.

Jamali, N., et al. (1999, Mar./Apr.). "An Actor-Based Architecture for Customizing and Controlling Agent Ensembles." *IEEE Intelligent Systems.*

James, R. (2000, Mar.). "Open Wide for the Latest Automation Advances." *PPI,* Vol. 42, No. 3.

Jamshidi, M., A. Titli, L. Zadeh, and S. Boverie (eds.). (1997). *Applications of Fuzzy Logic: Towards High Machine Intelligent Quotient Systems.* Upper Saddle River, NJ: Prentice Hall.

Jana, R. (1999, Sept. 13). "Getting the Most Out of Online Learning." *InfoWorld,* Vol. 21, No. 37.

Janvrin, D., and J. Morrison. (2000, Jan.). "Using a Structured Design Approach to Reduce Risks in End User Spreadsheet Development." *Information & Management,* Vol. 37, No. 1.

Jeng, B., et al. (1996). "Interactive Induction of Expert Knowledge." *Expert Systems with Applications.* Vol. 10, No. 3 and 4.

Jennings N. R. et al. (eds.). (1998). *Agent Technology: Foundation, Applications, and Markets.* New York: Springer-Verlag.

Jessup, L. M., and D. van Over. (1996, July/Aug.). "When a System Must Be All Things to All People: The Functions, Components and Costs of a Multi-purpose Group Support System Facility." *Journal of Systems Management,* Vol. 47, No. 4.

Jiang, J. J., G. Klein, and J. L. Balloun. (1998, Fall). "Systems Analysts' Attitudes Toward Information Systems Development." *Information Resources Management Journal,* Vol. 11, No. 4.

Jiang, J. J., G. Klein, J. L. Balloun, and S. M. Crampton. (1999, Jan. 25). "System Analysts' Orientations and Perceptions of System Failure." *Information and Software Technology,* Vol. 41, No. 2.

Jiang, J. J., W. A. Muhanna, and G. Klein. (2000, Jan.). "User Resistance and Strategies for Promoting Acceptance Across System Types." *Information & Management,* Vol. 37.

Johnson, D. G., and J. M. Mulvey. (1995, Dec.). "Accountability and Computer Decision Making." *Communications of the ACM,* Vol. 38, No. 12.

Johnson, J. (1999, Dec.). "Turning Chaos into Success." *Software Magazine.*

Johnson, R. C. (1999, Aug. 16). "Genetic Algorithms Adapt Fast ICs to Fab Variations." *Electronic Engineering Times,* No. 1074.

Jones, M., et al. (1995). "An Agent-based Approach to Spacecraft Mission Operations," in N. J. I. Mars (ed.), *Towards Very Large Databases.* Amsterdam: IOS Press.

Juan, P., Morant, J., and Gonzalez, L. (1999, Oct.). "Knowledge-based Systems' Validation: When to Stop Running Test Cases." *International Journal of Human–Computer Studies.*

Jung, C. (1923). *Psychological Types.* New York: Harcourt Brace.

Kalifa R., and R. Davidson. (2000, Mar.) "Exploring the Telecommuting Paradox." *Communications of the ACM.* Vol. 43, No. 3.

Kallman, E. A., and J. P. Grillo. (1996). *Ethical Decision Making and Information Technology,* 2nd ed. New York: McGraw-Hill.

Kandel, H. (1996). *Fuzzy Expert Systems Tools.* New York: Wiley.

Kaneshige, T. (2000, Feb. 1). "The Importance of Being Outrageous." *CIO.*

Kaplan, D., et al. (1998, Feb.). "Assessing Data Quality in Accounting Information Systems." *Communications of the ACM.*

Kaplan, R. S., and D. P. Norton. (1992, Jan./Feb.). "The Balanced Scorecard—Measures That Drive Performance." *Harvard Business Review.*

Kappelman, L. A., and E. R. McLean. (1991). "The Respective Roles of User Participation and User Involvement in Information System Implementation Success." *Proceedings of the Twelfth International Conference on Information Systems,* New York.

Kappelman, L. A., and E. R. McLean. (1994). "User Engagement in the Development, Implementation, and Use of Information Technologies." *Proceedings of the Twenty-seventh Annual Hawaii International Conference on System Sciences HICSS-27,* Wailea, HI, Los Alamitos, CA: IEEE Computer Society Press.

Karaboga, D., and D. T. Pham. (1999). *Intelligent Optimization Techniques: Genetic Algorithms, Tabu Search, Simulated Annealing and Neural Networks.* Heidelberg, Germany: Springer-Verlag.

Karat, C. M. (1998, Dec.). "Guaranteeing Rights for the User." *Communications of the ACM.* Vol. 41, No. 12.

Karimi, J., and P. L. Briggs. (1996, Sept.). "Software Maintenance Support for Knowledge-based Systems." *Journal of Systems and Software,* Vol. 34, No. 3.

Karimi, J., and M. K. Zand. (1998). "Asset-based System and Software Development—A Frame-based Approach." *Information and Software Technology,* Vol. 40, No. 2.

Kaski, S., J. Kargas, and T. Kohonen. (1997). "Bibliography of Self-Organizing Map (SOM) Papers," www.icsi.berkeley.edu.

Kaula, R. (1994). "Integrating DSS in Organizations: A Three-level Framework." *Industrial Management and Data Systems,* Vol. 94, No. 4.

Kearney, M. (1990, July). "Making Knowledge Engineering Productive." *AI Expert.*

Keen, P. G. W. (1980, Fall). "Adaptive Design for Decision Support Systems." *Data Base,* Vol. 12, Nos. 1 and 2.

Keen, P. G. W., and M. S. Scott Morton. (1978). *Decision Support Systems: An Organizational Perspective.* Reading, MA: Addison-Wesley.

Keirsey, D., and M. Bates. (1984). *Please Understand Me: Character & Temperament Types.* Del Mar, CA: Prometheus Nemesis.

Kelly, A. L. (1999, July 1). "Working Smart: United Airlines' Passenger Demand Forecasting System," *CIO.*

Kepner, C., and B. Tregoe. (1965). *The Rational Manager.* New York: McGraw-Hill.

Keyes, J. (1989, Nov.). "Why Expert Systems Fail." *AI Expert,* Vol. 4, No. 11.

Khoshafian, S., et al. (1998). *The Jasmine Object Database: Multimedia Applications on the Web.* San Francisco: Morgan Kaufmann.

Kidd, A. L., and M. B. Cooper. (1985). "Man–Machine Interface Issues in the Construction and Use of an Expert System." *International Journal of Man–Machine Studies,* Vol. 22.

Kilov, H., and L. Cuthbert. (1995). "Model for Document Management." *Computer Communications,* Vol. 18, No. 6.

Kim, S. K., and J. I. Park. (1996). "A Structured Equation Modeling Approach to Generate Explanation for Induced Rules." *Expert Systems with Applications,* Vol. 10, Nos. 3 and 4.

Kim, Y. J., Y. K. Kim, and Y. Cho. (1998, Feb.). "A Heuristic-based Genetic Algorithm for Workload Smoothing in Assembly Lines." *Computers & Operations Research,* Vol. 25, No. 2.

Kimball, R., and K. Strehlo. (1994, June 1). "Why Decision Support Fails and How to Fix It." *Datamation,* Vol. 40, No. 11.

King, D. (1990). "Intelligent Decision Support: Strategies for Integrating Decision Support, Database Management and Expert System Technologies." *Expert Systems with Applications,* Vol. 1, No. 1.

King, D. (1996). "Intelligent Support Systems," in R. H. Sprague and H. J. Watson, *Decision Support for Management.* Upper Saddle River, NJ: Prentice Hall.

King, D., and K. Jones. (1995, Jan.). "Competitive Intelligence, Software Robots and the Internet: The NewsAlert Prototype." *Proceedings of the Twenty-eighth Hawaii International Conference on Systems Sciences HICSS-28,* Wailea, HI. Los Alamitos, CA: IEEE Computer Society Press.

King, J. (1993). "Editorial Notes." *Information Systems Research,* Vol. 4, No. 4.

King, J. A. (1995, Feb.). "Intelligent Agents: Bringing Good Things to Life." *AI Expert,* Vol. 10, No. 2.

King, J. L., and S. L. Star. (1990). "Conceptual Foundations for the Development of Organizational Support Systems." *Proceedings of the Twenty-third Annual Hawaii International Conference on System Sciences HICSS-23.* Los Alamitos, CA: IEEE Computer Society Press.

Kiser, K. (1999, Nov.). "10 Things We Know So Far about Online Training." *Training,* Vol. 36, No. 11.

Kitamura, Y., et al. (1996). "A Method of Qualitative Reasoning for Model-based Problem Solving and Its Application to a Nuclear Plant." *Expert Systems with Applications,* Vol. 10, Nos. 3 and 4.

Kivijarvi, H. (1997). "A Substance-theory-oriented Approach to the Implementation of Organizational DSS." *Decision Support Systems.* Vol. 20, No. 3.

Klahr, P. (1997, Jan./Feb.). "Getting Down to Cases." *PC AI.*

Klahr, P., and E. Byrnes (eds.). (1993). *Innovative Applications of Artificial Intelligence 5.* Cambridge, MA: AAAI Press/MIT Press.

Klein, G., and J. J. Jiang. (1999, Oct. 15). "User Perception of Expert System Advice." *The Journal of Systems and Software,* Vol. 48, No. 2.

Klein, M. R., and L. B. Methlie. *Knowledge-based DSS with Applications in Business,* 2nd ed. Chichester, UK: Wiley.

Klir, G. J., and B. Yuan. (1995). *Fuzzy Sets and Fuzzy Logic: Theory and Applications.* Upper Saddle River, NJ: Prentice Hall.

Klusch, K. (1999). *Intelligent Information Agents— Agent-Based Information Discovery and Management on the Internet.* New York: Springer Computer Science.

Knapp, E. M. (1998, Jul./Sept.). "Knowledge Management." *Business and Economic Review,* Vol. 44, No. 4.

Koch, C., et al. (1999, Dec. 22). "The ABCs of ERP." *CIO,* www.cio.com.

Kogan, J. M. (1986). "Information for Motivation: A Key to Executive Information Systems That Translate Strategy into Results for Management," in Fedorowicz, J. (1986, April), *DSS-86 Transactions,* Washington, DC: The Institute of Management Sciences.

Kohonen, T. (1990). "The Self-Organizing Map." *Proceedings of the IEEE,* Vol. 78.

Kohonen, T. (1997). *Self-Organizing Map,* 2nd ed., Berlin: Springer-Verlag.

Kolonder, J. (1993). *Case-based Reasoning.* Mountain View, CA: Morgan Kaufmann.

Konsynski, B. R., and E. A. Stohr. (1992). "Decision Processes: An Organizational View." Chap. 2 in Stohr, E. A., and B. R. Konsynski, eds. (1992). *Information Systems and Decision Processes* Los Alamitos, CA: IEEE Computer Society Press.

Kopcso, D., et al. (1988, Summer). "A Comparison of the Manipulation of Certainty Factors by Individuals and Expert Systems Shells." *Journal of Management Information Systems,* Vol. 5, No. 1.

Kosko B. (2000). *The Fuzzy Future: From Society and Science to Heaven in a Chip.* New York: Harmony Books.

Koutsoukis, N. S., G. Mitra, and C. Lucas. (1999, July). "Adapting On-line Analytical Processing for Decision Modeling: The Interaction of Information and Decision Technologies." *Decision Support Systems,* Vol. 26, No. 1.

Koza, J. (1992). *Genetic Programming.* Cambridge, MA: MIT Press.

Kraff, A., et al. (2000, Jan.). "Agent-driven Online Business in Virtual Communities." *Proceedings of the Thirty-third Hawaii International Conference on Systems Sciences HICSS-33,* Hawaii, Los Alamitos, CA: IEEE Computer Society Press.

Kreie, J., and T. P. Cronan. (1998, Sept.). "How Men and Women View Ethics." *Communications of the ACM.* Vol. 41, No. 9.

Kroening, M. (1999, Mar./Apr.). "Weather on the Web." *PC AI.*

Krovvidy, S. (1999, July/Aug.). "Successful Knowledge Management Systems: An Expert Systems Approach." *PC AI.*

Krutchteen, P. (1998). *The Rational Unified Process: An Introduction.* Reading, MA: Addison-Wesley.

Kuechler, W. L., N. Lim, and V. K. Vaishnavi. (1995). "A Smart Object Approach to Hybrid Knowledge Representation and Reasoning Strategies." *Proceedings of the Twenty-eighth Annual Hawaii International Conference on System Sciences HICSS-28,* Hawaii, Los Alamitos, CA: IEEE Computer Society Press.

Kuhn, D., and A. Zohar (1995). *Strategies of Knowledge Acquisition.* Chicago: University of Chicago Press.

Kuipers, B. (1994). *Qualitative Reasoning and Simulation with Incomplete Knowledge.* Cambridge, MA: MIT Press.

Kuipers, B. J., and J. M. Crawford. (1994). *Short Algernon Reference Manual (Version 1.3.0).* Austin, TX: University of Texas at Austin.

Kulik, P. (1992, Nov./Dec.). "Automating the Helpdesk." *PC AI.*

Kumar, A., and Y. P. Gupta. (1995, Jan.). "Genetic Algorithms." *Computers & Operations Research.*

Kunnathur, A. S., M. U. Ahmed, and R. J. S. Charles. (1996, Jan.). "Expert Systems Adoption: An Analytical Study of Managerial Issues and Concerns." *Information & Management,* Vol. 30, No. 1.

Kuo, R. J., S. C. Chi, and S. S. Kao. (1999, Oct.). "A Decision Support System for Locating Convenience Store Through Fuzzy AHP." *Computers & Industrial Engineering,* Vol. 37, Nos. 1 and 2.

Kusiak, A. (ed.). (1988). *Artificial Intelligence, Implication for CIM, IFS.* New York: Springer-Verlag.

Kvassov V. (2000, Jan.). "Strategic Decisions and Intelligent Tools." *Proceedings of the Thirty-third Hawaii International Conference on Systems Sciences HICSS-33,* Hawaii, Los Alamitos, CA: IEEE Computer Society Press.

Lach, J. (1999, July). "Fraud Detectives." *American Demographics,* Vol. 21, No. 7.

Lais, S. (1999, Dec. 13). "CA Advances Neural Network System." *Computerworld,* Vol. 33, No. 50.

Lam, S. S. Y., K. L. Petri, and A. E. Smith. (2000, Jan.). "Prediction and Optimization of a Ceramic Casting Process Using a Hierarchical Hybrid System of Neural Networks and Fuzzy Logic." *IIE Transactions,* Vol. 32, No. 1.

Lane, P., and M. Lubatkin. (1998, May). "Relative Absorptive Capacity and Interorganizational Learning." *Strategic Management Journal,* Vol. 19, No. 5.

Lane, P. G., D. E. Doughlas, and T. P. Cronan. (1999, Fall). "LAN Configuration Decisions: An Expert Simulation (ESS) Approach." *Journal of Computer Information Systems.*

Lang, K. R., J. C. Moore, and A. B. Whinston. (1995). "Computational Systems for Qualitative Economics." *Computational Economics,* Vol. 8.

Larsen, N. C. (1999, Dec.). "Distance Learning: Linking the Globe through Education." *World Trade,* Vol. 12, No. 12.

Larson, J. A. (1995). *Database Directions: From Relational to Distributed, Multimedia and Object-oriented Systems.* Upper Saddle River, NJ: Prentice Hall.

Larson, M. (1999, Nov.). "New Software Tools Speed Analysis: Trade Your DOE Shotgun for a Rifle." *Quality,* Vol. 38, No. 12.

Lavington, S., N. Dewhurst, and E. Wilkins. (1999, June). "Interfacing Knowledge Discovery Algorithms to Large Database Management Systems." *Information and Software Technology.*

Lawton, G. (1999). "Chatterbots: the Web Gets Help from AI." *Computer,* Vol. 32, No. 7.

Lazzaro, J. J. (1993, July). "Computers for the Disabled." *Byte.*

Le Roux, B. (1996, Sept.). "Knowledge Acquisition as a Constructive Process: A Methodological Issue." *Decision Support Systems,* Vol. 18, No. 1.

Leake, D. B. (ed). (1996). *Case-based Reasoning: Experiences, Lessons and Future Directions.* Menlo Park, CA: AAAI Press/MIT Press.

Lechner, U., et. al. (1998). "Structuring and Systemising Knowledge on the Internet—Realising the Encyclopedia Concept as a Knowledge Medium." Institute for Media and Communications Management, University of St. Gallen, www.netacademy.org.

Ledlow, G. R., D. M. Bradshaw, and M. J. Perry. (1999, Mar./Apr.). "Animated Simulation: A Valuable Decision Support Tool for Practice Improvement." *Journal of Healthcare Management,* Vol. 44, No. 2.

Lee H., et al. (1999, Apr./June). "A View-based Hypermedia Design Methodology." *Journal of Database Management.*

Lee, H-Y., H-L. Ong, and L-H. Quek. (1995). "Exploiting Visualization in Knowledge Discovery," in V. M. Fayyad and R. Uthurusamy (eds.). *Proceedings of the First International Conferences on Knowledge Discovery and Data Mining (KDD-95).* Menlo Park, CA: AAAI Press.

Lee, J. W., et al. (1997, Jan.). "Intelligent Agents for Matching Information Providers and Consumers on the Web." *Proceedings of the Thirtieth Hawaii International Conference on Systems Sciences HICSS-30,* Hawaii, Los Alamitos, CA: IEEE Computer Society Press.

Lee, L. K., and H. G. Lee. (1987, June). "Integration of Strategic Planning and Short-term Planning: An Intelligent DSS Approach by the Post Model Analysis Approach." Vol. 3, No. 2. *Decision Support Systems.*

Leidner D., et al. (1999, Summer). "Mexican and Swedish Managers' Perceptions of the Impact of EIS on Organizational Intelligence, Decision Making and Structure." *Decision Sciences.* Vol. 30. No. 3.

Lemmon, H., and N. Chuk. (1995, May 15–18). "Cotton ++: A Cotton Crop Model and Expert System to Support On-Farm Decisions." *Proceedings of PACES.* Huangshan, China.

Lenat, D. B. (1982). "The Ubiquity of Discovery." *Artificial Intelligence,* Vol. 19, No. 2.

Lenat, D. B., and R. V. Guha. (1990). *Building Large Knowledge-based Systems. Representation and Inference in the Cyc Project.* Reading, MA: Addison-Wesley.

Lenz, M., et al. (1996). "CBR for Diagnosis and Decision Support." *AI Communications,* Vol. 9.

Leonard, D., and S. Sensiper. (1998, Spring). "The Role of Tacit Knowledge in Group Innovations." *California Management Review,* Vol. 40. No. 3.

Leonard, N. H., R. W. Scholl, and K. B. Kowalski. (1999, May). "Information Processing Style and Decision Making." *Journal of Organizational Behavior.* Vol. 20, No. 3.

Leontief, W. (1986). *The Future Impact of Automation on Workers.* Oxford, UK: Oxford University Press.

Leu, S-S., and H. Y. Chung. (1999, Nov.). "A GA-based Resource-constrained Construction Scheduling System." *Construction Management and Economics.* Vol. 17, No. 6.

Li, H., and P. E. D. Love. (1999, Mar.). "Combining Rule-based Expert Systems and Artificial Neural Networks for Mark-up Estimation." *Construction Management and Economics,* Vol. 17, No. 2.

Li, S. (2000, Jan.). "The Development of a Hybrid Intelligent System for Developing Marketing Strategy." *Decision Support Systems,* Vol. 27, No. 4.

Liang, D. B. (2000). *Applied Knowledge Acquisition.* San Francisco: Morgan Kaufmann.

Liang, T. P., and C. V. Jones. (1987, Summer). "Design of a Self-Evolving Decision Support System." *Journal of Management Information Systems.*

Liang, T. P., and B. R. Konsynski. (1993, Jan.). "Modeling by Analogy: Use of Analogical Reasoning in Model Management Systems." *Decision Support Systems,* Vol. 9, No. 1.

Liang, T. P., and E. Turban, eds. (1993, Jan./Mar.). "Case-based Reasoning and Its Applications," Special Issue. *Expert Systems with Applications.*

Liao, Z., and R. Landry, Jr. (2000). "An Empirical Study on Organizational Acceptance of New Information Systems in a Commercial Bank Environment." *Proceedings of the Thirty-third Hawaii International Conference on System Sciences HICSS-33.* Wailea, HI, Los Alamitos, CA: IEEE Computer Society Press.

Liberatore, M. J., and A. C. Stylianou. (1995, Aug.). "Expert Support Systems for New Product Development Decision Making." *Management Science,* Vol. 41, No. 8.

Liebowitz, J., (1999). *Building Organizational Intelligence: A Knowledge Management Primer.* Boca Raton FL: CRC Press.

Lightfoot, J. M. (1999, Aug.). "Expert Knowledge Acquisition and the Unwilling Expert: A Knowledge Engineering Perspective." *Expert Systems.*

Lin, C-T., and C. S. G. Lee. (1996). *Neural Fuzzy Systems: A Neuro-Fuzzy Synergism to Intelligent Systems.* Upper Saddle River, NJ: Prentice Hall.

Lindsey, C. S. (1998). "Neural Networks in Hardware: Architectures, Products and Applications." Royal Institute of Technology, Stockholm, Sweden, www.particle.kth.se/~lindsey/HardwareNNWCourse/home.html.

Lindstone, H., and M. Turroff. (1975). *The Delphi Method: Technology and Applications.* Reading, MA: Addison-Wesley.

Ling, X., and W. G. Rudd. (1989). "Combining Opinions from Several Experts." *Applied AI,* Vol. 3.

Lipp, A., and C. Y. Carver. (2000, Jan.). "Using Web Groupware and Cognitive Mapping in a CIS Department to Review and Revise the Assessment Process and Document Reasoning," *Proceedings of the Thirty-Third Annual Hawaii International Conference on System Sciences HICSS-33.* Los Alamitos, CA: IEEE Computer Society Press.

Little, J. D. C. (1970, Apr.). "Models and Managers: The Concept of a Decision Calculus." *Management Science,* Vol. 16, No. 8.

Liu, F-H. F. and S. Y. Shen. (1999, Oct.). "An Overview of a Heuristic for Vehicle Routing Problem with Time

Windows." *Computers & Industrial Engineering,* Vol. 37, Nos. 1 and 2.

Liu, J., and L. Tang. (1999, Oct.). "A Modified Genetic Algorithm for Single Machine Scheduling." *Computers & Industrial Engineering,* Vol. 37, Nos. 1 and 2.

Liu, N. K., and K. K. Lee (1997, Aug.). "An Intelligent Business Advisor System for Stock Investment." *Expert Systems.*

Liu, S. (1998). "Data Warehousing Agent: To Make the Creation and Maintenance of Data Warehousing Easier." *Journal of Data Warehousing,* No. 1.

Liu, S., et al. (2000, May) "Software Agents for Environmental Scanning in Electronic Commerce." *Information Systems Frontiers.*

Lloyd, B. (1996). "Knowledge Management: The Key to Long-term Organizational Success." *Long Range Planning,* Vol. 29, No. 4.

Loch, K. D., and S. Conger. (1996, July). "Evaluating Ethical Decision Making and Computer Use." *Communications of the ACM,* Vol. 39, No. 7.

Lockwood, S., and Z. Chen. (1994). "Modeling Experts' Decision-making Using Knowledge Charts." *Information and Decision Technologies,* Vol. 19, No. 4.

Lu, J., M. A. Quaddus, and R. Williams. (2000). "Developing a Knowledge-based Multi-objective Decision Support System." *Proceedings of the Thirty-third Hawaii International Conference on System Sciences HICSS-33.* Wailea, HI, Los Alamitos, CA: IEEE Computer Society Press.

Lucas, H. C. (1981). *Implementation: The Key to Successful Information Systems.* New York: Columbia University Press.

Lucas, H. C. (1995). *Information Systems Concepts for Management.* New York: McGraw-Hill.

Lui, H. C., et al. (1991). "Practical Application of a Connectionist Expert System—The Inside Story," in J. K. Lee, et al. (eds.). *Operational Expert Systems Applications in the Far East.* New York: Pergamon Press.

Lukose, D. (1996). "MODEL-ECS: Executable Conceptual Modelling Language." *Proceedings of the Tenth Knowledge Acquisition for Knowledge-based Systems Workshop,* www.ksi.cpsc.ucalgary.ca/KAW/KAW96/KAW96Proc.html.

Luther, R. K. (1998, Spring). "An Artificial Neural Network Approach to Predicting the Outcome of Chapter 11 Bankruptcy." *The Journal of Business and Economic Studies,* Vol. 4, No. 1.

Lyczak, R., and S. Weber-Russel. (1992). "An Expert Natural Language Interface for Statistical Packages." *Expert Systems with Applications,* Vol. 5, Nos. 1 and 2.

Machacha, L. L., and P. Bhattacharya. (2000, Feb.). "A Fuzzy-logic-based Approach to Project Selection." *IEEE Transactions on Engineering Management,* Vol. 47, No. 1.

Madhaven, R., and R. Grover. (1998, Oct.). "From Embedded Knowledge to Embodied Knowledge: New

Product Development as Knowledge Management." *Journal of Marketing,* Vol. 62, No. 4.

Maes, P. (1994, July). "Agents That Reduce Work and Information Overload." *Communications of the ACM,* Vol. 37, No. 7.

Maes, P. (1995). "Artificial Life Meets Entertainment: Life-like Autonomous Agents." *Communications of the ACM,* Vol. 38, No. 11.

Maes, P., et al. (1999, Mar.). "Agents that Buy and Sell." *Communications of the ACM.*

Magid, I. (1999, Dec.). "The Driving Forces in the Virtual Society." *Communications of the ACM.*

Mahapatra, R. K (1997/1998, Winter). "Case-based Reasoning: Extending the Frontiers of Knowledge-based Systems." *Journal of Computer Information Systems.*

Manago, M., and E. Auriol. (1995). "Integrating Induction and Case-based Reasoning for Troubleshooting CFM-56 Aircraft Engines." *XPS'95. Fourth German Conference on Expert Systems,* University of Kaiserslautern, Germany.

Mandry, T., et al. (1999, June). "Mobile Agents on Electronic Markets: Opportunities, Risks, and Protection." *Proceedings of the Twelfth International Bled EC Conference.*

Manheim, M. L. (1989). "Issues in the Design of Symbiotic DSS." *Proceedings of the Twenty-second Hawaii International Conference on System Sciences HICSS-22.* Wailea, HI, Los Alamitos, CA: IEEE Computer Society Press.

Maniezzo, V., et al. (1993, Aug.). "D-KAT: A Deep Knowledge Acquisition Tool." *Expert Systems.*

Mapleston. P. (1999, Aug.). "Real-time Process Control Is Said to Provide Perfect Shots." *Modern Plastics,* Vol. 29, No. 8.

Markel, M. (1999, Apr.). "Distance Education and the Myth of the New Pedagogy." *Journal of Business and Technical Communication,* Vol. 13, No. 2.

Markus, M. L. (1983, June). "Power, Politics and MIS Interpretation." *Communications of the ACM,* Vol. 26, No. 6.

Marlin, S. (1999, June). "Intelligent Telecentres." *Bank Systems & Technology.* Vol. 36, No. 6.

Mars, N. J. I. (ed.). (1995). *Towards Very Large Knowledge Bases.* Amsterdam: IOS Press.

Marshall, L. (1997, Sept./Oct.). "Facilitating Knowledge Management and Knowledge Sharing: New Opportunities for Information Professionals," *Online,* Vol. 21, No. 5.

Martin, P. (1996). "CGKAT: A Knowledge Acquisition Tool and an Information Retrieval Tool Which Exploits Conceptual Graphs and Structured Documents." INRIA, France, www.inria.fr/acacia/personnel/phmartin/cgkat.html.

Martin, P., and Eklund, P. (1999, May) "Embedding Knowledge in Web Documents." *Computer Networks.*

Mason, R. O., F. M. Mason, and M. J. Culnan. (1995). *Ethics of Information Management.* Thousand Oaks, CA: Sage.

Massetti, B. (1996, Mar.). "An Empirical Examination of the Value of Creativity Support Systems on Idea Generation." *MIS Quarterly,* Vol. 20, No.1.

Matsatsinis, N. F., and Y. Siskos. (1999, Mar. 1). "MARKEX: An Intelligent Decision Support System for Product Development Decisions." *European Journal of Operational Research,* Vol. 113, No. 2.

Matthews, D. (1999, Sept.). "The Origins of Distance Education and its Use in the United States." *T.H.E. Journal,* Vol. 27, No. 2.

May, J. H., and L. G. Vargas. (1996, Jan. 20). "SIMPSON: An Intelligent Assistant for Short Term Manufacturing Scheduling." *European Journal of Operations Research,* Vol. 88, No. 2.

Maybury, M. T. (1997). *Intelligent Multimedia Information Retrieval.* Boston: MIT Press.

McCaffrey, M. J. (1992). "Maintenance of Expert Systems: The Upcoming Challenge," in E. Turban and J. Liebowitz (eds.). *Managing Expert Systems.* Harrisburg, PA: Idea Group.

McCann, D. W. (1999, May/June). "Aircraft Icing Forecasts from Neural Networks." *PC AI.*

McCarthy, V. (1996, Feb. 15). "Nifco Lets Businesses Deal with NAFTA." *Datamation,* Vol. 42, No. 4.

McConnell, S. (1996). *Rapid Development.* Redmond, WA: Microsoft Press.

McCullough, S. (1999, Oct. 15). "On the Front Lines." *CIO.*

McDonald, M., and D. Shand. (2000, Mar.). "Request for Proposal: A Guide to KM Professional Services." *Knowledge Management.*

McFadden, F. R., J. A. Hoffer, and M. B. Prescott. (1999). *Modern Database Management.* Reading, MA: Addison-Wesley.

McFetridge, L., and M. Y. Ibrahim. (1998, Dec.). "New Technique of Mobile Robotic Navigation Using a Hybrid Adaptive Fuzzy-potential Field Approach," *Computers & Industrial Engineering,* Vol. 35, Nos. 3 and 4.

McGraw, K. L., and B. K. Harbison-Briggs. (1989). *Knowledge Acquisition, Principles and Guidelines.* Englewood Cliffs, NJ: Prentice Hall.

McGuire, C. (1999, Jan.). "The Next Level of Proprietary Protection." *Wall Street & Technology,* Vol. 17, No. 1.

McKeen, J. D. (1997, Fall). "Successful Strategies for User Participation in Systems Development." Journal of MIS, Vol. 14, No. 2.

McKenna, B. (1999, Feb.). "Growing Knowledge Organically." *Information World Review,* No. 144.

McNeill, D., and P. Freiberger. (1993). *Fuzzy Logic.* New York: Simon & Schuster.

McQuaid, M. M., et al. (2000). "Tools for Distributed Facilitation," *Proceedings of the Thirty-Third Annual Hawaii International Conference on System Sciences HICSS-33.* Los Alamitos, CA: IEEE Computer Society Press.

Meador, C. L., M. J. Guyote, and P. G. W. Keen. (1984a, June). "Setting Priorities for DSS Development." *MIS Quarterly,* Vol. 8, No. 2.

Meador, C. L., P. G. Keen, and M. J. Guyote. (1984b, May 7). "Personal Computer and Distribution Decision Support." *ComputerWorld,* Vol. 18, No. 19.

Medsker, L., and E. Turban. (1994). "Integrating Expert Systems and Neural Computing for Decision Support." *Expert Systems with Applications,* Vol. 7, No. 4.

Medsker, L., and J. Liebowitz. (1994). *Design and Development of Expert Systems and Neural Networks.* New York: Macmillan.

Medsker, L., et al., (1995). "Knowledge Acquisition from Multiple Experts: Problems and Issues." *Expert Systems with Applications,* Vol. 9.

Melymuika, K. (1999, June 21). "Coca-Cola: Marketing Partner," *ComputerWorld,* Vol. 33, No. 25.

Meredith, J. R. (1981, Oct.). "The Implementation of Computer-Based Systems." *Journal of Operational Management.*

Meso, P. N., and J. O. Liegle. (2000, Aug.). "The Future of Web-based Instruction Systems," *Proceedings of the Americas Conference of the Association for Information Systems,* Milwaukee, WI.

Milberg, S., et al. (1995, Dec.). "Values, Personal Information Privacy, and Regulatory Approaches." *Communications of the ACM,* Vol. 38, No. 12.

Mili, F. (1990, May). "Active DSS: Issues and Challenges." TIMS/ORSA Joint National Meeting, Las Vegas.

Mili, H., and F. Pachet. (1995). "Regularity, Document Generation, and Cyc," in Rada and Tochtermann (1995).

Min, D. M., et al. (1996, Sept.). "IBRS: Intelligent Bank Reengineering System." *Decision Support Systems,* Vol. 18, No. 1.

Min, H., and S. B. Eom. (1994). "An Integrated Decision Support System for Global Logistics." *International Journal of Physical Distribution and Logistics Management,* Vol. 24, No. 1.

Mintzberg, H. A. (1980). *The Nature of Managerial Work.* Englewood Cliffs, NJ: Prentice Hall.

Mintzberg, H. A. (1989). *Mintzberg on Management.* New York: Free Press.

Mintzberg, H. A. (1993). *The Rise and Fall of Strategic Planning.* New York: Free Press.

Miranda, S. M., and R. P. Bostrom. (1997, Jan.). "Meeting Facilitation: Process Versus Content Interventions," *Proceedings of the Thirtieth Annual Hawaii International Conference on Systems Sciences, HICSS-30* Wailea, HI, Los Alamitos, CA: IEEE Computer Society Press.

Mirchandani, D., and R. Pakath. (1999). "Four Models for a DSS," *Information Management.* Vol. 35, No. 1

Mitchell, M. (1999). *An Introduction to Genetic Algorithms.* Cambridge, MA: MIT Press.

Mitchell, T. M., et al. (1986). "Explanation-based Generalization: A Unifying View." *Machine Learning,* No. 1.

Mittman, B. S., and J. H. Moore. (1984, April). *Senior Management Computer Use: Implications for DSS Design and Goals.* Paper presented at the DSS-84 Meeting, Dallas, TX.

Mizell, I. R. (1998). *Invasion of Privacy.* Berkley: Berkley Publishing.

MMH (2000, Feb.). "Real Time Decisions, Instant Response." *Modern Materials Handling,* Vol. 55, No. 2.

Money, A., et al. (1988, June). "The Quantification of Decision Support Benefits Within the Context of Value Analysis." *MIS Quarterly,* Vol. 12, No. 2.

Moody, J. W., et. al. (1998/1999, Winter). "Capturing Expertise from Experts: The Need to Match Knowledge Elicitation Techniques with Expert System Types." *Journal of Computer Information Systems.*

Moon, Y. B., C. K. Divers, and H-J. Kim. (1998, Mar.). "AEWS: An Integrated Knowledge-based System with Neural Networks for Reliability Prediction." *Computers in Industry,* Vol. 35, No. 2.

Moore, C. (1999, Oct.). "Eureka! Xerox Discovers Way to Grow Community Knowledge." *KMWorld.*

Moore, J. H., and M. G. Chang. (1980, Fall). "Design of Decision Support Systems." *Data Base,* Vol. 12, Nos. 1 and 2.

Moran, P., and S. Ghoshal. (1996, Jan.). "Theories of Economic Organization: The Case for Realism and Balance." *Academy of Management,* Vol. 21, No. 1.

Morris, M. G., C. Speier, and J. A. Hoffer. (1999, Winter). "An Examination of Procedural and Object-oriented Systems Analysis Methods: Does Prior Experience Help or Hinder Performance?" *Decision Sciences,* Vol. 30, No. 1.

Motiwalla, L. F. (1995, Spring). "An Intelligent Agent for Prioritizing E-mail Messages." *Information Resources Management Journal,* Vol. 8, No. 2.

Mottl, J. N. (2000, Jan. 3). "Learn at a Distance." *Informationweek,* No. 767.

Munakata, T., and Y. Jani. (1994, Mar.) "Fuzzy Systems: An Overview." *Communications of the ACM,* Vol. 37, No. 3.

Murch, R., and T. Johnson. (1999). *Intelligent Software Agents.* Upper Saddle River, NJ: Prentice Hall.

Murphy, C. (1993). "The Southern Isle Financial Services Company: Amending the Gorry and Scott Morton Framework," in Holtham, C. (ed.), *Executive Information Systems and Decision Support.* London: Chapman and Hall.

Murthy, S., et al. (1999, Sept./Oct.). "Cooperative Multi-objective Decision Support for the Paper Industry." *Interfaces,* Vol. 29, No. 5.

Murthy, U. S., and D. S. Kerr. (2000). "Task/Technology Fit and the Effectiveness of Group Support Systems: Evidence in the Context of Tasks Requiring Domain Specific Knowledge." *Proceedings of the Thirty-Third Annual Hawaii International Conference on System Sciences HICSS-33.* Los Alamitos, CA: IEEE Computer Society Press.

Musen, M. A., et al. (1995). "PROTÉGÉ-II: Computer Support for Development of Intelligent Systems from Libraries of Components." *Proceedings of MEDINFO*

1995, Eighth World Congress on Medical Informatics, Vancouver, BC.

Musen, M. A., et. al (1999, Aug.)."Use of a Domain Model to Drive an Interactive Knowledge-editing Tool." *International Journal of Human–Computer Studies.*

Myers, I. B., and P. B. Myers. (1995). *Gifts Differing: Understanding Personality Type,* reprint ed. Palo Alto, CA: Consulting Psychologists Press.

Mykytyn, K., et al. (1990, Mar.). "Expert Systems: A Question of Liability?" *MIS Quarterly,* Vol. 14, No. 1.

Nagy, G. (2000, Jan.). "Twenty Years of Document Image Analysis in PAMI." *IEEE Transactions on Pattern Analysis and Machine Intelligence,* Vol. 22, No. 1.

Nahapiet, J., and S. Ghoshal. (1998, Apr.). "Social Capital, Intellectual Capital, and the Organizational Advantage." *Academy of Management Review,* Vol. 23, No. 2.

Nardi, B.A., et al. (1998, Mar.). "Collaborative, Programmable, Intelligent Agents." *Communications of the ACM,* Vol. 41, No. 3.

Nault, B. R., and V. C. Storey. (1998). "Using Object Concepts to Match Artificial Intelligence Techniques to Problem Types." *Information and Management,* Vol. 34, No. 1.

Neo, B. S. (1996). *Exploiting Information Technology for Business Competitiveness: Cases and Insights from Singapore-based Organizations.* Reading, MA: Addison-Wesley.

Neumann, S. (1994). *Strategic Information Systems.* New York: Macmillan.

Nevis, E. C., A. J. DiBella, and J. M. Gould. (1995, Winter). "Understanding Organizations as Learning Systems." *Sloan Management Review.*

Newell, A., and H. A. Simon. (1972). *Human Problem Solving.* Englewood Cliffs, NJ: Prentice Hall.

Newquist, H. P. (1996, Sept.). "Data Mining: The AI Metamorphosis." *Database Programming & Design* (Supplement).

Nezlek, G. S., H. K. Jain, and D. L. Nazareth. (1999, Nov.). "An Integrated Approach to Enterprise Computing Architectures." *Communications of the ACM,* Vol. 42, No. 11.

Nguyen H. T., and E. A. Walker. (1999). *A First Course in Fuzzy Logic.* Boca Raton, FL: CRC Press.

Ngwenyama, O. K. et al. (1996). "Supporting Facilitation in Group Support Systems: Techniques for Analyzing Consensus Relevant Data. " *Decision Support Systems,* Vol. 16, No. 1.

Niettinen K., et al. (1999). *Recent Advances in Genetic Algorithms.* New York: Wiley.

Niles, J. M. (1998). *Making Telecommuting Happen: A Guide for Telemanagers and Telecommuters.* New York: Wiley.

Nilson N. J. (1998). *Artificial Intelligence: A New Synthesis.* San Francisco: Morgan Kaufmann.

Ninios, P., K. Vlahos, and D. W. Bunn. (1995). "Industrial Simulation: System Modeling with an Object Oriented/DEVS Technology." *European Journal of Operational Research,* Vol. 81.

Nonaka, I., and H. Takeuchi. (1995). *The Knowledge-creating Company: How Japanese Companies Create the Dynamics of Innovation.* New York: Oxford University Press.

Nord, J. H., and D. Nord. (1995, Aug.). "Executive Information Systems: A Study and Comparative Analysis." *Information & Management,* Vol. 29, No. 2.

Nord, J. H., and D. Nord. (1996, Winter). "Why Managers Use Executive Information Systems." *Information Strategy: The Executive's Journal,* Vol. 12, No. 2.

Norman, B. A., and J. C Bean. (2000, May). "Scheduling Operations on Parallel Machine Tools." *IIE Transactions,* Vol. 32, No. 5.

Nunamaker, J. F., Jr. (1991). "Electronic Meeting Systems to Support Group Work: Theory and Practice at Arizona." *Communications of the ACM,* Vol. 34, No. 7.

Nute, D. E., et al. (1995). "A Toolkit Approach to Developing Forest Management Advisory Systems in Prolog." *AI Applications,* Vol. 9, No. 3.

Nwana, H. S., and D. T. Ndumu. (1999). "A Perspective on Software Agent Research." *Knowledge Engineering Review,* No. 2.

Nwosu, K. C., et al. (1997, July/Sept.). "Multimedia Database Systems: A New Frontier," *IEEE Multimedia.*

O'Brien, G., and J. Opie. (1999, Oct.). "What's Really Doing the Work Here? Knowledge Representation or the Higher-Order Thought Theory of Consciousness." *Behavioral and Brain Sciences.*

O'Dell, C., C. J. Grayson, Jr., and N. Essaides. (1998). *If Only We Knew What We Know: The Transfer of Internal Knowledge and Best Practice.* New York: Free Press (Simon & Schuster Inc.).

O'Hare, G., and N. Jennings (eds.). (1996). *Foundations of Distributed Artificial Intelligence.* New York: Wiley.

O'Keefe, R. M., and O'Leary, D. E. (1993). "Performing and Managing Expert System Validation," in Grabowski, M. and W. A. Wallace (eds.) *Advances in Expert Systems for Management.* Vol. 1; Greenwich, CT: JAI Press.

O'Keefe, R. M., et al. (1987, Winter). "Validating Expert System Performance." *IEEE Expert.*

O'Leary, D. (1996, Apr.). "AI and Navigation on the Internet and Intranet." *IEEE Expert.*

O'Leary, D. (1998, May). "Knowledge Management Systems: Converting and Connecting." *IEEE Intelligent Systems and Their Applications,* Vol. 13, No. 1.

O'Leary, D. E. (1993, Mar./Apr.). "Determining Differences in Expert Judgment: Implications for Knowledge Acquisition and Validation." *Decision Sciences,* Vol. 24, No. 2.

O'Leary, D. E. (1995, Apr.). "Some Privacy Issues in Knowledge Discovery: The OECD Personal Privacy Guidelines." *IEEE Expert,* Vol. 10, No. 2.

O'Leary, D. E., et al. (1997, Jan.). "Artificial Intelligence and Virtual Organizations." *Communications of the ACM,* Vol. 40, No. 1.

Oliver, J. R. (1996, Jan.). "On Artificial Agents for Negotiation in Electronic Commerce." *Proceedings of the Twenty-ninth Hawaii International Conference on Systems Sciences HICSS-29,* Wailea, HI. Los Alamitos, CA: IEEE Computer Society Press.

OR/MS Today. (1999, Dec.). "2000 OR/MS Resource Directory." *OR/MS Today,* Vol. 26, No. 6.

Orman, L. V. (1998, Summer). "A Model Management Approach to Business Process Reengineering." *Journal of Management Information Systems,* Vol. 15. No. 1.

Orzech, D. (1998, June). "Call Centers Take to the Web." *Datamation.*

Osyk, B. A., and B. S. Vijayaraman. (1995, Spring). "Integrating Expert Systems and Neural Nets." *Information Systems Management,* Vol. 12, No. 2.

Owen, S. (1990). *Analog for Automated Reasoning.* New York: Academic Press.

Owrang, M. M., and F. J. Groupe. (1996). "Using Domain Knowledge to Guide Database Knowledge Discovery." *Expert Systems with Applications,* Vol. 10, No. 2.

Oxman, S. W. (1991, May). "Reporting Chemical Spills: An Expert Solution." *AI Expert,* Vol. 6, No. 5.

Pal, K. and O. Palmer. (2000). "A Decision Support System for Business Acquisitions." *Decision Support Systems,* Vol. 27, No. 4.

Palma-dos-Reis, A., and F. Zahedi. (1999, July). "Designing Personalized Intelligent Financial Decision Support Systems." *Decision Support Systems,* Vol. 26, No. 1.

Palmer, B. (1999, May 10). "Click Here for Decisions." *Fortune,* Vol. 139, No. 9.

Palopoli, L., and R. Torlone. (1997, Nov./Dec.). "Generalised Production Rules as a Basis for Integrating Active and Deductive Databases." *IEEE Transactions on Knowledge and Data Engineering,* Vol. 9, No. 6.

Palvia, P., et al. (1996, Feb.). "Information Requirements of a Global EIS: An Exploratory Macro Assessment." *Decision Support Systems,* Vol. 15.

Panko, R. R. (1998, Spring). "What We Know About Spreadsheet Errors." *Journal of End User Computing,* Vol. 10, No. 2.

Panko, R. R. (1999, Fall). "Applying Code Inspection to Spreadsheet Testing," *Journal of Management Information Systems.* Vol. 16, No. 2.

Parker, S., et al. (1994, Sept.). "A DSS for Personnel Scheduling in a Manufacturing Environment." *Computers and Industrial Engineering.*

Parsaye, K., and M. Chignell. (1988). *Expert Systems.* New York: Wiley.

Parsaye, K., and M. Chignell. (1993). *Intelligent Database: Object-oriented, Deductive Hypermedia Technologies.* New York: Wiley.

PC AI. (1997, Apr. 15). "Blackboard Technology," www2.primenet.com/pcai/New_Home_Page/ai_info/ blackboard_technology.html.

PC Magazine. (2000, Feb. 8). "Pipeline: Enter the Third Dimension." *PC Magazine.*

Pendergast, M., and S. Hayne. (1999, Apr. 25). "Groupware and Social Networks: Will Life Ever Be the Same Again?" *Information and Software Technology,* Vol. 41, No. 6.

Peppers, D., et al. (1999). *The One-to-One Fieldbook.* New York: Bantam Books.

Pervan, G. P. (1999). "Intelligent Group Support Systems: Some Suggestions." *Proceedings of the Fifth International Conference of the Decision Sciences Institute.*

Piatetsky-Shapiro, G., et al. (1996). "An Overview of Issues in Developing Industrial Data Mining and Knowledge Discovery Applications," in J. Han and E. Ptyra, M. J. (ed.). (1996). *Fuzzy Logic: Implementation and Applications.* New York: Wiley.

Pinsonneault, A., and K. Kraemer. (1993, Sept.). "The Impact of Information Technology on Middle Mangers." *MIS Quarterly,* Vol. 17, No. 3.

Pinto, N. B., L. M. Stephens, and R. D. Bonnell. (1995). "A Case Study in the Use of Large-scale Knowledge-based Technology for an Environmental Application," in N. J. I. Mars, (ed.). *Towards Very Large Knowledge Bases.* Amsterdam: IOS Press.

Piramuthu, S., et al. (1993, Jan.). "Integration of Simulation Modeling and Inductive Learning in an Adaptive Decision Support System." *Decision Support Systems,* Vol. 9, No. 1.

Plamonden, R., and S. N. Srihari. (2000, Jan.). "On-Line and Off-Line Handwriting Recognition: A Comprehensive Survey." *IEEE Transactions on Pattern Analysis and Machine Intelligence,* Vol. 22, No. 1.

Poe, V. (1996). *Building a Data Warehouse for Decision Support.* Upper Saddle River, NJ: Prentice Hall.

Poh, H. L. (1994). "A Neural Network Approach for Decision Support." *International Journal of Applied Expert Systems,* Vol. 2, No. 3.

Poirier, C. C., (1999). *Advanced Supply Chain Management: How to Build a Sustained Competition.* Berkeley, CA: Publishers' Group West.

Pokras, S. (1989). *Systematic Problem-Solving and Decision-Making: Rational Methods for Problem-Solving and Decision-Making.* Los Altos, CA: Crisp Publications.

Polanyi, M. (1958). *Personal Knowledge.* Chicago: University of Chicago Press.

Polanyi, M. (1966). *The Tacit Dimension.* London: Routledge & Kegan Paul.

Port, O., and J. Carey. (1997, Nov. 10). "Getting to Eureka!" *BusinessWeek.*

Porter, M. E., (1985). *Competitive Advantage, Creating and Sustaining Superior Performance,* New York: Free Press.

Pounds, W. F. (1969, Fall). "The Process of Problem Finding." *Sloan Management Review.* Vol. 11, No. 1.

Powell, A. L. (2000, Aug.). "Commitment in a Virtual Team," *Proceedings of the Americas Conference of the Association for Information Systems,* Milwaukee, WI.

Powell, P. L., and J. E. V. Johnson, (1995, May). "Gender and DSS Design: The Research Implications." *Decision Support Systems,* Vol. 14, No. 1.

Prerau, D. S. (1990). *Developing and Managing Expert Systems.* Reading, MA: Addison-Wesley.

Principe, J. C., N. R. Euliano, and W. C. Lefebvre. (2000). *Neural and Adaptive Systems: Fundamentals Through Simulations.* New York: Wiley.

Proudlove, N. C., S. Vadera, and K. A. H. Kobbacy. (1998, July). "Intelligent Management Systems in Operations: A Review." *Journal of the Operational Research Society,* Vol. 49, No. 7.

Ptyra, M. J. (ed.). (1996). *Fuzzy Logic: Implementation and Applications.* New York: Wiley.

Qi, M. (1999, Oct.). Nonlinear Predictability of Stock Returns Using Financial and Economic Variables," *Journal of Business & Economic Statistics,* Vol. 17, No. 4.

Qi, M., and G. S. Maddala. (1999, May). "Economic Factors and the Stock Market." *Journal of Forecasting,* Vol. 18, No. 3.

Quah, T-S., et al. (1996, May 21). "Towards Integrating Rule-based Expert Systems and Neural Networks." *Decision Support Systems,* Vol. 17, No. 2.

Quarantiello, L. E. (1996, Jan.). "Gangs: Tracking the Homeboys." *Law and Order.*

Quenk, N. L. (1999). *Essentials of Myers-Briggs Type Indicator Assessment* Essentials of Psychological Assessment Series. New York: Wiley.

Quiroga, L. A., and L. C. Rabelo. (1995, Sept.). "Learning from Examples: A Review of Machine Learning, Neural Networks and Fuzzy Logic Paradigms." *Computers & Industrial Engineering.* Vol. 29, Nos. 1–4.

Rada, R., and K. Tochtermann, eds. (1995). *Expertmedia: Expert Systems and Hypermedia.* Singapore: World Scientific.

Raghunathan, N. (1994, Summer). "An Application of Qualitative Reasoning to Derive Behavior from Structure of Quantitative Models." *Journal of Management Information Systems,* Vol. 11, No. 1.

Rainer, R. K., Jr., and H. J. Watson. (1995a, June). "What Does It Take for Successful Executive Information Systems?" *Decision Support Systems,* Vol. 14, No. 2.

Rainer, R. K., Jr., and H. J. Watson. (1995b, Fall). "The Keys to Executive Information System Success." *Journal of Management Information Systems,* Vol. 12, No. 2.

Rainone, S. H., et al. (1998, Spring). "Ethical Management of Employee E-mail Privacy," *Information Strategy: The Executive Journal.*

Raju, K. S., and C. R. S. Pillai. (1999, Jan. 16). "Multicriterion Decision Making in River Basin Planning and Development." *European Journal of Operational Research,* Vol. 112, No. 2.

Ralha, C. G. (1996). "Structuring Information in a Distributed Hypermedia System," in N. Shadbolt, K. O'Hara, and G. Schreiber (eds.). *Advances in Knowledge Acquisition.* Berlin: Springer-Verlag

Ram, S., and S. Ram (1996, Jan.). "Validation of Expert Systems for Innovation Management: Issues, Methodology, and Empirical Assessment." *Journal of Product Innovation Management,* Vol. 13, No. 1.

Ramakrishnan, R., and J. Gehrke. (1999). *Database Management Systems,* 2nd ed. New York: McGraw Hill.

Ramsay, A. M. (ed.). (1996). *Artificial Intelligence: Methodology, Systems, Applications.* Amsterdam: IOS Press.

Rao, S. S. (1998, Jan. 12). "Evolution at Warp Speed." *Forbes,* Vol. 161, No. 1.

Rappaport, A., and R. Smith (eds.). (1990). *Innovative Applications of Artificial Intelligence 2.* Cambridge, MA: MIT Press.

Rasmus, D. W. (1995). "Creativity and Tools." *PC AI,* Pt. 1: May/June; Pt. 2: July/Aug.; Pt. 3: Sept./Oct.

Rayham, A. F. R., and M. C. Fairhurst. (1999, Feb.). "Enhancing Multiple Expert Decision Combination Strategies Through Exploration of A Priori Information Sources." *IEE Proceedings—Vision, Image and Signal Processing,* Vol. 146, No. 1, www.iee.org.uk.

Raynor, W. (1996). *The International Dictionary of Artificial Intelligence.* London: Glenlake Publishing.

Rayward-Smith, V. J., I. H. Osman, and C. R. Reeves (eds.). (1996). *Modern Heuristic Methods.* New York: Wiley.

Redman, T. C. (1998, Feb.). "The Impact of Poor Data Quality on the Typical Enterprises," *Communications of the ACM.*

Reed, R. D., and R. J. Marks II. (1999). *Neural Smithing: Supervised Learning in Feedforward Artificial Neural Networks.* Cambridge, MA: MIT Press.

Rees, J., and G. Koehler. (1999). "Brainstorming, Negotiating and Learning in Group Decision Support Systems: An Evolutionary Approach." *Proceedings of the Thirty-Second Annual Hawaii International Conference on System Sciences HICSS-32.* Los Alamitos, CA: IEEE Computer Society.

Reid, K. A. (1999). "Impact of Technology on Learning Effectiveness," Center for Excellence in Distance Learning (CEDL), Lucent Technologies, www.lucent.com/cedl.

Reinig, B. A., R. O. Briggs, and J. F. Nunamaker, Jr. (1997/1998, Winter). "Flaming in the Electronic Classroom." *Journal of Management Information Systems,* Vol. 14, No. 3.

Reiter E., and R. Dale. (2000). *Building Natural Language Generation Systems.* Cambridge, UK: Cambridge University Press.

Reiter, R. (1980). "A Logic for Default Reasoning." *Artificial Intelligence,* Vol. 13, 81–132.

Rettig, H. (2000). "3D Business Data Utilization VARs Are Helping Their Customers See Business Data More Clearly," pubs.cmpnet.com/vb/case/167drill.htm.

Rheingold, H. (1993*). The Virtual Community: Home-steading on the Electronic Frontier.* Reading, MA: Addison-Wesley.

Ribeiro, R. et al. (1995, Feb.). "Uncertainty in Decision Making: An Abductive Perspective." *Decision Support Systems,* Vol. 13, No. 2.

Rich, E., and K. Knight. (1991). *Artificial Intelligence,* 2nd ed. New York: McGraw-Hill.

Riesbeck, C. K., and R. L. Schank. (1989). *Inside Case-based Reasoning.* Hillsdale, NJ: Erlbaum Associates.

Robey, D. (1979, Sept.). "User Attitudes and MIS Use." *Academy of Management Journal,* Vol. 22, No. 3.

Robin, M. (2000, Mar.). "Learning by Doing." *Knowledge Management.*

Robinson, W. N. (1997). "Electronic Brokering for Assisted Contracting of Software Applets." *Proceedings of the Thirtieth Annual Hawaii International Conference on Systems Sciences HICSS-30,* Wailea, HI. Los Alamitos, CA: IEEE Computer Society Press.

Rockart, J. F., and A. D. Crescenzi. (1984, Summer). "Engaging Top Management in Information Technology." *Journal of Systems Management.*

Rockart, J. F., and D. W. DeLong. (1988). *Executive Support Systems: The Emergence of Top Management Computer Use.* Homewood, IL: Dow Jones–Irwin.

Roe, A. (1998, July 27/Aug. 3). "Water Distribution Engineers Apply Darwin's Theory to System Design." *Engineering News Record,* Vol. 241, No. 4.

Romano, N. C., Jr., J. F. Nunamaker, Jr., and R. O. Briggs. (1997). "User Driven Design of a Web-based Group Support System." *Proceedings of the Thirtieth Annual Hawaii International Conference on Systems Sciences HICSS-30,* Wailea, HI, Los Alamitos, CA: IEEE Computer Society Press.

Rosenschein, J. S., and G. Zlotkin. (1994, Fall). "Designing Conventions for Automated Negotiation." *AI Magazine,* Vol. 15, No. 3.

Rosenstein, A. H. (1999, Spring). "Measuring the Benefits of Clinical Decision Support: Return on Investment." *Health Care Management Review.* Vol. 24, No. 2.

Rosenwald, G. W., and C-C. Liu. (1997, Jan.). "Rule-based System Validation Through Automatic Identification of Equivalence Classes." *IEEE Transactions on Knowledge and Data Engineering,* Vol. 9, No. 1.

Rubenfeld, S., et al. (1994, Winter). "Caveat Emptor: Avoiding Pitfalls in Data-based Decision Making." *Review of Business.*

Rublin, L. R. (1999, Dec 13). "Neglected Gems." *Barron's,* Vol. 79, No. 50.

Rudenstein, R. (2000, Jan.). "A Bright Idea: HR Portal Helps Osram Sylvania See the Light." *Enterprise Systems Journal,* pp. 24–30.

Ruggiero, M. A., Jr. (1999, Mar.). "Birth of a Neural Network." *Futures,* Vol. 28, No. 3.

Russ K., and A. Wetherelt, (1999, Mar./Apr.). "Large Scale Mine Visualization Using VRML." *IEEE Computer Graphics and Applications.*

Russell, I. F., and A. N. Kumar (eds.). (2000, Feb.). "Special Issue: Tools and Techniques of Artificial Intelligence." *International Journal of Pattern Recognition and Artificial Intelligence,* Vol. 14, No. 1.

Russell, S., and P. Norvig. (1995). *Artificial Intelligence: A Modern Approach.* Upper Saddle River, NJ: Prentice Hall.

Ryan, J. (1988, Nov.). "Expert Systems in the Future: The Redistribution of Power." *Journal of Systems Management,* Vol. 39, No. 11.

Ryker, R., and N. Ravinder. (1995, Oct.). "An Empirical Examination of the Impact of Computer Information Systems on Users." *Information and Management,* Vol. 29, No. 4.

Saaty, T. L. (1995). *Decision Making for Leaders: The Analytic Hierarchy Process for Decisions in a Complex World,* revised ed. Pittsburgh, PA: RWS Publishers.

Saaty, T. L. (1996). *Decision Making for Leaders,* Vol. II. Pittsburgh, PA: RWS Publishers.

Saaty, T. L. (1999). *The Brain: Unraveling the Mystery of How It Works (The Neural Network Process).* Pittsburgh, PA: RWS Publications.

Saaty, T. L. (2000). *The Brain: Unraveling the Mystery of How it Works.* Pittsburgh: University of Pittsburgh Press.

Sadaranda, R., and S. K. Acharya. (1993, Oct.). "Modeling the Negotiation Paradigm for the Banking Industry." *Computers in Industry,* Vol. 22, No. 3.

Saitta, L. (1996). "Representation Change in Machine Learning." *AI Communications,* Vol. 9.

Sandahl, K. (1994). "Transferring Knowledge from Active Experts to End-user Environments." *Knowledge Acquisition,* Vol. 6.

Sanders, G. L., and J. F. Courtney. (1985, Mar.). "A Field Study of Organizational Factors Influencing DSS Success." *MIS Quarterly,* Vol. 9, No. 1.

Sandoe K., and A. Saharia. (2001). *Enterprise Integration.* New York: Wiley.

Sangster, A. (1994). "The Adoption of IT in Management Accounting: the Expert Systems Experience." *Journal of Information Technology,* Vol. 9.

Sarin, R. (1999, Sept.). "Debating Rationality: Nonrational Aspects of Organizational Decision Making." *Journal of Economic Literature.* Vol. 37, No. 3.

Satzinger, J. W., M. J. Garfield, and M. Nagasundaram. (1999, Spring). "The Creative Process: The Effects of Group Memory on Individual Idea Generation." *Journal of Management Information Systems,* Vol. 15, No. 4.

Sawyer, D. C., (1999). *Getting It Right: Avoiding the High Cost of Wrong Decisions.* Boca Raton, FL: St. Lucie Press.

Schantz, H. F. (1991, Spring). "An Overview of Neural OCR Networks." *Journal of Information Systems Management,* Vol. 8, No. 2.

Schein, E. (1997). *Organizational Culture and Leadership,* 2nd ed., San Francisco: Jossey-Bass.

Schein, E. (1999). *The Corporate Culture Survival Guide.* San Francisco: Jossey-Bass.

Schell, G. P. (2000, Aug.). "The 'Introduction to Management Information' Course Goes Online," *Proceedings of the Americas Conference of the Association for Information Systems,* Milwaukee, WI.

Schenk, K. D., N. P. Vitalari, and K. S. Davis. (1998, Summer). "Differences Between Novice and Expert Systems Analysts: What Do We Know and What Do We Do?" *Journal of Management Information Systems,* Vol. 15, No. 1.

Schmitt, L. J., and M. M. Amini. (1998, Aug. 1). "Performance Characteristics of Alternative Genetic Algorithmic Approaches to the Traveling Salesman Problem Using Path Representation: An Empirical Study." *European Journal of Operational Research,* Vol. 108, No. 3.

Schocken, S., and G. Ariav. (1994, June). "Neural Networks for Decision Support: Problems and Opportunities." *Decision Support Systems,* Vol. 11, No. 5.

Schrage, L. (1997). *Optimization Modeling with LINDO,* 5th ed. Pacific Grove, CA: Duxbury Press.

Schrage, M. (1995). *No More Teams!: Mastering the Dynamics of Creative Collaboration.* New York: Doubleday.

Schrage, M., and T. Peters. (1999). *Serious Play: How the World's Best Companies Simulate to Innovate.* Boston, MA: Harvard Business School Press.

Schultheis, R., and M. Sumner. (1994, Spring). "The Relationship of Application Risks to Application Controls: A Study of Microcomputer-based Spreadsheet Applications." *Journal of End User Computing,* Vol. 6, No. 2.

Schwartz, H. (1998). *Rationality Gone Awry? Decision Making Inconsistent with Economic and Financial Theory.* Westport, CT: Praeger.

Scott Morton, M. (1984, May 21–22). "Expert Decision Support Systems." Paper presented at a special DSS conference. New York: Planning Executive Institute and Information Technology Institute.

Scott, A. C., J. E. Clayton, and E. L. Gibson. (1991). *A Practical Guide to Knowledge Acquisition.* Reading, MA: Addison-Wesley.

Scott Morton, M. (ed.). (1991). *The Corporation of the 1990's.* Oxford, UK: Oxford University Press.

Scott Morton, M. S. (1971). *Management Decision Systems: Computer-based Support for Decision Making.* Cambridge, MA: Harvard University, Division of Research.

Seiler, T. M., and J. E. Aronson. (1995, June). "Using Interest Rate Parity in Simulated Artificial Neural Networks to Forecast the Movement of the Yen with Respect to the U.S. Dollar." *Proceedings of the Academy of International Business South Pacific Regional Meeting,* Perth, Australia.

Selic, B. (1999, Oct.). "Turning Clockwise: Using UML in the Real-time Domain." *Communications of the ACM,* Vol. 42, No. 10.

Sen, S., and J. L. Higle. (1999, Mar./Apr.). "An Introductory Tutorial on Stochastic Linear Programming Models." *Interfaces,* Vol. 29, No. 2.

Senker, P. (1989). "Implications of Expert Systems for Skill Requirements and Working Life." *AI and Society,* Vol. 3.

Shadbolt, N., K. O'Hara, and G. Schreiber (eds.). (1996). *Advances in Knowledge Acquisition.* Berlin: Springer-Verlag.

Shadbolt, N., K. O'Hara, and L. Crow. (1999, Oct.). "The Experimental Evaluation of Knowledge Acquisition Techniques and Methods: History, Problems and New Directions." *International Journal of Human–Computer Studies.*

Shafer, G. (1976). *A Mathematical Theory of Evidence.* Princeton, NJ: Princeton University Press.

Shafer, G. (1996). *Probabilistic Expert Systems.* Philadelphia: Society for Industrial and Applied Mathematics.

Shapira, Z. (1997). *Organizational Decision Making.* New York: Cambridge University Press.

Sharma, R. S., and D. W. Conrath. (1992, Aug.). "Evaluating Expert Systems: The Socio-technical Dimensions of Quality." *Expert Systems.*

Sharma, R. S., and D. W. Conrath. (1993). "Evaluating Expert Systems: A Review of Applicable Approaches." *AI Review,* Vol. 6.

Shaw, M. L. G., and B. R. Gaines. (1996). "WebGrid: Knowledge Elicitation and Modeling on the Web." KSI, University of Calgary, ksi.cpsc.ucalgary.ca.

Sheetz, S. D., D. P. Tegarden, L. F. Tegarden, L. Poppo, and D. Gynwali. (2000, Aug.). "A WWW-Based Group Cognitive Mapping Approach to Support Case-Based Learning," *Proceedings of the Americas Conference of the Association for Information Systems,* Milwaukee, WI.

Sheetz, S. D., et al. (1994, Summer). "A Group Support Systems Approach to Cognitive Mapping." *Journal of Management Information Systems,* Vol. 11, No. 1.

Sherif, K., and M. Mandviwalla. (2000). "Barriers to Actualizing Organizational Memories: Lessons from Industry." *Proceedings of the Thirty-Third Annual Hawaii International Conference on System Sciences HICSS-33.* Los Alamitos, CA: IEEE Computer Society Press.

Sheth J. N., and R. S. Sisodia. (1999, Nov. 15). "Are Your IT Priorities Upside Down?" *CIO.*

Shih, W., and K. Srihari. (1995). "DAI in Manufacturing Systems Control." *Computers and Industrial Engineering,* Vol. 29, Nos. 1–4.

Shim, S. J. (1999, Spring). "Exploring the Benefits of Expert Systems Use in Organizations." *Journal of Computer Information Systems.*

Shirani, A. I., M. H. A. Tafti, and J. F. Affisco. (1999, Sept.). "Task and Technology Fit: A Comparison of Two Technologies for Synchronous and Asynchronous Group Communication." *Information & Management,* Vol. 36, No. 3.

Siau, K. (1999, Oct.–Dec.). "Information Modeling and Method Engineering: A Psychological Perspective." *Journal of Database Management,* Vol. 10, No. 4.

Siegel, D. L. (1990, Summer). "Integrating Expert Systems for Manufacturing." *AI Magazine,* Supplement.

Silverman, B. (1995, Nov./Dec.). "Knowledge-based Systems and the Decision Sciences." *Interfaces.*

Silverstone, S. (1999, Dec.). "Innovate Creatively." *Knowledge Management.*

Simon, H. (1977). *The New Science of Management Decision.* Englewood Cliffs, NJ: Prentice Hall.

Singh, H. S., and H. Singh. (1998). *Interactive Data Warehousing.* Upper Saddle River, NJ: Prentice Hall.

Skyrme, D. J. (1997, Sept.). "Knowledge Management: Oxymoron or Dynamic Duo?" *Managing Information,* Vol. 4, No. 7.

Skyrme, D. J. (1999). *Knowledge Networking: Creating the Collaborative Enterprise.* Woburn, MA: Butterworth-Heinemann.

Skyrme, D. J., and D. M. Amidon. (1998, Jan./Feb.). "New Measures of Success." *Journal of Business Strategy,* Vol. 19, No. 1.

Slade, S. (1991, Spring). "Case-based Reasoning: A Research Paradigm." *AI Magazine.*

Slade, S. (1997). *Object-oriented Common LISP.* Upper Saddle River, NJ: Prentice Hall.

Slater, D. (2000, Feb. 1). "Loan Star." *CIO,* Vol. 13, No. 8.

Sleeman, D., and F. Mitchell. (1996). "Towards Painless Knowledge Acquisition," in N. Shadbolt, K. O'Hara, and G. Schreiber (eds.). *Advances in Knowledge Acquisition.* Berlin: Springer-Verlag.

Smeaton, A. F., and F. Crimmins. (1996). "Using a Data Fusion Agent for Searching the WWW." Glasnevin, Dublin, Ireland: School of Computer Applications, Dublin City University, lorca.compapp.dcu.ie/fusion/papers/fusion-wwwb.html.

Smith, G. V., and R. L. Parr. (1998). *Intellectual Property.* New York: Wiley.

Smith, K. T., and L. M. Smith. (1996, Apr.). "A Software Tool for Internet Operations Risk Analysis." *CPA Journal,* Vol. 66, No. 4.

Smith, M. (1999, July/Aug.). "Gender, Cognitive Style, Personality and Management Decision-making." *Management Accounting—London,* Vol. 77, No. 7.

Smith, P., et al. (1996). "Forecasting Short Term Regional Gas Demand Using an Expert System." *Expert Systems with Applications.* Vol. 10, No. 2.

Sonka, M., et al. (1998). *Image Processing: Analysis and Machine Vision.* Pacific Grove, CA: Brooks/Cole.

Sowa, J. F. (1997). *Principles of Semantic Networks: Exploration in the Representation of Knowledge.* San Francisco: Morgan Kaufmann.

Spector, L. et al. (eds.). (1999). *Advances in Genetic Programming.* Cambridge, MA: MIT Press.

Spivey, J. M. (1996). *Logic Programming: The Essence of Prolog.* Upper Saddle River, NJ: Prentice Hall.

Sprague, R. H., Jr., and E. D. Carlson. (1982). *Building Effective Decision Support Systems.* Englewood Cliffs, NJ: Prentice Hall.

Sprague, R. H., Jr., and H. J. Watson (eds.). (1996a). *Decision Support Systems,* 4th ed. Englewood Cliffs, NJ: Prentice Hall.

Sprague, R. H., Jr., and H. J. Watson. (1996b). *Decision Support for Management.* Upper Saddle River, NJ: Prentice Hall.

Stack, R. (1997). "Boston Central Artery/Tunnel Traffic Management Using an Expert System," www.transdyn.com/HTML/Papers/Traffic_Management_Expert_Sys.htm.

Stahl, S. (1999, Apr. 5). "Knowledge Yields Impressive Returns." *InformationWeek.*

Stamen, J. P. (1993, Oct.). "Structuring Databases for Analysis." *IEEE Spectrum.*

Steiger, D. M. (1998, Fall). "Enhancing User Understanding in a Decision Support System: A Theoretical Basis and Framework." *Journal of Management Information Systems,* Vol. 15, No. 2.

Stein, E. W. (1992, Fall). "A Method to Identify Candidates for Knowledge Acquisition." *Journal of Management Information Systems,* Vol. 9, No. 2.

Stein, L. A. (1996, Winter). "Science and Engineering in Knowledge Representation and Reasoning." *AI Magazine,* Vol. 17, No. 4.

Stewart, T. A. (1996, Nov. 27). "Getting Real About Brainpower." *Fortune,* Vol. 132, No. 11.

Stewart, V., and Mayes, J. (2000). "Business Applications of Repertory Grid" Enquire Within, www.Enquire-Within.co.nz/business.htm.

Stone-Gonzalez, J. (1998). *The 21st Century Intranet.* Upper Saddle River, NJ, Prentice Hall.

Strischeck, D., and R. Cross. (1996, Jan.). "Reengineering the Credit Approval Process." *Journal of Commercial Lending,* Vol. 78, No. 5.

Strong, D. M., et al. (1997, May). "Data Quality in Context." *Communications of the ACM.*

Studt, T. (1994, May). "Rapid Prototyping: Key to Fast Development," *R&D (RDV).*

Studt, T. (1998, Nov.). "Stat Systems Focus on Decision Making." *R&D,* Vol. 40, No. 12.

Sturman, M. C., and G. T. Milkovich. (1995, Jan./Feb.). "Validating Expert Systems: A Demonstration Using Personal Choice Expert, A Flexible Employee Benefit System." *Decision Sciences,* Vol. 26, No. 1.

Stylianou, A. C., G. R. Madley, and R. D. Smith. (1992). "Criteria for the Selection of Expert System Shells: A Sociotechnical Framework." *Communications of the ACM,* Vol. 35, No. 10.

Stylianou, A. C., R. D. Smith, and G. R. Madey. (1995). "An Empirical Model for the Evaluation and Selection of Expert System Shells." *Expert Systems with Applications,* Vol. 8, No. 1.

Sugumaran, V., and R. Bose. (1996, Feb.). "Expert System Technology in Organisational Process Domain Modeling." *Expert Systems,* Vol. 13, No. 1.

Suh, C. K., and E. H. Suh. (1993, Aug.). "Using Human Factor Guidelines for Developing Expert Systems." *Expert Systems,* Vol. 10, No. 3.

Suh, C. K., et al. (1995, Apr.). "Artificial Intelligence Approaches in Model Management." *Computers and Industrial Engineering,* Vol. 28, No. 2.

Sullivan, G., and K. Fordyce. (1990). "IBM Burlington's Logistics Management System." *Interfaces,* Vol. 20, No. 1.

Sun, M., J. E. Aronson, P. G. McKeown, and D. Drinka. (1998). "A Tabu Search Procedure for the Fixed Charge Transportation Problem." *European Journal of Operational Research,* Vol. 106, 441–456.

Sviokla, J. J. (1990, June). "An Examination of the Impact of Expert Systems on the Firm: The Case XCON." *MIS Quarterly,* Vol. 13, No. 1.

Sviokla, J. J. (1996, Summer). "Knowledge Workers and Radically New Technology." *Sloan Management Review,* Vol. 37, No. 4.

Swanson, B. D., E. Ralls, and J. E. Aronson. (1999, Feb.). "The Challenge of Information Systems Planning for Outcomes Systems in Managed Care." *Journal of Rehabilitation Outcomes Measurement,* Vol. 3, No. 1.

Swanson, E. B. (1988). *Information System Implementation.* Homewood, IL: Irwin.

Swanson, E. B., and R. Zmud. (1990, Jan.). "Distributed Decision Support Systems: A Perspective." *Proceedings of the Twenty-third Annual Hawaii International Conference on System Sciences HICSS-33,* Vol. III. Los Alamitos, CA: IEEE Computer Society Press.

Swenson, J. (1996, July 8). "Maps on the Web." *InformationWeek.*

Swink M., and C. Speier. (1999, Winter). "Presenting Geographical Information." *Decision Sciences.*

Taboada, M., et al. (1996, Nov.). "Integrating Medical Expert Systems, Patient Databases and User Interfaces." *Journal of Intelligent Information Systems,* Vol. 7, No. 3.

Tamiz, M., D. Jones, and C. Romero. (1998, Dec. 16). "Goal Programming for Decision Making: An Overview of the Current State-of-the-Art." *European Journal of Operational Research,* Vol. 111, No. 3.

Tanier, D. (1997). "Inheritance and Parallelization: Emerging Object-Oriented and Parallel Technologies for High Performance Database Systems." *Proceedings of the High-Performance Computing on the Information Superhighway, HPC—Asia 1997.* Piscataway, NJ: Institute of Electrical and Electronics Engineers.

Tavakkoli-Moghaddain, R., and E. Shayan. (1998, Dec.). "Facilities Layout Design by Genetic Algorithms." *Computers & Industrial Engineering,* Vol. 35, Nos. 3 and 4.

Tavana, M., and S. Banerjee. (1995). "Strategic Assessment Model (SAM): A Multiple Criteria Decision Support System for Evaluation of Strategic Alternatives." *Decision Sciences,* Vol. 26, No. 1.

Tecuci, G. (1998). *Building Intelligent Agents.* New York: Academic Press.

Teng, J. T. C. (1988, Jan.). "A Unified Architecture for Intelligent DSS." *Proceedings of the Twenty-first Hawaii International Conference on Systems Science HICSS-21.* Wailea, HI, Los Alamitos, CA: IEEE Computer Society Press.

Theodore, J. (1998, June). "Turn Data Puzzles into Perfect Pictures." *Business Geographies.*

Thiriez, H. (1992, Aug. 25). "Towards a DEISS." *European Journal of Operational Research,* Vol. 61, Nos. 1 and 2.

Thomas, H., et al. (1997, Nov./Dec.), "New Technology in Large Customer Call Center." *PC AI.*

Thuraisingham, B. (1989, Oct.). "Rules to Frames and Frames to Rules." *AI Expert.*

Tochtermann, K., and M. Fathi. (1994). "Making Use of Expertext to Enhance the Process of Knowledge Acquisition," in J. Liebowitz (ed.), *Proceedings of the Second World Congress on Expert Systems,* Lisbon.

Tochtermann, K., and V. Zink. (1995). "Artificial Intelligence and Hypermedia," in R. Rada and K. Tochtermann (eds.), *Expertmedia: Expert Systems and Hypertext.* Singapore: World Scientific Publishing.

Toffler, A. (1970). *Future Shock,* New York: Random House.

Toffler, A. (1991). *Powershift.* New York: Bantam Books.

Tolun, M. R., and S. M. Abu-Soud. (1998, Apr.) "ILA: An Inductive Learning Algorithm for Rule Extraction." *Expert Systems with Applications,* Vol. 14, No. 3, www.elsevier.nl/inca/publications/store/9/3/9/.

Torrance, E. P. (1988). "The Nature of Creativity as Manifest in its Testing," in *The Nature of Creativity,* Sternberg, R. J. (ed.). Cambridge, UK: Cambridge University Press, pp. 43–75.

Touchton, R. A., and S. D. Rausch. (1993, July/Aug.). "Putting Expert Systems to the Test." *PC AI.*

Trippi, R., and E. Turban. (1996a). *Neural Computing Applications in Investment and Financial Services.* Burr Ridge, IL: Irwin.

Trippi, R., and E. Turban. (1996b). *Neural Network Applications in Investment and Financial Services,* revised ed. Chicago: Probus Publishers.

Trippi, R., and E. Turban. (1996c). *Neural Networks in Finance and Investing.* Burr Ridge, IL: Irwin.

Trippi, R. R., and E. Turban (eds.) (1996d). *Neural Networks in Finance and Investing: Using Artificial Intelligence to Improve Real-world Performance,* 2nd ed. Chicago: Irwin.

Tsai, N., C. R. Necco, and G. Wei. (1994a, Oct.). "Implementing an Expert System: A Report on Benefits Realized (Part 1)." *Journal of Systems Management,* Vol. 45, No. 10.

Tsai, N., C. R. Necco, and G. Wei. (1994b, Nov.). "An Assessment of Current Expert Systems: Are Your Expectations Realistic?" *Journal of Systems Management.*

Tung, L. L., and E. Turban. (1996, Mar.). "Expert Systems Support Container Operations in the Port of Singapore." *New Review of Applied Expert Systems.*

Tung, Y., R. D. Gopal, and J. R. Marsden. (1999, Oct.). "HypEs: An Architecture for Hypermedia-enabled Expert Systems." *Decision Support Systems.* Vol. 26, No. 4.

Turban, E. (1992). *Expert Systems and Applied Artificial Intelligence.* New York: Macmillan.

Turban, E., J. K. Lee, D. King, and M. Chung. (2000). *Electronic Commerce: A Managerial Perspective.* Upper Saddle River, NJ: Prentice Hall.

Turban, E., and J. Liebowitz (eds.). (1992). *Managing Expert Systems.* Hershey, PA: Idea Group.

Turban, E., and J. Meredith. (1994). *Fundamentals of Management Science,* 6th ed. Homewood, IL: Irwin.

Turban, E., and P. Watkins. (1986, June). "Integrating Expert Systems and Decision Support Systems." *MIS Quarterly,* Vol. 10, No. 2.

Turban, E., et al. (2000). *Electronic Commerce: A Managerial Perspective.* Upper Saddle River, NJ: Prentice Hall.

Turban, E., et al. (2001). *Information Technology for Management,* 2nd revised ed. New York: Wiley.

Tyo, J. (1996, July 15). "Slicing Data on the Desktop." *InformationWeek,* 59–72.

Tyran, C. K., and J. F. George. (1993, Winter). "The Implementation of Expert Systems: A Survey of Successful Implementations." *Data Base.*

Tyran, C. K., and M. Shepherd. (2000, Aug.). "Collaborative Technology in the Classroom: A Research Framework," *Proceedings of the Americas Conference of the Association for Information Systems,* Milwaukee, WI.

Udo, G. J., and T. Guimaraes. (1994, July). "Empirically Assessing Factors Related to DSS Benefits." *European Journal of Information Systems.*

Ulrich, D. (1998, Winter). "Intellectual Capital = Competence × Commitment." *Sloan Management Review,* Vol. 39, No. 2.

Vaas, L. (1999, May 31). "Brainstorming." *PCWeek,* Vol. 16, No. 22.

Vahid, F., S. Narayan, and D. Gajski. (1991). "SpecCharts: A Language for System Level Synthesis." *Proceedings Computer Hardware Description Languages.*

Vahidov, R., and Elrod, R. (1999, Sept.). "Incorporating Critique and Argumentation in DSS." *Decision Support Systems,* Vol. 26, No. 3.

Van den Hoven, J. (1996, Mar./Apr.). "Executive Support Systems & Decision Making." *Journal of Systems Management.*

Van Harmelen, F., et al. (1996, Feb.). "Evaluating a Formal KBS Specification Language." *IEEE Expert,* Vol. 11, No. 1.

Van Horn, M. (1986). *Understanding Expert Systems.* Toronto: Bantam Books.

Van Weelderen, J. A., and H. G. Sol. (1993, May/June). "MEDESS: A Methodology for Designing Expert Support Systems." *Interfaces,* Vol. 23, No. 3.

Vance, M., and D. Deacon (1997). *Think Out of the Box.* Franklin Lakes, NJ: Career Press.

Vance, M., and D. Deacon (1999). *Raise the Bar: Creative Strategies to Take Your Business and Personal Life to the Next Level.* Franklin Lakes, NJ: Career Press.

Vedder R. G., et al. (1999, July). "An Expert System That Was." *Proceedings of DSI International,* Athens, Greece.

Venkatachalam, A. R., and J. E. Sohl. (1999, May). "An Intelligent Model Selection and Forecasting System." *Journal of Forecasting,* Vol. 18, No. 3.

Vieira, P., and F. Gomide. (1996, July). "Computer-aided Train Dispatch." *IEEE Spectrum,* Vol. 33, No. 7.

Volonino, L., H. J. Watson, and S. Robinson. (1995). "Using EIS to Respond to Dynamic Business Conditions." *Decision Support Systems,* Vol. 14, No. 2.

Von Altrock, C. (1996). *Fuzzy Logic and Neurofuzzy Applications in Business and Finance.* Upper Saddle River, NJ: Prentice Hall.

Von Krogh G., et al. (2000). *Knowledge Creation: A Source of Value.* New York: San Martin's Press.

von Oech, R. (1998). *A Whack on the Side of the Head.* New York: Warner Books.

Vranes, S., et al. (1996, May). "INVEX: Investment Advisory Expert System." *Expert Systems,* Vol. 13, No. 2.

Wagner, H. M. (1995, Nov./Dec.). "Global Sensitivity Analysis." *Operations Research.*

Wagner, J. (2001, Feb.). "Delivering DSS via ASP's," *Decission Support Systems.*

Wagner, W. P., and C. W. Holsapple. (1997, Feb.). "An Analysis of Knowledge Acquisition Roles and Participants." *Expert Systems,* Vol. 14, No. 1.

Walbridge, C. T. (1989, June). "Genetic Algorithms: What Computers Can Learn from Darwin." *Technology Review.*

Walden, P., C. Carlsson, and O. Kollonen. (2000). "Active Decision Support and Strategic Management—the Kirkniemi Fine Paper Mill Case." *Decision Support Systems.*

Wang, H., and H. K. O. Lee (1998, Mar.). "Consumer Privacy Concern about Internet Marketing." *Communications of the ACM.* Vol. 41, No. 3.

Wang, J. (1994, June). "Artificial Neural Networks vs. Natural Neural Networks." *Decision Support Systems,* Vol. 11, No. 5.

Wang, R. Y. (1998, Feb.). "Total Data Quality Management." *Communications of the ACM.* Vol. 41, No. 2.

Wang, S. (1999, Winter). "Analyzing Agents for Electronic Commerce." *Information Systems Management.*

Wang, W., S. Zhong, Q. Tian, and T. Wang. (1996). "An Agent Belief System for Multiagent Systems." *Proceedings of the Twenty-ninth Annual Hawaii International Conference on Systems Sciences HICSS-29,* Wailea, HI. Los Alamitos, CA: IEEE Computer Society Press.

Wareham, E. (1999, July 9). "Fraud-buster App Raises Concerns." *Computing Canada,* Vol. 25, No. 27.

Warkentin, M., et al. (1994, Nov./Dec.). "AI in Business and Management: Law and Legal Application (of AI)." *PC AI,* Vol. 8, No. 6.

Warkentin, M., L. Sayeed, and R. Hightower. (1999). "Virtual Teams Versus Face-to-Face Teams," in Kendell, K. E. (ed.), *Emerging Information Technologies.* Thousand Oaks, CA: Sage Publications, p. 8.

Warnock, S., M. R. Baren, and M. Barchilon. (2000, Aug.). "Collaborative Problem-solving with Listservs in a Long-distance Engineering Classroom," *Proceedings of the Americas Conference of the Association for Information Systems,* Milwaukee, WI.

Warren, J. R., et al. (1995, Fall). "Simulation Modeling for BPR." *Information Systems Management,* Vol. 12, No. 4.

Waterman, D. A. (1985). *A Guide to Expert Systems.* Reading, MA: Addison-Wesley.

Watkins, P. R., T. W. Lin, and D. E. O'Leary. (1992). "AI Integration for Enhanced Decision Support." *Proceedings of the Twenty-fifth Annual Hawaii International Conference on System Sciences HICSS-25,* Wailea, HI, Los Alamitos, CA: IEEE Computer Society Press.

Watson, H. J., et al. (1996, Summer). "Including Soft Information in EISs." *Information Systems Management,* Vol. 13, No. 3.

Watson, H. J., et al., (1997b). *Building Executive Information Systems.* New York: Wiley.

Watson, H. J., J. E. Aronson, R. H. Hamilton, L. S. Iyer, M. Nagasundaram, H. R. Nemati, and J. Suleiman. (1996). "Assessing EIS Benefits: A Survey of Current Practices." *Journal of Information Technology Management.* Vol. 7, Nos. 1 and 2.

Watson, H. J., G. Houdeshel, and R. K. Rainer, Jr. (eds.) (1997). *Building Executive Information Systems and Other Decision Support Applications.* New York: Wiley.

Watson, R. T. (1990). "A Design for and Infrastructure to Organizational Decision Making," *Proceedings of the Twenty-Third Hawaii International Conference on System Sciences HICSS-23,* Los Alamitos, CA: IEEE Computer Society Press.

Watson, R.T. (1998). *Data Management: Databases and Organizations.* New York: Wiley.

Weatherly, K. A. and L. R. Beach. (1996). "Organizational Culture and Decision Making," in Beach, L. R. (ed.). *Decision Making in the Workplace: A Unified Perspective,* 117–132. Mahwah, NJ: Lawrence Erlbaum.

Weber, A. (1996, Oct.). "Advanced Technology Propels Citgo Refinery Toward 21st Century." *Control Magazine.* Also at www.gensym.com. *Gensym Success Stories.*

Weber, E. S., and B. R. Konsynski. (1987/88, Winter). "Problem Management: Neglected Elements in Decision Support Systems." *Journal of Management Information Systems.*

Weiss, G., and S. Sen (eds.). (1995). *Adaptation and Learning in Multi-Agent Systems.* Berlin: Springer-Verlag.

Weitz, R. R. (1990, Summer). "Technology, Work and the Organization: The Impact of Expert Systems." *AI Magazine,* Vol. 11, No. 2.

Wellman, B. (ed.). (1999). *Networks in the Global Village.* Boulder, CO: Westview Press.

Wesphal C., and T. Blaxton (1998). *Data Mining Solutions: Methods and Tools for Solving Real-World Problems.* New York: Wiley.

White, A. P. (1995). "An Expert System for Choosing a Statistical Test." *New Review of Applied Expert Systems,* Vol. 1, No. 1.

Whitehead, S. D. (1995, Dec.). "Auto-FAQ: An Experiment in Cyberspace Leveraging." *Computer Networks and ISDN Systems,* Vol. 28, Nos. 1 and 2.

Whittaker, D. (1999, Oct.). "Spreadsheet Errors and Techniques for Finding Them." *Management Accounting,* Vol. 77, No. 9.

Whitten, J. L., and L. B. Bentley. (1997). *Systems Analysis and Design Methods,* 4th ed. Burr Ridge, IL: Irwin.

Wick, M. R., and J. R. Slagle. (1989). "An Explanation Facility for Today's Expert Systems." *IEEE Expert,* Vol. 4, No. 1.

Wierenga, B., and G. H. van Bruggen. (1998, Mar.). "The Dependent Variable in Research into the Effects of Creativity Support Systems: Quality and Quantity of Ideas." *MIS Quarterly,* Vol. 11, No. 1.

Wiig, K. M. (1993). *Knowledge Management Foundations.* Arlington, TX: Schema Press.

Williams, C., and B. D. Clayton. (1994). "Case Base Retrieval," White Paper. Inference Corporation, www.inference.com: m5.inference.com/products/cbrwp.html.

Williams, J. (1991). "Negative Consequences of Information Technology," in *Management Impacts of Information Technology: Perspectives of Organizational Change and Growth.* Harrisburg, PA: Idea Group.

Williams, S. R., and R. L. Wilson. (1999). "Group Support Systems, Power and Influence in an Organization," in Kendell, K. E. (ed.), *Emerging Information Technologies.* Thousand Oaks, CA: Sage Publications, p. 8.

Wilson, R. L., and R. Sharda. (1994, June). "Bankruptcy Prediction Using Neural Networks." *Decision Support Systems,* Vol. 11, No. 5.

Winarchick, C., and R. D. Caldwell. (1997, May). "Physical Interactive Simulation: A Hands-on Approach to Facilities Improvements." *IIE Solutions,* Vol. 29, No. 5.

Wise E. (1999). *Applied Robotics.* Indianapolis: H.W. Sams.

Wolf, G. (1994, May). "Schedule Management: An Object Oriented Approach." *Decision Support Systems.* Vol. 11, No. 4.

Wolfe, W. J., and S. E. Sorensen. (2000, Jan.). "Three Scheduling Algorithms Applied to the Earth Observing Systems Domain." *Management Science,* Vol. 46, No. 1.

Wolfgram, D. D., et al. (1987). *Expert Systems.* New York: Wiley.

Wong, B. K. (1996, July/Aug.). "The Role of Top Management in the Development of Expert Systems." *Journal of Systems Management.*

Wong, B. K., and J. K. S. Chong. (1992, Winter). "Averting Development Problems (in ES)." *Information Systems Management,* Vol. 9, No. 1.

Wong, B. K., and J. A. Monaco. (1995, Sept.). "Expert Systems in Business: A Review and Analysis of the Literature." *Information and Management.*

Wong, F. S., et al. (1992 Jan./Feb.). "Fuzzy Neural Systems for Stock Selection." *Financial Analysts Journal.*

Wright, G. P., A. R. Chaturvedi, R. V. Mookerjee, and S. Garrod. (1998, Mar.) "Integrated Modeling Environments in Organizations: An Empirical Study." *Information Systems Research,* Vol. 9, No. 1.

Wu, D. J. (1999, Nov.). "Discovering Near-optimal Pricing Strategies for the Deregulated Electric Power Marketplace Using Genetic Algorithms." *Decision Support Systems,* Vol. 27, Nos. 1 and 2.

Wu, X., (1995). *Knowledge Acquisition from Databases.* Norwood, NJ: Ablex Publishing.

Wyckoff A. et al. (2000). *The Economic and Social Impacts of Electronic Commerce.* Washington DC: Brookings Institute Press.

Yager, R. R., M. Fedrizzi, and J. Kacprzyk. (1994). *Advances in the Dempster–Shafer Theory of Evidence.* New York: Wiley.

Yan, Y. et al. (2000, Jan.). "A Multi-Agent Based Negotiation Support System for Distributed Transmission Cost Allocation." *Proceedings of the Thirty-third Annual Hawaii International Conference on Systems Sciences HICSS-33,* Wailea, HI. Los Alamitos, CA: IEEE Computer Society Press.

Yang, Z. R., M. B. Platt, and H. D. Platt. (1999, Feb.). "Probabilistic Neural Networks in Bankruptcy Prediction." *Journal of Business Research,* Vol. 44, No. 2.

Ye, L. R., and P. E. Johnson. (1995, June). "The Impact of Explanation Facilities on User Acceptance of Expert Systems Advice." *MIS Quarterly,* Vol. 19, No. 2.

Yen, J. (1999, Jan./Feb.) "Fuzzy Logic—A Modern Perspective." *IEEE Transactions on Knowledge and Data Engineering,* Vol. 11, No. 1.

Yen, J., and R. Langari. (1998). *Fuzzy Logic: Intelligence, Control, and Information.* Upper Saddle River, NJ: Prentice Hall.

Yongbeom, K., and E. A. Stohr. (1998, Spring). "Software Reuse: Survey and Research Directions. *Journal of Management Information Systems,* Vol. 14, No. 4.

Yoon, Y., et al. (1994, Jan.). "Integrating ANN with Rule-based Expert Systems." *Decision Support Systems,* Vol. 11, No. 5.

Yoon, Y., T. Guimaraes, and Q. O'Neal. (1995, Mar.). "Exploring the Factors Associated with Expert System Success." *MIS Quarterly,* Vol. 19, No. 1.

Yorman, D. (1988, May). "Success Factors for Expert Systems." *Capital PC Monitor,* Vol. 7.

Young, J. (1987, Nov. 4). "Ways to Win Top Brass Backing." *ComputerWorld.*

Yu, E. S. K., et al. (1996, Aug.). "AI Models for Business Process Reengineering." *IEEE Expert,* Vol. 11, No. 4.

Yueng, M. M. (ed.). (1998, July). "Digital Watermarking," Special Issue. *Communications of the ACM.* Vol. 41, No. 7.

Yun, W. Y., and Y. S. Choi. (1999, Mar. 20). "A Simulation Model for Container-terminal Analysis Using an Object-oriented Approach," *International Journal of Production Economics,* Vol. 59, Nos. 1–3.

Zack, M. H. (1999, Spring). "Developing a Knowledge Strategy." *California Management Review.*

Zadeh, L. A., (1994, March). "Fuzzy Logic, Neural Networks, and Soft Computing." *Communications of the ACM,* Vol. 37, No. 3.

Zahedi, F. (1987). "Qualitative Programming for Selection Decisions." *Computers and Operations Research,* Vol. 14, No. 5.

Zahedi, F. (1993). *Intelligent Systems for Business: Expert Systems with Neural Networks.* Belmont, CA: Wadsworth.

Zarri, G. P. (1995). "Knowledge Acquisition from Natural Language Documents for Large Knowledge Bases," in Mars, N. J. I., ed. (1995). *Towards Very Large Knowledge Bases.* Amsterdam: IOS Press.

Zarri, G. P., and S. Jacqmin, (1999). "WWW, Metadata and Knowledge Representation: A New Version, RDF-Compliant, of the Conceptual Language NKRL," www.apim.ens.fr/workshop_text_99/zarri_abstract. html. Abstract.

Zhang, G., M. Y. Hu, B. E. Patuwo, and D. C. Indro. (1999, July 1). "Artificial Neural Networks in Bankruptcy Prediction: General Framework and Cross-validation Analysis." *European Journal of Operational Research,* Vol. 116, No. 1.

Zhu, K., et al. (2000, Jan.). "Air Cargo Transport by Multi-Agent Based Planning." *Proceedings of the Thirty-third Annual Hawaii International Conference on Systems Sciences HICSS-33,* Wailea, HI. Los Alamitos, CA: IEEE Computer Society Press.

Zurada, J. M. (1995). *Introduction to Artificial Neural Networks.* Boston: PWS Publishing.

Note: Page numbers followed by t and f refer to tables and figures. Those followed by A and F refer to DSS in Action and DSS in Focus boxes, respectively.